Reference and Information Services

Library and Information Science Text Series

The Academic Library: Its Context, Its Purpose, and Its Operation. By John M. Budd.

The Collection Program in Schools: Concepts, Practices, and Information Services. 3d ed. By Phyllis Van Orden and Kay Bishop, with the assistance of Patricia Pawelak-Kort.

Developing Library and Information Center Collections. 4th ed. By G. Edward Evans with the assistance of Margaret R. Zarnosky

The Economics of Information: A Guide to Economic and Cost-Benefit Analysis for Information Professionals. By Bruce R. Kingma.

A Guide to the Library of Congress Classification. 5th ed. By Lois Mai Chan

The Humanities: A Selective Guide to Information Sources. 5th ed. By Ron Blazek and Elizabeth Aversa

Information Sources in Science and Technology. 3d ed. By C. D. Hurt

Introduction to Library Public Services. 6th ed. By G. Edward Evans, Anthony J. Amodeo, and Thomas L. Carter.

Introduction to Technical Services. 6th ed. By G. Edward Evans and Sandra M. Heft.

Introduction to United States Government Information Sources. 6th ed. By Joseph Morehead.

Library and Information Center Management. 5th ed. By Robert D. Stueart and Barbara B. Moran.

The Organization of Information. By Arlene G. Taylor.

Reference and Information Services: An Introduction. 3d ed. Richard E. Bopp and Linda C. Smith, General Editors.

The School Library Media Center. 5th ed. By Emanuel T. Prostano and Joyce S. Prostano.

The School Library Media Manager. 2d ed. By Blanche Woolls.

The Social Sciences: A Cross-Disciplinary Guide to Selected Sources. 2d ed. Nancy L. Herron, General Editor.

Systems Analysis for Librarians and Information Professionals. 2d ed. By Larry N. Osborne and Margaret Nakamura.

Wynar's Introduction to Cataloging and Classification. 9th ed. By Arlene G. Taylor.

REFERENCE AND INFORMATION SERVICES

An Introduction

Third Edition

General Editors:

Richard E. Bopp
University of Illinois
at Urbana-Champaign

Linda C. Smith
University of Illinois
at Urbana-Champaign

2001
LIBRARIES UNLIMITED
A Division of Greenwood Publishing Group, Inc.
Englewood, Colorado

LIBRARIES UNLIMITED
A Division of Greenwood Publishing Group, Inc.
P.O. Box 6633
Englewood, CO 80155-6633
1-800-237-6124
www.lu.com

Library of Congress Cataloging-in-Publication Data

Reference and information services : an introduction / general editors, Richard E. Bopp, Linda C. Smith. -- 3rd ed.
p. cm. -- (Library and information science text series)
Includes bibliographical references and indexes.
ISBN 1-56308-621-2 (cloth). -- ISBN 1-56308-624-7 (paper)
1. Reference services (Libraries) 2. Information services.
I. Bopp, Richard E. II. Smith, Linda C. III. Series.
Z711.R443 2000
025.52--dc20

CONTENTS

PREFACE

This new edition of *Reference and Information Services* takes the introduction to reference sources and services significantly beyond the content of the first and second editions. In Part I, "Concepts and Processes," most of the chapters have been completely rewritten and the remainder are significantly revised and updated. This has been necessary to keep up with new ideas and methods in the provision of reference service and the growing emphasis in the profession at large on the necessity of delivering service which is truly user-centered. In addition, the rapid development of the World Wide Web, with its myriad of reference sites, Web directories, and search engines, has greatly expanded the options available to reference librarians in their search for the information requested by their users. While not all reference sites on the Web are as authoritative as many traditional print sources, the increasing availability of current and reliable Web-based information has changed the search strategies employed by reference staff. For this reason, more search strategy boxes have been added to the chapters on sources in Part II, and many individual Web sites are discussed in the text. In addition, the two chapters in Part I which discuss electronic resources are, necessarily, dramatically different from those in the second edition.

The goal of this edition, however, remains the same. Like the first two editions, the third is designed primarily to provide the beginning student of library and information science with an overview both of the concepts and processes behind today's reference services and of the most important sources consulted in answering common types of reference questions. While this is the first edition in which Web sites providing various kinds of useful information play a prominent role, print and more traditional forms of electronic information continue to be extensively covered. In addition, this text offers chapter-length discussions of ethical dilemmas in reference interactions, of the principles and goals of library instruction, of training and continuing education for reference staff, and of the evaluation and management of reference services. It also includes a new chapter on ancillary services such as interlibrary loan and document delivery which, due to electronic advances, have assumed a more important role in the provision of comprehensive reference service.

In general, this edition gives relatively equal space to concepts and to sources. The first twelve chapters deal with concepts and are topical. Chapter 1 introduces and briefly describes important reference services as they are practiced in most general reference settings today. It also offers a brief history of reference services and a glimpse of likely future developments. Chapters 2 through 12 discuss important areas of reference activity and introduce the concepts which underlie their current practice. As already mentioned, all of these chapters have been either rewritten or extensively revised and updated to reflect the current literature and practice of reference librarianship.

Chapter 13 serves as an introduction to Part II of the text. It describes the general principles and sources for selecting and evaluating reference tools and the principles for building a reference collection. Chapters 14 through 22 discuss the characteristics and uses of particular types of reference tools; a number of general titles of each type are described, and where appropriate, electronic versions of these sources are noted. Significant electronic titles which have no print counterpart are discussed, as well. Authors of sources chapters have made special efforts to include reference tools commonly found in libraries of all kinds, to add discussions of important Canadian sources, and to identify and describe tools useful in the provision of reference service to the special populations of library users discussed in chapter 12. The description of reference sources in these chapters is based, generally, on the latest edition available in summer 2000. All URLs listed in the text were verified and updated in August 2000. The editors will compile updates to the text on a regular basis and make them available through the Libraries Unlimited Web site at http://www.lu.com/lu/idu.html.

Each of the sources chapters does more than merely describe the contents of the reference tools it includes. Each seeks to emphasize the formulation of strategies for the effective use of specific sources or groups of sources. Sources chapters conclude with a description of a librarian's strategy for answering a fictitious but realistic reference question in the context of a particular library setting.

The internal organization of the chapters also requires mention. Chapters 14 through 22 have nearly identical structures, with discussion generally falling under the following headings: Uses and Characteristics, Evaluation, Selection, Important General Sources, Search Strategies, and, following Notes and the List of Sources, Additional Readings. Chapters 1 through 12 also offer Additional Readings, which, along with the Notes, can be used to delve further into topics discussed in those chapters.

To complement the text and to highlight certain topics, boxes are used throughout the book (these are numbered consecutively within each chapter). In the chapters on sources, the boxes are used primarily to present scenarios which illustrate specific search strategies which can be followed when dealing with certain kinds of reference questions. In the chapters on concepts and processes, the boxes are of several types. Some present a situation or problem which the reader is invited to consider and, possibly, discuss in a group setting. Others highlight information which the author has chosen to present in outline form or as an extended quotation or definition. In the sources chapters, figures are used to illustrate important features of the reference tools discussed; these are also numbered consecutively within each chapter.

A goal of this text is to integrate discussion of related topics as much as possible. For instance, individual electronic reference sources are discussed, not in a separate chapter, but with other sources of the same type (as mentioned above, two chapters, 5 and 6, deal with types and uses of electronic sources and their integration into daily reference service). Many of the search strategies which are presented in the sources chapters attempt to show how print and electronic sources can be used together, in a complementary fashion, in the provision of reference service. There are also numerous cross-references throughout the book, referring the reader to chapters where other aspects of a given topic are discussed.

Throughout the text, terms which may be new to the reader are italicized and defined as they are introduced. The Subject Index provides comprehensive access to discussions of particular concepts and types of sources. The Author/Title Index includes all titles mentioned in the text, but does not include those found only in the Notes or in the lists of selected Additional Readings.

Some mention should be made of the multiauthored nature of this text. When the editors first planned this text more than twelve years ago, it was clear that the task was too large for two authors to complete successfully. Discussions with colleagues produced a number of additional individuals interested in the project, and others have joined since that time. The editors believe that the variety of perspectives the numerous authors bring to the text works to the advantage of the reader, who benefits from the unique experiences in reference work reflected in different chapters. While most authors are currently affiliated either with an academic library or with a graduate school of library and information science, several have worked previously in either public, special, or school libraries. While the general format in Part II has been imposed on the authors to provide overall consistency in the text, each author has a unique style and viewpoint. At the same time, each chapter has been read and edited by both editors, who have sought to eliminate any serious gaps or inconsistencies in the text which might result from the fact that so many individuals have been involved in its creation.

Reference and Information Services: An Introduction, third edition, reflects many of the comments and suggestions made by reviewers and by other library and information science professionals and educators. It is hoped that the text will be useful, not only to students of library and information science, but also to practicing librarians seeking to review basic reference principles and sources.

RICHARD E. BOPP
Associate Professor of Library Administration, Emeritus
University Library
University of Illinois at Urbana-Champaign

LINDA C. SMITH
Professor and Associate Dean
Graduate School of Library and Information Science
University of Illinois at Urbana-Champaign

ACKNOWLEDGMENTS

A number of individuals assisted the editors or one of the authors in the creation of this third edition of *Reference and Information Services*. We would like here to express our gratitude to them for their valuable contributions.

First we would like to thank the editorial and production staff at Libraries Unlimited, Inc. for their patience and support during a project that took much longer than we anticipated.

The authors of several chapters in the third edition built on the work of authors who contributed to the second edition. We would like to acknowledge our debt to Susan E. Bekiares, Leslie Edmonds Holt, David N. King, Martha Landis, Patricia F. Stenstrom, and Lizabeth A. Wilson for helping shape this text in its first two editions.

As was the case in the first two editions, Vincent Golden created the timeline for the American retrospective bibliography figure in Chapter 20. We thank him for his work.

John Dunkelberger suggested additional titles for inclusion in the third edition based on his work in reference at the Urbana Free Library. Laura (Carrie) Bissey did extensive bibliographic searches for several of the chapters, providing up-to-date lists of relevant literature for their authors and current bibliographic information for sources. We are grateful to them for their contributions.

Tina Chrzastowski and Josephine Z. Kibbee assisted in editing Chapter 7. Carol M. Tobin and Pamela C. Sieving provided valuable comments and suggestions in reviewing Chapters 5 and 6. Christine Forte offered excellent advice and helpful editing of Chapter 22. We appreciate their assistance to the authors of those chapters.

Finally, we express our gratitude to all others who have helped in any way in the revision of this text. We hope all mentioned here will take some pride in the finished product, to which they have been essential contributors.

LIST OF CONTRIBUTORS

Bryce Allen
Associate Professor
School of Information Science and Learning Technologies
University of Missouri-Columbia
Chapter 10

Richard E. Bopp
Associate Professor of Library Administration, Emeritus
University Library
University of Illinois at Urbana-Champaign
Chapters 1, 3, 16

Charles A. Bunge
Professor Emeritus
School of Library and Information Studies
University of Wisconsin-Madison
Chapter 1

David A. Cobb
Curator, Harvard Map Collection
Harvard University
Chapter 19

Holly Crawford
Assistant Professor
School of Communication, Information and Library Studies
Rutgers, The State University of New Jersey
Chapter 18

Prudence Ward Dalrymple
Dean
Graduate School of Library and Information Science
Dominican University
Chapter 4

Constance A. Fairchild
Assistant Professor, Emeritus
University Library
University of Illinois at Urbana-Champaign
Chapters 16, 17

Eric Forte
Social Sciences Librarian
University of California, Santa Barbara
Chapter 22

Lisa Janicke Hinchliffe
Library Instruction Coordinator
Milner Library
Illinois State University
Chapter 8

Frances F. Jacobson
University Laboratory High School Librarian
University of Illinois at Urbana-Champaign
Chapter 12

Josephine Z. Kibbee
Head of Reference and Associate Professor of Library Administration
University Library
University of Illinois at Urbana-Champaign
Chapter 11

Kathleen M. Kluegel
Reference Librarian and Associate Professor of Library Administration
University Library
University of Illinois at Urbana-Champaign
Chapters 5, 6

Laura R. Lucio
Reference/Electronic Resources Librarian and Assistant Professor
James C. Jernigan Library
Texas A&M University-Kingsville
Chapter 15

Mary Mallory
Head, Government Documents Library and Associate Professor of Library Administration
University of Illinois at Urbana-Champaign
Chapter 22

Susan Miller
Head of Information Services
Southern Connecticut State University
Chapter 14

Carol Bates Penka
Assistant Reference Librarian and Assistant Professor of Library Administration
University Library
University of Illinois at Urbana-Champaign
Chapter 20

Richard E. Rubin
Professor
School of Library and Information Science
Kent State University
Chapter 2

Linda C. Smith
Professor and Associate Dean
Graduate School of Library and Information Science
University of Illinois at Urbana-Champaign
Chapters 13, 21

Ellen D. Sutton
Associate Dean
College of DuPage Library
Chapter 12

Lynn Wiley
Head, Illinois Research and Reference Center
University of Illinois at Urbana-Champaign
Chapter 7

Sandra L. Wolf
Library and Information Science Library
University of Illinois at Urbana-Champaign
Chapter 15

Beth S. Woodard
Central Information Services Librarian and Associate Professor of Library Administration
University Library
University of Illinois at Urbana-Champaign
Chapters 8, 9

PART

I

CONCEPTS AND PROCESSES

CHAPTER

1

HISTORY AND VARIETIES OF REFERENCE SERVICES

Charles A. Bunge and Richard E. Bopp

DEFINITIONS AND DEVELOPMENT

Reference Services and the Reference Librarian

Anyone who has experienced the frustration of needing information but being somewhat overwhelmed or confused by the amount available and the complexities of finding what is needed can appreciate the value of personal assistance by an expert in working through these complexities. Such personal assistance is the essence of reference services and is the fundamental role of the reference librarian. This chapter provides an introduction to the nature and development of reference services in libraries and the role of the reference librarian. Other chapters in Part I expand on some of the concepts discussed in this chapter, and the chapters in Part II describe and discuss the use of the most basic tools that reference librarians employ to carry out their roles.

Libraries and producers of information sources try to make access to the information they contain "user-friendly," that is, capable of being used independently by those who need information. They design their sources based on their best knowledge and predictions of the needs, knowledge, and skills of their potential users. For some users, some of the time, this works quite well. However, most seekers of information and ideas, at some time or other, confront barriers to finding what they need, whether it be their own time limitations, lack of knowledge of what sources exist or how to find and use them, or the sheer size and complexity of the world of information. The reference librarian's primary task is to help such individuals overcome these barriers and to accomplish their goals using relevant information and ideas.

A good beginning definition of reference services is given in Box 1.1. In this text, the focus is on both personal assistance provided to individual library users (e.g., answering reference questions) and organized services provided to groups of users (e.g., bibliographic instruction). Attention is also paid to behind-the-scenes activities, such as staff development and evaluation of reference services, which are necessary components of the provision of quality services.

Box 1.1 One Definition of Reference Service

The Reference and User Services Association (the division of the American Library Association that has responsibility for supporting the development of reference services for library users of all ages) has issued guidelines for the development and delivery of such services. The guidelines state that "information services in libraries take a variety of forms including direct personal assistance, directories, signs, exchange of information culled from a reference source, readers' advisory service, dissemination of information in anticipation of user needs or interests, and access to electronic information."[1]

Reference librarianship, the professional specialty that has reference service as its focus, had its origins in the second half of the nineteenth century, partially in response to one of that era's most important accomplishments: the spread of education. As more people were educated, educational institutions grew in size, and the size and complexity of libraries grew as well. As the educational level of the general population rose, more people came to their local public libraries to use the collections there. Because these individuals were not skilled in library use, libraries gradually recognized the need for an intermediary between library users and library collections. That intermediary was a librarian, and within a short time, a *reference librarian*.

Developments in the History of Reference Services

Early History

Historians of reference services usually trace modern concepts of reference work to Samuel Green's 1876 paper, "Personal Relations Between Librarians and Readers," later published in *American Library Journal* (now *Library Journal*).[2] Until that time, libraries concentrated on acquiring and organizing materials, and library users were expected to find what they needed independently. Green's paper is both quaint and surprisingly modern in its concept of reference work. It is interesting to note that all three basic reference functions or approaches discussed later in this chapter—information, guidance, and instruction—are touched on in Green's paper. He advised librarians in public libraries that many users, particularly working men and businessmen, have neither the knowledge nor the time to search for the information they need, so the librarian should find the information and present it to them. When young people come to the library to work on school assignments, Green advised instruction in the use of encyclopedias and indexes to books, along with an invitation to ask for assistance if the needed information is not readily found. He also pointed out that librarians are frequently asked for guidance in the choice of recreational reading materials or in the conduct of research into specific topics. In all of these cases, Green observed, individuals do not know how to use a library effectively on their own, as do scholars. He also noted that friendly and effective assistance to users will bring citizens to the library and cause the community to view its public library as indispensable.

Green's ideas were presented at a time when printed library aids such as the dictionary catalog, the Dewey Decimal Classification system, and periodical indexes were also beginning to make it easier to find information in the library and within library materials. Although some librarians regarded these aids as sufficient, during the 1880s and 1890s the need for special full-time staff trained in the principles of assisting library users in their search for information gained wide acceptance. This new activity, initially called "assistance to readers," was known by the 1890s as "reference work." By 1883, public libraries in several large cities were offering classes for "reference assistants." In 1887, the first library school opened at Columbia College, and its curriculum gave attention to assistance to users. By 1900, many public libraries had reference rooms, where reference materials were available on open shelves and reference librarians were ready to provide assistance in the use of library materials.[3]

The Twentieth Century

During the first half of the twentieth century, the concepts and practices of reference work were expanded, and specialized services such as readers' advisory service and bibliotherapy (discussed below) were developed. Early in the century, public library reference departments began answering information requests by telephone. At about the same time, they offered reference services in branch libraries, in addition to those offered in the reference room of the central library. In public libraries, the establishment of separate collections, in areas such as business, science, music, and art, began as early as 1913. A similar trend in academic libraries had occurred by the 1930s, when some libraries created separate units to serve faculty and students in specific subject departments.[4] In both types of libraries, a consequence of this departmentalization was the need for reference librarians with appropriate subject backgrounds. This evolution of subject specialization has continued to the present day, contributing to a lively discussion about whether specialist or generalist reference librarians can offer the most effective mode of service.

At the same time, the growth of *special libraries*—libraries established to serve primarily employees of the institutions that created them—exerted a profound effect on the concepts and practices of reference work. The idea of special libraries developed in the early years of the century, beginning with the establishment of the Legislative Reference Service of the state of Wisconsin in 1900. Based on that example, special libraries were later created in industrial research laboratories, businesses, and health care institutions. The significance of special libraries for the development of reference service was that, unlike other libraries, special libraries existed primarily to provide service rather than to build and house collections.[5] This freed the special librarian to pursue a higher standard of reference service, based on a detailed knowledge by the librarian of the information needs of the clientele, a willingness to seek out needed information from any source, and an ability to synthesize or otherwise to prepare information for use by the client.

The delivery of reference services experienced dramatic changes in the twentieth century. In general, it increasingly became more efficient and effective—at times, and in certain settings—to deliver reference service by means other than face-to-face interactions at the reference desk. Originally, librarians answered questions and assisted library users from reference desks and readers' advisory desks. Then, reference service by telephone was added, followed by the acceptance of mailed or referred questions from users who had no direct contact with the library. During the last thirty years of the century, the library instruction movement brought academic librarians into the classroom to teach and answer students' questions. The growth of subject-based information services in academic and special libraries moved reference services into the offices of librarians as well as the offices, laboratories, and other working areas of their users. Today, the provision of reference service by fax and e-mail is expanding. Some libraries have eliminated their reference desks entirely, replacing them with a tiered system that offers ready-reference service at an information desk and in-depth reference services in the offices of reference librarians. Although face-to-face encounters at the reference desk are still the predominant mode of service delivery in most public and academic libraries, it is clear that other ways of delivering information, guidance, and instruction are gaining in popularity among both reference librarians and users.

The Literature of Reference Services

Discussion of reference services has generated a sizable body of literature over the years. Several textbooks have been written and edited by reference librarians and educators, from that of James I. Wyer in 1930 to William A. Katz's *Introduction to Reference Work, Volumes I and II,* now in its seventh edition, to the various editions of the present work.[6] As early as the 1890s and continuing to the present, reference librarians and teachers have compiled guides to reference sources (see Chapter 13). In addition to textbooks, there has been a considerable body of monographic literature on reference services, including the proceedings of important conferences, guides and manuals on the provision of various types of services, and reports of the results of research projects.

From the early article by Samuel S. Green mentioned above to the present, reference librarianship has been the subject of a vigorous literature in periodicals. All the major periodicals in librarianship have carried at least occasional articles on reference services. The bulk of these articles have been what might be called "philosophical," discussing issues, policies, and "theoretical" matters, or descriptive "how-we-do-it" articles, sharing practices and procedures with the wider reference community. A number of periodicals run regular columns that review reference tools (see Chapter 13). From the 1960s onward, there has been a sizable number of articles based on research, whether by practicing reference librarians, faculty and doctoral students at schools of library and information studies, or consultants and others.

Three important American journals specialize in reference services. The longest running (since 1960) has been *RQ* (now *Reference & User Services Quarterly*), the official journal of the Reference and User Services Association (RUSA) of the American Library Association, which carries articles based on research, along with columns that discuss trends, issues, and current practices in the various aspects of reference services. *Reference Services Review* began in 1972 and has been particularly important for its articles reviewing the information sources available on specific subjects on which library users are seeking assistance, as well as for its articles on technological developments and their applications to reference services. *The Reference Librarian* has been edited by Bill Katz since its beginning in 1981 and has had important theme issues and individual articles on every facet of reference services. Various specialties within reference work also have their periodicals, for example, *Research Strategies* for the bibliographic instruction community. The periodical literature on reference services is accessible through such indexes as *Library Literature*, *Library and Information Science Abstracts*, *Current Index to Journals in Education* (part of *ERIC*), and *Social Sciences Citation Index* (see Chapter 21).

Reference librarians share information about their work electronically, as well as in print. Most reference librarians have their favorite World Wide Web sites that list and provide links to useful sources to help answer reference questions. Many publishers and organizations offering services and information for reference librarians maintain Web sites; an example is RUSA, whose site includes links to those of its specialty sections (http://www.ala.org/rusa/). Listservs (e-mail discussion groups) are popular among reference librarians, and they exist for almost all of the specialties within the field, such as readers' advisory services or instruction. A listserv to which many reference librarians subscribe and which covers issues and concerns of general interest to the field is LIBREF-L (subscribe at listserv@listserv.kent.edu).

REFERENCE SERVICES: VARIETIES AND APPROACHES

Although reference services are changing in dramatic ways, their essence—the provision of assistance to individuals seeking information and ideas—remains stable. However, depending on the needs and goals of the individual, the reference librarian can take different approaches to the provision of assistance. For example, the user may need a fact, a piece of information, or a document to accomplish a task. Here the librarian's emphasis will be on the *information* and helping the user find it. Or, a user may have a longer term goal and wish to consult sources of information, ideas, or recreation on a more continuing basis, asking the librarian for advice on how to proceed. Here, the emphasis is on the user's need for *guidance* on how to find and use sources to meet an educational, recreational, or developmental goal. Sometimes the user is interested in knowing how the library or an information source works, to become more skilled or independent in finding information. Here, the librarian's approach is one of providing *instruction* in the use of libraries and information sources. In 1961 Samuel Rothstein called these basic approaches or emphases "the three primary colors in the reference work picture," and went on to say, "Almost every respectable library in the United States and Canada does some of each; almost no two libraries mix the colors in quite the same way."[7]

Information

Information services take a variety of forms, from the simple provision of an address or telephone number, to tracking down an elusive bibliographic citation, to the identification and delivery of documents about a specific topic. Although an increasing number of answers to information requests are retrievable by electronic means, information services in most settings still depend heavily on print tools for their effectiveness. The evaluation, selection, and maintenance of a collection of information sources suited to the information needs of the library's users, activities that are generally referred to as *collection development*, are discussed in Chapter 13.

Ready-Reference Questions

One of the most basic information services is answering *ready-reference questions*. A ready-reference question is considered to be one that can be answered quickly by consulting only one or two reference tools. It is generally a request for factual information, such as an address, the spelling or definition of a word, a date or place of an event, or something about the life or career of an individual. A ready-reference question could also be a request for brief information about an organization, such as a brief description of the organization's origin, purpose, and activities.

Ready-reference questions constitute the majority of questions received at most reference desks in public and academic libraries. The tools for answering these questions—both print and electronic—are quickly learned by the novice reference librarian, and providing answers to these questions soon becomes routine. In some libraries, two separate information service points are maintained: an *information desk* to handle ready-reference questions and a *reference desk* to deal with more difficult and time-consuming questions. Because ready-reference questions are such a major component of reference work, it is well to remember that each question, no matter how routine, is of importance to the user who asks it, and that meeting the information needs of each library user is the goal of an effective reference service. Also, experienced reference librarians know that questions that begin as ready-reference questions often evolve into more complex or detailed queries if even a simple reference interview is conducted (see Chapter 3).

Bibliographic Verification

Another frequently offered information service is *bibliographic verification*. This is similar to ready-reference, except that it provides facts about publications rather than about events, people, places, or organizations. Bibliographic verification typically requires the librarian to search the print or electronic versions of bibliographic tools, such as indexes, catalogs, bibliographies, and library and union catalogs (discussed in Chapters 5, 6, 20, and 21), to "verify" that the user's information about a document (i.e., a *bibliographic citation*) is correct and complete. The neophyte may well wonder why this is such an important part of reference work. The reason is that the habits of authors, publishers, students, researchers, and the general public often do not lead to the gathering of complete bibliographic citations. This problem is exacerbated by the vast number of information sources available via the Internet and the complexity of citing them appropriately. Unfortunately, publications such as newspapers and magazines, and even scholarly books and articles, do not always give complete information about the materials they discuss—complete enough to find those materials in a library, on the Internet, or at a bookstore. In addition, students working on assignments may not have written down complete or accurate information about the publication their teacher wants them to read, or the teacher may not have given them accurate information. Finally, because of the importance in the scholarly world of the "invisible college"—an informal network of colleagues with similar research interests—many citations are gathered by researchers in a context that does not always lead to their coming to the library with complete information. It becomes the librarian's job, in these situations, to try to find complete and accurate information, so that the user can gain access to the desired information source.

Bibliographic verification involves using what information is available to the librarian to find the missing information. This process can be much like putting together the pieces of a puzzle: Sometimes it is an interesting and enjoyable exercise, but, at other times, it can be very frustrating. Occasionally, the librarian will discover during the search that the information provided by the user was not only incomplete but inaccurate as well. At the end of the verification process, the user will generally have the information needed to locate the item in the library, obtain it on interlibrary loan, order it at a local bookstore, or access it electronically.

Interlibrary Loan and Document Delivery

Bibliographic verification often leads to an interlibrary loan request if it is determined that the library does not own the item needed by the user (see Chapter 7 for a full discussion of interlibrary lending). Interlibrary lending of materials has been practiced in libraries for many years. Because obtaining the document needed by the user is a logical extension of identifying that document (verification), interlibrary loan (ILL) has generally been regarded as a reference function, and it has often been handled by the library's reference department or by a separate department closely associated with the reference department. The ILL process itself includes an important reference function: The borrowing library must carefully verify the bibliographic information about the item requested before the request is forwarded.

The growth of electronic bibliographic utilities, such as OCLC, and cooperative networks among libraries (see Chapters 7 and 20) has made the interlibrary loan process faster and easier. Thirty years ago, most ILL transactions were manually verified and transmitted by mail. Today, however, when the borrowing and lending libraries both belong to such an electronic network, the borrowing library may be able both to verify the citation and place the ILL request electronically. When using a bibliographic utility or network to request a book, the cataloging record already in the network serves as verification (journal articles, of course, do not normally have cataloging records, so they still must be separately verified). Also, the request is transmitted instantly, and, as a result, the library user should receive the material faster. Even if the borrowing and lending libraries do not belong to the same network, electronic resources can be used to speed the transaction. If only the borrowing library belongs to a bibliographic utility, the necessary verification can be conducted electronically, a process that is generally faster than manual verification using print tools. If the two libraries both have access to an electronic mail system, the ILL request can be transmitted instantly. The increasing availability of telefacsimile devices (fax machines) and scanners to "convert" print materials into computer-readable form has made the transmission and receipt of materials requested via interlibrary loan much more rapid than had been the case before.

An alternative to the lending or transmission of materials between libraries is for the user (or the library on the user's behalf) to order periodical articles or other documents from a growing number of document delivery services, whether commercial or cooperative ventures among libraries. These services have access to large files of periodicals (and sometimes other documents), increasingly in electronic format, from which they can supply ordered items quickly. Sometimes these services are connected with electronic indexes, so that the user can order at the touch of a function key an article found in a search using the index. In such an environment, planning information services to users involves assessing costs and benefits of the library's paying for such services, requiring the user to pay for them, or using more "traditional" means of obtaining materials not owned by the library.[8]

The availability of published materials in electronic formats is completely changing what used to be called interlibrary loan. More and more publications, especially periodicals, are being published electronically. Also, groups of libraries and commercial producers of information sources are building large-scale collections of previously published materials that have been converted to electronic form. Libraries are increasingly substituting access to such electronic publications and collections for traditional purchase and subscriptions, often involving complex financial arrangements with commercial and library cooperative enterprises. Helping users get their hands on publications that are not physically in the library is no longer simply a matter of identifying the most appropriate library from which to borrow the material and initiating an interlibrary loan request. Rather, it involves verifying the bibliographic details as accurately as possible, identifying what might be numerous locations of the publication in a vast web of commercial and other sources, assessing costs (including time and effort) to the library and the users of accessing the publication at its various locations, and assisting users in making wise choices and effectively using the required technology to obtain and use the publication to serve their needs.[9]

Information and Referral Services

Just as reference librarians can identify resources in other libraries that can be borrowed for the user, they can also identify community resources and agencies that can provide the user with needed services. In the late 1960s and 1970s, the concept of an information and referral (I & R) service developed in a number of public libraries. As defined by Thomas Childers, I & R has as its goal "facilitating the link between a person with a need and the resource or resources outside the library which can meet the need."[10] Outside resources may include social service agencies, community organizations, government offices, or individuals. To support an I & R service, a library generally maintains a *resource file,* a current list of service agencies and information pertinent to them. This file may be a manual file or a locally produced database accessed by a computer. It is the major information tool that the reference librarian consults to refer users to the outside agencies that can assist them further (see Box 1.2).

Box 1.2 The Public Library as Information Center

There is an obvious need for some institution to be responsible for supplying information that will guide the public through the maze of government and private service agencies spawned by our complex society. Not knowing where to start in their search for information or direct assistance, all too commonly, people are shunted around from one waiting line or telephone number to another. Many become too discouraged to continue what seems like a futile pursuit. Whenever I & R service is introduced in public libraries, it proves to be extremely helpful and is invariably used extensively.

The public library has the capability of serving as the first-stop center for all information needs. Not only can it lend books, it can expand its reference service to link people to the information or practical assistance they need wherever the source exists, in or out of the library. The demonstrated need for this service, together with a growing recognition of the public library's broader information capability, are inspiring increasing numbers of public libraries to consider utilizing traditional professional skills to "index the community."

Clara Stanton Jones
"The Public Library as the Comprehensive Community Information Center"[11]

There are two basic levels or types of I & R services: those that only provide information about agencies and those that provide information and make direct referrals to agencies. Those that provide an agency name, address, and telephone number to the user, along with some information about the agency, are the easiest for a library to set up and maintain; however, the librarian does not know if the referral was or was not successful. I & R services that actually contact the agency to verify that it can and will assist the individual require much more time and effort in organizing material, training staff, and coordinating service with local agencies. However, the success rate of referrals using this approach—and, therefore, the effectiveness of this reference service—can be much higher in a service of this kind.[12] A national survey by Childers in the late 1970s found that most public libraries that offer I & R services provide information only, rather than actual referrals, although many libraries did acknowledge giving advice along with information about local agencies.[13]

Computer networks and the World Wide Web are powerful tools for bringing individuals together with social service agencies to meet their needs. Increasingly, libraries are participating in community efforts to enhance the development and use of these tools. Often called *community networks* or *freenets,* these collaborative efforts can add new dimensions to I & R services. Reference librarians can play a variety of roles in the development and operation of community networks, from initiating the planning, to providing technical knowledge and skills, to providing operational support. At the least, reference librarians should help their users gain access to and effectively use the resources of the community network to accomplish their goals.[14]

Research Questions

Both ready-reference and bibliographic verification interactions may evolve into yet another major information service, the provision of research assistance. This service, when compared to answering ready-reference questions, may require considerably more time and effort from the librarian. The user's information need is broader and/or the question asked is more complex or less concretely defined. Several sources may need to be checked before the complete answer is found. It may not even be immediately apparent to the librarian which type of information source is likely to contain the needed information. In this case, an intermediary source, such as a guide or index to information sources, must be consulted to obtain a list of likely sources.

The librarian must, when providing research assistance, carefully review the question with the user to ensure that the question is completely understood by both parties. This interactive process, called the reference interview, is described at length in Chapter 3. The reference interview is necessary to clarify many reference questions, because the user's information need may be broader than the user initially realizes. Or, the need may be of sufficient complexity that the librarian must ask a series of questions about it before understanding it enough to begin thinking of appropriate sources to search. As the search progresses, both the question and possible answers are further discussed. The conscientious librarian ensures that the user is completely satisfied with the information provided before ending the interaction.

Often, during a reference transaction of this nature, either the librarian or the user must interrupt the search process to attend to other activities. The handling of this situation depends to some degree upon the service policies of the individual library. The librarian may work further on the question as time permits and call or e-mail the questioner with the answer at a later time. If the user has more time but the librarian does not, the librarian may advise or instruct the user how to continue the search. This latter scenario is most likely in an academic or school library, but may occur also in a public library. In special libraries, it is generally assumed that the librarian will continue the search and deliver the information as soon as possible.

Fee-Based Services and Information Brokering

Some library users have needs for research and information assistance that require more time than can normally be provided by the reference librarian, at least without unduly taking time and resources away from other users. This leaves libraries with a dilemma: Either they serve these users, accepting the real or potential inequity to other users that such "extra" service entails, or they deny them valuable and needed service that could be provided from the information sources and staff of the library and that may not be available elsewhere. One response to this dilemma has been for libraries to establish fee-based services, so that those who need special research assistance can get it, while the library gains additional financial resources to overcome the potential inequities of providing in-depth assistance to some users.

Found in both public and academic libraries, most fee-based services in libraries serve the information needs of businesses, professionals, and other users who are willing to pay for extraordinary services. These include extensive database searching, document delivery, compiling bibliographies, expert consultation, and other such services. Fee-based operations in libraries range from separate units that handle thousands of transactions per year to infrequent services with no separate identity. Some of the units are supported entirely by funds generated from users, while others are expected to recover only direct staff costs.[15]

Fee-based information services can be exciting and challenging for reference librarians. Working on in-depth questions, without fearing that taking "extra" time will deprive the next user in line of help, and perhaps incurring charges (e.g., for long-distance telephone calls or use of expensive information sources) that the library could not afford to offer to all users can be very satisfying. On the other hand, the existence of such a service in a general library can raise complex questions of policy and practice, such as when to provide "free" service and when to charge, or how to work through potential conflict-of-interest issues involved in having a fee-based service within a library that is publicly supported and that is expected by the general public to provide its services without fees. Also, there is concern that library funders will come to see fee-based services as a "quick fix" for tight library finances.[16]

Services that are similar to fee-based services in libraries are offered by individuals and firms in the private, for-profit sector, as well. A common term for providers of such services is *information brokers*. These firms and "freelance" individuals recognize that businesses, professionals, and others consider information and information services so valuable that they will pay for them. Information broker operations range in size from one person, with billings in the hundreds of dollars per year, to large firms, with many employees and annual billings in the hundreds of thousands of dollars. Information brokers provide services similar to those provided by fee-based library services, including extensive searches of print and electronic information sources, compiling bibliographies, procurement and delivery of documents, consultation services, trademark and patent research, organization of files, building and maintaining company library or information services, and selective dissemination of information services (discussed later in this chapter).[17] Providing reference services through an information broker can be a satisfying "alternative" career for reference librarians.

Guidance

Some users consult reference librarians for assistance in finding information or materials relevant to a continuing interest, such as preparing to change jobs, facing retirement, carrying out a research project, or enjoying recreational reading. To provide such assistance, reference librarians take a somewhat different approach than that used to answer a factual reference question, an approach often called *guidance*. To provide effective guidance, the reference librarian usually needs to find out more about the user's interests, goals, and background than is typically necessary in answering reference questions. Also, rather than helping find an answer to a question, the librarian will assist the user in a process of finding a variety of sources and choosing among them, sometimes maintaining contact throughout the project or reading program.

The guidance approach to reference service, though not as often discussed in the literature of librarianship as the information and instruction approaches are, has just as long a history. During the first half of the twentieth century, it was prominently represented in public libraries in the form of readers' advisory services. Although such services have been less visible in recent years, the guidance function is still important in libraries in such forms as bibliotherapy and selective dissemination of information services in special libraries and term-paper counseling in school and academic libraries.

Readers' Advisory Services

It could be argued that readers' advisory services most clearly reflect the goals of the late nineteenth-century librarians who developed the concept of personal assistance to readers. Samuel Green, whose 1876 article was mentioned previously in this chapter, placed great emphasis on helping readers choose the books best suited to their interests, needs, and reading level.[18] The need for such a service was gradually recognized in public libraries. Although the first readers' advisory department was not established until 1923 (in the Chicago Public Library), there was a clear precursor of this service as early as 1885, when the St. Louis Public Library created the position of "library hostess."[19]

The classic readers' advisor interviewed library users to understand their needs and goals, then chose library materials that would fulfill those needs and goals. In many cases, a formal reading list was prepared for the user. Today, readers' advisors also sometimes provide current awareness services and library-use instruction to assist readers in using the library and keeping aware of new books in their fields of interest.[20] Readers' advisory services proliferated rapidly in the 1920s, had their "golden age" in the 1930s, declined in the 1940s, and all but disappeared in the 1950s, their essential functions taken over by general reference librarians or subject specialists.[21] In many libraries, because one-on-one readers' advisory service is so staff-intensive, bibliographies and resource lists on topics of common interest have been used to provide some guidance to users, while holding staff costs to a minimum.

Within the last decade or so, there has been renewed recognition of the importance of readers' advisory services. Numerous authors have argued that this approach can help the library reach important segments of its population and provide important service to its community.[22] Public libraries are establishing visible programs of readers' advisory service, and librarians with interests in this type of service are forming discussion and action groups within professional associations. Some librarians and libraries identify readers' advisory services almost exclusively with helping readers choose fiction for recreational reading.[23] However, helping users find useful materials to address problems and issues in their lives, continuing educational goals, or other nonfiction reading interests is still an important and satisfying service for reference librarians to provide. Youth services librarians find this a particularly good approach to helping young people find their way through their developmental stages or other changes in their lives. With so much information on current issues available from so many sources, including the Internet, today's readers' advisors face the challenge of helping users develop strategies for finding, evaluating, and using print and electronic resources, within the library and beyond, to achieve their goals.

Whether working with children or adults, fiction or nonfiction, books or World Wide Web sites, it is important that the readers' advisor keep the user's freedom of choice and privacy uppermost in mind. It is all too easy for librarians to assume that they know what is best for users and to impose their standards and values on the users' choice of resources. Reference librarians need to remind themselves frequently that each user's unique goals are the important ones and to help users in such a way that a variety of resources are discovered, leaving users free to choose among them, based on their own values and standards. Because users often ask the reference librarian for assistance in addressing issues that are considered sensitive, or even embarrassing, it is especially important in the guidance approach to honor the principles of privacy and confidentiality that are ethical standards in all reference services.[24] These issues are discussed further in Chapter 2.

Bibliotherapy

Bibliotherapy is a more specialized form of guidance, related in its goals to readers' advisory work but generally practiced in a group. Although not, strictly speaking, a reference service, it has been practiced alongside traditional reference services and readers' advisory services in programs such as the Counselor Librarianship Project at the Chicago campus of the University of Illinois in 1951.[25] Originally, bibliotherapy involved using directed reading to aid in a physical or emotional healing process. Today, bibliotherapists use literature, film, or other media, chosen for their appropriateness to the needs of the group, to assist the personal growth and/or rehabilitation of group members through discussion of the material read or viewed.

Practitioners have distinguished two primary types of bibliotherapy, clinical and developmental.[26] *Clinical bibliotherapy* is used by doctors and hospital librarians with persons with emotional or behavioral problems to encourage self-understanding or behavioral change. *Developmental bibliotherapy* is used with a wide variety of individuals in schools or in public libraries to promote self-knowledge, personal growth, and the successful completion of "developmental tasks" associated with various life stages. Clara Lack, who has practiced bibliotherapy in both a hospital and a public library setting, encourages public libraries to adapt the techniques of developmental bibliotherapy and create "readers' discussion groups" in which literature can be used as a basis for examining both individual and societal values and goals.[27] Although bibliotherapy requires specialized training and is not widely practiced, continuing interest in its techniques and goals is demonstrated in articles such as those by Arleen Hynes and Alice Smith.[28]

Term-Paper Counseling

Another form of guidance is *term-paper counseling* (sometimes called term-paper assistance or research consultation). Although generally discussed in the literature as a form of instruction, it is treated here as a guidance service because of its parallels to the readers' advisory services formerly offered extensively in public libraries. Term-paper counseling, like the readers' advisory service, is usually offered at a location other than the reference desk, where the librarian can spend more time guiding each student on an individual basis. Consumers of term-paper assistance approach the term-paper counseling desk or office on their own initiative to seek assistance in reaching a specific goal attainable primarily through the use of library materials (in this case, the completion of a research paper). The librarian considers each student's needs, assesses the student's understanding of library use and search strategies, and provides individualized guidance regarding which library tools should be consulted to find appropriate sources of information on the student's topic. The librarian will probably write down or print out a list of reference sources to be checked, much as the readers' advisor would compile a list of suggested readings on a topic.

Term-paper counseling programs are widespread in academic and school libraries. Some are offered throughout the school year, while others are offered only at the peak term-paper-writing times of each term. Either way, these programs offer a level of flexibility and individualized attention that is not usually available either at the reference desk or in group instructional programs.[29] *Term-paper clinics*, which consist of group instruction in library-use and research skills, may be offered in addition to or instead of the individual assistance provided in term-paper counseling sessions.[30]

Selective Dissemination of Information

Sometimes, reference librarians note newly received materials that they think would be of interest to individual users and let the users know of their availability. This is usually done informally and is a part of the readers' advisory relationship with users. A more formal or organized version of this kind of continuing contact between the reference librarian and the user is *selective dissemination of information* (SDI), a customized reference service offered most frequently to researchers by academic or special libraries. As in other guidance services, the librarian works closely with the potential user of SDI to ascertain his or her ongoing information need, typically associated with a research project. Then the librarian constructs a "profile" of this need, often consisting of subject terms that will be used to search indexes and other databases. This interest profile is matched against newly published or received information sources, or indexes to them, on some periodic basis (usually through the use of computer technology) and the user is notified of the results. Depending on the nature and funding of the service, the librarian can deliver to the user only the citations to materials, leaving the user to request or find desired articles, or the librarian can deliver the articles themselves.

SDI is sometimes called a *current awareness service*, because it is designed to keep users aware of current developments in their fields. Another popular current awareness service is providing to users copies of the tables of contents from journals, selected according to a profile of interests similar to that used in SDI. This allows users to stay current regarding what has appeared in journals of interest, without having to acquire and peruse the issues themselves.

Instruction

Some people who need to use information and ideas want to learn how libraries and information sources work, so that they can find and use resources independently. The reference librarian's response to this need is the *instruction* approach, which is discussed fully in Chapter 8. Instruction is a major component of reference service in academic and school libraries, is an important aspect of reference work in most public libraries, and can be found in varying degrees in different kinds of special libraries. Instruction is conducted with individual library users and also with groups of users. Depending on the library staff's assessment of user needs, the goals of instruction can range from simply orienting users to the library and its services, to helping users understand and use specific information resources, to teaching users how to find, evaluate, and use information sources in the library and beyond, as lifelong skills.

Some reference librarians have viewed instruction as a less desirable alternative to information services, feeling that users would generally prefer being helped to find information, rather than being taught how to find it themselves. In fact, sometimes reference librarians do feel forced to this alternative, for instance, with class research assignments, when the number of students seeking information exceeds the reference staff's ability to work on each question individually. However, instruction is now increasingly viewed in a broader context, in which it is complementary to information services. The sources of information in our society, both print and electronic, are rapidly growing in number and complexity. Users who are unaware of the existence, content, and organization of these sources may never know the extent of available information about a topic of interest to them. Some people prefer to find information for themselves, without being dependent on someone else for such an important and personal aspect of their lives. A policy statement adopted by the Council of the American Library Association in 1980 states that "it is essential that libraries of all types accept the responsibility of providing people with opportunities to understand the organization of information." The statement goes on to urge all libraries "to include instruction in the use of libraries as one of the primary goals of service."[31]

One-to-One Instruction

Helping an individual understand the organization and use of the library's collection is the oldest and still most commonly practiced form of instruction. It usually evolves naturally out of a reference interview, particularly in cases where the person is using the library for the first time or is conducting research that requires the use of unfamiliar reference tools. In the first case, the librarian typically explains the organization of the library and how to use the catalog that provides access to its collection. When instructing in the use of a reference tool, the librarian must inform the user about the organization and scope of the tool and explain how best to access the relevant information in it. This is best taught by example: The librarian demonstrates the use of the tool by finding relevant citations or data and makes sure the user understands the process well enough to continue the search or to conduct a similar search later.

Increasingly, one-to-one instruction involves helping users learn how to search electronic sources, such as the library's online catalog, a database at an electronic workstation, or the Internet. Although these electronic sources may be designed to be user-friendly, there are inevitable ambiguities or questions that cannot be answered by either online or printed aids (which, in any case, many users do not consult). Again, demonstrating a successful search is a more effective teaching technique than merely telling the user how to conduct one.

As is pointed out in Chapter 8, one-to-one instruction can now be accomplished effectively at a computer terminal, as well as in person. Computer programs can provide physical orientation to the library and instruction in the use of important library resources. Guides and "road maps" to specific types of information can also be stored in a computer's memory, from which they can be downloaded and/or printed out by users, either inside the library or at a remote location.

Group Instruction

In situations where a number of individuals are new to a community, whether that community be a city, an academic institution, or a private or public organization, it is most efficient to introduce these individuals to the library in a group, rather than one by one. Hence the popularity of the *library tour* or *orientation program.* It is important that new users learn the locations of important library units and equipment, and that, if possible, they meet the reference staff who are there to serve their information needs. Although printed guides, computer programs, and audio or video presentations can all add significant information to a library orientation, the "human touch" provided by a personal tour is the most effective way to welcome people to the library and encourage them to contact the librarian for assistance in the future.

In school and academic settings, librarians, working with teachers, often speak to all the students in a specific class who will be using the library for a research assignment. At its most basic level, *course-related* instruction, this talk may consist of a tour of the library, along with an introduction to reference sources in the subject areas covered by the course and suggestions as to their effective use in research. When teacher and librarian work together in designing the library-use activities of a course, a higher level of instruction, *course-integrated* instruction, can result. Here, the library instruction becomes a required part of the assignment, and the librarian acts more as a teacher—discussing the assignment, suggesting strategies for meeting the objectives of the assignment, and discussing reference sources as tools to be used in meeting those objectives.[32] Although course-related instruction is valuable and is still widely practiced, whenever possible, instruction librarians are moving away from talking about information sources as ends in themselves and toward "a problem-based approach to information gathering" in which sources "serve a secondary role . . . as examples of items useful to patrons in the search for information."[33] This kind of discussion is facilitated by course-integrated instruction, in which the librarian's expertise is recognized by both teacher and students as an essential component of the course.

Newer forms of group instruction have emerged in recent years. One example is workshops for faculty members to teach them concepts and methods of electronic database searching or to help them learn how to use the World Wide Web as a teaching tool.[34] Many colleges and universities also offer instruction, either for a group or one-to-one, to remote users (those who access the library and its resources from their homes or offices using electronic technology). Programs such as this are likely to increase in number, as more sources of information are accessible to users outside the confines of the library building. Instruction librarians are making more and more use of technology in their teaching, including sophisticated computer software and classrooms with the latest equipment to enhance instruction to students in the classroom or at remote locations.[35]

SOME CURRENT TRENDS AND ISSUES

Librarianship is a vibrant profession, constantly changing in response to new societal and technological developments. Reference librarians care deeply about providing services of a high quality, services that meet the information needs of their users and are perceived by the users as satisfying those needs. How best to achieve these objectives in a rapidly changing environment, with limited personnel and financial resources, is not always clear. Thus, reference librarians, like all professionals, have differing opinions about how their work should be conducted. These differences are reflected in the published literature of librarianship. This section introduces some recent trends and issues in reference services and discusses some of the concepts and strategies that librarians have developed to address these issues.

Library Systems and Networks

Reference work has been enriched in recent years by the growth of state, regional, and local library consortia and systems, by the development of local electronic community information networks, and by the creation of electronic cataloging utilities at the national level. These new networks have made it easier to locate needed sources in other libraries, and the electronic utilities in particular are very useful for bibliographic verification questions. Most recently, the ever-expanding kinds and amounts of information on the Internet have provided reference librarians with new options in their search for the information needed by users.

Library consortia and systems represent attempts by all kinds of libraries to improve their services to their users through cooperative activities in collection development, reference service, and document delivery. Reference service within this context is sometimes called *cooperative reference service* (see Box 1.3).[36] Very important to this process has been the growth of state and regional systems. The characteristics of these systems vary from one state to another. In some cases, membership is restricted to libraries of one type (e.g., public or academic libraries), but inclusion of all types of libraries is increasingly common. Whatever their composition, the intent is to make the entire world of information resources, in libraries and beyond, available to the users of any library in the system.[37]

Box 1.3 Cooperative Reference Service

Cooperative reference service extends a library's information service capability through interaction with other libraries or information centers. It is a process through which information assistance is provided, at least in part, by referring the user or the user's question to library/information personnel at another institution according to a system of formally established protocols.

Coöperative Reference Service Committee,
American Library Association[38]

Participation in cooperative reference arrangements makes the job of reference librarians both easier and harder. On the one hand, they are not restricted to the library's collection alone but can tap information resources in other local libraries, in libraries throughout the state, or across the entire Internet to help a user answer a question or fill a need for information and ideas. On the other hand, having the world of information sources available can make the reference interview more complex, exploring, for example, the user's willingness to wait for resources from another library, readiness to travel to a cooperating library to consult sources, or ability to use electronic equipment to access remote information sources. Reference librarians need to maintain some familiarity with and "command" of a wider range of information sources than is true of service based on the local library alone. Some reference librarians find it hard to "let go" of a reference question and refer it to another source, and some worry that having to turn to an "outside" source will reflect poorly on the local library, resulting in decreased respect or support by taxpayers or funders. Providing reference services through systems and networks can raise complex policy issues, such as how much service can be provided to users of other libraries without compromising service to one's primary user group. Most reference librarians would agree, though, that the increased quality of service brought to users by library systems and networks more than compensates for the challenges and complexities they also bring.

Electronic Reference Services

Many of the benefits of library systems and networks are due to the power and speed of electronic computer and communication technologies. Certainly, these technologies have revolutionized access to information in libraries of all kinds and sizes. The use of computer workstations to search the library's catalog and other databases obviates the need for users to search numerous card catalog drawers or annual volumes of periodical indexes in print format. The results of the search can be printed, saving users the drudgery of writing out each citation they wish to pursue. Increasingly, the catalog workstation, or another one nearby, can be used to access the vast amount of information available through the Internet. Some libraries receive and answer reference questions via e-mail and find other ways to serve users who cannot or do not wish to come to the library. These and many other developments and services are treated in depth in Chapters 5 and 6, so they are mentioned here only in the context of other trends and issues.

The continuing development of electronic reference services is having an impact on every facet of the reference librarian's work. The questions that users ask now include many that deal with how to operate the equipment and software systems that must be used to find information. The reference interview must often address users' unrealistic expectations of the Internet or their ability and willingness to use computer hardware and software. Perhaps the most dramatic impact of electronic developments is a vast increase in the number and types of information sources that are readily available to reference librarians and their users to address their needs. The many alternatives that exist for accessing information, along with the variety of financial arrangements that accompany them, make reference collection development increasingly complex.

Many reference librarians have found that working in this environment is very satisfying and that it has boosted their professional standing with their users and with other members of their communities. They answer a wide variety of questions faster and more easily than was the case previously. They participate as experts in complex decision making on computer systems and networking arrangements with administrative and governing officials in their institutions or cities. Their instructional programs help users learn how to thrive in the information age. On the other hand, the electronic environment also brings challenges to the reference librarian, especially the burden of gaining and maintaining an ever-widening range of skills and knowledge. The necessity of knowing and being able to use print sources does not diminish with the need to be knowledgeable and skillful with the almost limitless number of electronic sources that can be accessed with the stroke of the right computer keys. Helping users realize the importance of using the appropriate balance of electronic and "traditional" print sources can take special reference interview skills. The perception held by many users that "everything is available free on the Internet" makes gaining sufficient financial support for access to expensive databases all the more difficult. However, most reference librarians would agree that the benefits of electronic reference work are far greater than the challenges and problems it brings, and (at least most of the time) they look forward to working with new developments in this fast-moving environment.

Box 1.4 Reference Service Yesterday and Today

Comparing past and present reference practices can be both interesting and informative. One way to do this is to browse a reference services textbook from an earlier era and compare it to this text. A good choice might be Margaret Hutchins's *Introduction to Reference Work*, published in 1944.[39] Another valuable exercise is to think back to your childhood experiences in libraries. Do you remember times when a librarian in your school or public library assisted you in finding information or in using the library?

Based on these exercises, how do you feel reference work has changed in the past twenty years, or in the past fifty years? How has it remained essentially the same?

Stress and Burnout

Working with the public can be stressful, no matter in what profession or context, and reference librarians are not immune to the debilitating effect that such stress can have. Whether it is the feeling that the more one knows, the more one should know, or the feeling that limited time and resources do not allow one to provide satisfying public service, or being told that the World Wide Web makes reference librarians unnecessary, the reference librarian's psychological and physiological response to such perceptions can be painful and sapping of energy and enthusiasm.[40] Most of the time, most reference librarians find effective ways to cope with stress. However, sometimes the coping strategies chosen are ineffective and even contribute more stress, in a sort of "vicious circle." When this happens to a reference librarian, he or she is suffering from *burnout*. Box 1.5 describes some of the conditions that can contribute to burnout.

Box 1.5 The Downside of the New Technologies

(A) two-hour reference desk assignment may require an even longer time to recuperate due to the technostress and exhaustion caused by the demands of library patrons. With added technological developments, the orientation and instruction of individual library patrons have become tasks that require increasing amounts of time. . . . Understanding technology, searching skills, familiarity with online databases and CD-ROM products are all requirements for today's librarians. . . . The librarian must possess a split personality, adopting the machine's values when interacting with a computer and being what often seems the reverse when interacting with people.

Samuel T. Huang
"The Impact of New Library Technology on Reference Services"[41]

Many strategies for managing stress and avoiding burnout are suggested in the literature. Library and reference managers can assist by offering reference librarians options such as job sharing and job exchange and by encouraging librarians to undertake new and different assignments periodically to assure that their jobs do not become too routine or lacking in challenge. The training and development techniques described in Chapter 9 are designed to support employees and feed their self-esteem and self-confidence. The reference manager can also attempt to keep reference desk hours at a reasonable level, so that staff are not burned out by excessive contact with the public. The manager can also ensure that the reference service policy statement for the department recognizes reasonable limits to the service that reference librarians are expected to provide.

These methods depend on the concern and flexibility of the organization. Individuals also have the ability to heal themselves and to aid in maintaining the professional health of their colleagues. They can develop support systems with colleagues and avoid becoming overextended by learning to decline jobs and to give up overly demanding job responsibilities. They can also free themselves of timetables that are too rigid and from the trap of trying to live up to someone else's expectations. They can exercise regularly to dissipate job tensions and attend workshops and conferences to expand their professional contacts and exchange information and ideas.[42]

As Tina Roose has pointed out, those who are burned out were once on fire with enthusiasm and joy in their jobs.[43] Avoiding burnout requires thinking carefully and positively about oneself and one's work, avoiding excessive commitments while doing one's best to achieve reasonable yet challenging goals. Sharing both one's excitement and one's frustrations with trusted colleagues and maintaining an objective interest in serving the needs of users, while continually learning new ways to serve those needs, can help one stay on the course of job satisfaction and professional growth.

Staffing the Reference Desk

Many librarians (especially reference librarians) consider reference work to be the most complex and "professional" work in the library. They argue that "only professionally trained staff (1) can recognize the varying levels of need that clients bring to the desk, (2) can conduct the reference interview that is so often necessary to understand the real need behind the query as stated, and (3) can answer the complex questions that can come to the desk anytime it is open."[44] Such considerations have led many libraries to staff their reference desks exclusively with professionally trained reference librarians.

The widening range of duties at the reference desk that increasing computerization has brought (e.g., "troubleshooting" equipment and software problems), along with budget pressures, has brought scrutiny of the "conventional wisdom" that the reference desk should be staffed with only professional reference librarians. This approach can entail inflexible and inefficient use of staff resources, requiring highly skilled librarians to answer directional and simple reference questions, while important complex and high-level tasks are left undone, due to lack of staff time. A number of alternative staffing configurations for reference services are now being used in libraries of various types.[45]

The most common alternative staffing pattern is the use of paraprofessional or support staff at reference service points. Typically, paraprofessional staff are expected to handle directional questions and simple ready-reference questions, while referring more complex questions to professional staff. In the "tiered" arrangement, mentioned earlier in this chapter, the information desk is usually staffed by paraprofessionals, but general reference desks also often have some combination of professional and paraprofessional staff. Even though the use of paraprofessionals to staff reference service points is common now, issues such as appropriate limits on the questions they should answer, proper training, referral mechanisms, and supervision are still important and continue to be discussed in the literature.[46]

Another alternative to staffing reference services with only professional librarians is the use of specialists trained in other disciplines and technologies. At the support-staff or technical level, this might include the employment of a "technology assistant" at the reference desk to help users with such problems as booting computer workstations or making balky printers work. Some libraries have included subject specialists and computer specialists in their reference staffing arrangements.

Another reference staffing issue is whether certain "traditional" reference services should require staffing at all. As librarians study and analyze reference questions, they recognize that the information needs they reflect are recurring and repetitive. Perhaps the knowledge and skill required to respond to these needs (previously available only from reference librarians) might be encoded into computerized help systems and improved electronic interfaces for information sources. Such approaches in current use include computerized information kiosks, computer-assisted self-service instruction, self-guided building tours, and improved signage and maps.[47]

Evaluation and Performance Appraisal

Whether provided by professional reference librarians or paraprofessionals, face-to-face or indirectly, it is important that reference services respond quickly and accurately to the real information needs of its users. Evaluating reference services and the performance of the staff members who provide it is a very important current concern of reference librarians and managers. Evaluators have developed a variety of methods to collect and analyze data on various aspects of reference services, and a sizable body of literature has been generated reporting on the results. The most frequently evaluated elements of reference services have been instruction (see Chapter 8), the reference collection, and question-answering effectiveness (see Chapter 10).

Two of the most important issues in reference evaluation are the sources of data for evaluating question-answering effectiveness and methods of collecting the data. The use of the *unobtrusive* method, which involves having surveyors who pretend to be users ask questions of the reference staff and record data on the results (without the knowledge of the staff members involved), has generated considerable interest and even controversy.[48] A number of these studies have found that reference librarians seem to answer completely and accurately only some 50 to 60 percent of the questions they are asked. These findings have resulted in the so-called 55 percent rule, which some reference librarians and others have called into question.[49] More recent studies and evaluation efforts have attempted to develop useful alternatives to the unobtrusive method and to use the results of evaluation studies of all kinds to make changes and to improve services.[50]

Because most reference activity does not automatically result in records and data that can be used to measure the productivity or effectiveness of staff (as, for example, circulation or cataloging activities do), performance appraisal of reference staff is especially difficult. This problem has been exacerbated by a lack of agreement concerning what makes a good reference librarian and good performance by reference staff. Recent literature has taken two interrelated approaches to address these problems. First, there has been increasing recognition that emphasis should be placed on observable behaviors that have been shown to be associated with effective service (rather than on personality and other characteristics or traits that, even if possessed, may or may not lead to effective service). The reference community has developed guidelines regarding behaviors that seem to be essential or important for good service and has recommended their use in performance appraisal.[51] Second, reference librarians' peers and colleagues are thought to be an important source of data on the degree to which they consistently use these behaviors in providing service. Although it is not without problems and cannot be considered a panacea, *peer performance appraisal* is used successfully in a number of reference departments.[52]

Regardless of the method used to gather data, or of the findings, evaluation and performance appraisal will not be worth the time they take if the results are not analyzed and interpreted carefully, with the goal of improving service to users. Frequently, changes indicated include strengthening reference collections and facilitating ease of access to information, improving staff sensitivities and skills in communicating with users, and improvements in the overall reference environment. Of course, both the starting and ending points for evaluation and improvement should be the information needs of users and their perceptions of how well those needs are being met by reference services.

THE FUTURE OF REFERENCE SERVICES

What is the future of reference work? With all the information easily available from the Internet, from the mass media, from comfortable and well-stocked bookstores, will those seeking information still need personal assistance from reference librarians? Is reference librarianship a good career choice for the future? This topic is the subject of much discussion in the literature, and it might be useful to close this chapter with a brief summary of some of this discussion.

In large part, the future of reference services will depend on the future of libraries. There are those who argue that the wide and easy availability of information, especially on the Internet, will make libraries unnecessary and a poor investment for municipalities, educational institutions, and business enterprises. Certainly, modern communications have lessened the need for people to come to the library building for answers to questions and other services. However, the last half of the 1990s saw increasing agreement that the vast amount of essentially unorganized information on the Internet is just one more reason for the continuing need for libraries and librarians to organize and provide access to information, to help users find it, and to help them learn the critical thinking and information use skills that will be essential to survival in the increasingly complex information environment.[53]

Even if libraries continue to exist and develop, some people argue, they will provide access to information in very different ways from those of the past. The library's catalog will be easier to use and will have many more access points and self-help devices, obviating the need for the human assistance that was so necessary with the inflexible and complicated card catalog of the past. Reference tools will be user-friendly electronic sources, and access to a huge array of information sources outside the library will be enhanced by easy-to-use electronic interfaces that will require little or no human mediation. The role of the librarian, the argument goes, will become one of designing and "engineering" these interfaces and help systems, rather than personally helping users.[54] Indeed, some argue, the provision of personal assistance or reference service by a library will be an admission of failure to put appropriate emphasis on self-help and may even perpetuate such "inefficiencies."[55]

On the other hand, increasing experience with electronic information sources, including those on the Internet, has demonstrated to reference librarians and others that it is probably in the nature of complex information tools and systems that they will always develop faster than will self-help components and interfaces, making the personal assistance of experts necessary for the full use of the newest and most powerful information sources (and making the attempt to design a library where no human assistance is needed somewhat futile). Libraries and society at large are investing huge sums of money in the creation and provision of access to information sources. The provision of expert personal assistance to help users overcome the various barriers that exist to finding and using these sources effectively can add value to these sources by getting them used to increase the productivity and well-being of their users.[56] Feeling somewhat beleaguered by predictions of their eventual demise, reference librarians have been pleased to see articles outside of their own literature pointing out that the skills that reference librarians have for helping people articulate and focus their information needs, as well as skills in identifying, evaluating, and manipulating information sources to serve a particular information need, will continue to be needed in the foreseeable future.[57] One of these articles sums it up nicely: "The most critical and underestimated advantage librarians bring to bear is the most obvious—the human touch."[58]

But what will reference services look like in the future? In their basic elements, probably much like in the past. However, as discussions above on current issues and trends have intimated, there will be changes. Surely, there will be less emphasis on the library and the reference desk as the physical locale for reference services, as these services are offered from multiple, perhaps differentiated service points and as users can obtain services via e-mail, Web sites, and other means. Certainly, the tools used by reference librarians and their clients to gain access to information will represent a different mix of media and technologies than has been the case up to now, with an increasing integration of technologies and use of networking and collaboration across administrative and professional lines that previously have been separate. Differentiated service points, work with ever-more-complex and sophisticated systems, and collaboration with a range of specialists from within and outside the library will bring more complex and differentiated staffing patterns to reference services than has been the case with the general reference desk. And most reference librarians agree that, to make these changes benefit those who need to find and use information and ideas, reference librarians must be in constant pursuit of accurate knowledge regarding their users' needs and their information-seeking and use behavior, so that they can design and deliver services that respond to these needs and behaviors.[59]

DEFINING REFERENCE SERVICE: A REPRISE

The beginning of this chapter presented a rather broad and simple definition of reference service. Since reading that definition, the reader has been provided with more detailed information regarding specific types of assistance reference librarians provide to library users, a diverse variety of activities that, following a widely accepted practice, have been viewed under the general headings of information, guidance, and instruction. In addition, the reader has been given some indication of the kinds of tools (traditional and futuristic) the reference librarian employs in providing that assistance. In light of the reader's new knowledge, perhaps the definitions in Box 1.6 will also be useful in the ongoing attempt of reference librarians to define what they do. The remainder of this text adds much more information and provides both discussions of specific methods and issues and illustrative examples of reference tools, to supplement the definition presented here.

Box 1.6 Other Definitions of Reference Service

The best reference service combines mediated searching, formal and informal instruction in information-seeking skills (using hard copy sources, nonprint media, and automated systems), and assistance in the use of reference sources. It includes lessons in analysis and evaluation of the value of the information retrieved and the accuracy or correctness of the method of retrieval.

Rosemarie Riechel
Reference Services for Children and Young Adults[60]

The vision that should guide reference service . . . is that reference service is a value-added service that is tailored to the unique needs of each individual client. This puts the client and responsive, individualized service to him or her at the center of the value system that guides hour-to-hour, day-to-day reference practice.

Charles A. Bunge
"Vision and Values: Touchstones in Times of Change"[61]

Our society is in constant flux, and the characteristics and needs of library users are constantly changing in response to these societal changes. The task for reference services, in the present and in the future, is to help users meet their needs, emphasizing such core values as respect for users in all their diversity and complexity, equity and equal access to information, intellectual freedom, and freedom of choice for users in using information and ideas to achieve their own goals. Librarians thus face both opportunities and challenges. They must constantly find new and better ways of providing appropriate information, guidance, and instruction to the users they serve. In a changing world, this is not easy, but it is the unchanging goal.

NOTES

1. "Guidelines for Information Services" (July 2000). Available: http://www.ala.org/rusa/stnd_consumer.html.

2. Samuel Swett Green, "Personal Relations Between Librarians and Readers," *American Library Journal* 1 (October 1876): 74-81.

3. Louis Kaplan, "The Early History of Reference Service in the United States," *Library Review* 83 (Autumn 1947): 286-90; Thomas J. Galvin, "Reference Services and Libraries," *Encyclopedia of Library and Information Science* (New York: Marcel Dekker, 1977), 25:211.

4. Galvin, "Reference Services and Libraries," 214.

5. Ibid., 215-16.

6. An interesting discussion of reference textbooks and guides to reference tools is contained in John V. Richardson, Jr., "Teaching General Reference Work," *The Library Quarterly* 62 (January 1992): 55-89.

7. Samuel Rothstein, "Reference Service: The New Dimension in Librarianship," *College & Research Libraries* 22 (January 1961): 13.

8. Bill Coons and Peter McDonald, "Implications of Commercial Document Delivery," *College & Research Libraries News* 56 (October 1995): 626-31.

9. John H. Barnes, "One Giant Leap, One Small Step: Continuing the Migration to Electronic Journals," *Library Trends* 45 (Winter 1997): 404-15; Stephen P. Harter and Hak Joon Kim, "Accessing Electronic Journals and Other E-publications: An Empirical Study," *College & Research Libraries* 57 (September 1996): 440-56.

10. Thomas Childers, *Information & Referral: Public Libraries* (Norwood, N.J.: Ablex, 1983), 1; *see also* Marcia S. Middleton and Bill Katz, "Information and Referral in Reference Services," *The Reference Librarian* 21 (1988): entire issue.

11. Clara Stanton Jones, "The Public Library as the Comprehensive Community Information Center," in *Public Librarianship: A Reader*, ed. Jane Robbins-Carter (Littleton, Colo.: Libraries Unlimited, 1982), 128.

12. Robert Croneberger et al., "The Library as a Community Information and Referral Center," in *Public Librarianship*, 479.

13. Thomas Childers, "Trends in Public Library I & R Service," *Library Journal* 104 (October 1, 1979): 2035-39.

14. Elaine G. Toms, "Free-Nets: Delivering Information to the Community," *Public Libraries* 32 (September/October 1993): 311-15; Karen G. Schneider, "Community Networks: New Frontier, Old Values," *American Libraries* 27 (January 1996): 96.

15. Steve Coffman and Helen Josephine, "Doing It for Money," *Library Journal* 116 (October 15, 1991): 32-36.

16. Wendy Smith, "Fee-Based Services: Are They Worth It?" *Library Journal* 111 (June 15, 1993): 40-43.

17. Janet Gotkin, ed., "Information Brokering," *Bulletin of the American Society for Information Science* 21 (February/March 1995): 7-22; Sue Rugge and Alfred Glossbrenner, *The Information Broker's Handbook*, 3d ed. (New York: McGraw-Hill, 1997), 579p.

18. Green, "Personal Relations," 74-81.

19. Rhea Joyce Rubin, "Guidance," in *The Service Imperative for Libraries: Essays in Honor of Margaret E. Monroe*, ed. Gail A. Schlachter (Littleton, Colo.: Libraries Unlimited, 1982), 95.

20. Ibid., 96-97.

21. Ibid., 98-99.

22. Catherine Sheldrick Ross, "Readers' Advisory Service: New Directions," *RQ* 30 (Summer 1991): 503-18; Kathleen de la Peña McCook and Gary O. Rolstad, eds., "Developing Readers' Advisory Services: Concepts and Commitments," *Collection Building* 12, no. 3-4 (1993): entire issue.

23. Joyce G. Saricks and Nancy Brown, *Readers' Advisory Service in the Public Library*, 2d ed. (Chicago: American Library Association, 1997), 160p.; Ted Balcom, ed., *Serving Readers* (Fort Atkinson, Wisc.: Highsmith Press, 1997), 121p.

24. Rubin, "Guidance," 111-13.

25. Clara Richardson Lack, "Can Bibliotherapy Go Public?" *Collection Building* 7 (Spring 1985): 28; Rubin, "Guidance," 108.

26. Lack, "Can Bibliotherapy Go Public?" 28; Rhea J. Rubin, "Uses of Bibliotherapy in Response to the 1970s," *Library Trends* 28 (Fall 1979): 242-45.

27. Lack, "Can Bibliotherapy Go Public?" 27.

28. Arleen McCarty Hynes, "Bibliotherapy—The Interactive Process," *Catholic Library World* 58 (1987): 167-70; Alice G. Smith, "Will the Real Bibliotherapist Please Stand Up?" *Journal of Youth Services in Libraries* 2 (Spring 1989): 241-49.

29. Kathleen Bergen and Barbara MacAdam, "One-on-One: Term Paper Assistance Programs," *RQ* 24 (Spring 1985): 333-35.

30. Callie B. McGinnis, "Columbus College's Term Paper Clinic: A Ten-Year Tradition," *The Georgia Librarian* 25 (Winter 1988): 188-90.

31. Quoted in Carolyn A. Kirkendall and Carla J. Stoffle, "Instruction," in *The Service Imperative for Libraries*, 42.

32. Concise descriptions of course-related and course-integrated instruction are provided in Anne F. Roberts and Susan G. Blandy, *Library Instruction for Librarians*, 2d rev. ed. (Englewood, Colo.: Libraries Unlimited, 1989), 69-70.

33. Francesca Allegri, "Course Integrated Instruction: Metamorphosis for the Twenty-First Century," *Medical Reference Services Quarterly* 4 (Winter 1985/1986): 59.

34. Elaine Jane and Patricia Vander Meer, "The Library's Role in Academic Instructional Use of the World Wide Web," *Research Strategies* 15, no. 3 (1997): 123-50.

35. Caroline Rowe, "Modern Library Instruction: Levels, Media, Trends, and Problems," *Research Strategies* 12 (Spring 1994): 4-17.

36. Carl F. Orgren, "Cooperative Reference Service," *The Reference Librarian* 43 (1994): 63-70.

37. Sarah A. Long, "Systems, Quo Vadis?" *Advances in Librarianship* 19 (1995): 117-58; descriptions of two statewide networks can be found in Barbara Smith, "Maryland's Information Retriever," *Wilson Library Bulletin* 68 (March 1994): 37-40; and Maribah Mansfield, "Ohio's OPLIN: The Future of Library Service?" *Library Journal* 122 (October 1, 1997): 44-47.

38. Quoted in Orgren, "Cooperative Reference Service," 64.

39. Margaret Hutchins, *Introduction to Reference Work* (Chicago: American Library Association, 1944), 214p.

40. Charles A. Bunge, "Stress and Burnout in the Library Workplace," *Encyclopedia of Library and Information Science* (New York: Marcel Dekker, 1992), 49:349-61.

41. Samuel T. Huang, "The Impact of New Library Technology on Reference Services," *Illinois Libraries* 72 (November 1990): 601-2.

42. David S. Ferriero and Kathleen A. Powers, "Burnout at the Reference Desk," *RQ* 21 (Spring 1982): 277.

43. Tina Roose, "Stress at the Reference Desk," *Library Journal* 114 (September 1, 1989): 167.

44. Chris D. Ferguson and Charles A. Bunge, "The Shape of Services to Come: Values-Based Reference Service for the Largely Digital Library," *College & Research Libraries* 58 (May 1997): 255.

45. William L. Whitson, "Differentiated Services: A New Reference Model," *Journal of Academic Librarianship* 21 (March 1995): 103-10; Jackie Mardikian and Martin Kesselman, "Beyond the Reference Desk: Enhanced Reference Staffing for the Electronic Library," *Reference Services Review* 23 (Spring 1995): 21-28.

46. Chris Ferguson, "Reshaping Academic Library Reference Service: A Review of Issues, Trends, and Possibilities," *Advances in Librarianship* 18 (1994): 73-109.

47. Ferguson and Bunge, "The Shape of Services to Come," 257.

48. Peter Hernon et al., "Library Reference Service: An Unrecognized Crisis—A Symposium," *Journal of Academic Librarianship* 13 (May 1987): 69-80.

49. Terence Crowley, "Half-Right Reference: Is It True?" *RQ* 25 (Fall 1985): 59-68.

50. Charles A. Bunge, "Gathering and Using Patron and Librarian Perceptions of Question-Answering Success," in *Evaluation of Public Services and Public Services Personnel*, ed. Bryce Allen (Urbana-Champaign, Ill.: University of Illinois Graduate School of Library and Information Science, 1991), 59-83; Lillie S. Dyson, "Improving Reference Services: A Maryland Training Program Brings Positive Results," *Public Libraries* 31 (September/October 1992): 284-89.

51. "RUSA Guidelines for Behavioral Performance of Reference and Information Services Professionals," *RQ* 36 (Winter 1996): 200-203.

52. Geraldine B. King and Suzanne H. Mahmoodi, "Peer Performance Appraisal of Reference Librarians in a Public Library," in *Evaluation of Public Services and Public Services Personnel*, 167-203; Jane P. Kleiner, "Ensuring Quality Reference Desk Service: The Introduction of a Peer Process," *RQ* 30 (Spring 1991): 349-61.

53. An interesting World Wide Web site that has documents discussing these issues is at http://www.wils.wisc.edu/libpr/pr.html; see also *Buildings, Books, and Bytes: Libraries and Communities in the Digital Age* (Washington, D.C.: The Benton Foundation, 1996), 46p.; Steve Cisler, "Weatherproofing a Great, Good Place," *American Libraries* 27 (October 1996): 42-46.

54. Jerry D. Campbell, "Shaking the Conceptual Foundations of Reference: A Perspective," *Reference Services Review* 20 (Winter 1992): 29-35.

55. Alfred Willis and Eugene E. Matysek, Jr., "Place and Functionality of Reference Services from the Perspective of Total Quality Management Theory," in *Rethinking Reference in Academic Libraries*, ed. Anne G. Lipow (Berkeley, Calif.: Library Solutions Press, 1993), 185-89.

56. Charles A. Bunge, "A Reply to Willis and Matysek," in *Rethinking Reference in Academic Libraries*, 191-93.

57. David Pescovitz, "Reality Check: The Future of Libraries," *Wired* 3 (December 1995): 68; Cynthia N. James-Catalano, "Look to the Librarians," *Internet World* 7 (August 1996): 28-30; Bonnie A. Nardi et al., "Put a Good Librarian, Not Software, in the Driver's Seat," *Christian Science Monitor*, June 4, 1996, 18.

58. Nardi, "Put a Good Librarian . . . in the Driver's Seat," 18.

59. Ferguson and Bunge, "The Shape of Services to Come," 262-63.

60. Rosemarie Riechel, *Reference Services for Children and Young Adults* (Hamden, Conn.: Library Professional Publications, 1991), 3.

61. Charles A. Bunge, "Vision and Values: Touchstones in Times of Change," in *Rethinking Reference in Academic Libraries*, 33-35.

ADDITIONAL READINGS

Bushallow-Wilber, Laura, et al. "Electronic Mail Reference Service: A Study." *RQ* 35 (Spring 1996): 359-71.

The provision of reference services via e-mail is one element of delivering reference services to users without their having to come to the library. This report of a study at one library includes a useful discussion of the literature on this topic. The same issue of *RQ* includes an article on the e-mail reference interview.

Campbell, Jerry D. "Shaking the Conceptual Foundations of Reference: A Perspective." *Reference Services Review* 20 (Winter 1992): 29-35.

These musings on reference services by an admitted "outsider" who had not practiced as a reference librarian caused a lot of reference librarians and others to think anew about reference librarianship. Campbell argues that reference librarians should become "Access Engineers," analyzing the universe of knowledge and developing more efficient ways to deliver information to users.

Ferguson, Chris D., and Charles A. Bunge. "The Shape of Services to Come: Values-Based Reference Service for the Largely Digital Library." *College & Research Libraries* 58 (May 1997): 253-65.

Here, a practicing librarian and a library school professor discuss some of the technological dimensions of the largely digital library of the future, changes in reference service that are occurring, and the service values that reference librarians must advance to make this environment work effectively for all library users.

Fialkoff, Francine. "Reference 98." *Library Journal* 122 (November 15, 1997): special supplement, S1-S96.

This installment of the annual "Reference Announcement" issue of this periodical provides a kind of snapshot of some current developments in reference services and reference tools. Its overview of forthcoming reference sources points out that books continue to flourish, but that sources on CD-ROM might be declining in number, while the number of World Wide Web versions of reference tools increases.

Harris, Roma M. "Gender, Power, and the Dangerous Pursuit of Professionalism." *American Libraries* 24 (October 1993): 874-76.

This brief but provocative article summarizes Harris's position that, in its pursuit of professionalism, librarianship risks turning its back on important feminine values of service and collaborative relationships with users. Some of the values she discusses have been core values of reference librarians.

"Information Services Policy Manual: An Outline." *RQ* 34 (Winter 1994): 165-72.

The product of a committee of the Reference and User Services Association of the American Library Association, this outline is intended to help reference librarians and managers develop a policy manual to guide the provision of services. Perusal of it will give the reader an idea of the many facets of reference work and of the broad range of services and issues that must be considered in planning and delivering effective services.

Innovative Internet Applications in Libraries. Available: http://www.wiltonlibrary.org/innovate.html.

An interesting World Wide Web site that contains links to sites at libraries that, in the judgment of the compilers, are using the Internet effectively. There are sections on tutorials/guides and virtual reference desks (which includes a link to the Internet Public Library, a particularly interesting service).

Katz, William A., ed. *Introduction to Reference Work, Vols. I & II.* New York: McGraw-Hill, 1997. 730p.

This two-volume textbook covers reference sources and services. The first volume introduces some basics of reference librarianship, followed by discussion of reference sources arranged by type of source. The second volume addresses reference services and reference processes, covering such topics as the reference interview, bibliographical instruction, and document delivery and interlibrary loan.

Lipow, Anne Grodzins, ed. *Rethinking Reference in Academic Libraries.* Berkeley, Calif.: Library Solutions Press, 1993. 242p.

The institutes on which this volume is based explored the need for changes in reference services to respond to changes in user needs, information delivery, and society in general. Topics discussed include new staffing patterns, new administrative structures, new physical arrangements, and serving users who are at a distance from the library. Among several useful appendices is an annotated bibliography on the topic of "rethinking reference."

Maack, Mary Niles. "Toward a New Model of the Information Professional: Embracing Empowerment." *Journal of Education for Library and Information Science* 38 (Fall 1997): 283-302.

Using some of the same themes as Roma Harris (see above), this longer article points out that it is important that information professionals consider their core values and their relationships to their clients. Maack's discussion of the ethic of care in professional practice and the importance of activities with goals to diffuse knowledge, not to guard or control it, is highly relevant to reference librarianship.

Reference Service in a Digital Age: A Library of Congress Institute. Available: http://lcweb.loc.gov/rr/digiref/papers.html.

This institute, held in June 1998, brought together some 130 reference librarians and managers, along with expert speakers and panelists, to consider the impact of technology on the future of reference services. This Web site allows access to session content and bibliographies on such topics as the knowledge and skills needed by reference librarians to provide quality services in the electronic environment, strategies for providing appropriate and adequate digital information sources to provide quality service, working collaboratively with other agencies and institutions, and the appropriate balance between reference librarians and artificial intelligence technologies. Information about subsequent activities, including development of a collaborative digital reference service, can be found at http://lcweb.loc.gov/rr/digiref/digiref.html.

Rettig, James. "Future Reference—'Sired by a Hurricane, Dam'd by an Earthquake'." *The Reference Librarian* 54 (1996): 75-94.

Rettig, one of the most articulate current "philosophers" of reference services, discusses recent changes in the environment for reference services and summarizes some of the trends that he sees emerging. He believes that the common thread among them is a focus on the needs of the individual user. Other articles in this theme issue on "The Roles of Reference Librarians: Today and Tomorrow" are interesting, as well.

Schlachter, Gail A., ed. *The Service Imperative for Libraries: Essays in Honor of Margaret Monroe.* Littleton, Colo.: Libraries Unlimited, 1982. 215p.

Essays in this tribute to an outstanding teacher and conceptualizer of library public services provide one of the best treatments of the information-guidance-instruction paradigm for reference service (used earlier in this chapter) available in the literature.

Wood, M. Sandra, ed. *Reference and Information Services in Health Sciences Libraries.* Metuchen, N.J.: Medical Library Association and Scarecrow Press, 1994. 371p. (Current Practices in Health Sciences Librarianship, vol. 1).

Most of the literature of reference service relates to public and academic libraries. This informative and practice-oriented volume offers an excellent introduction to reference services in one type of special library. Its discussions of such topics as the reference interview and a wide variety of electronic resources would also be relevant to readers with interest in other types of special libraries.

CHAPTER

2

ETHICAL ASPECTS OF REFERENCE SERVICE

Richard E. Rubin

INTRODUCTION AND HISTORICAL BACKGROUND

On a day-to-day basis, librarians seldom focus their attention on the ethical implications of their professional actions. Nonetheless, ethical principles form an important framework that guides professional conduct. The ethical foundation of reference service shares, to a large extent, the general principles of library and information service. Therefore, this discussion embodies an analysis of the broader obligations of the profession as a whole. Understanding the ethical issues and principles of the field is best achieved by first providing an historical context. The values of a profession are not absent one day, only to appear fully formed the next; they are part of evolutionary changes in the profession and the society. For this reason, it is important to examine briefly the values that form the foundation of contemporary ethics for reference service.

When public libraries were first established in the mid- to latter part of the nineteenth century, library service was limited. "Closed shelving" restricted access to all but library staff. There were no reference desks. Desks, when present, served primarily as places where books were checked out or returned. It was probably not a particularly hospitable environment for asking questions. One library historian described the public library of this period as "inflexible, coldly authoritarian, and elitist."[1]If library users had questions, it was likely they left without asking any staff member to help them. These reluctant researchers were called "shy enquirers" by pioneering librarians, who recognized that the library was an important place to find information and that the librarian was obligated to provide it.[2] As Samuel Green, librarian of the Worcester Library and a former American Library Association president put it:

> The ideal library is one which invites everybody who has a question to ask . . . to come to the library and put his question, with the assurance that he will be kindly received, his question sympathetically considered, and every effort made to find the answer desired.[3]

Near the end of the nineteenth century, access to library collections was liberalized. Open shelves where library users could freely browse materials became increasingly common, and an information function separate from the circulation function emerged. A library worker was assigned to an "information desk."[4] This worker answered library users' questions, referred users to other departments, and prepared reference lists on various subjects.[5] In larger organizations, reference departments were headed by trained reference librarians aided by reference assistants. The importance of this new function in libraries led Samuel Green, in 1896, to refer to libraries as "Bureaus of Information."[6]

As reference work evolved, it was imbued with the moral cast of the latter half of the nineteenth century, an unabashedly moralistic period. It was not uncommon to read or hear public leaders, such as Andrew Carnegie, speak of the need for moral development among the citizenry and the obligation of those with wealth or power to direct this moral development. Public libraries were viewed as institutions through which this moral duty could be discharged. The nature of this duty has been described variously as helping Americans improve themselves and become educated citizens or socializing and controlling immigrant populations unfamiliar with American ways.[7] In any event, libraries and library service of the late nineteenth century were intended to educate and inculcate values, and librarians interpreted this function as a social or moral duty. This could be seen most conspicuously in careful control and selection of materials based on these beliefs. The modern concept of intellectual freedom played little or no role in library service.

According to Melvil Dewey, the civilizing power of librarians could hardly be exaggerated. If librarians performed their duty properly, they could guide library users from good to better. The moral power of librarians was so great that Dewey felt that they could shape the thinking of their entire community.[8] A young Winston Churchill echoed this view when he addressed the New Hampshire Library Association in 1903 on the unfortunate rising tide of mediocre books: "It is the duty of the library to separate this wheat from a mass of chaff. And to just such an extent—and it is a very great extent—is the librarian the custodian of public morals and the moulder of public men."[9]

The predominantly female composition of the library workforce was consistent with these moralistic views. Women were considered civilizers and domesticators of the society in general and of library users in particular. Their congeniality and gentility were expected to serve as models of proper library behavior.[10]

Such a heavy responsibility required a librarian of considerable moral character. The pressures must have been great. Corinne Bacon, a Connecticut reference librarian, noted in her address to the Connecticut Library Association in 1902:

> If anything is impressed upon us nowadays, it is the seriousness of our profession as librarians, the importance, nay, the necessity of attaining physical, mental and moral perfection.[11]

She also suggested that the reference librarian have the characteristics of "approachableness, omniscience, tact, patience, persistence, accuracy, knowledge of one's tools, knowledge of one's town, and familiarity with current events."[12] She added a "sense of humor" as well.

In 1904, G. T. Clark, librarian at the San Francisco Public Library, gave these paragons of virtue a heavenly quality:

> Many of those coming to the library are unaccustomed to the use of its tools, unfamiliar with the literature of the topic in hand and indiscriminating in the value of authorities. The reference librarian must make up for all these deficiencies and furthermore should be possessed of an angelic disposition, and be filled with an unquenchable desire to assist fellow beings.[13]

Providing good reference service was clearly important to reference librarians early in the twentieth century. These good intentions, however, were frustrated by the lack of professional training and resources. In 1926, Robert J. Usher reported a lack of in-depth reference books and a notable lack of articles on reference service. He lamented that poor training meant that

> the beginner in reference work must find his way, slowly, learning by doing, profiting by mistakes in which the innocent reader is, unfortunately, too often the loser. . . . I grant that not much more than an elementary knowledge of reference work can be expected from the new graduated library school student . . . without further training in research work the result must be an impaired service to the public.[14]

Other frustrations included the desire on the part of some library users to turn reference librarians into their "private secretaries or private tutors."[15] Some reference patrons were more exasperating than others. Bacon, for example, placed reference patrons into one of three classes:

1. The select few who know just what they want, state their want with clearness and expect you to meet it. It is a joy to work for them.
2. The people who expect nothing of you, apologize for disturbing you, and break out into a fever of gratitude over the slightest assistance. These are amusing.
3. The people who expect you to do all their work for them. These are irritating.[16]

Despite inadequate training and some difficult library users, librarians acknowledged and embraced the duty to provide good reference service. In 1904, McLoney, Librarian at the Des Moines Public Library, enumerated the primary elements of reference work:

1. A spirit of willingness on the part of the reference librarian which counts nothing too troublesome that will secure the desired result.
2. Having the resources of the library brought out to the fullest extent and made available.
3. Cultivation of the mental alertness which will quickly suggest possible sources of information upon obscure subjects concerning which catalog, index and bibliography may not offer what is needed.
4. Persistence. It very rarely is necessary to send inquirers away from the library without at least partial information upon the subject which they are looking up, and this never should be done until the fact is established beyond question that the library can not give the desired help.[17]

Although today's reference librarian is no longer considered an arbiter of moral conduct or poor thinking, many aspects of these "elements" are reflected in modern reference service: (1) a service-oriented perspective, (2) the responsibility to select and organize collections to maximize effectiveness, (3) strong knowledge of subjects and the principles and practices of fields, and (4) a commitment to either answering the question or referring to a source which can. These values are a strong foundation for any ethical code for information providers and resonate in the "Guidelines for Behavioral Performance of Reference and Information Services Professionals," adopted by the Reference and User Services Association (RUSA) in 1996.[18] (See Chapter 3 for additional discussion.)

ETHICAL GUIDANCE IN THE CONTEMPORARY ETHICAL ENVIRONMENT

Although it might be possible to impose a singular moral perspective on reference conduct, the heterogeneity of contemporary society and the increasing importance of tolerance of ideas as a guiding principle of our profession makes such an approach impractical and undesirable. Today's information environment and the reference librarian's role within it are increasingly complex and multifaceted. Consider some of the modern reference librarian's responsibilities:

- provides information to library users on request;
- evaluates, selects, and weeds reference materials;
- assists library users in their own searches to resolve information needs;
- counsels library users on effective search strategies;
- clarifies information queries and needs throughout the search process;
- instructs and educates users on search techniques and information resources;
- organizes print, nonprint, and electronic information to promote access;
- protects users' rights to privacy, confidentiality, and intellectual freedom;
- participates in professional activities to improve the profession and individual knowledge;
- participates in the improvement of local information systems;
- teaches fellow library staff to improve their skills;
- creates finding tools and Web sites to assist information seekers.

In addition, given the many types of libraries that exist today, there are many distinct ethical issues unique to each. Archivists, for example, confront issues regarding restricted access to records that might be in conflict with increased access in a public library. Information managers in private organizations might have greater restrictions on providing service than reference librarians working in a public setting. Given this variety, not all ethical standards can be applied or interpreted in the same way. Nonetheless, a general pattern regarding ethical obligations is evident in various professional codes.

Ethical or Professional Codes

Reference librarians, as well as librarians in general, are guided by a variety of professional codes or guidelines. These include the Reference and User Services Association (RUSA) "Guidelines for Behavioral Performance of Reference and Information Services Professionals," the American Library Association's (ALA) "Code of Ethics" (see Box 2.1), the American Society for Information Science's (ASIS) "ASIS Professional Guidelines" (see Box 2.2), the Society of American Archivists' "Code of Ethics for Archivists" (see Box 2.3), the Medical Library Association's "Code of Ethics for Health Sciences Librarianship" (see Box 2.4), and the American Association of Law Libraries' "AALL Ethical Principles" (see Box 2.5).[19]

Box 2.1 American Library Association Code of Ethics

As members of the American Library Association, we recognize the importance of codifying and making known to the profession and to the general public the ethical principles that guide the work of librarians, other professionals providing information services, library trustees and library staffs.

Ethical dilemmas occur when values are in conflict. The American Library Association Code of Ethics states the values to which we are committed, and embodies the ethical responsibilities of the profession in this changing information environment.

We significantly influence or control the selection, organization, preservation, and dissemination of information. In a political system grounded in an informed citizenry, we are members of a profession explicitly committed to intellectual freedom and the freedom of access to information. We have a special obligation to ensure the free flow of information and ideas to present and future generations.

The principles of this Code are expressed in broad statements to guide ethical decision making. These statements provide a framework; they cannot and do not dictate conduct to cover particular situations.

I. We provide the highest level of service to all library users through appropriate and usefully organized resources; equitable service policies; equitable access; and accurate, unbiased, and courteous responses to all requests.

II. We uphold the principles of intellectual freedom and resist all efforts to censor library resources.

III. We protect each library user's right to privacy and confidentiality with respect to information sought or received and resources consulted, borrowed, acquired or transmitted.

IV. We recognize and respect intellectual property rights.

V. We treat co-workers and other colleagues with respect, fairness and good faith, and advocate conditions of employment that safeguard the rights and welfare of all employees of our institutions.

VI. We do not advance private interests at the expense of library users, colleagues, or our employing institutions.

VII. We distinguish between our personal convictions and professional duties and do not allow our personal beliefs to interfere with fair representation of the aims of our institutions or the provision of access to their information resources.

VIII. We strive for excellence in the profession by maintaining and enhancing our own knowledge and skills, by encouraging the professional development of co-workers, and by fostering the aspirations of potential members of the profession.

Adopted by *ALA Council*—June 28, 1995

Box 2.2 ASIS Professional Guidelines

Dedicated to the Memory of Diana Woodward

ASIS recognizes the plurality of uses and users of information technologies, services, systems and products as well as the diversity of goals or objectives, sometimes conflicting, among producers, vendors, mediators, and users of information systems.

ASIS urges its members to be ever aware of the social, economic, cultural, and political impacts of their actions or inaction.

ASIS members have obligations to employers, clients, and system users, to the profession, and to society, to use judgement and discretion in making choices, providing equitable service, and in defending the rights of open inquiry.

Responsibilities to Employers/Clients/System Users

To act faithfully for their employers or clients in professional matters.

To uphold each user's, provider's or employer's right to privacy and confidentiality and to respect whatever proprietary rights belong to them, by limiting access to, providing proper security for and ensuring proper disposal of data about clients, patrons or users.

To treat all persons fairly.

Responsibility to the Profession

To truthfully represent themselves and the information systems which they utilize or which they represent, by

- not knowingly making false statements or providing erroneous or misleading information
- informing their employers, clients or sponsors of any circumstances that create a conflict of interest
- not using their position beyond their authorized limits or by not using their credentials to misrepresent themselves
- following and promoting standards of conduct in accord with the best current practices
- undertaking their research conscientiously, in gathering, tabulating or interpreting data; in following proper approval procedures for subjects; and in producing or disseminating their research results
- pursuing ongoing professional development and encouraging and assisting colleagues and others to do the same
- adhering to principles of due process and equality of opportunity.

Responsibility to Society

To improve the information systems with which they work or which they represent, to the best of their means and abilities by

- providing the most reliable and accurate information and acknowledging the credibility of the sources as known or unknown
- resisting all forms of censorship, inappropriate selection and acquisitions policies, and biases in information selection, provision and dissemination
- making known any biases, errors and inaccuracies found to exist and striving to correct those which can be remedied.

To promote open and equal access to information, within the scope permitted by their organizations or work, and to resist procedures that promote unlawful discriminatory practices in access to and provision of information, by

- seeking to extend public awareness and appreciation of information availability and provision as well as the role of information professionals in providing such information

- freely reporting, publishing or disseminating information, subject to legal and proprietary restraints of producers, vendors and employers and the best interests of their employers or clients.

Information professionals shall engage in principled conduct whether on their own behalf or at the request of employers, colleagues, clients, agencies or the profession.

(Adopted May 1992)
Reprinted with permission: American Society
for Information Science & Technology, Silver Springs, MD.

Taken as a whole, these codes suggest that ethical obligations occur on at least four levels: (1) *individual level*—librarians have an obligation to act ethically to each individual they serve; (2) *organizational level*—librarians have an ethical obligation to act in the best interest of their organization; (3) *professional level*—librarians have an ethical obligation to promote standards of professional conduct established by the accepted professional organizations; and (4) *societal level*—librarians, as do all individuals, have an ethical obligation to serve the best interests of the society as a whole.

The obligations noted in the codes manifest themselves in the manner in which reference work is conducted. They include the obligations to (1) provide the highest level of services to all library users/information seekers, treating all individuals with respect and courtesy; (2) protect the confidentiality and privacy of library users/information seekers; (3) respect the intellectual freedom of library users through equal, open, and nondiscriminatory access to information; (4) respect intellectual property or other proprietary interests; (5) pursue continuing education to improve professional skills; (6) advance the interest of the library user/information seeker over the interest of the librarian; and (7) improve the system or processes of the organization.

Professional codes are not magic formulas. Although the guidelines or precepts may be helpful, they are usually relatively brief statements. The many subtleties raised while discussing the code, and the reasoning behind the code, are usually lost in the final version. Consequently, attempts to interpret the code in the myriad situations that might arise are often difficult. In addition, ethical codes in the information professions are not supported by sanctions in case of violation. For example, violating the Code of Medical Ethics might lead to a physician's license being suspended or revoked. The information professions have no such sanctions.

Box 2.3 Code of Ethics for Archivists (Excerpts)

Archivists select, preserve, and make available documentary materials of long-term value that have lasting value to the organization or public that the archivist serves. Archivists perform their responsibilities in accordance with statutory authorization or institutional policy. They subscribe to a code of ethics based on sound archival principles and promote institutional and professional observance of these ethical and archival standards.

Archivists answer courteously and with a spirit of helpfulness all reasonable inquiries about their holdings, and encourage use of them to the greatest extent compatible with institutional policies, preservation of holdings, legal considerations, individual rights, donor agreements, and judicious use of archival resources. They explain pertinent restrictions to potential users, and apply them equitably.

Archivists endeavor to inform users of parallel research by others using the same materials, and, if the individuals concerned agree, supply each name to the other party.

Reprinted by permission of the Society of American Archivists

527 S. Wells St., 5th Floor, Chicago, IL 60607 (312) 922-0140

Nonetheless, professional codes are often a product of considerable thought and reflect professional consensus. They highlight many important ethical responsibilities of librarians in general, as well as reference librarians in particular. They provide important guidance in difficult situations, and despite the lack of sanctions, the general acceptance of such codes provides considerable normative support to regulate the conduct of information professionals.

Box 2.4

Code of Ethics for Health Sciences Librarianship

Goals and Principles for Ethical Conduct

The health sciences librarian believes that knowledge is the *sine qua non* of informed decisions in health care, education, and research, and that the health sciences librarian serves society, clients, and the institution, by working to ensure that informed decisions can be made.

Society

The health sciences librarian promotes access to health information for all and creates and maintains conditions of freedom of inquiry, thought, and expression that facilitate informed health care decisions.

Clients

The health sciences librarian works without prejudice to meet the client's information needs.

The health sciences librarian respects the privacy of clients and protects the confidentiality of the client relationship.

The health sciences librarian ensures that the best available information is provided to the client.

Institution

The health sciences librarian provides leadership and expertise in the design, development, and ethical management of knowledge-based information systems that meet the needs and obligations of the institution.

Profession

The health sciences librarian advances and upholds the philosophy and ideals of the profession.

The health sciences librarian advocates and advances knowledge and standards of the profession.

The health sciences librarian conducts all professional relationships with courtesy and respect.

The health sciences librarian maintains high standards of professional integrity.

Self

The health sciences librarian assumes personal responsibility for developing and maintaining professional excellence.

Box 2.5 AALL Ethical Principles

Preamble

When individuals have ready access to legal information, they can participate fully in the affairs of their government. By collecting, organizing, preserving, and retrieving legal information, the members of the American Association of Law Libraries enable people to make this ideal of democracy a reality.

Legal information professionals have an obligation to satisfy the needs, to promote the interests and to respect the values of their clientele. Law firms, corporations, academic and governmental institutions and the general public have legal information needs that are best addressed by professionals committed to the belief that serving these information needs is a noble calling and that fostering the equal participation of diverse people in library services underscores one of our basic tenets, open access to information for all individuals.

Service

We promote open and effective access to legal and related information. Further we recognize the need to establish methods of preserving, maintaining and retrieving legal information in many different forms.

We uphold a duty to our clientele to develop service policies that respect confidentiality and privacy.

We provide zealous service using the most appropriate resources and implementing programs consistent with our institution's mission and goals.

We acknowledge the limits on service imposed by our institutions and by the duty to avoid the unauthorized practice of law.

Business Relationships

We promote fair and ethical trade practices.

We have a duty to avoid situations in which personal interests might be served or significant benefits gained at the expense of library users, colleagues, or our employing institutions.

We strive to obtain the maximum value for our institution's fiscal resources, while at the same time making judicious, analytical and rational use of our institution's information resources.

Professional Responsibilities

We relate to our colleagues with respect and in a spirit of cooperation.

We distinguish between our personal convictions and professional duties and do not allow our personal beliefs to interfere with the service we provide.

We recognize and respect the rights of the owner and the user of intellectual property.

We strive for excellence in the profession by maintaining and enhancing our own knowledge and skills, by encouraging the professional development of co-workers, and by fostering the aspirations of potential members of the profession.

Approved by the AALL membership, March 1999
Reprinted by permission of the American Association of Law Libraries

The First Amendment

In addition to professional codes of conduct, librarianship as a profession is grounded in the ethical obligation to protect the First Amendment rights of library users and hence to protect the right of access to information. The First Amendment, among other things, protects the right of free speech and press. The right to speak or publish is hollow, however, unless citizens also have a right to gain access to the ideas that are spoken or otherwise produced. Public institutions whose primary purpose is to disseminate ideas play a critical role in protecting the First Amendment; attempts to restrict access to such ideas are violations of this right.

Libraries, especially public libraries, have consciously and concertedly associated themselves with protecting the First Amendment rights of American citizens, especially since the middle of the twentieth century. Protecting the right of access to ideas and information is a commonly accepted ethical obligation in the library profession, usually subsumed under the broader obligation to protect the intellectual freedom of library users. Although there are few First Amendment court cases that involve libraries, at least one federal appellate court recognized public libraries as defenders of First Amendment freedoms.[20]

SOME MAJOR ETHICAL ISSUES FACING REFERENCE LIBRARIANS AND OTHER INFORMATION PROFESSIONALS

There are many ethical issues confronting reference librarians. The brief discussions that follow are intended to identify some of the more common ethical concerns and challenge readers to think carefully about how they might deal with them.

The Tension Between Protecting the Right of Access and Protecting Individuals or Society from Harm

If an individual, who is unfamiliar to you, comes to the reference desk and requests material on how to build a bomb, do you provide it?
If an individual comes to the reference desk and asks if there is any material on how to freebase cocaine, do you provide it?
Should the library provide open access to the Internet for library users of all ages?

One of the most important ethical tensions in librarianship involves situations in which the rights of individuals come into conflict with their own welfare or that of others. As a rule, reference librarians are expected to withhold judgment regarding the nature of the inquiry. Foskett described this view in 1962 as the "Creed of the Librarian": in executing professional responsibilities, the librarian should have "no politics, no religion, no morals."[21] Such neutrality is considered essential to protect all information to which the citizenry has a constitutional right. There is little doubt that the ALA "Library Bill of Rights" (see Box 2.6) and the ALA "Code of Ethics" support this perspective. When an individual asks for information, it is the professional duty of the reference librarian to provide that information. But what if that information may cause direct harm to the individual asking for it or to others? (See Box 2.7.)

Box 2.6 Library Bill of Rights

The American Library Association affirms that all libraries are forums for information and ideas, and that the following basic policies should guide their services.

I. Books and other library resources should be provided for the interest, information, and enlightenment of all people of the community the library serves. Materials should not be excluded because of the origin, background, or views of those contributing to their creation.

II. Libraries should provide materials and information presenting all points of view on current and historical issues. Materials should not be proscribed or removed because of partisan or doctrinal disapproval.

III. Libraries should challenge censorship in the fulfillment of their responsibility to provide information and enlightenment.

IV. Libraries should cooperate with all persons and groups concerned with resisting abridgment of free expression and free access to ideas.

V. A person's right to use a library should not be denied or abridged because of origin, age, background, or views.

VI. Libraries which make exhibit spaces and meeting rooms available to the public they serve should make such facilities available on an equitable basis, regardless of the beliefs or affiliations of individuals or groups requesting their use.

Adopted June 18, 1948. Amended February 2, 1961, and January 23, 1980, inclusion of "age" reaffirmed January 23, 1996, by the ALA Council.[22]

Box 2.7 Case Study: To Be or Not to Be

Melissa, a 15-year old, comes into the Jonestown Public Library from time to time. None of the reference librarians in the Jonestown Public Library know her well, but when Melissa passes the desk she usually says, "Hi" as she goes by to any staff member who is stationed there. She is not a behavior problem, although rarely, a staff member may have to tell her to "keep her voice down." Some of the other students who come into the library have told a couple of the librarians that Melissa has some "problems," but they are not specific.

Melissa approaches the reference librarian. She looks like she has been crying because her eyes are a little red and her face is slightly puffy. In a slightly shaky voice she asks: "I've been looking for a book, but it's not on the shelf. It's called *Final Exit*. Can you tell me where it is?" You know that *Final Exit* is a book on how to commit suicide. You also know that it has just been returned and is on a cart ready for reshelving.

Questions

Should the librarian retrieve the book from the cart and give it to Melissa?

Should any other actions be taken?

Exactly what would you say to Melissa?

The issue of causing harm has recently been highlighted by debates over unrestricted access to the Internet. Because the Internet contains a variety of materials that may be considered sexually explicit, violent, or hateful, serious concern has been expressed about the common library policy that permits young people as well as adults to consult any part of a library collection. If such a policy is extended to the Internet, it is argued, detrimental effects could result to the young people exposed to such material. Consequently, a particularly active debate has ensued regarding the use of electronic filters that can block Web sites that contain offensive materials, especially those that are sexually explicit. On the face of it, such an argument seems sensible. Proponents of filters consider them appropriate in part because their use affirms and preserves the traditional character of library collections, that is, in general, libraries do not collect pornographic materials. Using filters that remove such sites makes Internet access consistent with other selection practices and protects young users from potentially harmful exposure.

There are, however, numerous ethical concerns. Filters violate fundamental tenets of reference work by denying access to information to some individuals but not others. Generally, the library profession has established the standard that all individuals have equal rights to information. Discriminating on the basis of age, for example, is expressly prohibited by the "Library Bill of Rights." This prohibition has been extended specifically to the electronic environment in the ALA policy, "Access to Electronic Information, Services, and Networks." In addition, filters have not been shown to be entirely successful, and their inability to distinguish appropriate sexual information from pornographic sites threatens constitutionally protected speech. Concern over the implementation of filters has led the American Library Association to issue a variety of official statements cautioning libraries against their use: "Resolution on the Use of Filtering Software in Libraries," the "Statement on Library Use of Filtering Software," and "Guidelines and Considerations for Developing a Public Library Internet Use Policy."[23]

Underlying the library profession's concern about filtering and the temptation to restrict materials because of their potential harm is the concept of intellectual freedom. The principle of intellectual freedom supports the belief that people have a fundamental right to the ideas produced in a society and that society functions best when the flow of ideas is unimpeded. Given this view, it is inappropriate for librarians to make judgments regarding the appropriateness of particular information for a particular individual. The reference librarian is not expected to guess to what use a particular piece of information will be put, but to provide the information to the information seeker. Otherwise, it gives license to the reference librarian to decide which reasons for use are valid and which are pernicious. Such a view would allow for considerable mischief.

Despite the strength of this argument, some writers maintain that there are even deeper issues at stake. Robert Hauptman, for example, argues that reference librarians, just like everyone else, have an ethical duty to protect others. Hauptman contends that "censorship is never warranted, but it should not be confused with a refusal to aid and abet egregiously antisocial acts."[24] Hauptman fears that professional education emphasizing the "Library Bill of Rights" becomes dogma that replaces thoughtful reflection on the specific situation and the ethical dilemmas that may arise.[25] In 1975, Hauptman conducted an experiment in libraries directly related to this issue. Self-described as "young, bearded, deferential," Hauptman visited thirteen public and academic libraries. After determining he was talking to a reference librarian, he indicated that he needed information on a "small explosive device" and wanted to know about the properties of cordite. He even indicated he was interested in whether a small amount would destroy a "normal suburban house." Hauptman reported that none of the librarians invoked ethical grounds for refusing to cooperate, and the vast majority tried to supply the information.[26] A similar finding occurred in a follow-up experiment conducted by Robert Dowd in 1989. Dowd asked reference librarians how to freebase cocaine.[27] The situations created by Hauptman and Dowd remind us that our ethical duty extends to the protection of others and the society at large, not just the library user. These dilemmas are difficult, because one must always weigh harm done to individuals and the society at large when the right to information is deprived based on the speculation of reference librarians.

Nonetheless, the issues Hauptman raises are good ones, and the implication that librarians as professionals have an obligation to be thoughtful and reflective is doubly important when dealing with ethical dilemmas. Whether they fear that information provided will be harmful to others, or to the individual, there will remain a residue of uneasiness when reference librarians provide information they suspect might be used to untoward purposes. At present the professional codes and guidelines—and professional education—offer the most solid framework for providing reference service.

Issues Related to Equality of Access to Information

Is the charging of fees for services ethical?
Is it ever appropriate to violate the confidentiality or privacy of library patrons?
Do children have the same rights to information as adults?

The central ethical principle guiding reference librarians is "equality of access." This notion is explicitly stated or inherent in the various codes and guidelines of the profession. For example, the ALA "Code of Ethics" calls for "equitable access," the ASIS "Professional Guidelines" exhort information scientists to "promote open and equal access to information," and the "Code of Ethics for Health Sciences Librarianship" "promotes access to health information for all." A variety of situations challenge this principle.

Charging Fees

Although libraries have often charged fees for various services, usually the charges have been small. With the rise of electronic information technologies, however, this situation has changed. Because information technologies are commonly used in reference services, these services are vulnerable to the increasing costs associated with these technologies. Charges for using databases have become a necessity for some libraries because of the prohibitive costs of accessing them. In addition, the costs of maintaining and constantly updating electronic technologies have placed significant burdens on libraries, and recovering these costs in some manner is reasonable.

The most obvious problem, however, is that fees represent a barrier to information access among those who cannot afford to pay them; they constitute a discriminatory practice, a violation of professional canons, and an abrogation of the constitutional obligation to provide access to information on an equitable basis. On the other hand, one could also argue that libraries could not provide the expensive technologies and access to expensive databases without charging and that it is inappropriate for the entire public to subsidize expensive services that are used by the few. In other words, if fees are charged, access may be denied to those who cannot afford it, but if fees are not charged, all access to information may be limited because the institution lacks the fiscal resources to provide it. Overall, however, it has been the collective opinion of the profession that library reference services should avoid the charging of fees because of its discriminatory character. This is clearly articulated in the ALA policy, "Economic Barriers to Information Access."[28]

Privacy and Confidentiality Issues

The concepts of privacy and confidentiality are explicit parts of many ethical codes in the information professions and are vital to the provision of information services. Although not specifically identified in the U.S. Constitution, a right to privacy has been recognized in a variety of court cases as an important right of citizens.

For individuals to feel comfortable seeking information, they must be confident that their queries and the answers given to their queries are confidential. There are significant First Amendment issues if such confidences are broken. Making reference inquiries and answers public creates what is referred to as a "chilling effect" on the First Amendment rights of library users. If library users feel that they could be subjected to public exposure, embarrassment, or sanction, they are not likely to pursue the information they need. Reference librarians are therefore ethically obligated to conduct their reference interviews in a manner that is minimally intrusive, and their queries should be directed only toward those factors that would help satisfy information needs.

Similarly, they must prevent, as far as possible, intrusions into the privacy of their users. This notion is linked to Fourth Amendment protections regarding unlawful search and seizure as well as to First Amendment rights. Generally speaking, the reference librarian is ethically obligated to keep the content of reference questions confidential, even when queried by government officials.

These rights were conspicuously challenged in the 1970s when the federal government made a concerted effort to investigate certain types of reference inquiries, especially in academic libraries. The FBI began the Library Awareness Program, the purpose of which was to try to identify foreign agents in the United States who were attempting to gather unclassified scientific and technical information that could give their countries a technological advantage. The FBI suspected that library collections were a perfect place for such agents to get this information. Consequently, they began making inquiries of librarians concerning individuals making such requests. The existence of this program was not revealed until 1987, when it was exposed by an incident at Columbia University. Following considerable protests by the American Library Association, the FBI decided to discontinue the program, although its revival is still a possibility.

Clearly, reference librarians have an ethical obligation to protect the privacy and confidentiality of library user inquiries, but is that obligation absolute? If a teenager who appears upset asks for information on committing suicide, is there any obligation to report the individual's apparent distress to a school counselor? If law enforcement investigators believe that the information requested and provided to a library user might reasonably cause harm to others, does the reference librarian have an obligation to reveal the content of the reference transaction?

As with most ethical dilemmas, no single answer produces perfect solutions. Under extraordinary circumstances one might imagine grounds for transgressing the basic ethical tenets of privacy and confidentiality, but it is clear that such tenets are fundamental to professional practice, and their violation must generally be considered a serious breach of the professional duty of reference librarians (see Box 2.8).

Box 2.8 Case Study: A Case of Honor or Privacy

Mary Smith is a reference librarian at the Martinville College Library, a small liberal arts college. Recently, a college student came into the library and requested help on the Internet terminal. The student indicated she was looking for help on preparing a term paper because she had to do one in Dr. Jones's introductory literature class. Mary knows Dr. Jones very well and considers her a good friend.

The student brought with her the name of a particular URL and she wanted to know how to find it. Mary recognized the URL because it had become popular among some of the students. It was a URL that provided access to copies of term papers prepared by students around the country.

Mary took the student to the terminal and briefly instructed her regarding how to enter a URL and how to use the search engines. The student stayed at the terminal for about twenty minutes. The last ten minutes were spent printing off a fairly lengthy document. Just before the student left, she approached the desk and thanked Mary for the help. Mary could see that she had a copy of a paper in her hand.

Not long after the student left, Mary went to the terminal, just out of curiosity, and saw that the student had printed off a term paper on James Joyce. It was called: "James Joyce: Portrait of an Artist as an Old Man." The paper was authored by Patricia Van Doren. Mary felt some pangs of guilt. There is a clear plagiarism policy at the college that says that students must report evidence of plagiarism. Mary wondered if she should say anything, but she didn't.

Several weeks later, Dr. Jones was having lunch with Mary at a local restaurant. Dr. Jones was talking about her classes when she commented that recently she had received a couple of term papers that really worried her. The style and quality of writing far exceeded the students' regular performances and she feared that someone had written their papers for them. She mentioned that one paper, prepared by a female student on James Joyce, was particularly troubling. The paper was finely written, and she simply didn't think that particular student could do that kind of work. Dr. Jones expressed frustration that she couldn't really do much about it.

Mary didn't know what to do about it either.[29]

Questions

What are Mary's obligations?

What is her primary responsibility?

What, if anything, should Mary say to Dr. Jones?

Should she mention the student specifically?

Should she mention the term paper database without mentioning the student?

If Dr. Jones had mentioned that she had heard of term paper databases, and asked Mary if she knew if they were being used by her students, what should Mary say?

Disparate Levels of Service

The reference librarian in most public libraries today encounters a wide variety of library users. Despite the differences in clientele, librarians are expected to provide equal library service. This was not always so. In 1911, for example, the highly respected librarian John Cotton Dana suggested that the amount of time devoted to a reference question depended on three things: (1) the significance of the query: whether the answers provided would add to the body of knowledge, be instructive to groups or individuals, or be merely of recreational interest or frivolous; (2) the claim of the inquirer: the status of the individual such as a library trustee or government official would likely receive greater time; and (3) the probability of success or ease in finding the answer.[30]

Although modern professional codes remind us to treat all individuals equally, today's reality suggests that Dana's criteria still prevail. For example, it is becoming more common today, given the difficult financial circumstances of many libraries, that special information services or special reference collections for special groups can only be offered if additional financial support is provided by them. Hence, libraries may provide special services to business and industry, but not fine arts. Although it is clear that providing services to an important part of the library community is ethically appropriate, it raises another important ethical dilemma: Devoting one's resources and energies to one group often means providing service of less quality to other groups. Because both fiscal and human resources are limited, if the technology "haves" are the groups emphasized by information services, then the technology "have-nots" might be deprived of resources and energy.

Sometimes concern has been expressed regarding the equality of service provided to certain groups, most notably children. Do children receive treatment equal to that given to adults? Do some reference policies discriminate against service for children? For example, in a public library, are homework questions treated the same way as if an adult had asked a similar question? In an academic library, are students' information queries treated the same way as a faculty member's? Are exceptions regarding library rules in the reference department more likely to be made for a faculty member, administrator, or board member than for a student?

The Internet has also raised the specter of differential treatment in regard to service. As noted earlier, Internet terminals may be restricted or filtered for young people. In the academic setting, different types of Internet services are available for some groups and not others. For example, students might be allowed access to both search and e-mail functions, but the general public may only be able to use the search functions.

The fundamental tenets of the profession suggest that providing unequal service is an unethical act, yet an ethical tension remains, reflecting the ethical obligation to protect and promote the survival of the library. Is it wrong to provide special services to those who are likely to influence, for better or worse, the future of the library? As information technologies increase in number and sophistication, it behooves reference librarians to consider who is being served, and why. Who is being included and who is being excluded or ignored?

Copyright Issues

Copyright is one of the most complex issues facing today's reference librarians (see Chapter 7 for a discussion of copyright in the context of interlibrary loan and document delivery). Copying information has been a service available in libraries for decades. The central issue regarding copyright centers on the idea of "fair use." Fair use is a concept under the copyright law that permits an individual, under specific conditions, to make a copy of something without the permission of the copyright owner. Four basic criteria are considered when determining if a particular use is a fair use:

1. the purpose and character of the use, including whether such is of a commercial nature or is for nonprofit educational purposes;
2. the nature of the copyrighted work;
3. the amount and substantiality of the portion used in relation to the copyrighted work as a whole; and
4. the effect of the use upon the potential market for or value of the copyrighted work.[31]

Use is more likely to be considered "fair use" when the purpose is educational, when it is a print item rather than a video, when only a small portion of the item is copied, and when the copy has little demonstrative effect on the profits that could be gained if the item were purchased from the copyright owner.

Copying, however, has become more complicated with the introduction of electronic technologies, especially access to the Internet and the World Wide Web (WWW). The Web provides vast amounts of otherwise unavailable information that can be rapidly copied or downloaded with little effort. This situation is both good and bad. It is good in that people and librarians have access to a tremendous amount of information. It is bad if librarians and library users do not respect the intellectual property rights of those who produce the information. This tension can be seen in the ALA "Code of Ethics," which asserts the intellectual freedom rights of library users, exhorts librarians to provide the highest levels of service, and insists that librarians concomitantly respect the intellectual property rights of information producers.

Reference librarians tend to take very liberal positions regarding the copying of material; "educational" use is often assumed, as is the trivial effect on the market for the creator or producer of the product. This is not surprising; after all, reference librarians ensure the information rights of library users. This seems like a manifestly ethical act. By the same token, it is reasonable to assume that copyright owners have a legal and moral right to protection from copying of their work and the right to benefit from the creation of their intellectual products. Excessive copying of materials is likely to be a violation of law, and violating the law is usually considered to be an unethical act. As information becomes more and more fluid and easily transferred, the ethical tensions in this area are likely to increase, and there will be greater and greater reliance on the reference librarian to act ethically.

CONCLUSION

Ethical considerations and obligations in reference work are many and are related in complex ways. Librarians bring to their workplace their own personal convictions and beliefs, and library users bring their own needs, purposes, and values as well. In this heterogeneous environment, the information professions provide some consistency regarding ethical conduct by identifying through their professional codes and education those behaviors that have been accepted as ethically responsible.

As a rule, the underlying ethical obligation of reference librarians, as of all library workers, is to provide the highest level of service to each library user. This not only entails providing accurate and complete information to every inquirer, it also requires that each library user be treated in an ethical and professional manner.

It is easy to think that ethical concerns only arise in particular circumstances or when dealing with particular library users or questions. Certainly these situations must be pondered carefully. It is equally important to realize that ethical obligations are fulfilled during each reference transaction. Every day, every time a question is asked, reference librarians fulfill or abrogate their ethical obligations. RUSA, in its "Guidelines," has identified clearly how these daily obligations are fulfilled. A brief restatement of these obligations represents an apt summary of what is meant by ethical and professional reference service. Reference librarians must

1. be approachable;
2. demonstrate a genuine interest in each library user's query;
3. listen carefully to each question and make the needed inquiries to truly understand what is being asked;
4. conduct thorough and accurate searches, or provide library users with the needed information to conduct the searches themselves; and
5. follow up with each library user to determine if the user's information needs have actually been met.[32]

In the broadest context, if reference librarians perform these functions, their ethical obligations will be satisfied and library users and the society as a whole will be well served.

NOTES

1. Michael Harris, "The Purpose of the American Public Library: A Revisionist Interpretation of History," *Library Journal* 98 (September 15, 1973): 2511.

2. James Duff Brown, "The Shy Enquirer," *The Library World* 13 (1911): 365.

3. Samuel S. Green, "Libraries as Bureaus of Information," *The Library Journal* 21 (July 1896): 324.

4. W. E. Foster, "The Information Desk," *The Library Journal* 19 (November 1894): 368.

5. Ibid., 368-69.

6. Green, "Libraries as Bureaus of Information," 324.

7. Harris, "The Purpose of the American Public Library," 2510-11.

8. Melvil Dewey, "The Profession," *Library Journal* 114 (June 15, 1989): 5.

9. Winston Churchill, "The Mission of the Public Library," *Library Journal* 28 (March 1903): 116.

10. Dee Garrison, "The Tender Technicians: The Feminization of Public Librarianship, 1876–1905," *Journal of Social History* 6 (Winter 1972–1973): 131-56.

11. Corinne Bacon, "Reference Work from the Librarian's Point of View," *The Library Journal* 27 (November 1902): 927.

12. Ibid., 929.

13. G. T. Clark, Librarian, San Francisco Public Library, in "Reference Work with the General Public," *Public Libraries* 9 (February 1904): 58.

14. Robert J. Usher, "Some Needs in Reference Work," *The Library Journal* 51 (September 15, 1926): 761, 762.

15. W. W. Bishop, "The Amount of Help to Be Given to Readers," *Bulletin of the American Library Association* 2 (September 1908): 327.

16. Bacon, "Reference Work from the Librarian's Point of View," 930.

17. Miss McLoney, "Reference Work with the General Public," *Public Libraries* 9 (February 1904): 64.

18. Reference and User Services Association, "Guidelines for Behavioral Performance of Reference and Information Services Professionals," *RQ* 36 (Winter 1996): 200-203.

19. Ethics policies for the American Library Association can be found at http://www.ala.org/alaorg/oif/ethics.html; for the American Society for Information Science at http://www.asis.org/AboutASIS/professional-guidelines.html; for the Society of American Archivists at http://www.archivists.org/governance/handbook/app_ethics.html; for the Medical Library Association at http://www.mlanet.org/about/ethics.html; and for the American Association of Law Libraries at http://www.aallnet.org/about/policy_ethics.asp.

20. *Kreimer v. Bureau of Policy for the Town of Morristown et al.* 958 F.2d 1242 (3d Cir. 1992).

21. D. J. Foskett, *The Creed of the Librarian—No Politics, No Religion, No Morals* (London: Library Association, 1962), 13p.

22. *Library Bill of Rights.* Available: http://www.ala.org/work/freedom/lbr.html.

23. "Internet Use Policies." Available: http://www.ala.org/alaorg/oif/internetusepolicies.html. "Internet Filtering." Available: http://www.ala.org/aasl/filtering.html.

24. Robert Hauptman, "Professional Responsibility Reconsidered," *RQ* 35 (Spring 1996): 329.

25. Robert Hauptman, "Professionalism or Culpability? An Experiment in Ethics," *Wilson Library Bulletin* 50 (April 1976): 626-27.

26. Ibid., 626.

27. Robert C. Dowd, "I Want to Find out How to Freebase Cocaine or Yet Another Unobtrusive Test of Reference Performance," *The Reference Librarian* 25/26 (1989): 483-93.

28. American Library Association, *Economic Barriers to Information Access* (Chicago: ALA, 1993). Available: http://www.ala.org/alaorg/oif/econ_bar.html.

29. For a discussion of term paper Web sites, see Gregory L. Anderson, "Cyberplagiarism: A Look at the Web Term Paper Sites," *College & Research Libraries News* 60 (May 1999): 371-73, 394.

30. John Cotton Dana, "Misdirection of Effort in Reference Work," *Public Libraries* 16 (March 1911): 108.

31. 17 U.S.C. Section 107.

32. Reference and User Services Association, "Guidelines," 200-203.

ADDITIONAL READINGS

Baker, Sharon L. "Needed: An Ethical Code for Library Administrators." *Journal of Library Administration* 16 (1992): 1-17.

Baker proposes that a separate code of ethics is needed for library administrators to supplement the ALA "Code of Ethics" and identifies the principles that should form the foundation of such a code.

Danielson, Elena S. "Ethics and Reference Services." *The Reference Librarian* 56 (1997): 107-24.

This article explores the ethical ramifications of reference service in the archival environment. Reference codes are discussed as well as issues related to the use of the Internet, responsibilities of ownership, equitable access, providing information about archives versus providing information from the archives, and privacy concerns.

Del Vecchio, Rosemary A. "Privacy and Accountability at the Reference Desk." *The Reference Librarian* 38 (1992): 133-40.

Del Vecchio explores the extent to which reference librarians are obligated to protect the privacy of library users and the expectations of library users regarding their privacy. The legal responsibilities regarding maintaining privacy are discussed as well as the obligations identified in professional codes.

Froehlich, Thomas J. "Ethical Considerations of Information Professionals." *Annual Review of Information Science and Technology* 27 (1992): 291-319.

This substantial literature review covers a number of issues on ethics and information professionals. Froehlich surveys the major concerns and examines such areas as privacy, confidentiality, and legal liabilities. He also includes discussions of the principles proposed for ethical action, the concerns of theoreticians and researchers, and the ethical code established by the American Society for Information Science.

Hauptman, Robert, ed. "Ethics and the Dissemination of Information." *Library Trends* 40 (Fall 1991): 199-375.

This collection of articles covers a wide range of topics on ethics in library and information science. Authors include Rosemary Ruhig Du Mont, Rhoda Garoogian, John Swan, Thomas Froehlich, Norman Stevens, and others. Among the topics discussed are ethical issues related to management, patron confidentiality, law librarianship, ethics in health sciences libraries, and ethical issues in technology transfer.

Hauptman, Robert. "Professional Responsibility Reconsidered." *RQ* 35 (Spring 1996): 327-29.

This essay reviews earlier articles by Hauptman and Dowd on the propensity of reference librarians to ignore the possible social ramifications of their actions and suggests that librarians remain insensitive to the possible harmful impact of their actions. Hauptman expresses concern that librarians fail to take responsibility for their actions and rely too heavily on their educational indoctrination.

Lindsey, Jonathan A., and Ann E. Prentice. *Professional Ethics and Librarians*. Phoenix, Ariz.: Oryx Press, 1985. 103p.

The authors review the historical and philosophical foundations of ethics codes in general. The text includes a detailed discussion of the development of the ALA "Code of Ethics," with verbatim reproductions of earlier versions of the code and commentary on the code by several notable librarians.

Mason, Richard O., Florence M. Mason, and Mary J. Culnan. *Ethics of Information Management*. Thousand Oaks, Calif.: Sage, 1995. 324p.

This text is a general treatise on the ethical and moral dimensions of handling information. Among the areas covered are the ethical challenges facing information professionals; understanding the nature of information; the relationship of information to decision making, power, and information policy; the foundations of ethical theory; and societal and organizational issues that relate to ethical decision making for information professionals.

Rubin, Richard E., and Thomas J. Froehlich. "Ethical Aspects of Library and Information Science." In *Encyclopedia of Library and Information Science*. New York: Marcel Dekker, 1996, 58: 33-52.

The authors provide an overview of the ethical responsibilities of librarians and information scientists and the ethical issues that they confront. The discussion covers the major areas of ethical concern such as privacy, selection, and copyright; it includes consideration of the values of information professionals and the factors that affect ethical deliberations.

Smith, Martha M., ed. "Information Ethics." *North Carolina Libraries* 51 (Spring 1993): 2-37. (Special issue).

This issue of *North Carolina Libraries* is devoted to information ethics. Articles have been prepared by Martha Smith, Gene Lanier, Susan Rathbun, Jennifer McLean, Lee Finks, and others. Topics covered include the general area of professional ethics as well as the unauthorized practice of law, archival management, and ethics in library and information science education. An ethics bibliography is also included.

CHAPTER

3

THE REFERENCE INTERVIEW

Richard E. Bopp

INTRODUCTION

The reference interview is essentially a conversation between a reference staff member and a user, the goal of which is to ascertain the user's information need and take appropriate action to satisfy that need through skillful use of available information sources. Although a conversation, it is not casual. It requires from the librarian a great deal of discipline. The librarian must concentrate on listening solely to the user, even when distractions such as ringing telephones, waiting users, or equipment malfunctions occur. Care is required to avoid misunderstanding the user's need or prematurely assuming one has fully understood it. Similar care must be taken in developing the correct strategy for a successful search of the available information sources to meet that need. Then the librarian must evaluate the information found and communicate its nature and value to the user in a helpful and understandable manner. Finally, the librarian must ensure that, in the opinion of the user, the information provided fully answers the question.

Of course, many users come to the reference desk with simple directional or informational questions, and the predominance of questions of this nature in reference service can cause library staff to underestimate the importance of the reference interview. Naturally, there are some questions that can be answered without negotiation. Many experienced librarians have found, however, that users who come to the reference desk with a seemingly simple question often have more complex information needs that they have not yet acknowledged or realized. In a widely quoted article, Robert Taylor labeled these "visceral needs," needs that are felt but not yet consciously formulated.[1] Without careful questioning and listening by the librarian, these questions may never be asked or answered.

In addition, some questions that the user regards as simple may require additional work later by the librarian if the specific information needed is not identified in the initial interview. For example, a question involving population may require the most current *estimate* or it might be answered by turning to the most recent *actual* count (decennial census for U.S. places), but the user may not tell the librarian which is desired. The librarian's ability to clarify the exact nature of the user's information need has been identified as a key element in user satisfaction with reference service.[2]

It is important to recognize that the principles of communication used in the reference interview are not entirely unique, but are analogous to techniques used by other professionals in helping roles. In many respects, as both Rachael Naismith and Carolyn Radcliff have observed, it is similar to a doctor's questioning of a patient regarding symptoms.[3] Among the most obvious similarities are a person in need of help and a professional who can help only when the need is fully revealed and understood by the helping professional. Because the client does not understand the structure of knowledge from which this need must be met, the professional must accurately ascertain the need and translate it into the structure of the specific information base that can satisfy that need. For reference librarians, this requires a desire to help people, a broad knowledge of information sources of all kinds, and a commitment to the ethical principles enunciated in Chapter 2. These are elements the librarian must bring to the reference encounter if it is to be a mutually satisfying experience and beneficial to the user.

Thus, it can be argued that the reference interview is at the center of reference service. It is the key to the library's mission of making information available and understandable to its user group. The reference librarian mediates between the user and the world of information (within and beyond the library), and guides the user—to the degree necessary—in the user's search to find appropriate, accurate, and complete information. In the reference interview, the reference staff demonstrate their commitment to the value of each user and the importance of each question. It is in the reference interview that the library most clearly and forcefully demonstrates to the public its value to them.

In this chapter, the reference interview is viewed as encompassing the human interaction between user and librarian throughout the reference transaction. Sometimes, the interview is treated as simply the conversation that takes place until the question has been fully defined. This approach, however, does not recognize the fact that the dialogue between user and librarian must continue throughout the process of finding the answer to the user's question, including, for example, the negotiation of the answer and any follow-up that occurs. Using the broader definition of the reference interview as including all interaction between user and librarian until the question has been answered, the reference interview is seen as generally following a pattern that includes the following steps:

1. Open the interview.
2. Negotiate the question.
3. Search for information.
4. Communicate the information to the user.
5. Close the interview.

This chapter identifies the principles of human interaction that contribute to the success or failure of reference interviews and examines in some detail each of the steps involved. Attention is given to actions reference staff can take to create a hospitable environment in which the reference interview can be conducted. In addition, the attitudes, behaviors, and skills on the part of the librarian that contribute to successful interviews are examined. Effective communication principles for each stage of the reference interview are discussed. Finally, specific situations that call for correspondingly unique approaches are examined.

Despite this discussion of steps and techniques, however, the underlying view of this chapter is that conducting a successful reference interview is essentially a straightforward matter. Pursuing three basic goals in a careful and disciplined manner should lead to success in most instances. These principles are:

1. Gain the trust of the user.
2. Ascertain from the user an accurate understanding of the question, so that it can be answered as completely as possible.
3. Make sure that the user is satisfied with the answer provided.

Successfully achieving the first goal will take the librarian a long way toward fulfilling the others, because user satisfaction has been found to depend on the interpersonal interaction with the librarian, and because a user who feels comfortable with a librarian is more likely to openly and completely reveal the information need. For this reason, the treatment here is intentionally practical in nature.

Of course, the librarian's search strategy also affects the success of the search. The principles guiding the actual search for answers to reference questions are discussed in Chapter 4.

OVERVIEW OF THE SUCCESSFUL INTERVIEW

Attitudes and Characteristics of the Reference Librarian

Just as not everyone could be a successful physician, not everyone is capable of providing effective reference and information services, even after appropriate study and training. Certain personal qualities and skills are required for good reference service, and not all can be learned. Various authors have listed the qualities of a good reference librarian; the lists are far from identical. What follows is discussion of one collection of the characteristics that contribute to successful performance in the reference interaction, the part of reference service involving the use of both human relations and intellectual skills.

Discipline

A disciplined mind is not always mentioned as a characteristic of good reference librarians, but without it reference interviews are essentially left to chance. The reference librarian must be capable of concentrating solely on one user and one information need, often in the midst of a variety of distractions in the reference environment (discussed below). At the same time, the librarian must apply any of a number of communication techniques necessary to understand the question and must also successfully develop an effective strategy for using available information sources to answer that question. This requires a strong dose of self-control, particularly in cases where time constraints exist or difficulties arise with the librarian's search strategy or the librarian's ongoing interaction with the user. Any negative emotions or false leads must be handled in a way that does not compromise the user's trust in the librarian as a competent information provider. An example of the use of discipline in the reference interview is the *choice* to listen carefully and fully to what the user has to say. This decision, as described by Mark Willis, is summarized in Box 3.1.

Box 3.1 Choose to Listen

This may sound silly at first, but many people are not good listeners because they don't want to be. They either don't care, don't see the value, or don't make the effort. One of the first and simplest steps we can take to improve our listening habits is to decide to be a better listener. Make it a priority to pay attention and learn what the speaker is truly trying to communicate. At the core of this is a decision to value the other person more than we had. To listen attentively, we have to make our own concerns and wants secondary to the speaker's.

Mark R. Willis
Dealing with Difficult People in the Library[4]

An organized mind is often a result of discipline, and it is essential for successful reference interactions. The librarian must always remember to ask appropriate questions, speak the user's language (not the jargon of librarianship), and assess the value of the information found before passing it on to the user. As for knowledge of interviewing techniques, it is useless if the librarian does not have the mental discipline to employ this knowledge in practice. For example, a common temptation is to deal with the user's question at face value, offer an easy, quick answer, and skip the reference interview altogether. It is only through discipline—through habitual attention to the user's verbal and nonverbal cues—that complex information needs can be uncovered behind simple questions. At the same time, some questions really are simple, and with practice and experience, one learns to tell the difference most of the time.

Mental discipline should also be used by the librarian to learn from experiences, both positive and negative ones. A user-centered reference service must respond to "failures" that occur because of gaps in the collection, services that are currently not provided, or gaps in the knowledge and skills of reference staff. Evaluation techniques for identifying these problems are noted in Chapter 10, but individual librarians can also work independently to improve their performance. It is particularly important to remember what was learned in a successful reference interview and to admit and seek to remedy failures that occur because of poor communication techniques or erroneous search strategies.

A Desire to Help

A commitment to helping people is the necessary correlate of a disciplined mind. Without it, the librarian risks appearing to be an uncaring robot, and many users will seek help elsewhere even if the answers provided by such a librarian are accurate. It is probably a desire to help that motivates many librarians to choose reference work as their specialty. "Helping" is not always easy, however. Some people, by their manner, make the reference librarian feel like a servant, and interactions with such users can be discouraging and disheartening. Here the combination of the desire to help with the quality of discipline makes it possible for the librarian to put such feelings aside and prepare for the next user, who will probably be more appreciative.

In any event, the desire to help should be expressed by the reference librarian in the form of approachability, friendliness, open-mindedness, and an interest in each user. An interest in people must be accompanied by the flexibility to work in the reference interaction with persons of widely variable personalities, appearances, and backgrounds. It has been pointed out that the more open and self-revealing the librarian is, the more open and forthcoming the user will be, and the more satisfied the user will be with the human relations aspect of the reference service provided.[5] Although some users prefer a totally anonymous librarian, most respond more positively to one who is open, courteous, and obviously interested in their unique needs.

Sensitivity

Sensitivity is the surest way to transform the desire to help into effective results, and with discipline it can be reconciled easily enough with the need to maintain a certain professional distance between librarian and user. It takes sensitivity to know how to proceed with the reference interview, because some users prefer a more formal and objective conversation while others will respond more positively to a librarian who is more casual or shows a real personal interest in the user's situation. The sensitive reference librarian realizes quickly which communication style is appropriate for the individual user.

Furthermore, reference librarians must show sensitivity in handling reference questions posed by certain groups, such as children, students (or parents) from other countries, persons with disabilities, and last, but not least, those individuals who are intimidated by computers or by libraries in general. Each user is an individual with unique characteristics and needs. The insensitive librarian could ruin any hope of success in the reference interaction by not perceiving the unique needs and concerns of each person who comes to the desk looking for assistance.

Patience

Patience is one of the most important qualifications for reference work. Anyone who works with other people in a service relationship needs patience to deal with cranky, arrogant, insensitive, or even overly timid individuals. People who need to unload their burden of frustrations will choose someone who is unlikely, due to the nature of the relationship involved, to respond in kind, whether that person is a supermarket checkout person or a reference librarian. Such encounters are the exception rather than the rule in the library, but the librarian must be able to withstand the storm without becoming flustered or angry. These days, the discomfort with computers and the maintenance associated with equipment such as printers can often be the trigger for user outbursts.

One must also be patient with oneself and with the "information universe" wherein the answer to the user's question is hidden. Some reference questions are very difficult, either from a bibliographic standpoint or from the nature of the topic that the user is pursuing. Good sources of information, or the exact bibliographic citation, can be difficult to find at times. It is important to remain calm and persistent, so that the user does not feel uncomfortable having asked the question or even sorry that it was asked of this particular librarian. At times it is necessary to tell the user that, given the complexity of the question, a return call later in the day or week is necessary. One can also mention that one will discuss the question with colleagues, to broaden the range of ideas brought to bear on it.

Broad Knowledge

Broad knowledge and varied interests help the librarian understand more quickly the user's question and translate it into the language of the bibliographic and factual universe of information. Unless one works in a specialized setting, such as a medical library, the more subject areas one feels comfortable with, the better one will be able to conduct a successful search of a specific body of literature.

Every reference librarian should read a good daily newspaper (and maybe a weekly newsmagazine as well), to keep up with current events.[6] In addition, it is helpful to read more specialized sources published for nonspecialists whenever possible; a good example is *Scientific American.* Particularly important for the many humanities graduates who end up at the reference desk is a passing interest in the sciences, because at general reference desks in public and academic libraries science-oriented questions will arise often. The librarian who follows this advice will feel more self-confident dealing with the broad range of questions that users ask and librarians need to understand.

This broad knowledge and wide range of interests naturally lead to a better knowledge of the information sources in a wide variety of subject areas. Understanding the terminology of a field makes it easier to learn and remember the reference titles in that field that seek to organize the knowledge of the field. Increasingly, this includes awareness of important Web sites in as many areas as possible.

Knowledge of Reference Sources

In football, coaches who are successful are often great motivators. But they also must possess a thorough knowledge of "the x's and o's," namely the individual offensive and defensive positions and strategies. For reference librarians, the "x's and o's" are their mastery of general and subject-specific information sources and their awareness of current world events or the substance and literature of subject fields. It takes time and experience—often aided by tips from colleagues—to acquire the grasp of reference resources necessary for efficient and effective answering of the questions that come to the librarian at a general reference desk. This knowledge is the subject of Part II of this text, and the strategies for putting this knowledge to use are discussed in Chapter 4. Here it might be added that for the new reference librarian, time to peruse the collection is usually helpful—even necessary—before that librarian is ready to staff the desk.

Interviewing Principles

A number of verbal and nonverbal communication techniques have been discussed in the library literature over the past 50 years. Many of these have proven, in either obtrusive or unobtrusive studies (see Chapter 10) of reference interactions, to improve the accuracy of the librarian's response and/or to have a beneficial effect on the user's feelings about the service provided by the reference staff member. These are discussed in the appropriate place in the following section.

Here, general principles that should guide all library staff when they interact with users are briefly presented. These principles enable the librarian to effectively utilize the attitudes and skills previously discussed. The principles are adaptations of commonsense guidelines for good human relations, and they give further substance to the three simple goals of the reference interview mentioned above.

1. Smile and greet the user in a friendly manner.
2. Listen carefully to, and take an interest in, what the user says.
3. Take each question seriously. Regard it as a learning experience, or if you prefer, as a helping experience.
4. Ask questions until you fully understand the user's information need.
5. Never think about the strategy you will use until you have fully understood the question.
6. Never think you know the answer. Let the reference tools and the user tell you when the question has been completely answered.
7. Invite the user to return if more help is needed, now or in the future.

These principles are stated simply, as befits general guidelines for reference service. Keeping them in mind will, by itself, improve one's reference interactions. Readers should also study the "Guidelines for Behavioral Performance of Reference and Information Services Professionals," prepared by the Reference and User Services Association (RUSA) of the American Library Association. The RUSA Guidelines are more detailed than the ones listed above, and include narrative summaries and examples of the various interviewing techniques. They are too lengthy to reproduce here, but excerpts are given in Box 3.2.

Box 3.2

Excerpts from RUSA Guidelines for Behavioral Performance of Reference and Information Services Professionals

1.0 Approachability

Approachability behaviors set the tone for the entire communication process between the librarian and the patron.... To be approachable, the librarian:

1.1 Is poised and ready to engage approaching patrons and is not engrossed in...activities that detract from availability to the patron....

1.3 Acknowledges the presence of the patron through smiling and/or open body language.

....

2.0 Interest

While not every query will contain stimulating intellectual challenges, the librarian should be interested in each patron's informational needs....To demonstrate interest, the librarian:

2.5 Appears unhurried during the reference transaction.

2.6 Focuses his or her attention on the patron.

3.0 Listening/Inquiring

Strong listening and questioning skills are necessary for a positive interaction. As a good communicator, the librarian:

3.2 Communicates in a receptive, cordial, and encouraging manner.

3.4 Rephrases the patron's question or request and asks for confirmation to ensure that it is understood.

3.7 Seeks to clarify confusing terminology and avoids excessive jargon.

4.0 Searching

As an effective searcher, the librarian:

4.9 Discusses the search strategy with the patron.

4.10 Encourages the patron to contribute ideas.

4.11 Explains the search to the patron.

....

5.0 Follow-up

The reference transaction does not end when the librarian walks away from the patron....For successful follow-up, the librarian:

5.1 Asks the patron if the question has been completely answered.

5.2 Encourages the patron to return to the reference service point.

5.8 Refers the patron to other sources or institutions when the query cannot be answered to the satisfaction of the patron.

"RUSA Guidelines for Behavioral Performance of Reference and Information Services Professionals"[7]

STEPS IN THE REFERENCE INTERVIEW

There is no law that says each interview with a user must follow the steps discussed here. Each librarian is unique, each user is unique, each question (beyond "where is the bathroom?") is unique, and just about every information source used to answer reference questions is unique. But the steps described in this chapter are basic enough that most interviews can be encompassed therein. General principles for the librarian to follow are presented; the exact manner in which they are applied is at the discretion of the reference staff member and will undoubtedly vary from one interview to the next.

Opening the Interview

The interview is usually opened by the reference librarian with a smile, a greeting, and an expression of interest in hearing the user's question (it is opened by the user if the librarian is surprised by the user, which should be avoided by attentiveness on the part of the librarian). To establish trust and openness, the librarian should be approachable, friendly, and focused solely on the user. This can be communicated nonverbally by sustained eye contact with the user, accompanied by a smile or leaning forward in one's chair. Some librarians sitting at low desks prefer to stand as a user approaches to indicate their readiness to meet the user's needs. It is important to continue to send positive nonverbal messages to the user throughout the interview to reassure the user that the librarian is interested in the specific question asked and also to encourage the user to continue to maintain a cooperative exchange of information with the librarian.

A general question, such as "How can I help you?" may begin the interaction. With experience, reference staff learn to adapt their communication style to the style preferred by the user—such as more friendly with outgoing and known users, or more formal with users who do not respond in kind to the librarian's initial friendliness. Although the interview is discussed here as a conversation, some users will exchange a few general remarks with the librarian to make themselves (or both parties) feel relaxed, while others will maintain a strictly "business only" posture.

Of course, the library setting or the characteristics of the user often dictate the nature of the opening of the interview. In a hospital or corporate library, the library users may have little time or interest in conversing, preferring instead that the librarian attend quickly and efficiently to their information needs from the beginning. However, in a public or academic library, when a young person comes to the reference desk, the librarian may want to talk with the person more (if time allows), particularly if the person appears to be shy. In similar fashion, senior citizens often like to converse with the librarian, obtaining some social interaction along with the answer to their question.

Whatever the nature of the opening of the interview, the goal is the same. The librarian seeks to establish that the library is a friendly place and that the library staff want to help users with their information needs. In addition, users should sense that the question they are about to ask has the complete attention of the reference librarian. This welcoming and informal attitude can be continued throughout the interview process, including such techniques as discussing the question and possible sources while one is walking from the desk to the appropriate shelf or table (see Box 3.3).

Box 3.3 The "Walking Technique"

Accompanying the person to the recommended source can be a valuable technique. It diffuses the stiffness, formality, and nervousness of inexperienced librarians and the users by providing a more informal situation for eliciting information. A casual, indirect exploration of a question and the individual's ability to pursue it may save time in the long run.

Diana M. Thomas, Ann T. Hinckley, and Elizabeth R. Eisenbach
The Effective Reference Librarian[8]

It should be no surprise that the most important point in the reference interview is the librarian's first response to the user's question. It is at this point that many users will make a judgment about the librarian's willingness and ability to satisfy their information need successfully. First, if the librarian shows any irritation with the question or any sign of being uncomfortable with its content, users will conclude that the librarian either does not want to help them or is unable to. Second, because users often ask questions before they have thought them out carefully, taking the first question at face value may easily lead to answers that users ultimately find incomplete.

Negotiating the Question

The negotiation of the user's question is the most important stage in the reference interview, and will consequently be discussed in some detail. Several communication techniques have been identified that allow user and librarian to get from the user's initial question to the precise information that is needed and the strategy that will be used to find that information. These techniques are discussed below; their use varies with the question asked, the type of library where it is asked, and a number of other variables. Library staff must, in each interview, decide which kind of question or communication technique is most likely to be successful.

The first step in understanding the user's need is to ascertain the scope of the question. A question such as, "What do you have on the Crusades?" might be answered with a general overview article in an encyclopedia, might require a book-length treatment of the topic, or might require specialized features such as a chronology or a map. Although it is important not to prejudge any user, the situation generally offers clues about what kind of information will be required. For example, college students will need scholarly books and articles on the Crusades, not the summary treatment found in a general encyclopedia.

Other areas to be negotiated in the reference interview include any limitations on format, language, date of publication, and similar factors that the librarian needs to know before the search begins, or at least in the early stages of the search. Also important is the matter of location: Does the user want to look only at materials in the library where the search is taking place, or will materials obtained by interlibrary loan or travel to another location also be part of the research being conducted? Of course, for many factual questions, consulting one or two reference tools will easily provide the answer, or information in other locations can be accessed by telephone or using the Internet.

Open and Closed Questions

Open questions are those that encourage the user to talk more about the information need. Examples are, "Can you tell me a little bit more about what you are looking for?" and "I think I understand what you want, but can you give me a little more detail?" Open questions are most useful in the early stages of the interview, when the librarian is seeking to define the scope and type of information needed. In a 1972 article, Geraldine King elaborated on this point at some length. An excerpt of that article is given in Box 3.4.

Box 3.4 The Value of Open Questions

The basic reason for using open questions is that they encourage the user to talk. . . . If the librarian uses a few open questions and lets the user talk, the user will often cover much of what the librarian needs to know and some important points the librarian would not have thought of asking about.

Geraldine King
"The Reference Interview"[9]

Conversely, closed questions generally lead to short answers, often a simple yes or no. Examples are, "Are you looking for a scholarly presentation or for a popular treatment?" and "Would a map or illustrations help you to visualize this?" Usually, closed questions are most helpful in the middle or latter stages of the reference interview, when the topic is well understood and only the format, time period, or some other variable needs to be determined. However, in those cases where the user knows exactly what is wanted and communicates this effectively to the librarian, a closed question may be the only negotiation required to find what the user needs. For example, the librarian usually needs to find out what level of detail is wanted, what format is preferred, and similar parameters of the user's information need.

Flexibility must guide the use of open and closed questions. Often a closed question early in the negotiation process is helpful. Asking the user whether this information is needed for a term paper or for a specific class assignment can be the quickest way of finding out what the librarian needs to know to help the user. Similarly, an open question at the end of the interview, such as "Is there any other information you need?" is a proper way to ensure that the librarian's work has been helpful and complete. There are no hard-and-fast rules about what kind of questions should be used at any point; it is up to the librarian's judgment and sensitivity to know how to proceed.

Neutral Questioning

Neutral questioning is a technique developed by Brenda Dervin as part of a broader approach to the reference interview called "sense making." Using this approach, the librarian strives to understand the user's question from the user's perspective by asking questions designed to elicit background information regarding the information need, such as why it is needed, to what use it will be put, and so on. In other words, the librarian tries to understand the *context* from which the information need arose.[10] However, this information is obtained by the librarian not by direct questions, which might offend the user, but through the use of neutral questions, such as "If you could tell me the kind of problem you are working on, I will get a better idea of what would help you."[11]

Neutral questions are open in nature, and they seek to get the user to talk more fully about the information need. They offer the librarian a chance to "see" the question the same way the user sees it. Neutral questions are most effective early in the interview process, but they can also be used when the librarian finds material that appears helpful but is not viewed as relevant by the user. In general, like active listening (see below), neutral questions help the librarian to avoid reaching premature and inaccurate conclusions about the user's need.

Encouragers

A specific class of open questions has been referred to as *encouragers.*[12] These questions overtly encourage the users to more fully reveal their information needs. Questions such as, "Can you tell me more about this topic?" and even short questions such as "Yes?" or "OK, what else?" can be very effective ways of getting the user to further explain the question so that the librarian can begin thinking about where to start in the search for an answer. As with neutral questioning, encouragers help the librarian see the question as much as possible from the viewpoint of the user and gain more insight into the background that produced the question. A fuller, more accurate understanding of this background is likely to lead to a more successful search strategy, because the success of the search strategy is ultimately determined by the user's need.

Active Listening

Active listening involves reflecting back to the user the librarian's understanding of the question to verify that it is being properly understood.[13] This usually takes the form of a tentative restatement of what the user has said, in terms that the librarian can work with, to get the user's agreement that this is what the user wants. The frequency with which the information need is restated will vary with the complexity of the topic the user is investigating. A question arising out of a lengthy research project in a field with which the librarian is unfamiliar may require that the librarian restate the question several times during the course of the interview and search process. More straightforward questions may require only that the librarian restate the question just before beginning to formulate a search strategy.

Asking Why

There is a considerable body of literature addressing the issue of whether or how the librarian should ask the user why the information being sought is needed. The question can quickly destroy any trust that the librarian has built up to that point in the interview. Many questions—health-related, about schools or camps, legal information, even term papers in certain types of courses—reflect very personal situations that the user might not wish to share with a stranger. For this reason, questions about why the user needs the information should be avoided whenever possible. Nonetheless, as Fred Oser (along with others) has pointed out, sometimes the use to which the information is to be put determines "the level of treatment and amount of information needed" and therefore helps the librarian better serve the user.[14]

Whenever possible, the best strategy for the librarian to follow is to deal solely with the question and any further information volunteered by the user. In those cases where the librarian needs to make a choice regarding type of tool and does not have the information to do it, a more roundabout method can be employed. One possibility is to ask how the information is to be used, but this is still very close to asking why; it is just not as blunt. Another method—which further points out the continuing nature of the interview throughout the search process—is to suggest that at this stage one of several alternatives must be selected and let the user choose which type of information is most suitable.

Alfred Benjamin, whose book, *The Helping Interview*, is often quoted in literature about the reference interview, has grave doubts about asking why in the counseling interview.[15] It inevitably causes a withdrawal by the interviewee and tension in the interview. However, Benjamin also believes, almost in spite of himself, that sometimes the question is necessary. His justification for using it is given in Box 3.5.

Box 3.5 Asking Why in the Helping Interview

Should the word "why," then, never be used? I know I wish I myself would employ it less.... I try to avoid it and am glad when I succeed, but often enough there it is to be dealt with again. The little word, however does have a justifiable place.... If the interviewee perceives that our attitude is unthreatening and if we use "why" simply to obtain factual information that we feel we need, then our use of the word should not cause undue damage.

Alfred Benjamin
The Helping Interview[16]

The Search Process

Once the librarian understands fully the user's information need, it is time to think about how and where the answer might be found. General approaches to searching for information are discussed in Chapter 4. More specific strategies to use with the different kinds of reference tools are outlined in the chapters in Part II. Here, the focus is on the human interaction that occurs while the librarian is searching for the answer to the user's question.

Except for those occasions when a return call will be made at a later time, the user will generally accompany the librarian in the search for the answer, either by observing the action on the computer screen or by following the librarian to the specific area the librarian has chosen as a starting point in the search. The search process should be a joint enterprise, with the librarian continually checking with the user to ensure that the information being gathered is appropriate as regards currency, intellectual level, precise focus, level of detail, and so on. Some users would rather be off doing something else while the librarian finds the answer for them, but this is not always the best method to employ if the question is a complicated one. At the very least, in such cases the librarian needs to conduct a more comprehensive reference interview before the user leaves to pursue other tasks.

As was pointed out in Box 3.3, the librarian can continue to discuss the question during the search process. In particular, the librarian should discuss with the user each tool chosen and the relevance of the information found there. If the user is one who wants only the answer and no information on how to use reference tools, then the librarian can confine the discussion to checking with the user to see if the information being found is what the user wants.

Communicating the Information to the User

When the librarian has found the answer to a user's question or has identified the research for the user to pursue, that information must be presented to the user in a manner that assures the user's satisfaction with the information provided. If the question is factual, it is only necessary to tell or show the user the source that provided the information and ensure that the information completely answers the user's question. If the user is a student, the librarian might reasonably ask if source information is a requirement, and if the answer is affirmative the librarian can help the student construct an appropriate bibliographic citation for the source.

With research questions, the librarian must make several decisions before communicating the "answer" to the user:

1. How much work is required for this research?
2. Can/should the librarian or the user take primary responsibility for this work (this varies with the library and its resources and policies)?
3. If the librarian will do the work, when and how will further information be communicated to the user?
4. If the user will do the work, how much instruction will the librarian need to provide before this can be carried out?

Once the librarian makes these decisions, they must be presented to the user and negotiated in a mutually satisfactory way. If the user is new to the particular library, this negotiation may be more difficult than it will be if the user is already familiar with the library's policies and research tools.

It should be obvious that information given to users must be at an appropriate intellectual level and free of jargon from either the field of librarianship or from any other field with which the user is unfamiliar. Users will not always say that the material presented to them is unclear or too difficult for them to master, so librarians must assess the user's abilities during the search process to avoid giving the user the right information in the wrong package.

Communicating the information to remote users presents its own problems, because the user cannot (in most cases) personally view the information. The issues that arise in telephone and e-mail communications with users are discussed later in this chapter.

Closing the Interview

How the interview is brought to an end is every bit as important as how it is opened, because the final exchange between librarian and user contributes greatly to the user's impression of the library's reference service, as well as to user satisfaction with the specific information provided. When the search has been successful and the interview pleasant, the librarian can again ask if the user's question has been completely answered, and if so, the librarian can simply encourage the user to return when another information need arises. Unfortunately, in too many cases the librarian lets the user leave, only to discover at a later time that important information was missed in the search process and the librarian does not know how to pass on this information to the user. This outcome leaves the librarian frustrated, and the user is probably not totally happy with the result, either.

The librarian can take any of a number of steps to try to avoid a premature or unsuccessful end to the reference encounter. One important rule recommended by Christopher Nolan[17] is to "always end an unsuccessful interview with a referral." If the librarian is unable to find the needed information, it is far better to seek help from a colleague in another department or library, or from a relevant community or national organization, than to send the user away empty-handed. The librarian and user can together decide who is better situated to consult the external source, based on convenience, time constraints, generally accepted procedures, and other factors. Whenever the librarian will do more searching or will consult with someone else after the user leaves, the interview should end with agreement on how and when the user will be contacted. The librarian should write down all pertinent information and have a standard procedure to ensure that it is not misplaced.

It should be emphasized that by no means should referrals be used to "get rid of" users because the reference desk is too busy or the librarian feels uncomfortable with the question. Proper referrals take time, and if the time is not taken, an unsatisfied user will often be the consequence. The best way to refer a user is to call the person or office to which the user is being referred to ensure that someone is there who can help with the question. It is important to be aware of resources available in other library units, nearby libraries, and other agencies and organizations. Sending a user to a place or person who cannot help with the information need wastes everyone's time and, in fact, often results in the user returning to the reference desk in a less friendly mood.

Another possible way to close the reference interview is to offer to continue the interview at another time when the librarian can devote more time and attention to the user's request. This might be an in-person interview held by appointment in an office setting, or it might simply be a more lengthy conversation after the librarian finishes the current shift at the reference desk. The interview could also be continued by e-mail if this is convenient for both parties.

Despite these guidelines to avoid premature closure, it should be said that, in most libraries, the majority of interviews concern topics that can be handled thoroughly in one brief interview and search process. In these cases, the librarian may simply pause for a minute to review the search to ensure that it has been comprehensive and accurate, then check with the user to see if the user also feels that the information need has been completely met. Even in such cases, however, it is important for the librarian to restate the offer to provide further assistance if the user discovers at a later time that more information is wanted.

THE REFERENCE ENVIRONMENT

Successful reference interviews do not depend only on the attitudes, knowledge, and skills of the librarian and the ability of the user to articulate the kind and level of information that is needed. They depend also on the physical and social environment in which the interview is conducted. If optimal conditions for a careful, thorough discussion of the user's needs are not present, the reference librarian faces difficult obstacles before the question is even asked.

Many professionals who need to question their clients have the option of conducting interviews in a private setting, such as an office, an examination room, or a room set aside for counseling. Except in cases where librarians have private offices in which to meet with researchers, reference staff must conduct their interviews at a public reference or information desk. This presents several problems. Other users may be standing at the desk waiting for service, giving the questioner little privacy and placing pressure on the librarian to finish the interview prematurely. If there is a telephone on the desk for incoming reference questions, the interruption of the phone ringing may be an irritant to the user and a distraction to the librarian. Even when librarians tell callers that they are busy and will call back when they can, the interview with the user who is at the desk has been adversely affected by the interruption. Taken together, the various problems associated with reference desk interviewing are a primary reason that the service provided there may appear to both user and librarian to be effectively limited to ready-reference questions that require little negotiation.

There are, however, steps that can be taken to improve the environment at the reference desk. In libraries where tiered service is provided (see Chapter 11), telephone calls can be answered by paraprofessionals at an information desk set up to handle ready-reference queries. If the reference desk is visible from this desk, staff there can forward complicated questions to the reference desk only if they see that a librarian is free to accept the call. If not, the information desk staff can take a message, and the call can be returned later. The problem of users standing at the reference desk waiting for service is more difficult to handle. The librarian may stop the interview in process long enough to assure the waiting user that the same attention will be available to that user in just a few moments. In cases where the interview leads naturally to an online search terminal or an index table, the librarian can use that less pressurized setting to continue to explore the needs of the user. Another solution is to have a reference staff member on "standby" duty during peak hours, available to handle waiting users or staff the desk while the librarian on duty continues the interview away from the reference desk.

INTERVIEWS FOR SPECIFIC SITUATIONS

The general principles and specific techniques of reference interviewing discussed above can be applied effectively to many user questions received at general reference desks. However, there are several specific situations that require adaptations of one kind or another to the general model of interviewing. Those that occur frequently in a variety of settings are discussed in this section. In addition, Chapter 12 presents specialized interviewing techniques required when dealing with groups such as children, young adults, or persons with disabilities.

Readers' Advisory Interviews

It was noted in Chapter 1 that readers' advisory services in public libraries have enjoyed a rebirth in recent years. In addition, the focus of these services has changed in ways that make them more helpful to more library users. Recreational or "escapist" novels no longer are viewed with distrust as they were earlier in the twentieth century, when education and self-improvement were considered the primary goals of reading. Readers' advisors now look upon the reading of popular fiction—or indeed, on reading itself—as intrinsically valuable and as serving an important function for the reader.[18] The readers' advisor, then, needs to discover why the reader finds certain types of literature interesting, then provide suggestions about books that might also be appealing to this particular individual. Joyce G. Saricks and Nancy Brown note that readers' advisory interviews, unlike other reference interviews, are at their best when they continue over a period of months or years, with the user gaining increasingly more trust in the librarian and the librarian understanding the user's reading interests more completely as they evolve over time.[19] This interaction generally occurs in public libraries, although the assistance reference librarians offer to scholars and others pursuing long-term research projects has many similarities to readers' advisory service.

As with other reference interviews, the success of the readers' advisory interview depends on the librarian's willingness to listen and to understand the user's tastes, along with the librarian's knowledge of a wide variety of fictional genres. In this type of interview, the information need is usually expressed as a desire to identify and read more books by a particular author, books in a specific genre, such as mystery novels, or simply for "another book like the one I just read." Neutral questioning, which is designed to help the librarian understand the context in which the information need arose, is particularly helpful here. Questions such as "What did you particularly like about that book?" are very helpful because they encourage users to discuss what is appealing to them at the present, or what kinds of plot, characters, settings, and other elements they have found enjoyable in the past.[20] The librarian needs to understand the user's current tastes and needs as thoroughly and objectively as possible, because, as Catherine Sheldrick Ross points out, suggestions that are based on the librarian's tastes rather than the user's will only be ignored.[21] Knowledge of fictional genres and titles is important here as well, because often a novel by a different author will actually turn out to be more appealing and satisfying to the user if it has a plot, setting, or protagonist much like the book recently enjoyed by that user. Annotated lists of titles in particular genres, although no substitute for good interviewing skills, can often help both the reader and librarian identify candidates for selection by the reader.[22]

In closing readers' advisory interviews, it is especially important to encourage the user to return for more assistance, and most important, with feedback regarding the book or books suggested by the librarian. If the recommended titles were not liked, further conversation may better clarify what the reader is looking for in a book. In addition, reasons for failure can be identified, and the librarian can better understand both the user and the title or genre involved.[23]

An excellent Web site for both readers' advisors and their users is *Reader's Robot* (http://www.tnrdlib.bc.ca/rr.html), maintained by the Thompson-Nicola Regional District Library System in Kamloops, British Columbia. This site collects reader and librarian input about books in 21 genres, both the usual fiction genres and some nonfiction categories such as travel and popular science. In August 2000, the site contained more than 3,300 reviews. The site also allows users to search the 21-genre databases using "appeal factors" (a concept used by Saricks and Brown, among others) such as length, plot, style, socio-economic level of characters, and others. *Reader's Robot* would make an excellent bookmark for librarians who serve as readers' advisors. Libraries may also subscribe to electronic readers' advisory resources such as *NoveList* (http://novelist.epnet.com).

For readers' advisory interviews involving nonfiction materials, nothing substitutes for a thorough knowledge of the subject field and the important works in that field—both those for specialists and those for the general reader. In this type of interview, the important characteristics of the needed materials are less subjective, and often revolve around the detail provided, the technical level of the writing, and the author's intended audience. However, non-specialists will sometimes be surprisingly well-versed in a particular field, while those with educational and work experience in a field may need only a summary treatment of the field as a whole or a brief, nontechnical overview of the latest trends. Guidance in choosing the best materials in a variety of subject areas has been provided for years by *The Reader's Advisor*, a frequently revised, multivolume work discussed in Chapter 20.

Remote Interviews: Telephone

When communicating with users over the telephone, the librarian must use a friendly tone of voice to compensate for the lack of visual nonverbal cues used in the face-to-face interview. Nor does the user get nonverbal cues from the librarian, except for the librarian's tone of voice. For this reason, it is particularly important that the librarian answer in a welcoming way, and not as though the caller is interrupting something more important. The librarian must often gain the user's trust even while telling the user that a return call is necessary due to the crush of in-person business at the reference desk. For this reason, the first impression made by the librarian is even more important than in face-to-face interviews.

On the other hand, the librarian can usually be more relaxed over the phone, because the question will often require a return call with the answer at a later time (trying to answer questions while leaving the caller on hold is not polite, except for the most routine requests quickly answerable by sources right at hand). Some in-person users unknowingly put pressure on the librarian by looking hurried, checking their watch, or continually interrupting with further comments that may not be germane (yes, it is possible to get users to volunteer too much information). Thus, it may be easier for the librarian, with a telephone caller, to listen carefully and ask questions adeptly, without being tempted to (or feeling pressure to) go to the search strategy stage too quickly. This assumes, of course, that the librarian does not have several users standing at the reference desk waiting for service. This latter situation is more common, unfortunately, and often negatively affects the reference interview with the calling user. For this reason, a separate center, away from public service points, is the ideal setting for telephone reference service, but this is more the exception than the rule.

With telephone requests, it is particularly crucial that the librarian fully understand what the user needs because the user is not physically present to participate in the search process. Before putting down the phone, the librarian should repeat the question to the user to be sure that it is understood; spellings of names and places, dates, and other details—such as the user's name and telephone number—should be verified with the user. It is generally best to write down as much as possible.

Of course, it often happens that the librarian needs to call back before the answer is found, to report on progress or to discuss the nature and value of what has been found to that point. When the answer is found, it is important to communicate the facts to the user carefully and deliberately, to make sure that the user understands everything correctly. It is also imperative to give the source of the information, for the user's benefit and also to prevent someone on the staff from repeating the entire search process should the user misplace the information or desire more detail at a later date.

Because of the complexity of telephone reference service, some libraries separate it entirely from desk service. The primary reason for doing this is that both operations are labor intensive, and if one or two librarians are trying to do both at once, it is difficult to give both in-person and telephone users the service they deserve. It is also difficult for librarians to maintain their friendly and composed demeanor when trying to juggle phone and in-person queries. Although e-mail reference service is less stressful for librarians, and probably also for users, some users will continue to prefer to use the telephone, if only to get a faster response for important but quickly answered questions.

Remote Interviews: Electronic

Unless one's reference service incorporates a telephone reference center that is separated from the reference desk, remote users will sometimes get less than optimal service. As more users have easy access to personal computers, however, electronic remote service options have become available that have distinct advantages over the telephone, while still allowing the user to access effective and timely reference service without having to come to the library building. In the 1990s, various libraries incorporated into their reference services the receiving of questions by e-mail or, most recently, by videoconferencing. E-mail reference service has since become routine, particularly in academic and special library settings, where accepting questions on the reference department's Web page has become popular as well. On the other hand, videoconferencing is still in its infancy but may very well become more common in the future.

The major drawback of accepting reference queries by e-mail or Web page is the asynchronous nature of the interaction: Library staff cannot interview the user in real-time. As Eileen Abels has pointed out, when e-mail is used to communicate, an interchange of questions and answers to clarify the question can result in substantial delays in providing the answer.[24] Consequently, the reference service must help users formulate better first questions by providing guidance ahead of time, through publicity about e-mail service and/or by instructions on the Web page. Questions that would occur in sequence during an in-person interview must be carefully selected and presented together at the outset when e-mail is the medium of communication. It is important to specify what types of questions can and cannot be answered using this service and also to stimulate the user to offer as much relevant information about the question as possible. Often, when the transaction is initiated through the reference service's Web page, a "search request form" is the vehicle through which the service is initiated. The form contains instructions and advice, along with boxes where the user types in the question and any other helpful information, requested or volunteered. When the form is completed and submitted, it is routed to an e-mail address where staff screen and handle the questions. Further discussion by e-mail or telephone may occur, or the staff may just use the information provided to answer the question and communicate that answer to the user by e-mail. Examples of such a search request form may be found in the Abels article[25] and on the Reference Web page of the Internet Public Library, a Web-based service of the University of Michigan School of Information (http://www.ipl.org/ref/QUE).

E-mail and Web-based reference requests appeal to some users more than to others. It is a perfect medium for the growing number of university students involved in distance education programs. It would also seem to fit the new approach to research in academic and business settings where e-mail is already a routine mode of communication between persons physically removed from their library or other staff. It is more convenient for users, who can submit questions at any time, while the librarians also find checking their e-mail when they are not at the desk more convenient than handling intrusive telephone calls. In her study of e-mail reference at Indiana University, Ann Bristow reported that one user suggested that the telephone be abandoned and all remote service be provided by e-mail.[26] It has also been reported that users formulate and present their questions more effectively if they write them down rather than speaking them in a face-to-face conversation.[27] However, other people will continue to prefer to come to the library and discuss their information needs in person with a librarian at the desk.

Several experiments with videoconferencing for remote reference service have been reported.[28] Videoconferencing offers the advantage of real-time discussion between the user and the librarian. The nonverbal cues unavailable by phone or e-mail might be helpful using this medium, assuming the use of video and computer equipment does not change the user's nonverbal behavior. The use of videoconferencing for real-time reference interviews requires expensive equipment (microphone, video equipment, and an appropriately configured personal computer), appropriate software, and intensive technical support, along with extensive training for staff and for the many users who will be, at least initially, intimidated by discussing their information needs on-camera.[29] In addition, users must come to the equipment, because at present most people do not have such devices in their homes or offices. However, in some special and academic libraries, particularly medical settings, where such technology is already in use or readily available, remote reference by videoconferencing may be more widely adopted in the future. Where remote branches, satellite locations, and similar organizational schemes necessitate and encourage improvements in electronic communication, videoconferencing for reference queries offers the big advantage of face-to-face, real-time interviewing.[30]

Imposed Queries

Imposed queries—questions asked by a user on behalf of someone else—have been recognized by reference librarians for many years, but have been carefully studied only recently in several articles by Melissa Gross.[31] Imposed queries are very common in reference work, because most student questions are imposed by their teachers and many other users come to the reference librarian for assistance with questions posed by friends, spouses, employers, or other individuals they are representing. These situations pose unique challenges (and opportunities) to staff conducting reference interviews, and are discussed separately here for that reason.

Gross discusses several aspects of imposed queries that require special care in the reference interview. Most obviously, because the person whose information need is presented by the user is not usually available at the time of the interview, the librarian must work with the user's often incomplete or even misunderstood information regarding the information requested. Techniques such as neutral questioning, encouragers, and other approaches that probe the origins of the question and the use to which the answer will be put may help the librarian understand the intent and purpose of the question in the context of the goals of the person who originated the request but is not present. Closed questions may also be needed to focus the information more precisely when the user is not completely sure on particular points. If the originator of the question is available by telephone, the librarian may need to talk to that person to clarify the question, or the user may need to check with that person and contact the librarian again later. As Gross points out, imposed queries point out better than most questions the need for the librarian to seek to understand the context from which the question arose.

Librarians and school media specialists need to identify questions arising from assignments, because steps can be taken to benefit future students with the same question and other librarians who will encounter the same or similar questions in later shifts. A call or e-mail to the teacher can clarify the assignment for library staff, can lead to group instruction for students who are expected to complete that assignment, and can lead—if appropriate—to setting aside relevant materials on reserve or in a special place where they can be securely and conveniently assembled for student use. Library staff can discuss the assignment if its difficulty or the size of the class warrants it, and may even prepare an instructional handout for student use. In short, the aspects of the imposed query that present problems, such as ambiguities or misunderstandings on the part of the user and librarian, can be reduced or eliminated.

Angry or Upset Users

Ideally, libraries would be places of relatively quiet activity and contemplation, and reference areas would be filled with users and librarians working together in perfect harmony in search of information and research materials. This is not the case, of course. The very nature of reference materials—their noncirculating status, the self-help component often necessary in large libraries, the difficulty of accurately using and interpreting computerized catalogs—and the very imperfect nature of human beings inevitably lead to expressions of frustration and even anger from library users. Sometimes it is restrictive library policies that irritate them, sometimes it is incomplete library collections or insufficient or inadequate service from library staff. Often it is frustrations that occurred before the visit to the library. It is common knowledge that people in public service positions are vulnerable to the person who is unhappy for some reason and reacts angrily to the first person who comes along. In any case, reference librarians will frequently face a user who is difficult to handle, and they need to be prepared to deal effectively with the encounter. Rarely, there will be encounters with mentally ill or deviant individuals, but only the much more common angry or irritated users are discussed here.

Several books and articles in the library literature offer help in preparing librarians to deal with angry or frustrated users.[32] The suggestions made basically involve applying to these specific situations the communication principles discussed throughout this chapter. The librarian confronted by an angry user needs to establish that the user's concerns are being heard, understood, and acted upon. This means that the librarian must listen carefully, attentively, and empathetically to the user. Active listening skills are especially important in conflict situations. Both the specifics of the problem and the user's feelings must be acknowledged by the librarian. Then the librarian must take some action to address the user's frustration, even if it cannot be the action the user initially wants. Often, alternative solutions can be identified that help the user deal with the situation. In other cases, the librarian can bring in a supervisor to speak with greater authority about the library's policies in a particular area. Even if no exception can be made, and no alternative approach can be found that will satisfy the user, the library can promise to review its policy in light of the user's frustration. Libraries cannot satisfy all requests, but they can assure their users that they are willing to rethink their policies and procedures in response to user needs.

Because conflicts between users and library staff are inevitable, it is important that libraries and reference departments have written policies that can be shown to angry users who question library practices.[33] This is particularly applicable to the situation where the user demands more than the library staff can provide. Some users try to intimidate librarians into deviating from established policies for their benefit. A commitment to empathy and a high standard of service should not require that one be subjected to such intimidation, or to any form of verbal abuse. Reference staff must be trained to remain firm in the face of such pressure, and it is immensely helpful to have written policies that have been approved by the library's director and/or governing body. Examples of such policies can be found in *Dealing with Difficult People in the Library*, by Mark Willis.[34]

It is also important for reference staff to discuss among themselves conflict situations and to look for ways such problems can be avoided in the future. Long after the complaining user is gone, the question "Could this have been avoided?" must be answered. Sometimes the user simply wants more than the library can provide, but repeated complaints—such as inadequate access to computers and electronic databases or unhappiness over canceled reference sources—should be referred to administrators for further consideration or review.

Whether or not expressions of frustration and anger are justified, a user-centered reference service will be willing to regularly re-examine its responses to expressed user needs.

CONCLUSION

The effectiveness of individualized reference service depends heavily on the ability of the library staff to conduct a successful reference interview. Successful interviews require a genuine interest in the user's information need, an ability to establish an atmosphere of trust with another person, and a sufficient grasp of communication principles to ask the right questions in the right way and at the right time. To begin with, this requires from the librarian an interest in helping people and the flexibility to deal with a variety of people and topics objectively. Armed with a strong ethic of service to individual users, the librarian will, over time, learn to employ consistently the communication skills that help users to articulate their information needs and make it possible for librarians to communicate the information they find to the user in a satisfactory manner. Also over time, the librarian will build the thorough knowledge of appropriate reference resources that, along with strong communication skills and a commitment to users, forms the basis for effective reference service.

In addition, successful reference interviews serve a broader goal of the reference or information service, namely user satisfaction. Recent studies by Joan Durrance indicate that a successful personal interaction during the reference interview is a strong predictor of user satisfaction with reference service.[35] Although librarians must always strive to provide the best possible information in response to user queries, in an imperfect world the knowledge that the personal interaction skills of the librarian can also convince users of the library's commitment to serving their needs should offer some incentive to constantly evaluate and improve these skills. The joy of reference work is experienced when the librarian's interaction skills and knowledge of reference tools mesh in a way that leaves the user satisfied both with the information provided and the mediator who provided it.

NOTES

1. Robert S. Taylor, "Question-Negotiation and Information Seeking in Libraries," *College & Research Libraries* 29 (May 1968): 182.

2. Various studies have documented this; see, for example, Patricia Dewdney and Catherine Sheldrick Ross, "Flying a Light Aircraft: Reference Service Evaluation from a User's Viewpoint," *RQ* 34 (Winter 1994): 217-30.

3. Rachel Naismith, "Reference Communication: Commonalities in the Worlds of Medicine and Librarianship," *College & Research Libraries* 57 (January 1996): 44-57; Carolyn J. Radcliff, "Interpersonal Communication with Library Patrons: Physician-Patient Research Models," *RQ* 34 (Summer 1995): 497-506.

4. Mark R. Willis, *Dealing with Difficult People in the Library* (Chicago: American Library Association, 1999), 91.

5. Marilyn J. Markham, Keith H. Stirling, and Nathan M. Smith, "Librarian Self-Disclosure and Patron Satisfaction in the Reference Interview," *RQ* 22 (Summer 1983): 372-73.

6. James Wyer advocated newspaper reading in his 1930 reference text, and others have since echoed this advice. For a more current view, see: Juris Dilevko and Elizabeth Dolan, "Reference Work and the Value of Reading Newspapers," *Reference & User Services Quarterly* 39 (Fall 1999): 71-81.

7. "RUSA Guidelines for Behavioral Performance of Reference and Information Services Professionals," *RQ* 36 (Winter 1996): 200-203. Also available: http://www.ala.org/rusa/stnd_behavior.html.

8. Diana M. Thomas, Ann T. Hinckley, and Elizabeth R. Eisenbach, *The Effective Reference Librarian* (New York: Academic Press, 1981), 116.

9. Geraldine B. King, "The Reference Interview: Open & Closed Questions," *RQ* 12 (Winter 1972): 159.

10. Brenda Dervin and Patricia Dewdney, "Neutral Questioning: A New Approach to the Reference Interview," *RQ* 25 (Summer 1986): 506-13.

11. Ibid., 511.

12. A useful discussion of encouragers can be found in Catherine Sheldrick Ross and Patricia Dewdney, *Communicating Professionally*, 2d ed. (New York: Neal-Schuman, 1998), 22-23.

13. A discussion of active listening that takes a slightly different approach than that described here is: Nathan M. Smith and Stephen D. Fitt, "Active Listening at the Reference Desk," *RQ* 21 (Spring 1982): 247-49.

14. Fred Oser, "Referens Simplex or the Mysteries of Reference Interviewing Revealed," *The Reference Librarian* 16 (1987): 72.

15. Alfred Benjamin, *The Helping Interview*, 3d ed. (Boston: Houghton Mifflin, 1981), 85-96.

16. Ibid., 91.

17. Christopher W. Nolan, "Closing the Reference Interview: Implications for Policy and Practice," *RQ* 31 (Spring 1992): 520.

18. Catherine Sheldrick Ross, "Readers' Advisory Service: New Directions," *RQ* 30 (Summer 1991): 507.

19. Joyce G. Saricks and Nancy Brown, *Readers' Advisory Service in the Public Library*, 2d ed. (Chicago: American Library Association, 1997), 57.

20. Ibid., 67-74.

21. Ross, "Readers' Advisory Service," 505.

22. Saricks and Brown, *Readers' Advisory Service*, 77.

23. Ibid., 71-72.

24. Eileen G. Abels, "The E-mail Reference Interview," *RQ* 35 (Spring 1996): 348.

25. Ibid., 357-58.

26. Ann Bristow, "Academic Reference Service over Electronic Mail," *College & Research Libraries News* 53 (November 1992): 632.

27. Abels, "The E-mail Reference Interview," 348. Abels quotes from a study by F. W. Lancaster published in 1968 by the Government Printing Office.

28. Two such studies are: Ruth A. Pagell, "The Virtual Reference Librarian: Using Desktop Videoconferencing for Distance Reference," *Electronic Library* 14 (February 1996): 21-26; and Robert B. McGeachin, "Videoconferencing and Remote Application Sharing for Distant Reference Service," *The Reference Librarian* 65 (1999): 51-60.

29. McGeachin, "Videoconferencing," 56.

30. See, for example Susan Lessick, Kathryn Kjaer, and Steve Clancy, *Interactive Reference Service (IRS) at UC Irvine: Expanding Reference Beyond the Reference Desk.* Available: http://www.ala.org/acrl/paperhtm/a10.html.

31. Melissa Gross, "The Imposed Query," *RQ* 35 (Winter 1995): 236-43, and "Imposed Versus Self-Generated Questions: Implications for Reference Practice," *Reference & User Services Quarterly* 39 (Fall 1999): 53-61.

32. An excellent example is: Rhea Joyce Rubin, "Anger in the Library: Defusing Angry Patrons at the Reference Desk (and Elsewhere)," *The Reference Librarian* 31 (1990): 39-51.

33. Ibid., 47; Willis, *Dealing with Difficult People*, 109-17.

34. Willis, *Dealing with Difficult People*, 164-86.

35. Joan C. Durrance, "Factors That Influence Reference Success: What Makes Questioners Willing to Return?" *The Reference Librarian* 49/50 (1995): 257.

ADDITIONAL READINGS

Benjamin, Alfred. *The Helping Interview*. 3d ed. Boston: Houghton Mifflin, 1981. 177p.

This little book, by a practicing rehabilitation counselor, is full of honest self-examination and important insights regarding the techniques that make an interview effective. Written in the first person, it contains many examples to illustrate its points. It is a marvelous introduction to the psychological aspects of the type of interviewing in which a professional seeks to help a client in some way.

Dervin, Brenda, and Patricia Dewdney. "Neutral Questioning: A New Approach to the Reference Interview." *RQ* 25 (Summer 1986): 506-13.

The authors present neutral questioning as a form of open question that helps librarians avoid premature diagnosis of user questions and understand the question from the user's point of view. The technique is based on a theory of the origination of information needs called the "sense-making model," which is also outlined in this influential article.

Dewdney, Patricia, and Catherine Sheldrick Ross. "Flying a Light Aircraft: Reference Service Evaluation from a User's Viewpoint." *RQ* 34 (Winter 1994): 217-30.

Dewdney and Ross employed library school students asking their own questions to test the effectiveness of reference librarians, using qualitative outcomes such as "user's willingness to return" (a measure developed by Joan Durrance) to measure the success of the reference transaction. Their study showed that sloppy interviewing techniques, such as unmonitored referrals and lack of follow-up, along with unapproachability and inadequate question negotiation, were too common.

Durrance, Joan C. "Factors That Influence Reference Success: What Makes Questioners Willing to Return?" *The Reference Librarian* 49/50 (1995): 243-65.

Durrance sought to expand the evaluation of reference encounters beyond the provision of successful information service (accuracy of answers) to include other aspects such as the quality of the reference interview and the provision of instruction and guidance. In her Willingness to Return Study, ongoing since 1986, she uses the willingness of users to return to the same librarian at a later time with another question to study what factors users consider important in the reference interaction. She found that such interpersonal qualities as approachability, ability to listen, and interest in the user's question were among the behaviors most often associated with success as judged by users.

Fine, Sara. "Reference and Resources: The Human Side." *Journal of Academic Librarianship* 21 (January 1995): 17-20.

In this short but thought-provoking essay, Fine discusses librarians' assumptions about themselves and their users, and how these assumptions can affect the service provided. She argues that better awareness of their own assumptions about themselves and their users will help reference librarians improve their service to those users.

Gross, Melissa. "The Imposed Query." *RQ* 35 (Winter 1995): 236-43.

———. "Imposed Versus Self-Generated Questions: Implications for Reference Practice." *Reference & User Services Quarterly* 39 (Fall 1999): 53-61.

In these two thought-provoking articles, Melissa Gross discusses reference interviewing when the question asked is posed not by the originator of the question but by an agent of that person, such as a secretary, student, family member, or other individual. In the first article, she reviews some of the relevant literature and develops a model for imposed queries. The second article delves more specifically into the problems associated with these questions and suggests solutions.

Howze, Philip C., and Felix E. Unaeze. "All in the Name of Service: Mediation, Client Self-Determination, and Reference Practice in Academic Libraries." *RQ* 36 (Spring 1997): 430-37.

Howze and Unaeze apply the concept of "client self-determination" (or self-empowerment), borrowed from social work, to the field of reference librarianship. They argue that the reference librarian's role as a mediator between users and information sources is best carried out when the librarian encourages users to "become full participants in their own outcomes."

Jennerich, Elaine Z., and Edward J. Jennerich. *The Reference Interview as a Creative Art*. 2d ed. Englewood, Colo.: Libraries Unlimited, 1997. 128p.

This book provides an excellent overview of the reference interview, including sections on skills, training, evaluation, and special kinds of interviews. It is thoroughly grounded in the literature, and the bibliography is extensive.

Radford, Marie L. "Communication Theory Applied to the Reference Encounter: An Analysis of Critical Incidents." *The Library Quarterly* 66 (April 1996): 123-37.

———. *The Reference Encounter: Interpersonal Communication in the Academic Library*. Chicago: American Library Association, 1999. 242p. (ACRL Publications in Librarianship, no. 52).

Both of these titles report qualitative studies of reference interactions, using detailed interviews with both the librarian and the user to understand their perceptions of the encounter. Among other conclusions, Radford suggests that users value highly the "relational messages that are communicated along with the information," and that librarians and library educators should focus more on the development of communication skills in training for reference service. She includes extensive quotations from users and librarians.

Ross, Catherine Sheldrick, and Patricia Dewdney. *Communicating Professionally*. 2d ed. New York: Neal-Schuman, 1998. 322p. (How-to-Do-It Manuals for Librarians, no. 58).

Ross and Dewdney discuss the skills required for effective communication and apply them to various library activities, from group activities and formal presentations to the one-to-one communication found in the reference interview. Of most relevance here are the sections on listening and question negotiation and on the types and stages of reference interviews. The book is very readable, and the annotated readings appended to each section are very helpful.

Taylor, Robert S. "The Process of Asking Questions." *American Documentation* 13 (October 1962): 391-96.

———. "Question-Negotiation and Information Seeking in Libraries." *College & Research Libraries* 29 (May 1968): 178-94.

These seminal articles are among the most frequently cited discussions of the application of communication principles to the reference interview. Taylor focused on the way in which questions are formulated by the user and how they are presented to the reference librarian. The second article, in particular, discusses principles of question negotiation that librarians should follow to accurately understand the user's information need.

CHAPTER

4

BIBLIOGRAPHIC CONTROL, ORGANIZATION OF INFORMATION, AND SEARCH STRATEGIES

Prudence Ward Dalrymple

INTRODUCTION

Students preparing for a career working to make information accessible to users face greater challenges today than they did even just a few years ago. The conceptual underpinnings and structure of the bibliographic universe as it has been organized by librarians and information specialists for decades are now being modified and adjusted to meet the tremendous demands of the information age. Procedures are being streamlined so that principles of bibliographic organization can be applied to ever-larger amounts of material. At the same time, material is being made available to the public through the Internet in unprecedented quantities, frequently without any regard to the principles that have been established by librarians. Today's library and information science students must deal with both universes—one that is carefully structured and organized, and another that often seems chaotic or assembled according to what appears to be a different set of rules. During the transition from traditional library organization to that based on digital models, librarians need to understand both worlds, and perhaps, begin to devise ways in which the librarian's traditional store of knowledge can be brought to bear on the multitude of information available electronically.

The premise of this chapter is that beginning librarians should understand the power and benefit of organizational schema, first by understanding the principles of traditional bibliographic organization of published materials. By gaining an understanding of these principles and how they can be exploited for information retrieval, librarians will be prepared to devise effective search strategies. They can also work to design organizational plans that can be applied to other emerging types of information and knowledge. Information professionals who are committed to providing access to information and materials directly to users can contribute to the creation of a more orderly and satisfying digital universe. Searching any information system is easier when the librarian is familiar with how it is organized (if it is organized). Conceptualizing the various strategies that can be employed to make searching effective and efficient can also be demonstrated to users through bibliographic instruction or point-of-access assistance, and they can be incorporated into the design of print and electronic materials to aid the user.

The process of organizing information to make it available to persons seeking to use it is known as *bibliographic control,* and it is an activity basic to librarianship. Indeed, the history of librarianship in the United States is closely associated with the development of bibliographic organization schemes, such as Melvil Dewey's classification scheme, and the extensive bibliographic activities of the nation's libraries, such as the Library of Congress, the National Library of Medicine, and the National Agricultural Library. Since the nineteenth century, considerable time, money, and effort have been expended to design, implement, and maintain local, regional, national, and international systems of bibliographic control to ensure that the universe of published information is made accessible. Today, the rapid growth of the Internet has led to a growing appreciation of the principles of organization that librarians have established and sustained. Although the Internet is far from organized in the traditional sense, several initiatives are underway that build upon librarians' traditional bibliographic practice; an understanding of the principles of bibliographic organization will enable reference librarians to use these enhancements and even to contribute to their growth and development. The purpose of this chapter is to introduce and explain these concepts and to indicate possible future directions.

The phrase *bibliographic universe* refers to the totality of published items, regardless of date, format, or location. *Bibliographic control* refers to the organizing of these items, or rather the organizing of the representations of these items, so that they may be identified and located. The most common methods of ordering and providing access in libraries have traditionally been by author, by title, and by subject. Other ways of organizing materials such as archives are interesting for comparative purposes, but are outside the scope of this chapter. Electronic formatting has also made virtually every character string in a record accessible, but for reasons that will become apparent, such expanded access can sometimes be a mixed blessing.

Although the concept of bibliographic control is simple, the practice of organizing information is complex and can be confusing to beginning librarians and library users. The universe of published materials may be partitioned in several ways: by publishing mode (e.g., books versus articles), by format (e.g., print versus electronic), or by subject area (e.g., general versus specific subject). These traditional types have been augmented by new categories of materials in hybrid and evolving formats such as Web sites, electronic journals, and consolidated sites consisting of resources hyperlinked to other sites and sources. For simplicity's sake, this chapter presents two main approaches to organizing these materials: catalogs and indexes. The bibliographic principles underlying their design and the ways they are evolving are discussed. The process of searching for information by applying the principles of bibliographic control is described, and general search strategies are explained.

Box 4.1 Defining Bibliographic Control

The bibliographical universe is not under effective bibliographical control until anyone can discover those of its inhabitants that will suit his or her purposes.

Patrick Wilson
"The Catalog as Access Mechanism"[1]

THE LIBRARY CATALOG

For many years, the library catalog was the primary means of locating and accessing items in a library's collection; indeed, the function of the catalog was to display the holdings of a particular library. Over the last several decades, however, the catalog's function has evolved so that it does not only reflect the library's collection, but also acts as an access mechanism to resources beyond the library. At the same time, as it has broadened its scope, it also has deepened to include sources that indicate the contents of items (e.g., journals) held by a library, such as indexes and citation databases. Although the records that make up a library's catalog may be drawn from one of the national cataloging databases such as OCLC (Online Computer Library Center) or RLIN (Research Libraries Information Network), the catalog itself is specific to that particular library's collection. Bibliographic records are selected from the national database and may undergo modifications, such as the addition of a local call number or volume holdings statement. Consulting a national database answers the question, "Does an item exist?" Consulting the catalog answers the questions, "Does the library own the item?" and "Where can the item be found?"

A library's catalog is cumulative, including all materials held in a collection, regardless of date of publication or date of acquisition. In large libraries or library systems, the contents of the catalog may be a combination of several libraries. In these instances, the catalog is known as a *union catalog.* (Local circumstances may preclude representation in the catalog of all holdings of all libraries within a system. When the catalog is not fully representative, this fact should be made clear to users and librarians.)

The catalog is composed of representations or surrogates of bibliographic objects, including books, journals, audio and video materials, maps, and other nonprint items. These representations are called *bibliographic records.* In a card catalog, the bibliographic record was printed on a set of cards; in an online catalog, the bibliographic record consists of machine-readable information encoded in digital format. The machine-readable version of a bibliographic record conforming to certain standards for content and structure of the data is called a MARC (Machine-readable Cataloging) record. When the whole universe of intellectual resources is taken into consideration, bibliographic records are seen to be only one component. To describe the resources available on the Internet, librarians (and others) are currently engaged in creating schemes for records describing materials that exist only in electronic format. These *metadata*, as they are known, are still evolving. Examples of these formats are the Dublin Core, the Electronic Archival Description, and the Text Encoding Initiative Guidelines for Electronic Text Encoding and Interchange. Many of these approaches are based on traditional principles, modified to take advantage of the electronic format, while others embody a whole new approach.

Historically, the catalog provided three major types of access points for a given item: author, title, and subject. In a card catalog, this meant that there was a card created for each author, title, and subject (usually two or three subjects as described by subject headings). The subject headings used in catalogs are selected from established subject heading lists—the *Library of Congress Subject Headings* (LCSH)[2] or the *Sears List of Subject Headings,*[3] for example—during the cataloging process. The use of standardized lists ensures that the terminology and format of the headings remain consistent. A *shelflist,* a file arranged by call number, provides control over the collection and access by classification number. It takes its name from the fact that it reflects the arrangement of items on the shelf; where no "shelf" exists, a shelf list offers the opportunity to browse by classification number. A single item, then, was represented by several cards in the catalog; to save labor and space, the number of cards was usually limited, and the listing of the various cards in the set appeared only on the main entry card.

As online catalogs gradually replaced card catalogs, cataloging principles began to change as well. Underlying the online catalog's structure is the MARC record (see Figure 4.1, page 72) showing which fields can be retrieved. All the bibliographic information associated with a specific piece is displayed in the various fields of the MARC record, along with the tag that identifies it. In Figure 4.1, the 100 field in the MARC record for the book *Medieval Knight, Read Me a Book!* shows that the main entry is the author, Adrienne Wigdortz Anderson. Catalogers consulted the cataloging rules to select one access point as the main entry—author or title, for example. Although the MARC record retains the concept of a main entry, which is reflected in the "100" field, some catalogers have now begun to question whether the concept of the main entry is outmoded.[4]

The shift from paper to electronic format has increased the number of possible subject access points. In Figure 4.1, the 650 fields are the subject headings; in this case, subject headings from two lists are displayed, the *Library of Congress* and the *Sears* lists. The source of the subject heading is indicated by the digit to the right of the 650. Five subject headings from each list are assigned to this book. When each subject entry necessitated the production and filing of a card, fewer subject headings were used—usually just two or three—but catalogers are no longer so limited in the number of subject headings they assign. More subject headings increase the possibility of retrieving that item using the authorized term from the subject heading list. This information, particularly the subject tracings, can be very useful because it shows how the cataloger chose to represent that particular item and can suggest terminology to use in searching. The ability to gain an overview of the full bibliographic record is often ignored by the catalog user (patron and reference librarian alike) when only the brief entry is displayed. Many systems allow the user to review brief listings, but then to request a display of the full record to determine the subject terminology that has been used to create the record and provide access to the item.

Figure 4.1 Example of a MARC record.

```
ÚÄÄÄÄÄÄÄÄÄÄÄÄÄÄÄÄÄÄÄÄÄÄÄÄÄÄÄÄÄÄ MARC Display ÄÄÄÄÄÄÄÄÄÄÄÄÄÄÄÄÄÄÄÄÄÄÄÄÄÄÄÄÄÄÄ¿
³ Find. . .  Options. . . Backup        Startover       Quit      Help. . . ³
ÄÄÄÄÄÄÄÄÄÄÄÄÄÄÄÄÄÄÄÄÄÄÄÄÄÄÄÄÄÄÄÄÄÄÄÄÄÄÄÄÄÄÄÄÄÄÄÄÄÄÄÄÄÄÄÄÄÄÄÄÄÄÄÄÄÄÄÄÄÄÄÄÄÄÄÄÄÄÄÄÄÄÄÄÄÄÄÙ
DTF-7799            Entered: 03/11/1999             Modified: 04/22/2000
Type: a Bib l: m Enc l:    Desc: a Ctry: mdu Lang: eng Mod:    Srce:
 Ill:       Audience:   Form:    Cont: b    Gvt:    Cnf: 0   Fst: 0 Ind: 1
 Fic: 0 Bio:    Dat tp: s Dates:  1999      Control:

  003;      ; a OCoLC $
  005;      ; a 19990310172134.0 $
  010;      ; a    98029284   $o 39477690 $
  040;      ; a DLC $c DLC $d UKM $d JNA $
  015;      ; a GB99-21079 $
  020;      ; a 0810835177 (pbk. : alk. paper) $
  043;      ; a n-us--- $
  050;    00; a LB1042 $b .A538 1999 $
  082;    00; a 372.67/7 $2 21 $
  049;      ; a JNAA $
  100;    1 ; a Anderson, Adrienne Wigdortz. $
  245;    10; a Medieval knight, read me a book! / $c Adrienne Wigdortz
             Anderson. $
  246;    30; a Medieval knight $
  260;      ; a Lanham, Md. : $b Scarecrow Press, $c 1999. $
  300;      ; a xi, 211 p. ; $c 22 cm. $
  504;      ; a Includes bibliographical references and index. $
  650;     0; a Storytelling $z United States. $
  650;     0; a Children's libraries $x Activity programs $z United States. $
  650;     0; a Activity programs in education $z United States. $
  650;     0; a History $x Study and teaching (Elementary) $z United States. $
  650;     0; a Historical reenactments $x Study and teaching (Elementary) $z
             United States. $
  650;     4; a Storytelling $z United States. $
  650;     4; a Activity programs in education $z United States. $
  650;     4; a Children's libraries $x Activity programs $z United States. $
  650;     4; a History $x Study and teaching (Elementary) $z United States. $
  650;     4; a Historical reenactments $x Study and teaching (Elementary) $z
             United States. $
```

INDEXES

Just as it is essential to understand some basic principles of cataloging, it is important to understand some basic principles of indexing. This need is even more critical when converting print to electronic media and merging indexing and cataloging files. It may be helpful to recall that the word *index* means "to point to." Indexes "point to" information located somewhere else; here, the term *index* refers to a tool that is used to locate information within a document. The most familiar index is the one found at the back of a book, which is used to find where certain topics are discussed within the text.

The indexes discussed in this chapter are indexes to published periodical literature. This kind of index is produced on a regular schedule (typically on a monthly, quarterly, or annual basis) and provides access to the topical contents of a group of publications. The group indexed may be determined by a variety of criteria; topic, language, publication type, and country of origin are some of the most common criteria. For example, the *Readers' Guide to Periodical Literature*[5] indexes a group of popular magazines published in the United States. *Education Index*[6] includes only publications whose primary focus is education, while *Index Medicus*[7] indexes medical journals published throughout the world in a variety of languages. The criteria used in selecting materials to include for indexing are usually explained in the introductory pages of the index and are essential reading for effective use of the index. When indexes are included in the catalog of the library, it is important to ensure that the appropriate explanatory materials are made easily accessible to the user. By the same token, explanations of the indexes in electronic form should be included in the systems presented to users. All too often, users are uninformed about what they are actually searching.

Indexes are published in book or electronic form and may be cumulative for a year or for longer time periods. Most print indexes are arranged in alphabetical order by subject, and some provide a separate listing by author. Some print indexes do not provide title access to materials. When indexes are published in electronic format, many more points of access are available. This is a definite advantage, but there are also costs, as will be pointed out in the section on search strategies.

Unlike a library's catalog, the domain of an index is unrelated to the library's collection. From the searcher's perspective, then, an index represents what has been published in a particular subject area during a specified time period; to determine whether a particular library holds an item, some additional searching must be undertaken. Although this may seem quite obvious, it becomes less clear when online or CD-ROM indexes are presented to the user alongside or through the same terminal as an online catalog. Such an index certainly is not necessarily located in the periodical section of the library, the traditional location of print periodical indexes. Many libraries now subscribe to services that provide full-text articles online even when they do not own the periodical itself, so it is important for reference librarians to inform users of what resources are available to them. Unless these distinctions are made very clear, users may expect to obtain all the items listed in an index, just as they would expect to locate all the items listed in a library's catalog. These distinctions become even less clear when a single interface is used to provide access to all materials (see below).

BEYOND CATALOGS AND INDEXES

Few reference librarians today would attempt to provide information to users without referring to the Internet. The wealth of materials available on the Internet makes it imperative to be comfortable searching in this environment. The way in which metadata schemes improve access to materials may not conform to traditional bibliographic principles, but there are similarities. The Dublin Core, for example, provides a set of descriptive elements not unlike those provided by the MARC record (see Figure 4.2, page 74). The Dublin Core, however, does not provide subject cataloging; that is, it does not select terminology from standardized lists to represent the topical content of the resource. Rather, it depends on keyword searching or "self-indexing" for this function. The extent to which materials on the Web will be brought into the bibliographic universe associated with the catalog is a topic of continuing philosophical and practical discussion.

Figure 4.2 Dublin Core definitions. Adapted from Dublin Core Metadata Element Set, Version 1.1: Reference Descriptions (http://purl.org/dc/documents/rec-dces-19990702.htm).

Each Dublin Core definition refers to the resource being described. For the purposes of Dublin Core metadata, a resource will typically be an information or service resource, but may be applied more broadly.

Element: Title
Definition: A name given to the resource.

Element: Creator
Definition: An entity primarily responsible for making the content of the resource.

Element: Subject
Definition: The topic of the content of the resource.

Element: Description
Definition: An account of the content of the resource.

Element: Publisher
Definition: An entity responsible for making the resource available.

Element: Contributor
Definition: An entity responsible for making contributions to the content of the resource.

Element: Date
Definition: A date associated with an event in the life cycle of the resource.

Element: Type
Definition: The nature or genre of the content of the resource.

Element: Format
Definition: The physical or digital manifestation of the resource.

Element: Identifier
Definition: An unambiguous reference to the resource within a given context.

Element: Source
Definition: A reference to a resource from which the present resource is derived.

Element: Language
Definition: A language of the intellectual content of the resource.

Element: Relation
Definition: A reference to a related resource.

Element: Coverage
Definition: The extent or scope of the content of the resource.

Element: Rights
Definition: Information about rights held in and over the resource.

PRINCIPLES OF BIBLIOGRAPHIC CONTROL

Despite the differences in scope between catalogs and indexes, some underlying principles of bibliographic control are addressed by both: arrangement, collocation and authority control, and depth and comprehensiveness of indexing. Each of these principles is defined and discussed in the following sections. Although much of the work of libraries is carried out through electronic means, the principles and terminology are best understood in the traditional format; once understood, they can be adapted and applied to the digital environment. In fact, some principles that appear to be nearly irrelevant in the digital world are included here not only for historical reasons, but because they exemplify utilitarian benefits that may be achieved in new and different ways as the digital environment evolves and matures.

Arrangement

The physical arrangement of the catalog has been used to improve retrieval capability for the user. For purposes of this discussion, the catalog is regarded as a file, a group of objects arranged in an arbitrary or meaningful order. An example of a file arranged in arbitrary order is a dictionary catalog, in which the records are arranged in alphabetical order. An example of meaningful order can be found in a classified catalog, in which the records are arranged by classification number to reflect a subject arrangement.

In classified catalogs, materials on similar subjects are filed together as they would appear on the shelf according to the classification plan. Users of a classified catalog must consult a schedule or plan to determine the appropriate class numbers for a particular topic before beginning to search, in much the same way as the index of a book is consulted to locate discussions of a particular topic. Classified catalogs are seldom used in the United States; they are more common in Europe. In a dictionary catalog, the searcher may approach the file directly, as one might consult an encyclopedia or a dictionary. In large libraries especially, dictionary catalogs were divided into two alphabets, one containing author/title entries and one containing subject entries only. This division, designed to reduce the number of cards that needed to be searched, often was invisible to the user, as illustrated in Box 4.2. In the online catalog, the same effect can be achieved by limiting the search key to a particular field.

Box 4.2 Undeserved Success in Catalog Searching

Although divided card catalogs have usually been understood to assist the user, particularly when files are large, this advantage sometimes goes unrecognized and unappreciated by catalog users. For example, in a study in which students were asked to search for topical information in a divided card catalog, one undergraduate conducted all five searches in the author/title catalog. The research assistant (a library school student) who observed this phenomenon later reported: "He never discovered that there was another section of the card catalog dealing with subjects. Based on his lack of understanding of the catalog, he shouldn't have been successful in finding materials. But the irony is, he found about as much as those students who conducted their searches in the subject catalog!" Can you think of a parallel example in online catalog searching?

Some of the characteristics of both dictionary and classified arrangements have produced interesting problems and attempts at new solutions in the online environment. This renewed interest in the use of classification as a tool for subject access is reflected in the research literature in subject analysis. For example, the ability to browse through a meaningful order (typical of a classified catalog) is supported in the Internet Public Library's (http://www.ipl.org/reading/books) provision of a classification schedule, such as the Dewey

Decimal System, along with the catalog records. Searchers can browse the classification schedule in order to gain a sense of related topics. In other catalogs, the related subject headings are displayed for browsing.

The physical arrangement of indexes reflects many of the same principles as the catalog. In most indexes, arrangement by subject is paramount. This is most often accomplished through a dictionary arrangement, although some indexes, such as *Library and Information Science Abstracts*,[8] use a classified arrangement. An example of a print index arranged by classification appears in Figure 4.3. Various methods of partitioning the file are employed in other indexes. For example, *Index Medicus* has a separate section of review articles, and separates author entries from subject entries in the print index; *Library Literature* lists book reviews separately. Partitioning of this type can be accomplished in the electronic environment by limiting the search key by field.

Figure 4.3

Entries from *Library and Information Science Abstracts* (September 2000). Reprinted with permission of Bowker (London, England).

12.21 SUBJECT INDEXING

9547

Indexing a local newspaper on the Web. B. Menk. *Library Computing,* 18 (2) 1999, p.151-9. il. refs.

Small town newspapers are not commonly indexed, leaving the public libraries in many communities with no reliable means of subject access to an important source of local information. With fairly minimal staff and a small expenditure on software, Lane Memorial Library in Hampton, New Hampshire, created a publicly accessible index to its local newspapers on its Web site. Reference staff members perform the indexing during slow times at the reference desk using Filemaker Pro software and the indexing guidelines and thesaurus developed in-house. Volunteers are being trained to expand the index retrospectively. (Original abstract - amended)

12.22 SEARCHING

9548

Topological models of distributed information retrieval systems. [In Chinese] M. Huang. *Journal of the China Society for Scientific and Technical Information,* 19 (2) Apr 2000, p.152-7. tbls. refs.

Introduces 3 topological models for distributed information retrieval systems: retrieval topology, pseudo metric topology and similarity topology. Shows that the retrieval topological model and the similarity topological model possess certain features which explain their practicability in the distributed setting. (Original abstract - amended)

12.23 INDEX LANGUAGES AND SYSTEMS

9549

Unified medical language system and its enlightenment to Chinese indexing language. [In Chinese] D. Hu and P. Fang. *Journal of the China Society for Scientific and Technical Information,* 19 (2) Apr 2000, p.158-63. refs.

Describes the history and present status, including all 4 knowledge sources and the development strategy and principles of the Unified Medical Language System. Discusses its impact on Chinese indexing languages. (Original abstract - amended)

Collocation and Name Authority Control

A basic tenet of cataloging is the principle of collocation, which means that similar materials are gathered together at a single location. In other words, one of the functions of cataloging is to ensure that all materials by Shakespeare are filed together and that all materials about aardvarks are located at the same point in the file. Although this may seem quite simple and obvious, the cumulative nature of the catalog, combined with the practice of using popular (and therefore changing) terminology for subject headings, makes total collocation difficult to achieve. At the same time, the experience of searching the Internet illustrates dramatically the potential benefit of "collocating" all materials in one place accessible to the searcher.

From their inception, catalogs were designed to be searched directly by the library user and are presumed to be self-explanatory. The use of popular words and terms as subject headings facilitates searching directly without first consulting a list of subject headings or requiring any specific training or subject expertise. Multiple-word phrases are sometimes combined and inverted for purposes of collocation; for example, "Insurance" and "Insurance, medical" appear together in an alphabetical display. The maintenance of linkages between terms is referred to as the *syndetic structure* of the subject headings. Cross-references are used to make intellectual links between the new and old terms; in electronic files, hyperlinks can be established between terms, terms can be mapped automatically to one another, or global changes can accomplish what previously required the addition of cards to the catalog.

Collocation works in a catalog because terminology can be confined to a specific field. That is, books *by* Shakespeare and books *about* Shakespeare can be differentiated because Shakespeare as an author is tagged differently than Shakespeare as a subject. A biography of Shakespeare would appear in the subject catalog, but if the title of the biography were *Shakespeare,* it would also appear in the author/title sequence. In libraries where the card catalog was divided, one alphabetical sequence included entries for authors and titles and another alphabetical sequence had entries for subjects (the "subject catalog"). Although this division was designed to assist the user by reducing the size of the file that needed to be searched, the benefit was sometimes not recognized by the user (see Box 4.2). In the online catalog, the same effect can be accomplished by limiting the search key to the subject field or the author field rather than simply using a keyword approach. By specifying the search key as "subject" or "author," the searcher can reduce the size of the retrieval set.

An essential requirement for achieving collocation is maintenance of *authority control,* whether of author's names, subjects, or titles. For example, author name authority control ensures that all existing permutations of an author's name—P. S. Winnicott, Pamela Smith Winnicott, Pamela S. Winnicott, or Pamela Smith if Winnicott were a name acquired or dropped by a change in marital status—are linked so that all the works written by this individual are gathered together at a particular location in the catalog. The sheer size of the bibliographic universe and the complexity of modern knowledge (the "information explosion") have made authority control one of the biggest challenges and controversies in cataloging today, driven in part by the mounting cost of comprehensive authority work. Some of the philosophical principles of the catalog and how they are changing in the digital world are articulately discussed in Jennifer Younger's article.[9]

Subject Authority Control

Subject authority control has as its objective the gathering together in one place of items on a particular topic. A few attempts at searching in a file that has no subject authority control should convince even the skeptic of the benefit that comes from assigning terms that represent the intellectual contents of an item. Although some titles may describe accurately the contents of some items, particularly in the scientific and technical world, titles of items in the humanities are not necessarily indicative of intellectual content. To retrieve these items, some method of naming or pointing to the contents of the piece is required. In cataloging this process is known as *subject cataloging* and is defined as the application of subject headings and the creation of subject entries. For periodicals, this process is known as indexing and consists of using terms called descriptors to "point to" the contents of the piece. Lists of *subject headings* such as the *Library of Congress Subject Headings* indicate those headings that are preferred and/or related (cross-references and see also references), while lists of *descriptors* are displayed in a *thesaurus* that indicates not only preferred terms through cross-references but also broader and narrower terms. These lists are referred to as *controlled vocabularies,* and the relationships among terms are known as the *syndetic structure* of the vocabulary.

Due to the richness of the English language, many similar terms can be used to represent a single idea; a system of controlled vocabulary links these many terms to a single term. All items that are about this topic are thus collocated together, improving retrieval for the user. This benefit obviously has economic implications both for indexing and for cataloging, but it is still a fundamental objective of bibliographic control. Correct, consistent use of authority control and controlled vocabulary provides quality control; that is, these techniques ensure that materials are represented reliably and consistently, so that the user may depend on consistent results when using proper search and retrieval techniques.

Classification, indexing, and subject cataloging have as their goal the grouping together of similar items for easy retrieval, but in electronic bibliographic systems the ways in which these various systems work together is beginning to shift. The distinctions between subject cataloging and indexing have blurred, although it is useful to recall the historical origins, as described in the next section on coordinate headings.[10] The benefits of syndetic structure can be overlooked and underutilized when the relationships among terms and the context of these terms are not made apparent to the user. The meaning of a particular term may vary considerably depending on the context. For example, the term "stress" can refer to psychological stress, mechanical stress, or the physical stress of a cardiac stress test.

Retrieval from a file will be much more precise if the person assigning the subject terms is able to specify which meaning is intended. Similarly, searchers will be able to focus their retrieval if they are able to select the appropriate meaning of the term by specifying the context. Some librarians are questioning the basic premise that the best (or only) way to achieve reliable subject access is to use standardized vocabulary.[11] Without standardized vocabulary, however, a greater burden is placed on the searcher—whether user or reference librarian—to construct a search that is both comprehensive and specific enough to meet the need. Other approaches, such as the Dublin Core, enable the creators of digital documents to select terms from a variety of terminology structures. The importance of indicating context both at the time of creating the indexing terms and at the time of retrieval will enhance the utility of this scheme. Nevertheless, the goal of grouping similar items together remains unchanged.

Depth and Comprehensiveness of Indexing

For many years, one distinctive feature of an index compared with a catalog was its depth and comprehensiveness of indexing. Indexing is most often associated with articles, whereas cataloging is associated with separately published works such as books. The bibliographic record for cataloging is standardized on a national or even international level, while the indexing record, known as the *unit record,* may differ from index to index. Despite these differences, however, one of the most important elements of the unit record is the set of descriptors used to describe the intellectual contents of the document. Before electronic catalogs and indexes became so prevalent, articles generally had many more descriptors attached to them than books had subject headings.

Descriptors in a thesaurus are linked by references indicating relationships, such as *broader* term, *narrower* term, and *related* term. Although recent editions of the LCSH include narrower term/broader term designations, LCSH was not originally designed to function as a true thesaurus.[12] Although the difference between a subject heading list and a thesaurus is debated among librarians, one difference is that the syndetic structure of a thesaurus is more rigorous and hierarchical than that of a subject heading list. Another difference lies in the way in which a thesaurus is constructed. Many thesauri are created a priori as reflections of the nature of the subject field. They are representations of knowledge within a specific subject area. The topics and their interrelationships are represented through terms regardless of the existence of documents within those areas. Other thesauri are more like subject heading lists, in that terms are introduced by virtue of *literary warrant;* that is, they are derived from the published literature of the subject field. When a term has been used sufficiently to warrant its use in a subject heading or as a descriptor, it is considered for inclusion in the list. These two approaches are portrayed vividly by Harold Wooster in his description of building a thesaurus (see Box 4.3).

Box 4.3 Two Approaches to Building a Thesaurus

There are, of course, two methods of thesaurus construction which I choose to call stalactitic and stalagmitic. The stalagmitic is the way Taube and I went about constructing our Index—down on the floor of the cave among the documents, slowly building towards the ceiling. The stalactitic seems to be much more fun—one convenes groups of experts who hang up on the roof of the cave, twittering and chirping among themselves, but as far away from the actual documents as they can get.

Stalagmitic thesauruses can be constructed either by humans or computers working with actual terms in text; stalactitic thesauruses only by committees of experts. And if a thesaurus has a smooth machine-produced regularity, with all terms expanded equally, it was probably produced by subject specialists jealous of the importance of their field; if it is full of charming irregularities, with some terms almost ignored and others expanded to almost tedious depth, it was probably produced by machine, faithfully reflecting the charming irregularities of the authors.

Harold Wooster
"A Naive Look at Subject Analysis"[13]

Subject headings sometimes capture more than one concept per heading by *precoordinating* the terms. For example, a book titled *Children's Books and Magazines: A Market Study* is about the children's book publishing industry. The subject heading for this book is "Children's literature-Publishing-United States." The concept "children" is precoordinated with the concept "literature" to make the subject heading "children's literature." Other types of literature may also be represented by precoordinated headings. Further, the subject heading for this book is composed of another term, "publishing," and finally, the geographical location "United States." Although all of these terms further describe what the book is about, they do not serve as access points except in electronic formats, such as an online catalog, in which keyword searching is available.

The concept of a precoordinated heading makes greatest sense when thinking about the challenges faced in preparing a print index. Precoordination performs the same function as the AND operator in a Boolean search (see Chapter 5). When Boolean searching (or its equivalent) was not available, precoordination saved the time of the searcher. When controlled vocabularies with precoordinated headings and syndetic structures are not available, a much greater burden rests on the ingenuity of the searcher. Terms may be precoordinated in various sequences to assist the searcher or indexer in selecting the appropriate term. By inverting the order of terms, similar terms can fall together; for example, "insurance, life"; "insurance, medical"; and "insurance, health," fall together when they are inverted. In another example, the order of terms is essential to the meaning: invert the terms in "venetian blind" and you get a "blind venetian!" The power that coordinated searching brought to the world of information retrieval is nicely presented in a history by Frederick Kilgour.[14]

In print indexes, unlike card catalogs, the descriptors attached to the item are not usually listed as part of the entry in the index. It is therefore impossible to see what other aspects of an article have been brought out by the indexer. In electronic systems, however, the searcher can request that the descriptors be displayed. Examining the descriptors can often provide insight into other aspects of a topic covered by an article, or can suggest additional terminology to be incorporated in a subsequent search. Figures 4.4 and 4.5 show the descriptors from the online version of *ERIC* and the subject headings for the same item in an online catalog.

Figure 4.4 Report listed in *ERIC*.

Citation 1

Accession Number
ED426712
Author
Bradburn, Frances Bryant.
Title
Output Measures for School Library Media Programs.
Availability
EDRS Availability: None.
Neal-Schuman Publishers, Inc., 100 Varick St., New York, NY 10013-1506; 800-548-2414 (Toll Free); Web site: http://www.neal-schuman.com ($45).
Date of Publication
1999
Country of Publication
U.S., New York
ERIC Subject Headings
Case Studies
Data Collection
Elementary Secondary Education
*Learning Resources Centers
*Library Administration
Library Development
*Library Services
Program Development
*School Libraries
Staff Development
Identifiers
*Output Measurements, Output Measures for Public Libraries, *Output Performance Measures.

Figure 4.5 Report listed in online catalog.

```
ÚÄÄÄÄÄÄÄÄÄÄÄÄÄÄÄÄÄÄÄÄÄÄÄÄ  Full Bibliographic Display ÄÄÄÄÄÄÄÄÄÄÄÄÄÄÄÄÄÄÄÄÄÄÄ¿
³ Find. . .  Options. . . Backup        Startover        Quit      Help. . . ³
ÄÄÄÄÄÄÄÄÄÄÄÄÄÄÄÄÄÄÄÄÄÄÄÄÄÄÄÄÄÄÄÄÄÄÄÄÄÄÄÄÄÄÄÄÄÄÄÄÄÄÄÄÄÄÄÄÄÄÄÄÄÄÄÄÄÄÄÄÄÄÄÄÄÄÄÄÄÄÄÄÄÄÄÄÄÄÄÄÄÄÄÚ
               Author: Bradburn, Frances Bryant.
                Title: Output measures for school library media programs /
                           Frances Bryant Bradburn.
            Published: New York : Neal-Schuman Publishers, c1999.
               Format: xx, 95 p. : ill. ; 28 cm.
              Subject: School libraries--Evaluation--Statistical methods.
                       Instructional materials centers--Evaluation
                           --Statistical methods.
                Notes: Includes bibliographical references (p. 89-91) and
                           index.
                 ISBN: 1555703267 (pbk. : alk. Paper)
          LC Card No.:     98045557
          OCLC ID No.: 39951734
```

THE CONCEPT OF SEARCH STRATEGY

A *search strategy* may be broadly defined as a conscious approach to decision making to solve a problem or achieve an objective. The typical library user may employ an approach to searching that may be more or less conscious, and more or less informed, but the professional librarian is expected to apply knowledge and judgment in approaching information work. In this chapter, search strategies are discussed in the context of librarians seeking to assist users to find information by consulting resources that have been brought under some form of bibliographic control. The purpose is to familiarize beginning librarians with the ways in which they can exploit the power of bibliographic control to find answers to reference questions more effectively. Although some reference will be made to search strategies for items not under bibliographic control, fuller discussion of this topic is included in Chapter 6.

These principles are described at a general level that differentiates them from heuristics or searching "tips" that apply to specific situations. For these, the reader is referred to the current library literature, wherein descriptions of such techniques appear regularly.[15] At the outset of any discussion of search strategy, it is useful to note that certain parameters will affect how any reference search is carried out; these are:

- What is wanted.
- What is known about what is wanted.
- What resources are available.
- How those resources are constructed.
- What is known about the structure of those resources.

Each of these questions is dealt with in different parts of this text. Because this chapter deals with the organization of information, the discussion of search strategy focuses particularly on how knowledge of bibliographic structures may be used to improve search results. Chapter 3 discusses ways for librarians to determine exactly what a user wants. It is worth noting, however, that this is not always clear at the time the search request is received or the reference question is posed. Rather, in the process of conducting an in-depth reference interview, the librarian and the user may come to understand more clearly what is wanted, and the focus of the search may change.

In 1936, Carter Alexander[16] proposed a model of searching, described in Box 4.4, that lays out the steps taken in conducting a manual search in a reference collection. The model describes six steps: clarify the question, select the type of materials to answer the question, prioritize the sources within the type, search and locate, evaluate, and repeat if necessary. The model assumes familiarity with the reference collection or at least the types of materials contained within that collection. In other words, this model assumes at least a working knowledge of the materials in Part II of this text. The reader will note that there is very little difference between the parameters specified in the paragraph above and the steps outlined by Alexander more than sixty years ago, when he could hardly have dreamed of the World Wide Web.

Box 4.4 A Model of the Search Process

A library user has come to the reference desk with the question, "I need to know about neural nets."

Step 1: *Clarify the question.* Find out what domain of knowledge the term comes from—physiology, psychology, or computer science? What does the inquirer plan to do with the information? At what level of detail is the information needed?

Step 2: *Select the materials.* Determine whether the term has been established long enough to appear in standard reference books, such as encyclopedias and dictionaries of the subject field, or whether recent issues of an index must be examined. Consulting the subject heading list to determine whether the topic appears as a subject heading that can be searched in a catalog is also appropriate. Consideration of a database search also occurs at this stage and may be appropriate if the term is too new to appear as a subject heading or descriptor. Knowledge of the reference collection and its contents is critical to success.

Step 3: *Prioritize the sources* identified in order of their likelihood of containing the answer. In the case of the neural nets question, one criterion for prioritizing might be the level of detail desired and the level of understanding exhibited by the user. For a layperson, a quick search in a general periodicals index or an up-to-date encyclopedia would be a good first priority.

Step 4: *Locate the sources.* Are they in the reference area? Are they owned by the library, or is it necessary to call another location or refer the user elsewhere?

Step 5: *Search the materials* you have selected until an answer is found or until you are sure that an answer cannot be found there. This process is evaluative, because the determination of suitability varies with the librarian's assessment of the user's information need.

Step 6: *Evaluate and repeat* if necessary. The searching process is cyclic and may require asking the person for further clarification, for more time, or whether a referral to another library would be desirable.

Examining the search patterns of both librarians and users to improve information access is an important research area in library and information science. Although early research focused primarily on patterns displayed by reference librarians answering questions from print sources, recent work has examined the search behavior of librarians conducting online searches. Studies have looked at such factors as individual differences, cognitive style, and differences between new and experienced searchers.[17] As users do more and more searching by themselves, a stream of research looking at how users access information on their own is continuing to grow. The study of both cognitive and affective aspects of the search process encourages librarians to become more aware of user needs at any given point, and enables librarians to make appropriate interventions to facilitate the searches. For example, research examining the need for users to engage in reformulating their requests based on feedback from an information system may lead to systems that prompt the user to examine subject headings as a source of additional search terms.[18] By studying how students feel at various stages of preparing a term paper, librarians may become aware that the search for information is not solely an intellectual process; it may be accompanied by a wide variety of feelings, including uncertainty, anxiety, confusion, relief, disappointment, or confidence.[19]

One of the benefits of electronic bibliographic information systems has been the opportunity to observe how people actually search. Many long-standing assumptions about the ways in which people look for information using the tools provided by librarians have fallen by the wayside. Fortunately, librarians have worked with system designers to provide enhancements based on these observations, and information system design has advanced dramatically in the last ten years. Many of the research studies that led to these advancements depended on users' ability to describe what they did, while they were doing it; others used the electronic "paper trails" known as transaction logs that captured users' interactions with systems.

The insights that have emerged from this research can be useful to beginning reference librarians because they illustrate ways in which various features of information systems can be exploited in creative ways to produce better results. These patterns can also provide guidance to librarians who are responsible for creating search aids to be used while searching in environments that are not organized according to bibliographic principles. Models of how individuals search the Internet are not fully developed yet, but early research suggests that searchers use a highly interactive approach. This makes sense, because there are few organizing principles used in putting items up on the Web, and the protocols used by search engines are usually not explicitly stated. Searchers must then interact with the system to deduce what works best for a given query and for a given search engine. Modeling search processes can be helpful in designing bibliographic instruction or in helping searchers improve their results. The growing availability of direct user access to electronic information systems has stimulated interest in modeling the search processes of casual (untrained) users as well as those of librarians.[20]

A critical component in search strategy is the selection of terminology. As discussed earlier in this chapter, the use of thesauri and controlled vocabularies lends power to the searcher who understands and can exploit them. Because search term selection is so powerful, research has explored how searchers select terms and how they monitor and correct their strategy based on feedback. This process has its origins in manual searching, as described in an early exploration of search strategy by Marcia Bates, and has been further developed in electronic environments.[21] For example, Bates's tactic, called TRACE, refers to using the information already found to derive additional search terms and to examine the way in which the document has been represented. In a catalog search, the searcher uses the subject headings as potentially relevant search terms in refining the search. As electronic retrieval systems have evolved, more and more of them facilitate the searcher's use of the subject terms (subject headings or index terms) to assist the searcher in coming up with additional search terms or in understanding the cataloger or indexer's approach. Just as examining the subject tracings on catalog cards improved manual searches, this same technique can be used in an online catalog by displaying the subject headings.

In print indexes, the list of descriptors is not displayed, and TRACE cannot be used. In an electronic environment, however, TRACE may be used by displaying the fields in the unit records that list the descriptors used. Some system designers have incorporated the TRACE tactic as a feature of the interface. In some systems, the user is prompted to ask for a listing of the descriptors with the suggestion that they can be incorporated into the search; in others, it is provided automatically. Such a feature is known as *automatic query expansion* and is an example of how a manual technique can inspire system enhancement.[22]

THE ELECTRONIC ENVIRONMENT

A useful concept in bridging the gap between print reference materials and electronic resources is to view the reference book as a file.[23] Files are composed of records and records contain fields: chunks of information that are directly accessible for searching. Files constitute the foundation of organized information. When a print reference tool is converted to electronic form, decisions must be made about how the records will be constructed, what fields will be searchable, and how they will be tagged. Otherwise, searching the file would simply be an exercise in matching strings of characters throughout the full text of the book.

Structured files possess certain variables and attributes that can be used as retrieval tools. For example, in a hardware store, the selection of paint for a room involves selection from the collection of possible paints available. Each paint has several attributes: color, texture, whether it is latex- or oil-based, and what kind of finish results. Each of these attributes of the paint may vary, and each of these attributes constitutes a field. If there is a field for each of the attributes, a searcher may limit the search term to a specific field or fields, thereby homing in on the specific aspect sought. A customer may come in wanting to paint a room blue, thus being able to specify the attribute color, but may not know enough to be able to specify the other attributes. If the person helping to narrow the choice has a structured file available, that person can search various attributes to find an appropriate paint. To be most effective, the searcher will know which fields are searchable, and base the interview with the customer on the fields that are searchable. If there is a field in the database called "finish," the searcher may be able to specify the type of finish. This will likely be a selection among three or four types, which may simply be tags: pre-specified terms that may even have a numeric code attached to them. Or, the searcher may have to put in a word that conforms to a specific vocabulary term, such as "eggshell" or "satin." Knowing that the file contains a searchable field called "finish," the searcher can search for the term "eggshell" in that field only. If the searcher simply uses the term "eggshell" without specifying the field, the retrieval will include paints that are the color "eggshell" as well as the finish "eggshell." Another attribute might be price, or price range. Depending on the circumstances, this may be searchable as a range as well as a specific value. The knowledge that the searcher has of the tools available—the imaginary databases described here—will determine the questions asked of the customer and what direction the search will take.

Translating this into a bibliographic realm, we see that certain fields or variables may have certain attributes, some of which may be pre-specified—author, title, series—or some of which may be pre-selected indirectly. For example, when searching *Education Index,* all the items will have to do with education; when searching a library's catalog, all materials are assumed to be in the collection. Knowing how the file is organized and what attributes are tagged and are searchable helps the reference librarian to design an effective strategy.

The preceding example illustrates how knowledge of the file structure facilitates effective searching. In becoming familiar with any reference source (file), one of the first questions to ask is, "What portions of the file are directly accessible for searching purposes?" Another way of putting this question is to ask, "What fields are searchable?" For example, in an electronic file, if one does not know the fields and which ones are searchable, one must resort to keyword searching throughout the file. Many false hits will likely occur. If the term "white," for example, is searched only in the names field, the retrieval will be much more accurate than if it were searched throughout the whole file, where it would pick up "white" in the title, subject headings, and possibly the publisher and imprint fields.

In a print reference tool, the analog for the searchable fields is the type of indexes to a given work that are available. Knowing in advance whether a reference book has a names index or only a subject index will determine how easily and effectively it can be searched. Some reference texts have numerous indexes that enable the librarian to identify just the right piece of information very quickly. For example, the *Physicians' Desk Reference*[24] has numerous indexes that are particularly effective in drug searching. Although reference librarians are expected to be able to search and retrieve information from sources that are not organized, searching unstructured files requires an extra measure of ingenuity to compensate for the lack of bibliographic organization.

The principles of bibliographic control in catalogs and indexes may differ on a number of dimensions because of fundamental differences in how each is expected to function for the user. However, assumptions about the function of catalogs and indexes have been challenged with the nearly universal adoption of online catalogs and wide availability of electronic indexes. As reference tools become more widely available in electronic form and the Web continues to grow in both size and sophistication, a discussion of search strategy based on the purpose of the tool becomes less relevant. What is of greatest concern to both user and librarian is how to exploit the power of the organizational principles in conjunction with the power of electronic retrieval. Because of the different functions of catalogs and indexes, the models used to describe a typical search have been assumed to differ as well. Generally speaking, the index search is conducted to identify items about a particular topic and is therefore inherently a subject or topical search. Both records loaded into a database and the format of a print index place primary emphasis on subject access. It has generally been assumed that catalog searches are known item searches, whereby users seek to locate particular items about which they possess some specific information—an author or a title, for example. The searcher enters the catalog, identifies the item, and goes to the shelf to locate it. The search may be broadened by browsing the shelves nearby, using the subject classification scheme to identify more items. This model may be described as moving from the specific to the general.

In an index, the searcher moves from the general topic to a specific aspect of the topic. In some indexes, the entries are arranged to reflect a hierarchical structure, with more general articles first, followed by more specific aspects listed underneath. Notice the specific aspects listed under the heading for "economic development" in Figures 4.6a & 4.6b, pages 86 and 87, from the *Social Sciences Index*.[25] The general to specific structure is readily apparent at first glance into the print index. The electronic version of *Social Sciences Index* does not reveal this structure so easily. By displaying the subject headings under "economic development," it can be seen that although there are a total of 488 items under economic development, a further breakdown by country, region, and time period is also available. What is not shown are the actual items themselves. A second step must be undertaken to display one or more items in each category. Furthermore, the novice user who does not recognize the availability of the various subheadings may not know how to further focus the search to show only the items dealing with a particular region such as Africa. Attempting to display all 488 items will almost surely end in frustration and an aborted search, with the searcher missing out on some potentially useful items. On the other hand, by using the power of coordinated searching (Africa AND economic development) the results can be reduced to 107.

Recently, some research has been done on the approach that most users take when searching the Web. Because there is no controlled vocabulary (descriptors or subject headings), search engines do not generally enable users to specify that the character string is to be searched only as a subject or only as a name. When a searcher is able to specify an exact name or phrase, this frequently helps reduce the retrieval, but there is little assistance in differentiating homographs or synonyms.

Another way of improving searching is through system design. Increasingly, librarians are taking an active role in creating or adapting systems to meet the needs of their users.[26] Appropriate didactic interventions, such as Help screens, can be built into the system interface, or the machine can be programmed to modify strategies automatically to achieve better results. Although such automated systems may vary in their quality, they are continually advancing the goal of providing more consistent and more effective user assistance. Some vendors have developed a consistent interface through which a variety of databases can be searched. For example, at a large metropolitan library, a single interface is used to search the online catalog and all the databases that are available to the library's users. There are, of course, both benefits and liabilities associated with this approach, not the least of which is the blurring between the function of a catalog and the function of an index (see above).

Figure 4.6a *Online display of subject headings from Social Sciences Index.* Reprinted with permission of The H.W. Wilson Company.

OVID

Subject Headings Index Display

Choose from among the following index entries:

SELECT	SUBJECT HEADINGS	# OF CITATIONS
___	economic conversion. sh.	97
___	economic councils. sh.	2
___	economic determinism. sh	6
___	economic development. sh.	488
___	economic development afghanistan. sh.	1
___	economic development africa. sh.	107
___	economic development africa history. sh.	2
___	economic development africa mathematical models. sh.	1
___	economic development africa research. sh.	1
___	economic development albania. sh.	3
___	economic development albania history. sh.	1
___	economic development algeria. sh.	5
___	economic development amazon river region. sh.	4
___	economic development amazon river valley. sh.	5
___	economic development amazon river valley history. sh.	1
___	economic development angola. sh.	1
___	economic development arab countries. sh.	5
___	economic development argentina. sh.	5
___	economic development argentina history. sh.	6
___	economic development asia. sh.	69
___	economic development asia history. sh.	3
___	economic development australia. sh.	2
___	economic development austria. sh.	2
___	economic development austria history. sh.	1
___	economic development bahrain. sh.	1

Figure 4.6b Entries from *Social Sciences Index* (June 1994). Reprinted by permission of The H. W. Wilson Company.

Economic development
See also
Developing countries
Gross national product
Industrialization
Infrastructure (Economics)
Linkages (Economics)
Organisation for Economic Co-operation and Development
Postindustrial society
Production (Economics)
Regional economic development
Rural development
United Nations. Economic and Social Council
Urban development

Economic growth and defense spending in developing countries: a causal analysis. N. K. Kusi. *J Confl Resolut* v38 p152-9 Mr '94
Global modelling in the 1990s: a critical evaluation of a new wave. B. van Steenbergen. *Futures (Engl)* v26 p44-56 Ja/F '94
Legal and economic development: the missing links [review article] E. A. Buscaglia, Jr. *J Interam Stud World Aff* v35 p153-69 Wint '93/'94
A question of linkage: capitalism, prosperity, democracy . . . I. Stelzer. *Natl Interest* no35 p29-35 Spr '94
The theory of the flying geese pattern of development and its interpretations. P. Korhonen. bibl *J Peace Res* v31 p93-108 F '94

Environmental aspects
See also
Sustainable development

Aid and the environment: outlook: cloudy. *Economist* v330 p42 F 12 '94
Carrying capacity: earth's bottom line. S. Postel. *Challenge* v37 p4-12 Mr/Ap '94
Environmental policy enactment under the military: some generalities between Brazil and Chile. M. Alario. bibl *Int J Comp Sociol* v34 p222-30 S/D '93
Growth and distribution under an environmental restriction. E. Hosoda. *Manchester Sch Econ Soc Stud* v62 p60-80 Mr '94
Rethinking the central institutions of modern society: science and business. W. W. Harman. *Futures (Engl)* v25 p1063-70 D '93; Discussion. v25 p1070-93 D '93
Travelling trash: Vietnam's environment under attack from all quarters. M. Hiebert. *Far East Econ Rev* v157 p21+ F 3 '94

International aspects

Coordinating the UN mission [interview with Nitin Desai] *UN Chron* v30 p40 D '93
Financing development in a world of market economics. Sir W. Ryrie. *World Today* v50 p15-18 Ja '94
Foreign debt and economic growth in the world system. D. S. Glasberg and K. B. Ward. bibl *Soc Sci Q* v74 p703-20 D '93
A new framework for development cooperation. *UN Chron* v30 p42 D '93
Thinking strategically about development: a typology of action programs for global change. E. A. Morgan and others. bibl *World Dev* v21 p1913-30 D '93

Mathematical models

Distribution and growth with an infrastructure constraint. J. M. Rao. bibl *Camb J Econ* v17 p369-89 D '93
Economic integration and endogenous growth. L. A. Rivera-Batiz and P. M. Romer. bibl *Q J Econ* v106 p531-55 My '91; Discussion. v109 p99-308 F '94
Money and growth: an alternative approach. P. N. Ireland. bibl *Am Econ Rev* v84 p47-65 Mr '94
New growth theory [symposium] *J Econ Perspect* v8 p3-72 Wint '94
Political economy, growth and convergence in less-developed countries. M. Chatterji and others. *World Dev* v21 p2029-38 D '93
Research and development expenditures and economic growth: a cross-country study. R. K. Goel and R. Ram. *Econ Dev Cult Change* v42 p403-11 Ja '94
Structural changes in agriculture: production linkages and agricultural demand-led industrialization. S. J. Vogel. bibl *Oxford Econ Pap* v46 p136-56 Ja '94

Social aspects

Bribonomics [summary of Corruption, by Andrei Shleifer and Robert Vishny] *Economist* v330 p86 Mr 19 '94
Does the human-capital/educational-sorting debate matter for development policy? K. Lang. bibl *Am Econ Rev* v84 p353-8 Mr '94
How economic development and family planning programs combined to reduce Indonesian fertility. P. J. Gertler and J. W. Molyneaux. bibl *Demography* v31 p33-63 F '94
Revisiting the relationship between growth and poverty. G. Azam and A. Redmon. *Rev Black Polit Econ* v22 p5-18 Summ '93
The urban complex in a world economy. S. Sassen. bibl il *Int Soc Sci J* v46 p43-62 F '94

Africa

Is Africa different? P. J. Conway and J. Greene. bibl *World Dev* v21 p2017-28 D '93
Monetary co-operation and economic growth in Africa: comparative evidence from the CFA-zone countries. D. Assane and A. Pourgerami. bibl *J Dev Stud* v30 p423-42 Ja '94

Amazon River region

Amazônia: democracy, ecology, and Brazilian military prerogatives in the 1990s. D. Zirker and M. Henberg. *Armed Forces Soc* v20 p259-81 Wint '94

Asia

Japanese capitalism and the Asian geese. W. K. Tabb. *Mon Rev* v45 p29-40 Mr '94
The price of liberty. G. Dalmia. *Far East Econ Rev* v157 p25 Mr 3 '94

Brazil

Environmental policy enactment under the military: some generalities between Brazil and Chile. M. Alario. bibl *Int J Comp Sociol* v34 p222-30 S/D '93

China

China in 1993: dissolution, frenzy, and/or breakthrough? D. Bachman. *Asian Surv* v34 p30-40 Ja '94
CITIC new development project [reprinted from Clippings] *Beijing Rev* v37 p25 Ja 17 '94

East Asia

Asia's fate: a response to the Singapore school. E. Jones. *Natl Interest* no35 p18-28 Spr '94
East Asian miracle [symposium] *Finance Dev* v31 p2-19 Mr '94
Industrial policy reform in six large newly industrializing countries: the resource curse thesis. R. M. Auty. bibl *World Dev* v22 p11-26 Ja '94
Locomotive of the world economy. Shi Min. *Beijing Rev* v37 p24-5 Mr 7 '94

Great Britain

Green but not heard [the British government has now produced its sustainable development strategy] V. Anderson. *New Statesman Soc* v7 p30-1 Ja 28 '94

India

Work participation, gender and economic development: a quantitative anatomy of the Indian scenario. A. Mathur. bibl *J Dev Stud* v30 p466-504 Ja '94

Indonesia

Hungry for land [villagers land ownership patterns cause problems for development] *Economist* v330 p39 Mr 5 '94
Indonesian development: the efficiency/equity debate regarding regional development [review article] C. Chifos and M. Romanos. *J Am Plann Assoc* v60 p116-21 Wint '94

Japan

The role of credit policies in Japan and Korea. D. Vittas and Y. J. Cho. *Finance Dev* v31 p10-12 Mr '94

Korea (South)

The role of credit policies in Japan and Korea. D. Vittas and Y. J. Cho. *Finance Dev* v31 p10-12 Mr '94

History

Transnational economic linkages, the state, and dependent development in South Korea, 1966-1988: a time-series analysis. Y. W. Bradshaw and others. bibl *Soc Forces* v72 p315-45 D '93

STRATEGIES FOR BIBLIOGRAPHIC SEARCHING

Two strategies, specific-to-general and general-to-specific, enable the searcher to exploit bibliographic structure to achieve an objective. These strategies may be applied to solving problems such as vocabulary selection and reference tool selection. Other strategies assist the searcher in capitalizing on specific system properties to improve the efficiency and quality of an information search. Two such properties are context and feedback.

The Specific-to-General Approach

The *specific-to-general approach* is defined as a search in which the searcher has a known relevant item or topic in mind and wishes to find others like it. For example, when a requester knows the author and title of a book and wishes to find similar books by different authors, the subject headings can be examined and then used to locate additional items. As pointed out earlier, this strategy works well in bibliographic systems that display descriptors, such as card catalogs and online databases and catalogs (see Box 4.5), but cannot be employed in most print indexes because they do not display descriptors.

Box 4.5 Finding Related Items

Suppose the user has just finished reading the book *Dreams of Reason: The Computer and the Rise of the Sciences of Complexity* by Heinz Pagels. She would like to continue reading in the same area, but she has no idea how to go about finding books on similar subjects. By looking up the book in the catalog, she discovers that the subject headings applied to the book are "Science—Philosophy," "Complexity (Philosophy)," and "Computers and civilization." Because her interest is really in the effects of computers on peoples' lives, she decides to look further under "Computers and civilization." Using the library's online catalog, she finds that there are 140 books with that subject heading. By browsing through the list, she finds the following books: *The Electronic Word: Democracy, Technology and the Arts; Competing Visions, Complex Realities: Social Aspects of the Information Society;* and *Computers, Ethics, and Society*. These will be a good start for further reading.

The first step is to locate the known item in the file. Assuming the information about the item is complete and correct, locating it in the file can usually be done through an author or title search. Although an author/title search is not always easy, especially when the file is large or the entry is complex (e.g., for corporate authors, such as those for U.S. government agencies), it is usually straightforward and unambiguous. Once the record is located, the searcher may examine the subject terms assigned to the work and immediately incorporate those terms in a subsequent search for more items. This direct entry into an information file eliminates the need to think of possible subject terms on one's own, and also makes consulting a thesaurus or list of subject headings optional. Of course, the terms located initially may also be used as entry terms into a thesaurus or list of subject headings. One of the reasons the specific-to-general approach works well is that it provides a specific, unambiguous entry point of known accuracy into an information file.

When used in an online database search, this technique is usually called *citation pearl growing*. The initial citation is the point of entry, or seed of the pearl, and the search is expanded outward by selecting subject terms from the descriptor fields of the unit record. The successive expansions constitute the layers of the pearl. Another example of this strategy in online searching is the most-specific-facet-first approach. For example, a proper name or a highly specialized term or phrase is used as the entry point. Because most online systems allow searchers to enter free text or keywords, almost any specific term can be used as an entry point. If the retrieval is sufficient and of good quality, the search can be terminated; if larger retrieval is desired, both free-text terms obtained from titles or abstracts and controlled vocabulary terms obtained from lists of descriptors can be added to expand the retrieval.

Citation indexing, discussed in more detail in Chapter 21, works on the same principle. A specific known item is used as an entry point to the index or database, and other items, assumed to be similar in subject matter because their authors cite the known item, can then be located. Citation searches may result in somewhat different retrieval, because it is the judgment of the authors of the works, rather than that of the indexers, upon which the links between items are established. Acknowledging the diversity of both indexing practices and citation habits, fully comprehensive results may be achieved by conducting multiple searches using both indexing and citation links.

Still another example of the specific-to-general approach is reflected in search request forms or in queries in reference interviews in which requesters are asked to supply a known citation as a starting point. Here, the requester makes the judgment as to the relevance of a particular item to the topic of the request (the information need). Such information may be invaluable to the searcher in fully understanding what is meant by the users' information request and in resolving any potential ambiguities.

General characteristics of the specific-to-general approach are its highly interactive quality and the need for continual review of results. The interactive nature of electronic information retrieval has been recognized in the research literature and has provided a locus for investigation of both mediated and end-user searches. A concomitant aspect of interactivity is the amount of feedback available to the searcher, and how the searcher uses the feedback to advance and refine the search.[27] With this degree of interactivity, however, there is always the danger that the searcher will become lost or distracted during the search; therefore, it is essential to know when to stop expanding the search and cycling through the process.

The General-to-Specific Approach

The key to effective searching when moving from the general to the specific is the syndetic structure that provides a logical overview or map of the concepts and vocabulary of a particular topic area. Because items are indexed to the most specific aspects of a topic, it is crucial to determine the correct level of specificity. This can be obtained quickly and easily by scanning a thesaurus. For example, the thesaurus used in indexing medical literature, known as *Medical Subject Headings* (MeSH)[28] provides terms for the leg bones of the human body. The four bone terms listed are *femur, fibula, patella,* and *tibia.* Articles dealing with fractures of the fibula would therefore be indexed at the most specific level: fibula and fractures. The femur, however, has an additional level of specificity that describes two particular locations on the femur: femur head and femur neck. A fracture of the femur that is located at the head of the femur must therefore be indexed at the most specific level: femur head and fractures. The best (and sometimes only) way to determine the level of specificity is to consult the thesaurus. The importance of the thesaurus to constructing a successful search has led some database producers to provide the thesaurus online. In addition, some thesauri (of which MeSH is an example) provide a display of terms in a hierarchical structure. In MeSH, this display is known as the *tree structure,* as shown in Figure 4.7, page 90.

The alphabetical listing and the tree structure can be used together to determine the correct level of specificity. In the alphabetical listing, an interpretive note is made at "leg bones," and the appropriate place in the tree structure is indicated by means of an alphanumeric code: A2.835.232.484. As pointed out earlier, some indexes incorporate syndetic structure either through classification or by the arrangement of items under a heading, or both.

A further enhancement to some online systems (e.g., *MEDLINE,* the online version of *Index Medicus)* is an Explode feature that captures several terms at various levels within the hierarchy below the starting term with a single command. Once a term is located in the hierarchy, it may be exploded, and the search expanded very quickly; this can be done without sacrificing precision, as it is possible to determine ahead of time which terms will be included. In the example used in the previous paragraph, an online searcher can explode the term "femur," thereby capturing all articles dealing with the femur, the femur head, and the femur neck. The explosion may also occur higher up in the tree, capturing all the terms for leg bones; in this case, the term "leg bones" is not a permitted descriptor, and so the numeric code A2.835.232.484 must be entered instead.

Figure 4.7 Tree structure from *Medical Subject Headings* (MeSH).

Musculoskeletal System	
Skeleton	
Bone and Bones	
Foot Bones (Non MeSH)	A2.835.232.262
Metatarsal Bones	A2.835.232.262.492
Tarsal Bones	A2.835.232.262.710
Calcaneus	A2.835.232.262.710.300
Talus	A2.835.232.262.710.780
Hyoid Bone	A2.835.232.409
Leg Bones (Non MeSH)	A2.835.232.484
Femur	A2.835.232.484.247
Femur Head	A2.835.232.484.247.343
Femur Neck	A2.835.232.484.247.510
Fibula	A2.835.232.484.321
Patella	A2.835.232.484.624
Tibia	A2.835.232.484.883

Unfortunately, not all bibliographic systems have thesauri, nor are the thesauri always readily available in libraries. Sometimes the list of subject headings used in a specific index is published in one section of the print index or can be purchased separately; all too frequently, it is not provided. Fortunately, more and more publishers have recognized the value of making their subject headings and thesauri available, especially in electronic sources. Without them, it is difficult to grasp the scope of the subject matter or the syndetic structure of the index. In print indexes, only those headings for items appearing in that volume are displayed in each volume of the index. Another problem is the number of subject heading schemes and controlled vocabularies that populate the bibliographic universe. These controlled vocabularies differ in degree of specificity, frequency of updating, availability, and structure. The librarian working in a general reference setting must cope with several different controlled vocabularies on a daily basis.

A single controlled vocabulary that encompasses many subject areas and is in widespread use (e.g., LCSH) provides consistency for librarians and users, but specialized thesauri developed by subject experts provide a greater degree of flexibility and specificity. In some specialized areas, there has been an attempt to rationalize controlled vocabulary to provide consistent access across a number of indexes. The Unified Medical Language System (UMLS) provides a systematic linking of terms from both clinical and bibliographic vocabularies.[29]

In addition to moving up and down a hierarchical list of descriptors, syndetic structure supports moving horizontally through the use of cross-references and see also references. As pointed out earlier, one of the advantages of a controlled vocabulary is collocation: gathering similar works together despite individual variance in title words or abstracts. Once the searcher has arrived at the correct location in an information source, the list of descriptors may be scanned to select more specific items.

One of the difficulties, however, is selecting the correct terminology to arrive at the desired spot in the file. In a system without cross-references, the searcher must use the allowed term (in the correct spelling and grammatical form) to locate any materials. Cross-references permit the searcher to move from an entry term that is not used to a controlled vocabulary term that is used. Using an incorrect term results in no retrieval (manual or online), creating the usually false impression that nothing exists on the given topic. Maintaining a cross-reference structure assists the user because it can increase the number of entry points; knowledge of the topic, a good imagination, and a large vocabulary can also be assets to the searcher.

The ability to allow users to match their terminology to the systems' is so important that various schemes for enhancing the number of entry points have been proposed. Some of these involve providing expanded lists of words that can be used as entry points (sometimes called "super thesauri"), encouraging reference librarians to add cross-references to catalogs, and allowing users to add their own terms to local databases. Although these ideas remain largely experimental, they serve to focus attention on an important problem in searching. A nearly universal problem when employing the general-to-specific approach in an electronic environment is the creation of large retrieval sets. The inexperienced searcher can risk losing important and valuable information if the size of the retrieval set is not reduced systematically and carefully. This can often be quite simple to do, as described by Michael Buckland and colleagues[30] in their proposal for enhancements to a catalog. Whether these enhancements are accomplished through functions programmed into the system or whether they are invoked by the librarian while searching, the end result is the same: The retrieval is more manageable in size, of better quality, and ultimately of more use to the requester.

Context and Feedback

The preceding discussion suggests that the specific-to-general approach is particularly well suited to electronic environments, while the general-to-specific approach works best when the searcher wants a quick overview of a topic by scanning a print source or when a screen display facilitates a quick and effective grasp of the materials retrieved. This contrasts the importance of context in developing a search strategy. In print sources, displays of syndetic structure inform the searcher of the context in which terminology is to be understood, as well as creating a visual map of the structure of a discipline. In online sources, however, these visual cues are often not available. As anyone familiar with the English language can attest, context plays a major part in resolving ambiguity when terms have several meanings. For example, stress can be understood in a psychological context ("stressed out" from exams), in a physical context (metals undergo stress), or in a medical context (stress as exertion).

The effect of ambiguity on searching can be substantial, particularly in large online systems (catalogs or databases that contain files covering many disciplines). Entering the term "stress" (meaning psychological stress) in an online catalog will retrieve a large number of items, but only a portion of them will deal with psychological stress. In some systems, the only way to determine which ones are relevant is to display all the items (no small task when 300 items are retrieved). Reviewing a few items and discovering that some of them deal with stress in metals will reveal semantic ambiguities, however, and indicate that another concept or term must be added to limit the search to the appropriate subject area. A very easy way to do this is to use Boolean AND with a psychological term such as "Role conflict," which fixes the search in the appropriate context where further refinements can take place. This model for searching is often called the *building-block approach* and is widely used in online searching.

In online databases where the subject content is consistent throughout the file, a different strategy is necessary. For example, in *PsycINFO* (the online version of *Psychological Abstracts)*[31] the use of a general psychological term would be unnecessary because the psychological context is implicit. In fact, including general psychological terminology in a search in *PsycINFO* may be counterproductive, because indexing of articles is done at a specific level. It is unlikely that such a general concept would be indexed, and therefore the search would retrieve little or nothing. Ironically, this tactic is sometimes referred to as *over-specifying* a search. What this means is that the searcher has not taken into account the implicit context of the file and has constructed a redundant search strategy (see Box 4.6 for an example).

Box 4.6

Effects of Failing to Recognize the Context of a Search

In looking for articles about the psychological effects of child abuse, the searcher selects an appropriate database (*PsycINFO*) but fails to recognize that virtually all articles in this file deal with psychological aspects of phenomena. The searcher correctly uses the descriptor "Child abuse," which retrieves 10,138 articles, but also chooses to create a free-text phrase "Psychological effects," which retrieves 1,954 articles. When the two search statements are combined, the result is 47 articles. These 47 articles might well be relevant, but it is likely that the number of relevant articles is much greater. The searcher's requirement that the words "Psychological effects" appear in the bibliographic record has resulted in an unrealistically restricted retrieval. Two alternative approaches should be considered. Either conduct a manual search of *Psychological Abstracts* under the descriptor "Child abuse" or attempt to gain greater understanding of additional parameters of the search through a more in-depth reference interview.

The importance of context is often overlooked, because it is often taken for granted. The tremendous growth of online and Web searching, wherein contextual clues are all but lost, has served to reemphasize the potential value of context in resolving ambiguity and providing clues as to meaning and direction in searching. The context supplies a kind of feedback that is invaluable to the searcher. Feedback about the progress of a search, particularly in an online environment, has come to be a valued component of system design. Features such as menus that assist the searcher in formulating (and reformulating) a search strategy, Help screens that can be invoked by the user as needed, and display of retrieved items in order of their relevance to the query are becoming more common as online system design continues to evolve.

Although online feedback may be more explicit, subtle forms of feedback can be observed in print formats. Hierarchical displays in indexes, evidence of the scope of an area, such as the amount of catalog space or the number of pages in an index allocated to a particular topic, and even the age of the catalog cards themselves often exert a subtle influence on the direction of a search. By recognizing the existence and value of feedback in refining or changing direction in a search, librarians can become aware of the role feedback plays in their own search strategies, and they can also incorporate feedback mechanisms in the programs and systems they provide to users.

Choice of Reference Tool

Little has been said so far in this chapter about the choice of reference tool. Selecting an appropriate reference tool or database affects the search strategy; together, tool selection and search strategy determine the effectiveness of the search. Strategies that are appropriate for the various types of tools discussed in Part II are presented along with the tools themselves. There are some intermediary tools, however, that deserve mention.

Print guides to reference works, such as the well-known *Guide to Reference Books*,[32] assist the searcher in identifying appropriate sources. Recognizing the value of syndetic structure, the *Guide* uses a classification by both subject area and type of tool. The approach employed by the *Guide* is general-to-specific, providing a visual map of a field through which one may navigate. Such an approach provides a good overview of the structure of a subject field and of the variety and scope of reference materials that are available.

On the other hand, the number of reference tools included in the *Guide* continues to expand rapidly, and only the most comprehensive reference collection is likely to own most of the tools described. Some libraries annotate the *Guide* with their holdings to simplify locating a tool in the reference collection. Other libraries create keyword indexes or small databases that contain descriptions of their reference holdings. These can be consulted quickly to determine which books are on hand to answer a particular type of question, and can be searched by keyword so that librarians can locate a book easily, even if they cannot recall the exact title.

On a more elaborate level, expert systems are being designed to lead the librarian or the user through a series of steps that will assist in locating the appropriate book to consult to find a particular piece of information. These developments stem from the recognition that librarians, like many professionals, have a limited capacity to remember all the resources available to them, and therefore wisely rely on intermediary assistance to ensure that they have not overlooked an important source of information.

Other tools are available to assist the online searcher in selecting the appropriate databases. They are discussed in depth in Chapter 13, but because they constitute a source of information parallel to print guides to reference sources and because tool selection is of critical importance to effective search strategy, they are mentioned briefly here. Sources such as the *Gale Directory of Databases*[33] provide a good overview of the growing number of databases available. In addition to these print tools, some systems such as Dialog allow a searcher to enter a specific term to see how many times that term appears in the various databases. By observing the frequency of occurrence of a term, the searcher can estimate the likelihood that a search on that topic will be fruitful in a particular database. As mentioned earlier, this strategy works best with a specific term, because more general terms are often implicit in a subject-specific database. Such implicit concepts are not indexed, and therefore no matches will occur.

SUMMARY AND CONCLUSION

An understanding of the way in which the bibliographic universe is organized is essential to effective, efficient searching. The two primary types of access mechanisms discussed in this chapter are library catalogs and indexes, each of which is presented as an ideal type—catalogs providing access to a particular library's collection of books, and indexes providing access to journal articles in a particular subject area. In actuality, each of these types exists in less pure forms, and the distinctions between them are becoming less clear-cut, particularly when they coexist in the same electronic environment. Despite—and perhaps because of—the increasing complexity of the bibliographic world, it is important to keep in mind the fundamental principles of bibliographic control such as access, physical arrangement, collocation and authority control, and depth and comprehensiveness of indexing.

Exploiting the power of bibliographic organization to conduct effective, efficient searches takes practice and experience. Thinking critically about the process as one goes along, as well as observing the behavior of others (librarians and users alike), can yield valuable insight into how best to assist and instruct others to find information. Although the searching process will vary from individual to individual, two general strategies for searching—specific-to-general and general-to-specific—can be used effectively. The selection of appropriate reference tools, a critical component to the success of a search, can be made easier by consulting bibliographies of reference works, and the selection of appropriate terminology can be facilitated by consulting sources that link various controlled vocabularies together. The application of online and computer technologies has affected the bibliographic world, both by making it more complex and by offering librarians the challenge and the means to improve access to information.

NOTES

1. Patrick Wilson, "The Catalog as Access Mechanism: Background and Concepts," *Library Resources & Technical Services* 27 (January/March 1983): 5-6.

2. U.S. Library of Congress, Cataloging Policy and Support Office, *Library of Congress Subject Headings,* 23d ed., 5 vols. (Washington, D.C.: Library of Congress, 2000).

3. Minnie Earle Sears, *Sears List of Subject Headings,* 17th ed., ed. Joseph Miller (Bronx, N.Y.: H. W. Wilson, 2000), 810p.

4. Michael Gorman, "Yesterday's Heresy—Today's Orthodoxy: An Essay on the Changing Face of Descriptive Cataloging," *College & Research Libraries* 50 (November 1989): 626-34.

5. *Readers' Guide to Periodical Literature,* 1900- . (New York: H. W. Wilson, 1905-).

6. *Education Index,* 1929- . (New York: H. W. Wilson, 1932-).

7. *Index Medicus* (Washington, D.C.: National Library of Medicine, 1960-).

8. *Library and Information Science Abstracts* (London: Library Association, 1969-).

9. Jennifer A. Younger, "Resource Description in the Digital Age," *Library Trends* 45 (Winter 1997): 462-81.

10. Marcia J. Bates, "Information Search Tactics," *Journal of the American Society for Information Science* 30 (July 1979): 205-14.

11. Alva T. Stone, "That Elusive Concept of Aboutness: The Year's Work in Subject Analysis, 1992," *Library Resources & Technical Services* 37 (July 1993): 277-97.

12. Mary Dykstra, "LC Subject Headings Disguised as a Thesaurus," *Library Journal* 113 (March 1, 1988): 42-46; and "Can Subject Headings Be Saved?" *Library Journal* 113 (September 15, 1988): 55-58.

13. Harold Wooster, "0.46872985 Square Inches—A Naive Look at Subject Analysis," in *Digest of 1970 Annual Meeting* (Philadelphia: National Federation of Science Abstracting and Indexing Services, 1970), 45.

14. Frederick G. Kilgour, "Origins of Coordinate Searching," *Journal of the American Society for Information Science* 48 (April 1997): 340-48.

15. Examples of such articles appear regularly in the journals *Online* and *EContent* (formerly *Database*), and a number have been reprinted in *Database Search Strategies & Tips: Reprints from the Best of Online and Database* (Weston, Conn.: Online, 1988), 94p.

16. Carter Alexander, "Technique of Library Searching," *Special Libraries* 27 (September 1936): 230-38.

17. Christine L. Borgman, "All Users of Information Retrieval Systems Are Not Created Equal: An Exploration into Individual Differences," *Information Processing & Management* 25 (1989): 237-51; Carol Hansen Fenichel, "Online Searching: Measures That Discriminate Among Users with Different Types of Experience," *Journal of the American Society for Information Science* 32 (January 1981): 23-32; and Tefko Saracevic and Paul Kantor, "A Study of Information Seeking and Retrieving. III. Searchers, Searches, and Overlap," *Journal of the American Society for Information Science* 39 (May 1988): 197-216.

18. Prudence W. Dalrymple, "Retrieval by Reformulation in Two Library Catalogs: Toward a Cognitive Model of Searching Behavior," *Journal of the American Society for Information Science* 41 (June 1990): 272-81.

19. Carol Collier Kuhlthau, "Inside the Search Process: Information Seeking from the User's Perspective," *Journal of the American Society for Information Science* 42 (June 1991): 361-71; "The Role of Experience in the Information Search Process of an Early Career Information Worker: Perceptions of Uncertainty, Complexity, Construction, and Sources," *Journal of the American Society for Information Science* 50 (April 15, 1999): 399-412.

20. Marcia J. Bates, "Indexing and Access for Digital Libraries and the Internet: Human, Database, and Domain Factors," *Journal of the American Society for Information Science* 49 (November 1998): 1185-1205; Carol Collier Kuhlthau, "Learning in Digital Libraries: An Information Search Process Approach," *Library Trends* 45 (Spring 1997): 708-24.

21. Bates, "Information Search Tactics," 205-14; Amanda Spink and Tefko Saracevic, "Interaction in Information Retrieval: Selection and Effectiveness of Search Terms," *Journal of the American Society for Information Science* 48 (August 1997): 741-61; Mirja Iivonen and Diane H. Sonnenwald, "From Translation to Navigation of Different Discourses: A Model of Search Term Selection during the Pre-Online Stage of the Search Process," *Journal of the American Society for Information Science* 49 (April 1998): 312-26.

22. Micheline Hancock-Beaulieu and Stephen Walker, "An Evaluation of Automatic Query Expansion in an Online Library Catalogue," *Journal of Documentation* 48 (December 1992): 406-21.

23. Marcia J. Bates, "What Is a Reference Book? A Theoretical and Empirical Analysis," *RQ* 26 (Fall 1986): 37-57.

24. *Physicians' Desk Reference* (Montvale, N.J.: Medical Economics, 1946-).

25. *Social Sciences Index* (New York: H. W. Wilson, 1974-).

26. Examples of librarian-designed systems may be found in Brian Nielsen, "Roll Your Own Interface: Public Access to CD-ROMs," *Database* 12 (December 1989): 105-9; and Linda C. Smith and Prudence W. Dalrymple, eds., *Designing Information: New Roles for Librarians* (Urbana-Champaign, Ill.: University of Illinois at Urbana-Champaign Graduate School of Library and Information Science, 1993), 222p.

27. Amanda Spink, "Study of Interactive Feedback during Mediated Information Retrieval," *Journal of the American Society for Information Science* 48 (May 1997): 382-94; and "Information Science: A Third Feedback Framework," *Journal of the American Society for Information Science* 48 (August 1997): 728-40.

28. U.S. National Library of Medicine, *Medical Subject Headings* (Washington, D.C.: National Library of Medicine, 1963-).

29. Betsy L. Humphreys et al., "The UMLS Project: Making the Conceptual Connections Between Users and the Information They Need," *Bulletin of the Medical Library Association* 81 (April 1993): 170-77.

30. Michael Buckland, Barbara A. Norgard, and Christian Plaunt, "Filing, Filtering, and the First Few Found," *Information Technology & Libraries* 12 (September 1993): 311-19.

31. *Psychological Abstracts* (Washington, D.C.: American Psychological Association, 1927-).

32. *Guide to Reference Books*, 11th ed., ed. Robert Balay (Chicago: American Library Association, 1996), 2020p.

33. *Gale Directory of Databases*, 2 vols. (Farmington Hills, Mich.: Gale Group, 1993-), semiannual.

ADDITIONAL READINGS

Bates, Marcia J. "Search Techniques." *Annual Review of Information Science and Technology* 15 (1980): 139-69.

In this review article, Bates provides a review and synthesis of literature in the field of search strategy, both manual and online, through 1980.

Cochrane, Pauline A. *Redesign of Catalogs and Indexes for Improved Online Subject Access: Selected Papers of Pauline A. Cochrane*. Phoenix, Ariz.: Oryx Press, 1985. 484p.

This collection draws together both indexes and catalogs, showing how the problem of subject access manifests itself in each.

Cochrane, Pauline A., and Karen Markey. "Catalog Use Studies—Since the Introduction of Online Interactive Catalogs: Impact on Design for Subject Access." *Library & Information Science Research* 5 (Winter 1983): 337-63.

This review focuses on methods and directions in research on searching online catalogs.

Cutter, Charles A. *Rules for a Dictionary Catalog.* 4th ed., rewritten. Washington, D.C.: Government Printing Office, 1904. 173p.

This early work sets forth the principles to which library catalogs still adhere.

Hafter, Ruth. "The Performance of Card Catalogs: A Review of the Research." *Library Research* 1 (Fall 1979): 199-220.

Krikelas, James. "Catalog Use Studies and Their Implications." *Advances in Librarianship* 3 (1972): 195-220.

———. "Searching the Library Catalog: A Study of Users' Access." *Library Research* 2 (1980-1981): 215-30.

An acquaintance with studies of catalog use as provided in these three literature reviews will serve to point out the challenges inherent in the study of search strategies. Because both catalogs and indexes are designed to be searched by library users as well as librarians, the insights gained from catalog use studies can introduce the ways in which librarians have conceptualized the relationship between design and use of bibliographic tools.

Mann, Thomas. *Library Research Models: A Guide to Classification, Cataloging and Computers.* New York: Oxford University Press, 1993. 248p.

By presenting a variety of models for searching, Mann raises the reader's awareness of the extent to which expectations affect results. The author focuses on the analysis of extensive information searches rather than short reference queries. His years of experience as a librarian in large research libraries led him to propose a "methods of searching" model that provides a lively counterpoint to traditional assumptions that have guided library practice.

Rosenfeld, Louis, and Peter Morville. *Information Architecture for the World Wide Web.* Cambridge, Mass.: O'Reilly & Associates, 1998. 202p.

The authors discuss how organization of Web sites affects navigation and use. They provide examples of both successful and not-so-successful sites, and raise provocative questions about the effectiveness of many characteristics currently popular in Web design.

Taylor, Arlene G. *The Organization of Information.* Englewood, Colo.: Libraries Unlimited, 1999. 280p.

This introductory text gives an excellent overview of the principles of organizing recorded information of various types. Within a broad context, the author enables the reader to see how organization facilitates use regardless of the specific set of principles used or the type of materials organized.

White, Howard D., Marcia J. Bates, and Patrick Wilson. *For Information Specialists: Interpretations of Reference and Bibliographic Work.* Norwood, N.J.: Ablex, 1992. 310p.

This collection of essays by three seminal writers in the field of storage and retrieval of bibliographic materials provides insight into the tools and processes of information work. The authors move between highly conceptual themes that are often provocative and idiosyncratic, and specific and practical suggestions for exploiting the principles and practice of bibliographic organization in strategic ways. The volume contains essays by Bates and Wilson that are expansions of the works cited in this chapter.

Younger, Jennifer A. "Resources Description in the Digital Age." *Library Trends* 45 (Winter 1997): 462-87.

This article provides the reader with an overview of the ways in which the library community is addressing the need for a comprehensive, updated approach to describing items in a digital environment. The author links the traditional accomplishments of cataloging and indexing to new approaches such as metadata, and does so in the context of the fundamental objectives of the library catalog.

CHAPTER

5

ELECTRONIC RESOURCES FOR REFERENCE

Kathleen M. Kluegel

INTRODUCTION

Many of the chapters in this book identify specific electronic resources for reference service. This chapter puts these resources into the context of the history and development of electronic information resources. If one can see the past, the future can be a little more understandable as well. Another goal is to show the structure that changes bits and bytes into information resources and the relation between structure and function. With this perspective, one can analyze how a tool works and how to identify its structure, then translate that structure into effective search strategies. These skills transcend any medium and any information delivery option.

The chapter also examines the end-user revolution in electronic information services. This revolution has transformed the role of the reference librarian in information delivery services. It is changing the fundamental definition of the reference collection as well. This has further ramifications in the design and organization of information services in and through the library.

HISTORY OF ELECTRONIC RESOURCES

In large part, the history of electronic resources for reference began with the development of computer-assisted typesetting and printing. The publishers of indexing and abstracting services first used computers to print their paper products. They created magnetic tapes that were interpreted by a computer and drove their printers. Computers could also read these magnetic tapes for other purposes. Companies and government agencies, such as the National Library of Medicine in the United States, developed computer software that could read and manipulate the information on these tapes in new ways. This software allowed reference librarians in those organizations to ask the computer to "search" for an indexed term or a group of terms to see if there were bibliographic citations to articles on these tapes that would meet the information needs of their users. Because the technology available at the time—magnetic tape and punch cards—processed the queries so slowly, these searches had to be done in batch mode. The query was keyed in during the day, the magnetic tape was run against the query at night, and the results were delivered the next day. Any typographical or logical errors in the query required re-doing the entire search and waiting for the new results. These single-agency search systems formed the foundation of the information retrieval industry in the 1960s.

Search systems that had been developed for use within a single corporation, such as Lockheed's Dialog and System Development Corporation's ORBIT, were next expanded in their scope to serve the research needs of other major research institutions such as universities, government agencies, and other large corporations. Modems allowed remote access to huge computers rather than limiting access to hardwired terminals. Magnetic tape was replaced by much faster disk stacks. These developments provided the first truly online searching, with the searcher and the search systems communicating interactively. The relatively slow communication technology inhibited online printing, so most search results were printed by the vendor and mailed to the searcher. These initial search services were limited to highly skilled reference librarians using a very limited set of databases in these select organizations.

As the number and variety of databases available through these search service vendors increased, the market for these services expanded as well, until it included most colleges, universities, corporations, and research libraries and institutions. The primary user for nearly all of the abstracting and indexing services available through these search systems was the professional reference librarian in these organizations. Librarians performed the searches to fulfill an information need presented by a member of the library's user community. These comprehensive searches done on behalf of a library user are termed *retrospective searches, bibliographic searches, online searches,* or *mediated searches.* Although still important for researchers with highly specialized, in-depth information needs, these searches are becoming less common elements of general reference service.

When a library has the kind of research needs best met by these specialized search services, it contracts with a large search service provider or vendor such as Dialog or STN to have access to the hundreds of databases with literally millions of citations across every subject. Several of the databases available on Dialog began during the earliest phase of electronic resource development and have nearly forty years of citations. More typically, these databases begin coverage in the mid-1970s. Each vendor has developed powerful search languages to support fast and precise retrieval of citations. The reference librarian masters the specialized command language needed to search the databases effectively and efficiently. The search services charge the library to search these databases on a per use basis, typically based on the time spent online, with additional charges for displaying or printing the citations. Because of the specialized search language and the charges based on time online, it is much more efficient for these searches to be done by a trained, experienced reference librarian than by the researcher who needs the information. Frequently in public and academic settings, the library passes along most or all of the direct charges for these searches to the person who requests the information. In special library settings, the costs may be absorbed by the organization to support the research needs of its members.

The usefulness of these mediated searches for researchers led to a demand for direct access to electronic resources. People who use search systems to interact with databases directly without the assistance of an intermediary are termed *end-users.* Because most end-users were unwilling to commit the time and energy required to learn the command languages, the information industry developed the first end-user systems. Some vendors created new services that were aimed specifically at this audience: Knowledge Index by Dialog and BRS AfterDark are just two examples. These systems were primarily menu-based in design rather than command-driven as were the full services. End-user systems typically offered a smaller group of databases and were sometimes available only during "off-peak" hours. Because of these factors, the vendors set the costs of these systems lower than those of the full-service versions they offered. The vendors based the charges on connect time or a flat fee. Some libraries chose to make these end-user online search systems available through the library, while other libraries chose to make only information about these systems available, leaving users to negotiate their own subscriptions. These initial end-user search services can be seen now as a transitional stage of development for electronic resources. The infrastructure, in terms of computers, networks, modems, and search systems, had not reached the stage of development necessary to support extensive end-user searching.

Parallel with online end-user development, CD-ROM systems were developed for end-user services. Libraries today purchase these systems, install them on workstations in reference rooms, and provide the instruction and support for their use, much as they have during the past decade. CD-ROM search software provides the user with much of the power of multiple indexes and Boolean logic available in the commercial online search environment, without its time and cost pressures. With these systems, the users are able to explore the database, following leads as they are discovered and printing out citations during the search. As an additional advantage, users appreciate being able to do the searching on their own. It allows them to be in charge of their own searches, relieves them of the burden of writing down their own citations (with their inevitable errors), and provides them with many citations in a very short time. These citations can be printed on paper or can be downloaded to the user's own diskette for later handling and printing. CD-ROM search software is designed to be *user friendly*, that is, to be easily understood and implemented by the searcher.

There has been a vast expansion of the world of end-user searching far beyond the scope of the local CD-ROM workstation and far beyond the walls of the reference room. The primary audience for current electronic information resources is the end-user. With the development of the World Wide Web, combined with the proliferation of low-cost computers and ready access to the Internet, the mass audience needed to support these expanded services now exists. The Web provides a common platform for the delivery of electronic resources to users: It is format-independent. One of the Web's primary attractions is the ability to provide access to electronic resources to any location on the globe. Libraries are now able to provide resources to their users wherever they happen to be.

To provide these services, each library subscribes to Web-based resources for the library's primary user community. These resources can reside on the providers' Web site or can be mounted on a local Web server. The ability to load resources locally with a standardized "turnkey" search system—a system that can be purchased, installed, and run with no local programming expertise—and yet provide global access to them is an important element in the development of user-centered information services.

When electronic resources are redesigned for the Web, much of the structure of the command-based search services is built into the search screen. In place of highly structured search command languages, most of these services provide a point-and-click interface with a "fill in the box" search window designed for easy searching by the end-user. The results are displayed on the screen for review. The user can select items to be printed or downloaded. In some cases, with a few more clicks, the user will be connected to a site with the full-text of the source online and ready to be printed. This system for providing electronic information services can be seen at thousands of workstations in homes, offices, and libraries throughout the world.

Box 5.1 The Law of the Instrument

If a new tool has been acquired, everything must be processed with that tool. This law is best demonstrated by a two-year-old and a hammer. The next best demonstration is the World Wide Web: If a library has a Web site, everything must go up on the Web.

One consequence of the change in the primary focus for electronic resources is the change in the way reference librarians use their expertise and understanding of databases. A few years ago, their role was to serve as an intermediary between the complex database search system and the person needing the information. Now it is to serve as coach and tutor for the end-user conducting the search. In either role, an understanding of the concepts and mechanics of information retrieval is essential for reference librarians. It can be argued that it is more important to fully understand a search system when one is a coach because of the consequences of an error. If, as a searcher, one mis-remembers a feature, the resulting search failure is readily apparent and can be corrected immediately. If one makes a similar error as a coach, the user may try to do searches and never understand why the search failed.

DATABASES

The term *database* needs to be explored more fully to gain an understanding of and appreciation for it. A database is a set of information formatted into defined structures. In this context, the information is likely to be text. The text can be a basic bibliographic citation including the authors' names and identifying the source, it can be an enhanced citation including subject headings and abstracts, or it could be the complete text of the article or report. Text can also include numbers and charts. In a database, these elements have been assigned to fields, which are defined and labeled according to the rules of the database. Frequently each field has a particular format for the elements within it. For example, an author's name is likely to be structured with the surname first, followed by a comma, and some elements of the forenames. This structure for names is ubiquitous, appearing in the telephone directory, personal address books, bibliographies, and the like, so that it is nearly invisible to us. However, it is the result of very deliberate decisions made by database producers and it has consequences for searching. Box 5.2 shows an example of how a typical entry from a telephone directory could be structured in the database.

Box 5.2 Sample Database Entry

Record Number=qs122333
Record Type=Residential
Surname=Hunkle
First Forename=Welkins
First Middle Initial=Q
First Title=DDS
Second Forename=Pat
Second Middle Initial=Q
Second Title=MD
Street Address=72798 South Broadleaf Boulevard
City=Hometown
Telephone Number=555-1234

In the telephone directory example above, the field labels allow the printing software to accomplish two essential tasks: sorting and formatting. The sorting can be imagined as a series of sets of slots. Each record will be sent through the appropriate slot at each level for further sorting. At each level, the sorting becomes finer. We are most familiar with telephone directories in which the following sorting and formatting rules are embedded: The initial sort would be at the record type, which determines the segment of the directory. The second level would be at the initial letter of the surname, and so forth. The sorting rules for the ordering of records in which the first several elements are identical would be complex. For example, with very common surnames, the differences between entries might occur at the street address level. With very unusual surnames, the sorting algorithm could stop at the surname level. Decisions about how to deal with compound surnames or hyphenated forenames would have to be built into the sorting software.

Once the records were sorted, the field labels would be used to determine formatting. The surname element would be in bold, at the furthest left place in the column. The forename and initials elements would then be set in lighter typeface, indented under the surname header. The street address would be abbreviated and put on the same line as the telephone number. From this simple example, one can see the kind of decision making that is required to build a database with enough structure for it to be functional. The developers have to anticipate all the forms of the information and take into account all the possible variations.

When applied to a database of bibliographic citations, this database-building process becomes very complex. Even a very basic bibliographic structure has to deal with the huge variety of names, journal titles, languages, abbreviations, volume and issue numbering, and pagination. All of the relevant data elements must have a field that supports their form; for example, ISSN numbers need to be eight characters long, ISBN numbers ten. To be of more use, the database structure must be explicitly built and labeled to support subject headings, descriptors, identifiers, and other elements that can also be added to the record. These elements are usually the results of human indexing.

SEARCHING CAPABILITIES

If a database remains a static set of information records, the structural elements identified above would determine how the information could be arranged and presented. For example, the telephone directory sorted, formatted, and printed for our hypothetical town can be viewed as a static database. As a static database, the telephone directory is useful but not very interesting. When the telephone directory or any other set of information becomes a dynamic and searchable database, it becomes more complex and interesting. The number of access points grows from one to many and one gains the power to manipulate the entries. How does the searching process work in databases? One of the more important capabilities of search engines is to create sets that meet user-defined criteria and manipulate them. Search engines use logic, algorithms, and character-string matching to accomplish this. "Searching" the telephone book with one's eyes involves similar processes. One looks for names that match the initial surname string in the query. Within that list, further searching looks for a match on the forename, even if it is there only as an initial. To choose among the possible matches, the address is checked to see if it matches what is known about the person. With search systems and databases, the fields, data elements, and structure of a database interact with the search engine capabilities in highly specific ways to create the information retrieval possibilities. One of the more important tools used in search systems is Boolean logic.

Boolean Logic

Boolean logic is a form of symbolic logic named after George Boole, the nineteenth-century English mathematician who developed it. Boolean logic uses common words as logical operators in very specific ways to create and manipulate sets. Some of these Boolean operators are AND, OR, and NOT.

The Boolean operator OR is used to create a set by making an item eligible for inclusion if it meets at least one of the stated criteria: An item would be included in a set if it meets the condition A OR the condition B OR the condition C, and so on. In creating a set of citrus fruit, one might use the Boolean string: oranges OR grapefruit OR lemons OR limes OR kumquats. This set is more inclusive than a set that has a single criterion for acceptance, for example, oranges. One way to visualize Boolean logic is with *Venn diagrams*. In these diagrams, shadings indicate the results of each of the operators. The Venn diagram for OR is shown in Figure 5.1.

Figure 5.1 The Boolean operator OR in a Venn diagram.

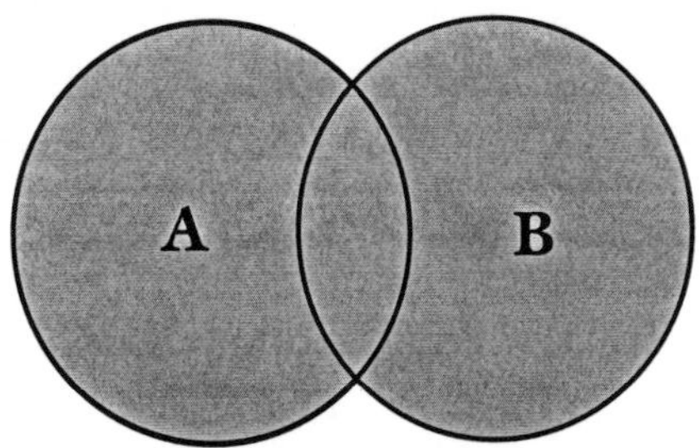

The Boolean operator AND is used to make a more restrictive set by requiring that an item meet both the conditions stated to be included in the final set: An item would be included only if it meets condition A AND condition B. One could use the Boolean AND to create a set containing only those books written by Isaac Asimov that contained the word *robot*. The Boolean string would be Isaac Asimov AND robot. The Venn diagram for AND is shown in Figure 5.2.

Figure 5.2 The Boolean operator AND in a Venn diagram.

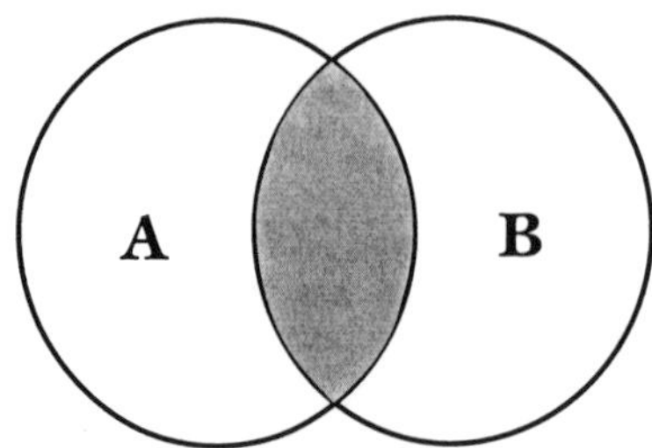

The Boolean AND and the Boolean OR are concepts that the beginning searcher may have trouble keeping straight. The use of the terms is somewhat at odds with the ordinary usage of the English words *and* and *or*. In ordinary English usage, *or* implies a choice—to select one item is to exclude the others—whereas the Boolean OR expands and includes all of the items. An example from a restaurant can highlight this difference. On a breakfast menu, one might be offered toast or a muffin or a bagel. From the customers' perspective, the English *or* means to select an item from the "breakfast bread" set. Viewing this menu from the restaurant's perspective, it has used the Boolean OR ("toast" OR "muffin" OR "bagel") to create the set "breakfast breads."

The Boolean AND and the English *and* produce different outcomes as well. The English *and* works through addition: It adds all the items joined by the *and*. The Boolean AND selects items that include all the named elements. To highlight this difference, one can look at another restaurant example. In a restaurant that allows one to choose one item from column A *and* one from column B *and* one from column C, the result of an order will be a plate that contains three items. The Boolean result of A AND B AND C is one item that contains all three elements (see Box 5.3), an unlikely dish in any restaurant.

Box 5.3 Results of a Boolean Search

If you send a reference librarian to the store with a Boolean list of "sugar" AND "flour" AND "eggs," you will get a *cookie*.

The Boolean operator NOT (sometimes AND NOT) is also used to make a more restrictive set. It first creates a set of items that meet the condition A and then removes from the set those items that also meet condition B. To create a set of trees that were not deciduous one would use the Boolean NOT to exclude deciduous from the set of trees. The Boolean string would be trees NOT deciduous. The Venn diagram for NOT is shown in Figure 5.3.

Figure 5.3 The Boolean operator NOT in a Venn diagram (A NOT B).

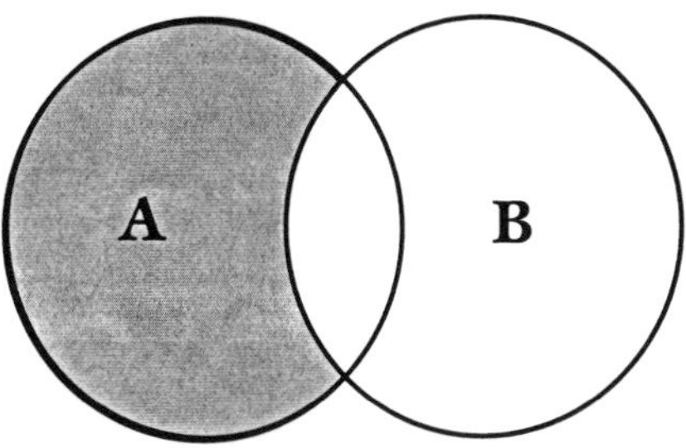

Boolean operators form the essential machinery for making computerized information retrieval precise and effective. With Boolean logic, one can manipulate databases containing a million records to produce the single item that contains all of and only the information specified by the user. It is most effective on databases that have a higher proportion of structured text and relatively little unstructured or free text.

Truncation

Another capability for database manipulation occurs because of the computer's vast list-making potential. It can compile a set of materials that meet multiple criteria simultaneously. The term *truncation* refers to shortening a word or eliminating some characters from a longer term to pick up variants. It is a form of the Boolean operator OR. In truncation, the computer is told to put into a single set all those items that share a common sequence of characters, even if they do not share all the same characters. This process can also be called a "wildcard" search or *stemming.* For example, in searching for the truncated term "librar," the computer is asked to make a set of items that contain the term "library" or "libraries" or "librarians" or "librarian" or "librarianship." The symbols used to indicate truncation will vary from system to system. The asterisk (*) is commonly used, but other symbols, including the question mark (?), the colon (:), and the plus sign (+), are also used in different systems.

Truncation can take place to the left, to the right, or in the middle of the core characters. Truncation can also involve the replacement of several characters or a single character. In the previous example, because the truncation occurred to the right of the core characters it is called right-hand truncation. It can be further described as a multiple-character truncation. If the truncation occurs to the left of the core characters, it is left-hand truncation. An example of left-hand truncation with the core characters "ship" would retrieve, at least, all the records containing any of the terms "librarianship," "guardianship," "statesmanship," "leadership," and "starship." When truncation occurs in the middle of the core characters, it is called *internal truncation.* An example of internal truncation would be "Labo#r," where the "#" is the internal truncation symbol. If this were a single-character substitution system, in which the symbol can stand for either nothing or a single character, this term would pick up items that contained the terms "labor" or "labour." If it is a multiple-character system, in which the symbol can stand for more than one alternate character, the set could include "labor," "labour," "laborer," or "labourer." Frequently, systems allow one to select a single-character or multiple-character truncation method to tailor the search to one's needs. Truncation allows the user to acknowledge and compensate for some amount of uncertainty in the source information, as well as for other, more predictable variations in the database. When using truncation, the searcher must take care to avoid unwanted hits, such as "readjustment" from a search for a truncated term like "read:".

In Web-based search engines, stemming or truncation is often applied without any express action on the part of the searcher. Each term input is matched to a set of terms that have the same stem. These multiple variants on the stem are then searched in the database or file.

Stemming and truncation are some of the ways to accomplish "fuzzy matches"; that is, to count as a match those terms that are close to the ones input. "Close" can be defined in several ways. With stemming and truncation, the definition is tied to matching the first several characters of the term. With other forms, the terms can be determined to be matching based on other factors.

The elements described above can be considered the essential retrieval aspects of search systems. Characters are input by the searcher and matched to characters contained within the database. A searcher, no matter how skilled, cannot retrieve citations that are not in the database. Items that meet the searcher's criteria are put into sets for possible further manipulation. Using these elements, the searcher does not learn anything about the content of the database except the number of items that match the criteria. The search works only as well as the searcher is correct in making assumptions about spelling, structure, and formatting of terms within the database, as well as about the content of the database. Most search systems also provide ways for the searcher to learn more about all these aspects of the database. Search systems provide a browseable display of terms that have a relationship with the term of interest.

Displaying the Index

An additional feature of some of the search engines used with electronic reference sources is the ability to display a range of terms in a context. This is a function of the computer's ability to build and display multiple indexes to a single database. A primary index, called the *inverted index* or inverted file, is built on an alphabetical basis, in which each retrievable word in the database is listed in a single sequence. This inverted index is part of the reason that a computer is able to manipulate the file at incredible speeds. It goes directly to the term requested, which is linked to the records containing that term. Without the inverted index, the computer would have to scan the entire database looking for the requested sequence of characters. The main inverted file is called the *basic index.* In an operation that may be called "browse" or "expand" or "neighbor," the computer displays the requested section of the basic index, as shown in Figure 5.4. This allows one to see a term while it is surrounded by the terms immediately preceding and succeeding it alphabetically. Often, there is an identification of the number of records in the database that contain that term. This feature allows one to identify the most productive terms to retrieve a concept. It brings to the eye some of the perhaps unanticipated terms that are in close proximity and allows one to preview the effects of truncation.

A variation of the basic index occurs in those databases that have a controlled indexing vocabulary. In these databases, the producers create and maintain a list of subject headings, called *descriptors,* which must be used by the indexers to identify the subject of the item. Frequently, these descriptors are linked with other related subject headings through the use of concepts such as "related term," "broader term," and "narrower term" (see also Chapter 4). When such relationships exist among the descriptors, the result is called a *thesaurus.* In some databases, an index of the descriptors is created. In others, the thesaurus itself is an index, with the related terms identified and directly retrievable. Figure 5.5, page 106, is an example of an online thesaurus display. The display identifies the subject heading and the synonyms it replaces, and it allows the searcher to manipulate each term further to explore related terms.

Figure 5.4 Basic index display from *Article1st* on FirstSearch. Note that: (a) OCLC owns the copyright rights in the reproduced Screen Shot; (b) the Screen Shot is used with OCLC's permission; and (c) FirstSearch and ArticleFirst are registered trademarks of OCLC Online Computer Library Center, Incorporated.

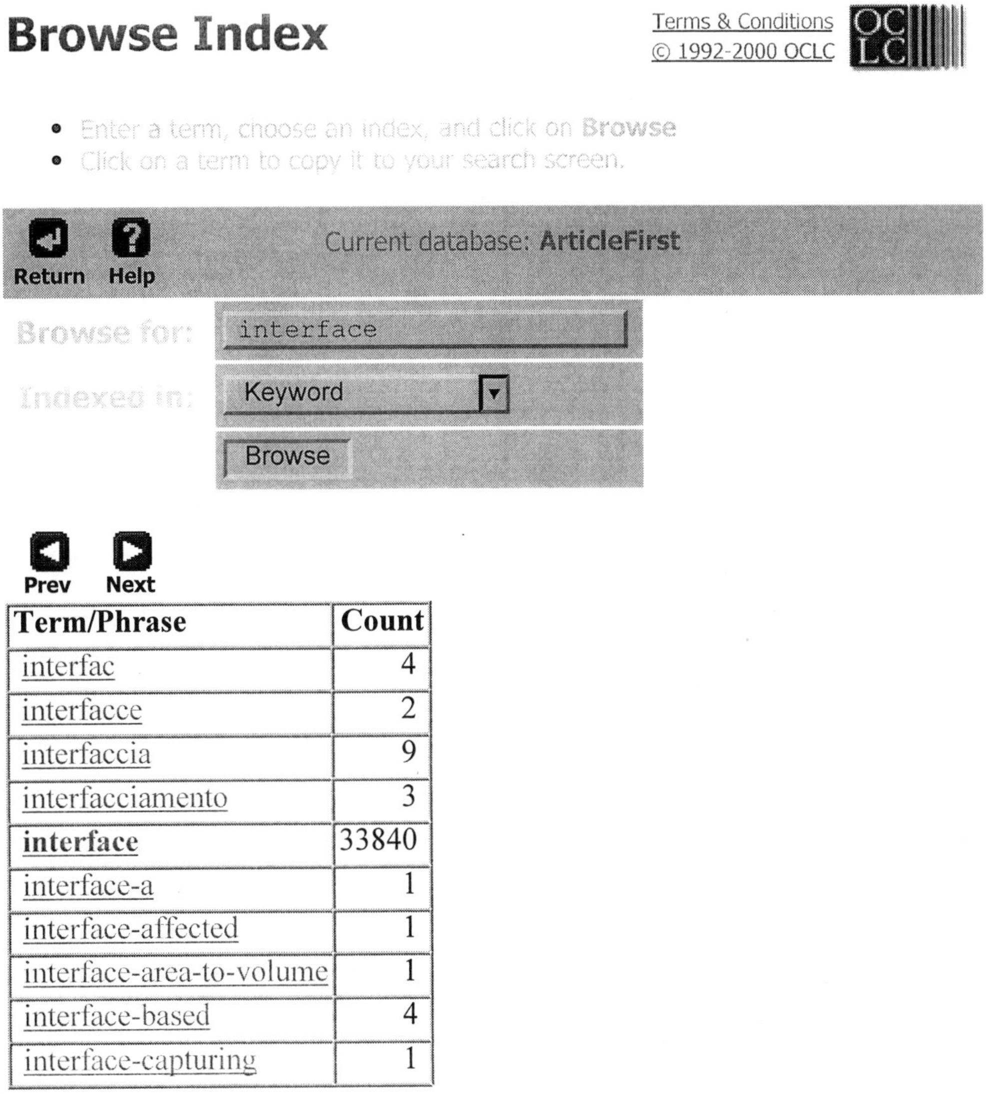

Browse Index

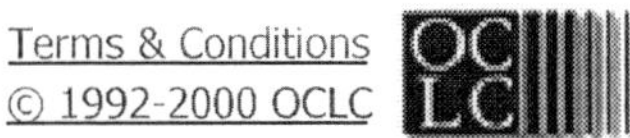

- Enter a term, choose an index, and click on **Browse**
- Click on a term to copy it to your search screen.

Current database: **ArticleFirst**

Browse for: interface

Indexed in: Keyword

Browse

Prev Next

Term/Phrase	Count
interfac	4
interfacce	2
interfaccia	9
interfacciamento	3
interface	33840
interface-a	1
interface-affected	1
interface-area-to-volume	1
interface-based	4
interface-capturing	1

Figure 5.5 Online thesaurus display from *PsycINFO* on Ovid. The number of records associated with each term is displayed in parentheses. Used with permission of Ovid Technologies, Inc. This material is reprinted with permission of the American Psychological Association, publisher of the *Thesaurus of Psychological Index Terms*, 8th Ed., © 1997, all rights reserved.

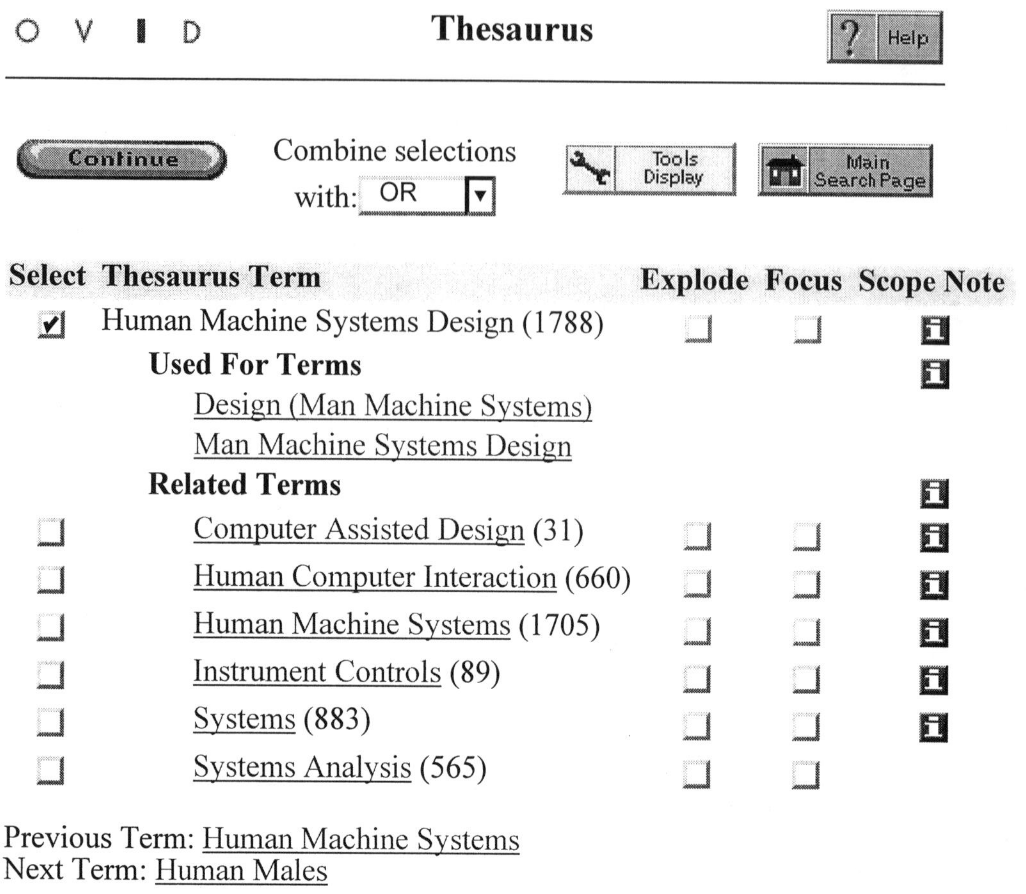

O V I D **Thesaurus** ? Help

Continue Combine selections with: OR ▾ Tools Display Main Search Page

Select	Thesaurus Term	Explode	Focus	Scope Note
☑	Human Machine Systems Design (1788)	☐	☐	i
	Used For Terms			i
	Design (Man Machine Systems)			
	Man Machine Systems Design			
	Related Terms			i
☐	Computer Assisted Design (31)	☐	☐	i
☐	Human Computer Interaction (660)	☐	☐	i
☐	Human Machine Systems (1705)	☐	☐	i
☐	Instrument Controls (89)	☐	☐	i
☐	Systems (883)	☐	☐	i
☐	Systems Analysis (565)	☐	☐	

Previous Term: Human Machine Systems
Next Term: Human Males

A database might also have terms in it that have more meaning if they are used to build yet another kind of index, one in which the function of the term is made explicit. For example, an author's name has more meaning and is more easily manipulated if it can be seen in the context of other authors' names. This can be seen most readily when imagining how to search for authors whose names are also nouns, for example, Hill, Stone, and Case. These names are much more useful when pulled into a separate formatted index with the standard rules for name display. One can pick out variations of a single author's name if this list is organized on a surname-first basis, as shown in Figure 5.6. Similarly, the name of a company might be more useful if it appears in a context of other company names or variants.

In addition, there can be other bases for indexes in a single database. In databases that contain numbers, some indexes may show these numbers in an ordinal list. For example, in business directories containing sales data, there may be an index that shows sales in order from largest to smallest, or there may be scales of magnitude for sales figures, showing the ranges. In other directories, zip codes or population figures may be more salient and could form their own indexes within a database.

Figure 5.6 Surname display from *ERIC* on Ovid. Used with permission of Ovid Technologies, Inc.

Select	Authors	# of Citations
☐	bungay h r.au.	1
☐	bungay henry.au.	1
☐	bunge annette l.au.	1
☑	bunge charles.au.	1
☐	bunge charles a.au.	17
☐	bunge mario.au.	2
☐	bungum timothy.au.	1
☐	bungum timothy j.au.	1
☐	bunish norbert t.au.	3
☐	bunke jennifer.au.	1
☐	bunker barbara b.au.	2
☐	bunker c a.au.	1
☐	bunker ellen l.au.	2

Positional Searching

An additional aspect of the basic index allows for great precision in identifying material. Each term in the basic index has markers that show its position in each of the records in which it appears. Most computer retrieval systems allow a searcher to specify a particular positional relationship between two terms, called *proximity.* A system will have a set of specialized proximity operators that name the positional relationship needed. For example, to specify that two terms must be right next to each other, one could use an "adjacency" operator. One could also specify that the terms be within a determined number of words, or in the same sentence, field, or paragraph. Proximity operators are a refinement on the Boolean AND operator. In this way, a searcher can specify that the system retrieve only those items that contain a phrase, such as "quality circles," even if that phrase is not a descriptor in the database.

Proximity operators use coded data about the word position of each searchable term in a database to determine retrieval. As each term from each document in the database is added to the basic index, it is coded with details on its position within the document. This would include its location in a document, field, paragraph, and sentence. An example of this type of coding is shown in Figure 5.7, page 108. This system of proximity coded searching is very fast,

Figure 5.7 Positional coding for proximity retrieval.

"Quality (RN1,P1,S1,W1) circles (RN1,P1,S1,W2) in (RN1,P1,S1,W3) database (RN1,P1,S1,W4) management (RN1,P1,S1,W5) and (RN1,P1,S1,W6) design (RN1,P1,S1,W7)."

The (RN1,P2,S1,W1) study (RN1,P2,S1,W2)....

In this hypothetical example, the coded numbers in the parentheses refer to the record number, the paragraph, the sentence, and the word within the sentence. To select the term *quality* in the same sentence as *design*, the search system will look at the record number for each term. If the record number matches, it will compare paragraph numbers for each term with the same record number. If both paragraph numbers match, it will look for matching sentence numbers. If all three numbers for both terms match, the document will be retrieved by the search system. For the system to select the phrase "quality circles," the numbers for record, paragraph, and sentence must match and the word numbers must differ by one. In most systems that offer proximity searching, the searcher can specify word order as well as degrees of closeness. This provides a great deal of precision in retrieval. It is critical to remember that each search system will have its own way to specify proximity. For many search systems, there is a special operator used to indicate proximity, such as *adj* or *near.* Other systems have two operators: One is used if word order is important and the other if word order does not matter. Typically, one is able to specify the number of words that can separate the terms. The searcher can specify that the first term has to be within one, two, three, or any other number of words of the second term. In such a system, the search statement could look like this: S *guide n/3 internet.* This would retrieve documents containing phrases like "a new guide to the Internet," "world wide Internet guide," and so on, because the two terms are within three words of one another.

In any search system, there are elements that are included in the record for display purposes but are not searchable. In an online catalog system, for example, the bibliographic record is likely to show the size and number of pages in a monograph. However, there are no online catalog systems that will allow one to search and retrieve items based on either the size of the pages or their numbers.

The power of the computer to create, manipulate, display, and retrieve these multiple indexes to a single file is very important to users. When this is combined with the power of Boolean logic, it multiplies the possibilities for creatively manipulating databases to retrieve the needed information. Multiple access points and the ability to combine them also allow retrieval of materials for which the information is incomplete. If one knows the author's surname, a word from the title, and a decade in which the book was published, combining these elements with a Boolean AND is very likely to produce a set that contains the needed item and very few others.

Beyond Boolean

Although Boolean logic is quite effective in many databases, it may be less effective in databases made up of full-text documents. These full-text databases tend to be quite unstructured, with natural language dominating whatever structured indexing language is associated with the text. In the course of a ten-page article, for example, many terms occur at least once and could therefore be retrieved in a simple Boolean search. Phrase searching, although more precise, will miss many documents because of the natural variations in expression in full-text materials. An alternative search design, which is more effective in these full-text databases, looks beyond mere occurrence and tries to measure the relative importance of the terms within a document, through *weighting*. In weighting, the frequency with which a term appears in the database and in a document forms a ratio that helps determine how important that term is in the search and how much weight to give its appearances. A term that occurs frequently in one document while occurring relatively infrequently in the database as a whole will be more heavily weighted than one that occurs with comparable frequency in both. In *relevancy rankings,* the higher the proportion of search terms in a document, the higher the ranking in predicted relevancy. This is based on the logical assumption that if one compares two documents of the same size, the document with a high number of occurrences of a term is likely to be more "about" that term than the one with a low number of occurrences of that same term. With these search parameters, documents will be retrieved and displayed based on the relative weights of the search terms.

In Figure 5.8, the sample sentence shows an example of a highly skewed document. The relevancy ranking for this document for the term "bird" is very high and for the term "seed" quite low.

Figure 5.8 A sample document that would rank high on a search for "bird".

"The word *bird* is used in a great many phrases in English, for example, bird bath, bird seed, bird feeder, bird song, song birds, bird brain, eat like a bird, bird's eye, birds of a feather, a little bird told me, bird of paradise, and bird nest."

Search Strategy

Understanding the search concepts discussed in this chapter is important in achieving effective and efficient searches. It is equally important to understand that these searching functions are expressed in different ways and combinations in each search system. Each system has an underlying set of operating assumptions that will govern the search and display process. These assumptions are called *defaults*. For example, a search system may have the Boolean AND as its default operator. In any search with two terms, it will search each term separately and combine the sets with the Boolean AND. Another search system will have a proximity operator as its default and look for each set of two terms as a phrase. Each of these default operators will produce substantially different results for the same two search terms. Similarly, each search system will have a default display option. In nearly every system, a searcher is able to override the default option on a search-by-search basis. Sometimes it is a matter of finding a search menu and changing the operator. In other cases, it is necessary to explicitly type in the search operator. In any case, it is essential to discover what the search system defaults are.

The steps that a searcher takes to find a set of materials that meet an information need make up the *search strategy*. The search strategy operates within the framework of the search system's mechanisms and the database structure and content. The goal of the search strategy to retrieve "all and only" the ideal set of relevant materials remains largely unattainable. Most of the decisions a searcher makes in the search strategy are made to achieve the appropriate balance between the two aims of information retrieval: precision and recall. *Precision* refers to getting only relevant material. *Recall* refers to getting all the relevant material. In a world in which language was unambiguous and where indexing was perfect, precision and recall would be the same. For the rest of us, because language is ambiguous and indexing imperfect, precision and recall are largely incompatible goals. For example, the word "program" is used to represent at least three rather different concepts. This affects precision, because a search on the term "program" for one of these concepts will retrieve unrelated material that refers to either of the other two meanings of the term, and thus reduces precision. On the other hand, because of synonyms and changes in terminology over time, there are often a multitude of terms to describe a single concept. Searching for every possible term to achieve perfect recall is a demanding task. As a result, search strategies are a compromise between precision and recall.

Information professionals learn these concepts as well as search-building techniques as part of their professional training and experience. A reference librarian develops the equivalent of a pre-flight checklist for databases, with features, structures, and logical elements forming a matrix to be checked against the new or revised database, interface, or delivery system. The experienced reference librarian approaches a new electronic resource with this set of expected functions and capabilities and investigates the ways in which they are supported, displayed, or invoked. An examination of the opening screen reveals some of the possibilities. A sample search or two will identify further answers. For example, a reference librarian might try to search for a compound surname, a surname with a prefix, or a hyphenated surname. The search system will respond with the desired item or will reveal how it deals with improperly formatted names. If the search screen is uninformative about the default search operators, a multi-word search with and without the Boolean operator explicitly typed in will be revealing. Help commands can be invoked to see if they illuminate effective search strategies. This is standard exploratory behavior for reference librarians and information specialists because they have these elements in their mental framework (see Box 5.4).

Box 5.4 Documenting Search Features

A new electronic resource has been acquired by the reference library. You have been asked to write preliminary documentation on its search interface for the other reference librarians to use. You might start with how to search simple and compound names. How to search for exact phrases in titles might be another element. Make a list of the other search functions and features that you would test in the development of this documentation.

ELECTRONIC RESOURCES AND THE END-USER

A walk around a typical reference room will reveal a number of computers with users working at them. This is not a big change. For more than two decades, library users have been using computer terminals to search the library's online catalog for materials of interest. What has changed is the size and shape of the information space available through the computer screen.

Electronic resources that were once the province of bibliographers and reference librarians are now essential parts of the end-user repertoire. One example of this transformation is the *bibliographic utility*. Its very name suggests heavy-duty work in the library. Utilities provide us with the essential resources we need: electricity, water, and heat. Bibliographic utilities at their center provide essential control over the library's collection through their large databases of shared cataloging. The records in the database are created by the combined efforts of large libraries, such as the Library of Congress, other national libraries, and contributing member libraries in many countries. The major bibliographic utilities in the United States are RLIN (from RLG) and WorldCat (from OCLC), which are discussed further in Chapter 20.

Bibliographic utilities have at the heart of their databases a set of bibliographic records in a specific machine-readable form, called MARC. MARC stands for *MA*chine *R*eadable

Cataloging, and it is both a standard format and a set of records conforming to that standard. In 1968, the Library of Congress developed the first MARC format for monographs in English. MARC standards for other languages and other materials followed. The members of the bibliographic utilities contribute their acquisition and cataloging records in MARC format to the databases. In this instance, libraries are database producers as well as database users. WorldCat had over 42 million unique records by July 2000.

WorldCat and RLIN began with cataloging and acquisitions librarians and staff as their primary creators and users. Although reference librarians were not the central focus of these bibliographic utilities, they soon discovered how useful the utilities were to find bibliographic records for materials that may have been cataloged anywhere in the country. These bibliographic utilities have broadened their role from cataloging through reference and on out to the public. Each service now provides an end-user version of the online union catalog. Only a few years ago, access to an online union catalog was as far from the experience of the typical library user as it could be; now it is a click away from anywhere.

Even further from the realm of everyday experience for most end-users was the exploration of online catalogs, national bibliographies, or union catalogs of other countries. Now, there are hundreds of individual library online catalogs from around the world. Ongoing cooperative efforts are producing national and international union catalogs accessible from computers anywhere in the world.

This transformation of bibliographic utilities and international union catalogs into end-user databases is emblematic of the changes in reference service. Where once a reference librarian had to walk back to the cataloging or interlibrary loan area to consult the database, now grade school students can dial up WorldCat from their home computers and discover new books by their favorite authors. Researchers can link to WorldCat and solve many bibliographic puzzles on their own, without consulting reference librarians. This direct access empowers users and gives them control over meeting their own information needs.

Direct access also escalates the level of questions brought to the reference desk. Now users are likely to say, "Can you help me find this? I couldn't find it in WorldCat." The bibliographic detective skill required to solve these problems is of a higher level. Instead of coming to the desk with a simple verification question about an English-language monograph, the researcher comes with a partial citation to a Hungarian-language conference proceeding. The ironic effect of having millions of bibliographic records available for all the library's users is to create more difficult challenges for reference librarians. Expectations about what is possible with electronic resources are very high. In addition, each reference librarian needs to develop a set of tactful explanations for how he or she was able to find something in WorldCat that the user had missed.

Structures Invisible to the Casual Observer

The expansion of the user base of electronic resources has ramifications for how search systems look and function. Many of the changes are positive ones, with some of the arcane requirements of command mode searching giving way to a simpler point-and-click system over the World Wide Web or on a CD-ROM workstation. For the most part, the search engine and its interface have taken on more of the work in the search process. Instead of typing in the code for the different fields, the searcher can click a button for that field. The interface interprets the different clicks and formats the search statement into the necessary codes that the search engine can understand. However, as the search engine migrates from command mode to a CD-ROM or the World Wide Web version, the search capabilities are often reduced. There is an assumption on the part of database producers and vendors that end-users either do not know or do not care about the kinds of distinctions that the highly structured database contains. Formerly distinct fields like descriptor, identifier, and titles are all merged into a single category and labeled as keyword searches. Although this tendency may increase the chances for retrieval of material from the database, it severely restricts the possibilities of refining a search. On the one hand, retrieving something rather than nothing is probably useful for the end-user. On the other hand, retrieving a great many items of only middling relevance can be equally frustrating.

Many of the codes and labels for internal structures of databases have become invisible. It is assumed that the user will recognize that this part is an author because it is a person's name, while that part is the author's affiliation because it is the name of an organization. Using explicit labels or even formatting the display to indicate different fields or structural elements is not very common in these database designs. The fact that the internal structure is invisible rather than nonexistent is more important than it might seem at first glance. In some cases, a trivial error in formatting a name can result in substantial differences in retrieval. These invisible structural elements tend to be focused on spaces and punctuation. For example, keeping or omitting a comma in a name search can be significant. The choice of hyphenating a compound word or separating the elements with a space can also yield substantial differences. If the user is fortunate, the search system will ignore the variation and retrieve the appropriate material. A less-sophisticated search system may recognize the error and suggest alternative input choices. An alternative response from the search engine would be to display the list of names that are closest to the one input, as interpreted and understood by the search engine. If the names look a bit odd—for example, if they are all hyphenated or are at the end of the alphabet—the alert user may be able to use the clues to devise a different strategy to produce a list of names that look more like the one desired. Not all search engines generate the kind of helpful feedback to assist the user in improving a search strategy. In the least-sophisticated systems, one receives no matches or an artificially low result without realizing that an error has occurred. Figure 5.9 illustrates the outcome of an author search on either "chomsky, noam" or "noam chomsky" in Biography and Genealogy Master Index on GaleNet. The search system yields several variant forms of the name rather than matching only on the terms entered, a very helpful feature for the user seeking all entries for this person in the database.

Figure 5.9 Name search on Biography and Genealogy Master Index. © Sociological Abstracts, LLC. Made available under an agreement with Cambridge Scientific Abstracts. Reprinted by permission.

BIOGRAPHY AND GENEALOGY MASTER INDEX   SEARCH | ABOUT | HELP

[Search] [About] [Help]

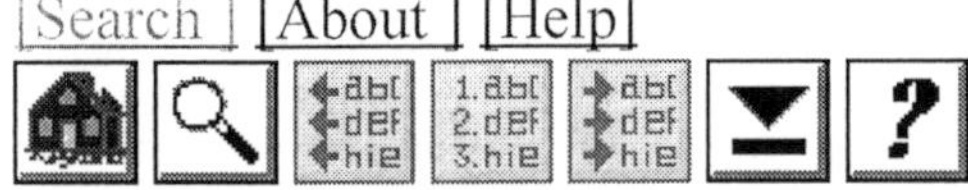

Documents: **1 - 7 of 7**

Ref	Cites	Name
1	42	Chomsky, Avram Noam (1928-)
2	13	Chomsky, Noam
3	73	Chomsky, Noam (1928-)
4	1	Chomsky, Noam (1929-)
5	3	Chomsky, Noam A (1928-)
6	14	Chomsky, (Avram) Noam (1928-)
7	1	Chomsky, (Avril) Noam (1928-)

Part of the reason that users may misinterpret the results of a search lies within the user. There is a significant amount of faith that the computer is providing help to the user; that is, that the computer "understands" what the user has asked for and has provided "the answer." When a user receives a set with one item in it due to the inadvertent matching of misspellings or receives a set of seven items out of a possible fifty that would match the user's needs, most of the time the user believes that these are the correct results and goes away. Few users come to the electronic resource with a well-developed sense of likely results, nor do they come with an effective yardstick with which to measure their success. Any results are the right results. That it was ever thus is a small comfort to reference librarians and interface designers alike.

Another potential area of miscommunication between the search system and the user is how the system handles words or phrases the user inputs. In some systems, there is automatic truncation of search terms or phrases. In others, the terms are searched exactly as input unless there is an explicit use of the system's truncation symbol. In some systems, the words are searched as a phrase, while in others there is an implicit Boolean AND between the terms. In still other systems, the terms are searched with relevancy ranking and weighting. Not all search systems make their searching choices apparent. The challenge for the user is to identify the search mechanism at work and to devise search strategies that are effective on this system. A problem for even the very alert user moving between two or more search systems is that these important search system features may be confounded or confused.

The internal organization of an electronic resource may not be evident to the user, nor might the user be aware that an electronic resource has internal organization. This is in contrast to a print reference source, which has to make its organization and arrangement clear to be used at all. A print source provides one or more structures to make the contents accessible. If it is organized along alphabetical lines, perhaps there will be an index providing additional terms to supplement the cross-references provided within the tool. One can think of an encyclopedia providing alphabetical entries supported by cross-references and a subject index. If a print tool is organized in a subject hierarchy, a table of contents will be provided outlining the arrangement. The *Handbook of Latin American Studies* is an example of this type. An alphabetical index is likely to be included in such a hierarchical tool. These alternative access structures can be a big help if the information one has about a question does not match the organizational pattern. In Bartlett's *Familiar Quotations*, for example, the body is arranged broadly by date, and within a date range alphabetically by the surname. However, because not everyone can correctly place a name in the appropriate era, an index by name is provided. As required by the nature of the tool, it also provides an extensive index by keyword in the quotation. In a reference tool on the World Wide Web, the context and the organization of the information are likely to be invisible. A piece of information will be brought to the screen in response to the search query. All that can be determined is whether the piece on the screen has the answer to the query. Internal structure can sometimes be discerned from the format of the query screen or the style of the displayed results. In any case, such structures may be irrelevant to the interaction because the searcher may not be able to use that knowledge as an alternative approach to the resource. Internal navigation within the tool is most likely to be limited to the query screen, rather than another access mechanism or browseable display.

The User and the Interface

Electronic resources differ from print materials in the way they are delivered to the user, whether the user is in the library, at home, in the office, or at an Internet café halfway around the world. Electronic resources exist as multiple potential realities rather than a single fixed reality. Just as water has no fixed shape or size, electronic resources have similar fluid properties. They arrive through an electronic "pipe" with a computer for a "faucet." The particular reality that exists for any user will differ in appearance and capabilities depending on the size of the pipe and the type of faucet being used to access the resource. The version one finds on the Web may differ in substantive as well as graphical ways from the version reached through TELNET (see Chapter 6). There may be an all-text option, or a low-graphics version of a resource. The fluid nature of the resource is a challenge for reference librarians as they seek to describe a resource helpfully and unambiguously for its users.

In addition, the resource itself is subject to change without notice. The interface can change markedly from one version to the next. New screens, new options, a new "look and feel" can leave a user unsure of how to proceed with a formerly familiar resource. A database may be made available through another provider. An abstracting and indexing resource can add links to full-text sites. A resource can do all these things simultaneously and throw in a name change at the same time. Again, the reference librarian seeking to describe an electronic resource is at a significant disadvantage in this task. Indeed, a description of a single database can begin to resemble a "rap sheet" for a career criminal, with an extensive list of "also known as" to describe the many possible names under which a user may recognize a particular resource. When corporate mergers or realignments are added to the mix, the task becomes truly daunting. Name changes are relatively uncommon in the world of print reference resources. When they occur, catalogers deal with them with a simple addition to the cataloging record. Users looking for the item under old or new names are successful. Likewise, the guides to reference resources, like Balay's *Guide to Reference Books* or *Walford's Guide to Reference Material*, provide access under previous names. With the slippery nature of the electronic resource, it is hard to pin down just what is to be named or described and how one might do this. To put it another way, one may not know a reference book by its cover, but at least it has one. What is the equivalent of an electronic resource's cover? How can the library make a label for a resource that is accurate, up-to-date, and durable in the face of all these changes?

When using electronic resources made available by the library, end-users will very likely have to switch from one interface to another. Figure 5.10 is an example of how the same database, *ERIC*, looks on the first screen of three different systems: Ovid, OCLC FirstSearch, and Cambridge Scientific Abstracts (CSA).

Both Cambridge Scientific Abstracts and OCLC FirstSearch offer an Advanced Search screen in addition to the basic search screen shown. So, in this case, for a single database, there are five different search screens offering different search capabilities and strategies, not to mention different citation handling and printing options. Most of the time, of course, each database will be available on a single system. However, because many libraries subscribe to several systems, the complexity of searching choices and strategies for the user trying to find information through multiple interfaces remains.

All the end-user systems, whether on CD-ROMs or over the Web, are intended to be user-friendly, but some are more successful in their design than others. Many systems offer two or more levels of searching, designed for both novice searchers and users with more searching experience. For the novice, there might be a series of menus with simple questions to answer that lead the user to select from a single displayed array of index terms. For the more experienced searcher, there might be a command-driven option or more expansive menu choices that provide more searching power, greater efficiency in handling citations, or just faster searching. F. W. Lancaster and colleagues compared end-user searches with mediated searches and confirmed other studies that found that end-users are very satisfied with their own CD-ROM searches, even when the actual quality is quite low.[1] Developing point-of-use instruction that can assist users in developing a better search strategy or expanding the search vocabulary is time-consuming and very hard to do well (see Box 5.5, page 116). It can be even harder to get the user to respond to these guides. In those systems that have different search levels, like Cambridge Scientific Abstracts and OCLC FirstSearch, the levels frequently have little in common, so the searcher moving from the basic to the advanced is faced with learning new terminology and new techniques. Search systems in which there is a "skills ladder" in which to build on skills and concepts from one level to the next are rare. As a result, it is difficult for the user to develop the skills needed to use the higher levels successfully. This results in the user either remaining at an unsophisticated level or needing individualized training and instruction in the higher-level search techniques.

Figure 5.10

One database and multiple interfaces—*ERIC* on CSA, Ovid, FirstSearch.
Used with permission of Ovid Technologies, Inc. This information is reprinted with the permission of CSA, 7200 Wisconsin Ave, Bethesda, MD 20814. www.csa.com. Note that: (a) OCLC owns the copyright rights in the reproduced Screen Shot; (b) the Screen Shot is used with OCLC's permission; and (c) FirstSearch and ArticleFirst are registered trademarks of OCLC Online Computer Library Center, Incorporated

CSA

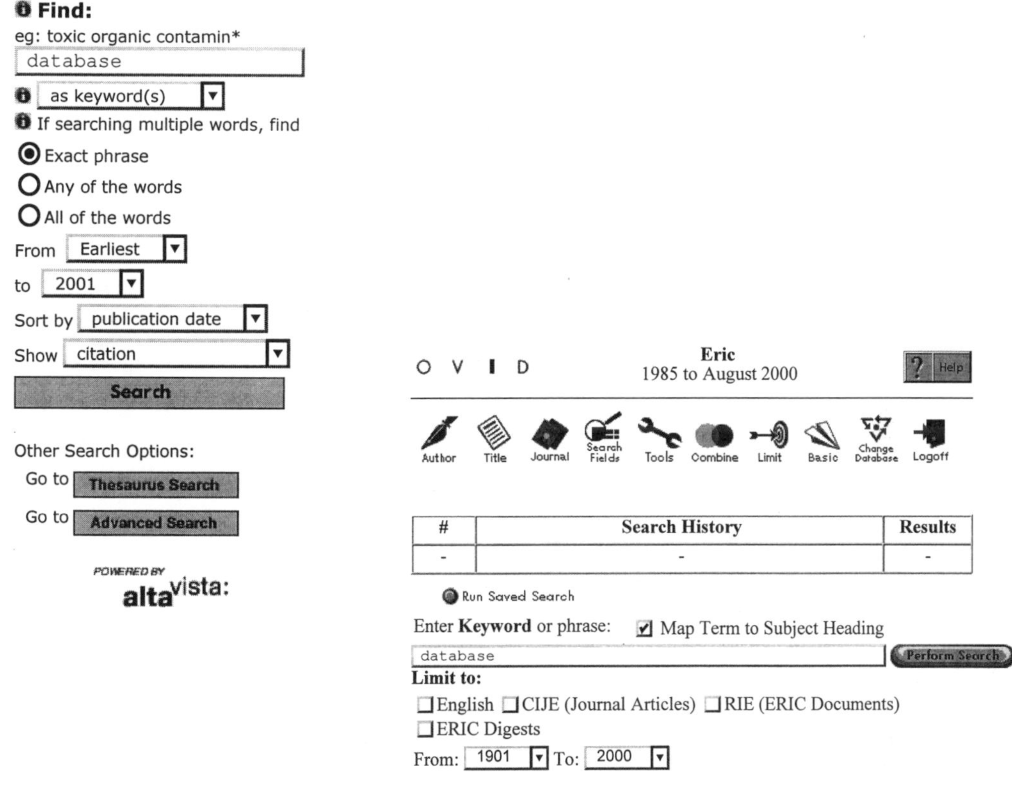

FirstSearch

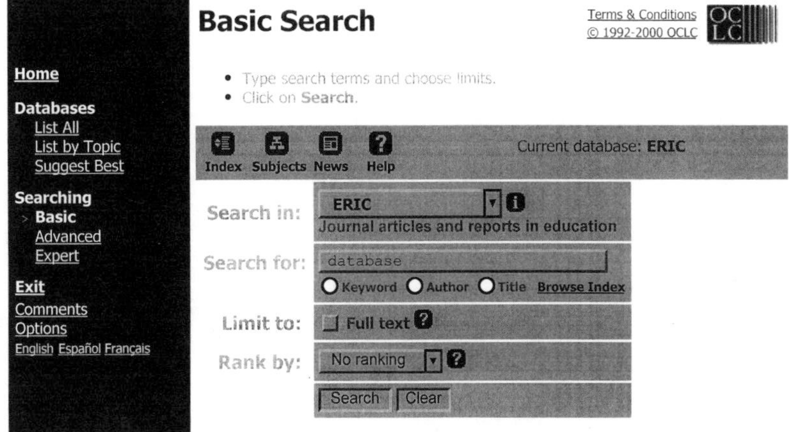

Box 5.5 Writing a Search Guide

A popular electronic resource has just come out in a new release. The new version has two levels of searching instead of the single basic search it formerly had. You are going to be writing a new user guide for the resource. Knowing that most users will use a guide only if it is very short, you need to make some early choices. Will you write a guide for the basic level and add a note that users should ask at the reference desk if they need help with the advanced search or will you write a guide that will assist users in determining which kind of search they will need to use, with some examples of correct searches? Will your decisions be the same if you intend to mount the guide on the Web as well as have a print version available?

As the discussion of search capabilities indicated, the concepts that enable efficient and effective searching are not necessarily known, recognized, or understood by the end-user. If a search window offers Boolean searching, how likely is it that the user will know whether this function is needed for an effective search? Nor does the average user have the kind of sample searches at the ready that would reveal the search mechanisms at work in the database. It is hard to imagine a user who has the "Top Ten List of Things to Learn About Database Searching" in a shirt pocket, briefcase, or backpack. It is almost equally hard to imagine that the end-user understands the need for such a list.

Not all electronic information resources make it clear to the casual user (or the reference librarian) what the database contains, in terms of degree of coverage of the listed journals, the dates of coverage, and the like. Users may start with very optimistic expectations of the online coverage based on the enthusiastic descriptions of the possibilities of electronic resources as portrayed by television and its commercials. Very often different versions of the same database vary significantly from one another and from the print version as well. One of the ways in which they vary is in frequency of updates. The Web-based version of the database may be updated frequently, while the CD-ROM version is typically updated on a monthly or quarterly basis.

INTEGRATING END-USER RESOURCES INTO USER-CENTERED REFERENCE SERVICES

Paying for access to electronic resources is just one step in developing effective reference service. Systems and services must be created and implemented that allow the user to identify the resources available, select the appropriate resources, access them, search them to discover the needed information, handle the output, and ultimately use the information discovered. These systems and services need to be site-independent; that is to say, the remote user and the user in the library should be able to follow the same path with the same ease and the same chance of success.

Reference Service Environment

For the purposes of this discussion, the reference service environment consists of the physical surroundings of the reference service point, the reference presence in the library Web space, the equipment used in the provision of the service, the reference staff, the reference collection, and the reference service policies. This reference matrix is a dynamic, interlinked one, with changes in any area affecting and shaping each of the others. At the very center of this reference service matrix is the user. Each element of the environment must be designed with the user's needs in mind. It is essential that the different user groups that make up a reference library's community be considered in this design.

One user group to be considered in the design is reference librarians themselves. They are the most intensive users of the resources. It would be much easier to design reference environments if reference librarians were the only user community. If this were the case, when physical reference environments were designed in libraries, the tools could be put wherever the reference librarians needed them. They could be moved as often as needed. If a "professionals only" information space were designed for the Web, the same principles would apply. Librarians know their own strengths and weaknesses and can evaluate the success of the design in real time. If something did not work the way it was intended, this would make itself evident to the developer—often the same person as the user—right away. Modifications could be undertaken on the fly to remedy the situation. Communicating to those affected by the change would be straightforward—an e-mail to one's colleagues or a note left at the reference desk would suffice.

When the reference environment is opened to the many user communities served, this has consequences for the ability to design the information space. In the physical reference room, the needs of the independent user of the reference tools must be balanced against the needs of the reference staff. It might be very convenient for reference librarians to have all the almanacs at the reference desk, but it would not be a successful location for the users. Similarly, as the many elements of the physical reference collection migrate to the information space on the Web, reference librarians seek to arrange the electronic resources for ready access by virtual users. To direct those users who may not know the formal names of different kinds of reference tools, the reference space may use the language of questions to identify resources by function. For example, the reference space could pose these choices: "Looking for a quick fact or definition? Click here for almanacs and dictionaries." "Trying to find a longer explanation for a concept? Click here for general and specialized encyclopedias." In this way, those users who know the type of tool they need can recognize it, while those who are less familiar can try to select the appropriate resource by the kind of question they have in mind. In any design, it is essential to provide a link to real help, such as a telephone number for the reference desk, with hours of service, in addition to a link for "ask a reference question" e-mail service.

With the translation of reference resources to the World Wide Web, another aspect of the reference environment changes. As opposed to traditional print reference tools, which are located within a physical environment and provide a context for the information they contain, Web-based tools exist without a frame of reference. Typically, a print source has a call number that simultaneously identifies its subject matter and locates it next to other reference tools on the same subject. Print tools are often clustered by function within the reference room, with atlases collected together and perhaps indexes arranged on tables. This physical co-location can provide some benefits through serendipity, bringing to the user's attention an unknown or forgotten title. These features of location and context are largely or entirely absent from the Web. Most Web-based tools exist in complete isolation from one another. Perhaps titles that are produced by a single publisher or that are made available through an aggregator will be identified on a single selection screen. More often, the URL is a context-less anchor to a single tool. Some reference tools may lend themselves to a post hoc consumer clustering through bookmarks and the like, but these are frail structures in contrast to the rugged and durable outlines of the LC or Dewey classification schemes. In addition, these post hoc groupings require constant updating.

Managing Access

Electronic resources can come to a library and its users through many different consortial arrangements. A library can be a member of a state-wide consortium, a regional consortium, a consortium based on type of library, or other bases. Each of these consortia may provide electronic resources to its member libraries for use by the libraries' user communities. These arrangements greatly expand the pool of resources available to the members of the consortium. Typically, there are substantial discounts for the resources acquired by consortia.

This results in more effective expenditures of scarce resource dollars. The benefits of these arrangements are clear, but there are some complications that arise as well. The licensing arrangements for each consortium can divide a reference library's users into groups with differing access rights and different service options. With overlapping domains of "citizenship" in different cooperative agreements, different users may find that some resources are available only under certain conditions, for example when they are in the library, while other resources are not available at all.

Managing access for these multiple user communities is a challenge. The library seeks to make as many resources available to as many of its users as possible while not violating the licensing terms. A library can develop alternative strategies to deal with these multiple and overlapping citizenship issues. Many libraries define their licensed primary user community to include all those who use the resources in-person at the library. These users may be thought of as wearing a temporary identification badge. For the length of their visit, they are part of the organization.

The extension of temporary citizenship works for those who use licensed resources in-person. For remote users, the library must be able to ascertain their eligibility to use the resource. One way to do this is through Internet addresses associated with the library. The library identifies the set of Internet addresses, called IP ranges, that belong to its primary user group. Anyone using a computer with an IP address in the correct range is allowed access to the resource. Others will be turned away. This is most effective for a campus or a company with a unique set of IP domains. It can also be used for some broad-based electronic resources. For example, Indiana has made some electronic resources available to everyone in the state through its INSPIRE program. All the public IP ranges that are in Indiana are allowed access to these resources.

The other way to determine membership in a group is through authentication. *Authentication* is a two-step process for assuring that the person is truly the person and is on the list of eligible users, typically through matching a name and password with an entry in the user database. For example, in the INSPIRE program, if Indiana residents want to use the service through a national Internet service provider, they need to register and get added to the INSPIRE user database. When they logon, their computer is checked against the database before being allowed to use the service. It is a challenge to make the authentication process reliable, efficient, and unobtrusive. It is nearly impossible to make the properly authenticated session also anonymous. Many of the library's users are aware that the library is committed to keeping the activities of its users confidential, but they are also aware that there is a difference between confidential and anonymous. Because of authentication, there is a chance that these sessions will not remain confidential. Users who wish to maintain anonymity may have to do their research in the library on computers that have direct access to the needed resources.

EXPANDING RESOURCES

The changes in technology can be summed up in one word: more. More speed, more images, more formats, more channels, and more resources. The future is likely to be more of the same. Is the result just more reference service, or are there some fundamental differences in how these resources are developed and used?

In the beginning of the end-user revolution, there were relatively few resources available. Most of them were known to the user in their print format. The move to electronic form meant faster, easier, more flexible searching within familiar boundaries. The users had some idea about the kind of material that they would receive from their searches. One of the roles of the reference librarian was to guide the user from the print to the electronic version. User instruction was largely one-to-one and took place in the reference room or at the information desk.

By 2000, the tidal wave of electronic resources had washed away virtually all knowledge of the existence of print resources and swept all signposts from the emerging reference resource landscape. The end-user's information universe has expanded from a tidy solar system to an immense and expanding galaxy. Just as a galaxy is filled with neutron stars, supernovas, quasars, suns, and planets beyond counting, the end-user's information space has become much more complex. It begins with indexes and abstracts and includes full-text electronic journals, dictionaries, encyclopedias, directories, and datasets, to name just a few resources. This has transformed the role of reference librarians in helping users navigate this space.

As the number and type of electronic resources grows, the challenge becomes one of assisting users in identifying and selecting the appropriate resource for their needs. In person, the reference librarian can guide the end-user from source to source, pacing the information flow to suit the user's knowledge and experience. The reference librarian is also able to see if the user is working successfully alone or if some additional guidance is needed. When reference librarians think about developing and delivering the same guidance to those users who are far beyond the walls of the reference room, they have provided *gateways* or *portals.* These gateways on the World Wide Web can be thought of as maps to the library's information space and are designed to guide the user to the correct resources. They attempt to divide resources into familiar categories and keep similar kinds of resources together. In some ways, the gateways work to simulate the arrangement of a reference room on the screen. Creating a set of virtual index tables, encyclopedia cases, and dictionary stands on the library's gateway page may help the user identify where to begin.

Some gateways may be built as a series of branching menus with multiple layers of choices. Each choice brings a new set of choices to the screen until the user reaches the final layer. This strategy assists the user by breaking down an enormous amount of information into smaller, more manageable pieces. Instead of having to deal with 250 electronic resources of all types in one long list, one can choose among perhaps five categories. These could be arranged on a subject basis or on another functional basis. This approach has some distinct advantages over scrolling through screens of resources. It is important that the menus are very well designed, with clear, unambiguous, and comprehensive choices and very flexible detours back to previous levels for an alternate set of choices.

If gateways are based on a database of databases, they can provide a kind of flexibility and responsiveness that is unavailable in traditional guides to reference sources. A carefully designed database of databases can include inclusive and exhaustive lists of subjects and topics for each of the resources, based on the vocabulary of that discipline. The gateway can be built "on the fly" in response to a user's query. For example, a user may come to the gateway and be invited to type in some words from a topic of interest. The gateway software will search for resources that contain that topic and present to the user tools such as subject encyclopedias, abstracting and indexing sources, and even Web sites of possible interest. This approach, although an interesting and valuable alternative to a more static style of gateway, has a problem that may be termed the "Salvador Dali" problem. That is, a user may type in a term like "Salvador Dali" rather than "Art History" or "Modern Art" or "Twentieth Century Art" or other more generalized description of the subject. The converse problem, the "History" problem, occurs when a user types in a topic that is so broad it matches nearly every resource in the system. Devising appropriate guidance mechanisms for these searches will be a long-term challenge for reference librarians, as will be the development of the descriptors for each of the resources.

Of course, the users of the virtual reference room are similar to the users of the physical reference room. They may not know where to start or how to frame their question. They may not understand the relationship between and among different kinds of reference resources. So to supplement the electronic gateway to the virtual reference room, some libraries have created research guides on their Web pages to assist users. Some of these are virtual "pathfinders" with step-by-step guides to research in an area. The University of Iowa (http://explorer.lib.uiowa.edu/) and Cornell University (http://www.library.cornell.edu/okuref/research/tutorial.html) libraries have developed research guides on the Web.

Translating the intellectual and functional concepts of information resources into the visual and verbal structures of the computer screen will take good imagination and design skills. Providing enough information to support intelligent decision-making processes within the constraints of computer screens is a challenge. This challenge is addressed through a variety of mechanisms. "Layering" the screen so that additional information about a resource is accessible through a mouse-over or as a pop-up is one strategy. Creating an "About This Database" icon that links to fuller descriptions of the resources is another strategy. Adding to the challenge is the constantly changing array of reference resources. Reference collections have always been dynamic. Reference librarians add resources as they become available, replace older editions with new ones, and de-accession materials as they lose their utility. However, the rate of change for electronic resources is substantially higher than for traditional print resources. In addition to the "changes by choice" in which a library changes its subscriptions to add or delete a title, there are the changes in the nature of the resources that remain in the collection. Given the very fluid state of electronic resources, how can the library's gateway service lead novice users to the "new" resource while helping experienced users recognize that it is a new incarnation of the one they used last week?

DEFINITION OF THE REFERENCE COLLECTION

The revolution in reference is causing some fundamental changes in the way reference librarians acquire, describe, think about, and use their collections (see Chapter 13). In times of rapid transition, it can be helpful to see both the past and the present as preludes to discovering possible routes to the future. Following is a description of the "classic" reference collection.

The reference collection is a distinct set of print and electronic resources selected and acquired by reference librarians and made available within a recognizable space to local user communities. Reference librarians thrive on the challenge of identifying the right set of reference resources that they can consult to deal with the information needs of their users, within budgetary and space constraints. Reference librarians have developed the criteria for assessing the quality of these tools, and they apply these criteria in choosing items for the reference collection. The crucial challenges for reference librarians are establishing intellectual control over the content of the collection and reflecting that control in ways that benefit users. These challenges are more readily met because of the rigorous selection and evaluation process for each resource as it is acquired. Because the reference collection has a structure and a shape built by the reference librarians who use it, integrating new tools and resources into the working collection is a nearly automatic process. The reference librarian's mental map of the intellectual content of the reference collection is well developed and well maintained. This mental map is reflected in the physical arrangement of the room, with materials organized for effective use.

As the reference collection migrates to electronic form, what elements of the earlier definition remain? Some of them remain virtually unchanged, others continue in modified form. There is one area that warrants extensive exploration: selection and acquisition. This is where the traditional orderly reference collection development processes have changed the most.

The first step of selection is the identification of forthcoming tools of possible interest. The reference librarian tries to be aware of new tools that will be released in the near future. However, because electronic resources are so fluid in nature, this identification is an amorphous process. Between the time of announcement and the time of appearance in the marketplace, many resources have undergone extensive revisions of concept and execution. Some resources are offered on a basis that is similar to a prospectus. If the proposed tool generates enough interest and orders, it will continue through the development cycle to a production version. If not, it may be withdrawn for redesign or delayed until there are sufficient purchasers. A tool that was identified as being of some interest in April might be of much greater or lesser interest by September when it is released. The version that was available for evaluation might be very different from the version that is delivered. Much of the time it is an improved version, but not always.

Another factor that is important in the selection of electronic resources, although it played a negligible role in the print collection, is the availability of a resource from multiple sources. Many resources are available in different configurations at a substantial difference in price. For example, in the discussion of interfaces, it was noted that *ERIC* is available through at least three vendors. The same original *ERIC* database forms the core of these different products. However, in some very real sense, *ERIC* is not the same database in all these cases. It may be too much to assert that the interface IS the product. It is not too much to assert that it is impossible to evaluate a resource without evaluating the interface. For some tools, evaluation of a resource for selection into the reference collection is based at least as much on the interface as on the content. This represents a change in emphasis from the selection for the print collection. In the print world, nearly all reference collections have at least one reference tool that is nearly impossible to use. Reference librarians put up with the difficulties of use because the content comes in only one print package. The economies of print publishing ensure that. In the reference room, the reference librarian is available to serve as the intermediary between the print tool and the user. There is no expectation that the user will learn the eccentricities of its arrangement and access. By contrast, in the electronic reference collection, the expectation is that the end-user will be using the electronic resource independently, without a reference librarian to serve as an intermediary. If the resource content is offered with an interface that is difficult for end-users or confusing or lacks important features, many librarians will pass. They will wait with some assurance that another company will offer the same content in a package that has better features. If it is a crucial resource, then perhaps it will be selected but kept on a "wait and see" basis until it improves or there is an alternative.

In weighing one version of a resource against another, some factors are difficult to balance. Perhaps one source offers a longer run of the database, while another may offer a smaller subset of the database at a significant discount. It is very hard to weigh the "costs" of not offering the older citations. A third source provides the users with more options for citation handling, which is a popular feature for the library's many remote users. Perhaps a fourth source is the least expensive to acquire, but requires that the library mount the database on its own server. If the library already owns a server, the marginal costs for mounting and maintaining an additional database may be fairly low. Perhaps the library is in a consortium that is considering a multi-database package that includes the database but with an interface that is less user-friendly than one of the alternatives. Finding ways to evaluate the array of choices on all these factors is one of the continuing challenges faced by the reference librarian.

After the rigorous evaluation process, each electronic resource is considered for addition to the collection. The process of adding resources to the collection is called *acquisition*. However, in the realm of electronic resources, the concept of acquisition has been redefined into something more equivalent with leasing than with ownership. Although some titles in some electronic formats can be purchased on a permanent basis, most are acquired on much more temporary terms. Electronic resources are made available to a defined group of users for a defined period of time. It is this increasingly ephemeral nature of the reference collection that has created some cognitive dissonance among reference librarians. The concept of reference collection used to carry with it a notion of permanence. There is nothing temporary in the impression given by the hundreds of sage and gold volumes that make up the *National Union Catalog of Pre-1956 Imprints*, for example. The *Dictionary of National Biography* will be of interest and value well into the next century, at least. Any library that owns these reference tools will keep them available for decades. By contrast, a reference librarian can look at a computer screen and realize that a tool that was there yesterday is gone today. That is an unsettling moment. These moments are occurring with great frequency at reference desks everywhere. Because this is the new reality, it pays to approach the reference desk with an open mind, ready to adjust one's strategies to the day's resources.

If a reference tool meets the selection criteria and has been added to the collection, its role in reference service needs to be settled. The reference librarians decide just how and where an item is to be "virtually shelved," that is to say, into which synthetic context the tool will be added. The electronic map of the virtual reference room will be updated. The new resource will be listed or linked from the cluster of electronic tools that it is most like, for example, with dictionaries or indexes or biographical sources. While the new item is being linked and listed, it is likely that the other tools of its kind will be re-assessed in light of the new resource. Perhaps a realignment of resources is in order. A single category might be divided into two if the original list gets too long to be easily managed or navigated. It is understood that this intellectual integration of the electronic resource is a critical step in the continuing management of the reference collection.

The impermanence of electronic resources can lead to some caution in the intellectual integration process. It is hard to invest much scarce human capital in developing aids and guides for yet another resource whose time in the collection may be measured in months rather than years. On the other hand, it is essential to make each reference tool fully accessible and available for use while it is part of the collection. With the transformation of the reference room and the reference collection into an access node rather than a depository, developing a comprehensive access system is essential. One can claim a distinction between a tool that is not owned and one that is unavailable, but it is a distinction without a difference for the user.

In evaluating a reference tool, one factor to consider is cost. A more important factor is value. One can measure the price of a reference tool in terms of absolute cost. This is easy to do by just reading the invoice. It is harder to measure the value of a reference tool. One way to begin to measure value is to look at cost per use. In terms of cost per use, a $40 item that is not used in a year is more expensive than the $4,000 database that is used once a day. The costs of making the resource more usable through training sessions, user guides, publicity, or demonstrations may very well be recovered in the added value of the resource for its users. The cost per use will go down because of the increased number of users. It is nearly impossible to accurately measure the number of times a print tool is used, but most reference librarians have a general sense of use. Usage is likely to be expressed in general terms such as very frequently, occasionally, and rarely or never. This is in contrast with electronic tools that are typically set up to produce usage reports. Thus, comparing print and electronic tools on cost per use is a somewhat speculative process, but it can help clarify the evaluation of their utility for the users of the reference collection.

When evaluating an electronic reference tool, there is at least one other cost factor to consider as well. It is called "soft costs." Unlike "hard costs," soft costs cannot be measured in dollars and cents. Soft costs are paid in time, energy, and frustration. They are paid by the users who spend excessive time trying to figure out a search system. Users pay soft costs whenever they fail to find an item that is in the system. It can be helpful to think about a hypothetical interface in which the search button is just an unlabeled arrow. Some users will figure out that this means search. Other users will try other buttons first and then try the arrow. Still other users will ask for help. Other users will quit. Every library that owns this resource will create a guide of some kind indicating that the arrow button means search. Each individual action that is needed to compensate for the unclear button adds a little bit to that system's soft costs. Perhaps for any one library, it is not that much, but when multiplied by the number of users of all the libraries, it adds up. At some point, the soft costs exceed the "hard costs" of the system. All systems come with soft costs, but it is useful to keep in mind that these will vary across systems. It is worthwhile to evaluate the interface for a resource in terms of likely soft costs as well as hard costs. Whether the soft costs outweigh the value of the resource is a question that may have a different answer in each library.

Another factor in evaluating an electronic reference tool is accessibility. For electronic resources, one form of accessibility is greatly improved: physical access. Consulting an electronic reference tool can be accomplished without a visit to the physical reference room. This eliminates a variety of architectural and meteorological barriers to access. It also removes time barriers. A tool may be consulted whenever electricity is available, rather than when a library is open and staffed. It requires a computer (or a TV set with a Web box) and a telephone connection. These are not free but are rapidly becoming available for a minimal investment. The library and its resources are able to reach a much larger portion of its user communities than ever before. However, electronic resources bring their own accessibility challenges. Some Web-based resources' primary interfaces are highly dependent on good vision and fine-motor skills. Maneuvering a mouse and clicking the buttons can be difficult for some users. There are widely available assistive computer programs as well as other kinds of adaptive technology that address these issues. An example of these assistive programs is StickyKeys, which makes it possible to do the two- and three-key combinations that are often required for computer operations. The all-too-familiar "Control-Alt-Delete" key combination requires significant two-handed dexterity. StickyKey makes it possible to do this one keystroke at a time. Not all interface accessibility concerns are fully addressed by the technology, however. An all-text version, for example, works better with most screen-reading technology than an image-based interface. Some resources come with alternative interfaces that can meet the needs of a variety of users. In evaluating electronic resources, those that come with alternative interfaces are preferable to those that depend on assistive and adaptive technologies.

An essential element of the evaluation of reference resources is the involvement of the end-user. Experienced reference librarians have a great deal of information about how end-users interact with information resources. They have developed insights into how the user views the information universe. However, this knowledge is necessarily limited in a variety of ways. More is known about the users with whom librarians have contact than those who do not come in or call. More is known about those users who have overcome the barriers to access reference service than those the barriers have turned away. Not all barriers may even be known.

In trying to evaluate a reference tool or interface from an end-user point of view, the librarian's experience is a two-edged sword. On the one hand, this experience has revealed how some users approach and use a reference tool. On the other hand, it has made some parts of the experience opaque. It is nearly impossible to recapture that original feeling of innocence in the face of an electronic reference tool. Librarians can see the information on the screen in a way that the novice cannot. Some parts of the screen may as well be empty for as much as a new user is able to glean from them. In any interface, no matter how a "fill in the blank" option is phrased or labeled, a reference librarian will have a clue as to what to do next. At a minimum, the librarian will know to check that the little cursor bar is inside the box before trying to type. This knowledge is far from universal. A librarian will likely notice that some symbol or icon is a toggle switch and be able to make a reasonable estimate of its function and impact. Many of the new users do not see the buttons or do not fully understand the ramifications of these choices. As librarians evaluate these tools, it is critical to be aware how these differences in experience affect perceptions of usability. With those real limits on knowledge of user behavior, it would be a foolhardy reference librarian indeed who feels competent to fully assess and evaluate the usability of any reference resource for end-users.

In view of these factors, it becomes critical to develop and use formal and informal pathways for user feedback on electronic reference tools. For those tools that are available from different sources, setting up a formal evaluation process where users can test and compare the interfaces as part of the initial selection process would be an excellent start. For a modest outlay of library resources to pay a set of willing subjects and to hire recorders and transcribers to capture the interactions, one can gain an enormous amount of information on which to base a decision. If paying volunteers is not feasible, perhaps groups like the Friends of the Library could be invited to participate in the evaluation. Library staff members could take notes of their observations. The volunteers' reward would be information on topics of interest and a sense of contribution; the librarians' reward would be insight into how well the interfaces matched their users' needs. In either scenario, one could be assured that the evaluation and selection process had included the most important stakeholders, the users themselves. Providing feedback to the database producers is an effective way to close the development loop and encourage more usability in the next version of the interface.

For internally developed electronic resources like Web pages and gateways, this user evaluation needs to be incorporated into the design and development phase. It also needs to be a periodic feature of the implementation phase. This is one area where the flexibility and impermanence of the electronic medium is an overlooked feature. Libraries would like to view their gateways, portals, and guides as finished products, whereas they need to be viewed as permanently under construction. Although no one likes a Web site that is in constant flux, one that evolves over time to a more usable version is welcomed.

If "user-centered information services" is to be anything but a slogan on annual reports, reference librarians and reference departments need to develop and maintain an active user perspective on their resources and services. This can involve user surveys and interviews, as well as surveys and interviews with people who do not use the library. Identifying barriers to use is an important step toward removing them.

CONCLUSION

Reference librarians find themselves trying to manage the fire-hose flow of information into drinking-fountain streams of information that the user can handle. The step-down mechanisms of gateways, searchable databases of databases, menus, guides, and links are demanding all the imagination, skill, research, energy, work, and luck that can be mustered. The rewards for this effort have been substantial and widespread. Millions of users who connect to the library's computer system can initiate a set of activities that go far beyond the answers reference librarians once provided following the question, "May I help you?"

From the library's gateway, the system authenticates the user's status within the library's service communities, queries the user about information needs, provides access to specialized information resources, identifies electronic abstracting and indexing resources, links to the full text of the documents, allows desktop delivery of articles that are from collections a thousand miles away, connects with the local, expanded online catalog, identifies a variety of print and digital resources available, sends the print resources to the user's location, provides access to a very large portion of the monographic works of the world, and interacts with an interlibrary lending component to arrange delivery of those works not held by the local library. All these functions can happen in less time than it takes to drive to the library, find a parking spot, dig under the front seat for change for the parking meter, climb the marble stairs to the library, and approach the reference desk looking hopeful.

NOTES

1. F. W. Lancaster et al., "Searching Databases on CD-ROM: Comparison of the Results of End-User Searching with Results from Two Modes of Searching by Skilled Intermediaries," *RQ* 33 (Spring 1994): 370-86.

ADDITIONAL READINGS

Coffman, Steve. "Building Earth's Largest Library: Driving into the Future." *Searcher* 7 (March 1999): 34-47. Also available: http://www.infotoday.com/searcher/mar99/coffman.htm.

In this article, Steve Coffman offers a challenge for libraries and librarians to develop a cooperative union online catalog and circulation system as helpful and easy to use as Amazon.com. Read this article and imagine a different kind of OPAC in the future.

Crawford, Walt. *Being Analog: Creating Tomorrow's Libraries.* Chicago: American Library Association, 1999. 245p.

Walt Crawford presents a probably necessary antidote to the digital fever of the times. Perhaps "The Law of the Instrument" is being taken too literally by libraries and librarians. There is as much danger in believing the overly optimistic predictions of the future as the overly pessimistic ones. Critical thinking never goes out of style.

LIBLICENSE: Licensing Digital Information: A Resource for Librarians. Available: http://www.library.yale.edu/~llicense/index.shtml.

This Web site focuses on the topic of licensed electronic resources in libraries. As the introduction states: "[T]hese materials will serve as a useful starting point towards providing librarians with a better understanding of the issues raised by licensing agreements in the digital age." Although the site makes clear that these resources are not a substitute for legal advice and opinion, they can be used as a starting point in examining any potential license. Examples of model licensing principles and preferred licensing language offer solid help to the reference librarian working with these increasingly important issues.

Lipow, Anne G. " 'In Your Face' Reference Service." *Library Journal* 124 (August 1999): 50-52.

This article can be seen as a wake-up call to reference librarians to develop methods to deal with the information needs of the remote user wherever and whenever they arise. Lipow proposes some thought-provoking organizational and technological innovations as ways to make reference service more visible and available.

Mates, Barbara T. *Adaptive Technology for the Internet: Making Electronic Resources Accessible to All.* Chicago: American Library Association, 2000. 192p.

This volume provides a snapshot of available adaptive and assistive technology that can bring the promise of the World Wide Web and the Internet to the widest possible audience. Doug Wakefield and Judith Dixon are contributors who bring experienced voices to the discussion. It includes information on Web sites, vendors, manufacturers, and consultants that can help a library on its path to full accessibility.

Virtually Yours: Models for Managing Electronic Resources and Services. Edited by Peggy Johnson. Chicago: American Library Association, 1999. 165p.

This volume is an edited set of papers presented at the RUSA/ALCTS Joint Institute in 1997. Collection development librarians and reference librarians shared their visions for a future in which seamless, integrated, dynamic collections are acquired, processed, and made available to the user through the collaborative efforts of the entire library staff.

Walker, Geraldene, and Joseph Janes. *Online Retrieval: A Dialogue of Theory and Practice.* 2d ed. Englewood, Colo.: Libraries Unlimited, 1999. 312p.

Although it focuses on the traditional search services and systems, this comprehensive book includes searching techniques for the World Wide Web. Extensive examples and illustrations help illuminate the concepts and commands of efficient searching.

CHAPTER

6

UNDERSTANDING ELECTRONIC INFORMATION SYSTEMS FOR REFERENCE

Kathleen M. Kluegel

INTRODUCTION

Chapter 5 presented the history and development of electronic resources for reference, exploring the expansion of these resources far beyond the reference room walls and the consequences for reference service. This chapter examines the structures that underlie the creation and distribution of these resources, beginning with a look at the history of the Internet. Next the terms and concepts of the Internet needed to understand the current generation of electronic resources and services are introduced. An analysis of Internet and World Wide Web tools and how they work follows, creating a framework for understanding and developing the next generation of products and services. The final section focuses on some of the fascinating challenges facing reference librarians in the emergent digital information age.

HISTORY OF THE INTERNET

The Internet has a brief but explosive history. What has become the Internet began as ARPANET, an experimental high-speed network linking computers at Department of Defense research sites in the early 1970s. Its major goal was to develop a distributed computer network that could withstand disruptions. The only computers on ARPANET belonged to the Department of Defense and its major contractors. In the mid-1980s, the National Science Foundation developed its own network, NSFNET, to link its five supercomputer sites around the country. Many universities wished to connect to one of these supercomputer sites to do research. Because of the enormous costs it would take to run telephone lines crisscrossing the country, a series of regional networks was developed around each of the supercomputer sites. These regional networks were designed along the same lines as ARPANET and interconnected with one another. Any computer connected at any point on any of the regional networks could communicate with any other computer. These regional networks have continually upgraded the speed and reliability of the communication equipment and the computers running them to provide an effective networking environment. Together these networks and similar networks around the world form the Internet. The Internet has become a ubiquitous phenomenon that is growing at an unbelievable rate. Various means are used to assess the size of the Internet and the World Wide Web. One set of current statistics can be found at the site of the Internet Software Consortium. As of January 2000, there were 72,398,092 top-level domain name hosts.[1] An article by Hal Kirkwood identifies several Web sites that measure different aspects of the World Wide Web.[2]

INTERNET TERMS AND CONCEPTS

In spite of the nearly universal presence of the Internet and the World Wide Web in daily life, there is little awareness of the elements that make them possible. The following discussion focuses on the underlying concepts, structures, and services that make up the Internet. Understanding these fundamental Internet concepts prepares one to assimilate future developments and innovations. These concepts also are useful in interpreting the sometimes-cryptic messages that computers display when accessing the Internet and the World Wide Web. Knowing the terminology of network structures facilitates communication with the technical systems staff as well.

Protocols

It can be helpful to think of the Internet as a many-layered information environment. Some concepts form the foundation on which the other layers depend. The most critical element in the understanding of the Internet and the World Wide Web is the concept of protocols. *Protocols* are formal agreements on the form and style of communication to assure reliable information transfers. In diplomatic circles, protocols are rules of speech and behavior that have been codified to ensure clear communication across cultural or linguistic boundaries. These rules facilitate diplomatic interactions and reduce areas of possible confusion. On a more familiar level, a protocol is an agreement such as, "We will all use the twenty-four hour clock when we talk about time."

By establishing and using this and other protocols, one can ensure clear and unambiguous communication. Computers connected to the Internet transfer information using protocols. It is almost impossible to overstate the importance of protocols in the area of electronic networks. Without protocols, there could be no computer network, because information created in one computer environment could not be used, shared, transferred, or seen by someone using a different computer.

The essential protocol for national and international networks is TCP/IP (Transmission Control Protocol/Internet Protocol). TCP/IP governs the transport of information from one computer to another, independent of the kind of data. It ensures that information created in one computer will be received by another, unchanged by the process. TCP/IP forms the fundamental transport level for the Internet. It can be thought of as the foundation for the Internet. Specialized kinds of information may require that additional protocols be defined to enable successful exchanges. These protocols form layers that are carried on top of TCP/IP layers. The railway system provides a useful analogy. TCP/IP forms the railroad tracks. The various kinds of additional protocols are the different kinds of engines and cars that can ride those rails. The content is carried in the appropriate rail cars.

The TCP/IP protocol provides the rules that allow one computer to establish a connection to another computer on the Internet. The TCP/IP protocol is incorporated into TELNET programs such as WinQVT or Kermit. It links the remote computer to the user's display and keyboard as if the user's computer were directly connected to it. Once the connection has been established, the TELNET program serves as an invisible intermediary between the user's workstation and the remote system. One of the important features of TELNET is the power to link disparate computers together, through shared protocols. To the users of the Internet, TELNET is rather like riding on a swan; that is, the user gets a very smooth ride, but the TELNET swan is paddling like crazy beneath the surface, making links, exchanging protocol parameters, and transferring information across multiple boundaries.

TELNET allows the wider use of resources without the need to transfer the resource from one environment to another. Large databases can be built and reside on a single host computer with multiple remote users. Because TELNET provides remote access to the resource that is identical to the local access, no loss of functionality occurs. Typically, the TELNET host computer asks for users to logon. This logon allows the host computer to allocate a portion of its resources to each session.

TELNET is called a *stateful* protocol because the user's computer and the server computer maintain an active connection. TELNET sessions are also known as online sessions. Command-mode interfaces are generally TELNET-based and stateful. As a rule, stateful search systems support the creation of discrete sets that can be manipulated by the user. The user can refer to previous elements of the interaction and re-use information without re-entering it. Logical operators such as the Boolean AND can be employed to combine sets. Modifying the sets by language, date, or other element is also supported in typical stateful search sessions.

Client-Server Computing

The client-server model is another important element of networked computing systems. In client-server programs, the functions of the program are split into two components. The client is the "face" of the program. It is the part of the program the human user sees on the screen and interacts with. The client accepts the commands of the user and then interacts with the server portion of the system, using the protocols incorporated into its design to translate the commands into the language of the computer performing the task. After the server completes the task, it provides the results to the client to translate them into the response the user sees on the screen. Typically, the client program is first designed to work with one set of machines or on one operating system, called the platform. The primary platforms for personal computers are Microsoft Windows, Macintosh OS, and Linux. Because each of these platforms is unique in its programming language and rules, client programs have to be modified to work on the other platforms. The process of modifying software to work on different platforms is called *porting.* (See Box 6.1 for another illustration of these concepts.)

Box 6.1 The Screwdriver as a Client-Server Model

The screwdriver handle takes the user input—gripping and twisting—and translates that energy into an input the screw understands—the bit. The screw and screwdriver also demonstrate the importance of standards and protocols: The slot in the screw is machined to a standard shape, width, and depth to match the standard dimensions of the screwdriver. One could further stretch the model by positing the changeable-bit screwdriver as an example of porting.

The client-server model of computer systems allows different tasks to be allocated to the different modules. For example, in search systems, the user interface is typically a client-supported activity. The client provides a screen designed to assist the user with the desired task. It may further provide help screens. By shifting these functions to a local client, the server has more free resources to support the primary function. An online public access catalog (OPAC) is an example of a client-server system. In a typical OPAC, the interface is a client program that is loaded and runs on the computers used to access the catalog. It shows the user a screen with search options and help screens. The user interacts with the interface and enters information about the needed materials, such as a title, an author, or a topic. Acting as a silent, behind-the-screen, "invisible butler," the interface translates the user information into the precise search commands used by the OPAC's search engine and sends the command to the server. The server responds with a stream of coded bibliographic and circulation information about the item. The client translates this stream of bits and bytes into a formatted display that the user can understand. Typically, the display will have additional options for locating a particular item, searching for related items, and the like. The client portion of the program supports all of these activities. The advantages to the user of this "invisible butler" acting as interpreter are substantial. The user does not have to spend time and energy learning the precisely formatted search commands. This frees the user to focus on accomplishing the task of finding the needed materials in the OPAC. The search interface screen can be designed to provide a helpful and supportive search environment with user-friendly features like pop-up help screens or interpretive glosses.

There are advantages for the search system as well. Because the client serves as the translator between the user and the server, the server can operate more efficiently on the actual search and retrieval functions. Thus, the workload is shared across the processors, resulting in faster search response time and the ability to support a larger number of users.

The diversity of the computers that make up the Internet and the World Wide Web make the client-server model the only feasible one. The millions upon millions of personal computers from a myriad of manufacturers use a wide range of client programs to access the Internet. A wide variety of Web servers run a number of server software programs. Both the client programs and the server programs are designed around the Internet protocols.

The specialized client programs developed for the Web are called *browsers.* Browsers such as Netscape Navigator and Internet Explorer are programs or a cluster of inter-related programs and applications that are developed to work with the different protocols and conventions that make up the Web. Browsers interact with the Web servers that hold the millions of files that make up the pages, images, sounds, and data of the Web.

Hypertext Transfer Protocol

The most important protocol in the World Wide Web is HTTP (Hypertext Transfer Protocol). *Hypertext* is the term used to describe files of two main types. The original meaning refers to any document that can be read in a non-linear manner with different paths through the text. This results in a different experience for each reader depending upon the choices made at each juncture. The other, more common, meaning of hypertext, and its extension *hypermedia,* is a file or document that contains links to other files. These linked files can contain text, data, sound, and/or images and can reside on one or many computers connected to the Web. HTTP provides the support for moving or viewing these files across the Web.

Files and documents on the Web are coded to protocols. In the case of text, the most widely-used Web protocol at this time is HTML (Hyper Text Markup Language). HTML is an application of the SGML (Standard Generalized Markup Language) ISO (International Standards Organization) standard. Markup languages provide a consistent and unambiguous way to describe the structural parts of a document, independent of content. These descriptions, or tags, can be thought of as a particular kind of editing code, related to the codes that have been used by blue-pencil wielding editors for years. HTML and SGML tags can be read and understood by humans as well as by machines. The HTML protocol includes a set of predetermined codes for the functional parts of a document. These codes have been incorporated into the standard Web browser and include header, paragraph, list, and so forth. Web browsers interpret these codes to display the documents or files correctly. Typefaces, font size, placement on page, blank spaces, indentations, and other display elements are implemented according to the HTML protocol as interpreted by the particular Web browser of the user. Specialized programs can be used to create HTML-coded documents. HTML coding is supported by major word processing programs, such as Microsoft Word, as well. The value of adding HTML codes to a document goes beyond the aesthetics of the display. These codes turn a page of undifferentiated plain text into a structured document that is much easier to read and interpret.

META Tags

A special category of HTML tags, called META tags, deserves some initial explanation here. HTML META tags are the World Wide Web implementation of *metadata,* a term that can be translated as "data about data." HTML META tags are a set of tags that can be used to describe the content of the Web page without affecting its appearance in any way. The information contained in HTML META tags is understood and used by the servers and clients that make up the World Wide Web.

URL

Other HTML codes also support the existence, formatting, and utilization of the hypertext links to other documents. These interconnected, linked documents, and files form the World Wide Web. Each document or file has a unique address, the URL (Uniform Resource Locator). The URL is built by following another protocol. Each element of the URL has a specific function and can be parsed. The part of the URL that is before the colon specifies the type of access protocol. For example, the URL can begin with "http:", which indicates that the resource is a hypertext/hypermedia file and will be retrieved using the HTTP protocol. Another common access protocol is "telnet:", which indicates that the resource will be accessed with the TELNET protocol. The part of the URL after the colon is interpreted in ways that are specific to the access method. In general, two slashes after the colon indicate that the elements that follow identify the machine where the resource is located. The term *machine* as used here can be a single computer or a cluster of computers working together as if it were a single machine. The address part of the URL following the slashes is called the domain name. Each address on the World Wide Web must be registered to assure its uniqueness. There are naming conventions that govern the appearance of the domain name. In the United States, the domain names have one of five main endings: edu, org, com, gov, and net. Each ending lets the user anticipate the kind of organization or service that is available through that Web site. Although the categories are not absolute, in general, ".edu" stands for an education organization, ".org" for a nonprofit organization, ".com" for commercial sites, ".gov" for units of government, and ".net" for organizations that support Internet access and Web services. It is likely that the number of domain name endings in the United States will expand soon to provide more specificity of the type of service each provides. In other parts of the world, there are similar patterns governing domain name conventions. In countries outside of the United States, domain names generally include an abbreviation for the country of origin as well as an element designating the kind of service provider.

As an example of a URL that follows the current domain naming conventions, a URL such as http://www.ala.org tells the user that the resource is a hypertext one and that it is located on the machine registered to the American Library Association, a not-for-profit organization. Similarly, an example of a fictitious address that looks like telnet://myemail.email-mail.com tells the user that the resource is one which must be accessed through the TELNET protocol and is on a machine registered with the imaginary Email-Mail Company in the corporate sector of the World Wide Web.

An example of the pattern for a URL from another country is http://auniversity.ac.uk, identifying a fictitious academic site in the United Kingdom. A URL for a commercial site in Australia might look like this: http://mycompany.com.au.

Browsers for the World Wide Web present the user with an interface that allows the direct input of a known URL or a search of the content of the Web to discover documents that meet the user's needs. Once a URL has been selected, the browser goes to the appropriate Web server, finds the requested file, delivers it to the user's desktop, and displays it according to the HTML coding included in the file.

The power of HTTP and URLs combines to transform the product of publication from a static, linear document to a dynamic, hypertext one (see Box 6.2). For example, if an author is creating an international travel guide, it can be done as a printed book or as a document on the Web. In a book or other fixed text format, the author would have to include as much information as possible while providing readers with contact information such as telephone numbers and addresses of organizations that may have additional material. Constraints of size would determine some choices for the author.

In contrast, on the Web, the author would be able to incorporate much of the information through links to relevant Web sites anywhere in the world. For example, the author could provide a link to the United States Department of State Travel Advisories page (http://travel.state.gov/travel_warnings.html). This link would bring the user directly to the most complete and up-to-date information about places that may present difficulties to the traveler. This hypertext travel publication would provide each user with a unique experience, as some links will be explored by some readers but not others, or may be explored in a different sequence. Many of the linked pages will be part of other hypertext documents on the Web, which can themselves be explored or not as the reader chooses.

Box 6.2 The Power of Hypertext

In writing this chapter, for example, the author wished many times that it could be created as a hypertext document, with links from terms and concepts to pages of explanation and examples. Using hypertext would also provide an opportunity to link to relevant Web sites.

Stateful or Stateless?

The most commonly deployed version of HTTP is HTTP/1.0. HTTP/1.0 is called a stateless protocol because each HTTP request opens a new TCP connection, starts the session, interacts with the server, fills the request, and closes the TCP connection. Web pages that have embedded images, for example, fill each image request as a separate TCP connection to the server. Each HTTP request is executed as an independent interaction without any knowledge of the requests that came before it. Consequently, browsers are limited in their ability to incorporate previous information into their searches or other World Wide Web interactions. Statelessness has far-reaching implications for searching on the Web and for manipulating the results of that search.

If one looks at the full URL in the browser window during successive steps of a Web interaction, it can be very revealing. At each stage of the process, the browser adds elements to the URL to produce a particular address string that will be translated into the needed next action (see Box 6.3). For example, if one clicks a button to see items 11–20 from the results of a Web search, the URL may show additional codes added to the search string to retrieve items 11–20. The search engine re-executes the entire search with these additional codes to produce the next page of items. This stateless search process is not particularly efficient when compared with a typical stateful search. In a stateful system, all the items would be retrieved into a set on the server, and they can be displayed in any order in any format with a simple display command.

Box 6.3 URL Examples

This example of URLs is patterned after the Northern Light search system for an original search and for the second page of results. The hypothetical search term is "peanut butter".

Original query:

http://www.northernlight.com/nlquery.fcg?cb=0&qr=peanut+butter& orl=

Request for second page of results:

http://www.northernlight.com/nlquery.fcg?ho=zeppo&po=5128&qr= peanut+butter&cb=0&db=122492288&nth=14&orl=

There are "overhead costs" to the World Wide Web in the relatively inefficient TCP connections that must be re-established with every interaction. Everyone using the Internet and the World Wide Web pays these costs through reduced speed of response and lost bandwidth. In ordinary Web usage, the implications of statelessness for most activities are relatively minor. One becomes accustomed to the sometimes lengthy waits for the next set of possible sites of interest. Or the converse occurs when one waits for a very large document to be transmitted in its entirety, although only a small segment is of actual interest.

Statelessness has much larger implications for database searching. The self-contained nature of a stateless interaction is at odds with the kinds of step-by-step searches that are typical of a command-line database search. Concept building, searching for synonyms, and combining concepts are all components of a traditional, stateful database search. Traditional online search systems provide the mechanisms that allow searchers to create very complex searches with several parameters to retrieve a very focused body of materials. It is more cumbersome and more difficult to achieve these same results in a stateless search environment. To support these complex search activities, some of the commercial database sites have developed search programs that achieve pseudo-statefulness using technologies such as cookies and JavaScript. The servers use these mechanisms to keep track of search results and documents. This results in a search experience that is very similar to a stateful one. These pseudo-stateful systems have their own associated costs and inefficiencies for the server and for the user, but these costs are more than balanced by the effective retrieval of relevant materials.

The current statelessness of the World Wide Web is both a feature and a flaw. On the one hand, statelessness allows many more people to use a single resource than a stateful session would. The Web server can send out the little packets of information very quickly without having to expend any internal resources on keeping track of the transactions. One can think of the stateless Web server as a Pez dispenser, sending the little candies down a chute as quickly as it can flip its top. A stateful session would require the Web server to keep track of which user had seen which page and to keep the pages in order. The server would have to allocate internal resources such as memory and programming for these management tasks. In stateful sessions, each user is allocated an amount of memory or disk space on the server machine to store the intermediate results of searches. The sets have to be numbered and counted and ordered. In addition, stateful sessions require a one-to-one match between a user and a port or socket. When the server is out of ports, no more users can logon.

Stateless servers open and close sessions so quickly that a queue of browser requests can move along briskly. This statement is put to the test during busy times at very popular sites. But very large commercial Web sites can be designed to handle a million hits, while stateful servers reach their limits at much lower levels. In addition, once the Web resource has been transferred to the user's computer, it is a local resource, which can be quickly accessed without interacting with the Web server. It can be stored on a temporary basis in a cache or on a permanent basis on the user's computer.

Researchers who study traffic over the World Wide Web have determined that, on the whole, persistent TCP connections would be around 20 % more efficient than temporary TCP connections and statelessness on the Web. Consequently, the HTTP Working Group of the Internet Engineering Task Force has developed a new HTTP draft protocol called HTTP/1.1, which supports persistent connections. This means that once a browser connects to a Web server, it can receive multiple files through the same connection. HTTP/1.1 also supports pipelining, which is the sending of multiple requests over a single persistent TCP connection. Balachander Krishnamurthy and colleagues discuss the development of HTTP/1.1 and the implications of the new protocol in a recent article.[3]

Because of the demands placed on server resources by persistent TCP connections, HTTP/1.1 incorporates rules that allow servers or clients to terminate the connection as needed. One of the important factors in the development of the new hypertext protocol is the requirement that HTTP/1.1 maintain backwards compatibility with HTTP/1.0. This means that the functions, commands, and codes that were used in HTTP/1.0 will still be correctly interpreted by browsers and servers using HTTP/1.1. This backwards compatibility is essential because while most newer versions of Web browsers support HTTP/1.1, there is a large installed base of older clients that do not. In addition, not all Web servers support HTTP/1.1. The requirement of maintaining backwards compatibility adds to the complexity and inconsistencies within HTTP/1.1 that would not be present if the developers had been free to develop the protocol in isolation.

Other Significant Protocols

There is a variant of the regular HTTP protocol, called S-HTTP, for Secure HyperText Transfer Protocol. This protocol assures that the information submitted is secure and protected. This protocol is usually represented to the Web browser as https://. One will normally encounter the S-HTTP protocol when completing a form that requires important personal or financial information. One use for S-HTTP is authentication, certifying to the Web server that one is authorized to use a particular Web resource. If the user has to logon to use a Web resource, the process is likely to be conducted with the S-HTTP protocol.

Web browsers can be configured to alert a user when entering and leaving a secure Web space, so the user does not inadvertently submit sensitive information over an insecure connection. The site or server that performs the authentication may have www-s as the first element of the URL to identify it as a secure server. There are other kinds of security protocols in use throughout the Web. Some of them involve encryption, which scrambles the information so thoroughly that even if the data are intercepted they cannot be interpreted without the decryption key. Different encryption programs have different levels of protection. Commercial Web sites will frequently identify the strength of their encryption protection as a way of clarifying the level of safety of the information transmitted.

Other significant protocols are supported by browsers on the Web. One of the important services of the Internet is support for file transfers from one machine to another. The FTP (File Transfer Protocol) is the Internet standard, high-level protocol for transferring files. It is less well known now than some of the other Web protocols because the common Web browsers provide transparent support for it, typically calling it a download or a save. FTP enables users at any Internet site to retrieve files, documents, data, or programs from many other Internet sites. It is the way that shareware and other programs are delivered from a server and downloaded to the user's computer. Many users of the World Wide Web have used FTP to download the programs, plug-ins, or other files that update or enhance their Web browsers.

As the above discussion has documented, each resource on the Internet and the World Wide Web is created with a set of rules based on common protocols. HTTP, for example, is designed to format plain text. But plain text must itself be based on common standards to be understood and interpreted correctly. The most basic format for text is plain ASCII, which is an international standard for representing letters and numbers. ASCII includes upper- and lowercase letters, punctuation marks, and numbers from 0 to 9 (essentially all the characters represented by an English-language typewriter keyboard). Each character is a seven-bit combination with numeric values from 32 to 128. Plain ASCII text does not contain any formatting information beyond spaces and line breaks. To include features such as underlining or boldface or different type fonts requires encoding elements beyond the seven-bit limit, as does representing non-ASCII characters from other alphabets or characters from languages such as Japanese, Chinese, and Korean. Computer programs use characters beyond the basic ASCII set, namely the full binary character set, and these must be encoded as well, if they are to be transmitted across the Internet.

Beyond information that is communicated through plain text or numbers, there is information that relies on patterns or relationships among the elements. For example, spreadsheets and other databases contain information in the formatting, with cells, rows, and columns carrying vital elements that must be maintained in transferring data from one setting to another. Because several of the Internet protocols are built on the seven-bit limit for file transmission, various encoding systems have been developed to allow the transmission of complex text files and binary files within these constraints. In each of these systems, ASCII characters are used to represent non-ASCII information. The HTML markup language is an example of complex formatting codes being carried through regular seven-bit ASCII characters. The following is an example of HTML code that a Web browser will understand and use to turn the regular font ASCII text phrase "Web-Based Reference Sources" into a larger, bold font heading for a Web page: < font size = + 2 > < b > Web-Based Reference Sources < /b > < /font > < br >.

One of the more well-known mechanisms for supporting distribution of graphic, nontextual, or complex text files is MIME, the Multipurpose Internet Mail Extensions specification. MIME allows for the use of an extended set of characters and the representation of contents other than plain text. This protocol makes it possible to represent arbitrarily complex data structures based on a standardized meta-language. MIME compliance has been built into some of the major e-mail packages and Web browsers, allowing users of those packages to receive these complex files with their formatting and images intact.

Beyond HTML

As noted in the earlier discussion, HTML is a specialized form of SGML (Standard Generalized Markup Language) designed to operate over the World Wide Web. HTML uses a pre-defined set of markup tags that are incorporated into Web browsers. It is well suited to the handling and display of relatively simple documents over the Web. However, complex documents need more structure than is supported by the limited set of HTML tags. Knowing that the full-sized edition of SGML can handle even extremely complex, multi-layered documents, one might propose that the full-sized SGML set would be the solution for handling these documents in the Web environment. However, SGML cannot be used to markup or tag documents for transmission over the Web, because the standard full-featured SGML parser (the program that reads and interprets the tags) is too large to be incorporated into Web browsers.

Recognizing the need for encoding complex document structure and the limitations of even an expanded HTML set of tags, an alternative coding solution is needed. Another markup language designed to handle complex documents and other data sets over the World Wide Web is being developed. Like HTML, XML (Extensible Markup Language) is based on SGML. The "extensibility" of XML refers to the ability of users to define specialized tags as needed. However, it is important to realize that XML is not created by adding a larger set of HTML-like tags to those currently available. Instead, XML needs to be understood as a simplified form of SGML. The first XML is designed to function with a streamlined SGML parser that can be included in every Web browser. It may seem contradictory to say that XML is designed to handle extremely complex documents and yet is referred to as a simplified version of SGML. XML transcends the contradiction by creating a streamlined parser with few, if any, pre-defined tags. The definitions of the tags for each document will have to accompany it, either through scripts or through style sheets. This allows the parser to remain small while allowing it to deal with the potentially infinite variety of tags that a user can create in XML.

Although XML is not backwards compatible with HTML, HTML documents can be readily converted to XML. XML is designed to be a platform-independent, vendor-independent, and media-independent language for publishing. XML will also support the interchange of data and information between dissimilar databases. Jon Bosak describes some of the ways that an XML system could enhance client-side manipulations of data.[4] Customized displays of documents and a phone book sorted by first name instead of by last name are just two of the examples. XML is being tested as part of the Digital Libraries Initiative project at the University of Illinois at Urbana-Champaign.[5] Because XML creates the possibility of a standardized system of publishing that would support formats as dissimilar as books, printed newspapers, complex data structures, and World Wide Web documents, XML is likely to be of increasing importance in the years to come.

Future Developments

Protocols for the World Wide Web are constantly being created. The success of a protocol depends on the number of applications like Web browsers that adopt it. For example, in 1999, MP3 was developed as a new protocol for compressing digital audio files for distribution over the Web. Because it is very effective at reducing the size of audio files without a significant loss of quality, it has rapidly become a very popular Web format. Because of its popularity, small portable MP3 players for these files are being developed and sold. Although MP3 is the current emerging informal standard for compressed audio files, it is not clear at this time if MP3 will be adopted as a formal international standard. At some point, a protocol can assume the de facto status of a standard if it effectively functions as one.

Box 6.4 If You Build It, They Will Come

If you design a protocol that solves a problem more efficiently and more elegantly than previous solutions, the applications will follow.

As this discussion of file formats demonstrates, the Internet and the World Wide Web have to be learned simultaneously as medium and as message, as protocol and as content. A resource that can be imported through FTP has to be understood as resource and as format. Using TELNET to manipulate a distant resource can be understood both as local and as distant process. Digitized images or multimedia that are on the Internet can best be understood and manipulated as intrinsically part of the protocols and standards used to create and support them. The closest analogy might be a person encountering the printed word for the first time in the form of a book. Comprehending the book as simultaneously format, content, protocol, and standard would be necessary to assimilate and use it. Learning to "read" the structure of the Internet and the Web follows the same pattern.

PROLIFERATING RESOURCES

The Internet is so vast that knowing what is on it is literally impossible. It contains resources that did not exist even in the imagination ten years ago. It is a self-determining entity that is growing and developing in many directions simultaneously. Many of the millions of users are contributors to the Internet, formally through database projects, or more informally through personal Web pages, listservs (electronic discussion groups), and forums. One way to imagine this is as a gigantic supermarket bulletin board, with everyone free to contribute postings on any topic at any time. The World Wide Web proves the old axiom that there is freedom of the press for anyone who owns one. The Web has made it possible for nearly everyone to be a publisher (see Box 6.5).

Box 6.5 Everyone Is an Author

It has been said that more people write poetry than read it. Is this true of the World Wide Web as well? If true, is it a problem?

INTERNET SOLUTIONS

People seeking to understand the Internet and use it effectively have a variety of options available. Several print guides aid in the discovery of Internet and World Wide Web resources. These include the column "Internet Resources," published in each issue of *College & Research Libraries News.*[6] Each of the columns focuses on a particular subject area. There are columns in newspapers and magazines that identify sites that address consumer, health, travel, entertainment, and other information needs. However, the vast majority of such aids are contained within the Internet itself. It may seem paradoxical to turn to the Internet for help in solving Internet problems, but it can be a very effective strategy. In this section, some of the most widely available systems for navigating the Internet and Web are described.

Web search engines and Web directories are the primary ways that people discover resources on the World Wide Web. Yet, there is a nearly universal feeling of uncertainty in using them. Some of the questions that arise include: Should I start with a directory or a search engine? Which one works best for this request? Is the coverage complete? How can the search be made more effective? There are no hard-and-fast answers to any of these questions, but learning the principal mechanisms behind the search engines can help determine the proximate answers for any given question on any given day. It can also help formulate more effective search strategies. This is illustrated first by focusing on search engines.

Search Engines

What is commonly called a Web search engine is really a World Wide Web search system consisting of three major components: the crawler (or spider), the index, and the search engine itself. The *crawler* is a robot program that is sent out on the World Wide Web to discover new Web pages and explore the other Web pages at each site. The crawler brings this information back to the base. The information for each Web page (the URL, the title, words and phrases from the page, etc.) is added to the *index.* The *search engine* operates on the information contained in the index. When a search is conducted, the search engine looks through its index and identifies all the pages that "match" the search query.

If all search engines are based on these same three components, how does one explain their differences in action? This chapter discusses the differences in general. For a more thorough examination, see the Web site *Search Engine Showdown: The Users' Guide to Web Searching*, created by Greg R. Notess, which provides very useful descriptions, comparisons, and reviews of search engines.[7]

One difference in search engines lies in the number of pages at each Web site that are selected for indexing. Some Web crawlers identify only the top-level page or top- and second-level pages at each site; others follow all the URL extensions for each site. For example, although all Web crawlers would index a page with the hypothetical URL http://theuniversityofwonderful.edu, some would omit the third-level URL http://theuniversityofwonderful.edu/library/information.html page. This leads to some difficult choices for Web site developers. On the one hand, a single main URL gives all the pages a unifying identity and clearly marks all the pages, regardless of level, as belonging to the overarching organization. On the other hand, it can make most of the pages invisible to at least some search engines. If each sub-unit of the main organization has its own top-level URL, it makes more Web pages retrievable, but makes it more difficult for users of the page to recognize the internal relationships of the pages with one another and to explore the organizational hierarchy. This alternative approach would yield URLs that followed this pattern: http://home.universityofwonderful.edu, http://library.universityofwonderful.edu, http://englishdepartment.universityofwonderful.edu, and so forth.

Another difference lies in how each search engine indexes a page that the crawler identifies. Some search engines select every word from the entire Web page for their indexes. Other search engines use formulas that determine what words from which parts of the page are included in the index. For example, a search engine might select all the words from the title and the first twenty lines of the text, supplemented by the most frequent words in the entire document.

The relative position of terms and phrases within the document is an important element in determining content. A document is likely to put its primary subject in the title and the first paragraph of the document rather than the last paragraph. Terms one encounters for the first time in the last paragraph are not very likely to have received a comprehensive treatment.

Another difference among search engines is the way they determine what a Web page is about. As discussed in Chapter 5, it is a reasonable operating assumption that a document that uses a term many times is more "about" that term than one that uses it only once or twice. Some search engines count the words and phrases contained in the page and use ratio formulas to determine the most important terms. As an additional strategy to try to identify key concepts, Excite uses statistical frequency to analyze clusters of terms in relation to one another to see if meaningful patterns emerge. Other search engines look at the titles and keywords of pages that are linked to the original page to further reinforce or refine the subject of the page. A page that has the keyword *spider,* for example, and also has links to pages that have the words *spider, silk,* and *arachnids* is more likely to be about the eight-legged creatures than about Web search crawlers.

Some search engines provide another layer of structure for their indexes by identifying the field for selected terms. Typical fields that some search engines include are title, named person, URL elements, and dates associated with the page. These search engines allow the search to specify the kind of information needed to satisfy the search request. These search engines function a bit like the database search systems discussed in Chapter 5. Like those database search engines, the Web search engines require that field limits be constructed according to specific patterns to work correctly. As Ran Hock notes, some search field elements are interpreted differently by different systems.[8] The date field in particular is one which can mean any one of several dates associated with a page: date updated, date created, date indexed, and so forth. Each search engine has a link to a help screen or a guide for advanced searching that will clarify how to format a field search and provide examples of its correct use.

Search engines strive to achieve the goals of recall and precision while dealing with the millions of pages and hundreds of millions of indexing terms contained within the World Wide Web. In the context of searches, *recall* refers to the retrieval of *all* the pages that are relevant to the query, while *precision* refers to retrieving *only* the pages that are relevant to the query. The challenges to be faced by search engines in achieving these incompatible goals are substantial. One often hears the phrase "comparing apples and oranges" when describing the difficulty of comparing the relative merits of disparate objects. On the World Wide Web, this challenge can be described as "comparing apples, oranges, eagles, mountains, elephants, and petunias." Pages differ in their size, audience, design, content, and structure. They are created by earnest third-graders and eminent professors. They vary in accuracy, reliability, availability, and readability. The language each uses in its content differs from another. Like snowflakes, no two Web pages are alike. However, Web pages, unlike snowflakes, are made up of a variety of elements. A Web page may be all text or mostly images; full of sound or completely silent. A search engine combing the indexes of the World Wide Web has to develop strategies for dealing with this overwhelming diversity in ways that allow the users to take advantage of the rich resources available. All the decisions on depth of indexing, patterns, field labels, and other indexing algorithms have an impact on how each search engine achieves this goal.

To achieve recall, Web search engines use a variety of techniques. One of the principal methods is *truncation,* or *stemming.* The search words that are input are stripped of their endings and all the words in the index that match the stem are added to the retrieval results. For example, if the search query includes the term "swimmers," the search engine would stem the word and search for those terms in the index that begin with the root "swim-." Thus "swims," "swimming," "swim," and "swimmer" would all be counted as a match for the search term and be retrieved. This is just one matching rule that each search engine defines for itself. Another rule concerns capitalization of search terms. Some search engines disregard the case of the search query, and both capitalized and lowercase terms are considered a match. Other search engines are case-sensitive and include the case of the search term as an element in determining a match. In concept-based search engines, terms from the search query are processed in a similar way that one might look through a thesaurus, and a set of synonyms is searched in the index. In these systems, the list of terms to be searched is developed through statistical analysis of Web pages and thus is subject to a degree of imperfect assumptions about the exact relationship between any one term and a concept. All of these search rules and algorithms have as their aim retrieving a comprehensive set of Web pages for each search query.

To achieve precision, each Web search engine tries to ensure that the documents retrieved are focused on the search query. Relevancy scores and ranking are the two primary ways to achieve this precision. Frequency of occurrence of a term is one way of calculating relevancy. Another factor that Web engines take into account in determining relevancy is the degree to which other Web pages with the same search terms link to one another. In addition, in general, Web pages with more links to them are likely to have been found valuable by their users.

Web search engines that provide searches limited to particular fields can be effective in improving precision on search terms that might otherwise be too generic to be useful. For example, a search for the radio show "This American Life" as a basic search on Northern Light produced over three million hits. When restricted to a title search, it produced fewer than two hundred hits, and the main home page for the show is the first item retrieved. However, even this strategy is not always effective. In spite of the simple-looking interface with its little search box, each Web search engine is supremely sensitive to the formatting of search queries. Seemingly minor differences in search string construction, such as the presence or absence of quotation marks, plus signs, and spaces, can produce disproportionate differences in results. For example, in a sample search on AltaVista, when using the basic search page, the field-limited, exact phrase query, *title:"this american life"* produced thirty-four pages, while the field-limited keyword query, *title:this american life* produced over four million pages, and the plain keyword query, *this american life* produced two thousand pages. Experimentation with these and many other formulations in several search engines produces results that are sometimes difficult to understand in the context of how the search engine is expected to handle these searches.

The above example is focused on what might be called the "known item search," in which the searcher is seeking one particular page. This type of search might also be called a closed-end search. It is a search for an item that will be recognized if retrieved. The hoped-for page may or may not exist on the Web, but the search statement is constructed to find it if it exists. This type of search is common when trying to find a corporation or an organization home page, for example. When one is searching for the Folger Shakespeare Library's home page, it will be clear if one has found it or not. By contrast, the more open-ended search is one in which the user is looking for information about a topic. The searcher may have to retrieve and examine many pages and make comparisons among them to determine which best serves the information need. The search engines' indexing and retrieval decisions can have a profound effect on these searches as well. Stemming or synonym searching is likely a more helpful feature when trying to find information on a topic than when searching for a single known page. The open-ended search needs a different formulation of its search query than a closed-end search. In contrast to the tightly focused query for the known-item search, the open-ended search is likely to be more broadly constructed. It might include fairly general terms describing the topic and perhaps some synonyms for the key concept. As an example, a search for resources that discuss privacy issues on the World Wide Web will look different from a search for the privacy watchdog group, The Center for Democracy & Technology.

It is useful to realize that search engines are not working in isolation as they develop and refine their indexing and retrieval rules. With the increased importance of the World Wide Web for business and organizations, there is a dynamic interplay between search engines and the Web page designers. The search engines want to serve their users by providing the best, most relevant sites for each search. Web page designers want to assure their clients that their pages will be retrieved and displayed as many times as possible. Understanding that Web search engines look for frequency and density of keywords as part of their measures of relevancy, some Web page designers will repeat keywords and phrases many times throughout a document to assure their pages get indexed with these terms. To counteract this ploy, some Web search engines apply reduction formulas in their relevancy measures if search terms are repeated excessively. Although some search results may be affected somewhat by these competing strategies, the overall impact is relatively small.

It is important to remember that there are new Web search engines introduced and new features are added to current search engines nearly every other week. In addition, there is a growing set of metasearch sites, which simultaneously search on several search engines.

In the face of all this simultaneous choice and change, reference librarians seeking to use search engines more proficiently may need to pursue their goal through the parallel strategies of intensive and extensive searches. The intensive part of the strategy is to learn one or two search engines very well, so that the underlying logic of the indexing and retrieval system becomes clear. This quest can be facilitated by using some of the search engine tutorials available over the World Wide Web.[9] The extensive part of the strategy is to selectively explore a new search engine or metasearch site regularly. For example, one could conduct the same search on a familiar search engine and a completely new search engine. Comparing the results and the facility with which each one identified useful resources can expand and sharpen one's search skills. With this approach, one gains the ease and skills with searches that will produce efficient and effective search techniques (see Box 6.6).

Box 6.6 Flaw or Feature?

Discussions of the World Wide Web and its search engines and directories usually end up revolving around a question: Is it a flaw or is it a feature? Frequently, an aspect of a search engine, automatic stemming for example, will be a flaw for one search and a feature for another.

Web Directories

Web directories, such as Yahoo!, do not have robot Web crawlers to seek out new Web pages. Information about new or revised Web pages comes to Web directories through submission forms filled out by the Web page creators. The submission forms contain the title, URL, and the descriptions, which are processed by the directory. The Web directories use this information to classify the Web pages into the appropriate subject area within a larger subject hierarchy.

In most cases, there are Web sites listed for each level, in addition to choices for more specialized topics. This allows users of the site to click down through the categories until the right level of specificity is reached. In addition to this hierarchy browsing, Yahoo! allows users to search for specific terms within each category or to search all of Yahoo! This feature helps address one of the major challenges of hierarchical subject classifications, namely the multifaceted nature of many subjects. Tennis is both a sport and sporting equipment, so at a minimum it will appear in Yahoo! under "Recreation" and under "Business and Economy." The search results will display the different hierarchies for each term or phrase. To discover resources for each facet of the topic, the user will need to explore the topic under several headings.

Following are the Yahoo! hierarchies in which the term "meta tags" was listed:

1: Business and Economy > Companies > Internet Services > Web Services > Marketing > Promotion > Search Engine Placement Improvement >

2: Computers and Internet > Information and Documentation > Data Formats > HTML > META Tag

The two hierarchies reflect the different emphases of the concept. Meta tags are one implementation of the intellectual concept of metadata. In the first hierarchy, the business importance of meta tags for the way pages are ranked by search engines is the main focus. In the second, the focus is on the mechanics and implementation of meta tags, although the impact on search engines is also present. One consequence of the Yahoo! presentation is to bring to the user's attention some alternative perspectives for a concept. This expansion can come at the expense of speed or ease, but it can also enrich the user's understanding of a concept.

One point that is necessary to understand is that none of the Web search engines or Web directories offers 100 % coverage of the resources on the Web. At an absolute minimum, none of them will include pages that are marked "do not index" or its equivalent. Web directories will list only those sites that have submitted a form. In a study published in the July 1999 issue of *Nature,* Steve Lawrence and C. Lee Giles report that around 50 % of the World Wide Web is indexed by any of the major search engines.[10] The best search engine, Northern Light, included approximately 16 % of total estimated Web pages at the time of the study. Search engines may have changed their totals for pages indexed in the interval, but it is likely that the proportion of Web pages indexed remains substantially below the 75 % mark.

INTERNET CHALLENGES

This section describes some of the challenges for reference librarians in using the Internet and its resources for reference. Many of the challenges of the Internet can be expressed as questions: Who created the resource? How can these resources be identified and cataloged? What is the authority of the resource? How can one be sure that the resource received or used is identical to the original? What are the intellectual property rights of the resource creator? How are these rights recognized and supported? Who is eligible to use these resources? The following section identifies some solutions being developed to help librarians answer these questions.

Internet Resource Description

One of the implementations of metadata is focused on a standard description of Internet and World Wide Web resources. The Online Computer Library Center (OCLC) and the National Center for Supercomputing Applications (NCSA) have worked together to help develop a standard set of metadata elements called the Dublin Core Metadata Element Set. It is named after OCLC's home city of Dublin, Ohio, where the initial conferences took place. As it describes itself on its home page, the Dublin Core is a "simple content description model for electronic resources."[11] This cooperative effort is designed to assist in the identification, description, and retrieval of Web resources. The Dublin Core defines a set of structured elements that are intended to be used by authors to describe their Web resources. The current set of metadata elements (see Chapter 4) includes the Web resource title, creator, subject, description, publisher, contributor, date, type, format, identifier, source, language, relation, coverage, and rights. If the Dublin Core is adopted by a large number of Web resource developers, it will facilitate consistent identification and retrieval of these resources.

Metadata elements associated with Web resources form two classes of META tags. One group, META HTTP-EQUIV tags, are so called because, like regular HTTP tags, they guide the actions of the Web browser in the formatting and display of the Web resource. The other group, META NAME tags, are tags that are unrelated to the formatting and display functions. The Dublin Core is one set of META NAME tags. Search engine rules vary in their treatment of META NAME tags on Web pages. Some engines use them to index the page and its content, while others index the information contained in some META NAME tags, like a keyword tag, but ignore others. Still others ignore all META NAME tags. Because META NAME tags do not affect the display of Web resources, they can be used to provide meaningful content and description for a Web page that does not have extensive text. For example, many Web resources do not have meaningful titles. As one guide to META tags puts it, if a Web page is titled, "My World," it does not tell the search engines or directories anything about the content.[12] If the rest of the first page is equally lacking in semantic content, perhaps because it is covered with images of your world, or because it just has the first names of the members of a circle of friends, for example, there is nothing for a Web search engine to index or retrieve. A Web page developer can use META NAME tags to provide meaningful contents and description while leaving the visual design elements uncluttered by text.

Standards

The Internet and the World Wide Web provide reference librarians with the connectivity to a wide variety of electronic bibliographical resources. Many of these resources, like online catalogs and indexing and abstracting services, are supported through proprietary systems developed by vendors and suppliers. These proprietary systems require that the resources be searched using the disparate search interfaces provided by each system developer. The multiplicity of search interfaces is a barrier to efficient use of the resources. The solution to the problem is a third-party system that can interoperate with disparate systems and provide a single-user interface. This is an information retrieval standard, known in the United States as the ANSI/NISO Z39.50-1992, Information Retrieval Service and Protocol, internationally as the ISO 23950, and informally as Z39.50.

The Z39.50 standard provides a client-server electronic information system design "blueprint." Information system and database developers are using this blueprint to design their systems in ways that make it possible for users of one system to access databases in another system using one set of commands, without regard to the hardware or software of the host system. Each system or database can be designed with its own unique features and search functions and search interface, but each of these is mapped to a corresponding Z39.50 element. Because Z39.50 includes the information needed to program an encoder/decoder for translating commands from one system to another, it provides a translating function that allows one system to correctly interoperate with another. When each uses Z39.50, it allows users of each of these OPACs to maximize the search options supported by the other and creates the largest possible common ground. It also provides for the translation of the incoming record(s) to a standard format that will be readily understood by the user. Although Z39.50 maximizes the common ground between dissimilar or different systems, it cannot supply the missing pieces from either. An option has to exist in both systems to be available through the Z39.50 interface. For example, if one OPAC supports adjacency searching, and another does not, the option to do adjacency searching will not be offered through the Z39.50 interface.

Z39.50 shows the promise and the limitations of interoperability. It is a big advance in the move toward mutual intelligibility of disparate systems. However, as with any translating device, Z39.50 cannot be truly idiomatic. Each system has variations in the search engine and in the specific search choices in system design and implementation. It is important that reference librarians understand that variations in indexing and retrieval decisions will have real impacts on the search results. This is a particularly subtle and important area of user education as well. As Sylvia Carson and Dace Freivalds note from their experience at Pennsylvania State University, "the perception that indexing and retrieval is the same across all servers will be one of the thorniest issues trainers will face. They will need to familiarize themselves with the indexing and retrieval conventions of the other database so that they can interpret the search results for users and have ready answers for the question 'But I can do this on LIAS—why not here?'."[13] Because Z39.50 can provide a familiar "look and feel" to a variety of resources, highlighting this distinction for the users will be a formidable challenge indeed.

Within the TELNET-based electronic information sphere, there are efforts at standardization or consistency as well. One example is ANSI/NISO Z39.58—Common Command Language for Online Interactive Information Retrieval. It defines nineteen terms used in command-line search systems. There is reason to believe that the next generation of search software will likely have full recognition of the Common Command Language built in, so that the individual searcher can use it to search in any environment. The translating aspect of the program will result in all supported commands being executed appropriately by the system. This built-in translation will be done behind the screen and the user will not be aware that the terms and commands being input are in need of translation. In this way, the command "DISPLAY" will be understood in all the systems as a command to show the record. Currently, there are many terms for this activity—TYPE, SHOW, ..P, D, and PRINT among others—across the search systems. If Z39.58 is built into the system, each of these commands will be translated into DISPLAY. There is still the remaining challenge of some search and/or display functions being available in one system and not in another. Some companies build recognition of alternate commands into their software, so that, even in the absence of the Common Command Language, one can use the same language across multiple systems. Standardization of the commands will assist end-users and reference librarians by reducing the cross-system-interference and learning curve of multiple system use. There is growing recognition on the part of the information industry that standardization of terminology and command structure can lead to increased user satisfaction.

It is highly likely that standardization of terminology or formats or, more likely, mutual recognition of variants of terminology and resource formats will become more widespread in the years ahead. The World Wide Web has provided both the means and the necessity for this standardization. These standards and associated protocols will foster the development of compatible information resources and the integration of information from disparate sources. The reference librarian will be able to master the standard formats and standard retrieval languages and be in a position to navigate the networks with expectations of success.

Technological Ripples

With each new shift and development in information technology, reference librarians face another challenge, the challenge of innovation. Each new technology provides solutions that previous technologies did not or could not provide. Each new technology also brings its own set of problems seeking resolution, although these may be hidden from view. No doubt, the typewriter instituted a substantial change in the way many tasks were accomplished at the time of its adoption throughout libraries. It was the first step in providing full catalog information at each access point. In earlier times, due in part to the laborious nature of writing catalog cards with pen and ink, full information was provided only at the main entry card, and brief information at all other access points. Because of the higher transcription speeds possible with the typewriter, labor-saving policies of this kind became less necessary. The benefit of this technology for reference was substantial. Consistently formatted cards with more information at each access point saved the time and energy of reference librarians with every use of the catalog. These benefits had to be weighed against the costs of adopting the new technology. The costs of adoption included the expense of acquiring the typewriters, but also included training costs and maintenance costs. There were policy issues as well. Although each member of the library staff was likely to be able to write on catalog cards, it is likely that not all of them would be able to have a typewriter.

The problems the technology presented are somewhat less apparent. Each user of the typewriter had to be trained to be proficient with the machine. In the beginning, layouts of the keyboard were not standard. The QWERTY keyboard became standard, neither because of its "user friendliness" nor its "human-factors design" but because it reduced the jamming of the mechanical keys. The QWERTY keyboard shows some of the long-term consequences of standard development. The standard can long outlive its origins in necessity and can, in some cases, actively slow the pace of development. If the typewriter had been invented in an English-speaking country after the invention of the transistor, for example, its keyboard would likely be standardized according to the frequency of use of letters in the English language. Typographical errors would likely be much less frequent in this case, and the average speed of typing would likely be much higher, as well.

Technical innovations create policy issues as well. Each library had to weigh the cost and benefit factors about typewriters and determine the best distribution. Typewriters were relatively expensive machines. How few could be purchased and still gain the advantage of the technology? As in any early innovation, not every manufacturer survived. Thus, some libraries had a variety of typewriters for which there were no longer parts or service available. These are some of the costs of adoption of new technologies.

In any environment, there will be early technology adopters, who usually pay substantial premiums in terms of human resources to learn and manage new technologies. The expectation is that these costs will be recovered in the advantages offered by the change. Often this strategy pays off, but in other situations, the investment has to be written off as a learning experience.

There are costs associated with late adoption of new technologies as well. Staff time and energy have to be expended to keep the old system functional. Technical support becomes more difficult to find as those with expertise in the old system move on. There are the costs of being out-of-step with the rest of the library systems. Cooperative arrangements are more difficult, expensive, or just impossible because of the incompatibility of the old technology with the new. Effective management of technology requires a careful balance between the costs of adoption and the costs of non-adoption. It is likely that the organization's experience with previous generations of technology will shape the corporate culture in this regard. One position may be described by the old saying, "Once burned, twice shy," which suggests caution and delay as important elements in the technology adoption policy. On the other hand, as Mark Twain noted, "We should be careful to get out of an experience only the wisdom that is in it—and stop there; lest we be like the cat that sits down on a hot stove lid. She will never sit down on a hot stove lid again—and that is well; but also she will never sit down on a cold one any more."[14] This suggests that adoption assessment needs to focus on the particular strengths, weaknesses, costs, and benefits of each opportunity rather than the number of months since first deployment. There are lessons that can be learned too well.

Orphan Technologies

One of the continuing challenges of electronic resources is that technological innovation often leads to technological obsolescence. Most technological innovations have one of two relationships with the previous generation of hardware and software. The relationship can be one of backward compatibility, in which the new technology accommodates the old. As one example, newer CD-ROM drives usually play CD-ROMs compiled under older standards. This is largely a result of the size and importance of the installed base of the older technology. It would take a brave standard to render millions upon millions of CD-Audio and CD-ROM discs obsolete. It is likely to happen someday, but not yet. One complication of backward compatibility is the likelihood that the newer technology is unable to be as innovative, efficient, or radical as it could be. It represents a compromise between the possible and the achievable.

With many technologies, the relationship is succession, in which the new technology supersedes the older technology and leaves it behind. This is the result when the projected improvements cannot be achieved within the framework of the old. For example, the larger capacity of the 3.5-inch disks depends on a change in the way data are written and read that is incompatible with the old 5.25-inch floppy disks. Therefore, the newer disks superseded the old and produced a large number of old diskettes that cannot be read on any current computer. At the time of the introduction of the smaller diskette size, most computers came with two disk drives, one for each size. Those users who had stored important data on the larger floppies had to migrate their data to the new format while the equipment supporting the old format was available. Not everyone took advantage of this migration window. Consequently, there are offices and desk drawers throughout the land that have floppies which are for all practical purposes unusable. There may be large computer labs and specialized data recovery companies that can transfer the content to a more modern format, but this is an undertaking that most users do not pursue. The floppy diskette is just one more step in a long line of orphan technologies, ranging from the original 80-column punch cards to computer tapes of various outmoded sizes, as well as a variety of other computer disk sizes. It is likely that some of the more capacious portable storage media, including re-writeable CDs, will supersede the current 3.5-inch diskette as well.

A topic related to orphan technology is electronic archiving. At this time, *electronic archiving* is essentially an oxymoron. As the examples above show, just because data continue to exist in a physical sense on an uncorrupted disk or a perfectly preserved CD-ROM does not mean that the data have been archived. If the data exist on only one medium, and if the last machine to read that particular format has broken beyond repair, the existence of the physical medium does not equal preservation. At this time, preservation of electronic content consists of a series of migrations from medium to medium. This requires a serious commitment of resources to set up a regular review and updating of all the electronic formats held in a collection. Decisions about what to keep will vary with the library's mission.

When it comes to content that is on the World Wide Web, archiving becomes even more problematic. To begin with, archiving has two different meanings within the context of the Web. One meaning refers to making the collected communications of a listserv or other discussion group available as a searchable file. One such archive is the Liblicense-L archive at Yale (http://www.library.yale.edu/~llicense/ListArchives/). One can go to the archive and search on a topic related to the licensing of electronic resources by libraries. It will list the items that contain that term and provide a list of threaded discussions. This type of Web archive is straightforward. It requires an investment of time and equipment to maintain, but each message is a self-defined, self-contained unit. A message may refer to previous messages, often by incorporation, but is itself the unit of analysis.

As more and more of the world's cultural and intellectual content migrates to the World Wide Web, there is concern about the impermanence of the record. This issue is the focus of the other kind of archiving of Web content. Some of the issues associated with this broader aspect of archiving of the Web are discussed by Peter Lyman and Brewster Kahle.[15]

Some organizations do a periodic preservation of their Web sites, as a "snapshot." A copy is made and saved of all the current pages of a site. One fundamental issue that confronts the library wishing to archive the content of its Web site is defining what is meant by a Web page. Most Web pages contain links to other pages. Some of these linked Web pages contain a substantial portion of the content of the linking page. However, retrieving these related pages and including them in any preservation process is beyond the scope of these Web site projects. Even if it were technically possible, intellectual property rights issues would greatly impede the inclusion of these linked pages. In any case, because of the tremendously dynamic nature of the Web, any decision concerning a linked page is subject to a de facto veto by changes in the linked page itself. The life span of Web pages can be measured in days or weeks. Although many of these pages might be considered ephemeral in the sense of referring to occasions that have come and gone, the occasion may be worth remembering as part of our shared cultural experience (see Box 6.7). Some of what we know about William Shakespeare is from the preserved playbills and other ephemera. If a new play by a novice playwright is produced by a small theater company, but the only record of this is on the Web, what will the future know of it?

Box 6.7 Preservation and the World Wide Web

The digital library has been described as a library without walls. Stuart Weibel noted that, "It has no walls. Unfortunately, the roof is gone, too."[16]

Is Weibel correct? If so, what are some of the consequences for preservation?

During this period of transition from mostly paper to mostly digital publication, some issues of identity are emerging. In the recent past, it has been possible to refer to a journal or a reference book and have an expectation that all users of the journal or reference book will have the same experience with items of identical content. The title, *Statistical Abstract of the United States,* for example, has existed in paper for over one hundred years. A user of the 1978 volume in Namibia will see the same pages as a user in Virginia. The same is true for such standard reference titles as *Contemporary Authors.* However, as these titles migrate to the World Wide Web, the constancy of their content and the ability to reliably predict the information that will be found at the Web site is no longer a certainty. Some journals have a print version and an electronic version that differ substantially from one another. The electronic version has no page limits, perhaps, or allows for a fuller presentation of the statistical analysis of the data. The electronic version may contain links to the full text of the cited articles. It is reasonable to ask the question, which is the REAL journal? It is also reasonable to ask about the preservation of the full content of both versions. It is likely that major research libraries will maintain a copy of the print version for as long as it is published. It is likely that the major publishers of journals will keep copies of the electronic versions as well. Mechanisms for maintaining permanent access to the preserved copies are still being developed. OCLC Electronic Collections Online has committed the considerable resources of OCLC to permanently preserving content and access to the electronic journals in its collection. Other organizations such as JSTOR are committed to developing a permanent collection of digitized journals. All of these efforts are commendable and will result in the preservation of a significant number of the published electronic journals and electronic versions of journals. An article by Brunelle offers a fuller discussion of the current models of preservation.[17] There are still concerns about the material that is less mainstream. Which organizations have sufficient resources to spend on developing and maintaining permanent access to the smaller, experimental, and short-lived journals and other publications on the World Wide Web?

PUBLIC INFORMATION RESOURCES AND THE REFERENCE LIBRARIAN

The consequences for reference librarians of the growth of the personal delivery of information services are hard to determine. People have always had alternative sources of information on any topic. Typically, the primary source is the circle of family and friends. Local and national news sources are likely the second most important information source. Perhaps now many people depend on the news preferences they have configured for their World Wide Web portal. Where libraries and reference departments fit into the strategy depends on the education and experience of the person seeking the information. Will the wiring of the world's living rooms change the fundamental nature of reference work, or will it change it only on the margins? As reference librarians expand the scope of their resources and services, will they also expand the audience? Will there be a twenty-four-hour TV librarian on Channel 411? Will the person at home punch in a question and the answer appear as an e-mail message on the person's own Channel One? Or will the inquirer turn on the interactive camera on the television set and ask the librarian a question live and get a personal video reply? These are some possible roles for reference librarians.

One can envision other roles for reference librarians in the digital information industry. Some are relatively easy to identify, if hard to create, such as the need to reach and teach the remote user of the library's resources. Others are more elusive, such as imagining and creating the new role of the library in the planning and implementation of these technologies, nationally and locally.

THE FUTURE OF REFERENCE TECHNOLOGY

One aspect of technological innovation is the fact that the people who interact with the new technology have a mental framework shaped by their previous experience. The ways in which we think about the new are shaped by the old. It takes some maturing of technology before we can start to think about it in entirely new ways. The initial implementation of NCSA's Mosaic Web browser was shaped at least in part by the developers' experiences with Gopher, Archie, and Veronica. An experienced reference librarian initially approached the World Wide Web from the perspective of a skilled command-line searcher. The two technologies share a common base of electronic information with associated retrieval software. However, the Boolean approach is not an ideal match for searching millions of pages of full-text resources, and orderly sets are not the likely outcome of a Web search. With an examination of the Web on its own terms as a reference resource, reference librarians have adopted new strategies and new skills.

The growing body of electronic texts and multimedia resources available over the Internet and the Web requires a fresh look at how information is organized and retrieved. An examination of how users find and utilize information may lead to the conclusion that the traditional lines that are drawn between different types of materials are not understood by users. For example, do the boundaries drawn between journal articles and books reflect useful distinctions about intellectual activities, or do they reflect the traditional methods of material production and distribution? If a growing understanding of users' needs reveals it to be a distinction that hinders access and use, it is likely that an integrated system of access to all forms of library resources will be developed. Z39.50 is just one mechanism that can be implemented to provide a single, unified interface to a wide variety of information resources.

This example can serve as a model for the re-examination and re-imagining of other reference tools and systems and how they serve their users. Reference librarians have a vital role to play in designing and conducting the research that will inform the new system designs and in interacting with system developers to ensure that the needed functionalities are built-in from the start. These re-designed information systems will provide reference librarians with the real tools needed to answer the question, "May I help you?"

NOTES

1. *Internet Domain Survey, January 2000.* Available: http://www.isc.org/ds/WWW-200001/report.html.

2. Hal P. Kirkwood, Jr., "Internet Surveys, Statistics, and Geography," *Online* 23 (September-October 1999): 90.

3. Balachander Krishnamurthy, Jeffrey C. Mogul, and David M. Kristol, "Key Differences Between HTTP/1.0 and HTTP/1.1," *Computer Networks* 31 (1999): 1737-51.

4. Jon Bosak, *XML, Java, and the Future of the Web* (March 10, 1997). Available: http://metalab.unc.edu/pub/sun-info/standards/xml/why/xmlapps.htm.

5. *Digital Libraries Initiative.* Available: http://dli.grainger.uiuc.edu/.

6. *College & Research Libraries News* (Chicago: Association of College and Research Libraries).

7. Greg R. Notess, *Search Engine Showdown: The Users' Guide to Web Searching.* Available: http://www.searchengineshowdown.com/.

8. Ran Hock, "How to Do Field Searching in Web Search Engines: A Field Trip," *Online* 22 (May/June 1998): 18-22.

9. Angela Elkordy, *Web Searching, Sleuthing, and Sifting.* Available: http:// www.thelearningsite.net/ cyberlibrarian/searching/ismain.html; Debbie Flanagan, *Web Search Strategies.* Available: http://home. sprintmail.com/ ~ debflanagan/main.html; Linda Barlow, *The Spider's Apprentice: A Helpful Guide to Web Search Engines.* Available: http://www.monash.com/spidap.html.

10. Steve Lawrence and C. Lee Giles, "Accessibility of Information on the Web," *Nature* 400 (July 8, 1999): 107-9.

11. *Dublin Core Metadata Initiative.* Available: http://purl.oclc.org/dc/index.htm.

12. *How to Use HTML Meta Tags.* Available: http://searchenginewatch.internet.com/webmasters/meta. html.

13. Sylvia MacKinnon Carson and Dace I. Freivalds, "Z39.50 and LIAS: Penn State's Experience," *Information Technology & Libraries* 12 (June 1993): 236.

14. John Bartlett, *Familiar Quotations,* 14th ed. (Boston: Little, Brown, 1968), 762.

15. Peter Lyman and Brewster Kahle, "Archiving Digital Cultural Artifacts: Organizing an Agenda for Action," *D-Lib Magazine* 4 (July/August 1998). Available: http://www.dlib.org/dlib/july98/07lyman. html.

16. Stuart Weibel, *Mending Our Net: Gathering, Describing, and Preserving Information in the Digital World* (May 1996). Available: http://www5conf.inria.fr/fich_html/slides/invited/IS1/all.htm.

17. B. Brunelle, "Models for Electronic Full Text: Choices and Challenges," in *Online Information 98, Proceedings of the 22nd International Online Information Meeting*, London, 8-10 December 1998 (Oxford: Learned Information Europe, 1998), 249-52.

ADDITIONAL READINGS

Conner, Kiersten. *The Whole Internet: The Next Generation.* 1st ed. Cambridge, Mass.: O'Reilly, 1999. 542p.

This revision of Ed Krol's classic, *The Whole Internet User's Guide & Catalog,* maintains the focus on the user. It provides an understanding of the tools needed to make the World Wide Web and the Internet work for the user. It also shows some of the less-well-known Web developments, like push technologies.

Current Cites: An Annotated Bibliography of Selected Articles, Books, and Digital Documents on Information Technology. Edited by Teri Andrews Rinne. Available: http://sunsite.berkeley.edu/ CurrentCites.

This is a current awareness service offered by a team of librarians and library staff. The editors select articles, reports, and some monographs, print and electronic, on a wide range of topics under the broad umbrella of electronic information technology. They add clear, evaluative, and helpful annotations and distribute the list monthly to subscribers. There is an accessible archive of the database from January 1994 to the present that offers dynamically created bibliographies on demand.

Hock, Randolph. *The Extreme Searcher's Guide to Web Search Engines: A Handbook for the Serious Searcher.* Medford, N.J.: CyberAge Books, 1999. 212p.

Hock presents a current description of the capabilities and limitations of Web search engines. It offers a general discussion of common search engine functions and then provides a chapter for each major search engine. The chapters reveal some of the less-obvious search and ranking algorithms at play. The systematic analysis gives a clear understanding of how things really work on the Web.

Miller, Paul. "Z39.50 for All," *Ariadne* 21 (September 1999). Available: http://www.ariadne.ac.uk/ issue21/z3950.

This article is an excellent introduction to Z39.50. It draws together the concepts and implementation of Z39.50 in libraries and in other environments. The examples are well selected and clear. A comprehensive list of references to the active participants in the development of Z39.50 is included.

Online. Special Search Engine Section. 23 (May/June 1999): 20-86.

This special issue featuring search engines brings together articles from the experts on Web search engines. Articles on search engine technology, search features, and search results ranking provide insights into the current search engine capabilities, while the articles on natural language searching and on metasearch engines look ahead to future developments.

Preserving Digital Information. Report of the Task Force on Archiving of Digital Information. Commissioned by The Commission on Preservation and Access and The Research Libraries Group. Washington, D.C.: Commission on Preservation and Access, 1996. 62p. Also available: http://www.rlg.org/ArchTF.

This report presents the history, issues, and challenges of creating a comprehensive archive of the cultural heritage represented in digital form. It identifies the essential elements of a preservation undertaking and highlights some current digital projects.

CHAPTER

7

ACCESS-RELATED REFERENCE SERVICES

Lynn Wiley

INTRODUCTION: AFTER THE SEARCH

A library user approaches the reference desk to say: "Thanks for your help earlier when I was looking for book titles and journal articles, but now I need advice on where to get them. I've checked the catalog and the shelves and they're just not available here."

Reference personnel find facts or information sources and teach information retrieval skills to the library user. Bibliographic searching and verification are critical reference services. With this help, users can identify those titles covering their topic or learn to use the tools to help them select citations for items that will fulfill their particular research need. But what about that next step—actually getting the materials? Reference librarians can open doors to the world of information, but does the local public library have the title required? Or is it in an academic institution down the road or in a major research library 50 miles away? If another library owns the title, will that institution loan or copy it? When and where will it be delivered, and at what cost? Librarians know that a large gap exists between the identification of a title and actually obtaining it. Getting it elsewhere is an option, but often involves a lengthy process including a referral to yet another service desk. In today's world, the expectations for fast access to any identified item are high. Can libraries meet the challenge?

This chapter is devoted to the issues surrounding access to materials—all formats of items—and how libraries are striving to obtain these for their users. Reference librarians need to know how interlibrary loan and document delivery services work. They must understand the range of alternatives to help select the best options to achieve success in providing these services. Finally, their expertise in both building better access services and teaching library users how to take advantage of access programs is critical in ensuring that libraries will bridge the gaps in their collections.

Access Needed: Now More Than Ever

The need for better access to library material is high, particularly for the substantial population of users choosing to access the library remotely, from home or office (see Box 7.1, page 150).

Box 7.1 Service Expectations

Consider these scenarios:

With more users tapping into services remotely, the demand for new services is increasing. Users want one easy search-and-order online interface to cover all their information needs. Ideally, they want it all available as full text online or, if not, then direct delivery. "I don't need to come in to place an order, why do I need to come all the way in to pick the volume up?"

How about the student taking classes through a distance education program? The home institution's library facilities are 100 miles away. How can this user's library material needs be met? Is the user allowed to use material available at local libraries? Will interlibrary loan staff order and deliver material? What about items in the local collection—who is responsible for handling these materials and making sure the student has good access to required material?

No single library in recent times has been able to serve all its readers' needs. Other library collections are constantly tapped to fill user requests. Libraries have utilized interlibrary loan (ILL) for years with as simple a mechanism as a letter introducing a scholar or requesting a book be lent for a brief time for a reader's use. *Document delivery*, defined here as that aspect of ILL services that obtains a copy of an article, report, or chapter, has been available on a large scale since the advent of photocopiers. Interlibrary loan and document delivery requests have grown exponentially in the past few decades. Libraries have turned to this kind of access to fill the needs of their users and do so at an ever-accelerating rate. The Association of Research Libraries (ARL) statistics graphically illustrate the tremendous growth of ILL requests in just ten years (see Figure 7.1). The use of ILL reflects the growing need for access to a wider group of collections. Although the ARL borrowing statistics cover only the major research libraries, libraries of all types are relying heavily on interlibrary loan.

Many factors contribute to this increased reliance on other collections. More materials are being published than ever before, and they are harder to identify and acquire. Titles are missed, often going out of print before being noticed by many libraries. Library budgets are overextended in meeting new technological challenges, leaving less money to acquire and process materials. Budgets were stagnant during times of high inflation and low dollar values and have not recovered in the economic boom years. Serial prices have increased exorbitantly, resulting in subscription cancellations while also eroding monograph budgets. Space is at a premium, and libraries cannot expand to meet the shelving demands of a larger collection. Libraries today are spending more to keep less. It is clear that there is not enough money in *any* library's budget to collect at the rate now required.[1]

At the same time, libraries have been very successful in networking online catalogs and bibliographic databases that users can access from home or office, often after regular library hours. As a result, users are finding more information sources than their local libraries can immediately supply online. Full-text options do not yet offer any large-scale relief. They can be very expensive and may require paper subscriptions, which increases the costs. Moreover, they may have restrictions embedded in licensing agreements that prohibit sharing among libraries. Heavily requested materials or unique and rare titles may be digitized, but the moderately used and older back files of titles may not. Analyses of interlibrary serial article requests such as those by Chandra Prabha and Elizabeth Marsh[2] and Eve-Marie LaCroix [3] have revealed that a large percentage of requests are for articles from a single title. Frequently requested titles can be imagined as a comet and those with fewer requests as the tail, which becomes thin but very long, stretching far behind the comet itself. This very large list of low-use titles may not be available in full text soon. The need for widely diverse collections is even more apparent with monographs. Greg Byerly's 1996 report on OhioLINK[4] reveals how little overlap there is for monographs in Ohio academic libraries' collections, reaffirming a classic study on collection overlap done by William Potter in 1986.[5] Users need access to a wide variety of materials. Who has these titles and who will maintain access to them in the future?

Figure 7.1 Supply and demand in ARL libraries, 1986–1999. Source: *ARL Statistics 1997-98*, Association of Research Libraries, Washington, DC, p. 12.

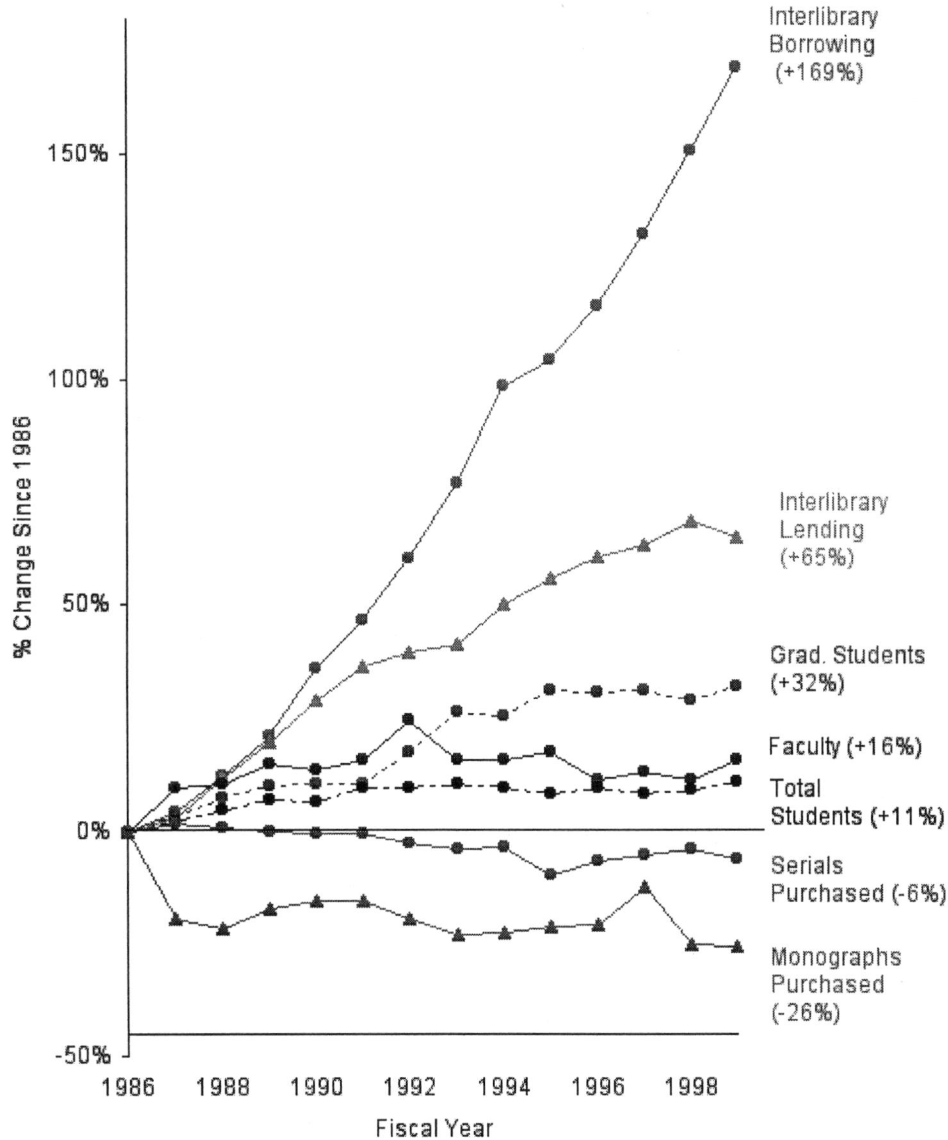

http://www.arl.org/stats/arlstat/1999t3.html.

LIBRARY RESPONSES

Interlibrary Loan

One must understand the basic process and also the history and development of ILL to better understand how it is evolving. At one time, gaining access to other library collections was a privilege only scholars had. They were likely to be familiar with the literature of their discipline and knew the titles required as a result of much research. They were often the only ones who knew where a title might be located, based on correspondence with their colleagues at institutions around the world. With the advent of national bibliographies, librarians were able to find locations more readily, but ILL was still a limited service. A combination of factors began to change that, beginning with the demand for more education and the parallel growth of research materials. Interlibrary loan processes became more formalized, with standardized request forms. These forms were completed on paper, with multiple copies for the home library, lending institutions, and requester. They required laborious filing and tracking and are still used today. The evolution of the National Interlibrary Loan Codes in the twentieth century reveals how interlibrary loan service perceptions have changed in the library community. Once seen as a privilege for the elite few, it became a formalized library process but still with restricted access. Borrowing library responsibilities were emphasized and lending guidelines encouraged. The last approved code includes language that clearly views interlibrary loan as an integral part of a full-access program and reminds lenders of their responsibilities. This code is even now under revision and will continue to emphasize how to address users' need to obtain material unavailable in their local collections.[6]

From an outsider's perspective, ILL seems to be production based: Get an order and fill it. It is not like retail ordering from a mail-order catalog, however. There is no central supply source, no one comprehensive database of products described, and no indication of whether the "stock" is available. Ordering options are many, although an order may not result in delivery. Supplier fees vary, and the means and expected time of delivery are unpredictable or unknown. The steps seem straightforward, but because requests can cover any format from any time period, the work involved in verifying a citation and locating supplying sources can be extensive. The whole process is labor-intensive, resulting in substantial costs. The ILL/DD Performance Measures Study, conducted by the ARL, yielded baseline average indicators of cost, turnaround time, fill rates, and user satisfaction:

> [O]n average, a research library spends $18.35 to obtain an item for a local patron. A borrowing request takes on average 16 calendar days to be filled, and the borrowing fill rate is 85%. The patrons who used ILL during a six-week sampling period were overall very satisfied with ILL services. . . . On average, a research library spends $9.48 to fill a lending request from another library, and has a 58% fill rate as a lender. Therefore, assuming that both the borrower and lender are research libraries, the average cost for a completed ILL transaction in 1996 was $27.83.[7]

ARL further examined the top performers in borrowing and lending activities to determine some best practices demonstrated by these institutions. Based on these practices, ARL has designed and is now offering workshops for ILL practitioners designed to help them improve their local practices. More information is available on the Web at the ARL access page (http://www.arl.org/access/index.shtml). Other ILL practitioners have shared their knowledge with their colleagues. Virginia Boucher's *Interlibrary Loan Practices Handbook* (see "Additional Readings") does a superb job in identifying all the tools and processes required for a successful ILL operation.

The basic ILL cycle is illustrated in Figure 7.2. The cycle can be described as covering three areas: The part where the user identifies a title and submits a request is the first or "Front" end. In the second or "Middle" process, the ILL order is submitted to a supplier and the request is tracked for fulfillment. The third, "End," step includes the procedures to receive and process the material for the user.

Figure 7.2 ILL cycle.

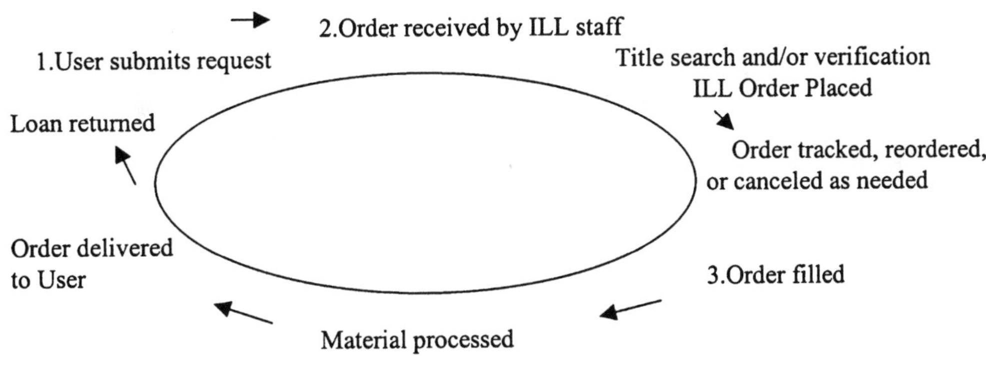

The basic cycle of ILL processes described above does have variations based on the services libraries have implemented. ILL order mechanisms are being set up on the library catalog, on Web pages, or via an online index Web link. In some cases users place their own orders, which may go directly to a lender. Material may be delivered directly to the user, or the processing is integrated with the local automated system, making receipt simple and allowing for quick handling.

In an ideal ILL world, all material would be accessible and options customized to fit the user's needs. One such scenario has been used effectively to raise the bar for better ILL services[8] (see Box 7.2).

Box 7.2 An ILL Vision

A researcher logs into his or her network and simultaneously searches several catalogs and indexes. Scanning the results, several are marked for ordering. Local resources are searched automatically and the researcher sees what is owned and available for delivery. Links to additional sources appear for the other titles, prompting the researcher to select the most appropriate order option. Some articles are ordered from a commercial supplier for a fee, others are routed to a library service to be copied and delivered back as full text. Books are requested from partner libraries with pick up or delivery option specified. Minutes later, the researcher signs off, secure in the knowledge that the material will soon be on its way. The system has identified the user, refers to a profile of delivery preferences, and records the transactions in a log for future reference. The user can log in and track the progress, allowing for better information about and therefore control of the research process.

Figure 7.3, pages 154-55, shows an example of an online request form library users may call up and fill out anytime from any workstation with a Web browser: The forms are downloaded daily and the materials are ordered by ILL staff.

Figure 7.3 Example of a Web-based online ILL order form.

Information Resource Retrieval Center	**REQUEST FORM - LIBRARY USER INFORMATION** Please fill out the form below completely. Photocopies may be mailed to the address you provide if they are not delivered electronically. Be sure to check for a valid campus or home address to ensure delivery. The phone number and e-mail may be used to contact you if there is a question about your request.

Name:	Last, First, M.I.:
Delivery & Contact Address:	Street Address: City, State, Zip:
Phone:	
E-Mail Address:	
Department:	
Status:	
Your ID's 14-digit barcode:	(Hint: it begins with 2011)

Select the **Request Photocopy** button for journal articles, book chapters, patents, and standards.
Select the **Request Loan** button for books, microforms, videos, dissertations, and theses.

Request Photocopy | Request Loan | Reset This Form

Information Resource Retrieval Center	**REQUEST FORM - LOAN INFORMATION** This form can be used to order books, dissertations, and audio-visual materials. Loans are items that the patron can borrow, but they are returned to the owning institution after a 21 day circulation period. Fields that have an asterisk* beside them are required. If you don't know the information, type the word "unknown" in the field and we will do our best to locate your material without the complete citation. Be sure to press the submit button when you are finished.

***Author:**	Last, First, M.I.:
***Title:**	
Publication Information:	Publisher/Place of Publication: *Date of Publication / Edition:
Source of Citation:	
Notes:	
***Need By Date:**	This must be a date (mm/dd/yy).

Submit Loan Request | Reset This Form

Information Resource Retrieval Center	**REQUEST FORM - PHOTOCOPY INFORMATION** Please read through the copyright restrictions and click in the checkbox to indicate that you accept them. Fields in the request form that have an asterisk* beside them are required information. If the information is unknown, type the word "unknown" so the request will be accepted. We will do our best to locate the material without the complete citation. Don't forget to press the submit button when you are finished.

Warning Concerning Copyright Restrictions

The Copyright Law of the United States (Title 17, United States Code) governs the making of photocopies or other reproductions of copyrighted material. Under certain conditions specified in the law, libraries and archives are authorized to furnish a photocopy or other reproduction. One of these specified conditions is that the photocopy or reproduction not be "used for any purposes other than private study, scholarship, or research." If a user makes a request for, or later uses, a photocopy or reproduction for purposes in excess of "fair use," that user may be liable for copyright infringement.

☐ **CLICK in the box to indicate that you understand and accept the Copyright restrictions as outlined above.**

***Journal Title:**	
***Article Author(s):**	Last, First, M.I.:
***Article Title:**	
Publication Information:	*Volume *Issue *Date *Pages Publisher/Place of Publication:
Patent Number or Standard:	Number:
Source of Citation:	
Notes:	
***Need By Date:**	This must be a date (mm/dd/yy).

[Submit Photocopy Request] [Reset This Form]

IRRC Home | University Library | University of Illinois at Urbana-Champaign

Email comments to: IRRC
10/08/2000 clw

Problems and Issues in Interlibrary Loan

Shirley Baker and Mary Jackson describe problems with ILL in their ARL White Paper on access, published in 1992.[9] They also outline possible directions in which to move. Their work inspired the creation of the ARL North American Interlibrary Loan Document Delivery program (NAILDD). NAILDD was established in 1993 to help develop new systems and services to deal with the problems evident in handling the increasingly larger volume of interlibrary loan activity. The project work centered on three major areas: management software for tracking requests, accounting/financial tracking, and standards for better communication and interoperability between systems. If ILL services were speedier, more successful, and easier to do, then a more complete resource-sharing program might be possible. Some of the NAILDD success stories are mentioned in this chapter, but the work is ongoing today. Libraries are finding some interim and long-term solutions to problems, such as those outlined in Box 7.3, while vendors, including the utilities, are responding to the demand for better ILL access.

Box 7.3 Examples of Typical ILL Problems

A loan is submitted to a potential supplier but no response is given; the order must be resubmitted, sometimes several times before a lender sends the title or a reason for non-supply is identified.

A borrowing library wishing to avoid sending to a charging supplier tries all free sources before finally sending to a lender who does supply for a fee. Now the request has taken much longer to fill.

Article requests are supplied with missing or illegible pages.

Loans are shipped but never received due to improper addresses, errors in packaging or processing on the lender side, receiving problems at the borrowing library, and mail carrier problems.

A library user wants to check on the status of requests and can only do that in person.

The good news is that the same technology that has opened up a host of resources for library users may also be harnessed to provide a better means to obtain requested items. The tools used in ILL to verify a title, find locations and holdings, and then place an order have become easier to access and use. This has been true for ILL office staff and can be for other library staff and library users. Better interfaces are being built using Web technology so users are guided more effectively to sources and choices. Library automation vendors and the bibliographic utilities are developing ways to allow for more effective ILL processes. The utilities have been more successful in some innovations. Few integrated system vendors have working products that can handle the entire ILL cycle from order to delivery without requiring libraries to share systems. Many are at least now including a search and order utility allowing users to do this themselves.

Resource Sharing

Resource sharing seems an obvious solution for libraries, to share the responsibility for acquiring needed information and then to share the actual material. Indeed, libraries have been poised for a full resource-sharing program since the creation of print union catalogs (see Chapter 20). The reality is different because libraries are accountable to their school, university, company, hospital, or community and are reluctant to cut core titles because a guarantee of physical access to materials found elsewhere may be difficult to ensure. Today's networked environment with easily accessible distributed systems makes it harder to define what a local core collection really is. Libraries can design online systems that provide easy remote access and allow the user to link to any number of information sources. Should it matter where something is located if a user can easily link to a resource? It does when physical access is demanded. Library managers look to ILL to supplement their collections, but they want better guarantees and consistent service. The lack of reliability, the labor-intensive nature of the work, and the length of time a transaction takes are all drawbacks. Increases in ILL mean that ILL offices are hard pressed to keep up, even with new technology available to streamline processes. ILL staff is left identifying with Alice's predicament in the *Through the Looking Glass* (see Box 7.4).

Box 7.4 Running in Place

Alice: "Why I do believe we've been under this tree all the time! Everything is just as it was!" The Red Queen replies "Of course" and Alice remarks that "Well, in our country, you'd generally get somewhere else, if you ran very fast for a long time as we've been doing." "A slow sort of country!" said the Queen. "Now, here, you see, it takes all the running you can do, to keep in the same place. If you want to get somewhere else, you must run at least twice as fast as that."[10]

Evolutionary biologists actually use the term "Red Queen principle" to describe a rapid evolutionary process. The truth is that increased demand causes a more rapid evolution of ILL processes. By streamlining these processes with better automation techniques, reliability and turnaround improve significantly.

Library Networks

Library networks have played a critical role in creating access to collections. The growth and development of these networks, local and national, and even international, have made possible the volume growth of ILL activity. Once online bibliographic records were available through the creation and adoption of machine-readable records, library networks grew at a rapid rate. Libraries immediately realized the benefits of sharing access to bibliographic records and then the ability to share the actual items by interlibrary loan.

Local Networks

Local and regional networks based on one union catalog provide easy and efficient ways to share. Libraries join together to develop or buy programming to create one large bibliographic database of all their holdings. With the addition of circulation capabilities, loan transactions between members are greatly facilitated. Information on item availability is an added benefit. No time is wasted requesting those titles that are charged out or non-circulating. Volume or summary holdings for serial titles are also available. This helps staff and users to determine who owns a particular volume or issue. There are many local variants to the structure and details of the programs built by networks. Some networks are restrictive in membership requirements; some have more stringent controls over record contribution than others do. Some offer free book loans with item delivery backed up by courier services for their member organizations. Others also allow for their own separately maintained union lists and expedited copy arrangements.

One example of a local network is Illinet Online. It began with a handful of libraries that in 1978 shared a homegrown circulation system. It is now part of a 45-member library system called the Illinois Library Computer System Organization (ILCSO). Members share a union catalog of 22 million items. More than 600,000 users in the system enjoy full access to all the circulating titles and may request them online regardless of location. An unusual feature is that public libraries across the state may also request items on behalf of their users. These libraries do not have to be part of ILCSO to gain easy access to both the online requesting and delivery of *returnables* (book loans). All of these loans are delivered via a network of state-supported delivery routes for cost-effective transport. ILCSO libraries also contract with vendors to offer cost-effective access to online indexes accessible to all member library users.

OhioLINK, serving more than 500,000 students, faculty, and staff at 76 institutions, is another example of a regional network. It offers access to more than 31 million library items statewide and also provides access to 76 research databases. The membership includes 17 public universities, 23 community/technical colleges, 35 private colleges, and the State Library of Ohio. OhioLINK requires each member to use the same system vendor, while each library retains local control of its own materials. These local records are merged to form one central catalog used for interlibrary loan. OhioLINK users may access this database to request any circulating item. As with Illinet Online, delivery is supported with a courier service.

These systems offer easy access to item records and, with *patron-initiated borrowing*, provide a huge collection of material to affiliated borrowers while minimizing the labor involved in the loans. Patron-initiated borrowing systems allow users to make their own requests and monitor them online. These systems see a higher volume of use because more titles are available to the user and the procedures are integrated into the online catalog. Users search, and when an item is not owned or is unavailable locally, may place a request. Barbara Preece and Thomas Kilpatrick describe how request volume increased when users were allowed to make their own orders for titles unavailable at their local library.[11] Requesting is easy, and so is processing. The labor shifts to the circulation departments from ILL offices, because these loan transactions are handled with familiar local system processes. Because online circulation processes govern the loan transactions, users may manage their own request tracking. Reference librarians are called upon to teach users how to access their accounts and to interpret the status of their requests.

There are many other local systems running or developing similar projects. These networks require good governance, with formal agreements and shared policies and procedures to build the shared catalog. The benefits are many, beginning with the economic ones, because the members share system costs. ILL fill rates are high, and resource sharing with cooperative collection development programs can be extended easily. The drawbacks include the investment of time necessary to coordinate such organizations. All members must agree on basic policies, and local issues may be subordinated to larger consortium needs. These networks have provided models illustrating how easily and economically materials may be shared. Other libraries may want to emulate this integrated ILL process but look for technological solutions rather than organizational ones.

Bibliographic Utilities or Networks

The networks synonymous with resource sharing across the nation—OCLC, RLIN, and WLN (now OCLC/WLN[12])—originated as local or statewide networks that evolved over time to become large nonprofit corporations. These corporations sell services that are anchored in the large bibliographic databases they support. The utilities have since broadened their services to include integrated access to a variety of online indexes, but the databases are still central to resource sharing. OCLC and RLIN offer access to the closest thing we have to online national bibliographies in the United States.

More than any other utility, OCLC has helped to shape interlibrary loan in the United States and has provided the tools that allow the large volume of lending and borrowing that occurs today. Statistics reveal that more than 100 million ILL requests have been generated on the ILL subsystem since 1979. The union catalog, formerly known as the Online Union Catalog, now referred to as WorldCat, contains more than 43 million records in eight bibliographic formats representing more than 400 languages, with more than 775 million location holdings as of September 2000.[13] Networks and services link more than 37,000 libraries in 67 countries and territories. These services reach into every area of librarianship and have helped to transform them.

OCLC began in 1967 as a simple nonprofit corporation, the Ohio College Library Center, a group of 54 libraries interested in sharing resources. An online shared cataloging system was in place in 1971. OCLC quickly expanded to nonacademic libraries with the offer of attractive membership options. By 1973, it was no longer regional in scope, and in 1981 the name was changed to Online Computer Library Center. Today, it is simply OCLC. The ILL subsystem was implemented in 1979, forever changing the laborious, time-consuming mechanisms previously necessary to transact a remote loan:

> I still remember the first time I used the OCLC Interlibrary Loan Subsystem: the sun was shining, the birds were singing, and a simple OCLC system search revealed the correct bibliographic citation and holdings for a book requested by a patron. An online request form was sent easily to the holding libraries and the item appeared in my library within a week.[14]

Begun as a way to share cataloging records, OCLC has grown in so many directions that the use of that system is just a small part of its suite of services, representing only 36% of its total operation. OCLC is now well known for its FirstSearch databases, which offer one interface to a multitude of databases developed by various publishers. OCLC and RLIN (described below) have helped to bridge the access gap by linking indexes to potential sources for the material (see Box 7.5). OCLC has been working with several library consortia to develop an interface and software that allow users to place orders directly after searching the member library catalogs. This is described more fully in the section on standards.

Box 7.5 OCLC ILL Innovations

Since 1979, a number of time-saving enhancements have been added to the resource-sharing services. For example, OCLC has integrated the ILL function with databases so that an order may be made directly from WorldCat and a number of other databases. Library users may find their citations, and if the facility has been enabled, may place an order for the title. Libraries may then choose to look at these or may elect to set up the ILL Direct function, which will separate out requests that match criteria selected by the borrowing library and send them to preferred lenders. These lenders are identified with a profile that the requesting library sets up under the OCLC Custom Holdings option. Libraries may also choose to take advantage of an ILL fee management system (IFM) set up by OCLC. This service frees libraries from having to worry about billing and paying ILL invoices. All of these innovations have freed up staff to spend more time on problem requests and to meet the higher volume of requests.

The Research Libraries Group (RLG), which began in 1974, founded RLIN, a database of bibliographic records for materials in major research library collections. This critical database provides access to a wealth of unique research material essential for graduate students and scholars. A user-friendly interface, Eureka, makes searching the database easy. RLIN is available for searching even for nonmembers, for a fee, and many libraries use it to search for elusive records not found on OCLC.

RLG membership initially required that institutions be affiliated with a major research organization. Qualifying groups included IRLA (International Research Library Association), AAU (Association of American Universities), and ARL (Association of Research Libraries). This restriction limited the growth of RLG until the membership structure was expanded with new categories.[15] Membership in 2000 totals 161 institutions, including libraries, museums, archives, and research institutions. This membership structure ensured that the database covered important research material, but it also hampered growth and subsequent resource sharing, as the number of participants is much smaller than OCLC's membership base.

RLG members, as research libraries with large scholarly collections, built the database to fit their requirements. Very early on, it provided for the character sets necessary for cataloging in a variety of non-roman languages. The physical formats supported also reflect the research collections of the members. RLIN helped set the standard for describing musical scores, manuscripts, and visual resources: all the wide variety of materials found in a major research library.

RLIN, like OCLC, supports interlibrary loan with an electronic request facility. Members of RLG may also elect to belong to the SHARES program that provides for reciprocal borrowing and priority handling of members' requests. RLG has been as responsive as OCLC to the need for innovative services and has introduced enhancements such as the preferred partners customizing feature. In addition, RLG developed a facility to manage ILL requesting—ILL Manager—that provides for tracking and control of requests as well as the ability to search and order across multiple platforms. This new service was recently introduced and may address the problems many offices have in working with several ILL order mechanisms.

RLG is well known for the indexes provided through the CitaDel citation order service. These indexes cover important research tools, some of them primary to the discipline covered. CitaDel provides order or source information for the actual material indexed, making access that much easier. A new project to allow for patron-initiated borrowing (Borrow Direct) was tested by three RLG institutions beginning in 1999. A very popular product developed by RLG is the Ariel article transmission software. This innovative software has dramatically improved delivery times for documents while cutting supply costs of lenders. Ariel is described in the document delivery section below.

WLN, recently merged with OCLC, began as the Washington Library Network, a regional system with goals similar to OCLC and RLG, but with different participants. WLN's database was particularly well known for its rigorous standards for cataloging. The merger with OCLC brings more breadth and depth to the WorldCat database. It also provides for better sharing of those materials located in the western part of the United States.

The competition between RLIN and OCLC has been useful because it helped to create new services as each has sought to serve a segment of the marketplace. It is frustrating to have to switch systems when a monograph is verified on RLIN but the order must be transferred manually to OCLC because the library is not part of the RLIN ILL program. Both utilities are now addressing this lack of interoperability, a key issue facing all libraries today using any ILL mechanism. Another reality is that libraries' local systems are not linked directly with the utilities' databases. To determine a title location, status, and often volume holdings, the local system must be consulted. The local system is also used to loan material, so ILL staff are often keying in their record updates in two places, on the circulation module and on the utility system.

Resource Sharing Issues

The networks offer greater opportunities for enhanced sharing. Better resource sharing requires a basic infrastructure that goes beyond the networks. Library material has to be uniquely described to be identified and located. In addition, the material location and status, along with holdings and additional copy information, provide the user with valuable information on local availability. Networks allow users to tap into library resources remotely and have greatly expanded access to library materials online. A successful access services program requires a coordinated effort in all areas of librarianship: cataloging, serials control, circulation, collection management, reference, systems, administration, and interlibrary loan. This infrastructure seems fairly obvious, but it can be complex even in a small library. When many libraries are involved (as of course is the case with ILL) the complexities can be overwhelming. Access services are more successful when standards are applied.

STANDARDS

Individuals rely on standards every day in going about their daily business. Standards allow us to use our electronic appliances, drive our cars, pay for goods, and communicate by phone or e-mail, just to name a few daily occurrences. Libraries also rely on standards. In the ILL world, some of the most important include:

MARC, a consistent way to describe material for online access

Z39.50, protocols to search across different databases and networks

ISO ILL, guidelines for communicating borrowing and lending messages consistently while offering opportunities for streamlined work processes

Circulation Interchange, for availability/location information as well as a way to integrate user database and item processes no matter what local system is used.

MARC: Records to Access

For items to be found in the collection, they must be cataloged in such a way as to ensure consistent retrieval. Much progress has been made in that regard, but the situation is still not perfect (see Box 7.6).

Box 7.6 Ideal Cataloging

In an ideal world, each unique bibliographic entity would be cataloged only once. It would have attached to it a unique bibliographic record that could be shared electronically with every other library that acquired the work. The cataloger would know the language or languages in which the item was produced, would have in-depth knowledge of the subject matter, and would adhere strictly to an accepted world standard for description, subject analysis, and classification. This complete and perfect bibliographic record would be recorded in an electronic format that was shared by all the world's libraries. It would be distributed instantly to a single global bibliographic database, from which any other library could draw the record instantly for local use. The notes and subject terms could be translated automatically into a chosen language. The entire record would be transliterated into a chosen script if desired. Nirvana would be reached.

Jay H. Lambrecht
"International Cooperation in Cataloging: Progress and Constraints"[16]

The problems that plague cataloging will challenge resource-sharing efforts also (see Box 7.7). Users with access to self-initiated requesting systems will not find records if material is not consistently cataloged. Duplicate records confuse users, ones that obscure a format frustrate, and inconsistent application of rules means users may overlook holdings when a record does not get selected. Entering "Proceedings of the Zoological Society of London," for example, in some catalogs retrieves some holdings, and "Zoological Society of London, Proceedings," retrieves others. This confounds the user. Different search strategies yield different results, depending on the cataloging practice in place. Reference librarians understand these variations, but users do not. Reference librarians will continue to help users search effectively and may even do so at a higher volume as request failures and delays bring users back to staff for help. These types of problems occur with local OPACs and union catalogs, from regional networks to national utilities. Reference librarians must be aware of record inconsistencies in the catalogs used and work to identify and resolve the problems. Projects to link catalogs with one search interface will be problematic, both because of the inconsistencies inherent in the cataloging processes and local variants in search and retrieval protocols.

Box 7.7 A Change of Heart

I have been one of the wild men of the profession who have told catalogers to get with it: any old record will do as long as it serves to get the item on the shelf quickly. In an electronic resource sharing environment, this simply won't do. Bad records waste the time of the reader. As librarians working to a budget, we need faster, cheaper, better records, but our users need fuller records, too, when they can't browse the shelf to see whether what is described is what they are actually looking for. When we acquire irrelevant material for users, we waste not only their time but our own and we are very likely to be wasting the money in interlibrary loan that we are saving in cataloging.

Marshall Keys
"Both Borrower and Lender Be"[17]

New solutions for ILL requesting combine some of the best functions of the shared union catalog approach, where status and location are easily identified, and those of bibliographic utilities, where one search and order mechanism can be used for a very large number of library holdings. It is not an option for many libraries to be part of a larger shared catalog. Individual libraries have implemented their own stand-alone systems over time and have relied on OCLC or RLIN for ILL. With the advent of fairly new standards, it is now possible to link totally different OPACS and include an order facility for users.

Z39.50: Information Retrieval Protocols

Library online catalogs worldwide are now accessible via the Web to a much wider user community. Web interfaces and one common search command have made it much easier for any user to link to and search a remote database. Systems can be set up to search multiple catalogs with one command, eliminating both the need to learn system-specific searching commands and the time spent in repeating that search with different commands down a list of databases. The Z39.50 search standard has helped to alleviate those problems (see Chapter 6). Increased access can also be frustrating. Once an item is found, how can it easily be ordered? The Z39.50 information retrieval standard, combined with new order interfaces, has the potential to revolutionize access for staff and users. Widely disparate systems separated organizationally and geographically may now be linked together. Users may select and search another database using a local interface and retrieve records displayed in that familiar interface. An added bonus is that the records have the potential to indicate availability and shelf location. The user then selects the record and submits an order that transfers data elements of that bibliographic record. Depending on how the user is identified, specific data on the individual may be transferred or be input by the requester. Resulting orders may go to an ILL office, be sent on to partner libraries, or be handled by a utility. Response time is an issue when multiple databases are searched, especially when result sets are large.

A more problematic area, because it is difficult to control, lies in the Z39.50 protocol itself. System vendors have implemented different versions of the protocol. How fields are indexed varies in online catalogs utilizing different integrated systems. How the protocol is set up to work with the indexing may also vary. One query input by a user may get fine results for a name search in one database and a puzzling response from another. It may be difficult to merge set results. Which record should all the others be compared to, and what will be the unique identifier used to match and delete duplicates? Catalogs that users select to search may change, requiring maintenance of the Z39.50 set-up. This can be difficult to achieve when many library catalogs are involved. Clifford Lynch points out the problems still evident in Z39.50 implementations of distributed systems and contrasts these with the level of resource sharing possible in union catalogs where indexing, retrieval, and cataloging standards are more consistent. Searching and indexing, performance and management and consolidation of search results are areas where Z39.50 linked system approaches may confuse users and librarians alike.[18]

The distributed system approach using Z39.50 does show great potential. Reference librarians must learn how these systems are set up in their libraries and work with systems personnel in reporting problems. They can advise on the search options given and how interfaces can be designed to best instruct the remote user. They will also train users how best to utilize these new search and order options.

The Committee on Institutional Cooperation (CIC)—a consortium of the Big Ten schools plus the University of Chicago—Library Initiatives program uses Z39.50 to extend online access for all CIC library users for the over 60 million holdings of the CIC libraries. OCLC was selected as the vendor for the U.S. Department of Education grant to create a Virtual Electronic Library (VEL). OCLC designed the WebZ interface that utilizes the Z39.50 protocol. Technology staff from the member libraries customized the interface to best fit their users' needs. No one WebZ interface may look exactly like another, but they all have in common the ability to search the Z39.50-compatible online catalogs of all the CIC libraries. This allows users to select and order both loans and article copies easily. Presently, the system routes these requests through the OCLC ILL subsystem, where they may be candidates for OCLC Direct request handling and therefore go directly to the lender, or be sent to the review file of the user's home library to be mediated by ILL staff. Local staff handle all article requests, because users cannot easily verify holdings of the libraries and may forget to key in critical parts of the article citation. The service has allowed CIC institutions to offer patron-initiated borrowing, some for the first time. Users, when properly instructed, can log in to the system, search the catalogs, browse the results, select the records for the items needed, determine availability, and order the materials themselves. This system, coupled with the private courier service the CIC institutions employ, allows for better access, more success in finding available titles, and speedier delivery of items. The end result is enhanced access for library users.

Figure 7.4, page 164, shows the result of a search on CICVEL. A user logged in, searched the combined catalogs, and selected a record to order. Note the ILL request link at the top right. Choosing this prompts the system to do several things: transfer the bibliographic information to a form, authenticate the requester, and transfer specific user information to the form. Instructions on the form can be customized.

CIC continues to work on future developments of the VEL, working to build one system to handle all ILL needs. Other organizations are using this distributed system approach, and it is not just limited to the academic model. Six hundred public libraries in Illinois are now linking their catalogs using the OCLC WebZ approach. Information about the Virtual Illinois Catalog (VIC) is available on the Web (http://vic.sos.state.il.us/aboutvic.html). Another academic consortium, the Pennsylvania Academic Libraries Connection Initiative (PALCI), has designed its own distributed system to enhance interlibrary loan among its libraries. Information about the project and a demo can be found at http://www.lehigh.edu/ ~ inpalci/abtmenu.htm.

Figure 7.4 Example of CICVEL record. Committee on Institutional Cooperation (CIC).

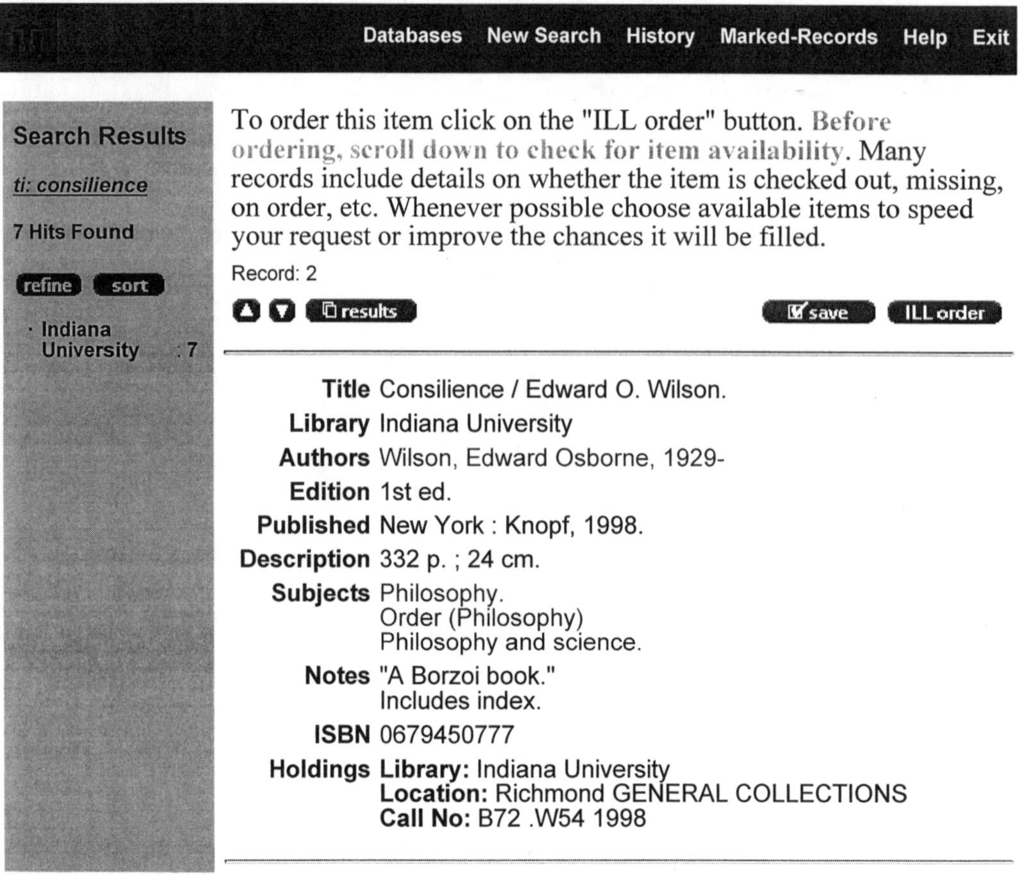

Interoperability and Communication: The ISO Protocols

The current inability to send requests anywhere regardless of the system platform is frustrating to ILL staff. In addition, ILL staff interact with many suppliers, both libraries and commercial, all potentially using different terminology subject to different interpretations. Consider these examples:

- Library A requests a loan only to be told it is unavailable. Does this mean it is charged already, identified as missing, non-circulating, or simply not found on the shelf? The answer guides the library as to the next step in obtaining the loan, but inconsistent responses delay the process.
- ILL staffs send ILL orders via the utilities, by fax, mail, and over the Internet. Each vehicle requires its own process, and each then must be tracked differently. One order interface that automates the ordering for all systems used, and then tracks that order with consistent statuses in a central database, would reduce errors, speed up requests, and enhance fill rates.

- Requesting staff could help speed up a loan if the local call number and location could be supplied consistently to the lender.

The ISO ILL Protocol is an evolving standard that may offer some relief. There are in fact two standard documents, ISO 10160 ILL Loan Application Service Definition and ISO 10161 ILL Application Protocol Specification. The ISO ILL Protocols were developed in Canada by the National Library of Canada to provide a way to handle messaging consistently, which is important in processing complex ILL transactions. The standard was published in 1993, with the second edition issued in 1996. ISO ILL provides for a central messaging system. All possible messages regarding an ILL status are predefined. Rules for proper sequence of these statuses are set up for appropriate updating. For example, the system will not allow an item not yet loaned to be renewed. The messages are set up to allow great flexibility in exchange between communication networks. The application has the capability to cover the entire interlibrary loan cycle from request processing to tracking and management, giving ILL units the potential for much greater control over all requests. A central database of order transactions is created and can be used for financial, statistical, and copyright record keeping. The protocol does this across different hardware and software applications. ISO ILL can replicate current ILL models from the very simple request from one library to another, to a complicated patron-initiated request that is forwarded to a set of lenders. One part of the protocol can also work with local circulation systems—checking availability automatically, for example, before submitting the request.

With ISO ILL on the horizon, vendors can begin offering more interlibrary loan capabilities in their systems. Some will only offer ways to integrate the new protocols into existing systems, but that in itself will offer groups of libraries more flexibility in building modules to suit their needs. Libraries may link their catalogs and purchase ISO-compliant software (see Box 7.8) to link their resource sharing, allowing for direct user access to loan or perhaps even article requesting, all managed automatically and consistently.

Box 7.8 ILL New Software Options

Several new companies are now offering ISO-compliant products to help libraries build better resource-sharing programs. Some of these companies are partnering with other library vendors, linking products together to better integrate user access options. Some products are stand-alone management tools. This is just a sampling of the newer software options now available to libraries looking for enhanced ILL solutions:

- CPS Systems Inc. developed the Universal Resource Sharing Application (URSA) that Epixtech now uses for their Resource Sharing System. Libraries may link with partners and allow users to order material directly from those catalogs.
- CLIO is an ILL manager product developed by Perkins and Co. They have joined with the Endeavor company, allowing that vendor to offer an ILL module that provides for order monitoring and tracking.
- Fretwell-Downing Informatics' Virtual Document Exchange (VDXrequest) allows users to order and ILL staff to transmit and track orders effectively.
- AVISO, offered by A-G Canada Ltd., is ILL management software that can work with an online order interface that a library may customize for its users.
- Pigasus Software markets a request management system called WINGS that simplifies ILL ordering while allowing for the many order options required.

Why should reference librarians be concerned about these protocols? Libraries can now be expected to migrate to new systems perhaps every decade. The ISO ILL developments are helping to push new ILL services that vendors are now including in their systems. There are also separate products available, and reference staff can support their purchase for ILL operations if they understand how these may ultimately help serve their users. Reference staff can also work within consortia organizations to see if these new products may enhance resource sharing.

Circulation Interchange Protocol

This is a relatively recent standard under development by the National Information Standards Organization (http://www.niso.org/commitat.html). Libraries want circulation status to be integrated with ILL functionality for ease of use and better service. Staff wants to be able to process material consistently. Users want to manage their requests in one comprehensive interface. Libraries want to be able to define privileges for user categories and also control subsequent use and allow for options for fees. This developing standard will help to bridge the gaps in the distributed systems that hope to emulate shared union catalog requesting services. The group defining the process and guidelines includes vendors and librarians, who will determine its realistic use.

Standards are especially important in interlibrary loan, because these processes cover so many areas of librarianship and because so many interested parties are involved. With resource sharing critical to library access and with vendors responsive to that need, it is hoped that the standards will indeed be well developed and adopted to maximize access for all library users.

EVOLVING ACCESS SERVICES

Patron-Initiated Ordering

There is a growing trend to put more material-requesting options directly in the hands of users. OhioLINK and ILCSO libraries are two consortia that have offered this option to their users for loans for some time. There has been much greater interest in these systems lately as library administrations react to the pressure for better access. A group of libraries in Missouri (MOBIUS consortium) is implementing a new Innovative Interfaces Inc. (III) system that will utilize the III INN-Reach software to allow users to place their own requests (http://mobius.missouri.edu/). The 71 libraries on 64 SUNY campuses in New York State are in the process of contracting with Ex Libris for a system to manage all their merged holdings. Patron-initiated requesting will be a feature on the new system (http://www.sunyconnect.suny.edu/). OCLC offers some revolutionary options in their FirstSearch ILL links. The distributed system approach, as exemplified by the CICVEL and the PALCI order interface, is the latest approach to patron-initiated ordering. All of these are appropriate ways to expand the access options for library users. Use of these systems relieves ILL staff from the more routine requests. Users can select and order the title they need, eliminating the front-end processing or staff-mediated backlogs. At the minimum, the library user saves the time of the ILL staff by choosing the record and eliminating the bibliographic verification work, submitting an electronic form, fully verified, to the ILL office. Then that request goes through the ILL cycle. The maximum approach includes the facility to send the request directly on to an automatically selected lender, where it is handled as a circulation transaction.

Self-initiated requesting online is still regarded as a fairly new and innovative service. The full potential of this option has not been realized, for several reasons. Libraries are loath to lose the control they exercise over user requests, fearing local resources will be overlooked. ILL materials can be expensive and may not come in time to meet a user deadline. Infrastructure pieces may be lacking, such as a reliable and secure way to authenticate users. Not every library user may be allowed interlibrary loan access. One example could be alumni who may obtain a library card but are restricted to local collection access. Mounting electronic forms without an authentication process will result in misunderstandings and conflict. Library staff may lack the knowledge or skills in automating basic processes, and the technology support can be uneven. Library users also need to be educated about their options and directed to the access sources.

Volume is likely to go up as users explore these options. Libraries, recognizing the need for more direct options for their users when local resources have been exhausted, will be experimenting with any or all of these approaches for some time to come.

Document Delivery

Much of the material covered so far in this chapter has focused on all interlibrary loans, with some of the newest trends focusing on returnables. But article or document delivery has its own special issues. The nature of serials sets article requesting apart. Obtaining accurate article citations can be a complex and time-consuming process. Photocopy orders require the location of a source that has that particular volume. Cost is another factor and is predicated on supplier policy, supplier options for speedier delivery, and copyright fees that may be applied either by the supplier or due to the publisher if the title is heavily requested (see discussion of copyright below). Delivery options are also important because they will decide the turnaround time required and how users may be able to read or pick up their material. Document delivery is an important issue as libraries increasingly rely on it instead of continuing to subscribe to serial titles that are no longer cost effective to own. This option can work if library users are well served by access rather than ownership. This requires a program with good guarantees of high-quality documents delivered in a timely and cost-effective manner.

Approaches to Document Delivery

Libraries as Suppliers. Traditional ILL methods are still heavily used to obtain articles not owned by libraries. Here the library user has already identified an article from a title not owned and has submitted an order for it. Libraries may require users to verify the source so as to be sure the citation is accurate before passing it on to a potential lender. Then, typically, staff will determine the location and set up an order on one of the bibliographic utilities. Holdings verification is a real problem because several sources may need to be consulted. For example, OCLC offers union list capabilities, but many libraries do not contribute to it. Large shared union catalogs may have to be searched as well as the unique serial union lists produced and maintained by state or regional consortia. Older material (requests for copies from volumes that predate many online initiatives) requires yet another check in print sources such as the *Union List of Serials.* Delivery options may be specified but cannot be guaranteed because the lender will not always want, or be able, to comply. Supplier errors in copying or mailing incorrectly may delay or derail a request.

Commercial Suppliers. Commercial suppliers have been around for a number of years, although individual suppliers may come and go. These are companies or institutions that have dedicated staff and resources to services that provide copies of material for a fee. Some of the biggest and best known include the British Library Document Supply Centre (BLDSC), Bell and Howell's UMI service, UnCover (which grew out of the CARL company), The Institute for Scientific Information's (ISI) Document Solution, and the Canadian Institute for Scientific and Technical Information (CISTI). There are many others focusing on one discipline or one collection of material. Their services have seen considerable interest and growth of use in the past few years.

If library constituencies can be convinced that document access is almost as effective as ownership, then selected serial titles may be obtained this way, freeing libraries to explore more resource sharing or innovative new services. For some libraries, this option of access has been the only way that their community of users could continue to have access to material once available locally. Louisiana State University, for example, went through some major budget cuts in the 1990s, but the library was able to build an access program using a commercial supplier.[19] The costs of the document delivery system were far less than the total costs of subscribing to the journal titles.

Commercial suppliers can be a very reasonable alternative to owning low-use titles when service is backed by an excellent and available collection with high-speed delivery options. There are many suppliers available to choose from. Sheila Walters addresses some of the factors to consider:

- What is needed?
- What are the capabilities of the suppliers?
- Compare the products and services.
- Evaluate local needs using prioritized guidelines such as cost, speed, coverage, and fill rate.
- Test!
- Consider staff and user needs when evaluating results of the test.[20]

One very important factor to consider is how users can use the document delivery service to replicate on-site access. Suppliers with well-designed tables of contents (TOC), allowing users to easily browse titles not subscribed to, select, and then order them without mediation, will help to ensure a high level of access. UnCover, the BLDSC, CISTI, and ISI are examples of suppliers with these services. Users in some cases can set up an automated current awareness profile by subject or journal title to be alerted to new documents in their areas of interest. The results can be e-mailed directly to the researchers, who will select and order the articles themselves. Perhaps the most compelling reason to use a supplier rather than a library is the greater guarantee of a successful fill in a predictable time period. Libraries can rely on these services and depend on them when canceling titles. Libraries must also be sure to select suppliers who show evidence of a long and stable service for better guarantees of long-term access. Libraries can also facilitate access to these services on behalf of those users who want the option to order (and pay) for articles they would rather not wait for. The range of options available from the major suppliers makes it possible for libraries to design an array of options for their users. For example, the BLDSC offers several delivery options, including air mail, 2 hour or 12 hour fax, courier, and 2 hour or 12 hour Ariel (Internet delivery).

A user has selected an article for ordering. The service may be set up to allow the user to confirm the order, thereby sending it to the BLDSC, or it may be confirmed later by an authorized library staff member who checks for these orders routinely.

DOCLINE. There is one document delivery service that serves as a model for others. DOCLINE is a unique library-to-library document delivery service. This is an integrated approach to the problems inherent in ordering articles and so is quite unlike the ILL offered by the major bibliographic utilities. It is unique in streamlining the process by linking the article itself to the source. The National Library of Medicine (NLM) built the system to handle access by one standard citation number to one standardized serial holding list (SERHOLD). Orders are easily identified from the *MEDLINE* index, which is central to all biomedical journal literature and utilizes unique record identifiers. Participating libraries first enter their own biomedical serial holdings into the SERHOLD database and then build a profile of their preferred lenders. When requests are input using the unique record identifier, the system matches the serials needed from that identifier and routes them to the specified hierarchy of lenders who have also all entered their serial holdings. The lender then receives the request and acts on it. This service has eliminated the need to re-verify or re-enter citations or search for bibliographic records and holdings. The system is also superb in tracking rerouting and order history, detailing why particular articles could not be sent. Library users may generate their own online requests via the NLM Loansome Doc order service, which operates with the user-friendly Grateful Med interface to *MEDLINE*. New enhancements in the ease of serial holdings updating and order management make this an excellent system. Its one major drawback is that it includes only biomedical literature. The use of the record identifiers has prompted more attention to how such a standard number for any article could enhance access if included in an index. Imagine how a library user could browse an index and choose an article with such an identifier. The unique number would identify not only the citation, but also the potential supplier, eliminating any need for a staff-mediated order.

Delivery to the User

Library users can easily make their orders online now, but how does the material ordered and received at the home library actually reach the user? Returnables, once processed, most often must be picked up at the users' library. Some campuses do have delivery programs allowing the received volumes to be mailed to campus addresses after passing through a central site. Distance education programs are forcing an examination of user access where cooperating libraries may allow users to define a pick-up or delivery point closer to their homes for optimal convenience. Another idea, not yet adopted by a large number of libraries, is direct delivery to the user's address. Here the lender bypasses the borrowing library central receive site and sends the requested loan directly to the user. This service generally requires some proof of delivery, so courier mail services are utilized and packages are signed for. AMIGOS (a network of libraries in the Southwest) and some academic libraries in Colorado are two distinct groups exploring direct delivery to determine the problems and test the turnaround time.[21] Cost is certainly an issue, along with tracking. Libraries can hope to join together to obtain discounts from couriers, but this can be very complex due to the courier's reluctance to deal with many disparate groups over geographically separate areas. Direct delivery will be limited until a cost solution is found. Well-defined groups of libraries have been successful in contracting with private courier services to expedite delivery with partner or consortia member libraries.

A number of states support statewide library delivery routes. These services are very economical because fees are often based on pick-up and drop-off sites rather than by the piece. Items do not have to be wrapped separately, minimizing the need for mailing supplies and the labor of individual handling. One drawback, however, is that the items cannot be tracked when missing. These services cannot be extended to direct end-user delivery if tracking is required. Delivery is one part of the ILL cycle where innovation could dramatically improve service and where reference help is needed to guide users to their best options. A new twist is article delivery through electronic means.

Electronic Delivery

Facsimile transmission was one of the first enhancements for article delivery. It provides for fast access to text pages, but resolution is poor and any graphical images or photographs in the article may be rendered illegible. Advances in image technology have now allowed for new delivery service over the Internet with excellent resolution on screen and when printing. RLG developed a software product, now in use at many interlibrary loan offices, that makes it easy to deliver high-quality articles quickly and cost effectively. The software, named Ariel, works with a variety of widely available scanners and printers. It allows easy scanning of text into standard images that are compressed and delivered over the Internet. This software has seen wide use in the eight years it has been available. An article detailing the speed in delivery and cost benefits of using Ariel is available on the Web.[22] Ariel has seen many enhancements in the last few years. Now, images may be sent as e-mail attachments, eliminating the need for end-users to have Ariel loaded at their "receive" stations.

However, the images are large and many libraries have not yet been able to direct incoming material to users this way, because local networks may restrict file sizes or users may find their individual workstations disabled by the memory-intensive files.

Another product that allows the image to be converted to a more readily accessible format for easy viewing is Prospero. Prospero is available as freeware from the developers under the GNU or General Public License (http://www.gnu.org/home.html). Prospero provides for utilities to convert the incoming images to Portable Document Format (PDF) and transfer them to a server space where a user may view it. PDF can be used independent of the hardware or operating systems on a workstation. The files can be viewed using a viewer such as Adobe Acrobat. Prospero provides document security to prevent copying and file changes. The software includes programming for an automatic e-mail message to be sent to the user giving the user the address, a password, and instructions on how to retrieve the article. The home library may customize the service easily to both control access to the text and do daily maintenance to delete articles after a set period of time. More information about this product may be obtained from the developer's home page (http://bones.med.ohio-state.edu/prospero). Desktop delivery is now a possibility on a large scale with no inconvenience to the end user. The control and maintenance features included in Prospero are a great relief because they allow libraries to deal effectively with copyright law and guidelines.

In all the delivery programs mentioned, users will turn to reference librarians for explanations of the service and to clarify the delivery options, as presented in Box 7.9, or as in the last case, help in opening and viewing a file.

Box 7.9 To Pay or Not to Pay

Consider the library user looking for a rush order for an article from a medical journal. It may seem expedient to go directly to a supplier offering a guaranteed delivery time, but the cost may be overly high. This is when reference staff should establish the user's time frame to rule out alternatives. It may also be the time to think of establishing a fee-based service offering expedited delivery. Under those circumstances, the user has the choice of obtaining the article knowing the deadline can be met, or of first exhausting less expensive or even free sources but taking the chance that the article may be delivered late.

COPYRIGHT

Copyright legislation protects the holders of copyright from loss of revenue and from unauthorized uses of their material, including adaptations of it. Society protects the investment the copyright holders have made in creating the work. However, U.S. copyright law also balances that protection by providing for some exceptions, which allow the citizens of the United States to have access to materials needed to learn and add to our collective knowledge. When, in 1790, George Washington asked Congress to enact copyright legislation, he argued that it would increase the national stock of knowledge. And knowledge, he said, is "the surest basis of public happiness."[23]

Access to copyrighted material is much easier in our networked environment, where copies are but a click way. All librarians must be familiar with the provisions of copyright law and guidelines, as well as the ethical implications discussed in Chapter 2. Libraries must abide by the law and must also protect the rights allowed them in obtaining copies for users and in maintaining collections. Reference librarians help guide users to access copyrighted material based on their knowledge of the law and the fees that might have to be paid directly as a result of a copy being made.

The Copyright Law of 1976 (Title 17 U.S. Code) was groundbreaking in the exceptions allowed for copying. The Digital Millennium Copyright Act of 1999 is the latest update to this copyright legislation, although several issues are still under review. There are several excellent guides to copyright legislation, some of which are included in the "Additional Readings" section.

Section 106 of Title 17 describes the copyright owner's rights. The Fair Use clause is in section 107. This section allows for copying of copyrighted material for purposes of criticism, comment, news reporting, teaching, scholarship, or research. These uses are qualified by a number of factors:

> (1) the purpose and character of the use, including whether such use is of a commercial nature or is for nonprofit educational purposes;
>
> (2) the nature of the copyrighted work;
>
> (3) the amount and substantiality of the portion used in relation to the copyrighted work as a whole; and
>
> (4) the effect of the use upon the potential market for or value of the copyrighted work. The fact that a work is unpublished shall not itself bar a finding of fair use if such finding is made upon consideration of all the above factors.[24]

Fair use interpretation can be extreme, from those who say the law allows any copying done for any educational use, to the reverse stance taken by copyright holders, who would like to see this clause removed. For that reason, it is perhaps not surprising that attempts to provide guidelines have not been successful. A commission had been set up by Congress to develop guidelines for fair use (Commission on Fair Use or CONFU), but it was disbanded after several years' work. The panel of educators, scholars, publishers, and librarians could not agree. One of the guidelines was to have covered interlibrary loan.

ILL processes are concerned with fair use, but also with very specific sections of the law dealing with systematic reproduction, public domain, and the education of library users. Libraries were given certain rights to make copies under section 108 of Title 17. These rights are spelled out in great detail. The part most concerned with interlibrary loan is 108(g)(2), which covers systematic reproduction of materials:

> (g) The rights of reproduction and distribution under this section extend to the isolated and unrelated reproduction or distribution of a single copy or phonorecord of the same material on separate occasions, but do not extend to cases where the library or archives, or its employee—
>
> > (1) is aware or has substantial reason to believe that it is engaging in the related or concerted reproduction or distribution of multiple copies or phonorecords of the same material, whether made on one occasion or over a period of time, and whether intended for aggregate use by one or more individuals or for separate use by the individual members of a group; or
> >
> > (2) engages in the systematic reproduction or distribution of single or multiple copies or phonorecords of material described in subsection (d): Provided, That nothing in this clause prevents a library or archives from participating in interlibrary arrangements that do not have, as their purpose or effect, that the library or archives receiving such copies or phonorecords for distribution does so in such aggregate quantities as to substitute for a subscription to or purchase of such work.[25]

Systematic reproduction was deliberately not defined here. Congress appointed the U.S. National Commission on New Technological Uses of Copyrighted Works (CONTU) to wrestle with this issue. This group made recommendations to Congress that are not law (although appended to the law) but are guidelines to follow. These guidelines have not been tested in court. The full text can be read in the U.S. National Commission on New Technological Uses of Copyrighted Works, *Final Report.*[26] The guidelines offer help in limiting or allowing copying under certain conditions. Periodical copying in any one year is limited to five articles from one title from the last five years' worth of issues, counting back from the date of the request ("five in five"). Libraries must indicate when they follow the Commission guidelines (CCG) on the request and also must retain their records for three calendar years. Libraries that do not follow through on the guidelines when making requests will see requests delayed or not filled, and in extreme cases they may be subject to investigation.

Once the limit of "five in five" is reached, the requesting library must seek other options for obtaining a copy. Some of those options include seeking permission from the copyright holder (the publisher in the case of most periodicals), which often means paying for permission with a "royalty" fee. These fees may also be paid indirectly through a clearinghouse center or commercial supplier. Many ILL offices use the Copyright Clearance Center (CCC) to pay the fees due publishers by keeping track of the requests and submitting a record of use for the sixth and later copy. Another option is to not request the sixth or later copy from a library but instead use a commercial supplier to obtain the article. The supplier will collect the fee on behalf of the publisher. The fees vary widely from publisher to publisher, with the more expensive journals requiring the highest fees. Reference librarians, in seeking the best source for a needed copy, should be aware of these fees; they can easily bring the price of a copy to $50.00.[27]

Full-text sources come with licensing agreements that may have certain ILL restrictions. Librarians are aware of the prohibitive restrictions, however, and will work with publishers to adjust the language to be sure cooperative sharing can continue when a resource is full text online rather than in print and on a shelf.

SUMMARY: ACCESS ANYWHERE, ANYTIME

The ILL process is a complicated one, but new tools and approaches to resource sharing are available to provide seamless access to remotely located materials. Reference librarians have critical roles to play in setting up new services and in ensuring that users can make effective use of them. With change now a constant in libraries, it is important that librarians keep up with evolving technology and the resulting products, because they will help to select and implement new systems that allow for the best options in access. They will also provide for the training and documentation that the users need to be aware of and best realize the benefits of the services. With better delivery options, reference librarians will be called to help finish that ILL cycle by ensuring that the user has the material in hand in a way not possible before.

Just as online systems integrated library operations, new tools will help to integrate access service programs. The reference librarian will help to broker all aspects of the information-seeking process from title identification to delivery (see Box 7.10).

Box 7.10 Final Product—Satisfied Users

There are many compelling reasons to develop enhanced ILL programs; the best are library user success stories:

A hospital librarian needed rush access to an article on rare fungi, which a local doctor suspected as a culprit in a patient's strange disorder. The serial title, an obscure agricultural publication, was held at only a few research libraries. One was able to retrieve it and send it over the Internet in less than four hours.

The natural history curator was ecstatic to receive a loan of an older museum bulletin that contained beautiful color plates needed for research. The journal generally did not circulate but an exception was made for this researcher.

The doctoral candidate was able to obtain copies of theses on one particular subject area, allowing for better focus on that user's own thesis.

A music teacher was looking for that perfect score that would bring out a student's potential in an important competition and located it in a library 300 miles away. ILL services provided for a loan and the student received the piece in ample time to practice, with much appreciation from the teacher.

Access to the world's library collections is important to all. Reference librarians play an integral role in the processes that provide this access.

NOTES

1. Brian L. Hawkins, "The Unsustainability of the Traditional Library and the Threat to Higher Education," in *The Mirage of Continuity: Reconfiguring Academic Information Resources for the 21st Century*, eds. Patricia Battin and Brian L. Hawkins (Washington, D.C.: Council on Library and Information Resources, 1998), 129-53.

2. Chandra Prabha and Elizabeth G. Marsh, "Commercial Document Suppliers: How Many of the ILL/DD Periodical Article Requests Can They Fulfill?" *Library Trends* 45 (Winter 1997): 551-68.

3. Eve-Marie LaCroix, "Interlibrary Loan in U.S. Health Sciences Libraries: Journal Article Use," *Bulletin of the Medical Library Association* 82 (October 1994): 363-68.

4. Greg Byerly, "Ohio: Library and Information Networks," *Library Hi Tech* 14, no. 2-3 (1996): 245-54.

5. William Gray Potter, "Collection Overlap in the LCS Network in Illinois," *The Library Quarterly* 56 (April 1986): 119-41.

6. The National Interlibrary Loan Code has been revised multiple times. The 1940 version clearly describes the service as one for scholars and researchers only, going so far as to say that graduate students must be careful to pick only those fields of study supported by their institution's library. A progression of revisions is available from: "Revised Code," *Library Journal* 65 (October 1, 1940): 802-3; "National Interlibrary Loan Code," *RQ* 20 (Fall 1980): 29-31; "National Interlibrary Loan Code," *RQ* 33 (Summer 1994): 477-79. Available: http://www.ala.org/rusa/stnd_Inc.html.

7. Mary E. Jackson, "Measuring the Performance of Interlibrary Loan and Document Delivery Services," *ARL: A Bimonthly Newsletter of Research Library Issues and Actions* 195 (December 1997). Available: http://www.arl.org/newsltr/195/195toc.html.

8. These authors were among the first to formally describe an ideal for ILL access. Harry S. Martin III and Curtis L. Kendrick, "A User-Centered View of Document Delivery and Interlibrary Loan," *Library Administration & Management* 8 (Fall 1994): 223-27.

9. Shirley K. Baker and Mary E. Jackson, *Maximizing Access, Minimizing Costs: A First Step Toward the Information Access Future.* Report to the ARL Committee on Access to Information Resources (Washington D.C.: Association of Research Libraries, 1992), 17p.

10. Lewis Carroll, *Alice's Adventures in Wonderland & Through the Looking Glass* (New York: Schocken Books, 1978), 221p.

11. Barbara G. Preece and Thomas L. Kilpatrick, "Cutting out the Middleman: Patron-Initiated Interlibrary Loans," *Library Trends* 47 (Summer 1998): 144-57.

12. "OCLC and WLN Have Now Merged (and Formed the OCLC/WLN Pacific Northwest Service Center, a Division of OCLC)," *Information Today* 16 (February 1999): 45.

13. *OCLC System Statistics.* Available: http://www.oclc.org/oclc/new/stats.htm.

14. Kate Nevins, "An Ongoing Revolution: Resource Sharing and OCLC " *Journal of Library Administration* 25, no. 2-3 (1998): 65.

15. William Saffady, "Commercial Sources of Cataloging Data—Bibliographic Utilities and Other Vendors," *Library Technology Reports* 34 (May/June 1998): 279-432.

16. Jay H. Lambrecht, "International Cooperation in Cataloging: Progress and Constraints," *Advances in Librarianship* 19 (1996): 217.

17. Marshall Keys, "Both Borrower and Lender Be: Reference and Resource Sharing During the Transition to a Ubiquitous Electronic Environment," in *The Future Is Now: The Convergence of Reference and Resource Sharing* (Dublin, Ohio: OCLC Online Computer Library Center, 1996), 28p.

18. Clifford A. Lynch, "Building the Infrastructure of Resource Sharing: Union Catalogs, Distributed Search, and Cross-Database Linkage," *Library Trends* 45 (Winter 1997): 448-61.

19. Janellyn Pickering Kleiner and Charles A. Hamaker, "Libraries 2000: Transforming Libraries Using Document Delivery, Needs Assessment, and Networked Resources," *College & Research Libraries* 58 (July 1997): 355-74.

20. Sheila A. Walters, "Commercial Document Delivery: Vendor Selection Criteria," *Computers in Libraries* 14 (October 1994): 14-15.

21. Two discussions on direct delivery were reported on the ILL-L listserv. The first is a brief report on the Auraria Library's experience in Colorado: Eveline Yang, *Re: Direct mailing copies* (April 7, 1997). The second details the AMIGOS network direct mailing option in Texas: Ron Glass, *Re: Direct mailing copies* (April 14, 1997) [Online]. Available e-mail: listproc@listserv.acns.nwu.edu.

22. *Cost-Effectiveness of Ariel for Interlibrary Loan Copy Requests: Summary of a Report to RLG SHARES Participants* (March 6, 1996). Available: http://www.rlg.org/ariel/arifax.html.

23. Charles C. Mann, "Who Will Own Your Next Good Idea?" *Atlantic Monthly* 282 (September 1998): 58.

24. U.S. Copyright Law of the United States of America, *Circular 92* (Washington, D.C.: Government Printing Office, 1995), 9p.

25. Ibid.

26. U.S. National Commission on New Technological Uses of Copyrighted Works, *Final Report,* July 31, 1979 (Washington, D.C.: Library of Congress, 1979), 55.

27. Nancy J. Chaffin, "Examining Copyright Fees for Article Delivery," *Serials Librarian* 31, no. 3 (1997): 67-78.

ADDITIONAL READINGS

Baker, Shirley K., and Mary E. Jackson, eds. *The Future of Resource Sharing.* New York: Haworth Press, 1995. 210p.

This book documents the reasons behind the need for libraries to work collaboratively to share resources. It includes examples of a variety of approaches to share more effectively and covers projects that are addressing the need to change ILL processes.

Boucher, Virginia. *Interlibrary Loan Practices Handbook.* 2d ed. Chicago: American Library Association, 1997. 249p.

An excellent manual on interlibrary loan processes, this volume covers everything from ordering to delivery.

Chrzastowski, Tina E., and Karen A. Schmidt. "Collections at Risk: Revisiting Serial Cancellations in Academic Libraries." *College & Research Libraries* 57 (July 1996): 351-64.

The authors reveal the tendency for research libraries to cancel the same serial titles, leaving them holding the same core of titles rather than maintaining a diverse group of titles.

Crews, Kenneth D. *Copyright, Fair Use, and the Challenge for Universities: Promoting the Progress of Higher Education.* Chicago: University of Chicago Press, 1993. 247p.

The author emphasizes the point that higher education is a key player in maintaining fair use. These institutions' researchers and scholars are adding to the volumes of copyrighted material even as they seek to make use of them. Institutions must work to promote good copyright guidelines and the fair use necessary for access to information.

Gasaway, Laura, and Sarah K. Wiant. *Libraries and Copyright: A Guide to Copyright Law in the 1990's.* Washington, D.C.: Special Libraries Association, 1994. 271p.

The authors offer a complete review of copyright law and libraries in the United States, with a brief section on international copyright law. Librarians may find many of their questions on copyright handled here, along with practical guidance on libraries' use of copyrighted material.

Grosch, Audrey. *Library Information Technology and Networks.* New York: M. Dekker, 1995. 385p.

Grosch gives an interesting historical overview of networks from local to national/international bibliographic utilities.

Higginbotham, Barbra Buckner, and Sally Bowdoin. *Access Versus Assets: A Comprehensive Guide to Resource Sharing for Academic Librarians.* Chicago: American Library Association, 1993. 399p.

This is a classic work on the new emphasis on access to collections rather than ownership.

Jackson, Mary E. *Maximizing Access, Minimizing Cost: The Association of Research Libraries North American Interlibrary Loan and Document Delivery (NAILDD) Project, a Five Year Status Report.* Washington, D.C.: ARL, January 1998. Available: http://arl.cni.org/access/naildd/overview/statrep/statrep-9801.shtml.

Mary Jackson describes the NAILDD project, the goals set forth, and the accomplishments thus far.

Lutzker, Arnold P. *Primer on the Digital Millennium: What the Digital Millennium Copyright Act and the Copyright Term Extension Act Mean for the Library Community.* Washington, D.C.: Lutzker & Lutzker LLP, July 4, 1999. Available: http://arl.cni.org/info/frn/copy/primer.html.

This report provides an update on the most significant change to the copyright law since 1978.

McCallum, Sally H. "What Makes a Standard?" *Cataloging & Classification Quarterly* 21, no. 3-4 (1996): 512-15.

McCallum gives a good overview of standards, which can help to clarify the use of that term in the library profession.

Michael, James, and Mark Hinnebusch. *From A-Z39.50 Networking Primer.* Westport, Conn.: Mecklermedia, 1995. 166p.

The authors provide a good explanation of the Z39.50 protocol, its history, and its importance to libraries.

Mitchell, Eleanor, and Sheila Walters. *Document Delivery Services: Issues and Answers.* Medford, N.J.: Learned Information, 1995. 333p.

The authors look at the subject of document delivery from all angles: technology, copyright, evaluation, and new directions.

Potter, William Gray. "Recent Trends in Statewide Academic Consortia." *Library Trends* 45 (Winter 1997): 416-34.

Potter documents how statewide consortia are combining forces to buy new systems, purchase online resources, and enhance ILL.

Sapp, Greg, ed. *Access Services in Libraries: New Solutions for Collection Management.* New York: Haworth Press, 1993. 245p.

This volume examines how internal library procedures in circulation and reference affect access. Access departments are phenomena of the late twentieth century. The volume includes contributions from access librarians and their approaches to this new type of organization.

Turner, Fay. "Document Ordering Standards: The ILL Protocol and Z39.50 Item Order." *Library Hi Tech* 13, no. 3 (1995): 25-38.

Fay Turner describes the ISO ILL protocol and how it works with ordering.

Weaver-Meyers, Pat L., Wilbur A. Stolt, and Yem S. Fong, eds. *Interlibrary Loan/Document Delivery and Customer Satisfaction: Strategies for Redesigning Services.* New York: Haworth Press, 1996. 265p.

Are users satisfied with interlibrary loan; what do they need and want for the service? What are ILL staff doing to meet these needs? These questions are addressed by the papers in this volume.

CHAPTER

8

INSTRUCTION

Lisa Janicke Hinchliffe and
Beth S. Woodard

INTRODUCTION

Instruction is a fundamental function of librarianship. Rare is the reference librarian, bibliographer, or even cataloger who does not have some responsibility for staff or user education. As libraries move into an age when one no longer needs to be physically within a library's walls to locate and use information, librarians are increasingly involved in education. At one time, users were required to visit the library building to use the card catalog, to leaf through periodical indexes, and to browse the bookshelves. With the increasing availability and sophistication of library computer networks, expanded availability of personal computers, and the proliferation of information resources outside the domain of the library, greater and greater capability for information retrieval is put in the hands of the independent library user. Librarians are taking on increased responsibility for educating users in retrieval, use, and management of information so that users can be successful in meeting their information needs.

WHAT IS INSTRUCTION?

In defining *instruction*, a statement on librarians and the teaching role of librarians made in 1876 by Otis Hall Robinson is as applicable today as it was more than 120 years ago. During the Conference of Librarians (the forerunner of the American Library Association's conferences) held in Philadelphia in 1876, a group of distinguished librarians were asked to respond to the paper, "Personal Intercourse and Relations Between Librarians and Readers in Popular Libraries," authored by Samuel Green, the librarian of the Worcester Free Public Library. In his paper, Green put forth a philosophy of personalized reference service for library users, including the admonition to "give them as much assistance as they need, but try at the same time to teach them to rely upon themselves and become independent."[1] Robinson, then head of the University of Rochester Library, responded in what was a visionary statement on librarians as teachers:

> I wish his paper could be read by every librarian and every library director in the country. A librarian should be so much more than a keeper of books; he should be an educator. It is this that I had in mind yesterday when I spoke of the personal influence of a librarian to restrain young persons from too much novel-reading. The relation which Mr. Green has presented ought especially to be established between a college librarian and the student readers. No such librarian is fit for his place unless he holds himself to some degree

> responsible for the library education of the students. They are generally willing to take advice from him; he is responsible for giving them the best advice. It is his province to direct very much of their general reading; and especially in their investigation of subjects, he should be their guide and friend. I sometimes think students get the most from me when they inquire about subjects that I know least about. They learn how to chase down a subject in a library. They get some facts, but especially *a method*. Somehow I reproach myself if a student gets to the end of his course without learning how to use a library. All that is taught in college amounts to very little; but if we can send students out self-reliant in their investigations, we have accomplished very much.[2]

Many years after the 1876 Conference of Librarians, the American Library Association echoed the emphasis on instruction in affirming the importance of instruction services in all libraries. According to the *ALA Policy Manual,*

> 52.6 Instruction in the Use of Libraries
>
> In order to assist individuals in the independent information retrieval process basic to daily living in a democratic society, the American Library Association encourages all libraries to include instruction in the use of libraries as one of the primary goals of service. Libraries of all types share the responsibility to educate users in successful information location, beginning with their childhood years and continuing the education process throughout their years of professional and personal growth.[3]

Instruction is, then, the teaching of individuals to become "successful bibliographic problem-solvers who learn through information use"[4] who also know when they need help. Instruction goes beyond the walls of the library, individual research tools, and search methods to the broader concept of information literacy. As the amount of information available continues to expand, and as radical changes continue to affect the ways that information is stored, organized, accessed, and used, it has become increasingly apparent that individuals need instruction, not only in the use of libraries, but also in the general handling and use of information throughout their lives.

Theoretical Approaches to Instruction

Numerous terms have been developed for instruction in the use of libraries and information, most notably *library orientation*, *library instruction*, *bibliographic instruction*, and *information literacy instruction*. At first glance, the various terms may appear to be semantic hairsplitting and, in practice, the terms are used almost interchangeably without mention of the distinctions among them. Indeed, in 1995, the Bibliographic Instruction Section of the Association of College and Research Libraries changed its name to the Instruction Section, perhaps indicating that what is of most importance is *instruction* per se.

To claim that each term is completely distinct from the others and that no overlap exists would be misleading. As the terms came into use, the programs that were described by the newer term often included everything indicated by the previous term, in addition to newer developments and initiatives. What the various terms do point to is the evolution of the theory of educational services in libraries and the different approaches that different libraries may use in providing instructional services. As such, each instruction term is worth some attention.

Library Orientation

Library orientation comprises activities designed to welcome and introduce users and potential users to services, resources, collections, building layouts, and the organization of materials. Although users may develop some research skills through these activities, the primary purposes are to increase user comfort and to welcome users. Goals for library orientation might include introducing users to the physical facilities of the building (service desks, staff members, and library policies), motivating users to come back and make use of resources, and communicating an atmosphere of service and friendliness.[5]

Library Instruction

Library instruction refers to instruction in the use of libraries, with an emphasis on institution-specific procedures, collections, and policies. The term emphasizes the library as defined by its physical parameters. The focus of library instruction is on in-depth explanation of library materials; it concentrates on tools and mechanics, including techniques in using periodical indexes, reference sources, card and online catalogs, and bibliographies. Sample objectives of a library instruction program include learning to use the *Readers' Guide Abstracts*, finding books on a subject through the library catalog, using microforms and networked information resources, and using specific reference tools such as the *Columbia Gazetteer* or *Facts on File*.[6]

Bibliographic Instruction

Bibliographic instruction began to be used in the mid-1970s to refer to any educational activities designed to teach learners how to locate and use information.[7] In contrast to library instruction, bibliographic instruction goes beyond the physical boundaries of the library and beyond institution-specific confines.

Proponents of bibliographic instruction have suggested that the term better reflects the teaching that is undertaken. Librarians were moving toward critical thinking and problem solving rather than tool-based or institution-specific approaches to instruction. In particular, the 1980s saw the emergence of an emphasis on a conceptual approach to instruction based on learning theory.[8] The more conceptual approach to bibliographic instruction focuses on teaching principles rather than specific tools, for example, the concept of the scholarly publishing cycle rather than the mechanics of a particular database.[9] The intent of teaching principles of information organization and retrieval is to provide learners with the knowledge to function in a broad range of information situations and environments. Such instruction emphasizes developing and using a *search strategy*—a systematic approach to identify, locate, and evaluate information.

Information Literacy Instruction

The most recent development in the theory of instruction is the theory of *information literacy* instruction. Paralleling the developing emphasis on information literacy has been an increasing focus on the process of learning rather than the process of teaching.

In 1989, the American Library Association Presidential Committee on Information Literacy called for individuals to develop information literacy to fully participate in the information society. Key to this document is its definition of information literacy (see Box 8.1).

Box 8.1 Definition of Information Literacy

To be information literate, a person must be able to recognize when information is needed and have the ability to locate, evaluate, and use effectively the needed information. Producing such a citizenry will require that schools and colleges appreciate and integrate the concept of information literacy into their learning programs and that they play a leadership role in equipping individuals and institutions to take advantage of the opportunities inherent within the information society. Ultimately, information literate people are those who have learned how to learn. They know how to learn because they know how information is organized, how to find information, and how to use information in such a way that others can learn from them. They are people prepared for life-long learning, because they can always find the information needed for any task or decision at hand.

American Library Association Presidential Committee on Information Literacy *Final Report*[10]

This definition sparked a sometimes vigorous and confused debate in librarianship about the implications of embracing the notion of information literacy.[11] To some extent, this debate continues. Loanne Snavely and Natasha Cooper summarize the main points of the debate in their article, "The *Information Literacy* Debate." After considering various pro and con arguments, Snavely and Cooper conclude with a recommendation for "embracing the term *information literacy*, using it carefully and with clarity."[12] Indeed, the profession seems to have followed that recommendation for, in 1997, the Association of College and Research Libraries established the Institute for Information Literacy, (1) to train instruction librarians, (2) to develop and provide programming for library administrators on information literacy issues, and (3) to support the Association of College and Research Libraries and the National Forum on Information Literacy in various higher education initiatives.[13]

Not surprisingly, while the debate about the term *information literacy* continued, librarians accepted the definition as stated in the *Final Report* of the Presidential Committee and set to work establishing information literacy programs. Indeed, Christine Bruce points out that "in the late 1980s and 1990s, interest in information literacy mushroomed on all continents."[14] Because information literacy instruction includes instruction in the use of information broadly defined, it is necessarily broader than library or bibliographic instruction activities. Librarians engaged in information literacy instruction become involved with a wide variety of educational activities both in the traditional library setting as well as in non-traditional settings. In many cases, this has led to increased collaboration with other educators and, at some institutions of higher education, librarians have become campus leaders in information literacy efforts across the curriculum.

School librarians have been active in developing instruction programs that replace the traditional library instruction goals of merely teaching physical access to information with information literacy goals. Michael Eisenberg and Robert E. Berkowitz provide a detailed curriculum for teaching library and information skills in *Information Problem-Solving: The Big Six Skills® Approach to Library and Information Skills Instruction.*[15] In 1998, the American As sociation of School Librarians and the Association for Educational Communications and Technology articulated "The Nine Information Literacy Standards for Student Learning" in *Information Power: Building Partnerships for Learning* (see Box 8.2) and in early 2000, the Association of College and Research Libraries approved the *Information Literacy Competency Standards for Higher Education* (see Box 8.3). These documents and many others provide excellent direction for school librarians developing information literacy instruction and can also serve as a source of ideas for developing standards and curriculum for other types of learners.

Box 8.2 The Nine Information Literacy Standards for Student Learning

Information Literacy

Standard 1: The student who is information literate accesses information efficiently and effectively.

Standard 2: The student who is information literate evaluates information critically and competently.

Standard 3: The student who is information literate uses information accurately and creatively.

Independent Learning

Standard 4: The student who is an independent learner is information literate and pursues information related to personal interests.

Standard 5: The student who is an independent learner is information literate and appreciates literature and other creative expressions of information.

Standard 6: The student who is an independent learner is information literate and strives for excellence in information seeking and knowledge generation.

Social Responsibility

Standard 7: The student who contributes positively to the learning community and to society is information literate and recognizes the importance of information to a democratic society.

Standard 8: The student who contributes positively to the learning community and to society is information literate and practices ethical behavior in regard to information and information technology.

Standard 9: The student who contributes positively to the learning community and to society is information literate and participates effectively in groups to pursue and generate information.

From *Information Power: Building Partnerships for Learning by American Library Association of School Librarians and Association for Educational Communications and Technology*. [16]

Box 8.3 Information Literacy Competency Standards for Higher Education

Standard 1: The information literate student determines the nature and extent of the information needed.

Standard 2: The information literate student accesses needed information effectively and efficiently.

Standard 3: The information literate student evaluates information and its sources critically and incorporates selected information into his or her knowledge base and value system.

Standard 4: The information literate student, individually or as a member of a group, uses information effectively to accomplish a specific purpose.

Standard 5: The information literate student understands many of the economic, legal, and social issues surrounding the use of information and accesses and uses information ethically and legally.

From *Information Literacy Competency Standards for Higher Education.* [17]

The shift to focusing on the literacy of the learner parallels a shift in education more generally from an emphasis on teaching to an emphasis on learning. Many colleges and universities are refocusing their missions to be institutions of learning rather than teaching. Likewise, developments in corporate training are emphasizing the process of learning rather than the production of training events. The continued development of computer networking technologies points to a future of learning on demand, with lifelong development of knowledge and skills, including information literacy.

Relationship to Reference Services

Although many assume that instruction is a recent outgrowth of reference services, instruction and reference philosophies developed simultaneously as responses to individuals who were unable to use libraries organized for the specialist or scholar. It is certainly true that the last thirty years have seen accelerated advances in the theory and practice of instruction. The resulting separation of instruction programs from reference services has caused some to wonder about the relationship between reference services and instruction. Are reference and instruction diametrically opposed? Must it be either reference or instruction? Does instruction detract from or enhance the quality of reference service? Is instruction merely an adjunct service to the reference desk? Or is reference an adjunct to instruction? In considering these questions, it is best to return to the roots of instruction and reference and remember that reference and instruction are intrinsically linked, complementary, and intertwined services. One study of academic library positions noted that "every announcement for a reference librarian position also mentioned instruction."[18] To separate instruction from reference or reference from instruction is to do a disservice to users.

Reference as a Form of Instruction

Some suggest that reference service is the most intimate form of instruction. Indeed, Samuel Green's approach was one of instruction through individualized and personalized reference service. In some instances, the one-to-one assistance a user receives from a librarian may be the most effective form of instruction. Ideally, individualized and personalized reference service would be available to everyone, whenever and wherever it is needed; however, leaving instruction solely to the reference desk is not always possible or practical.

Instruction at the reference desk presupposes that a user will approach the desk and ask a question and that the librarian on duty will have the time to provide instruction. What happens if one librarian is on duty and ten individuals are in line? Instruction might be abandoned in favor of the expedient answer. In-depth reference service is typically tied to a place and set hours. If dependent on reference services for assistance, how will users get help when they remotely access the online system and they do not get the desired results, or when the library is open but the reference desk is closed? The limitations of the reference desk can create barriers to educating users.

An Instructional Philosophy of Reference Service

One philosophical approach to reference work is that instruction is a part of reference. When reference librarians approach a reference question with an instructional philosophy, not only do they provide the information that users need, they also capitalize on the opportunity to utilize the experience as a "teaching moment." The old Chinese proverb—"Give a man a fish, feed him for a day; Teach a man to fish, feed him for a lifetime"—certainly describes this approach.

Every reference encounter requires a decision along a spectrum, with providing the complete answer on one end and teaching a search strategy on the other end. Most encounters fall somewhere in the middle. Even individuals who feel very strongly about their teaching role may provide "information" without elaboration when it is appropriate for that situation.

Creating handouts, bibliographies, and Web pages; providing better signage; and improving library layout are all reference services within an instructional framework. Providing the information and strategy to the user at the point of need allows users to access library materials and information resources independently, if they so desire. One-on-one instruction at the reference desk provides personalized strategies for research as well as advice on how to use specific skills.

Instruction as a Separate Service

Instruction services provide solutions for overcoming the limitations of the reference desk while meeting the needs of users. Moving away from a focus on the librarian as a continuous provider of information, instruction emphasizes information independence for users. This emphasis is important for several reasons:

- An information society requires a citizenry capable of accessing, evaluating, and using information independently.[19]
- Computer networking technologies enable users to complete vast amounts of research without physical presence in a library. The breakdown of geographic boundaries for access to information resources demands an alternative to traditional reference desk service.[20]
- Libraries have recognized that not all user needs can be addressed through traditional reference services because those services cannot effectively handle the ever-increasing demands for assistance given current and expected staffing levels.[21]
- Institutions of higher education, corporate training, and continuing education programs are emphasizing learning as an outcome rather than teaching, which is a method.[22]

As professionals, librarians are always reexamining and questioning library services, including instruction. Many questions exist and will continue to exist. How do libraries provide services to "invisible" users remotely accessing information systems? How are electronic retrieval skills best taught? How can technology and Internet resources be integrated into education programs? What impacts do networks, resource sharing, and electronic mail have on reference services and instruction and on how people learn? Both traditional reference desk service and instruction will continue to undergo dramatic changes as technology influences the relationship between librarians, users, and information resources.[23]

DEVELOPING AND IMPLEMENTING INSTRUCTION

As explained earlier in this chapter, library orientation, library instruction, bibliographic instruction, and information literacy instruction are terms used to describe various theoretical approaches to instruction in libraries. Like most educational theories, these various theoretical approaches do not necessarily translate directly into practice but rather serve as the underlying philosophical foundations of instructional practices. Regardless of the underlying theoretical approach, developing and implementing instruction is a complex and multifaceted process. The process of developing instruction is called *instructional design*.[24]

One caveat is in order. The instructional design process is often presented as a series of sequential stages distinct from one another, and this is how it will be presented here. In reality, the process is much less sequential and the issues are far less distinct from one another. Instruction librarians must use their knowledge of the theory of instructional design to guide them through the reality of their work life and organizational circumstances. Six scenarios posing circumstances requiring the application of instructional design are interspersed in boxes throughout the text in this section.

Needs Assessment

Conducting a *needs assessment* prior to developing and implementing a specific instructional program is crucial to ensuring a responsive and appropriate educational program. A need is a discrepancy "between an actual condition or state and a desired standard"[25] and should not be confused with a want or a demand, neither of which is necessarily indicative of a discrepancy between *what is* and *what should be*. A *needs assessment* is the process of identifying existing discrepancies, prioritizing discrepancies, and then selecting discrepancies to be addressed.[26] According to Donna S. Queeney, the "most fundamental value of needs assessment is in determining which programs should be offered and what content should be included."[27] Needs assessment must be ongoing to respond to changes in user groups, information structures, and resources. Both external and internal factors need to be assessed to ascertain the educational needs of users and the library's ability to meet them.

Strategies for needs assessment are numerous, including literature reviews, surveys and questionnaires, observations, and testing. Literature reviews include research into local and institutional sources, such as archives, college catalogs, annual reports, statistical summaries, and promotional brochures, as well as use of national and international sources, such as clearinghouses,[28] discussion groups, and publications in library science and related fields. Surveys can be conducted that ask users about their needs and preferences or that ascertain staff attitudes toward instruction. Astute observation at the reference desk, in the stacks, or near computer terminals can also provide strong anecdotal evidence of user needs. Finally, users can be tested on their knowledge and skills. User surveys and observation are probably the most commonly used approaches in conducting needs assessment for library instruction.

After gathering and analyzing information about existing needs, the instruction librarian must determine which needs are highest in priority, which can be addressed through instructional interventions (not all needs are appropriate for educational solutions), which are politically acceptable to address, and so forth. After selecting the needs to be addressed, a general statement of the broad aim of the instruction to be developed should be formulated. This broad aim will serve as a touchpoint and focus throughout the remaining stages in developing and implementing instruction.[29]

Box 8.4 Scenario: The Needs of Genealogists

You are one of five reference librarians in a medium-sized public library. Each time you work a weekend shift at the reference desk you notice that you are asked a large number of questions about genealogy research. Raising this observation with your reference colleagues, you learn that they too have noticed this pattern in reference questions on the weekends. The head of the reference department suggests that the library consider offering a genealogy research workshop. You are assigned to conduct a needs assessment to determine whether such a workshop would be useful, who would attend, and what information should be taught. Outline your approach.

Structures of Instruction Programs

The particulars of program structures are somewhat dependent on the type of library—that is, whether a library is academic, school, special, or public; however, all program structures can be thought of as being on a continuum of collaboration. At one end of the continuum is instruction that is developed and offered by the library alone. At the other end of the continuum is instruction that is developed and offered by the library in full collaboration with another organization, group, or institution. Between the two ends exist a variety of collaborative structures.[30]

After identifying the existing instructional needs through an informal or formal needs assessment process, an instruction librarian should consider the available opportunities for collaboration and the desirability of those opportunities. In pursuing a particular structure for an instruction program, librarians must consider the political environment, administrative support, and the degree of interdepartmental and interinstitutional cooperation that exists. In some circumstances, a solo venture by the library may be more effective or more desirable than a joint effort. Neither end of the continuum of collaboration is inherently better than the other; what is important is that the structure implemented in a particular setting is the most appropriate and effective given the circumstances and instructional needs. The structure of the program should be decided upon before other instructional design decisions are made, to involve any collaborative partners early on in the instructional design.

The particular mix of instruction offerings and collaborations that exist in a particular library will be unique to that library's situation and mission. In "Structures of Bibliographic Instruction Programs: A Continuum for Planning," Lori Arp and Lizabeth A. Wilson detail a continuum of cooperation for academic libraries.[31] Defining the continuum is the level of cooperation required among librarians, departmental faculty, and university administrators. Orientation activities require little to no cooperation, whereas course-related instruction, course-integrated instruction, and team teaching require increasing levels of departmental faculty cooperation, and separate courses require the cooperation of university administrators as well. *Course-related instruction* occurs during class time with the support and cooperation of the course instructor and provides learners in a given course with the information skills needed to carry out one or more activities of that course.[32] *Course-integrated instruction* is developed at the time that the course is designed, is part of the objectives of the course, and is essential to knowledge of the subject.[33] At its most developed stage, course-integrated instruction takes the form of *team teaching,* where the instruction is designed, delivered, and evaluated by the librarian and classroom teacher together. According to Arp and Wilson, as an academic library instruction program develops and cooperation increases, librarians can move toward structures more fully integrated into the institution's educational mission and goals.

The program structures that develop in school libraries will be similar to those in academic libraries; however, curriculum guidelines, state education regulations, and staff certification requirements will also likely affect the types of collaboration that develop. In schools that embrace resource-based teaching, which uses a variety of primary resources rather than textbooks, high levels of collaboration are likely to develop and librarians will work closely with teachers and administrators to integrate library instruction into the curriculum.

In public libraries, potential collaborative partners are quite varied. In addition to schools and other educational institutions, public librarians might partner with businesses, nonprofit organizations, local governments, church groups, civic groups, or similar groups in developing instructional programs to meet the needs of different user groups. Likewise, special librarians have many opportunities to collaborate with other professionals within their larger institutions.

Even when extensive collaboration is in place, many libraries offer at least some instruction that is developed and sponsored by the library alone without any collaborative partners. For example, most libraries offer some form of library orientation designed to introduce and orient users to services, facilities, and resources, often in the form of guided building tours. Another type of library-sponsored instruction uses workshops to introduce users to methods and strategies for using particular resources; however, the workshops are developed for a walk-in clientele rather than for a particular group.

Goals and Objectives

After a needs assessment has been conducted and any collaborative partners identified, the instruction librarian is ready to identify the desired learning outcomes: the goals and objectives of the instruction. Goals and objectives do not guarantee successful instruction, but the lack of them could mean failure. Writing goals and objectives is a skill that may be frustrating and time-consuming to acquire at first, but it is an essential skill for good teaching.[34]

Written objectives for instruction are expressions of the intended outcomes or results of learning. Instructional objectives serve both the instructor and learner. For the instructor, objectives focus and guide instruction, provide consistency in structuring content, facilitate choices of media and methods, assist in determining supplemental learning aids and/or approaches for student activities, and provide a mechanism for evaluation. For the learner, objectives give direction, set clear expectations, increase motivation, focus time, and allow for self-monitoring. For both the learner and the instructor, objectives create a mutual understanding of content, expectations, and outcomes. Objectives help make learning more effective and efficient.

Levels of Objectives

There are three levels of objectives: general, terminal, and enabling.[35] *General objectives* describe the overall goals of a program and what the entire program is designed to achieve in broad terms. Often these are expressed in fuzzy terms such as, "understands," "appreciates," or "believes." *Terminal objectives* break the general objectives into more specific, meaningful units that are the intended outcomes of instruction. *Enabling objectives* define the specific knowledge or skills necessary to achieve the terminal objective; they describe the behavior of a person who has mastered the material. Enabling objectives have three characteristics: the performance (observable behavior), conditions (situation statement), and criterion (acceptable behavior and who judges the performance of that behavior).[36] See Box 8.5 for examples.

Box 8.5 Examples of General, Terminal, and Enabling Objectives

General: "The user understands how information is defined by experts, and recognizes how that knowledge can help determine the direction of his/her search for specific information."[37]

Terminal: "The user understands the processes through which information sources are accepted and disseminated in the research community."[38]

Enabling: Given a stack of general magazines and a stack of scholarly journals, clearly labeled (conditions), the student (the learner) can identify (the performance) at least five differences between articles in general magazines and those in scholarly journals (criterion).

Considerations in Writing Objectives

Some instructional designers insist that objectives be "stated carefully early in planning, specifically right after the goal or statement of general purposes is formulated for a topic. Sequentially, this may sound correct, but in actual practice it does not often work."[39] There are times when the design sequence is reversed. For example, a librarian may "inherit" a project to help students learn to use the online catalog using a Web-based tutorial. The general goals and the method have already been chosen. In other circumstances, the instructor's thinking is not clear until later in the process. Norman E. Gronlund advocates writing objectives that are "specific enough to provide focus for both teaching and the assessment of learning, without limiting the teacher's flexibility in selecting instructional methods and materials."[40]

Critics of writing objectives in behavioral terms argue that student performance may reflect less than what the student has learned.[41] Others note that it is difficult to isolate specific behaviors in affective areas and for the higher levels of cognition because, at higher levels, "overt responses are less dependable as evidence of internal states."[42] For example, an individual may act confident, but feel insecure. Others suggest that "specific learning outcomes simply serve as a *sample* of the types of performances we are willing to accept as evidence of the attainment of our general instructional objectives."[43] In the example of a terminal objective in Box 8.5, the student could just as easily have been asked to separate a pile of magazines and journals into two separate categories, telling why each periodical was put into a specific pile. (Note that neither of these two objectives asked the students for recall, or mere memorization, of the differences, but required application of what the student had learned.) Either performance—to list or to separate—gives evidence that the student can distinguish between the two types of periodicals. The specific performance is not needed to select a teaching method or to sequence learning events, but is necessary once the learning is to be assessed. Thus, an enabling objective without criterion might be stated as: "The student can distinguish between a general magazine and a scholarly journal."

Possible Frames of Reference for Objectives

Gronlund also suggests "using an overall classification of possible learning outcomes to serve as a frame of reference" to help broaden the possible areas considered, to aid in stating and organizing objectives, and to check for possible omissions.[44] Benjamin Bloom's *Taxonomy*[45] gives a hierarchical organization of learning in the cognitive domain (thinking skills) in six levels: knowledge, comprehension, application, analysis, synthesis, and evaluation, with the last three identified as higher-level thinking skills. Similarly, David R. Krathwohl and colleagues[46] have done the same for the affective domain, and Elizabeth S. Simpson[47] has detailed the psychomotor domain. A. Dean Hauenstein[48] takes a holistic approach to the three domains in rewriting the taxonomies as a unified whole. In applying objectives to libraries, instruction librarians will find assistance in the *Model Statement of Objectives for Academic Bibliographic Instruction,*[49] developed by the former Bibliographic Instruction Section of the Association of College and Research Libraries under the leadership of Lori Arp. The *Model Statement* can be customized to a particular library regardless of type and to individual learners regardless of experience, age, or background. As a unique blend of several theoretical traditions, this document presents an excellent framework for thinking about instruction in libraries.[50]

Appropriateness of Objectives

To determine if the objectives are well written and appropriate, instruction librarians should consider the following questions:

- Are the learning outcomes appropriate?
- Are the objectives attainable?
- Are the objectives in harmony with the philosophy of the library?
- Are the objectives in harmony with the principles of learning theory?
- Is the learner the subject of the objective statements?

Box 8.6 Scenario: The Online Catalog Workshop

You have been hired as the instruction librarian at a small liberal arts college that has not previously had an instruction librarian. Your first task is to develop a series of one-hour open workshops for faculty and staff of the college to be held in the library's new hands-on electronic classroom. Because the library is bringing up a new online catalog interface, which has caused numerous faculty members to express frustration with not knowing how to use the new system, you decide that the first workshop you will develop will be an introduction to the online catalog. Describe the general, enabling, and terminal objectives that express the intended learning outcomes of the workshop.

Learning Theory and Styles

The most effective instruction efforts take into account learning theory and consider individual styles of learning. Therefore, it is essential that instruction librarians become and stay conversant with current learning theory.

Views of Learning and Knowledge

What is learning? What is knowledge? Although these may seem like easy questions, the answers are actually very complex and depend on how one looks at the world and views the nature of knowledge. Robert M. Gagné defines learning as "a change in human disposition or capability that persists over a period of time and is not simply ascribable to processes of growth."[51] Theories on how individuals learn continue to be developed and modified. As theories are proposed and become accepted, older ones are not necessarily discarded. Divergent theories exist simultaneously and are often considered equally valid in different situations. Although there is not one definitive, exclusive learning theory, the major schools of behaviorism, cognitivism, and constructivism have had particular impact on the field of library instruction.[52]

Behaviorists view knowledge as passive, largely automatic responses to external factors in the environment. Ideas are fixed and immutable. The learner adapts or responds to changes in the environment. Learning is largely seen as a passive process that focuses on new behavioral patterns being repeated until they become automatic. For behaviorists, the emphasis is on the *outcome* of learning. B. F. Skinner studied behavioral conditioning, in which reinforcement—positive, negative, or lack of—shapes behavior. Positive reinforcers help one to make connections, negative reinforcers cause learners to avoid undesirable responses, continuous reinforcement increases the rate of learning, and intermittent reinforcement contributes to longer retention. Edward Thorndike theorized that learning is the formation of connections or bonds between stimuli and responses.

Cognitivists view knowledge as symbolic, mental representations in the minds of individuals. The emphasis is on active mental processing or information processing. Changes in behavior are observed, but only as an indicator of what is going on in the learner's mind. Knowledge is still viewed as given and absolute but is formed and reformed through experience. For cognitivists, the emphasis is on the *process* of learning. Gagné's information processing theory argues that people can reason with higher-level concepts if they have learned all of the prerequisite lower-level information. Jean Piaget and R. C. Anderson independently advocated schema theories that view organized knowledge as an elaborate network of abstract mental structures that represent one's understanding of the world. Learners build schemata and make connections between ideas.

Constructivists view knowledge as a constructed entity made by each and every learner independently through the learning process, based on individual experiences and schemata. By reflecting on experiences, individuals construct their own understandings of the world;

learning is the process of adjusting and restructuring mental models to accommodate new experiences. Constructivists argue that teaching should focus on preparing the learner to solve problems in ambiguous situations. There are two schools of constructivist thought: cognitive constructivism, which focuses on the individual, and social constructivism, which focuses on social interaction. Piaget discussed situated (or shared) cognition, in which learning is viewed as the process of entry into a community of practice.

Humanists view knowledge as the acquisition of information and the personalization of that information. Learning occurs primarily by reflecting on personal experience and as a result of intrinsic motivation; it is defined as an increasing capacity to be self-directing. The role of instruction is to help learners extract the knowledge from their own insights and experience and *personalize* it. Humanist teachers focus on problem solving, development of human potential, and greater self-direction, making use of self-discovery, goal setting, esteem building, and relationship building activities.

These views of learning affect instruction in libraries. The influence of behaviorists can be seen in the writing of behavioral objectives, workbooks, linear computer-assisted instruction, and institution-specific instruction. The cognitivist theory is reflected in the use of conceptual frameworks and guided design, and in an increased awareness of learning styles.[53] Constructivist theory is reflected in the use of collaborative learning, synchronous and asynchronous online learning environments, and problem analysis.

Styles of Learning

Individuals also develop their own personal preferences for learning. Each individual develops a learning style or a habitual manner of problem solving. Educators have divided and analyzed these learning styles using a variety of measurements.[54]

One way that educators divide learning styles is into *field-dependent* and *field-independent*.[55] A field-dependent learner prefers learning by observing, is distracted by surroundings, seeks guidance, and likes learning in groups. A field-independent learner tends to learn through question and answer, likes to work alone, and is analytical in problem solving. Cerise Oberman has used "Petals Around a Rose," a dice game predicated on this distinction, to illustrate the importance of teaching problem solving.[56]

David Kolb found that individuals have tendencies to both perceive and process information differently. Learners can be *concrete* or *abstract* perceivers and *active* or *reflective* processors. Concrete perceivers absorb information through direct experience, by doing, acting, sensing, and feeling. Abstract perceivers, on the other hand, take in information through analysis, observation, and thinking. Active processors make sense of an experience by immediately using the new information. Reflective processors make sense of an experience by reflecting and thinking about it. (See Box 8.7, p. 190.) Traditional education practices tend to favor abstract perceiving and reflective processing.[57]

Another theory suggests that the two different sides of the brain control two different modes of thinking and that each individual prefers one mode over another. Left-brain thinkers are logical, sequential, rational, analytical, objective, and look at parts. Right-brain thinkers are random, intuitive, holistic, synthesizing, subjective, and look at wholes. In general, traditional school settings tend to favor left-brain modes of thinking and downplay right-brain ones.[58]

With so many views of how people learn,[59] it should not be surprising that there are also many debates about the validity and usefulness of teaching to so many different styles. "Using only one measure assumes that one inventory is more correct than others. At this time that assumption cannot be made. It may be assumed that, with human individuality, multiple descriptions of learning style are necessary."[60] It is rare for instruction librarians to be able to test learners before instruction, so they often must use aggregate data and research studies to make reasonable assumptions about student populations. Also, many psychological instruments are not available for administration by librarians. As such, instruction librarians must be prepared to address a variety of learning styles in any learning experience.

Classroom presentations must be supplemented with other experiences, case studies, class discussion or group work, time for reflection and practice, and so on. Similarly, Web-based instruction can also support different learning styles. For example, hypertext environments allow user choice in exploring instructional content as well as encouraging user interaction with the material. Electronic mail and other messaging systems can expand group interaction beyond the constraints of a fifty-minute session and give time for reflection before discussion.

Box 8.7 Kolb's Model of Experiential Learning with Examples of Appropriate Instructional Methods[61]

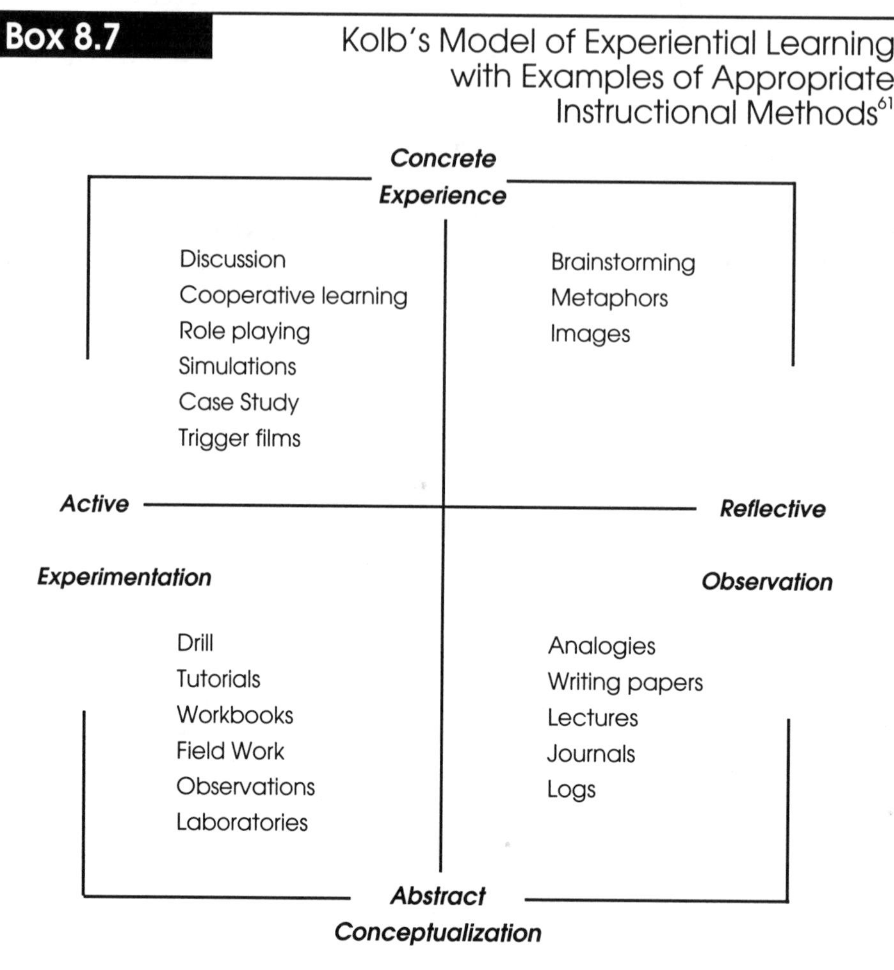

Instructional Methods

After a needs assessment is completed, learning goals are articulated, and learning theory and styles are examined, the instruction librarian begins the process of deciding what *instructional method* to employ. No one instructional method serves all situations, and the effectiveness of an instructional method is contingent on the learning objectives to be achieved, the learning styles of the participants,[62] and the instructor's facility with the method. Commonly, more than one method is used during a single session; for example, a class might begin with a short lecture that incorporates multimedia, go on to student brainstorming in small groups, and end with the entire class discussing solutions. A variety of teaching methods keeps learners involved and responsive, and every instructional strategy has certain advantages and disadvantages. It is essential that careful consideration be given to these advantages and limitations to ensure that the strategy selected for a specific instructional setting is one that will be effective and efficient.

Strategy decisions must be based on careful analysis of instructional objectives, subject matter, learner populations, instructors, instructional space, facilities, equipment and materials, time, and costs. "In reality, no one method or combination of methods can be applied with equal success in all circumstances. The instructor will often have to experiment with several different approaches to find the right one for a particular course and class."[63] The overriding consideration in the selection of strategy is the objectives of instruction—what the student will be required to do. Beginning librarians should explore their teaching strengths as well as methods that are most effective for their learners. Instructors should also consider the "Seven Principles for Good Practice in Undergraduate Education" (see Box 8.8), which are easily adaptable to other instructional settings.

Box 8.8

Seven Principles for Good Practice in Undergraduate Education

1. Encourages student-faculty contact
2. Encourages cooperation among students
3. Encourages active learning
4. Gives prompt feedback
5. Emphasizes time on task
6. Communicates high expectations
7. Respects diverse talents and ways of learning

Arthur W. Chickering and Zelda F. Gamson,
"Seven Principles for Good Practice in Undergraduate Education"[64]

Lecture/Discussion

A *lecture* is a semiformal discourse in which the instructor presents a series of events, facts, or principles; explores a problem; or explains relationships.[65] It is basically a means of "telling" and is used to inform. Lectures are presented by experts and are one-directional; that is, there is little interaction between the instructor and the students, with little or no interchange of ideas permitted. It is difficult to perceive student reactions, misconceptions, inattention, or difficulties during a lecture. On the other hand, lectures have the benefit of transmitting large amounts of information at one time to a large number of students. The length and content are easily modified and the largest amount of information can be conveyed in the shortest amount of time.

Discussion includes questions, answers, and comments from instructors and students. Discussion can be instructor-centered to "clarify content, define terms, identify assumptions, motivate participation, recognize contributions"; group-centered to "build on experience, explore hypotheses, strengthen relationships, raise questions, formulate ideas, examine assumptions"; or collaborative to "solve problems, share responsibilities, compare alternatives, test hypotheses, modify assumptions."[66] Leading discussion requires more instructor resourcefulness, initiative, and ability than does lecturing and also requires advance preparation of the participants in the form of reading assignments, thinking, and study. There are size limits, although small group discussion can be used effectively in large classrooms with advanced preparation on the part of the instructor. Relatively large blocks of time are needed for discussion to be effective. A high degree of student participation and their active involvement promotes better and more permanent learning.

Demonstration

In *demonstration*, the instructor actually performs a skill, showing the students what to do and how to do it, usually accompanied by explanations to point out why, where, and when it is done. Demonstrations give concreteness to oral explanations, helping students learn faster and more permanently and preventing misunderstandings. The student is usually expected to be able to repeat the task or activity after the demonstration. Students must clearly see every part of the demonstration, so environmental factors such as lighting, size of group, or the ability to project screens or pages are important. Equipment must function adequately; instructors need to consider backup approaches if equipment malfunctions. Models or mock-ups can be costly.[67] Because sequencing is usually important in demonstration, situation, timing, and pacing are also critical. Students must be given time to see the action, think about it, and then perform the task themselves.

Active Learning

The literature suggests that students should do more than just listen for effective and efficient learning to take place.[68] According to Charles C. Bonwell and James A. Eison,

> They must read, write, discuss, or be engaged in solving problems. Most important, to be actively involved, students must engage in such higher-order thinking tasks as analysis, synthesis, and evaluation. Within this context, it is proposed that strategies promoting active learning be defined as instructional activities involving students in doing things and thinking about what they are doing.[69]

Active learning provides time for learners to process information and transfer learning to long-term memory and thus promotes greater retention of information and skills and higher cognitive learning. Learners have more opportunities to integrate new information with existing knowledge, so they are better able to translate what they have learned into their own schema. Active learning can be used to reinforce other methods. For example, students can be given a short lecture on Boolean operators followed by an active learning exercise in which they group themselves using individual characteristics like hair or eye color to demonstrate their understanding of Boolean concepts.[70]

Collaborative Learning

Collaborative learning is an umbrella term for a broad array of teaching methods that are learner-centered and based on the premises that learning is an active, constructive process; learning depends on rich contexts; learners are diverse; and learning is inherently social. The most structured form of collaborative learning is cooperative learning—a systematic instructional strategy in which "small groups work together toward a common goal."[71] Cooperative learning has been used successfully in library instruction.[72]

Five attributes must be present for collaborative learning to be successful: positive interdependence, face-to-face communication, individual responsibility, social skills, and time for reflection.[73] Obviously, establishing this kind of environment in a "one-shot lecture" opportunity can be extremely difficult, unless the learners are already comfortable in collaborative learning environments. Instruction librarians must learn to feel comfortable with giving up total control of the learning process, sharing that control with the students, and taking risks. When collaborative learning environments are established appropriately, they help students personalize knowledge and apply learning, thus improving student attitudes, retention, performance, and levels of success. In addition, students develop problem-solving skills and more effective communication skills.[74] Box 8.9 provides a framework for analyzing how time is allocated among different activities in an instructional session.

Box 8.9 Student Activities During Instruction[75]

What percentage of instructional time in a typical classroom period is focused on the following activities?

	Percent
Students reading	_____
Students watching	_____
Students listening	_____
Students talking	_____
Students writing	_____
Students reflecting	_____
Students acting	_____
Other	_____
Total =	100%

Include all time spent on instructional activities but excluding activities such as passing out handouts, taking roll, etc. Do not total above 100%. Even though students are probably thinking and writing while the instructor is speaking, count only the times when students are thinking or writing with no other activity going on.

What percentage of time in a typical classroom period do students spend doing the following?

Working independently	_____
Working in groups	_____
Total =	100%

Instructional Materials

Instructional materials include any and all resources that are created to assist with teaching and learning, including guides, worksheets, videotapes, tutorials, Web sites, and textbooks. Some instructional materials are designed to be used by the learner without formal instruction, whereas others are designed to be used within the context of an instructional presentation.

Handouts

Perhaps the most common type of instructional material is the handout. Handouts are used as stand-alone instructional opportunities as well as supplements to point-of-use instruction at the reference desk and during instruction sessions. Plain or fancy, simple or complex, handouts provide information and instructions that are needed by the learner but not easily committed to memory without practice. In some cases, the information might be needed only on rare occasions. In others, the handout supports the learner until a given procedure or informational detail is committed to memory. The handout is very flexible.

Regardless of their intended purpose, handouts must be well designed if they are to be useful to the learner. A poorly developed handout may actually make a given task more difficult than if no handout were available at all. When developing handouts, consider the following:

- Content: Systematic and careful decisions about the information that is included in a handout must be made; equally important to consider is what information will not be included. The type of information to be presented should also be considered in light of instructional objectives—Is the content declarative (knowledge that or knowledge about), procedural (knowledge how), or conditional (knowledge when or knowledge why)?[76]—as well as the structure of the content.[77] These factors will help determine how the information should be presented.
- Relationships: The relationship between the handout in development and other handouts and instructional content should be considered.
- Permanence: Decide whether the handout is for one-time use or will be used in multiple situations.
- Design: Size, orientation, white space, line width, typography, justification, fonts, and institutional standards are among the many design issues an instruction librarian should consider.[78]

Box 8.10 Scenario: Call Numbers

You are the school library media specialist in a suburban high school that uses the Dewey Decimal system. The teachers in your school have requested a handout explaining what call numbers are and how to use them in locating books in the library. Create this handout taking into consideration the following factors: content, relationships, permanence, and design.

Exercises and Assignments

Unlike handouts, which are often distributed to learners during instruction as well as at various public service points within the library, exercises and assignments are unique to instruction sessions. The purpose of an exercise is to provide learners with an opportunity to practice with new resources or skills. Assignments are similar in purpose but with the additional requirement that the learner is in some way responsible for demonstrating skill or knowledge through completion of the assignment, often to receive a grade or credit for the instruction. Although worksheets and research term papers are common assignments, there are many exciting alternative projects such as mock trials and editorials that should be considered as well.[79]

Like handouts, exercises and assignments must be well developed to be effective. When developing exercises and assignments, consider the following:

- Content: Instructional goals and objectives should direct the development of every exercise or assignment.[80] This will ensure that the activities required of the learners are directly related to the learning outcomes expected from the instruction and that the exercise or assignment is not "busy work."
- Realistic expectations: Overly complex activities that fail to provide for the developmental processes of learning will frustrate students. If an exercise or assignment is complex, break the activity into parts and provide students with opportunities to "check their work" before completing, perhaps incorrectly, an entire activity.

- Grading and feedback: Up-front consideration of how exercises and assignments will be graded or how other feedback will be provided to students will prevent situations in which learner performance cannot be assessed.

Both exercises and assignments can indicate the extent to which learners have accomplished the goals and objectives of the instruction session. Such assessment of learning is vital to evaluating the effectiveness of instruction and identifying areas where student achievement is less than expected or hoped.

Box 8.11 Scenario: The Persuasive Speech

You are one of two reference librarians at a community college. At the beginning of each semester, all 200 students in Speech Communication 109: Principles of Communication are required to do library research in preparation for a persuasive speech. Each student selects a general speech topic from a list of broad social issue topics (e.g., capital punishment, abortion, legalization of drugs, euthanasia, gun control, and pornography). Each student is then required to choose a specific position within the broad topic area and to find three scholarly journal articles. Presently, the students receive no library use instruction and often fail to narrow their topics and/or locate appropriate library resources. More often than not the result is frustrated students, edgy librarians, and disappointed instructors. As part of the institution's recently articulated commitment to information literacy, the department chair offers to schedule one and one-half hours of class time for a librarian to instruct the students in the use of library resources, provided that the students complete a graded exercise as part of the session. Develop objectives for this library instruction session and then, using those objectives as a guide, create an exercise for the students.

Instructional Technology

New educational technologies have given instruction librarians incredible promises—increased work speed through instantaneous transmissions, increased work efficiency, removal of possibilities of human error, provision of access to those outside the library's walls,[81] accommodation of different learning styles,[82] and improved interactions with others[83]—at less cost than the traditional methods. Instruction librarians should use technology in combination with other modes of delivery and teaching methods to make learning more active and interactive but must be careful that the glitz of the technology is not the primary reason for the changes. Often the old technology or method is equally, or even more, effective. For example, online tutorials may require less staff time for instruction, but by removing learners from the library environment, the learners are divorced from viewing the librarian as mentor and guide for their research.

Many libraries start by replicating existing materials within a new technological context, such as making paper handouts available on the library's Web page. However, instructional designers warn that "just making content available is not education. Learning requires action, interaction, and application."[84] The next phase of adopting new technology is to more fully utilize the technology's capacity for new and better ways of teaching by creating cooperative and independent learning systems. Developers of library instruction programs should take advantage of opportunities for high-speed, two-way, multimedia communication in delivery of instruction when appropriate for the learning objectives and student populations. The ultimate phase of incorporating technology into instruction involves a redesign of programs characterized by unmediated user access to source materials and tools, opportunities for apprenticeships and cooperative learning, and opportunities for self-paced learning where appropriate.[85]

Utilizing the full potential of instructional technology takes a great deal of time and requires that instructors learn new skills, develop support systems, and work collaboratively with colleagues to avoid redundancies and costly mistakes. The University of Washington UWired project,[86] which created electronic learning communities and provided a coordinated institutional approach to teaching and technology, is an example of a reconfigured learning environment in library instruction. Important to note is that UWired is not about technology, but about learning and community, with technology as the "lubricant."[87] In the final analysis, pedagogy must come before technology.

Evaluation

Evaluation is "a process involving the collection and presentation of information in a manner intended to increase the credibility and usefulness of that information."[88] Librarians regularly make observations and judgments about the effectiveness and value of instruction initiatives; however, evaluation is set apart from the everyday activity of making decisions by the purposive nature of the collection and analysis of data in evaluation. Although the same conclusions might be reached through everyday observation, conclusions reached through systematic data collection and analysis are likely to be perceived as more reliable and trustworthy.

The primary purpose of evaluation is the improvement of instruction for the benefit of learners. By investigating the success (or the lack of success) of past instruction efforts, an instruction librarian will be prepared to make sound decisions about future initiatives. Without the information that an evaluation provides it may be difficult to ensure that instruction efforts are responsive to needs and continue to improve. In the current era of accountability, evaluation results can also be used to answer queries from library administrators, legislators, or accrediting bodies about the impact of libraries on the information literacy of users.

In conducting a program evaluation, the instruction librarian must return to the goals of the instruction program. Put most simply, a program evaluation will investigate whether the program has met its goals.[89] Specific questions for investigation might include whether teaching methods are effective, program resources are used efficiently, learners develop intended skills, faculty perceive the instruction as valuable, students can transfer skills to another research tool, learners feel more comfortable,[90] and appropriate goals and objectives were selected for the program. Selecting appropriate methods, instruments, data, and conclusions are dependent on which particular question or set of questions is under investigation.[91]

Librarians who are not responsible for overall program evaluation may also be interested in using learner feedback to improve their own teaching. Assessment techniques such as The Minute Paper (see Box 8.12), The Muddiest Point, and The One-Sentence Summary can provide a wealth of information through relatively low-risk and simple procedures.[92] The results of such assessments can also inform and strengthen program evaluation conclusions.

Box 8.12 The Minute Paper

Directions to Learners: Please take one minute and respond to the following two questions:

1. What was the most important thing you learned during this session?
2. What important question remains unanswered?

Direction to Instructor: Tabulate the responses and reflect on any patterns. Use responses to guide subsequent instructional sessions. In particular, use learner questions to clarify content before moving on to new learning objectives.

ADMINISTRATION AND MANAGEMENT OF INSTRUCTION

Administering instructional services involves many issues, including organizational structures; personnel; budgets and funding; facilities; and promotion, marketing, and public relations. The beginning librarian may not be responsible for the management of a program; however, how and how well the program is managed will greatly affect the ability of all participating librarians to implement effective instruction.

Organizational Structures

The instruction librarian works within at least two organizational structures: that of the library and that of the larger institution. Both organizational structures have the potential to facilitate or hinder instructional efforts. The successful instruction librarian learns how to maneuver within the structures, pinpoint how and where decisions are made, and influence those decisions.

The greater institution may be a college, school system, public library board, community, or company. Within that structure, decisions about policies, procedures, budgets, and personnel are made that will affect the instruction program either directly or indirectly. The instruction librarian needs to determine where various decisions are made, who makes the decisions, and what information and processes are used in making the decisions. Some answers may be readily available and easily determined from the institution's organizational chart; others might be mired in institutional lore or affected by personalities. To effectively manage an instruction program, the librarian responsible must work within both the official structure of an organization as well as the informal networks of influence that exist in every institution.

Within the library, organization of the instruction program may take a variety of forms depending on the type and size of the institution. Instruction may be the responsibility of a separate department, the reference department, subject specialists, or any combination of these.[93] Each approach has advantages and disadvantages.

A separate department allows instruction librarians to concentrate on instructional design and delivery without the distraction of conflicting priorities and responsibilities. Although a separate department establishes visibility for educational services, it can also isolate instruction librarians from related service areas such as reference and collection development.

More typical is for instruction to be the responsibility of reference librarians or subject bibliographers led by a single coordinator of instruction, rather than an entire instruction department. Responsibility for instruction is a reasonable extension of the role of reference librarians and subject bibliographers; however, overwork and confusion of priorities can result when reference librarians or subject bibliographers take responsibility for instruction.[94] In such settings, an instruction coordinator is usually responsible for monitoring the instruction load and providing some type of leadership for the instruction program. In smaller libraries, the instruction coordinator may be a reference librarian with particular instruction coordination duties. In larger libraries, the instruction coordinator is likely to be a separate position filled by an individual specializing in library instruction.

In a one-person library, it goes without saying that the same person who selects and catalogs materials and provides reference services is also responsible for instruction. In many school and corporate libraries, the organizational structure of the "holistic librarian" is the norm.

Box 8.13 Scenario: Library Instruction and the Freshman Year Experience

You are a reference librarian at a research university which is developing a new program to support undergraduate students. This freshman year experience program divides students into learning communities. All twenty students in a given learning community will meet in a weekly success seminar and take at least two classes together in the fall and one in the spring. The success seminar will include instruction in library and research skills. The Head of Public Services has asked you to investigate different organizational approaches for providing this instruction. Specifically, you are to recommend whether the library should (1) hire librarians who will be solely responsible for providing the instruction to the 100 learning communities, (2) create a team of librarians who focus on this instruction but have other responsibilities as well, or (3) hire a coordinator and require that current reference librarians each provide instruction for some of the learning communities. Write a report that compares the advantages and disadvantages of each approach and then recommends a course of action.

Personnel

Instruction services, like most reference services, are personnel-intensive. Regardless of the organizational structure, staff with appropriate education, experience, and expertise are needed for an instruction program to be successful.[95] Without appropriate personnel, designing and implementing instruction is impossible.

The skills needed by a librarian with instruction responsibilities differ from those needed by the coordinator of an instruction program. In 1984, the Education for Bibliographic Instruction Committee of the ALA/ACRL Bibliographic Instruction Section identified the following proficiencies as required for entry-level librarians to perform instructional activities:

- Ability to select educational objectives for specific activities.
- Ability to select appropriate educational methods.
- Knowledge of evaluation techniques.
- Teaching ability.
- Instructional media skills.[96]

The same committee also identified the following proficiencies as needed for administrative instructional activities:

- Conduct needs assessment.
- Devise policies and plans.
- Acquire necessary staff and budget.
- Train and evaluate staff.
- Market bibliographic instruction.
- Conduct program evaluation.[97]

Instruction responsibilities, however, are not the sole domain of public service librarians. Technical services librarians may participate in the instruction program. Library support staff are also involved in the implementation of instruction programs, in activities such as handout compilation, scheduling, marketing, and, in some cases, delivery of the instruction.

Staff outside of the library in the larger institution may also do work that supports the library instruction program. For example, a university's multimedia development unit might assist with the creation of a Web-based library tutorial or a company's marketing department might provide guidance in developing eye-catching handouts and signage.

Recruitment of qualified professionals and continuing education are major issues for instruction administrators. Because relatively few library schools have provided education for instruction, librarians may feel ill-prepared for instruction responsibilities.[98] School librarians with teacher preparation may fare better, but they often still lack specific background in library instruction and its development. Because of this lack of expertise, some libraries have established in-service training programs,[99] and many individuals—even those with extensive instruction experience—seek out continuing education opportunities such as the LOEX and WILU[100] conferences and the programs offered by the Institute for Information Literacy.[101]

Box 8.14 Scenario: A Position Announcement

You are one of four reference librarians at a private college. The two most senior reference librarians have announced that they are retiring. The reference coordinator has asked you to write two draft position advertisements—one focusing on reference and the other on instruction—for discussion at the staff meeting next week. Review the job advertisements listed on the *C&RL News Classified Advertising* Web site, create the two advertisements, and then draft a cover memo to the reference coordinator detailing the differences between the positions.

Funding

All aspects of designing, implementing, and managing a library instruction program will require financial support. A library instruction program must have ongoing funding to accomplish the program's goals and objectives.[102] Funding is needed for staff, equipment, supplies, facilities, instructional materials, promotion and marketing, and training. Without money, not much happens.

The library's budget for instructional activities should be integrated in the operating budget. In some cases, this will mean funds specifically allocated to the instruction program and managed by the instruction coordinator. In other cases, funding for instruction will be included as appropriate throughout the library's budget, such as funding for instructional equipment in the equipment budget or funding for training in the continuing education and travel budgets.

Funding may also be available for special projects through sources external to the library. A larger institution may provide funds through internal competitions. For example, a college may sponsor curriculum innovation grants or provide technology-enhancement funds. Instruction librarians might also apply for grants from state and federal government agencies and charitable foundations.

Facilities

Instruction programs have a variety of space needs, including space for instruction, preparation, storage, and staff offices.[103] With respect to the goals of an instruction program, the most important space is the space for instruction—the classroom. In *Designing Places for People*, C. M. Deasy explains that, because teaching is fundamentally about communication, "classroom design must therefore focus on providing the proper setting for effective and accurate communications."[104] In other words, the classroom environment itself affects the ability of students to learn. Whether a computer classroom or a traditional lecture or seminar room, layout, seating configuration, furnishings, heating, ventilation, air conditioning, lighting, and acoustics are some of the many elements to consider in designing classrooms.[105] Spaces in the reference room, microforms area, and other locations in the library may also serve as instruction spaces as demanded by the instructional needs of a particular group of learners.

Space for preparation is needed for the development of instructional materials, testing new technologies, and duplicating materials. Space for storage is necessary for equipment and supplies as well as instructional materials already duplicated and awaiting distribution. Finally, staff of the library instruction program must have office space and equipment to complete their tasks effectively and efficiently.

Publicity and Public Relations

Promoting and marketing instruction involves educating potential users regarding the availability of instructional services[106] and convincing those users to take part in instructional offerings. Publicity can take place through a variety of mechanisms, including formal liaison relationships, brochures, signage, the library Web page, personal letters, newspaper advertisements, an eye-catching logo, and word of mouth.[107]

As has been emphasized with respect to designing and implementing instruction, designing and implementing a program of publicity for instruction should be guided by the development of goals and objectives.[108] Developing marketing and promotional materials demands similar considerations to those that guide the development of instructional materials. Because library instruction programs primarily comprise services and not products, the instruction librarian should consult the general literature on nonprofit services marketing.[109] In addition to promoting instructional services, publicity should also portray librarians as educators and libraries as educational institutions. Finally, the results of the program of publicity should be evaluated for effectiveness.

FUTURE TRENDS AND CHALLENGES

The ongoing challenge of instruction is teaching the content—tools, skills, competencies, attitudes, and processes—that users need to know to be independent, information literate individuals in the current information environment and to be able to adapt to the environments that develop in the future. As libraries and information resources change and develop, so too must library instruction.

Networking and computer technologies are changing fundamental information structures and organizational principles. Librarians cannot teach a "one size fits all" strategy to all users (or even a few well-constructed strategies) as the "information" environment is constantly transformed into something less familiar. Users must apply knowledge in different environments, so librarians must emphasize concepts rather than teaching individuals to use specific tools.

Instructional technologies are altering the very nature of the learning environment. Distance learning environments are becoming increasingly commonplace; and even "on campus" students and "local" public library users are accessing materials remotely and are demanding that instructional programs be delivered in the same venue. As fewer individuals come in person to request assistance or to attend workshops held in the library, librarians must find ways to instruct users where they need help. Not only does this mean creating tutorials and online instructional materials, but it means becoming involved in the development of "Help pages," search software, and front-end library Web pages.

Instruction librarians are challenged to change the focus from *teaching* to *learning.* Although it is important for the teacher to plan instruction, the instructional activities themselves are not as important as what happens to the learners through the activities. This shift to emphasize learning implies that one must assess the impact that instruction has on the ability of the student to accomplish the task.

It is not enough just to make instructional materials "available." These materials must also engage users and provide mechanisms to actually involve the users with the materials and increase student time on task. Learning is often a collaborative activity, and librarians need to help students learn collaborative problem solving and interactive decision making in the classroom or asynchronously. The instructor must use a variety of instructional approaches: behaviorism to condition learners to do things in certain ways, cognitivism to teach problem-solving tactics where defined facts and rules apply to unfamiliar situations, and humanism to deal with problems that need formulation and reflection.

Librarians involved in instruction are challenged to take on a wider variety of roles. Not only do librarians model search strategies, coach users in their own search strategies, and facilitate group interaction, but they also need to develop skills as advocates for users, developers of collaborative communities, and trainers for other instructional librarians and for volunteers or students involved in peer tutoring. Librarians must seek out institutional partners in recognition that users cannot become information literate in an isolated environment.

Probably the biggest challenge to instruction librarians is to manage these changes. The challenges today are the opportunities for tomorrow. Instruction librarians must be ready to take on these challenges in educating users for today and for their lifetimes.

NOTES

1. Samuel S. Green, "Personal Relations Between Librarians and Readers," *American Library Journal* 1 (1876): 80.

2. Otis H. Robinson, "Proceedings: First Session," *American Library Journal* 1 (1876): 123-24.

3. "ALA Policy Manual," in *ALA Handbook of Organization, 1998–99* (Chicago: American Library Association, 1998), 43.

4. Harold W. Tuckett and Carla J. Stoffle, "Learning Theory and the Self-Reliant Library User," *RQ* 24 (Fall 1984): 58.

5. James Rice, Jr., *Teaching Library Use* (Westport, Conn.: Greenwood Press, 1981), 5.

6. Ibid., 6.

7. Association of College and Research Libraries, Bibliographic Instruction Section, Policy and Planning Committee, *Bibliographic Instruction Handbook* (Chicago: American Library Association, 1979), 69p. Interestingly, the term *bibliographic instruction* was unknown in the field or the literature when the Association of College and Research Libraries Ad Hoc Committee on Bibliographic Instruction was formed in 1971. The term appears to have been coined by the original organizers. Cerise Oberman, in "What's in a Name? The Search for *Bibliographic Instruction*," *Bibliographic Instruction Section Newsletter* (Fall 1993): 2, states: "Where did the term *bibliographic instruction* come from? It is difficult to say. I have offered the honor to Tom Kirk, but he refuses this distinction. Perhaps it emerged from the intense need of a group of librarians fervently seeking an expression to capture the new spirit that was emerging and at the same time distance themselves from old terms. Whatever the origin, it was apparently right. *Bibliographic instruction* not only became the label used to describe the library instruction programs, but it was soon used to characterize a new specialist—a bibliographic instruction librarian."

8. Constance Mellon, ed., *Bibliographic Instruction: The Second Generation* (Littleton, Colo.: Libraries Unlimited, 1987), xiii. See also Cerise Oberman and Katina Strauch, eds., *Theories of Bibliographic Education: Designs for Teaching* (New York: R. R. Bowker, 1982), 233p.

9. Pamela Kobelski and Mary Reichel, "Conceptual Frameworks for Bibliographic Education," *Journal of Academic Librarianship* 7 (May 1981): 73-77. Also reprinted as Pamela Kobelski and Mary Reichel, "Conceptual Frameworks for Bibliographic Instruction," in *Conceptual Frameworks for Bibliographic Education*, eds. Mary Reichel and Mary Ann Ramey (Littleton, Colo.: Libraries Unlimited, 1987), 3-12.

10. American Library Association Presidential Committee on Information Literacy, *Final Report* (Chicago: American Library Association, 1989), 1. Also available: http://www.ala.org/acrl/ili/ilit1st.html.

11. Lori Arp, "Information Literacy or Bibliographic Instruction: Semantics or Philosophy," *RQ* 30 (Fall 1990): 46-49; Christine Bruce, *The Seven Faces of Information Literacy* (Adelaide, Australia: Auslib Press, 1997), 10-13.

12. Loanne Snavely and Natasha Cooper, "The *Information Literacy* Debate," *Journal of Academic Librarianship* 23 (January 1997): 9-14. For additional readings and discussion, see Trish Ridgeway, "Information Literacy: An Introductory Reading List," *College & Research Libraries News* 51 (July/August 1990): 645-48; and Esther Grassian and Susan E. Clark, "Information Literacy Sites: Background and Ideas for Program Planning and Development," *College & Research Libraries News* 60 (February 1999): 78-81, 92.

13. Additional information about the Institute for Information Literacy is available at http://www.ala.org/acrl/nili/nilihp.html. See also Cerise Oberman, "The Institute for Information Literacy: Formal Training Is a Critical Need," *College & Research Libraries News* 59 (October 1998): 703-5. Also available: http://www.ala.org/acrl/iiltrain.html.

14. Bruce, *Seven Faces of Information Literacy*, 5.

15. Michael Eisenberg and Robert E. Berkowitz, *Information Problem Solving: The Big Six Skills® Approach to Library and Information Skills Instruction* (Norwood, N.J.: Ablex, 1990), 156p.

16. American Association of School Librarians and Association for Educational Communications and Technology, *Information Power: Building Partnerships for Learning* (Chicago: American Library Association, 1998), 8-9.

17. Association of College and Research Libraries, *Information Literacy Competency Standards for Higher Education* (2000). Available: http://www.ala.org/acrl/ilcomstan.html.

18. Chris Avery and Kevin Ketchner, "Do Instruction Skills Impress Employers?" *College & Research Libraries* 57 (May 1996): 258.

19. American Library Association, Presidential Committee on Information Literacy, *Final Report.*

20. Cheryl LaGuardia, ed., *Recreating the Academic Library: Breaking Virtual Ground* (New York: Neal-Schuman, 1998), 291p.

21. Cheryl LaGuardia, Stella Bentley, and Janet Martorana, eds., *The Upside of Down-Sizing: Using Library Instruction to Cope* (New York: Neal-Schuman, 1995), 249p.

22. Barabara Wittkopf, "Learning Paradigm," *Research Strategies* 14 (Spring 1996): 66-67; Robert B. Barr and John Tagg, "From Teaching to Learning," *Change* 27 (November/December 1995): 13-25.

23. For continued discussion of this issue, see "The Future of Reference II," *College & Research Libraries News* 50 (October 1989): 780-99; Joanne Euster, "Technology and Instruction," in *Bibliographic Instruction*, ed. Constance Mellon (Littleton, Colo.: Libraries Unlimited, 1987), 53-59; Anne Grodzins Lipow, ed., *Rethinking Reference in Academic Libraries* (Berkeley, Calif.: Library Solutions Press, 1993), 242p.; and Cheryl LaGuardia, ed., *Recreating the Academic Library.*

24. Mary Ellen Litzinger, "Instructional Design," in *Sourcebook for Bibliographic Instruction* (Chicago: Association of College and Research Libraries, 1993), 17-27.

25. Donna S. Queeney, *Assessing Needs in Continuing Education: An Essential Tool for Quality Improvement* (San Francisco: Jossey-Bass, 1995), 3.

26. Roger A. Kaufman and Fenwick A. English, *Needs Assessment: A Guide to Improve School District Management* (Arlington, Va.: American Association of School Administrators, 1976), 20.

27. Queeney, *Assessing Needs,* 14.

28. The National Library Orientation Exchange (LOEX Clearinghouse) serves as a clearinghouse for library instruction materials. Upon request, LOEX will send practitioners at member institutions sample scripts, videotapes, handouts, and the like. For more information, see the LOEX Web site (http://www.emich.edu/~lshirato/loex.html).

29. Charles K. West, James A. Farmer, and Phillip M. Wolff, *Instructional Design: Implications from Cognitive Science* (Englewood Cliffs, N.J.: Prentice Hall, 1991), 238-41.

30. For specific examples, see Jean Sheridan, ed., *Writing-Across-the-Curriculum and the Academic Library: A Guide for Librarians, Instructors, and Writing Program Directors* (Westport, Conn.: Greenwood Press, 1995), 240p.

31. Lori Arp and Lizabeth A. Wilson, "Structures of Bibliographic Instruction Programs: A Continuum for Planning," in *Integrating Library Use Skills into the General Education Curriculum,* eds. Maureen Pastine and Bill Katz (New York: Haworth Press, 1989), 25-39.

32. ACRL, *Bibliographic Instruction Handbook*, 58.

33. Ibid.

34. Librarians new to writing objectives should consult Robert F. Mager, *Preparing Instructional Objectives* (Belmont, Calif.: Fearon, 1975), 136p., for a lively, self-paced lesson.

35. Jerrold E. Kemp, *The Instructional Design Process* (New York: Harper & Row, 1985), 88.

36. Mager, *Preparing Instructional Objectives*, 21.

37. Association of College and Research Libraries Bibliographic Instruction Section, *Read This First: An Owner's Guide to the New Model Statement of Objectives for Academic Bibliographic Instruction* (Chicago: American Library Association, 1991), 8.

38. Ibid.

39. Kemp, *Instructional Design Process,* 78.

40. Norman E. Gronlund, *How to Write and Use Instructional Objectives* (Englewood Cliffs, N.J.: Merrill, 1995), 4.

41. William D. Rohwer, Jr., and Kathryn Sloane, "Psychological Perspectives," in *Bloom's Taxonomy: A Forty Year Retrospective,* eds. Lorin W. Anderson and Lauren A. Sosniak (Chicago: National Society for the Study of Education, 1994), 44.

42. Gronlund, *How to Write and Use Instructional Objectives*, 57.

43. Ibid., 9.

44. Ibid., 31.

45. Benjamin S. Bloom et al., eds., *The Taxonomy of Educational Objectives. The Classification of Educational Goals, Handbook I: Cognitive Domain* (New York: Longmans, Green, 1956), 207p.

46. David R. Krathwohl, Benjamin S. Bloom, and Bertram B. Masia, *The Taxonomy of Educational Objectives. The Classification of Educational Goals, Handbook II: Affective Domain* (New York: David McKay, 1964), 196p.

47. Elizabeth J. Simpson, "The Classification of Educational Objectives, Psychomotor Domain," *Illinois Teacher of Home Economics* 10 (1966): 111-44. (Also available as ERIC Reproduction Service Document No. 010368). Others besides Simpson have written taxonomies for the psychomotor domain, for example, Anita J. Harrow, *Taxonomy of the Psychomotor Domain: A Guide for Developing Behavioral Objectives* (New York: David McKay, 1972), 190p.

48. A. Dean Hauenstein, *A Conceptual Framework for Educational Objectives: A Holistic Approach to Traditional Taxonomies* (New York: University Press of America, 1998), 151p.

49. Association of College and Research Libraries, Bibliographic Instruction Section, "Model Statement of Objectives for Academic Bibliographic Instruction: Draft Revision," *College & Research Libraries* 48 (May 1987): 256-61.

50. Lori Arp, "An Introduction to Learning Theory," in *Sourcebook for Bibliographic Instruction* (Chicago: Association of College and Research Libraries, 1993), 10.

51. Robert M. Gagné, *The Conditions of Learning and Theory of Instruction* (New York: Holt, Rinehart & Winston, 1985), 2.

52. Discussions of contributions by Robert M. Gagné, B. F. Skinner, Edward Thorndike, Jean Piaget, and others can be found in: Greg Kearsley, *Explorations in Learning and Instruction: The Theory into Practice Database* (http://www.gwu.edu/ ~ tip/); *Guide to Theories of Learning* (http://commhum.mccneb.edu/PHILOS/learntheo.htm); *How Do We Learn?* (http://www.eiu.edu/ ~ edtech/teamTeach_Ex/index.htm); *CSCL: A Brief Overview and Interesting Links for Further Study* (http://www.uib.no/People/sinia/CSCL/); *Funderstanding's About Learning* (http://www.funderstanding.com/theories1.html).

53. See Kobelski and Reichel, "Conceptual Frameworks" and Oberman and Strauch, *Theories of Bibliographic Education.*

54. See Joan Kaplowitz, "Contributions from the Psychology of Learning: Practical Implications for Teaching," in *Learning to Teach: Workshops on Instruction* (Chicago: American Library Association, 1993), 57-70; Blue Wooldridge, "Increasing the Effectiveness of University/College Instruction: Integrating the Results of Learning Style Research into Course Design and Delivery," in *The Importance of Learning Styles: Understanding the Implications for Learning, Course Design, and Education*, eds. Ronald R. Sims and Serbrenia J. Sims (Westport, Conn.: Greenwood Press, 1995), 50.

55. Herman A. Witkin, Carol Ann Moore, Donald R. Goodenough, and Patricia W. Cox, "Field Dependent and Field Independent Cognitive Styles and Their Educational Implications," *Review of Educational Research* 47 (1977): 1-64.

56. Cerise Oberman, *Petals Around a Rose: Abstract Reasoning and Bibliographic Instruction* (Chicago: Association of College and Research Libraries, 1980), 23p.

57. See David A. Kolb, *Experiential Learning: Experience as the Source of Learning and Development* (Englewood Cliffs, N.J.: Prentice-Hall, 1984), 256p.; Carl Jung, *Psychological Types: or, The Psychology of Individuation* (New York: Harcourt Brace, 1923), 654p.; Gordon Lawrence, *People Types and Tiger Stripes: A Practical Guide to Learning Styles* (Gainesville, Fla.: Center for Applications of Psychological Type, 1982), 101p. See *Learning-Style Inventory: Self-Scoring Inventory and Interpretation Booklet* (Boston: McBer & Company, 1985), 14p. for one example of an instrument measuring individual learning style.

58. Bernice McCarthy, *The 4-MAT System: Teaching to Learning Styles with Right/Left Mode Techniques*, rev. ed. (Barrington, Ill.: EXCEL, 1987), 220p.

59. For more information on learning styles, see *Teaching Resources*. Available: http://www.studyweb.com/teach/trlearnstyle.htm.

60. Leslie K. Hickcox, "Learning Styles: A Survey of Adult Learning Style Inventory Models," in *The Importance of Learning Styles: Understanding the Implications for Learning, Course Design, and Education*, eds. Ronald R. Sims and Serbrenia J. Sims (Westport, Conn.: Greenwood Press, 1995), 44.

61. Based on Kolb, *Experiential Learning.*

62. Wooldridge, "Increasing the Effectiveness," 64.

63. Ronald R. Sims and Serbrenia J. Sims, "Learning Enhancement in Higher Education," in *The Importance of Learning Styles: Understanding the Implications for Learning, Course Design, and Education*, eds. Ronald R. Sims and Serbrenia J. Sims (Westport, Conn.: Greenwood Press, 1995), 22.

64. Arthur W. Chickering and Zelda F. Gamson, "Seven Principles for Good Practice in Undergraduate Education," *AAHE Bulletin* 39 (1987): 3-7.

65. William R. Tracey, *Designing Training and Development Systems* (New York: AMACOM, 1994), 253-55.

66. See Jodi Reed, "Engage Students with Variety and Interaction," *Videoconferencing Instructional Strategies* (1999). Available: http://www.kn.pacbell.com/wired/vidconf/instruct.html#Engage.

67. Tracey, *Designing Training,* 253-55.

68. A bibliography of active learning articles can be found at *The Active Learning Site.* Available: http://www.active-learning-site.com/bib1.htm.

69. Charles C. Bonwell and James A. Eison, *Active Learning: Creating Excitement in the Classroom* (Washington, D.C.: The George Washington University School of Education and Human Development, 1991), iii.

70. Paula Dempsey and Beth Mark, "Human Boolean Exercise," in *Designs for Active Learning: A Sourcebook of Classroom Strategies for Information Education*, eds. Gail Gradowski, Loanne Snavely, and Paula Dempsey (Chicago: American Library Association, Association of College and Research Libraries, 1998), 117-18. *Designs for Active Learning* contains more than fifty activities. For more active learning activities, see Jeanetta Drueke, "Active Learning in the University Library Instruction Classroom," *Research Strategies* 10 (Spring 1992): 77-83.

71. Robert E. Slavin, "Cooperative Learning," in *Encyclopedia of Educational Research,* ed. Marvin C. Alkin (New York: Macmillan, 1992), 1:235.

72. Marjorie Markoff Warmkessel and Frances M. Carothers, "Collaborative Learning and Bibliographic Instruction," *Journal of Academic Librarianship* 19 (March 1993): 4-7, found that pairing students allowed them to share ideas and helped alleviate computer anxiety; Kim N. Cook, Lilith R. Kunkel, and Susan M. Weaver, "Cooperative Learning in Bibliographic Instruction," *Research Strategies* 13 (Winter 1995): 17-25 (Note: the benefits of cooperative learning were not conclusive in this case); David W. Johnson, Roger T. Johnson, and Edythe Johnson Holubec, *The New Circles of Learning: Cooperation in the Classroom and School* (Alexandria, Va.: Association for Supervision and Curriculum Development, 1994), 111p., describes four levels of cooperative skills: forming, functioning, formulating, and fermenting.

73. Lizabeth Wilson, Sharon Mader, Lori Arp, and Mary Jane Petrowski, "Cooperative Learning: A Guided Discovery Workshop," in *The Impact of Technology on Library Instruction,* ed. Linda Shirato (Ann Arbor, Mich.: Pierian Press, 1995), 24.

74. Slavin, "Cooperative Learning," 236-37.

75. Adapted from a workshop by Trish Ridgeway, *Integrating Active Learning Into Library Instruction: Practical Information for Immediate Use,* A Pre-Conference sponsored by the Bibliographic Instruction Section of the Association of College and Research Libraries (Miami, Fla.: June 24, 1994).

76. West et al., *Instructional Design,* 15-16.

77. Ibid., 36-57.

78. Mary Jane Walsh, "Graphic Design for Library Publications," in *The Impact of Technology on Library Instruction,* ed. Linda Shirato (Ann Arbor, Mich.: Pierian Press, 1995), 141-58.

79. See Kris Huber and Patricia Lewis, "Tired of Term Papers? Options for Librarians and Professors," *Research Strategies* 2 (Fall 1984), 192-99; Miriam E. Joseph, *Term Paper Alternatives; Or . . . So You'd Like Your Students to Use the Library But Don't Want to Assign a Research Paper?* Available: http://www.lib.berkeley.edu/TeachingLib/PaperAlternatives.html; Marilyn Lutzker, *Research Projects for College Students: What to Write Across the Curriculum* (New York: Greenwood Press, 1988), 141p.

80. Christina J. Woo, "Developing Effective Library Assignments," in *Learning to Teach: Workshops on Instruction* (Chicago: American Library Association, 1993), 30.

81. Cheryl LaGuardia, et al., *Teaching the New Library* (New York: Neal-Schuman, 1996), 139-54, discusses instruction for remote users.

82. Po-Ching Wang, "Gardner's Multiple Intelligences," *Penn State Educational Systems Design Home Page: Penn State University* (http://www.ed.psu.edu/insys/ESD/Key/Keyschoo/key1.htm), gives examples of how instructional strategies can accommodate different learning styles. See also Arthur W. Chickering and Stephen C. Ehrmann, *Implementing the Seven Principles: Technology as Lever*. Available: http://www.aahe.org/technology/ehrmann.htm.

83. Morten Flate Paulsen describes possible technology-based teaching methods based on the number and type of interactions in *The Online Report of Pedagogical Techniques for Computer-Mediated Communication* (1995). Available: http://www.nettskolen.com/alle/forskning/19/cmcped.html. He describes several communication approaches: (1) One-Alone (online resources paradigm): online databases, online journals, online interest groups; (2) One-to-One (the e-mail paradigm): learning contracts, apprenticeships, correspondence studies; (3) One-to-Many (the bulletin board paradigm): lectures, symposia, skits; and (4) Many-to-Many (conferencing paradigm): discussion groups, debates, simulations, case studies, role plays, brainstorming, group projects.

84. Rick Ells, "Basic Premises of This Workshop," in *Effective Use of the Web for Education: Design Principles and Pedagogy* (1998). Available: http://staff.washington.edu/rells/effective/premises.html.

85. Barbara O'Keefe, "Learning Communities, A Paper Presented at the 1997 UIUC Faculty Retreat on College Teaching," in *Tradition, Innovation, and Technology: Teaching for Active Learning* (Urbana, Ill.: February 6, 1997).

86. See *UWired Web Page* (http://www.washington.edu/uwired) for more information.

87. Lizabeth A. Wilson, "The Way Things Work," in *Programs That Work*, ed. Linda Shirato (Ann Arbor, Mich.: Pierian Press, 1997), 9.

88. David N. King, "Evaluation and Its Uses," in *Evaluating Bibliographic Instruction: A Handbook* (Chicago: American Library Association, 1983), 5.

89. Litzinger, "Instructional Design," 24.

90. Carol Collier Kuhlthau, *Seeking Meaning: A Process Approach to Library and Information Services* (Norwood, N.J.: Ablex, 1993), 199p.

91. For more information on evaluation as well as information about specific evaluation methods and instruments, see American Library Association, Library Instruction Round Table, Research Committee, *Evaluating Library Instruction: Sample Questions, Forms and Strategies for Practical Use*, ed. Diana D. Shonrock (Chicago: American Library Association, 1996), 174p.; F. Wilfrid Lancaster, *If You Want to Evaluate Your Library* (Champaign, Ill.: University of Illinois, Graduate School of Library and Information Science, 1988), 193p.; and Mignon Adams, "Evaluation," in *Sourcebook for Bibliographic Instruction*, ed. Katherine Branch (Chicago: Association of College and Research Libraries, 1993), 45-57. More experienced evaluators may wish to evaluate the effectiveness of the evaluations that are in place using The Joint Committee on Standards for Educational Evaluation, *The Program Evaluation Standards: How to Assess Evaluations of Educational Programs* (Thousand Oaks, Calif.: Sage, 1994), 222p.

92. Thomas A. Angelo and K. Patricia Cross, *Classroom Assessment Techniques: A Handbook for College Teachers* (San Francisco: Jossey-Bass, 1993), 427p. See also Maryellen Weimer, Joan L. Parrett, and Mary-Margaret Kerns, *How Am I Teaching? Forms and Activities for Acquiring Instructional Input* (Madison, Wis.: Magna, 1988), 100p.

93. Anne K. Beaubien, Sharon A. Hogan, and Mary W. George, *Learning the Library: Concepts and Methods for Effective Bibliographic Instruction* (New York: R. R. Bowker, 1982), 230.

94. William Miller, "What's Wrong with Reference: Coping with Success and Failure at the Reference Desk," *American Libraries* 15 (May 1984): 303-6, 321-22.

95. Association of College and Research Libraries, Instruction Section, "Guidelines for Instruction Programs in Academic Libraries," *College & Research Libraries News* 58 (April 1997): 264-66. Also available: http://www.ala.org/acrl/guides/guiis.html.

96. Reported in Rao Aluri and June Lester Engle, "Bibliographic Instruction and Library Education," in *Bibliographic Instruction*, ed. Constance Mellon (Littleton, Colo.: Libraries Unlimited, 1987), 117.

97. Ibid.

98. See ibid., 111-24; and Diana Shonrock and Craig Mulder, "Instruction Librarians: Acquiring the Proficiencies Critical to Their Work," *College & Research Libraries* 54 (March 1993): 137-49. Bridgit Shea Sullivan, "Education for Library Instruction, A 1996 Survey," *Research Strategies* 15 (1997): 271-77 reports evidence that an increased number of library schools are offering separate courses in library instruction, although no evidence of a large overall increase in the number of library schools including library instruction in the curriculum in some way.

99. For information on implementing in-house staff development programs, see Mary Jane Petrowski and Lizabeth Wilson, "Avoiding Horror in the Classroom: In-House Training for Bibliographic Instruction," *Illinois Libraries* 73 (February 1991): 180-86; Association of College and Research Libraries, Bibliographic Instruction Section, *Learning to Teach: Workshops on Instruction* (Chicago: American Library Association, 1993), 76p.; Alice S. Clark and Kay F. Jones, eds., *Teaching Librarians to Teach: On-the-Job Training for Bibliographic Instruction Librarians* (Metuchen, N. J.: Scarecrow Press, 1986), 232p.

100. WILU (the annual Workshop on Instruction in Library Use) alternates in location between Quebec and Ontario and offers sessions in both French and English. Information about the 2000 conference is available: http://www.lib.uwo.ca/wilu2000.

101. The Institute for Information Literacy offers an Immersion Program with two tracks, one for new librarians and librarians new to teaching and the other for experienced instruction librarians who seek to further develop, integrate, or advance an information literacy program within their institution. Additional information is available: http://www.ala.org/acrl/nili/nilihp.html.

102. ACRL, "Guidelines for Instruction Programs in Academic Libraries," 266.

103. Ibid., 265.

104. C. M. Deasy, *Designing Places for People: A Handbook on Human Behavior for Architects, Designers, and Facility Managers* (New York: Whitney Library of Design, 1985), 105.

105. For a detailed discussion of these elements and much more, see Robert L. Allen et al., *Classroom Design Manual* (College Park, Md.: University of Maryland Academic Information Technology Services, 1996), 90p. A useful "Sample Facilities Assessment Form" is included in May Brottman and Mary Loe, *The LIRT Library Instruction Handbook* (Chicago: American Library Association, Library Instruction Round Table, 1990), 39.

106. Patricia Breivik, *Planning the Library Instruction Program* (Chicago: American Library Association, 1982), 119.

107. LaGuardia et al., *Teaching the New Library*, 73-74.

108. Breivik, *Planning the Library Instruction Program*, 121.

109. See, for example, Alan R. Andreasen and Philip Kotler, *Strategic Marketing for Nonprofit Organizations*, 5th ed. (Upper Saddle River, N.J.: Prentice Hall, 1995), 632p.

ADDITIONAL READINGS

American Association of School Librarians and Association for Educational Communications and Technology. *Information Power: Building Partnerships for Learning*. Chicago: American Library Association, 1998. 205p.

Information Power is a valuable handbook for librarians engaged in the development of school library media programs. Reflective of the leadership school librarians have taken in instruction, the book addresses missions and challenges of school libraries, the roles and responsibilities of school library media specialists, leadership, planning, management, personnel, resources, and association support.

American Library Association. Presidential Committee on Information Literacy. *Final Report*. Chicago: American Library Association, 1989. 17p. Also available: http://www.ala.org/acrl/nili/ilit1st.html.

The report of the Presidential Committee on Information Literacy convincingly presents the case for librarians taking a leading role in information education. Well-written and engaging, the report creates a compelling case for information literacy in personal life, business, and citizenship. The committee's recommendations have far-reaching implications for all librarians, not just those explicitly involved with education.

Branch, Katherine, and Carolyn Dusenbury, eds. *Sourcebook for Bibliographic Instruction*. Chicago: Association of College and Research Libraries, 1993. 89p.

The *Sourcebook* provides a desktop tool for the practitioner or library school student. The text has overview articles on the theory and practice of instruction and directs the reader to additional sources of information. The five main chapters include learning theory, instructional design, teaching methods, evaluation, and management of instructional programs. Appendices on setting up and managing a program, evaluating lecture presentations, and identifying associations that promote bibliographic instruction are of particular value.

Breivik, Patricia Senn. *Student Learning in the Information Age*. Phoenix, Ariz.: Oryx Press, 1998. 173p.

Breivik emphasizes resource-based learning as a strategy for helping students assume more responsibility for their own learning, especially in the area of information literacy, and for strengthening partnerships between faculty and librarians. Rich in examples already successfully implemented, this work outlines steps for developing a campus information literacy program.

Eisenberg, Michael B., and Robert Berkowitz. *Information Problem Solving: The Big Six Skills® Approach to Library and Information Skills Instruction*. Norwood, N.J.: Ablex, 1990. 156p.

This text presents a conceptual framework for information and library skills programs in school media centers. The Big Six Skills Curriculum is predicated on information problem-solving and critical thinking skills as key to library and information use by students. The book presents a thorough description of how to use a simple yet integrated approach to library and information skills instruction in the schools.

Kirby, John, Lucy Liddard, and Kay Moore. *Empowering the Information User: New Ways into User Education*. London: Library Association Publishing, 1998. 76p.

The authors define *empowerment* as "providing users with the necessary skills to find and exploit information that they need for work, study and leisure," and see it as a more encompassing term than *bibliographic instruction* or *user education*. Four case studies from different library settings are used throughout the book to illustrate how empowerment can be used in any information service. The processes of identifying user groups and their needs, analyzing and devising learning outcomes, designing the content of learning opportunities, delivering the program and choosing appropriate media, and monitoring and evaluating are summarized in this slim volume.

LaGuardia, Cheryl, Michael Blake, Lawrence Dowler, Laura Farwell, Caroline M. Kent, and Ed Tallent. *Teaching the New Library: A How-To-Do-It Manual for Planning and Designing Instructional Programs*. New York: Neal-Schuman, 1996. 171p.

The authors provide a practical guide to transforming teaching in evolving information environments, given new definitions of users, changing roles for librarians, and mixed information formats. Step-by-step they guide "the perplexed" through the process of creating a teaching program, including prioritizing instructional needs, drumming up support, analyzing teaching formats, recruiting and training teachers, and evaluating the program. Of particular note are the sections dealing with instructional settings, including alternatives to traditional forms with sample electronic classroom floor plans and an "unglossary" (a list of terms that should be left out of instruction).

Leckie, Gloria J. "Desperately Seeking Citations: Uncovering Faculty Assumptions about the Undergraduate Research Process." *Journal of Academic Librarianship* 22 (May 1996): 201-8.

Leckie describes information-seeking problems created by the typical research paper assignment. The large "disjuncture" between the expectations of faculty members as expert researchers and undergraduates as novice researchers are revealed in the research paper assignment. Undergraduates are more likely to use whatever sources are familiar even if those sources are not relevant. Leckie advocates a stratified approach with a six-part structure for the research paper process. She urges faculty to take responsibility for teaching library-based research skills, with librarians taking supportive roles as mentors.

GUIDELINES

Association of College and Research Libraries, Bibliographic Instruction Section. "Model Statement of Objectives for Academic Bibliographic Instruction: Draft Revision." *College & Research Libraries News* 48 (May 1987): 256-61. Also reprinted in Association of College and Research Libraries, Bibliographic Instruction Section, *Read This First: An Owner's Guide to the New Model Statement of Objectives for Academic Bibliographic Instruction.* Chicago: American Library Association, 1991. 45p. Also available: http://www.ala.org/acrl/guides/msobi.html.

Association of College and Research Libraries, Instruction Section. "Guidelines for Instruction Programs in Academic Libraries." *College & Research Libraries News* 58 (April 1997): 264-66. Also available: http://www.ala.org/acrl/guides/guiis.html.

CHAPTER

9

REFERENCE SERVICE IMPROVEMENT

Staff Orientation, Training, and Continuing Education

Beth S. Woodard

INTRODUCTION

In "The Making of a Reference Librarian,"[1] Samuel Rothstein argues that whether one believes that reference librarians are "made" or "born," a small industry has been devoted for over a hundred years to improving their performance at the reference desk. Most librarians agree that merely working with library users and reference sources on a daily basis does not ensure that reference librarians will acquire a thorough knowledge of a wide variety of sources, that they will understand users' requests accurately, or that they will translate the users' requests appropriately. Although some people have natural abilities in working with others and good instincts regarding how to approach reference questions—both asking appropriate questions and listening for what is not expressed—all reference librarians need nurturing and training to expand and complement these innate abilities.

New reference librarians often begin their careers with only the required library and information science courses to support them, occasionally reinforced with paraprofessional or preprofessional work.[2] Beginning reference courses generally cover specific reference sources, types of print and electronic sources, reference query negotiation, selection and evaluation of reference sources, and manual searching strategies.[3] Only one of these five topics is directly related to the service aspect of reference work. To use this basic knowledge effectively, reference librarians must be trained to apply their professional education to a particular library setting. A survey conducted in 1992 indicates that actual reference work is rarely integrated formally into reference courses.[4] It is unreasonable to expect new graduates to perform today's sophisticated reference services successfully, or even adequately, without an investment of time and effort on the part of the employing library. These graduates need careful orientation, training, retraining, development, and continuing education to maximize their potential for providing effective reference service. In a pilot study conducted in Ohio, almost all librarians surveyed felt that the skills needed to conduct a reference interview successfully can be taught. Most indicated that their formal training in conducting interviews had been given by their employers.[5]

Reference librarians rarely see themselves as educators or administrators, even though they often perform traditional educational and administrative functions, such as teaching individuals how to use the library catalog or an index and supervising clerks, students, paraprofessionals, volunteers, or other librarians. These supervisory responsibilities usually include training in some capacity. The average reference librarian is generally only vaguely aware of this role in training, either as a recipient or as a facilitator for others. This chapter describes the role of training in preparing reference staff to provide effective service and in maintaining skill levels.

As reference departments recognize limitations on the roles that professionals can play in providing reference service, there has been more of an emphasis on the use of paraprofessionals in reference services. Subsequently, there has been greater interest in designing training programs and in sharing information about the training process.[6] In addition, there has been enormous interest in training generated as a result of studies indicating that reference service is not always accurate (see Chapter 10).

When reference departments rely only on informal apprenticeships, serious gaps in reference staff training occur. Commonly, trainees—whether new reference librarians, reference assistants, student shelvers, or volunteers—learn a few specific tasks and never understand the rationale for what they are doing or how these tasks fit into the overall mission of the library. Employees not only need to be trained in specific skill areas related to their direct responsibilities, they must also have a knowledge base broad enough to understand the larger context. A broad knowledge base also allows them to learn the new skills they need to respond to the rapidly changing environment of reference and information services.

Today's reference staff are expected to handle changes that occur with increasing frequency. Reference personnel must live with uncertainty and must adapt to new management styles, changing user demands, advances in technology, and their own expanding roles in creating Web pages or participating in networked campuses or organizations, community outreach, and distance education. Unless training ensures that librarians are committed to the value of reference service, are able to provide instruction to users regarding available services, and are flexible in responding to changes, reference librarians will be limited to using traditional tools, and they will not be able to approach reference service in the context of changed user needs or new technologies.[7]

The terms *training*, *education*, and *development* are often used interchangeably. Leonard Nadler introduced the term *human resource development* in 1969, defining it as "organized learning experiences in a definite time period to increase the possibility of improving job performance growth."[8] He went on to make fine distinctions between training, education, and development, which Suellyn Hunt further clarified for librarians: "Training = job-related learning experiences; Education = individual-related learning experiences; Development = organizational-related learning experiences."[9] The various aspects of these three activities are explored in this chapter.

ORIENTATION

All staff members, whether part-time employees, temporary workers, or experienced individuals who plan to stay for a while, need *orientation*, or an introduction to the job environment. *Staff orientation* is "an initial training process designed to acquaint new employees with various aspects of the organization, including established goals, policies, and procedures; the physical environment; other personnel and working relationships, job duties and responsibilities; and fringe benefits."[10] Typically, this type of training is not transferable to another setting and provides little that employees could use if they took jobs in other libraries. Box 9.1, page 212, provides an example of an orientation program.

Box 9.1 Sample Orientation Checklist

General Orientation Checklist

Employee's Name: ______________________________

Weeks 1–2

Orientation to Reference Department

1. Meet with library personnel office representative
2. Meet with trainer to cover such things as training plan schedule, employee's work area, position's duties based on job description, and job conditions and benefits; hours, vacations, sick leave, and other matters
3. Organization and Goals of Reference Department
    - Reading material, such as New Employee Orientation Packet: IV. Reference, Reference Department Policies and Procedures Manual, and last year's departmental annual report. Explanation of Reference's mission, goals, and expectations
4. Tour of Reference, introduction to each staff member below: (list departmental staff, with job titles or areas of responsibility)
    - Location of important files or reading materials such as meeting minutes and staff newsletter

Orientation to Public Services

1. Read New Employee Orientation Packet: III. Public Services
2. Meet with assistant to head of public services—introduction to Public Services mission, goals, and policies
3. Tour of Public Services—introduction to key staff, including heads of documents, circulation, and interlibrary loan
4. Location of facilities, files, etc., including Photoservices and Microforms

Weeks 3–4

Orientation to General Library System

1. Read New Employee Orientation Packet: II. The General Library and Library Brochure
2. Tour of the Main Library, Branch Library I, and Branch Library II
3. New Employee Coffee

Orientation to the Campus/Community

1. Read New Employee Orientation Packet: I. The Campus/Community
2. Attend the Campus Personnel Office's new employee orientation session

Donnagene Britt, Patricia Davison, and Judith Levy, eds.,
Painlessly Preparing Personalized Training Plans[11]

Enculturation

Orientation provides a sense of support, defines the employee's singular role in the library, and establishes the individual as a part of the team. Dorothy Jones stresses that the training of new librarians should address the political setting, the work organization of the department, the details of each task, and the path to promotion and job retention.[12] The orientation program's ultimate goal is to promote a feeling of self-worth, a sense of belonging, an attitude of pride and confidence in both self and the library, and a desire to succeed. H. Scott Davis stresses that research has indicated that the first few weeks in a new job are important to establishing future job satisfaction and productivity in new employees and in capitalizing on the excitement and anticipation felt in the first few days.[13] One objective should be to address typical issues and answer typical questions before they cause frustration or inhibit productivity. *Enculturation* should be a part of orientation programs, communicating the culture, the expectations for dress and behavior (both the formal and the informal rules of behavior), and the importance of each individual in the organization.

To give the new staff member a sense of the organizational culture, including areas of authority and expertise, the individual should meet with key personnel throughout the organization. This allows him or her to discover how each unit functions and the interrelationships between units.[14] The personal connection also allows the individual to feel comfortable in returning to the expert to ask questions when needed.

Socialization

Socialization is also an important aspect of the reference orientation session. Employees need time to get acquainted with their coworkers in an informal setting, to discuss their activities in an unstructured environment, and to reflect on and absorb what they have already been told. In any training program, reference staff, as well as staff in other departments with which the trainee comes in contact on a daily basis, should be formally introduced, but they should also have some opportunity to meet on a less formal basis, such as a coffee hour or other informal gathering. This is particularly important for reference staff who must work together as a team and make referrals to other service points in the library.

Expectations

The first day of orientation is the appropriate time to discuss both the employee's expectations and the employer's. "Time spent here can prevent many misunderstandings and counterproductive situations later."[15] Anne May Berwind stresses the need for staff to discuss the local philosophy of reference service. This discussion should include the nature of the population of users served and the primary purpose of the reference service—whether it is to find answers as rapidly as possible or to teach users how to find information independently. Priorities for service should be agreed upon, and reference librarians need to know if they are expected to work independently or together to provide service.[16]

Orientation is only the first step in a continuing process. A positive, upbeat orientation program extending over a period of several weeks or even months can be very effective in helping the new employee to become an efficient, productive member of the library staff.[17] An effective period of induction will help the new staff member become more receptive to continuing training, absorb the details of the job, become a better team player, and feel comfortable in the new position.

Box 9.2 Library Orientation Outline

Organizational Values		
FIRST WEEK	**FIRST MONTH**	**FOURTH MONTH**
Institution's mission Library's mission Individual's role in mission Relationship between mission and evaluations and budget priorities	Library's approach to rules Departmental rules that may frustrate patrons Goals behind key policies	How and when to bend rules Problem solvers in other units How and when to gather patron concerns and suggestions and what to do with them

General Orientation		
FIRST WEEK	**FIRST MONTH**	**FOURTH MONTH**
Location of primary resources and services Basic desk procedures Library hours Emergency procedures	How to operate equipment How to complete necessary forms Phone system tricks Locations of smaller library units	The sequence of processing orders Directions to popular locations on campus or in the city The importance of continuing education and the types of programs that are available

Reference		
FIRST WEEK	**FIRST MONTH**	**FOURTH MONTH**
How to do simple searches in the catalog Types of reference sources Analyzing reference questions Location of the most frequently requested sources	How to do complicated keyword searches Desk reference collection How to use primary indexes How to use the sources in one popular academic subject area, such as education, that has "user friendly" reference sources	How to use the more-complex sources in various academic disciplines and special collections, such as government documents, business, and law How to tap informational resources that extend beyond the local collection by using sources such as OCLC, the Internet, or online table of contents services

Interpersonal skills		
FIRST WEEK	**FIRST MONTH**	**FOURTH MONTH**
Greeting patrons Encouraging patron follow-up Phone techniques Treating staff as patrons	Listening skills Making referrals Receiving referrals Coping with stressful individuals and situations	Dealing with irate patrons Saying "no" Dealing with patrons with special needs Intervening when another staff member is misinforming a patron

Joanne M. Bessler. *Putting Service into Library Staff Training*[18]

Conducive Learning Environments

A planned orientation also helps to establish an atmosphere that facilitates learning. Orientation reduces stress when opportunities are given for individuals to share work-related problems and questions. When similarly situated individuals share feelings of frustration and isolation, those feelings are reduced, and work relationships can also improve. Orientation can also be a motivator. When individuals see the library as an organization that is willing to put time and effort into orientation and training, they are likely to feel more a part of the organization and make a commitment to it.

When planning orientation and training activities, trainers should attempt to create learning environments that facilitate learning. Trainers need to remember that research about how adults learn suggests that the following elements need to be incorporated into the design of a training program:

- involve participants in mutual planning
- provide for active involvement
- promote individual discovery
- recognize the personal and subjective nature of learning
- accept differences
- recognize people's right to make mistakes
- tolerate ambiguity
- allow cooperation and self-evaluation
- permit confrontation[19]

BASIC TRAINING: LEARNING THE ESSENTIALS

Basic training in job requirements is mainly concerned with helping staff members learn fundamental job skills, but it also covers some skills that employees may be able to take to other jobs. The *ALA Glossary* defines training as "the process of developing the knowledge, skills, and attitudes needed by employees to perform their duties effectively and to meet the expectations and goals of the organization. This diverse process, which may be performed by supervisors, fellow employees, and personnel officers, involves planning, preparation, execution, and evaluation."[20]

Defining Competencies

If supervisors fail to define performance expectations, employees will establish their own acceptable performance levels, either individually or as a group. Studies have shown that employees set unofficial guidelines for productivity for the group.[21] Staff members will observe colleagues and draw their own conclusions regarding the kind of behavior that is expected if expectations are not clearly articulated.

The mutual development of performance expectations and objectives will avoid hidden expectations of standards. If clear standards and specific models of performance are described, individuals will know what is expected of them and how they are to be evaluated. If librarians, or any group of library workers, are asked to participate in establishing these objectives, the objectives are more likely to be accepted by the group.

After a consensus of what constitutes adequate performance has been established, the next important step is to write a competency description, which describes the correct performance of a job and delineates behaviors that signal when it is done right. *Competencies* are knowledge, skills, or attitudes that enable a person to function satisfactorily in a work situation, either alone or with others. Unfortunately, the profession as a whole has not come to a consensus about just what these competencies are for reference service.[22] However, a number of competencies necessary for effective reference service have been identified. One study has identified behavioral attributes that can be correlated with positive user perceptions of reference performance: approachability, interest, listening, searching, and follow-up.[23] See Box 9.3 for an example.

Box 9.3 A Portion of the RUSA Guidelines for Behavioral Performance for Follow-Up

5.0 Follow-up

The reference transaction does not end when the librarian walks away from the patron. The librarian is responsible for determining if the patron is satisfied with the results of the search and is also responsible for referring the patron to other sources, even when those sources are not available in the local library. For successful follow-up, the librarian:

5.1 Asks the patron if the question has been completely answered.

5.2 Encourages the patron to return to the reference service point.

5.3 Returns to the patron after the patron has had time to study the information source(s).

5.4 Consults other librarians when additional subject expertise is needed.

5.5 Makes arrangements, when appropriate, with the patron to research a question even after the patron has left the library.

5.6 Tries to ensure that the patron will get appropriate service after a referral by providing accurate information to the other department, library, or organization about the question, the amount of information required, and sources already consulted.

5.7 Facilitates the process of referring a patron to another library or information agency through activities such as calling ahead, providing direction and instructions, and providing the library and the patron with as much information as possible.

5.8 Refers the patron to other sources or institutions when the query cannot be answered to the satisfaction of the patron.

RASD Ad Hoc Committee on
Behavioral Guidelines for Reference and Information Services,
"RUSA Guidelines for Behavioral Performance of Reference and
Information Services Professionals"[24]

Some other reference competencies can be derived from the various functions performed by reference librarians. In the reference interview, reference staff need to have excellent communication skills, including listening, instructing others, and giving clear directions. Virginia Massey-Burzio emphasizes that reference librarians need communication skills, "In addition to verbal skills, writing skills are also needed since a considerable part of a reference librarian's life is spent preparing brochures, pathfinders, flyers, point-of-use instruction guides, grant proposals, articles in the campus newspaper and in library newsletters, and other written communication."[25] Reference staff need to be able to work well in teams and foster ways of sharing knowledge. They must deal with angry and frustrated users as well as diversity issues. They must prioritize when confronted with multiple demands and long lines of users. They must know when to give information, how far to go in providing information, when to stop, when to refer, and when to teach. Reference staff increasingly must develop presentation skills for dealing with groups.

When answering questions, librarians must know about available reference sources (both electronic and print), be able to find proper sources to answer the questions, be familiar with the library's collection and local resources, and use appropriate technology. They also have to maintain awareness of community resources and optional delivery services through interlibrary loan, consortial agreements, FAX, and full-text services. They have to maintain at least minimal skill levels in searching online systems and the Internet. Mary Nofsinger identifies six major categories of competencies: reference skills and subject knowledge, communication and interpersonal skills, technological skills, analytical and critical thinking skills, management and supervisory skills, and commitment to user services.[26] Although these are only a few of the functions that reference librarians perform, they illustrate the diversity of competencies required.[27]

Competencies can be identified for specific staff levels or for particular services. For example, certain groups of staff may provide all levels of reference service, from providing directional assistance to complex bibliographic verification and research consultation. Other staff members may only provide directional and ready-reference assistance, and refer all other queries to a more experienced staff member, a different level of staff, or to another service point. These levels can be by service point or may all be located at the same desk. Box 9.4, page 218, provides an example of core competencies needed in an academic library.

Assessing Training Needs

Reference departments frequently hire new staff members. Because no department has unlimited time or funds to train, it needs to determine how to get the most from training. Therefore, it is essential to conduct a *needs assessments*. Needs assessment is important to plan, manage, and allocate scarce training dollars, as well as to evaluate training results. Training needs are competencies required or desired but which have not yet been developed. Training should never be conducted without identifying its purpose or need.

There has been a great deal of discussion about what reference librarians need to know, from a general liberal arts and sciences background that gives a basis of knowledge to comprehensive knowledge of reference sources. A public service attitude, communication skills, teaching ability, an ability to evaluate information, a knowledge of the structure of literature, and the ability to formulate search strategies effectively are all aspects of reference service that most reference librarians would include as requirements.

Analyzing Tasks

Analyzing what goes on at the reference or information desk can be a good beginning for identifying needs of reference librarians or paraprofessionals. Reference interview techniques; knowledge of reference sources; ability to manipulate online and card catalogs, local files, community information, CD-ROM stations, online databases, or networked resources; and working as a team with colleagues, sharing knowledge in a constructive way, are all areas in which any staff member who works at a reference or information desk should be competent. Although analysis of reference desk activities is a good way to identify basic training needs for new reference desk workers, many other techniques are available.[28]

Box 9.4 Core Competencies, University Libraries, University of Nebraska-Lincoln

Analytical Skills/Problem Solving/ Decision Making

Recognizes patterns, draws logical conclusions, and makes recommendations for action. Uses a well-ordered approach to solving problems and sound judgment in making decisions despite obstacles or resistance.

Communications Skills

Listens effectively, transmits information accurately and understandably, and actively seeks constructive feedback.

Creativity/Innovation

Looks for opportunities to apply new and evolving ideas, methods, designs, and technologies.

Expertise and Technical Knowledge

Demonstrates broad, in-depth, and up-to-date knowledge of pertinent fields and awareness of current technology.

Flexibility/Adaptability

Performs a wide range of tasks, responds to changes in direction and priorities, and accepts new challenges, responsibilities, and assignments.

Interpersonal/Group Skills

Builds strong work relationships with a sensitivity to how individuals, organizational units, and cultures function and react. Establishes partnerships at all levels and across department and functional lines to achieve optimum results.

Leadership

Sets and models high performance standards characterized by integrity. Earns trust and respect of others by coaching, inspiring, and empowering teams of people to achieve strategic objectives.

Organizational Understanding and Global Thinking

Demonstrates an understanding of the institution in its entirety and works to achieve results across disciplines, departments, and functions. Develops and maintains supportive relationships across the organization.

Ownership/Accountability/ Dependability

Accepts responsibility for actions, results, and risks. Gets the job done.

Planning and Organizational Skills

Anticipates and predicts internal and external changes, trends, and influences in order to effectively allocate resources and implement appropriate library initiatives.

Resource Management

Demonstrates a consistent focus on minimizing expenses while maximizing results.

Service Attitude/User Satisfaction

Understands and meets the needs of users and addresses their interests and concerns of those affected.

Joan Giesecke and Beth McNeil. "Core Competencies and the Learning Organization" *Library Administration and Management*[29]

Interviews

Interviews, either with individuals or in groups, are particularly useful in determining the needs of experienced librarians.[30] From interviews, it may be determined that librarians have specific ongoing training needs, such as further practice in asking open-ended questions and achieving closure in the reference interview. Other areas in which experienced personnel generally identify training needs are in using new equipment or systems, learning new sources and tools, and reviewing little-used reference sources. Box 9.5 provides a sample list of the training needs of a reference assistant.

Box 9.5 Sample List of Training Needs of a Reference Assistant

Task: "Responds to patron information needs through the use of reference sources"

Needs to know:

Where things are in the building, emphasizing reference area

Understand library policies regarding amount of help given to each category of patrons

How to conduct a reference interview

What is in the reference collection

What are the types of reference sources (almanacs, dictionaries, etc.)

How to use the local "hard to answer" file

Understand to whom and how to refer difficult questions

How to use the telephone system

Julie Ann McDaniel and Judith K. Ohles, *Training Paraprofessionals for Reference Service*[31]

When Needs Don't Point to Training

When skill deficiencies exist, certain questions must be answered to determine the best course of action. If the job is one the employee used to do, have procedures changed? If not, then feedback and practice may be the answer. If procedures have changed or it is a new job, then procedures may be simplified, training may be done on the job, or formal training may have to be arranged. If there is no skill deficiency, then the obstacles to adequate performance must be examined and corrected. One obstacle may be that procedures are unrealistic or have not been clearly communicated. Creating practice sessions, a job aid, or a finding guide, or combining them, can be a more practical approach to helping people to perform infrequent complex tasks. Not all deficiencies in performance can be addressed with training; some performance problems are associated with environmental or attitudinal factors that prevent or discourage optimum performance. Other techniques, such as providing feedback on observed behaviors or planning practice sessions, can also be used to improve performance at the reference desk.

Box 9.6 Scenario: Is This a Training Problem?

A large university reference department provides occasional reference assistance in using the library's collection of British Parliamentary Papers. The staff has received training, which consists of reviewing the types of access tools, discussing formats, and examining a bibliography prepared by an experienced librarian. One particular staff member has trouble dealing with these questions. She ordinarily panics and turns to the person who prepared the bibliography. When that person is not available, she can generally muddle through to answer the question.

Is this a training problem? What are the obstacles to adequate performance?

Training Needs of Staff Groups

Every reference department has a variety of individuals who make up the staff and provide varying levels of service. From the student shelver and clerical person who checks in the books, to the paraprofessional who works the reference desk a few hours a week, to the senior reference librarian or head of the department, everyone has training needs that need to be addressed.

Volunteers

Although the use of volunteers to provide reference service is a managerial decision that may or may not come under the purview of the individual entrusted with training, the training of volunteers requires flexibility and individuation. Volunteers can range from unemployed librarians, to staff members in other departments, to well-meaning community members with little or no skills or background in libraries. Consequently, this makes it extremely difficult to lump them into a category. The kind of responsibilities they have in the department will determine the kind of training they will need. Museums and other nonprofit organizations use volunteers very successfully in their educational programs, and there is certainly no reason why libraries cannot do the same.

Students and Clerical Workers

Students and clerical workers have needs similar to volunteers in that they often come to their jobs without library backgrounds or familiarity, so they often need more than basic orientation to know where they fit into the system. They need to understand the terminology and the service mission of the department, with the understanding that they represent the library to many users.

Paraprofessionals

Paraprofessionals often come with a wide variety of backgrounds and skills. Some may have little or no library experience and little formal education; others may have extensive library experience; yet others may have advanced degrees in other subject areas. With such inconsistency, trainers must either test for each person's knowledge or assume no knowledge and begin from scratch.

Reference interview behaviors, as well as general information on how materials are physically and intellectually accessed in the library, need to be included, along with specific tools and sources paraprofessionals are expected to know. Generally, training needs to include an introduction to and practice sessions on the library's catalog and specific tools such as indexes in all formats that are appropriate (CD-ROM, online, Web-accessible, or print). In addition, types of information frequently in demand, such as biographical information, statistics, government information, newspapers or current events, or special types of materials such as newspapers and government publications, should be covered in a manner determined by the individual library. The sources chapters of this book can provide suggestions for these sessions or modules of training. Paraprofessionals also need guidance regarding how to examine a new reference source and how to identify strengths and weaknesses of specific sources. In addition, paraprofessionals will need written policies and procedures indicating when it is appropriate to refer users to professional librarians in the department or in other departments, other libraries, or outside agencies.

Because most paraprofessionals do not have the benefit of a library school education, they will need guidance in the process of approaching a reference question. For example, they need to learn how to analyze a question so that when they do not find the answer in the first source they try, they can devise an alternate strategy.

Writing Objectives for Training

If training objectives are to be useful, they must describe the kind of performance that will be accepted as evidence that the learner has mastered that particular task. This definition by behavior is used to measure whether the trainees have achieved the goal of the training and whether the training is successful.

There are three kinds of objectives: *acquiring knowledge, learning skills,* and *reinforcing attitudes.* Examples of knowledge in the reference setting include information and understanding about the reference collection, the general collection, library services, and policies. Skills of reference librarians include the ability to translate that knowledge into performing tasks, such as conducting reference interviews, instructing users, and communicating in a clear and concise way. Attitudes such as commitment and motivation are observable in the behavior of the reference librarian.[32]

With training as with other educational sessions (see Chapter 8), if objectives are to be useful, three elements are necessary: *performance, conditions,* and *criteria.*[33] Performance describes what is to be done—what the trainee should be able to do. Conditions describe the situation and the kinds of tools that can be used. Criteria describe the quality and quantity of work expected and the time allowed to complete the job. In reference work, this means the quality of service, including accuracy and completeness.

Selecting Methods

Selection of the most suitable instructional strategy is based on several considerations. One of the most important is congruency with the stated training objective. The strategy should recognize the need for trainees to respond and to receive feedback, should adapt to individuals' different learning styles, and should approximate what happens on the job. Factors that restrict the choice of strategy include the instructor's level of skill, the size of the group, costs, time, and equipment available.

Knowledge

Some methods are more suitable than others in helping trainees attain the objective. Objectives that stress knowledge acquisition, such as "describe the structure of biological literature," are appropriately reached through lecture, discussion, and assigned readings. Lectures and films require only that people listen and watch, while programmed texts and computer-aided instruction are specifically designed to require that a choice be made before the trainee can move to the next question, page, or screen. Research has shown that programmed texts are the first choice of trainers for knowledge retention.[34]

Skills

The use of videos has been increasingly popular in training. For communication and management skills it can model appropriate behavior. For technical procedures that apply step-by-step processes, videos not only demonstrate appropriate techniques but also allow slow motion and replay functions that will deepen comprehension. Used to record trainees' behaviors, video can provide opportunities for self-observation and evaluation.[35] *Trigger videos,* or short episodes, can raise a large number of issues, including sexual harassment, handling aggression or other problems, or behaviors that affect the image of the library,[36] and stimulate or trigger discussions.

Skills generally cannot be learned and applied without some sort of practice. Although the general concepts behind the application of skills, such as the steps involved in the reference interview, can be learned through lectures, demonstrations, or other passive forms of teaching, reference staff must *use* a skill if they are to apply it consistently.

Role playing, in which situations are outlined and individuals assume roles to try out behaviors in a realistic manner, is one technique that simulates the job environment. Other methods that simulate job behavior include case studies, management games, practice sessions, and workshops. Often, reference departments compile questions that have really been asked at their desks and ask trainees to identify sources to answer these questions.[37] If the training objective is to select an appropriate search strategy to find a known item in the online catalog, effective methods might include programmed instruction or a combination of reading, lecture, and discussion, as well as practice sessions. Because this objective requires that a choice be made, a method requiring a response will be more effective.

When introducing new staff to database searching, general searching techniques can be explained through lecture/demonstration. This can be followed by a set of practice searches for specific databases. Other databases, search software, and more specific search techniques can again be demonstrated with lectures and demonstration and followed by hands-on practice. As training proceeds over the course of several days with several different databases, trainees should start to ask when they would go to a particular source. Training people *how* to use a particular resource does not guarantee that they will know *when* to use it appropriately. After a discussion of the advantages and disadvantages of each system, the trainees can be divided into small groups and given a series of questions. They can be asked to try them in the different systems and report back to the group what worked and what did not. Providing an environment in which it is acceptable to make mistakes, but simulating the kinds of questions they will be asked at the information or reference desk, helps trainees learn for themselves when it is appropriate to examine a particular tool.

The best training promotes self-discovery, recognizing that "the most important things cannot be taught but must be discovered and appropriated for oneself."[38] As an ancient proverb puts it: "Tell me, I forget. Show me, I remember. Involve me, I understand." Adults learn best with active involvement, by solving realistic problems. If adults work things out for themselves, they are more likely to be able to work out a similar problem on the job. Active learning promotes the use of ingenuity and imagination rather than performance of a task in a set manner. Problem-solving skills can be learned effectively in this way, using case studies or in-basket exercises to simulate decisions that must be made on the job. Asking staff to take on training another person can have similar benefits.

Box 9.7

Scenario: Write Guidelines for Preparing Training

The introduction to and updating of the information staff, which consists of 12 library assistants, to online databases has gotten out of hand. There are just too many databases and too many software vendors for one person to keep track of. The reference training coordinator has decided to ask each of the 12 library assistants to be responsible for training the others. A small committee of reference librarians has been assigned to help the training coordinator come up with guidelines for the training. What should be included in the documentation that each assistant develops? Should they also be asked to develop handouts for users? How much autonomy will each assistant have in creating these training materials?

Attitudes

Attitudes can be influenced in a variety of ways, and experts differ in the approaches they suggest. With adults, interaction again is important, so sensitivity training, role playing, and discussion groups are useful means of changing attitudes.

Factors in Strategy Selection

The availability or lack of experienced trainers, instructional space, facilities, equipment, and materials can do much to facilitate or hinder the training process, and all influence the choice of instructional strategy. The time and costs of development, the size of the group, and the learning styles of the trainee population also restrict the choices the trainer can make. A number of training experts have written excellent guides to facilitate selection of training methods for the new trainer.[39] Instruction experts have also identified approaches to teaching library skills to users; these approaches transfer well to training situations.

Box 9.8 Scenario: Identify Training Activities

The reference librarian and the circulation librarian at a small college library have been asked to improve the staff's dealings with angry patrons. In doing research, they identified three steps: (1) calming the patron, (2) identifying the problem, and (3) providing relief. Staff have more difficulty with steps one and three. Brainstorm about possible training activities. What are the strengths and weaknesses of each?

Box 9.9 Develop a Case Study

In small groups, identify a problem area in reference services training and develop a case study. Share the case study with another group, asking them to actually work through the problem. Consider the perspectives of both staff and users in considering approaches. Ask the group to identify the strengths of this case study and offer suggestions for improvement.

Sample case study:

You are working alone at a very busy information desk at Green County Public Library. The mayor's secretary calls and says that the mayor needs the names and addresses of the publishers of about twenty periodicals and that she needs it now. Although the source of this information is at your service desk, the information will require multiple look-ups. Furthermore, you see three restless patrons circling your desk area. Identify three ways to handle this call that could satisfy the mayor and tend to your on-site patrons.

Joanne M. Bessler, *Putting Service into Library Staff Training*[40]

Facilitating Retention of Skills

In learning almost any skill, people go through an awkward phase when the newly acquired skill does not feel natural and does not achieve results. This period, called the "results dip" or "incorporation lag," is particularly difficult.[41] Initially, when reference librarians attempt to substitute a new behavior for an old one, it feels uncomfortable and results suffer. Some studies have found that up to 87 percent of the skills actually acquired by a training program may be lost if attention is not paid to making sure that these skills are retained.[42] Combating the problem of transferring learned skills to the job environment can take several forms, both during the training itself and back on the job.

Practice

Techniques that simulate the behavior used on the job are more likely to teach skills that will actually be used in that setting. The training program itself should include a sufficient amount of time to practice, which may be as much as a third of the instruction time.[43] Practice away from the job provides an opportunity to fail in a controlled environment without the normal consequences, a frame of reference for tasks to be performed in, and an ability to apply new skills learned more easily and readily.

Role-plays, although not a particular favorite with trainees, continue to be one of the best approaches to allow the learner to take part in a realistic, but simulated and therefore non-threatening, situation. Role-plays are excellent ways to demonstrate appropriate techniques to use with problem patrons and in question negotiation. Role-plays in isolation do not produce skilled performers. They do, however, help ensure that trainees learn the steps appropriate for skilled performance. This technique has been used successfully at Baylor University, where Janet Sheets has developed a role-play she calls "The Reference Game."[44] In this game, the emphasis is on the interaction with users rather than on the selection of a particular reference tool.

Drills, or short, repetitive exercises, can be used to master skills in small steps. As skills are practiced under a variety of circumstances, the trainee's ability to perform consistently improves. During these drills, trainees function as coaches for each other, helping to critique as each element or move is practiced and then combined into a series of moves. Drilling then provides confidence and "confidence builds 'ownership' of the skill. And ownership must occur *during* the training course in order for the skill to transfer to the real job."[45]

Several other techniques can be used during the training session to facilitate retention of skills learned. *Action plans*, where the participants reflect on program content and write goals of intended implementation, are useful techniques for maintaining behavior. These can take the form of a letter to oneself or an ideas and applications notebook. Other activities that can be incorporated into training sessions include *guided practicing* (as opposed to turning trainees loose for independent practice), and *question-and-answer sessions* that involve some sort of systematic pattern to include everyone.

Feedback

One of the most important methods of facilitating retention of skills on the job is *feedback*. There are two basic types of feedback. The first recognizes good work, general competence, or exemplary performance, and encourages employees to keep up the good work. This kind of feedback is important in maintaining skill levels, because behaviors can lapse through lack of reinforcement. Addressing the upkeep of these strengths is as important as fixing problems. The other kind of feedback is *improvement feedback*, which sends the message that change is needed. This feedback calls attention to poor work, areas of incompetence, or problem behavior.

Effective feedback is immediate, clear, accurate, specific, and positive. Behaviors should be reinforced as quickly as possible. Trainees need to be informed of the trainer's awareness of their behavior as soon as it happens, through attention, recognition, or praise. Negative feedback is better than no feedback at all, but positive feedback produces the best results. Employees tend to remember longest what they hear first and last in a message, and are more likely to apply suggestions if the feedback is personal and private. Approval of or agreement with ideas and behavior is communicated by the absence of feedback, so it is very important for people to be informed when their behaviors are not appropriate.

There are several ways to provide feedback on the job. Performance can be examined through personal diaries and self-reporting by individuals; through observations and interviews with supervisors, either informally or in a performance appraisal; or through buddy systems, support groups, coaching, or job aids. Very few of these methods have been reported as having been applied in reference settings. *Coaching*, which is basically one-on-one counseling, is one technique that has been used to provide feedback on reference staff performance in reference interviews, notably in public libraries. Coaching is one of the best ways to make sure that newly learned skills are transferred and maintained on the job, but it is a feedback technique that has only recently been applied in reference situations. Informal coaching situations can be established, however, merely by providing an environment in which an experienced person works with an inexperienced one. At one academic library with both an information desk and a reference desk, during the first month reference librarians work alongside newly hired graduate assistants at the information desk to ease them into their new environment and to give them additional opportunities for feedback.

Box 9.10 Scenario: Giving Effective Feedback

Mary, a new reference assistant, is handling the reference desk while the reference librarians are in an extended meeting. An abusive caller telephones the reference desk and demands to speak to a reference librarian. Mary tells the caller that none are available and asks if she can help in any way. He curtly says no and continues to be abusive without actually swearing. Mary hangs up.

When the reference librarians return from their meeting, the abusive individual immediately calls the reference head. After taking the call, John, the reference head, calls Mary into his office and says, "I hear you hung up on one of our users; tell me about it." Mary relates the story in detail. John says, "I think you did the right thing. No one should have to put up with that kind of abuse. However, based on what you told me, I think there may have been a better way to handle the situation. What do you think it might be?"

Was this feedback effective?

Other Interventions

Alternatives to giving feedback include *review sessions*, which give trainees opportunities to refine and polish skills learned and encourage continued use of the skill; *further practice time*, such as that provided by database vendors who give free time or reduced rates on selected databases; or the use of *job aids*. The use of informational job aids or performance aids helps to transfer skills learned in training. The idea behind job aids is to eliminate the need for people to remember details by providing assistance in the form of checklists, reference manuals, flowcharts, computer databases, templates for keyboards or telephones, and so forth.[46] These performance aids give trainees a better chance to use new skills by providing the minimal guidance so badly needed in the early stages of attempting to apply a newly learned skill on the job. See Figure 9.1, page 226, for more intervention techniques.

Assessing and Evaluating Training

Without evaluation, it is impossible to know whether the training program has done what it was designed to do. Has the performance of the reference staff member improved? If so, is it because of the training program? It is important to build evaluation into the program from the very beginning.

Who Evaluates?

Experts suggest that evaluation be done by as many people as possible to eliminate biases. This means that the supervisor, the trainer (if not also the supervisor), the employee who received the training, coworkers, and outsiders (who could be library users) may be involved in evaluation.

Figure 9.1 Sample interventions for performance problems. Source: Danny G. Langdon, Kathleen S. Whiteside, and Monica M. McKenna, eds., *Intervention Resource Guide: 50 Performance Improvement Tools.*[47]

IMPROVE PERFORMANCE	ESTABLISH PERFORMANCE
Action research	Employee selection
Business planning	Job aids
Coaching	Mentoring
Feedback	Modeling
Training	Training
MAINTAIN PERFORMANCE	**EXTINGUISH PERFORMANCE**
Compensation	Outplacement
Feedback	Upward evaluation
Performance standards	Withholding information
Work schedules	Withholding rewards

Trainee Evaluation. Otherwise excellent staff development programs often fail to provide built-in opportunities for participants' self-assessment. Thomas Shaughnessy argues that "staff development programs which include a self-assessment component should focus on providing each participant with the tools and materials necessary for the individual to test himself or herself and to score the test."[48] Programs that provide for self-assessment ease staff anxiety concerning test results and increase accuracy of results. Videotaping has been suggested as "a useful, and surprisingly comfortable, self-evaluation technique, because it captures actions in context otherwise lost to the person acting."[49] The results of self-evaluation are difficult to validate, however, and should be used in conjunction with other approaches.

Peer Evaluation. William Young believes that peers working together at a reference desk are those in the best position to judge reference behaviors, and that this is the most promising and realistic approach to evaluating reference desk performance.[50] *Behaviorally anchored rating scales* (BARS) are frequently used to assist in defining degrees of performance on the job. Several libraries have used these satisfactorily. Most have extracted behaviors, skills, and knowledge from a service standard to create a checklist of desirable behaviors, such as a reference librarian asking for assistance in certain situations or suggesting alternative sources of information to the user.[51] Figure 9.2 shows behaviorally anchored rating scales that are a portion of an instrument used in peer evaluations of an information desk staff of an academic library.

Supervisor Evaluation. The supervisor's evaluation is the most subjective, and can be difficult to rely on in training situations, unless testing, observation, or interviews accompany it. Also, because supervisors have a number of other areas of job performance to attend to, the particular performance concerned with training may be difficult to determine.

Figure 9.2 A portion of an instrument used in peer evaluations by staff at an information desk.

II. Interactions with Users	Seldom	Not Frequently Enough	Sometimes	Frequently	Almost All the Time	Cannot Respond
Maintains a Professional Posture						
1. Looks alert, confident, and interested						
2. Manifests openness (e.g., is approachable)						
3. Works to minimize initial barrier between patron and staff member						
4. Establishes good eye contact (e.g., looks up as patron approaches desk)						
Desk Service Priorities						
1. Gets people started						
2. Acknowledges the presence of users not yet served						
Effective Communication						
1. Uses good grammar						
2. Gears expression to user's understanding						
3. Avoids unexplained or unnecessary jargon						
4. Speaks in a positive, relaxed, appropriately loud tone of voice						
Helps Shape Questions						
1. Listens well						
2. Seeks definitions						

Library User Evaluation. Although library users' consistently high ranking of satisfaction with reference services calls into doubt their ability to evaluate reference performance,[52] it has been suggested that library users can evaluate librarians' attitudes, degree of self-confidence, and ability to instruct individuals in the use of reference sources.[53]

What Is Evaluated and How?

Evaluating training can be very difficult. Decisions have to be made not only concerning how to evaluate but also on what can and should be evaluated. Four different levels can be evaluated in a training program: *reactions, learning, job behavior,* and *results.*[54]

Reactions. Although attendees do not necessarily have to enjoy a session, it is important that a positive reaction to the training sessions occur if learning is to take place. A positive reaction to training is a precondition to learning, but it is not a guarantee that learning will transpire. Participants must feel a commitment to training—must feel it is valuable—in order to learn. Most often, reactions are assessed by asking trainees to complete rating scales for individual sessions. Verbal comments or nonverbal cues can also be observed. To supplement the attendees' comments, the supervisor or an observer should also record comments.

Learning. Learning—the acquisition of knowledge, skills, or attitudes—within the training context can be tested through programmed instruction, objective tests, essays, and pen and pencil tests. Testing may also be built into the training, such as judgment of performance in practice sessions or in-class exercises. To determine if skill improvement can indeed be attributed to the training program or if it results from outside influences, training experts recommend the use of *pre-tests, post-tests,* and *control groups.*[55] All those attending a training session, as well as those in a control group that does not receive training, are given a pre-test, to see what skills and knowledge they already possess. After a period of time has elapsed since training was administered, both groups are again tested to see if skills improved through training or merely from working on the job. Most librarians, unfortunately, have difficulty finding the time to administer tests in this way.

On-the-Job Behaviors. Although trainees may learn the skills and be able to perform them in the training session, they may not be able to perform them on the job. If the trainee did achieve the criteria during training sessions, the application exercises may not have been similar to the on-the-job environment. For example, when given citations with the author and title identified, reference assistants may be able to search the online catalog correctly. However, they may not be able to do so effectively on the job because they are unable to identify those key items from a citation that does not have the elements labeled. The evaluation itself can affect the result of training, so if trainers or supervisors wish to reinforce that training, they should use *obtrusive methods,* or testing that is known to the trainee. If it is important that outside factors be limited, *unobtrusive methods,* in which the trainees do not know they are being tested, should be used. Terry Weech and Herbert Goldhor have shown that reference librarians correctly answer a larger proportion of reference questions when they know they are being evaluated.[56] Chapter 10 discusses the advantages and disadvantages of unobtrusive and obtrusive methods in more detail.

When on-the-job benefits of training programs are hard to measure or are unclear, or when outcomes are not adequately measured with simple quantitative methods, as is the case in reference librarianship, interviews can be useful. Interviews and group discussions are more informal ways of assessing the effectiveness of a training program.[57]

Organizational Benefits

The final results, or benefit to the organization, should be the last stage of evaluation. Benefits such as users' satisfaction with library service, or their ability to access needed information, are difficult to measure. If the goal is to determine the effect that training has had on these outcomes, it becomes even more complicated; for this reason, libraries rarely evaluate at this level.[58]

BEYOND THE BASICS: CONTINUAL LEARNING

Training for reference staff should be a continuous process that is never really finished. Although the library can complete its induction phase to orient new staff members and finish on-the-job training for basic job skills, the basic level of skills constantly changes as resources, technology, customer needs, and services evolve. There is an additional need for reference staff to go beyond basic level competencies to mastery of their field, or expertise in a particular area.

Two different approaches to continual or lifelong learning can be identified. Although the two approaches use similar methods and have similar purposes of improving the competence of individuals, each has a different focus. *Staff development* is organizationally centered and directed, whereas *continuing education* is individually centered and directed. They are, however, not mutually exclusive, and are in fact complementary approaches. Both approaches are actually beneficial in helping staff members avoid technological obsolescence, develop expertise and knowledge in specialized areas, and widen experiences and practical knowledge.

Mastery or Expertise

A common practice in new employee orientation and training efforts is to have the new employees spend a lot of individual time with other staff members at the beginning of the employment period. Once the overview is given and a foundation laid, they are often left to jump in and "sink or swim." Because they do not know yet how to choose the most important information out of all they are hearing, they often reach information overload, and "later portions of the orientation process may not even be heard."[59] Alternating tasks with early orientation sessions and providing continuing training and review sessions can help new staff members build full knowledge or mastery of the content more gradually and more interactively.

Expertise in specific areas should also be encouraged. In developing expertise in reference, staff members deepen their understanding of resources and technology and learn how to transfer existing skills to a new environment,[60] a crucial skill in a constantly changing environment.

Change Management

Multiple paradigm shifts in the world economic, political, and cultural order, and simultaneous shifts in organizations, businesses, and information technology, are having a significant impact on library and information services. Howard Harris suggests that, "To succeed, libraries must now be agile, flexible, and able to adjust to a world that resembles an amusement park roller-coaster ride or white-water rafting."[61]

The sources that record information and the tools that provide access to these sources are revised and updated or appear in different forms. In such a time of profound change, the knowledge that individuals bring initially to their work can become obsolete rapidly. The effort required to maintain current knowledge and understanding is immense.

"In the print era the reference librarian could turn to the Mudge/Winchell/Sheehy *Guide to Reference Books*, or locate an index for a given journal through the listings in Ulrich's or other specialized guides. In the online era, new tools will have to be built that can deal comprehensively with a dynamic environment."[62] Reference librarians will always have to keep up with new information, new reference sources and access tools, and the changing needs of their users.[63]

Reference librarians have traditionally been conservators or caretakers of the library's collections. These roles are evolving as reference librarians become mediators between users and materials, information counselors, and educators and guides in teaching how to find and evaluate information. "[T]he reference librarian must not only be able to find relevant information or documents, but must be able to evaluate them on the criteria of availability, ease of access, authority, presence of biases, scope, and timeliness—regardless of electronic or print format or location. In addition, a critical thinking librarian must estimate the quantity and intellectual level of information required by the user."[64]

"Clearly, ongoing training is necessary to enable staff to keep up-to-date with changes. In responsive service, processes and procedures will be constantly monitored and modified to meet changing needs. Managers and supervisors need to ensure that staff understand new procedures and are able to put them into practice."[65]

Job Stress

Continual learning should help reference librarians deal with the stress that accompanies any kind of front-line position (see Box 9.11). Tina Roose points out that "reference librarians are among the few researchers of this world who are expected to perform with an audience in the midst of many other demands and distractions."[66] Four factors contribute to stress at the reference desk: technology, users, environment, and staffing.

Box 9.11

Reference Service as Combat: Fighting Job Stress

Some experts suggest that jobs with a high emotional labor content, jobs where the performer's persona goes on the line time and time again at the customer interface, should be treated as combat. And like combat soldiers, people in high-stress service jobs need to be rotated off the front line frequently—and sometimes permanently. As one expert puts it, "In Vietnam we *knew* come hell or high water, that after so many months, we were out of there. You need to do that for service people. They have to know there is a light at the end of that tunnel—and it isn't from an oncoming train."

Ron Zemke, "Contact! Training Employees to Meet the Public"[67]

Technology

Computers have assumed a central role in librarianship. Librarians need to maintain basic knowledge of operating systems, learn basic hardware and communications troubleshooting techniques, and develop deep understanding of software used every day.[68]

> When libraries dealt with only one or two database vendors, it was comparatively simple for an individual to remember what databases were available.

> For unfamiliar subject areas, a quick reference to the paper directories supplied by the online vendor yielded the needed information. As the sources of online information have multiplied one person can no longer keep a mental catalog of the likely places where individual pieces of information may be found.[69]

In addition to the variety of sources available, in an online environment available resources can change overnight. Technological obsolescence can occur when individual competence holds constant while professional standards advance.[70]

Users

The technological age has brought further complications in raising the expectations of users about libraries and the ability of library staff to provide information immediately. Users often expect reference staff to provide data that may not be collected, or which by nature is confidential. When advised by reference staff on a course of action, the user may not be willing to follow that advice if it seems like too much work. For example, individuals wanting information on a topic from the 1960s are incredulous when told they will have to use print indexes to find information. They may go to the next person on duty in the hope of getting a different answer to their question.

Reference staffs are increasingly dealing more directly with diverse populations—individuals with physical, emotional, and health limitations who may have been served by special agencies before or individuals with different cultural expectations (see Chapter 12). Although recognition of the needs of a diverse population is important, it brings further stresses to a service desk in the amount of knowledge required to handle a particular question and the amount of patience or tact needed.

Environment

Local collections necessarily have limitations, and with today's information explosion, no one institution can be expected to acquire everything its users could reasonably ask about. Additionally, the arrangement of the reference collection, the physical desk(s), and equipment can negatively affect the reference transaction.[71] If desks are cumbersome to use or inhibit the use of a particular kind of source, service is affected. Aging or constantly malfunctioning equipment can also be a stress factor. Service philosophies can vary tremendously from one service desk to another even within the same institution. This, too, can contribute to users' expectations or frustrations and thus the librarian's stress.

Staffing

There is a limit on how much individuals can work with the public, and this factor is different for each person. Some individuals work better in small stretches of time, while others do well working on the desk for longer periods of time. Departments should limit the number of hours that staff members are expected to work. Inappropriate staffing can also create stress. Boredom from staffing professionals during slow periods or anxiety from single staffing during busy times is equally problematic. Lack of technological backup, especially on nights and weekends, can be another problem.

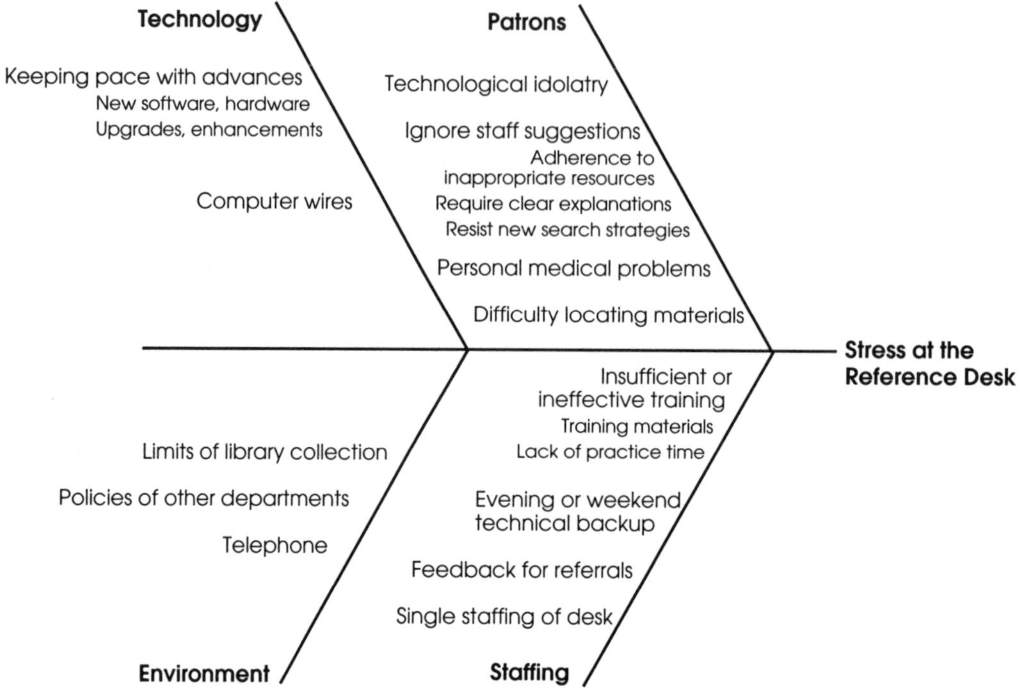

Figure 9.3 Fishbone diagram: factors producing stress at the reference desk. Source: Pamela M. Rose, Kristin Stoklosa and Sharon A. Gray, "A Focus Group Approach to Assessing Technostress at the Reference Desk."[72] Permission granted by the American Library Association.

Burnout

Burnout as introduced in Chapter 1, is an overwhelming feeling of frustration, apathy, and exhaustion regarding one's work.[73] It is not a problem unique to reference service providers, but it is very intense and pervasive.[74] "Reference librarians seem most particularly at risk for burnout because of their assignment of general direct availability for an unpredictable stream of requests and demands and their high visibility in most libraries."[75] Various individuals have attributed the problem to:

- too many new services and activities added to traditional reference desk service with no increase in staff to handle the new activities,[76]
- a gap between the ideals of reference librarianship that [librarians] believe and espouse and the realities of reference service that can be practiced,[77] or
- *technostress*, or the anxiety and psychological pressure created by the continually expanding range of electronic tools that reference librarians must master.[78]

It is important to note that the four stages of burnout—*enthusiasm, stagnation, frustration*, and *apathy*—start with enthusiasm. The challenge to libraries and to individuals is to rekindle the fire of enthusiasm and not let it burn out, but to feed it with challenges, new environments, new information, and new techniques, without letting it engulf reference staffs. Staff development and continuing education can provide the kindling for the fire by presenting new information and techniques of approaching the reference process. When someone is removed from the desk, even temporarily, to attend a development activity, it gives that person breathing room and a chance to reflect upon what has happened. The sessions are intended to provide new insights into desk service and new ways of coping with stress by improving knowledge, skills, or attitudes.

Organizational Responses

"The organizational costs of burnout are high. Lost motivation, increased staff turnover, poor delivery of services, increased employee theft, increased tardiness, and greater absenteeism all result in significant indirect costs to organizations."[79] Luckily, the organization has a variety of ways to prevent burnout and to help combat it once it has developed.

Managerial Decisions

The library reference manager can take control of some of the issues that contribute to stress and burnout. By establishing an atmosphere of support and trust, by balancing the kinds of service activities in which reference librarians are engaged, by establishing service standards and policies and communicating them effectively, the reference department head can help keep burnout from developing. Once burnout has occurred, the department head can change job assignments or institute cross-training to change the environment in which the burnout was initiated.

Developing Trust. Janette Caputo identifies "a high level of mutual trust"[80] as the single most important facet to the effective supervisory relationship in terms of burnout prevention. "Supervisors who see themselves as trainers or coaches have the best success in counteracting burnout, as they encourage individual growth and development and open the door for group applications of theoretical knowledge to practical situations."[81] Individuals with good support systems with colleagues develop better coping mechanisms.

Balancing Activities. Supervisors can keep reference desk hours at a reasonable level, minimizing excessive contact with the public. Reference managers need to respond when demands are high. Joanne Bessler suggests using a "floater" position to assist in areas with higher workloads, identifying low-priority work that can be deferred or eliminated, and creating a team that can work across units when needed.[82]

Service Statements. Department heads can develop reference service policy statements that recognize reasonable limits to service that librarians are expected to provide. "When training staff to apply policies, you should also prepare staff for likely challenges and exceptions. Discussing exceptions at staff meetings is helpful. A staff member who knows why a policy was written and how it has been interpreted is well prepared to make a reasonable judgement."[83] Explicitly stating to staff at all levels when rules can be modified in providing help to users is important in defining levels of empowerment. For example, volunteers or student staff who work very limited schedules may not have the comprehensive understanding of overall library operations to be able to judge special user requests, while nonsupervisory staff may be able to bend policies within certain guidelines.

Redesign Job. Managers can redesign the content of a job through job rotation or exchange, or provide assignments that allow individuals to gain authority, personal achievement, recognition, growth, responsibility, and advancement. They can encourage employees to undertake new and different assignments periodically to assure that their jobs do not become too routine or lacking in challenge.[84] Staff development programs that help service providers see their job as playing a role for the organization can also provide concrete assistance with job burnout and stress.

Cross-Training. "Cross-training is valuable because it helps employees become familiar with co-workers' contributions and get a better idea of how the institution works as a whole. In addition, cross-trained staff members can pinch-hit for each other when the need arises."[85] Lothar Spang states that, "Librarian participants have agreed that the cross-training opportunities have substantially improved their ability to provide accurate and convenient service to an increasingly cross-discipline user population."[86]

Staff Development

Staff development's goal is to improve the organization's effectiveness, or service to its users, by increasing the competence of its staff. Much of the training that has been discussed up to this point is encompassed by the term *staff development*; orientation and on-the-job training are certainly included. The library has a responsibility to improve staff performance, and it is to the library's benefit to produce employees who are committed to the library.

Merely providing the training for basic job skills is not enough. The library administration should provide continual training for reference librarians that develops and maintains competence, updates basic professional foundations, and introduces new concepts. Staff development should emphasize attitude shaping, people-handling skills, dealing with users' feelings, listening skills, and thinking on one's feet. "Given the scope and pace of present and prospective change, training, by itself, will not provide librarians with a satisfactory framework for new understandings, or the basis for responding to the changed environment."[87] An ongoing development program is necessary.

Libraries as Learning Organizations

Although individual learning is important, it needs to affect the overall organizational performance to have a long-range benefit. Although a particular individual may become an expert in a specific area, if that information and expertise is not shared with the organization, the organization will lose that expertise when the individual leaves. On the other hand, if the individual shares this expertise in such a way that he or she trains others and the information learned is incorporated into organizational documentation, then the expertise remains in the organization after the individual leaves. Libraries that promote this kind of transfer of knowledge and expertise can be called *learning organizations.*

A learning organization is one that has an enhanced capacity to learn, adapt, and change, and is "skilled at creating, acquiring, and transferring knowledge and insights."[88] It is characterized by:

- using information technology to inform/empower the many rather than the few;
- collaboration rather than competition; making comparisons of the organization's best practices with the practices of others;
- encouraging self-development opportunities for everyone in the organization and encouraging individuals to take responsibility for their own learning and development;

- exchanging information—getting closer to customers and suppliers;
- using the people in contact with customers to bring back useful information about needs and opportunities.[89]

Personal Responses: Continuing Education

Individuals must also accept some of the responsibility for refueling the fire by planning their own continuing education activities. Continuing education activities center on the individual's personal interests, and include those that promote personal development and growth as an individual, whether to increase personal job satisfaction or to prepare for a promotion. Continuing education includes learning experiences that will introduce new concepts and skills, update basic professional foundations, refresh or reemphasize aspects of professional training, provide additional competencies to make career advancement or change possible, and furnish the individual with an overview of his or her profession as a changing and evolving discipline.[90]

Charles Bunge discusses methods that reference librarians use to update their reference knowledge and skills. The most frequently mentioned strategy is reading professional literature, followed by reference staff meetings and staff sharing. He also identifies attendance at conferences, workshops, and other meetings outside the individual's library as much-used methods for reference librarians.[91] One librarian has started a "journal club" where individuals share what they have learned through professional reading. Another relies heavily on electronic bulletin boards, claiming that it is like "a professional conference online without the airfare."

Opportunities for continuing education originate from many different sources. Courses offered at local community colleges, colleges, or universities range from computer and software management courses and supervisory and teaching skills to subject-related topics that may or may not lead to an advanced degree. Outside groups, such as online database vendors, often offer basic and advanced training in the use of their software, with refresher courses and updates on specific databases. Library professional organizations make many contributions to continuing education for reference librarians. Local interest groups often provide forums for discussing mutual problems, challenges, and potential solutions with peers. State associations sponsor conferences, workshops, and programs in more convenient locations than many nationally sponsored programs. The American Library Association, and associations of special groups provide numerous activities that can promote the individual reference librarian's development. As outlined in *Continuous Learning*,[92] a report to the ALA Executive Board, these opportunities include: programs and exhibits at conferences, preconferences, regional and national institutes, chapters, traveling exhibits, teleconferences, publications, electronic discussion lists, Web sites, online courses, fax-on-demand, speakers' bureaus, and networking and mentoring. The report goes on to recommend that ALA become involved in post-master's certification programs, explore the development of a distance education service, establish a continuing education clearinghouse, enhance public programming, and build library roles in public education. See the *ALA Handbook of Organization* for the names of groups emphasizing staff development and continuing education.[93]

CONCLUSION

The results of a thorough and responsive training program that involves the staff in decision making and uses participatory educational methods will be a highly motivated staff who have high morale and good self-esteem, identify with their peers, cope with changes and stress, make fewer mistakes, and solve problems. On the other hand, unplanned on-the-job training may result in ill-trained, unmotivated employees. There are dangers that necessary skills may not be learned or that undesirable methods and approaches will be reinforced and low standards set. "Employees (new or old) learn, whether we wish it or not. If we are disorganized, indifferent, or sloppy in our approach, the employee will absorb the standards. No amount of future lecturing will erase these standards."[94]

The act of training itself motivates and builds employee confidence and self-esteem, regardless of the actual content of training. Training reduces stress and turnover, improves work relationships, and increases adaptability. Without training, reference librarians cannot keep up with change, develop expertise, or learn how to transfer what they already know to new environments.

Reference librarians are truly in the knowledge business, both on behalf of their users and for themselves. Librarians cannot help the users fulfill their information needs if they themselves are ignorant of the sources, lack the ability to access the information they know exists, or are unwilling to go that extra step to gain that knowledge and skills. A well-planned program of training, development, and continuing education will give the reference staff the tools they need to tackle the tasks at hand and strategies for approaching new problems as they arise.

NOTES

1. Samuel Rothstein, "The Making of a Reference Librarian," *Library Trends* 31 (Winter 1983): 375-99.

2. Ronald R. Powell and Douglas Raber, "Education for Reference/Information Service: A Quantitative and Qualitative Analysis of Basic Reference Courses," simultaneously co-published in *The Reference Librarian* 43 (1994): 145-72, and *Reference Services Planning in the 90's*, ed. Gail A. Eckwright and Lori M. Keenan (Binghamton, N.Y.: Haworth Press, 1993), 145-72.

3. Marsha D. Broadway and Nathan M. Smith, "Basic Reference Courses in ALA-Accredited Library Schools," *The Reference Librarian* 25-26 (1989): 431-48.

4. Kimberly L. Nakano and Janet Morrison, "Public-Service Experience in the Introductory Reference Course: A Model Program and Survey of Accredited Library Schools," *Journal of Education for Library and Information Science* 33 (Spring 1992): 110-28; Shelly L. Rogers, "Orientation for New Library Employees: A Checklist," *Library Administration and Management* 8 (Fall 1994): 213-17.

5. Michele M. Deputy, "A Study of Librarians' Attitudes Towards the Reference Interview," ERIC Document ED 401919, December 1995, 42p.

6. Julie Ann McDaniel and Judith K. Ohles, *Training Paraprofessionals for Reference Service*, How-To-Do-It Manual for Libraries, no. 30 (New York: Neal-Schuman, 1993), 1-5.

7. Sheila D. Creth, *Effective On-the-Job Training: Developing Library Human Resources* (Chicago: American Library Association, 1986), 6.

8. Leonard Nadler and Zeace Nadler, *Handbook of Human Resource Development*, 2d ed. (New York: Wiley, 1990), 1.3.

9. Suellyn Hunt, "A Structure and Seven-Step Process for Developing In-House Human Resources Programs," *Bookmark* 41 (Summer 1983): 227.

10. Heartsill Young, ed., *The ALA Glossary of Library and Information Science* (Chicago: American Library Association, 1983), 214.

11. Donnagene Britt, Patricia Davison, and Judith Levy, eds., *Painlessly Preparing Personalized Training Plans* (Berkley, Calif.: University of California Library, April 1982), 7-9.

12. Dorothy E. Jones, "I'd Like You to Meet Our New Librarian: The Initiation and Integration of the Newly Appointed Librarian," *Journal of Academic Librarianship* 14 (September 1988): 22.

13. H. Scott Davis, *New Employee Orientation*, How-To-Do-It Manual for Libraries, no. 38 (New York: Neal-Schuman, 1994), v.

14. Sandra Weingart, Carol A. Kochan, and Anne Hedrich, "Safeguarding Your Investment: Effective Orientation for New Employees," *Library Administration and Management* 12 (Summer 1998): 157.

15. Ibid.

16. Anne May Berwind, "Orientation for the Reference Desk," *Reference Services Review* 19 (Fall 1991): 51-54, 70.

17. Mary W. Oliver, "Orientation of New Personnel in the Law Library," *Law Library Journal* 65 (May 6, 1972): 140.

18. Joanne M. Bessler, *Putting Service into Library Staff Training* (LAMA Occasional Paper Series) (Chicago: American Library Association, 1994), 15.

19. Susan Imel, "Guidelines for Working with Adult Learners," *ERIC Digest* 154, 1994. Available: http://www.ed.gov/databases/ERIC_Digests/ed377313.html; and Malcolm S. Knowles, "Adult Learning," in *ASTD Training and Development Handbook: A Guide to Human Resource Management,* 4th ed., ed. Robert L. Craig (New York: McGraw-Hill, 1996), 253-65.

20. Young, *ALA Glossary*, 231.

21. F. J. Roethlisberger and W. J. Dick, *Management and the Worker* (Cambridge, Mass.: Harvard University Press, 1939), 522.

22. A number of individuals have made attempts to put together lists of competencies: *Future Competencies of the Information Professional*, SLA Occasional Papers Series, 1 (Washington, D.C.: Special Libraries Association, 1991), 24p.; Joan Giesecke and Beth McNeil, "Core Competencies and the Learning Organization," *Library Administration and Management* 13 (Summer 1999): 158-66; *Self-Assessment Guide for Reference* (St. Paul, Minn.: Office of Library Development and Services, revised 1986), 1-52; Lois Buttlar and Rosemary Du Mont, "Library and Information Science Competencies Revisited," *Journal of Education for Library and Information Science* 37 (Winter 1996): 44-62; Marydee Ojala, "Core Competencies for Special Library Managers of the Future," *Special Libraries* 84 (Fall 1993): 230-34; Ilene F. Rockman, "Reference Librarian of the Future," *Reference Services Review* 19 (Spring 1991): 71-80; RASD Ad Hoc Committee on Behavioral Guidelines for Reference and Information Service, "RUSA Guidelines for Behavioral Performance of Reference and Information Services Professionals," *RQ* 36 (Winter 1996): 200-203; Cecilia D. Stafford and William M. Serban, "Core Competencies: Recruiting, Training, and Evaluating in the Automated Reference Environment," *Journal of Library Administration* 13 (1990): 81-97; RASD MARS Education, Training and Support Committee, *Electronic Resources Skills: An Assessment and Development Log for Reference Staff,* RASD Occasional Paper, no. 17 (Chicago: American Library Association, 1995), 16p.

23. "RUSA Guidelines," 200-203.

24. Ibid., 202.

25. Virginia Massey-Burzio, "Education and Experience: Or, the MLS Is Not Enough," *Reference Services Review* 19 (Spring 1991): 73.

26. Mary M. Nofsinger, "Training and Retraining Reference Professionals: Core Competencies for the 21st Century," co-published simultaneously in *The Reference Librarian* 61 (1999): 9-19, and *Coming of Age in Reference Services: A Case History of the Washington State University Libraries*, ed. Christy Zlatos (Binghamton, N.Y.: Haworth Press, 1999), 9-19.

27. For further discussion of areas of competency, see Anne F. Roberts, "Myth: Reference Librarians Can Perform at the Reference Desk Immediately Upon Receipt of MLS. Reality: They Need Training Like Other Professionals," in *Academic Libraries: Myths and Realities. Proceedings of the Third National Conference of the Association of College and Research Libraries* (Chicago: ACRL, 1984), 402.

28. See Geary A. Rummler, "Determining Needs," in *Training and Development Handbook,* 3d ed., ed. Robert L. Craig (New York: McGraw-Hill, 1987), 217-47, for a discussion of alternative needs assessment techniques; and Mel Silberman, *Active Training: A Handbook of Techniques, Designs, Case Examples, and Tips* (Lexington, Mass.: Lexington Books, 1990), 16-19, for a list of advantages and disadvantages of nine basic needs assessment techniques.

29. Joan Giesecke and Beth McNeil, "Core Competencies and the Learning Organization," *Library Administration and Management* 13 (Summer 1999): 160.

30. Barbara Conroy, "The Structured Group Interview: A Useful Tool for Needs Assessment and Evaluation," *Mountain Plains Journal of Adult Education* 4 (March 1976): 19.

31. McDaniel and Ohles, *Training Paraprofessionals for Reference Service,* 18.

32. Creth, *Effective On-the-Job Training*, 31.

33. Robert F. Mager, *Preparing Instructional Objectives*, 2d ed. (Belmont, Calif.: Fearon Publishers, 1975), 21.

34. John W. Newstrom, "Evaluating the Effectiveness of Training Methods," *Personnel Administrator* 25 (January 1980): 58.

35. Gwen Arthur, "Using Video for Reference Staff Training and Development: A Selective Bibliography," *Reference Services Review* 20 (Winter 1992): 63-68.

36. Phillipa Dolphin, "Interpersonal Skill Training for Library Staff," *Library Association Record* 88 (March 1986): 134.

37. Julian M. Isaacs, "In-Service Training for Reference Work," *Library Association Record* 71 (October 1969): 301.

38. Donald A. Schon, *Educating the Reflective Practitioner: Toward a New Design for Teaching and Learning in the Professions* (San Francisco: Jossey-Bass, 1987), 92.

39. The following sources are extremely useful: Chip R. Bell, "Criteria for Selecting Instructional Strategies," *Training and Development Journal* 31 (October 1977): 3-7; Vernon S. Gerlach and Donald P. Ely, *Teaching and Media: A Systematic Approach,* 2d ed. (Englewood Cliffs, N.J.: Prentice Hall, 1980), 420p.; John W. Newstrom, "Selecting Training Methodologies: A Contingency Approach," *Training and Development Journal* 29 (October 1975): 12-16; William R. Tracey, *Designing Training and Development Systems*, 3d ed. rev. (New York: AMACOM, 1992), 532p.; Marilla D. Svinicki and Barbara A. Schwartz, *Designing Instruction for Library Users: A Practical Guide* (New York: Marcel Dekker, 1988), 249p.; and *The ASTD Handbook of Training Design and Delivery,* ed. George M. Piskurich, Peter Beckschi, and Brandon Hall (New York: McGraw-Hill, 2000), 530p.

40. Bessler, *Putting Service into Library Staff Training*, 30.

41. Neil Rackham, "The Coaching Controversy," *Training and Development Journal* 33 (November 1979): 14.

42. Ibid.

43. Susan N. Chellino and Richard J. Walker, "Merging Instructional Technology with Management Practices," in *Strengthening Connections Between Education and Performance*, ed. Stanley M. Grabowski (San Francisco: Jossey-Bass, 1983), 12.

44. Janet Sheets, "Role Playing as Training Tool for Reference Student Assistants," *Reference Services Review* 26 (Spring 1998): 37-41.

45. James C. Georges, "Why Soft-Skills Training Doesn't Take," *Training* 25 (April 1988): 46.

46. Ron Zemke and John Gunkler, "28 Techniques for Transforming Training into Performance," *Training* 22 (April 1985): 62.

47. Danny G. Langdon, Kathleen S. Whiteside, and Monica M. McKenna, eds., *Intervention Resource Guide: 50 Performance Improvement Tools* (San Francisco: Jossey-Bass, 1999), 20.

48. Thomas W. Shaughnessy, "Staff Development in Libraries: Why It Frequently Doesn't Take," *Journal of Library Administration* 9 (1988): 7.

49. Judith Mucci, "Videotape Self-Evaluation in Public Libraries: Experiments in Evaluating Public Service," *RQ* 16 (Fall 1976): 33.

50. William F. Young, "Methods for Evaluating Reference Desk Performance," *RQ* 25 (Fall 1985): 73.

51. Diane G. Schwartz and Dottie Eakin, "Reference Service Standards, Performance Criteria, and Evaluation," *Journal of Academic Librarianship* 12 (March 1986): 6; and Mignon S. Adams and Blanche Judd, "Evaluating Reference Librarians Using Goal Analysis as a First Step," *The Reference Librarian* 11 (Fall/Winter 1984): 141.

52. William F. Young, "Evaluating the Reference Librarian," *The Reference Librarian* 11 (Fall/Winter 1984): 123-24.

53. Schwartz and Eakin, "Reference Service Standards," 4-8.

54. Donald L. Kirkpatrick, "Techniques for Evaluating Training Programs," *Training and Development Journal* 33 (June 1979): 78-92.

55. A. C. Hamblin, *Evaluation and Control of Training* (London: McGraw-Hill, 1974), 8.

56. Terry L. Weech and Herbert Goldhor, "Obtrusive Versus Unobtrusive Evaluation of Reference Service in Five Illinois Public Libraries: A Pilot Study," *The Library Quarterly* 51 (1982): 305-24.

57. See Robert O. Brinkerhoff, "The Success Case: A Low-Cost, High Yield Evaluation," *Training and Development Journal* 37 (August 1983): 58-59, 61; and Sumru Erkut and Jacqueline P. Fields, "Focus Groups to the Rescue," *Training and Development Journal* 41 (October 1987): 74.

58. Kirkpatrick, "Techniques for Evaluating Training Programs," 89.

59. Janette S. Caputo, *Stress and Burnout in Library Service* (Phoenix, Ariz.: Oryx Press, 1991), 134.

60. Nina Stephensen and Deborah J. Willis, "Internet In-Service Training at the University of New Mexico General Library," co-published simultaneously in *The Reference Librarian* 41/42 (1994): 211-14, and *Librarians on the Internet: Impact of Reference Services,* ed. Robin Kinder (Binghamton, N.Y.: Haworth Press, 1994), 211-14.

61. Giesecke and McNeil, "Core Competencies," 158.

62. Ron Force, "Planning Online Services for the 90s," simultaneously co-published in *The Reference Librarian* 43 (1994): 113 and *Reference Services Planning in the 90s,* ed. Gail A. Eckwright and Lori M. Keenan (Binghamton, N.Y.: Haworth Press, 1994), 113.

63. Charles A. Bunge, "Strategies for Updating Knowledge of Reference Resources and Techniques," *RQ* 21 (Spring 1982): 228.

64. Nofsinger, "Training and Retraining," 15.

65. Julie Parry, "Continuing Professional Development," in *Staff Development in Academic Libraries: Present Practice and Future Challenges,* ed. Margaret Oldroyd (London: Library Association Publishing, 1996), 23.

66. Tina Roose, "Stress at the Reference Desk," *Library Journal* 114 (September 1, 1989): 166.

67. Ron Zemke, "Contact! Training Employees to Meet the Public," *Training* 23 (August 1986): 44.

68. Dan Marmion, "Facing the Challenge: Technology Training in Libraries," *Information Technology & Libraries* 17 (December 1998): 216-18.

69. Force, "Planning Online Services," 112-13.

70. Elizabeth W. Stone, "Towards a Learning Community," in *Continuing Education for the Library Information Professions*, ed. William G. Asp et al. (Hamden, Conn.: Library Professional Publications, 1985), 65.

71. See Anna M. Donnelly, "Reference Environment," *The Reference Assessment Manual* (Ann Arbor, Mich.: Pierian Press, 1995), 47-50.

72. Pamela M. Rose, Kristin Stoklosa, and Sharon A. Gray, "A Focus Group Approach to Assessing Technostress at the Reference Desk," *Reference & User Services Quarterly* 37 (Summer 1998): 315.

73. Roose, "Stress at the Reference Desk," 167.

74. See the following articles for discussions of burnout in librarians: Mary Haack, John W. Jones, and Tina Roose, "Occupational Burnout Among Librarians," *Drexel Library Quarterly* 20 (Spring 1984): 46-72; William Miller, "What's Wrong with Reference: Coping with Success and Failure at the Reference Desk," *American Libraries* 15 (May 1984): 303-6, 321-22; Sandra H. Neville, "Job Stress and Burnout: Occupational Hazards for Service Staff," *College & Research Libraries* 42 (May 1981): 242-47; David S. Ferriero and Kathleen A. Powers, "Burnout at the Reference Desk," *RQ* 21 (Spring 1982): 274-79; Nathan M. Smith and Veneese C. Nelson, "Burnout: A Survey of Academic Reference Librarians," *College & Research Libraries* 44 (May 1983): 245-50; Nathan M. Smith, Nancy E. Birch, and Maurice Marchant, "Stress, Distress, and Burnout: A Survey of Public Reference Librarians," *Public Libraries* 23 (Fall 1984): 83-85; and Ron Blazek and Darlene Ann Parrish, "Burnout and Public Services: The Periodical Literature of Librarianship in the Eighties," *RQ* 31 (Fall 1992): 48-59.

75. Caputo, *Stress and Burnout*, 59.

76. Miller, "What's Wrong with Reference," 303.

77. Charles Bunge, "Potential and Reality at the Reference Desk: Reflections on a 'Return to the Field'," *Journal of Academic Librarianship* 10 (July 1984): 131.

78. John Kupersmith, "Technostress and the Reference Librarian," *Reference Services Review* 20 (Summer 1992): 7-14.

79. Caputo, *Stress and Burnout,* 32.

80. Ibid., 136.

81. Ibid.

82. Bessler, *Putting Service into Library Staff Training,* 33.

83. Ibid., 38.

84. Samuel T. Huang, "The Impact of New Library Technology on Reference Services," *Illinois Libraries* 72 (November 1990): 601-2.

85. Weingart, Kochan, and Hedrich, "Safeguarding Your Investment," 157.

86. Lothar Spang, "A Staff-Generated Cross-Training Plan for Academic Reference Librarians: The TQM Approach at Wayne State University Libraries," *Reference Services Review* 24 (Summer 1996): 84.

87. Howard Harris, "Retraining Librarians to Meet the Needs of the Virtual Library Patron," *Information Technology & Libraries* 15 (March 1996): 48.

88. David Garvin, "Building a Learning Organization," *Harvard Business Review* 70, no. 4 (July/August 1993): 80.

89. Harris, "Retraining Librarians," 51.

90. Stone, "Towards a Learning Community," 62.

91. Bunge, "Strategies for Updating Knowledge," 229-31.

92. *Continuous Learning: A Report to the ALA Executive Board*, photocopy, Summer 1998, 7p.

93. *ALA Handbook of Organization* (Chicago: American Library Association, annual).

94. Gordon F. Shea, *The New Employee: Developing a Productive Human Resource* (Reading, Mass.: Addison-Wesley, 1981), 61.

ADDITIONAL READINGS

Allan, Ann, and Kathy J. Reynolds. "Performance Problems: A Model for Analysis and Resolution." *Journal of Academic Librarianship* 9 (May 1983): 83-88. Reprinted in *Performance Evaluation: A Management Basic for Librarians*, edited by Jonathan A. Lindsey. Phoenix, Ariz.: Oryx Press, 1986. 198-208.

Allan and Reynolds describe a flowchart for identifying appropriate solutions to performance problems in libraries. A series of questions helps identify major issues.

Allan, Barbara. *Developing Information and Library Staff Through Work-based Learning: 101 Activities.* London: Library Association Publishing, 1999. 191p.

"Work-based learning may involve *learning at work* as well as *learning through work*" (p. 5). Techniques used on the job—such as structured learning in the workplace and on-the-job training/learning opportunities—complement short courses and gaining academic and/or vocational qualifications. Activities identified as work-based include information discussions with colleagues, taking an active part in staff meetings, giving talks to groups outside the profession, visiting other libraries, writing guides/aids for users, reading library literature, attending conferences and meetings, receiving in-service training, coaching, mentoring, job rotation, guided reading, and group work.

Arthur, Gwen. "Using Video for Reference Staff Training and Development: A Selective Bibliography." *Reference Services Review* 20 (Winter 1992): 63-68.

Arthur's selective bibliography reviews the literature of video for reference staff training and development, emphasizing the use of video to develop communication skills, aid in service encounters, and improve instructional and presentation skills, electronic searching, and computer applications.

Bessler, Joanne M. *Putting Service into Library Staff Training.* Chicago: American Library Association, 1994. 72p. (LAMA Occasional Papers Series).

This guide aims to help library managers teach staff in all areas of library work—public, technical, and administrative services—the attitudes and skills to make their library a service-oriented organization. Developing a mission statement, recruiting employees with service attitudes, preparing staff to give quality service through orientation and continuous training, and empowering staff are areas addressed.

CLENExchange (newsletter of the American Library Association Continuing Library Education Network and Exchange Roundtable). Available: http://www.ala.org/alaorg/rtables/clene/clenexchange.html.

This newsletter provides reviews of training books, summaries of training workshops, and helpful training tips.

Craig, Robert L., ed. *The ASTD Training and Development Handbook: A Guide to Human Resource Development.* 4th ed. New York: McGraw-Hill, 1996. 1071p.

This extensive manual provides hundreds of practice-proven techniques from industry experts. Chapters cover the instructional design process, measuring and evaluating training results, facilitating learning and coaching, encouraging self-directed learning, and customer service training.

Creth, Sheila D. *Effective On-the-Job Training: Developing Library Human Resources.* Chicago: American Library Association, 1986. 121p.

Creth presents a very concise overview of training needs, planning, implementation, and evaluation, with exercises and examples drawn from libraries. The two appendices are particularly useful, containing excerpts of actual job training plans in libraries for various kinds of positions and an orientation checklist.

Davis, H. Scott. *New Employee Orientation* New York: Neal-Schuman, 1994. 144p. (How-To-Do-It Manuals for Libraries, no. 38).

The author, a practicing librarian, wrote this book to fill a gap in the professional literature by providing a practical guide to the process of effectively orienting new library employees. A menu of program options and activities is presented. Good examples of gathering staff suggestions through surveys, brainstorming, and focus groups for determining the content of and need for orientation are included.

Scott includes an excellent section on anticipating and handling problems such as ineffective participants, short notice, dropouts, resistance, and mismatching of mentors. Some examples from the Indiana State University mentor orientation program are included as a model. Some noteworthy suggestions include creating a glossary of common library terms and abbreviations and maintaining a staff photo album. Participant input is suggested as of primary importance in the evaluation phase.

Jones, Dorothy E. " 'I'd Like You to Meet Our New Librarian': The Initiation and Integration of the Newly Appointed Librarian." *Journal of Academic Librarianship* 14 (September 1988): 221-24.

Jones discusses the importance of introducing new librarians to the organizational culture, departmental objectives, work organization within the department, task details, and the path to promotion and job retention. She advocates careful preparation for and supportive introduction to the policies, procedures, methods, relationships, and attitudes of each unique situation.

Katz, Bill, ed. "Continuing Education of Reference Librarians." *The Reference Librarian* 30 (1990): 1-273.

This issue of *The Reference Librarian* covers a range of topics concerning training and continuing education of librarians. Several articles stress the need for adaptability and critical thinking skills.

Lipow, Anne Grodzins, and Deborah A. Carver, eds. *Staff Development: A Practical Guide.* 2d ed. Chicago: American Library Association, 1992. 104p.

The first five chapters, new to this edition, provide theoretical background on adult learning, transfer of skills, and instructional design. The subsequent chapters are descriptions of the stages of planning, preparing, and implementing staff development programs. The last chapter includes a good bibliographic guide for additional practical information on staff development.

McDaniel, Julie Ann, and Judith K. Ohles. *Training Paraprofessionals for Reference Service.* New York: Neal-Schuman, 1993. 180p. (How-To-Do-It Manuals for Libraries, no. 30).

McDaniel and Ohles provide a practical approach to assist librarians in training paraprofessionals for library reference work. Reviewing briefly the planning process, they focus on giving checklists, examples, case studies, and actual practice questions for eight training modules that would be appropriate in most libraries. Lists for further reading, training tips, chapter reviews, and discussion topics make this an extremely useful source.

Messas, Kostas. *Staff Training and Development.* Washington, D.C.: Association for Research Libraries, 1997. 199p. (SPEC Kit 224).

This survey examines the state of formal staff training and development programs in ARL libraries, finding that only 56% of the fifty respondents had such a program in place. The most frequently used formats are small group discussions and on-site workshops, followed by off-site workshops, videotapes and films, and lectures. This SPEC Kit includes the best representative supporting documents and materials from the survey, including mission statements, guidelines, needs assessments, training activities, training course catalogs, and evaluations. Another valuable feature is a good bibliography of library staff training materials written since 1990.

Nofsinger, Mary M., and Angela S. W. Lee. "Beyond Orientation: The Roles of Senior Librarians in Training Entry-Level Reference Colleagues." *College & Research Libraries* 55 (March 1994): 161-70.

The authors suggest that more experienced staff members can play four vital roles in training entry-level reference librarians: as teachers or coaches, as interpreters or advisers for the institution's culture, as role models for interpersonal skills and cooperation among professional colleagues, and as mentors in professional development.

Oldroyd, Margaret, ed. *Staff Development in Academic Libraries: Present Practice and Future Challenges.* London: Library Association Publishing, 1996. 148p.

This work explores staff development in relation to change management at organization, library, and individual levels.

Parry, Julie. *Induction.* London: Library Association, 1993. 57p.

Parry's stated purpose is to "demonstrate the benefits of adopting a systematic approach to the design and delivery of induction programmes for new staff in library and information services." This publication provides a comprehensive guide without being prescriptive. Examples from actual orientation schemes are included.

Piskurich, George M., Peter Beckschi, and Brandon Hall. *The ASTD Handbook of Training Design and Delivery: A Comprehensive Guide to Creating and Delivering Training Programs—Instructor-Led, Computer-Based, or Self-Directed.* New York: McGraw-Hill, 2000. 530p.

Replacing the 1993 edition of the *ASTD Handbook of Instructional Technology*, this book serves as a companion to the *ASTD Handbook of Training and Development* by focusing on the design and implementation of classroom instruction, technology-based training, and self-directed learning. It provides a comprehensive guide to the strengths and weaknesses of every important training technique, from preparing a traditional classroom lecture to designing a completely self-directed Web-based training program.

Robles, Kimberley, and Neal Wyatt. *Reference Training in Academic Libraries.* Chicago: American Library Association, Association of College and Research Libraries, 1996. 171p. (CLIP Note no. 24).

A survey gathered data on reference training programs from 206 small and medium-sized academic libraries. This book represents a selection of these programs. Libraries with larger student bodies and higher numbers of full-time librarians tended to have training programs in place. Those libraries that did not have training tended to have fewer reference librarians, averaging two per department.

Stabler, Karen. "Introductory Training of Academic Reference Librarians: A Survey." *RQ* 26 (Spring 1987): 363-69.

Stabler surveyed 116 newly appointed reference librarians concerning the effectiveness of introductory training programs. The study found that many new reference librarians felt that their orientation programs were poorly organized, and listed the availability of a policies and procedures manual as the most frequent suggestion for improvement.

Tracey, William R. *Designing Training and Development Systems.* 3d ed. New York: AMACOM, 1992. 532p.

This lengthy and detailed overview of every conceivable aspect of training is particularly useful for writing objectives, selecting appropriate media, and constructing evaluative instruments.

TRAINING MATERIALS

Customer Friendly Libraries in a High Tech Age: Being Prepared for Potential [videorecording]. Towson, Md.: Baltimore County Public Library/Library Video Network, 1998. (23 minutes).

Technology is rapidly changing the way libraries operate, both internally and externally. Maintaining the excellent customer service traditionally supplied by libraries is the focus of this video. It reviews basic customer service strategies and how they can be applied in today's libraries. The tape covers issues common in libraries today: making time for adequate staff training, managing computers for public use, helping customers feel comfortable with new technology, and preparing for potential problems.

Customer Service: More Than a Smile [videorecording]. Produced by Library Video Network. Chicago: ALA Video, 1991. (13 minutes).

This video demonstrates techniques for improving customer service in the library, helping library staff become more aware of the importance of customer service, and equipping them with the skills they need to provide that service. It is recommended for all library employees, as well as other groups interested in improving their customer service delivery. The training package includes a step-by-step guide for leading a half-day workshop, as well as reproducible worksheets and handouts for participants.

Dealing with Angry Customers [videorecording]. Santa Monica, Calif.: Salenger Education Media, 1995. (18 min. 25 sec.).

This video shows front-line people how, when confronted with angry customers, to deal first with the customer's feelings, then deal with the person's problems.

The Difficult Reference Question [videorecording]. Produced by Library Video Network. Baltimore, Md.: The Network, 1986. (19 minutes).

This video introduces the skills needed to handle difficult or unusual inquiries, offering specific guidelines for dealing with each user in a patient, nonjudgmental, compassionate manner. A discussion guide is included.

Does This Completely Answer Your Question? [videorecording]. Towson, Md.: ALA Video/Library Video Network, 1992. (19 minutes).

The reference interview is broken down into five stages: set the tone, get the facts, give information, cite the source, and provide follow-up.

If It Weren't for the Patron: Evaluating Your Public Service [videorecording]. Baltimore, Md.: Library Video Network, 1988. (17 minutes).

This video is designed to stimulate a discussion of good communication techniques and public service practices. The start-stop format allows for discussion after each segment before showing the better way to handle a certain situation. A discussion guide is included.

Nolan, Anne Certsvick, and Marilyn P. Whitmore, eds. *Instruction and Training for Enhanced Reference Service: Using Hands-On Active Learning Techniques.* Volume 1, Categories of Fact and Finding Reference Resources, 220p.; volume 2, pt. 1, Reference Resources of the Disciplines, 267p.; volume 2, pt. 2, Major Topics and Their Reference Resources, 220p. plus disk. Pittsburgh, Pa.: Library Instruction Publications, 1998–1999. (Active Learning Series, no. 3).

The editors, affiliated with large institutions using a variety of staff to provide reference service, recognized a need for reference training materials that can be shared across libraries. Each chapter in this three-part series includes an introduction, lesson plans, suggestions for preparation and presentation, and hands-on exercises.

People First: Serving & Employing People with Disabilities [videorecording]. Produced by Library Video Network. Chicago: ALA Video, 1990. (38 minutes).

This video describes different disability levels and how they can influence service the library provides. It presents suggestions on how libraries can eliminate physical and psychological barriers. Staff sensitivity training is one alternative described.

Soaring to Excellence [videorecordings]. Glen Ellyn, Ill.: College of Du Page Satellite Network, 1995–2000.

This series of videos ranging in length from 45 minutes to almost three hours consists of recordings of teleconferences held from 1995 to the present. Topics covered include proactive internal relations, positive morale, disaster planning, technostress, creative thinking, success in the workplace, Internet searching, and many others. A list of current teleconferences is available: http://www.cod.edu/teleconf.

The Telephone Doctor [videorecordings]. St. Louis, Mo.: Telephone Doctor, 1983-1999. (see http://www.teldoc.com/video.asp for a list of available videos).

With hundreds of ideas, skills, and techniques, the Telephone Doctor® sixteen-video customer service training library includes skill-driven training videos ranging in running time from 7 to 33 minutes. Each video module includes a leader's guide, five participant workbooks, twenty-five desktop reminder cards, and a "Getting Started" guide.

CHAPTER

10

EVALUATION OF REFERENCE SERVICES

Bryce Allen

INTRODUCTION

"Evaluation" of reference services literally means to establish the value of the services offered. One can sometimes establish value in quantitative terms; for example, business information services may place a dollar value on the information they provide.[1] In general, however, evaluation of reference and information services relates to the quality of the service, even when librarians or users cannot easily measure quality in quantitative or monetary terms. Improving the quality of service (as opposed to the narrower idea of enhancing the value of service) is the objective of the evaluation of reference services. This chapter outlines techniques that reference librarians can use to establish the quality of their services.

Before examining these techniques in detail, it should be emphasized that quality of service is an everyday, commonsense idea. It is not too difficult to decide if one has received good service, whether it is in a retail establishment, a restaurant, or a library. Users soon form opinions that some librarians give better service than others, that some libraries are easier to use than others, or that some sources are more reliable than others. Evaluation of reference services can make use of this critical judgment on the part of users to improve the quality of service.

Managers of reference and information departments are concerned with evaluating the services provided by their departments. But it would be wrong to think of evaluation as strictly a management function. In some industrial operations, quality control is a separate department, intended to check on the work done by line workers. However, in other companies, Total Quality Management (TQM) and Continuous Quality Improvement (CQI) have supplanted this separation of quality control from production. Industry has come to recognize that line workers have a primary responsibility for the quality of the product and that the entire organization shares a focus on quality. In professional services, separating evaluation from service provision is inappropriate, as the widespread interest in quality programs in libraries indicates.[2]

Specific management techniques such as TQM are not necessary to ensure that library professionals are constantly concerned about the quality of the service they provide. James Shedlock has written that, "Most professionals routinely ask themselves, 'Am I giving quality service?' This concern for quality is generally considered a mark of professionalism."[3] A concern with evaluation is an important part of a professional attitude, or a professional approach, to library and information services. Reference and information staff must continually ask themselves (and their coworkers) questions about their work and about the tools they are using. Every time a librarian comments on the relative usefulness of a reference work, evaluation occurs. Every time a librarian wonders, "How might I have handled that question better?", an evaluative attitude is being displayed. If, on occasion, an information worker asks,

"Should we really be answering that kind of question?", a more profound evaluation of service provision is being accomplished.

This professional concern for evaluation can be traced throughout the history of reference librarianship. Reference departments have always kept reference statistics. Such statistics provided a means to measure reference services, but more sophisticated means of evaluating reference work were not developed until the 1940s. It is not a coincidence that this period also marked the emergence of program evaluation in a variety of social programs.[4] In 1939, Edward Henry proposed criteria for evaluating reference collections and personnel,[5] and G. L. Gardiner has traced empirical studies of reference back to 1943.[6] But large-scale awareness of the importance of reference evaluation really began in the 1960s. Samuel Rothstein played a major role in articulating this awareness in an important article in 1964.[7] Later in that decade, more sophisticated evaluation techniques such as unobtrusive testing (discussed in more detail below) began to evolve, and since then reference librarians have employed a variety of means of evaluating the quality of reference services.

In summary, professionals who are concerned about the services they provide are constantly evaluating reference services. It is an essential component in a professional attitude toward library and information work. When managers of library and information departments become concerned with evaluation, they put mechanisms in place to channel and direct this concern about the quality of service. Structures for evaluation become part of the formal organization of the department. Procedures are established to carry out the evaluation in a regular and consistent manner, so that quality of service can be compared over time. The natural concern for quality that is a part of a professional attitude is channeled into techniques that accomplish evaluation in efficient and effective ways.

WHY EVALUATE REFERENCE?

Sometimes, librarians take for granted the importance of evaluation of reference and information services. But evaluation is a costly activity. It uses resources that might be employed in other ways. One of the most costly aspects of evaluation is the staff time required to accomplish it. A librarian who is evaluating some portion of the collection, or who is analyzing the results of user questionnaires or conducting a community survey, is not available to deal with users' queries.

The benefits to be achieved by evaluation must be weighed against these costs. The most important motive for evaluating library services is to improve the services. It follows that techniques must be used that will provide insights into how services can be improved. It is essential that all evaluation efforts be driven by a serious desire to provide better service to library users. Evaluation that is not followed by improvement may be wasted effort.

A second motive that can justify the effort, and the cost, of evaluation is that of managing resources effectively. Both human and physical resources are essential to reference and information services. But there are frequently alternative ways of employing these resources in providing services. It may be possible to use paraprofessional staff instead of professional staff in some aspects of service provision or to substitute a lower cost reference source for an expensive one. Evaluation can provide insights into the most efficient way of running a reference or information service.

Another motivation, one that Samuel Rothstein called a "hidden agenda" in reference evaluation, is political.[8] It is important that those who are responsible for providing funding for reference and information departments be made aware of the benefits achieved by those services. Those who are involved in service provision see evidence of the value of the service daily, as users are able to meet their information needs. They may take for granted that the service is worthwhile and that it should be adequately funded. However, libraries seldom have a surfeit of funds. Instead of taking for granted the benefits of reference and information services, reference staff may be asked to justify their existence with hard data. The techniques of evaluation discussed in this chapter can provide the kind of evidence that will convince funding agencies to make adequate resources available.

WHAT CAN BE EVALUATED?

The first task facing reference and information departments that want to establish a program of evaluation is to decide what aspects of their services are to be evaluated. One concept that may help in this decision is F. W. Lancaster's distinction between the *inputs* that go into provision of services, the *outputs* in terms of service actually provided, and the ultimate *outcome* from services.[9] Box 10.1 illustrates these distinctions for reference services.

Box 10.1 What Can Be Evaluated?

1. Inputs:

   Reference Materials:

   - Printed information resources
   - Electronic information resources

   Staff:

   - Reference librarians
   - Reference assistants

2. Outputs:

   Factual questions answered (correctly, promptly)

   Instruction given

   Assistance in using information resources provided

3. Outcomes:

   Information needs satisfied

   Library skills and knowledge improved

In many reference and information departments, there may already exist programs to evaluate some of the inputs (the components that go into providing reference services). In particular, the departments may have established mechanisms for evaluating information resources (the reference sources) in terms of their quality and coverage and the human resources (the reference staff) in terms of their performance in providing reference services. This evaluation of resources constitutes the first level of evaluation.

Making use of high-quality resources does not necessarily guarantee that high-quality service will be provided. A variety of libraries have tested a number of mechanisms to measure directly the quality of service (the outputs). Typically, these measures focus on the reference transaction, in which questions are answered or instruction and assistance are provided. Evaluation of reference transactions constitutes the second level of evaluation.

Finally, there is a third level of evaluation. Even if the service is using high-quality resources (the first level) and doing a good job of dealing with individual transactions (the second level), it may not be meeting the needs of its user community in an effective and efficient manner. Again, mechanisms exist that enable a library to assess the extent to which it is meeting the information needs of its community: in other words, the outcomes of the service.

The section below on evaluation techniques provides a more detailed outline of the ways librarians can assess the quality of their reference services at each of these three levels.

STANDARDS FOR REFERENCE SERVICES

An important question in establishing a program of evaluation for reference services relates to the standards against which services can be judged. In some industries, for example, it is possible to establish "standard times" for the various tasks involved in manufacturing products. These standards enable productivity to be measured. Similarly, quantitative standards can be established for the quality of the manufacturing (for example, machining a part to within 1/1000 of an inch). In some library tasks, similar productivity and quality standards can be established, such as standard times or standards of accuracy for entering a record into a database. But because of the nature of the work, it is difficult to establish quantitative standards for reference work. Most reference librarians would agree that service should be accurate and complete, and that users' information needs should be satisfied. The difficulty comes in establishing a quantitative standard for each of these characteristics. Should accuracy attain 90% or 95%? Should the standard for user satisfaction be set at 95% or 99%? Even when evaluation methods are used for measuring the accuracy of responses or the satisfaction of users, there is no clear way of establishing an accepted minimum standard of performance.

Associations concerned with reference services, and state and regional authorities, have devised a number of standards for reference services.[10] But these are usually very general in nature, and although they may sometimes suggest quantitative goals, they seldom provide a basis for the detailed evaluation of a particular reference service. This means that libraries must set their own standards for quality reference services. One way of establishing such standards is to examine the results obtained by similar libraries (see, for example, Box 10.2). This in turn implies that similar or identical evaluation techniques must be used by a number of libraries, so that the results can be compared. In the absence of detailed standards for reference services, these comparative data are very important in understanding the significance of the results of evaluation.

Box 10.2 Standards for Reference Service

The Ohio Public Libraries Standards for Reference Service has a provision that 80% of all reference questions should be answered on the same day. How do you suppose that percent was chosen as a standard? Suppose a library attains a same-day response rate of 75%. Does it follow that the library is providing inadequate service? Suppose a library provides a same-day response rate of 90%. Does this mean that the librarians need not be concerned about improving the timeliness of their service? How would you go about evaluating the service of a public library reference department to see if the standard was reached?

TECHNIQUES OF EVALUATION

Reference librarians and researchers have developed and tested a variety of techniques for evaluating their services. The following discussion highlights those that have been found particularly useful. Although these techniques represent the state of the art in reference evaluation, they all have drawbacks and limitations. No single technique can provide a complete picture of reference quality, and reference librarians may wish to select several techniques to assess their information services.

Level 1: Evaluation of Resources

Evaluating Reference Collections

In Chapter 13, criteria for the selection of high-quality reference materials are introduced. A reference collection should consist of the best tools the library can afford. But selecting high-quality materials is not enough to ensure that the collection as a whole has a high quality. The quality and usefulness of materials must be assessed on a regular basis after they have been added to the collection. Three criteria are useful in this ongoing evaluation of reference collections: the extent to which the information included is up-to-date, the use that is made of the materials, and the reputation of the materials as indicated by their inclusion in standard lists (see Box 10.3).

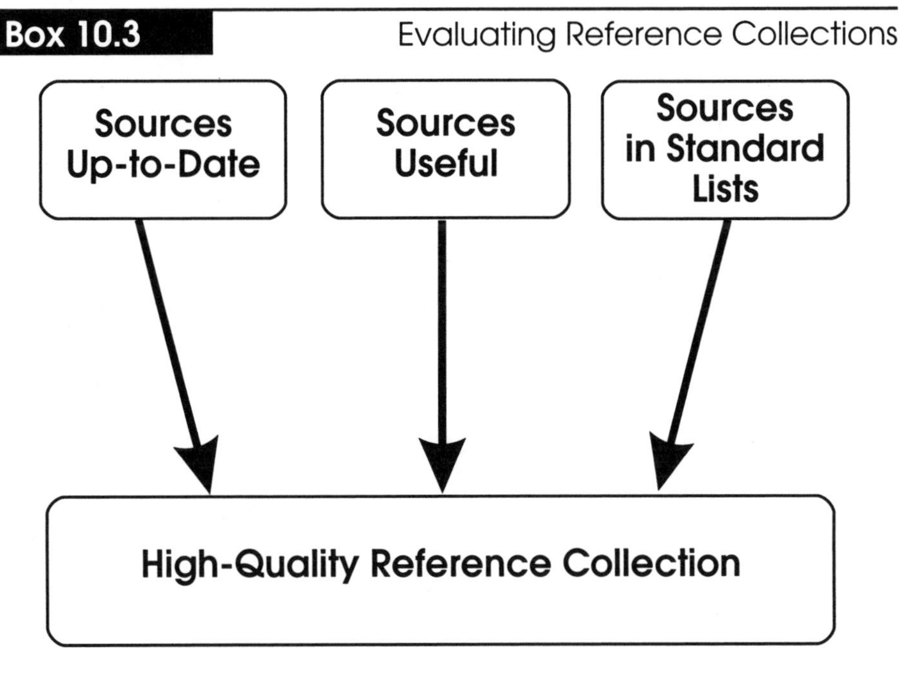

It should be emphasized that these criteria, developed initially to facilitate the evaluation of print materials, also apply to the wide variety of electronic resources available to reference librarians. In addition, special criteria can be applied to electronic resources, and these are discussed in the following section.

The first criterion for reference collection evaluation, the extent to which the materials are up-to-date, is important because the quality of reference materials can change over time. The information they contain may have been accurate when they were acquired, but may now be incorrect. New titles may supersede older reference works. Superseded editions are candidates for removal from the collection, and all older materials should be carefully scrutinized to ensure that the information they present is still accurate and useful. With electronic resources, the frequency of updating of the databases is an important consideration. Sometimes, the updating schedule differs for online and CD-ROM versions of the same databases. Although electronic sources are usually more up-to-date than their print counterparts, occasionally the opposite occurs, and print sources provide the most current information or citations. This confused state of affairs means that librarians must be careful to ensure that their collections provide the most up-to-date information to users. Web pages may be updated very frequently (sometimes on a daily or weekly schedule). There are also Web pages that are still active whose content may not have been altered for a period of months. One mark of a high-quality Web page is a "last updated" note, displayed in some prominent location. This information is important in assessing the currency of the information contained on the page.

The second criterion, the usefulness of the materials in the collection, is more general than the first criterion and more difficult to assess. In addition to scanning the collection to ascertain the currency of its materials, it is possible to measure directly the usefulness of the titles in it. A tally of materials being reshelved can be used to obtain an approximate measure of the use of those materials. Alternatively, reference staff can insert a form into each reference book and make a check on it every time they consult that title. Another technique is to affix adhesive colored dots to the spines of materials to indicate either reshelving or consultation by a reference staff person. These methods can give a helpful quantification of the use of the materials in the collection.

Frequency of use of electronic resources accessed via dedicated workstations can be assessed by using sign-up sheets or by tallying the numbers of users who visit each workstation. When many databases are accessed through a single terminal, transaction logs can provide data on frequency of use. This technique is discussed in more detail below. Similar transaction logs are created by the "history" features found in many Web browsers that record the Web pages consulted by users.

One can never rely solely on the demonstrated use of materials in evaluating materials in a collection. For example, users may be consulting obsolete materials because the library has not acquired more current tools. Or materials may be little used because of lack of familiarity by reference staff or inadequate subject access provided by the library catalog. Demonstrated use should always be taken as only one input along with others in deciding whether to retain an item in the collection.

The third criterion is the reputation of the materials in the collection. This can be established by comparing the contents of the collection with standard lists. For example, Kim Dority edits *A Guide to Reference Books for Small and Medium-sized Libraries,*[11] and Barbara Ripp Safford edits *Guide to Reference Materials for School Media Centers.*[12] Also useful is a compilation of reference books edited by Bohdan S. Wynar, *Recommended Reference Books for Small and Medium-sized Libraries and Media Centers.*[13] Other standard lists of reference materials are covered in Chapter 13. In all cases, these standard lists can be used to improve the quality of the collection, either by adding or removing titles. It is, however, important to exercise caution in using these lists. They are designed to be used by many libraries and so do not take into account local variations in user populations and needs. Thus, the standard lists may omit items that are invaluable to a particular collection while including materials that would be superfluous in that collection.

One basic assumption that guides the idea of reference collection evaluation is that there is an optimal size for such a collection. A reference collection should be small enough that reference staff can have a reasonable familiarity with all of the tools, the kinds of information they contain, and the kinds of questions they can answer. On the other hand, a reference collection should be large enough so that a reasonable proportion of inquiries can be resolved and answered quickly. Experience indicates that, especially for factual reference questions, a small, high-quality collection with which the reference staff is thoroughly familiar can be more effective than a larger collection. As high-quality materials are added to the collection, it is important to survey the collection and remove materials that are superseded, unused, or not recommended, so that the collection can remain at its optimal size, and books that are not frequently consulted in the reference collection can be made available for circulation to library users.

Mechanisms for reference collection evaluation will differ from one library to another, but it is always desirable to make the reference staff responsible for the task. Frequently the collection is divided by topic area, with the staff member most familiar with a topic being given responsibility for that section. These specialists may suggest items for withdrawal from the collection or for transfer to another part of the library. Some mechanism for consultation with the rest of the reference staff is important so that all reference staff will know what is happening to the collection.

Box 10.4 Scenario: Evaluating Reference Books

A university library reference department has in its collection a multivolume encyclopedia published in the 1950s in the European duchy of Transmogrania. Of course it is written in Transmogranian, a language that none of the reference staff can read. This encyclopedia remains in the lists of reference works because it is a standard, authoritative work on all aspects of Transmogranian life and culture. A survey of the reshelving of reference works in the department shows that no volumes of this work were reshelved during the six months in which the survey was conducted. As always, the reference library is finding that its shelf space is inadequate, and one reference librarian suggests removing the encyclopedia from the reference collection. Would you (a) keep the encyclopedia in reference, because it is a standard reference work; (b) transfer the encyclopedia to the general stacks, where it will become a circulating title; or (c) get rid of the encyclopedia by donating it to the only faculty member on campus who can read Transmogranian? Are there alternative solutions?

Now suppose that one of your expert Web-surfing librarians has discovered that the government of Transmogrania has established a Web site that contains very thorough current information about the duchy of Transmogrania in Transmogrania and imperfect English. Does the availability of this resource affect your decision about the encyclopedia?

Evaluating Electronic Sources

With the introduction of electronic information storage and retrieval into the reference process, evaluation of reference sources has acquired new dimensions (see Box 10.5, p. 252). Librarians can evaluate the content of online databases using the same criteria as for print reference tools: accuracy, scope, authority, and so forth. However, some databases are available through a number of vendors, each of which uses a different interface or command structure. This proliferation of database vendors has increased dramatically with the widespread use of CD-ROM systems and the possibility of providing access to databases over the Internet. Thus, as described in Chapter 13, librarians frequently have the opportunity to evaluate not only the content of the databases, but also the interface, access points, and command structure through which they and their users search the databases. This means that librarians should be paying particular attention to the ease of use and effectiveness of interfaces and command structures when they are deciding which sources should be used in their reference services. Andrew Large provides a good outline of the criteria for evaluating these sources, including such considerations as the retrieval approaches provided by search software and the support services offered by CD-ROM vendors.[14]

The World Wide Web places many new information resources at the fingertips of both reference librarians and users. The quality of the information resources on the Web varies considerably, so the evaluative approaches outlined here are even more crucial if quality of reference services is to be maintained. In addition to standard criteria, Alastair Smith suggests that usability factors such as graphic and multimedia design, browsability, and organization be considered when rating Web sites. These criteria are amplified in an article by Kevin M. Oliver and others.[15] The task of evaluating Web sites places additional demands on reference librarians; increased use of such information resources in reference service places the onus for such evaluation firmly on the information specialists who provide that service.

Box 10.5 Evaluating End-User Searching

End-user searching provides tremendous opportunities for library users to satisfy their information needs. However, not all electronic resources are equally effective, reliable, or usable. Your library has been offering end-user searching of bibliographic databases on CD-ROM for the past five years. How can you evaluate the success of this technology in meeting information needs? How can you evaluate the quality of the training that is being offered to individuals who make use of this service? What information will you need to justify the continuation of this program of end-user searching? How might this information be derived from your evaluation of the service?

There is one type of electronic resource for which reference librarians have a special responsibility: the online public access catalog. Once considered primarily the responsibility of technical services librarians, catalogs have become a matter of joint responsibility in many libraries. Reference librarians are ideally located to assess the usability of online catalogs and to identify problems experienced by library users. One technique that librarians can use to evaluate an online catalog is transaction log analysis. Many systems have the capability of recording (logging) the commands, menu selections, and features used by searchers. These records can then be printed and analyzed in detail to identify areas for potential improvement.[16] Many online catalogs have expanded to incorporate access to periodical indexes and similar electronic information and to offer Web-based browsable access to these information resources. It is essential that reference librarians use their expertise in evaluating electronic information resources to suggest how the usability of this important tool can be improved for all library users.

Evaluating Reference Staff

Any library with a thoroughly developed personnel function will already have in place one of a number of techniques for conducting annual or periodic evaluations of its employees. Although a variety of personnel evaluation techniques exist and can be found in any of the standard textbooks on library management or library personnel administration, evaluation of reference personnel poses special problems and challenges. Personnel evaluation normally takes into account two different criteria: the characteristics of the employee (in terms of qualifications for the position) and the employee's performance of the job itself.

The first criterion for reference staff evaluation is the extent to which employees possess characteristics that will make them good reference staff. However, it is difficult to establish a suitable list of employee characteristics against which reference staff can be evaluated. The reference literature provides several lists of possible criteria.[17] Examples include approachability, knowledge of reference resources in the collection and on the Web, and the ability to investigate a problem thoroughly. But even if a list of employee characteristics has been developed, it is sometimes difficult to test the extent to which librarians have those characteristics. How can one test such characteristics as approachability, or even something less subjective, such as the employee's knowledge of the reference collection?

The second criterion is how staff are performing in their jobs. The main problem with this criterion appears to be one of observation. Usually, an employee's supervisor is the one who conducts the evaluation, but it is frequently difficult for the supervisor to observe directly how well a reference librarian is performing. It may not be possible to observe in detail the interaction between a reference librarian and a user without intruding upon that interaction. Other individuals, such as the librarian's coworkers or the users who are served by the librarian, may be in a better position to observe how well the librarian is performing, but obtaining the evaluations of these individuals may be difficult because of concerns about personal bias and confidentiality. It seems likely that in many situations the librarians themselves are in the best position to observe the quality of the service they are providing. Some libraries ask employees to evaluate themselves and include this self-evaluation in the performance evaluation scheme.

The objective of reference staff evaluation is to help reference librarians and other reference staff to improve the level of their performance, and thus to improve the service offered. The evaluation function should provide feedback to reference staff about their performance, so that their natural concerns about providing high-quality service can motivate them to improve their performance. One model that has great potential in reference services is the Management by Objectives (MBO) model. This process takes into account the capabilities of each worker and uses an iterative process of feedback to create a high-quality reference staff. In MBO, the workers' characteristics and performance are evaluated by themselves and by others such as supervisors or coworkers. As part of the evaluation process, areas for possible improvement are identified, and concrete objectives are set for the coming year. The next performance evaluation takes into account the workers' objectives from the past year and provides feedback on how well those objectives have been achieved. Reference staff members and their supervisors then set new objectives for improved service in the following year.

Box 10.6 Scenario: Evaluating Reference Librarians

In some libraries, salary increases are determined, at least in part, on the basis of "merit." The theory behind merit increases is that the best employees are rewarded for their efforts, while those who are providing less excellent service are given an incentive to improve. How might this work in practice? Suppose you are supervising a reference staff of ten, and only three of them can have merit increases. How would you go about selecting the three best employees? How would you explain to the rest of the staff the criteria upon which they were being judged? Could you implement a merit pay system in a fair and objective manner?

Level 2: Evaluation of Reference Transactions

Although the ongoing evaluation of resources such as collections and personnel is important, it provides only a partial perspective on the quality of reference services. To get a more complete picture, it is essential to evaluate what happens when the service is being provided. Katherine Emerson has defined the reference transaction as "an information contact that involves the use, recommendation, interpretation or instruction in the use of one or more information sources, or knowledge of such sources, by a member of the reference or information staff."[18] This transaction involves a complex encounter between the librarian and the user.

A typical reference transaction starts when a library user asks for some information or assistance. The information need may be clarified through a reference interview, and then the reference librarian performs one or more of a wide range of activities: instruction, explanation, bibliographic searching, and examination of sources and tools. Finally, if all goes well, the information or assistance is obtained by the user. Evaluation of such a complex transaction is difficult, and it is made more difficult by the fact that several transactions may be occurring simultaneously in a busy reference department. However, a number of techniques have been developed to try to evaluate the effectiveness of reference transactions in any library. These include unobtrusive evaluation, obtrusive evaluation by user surveys and other methods, and compilation of reference statistics.

Unobtrusive Evaluation

One way of simplifying the evaluation of reference transactions is to concentrate on one component of the transaction, or on one particular kind of transaction. One example of this simplification has occupied a great deal of the literature on reference evaluation in the past twenty years: *unobtrusive evaluation.* Terence Crowley, in his 1968 doctoral thesis, developed a technique of unobtrusive evaluation of reference services, and Thomas Childers's thesis two years later refined the technique.[19] Proxy users were hired to approach library reference desks, either in person or by telephone, and to ask factual questions for which the correct answers had previously been established. From the responses received, it was possible to ascertain the proportion of correct responses given by various libraries. This evaluation was unobtrusive because the library staff being evaluated did not know that the experiments were being conducted. Later research by Terry Weech and Herbert Goldhor[20] established the value of this technique in providing an accurate picture of service provision by demonstrating that when reference staff were aware that they were being evaluated, they correctly answered a larger proportion of the questions.

Since the pioneering work of Crowley and Childers, a large number of studies using unobtrusive evaluation have appeared in the literature. Kenneth Crews provides a good overview of this research.[21] A consistent pattern of responses has emerged. In responding to questions about facts, library reference departments give correct answers about 55% of the time. Naturally this result has been a cause of considerable discussion among librarians who are concerned about the quality of service. It has also led to increased interest in methods of improving performance of reference staff (see Chapter 9).

Researchers have applied unobtrusive techniques to studies of other aspects of the reference transaction. Proxy users have asked questions requiring more detailed analysis, as well as questions that draw on specialized sources such as government documents. Similar techniques have studied the extent to which reference staff conduct reference interviews and the quality of those interviews. Unobtrusive studies directed toward different classes of reference staff (librarians, library technical assistants, and student assistants) have been completed. A number of studies have used unobtrusive testing as a diagnostic tool within one library, for example, to determine areas in which staff training may be required. Because e-mail reference services so closely resemble the telephone reference services that were the first to be unobtrusively evaluated, such services seem good candidates for this evaluation technique.

Unobtrusive testing is now an established element in the evaluation of reference transactions. A number of concerns about the technique exist, however. Some feel that it is unethical to test reference services in this way without informing the reference staff that such an experiment is being conducted. This concern may be more substantial when the results of unobtrusive testing are applied to individual staff members rather than to the service as a whole. Another major concern relates to the fact that unobtrusive testing has been used primarily to examine one aspect of the reference transaction: the accuracy of responses to factual questions. It is important that the ability of reference departments to answer factual questions not be taken as indicative of all of the services they provide. For example, other activities, such as providing detailed bibliographic assistance or instruction in library use, may be just as important in the reference department's service.

It is difficult to escape the consistent finding from more than twenty studies that has come to be called the "55% rule." Many comments about the "crisis" in reference services are based on the widely held opinion that reference services should be doing better than this. The results of unobtrusive testing have pointed out areas in which substantial improvement can be made in the service provided by library reference departments. Libraries are now turning their attention to staff training, collection improvement, and other techniques to improve the accuracy of responses to factual questions.

Box 10.7 Scenario: Unobtrusive Evaluation

As the supervisor of a reference department, you are concerned about the quality of service being offered. After reading the accounts of a number of unobtrusive tests of reference services, you decided to conduct such a test yourself. It has now been completed, and you have communicated the results to the reference staff. One of the reference librarians, discovering that his service has been evaluated unobtrusively at some time in the past two months, expresses considerable anger about the unobtrusive evaluation. First of all, he says that they are busy enough in the reference department without having these phony patrons to deal with as well. Second, he feels that the university students hired to ask the questions are not like real users: They do not have a real information need, so they cannot provide a realistic test of the librarians' ability to meet users' needs. In addition, the unobtrusive test pays attention to only one aspect of his work: the accuracy and completeness of the response. He feels that this is not a fair evaluation of his abilities as a reference librarian. But the thing that bothers him most about it is the sneakiness of the technique. Why can't they let people know before doing something like this?

What responses would you, as the supervisor, make to these criticisms? Do you think you could convince the librarian that unobtrusive evaluation is in fact a good idea?

Obtrusive Techniques: User Surveys

Among the obtrusive techniques of evaluating reference transactions, perhaps the most widely employed is user surveys. Here there is no element of surprise: The library staff know that a survey of users is being conducted. In fact, in most cases the library staff conduct the survey. Generally speaking, such surveys have asked users whether they found what they needed, whether they were satisfied by the service provided by the reference department, and whether the reference staff appeared efficient, friendly, and so forth.

This approach shares the weaknesses of other survey techniques. First, what is being solicited are opinions, rather than facts. Such opinions may be helpful and interesting, but they are not necessarily a reflection of reality. If 75% of users say they found what they needed, we should not assume that the reference department is functioning at 75% effectiveness. Users may understate or overstate their success depending on the state of their knowledge, the feeling they have about libraries or about the library staff, and other variables. User satisfaction questions are particularly prone to response bias on the part of users (i.e., the respondents reply as they think they are expected to reply, not as they really feel).

Despite these shortcomings, user surveys can provide useful detail about the workings of the reference service. One of the best surveys has been developed and tested over a number of years in a wide variety of libraries: the Wisconsin-Ohio Reference Evaluation Program.[22] In this survey, after each reference transaction the user answers one set of questions while the library staff member answers a set of matching questions. The first advantage of this technique is that it provides a comparison between the opinions and perceptions of users and library staff about the transaction. The second advantage is that the questions are tied to a specific transaction, rather than being asked about service in general. This seems likely to reduce the chance of response bias. The third advantage is that this survey instrument has been used in a variety of libraries. The survey results from all of these libraries are available in a database, and it is possible to determine how the results from one library compare with those of similar libraries. Instead of having only a general idea about the reference service, a reference librarian can identify areas that need improvement, or areas of particular strength, compared with other libraries serving similar user groups.

In general, the task of questionnaire design is so tricky, and the likelihood of response bias so great, that libraries are well advised to avoid trying to create their own survey instrument. Using an expertly designed and well-tested survey instrument such as the Wisconsin-Ohio form can produce useful results, whereas in-house forms may be difficult to interpret and may produce only vague and uncertain results (see Box 10.8).

Box 10.8 Evaluation by Questionnaire

One questionnaire used to evaluate the service in an academic library contained the following item: "Please give a brief description of your last encounter with a reference librarian. What did you do? What did the librarian do?" The questionnaire allowed about half a page for a written response. What kind of responses do you think would be obtained from this item? How would you go about analyzing the responses to find out whether the reference department was providing high-quality service? What other purposes might this item serve? Try answering this item yourself. Do you think response bias might affect what you say?

Other Obtrusive Evaluation Techniques

Researchers have tested some suggestions of other obtrusive techniques for evaluation of reference work. Some researchers have made recordings of reference transactions and have analyzed the recordings to ascertain the extent to which interview techniques such as open and closed questions have been used (see Chapter 3 for a discussion of these techniques) and how these techniques are associated with success in reference transactions. In other experiments, reference transactions have been videotaped and the effectiveness of the reference staff member has been evaluated by peer judges. Although such techniques provide an unprecedented opportunity to observe and analyze in depth the performance of reference librarians and the quality of the service they are providing, a number of ethical and practical concerns have prevented the use of these obtrusive techniques in the working environment of reference departments.

Reference Statistics

Probably the oldest and most widespread technique of assessing reference work is to keep a tally of the number of questions that are answered during a given period at a given service point. Sometimes these tallies are analyzed by type of question asked (subject queries vs. directional), and a few details may be recorded about the kind of answer that was given (for example, the time taken to answer the question). Reference statistics that result from the compilation of such tallies are useful for managers. They may provide the input needed to improve the scheduling of staff at service points, and they may provide data to justify the extension of reference services. But it is questionable whether reference statistics really provide any solid evaluation of the service provided. Box 10.9 shows an example of a reference statistics tally sheet. Managers can use data collected on such a sheet to identify busy times so that additional staff can be scheduled or to identify the amount of individualized library instruction that is required at different times during the year so that group bibliographic instruction can be implemented during those periods of high demand.

Reference statistics, and their byproducts such as reference fill rates (the proportion of reference questions successfully answered) and reference completion rates (the number of reference questions completed on the same day), make assumptions about the quality of the reference work, but do not really measure that quality. Reference statistics cannot distinguish between a transaction that is successfully completed and one in which the user is not helped. Accordingly, it is correct to think of reference statistics and output measures as an important type of data collection for management of the service, but not as an evaluative tool (see Box 10.10, page 258).

Box 10.9 Example of a Reference Statistics Tally Sheet

Reference Desk
Daily Statistics

Day:
Date:

Record All Questions Here	**9am-1pm**	**1pm-6pm**	**6pm-9pm**
Reference			
Directional			
Additional Data: Mark When Appropriate			
Telephoned Questions			
Instruction			
Online Catalog			
Internet Search			
Research Question			

Box 10.10 Reference Statistics

Output Measures for Public Libraries[23] suggests the use of "reference completion rate" as a tool for assessing reference output. Is it possible that reference librarians might judge a question as completed but that the user might regard the response as incomplete? Paul Kantor[24] suggests a measure that relies on reference librarians' estimates of the success of the reference process. Again, is it possible that librarians might regard a transaction as being successfully completed, but the user's opinion might differ? How might you try to improve these measures to get a more objective idea of completion rate or success rate?

Level 3: Evaluation of Reference Services

The third level of evaluation of reference moves beyond individual reference transactions and attempts to evaluate the extent to which reference services are meeting their overall objectives. For this kind of evaluation to be possible, a statement of the goals and objectives of the reference department must exist. A typical statement of goals and objectives might include meeting the information needs of the user community and teaching the user community about the library and its services. The task of this third level of evaluation is to ascertain the extent to which the reference service is meeting its goals and objectives.

To evaluate how well the reference service is meeting the information needs of the user community, it is necessary to survey the entire community in some reliable way to find out what its information needs really are and whether the members of the community perceive the library as a source that can provide the information they need. Similarly, to find out the effectiveness of the reference service in teaching the community about the library, it is necessary to ascertain the extent of community knowledge about the library's services.

In dealing with these larger questions, other concerns may be addressed as well. It may be possible to identify population segments whose information needs are not being met by reference services, or parts of the user community that show little awareness of the library's services. All of these concerns are addressed by a community needs analysis. A number of different techniques can be used to analyze the information needs of a community. *A Planning Process for Public Libraries*[25] gives an example of a telephone survey that can be used by a public library to ascertain the extent to which the citizens in the community know about and use the library's reference services. Other, less formal techniques can also be used. For example, key informants from within the user community can be interviewed to determine the extent to which there are user needs that are not currently being met by the library's reference services. Focus groups can also be used in this type of evaluation, as introduced by Massey-Burzio.[26]

One way of thinking about this level of evaluation is to see it as part of an ongoing planning process, in which all of the possible kinds of library service are considered along with the existing service. The kinds of questions that might be asked are: "Should we be answering the kinds of questions that we are currently answering?" and "Are there questions that we should be answering that we are not currently answering?" The community survey will give an idea of the level of use currently made of existing reference services, and it should also identify areas of information need that reference services are not currently meeting. This information can serve as input to the library's ongoing strategic planning process (see Box 10.11).

Box 10.11 Community Surveys

A public library's community needs analysis ascertains that 90% of the citizens of the community know about reference services, and 75% of the citizens approve of the work that the service is doing. But only 23% of the citizens indicate that they have made use of the service in the past three years. What does this tell the library about the quality of its service? What additional questions does it raise? How might the library try to answer those questions?

The same survey shows that one of the main problems facing citizens in the community is obtaining affordable rental housing. Landlord-tenant disputes were frequently cited as an area where the citizens find they need information. Should the library try to respond to this problem? What sort of information service might be helpful?

RELATED ISSUES

How reference evaluation is implemented in specific libraries depends on a variety of factors. Differences between the communities served by different types of libraries can limit the usefulness of some of the evaluation techniques discussed above. At the same time, the organizational structure within which reference services are provided can influence how evaluation occurs.

Evaluation of Service to Specific Populations

The unique nature of the user population being served by the reference or information services can influence the process of evaluating these services. The example used here is services to children and young adults, but similar concerns may be raised about services to a wide range of specific populations, from homebound seniors to the socially disadvantaged. The special needs of these populations provide new criteria against which services can be evaluated. For a fuller discussion of the needs of specific populations, see Chapter 12.

In the area of evaluation of resources, librarians need to consider how appropriate the reference tools are to meeting the information needs of children. White found that many children's reference tools have inappropriately high reading levels.[27] Evaluation of human resources (i.e., children's reference librarians) requires consideration of special criteria such as patience and empathy with children. In an evaluation of reference transactions, some of the techniques discussed above may require adaptation. For example, children may not be able to complete a traditional user survey or to act as surrogates in unobtrusive testing. Interviews with users may be the best way to evaluate the success of reference transactions in the children's reference department. At the third level of evaluation, evaluation of services in the aggregate, each of the programs of the children's department can be assessed in relation to the department's goals. Some of the data used in this kind of evaluation can come from the children themselves—for example, from their willingness to return for additional programs. It may also be possible for library staff to assess how children's cognitive skills are developing as a result of library programs and activities. But the evidence of others who deal closely with the children is also important, such as parents' opinions about the importance of library programs in the lives of their children and teachers' assessments of the effectiveness of library programs in enhancing students' cognitive and academic skills.

Electronic reference resources have made their presence felt in services to children as well. Here, the usability of information technology is a particularly important issue, and reference librarians have a special responsibility to ensure that the technology does not become a barrier to information seeking and use by children. For example, some research in the success children have in using online catalogs suggests that these tools need to be specially customized for their use.[28]

This example demonstrates that reference services to specific populations present challenges for evaluators. Although the need for evaluation is as great as for general reference services, evaluation techniques may have to be adapted for effective use with the specific population being served (see Box 10.12).

Box 10.12 Evaluating Reference Services for Children

In many schools, students are given assignments that require them to make use of the school library. By examining completed assignments, a school librarian can ascertain the extent to which students are making successful use of the library. This provides a direct means of evaluating the quality of the information and instruction services of the school library. In a public library children's department, the librarian does not have such a convenient mechanism for evaluation. How would a children's librarian ascertain the quality of information and instruction services being provided by the library? What evidence could be used to evaluate these services?

Organizing for Evaluation

There is no ideal organizational structure or mechanism for implementing reference evaluation. In a small library, one or two individuals may have responsibility for the entire array of reference services. At the other end of the spectrum, a large library may have dozens of staff members providing reference services through a large number of service points. But there are some necessary conditions for the evaluation of all reference services. It is necessary for reference staff to have time to step back from the daily provision of service and to examine the service as a whole. There must be an opportunity for the setting and regular reexamination of the goals and objectives of the reference services. From this can come an understanding of the aspects of the service most in need of evaluation and of evaluation techniques that can be applied to those areas.

It is also necessary to have the responsibility for evaluation clearly delineated, and written into job descriptions wherever appropriate. If this does not happen, the reference staff will tend to think of evaluation as a good idea, but one that someone else will deal with. When any reference program is developed, an evaluation component must be included in the planning. For example, if a bibliographic instruction program is being developed, the librarians in charge must have, from the beginning, a clear idea of how the success of the program will be measured. Similarly, if the library is thinking of acquiring a new technology, an evaluation scheme that will assess the effectiveness of that new technology must be incorporated from the beginning of the planning process. If a branch library is being opened in a new community, a plan for community needs analysis (with regular follow-up analysis) should be included in the planning for that branch.

If a library is providing services that are not being evaluated, library staff have a responsibility to develop techniques to evaluate them. Some libraries have started to do unobtrusive evaluation of their telephone reference service on a regular basis and to chart the accuracy and completeness of the responses given over time. Other libraries have adopted a questionnaire approach to the regular evaluation of reference transactions. The key point is that evaluation should be an ongoing, regular part of the functioning of the reference department. Single, isolated attempts at evaluation can produce interesting results, but the value of these projects is soon lost. Ongoing evaluation provides the input that is necessary for the continual improvement of the service.

Finally, it is necessary to bring together those librarians who are responsible for evaluation of reference services on a regular basis so that they can share their perceptions of the quality of service. In such meetings it is possible to develop means by which evaluation can be translated into improved services. This ties the results of evaluation directly to the ongoing planning process of the reference department. All planning efforts, including financial planning and budgeting, must be influenced by evaluation. As indicated at the beginning of this chapter, evaluation that does not lead to service improvement may be a waste of effort. It is important for the library staff to be able to take the time to obtain a perspective on the quality of the existing services and to plan for ways in which services can be improved.

CONCLUSION

All of the techniques and approaches to the evaluation of reference services described in this chapter have shortcomings. None of them provides a complete picture of the quality of services. Accordingly, a thorough evaluation program will make use of a number of these techniques in an integrated manner to build up an overview of the effectiveness and quality of reference services.

A multimethod approach to reference evaluation will include elements from all levels of evaluation. It is important to evaluate the inputs to reference services, including the reference collection and the reference staff. Similarly, it is important to obtain some idea about how well the reference transactions are being completed. Finally, it is essential that the success of reference services in meeting overall goals and objectives be considered from time to time through some sort of community needs analysis. Many libraries have some or all of these elements in place, and the challenge is to integrate the results of the different kinds of evaluation and to respond to these results with effective action.

When one selects a particular aspect of reference services to evaluate, one places a great deal of value and emphasis on that aspect. For example, a library that chooses to evaluate accuracy in answering simple, factual, and unambiguous questions sends a message to its staff that this kind of service is important. Some libraries have chosen to reevaluate reference accuracy repeatedly, thus reinforcing the message that this is the most central aspect of reference services. Only a balanced, multimethod evaluation program can avoid this undue emphasis on one type of service and give librarians a balanced understanding of the quality of the services they provide.

There are many questions still to be answered about assessing the quality of reference services. For example, James Rettig has suggested that librarians should place their evaluation of reference in the context of a better understanding of what users expect of reference services.[29] In another provocative article, Jo Bell Whitlatch lists many questions that are not completely addressed by current methods of evaluation.[30] Many of these questions relate to user motivations and behaviors. Systematic research into user expectations and behaviors, such as Rettig and Whitlatch suggest, may indeed give reference librarians a better basis for assessing the quality of their services. Although much research remains to be completed, reference evaluation has become an essential component of service provision. It is the responsibility of every professional librarian to ensure that adequate resources are available to the evaluation and improvement of service so that reference services can fulfill their mandate of providing information that will be of value to users.

NOTES

1. Readers interested in pursuing further the concept of the value of information can begin by examining these survey articles: Aatto J. Repo, "The Value of Information: Approaches in Economics, Accounting, and Management Science," *Journal of the American Society for Information Science* 40 (March 1989): 68-85, and Joan Parker and Janice Houghton, "The Value of Information: Paradigms and Perspectives," *Proceedings of the ASIS Annual Meeting* 31 (1994): 26-33.

2. The entire issue of *Library Trends* 44 (Winter 1996) is devoted to quality improvement in a range of libraries.

3. James Shedlock, "Defining the Quality of Medical Reference Service," *Medical Reference Services Quarterly* 7 (Spring 1988): 49.

4. Jack L. Franklin and Jean H. Trasher, *An Introduction to Program Evaluation* (New York: Wiley, 1976), 233p.

5. Edward A. Henry, "Judging Library Reference Service," *Library Journal* 64 (May 1, 1939): 358-59.

6. G. L. Gardiner, "The Empirical Study of Reference," *College & Research Libraries* 30 (March 1969): 130-55.

7. Samuel Rothstein, "The Measurement and Evaluation of Reference Service," *Library Trends* 12 (January 1964): 456-72.

8. Samuel Rothstein, "The Hidden Agenda in the Measurement and Evaluation of Reference Services: Or, How to Make a Case for Yourself," *The Reference Librarian* 11 (Fall/Winter 1984): 45-52.

9. F. W. Lancaster, *If You Want to Evaluate Your Library*... (Champaign, Ill.: University of Illinois Graduate School of Library and Information Science, 1988), 193p.

10. See, for example, Suburban Library System, "SLS Minimum Reference Standards for Public Libraries," *Illinois Libraries* 70 (January 1988): 16-19; Marjorie E. Murfin and Charles Albert Bunge, "Responsible Standard for Reference Service in Ohio Public Libraries," *Ohio Libraries* 1 (March/April 1988): 11-13; Joanne G. Marshall and Holly Shipp Buchanan, "Benchmarking Reference Services: An Introduction," *Medical Reference Services Quarterly* 15 (Spring 1996): 1-13.

11. G. Kim Dority, ed., *A Guide to Reference Books for Small and Medium-sized Libraries, 1984–1994* (Englewood, Colo.: Libraries Unlimited, 1995), 372p.

12. Barbara Ripp Safford, *Guide to Reference Materials for School Library Media Centers,* 5th ed. (Englewood, Colo.: Libraries Unlimited, 1998), 353p.

13. Bohdan S. Wynar, ed., *Recommended Reference Books for Small and Medium-sized Libraries and Media Centers* (Englewood, Colo.: Libraries Unlimited, annual).

14. J. Andrew Large, "Evaluating Online and CD-ROM Reference Sources," *Journal of Librarianship* 21(April 1989): 87-108.

15. Alastair G. Smith, "Testing the Surf: Criteria for Evaluating Internet Information Resources," *Public-Access Computer Systems Review* 8 (1997): 1-14. Also available: http://info.lib.uh.edu/pr/v8/n3/smit8n3.html; Kevin M. Oliver, Gene L. Wilkinson, and Lisa T. Bennett, "Evaluating the Quality of Internet Information Sources," in *Proceedings of Ed-Media 97 and Ed-Telecom 97—World Conference on Education Multimedia and Hypermedia & World Conference on Education Telecommunications,* eds. Tomasz Müldner and Thomas C. Reeves (Charlottesville, Va.: Association for the Advancement of Computing in Education, 1997), 971-77.

16. Good examples of the use of transaction log analysis are reported by Steven D. Zink, "Monitoring User Search Success Through Transaction Log Analysis: The WolfPAC Example," *Reference Services Review* 19 (1991): 49-56; Rhonda N. Hunter, "Successes and Failures of Patrons Searching the Online Catalog at a Large Academic Library: A Transaction Log Analysis," *RQ* 30 (Spring 1991): 395-402; and Thomas A. Peters, "When Smart People Fail: An Analysis of the Transaction Log of an Online Public Access Catalog," *Journal of Academic Librarianship* 15 (November 1989): 267-73. An excellent overview of techniques and findings is Thomas A. Peters and others, "Special Theme: Transaction Log Analysis," *Library Hi Tech* 11, no. 2 (1993): 37-106.

17. Brian Quinn, "Beyond Efficacy: The Exemplar Librarian as a New Approach to Reference Evaluation," *Illinois Libraries* 76 (Summer 1994): 163-73; Carole A. Larson and Laura K. Dickson, "Developing Behavioral Reference Desk Performance Standards," *RQ* 33 (Spring 1994): 349-57; RUSA, "Guidelines for Behavioral Performance of Reference and Information Services Professionals," *RQ* 36 (Winter 1996): 200-203.

18. Katherine Emerson, "Definitions for Planning and Evaluating Reference Services," *The Reference Librarian* 11 (Fall/Winter 1984): 67.

19. These theses were subsequently published as Terence Crowley and Thomas Childers, *Information Service in Public Libraries: Two Studies* (Metuchen, N.J.: Scarecrow Press, 1971), 210p.

20. Terry L. Weech and Herbert Goldhor, "Obtrusive Versus Unobtrusive Evaluation of Reference Service in Five Illinois Public Libraries: A Pilot Study," *The Library Quarterly* 52 (October 1982): 305-24.

21. Kenneth D. Crews, "The Accuracy of Reference Service: Variables for Research and Implementation," *Library & Information Science Research* 10 (July–September 1988): 331-55.

22. For a description of the development of this questionnaire, see Charles Albert Bunge, "Factors Related to Reference Question Answering Success: The Development of a Data-Gathering Form," *RQ* 24 (Summer 1985): 482-86; and Marjorie E. Murfin and Gary M. Gugelchuk, "Development and Testing of a Reference Transaction Assessment Instrument," *College & Research Libraries* 48 (July 1987): 314-38.

23. Nancy A. Van House and others, *Output Measures for Public Libraries: A Manual of Standardized Procedures,* 2d ed. (Chicago: American Library Association, 1987), 99p.

24. Paul Kantor, "Quantitative Evaluation of the Reference Process," *RQ* 21 (Fall 1981): 43-54.

25. Vernon E. Palmour, Marcia C. Bellassai, and Nancy V. DeWath, *A Planning Process for Public Libraries* (Chicago: American Library Association, 1980), 304p.

26. Virginia Massey-Burzio, "From the Other Side of the Reference Desk: A Focus Group Study," *Journal of Academic Librarianship* 24 (May 1998): 208-15.

27. Marilyn Domas White, "The Readability of Children's Reference Materials," *The Library Quarterly* 60 (October 1990): 300-319.

28. Leslie M. Edmonds, Paula R. Moore, and Kathleen Mehaffey Balcom, "The Effectiveness of an Online Catalog," *School Library Journal* 35 (October 1990): 28-32; Paul Solomon, "Children's Information Retrieval Behavior: A Case Analysis of an OPAC," *Journal of the American Society for Information Science* 44 (June 1993): 245-64.

29. James R. Rettig, "Reference Research Questions," *RQ* 31 (Winter 1991): 167-74.

30. Jo Bell Whitlatch, "Research Topics from the Program—Unanswered Questions," *RQ* 31 (Spring 1992): 333-37.

ADDITIONAL READINGS

American Library Association, Reference and Adult Services Division (RASD), Evaluation of Reference and Adult Services Committee. *The Reference Assessment Manual.* Ann Arbor, Mich.: Pierian Press, 1995. 372p.

This book represents a major attempt to bring together the theory and practice of reference evaluation in libraries. Of particular interest is the final section, which contains reviews of a large number of reference evaluation instruments.

Bunge, Charles A. "Factors Related to Output Measures for Reference Services in Public Libraries: Data from Thirty-Six Libraries." *Public Libraries* 29 (January–February 1990): 42-47.

This article gives a good summary of some of the data collected by libraries using the Wisconsin-Ohio Reference Evaluation Program and illustrates the usefulness of this evaluation technique, particularly in diagnosing how performance might be improved.

Crews, Kenneth D. "The Accuracy of Reference Service: Variables for Research and Implementation." *Library & Information Science Research* 10 (July–September 1988): 331-55.

Crews provides an overview of reference accuracy studies that illustrates the great variety of research into this particular aspect of reference quality. He then shows how the variables in these studies can be standardized.

Dewdney, Patricia, and Catherine Sheldrick Ross. "Flying a Light Aircraft: Reference Service Evaluation from a User's Viewpoint." *RQ* 34 (Winter 1994): 217-30.

This is one of several reports of unobtrusive observation of reference interactions from these authors, all of which illustrate the complexities of successful reference practice and the pitfalls that can lead to lower quality performance.

Durrance, Joan C. "Factors That Influence Reference Success: What Makes Questioners Willing to Return?" *The Reference Librarian* 49/50 (1995): 243-65.

Durrance discusses a qualitative adaptation of unobtrusive methods that provides important insights into the reference behaviors that lead to successful transactions, as measured by "willingness to return" to the same service provider for help in the future.

———. "Reference Success: Does the 55 Percent Rule Tell the Whole Story?" *Library Journal* 114 (April 15, 1989): 31-36.

Recognizing that accuracy of answers as revealed by most unobtrusive testing provides only a partial view of the quality of reference service, Durrance used unobtrusive observation to evaluate the setting of the reference transaction, the use of interviewing skills by reference librarians, and the interpersonal behavior of reference librarians.

Hernon, Peter, and Charles R. McClure. *Unobtrusive Testing and Library Reference Services.* Norwood, N.J.: Ablex, 1987. 240p.

This is an important text on unobtrusive testing methods, providing a full discussion of many of the issues surrounding this type of evaluation. It also provides findings from the unobtrusive tests conducted by the authors.

Hernon, Peter, and Ellen Altman. *Assessing Service Quality: Satisfying the Expectations of Library Customers.* Chicago: American Library Association, 1998. 243p.

This broadly based approach to service quality includes many helpful examples of evaluation techniques. Written in a readable style and with an emphasis on practical aspects of service evaluation, this manual will be useful to both library practitioners and students considering how best to evaluate reference services.

Pierce, Sydney J., ed. "Weeding and Maintenance of Reference Collections." *The Reference Librarian* 29 (1990): 1-173.

This entire issue is devoted to reference collection evaluation and maintenance. It is an excellent resource for people interested in exploring all facets of this important activity.

Robbins, Jane, Holly Willett, Mary Jane Wiseman, and Douglas L. Zweizig. *Evaluation Strategies and Techniques for Public Library Children's Services: A Sourcebook.* Madison, Wis.: School of Library and Information Studies, University of Wisconsin-Madison, 1990. 302p.

The editors have compiled an impressive collection of articles about evaluation of children's services. See particularly the articles by Adele Fasick, Diane Young, and Mary K. Chelton for good approaches to this kind of evaluation.

Van House, Nancy A., Beth T. Weil, and Charles R. McClure. *Measuring Academic Library Effectiveness: A Practical Approach.* Chicago: American Library Association, 1990. 182p.

The counterpart of the well-received *Output Measures for Public Libraries,* this handbook provides good practical advice on developing measures to assess the effectiveness of academic libraries. Many of the measures rely on perceptions and self-reports from librarians.

Van House, Nancy A., Mary Jo Lynch, Charles R. McClure, Douglas L. Zweizig, and Eleanor Jo Rodger. *Output Measures for Public Libraries: A Manual of Standardized Procedures.* 2d ed. Chicago: American Library Association, 1987. 99p.

This is the standard handbook for data collection on the "outputs" of public libraries. It is worth reading critically to assess how the suggested procedures can measure the quality of reference service. Another aspect worth noting is the extent to which the output measures are based on self-reporting by librarians about their service.

CHAPTER

11

ORGANIZING, DELIVERING, AND MANAGING REFERENCE SERVICES

Josephine Z. Kibbee

INTRODUCTION

As discussed in Chapter 1, American libraries have provided "assistance to readers" since the late nineteenth century. From its inception, this assistance has generally been available in the reference room (or otherwise designated area in the library), at a desk staffed by librarians. In recent years, however, this model has come under attack on several fronts. Networked information access has reduced dependence on the reference room as the place where library research begins, users are not necessarily best served by a librarian presiding at a reference desk, and managers question whether providing undifferentiated "assistance" is the optimal use of professional staff. In response, many libraries have implemented variations on the model, such as tiered service or roving, and may offer subject-specific service points or research consultation. More important, a growing realization that reference is more than answering questions has broadened the role of reference librarians who play an increasingly critical role in identifying user needs, mediating between the users and systems, and providing outreach services to the library's diverse user communities.

This chapter highlights key issues in the organization, delivery, and management of reference services as they retool for the future. A review of the traditional model of reference services is followed by a discussion of the movement to "rethink reference" and consider alternative models for the delivery of information services. Central to this discussion is the evolving role of the reference librarian and the corresponding evolution of the reference department. Management issues are discussed, particularly in the context of the increasing emphasis on teamwork and user service. The chapter concludes with a model of service that puts the user—rather than the reference desk—at the center.

TRADITIONAL ORGANIZATION OF REFERENCE SERVICES

The Reference Department Within the Library

Libraries have traditionally been divided into public services and technical services units. As a component of public services, the reference department is primarily responsible for providing information and instructional services. Other public services units typically include circulation, interlibrary loan, outreach services, and special collections. Owing to differences in the size and organization of libraries, a single reference department is not necessarily a given. In smaller libraries, a single librarian holds multiple responsibilities and most likely does not operate a separate reference desk. Larger libraries might be divided into subject-specific departments (e.g., business, local history, music) and operate separate reference desks within these units.

For years, the question of centralized versus decentralized services has been hotly debated. Proponents of centralization cite advantages to library users, who are served with greater efficiency and receive fewer referrals elsewhere. Additional advantages include extended service hours, more consistent availability of professional staff (particularly on nights and weekends), and reduced duplication of resources.[1] Proponents of decentralized reference services likewise cite advantages to library users. They argue that the quality of reference assistance is improved because subject specialists are better equipped to provide in-depth, subject-based service. Within a smaller and more homogeneous unit, librarians enjoy greater autonomy and control, and cite preferences of users for more focused units of library service and small, client-centered work groups.[2]

It is interesting to note that this debate has cooled considerably in recent years as electronic networking has shifted emphasis from the *location* of services to the *delivery* of services. Nonetheless, the question of optimal organization of the library has yet to be resolved. As discussed below, the organization of reference services, like the organization of the library, is evolving in response to the changing format of information and expanding user needs and expectations.

Organization of the Reference Department

Depending on the size of the library and the librarians' additional responsibilities, reference departments generally number from two to twenty professionals. The focal point of the department is generally a desk with a networked workstation, staffed by one or more librarians, in proximity to a reference collection that holds many of the titles described in this book. The information services provided, discussed in Chapter 1, typically include ready reference, bibliographic verification, information and referral, research consultation, and individual instruction, and are delivered in person, over the phone, and via e-mail. Reference departments strive to provide the maximum number of hours of service they can realistically accommodate, including evening and weekend hours.

Although the reference desk is the department's focal point, direct information service to users is only part of the librarian's responsibilities. As discussed in Chapter 8, instruction is intrinsic to reference, and instructional programs are usually administered through reference departments. In many libraries, reference librarians also serve as subject specialists and hold responsibility for collection development and faculty or community liaison. In academic libraries, reference departments may be responsible for the administration of interlibrary loan, government documents, and periodicals or microforms collections. In public libraries, reference departments manage community information and referral services, readers' advisory, and outreach programs.

The traditional organizational model reflects the realities of the library's historical role, the physical layout of most library buildings, and deeply held professional values. Charles Bunge and Chris Ferguson identify these values as equity and ease of access, personal service, and high standards for the delivery of quality professional service.[3] Notably absent from the reference department's responsibilities just less than a decade ago, however, are the multitude of responsibilities resulting from electronic networking, such as the collection and management of electronic resources, Web site development, and service to remote users (see Box 11.1). It is important to refit these values to the realities of an increasingly digitized environment and shifting user needs and expectations.

Box 11.1 Position Open

Reference Librarian. Old Faithful University Library invites applications for the position of reference librarian. Under the direction of the head of reference, the successful applicant will provide reference desk services (including evening and weekend rotation), database searching, class lectures on reference tools and research methods, collection development, faculty liaison, assistance with interlibrary loan, and preparation of bibliographies and informational handouts. QUALIFICATIONS: accredited MLS; second master's in an appropriate area preferred; working knowledge of standard reference materials and relevant computer skills; knowledge of trends in academic library service and library automation.

Composite Classified Ad, *Library Journal*, circa 1990

RETHINKING REFERENCE

A quick glance through library literature since the mid-1980s reveals a serious concern with "traditional" reference service. Articles raising the alarm, and even tolling the death knell for reference, appeared with increasing frequency, and challenges to "rethink" reference became more urgent.[4] Critics questioned the accuracy of the information provided by reference librarians,[5] the utility of the reference desk,[6] staffing models,[7] and the very conceptual foundation upon which reference is built.[8] At the heart of these concerns lay not only the impact of electronic information sources, but the need for a better understanding of user needs and improved responsiveness in an increasingly technological environment.

The Reference Desk: Critical Mass or Trivial Pursuit?

Long a cornerstone of reference service, in theory the reference desk reflects the values that Bunge and Ferguson identify as being core to reference librarianship: convenient and equitable service to users, individually tailored personal assistance, and high professional standards.[9] Patricia Swanson describes the reference desk as representing a "critical mass of resources—human, printed, and now electronic, so configured for a convenient and predictable location so that library patrons can find the service and can find someone to help them."[10] Yet, a review of library literature over the past decade indicates that the desk has come to represent much of what can be considered wrong with reference: undifferentiated service, questionable use of staff expertise, dependence on a physical location, and insensitivity to user needs. Critics charge that the ideal of the reference desk, staffed by competent professionals whose expertise is consistently challenged by informed library users, is elusive at best. Repetitive and routine questions—such as how to locate a book or how to print citations from a database—ignore librarians' expertise and contribute to job dissatisfaction (see Box 11.2, page 268). Thelma Freides asserts that "by establishing the desk as the focal point of reader assistance, libraries not only expend professional time on trivial tasks, but also encourage the assumption that the low-level, undemanding type of question handled most easily and naturally at the desk is the service norm."[11] Her studies of user behavior indicate that users do, in fact, perceive the reference desk as intended for quick replies. When the opportunity arises for providing detailed bibliographic assistance or research consultation, both user and librarian experience frustration when ringing phones and queues of users with short-answer questions compete for the librarian's attention. Some have questioned whether the reference desk has made general users less self-sufficient and more dependent on library staff. Others argue that because well-designed signage systems and user-friendly interfaces to the online catalog and other databases would go far in reducing demand on reference, librarians should concentrate their efforts in these directions.

Box 11.2 A Question of Gender?

Although those few workers in other fields who offer help at odd times (and fancy prices) distinguish among requests on the basis of urgency . . . librarians resist making distinctions and in some libraries can be seen scurrying about at all hours of weekday and weekend. . . . Perhaps this servile attitude derives from the gender makeup of librarianship, for women are socialized to sacrifice self, do what is asked, and accept endless workdays. . . . Has the sex of our majority helped shape our service assumptions?

Mary Biggs
"Replacing the Fast Fact Drop-in with
Gourmet Information Service"[12]

Tiered Service

Despite its drawbacks and limitations, however, most librarians will attest that the reference desk is alive and well. Judging from the volume of action seen by most reference troops on the front lines, a retreat from this service could hardly be justified under current circumstances (see Box 11.3, page 270). Alternative models, therefore, generally do not focus on dismantling the reference desk as much as offering differentiated service: different levels of service that take into consideration factors such as complexity of the query and appropriate level of staff expertise.

A common example is *tiered* service, wherein a separate information desk is established to address directional and quick-answer queries, while complex or in-depth questions are handled at a reference desk or by consultation. Ideally staffed by well-trained paraprofessionals who make informed referrals, a separately staffed "ready-reference" query point can relieve pressures on the reference desk by answering the telephone, handling directional questions, and answering routine online catalog and ready-reference questions. Librarians are thus free to focus on questions that require professional expertise. Tiered models have become increasingly common, and the arrangement is generally effective for successfully handling "routine" queries. Experience shows, however, that a separately staffed information desk requires a clearly defined mission and a considerable investment in training to operate successfully.[13]

Tiered service is not a panacea, however. Smaller libraries cannot always afford the luxury of designating separate staff and facilities for reference, let alone establishing two or three service points. Availability of qualified assistants is another consideration, because public libraries and academic libraries without programs in library and information science are at a disadvantage in recruiting and hiring qualified student assistants. More important, users are faced with increasingly sophisticated library resources such as expanded online catalogs and a daunting array of electronic databases, so the "simple/complex" dichotomy that drives tiered service grows increasingly blurred.

Although tiered service departs from the "one size fits all" service represented by a single reference desk, one can argue that it still remains basically librarian-centered rather than user-centered. Underlying the notion of tiered service are concerns about the optimal use of the librarian's time and expertise, reduction of stress and burnout, appropriate professional image, and more efficient use of human resources. Thus, although tiered services may address the issue of appropriate use of staff, they do not address the full spectrum of users' information needs that contemporary libraries face.

Research Consultation

A third level of service, often referred to as *research consultation*, has also been implemented in many libraries. In this scenario, questions involving research sources and strategies are handled during scheduled appointments, or complex questions are referred to a librarian who holds office hours rather than handling them at the desk. Although staff-intensive, research consultation makes optimal use of professional staff expertise, eliminates the intrusions and stresses that often accompany "on the fly" reference encounters, and offers librarians and users a more satisfying and productive encounter.[14] In a much-discussed reorganization at Brandeis University Library, the reference desk was eliminated in favor of an information desk, staffed by paraprofessionals, and a research consultation service drawing exclusively on librarians through a combination of office hours and appointments. In an article evaluating the Brandeis model, Douglas Herman concludes that the project is a "mildly qualified" success: Informed referrals remain a problem at the information desk, but faculty and students enthusiastically endorse the consultation service.[15]

Roving

On the other end of the spectrum, many reference departments encourage librarians to move from behind the desk and approach users (rather than vice versa), offering assistance to those who are staring blankly at a terminal or randomly eyeing shelves. Generally known as *roving*, this service operates on the assumption that many users do not ask for assistance, and that users can benefit from the librarians' expertise in clarifying research strategies, suggesting additional resources, and otherwise enhancing the user's skill in finding information. A detailed study by Ellen Kramer concludes that these spontaneous contacts indeed multiply opportunities to use professional skills and reach users who might not otherwise solicit assistance.[16] James Rettig cites the positive message that the librarian is available and willing to help—where the user is working, not where the desk and librarian are located.[17] With increasingly sophisticated online catalogs, a multitude of databases and interfaces, and a blend of print and electronic resources, few users fail to benefit from direct mediation.

Differentiated Service

Incorporating aspects of tiered service, research consultation, and roving, William Whitson proposes establishing a *differentiated service* model. He identifies five distinct but interrelated services: directional and general information, technical assistance, finding answers for users, research consultation, and instruction. Each of these services should operate separately, fitting staff skills and hours of service to user needs and library priorities.[18] Whitson argues, as have others before him, that reference is a composite service and requires an alternative to the "one size fits all" desk. Providing information about the library—services, hours, facilities—for example, requires no specialized knowledge or personnel and should be delivered via signs, automated kiosks, Web sites, etc. If a separate information desk is designated, it should be staffed with student workers who are not expected to provide more substantive assistance. Technical assistance—helping users negotiate through online systems—should be provided by staff who are roving on site, at the point of use. Whitson contends that "knowledge of a specific [electronic] reference tool is a technical skill, and is not the same as having a broad understanding of the organization of published knowledge,"[19] and therefore does not necessarily require a professional librarian.

Providing factual information and research consultation, on the other hand, do involve the broader depth of knowledge and array of skills that a librarian brings, but these services likewise should be differentiated. Whitson suggests that the former can be established along the lines of an "information broker" model, where the user leaves the question and receives a response within a reasonable period of time.[20] Research consultation follows the professional services model, with scheduled appointments. Instruction would be incorporated into research consultation and technical assistance or could be a separate adjunct service.

Box 11. 3 Defend or Refute

The reference desk, staffed by professional librarians, is an essential feature of public and academic libraries and represents the best means of providing:

- Convenience to users, who can make inquiries at one central point and at the time they need the information.
- Maximum benefit to users of librarians' professional expertise in conducting reference interviews and efficiently finding information.
- Personalized contact and opportunity for individualized instruction.

MOVING BEYOND LIBRARY WALLS

Although the alternative service models described above reflect more proactive and user-centered approaches, they address only the needs of users in a particular location at a given time and are predicated on users being physically within the library. With the ubiquitous Internet and the ability of networks to deliver online catalogs, periodical indexes, full-text articles, and reference works to users outside the library, users are becoming less dependent on being *in* the library to do their research. Consequently, reference librarians are also challenged to serve users beyond library walls. The following section describes initiatives to provide information services to remote users, primarily utilizing e-mail and videoconferencing.

E-Mail Reference Service

Providing reference via e-mail represents one of the first attempts (besides the telephone) to provide assistance to users outside the library. Initially, librarians were concerned about unrealistic user expectations, high volume of use, and the loss of the reference interview in this asynchronous environment. Fears were allayed as studies indicated that the majority of the questions are straightforward and can be answered using standard reference tools, users approach e-mail with much the same expectations as face-to-face encounters, and usage has not proved overwhelming to library staffs.[21] Moreover, the reference interview can be adapted to this medium without subsequent loss of the advantage of face-to-face encounters.[22] Consequently, e-mail reference has become a commonplace practice and a logical extension of information services.

Electronic Conferencing

Although offering a convenient means of asking a question, e-mail is only a partial solution to meeting information needs of remote users. Constrained by an unsophisticated technology and divorced from a larger context (e.g., research project, working group), e-mail is distinctly limited. A review of library literature reveals that few libraries are currently utilizing e-mail's synchronous cousin, conferencing technology. Although "chat" tends to connote a casual approach to communication, in its more sophisticated incarnations, conferencing software provides a powerful communication and learning tool. Useful as a means of humanizing online communications, Internet-based collaborative software establishes real-time connections and facilitates the development of learning communities through online collaboration (see Box 11.4). As information professionals, librarians have a great deal to contribute to and learn from participating in online learning communities. The challenge is to acquire and understand the technology; establish partnerships with user groups; and apply traditional reference skills to a synchronous, digital environment. Inga Barnello writes, "For the most part, inquirers will not look for librarians at the reference desk in the next century. Librarians need to be at the opposite end of researchers' keyboards."[23]

Box 11.4 Electronic Conferencing for Reference

In one future scenario, users will call librarians into their online searches when they need assistance, via electronic conferencing. Describe other scenarios in which reference librarians might use conferencing technology.

Videoconferencing

Although conferencing applications are in their infancy, the software and hardware demands are relatively straightforward. Videoconferencing, on the other hand, requires a more sophisticated infrastructure. In a 1998 article, Bernie Sloan reviews several reference videoconferencing initiatives, including the University of Michigan's Interactive Reference Assistance and the University of California at Irvine's Interactive Reference Service. Typically, these initiatives involve installing videocameras and desktop conferencing software at the reference desk and at a remote location such as residence halls or labs to provide users with real-time consultation with a librarian.[24]

These initiatives experienced moderate success. Although users appreciated the service, some felt uncomfortable or self-conscious in front of a camera. The quality of the video and sound communications was not always consistent, and participants were constrained by not seeing each other's keyboards. Finally, many of the users still needed to go to the library to get the materials they needed.[25] Important lessons are being learned by these pilot studies, however: the need for high-level technical support, enhanced interactive capabilities (e.g., whiteboards that enable participants to view each other's screens), and the interdependence of remote services and remote resources. Although results are inconclusive and more work is clearly needed, these initiatives represent innovative efforts to extend the reach of information services beyond the library building.

NEW ROLES, NEW RESPONSIBILITIES

E-mail reference and videoconferencing basically deliver information services via nontraditional means and involve direct (albeit remote) interaction between the librarian and the user. In other words, they are a logical extension of the reference librarian's traditionally central function of answering questions. This model, however, does not reflect changes in information-seeking behavior (i.e., users accessing information directly through the Internet); user needs, such as technical assistance with hardware and software; and the need for user-friendly navigation systems. The reference librarian's job has always involved "behind the scenes" work such as building community information and referral files, preparing instruction, developing pathfinders and finding aids, constructing local databases, and developing virtual reference collections. An electronic environment extends the reach of these services and resources by delivering them to a wider audience and expands the reference librarian's role as creator and organizer of information. Moreover, just as librarians mediated between users and the collection, so must they mediate between users and electronic resources by facilitating technical and intellectual access. A logical extension of "rethinking reference" involves not only reconceptualizing how reference services are organized within the library but also redefining the role of the reference librarian to embrace a model of the librarian as information organizer/creator and technology facilitator, whose services are largely delivered through a network. A possible position announcement for finding such a librarian is given in Box 11.5, page 272.

Box 11.5 Position Open

Information Access Librarian: Digitopia Public Library invites applications for the position of Information Access Librarian. As part of the Information Access Team, the successful applicant will provide reference service in person and through the network; select and organize electronic resources; design expert systems for selecting among Digitopia's numerous electronic resources; facilitate access to information technology for members of the community; and establish partnerships with local institutions and organizations to develop full text and multimedia community information databases. QUALIFICATIONS: Accredited MLIS; second master's in information technology preferred; experience with database and Web site design and construction; excellent automation skills; must be flexible, innovative, and dynamic.

Classified Ad, *Library Journal,* 2005

Information Organizer/Creator

Despite the proliferation of relatively sophisticated search engines (see Chapter 6), efficiently finding reliable and well-organized information on the Internet is not always easy. Consequently, reference librarians have applied their selection and organization talents by culling useful resources on the Web and developing virtual reference desks. The Internet Public Library (http://www.ipl.org) is a good example of a collection of Web sites that attempts to replicate the content and organization of a traditional reference collection. Although not all of the sites resemble reference books in format and authority (there are few encyclopedias, handbooks, etc.), they nonetheless provide useful online information. Through the efforts of professionally trained librarians, virtual reference desks represent a value-added service by distilling out and organizing the more useful Internet resources. The Internet Public Library is also an example of how reference librarians are *creating* information resources.

Projects such as *Presidents of the United States* (http://www.ipl.org/ref/POTUS) combine factual information in almanac format with links to related Web sites. Other libraries are digitizing local information files for distribution to a wide audience, such as the Hennepin County Library Job and Career Information Center (http://www.hennepin.lib.mn.us/jacic). Finally, libraries are creating significant new resources, such as the notable *American Memory Project* (http://www.memory.loc.gov), compiled under the auspices of the Library of Congress. Through these projects, librarians are actively involved in creating unique resources and delivering them to users.

Facilitator of Technology and Information Access

The phrase "technical consultant" may make the blood run cold for "non-techies," as it calls to mind images of screwdrivers, impenetrable installation manuals, and incomprehensible language. Although the librarian of the future will not necessarily need to speak in C + + language, understanding the basic technological underpinnings of information delivery, such as telnet, authentication, or Java, becomes increasingly critical in satisfying a user's information needs if technical barriers impede access. As Bunge and Ferguson observe, library users are increasingly coming to expect that all the tools and resources they need will be available from a single workstation. Consequently, libraries will develop "holistic computing environments," which include electronic bibliographic tools, network navigation and communication tools (Web browsers, ftp, etc.), and productivity tools (word processing, spreadsheets), to allow for information retrieval and manipulation at a single workstation. As an extension of their "long-standing traditions of personalized service and equity of access," librarians will be increasingly responsible for "making technology work for everyone."[26]

A related concern is the selection or design of user-friendly navigation systems, online help for electronic information resources, and expert systems to facilitate access to information. In this capacity, the reference librarians function less as *mediators* than as *facilitators*, enabling users to function independently. The challenge is considerable because libraries now offer an astonishing range of resources with a dizzying array of interfaces. Increasingly librarians must present these resources in a way that makes sense to users and facilitates their access. They must design navigation systems that enable users to make informed choices among databases and ultimately to access the book, article, or fact they are seeking.

CHANGING MANAGEMENT TO MANAGE CHANGE

As libraries change, so must the organizational and management structures that support them. Hierarchical management—from the top down—has been the prevailing model for libraries and consequently for reference departments throughout much of their history. This model offers the advantages of clear lines of authority and responsibility, centralized budgetary control, and straightforward decision making and personnel management. The tradeoff, however, is reduced communication and participation and less flexibility in adapting to new environments (see Box 11.6). On the other hand, flexibility is encouraged by breaking down traditional distinctions between public services, systems, and technical services, and establishing workgroups or teams along functional lines. Consequently, libraries are increasingly looking toward management models that facilitate making the changes necessary for success in a digital environment.

Flattening the Organizational Structure

Flattening the hierarchy to reduce the number of reporting levels is considered by many as a key to facilitating change. In the resulting configuration, the staff has no more than one manager between them and the director. The manager functions not as a supervisor but as a team leader, responsible for overseeing decision-making processes and communication and coordinating resource allocation and support services. Management of specific functions such as instruction or information services can be rotated, and task teams can be established to develop new programs or services.[27]

Box 11.6 Heaviest Element Discovered

The heaviest element known to science was recently discovered at one of the national laboratories. The element, tentatively named administratium (Ad) has no electrons or protons...it does, however, have one neutron, 75 associate neutrons, 125 deputy associate neutrons, and 11 assistant deputy associate neutrons. This gives it an atomic mass of 212. The 212 particles are held together in the nucleus by a force that involves the continuous exchange of mesonlike particles called memoöns. Because it has no electrons, administratium is inert. Nevertheless, it can be detected chemically because it seems to impede every reaction in which it takes part.

Thomas G. Kyle
"Heaviest Element Discovered"[28]

As David Lewis observes, "In many cases, the roles reference librarians are asked to play are incompatible with the way their work lives and their organizations are structured."[29] For example, most reference work is structured around a reference desk, instruction classroom, and physical collection. To bring about the changes necessary to function in a more networked environment, the unit must have the authority to redefine itself and establish functional groups of specialists whose work cuts across traditional distinctions between public services, systems, and technical services. Goal setting, strategic planning, revising or establishing policies, collecting data on user behavior, and staff development and training become critical to move forward with new initiatives and programs, such as providing reference via videoconferencing to campus housing or offices.

The bottom line is that the reference department may cease to function as a discrete operational unit. Instead, it may give way to a team or teams whose primary responsibility is ensuring access to information, whether through personal assistance, by troubleshooting hardware or software problems, or by expediting interlibrary loan. As Chris Ferguson writes, "public services are converging in ways that are rendering insignificant such conventional distinctions as reference, instruction, liaison, document delivery, and database searching."[30]

Total Quality Management

The team approach mentioned above is most closely associated with a management technique known as Total Quality Management (TQM). More than a philosophy of service, TQM is a highly structured process that relies on gathering quantifiable data, encouraging intensive employee participation (in the form of "quality circles" or teams), and requiring rigorous measurement and evaluation. Basically, the pursuit of "quality" must become the primary responsibility of everyone in the organization and continuous improvement of customer-driven service their goal.[31]

Because of TQM's heavy reliance on refining processes and procedures—flowcharts are particularly popular—its application to reference is not clear-cut. Moreover, many librarians are not comfortable with a management model developed primarily for business and industry (hence the preference of many librarians for the term "user" rather than "customer"). Nonetheless, the principles driving TQM are fast becoming the principles that need to drive libraries: accountability through the collection of quantifiable data, or "managing by fact"; an organizational structure that facilitates change; and above all, a focus on determining user needs and providing user satisfaction.

SUMMARY

Reference service has historically centered around a desk staffed by professionals, surrounded by a core collection of reference books. With advances in technology, the card catalog gave way to the online catalog and the reference desk was no longer bound to a particular location. Next to migrate were periodical indexes, which were no longer confined to the reference room. And finally, the Internet opened a host of licensed and "free" resources for use at a user's desktop. This evolution challenged the traditional organization and delivery of reference services and prompted the need to "rethink" reference, which continues today. Libraries have responded with diverse and flexible configurations, based on the desire to respond to a variety of user needs (e.g., ready reference, software troubleshooting, research consultation) with the appropriate personnel level, in a suitable environment. With advances in communications technology, that environment is fast becoming the user's home, classroom, or office.

Reference librarians are becoming more proactive not only in the way they deliver services but also in the services they provide. Organizing networked information for easy access and digitizing local information files are efforts to address community information needs. Moreover, the traditional role of mediating between the user and the library now extends to facilitating the use of technology to access information anywhere. The newly evolving role of the reference librarian clearly outstrips the capacity of one individual, or department, to deliver this type of service. Consequently, the notion of developing functional teams whose members bring expertise from public and technical services and systems is gaining in popularity. To facilitate these changes, libraries are using management models, such as

Total Quality Management, that encourage change through a flatter hierarchy and increased participation of staff.

Although the challenges of the future appear daunting, reports of the death of reference services are greatly exaggerated, and reference librarians are unlikely to become an extinct species. Quite the contrary. According to Bonnie Nardi, "in the information society, librarians are a keystone species. With the advent of massive amounts of information available on the Internet, librarians are increasingly important. . . . The intelligent search and filtering provided by human agents needs to be part and parcel of the electronic world."[32] As reference librarianship begins its second century, "personal assistance to readers" takes on a new meaning.

NOTES

1. Jane P. Kleiner, "The Configuration of Reference in an Electronic Environment," *College & Research Libraries* 48 (July 1987): 302-13.

2. See Snunith Shoham, "A Cost-Preference Study of the Decentralization of Academic Library Services," *Library Research* 4 (1982): 175-94; and Charles Martell, *The Client-Centered Academic Library: An Organizational Model* (Westport, Conn.: Greenwood Press, 1983), 136p.

3. Charles A. Bunge and Chris D. Ferguson, "The Shape of Services to Come: Values-Based Reference Service for the Largely Digital Library," *College & Research Libraries* 58 (May 1997): 258.

4. See, for example, William Miller, "What's Wrong with Reference: Coping with Success and Failure at the Reference Desk," *American Libraries* 15 (May 1984): 303-6, 322; Keith Ewing and Robert Hauptman, "Is Traditional Reference Service Obsolete?" *Journal of Academic Librarianship* 21 (January 1995): 3-6; and David W. Lewis, "Traditional Reference Is Dead, Now Let's Move on to Important Questions," *Journal of Academic Librarianship* 21 (January 1995): 10-12.

5. Peter Hernon and Charles R. McClure, "Unobtrusive Reference Testing: The 55 Percent Rule," *Library Journal* 111 (April 15, 1986): 37-41.

6. Barbara J. Ford, "Reference Beyond (and Without) the Reference Desk," in *Energies for Transition: Proceedings of the Fourth National Conference of the Association of College and Research Libraries* (Chicago: American Library Association, 1986), 179-81.

7. Larry R. Oberg, "The Emergence of the Paraprofessional in Academic Libraries: Perceptions and Realities," *College & Research Libraries* 53 (March 1992): 99-112.

8. Jerry D. Campbell, "Shaking the Conceptual Foundations of Reference: A Perspective," *Reference Services Review* 20 (Winter 1992): 29-36.

9. Bunge and Ferguson, "The Shape of Services to Come," 258.

10. Patricia K. Swanson, "Traditional Models: Myths and Realities," in *Academic Libraries: Myths and Realities: Proceedings of the Third National Conference of the Association of College and Research Libraries* (Chicago: American Library Association, 1984), 89.

11. Thelma Freides, "Current Trends in Academic Libraries," *Library Trends* 31 (Winter 1983): 466-67.

12. Mary Biggs, "Replacing the Fast Fact Drop-in with Gourmet Information Service: A Symposium," *Journal of Academic Librarianship* 11 (May 1985): 69.

13. Beth S. Woodard, "The Effectiveness of an Information Desk Staffed by Graduate Assistants and Non-Professionals," *College & Research Libraries* 50 (July 1989): 455-67.

14. Virginia Massey-Burzio, "Rethinking the Reference Desk," in *Rethinking Reference in Academic Libraries,* ed. Anne Grodzins Lipow (Berkeley, Calif.: Library Solutions Press, 1993), 43-48.

15. Douglas Herman, "But Does It Work? Evaluating the Brandeis Reference Model," *Reference Services Review* 22 (Winter 1994): 17-28.

16. Ellen H. Kramer, "Why Roving Reference: A Case Study in a Small Academic Library," *Reference Services Review* 24 (Fall 1996): 67-80.

17. James Rettig, "Future Reference: Sired by a Hurricane, Dam'd by an Earthquake," *The Reference Librarian* 54 (1996): 87-88.

18. William L. Whitson, "Differentiated Service: A New Reference Model," *Journal of Academic Librarianship* 21 (March 1995): 103-10.

19. Ibid., 105.

20. Ibid., 106.

21. Ann B. Bristow, "Academic Reference Service over Electronic Mail," *College & Research Libraries News* 53 (November 1992): 631-32, 637.

22. Eileen G. Abels, "The E-mail Reference Interview," *RQ* 35 (Spring 1996): 345-58.

23. Inga H. Barnello, "The Changing Face of Reference: A History of the Future," in *The Changing Face of Reference,* eds. Lynne M. Stuart and Dena Holiman Hutto (Greenwich, Conn.: JAI Press, 1996), 14.

24. Bernie Sloan, "Service Perspectives for the Digital Library: Remote Reference Services," *Library Trends* 47 (Summer 1998): 117-43.

25. Ibid., 126-29.

26. Bunge and Ferguson, "The Shape of Services to Come," 259-60.

27. David W. Lewis, "Making Academic Reference Services Work," *College & Research Libraries* 55 (September 1994): 451-52.

28. Thomas G. Kyle, "Heaviest Element Discovered," *Journal of Irreproducible Results* 35 (January/ February 1990): 31.

29. Lewis, "Making Academic Reference Services Work," 445.

30. Chris Ferguson, "Reshaping Academic Library Reference Service: A Review of Issues, Trends, and Possibilities," *Advances in Librarianship* 18 (1994): 102.

31. For a more detailed discussion, see Rosanna M. O'Neil, *Total Quality Management in Libraries: A Sourcebook* (Englewood, Colo.: Libraries Unlimited, 1994), 194p.

32. Bonnie A. Nardi, "Information Ecologies," *Reference & User Services Quarterly* 38 (Fall 1998): 49.

ADDITIONAL READINGS

Ferguson, Chris. "Reshaping Academic Library Reference Service: A Review of Issues, Trends, and Possibilities." *Advances in Librarianship* 18 (1994): 73-109.

Ferguson provides an excellent overview of the issues fueling the current debate on the theory and practice of reference services in academic libraries. Beginning with an anatomy of the "crisis" in reference, he examines factors such as funding, the impact of technology, organizational structures, quality of service, and burnout, which call into question the efficacy of the traditional model. He concludes with a prediction that future libraries will see a more fully integrated and user-centered service.

Kleiner, Jane P. "The Configuration of Reference in an Electronic Environment." *College & Research Libraries* 48 (July 1987): 302-13.

In this well-researched article, Kleiner examines the centralization versus decentralization debate in light of electronic technologies. Both the positive and negative impacts of centralization on staff and services are reviewed, and the rationale is presented for the move to centralized reference services at Louisiana State University Library.

LaGuardia, Cheryl, and Barbara A. Mitchell. *Finding Common Ground: Creating the Library of the Future Without Diminishing the Library of the Past.* New York: Neal-Schuman, 1998. 478p.

The contributors to this collection of papers from the Finding Common Ground symposium, held at Harvard University in 1997, represent a veritable "who's who" among librarians. Articles discuss the impact of networks and the changing face of research. Reference issues feature prominently in the section "Satisfying our Users."

Lewis, David W. "Making Academic Reference Services Work." *College & Research Libraries* 55 (September 1994): 445-56.

Lewis focuses on the organizational changes that are required if reference librarians are to assume new roles and responsibilities. He proposes giving reference librarians clear budgetary and programmatic authority, flattening the hierarchy, providing adequate support services, consolidating reference staffs and service points, and involving reference librarians in public services planning and priority setting.

Mardikian, Jackie, and Martin Kesselman. "Beyond the Desk: Enhanced Reference Staffing for the Electronic Library." *Reference Services Review* 23 (Spring 1995): 21-28.

Focusing on new ways of thinking about and organizing reference services, Mardikian and Kesselman propose three levels of service to conform to the level of need: minimum human intervention, trained paraprofessional staff, and librarians. They also discuss new opportunities offered by the electronic library, including cooperative reference and instruction over the network, access development and interface design, developing reference expert systems, and librarians as knowledge managers.

Massey-Burzio, Virginia. "Reference Encounters of a Different Kind: A Symposium." *Journal of Academic Librarianship* 18 (November 1992): 276-86.

Massey-Burzio describes the rationale behind the elimination of the reference desk at Brandeis University and contends that the traditional reference model needs to be seriously reevaluated. Five respondents provide reactions to her thought-provoking argument.

O'Neil, Rosanna M. *Total Quality Management in Libraries: A Sourcebook.* Englewood, Colo.: Libraries Unlimited, 1994. 194p.

This volume of readings presents a good overview of the application of Total Quality Management (TQM) principles to libraries. The emphasis on identifying user needs, measuring satisfaction, and adopting a teamwork approach has relevance for structuring and managing reference services.

"Reference Service in a Digital Age." *Reference & User Services Quarterly* 38 (Fall 1998): 47-81.

This collection of seven articles is derived from the Library of Congress Institute, Reference Service in a Digital Age, held in June 1998. Papers focus on issues such as the impact of Internet-based information services (AskA...'s) on reference, transitioning from print to electronic resources, electronic reference service guidelines, and copyright.

Ridgeway, Trish, Peggy Cover, and Carl Stone, eds. *Improving Reference Management.* Chicago: Reference and Adult Services Division, American Library Association, 1986. 73p.

This collection of papers is based on a workshop sponsored by the Southeastern Library Association and the Reference and Adult Services Division of the American Library Association. Seven articles address management concerns such as establishing standards, evaluation, burnout, utilization of paraprofessionals, and management techniques.

Schloman, Barbara F. "Managing Reference Services in an Electronic Environment." *The Reference Librarian* 39 (1993): 99-109.

Schloman explores the new demands on managing reference services in light of an increasingly electronic environment and proposes an organization of reference staff based on functional and disciplinary teams.

Stuart, Lynne M., and Dena Holiman Hutto, eds. *The Changing Face of Reference.* Greenwich, Conn.: JAI Press, 1996. 238p.

This collection of sixteen articles identifies and describes the causes and effects of changes that have forced librarians to reexamine reference service. Sections include changing approaches to reference service, the impact of technology, reference service for changing user populations, and reference service beyond library walls.

"Symposium on Reference Service." *Journal of Academic Librarianship* 21 (January 1995): 3-16.

Leading off with the provocative article, "Is Traditional Reference Service Obsolete?," followed by four responses, this series of essays calls into question the notion of "reference librarians answering questions at a reference desk." Evolving responsibilities include the design of user-friendly retrieval systems, negotiation of complex automated reference environments, and continued human mediation.

Tyckoson, David A. "What's Right with Reference." *American Libraries* 30 (May 1999): 57-63.

Assessing the impact of the reference reform movement that began in the mid-1980s, Tyckoson reaffirms the centricity of one-on-one reference service and underscores the need for adequate resources to do the "real work" of reference.

Whitson, William L. "Differentiated Service: A New Reference Model." *Journal of Academic Librarianship* 21 (March 1995): 103-10.

Whitson conceptualizes reference as a composite of five interrelated services: directional and general information, technical assistance, provision of factual information (ready reference), research consultation, and instruction. He recommends that these services be maintained separately, matching staffing level and hours of service to user needs and library priorities.

CHAPTER

12

REFERENCE SERVICES FOR SPECIFIC POPULATIONS

Frances F. Jacobson and Ellen D. Sutton

INTRODUCTION

An underlying philosophy of this book, articulated most explicitly in Chapter 2, is a commitment to quality reference service for *all*. Because "all" encompasses individuals with a variety of needs, successful reference service must accommodate those needs. There is no standard blueprint for reference services that is appropriate in all situations. Developing specialized reference services for specific populations within our society is an essential corollary to developing service for the majority. Beyond the provision of basic reference services to an obvious, primary group of users, librarians need to identify significant secondary or special groups of users with common needs and adjust reference service to these groups.

The basis of concern for reference service to specific populations is ethical as well as legal. Reference librarians often must be advocates for members of these groups to ensure them equitable access to information and materials. In addition, libraries supported by public funds have a legal obligation to provide service without discrimination based on class, race, gender, or other defining social or physical characteristics. As noted in Chapter 2, the profession has created the *Library Bill of Rights* to emphasize its commitment to fair use of resources and openness to all users (see Box 12.1).

Box 12.1 Library Bill of Rights

Article V of the Library Bill of Rights states that:

> A person's right to use a library should not be denied or abridged because of origin, age, background, or views.[1]
>
> (Adopted June 18, 1948. Amended February 2, 1961; June 27, 1967; and January 23, 1980, by the ALA Council)

Broadly interpreted, this article includes all persons, regardless of characteristics or circumstance. In the Interpretation of Article V, *Free Access to Libraries for Minors*, the right of minors is explicitly defended:

Librarians and governing bodies should maintain that parents—and only parents—have the right and the responsibility to restrict the access of their children—and only their children—to library resources. Parents or legal guardians who do not want their children to have access to certain library services, materials or facilities, should so advise their children. Librarians and governing bodies cannot assume the role of parents or the functions of parental authority in the private relationship between parent and child. Librarians and governing bodies have a public and professional obligation to provide equal access to all library resources for all library users.[2]

(Adopted June 30, 1972; amended July 1, 1981, and July 3, 1991, by the ALA Council)

This chapter examines models of reference service delivery to a selection of groups whose needs are especially well defined, although not always met. The chapter does not address the reference needs of those in the business or technical sector, who would typically be served by special libraries. Instead, the focus is on groups who are defined in terms of socioeconomic, ethnic, or physical characteristics. The specific groups discussed are differentiated on the basis of age (children, young adults, and the elderly); disabling conditions (physical and developmental disabilities); and cultural identity, which may include language facility (non-English-speaking and the adult illiterate). For each of these groups, defining characteristics of the group are described, and reference techniques and policy issues associated with the group are discussed.

Within any library service community, there are certainly other groups to consider (e.g., institutionalized populations, specific ethnic or religious groups, members of the gay and lesbian communities, etc.), and not every group discussed here may be part of a given library's service population. The intent of this chapter is to give an overview of issues associated with reference service to individual groups. The assumption is that service to any one group is a microcosm of general reference service—that the basics of reference service are present, and the task is to adapt good reference skills and collections to serve each group. The model for adapting reference service includes:

1. Assessing the problems a member of a specific group experiences when trying to access information and services provided by the library.
2. Conducting research that includes contact with associations and service providers about how to improve services for specific categories of users (and how to attract nonusers).
3. Planning how to adapt the reference interview, collection development, and delivery of service.
4. Training staff to work with users with special needs or cultural differences.
5. Implementing periodic evaluation of reference services to members of specific groups.

Although school, public, academic, and special libraries may vary in the degree to which certain reference services are provided, elements to be considered in an adequate configuration of reference services to specific groups include:

1. Informational services commensurate with the group's needs and abilities, such as ready-reference, homework assignment help, personal research assistance, and information and referral services (see Chapter 1).
2. Readers' advisory service (see Chapter 1).
3. Instructional services that include assistance both in finding materials and in understanding the information found (see Chapter 8).
4. Collection development to support the informational and developmental needs of each group, including a good reference and circulating collection of materials at appropriate reading and cognitive levels in book and nonbook formats.
5. Interlibrary referral and loan services to supplement local sources when necessary.
6. Solutions to problems of access caused by physical, cognitive, or emotional barriers.[3]

REFERENCE SERVICE IN A PLURALISTIC SOCIETY

Ethnic Diversity

A demographic profile of the United States and Canada reveals a highly diverse, culturally rich picture. Population projections from the U.S. Census Bureau indicate that by 2010, Hispanics will make up 13.8 percent of the U.S. population, African Americans 12.6 percent, Asians 4.8 percent, and Native Americans 0.7 percent. Hispanics will have replaced African Americans as the country's largest minority group. The percentage of non-Hispanic whites in the population will continue to decrease, and by 2050, non-Hispanic whites will barely be holding on to their majority status.[4] In 1997, 13.3 percent of the total population lived below the poverty level; only 11 percent of the white population shouldered this burden, while 26.5 percent of African Americans and 27.1 percent of Hispanics lived below the poverty line.[5]

Such overwhelming data compel librarians to consider providing reference service that is responsive to different needs and, as stated earlier, does not have a formulaic, one-size-fits-all approach. Marcia Nauratil observes that "the [relatively small] size and composition of the library's traditional clientele might be due more to a library's own middle-class orientation than to various inadequacies on the part of nonusers."[6] Mengxiong Liu notes that nontraditional clientele may not have a conceptual awareness of library services or may come from a culture that embraces an entirely different philosophy of education.[7] As individuals, their information-seeking behavior is affected by "different cultural experiences, language, level of literacy, socioeconomic status, education, level of acculturation and value system."[8]

Phoebe Janes and Ellen Meltzer advocate training that specifically addresses the need to individualize and adapt reference service.[9] They state that training is necessitated by invisible barriers and implicit assumptions of which many librarians are not consciously aware. For example, library staff are often guilty of assuming that users share common experiences in libraries and similar communication styles. Special training in racial and cultural sensitivity may be useful in learning to recognize and overcome assumptions and in learning not to classify user difficulty as weakness or deficiency. To deliver effective reference service, librarians need to recognize their own values, set aside judgmental behavior, learn to see through other perspectives, be adaptable and service-oriented, and anticipate change. Patrick Andrew Hall argues that the role of *affectivity*—"the more intangible qualities of personal rapport and empathy"—is just as important as familiarity with specific cultural experiences and sensitivity to diversity.[10] Thus, while it is useful to know that people of color may regard professional distance as "a sign of rudeness or contempt,"[11] it is the specific *relationship* between librarian and user that builds an effective interaction, more so than the generic, "culturally correct" approach.

Non-English Speakers

Non-English (or new-English) speakers represent every age group and every level of the socioeconomic spectrum and make use of all types of libraries. In 1990, almost 20 million persons living in the United States (7.9 percent of the U.S. population) were foreign-born;[12] between 1991 and 1997, almost 7 million more immigrants arrived in the United States.[13] In 1998, there were more than 30 million Hispanics in this country (Hispanics made up almost 11 percent of the population),[14] and there were more than 481,000 international students enrolled in institutions of higher education.[15] Clearly, ethnic diversity continues to be a major factor in the composition of the U.S. population.

New or non-speakers of English fall into three general categories: long-term residents or citizens; immigrants or newly arrived persons, both permanent and transient; and international students attending institutions of higher education. At issue is not only mastery of the

English language but also individual background and experience with the U.S. system of libraries.

Although types of libraries vary in the exact nature of reference services provided, all libraries should adapt their standard reference services to their non-English-speaking users. Particular attention should be paid to collection of materials in different languages, as appropriate, and to materials that describe or reflect the cultures of the library's users. Public libraries in particular should provide access to materials for teaching and learning English[16] and to continuing education opportunities, such as literacy programs, study programs for citizenship, or high school equivalency courses.[17] In her library's English as a second language (ESL) classes, Lena Gonzalez makes an ally of technology. In addition to ESL software, she has students use word processors to write or dictate stories that become part of the class curriculum. She notes that Internet access to information about her students' home countries is very meaningful to those who are homesick or wish to share their experiences with others.[18] In libraries where this kind of comprehensive programming is not feasible, access to such services should be provided by means of referral or liaison work. When possible, libraries should also provide bilingual or bicultural reference staff or solicit the aid of volunteer groups for translation purposes or peer support.

However, all types of libraries share the responsibility of provision of reference services to non-English speakers. School library media centers may serve multiple groups of bilingual children, and librarians need to develop communication skills based on cultural awareness and provide materials in all of the native languages of their students. School libraries can also form effective partnerships with ESL teachers, which will strengthen students' experiences and expand their understanding of library services.[19] Academic libraries need to include in their reference program bibliographic instruction that is accessible to students for whom English is a second language. For example, international students have been recruited to conduct orientation tours in target languages and to act as peer tutors.[20]

Reference services to non-English-speaking groups are more expensive in terms of required staffing and materials than are services to the general U.S. public. But such services facilitate retention of native languages and traditions while easing integration into the new culture. Such citizens move more quickly to a position to contribute to the economy and the culture of their surroundings and to "pay back" the society that supported their transition.[21]

Cultural Differences and Reference Service

Libraries, as Americans know them, are rather unusual in their approach to library service. In many countries, academic libraries are nothing but vast study halls, or their limited collections are locked in closed stacks. Access to these warehouses is obtained through the beneficence of retrieval clerks who are not trained librarians. Collections are often noncirculating, or users may have to pay fees to check books out. A comparable public library system for the general population may not exist. Reference service is neither provided nor understood in the way that it is practiced in the United States. In support of this type of library service are educational traditions that are often based on rote learning, where the teacher is regarded as the repository of all knowledge; no independent investigation is required, and it may in fact be strongly discouraged.[22]

The characteristics of the U.S. library system are simultaneously wonderful and daunting to many non-English speakers. In these libraries one is permitted direct access to a seemingly unlimited supply of materials and, most exciting of all, one is allowed to take materials home. On the other hand, open access implies independent negotiation of a confusing and unfamiliar environment. Asking for help does not always seem to be a viable option. From some cultural perspectives, library staff members may be suspect as representatives of the institution, as figures of authority (see Box 12.2). Librarians may exhibit what appears to be confusing body language, or by their gender or perceived social status be deemed unapproachable. From this vantage point, the users must ask questions, not about something they know, but about something they do *not* know, a task that is difficult enough to accomplish when English is one's first language.[23]

Box 12.2 In the Words of a Foreigner

In some foreign countries the librarian at the reference desk still possesses the image of the person with the power to claim monopoly of all knowledge, and thus is not to be disturbed. Further, societal demands in some countries require that people of a certain social status, or age, or gender ask nothing but intelligent questions. Thus, with this same perception of the librarian, and the concomitant potential for ridicule, some foreign students will not approach the librarian. And if they have a first (bachelor's) degree, and are large males, they will certainly shy away from the reference desk, abiding by the norm that intelligent people (as shown by possession of a first degree), and mature beings (as shown by size and/or age) do not ask silly questions, even if this is the only way to get much-needed answers. Sometimes it is not easy for foreign students to realize that certain types of ignorance are acceptable, and that librarians are there to help.

Kwasi Sarkodie-Mensah
"In the Words of a Foreigner"[24]

The Reference Interview

Fundamentally, the librarian's conduct during the reference interview is no different with non-English speakers than it is with other users. As stressed in Chapter 3, the librarian should treat all people and queries with respect and seriousness. However, with non-English speakers it is especially important to "understand their timidity; their ignorance of [the] system; their reticence toward public institutions; and their awe."[25] It is crucial to be aware of and to understand both cultural and individual differences. For example, Latin America is composed of 45 political units, making the term *Hispanic* hardly descriptive of the very different cultural traditions represented.[26] Furthermore, every cultural group is composed of individuals who have their own unique needs and questions.

It is important to make no assumptions regarding what non-English-speaking users know about libraries. Depending upon circumstances, they may not understand the concept of call numbers, be able to decipher commonly used library terms, or know how to distinguish between printed U.S. first names and surnames.[27] In answering reference questions, slang should be avoided and use of the materials explained and demonstrated, giving users the opportunity to observe and then to imitate. Whenever possible, the librarian should escort a new library user through to the end of the process, such as locating a book or a magazine on the shelf. It is easy to mistake nods and smiles as signifying comprehension. This pitfall can be avoided by asking questions that allow users to communicate more precisely what they do or do not understand. Even apparent English-language fluency may not produce an outcome of successful communication and cultural understanding.[28] It is also possible to misunderstand body language or perceived gruffness; the librarian must instead concentrate on the intent of the user's question. After a question is answered, follow-up is especially important and vital to proper closure of the interview.

Illiterate/Low-Literate Adults

The first international survey of illiteracy was published in 1995 by Statistics Canada and the Organisation for Economic Co-operation and Development (OECD).[29] Results show that 46.6 percent of the adult population of the United States is unable to perform Level 3 prose literacy tasks, such as reading a set of four movie reviews to determine which review is least favorable.[30] Of those who are only at the first level of prose proficiency (20.7 percent), 44.2 percent have no income and 25.9 percent are in the lowest income quintile[31] (see Box

12.3). These statistics suggest that delivery of reference service may need to be adapted for significant numbers of adults, in any community, who do not read well.

Box 12.3

A Third of the Nation Cannot Read These Words

Twenty-five million American adults cannot read the poison warnings on a can of pesticide, a letter from their child's teacher, or the front page of a daily paper. An additional 35 million read only at a level that is less than equal to the full survival needs of our society.

Together, these 60 million people represent more than one-third of the entire adult population.

Jonathan Kozol
Illiterate America[32]

Many libraries, particularly public libraries, offer special services to nonreading adults. One such service is appropriate referral to community agencies or literacy councils that provide testing and tutoring. Some libraries house such services in the library or provide space for tutoring. Many community colleges or public and school libraries support programs such as GED (General Educational Development—high school equivalency) or formal adult basic education programs, or offer special tutoring services to nonreading adults. Materials explaining tutoring and other services should be written at no higher than a fourth-grade level, and such services should be promoted through other media, such as television and radio, as well.

In its analysis of the OECD survey, the Educational Testing Service noted that "adults with low literacy levels do not usually acknowledge or recognize they have a problem."[33] Three Lila Wallace-Reader's Digest Fund-supported programs in New York City attract adults by emphasizing other high-interest topics.[34] The Brooklyn Public Library focuses its program on technology: use of the Internet, e-mail, and CD-ROMs. The New York Public Library has created a thematic curriculum around immigration and the history of people who have lived in the Bronx. The Queens Borough Public Library relies on student committees to advise on curriculum and collection development. Unconventional approaches such as these are more likely to attract those in need.

Library reference collections should contain the types of information needed by adolescents or adults who do not read well, in formats or reading levels accessible to them when possible. Because poor reading skills are frequently associated with poor earning power, this information should include coping or basic life skills information, such as health, consumer, employment, and money management data. The general library collection should include materials for developing basic reading skills (materials on a beginning to fourth- or fifth-grade reading level), GED materials (reading level of grades five to seven), and leisure reading.[35]

It is important to be aware that adults with reading problems may be unwilling to explain those problems. As in any reference transaction, it is important to listen carefully and to observe not just the literal spoken words but also other available cues. In answering specific queries, reference librarians should be prepared to offer materials on a low reading level, when available, and to read or paraphrase the information contained in them to the user. A variety of associations and publishers provide materials for the new adult reader, including Laubach Literacy and the Literacy Volunteers of America.[36] Smaller libraries might choose to integrate adult and children's nonfiction collections "to reduce the stigmatization of the adult new learner when selecting materials."[37] Educators who specialize in adult basic education can advise librarians of available materials for the new adult reader, as well as provide training for reference librarians in interviewing and assessing the needs of the nonreading adult.

REFERENCE SERVICE TO DISABLED INDIVIDUALS

Among the special populations for whom librarians need to develop a full range of reference services are individuals with disabilities. In 1990, the Americans with Disabilities Act (ADA) was signed into law, representing "a milestone in America's commitment to full and equal opportunity for all its citizens."[38] Title II of the ADA governs public services for disabled individuals. It states that "library services must be provided in a manner that allows *each* eligible user with a disability to equally benefit from the local library. . . . Every decision about ADA compliance must be made on a case-by-case basis, taking into consideration the elements involved in the service or program and the needs of the library patron with a disability."[39] A particular service for persons with disabilities can be denied only if a library can prove that it would incur an undue burden were it to be required to offer the service. However, thinking in terms of "requirements" masks a simple reality. As Katy Lenn observes, it "is important to remember that the purpose of legislation for the disabled is not to create special rights but equal rights."[40]

Developments in adaptive technology have transformed many dreams into realities, such as speech recognition systems, CCTV (closed circuit television for enlarging texts), and computer-driven Braille embossers. But lack of funding for high technology should not inhibit service to disabled users. As Jill Mendle notes, "Many aspects of ADA compliance are not technology-intensive, and although less dramatic than voice catalogs, are no less important to the individuals involved."[41]

Each library needs to formulate its own service policies, using the ADA as a guideline. A library, for example, may adopt the policy that when its employees are unable to provide equal, immediate delivery of service, such as photocopying the information in answer to a reference question, they will provide the material within 24 hours. The goal to work toward in the future is equal treatment of all persons, the key ingredient being a positive attitude on the part of the staff. At many academic libraries, the reference department coordinates specialized services for users with disabilities.[42] In any library, the reference department will certainly play a central role in developing and implementing services for disabled persons.

Both legally and ethically, librarians should evaluate the reference services they offer from the perspective of the user with a disability. This is a challenging task, as there are numerous disabling conditions, and, in any community served, the incidence of any one disabling condition may be relatively low. The general groups considered here are individuals with physical disabilities and those with developmental disabilities.

Persons with Physical Disabilities

The physically disabled population includes persons who are blind and visually impaired, individuals who are deaf and hearing-impaired, and persons with mobility impairments. Each of these groups requires somewhat different adaptations of reference service. The uniting theme, however, is realistic access to resources and services so that these items are usable by the individual with a physical disability.

Visually Impaired Persons

People who are blind or visually impaired have had the longest tradition of special services from libraries. The Library of Congress developed a special reading room for blind persons in 1897.[43] In the 1930s, the Library of Congress developed a national network of libraries to serve blind persons, and in the mid-1960s other disabled individuals became eligible for this service. The services of the Library's National Library Service for the Blind and Physically Handicapped are available though public libraries and regional centers. For eligible individuals, the service includes the loan of talking books; a large-print reference collection of books, magazines, and vertical-file materials; and a system of interlibrary loan and technical assistance available through regional libraries for the blind and physically handicapped. The Library is currently planning the migration from analog to digital format for its talking book collections.[44]

In addition to the Library of Congress programs, there are many other programs and agencies whose products and services are useful in helping the person with visual impairment gain access to information. A variety of vendors distribute large-print books and magazines, and the quality and quantity of recorded materials are increasing. Many larger communities have radio stations for blind and other disabled individuals, as well as organizations that arrange for recording text and other materials. A number of innovative adaptations of computer workstations have reduced the need for human readers for the blind, except for handwritten materials. Libraries should provide visually impaired users with an Optical Character Recognition (OCR) system, which scans printed text and either yields speech output or stores information on diskette for alternate output (e.g., Braille, large print). If a library already has a personal computer and screen access equipment (i.e., a scanner), the price range in 1999 for an OCR system was $1,500 to $2,500. A self-contained bundled system was in the $3,500 to $5,500 range.[45] Other devices are available that translate the spoken word to print; these are useful in reference transactions with individuals who are either visually or hearing-impaired. Paperless Braille display units and Braille embossers can interface with a personal computer to give the library user access to information from CD-ROM products or the online catalog.[46]

As reference services become more Web-driven, librarians must consider whether their Web pages are accessible to visually impaired users and the technical reading devices they employ.[47] Special software is available that interacts directly with appropriately designed HTML information on a Web page and translates it into speech, making it useful to the learning disabled and learners of new languages as well as the visually impaired. A number of prescriptions will ensure Web-compliant design:

- Provide alternative text for images and Java applets, especially the "hot-spots" in image maps.
- Use contrasting colors for text, image, and background, and standard style sheets and encoding.
- Provide summaries for tables of data.
- Avoid blinking and scrolling text and make pages function without frames.

Standards for Web-compliant design have been developed by the W3C's Web Accessibility Initiative (http://www.w3.org/WAI). However, a relatively easy way for librarians to check the compliance of their Web pages is to run them through *Bobby*, a Web-based service that analyzes Web pages for their accessibility as well as their compatibility with various Web browsers. Developed by the Center for Applied Special Technology, *Bobby* is found at http://www.cast.org/bobby.

Reference librarians, particularly those in public libraries, should know how to register users for the Library of Congress program and how to make the various services and devices known to persons in the community who would benefit from their use. The ADA will prompt more libraries to supply readers and reading devices for people with visual impairments. In reference service it is important to provide requested information in a readable form as quickly as possible. This may mean reading lengthy passages to the user or requesting documents in a format readable by the user.

Hearing-Impaired Persons

Individuals with hearing impairments have traditionally been less well served by libraries. The language impairment of deaf persons requires both sensitivity and skill on the part of reference staff to provide effective service. It is important to note that needs and communication techniques will vary depending on whether a person is prelingually deaf, profoundly deaf, deafened late in life, or hard of hearing. Several steps can be taken to provide access for users with hearing impairments. First, in the area of collection development, information about hearing impairment, products for hearing-impaired individuals, community resources, and captioned films and videos are important (including the availability of closed caption decoders where there are also viewing facilities). Additionally, clear signage to lead users to these materials is essential.[48] The second step is to provide ways by which the person who is hearing-impaired can communicate with the reference staff. This can include employing librarians who know American Sign Language (or having an interpreter available by appointment); providing TDD (Telecommunication Devices for the Deaf) machines, which can be attached to a regular telephone; and setting up e-mail reference service and electronic bulletin boards that are accessible to hearing-impaired individuals with personal computers. The third step is publicizing references services, through brochures and other means, to the hearing-impaired community, as well as to families and service providers.

Mobility-Impaired Persons

Reference librarians serving mobility-impaired persons should employ appropriate means of communication and document delivery. For example, answering reference questions might entail note-taking, retrieval of books from higher shelves, or photocopying for the user. The reference area itself should be evaluated to ensure that it is barrier-free. Appendix B of the *Americans with Disabilities Act [ADA] Handbook* contains the "ADA Accessibility Guidelines for Buildings and Facilities."[49] Additionally, specific information on adaptations to the environment are part of municipal or state building codes or accessibility standards. Librarians need to start by looking at Appendix B of the *ADA Handbook* and at state and local codes to determine what needs to be done to come into compliance. In addition, state and national advocacy groups may be able to supply information on adapting environments, or local individuals with physical disabilities may be able to help by personally assessing the library's space.[50] Telephone reference services and communication by computer may help homebound individuals gain access to reference service.

It is also important to publicize to the physically disabled community that the library is accessible. People who are mobility-impaired need information about disabling conditions, available community services and resources, and current legal and medical information. Such guides as *Resources for People with Disabilities: A National Directory*,[51] or more specialized titles such as *Financial Aid for the Disabled and Their Families*,[52] will direct users to sources of information, advocacy, and services.

Persons with Developmental Disabilities

Persons who have *developmental disabilities* fall into a wider variety of categories than generally assumed. Developmental disabilities include broad categories such as learning disabilities, mental retardation, and attention deficit disorder with hyperactivity. Characteristics that are often common to these disabilities are difficulties with language, communication, perception, and cognition. Some individuals may also experience problems with emotional and social development. In their book on information services for people with developmental disabilities, Linda Lucas Walling and Marilyn M. Irwin include in their definition such specific labels as autism, Down syndrome, epilepsy, deaf-blind, multiply disabled, spina bifida, medically fragile, Tourette syndrome, fetal alcohol syndrome, and cerebral palsy.[53] Because of the potential for confusion and misunderstanding, they recommend that the term "developmentally disabled" be defined whenever it is used. Obviously, with such a variety of characteristics, reference needs will vary and librarians need to plan accordingly. The comments in this section are primarily directed toward service to individuals with cognitive difficulties.

Despite a limited ability to manipulate information, individuals with cognitive disabilities have a right to information, and reference librarians can adapt services to meet their needs. Reference interview sessions will need to be short and focused. Rephrasing or repetition may be necessary, and listening creatively will facilitate communication. The most successful materials are those that have large print, brief texts, and uncluttered pictures. Although children's materials often prove to be good reference tools, mentally disabled adults have the full range of adult concerns, such as vocation, social relationships, sexuality, money management, and parenting; thus, they frequently need to go beyond the resources of a children's reference collection. The adult reference collection can include titles from among the increasing number of materials available for the adult new reader. Because the mentally impaired user may be slow in processing information, it is important to have useful reference materials that circulate, or space so that the materials may be used for extended periods of time in the library.

It is important to provide information about developmental disabilities, including the identification of relevant local and national organizations and agencies, so that family and caregivers can understand the conditions as well as make appropriate decisions about care. Reference librarians may offer to create bibliographies and special informational brochures about library services to be used by care providers, special schools, and organizations for individuals with developmental disabilities.

Another category of mental disability is mental illness, which is included in the ADA's definition of disability. With the deinstitutionalization of large numbers of seriously mentally ill individuals without the provision of sufficient community resources to accommodate them, many have become marginalized in our society, and even homeless. Libraries have seen an influx of these displaced people in their reference and reading rooms. Thomas Hecker suggests that libraries' "problem patron" response be replaced by casting the situation in terms of disability, where services and protections are provided as appropriate.[54] But he does not intend for libraries to serve as social service agencies in the face of extreme situations:

> Rather, I suggest that librarians apply the disability model to patrons with mental illness who have retained, or who have regained, a level of functioning which is still within the pale of society. Such people may exhibit symptoms which 'stretch the envelope' of our tolerance, but if tolerance will allow them to live an acceptable life within society, tolerance is the accommodation which must be accorded them.[55]

REFERENCE SERVICES FOR SPECIFIC AGE GROUPS

Three age groups are discussed in this chapter. As an introduction to thinking about differences in reference services called for because of age, the focus is on children, young adults, and the elderly. Service to adults is not addressed because the basic reference services described elsewhere in this book focus on services to the general adult audience. For this discussion, *children* are defined as persons from birth to age 14, or infancy through junior high school, while *young adults* are defined as persons from age 12 through 18, or junior high and high school students. There is an intentional overlap in the definitions of children and young adults to account for the variety of ways in which public libraries and schools choose to serve persons of junior high or middle school age. The *elderly* include persons who are 65 years of age or older. Although there is little literature on special needs of the elderly for library service, this is one of the fastest-growing segments of our population, constituting 12.7 percent of the population in 1998.[56] Undoubtedly, the library profession should begin to adapt reference services to meet the needs of this growing population.

Children and Young Adults

There are some underlying assumptions that provide a useful framework for understanding reference service to children and young adults. First and most fundamental is that children progress through a series of developmental stages as they mature. These stages define what type of reference service is appropriate to match a child's cognitive capabilities. For example, most third-graders can categorize and use basic classification systems. Carol Kuhlthau found that this ability means that third-graders are capable of understanding the difference between fiction and nonfiction and that the purpose of call numbers is to bring together books on the same topic.[57] However, their use of a library catalog must be guided, as well as their journey from the catalog to the books on the shelf. Children labor under a real handicap in having to use a library system designed for adult users. Vicky Crosson notes that "most subject terms used in library catalogs are on a sixth grade or above reading level and often use words not commonly used by children."[58] Clearly, all reference service to children must be conducted within the context of developmental parameters.

Christine Behrmann and Dolores Vogliano assert that a good children's librarian demonstrates two types of skills: cognitive and affective.[59] *Cognitive skills* provide for competence and qualification in fulfilling children's information needs. *Affective skills* are those that enable the librarian to respect and understand the needs of young people. The librarian providing reference service to children has a special responsibility for mastering these affective skills, because there is more at stake in these transactions than simply answering questions correctly. It is at this stage in their lives that children often form lifelong attitudes about libraries. Young people can feel empowered by the library and its resources or intimidated and excluded by those same riches.

A final theme that underscores reference service to youth is the effect of recent educational reform movements on library use in both school and public libraries. There has been a trend away from textbook-based teaching and toward *information literacy*, which relies on the constructivist ideals of resource-based teaching and learning.[60] In this educational model, students take more responsibility for their own learning. Information seeking and analysis become an integral part of the curriculum, resulting in an increased use of the library and a greater need for reference services.

Reference Services for Children

In addition to helping the children themselves, most reference service to children includes assistance to parents, teachers, and other care providers. In her case study, Janice Harrington found that 29 percent of the requests for information at the children's reference desk came from adults.[61] Often, an adult is the intermediary for the child's questions and needs guidance in the use of materials housed in the youth services area of the public library or the school library media center.

Harrington found definite differences in the types of questions asked by adults and those asked by children.[62] Children tend to ask questions of a locational or mechanical nature, and their questions are overwhelmingly school-related. Adults ask more policy- or program-oriented questions, more complex readers' advisory questions, and more questions involving bibliographic verification and other informational needs. Unfortunately, not all adults are clear or skilled translators of children's needs, and the reference librarian must develop a range of interviewing skills to determine what the child really wants to know or read. In any case, children's reference service includes users of all ages.

Information Services. Information service to children is a central part of library services to children and is not secondary in importance to programming for children. Consider this observation made by Janice Harrington: "Approximately 576 persons attended programs at the Urbana Free Library during the same period of time as the study of its children's information service, while at least 2,158 requests were made by adults and children at the question desk.

In these terms, it becomes apparent that information service is the largest 'program' offered by the children's department."[63] Children have limited choices for gathering information and may logically turn to the librarian at the public library or at school for help. Young children's information needs are especially likely to be overlooked because of an emphasis in service to preschoolers on programming and fiction collection development. It is important to supply to young children information that is stated simply. Librarians need to have commercially or locally produced bibliographies of picture book and easy-to-read titles available for both reference staff and users to consult, as subject cataloging of these materials is often inadequate.

As noted above, various studies of children's reference questions show that they are predominantly school-related or stimulated by popular culture (e.g., television, movies, sports).[64] Thus, there is a certain predictability in much reference work with children, although it is important not to become complacent. Elizabeth Overmyer observes that children's librarians do not tend to consciously develop their reference skills in the same way that they prepare for the other activities they are responsible for, such as story hours and booktalks. As a result, they are more likely to have limited access to and knowledge of some of the newer tools and techniques of reference work.[65]

It is not easy to get teachers to warn librarians about the assignment needs of children, but often librarians can set up a system of communication whereby assignment sheets are copied and kept on file. Public and school librarians can telephone teachers or approach them informally with questions and can keep notations from year to year about major assignments that are likely to recur perennially. Strong communication links between school library media specialists and public library reference staff can help both institutions provide better reference service to school children (see Box 12.4 for an example of a form that school librarians can use to alert public library reference staff of classroom assignments).

Local or state-mandated curriculum requirements can also be used to identify courses that may involve library use. Also, some time spent reading local newspapers and school newsletters and keeping up with movies, music, and youth culture will help librarians predict and relate to reference questions on personal interest topics. A community resource file that contains a section on children's activities will be extremely useful in answering questions about local events and issues.

Automated reference tools are finding increasing application in children's reference service. Until just a few years ago, most available online catalogs, as well as commercially produced electronic reference tools such as CD-ROM encyclopedias, were not developed with the needs of children in mind. Typing a string of correctly spelled words, often preceded by an arcane code defining a search type, is difficult enough for an adult to accomplish, let alone a child with elementary reading skills. Successful electronic systems share important characteristics, such as multiple search modes, which provide the flexibility of meeting the needs of varying levels of cognitive development, and interface designs that capitalize on recognition skills and natural browsing search strategies. For example, the Kid's Catalog from CARL Corporation is a graphical user interface that provides age-appropriate searching software that links to the bibliographic data on a public access catalog.[66] Children can identify and select topics by browsing colorful icons that represent the Dewey hierarchy as well as popular topics that cross strict Dewey categories. Children who are adept typists and spellers can use a mode that allows them to type in their search strategies. From each book record, a library map is available that flashes the location of the book on the screen.

In this era of shared catalog systems and consortial agreements, interlibrary loan is more accessible to children than it ever has been before. Children can often initiate transactions themselves, with "their" de facto library being the extensive network of libraries on a shared database. However, some local interlibrary loan services may have special limitations with regard to persons below a designated age. Sometimes schools are excluded from interlibrary loan policies and agreements.

Box 12.4 Sample Assignment Alert Form

Mass-Assignment Alert!

TO: , Public Librarian

Fax #:

(Date)

Dear Public Library Colleague,

We wanted to alert you to a major research project that has been assigned in our school. You may want to keep some of your material on reserve to meet student demand and more equitably distribute your resources. Here are some details you may find helpful.

Teacher ____________________ Subject/Class ________________

Grade ______________________ Date Due ____________________

Project/Assignment ____

Expected Product ____

A copy of the student assignment sheet is attached for your convenience. Please feel free to contact us with any questions.

Librarian ____

School ____

Phone ____

E-mail ____

Fax # ____

Joyce Kasman Valenza, *Power Tools: 100+ Essential Forms and Presentations for Your School Library Information Program*[67]
Reprinted by permission of ALA

The Internet has, without doubt, made a bigger impact on reference service to children than any other advancement in recent technology history. Not only do vendors use it as a standard way of delivering information products, but nonprofit and public sector information providers have found it to be an inexpensive and effective means of dissemination—usually without having to charge fees. But finding information on the Internet can be extremely problematic for a child. Search engines and Internet directories all use different protocols and retrieve from different parts of Internet space. Commercial sites are mixed in with educational sites, and personal Web pages pop up alongside government agencies.

Reference librarians are important advisors in the Web searching process. They should assist the young user by creating supportive library home pages that provide links to "jumping off" sites specifically designed for children. An example of this type of service is *Yahooligans!* (http://www.yahooligans.com), a hierarchical category search tool that links to sites built for children. Another example is the Youth Division of the Internet Public Library (http://www.ipl.org/youth), which is maintained by a librarian and even has child-oriented Web links organized by Dewey Decimal classification. Librarians also need to help users evaluate the results of their searches, redefine search strategies, and assess the authority and depth of individual Web sites.

Community concerns about children's access to inappropriate materials on the Internet have spawned the development of Internet filtering software, often installed on computers that serve children in libraries. Filtering software has enormous implications for students' ability to access information. Filters are known to prevent successful searches for information on topics such as breast cancer, which fail because the word "breast" is blocked. The American Library Association has taken the position that the use of filtering software by libraries to block protected speech violates the *Library Bill of Rights.*[68]

Ethics and Confidentiality. Children may request information on sensitive topics, such as sex or drugs. Reference librarians need to consult and interpret—and in some cases formulate—local policy related to the provision of information to minors on controversial topics. Some institutions are required to act *in loco parentis* (in the place of the parent) unless released from this status by particular parents with respect to their own children. The political or religious affiliation of some libraries may dictate local policy with regard to minors and require library personnel to provide less than the *Library Bill of Rights'* intended level of access to information. For example, in a parochial school library, librarians may be restricted from providing information about abortion. They may also be required to install Internet filtering software on their Web server.

The ability to maintain confidentiality in a user-librarian relationship is inextricably tied to legal issues. In a school library setting, the librarian is typically governed by the same regulations that govern all personnel, designating them mandated reporters of certain kinds of information. For example, the Abused and Neglected Child Reporting Act of Illinois specifically states that the privileged quality of communication between designated employees and children does not apply in situations involving abuse and neglect.[69]

The Reference Interview. The reference interview is important for all users, but it is "particularly problematic when dealing with children who form their questions through limited vocabulary and sphere of experience."[70] The main vehicle for determining the child's need for information and fulfilling that need is the reference interview. A friendly, open demeanor and careful listening to children will help them express their needs. Children frequently lack an intellectual context for their questions, so interviews with children may need to be more directive, with more explanations and fewer open-ended questions than interviews with adults. For example, children often come with a homework assignment question that is essentially the teacher's—the student acts as a messenger, not as a thoughtful (or even interested) inquirer.

Children's questions may contain inaccurate information. Verification of spelling, proper names, and facts presented in a child's questions may be a good first step in an interview to ensure that both the librarian and the child are on the right track. Children also have difficulty following directions in sequence. A seemingly reasonable suggestion to a middle-grade child that includes three or four steps (e.g., go to the catalog, find the call number of this book, go to the proper place in the stacks, find the book, look in the index for your topic) may be too difficult for the child to remember at this stage of development. The reference interview may have to be done gradually as the child works through the search step by step. Reference librarians frequently follow a child all the way to the source.

In addition to the problems of getting information from the child and helping the child absorb information from the librarian, time is a factor. Children have a short attention span and are easily discouraged if the search is not successful in the first few attempts. Again, a series of short exchanges may be more successful than one longer, more complete interview. The reference librarian needs to be good at juggling several simultaneous searches, keeping track of each child's progress. Children react to a positive attitude and praise; although efficiency may sometimes seem to be sacrificed for friendliness, reference service ultimately will be more effective if presented in this manner.

Readers' Advisory. Although libraries vary in the provision of readers' advisory services to the general adult population (see Chapter 1), readers' advisory is an essential reference service for children. Whether asking for school-related information or a good book to read, children usually need some guidance in choosing materials. Readers' advisory service to children is enhanced when the librarian knows the local collection well, has specialized training in library materials for children, and is an active reader of the literature. When helping children with book selection, the librarian should determine the child's interests or needs, age or grade level, and approximate reading level. Often the child can articulate an interest and age or grade level, but it may be a little more difficult to assess actual reading level. School library media specialists may be able to check school records, while public librarians may have to ask what books the child has been reading recently to get some idea of where to start. It is always wise to give children several choices of titles and encourage personal selection. This gives the child practice in independent book selection but also answers the child's need for some guidance from a knowledgeable adult.

Instruction for Children in the Use of Libraries and Materials. Both formal group instruction and individual instruction are generally considered part of reference service to children. Traditionally, formal library instruction has been the responsibility of the school librarian. Integrating library skills in all areas of the curriculum, cooperation between librarian and teacher, and creative learning activities will provide children with the skills they need to succeed in school and become lifelong learners. Unfortunately, library time in many elementary schools is still scheduled in a fixed manner apart from any consideration of what is going on in the classroom. Fixed scheduling is an administrative convenience that allows teachers to use library time as planning time and ensures that students come to the library on a regular basis. The new edition of *Information Power* notes that:

> In a student-centered school library media program, learning needs take precedence over class schedules, school hours, student categorizations, and other logistical concerns. To meet learning needs, the program's resources and services must be available so that information problems can be resolved when they arise.[71]

Fixed schedules inhibit the integration of library instruction into the curriculum. Students may learn library skills in this environment but do not generally have the opportunity to *apply* what they have learned in the context of real educational problems. Even if students are allowed access to the library outside of designated library time, the librarian is generally busy with another scheduled class. These limitations, as well as the natural boundaries of different stages of cognitive development, may explain why discrete skills learned in formal library instruction are not effectively transferred by children to academic libraries when students reach higher education[72] and why students have difficulty transferring skills from school to public libraries.[73]

Library skills that are abstracted from situations where they can be meaningfully applied are difficult for children (or anyone) to generalize to other situations. Instead, learning how to use the library is more meaningful if it is viewed as a *process that occurs in context* rather than as a set of specific discrete skills. To achieve this aim, more school libraries are turning to a system of flexible scheduling. Instruction in this type of environment includes a combination of generic information and library-specific information, taught in the context of a particular application rather than as ends in themselves. Children receive multiple exposures of this process through many trips to the library for different school projects, developing a rich view of how to access information. Again, this approach reflects the values expressed in the *Information Literacy Standards for Student Learning*[74] (see Box 8.2) and the general educational trend toward project and resource-based learning that integrates and situates knowledge.

Individual instruction also takes place during the reference interview in both school and public libraries. By discussing a question during the reference interview and explaining why and how particular reference tools are used to answer the question, the librarian provides models of search strategies that the young person can emulate. Drawing the user into active involvement in answering the question (e.g., encouraging the child to find an index entry during the reference interview, letting the child lead the way to the book on the shelf) means that the child is immediately applying the new knowledge with the support and encouragement of the librarian/instructor. Children may also need help in interpreting information once it is found. It is often a creative process to determine at what point library instruction related to homework assignments becomes doing the homework itself!

Reference Services for Young Adults

Young adult (YA) reference services are composed of essentially the same components as children's reference services, with some salient age-related differences. For example, young adults require access to adult-level materials as well as to children's collections. They are also less dependent upon parents or other adults to act as intermediaries or to assist with the use of materials. Two major components of reference work with young adults, readers' advisory and school-related information needs, are discussed in this section. Young adults are served by public libraries, school libraries, and, in many cases, college and university libraries. They constitute a prominent service group in these libraries. Sixty percent of the people entering public libraries during a typical week in the fall of 1993 were children and young adults. Twenty-three percent of the total were young adults.[75] However, only 11 percent of public libraries had an in-house young adult librarian.[76] Somewhat fewer than 40 percent reported having either a young adult specialist or a "youth services specialist,"[77] a "specialist" being a staff member who has education or training in services to children and young adults.

Adolescence is a time of transition. Public libraries typically purchase unique as well as duplicate copies of selected titles for their young adult users, but manage these materials in different ways. Fifty-eight percent of public libraries provide a section or special collection of materials specifically designated for young adults.[78] Another 15 percent collect young adult materials, but shelve them with the adult collection, while 16 percent shelve these materials in the children's section.[79] The concept of giving young adults a separate library space of their own came into favor during the 1940s and 1950s,[80] but has proven to be expensive in terms of staffing and has not decreased the need for duplication of materials among departments. Current thinking judges the separation of services to be developmentally counterproductive; rather than segregating young adults, libraries should assist them in learning adult behavior in an integrated environment conducive to promoting this apprenticeship. At the same time, targeted services should still be offered. Teenagers are particularly attracted to online alternatives, such as chat groups and special teen Web "spaces."

Information Services. School-related queries account for the majority of the informational activities of young adult reference work. The trend toward resource-based education is also thriving at the secondary level. Students progressing to junior or middle and then senior high school are faced with assignments of increasing number and complexity. In the school library, the librarian's best ally in providing assignment-related assistance is a good instruction program that is integrated into the school curriculum. In this way, the intent of such assignments—to teach students how to locate and use information independently—is directly reinforced by the person most qualified to see that this actually happens. Reference service is inextricably linked to the teaching role for school library media specialists, as supported by *Information Power* and *Information Literacy Standards for Student Learning.*[81]

In the public library, librarians have much less control over library-related assignments, although these generate a great deal of their reference activity. For frequently requested topics, many libraries prepare *reference pathfinders* (suggested search strategies that include standard reference tools and their appropriate subject headings). For recurring and popular topics, pathfinders provide a kind of one-on-one instruction in high-use environments where a librarian may not always be readily available. They are especially effective for young adults who are too shy to ask for help or who appreciate the opportunity to work independently.

There are many variations on the pathfinder theme. Anita Bell describes a term-paper resource center concept where commonly needed tools such as style manuals, dictionaries, and even extra note cards and other supplies are kept, along with handouts on term-paper writing skills and a notebook full of pathfinders.[82] Something as simple as Web browser bookmarks with links to homework help sites may satisfy many students' needs. Robust sites now exist to help students direct their Web searches. The Internet Public Library (http://www.ipl.org) is one such example, as is the Homework Center created by the Multnomah County Library (http://www.multnomah.lib.or.us/lib/homework).[83] However, students tend to sit down at a Web search engine and type in keywords and may need to be directed to bookmarks or other customized Web homework tools. If Internet filtering software is installed, it can prove to be a real liability, as students conduct research on topics ranging from drug legalization to assisted suicide.

Finally, it is important to establish a library policy for young adult reference services that delineates what the library can and cannot do in terms of homework assistance. Telephone support of assignments, for example, is an amorphous issue; it is difficult enough to define limits of telephone reference service among professionals and even more difficult to explain them to an adolescent.

Interlibrary loan service presents special challenges for young adults as well as for children. In practical terms, tight deadlines and the human tendency to procrastinate, coupled with increased mobility on the part of teenagers, usually suggest that direct reciprocal borrowing from nearby libraries is a more viable option than interlibrary loan for young adults. The reference librarian can assist by providing location information to the user. Debra Kachel describes improvements in resource sharing access tools as well as document delivery methods.[84] She also argues that the move away from textbook-based, outcome-driven curricula has increased the need for interlibrary loan. Fortunately, the growing availability of electronic full-text sources has also decreased dependence on interlibrary loan services. Even small libraries can take advantage of these subscriptions if they belong to a consortium or district that negotiates group rates. From a student's perspective, however, there is often no difference between the sources they retrieve from a respected information vendor and those they retrieve from the results screen of a Web search. Reference intervention is a critical component at this juncture, helping students to determine the reliability and authority of online sources.

Ethics and Confidentiality. As a part of growing up, young adults are naturally interested in information of a personal or sensitive nature. In the library, they face the prospect of going through an intermediary to find information on topics like sexuality or troubled family relationships. The librarian must be seen as a neutral resource, yet appear sympathetic and understanding. A school librarian may be in the privileged position of knowing the individuals better, of being the trusted counselor. On the other hand, a student in search of sensitive information may prefer to ask for it where anonymity is more likely. Helma Hawkins suggests that teens searching for information about homosexuality may be afraid to be seen buying a book on the topic, especially in a gay book store, "but they might sit in a quiet part of the public library and read."[85] Some libraries have established anonymous question and answer services as a way to satisfy those unasked reference questions.[86] The exchanges can be posted in a publicly accessible area of the library, or even electronically, as fits the situation.

The ability to maintain confidentiality in the user-librarian relationship, however, is dependent on legal issues, as outlined in the previous section regarding confidentiality and children. In a public library, the written reference policy can provide the opportunity to make an explicit statement regarding open access and the library's commitment to confidentiality. By doing so, the library is released from the *in loco parentis* role and can grant young adults independent and adult status in their pursuit of information. In any case, it is incumbent upon the librarian to find out what local laws or policies govern this issue before stumbling into a compromising situation (see Box 12.5).

Box 12.5 — What Would You Do?

David, a quiet 15-year-old, is a regular library user. The staff notices that lately he has been visiting the Web sites of white supremacy organizations and gun owners' interest groups. When he asks for help finding information that denies the existence of the Nazi Holocaust, the librarian, who happens to be Jewish, hesitates at his request. She also wonders if she should inform David's parents.

What should the librarian do in this situation?

Are there legitimate limits or larger responsibilities when it comes to certain types of reference requests?

Readers' Advisory. Young adult reference service began largely as an out-of-school, extracurricular effort to emphasize reading guidance in an era when school courses were taught solely from textbooks.[87] This orientation continued even after teachers began expecting students to use outside sources. In libraries without a young adult specialist, the readers' advisory role is often subsumed by the school-related informational role, one with which reference generalists may be more comfortable and where the techniques and tools more readily translate across age levels.

Readers' advisory service is an aspect of reference work that is of critical importance in the young adult arena. Books present young adults with options, allowing them to glimpse models of conflict resolution and decision making and, in the process, to develop their own critical-thinking skills. Librarians who serve young adults need to know the literature, to be able to suggest titles that are similar to other titles a young library user has enjoyed, and to discuss the issues raised therein. Dorothy M. Broderick admonishes today's librarians with the example of Margaret Edward of the Enoch Pratt Free Library, who required a librarian to read and orally report on 300 titles from the New York Public Library's *Books for the Teen Age* before being granted the title of Young Adult Librarian.[88] Because teens sometimes are reluctant to talk to adults, electronic subscription products are now available that may help bridge the gap. *NoveList* (http://novelist.epnet.com) allows the user to search for titles at the adult and/or the young adult level. GaleNet's (http://www.gale.com) *What Do I Read Next?* includes titles from the volumes in their print series, including *What Do Young Adults Read Next?*[89]

The Reference Interview. As young adults begin to move away from the children's department and to ask questions at the adult reference desk, they encounter many librarians who are helpful and friendly, take their needs at face value, and treat them as individuals. They also encounter librarians who are uncomfortable with them, see them as potential problems, and judge their needs to be less serious than those of adults and therefore less important. In a study of reference service success rates in 36 public libraries, Charles Bunge reported an overall success rate of 61.74 percent.[90] But for high school students, the success rate dipped to 55.11 percent, the lowest of any demographic category. Complicating the situation, developmental differences often make it extremely difficult to determine a young person's age. Some young adults still look juvenile, yet consider themselves beyond that stage. Because publishers package most curricular material for the juvenile market, a lot of information very appropriate for adolescents is housed in the children's department. Clearly, navigating between the adult and juvenile departments during the reference process calls for tact and discretion.

During any reference interview, the librarian must determine a user's actual need, as opposed to the need as it is initially expressed. In the case of young adults, vocabulary and self-concept are still developing.[91] Young adults may not yet possess the analytical skills to identify the components of their information need or to approach a problem systematically and sequentially. They tend to be literal-minded, focusing on the end product rather than the process, asking questions such as: "I need a book that compares revenge in *Hamlet* with revenge in Stephen King's books."[92] They have to articulate their needs to a figure of authority in a strange environment. The librarian must therefore take special pains to be approachable, friendly, nonjudgmental, and above all, not condescending. A user's reluctance to come forward must also be respected. Mary K. Chelton and James M. Rosignia note that "conducting a reference interview with young adults has been likened to dental extraction" and advocate a "we're in this together" approach.[93] However, when a question is obviously school-related, it is often possible to ask more pointed, direct questions than one normally would: "Can I ask you what your assignment is? Do you have a copy of it with you?" It is always helpful to rephrase the question to make sure both parties are working under the same assumptions.

Some Final Thoughts on Reference Services for Youth

In *Output Measures for Public Library Service to Children* and *Output Measures and More: Planning and Evaluating Public Library Services for Young Adults*, Virginia Walter provides formulas for measuring and evaluating reference requests, as well as information on how to interpret and use the data.[94] Rosemarie Riechel supplies detailed instructions for qualitative and quantitative evaluation of reference service to youth in both school and public library settings.[95] Her definition of reference service to youth bears repeating: "The best reference service combines mediated searching, formal and informal instruction in information-seeking skills (using hard copy sources, nonprint media, and electronic systems), and assistance in the use of reference sources. It includes lessons in analysis and evaluation of the value of the information retrieved and the accuracy or correctness of the method of retrieval."[96]

However, the results of Riechel's extensive surveying of public and school libraries paint a radically different picture of actual levels of service. She reports on inadequate reference collection budgets, limited staffing, differential service policies based on age, and lagging implementation of technological advancements in youth service areas. Others, such as Bunge, report similar observations. Computer technologies are in heavy demand by children and young adults, yet in 1995 only 30 percent of public libraries had them available for this user group.[97] Finally, in her study of New York State school library media centers, Nancy Zimmerman found that 22.5 percent did not even have a telephone, which is perhaps the most basic reference tool of all.[98] Riechel exhorts librarians not to be passive in their acceptance of the status quo, and to instead "become active leaders and lobbyists for their cause. The future of reference service to children and young adults depends on professional initiative and dedicated activity."[99]

Older Adults

Although the other special age groups (children and young adults) have both a body of professional literature and an established separate place in libraries, the elderly often lack recognition as a group with special needs. Because the elderly are a fast-growing population, it is likely that their special needs and services will come to the forefront in the next 25 years. In 1998, 12.7 percent of the American population was age 65 or over.[100] By 2025, it is estimated that those 65 or older will have become 18.5 percent of the nation's population.[101] It is also anticipated that because of improved health care, older adults will be more active. Box 12.6 points out the challenge these facts present to libraries.

In working with older adults, it is important to approach each person as an individual who may not share the characteristics or interests commonly associated with the elderly. One should avoid assuming that older adults experience a decline in cognitive ability, because many do not. Indeed, some researchers have identified intellectual capacities that improve with age.[102] Other assumptions must also be avoided. For example, reading interests may or may not change as individuals grow older. Older persons are not necessarily retired; in 1998, 11.6 percent of persons 65 or older were employed in the labor force.[103] Finally, many grandparents are now raising their own grandchildren; 1.4 million children lived with their grandparents in 1998, without any parents in the household.[104] These older adults have reference needs that do not fit the mold of the "typical" senior citizen.

Box 12.6 If Librarians Won't Do It, Who Will?

Librarians have, through the years, not done enough for elders within the walls of libraries. But such staff cannot allow this to continue if their job is to be done right. Library services and programs to elders will become more and more important as the years go by. As elders increase in numbers, their advocacy will increase, and other agencies will step in to provide the services, probably for a fee. The library is uniquely suited for providing the informational undergirding of our society—a role that sometimes only librarians take seriously.

Celia Hales-Mabry
The World of the Aging: Information Needs and Choices[105]

Good reference service for elderly individuals includes all the basic components of good reference service for the general adult population, with particular attention to the individual needs of elderly users. In its guidelines for library service to older adults, the Reference and User Services Association of the American Library Association exhorts libraries to provide a full slate of integrated library services to the elderly.[106] Reference librarians need to avoid stereotyping or patronizing older users and should develop effective communication skills so as to encourage them to ask questions and to ensure that each answer is fully understood by the user. Many older adults, for example, have had limited exposure to computers and may experience more computer anxiety than younger library users. Where the library was once a friendly, welcoming place, it now feels intimidating and impersonal. Special online catalog instruction sessions tailored for older individuals will create a comfortable atmosphere where users can ask questions and experience self-paced practice and one-on-one coaching. In general, informational programs are among the most popular of the range of programs offered to older adults in public libraries.

Collections should be developed that deal with common concerns such as income, social security, transportation, housing, and health, all from the point of view of older adults as well as from the point of view of their children or other caregivers. It is important to have current directories (local, state, and federal) of services for the elderly, as well as materials that discuss the aging process and how to obtain adequate medical, legal, financial, and psychological help. Libraries can use directories to provide information and referral to appropriate government and private agencies serving the elderly. Online, searchable databases, such as the AARP's fee-based *AgeLine* (http://research.aarp.org/ageline/home.html), are frequently updated. Sources such as Ken Skala's *American Guidance for Seniors . . . and Their Caregivers*[107] and the National Institute on Aging's *Resource Directory for Older People*[108] are examples of titles that provide an overview of current issues and list sources of services for older adults. Regional and, less frequently, local directories of this type are available also. A community resource file should include information about rights, organizations, local transportation, housing, educational and recreational opportunities, tax changes, social security, and Medicare. A centralized reference collection of this type of information will prove invaluable to older library users and service providers.

To provide reference service to older adults, it may be necessary to offer remote delivery of materials and service. Certainly the most common form of remote delivery of reference service is by telephone. In libraries where in-person reference service is busy and takes precedence over answering questions over the telephone, special provisions must be made to serve the homebound and the institutionalized elderly. The general rule of serving walk-in users before answering the telephone is logical but may make it difficult for the older adult to access the library. It may be necessary to set up a special telephone service for elderly (or disabled) persons who cannot easily get to the library. Also, it may be possible to take reference service to elderly individuals by including reference materials in the bookmobile collection when making stops at retirement homes, nursing facilities, or senior citizen centers. Training bookmobile staff in basic reference service would ensure that questions could be answered in a timely and predictable fashion.

It is important to communicate to older adults the reference services that are available to them and to make them feel welcome. The library can effectively market services of particular interest to older persons through library brochures, specific informational programs held in the library, and outside agencies. Reference librarians should cultivate communications with other service agencies in the community; often, specialists in services to the elderly can provide training for library staff in working with the elderly and make appropriate referrals to the library if interagency cooperation is practiced. Careful assessment of what use older citizens make of a library may reveal a need to publicize existing reference services or a way to adapt services to meet the needs and capacities of older adults.

CONCLUSION

Reference services should be offered to all persons in a library's service community regardless of their circumstances or identifying characteristics. There are several issues to be addressed by librarians responsible for ensuring that specific groups in their service community have equal access to reference service. First, librarians need to acknowledge that reference services do need to be adapted, or at least assessed, with respect to the needs and abilities of particular groups. Librarians need to identify groups within their community that might face obstacles to free access to information. It should be stressed that this assessment needs to go beyond polling or observing current users of library reference materials or services. If impediments such as physical or communication barriers exist, members of a group affected by the barriers often are nonusers of the library and thus invisible to the librarian who only observes the behavior of the user group.

Once groups are identified, librarians need to create a plan of service for meeting the special needs of individuals in each. This plan would include determining the adaptations needed by each group, assessing the library's ability to meet identified needs, and establishing priorities for actions to be taken by the library. It is important to work with other agencies, including local ones and regional or national organizations, both to identify needs of special users and to design collections and services that meet the groups' reference needs. The library should have policies and procedures, including staff training, that enhance access to full reference services. Special adaptations to library procedures to accommodate the needs of identified groups should be incorporated in library handbooks or manuals. Finally, librarians should plan regular evaluation of services and facilities for targeted groups, so they can keep up with—or even anticipate—changes in the population of those groups as well as relevant changes in library technology.

Librarians need to plan reference services, assemble reference collections, and develop reference skills appropriate to the various groups in their community of users. This planning process must begin with an understanding of the diverse groups that constitute that community.

NOTES

1. American Library Association, *Intellectual Freedom Manual,* 5th ed. (Chicago: American Library Association, 1996), 3.

2. Ibid., 84-85.

3. Based in part on a list from Shirley Fitzgibbons, "Reference and Information Services for Children and Young Adults: Definition, Services, and Issues," *The Reference Librarian* 7/8 (Spring/Summer 1983): 5-6.

4. *Statistical Abstract of the United States 1999* (Washington, D.C.: U.S. Bureau of the Census, 1999), table 19.

5. Ibid., table 763.

6. Marcia J. Nauratil, *Public Libraries and Nontraditional Clienteles: The Politics of Special Services* (Westport, Conn.: Greenwood Press, 1985), 12.

7. Mengxiong Liu, "Ethnicity and Information Seeking," *The Reference Librarian* 49/50 (1995): 123-34.

8. Ibid., 124.

9. Phoebe Janes and Ellen Meltzer, "Origins and Attitudes: Training Reference Librarians for a Pluralistic World," *The Reference Librarian* 30 (1990): 145-55.

10. Patrick Andrew Hall, "The Role of Affectivity in Instructing People of Color: Some Implications for Bibliographic Instruction," *Library Trends* 39 (Winter 1991): 316-26.

11. Ibid., 322.

12. *Statistical Abstract of the United States 1999,* table 56.

13. Ibid., table 5.

14. Ibid., table 19.

15. Ibid., table 310.

16. Janet Hansen, Deborah Barabino, and Debra Floyd, "English Without Tears: ESL Materials," *Library Journal* 117 (September 1, 1992): 139-42.

17. Robert P. Haro, *Developing Library and Information Services for Americans of Hispanic Origin* (Metuchen, N.J.: Scarecrow Press, 1981), 286p.

18. Steve Sumerford, "Creating a Community of Readers to Fight Functional Illiteracy," *American Libraries* 28 (May 1997): 44-48.

19. Anne H. Filson, "Librarian-Teacher Partnerships: Serving the English-as-a-Second-Language Students," *Journal of Youth Services in Libraries* 5 (Summer 1992): 399-406.

20. Manuel D. Lopez, "Chinese Spoken Here: Foreign Language Library Orientation Tours," *College & Research Libraries News* 44 (September 1983): 265-69.

21. Leonard Wertheimer, "Library Service to Ethnocultural Minorities: Philosophical and Social Bases and Professional Implications," *Public Libraries* 26 (Fall 1987): 98-102.

22. Ziming Liu, "Difficulties and Characteristics of Students from Developing Countries in Using American Libraries," *College & Research Libraries* 54 (January 1993): 25-31; Sally G. Wayman, "The International Student in the Academic Library," *Journal of Academic Librarianship* 9 (January 1984): 336-41; Louise Greenfield, Susan Johnston, and Karen Williams, "Educating the World: Training Library Staff to Communicate Effectively with International Students," *Journal of Academic Librarianship* 12 (September 1986): 227-31.

23. Karen M. Moss, "The Reference Communication Process," *Law Library Journal* 72 (Winter 1979): 48-52.

24. Kwasi Sarkodie-Mensah, "In the Words of a Foreigner," *Research Strategies* 4 (Winter 1986): 31.

25. Tamiye Fujibayashi Trejo and Mary Kaye, "The Library as Port of Entry," *American Libraries* 19 (November 1988): 890-92.

26. Ibid., 890.

27. Greenfield, Johnston, and Williams, "Educating the World," 230. See also Kwasi Sarkodie-Mensah, "Dealing with International Students in a Multicultural Era," *Journal of Academic Librarianship* 18 (September 1992): 214-16; and Joan Ormondroyd, "The International Student and Course-Integrated Instruction: The Librarian's Perspective," *Research Strategies* 7 (Fall 1989): 148-58. Appendix A of the latter contains "Rules for Effective Communication with International Students."

28. Yoshi Hendricks, "The Japanese as Library Patrons," *College & Research Libraries News* 52 (April 1991): 221-25.

29. *Literacy, Economy and Society: Results of the First International Adult Literacy Survey* (Ottawa, Ont.: Statistics Canada and the Organisation for Economic Co-operation and Development, 1995), 199p.

30. Ibid., 57.

31. Ibid., 61.

32. Jonathan Kozol, *Illiterate America* (New York: New American Library, 1985), 4.

33. "International Adult Literacy," *ETS Policy Notes* (Princeton, N.J.: Educational Testing Service, 1996). Available: http://www.ets.org/research/pic/ials.html.

34. "Library-Based Literacy Programs Enrich Cultural Life of Communities," *Literacy Update* 7 (March/April 1998). Available: http://www.lacnyc.org/pubs/update/Apr98/library13.htm.

35. Debra Wilcox Johnson with Jennifer A. Soule, *Libraries and Literacy: A Planning Manual* (Chicago: American Library Association, 1987), 31.

36. Laubach Literacy, 1320 Jamesville Avenue, Syracuse, N.Y. 13210, 315-422-9121. Available: http://www.laubach.org; Literacy Volunteers of America, 635 James St., Syracuse, NY, 13203-2214, 315-472-0001. Available: http://www.literacyvolunteers.org.

37. Nauratil, *Public Libraries and Nontraditional Clienteles,* 90.

38. U.S. Equal Employment Opportunity Commission and the U.S. Department of Justice, *Americans with Disabilities Act Handbook* (Washington, D.C.: Government Printing Office, 1992), 1.

39. Michael G. Gunde, "Working with the Americans with Disabilities Act," *Library Journal* 116 (December 1991): 99.

40. Katy Lenn, "Library Services to Disabled Students: Outreach and Education," *The Reference Librarian* 53 (1996): 14.

41. Jill Mendle, "Library Services for Persons with Disabilities," *The Reference Librarian* 49/50 (1995): 118.

42. Association of Research Libraries, "Library Services for Persons with Disabilities," *SPEC Kit* 176 (July/August 1991): 7.

43. Steven J. Herman, "Information Center Profile: Library of Congress Division for the Blind and Physically Handicapped," in *Library Services to the Blind and Physically Handicapped*, ed. Maryalls G. Strom (Metuchen, N.J.: Scarecrow Press, 1977), 5.

44. National Library Service for the Blind and Physically Handicapped, *Digital Talking Books: Planning for the Future* (Washington, D.C.: Library of Congress, July 1998). Available: http://www.loc.gov/nls/dtb.html.

45. American Foundation for the Blind, *Optical Character Recognition Systems* (New York: AFB, May 1999). Available: http://www.afb.org/technology/fs_ocr.html.

46. Barbara T. Mates, *Library Technologies for Visually and Physically Impaired Patrons* (Westport, Conn.: Meckler, 1991), 190p.

47. Carol Casey, "Accessibility in the Virtual Library: Creating Equal Opportunity Web Sites," *Information Technology & Libraries* 18 (March 1999): 22-25.

48. Kieth C. Wright and Judith F. Davie, *Library and Information Services for Handicapped Individuals*, 2d ed. (Littleton, Colo.: Libraries Unlimited, 1983), 66.

49. *American with Disabilities Act Handbook,* [n.p.]

50. Ibid., 123-24.

51. Elizabeth H. Oakes and John Bradford, eds., *Resources for People with Disabilities: A National Directory* (Chicago: Ferguson Publishing, 1998), 2 vols., 1026p.

52. Gail A. Schlachter and R. David Weber, eds., *Financial Aid for the Disabled and Their Families: 2000–2002* (El Dorado Hills, Calif.: Reference Service Press, 2000), 483p.

53. Linda Lucas Walling and Marilyn M. Irwin, eds., *Information Services for People with Developmental Disabilities: The Library Manager's Handbook* (Westport, Conn.: Greenwood Press, 1995), 4.

54. Thomas E. Hecker, "Patrons with Disabilities or Problem Patrons: Which Model Should Librarians Apply to People with Mental Illness?" *The Reference Librarian* 53 (1996): 5-12.

55. Ibid., 10.

56. *Statistical Abstract of the United States 1999,* table 14.

57. Carol Collier Kuhlthau, "Meeting the Informational Needs of Children and Young Adults: Basing Library Media Programs on Developmental States," *Journal of Youth Services in Libraries* 2 (Fall 1988): 51-57.

58. Vicky L. Crosson, "Hey! Kids Are Patrons, Too!" *Texas Libraries* 52 (Summer 1991): 50.

59. Christine Behrmann and Dolores Vogliano, "On Training the Children's Reference Librarian," *Illinois Libraries* 73 (February 1991): 152-57.

60. See, for example, American Association of School Librarians and Association for Educational Communications and Technology, *Information Literacy Standards for Student Learning* (Chicago: American Library Association, 1998), 48p.; Patricia Senn Breivik, *Information Literacy: Educating Children for the 21st Century* (New York: Scholastic, 1994), 198p.; James C. Thompson, "Resource-Based Learning Can Be the Backbone of Reform, Improvement," *NAASP Bulletin* 75 (May 1991): 24-28; Carol-Ann Haycock, "Resource-Based Learning: A Shift in the Roles of Teacher, Learner," *NAASP Bulletin* 75 (May 1991): 15-22; and Michael B. Eisenberg and Ruth V. Small, "Information-Based Education: An Investigation of the Nature and Role of Information Attributes in Education," *Information Processing & Management* 29 (March-April 1993): 263-75.

61. Janice N. Harrington, "Reference Service in the Children's Department: A Case Study," *Public Library Quarterly* 6 (Fall 1985): 65-77.

62. Ibid., 73.

63. Ibid., 75.

64. Gertrude B. Herman, "What Time Is It in Antarctica? Meeting the Information Needs of Children," *The Reference Librarian* 7/8 (Spring/Summer 1983): 77; Harrington, "Reference Service," 73.

65. Elizabeth Overmyer, "Serving the Reference Needs of Children," *Wilson Library Bulletin* 69 (June 1995): 141.

66. Paula Busey and Tom Doerr, "Kid's Catalog: An Information Retrieval System for Children," *Journal of Your Services in Libraries* 7 (Fall 1993): 77-84. See also the CARL Web site at http://www.carl.org.

67. Joyce Kasman Valenza, *Power Tools: 100 + Essential Forms and Presentations for Your School Library Information Program* (Chicago: American Library Association, 1998), 1.16.

68. American Library Association Intellectual Freedom Committee, *Statement on Internet Filtering,* (July 1, 1997). Available: http://www.ala.org/alaorg/oif/filt_stm.html.

69. "Abused and Neglected Child Reporting Act," *Illinois Revised Statutes*, 1987 23: 2054.

70. Linda Ward Callaghan, "Children's Questions: Reference Interviews with the Young," *The Reference Librarian* 7/8 (Spring/Summer 1983): 55.

71. American Association of School Librarians and the Association for Educational Communications and Technology, *Information Power: Building Partnerships for Learning* (Chicago: American Library Association, 1998), 89.

72. Patricia Payne, "Narrowing the Gap Between Library Instruction and Functional Library Literacy," *The Reference Librarian* 7/8 (Spring/Summer 1983): 115.

73. Leslie Edmonds, Paula Moore, and Kathleen Mahaffey Balcom, "The Effectiveness of an Online Catalog," *School Library Journal* 36 (October 1990): 28-32.

74. AASL and AECT, *Information Literacy Standards for Student Learning.*

75. Sheila Heaviside et al., *Services and Resources for Children and Young Adults in Public Libraries* (Washington, D.C.: National Center for Education Statistics, Office of Educational Research and Improvement, August 1995), 3.

76. Ibid., 11.

77. Ibid., 10

78. Ibid., 37.

79. Ibid.

80. Mary K. Chelton, "Young Adult Reference Service in the Public Library," *The Reference Librarian* 7/8 (Spring/Summer 1983): 35.

81. AASL and AECT, *Information Literacy Standards for Student Learning.*

82. Anita C. Bell, "A Term Paper Resource Center," *School Library Journal* 38 (January 1992): 34-36.

83. See Walter Minkel and Roxanne Hsu Feldman, *Delivering Web Reference Services to Young People* (Chicago: American Library Association, 1999), 121p., for an in-depth description of designing a homework reference site.

84. Debra Kachel, "Document Delivery and School Libraries," *Wilson Library Bulletin* 67 (February 1993): 45-48, 112.

85. Helma Hawkins, "Opening the Closet Door: Public Library Services for Gay, Lesbian, & Bisexual Teens," *Colorado Libraries* 20 (Spring 1994): 28.

86. Tom Hindman, "Dear Amy," *Voice of Youth Advocates* 13 (June 1990): 91-92.

87. Chelton, "Young Adult Reference Service," 32.

88. Dorothy M. Broderick, "On My Mind," *Voice of Youth Advocates* 11 (August 1988): 116.

89. Pam Spencer, *What Do Young Adults Read Next? A Reader's Guide to Fiction for Young Adults*, 3 vols. (Detroit: Gale, 1994-1999).

90. Charles A. Bunge, "Factors Related to Output Measures for Reference Service in Public Libraries: Data from Thirty-Six Libraries," *Public Libraries* 29 (January/February 1990): 42-47. For further commentary related to young adult reference services, see Carolyn Caywood, "Quality Reference Service," *School Library Journal* 37 (November 1991): 62.

91. David P. Snider, "Eggs to Omelets Without Eggshells," *The Reference Librarian* 7/8 (Spring/Summer 1983): 99.

92. Mary K. Chelton and James M. Rosignia, *Bare Bones: Young Adult Services Tips for Public Library Generalists* (Chicago: American Library Association, 1993), 30.

93. Ibid., 32.

94. Virginia A. Walter, *Output Measures for Public Library Service to Children: A Manual of Standardized Procedures* (Chicago: American Library Association, 1992), 50-54; and Virginia A. Walter, *Output Measures and More: Planning and Evaluating Public Library Services for Young Adults* (Chicago: American Library Association, 1995), 68-72.

95. Rosemarie Riechel, *Reference Services for Children and Young Adults* (Hamden, Conn.: Library Professional Publications, 1991), 219p.

96. Ibid., 3.

97. Heaviside et al., *Services and Resources for Children and Young Adults,* iii.

98. Nancy P. Zimmerman, "Compromise in the Information Age: The Attitudes of School Library Media Specialists Toward Technology," *Journal of Youth Services in Libraries* 6 (Spring 1993): 307.

99. Riechel, *Reference Services for Children and Young Adults,* 127.

100. *Statistical Abstract of the United States 1999,* table 14.

101. Ibid., table 24.

102. Diana S. Woodruf-Pak, "Aging and Intelligence: Changing Perspectives," in *Information and Aging,* ed. Betty J. Turock (Jefferson, N.C.: McFarland, 1988), 18-19.

103. *Statistical Abstract of the United States 1999,* table 50.

104. Ibid., table 85.

105. Celia Hales-Mabry, *The World of the Aging: Information Needs and Choices* (Chicago: American Library Association, 1993), 126.

106. Reference and User Services Association, American Library Association, *Library Services to Older Adults Guidelines* (1999). Available: http://www.ala.org/rusa/stnd_older.html.

107. Ken Skala, *American Guidance for Seniors . . . and Their Caregivers* (Chevy Chase, Md.: Key Communications Group, 1998), 560p.

108. *Resource Directory for Older People.* (Bethesda, Md.: National Institute on Aging). Available: http://www.aoa.dhhs.gov/aoa/resource.html.

ADDITIONAL READINGS

Alire, Camila A., and Orlando Archibeque. *Serving Latino Communities: A How-To-Do-It Manual for Librarians.* New York: Neal-Schuman, 1998. 253p.

This book is an excellent practical introduction to library services for the Latino community. Chapter 7, "May I Help You? The Important Role of Library Personnel," provides valuable guidance on staff recruiting and training practices.

American Association of School Librarians and Association for Educational Communications and Technology. *Information Power: Building Partnerships for Learning.* Chicago: American Library Association, 1998. 205p.

Information Power includes the nine "Information Standards for Student Learning," which guide the development of school library media services, including reference service.

Beck, Susan Gilbert. "Technology for the Deaf: Remembering to Accommodate an Invisible Disability." *Library Hi Tech* 13, nos. 1-2 (1995): 109-22.

Beck provides an exhaustive overview of technologies, guidelines, and strategies to use in serving a population that is too often overlooked.

DeCandido, GraceAnne A. *Services to People with Disabilities.* Washington, D.C.: Association of Research Libraries, 1999. 31p. (SPEC Kit 243).

This report profiles services to users with disabilities in selected university libraries and identifies online resources.

Deines-Jones, Courtney, and Connie Van Fleet. *Preparing Staff to Serve Patrons with Disabilities.* New York: Neal-Schuman, 1995. 143p.

Chapter 2 of this volume in Neal-Schuman's How-to-Do-It series covers readers' advisory and reference services. Chapter 7 is on the special needs of senior citizens.

Gough, Cal, and Ellen Greenblatt, eds. *Gay and Lesbian Library Service.* Jefferson, N.C.: McFarland, 1990. 355p.

The main focus of this book is collection development, but chapter 9 addresses service issues and the "user-friendliness" of the library to gay and lesbian users. In this chapter as well as in chapter 7, which is on the evolution of gay and lesbian-related topics in the Library of Congress Subject Headings, the authors discuss intellectual access issues.

Hales-Mabry, Celia. *The World of the Aging: Information Needs and Choices.* Chicago: American Library Association, 1993. 187p.

Hales-Mabry provides comprehensive coverage of the information needs of older adults. She considers the information-seeking patterns of older adults, ways to serve older adults with special needs, and how information receipt is affected by physiological, psychological, and sociological influences.

"Information Literacy." *NASSP Bulletin* 83 (March 1999): 1-90.

This theme issue describes the AASL Information Literacy standards for an audience of school leaders and administrators. Eleven articles contributed by distinguished practitioners and researchers present topics such as the collaborative role of the school library media specialist and the importance of integrating information literacy skills into the curriculum.

Katz, Bill, ed. *Information Seeking Patterns: Diverse Populations.* New York: Haworth Press, 1995. 346p. (Also published in *The Reference Librarian* 49/50 [1995]: entire issue.)

This collection includes several important articles: "Library Services for Persons with Disabilities," by Jill Mendle; "Ethnicity and Information Seeking," by Mengxiong Liu (see annotation below): "Knowledge Gap, Information-Seeking and the Poor," by Elfreda A. Chatman and Victoria E. M. Pendleton; "A Matter of Focus: Reference Services for Older Adults," by Connie Van Fleet (see annotation below): "Kids Count: Using Output Measures to Monitor Children's Use of Reference Services," by Virginia A. Walter; and "Women Library Users and Library Users of Traditional Women's Subjects," by Geraldine B. King.

Katz, Bill, ed. *Reference Services for the Unserved.* New York: Haworth Press, 1996. 157p. (Also published in *The Reference Librarian* 53 [1996]: entire issue).

Guest edited by Fay Zipkowitz, this volume includes articles on library services to students with disabilities, individuals with mental illness, and battered women. It also contains an annotated bibliography on library services to traditionally underserved groups.

Liu, Mengxiong. "Ethnicity and Information Seeking." *The Reference Librarian* 49/50 (1995): 123-34.

This article summarizes characteristics of multi-ethnic groups in the information-seeking process and suggests effective techniques for improving communication, meeting goals of diversity in reference service, developing needs assessments and outreach programs, improving staff training and recruitment, and planning other special programs.

Minkel, Walter, and Roxanne Hsu Feldman. *Delivering Web Reference Services to Young People.* Chicago: American Library Association, 1999. 121p.

Minkel and Feldman offer a no-nonsense guide designed to help librarians hone their Web reference skills and provide developmentally appropriate Web services for youth. Their guidance on developing "Webliographies" for public library Web pages is especially valuable.

Quezada, Shelley. *Developing Literacy Programs in Small and Medium-Sized Libraries.* Chicago: Library Administration and Management Association/American Library Association, 1996. 14p.

This brief guide presents a rationale for the provision of literacy programs in libraries and outlines specific steps in the development of this service. Quezada covers issues ranging from staff training to materials selection.

Riechel, Rosemarie. *Reference Services for Children and Young Adults.* Hamden, Conn.: Library Professional Publications, 1991. 219p.

Riechel provides a portrait of reference service practices, policies, and procedures for children and young adults in school library media centers and public libraries. She identifies the problems and service shortcomings that were revealed during the course of her research.

Van Fleet, Connie. "A Matter of Focus: Reference Services for Older Adults." *The Reference Librarian* 49/50 (1995): 147-64.

Van Fleet covers reference interview skills, the information needs of older adults, and targeting special library services for users over the age of 50.

Walling, Linda Lucas, and Marilyn M. Irwin, eds. *Information Services for People with Developmental Disabilities: The Library Manager's Handbook.* Westport, Conn.: Greenwood Press, 1995. 344p.

This volume describes developmental disabilities as well as the range of existing support systems before launching into a thorough treatment of library and information systems for this user group.

Weibel, Marguerite Crowley. *The Library as Literacy Classroom: A Program for Teaching.* Chicago: American Library Association, 1992. 300p.

This detailed handbook opens with an insightful quote from a literacy student who wonders why class is held at the library and then realizes that the library is "where you go to read." Weibel describes methods that draw on the full richness of library services and collections.

PART

II

INFORMATION SOURCES AND THEIR USE

CHAPTER
13

SELECTION AND EVALUATION OF REFERENCE SOURCES

Linda C. Smith

REFERENCE SOURCES

Part I of this text introduces the variety of services provided by reference librarians in all types of libraries and information centers. Essential to the provision of services is a carefully selected collection of sources. This chapter introduces the types of sources used most frequently in reference work and discusses reference collection development and maintenance. This includes consideration of the criteria used to evaluate sources as well as reviewing media and guides to reference materials useful in collection development. Discussion encompasses both well-established reference sources and approaches to collection development, as well as responses to the newly emerging challenges posed by freely available Internet resources. The remaining chapters in Part II discuss the characteristics and uses of particular types of reference sources.

What Is a Reference Source?

In considering selection and evaluation of materials for the reference collection, it is helpful first to attempt to characterize the types of materials most commonly included in reference collections. *The ALA Glossary of Library and Information Science* offers the following definitions of *reference book*: "1. A book designed by the arrangement and treatment of its subject matter to be consulted for definite items of information rather than to be read consecutively. 2. A book whose use is restricted to the library building."[1] Marcia Bates labels these definitions *functional* and *administrative*.[2] She further clarifies the concept of a reference book by describing in greater detail the arrangement and indexing that typically characterize the presentation of information in reference books. Bill Katz provides a history of the development of each of the standard categories of reference books, from encyclopedias to bibliographies, showing the relationship to intellectual and technological developments.[3]

As described in Chapter 1, reference librarians must be able to respond to a wide variety of questions, such as ready-reference or research, depending on the needs expressed by library users. Increasingly, the concept of a *reference collection* made up of reference *books* is an inadequate characterization of the resources most frequently used by reference librarians. *Harrod's Librarians' Glossary and Reference Book* defines the broader concept of *reference source*: "any material, published work, database, web site, etc. which is used to obtain authoritative information."[4] Thus, although print materials continue to be important, they are supplemented by materials in microform, CD-ROM, or electronic resources accessed via computers and network connections. With the availability of a growing number of freely available resources on the Internet, it is limiting to think of the reference collection as only those materials that are purchased or licensed by the library. Nevertheless, reference librarians still have a responsibility to identify resources of value for reference work, possibly selecting a "virtual reference collection" to supplement the material housed in the reference section of the library. Where the same title is available in alternative formats, a choice must be made as to which one(s) will be most useful. Reference librarians must also monitor the growing availability of all types of materials in electronic form, as their enhanced searching, retrieval, and display capabilities may make them useful in answering reference questions even though they are not reference sources per se.

Types of Sources

As noted, one way to categorize reference sources is by format: print, microform, distributed electronic format such as CD-ROM, or electronically accessible over a network. Alternatively, it is possible to divide reference sources into two main classes: compilations that furnish information directly and compilations that refer to other sources containing information, merely indicating places in which information may be found. In practice, this distinction becomes blurred because sources of the first type often refer to others for fuller information, and those of the second type are adequate for answering some questions. Sources of the first type include encyclopedias, dictionaries, almanacs, handbooks, yearbooks, biographical sources, directories, atlases, and gazetteers; sources of the second type include catalogs, bibliographies, and indexes. Each of these is the subject of one of the remaining chapters in this book. In addition, government publications, which frequently constitute unique sources of information, are treated in a separate chapter. Although not the subject of a separate chapter in this book, pamphlets and clippings files are often part of the reference collection, organized by subject in a vertical file. Such collections tend to feature items of local interest, selected for their potential reference value.[5] Increasingly reference librarians are building Web sites to link to this type of information in electronic form.

REFERENCE COLLECTION DEVELOPMENT AND MAINTENANCE

The work of reference librarians includes selection of an adequate and suitable collection of reference sources and arrangement and maintenance of the collection so that it can be used easily and conveniently. Unplanned collection development and neglect of weeding can impair the efficiency of reference services. Records of unanswered questions are one means of identifying deficiencies in the existing collection.

Components of the Collection

Because reference collections now include materials in a variety of formats, the reference librarian must decide whether to acquire particular titles in more than one format. At present, many titles exist in only one format, be it print, microform, or electronic. Others are available in several different formats. For example, to aid in locating residential telephone numbers, one can purchase print telephone directories, *Phonefiche* in microform, a compilation of directories on CD-ROM, or use one of the many freely available telephone directory services on the Web. Although the different formats may be identical or at least overlapping in content, they may differ in search capabilities.

The greater flexibility of searching electronic resources has led some to predict that there will be increasing migration from print to electronic sources, with libraries canceling subscriptions to print indexes, for example, in favor of online or CD-ROM access. Librarians must weigh such factors as relative costs, amount of use, and likely users and uses in deciding which formats to acquire. These decisions must be continuously reviewed as new titles become available in electronic formats.[6]

Reference Collection Development

Increased costs of reference sources and proliferation of formats and titles have focused attention on the importance of a systematic approach to reference collection development. Librarians have more options than ever before in creating a reference collection that is responsive to the needs of the community served. Many of the sources described in this text commonly form the core of a library's reference collection, but other titles in a specific collection will vary depending on local needs.

Decisions in collection development include whether to buy newly published titles, buy new editions of titles already in the collection, cancel a title that is now freely accessible on the Web, continue serials such as indexes, contract with vendors for online access or acquire CD-ROMs or load databases locally, and coordinate collection development with other libraries to ensure the availability of at least one copy of an expensive set in a particular geographic area or take advantage of consortial pricing arrangements. A written collection development policy can provide guidance in making these decisions and will help in establishing and maintaining an effective reference collection. Sydney Pierce suggests that developing a reference collection development policy requires the reference staff to identify the objectives to be met by the collection and to define the content of the collection: the nature and organization of its different parts, criteria for placing materials in each part, and formats and degree of duplication desired for reference materials.[7]

Surveys indicate that many libraries do not have written collection development policies.[8] Chapter 2 of Christopher Nolan's text on managing the reference collection outlines possible elements of a reference collection development policy,[9] including: (1) an introduction, relating reference collection development to the library's overall collection development plan; (2) scope of the collection; (3) staff responsibilities; (4) selection criteria; (5) any special policies; (6) sources of funds for the purchase of reference sources; and (7) external relationships, the library's position on working with other libraries for reference collection support. Examples of policies are available in the literature to provide some guidance.[10]

Maintaining the collection is an ongoing process. For example, to provide accurate information in response to questions regarding current addresses, telephone numbers, and statistical data, it is important to have the latest available edition of a tool in the collection and to be aware of the Web resources that may have even more current information. Publishers' announcements and reviews can alert the librarian to the availability of new titles and new editions; publishers' Web sites can also be perused.[11] Regular inventory of the reference collection is needed to identify areas that require updating or strengthening. Chapter 10 provides more discussion of the evaluation of reference collections.

Arrangement of the Collection

Just as different libraries have somewhat different sets of titles making up their reference collections, there are different possible arrangements of titles. One possibility is to maintain a classified arrangement regardless of type. An alternative is to group types of sources together, creating sections for encyclopedias, biographical sources, directories, indexes, and so forth. Most collections designate a portion of the titles as ready-reference because of the frequency with which they are consulted and the need for rapid access to their contents. These titles are often kept at or near the reference or information desk.

It is difficult to integrate sources requiring special equipment, such as microform readers or computer workstations and CD-ROM drives, with other titles of the same type or in the same subject area. Whatever arrangement is chosen, consideration must be given to ease of access by the library user as well as the reference librarian. Special signage or handouts may be required to orient the library user to the location of particular sections of the collection.

With the increasing availability of resources in electronic form, reference librarians are often involved in library projects to design the interface or gateway to orient library users to available resources and aid in their selection. As discussed in Chapter 5, the familiar orienting devices of physical collections now need to be supplemented by approaches to guiding navigation and selection via the interface to these electronic resources.

Weeding the Collection

There must be a systematic basis for weeding (i.e., deselection, pruning, deacquisition[12]) as well as for adding new titles to the collection. A reference librarian should discard materials in the same way that they are chosen: by taking into account what is already in the collection and what is actually needed for reference work. Weeding keeps the collection from becoming a depository of out-of-date materials and reduces the danger of giving incorrect information from dated sources. Factors affecting weeding include frequency of use, age of material, physical condition, arrival of a new edition that supersedes a volume already on the shelf, and the need for space. Weeded materials may be placed in the circulating collection or discarded, depending on their possible continuing value to users. For example, old directories might be used for historical research. Different types of materials will require different guidelines for retention. Lynn Westbrook provides guidelines for weeding reference serials,[13] and William Katz lists general guidelines for various types of reference sources.[14] For example, Katz notes that almanacs, yearbooks, and manuals are usually superseded by the next edition. However, because the information in each is rarely duplicated exactly, he suggests keeping old editions for at least five years and preferably ten. With the growing emphasis on electronic resources in reference collections, librarians must devote increasing attention to policies for retaining access to materials in this form.[15]

EVALUATION OF SOURCES

In building the reference collection, the librarian must evaluate the quality of individual sources and their suitability for inclusion in the library's reference collection. Although evaluation criteria were originally developed for print sources, they are also applicable to nonprint sources, such as microforms and databases. It may be more difficult to apply some of the criteria to electronic and other nonprint sources, however, because such media cannot be examined directly in the same way that one handles print sources. The criteria covered in this chapter and listed in Box 13.1 apply to all types of reference sources; Chapters 14 through 22 include sections on evaluation of particular types of sources and highlight the criteria of special importance for those types. By considering these evaluation criteria, the librarian will be better able to judge whether a particular source meets the needs of the library and its users and is worthy of purchase or licensing using the limited funds available for reference collection development.

The focus in this chapter is on evaluation of individual titles. Although databases are not yet reviewed as extensively as print sources, a number of authors have proposed criteria for evaluating CD-ROM and online databases, as well as Web resources, and these are incorporated in the following discussion.[16] Lynne Martin provides an interesting evaluation of online catalogs as reference tools using similar criteria.[17]

Box 13. 1 Evaluation Criteria

Format
 print/microform/electronic, physical makeup, illustrations

Scope
 purpose, coverage, currency

Relation to similar works
 uniqueness, spinoffs, new editions

Authority
 authorship, publisher/sponsor, sources of information

Treatment
 accuracy, objectivity, style/audience

Arrangement
 sequence, indexing

Special features

Cost
 price, licensing conditions

Format

When reviewing print sources, one is concerned with the physical makeup and features of the book, such as binding, paper, typeface, and layout. If a print source includes illustrations, one must judge their quality and relationship to the text. Recent reference publishing has placed increasing emphasis on visual material.[18] Print sources have the advantages of being straightforward to use, predictable in cost, and usable by more than one person simultaneously if a multivolume set. Disadvantages include the space required to house print sources, the problem in maintaining their currency, and the limitations on search strategies.

Microform formats may prove satisfactory for sources with short entries and alphabetical arrangements, such as bibliographies and directories. Microforms can save space and are a recognized medium for preserving content that has continuing value. Disadvantages include equipment costs and maintenance, the need for user orientation, the limit to one user at a time per viewer, and the limitations on search strategies.

CD-ROMs allow complex searching and store large amounts of information. The introduction of multimedia CD-ROMs and DVD technology means that they now can store images and sound in addition to text and numerical data.[19] (As with illustrations in print sources, the quality and reference value of such images and sound should be assessed.) On the other hand, CD-ROMs may be expensive, somewhat slow to search, and variable in ease of use because interfaces are not standard. They may lack currency, and they require work space for equipment.

As do CD-ROMs, online databases and Web resources support flexibility and complexity in searching and may contain large amounts of information. In addition, they can be updated more frequently than CD-ROMs. Limitations of online access to commercial databases include unpredictable costs (unless databases are locally loaded or licensed to allow unlimited use), the need for equipment, and the frequent need for special training to use search systems effectively. Web resources may vary in usability and stability. These advantages and disadvantages must be weighed when evaluating a reference source in one or more formats.

Scope

One indication of scope is the statement of purpose, generally found in the preface of print reference sources. In evaluating a source, it is necessary to judge to what extent the statement of purpose is fulfilled in the text. Has the author or editor accomplished what was intended? Aspects of scope include subject and geographical coverage. Time period coverage is also important for many reference works. How current are the contents? For a serial publication, how frequently is it updated? What is the language of publication? Print sources can be examined to assess the various parameters that define the work's scope, but evaluations of electronic sources may have to rely more on documentation—written descriptions that attempt to characterize the coverage of the source. Sample searches can be done to probe various aspects of the scope, but it may be difficult to develop as thorough an understanding of the source's scope as is possible with a print tool, where this "metainformation" about scope is contained in a clearly identifiable preface. Péter Jacsó provides a thorough review of approaches to assessing database scope.[20] Factors to consider include size of the database, the number of sources and time period covered, unique content when compared to other databases, and geographic and language coverage.

When the same source exists in different formats, currency may vary. Online sources are often more current than print and CD-ROM sources. There are many exceptions, however, so the librarian should investigate relative currency for each source being evaluated. Resources providing links to Web sites can suffer from "linkrot" (when URLs given are no longer correct) unless an effort is made to update them on a regular basis.[21]

Relation to Similar Works

A newly published title may have different types of relationships to sources already in the collection. These need to be taken into account when assessing the potential value of a new title to the collection. One obvious category is a new edition of a title already held. In this case, it is necessary to assess the extent of revision in the new edition. Is it sufficient to warrant purchase? Another category is works of similar scope. To what extent is there overlap in content, and to what extent is there unique information? If there is overlap in content, is information more easily found in the new source? Is it written for a different audience? Reference book publishers may issue spinoffs from large sets, such as a one-volume physics encyclopedia with articles selected from a multivolume encyclopedia of science and technology. Although the one-volume encyclopedia might be useful in a branch library that does not own the parent set, it would duplicate information already found in a collection that contains the original set.

With the availability of electronic counterparts, whether online or on CD-ROM, for many print tools, it is important to assess the extent to which the content corresponds. For example, there are often differences in time period covered. At times, there is more information in electronic formats because it is easy to store additional information in them. In some cases, the same database is available from different publishers of CD-ROMs or online vendors; thus, it is necessary to consider differences in search capabilities and coverage.

Authority

Indicators of authority include the education and experience of the editors and contributors, as indicated by degrees earned and organizational affiliations. The reputation of the publisher or sponsoring agency is also an indicator. Certain publishers are well established as sources of quality reference materials. Many reference sources include lists of material used in compiling the source. These lists can be used as an indicator of the authority of the work, as well as being leads to additional sources of information. It may be easier to evaluate the authority of print reference sources, because statements of authorship and lists of references can be easily identified. If a CD-ROM or online database has a print counterpart, authority can likewise be judged. When there is no print counterpart, it may be necessary to judge authority from statements presented in the documentation describing the electronic source.

Treatment

Accuracy is important in reference works. How reliable are the facts presented?[22] How "dirty" is a database? Are there misspelled words,[23] missing data elements, or inconsistent formatting of parts of the record such as author names? Objectivity can be assessed by examining the coverage of controversial issues and the balance in coverage given to various subjects. Because reference works can be addressed to particular audiences, it is important to determine who can best use the work: layperson or scholar, adult or child.[24] Reviewing topics on which one has personal knowledge allows one to assess the accuracy and quality of writing.[25] Again, this type of review may be easier to accomplish with print sources than with those on CD-ROM or online.

Arrangement

Print and microform sources arrange entries in a particular sequence, such as alphabetical, chronological, or classified. If the sequence is a familiar one, such as alphabetical, the user of the source may be able to directly find the information sought rather than first having to look up the location in an index. The flexibility of a reference source is typically enhanced by the availability of indexes offering different types of access to the information. In addition, the text itself may offer leads to additional information in the form of cross-references to related entries. In general, electronic sources offer many different indexes to the contents of a database. These may allow the reference librarian to answer questions that cannot be answered in a print source because neither the primary arrangement of entries nor the indexes offer the needed point of access. For example, although a print bibliography may allow one to search by author, title, and subject, a publisher index is not likely to be provided. In an online or CD-ROM version of the bibliography, however, *publisher* could be a searchable data element, allowing one to locate easily the list of items in the bibliography issued by a particular publisher.

Special Features

One will always be interested in identifying any special features that distinguish a given reference source from others. CD-ROM sources have many possible variations in design because the databases are sold with software for searching the contents and displaying the information. A further complicating factor is that many publishers attempt to improve their existing products by identifying factors that might enhance their usability. Any new developments that make database searching easier and more accessible to users will affect the choice among products. In addition, in the case of electronic sources, one must consider the quality of available documentation,[26] training, and customer support. For Web resources, effective use of hyperlinks may add to a source's value.

Cost

The costs of print sources and sources in distributed electronic formats (e.g., CD-ROM) are similar in that a copy is acquired for in-house use in the library, and the purchase or subscription price buys unlimited access to the contents of the source. Pricing of online databases follows a variety of models, from a charge per use to subscription with unlimited access for authorized users. Pricing may depend on the size of potential user populations, ownership of print equivalents, number of simultaneous users of the resource, and whether the library is licensing the database as part of a consortium or individually. In assessing cost, the reference librarian must try to determine if the price is appropriate in relation to the need and the anticipated frequency and length of use. In the case of nonprint sources, costs include purchase and maintenance of equipment to make the contents accessible. One may also want to consider the costs in terms of the staff support needed to allow users to make use of a nonprint source.

Access to electronic resources often takes place within the confines of a license that defines appropriate use over a specific period of time. Selection of such resources and negotiation of licensing agreements should consider whether the rights assigned by the license are adequate for the library's purposes.[27] Although reference librarians may not be involved directly in negotiating licenses, they should provide input reflecting the needs of library users. Once resources have been licensed for use, reference librarians need to understand how the content may be used (i.e., what is considered fair use), how the content may be accessed (only within the library or also remotely), and who is defined as an authorized "user." As electronic resource publishers try to earn revenue based on levels of use of their products, libraries are having to make decisions about how many simultaneous users they can afford to support as they negotiate licensing agreements for database access. Usage data can help fine-tune these decisions as licenses come up for renewal.[28]

VIRTUAL REFERENCE COLLECTION DEVELOPMENT

Discussion to this point has emphasized the key role of the reference librarian in building collections of purchased or licensed materials. As explained in Chapter 5, with the advent of the open environment of the Web, where many different organizations and individuals create sites that are freely accessible, it is necessary to expand the well-established notions of reference sources and reference collections to encompass these new resources. When connecting to the Web via a browser and Internet connection, one has access to everything that has been made freely available on the Web.

Two examples can be used to illustrate this change. *Books in Print*, long a standard tool for verifying basic bibliographic information about books in print, now competes with the descriptive and review information about books found on the Web at the sites of Internet booksellers such as Amazon.com (http://www.amazon.com) or Barnes & Noble (http://www.books.com).[29] Many associations of all types now have their own Web sites with much more detailed information than that found in widely used directories of associations such as *Encyclopedia of Associations*. Elizabeth Thomsen suggests that librarians need to examine all areas of their collections to make sure that they are still worth the time and money invested to maintain them.[30] Reference librarians must determine whether such special collections as vertical files, college catalogs, company annual reports, and telephone books can now be replaced with access to resources available on the Web.

Rather than relying solely on search engines, which do not automatically differentiate the authoritative sites from the rest, reference librarians can exercise the same type of selectivity that they do in building physical reference collections by building virtual collections. Librarians can develop special guides for users of their own libraries. Once published on the Web, they are available to a much wider audience as well. There is a growing body of literature providing guidance on developing such virtual reference collections.[31] For example, Diane K. Kovacs identifies tools helpful in developing such a collection and lists a core ready-reference collection of Web resources including directories, dictionaries, encyclopedias, news sources, and legal and statistical information.[32] The Internet Public Library Ready Reference Collection (http://www.ipl.org/ref/RR) is one example of a virtual reference collection; furthermore, many different subject areas now have their own quality-controlled subject gateways.[33]

SELECTION AIDS

A number of tools are available to assist the reference librarian in evaluating sources for possible inclusion in the library's reference collection. Reviewing sources, varying in frequency from semimonthly to annual, offer critical reviews of newly published titles. Although most titles covered are in print format, reviewing sources are including increasing numbers of nonprint titles as well. To identify gaps in existing collections, guides to reference sources can be used. These guides are also valuable as aids in identifying likely sources for answering particular reference questions (as described in Chapter 4). Both current reviewing media and guides to reference sources are helpful to librarians in developing collections on which effective service is based, but they are no substitute for informed judgment in selection of titles best suited to the library's users. This requires a thorough knowledge of the library's existing reference collection and user needs.

Reviewing Sources

Because it is impossible to examine all books before purchase, several reviewing sources are useful to the librarian in identifying and evaluating new titles. Analyses of these sources demonstrate that they differ in number of titles covered and that each covers some unique titles.[34] Thus, it is worthwhile to monitor several of these sources for reviews of reference materials. One difficulty with reviews is the time lag in appearance of reviews following publication of the reference work. Generally, the more thorough the review, the longer the time lag. The frequency of publication of the reviewing sources also influences time lag.

Reference Books Bulletin appears in the semimonthly issues of *Booklist.* It provides long, comprehensive, and evaluative reviews prepared by members of the American Library Association's Reference Books Bulletin Editorial Board or by guest reviewers and revised by the board as a whole.[35] Major new reference sources in English are analyzed at length, and many additional titles, as well as selected revisions of standard works, are also evaluated. In recent years, an annual review of general encyclopedias has been included, and reviews of selected electronic sources have been introduced. Reprints of *Reference Books Bulletin* are issued annually, and selected reviews can be found on the *Booklist* Web site (http://www.ala.org/booklist/index.html).

In contrast to the lengthy reviews found in *Reference Books Bulletin*, *Library Journal* includes a section of brief, signed reference book reviews in each issue. Books reviewed are generally suitable for public and college libraries. There is a regular column on "Database & Disc Reviews" for commercial products, as well as "WebWatch," which highlights free quality Web sites in a particular subject area (also found on the *Library Journal* Web site at http://www.libraryjournal.com). A supplement to the November 15 issue now highlights new and forthcoming reference sources in both print and electronic formats. *Choice*, focusing on books suitable for undergraduate collections and published eleven times per year, often reviews more specialized titles than does *Library Journal.* Each *Choice* issue has a section of signed reviews of reference books and electronic resources, and reviewers are encouraged to compare the title being reviewed with related titles. Since 1997 *Choice* has published an annual issue supplement in September devoted to Web sites of value to academic libraries. The 1999 supplement included nearly 600 sites carefully selected for quality of content and design. *Choice* is also available on the Web for a fee as *ChoiceReviews.online* (http://www.choicereviews.org) with coverage from 1988, and on CD-ROM from SilverPlatter with quarterly updates. Search options of the Web version include keyword, author, title, ISBN, reviewer, year of publication, format, and readership level. The CD-ROM product *Books in Print with Book Reviews on Disc* incorporates reviews from a number of sources, including *Booklist*, *Choice*, and *Library Journal. Reference & User Services Quarterly* (formerly *RQ*) includes critical reviews of reference books and databases in each quarterly issue. There is also a list of books received but not reviewed. Lists of titles reviewed in each issue are on the Web (http://www.ala.org/rusa/rusq/index.html).

The most comprehensive source of reviews is *American Reference Books Annual* (*ARBA*). The annual volumes aim to review all reference books published and distributed in the United States and Canada in a given year. Reference sources that are revised on a regular or continuing basis are periodically reassessed, and some CD-ROM titles are now covered. Following many of the reviews are references to additional reviews appearing in selected journals. Arrangement is classified in thirty-seven chapters in four broad categories: general reference works, social sciences, humanities, and science and technology. General reference works are further subdivided by form, such as dictionaries and encyclopedias. Subject areas are subdivided by topic, such as history and law within social sciences. The reviews, written by a pool of more than 400 subject specialists, critically evaluate each work. Each entry includes a full bibliographic citation with price, a description of the reference work, and an evaluation of content. Each volume is indexed by author/title and subject. Indexes cumulate every five years; to date, cumulations for the periods 1970–1974, 1975–1979, 1980–1984, 1985–1989, 1990–1994, and 1995–1999 are available. The 2000 volume included 1,543 reviews, bringing the total number of reviews since 1970 to 53,319.

Since 1981, a selection of reviews from *ARBA* has been published as *Recommended Reference Books for Small and Medium-sized Libraries and Media Centers*, which reprints about one-third of the year's *ARBA* reviews and tags them for type of library (college, public, or school media center). These sources allow librarians to locate new works in a given field through the subject arrangement, to consult other published reviews from citations provided, and to compare the price and coverage of reference books in a particular subject area. Multiyear compilations, highlighting titles of lasting value from *ARBA*, have also been published in a series on *Best Reference Books*, covering the periods 1970–1980, 1981–1985, and 1986–1990. *Reference Reviews Europe Annual* complements *ARBA* coverage by providing English-language reviews of European reference titles. Subscribers also have access to reviews on the Web (http://www.rre.casalini.com).

More selective lists of recommended reference sources appear annually in *American Libraries* and *Library Journal*. The list in *American Libraries* is selected by the Reference Sources Committee of the Reference and User Services Association of the American Library Association and appears in the May issue. The list in *Library Journal* is selected by experienced reference librarians and appears in the April 15 issue. These lists are helpful in identifying outstanding reference sources of potential value in many libraries. Both lists now include electronic resources in addition to print titles. The Web is also being used as a medium for distributing reviews of reference sources. *Reference Reviews*, hosted at the Gale Group Web site, currently has four parts: "Péter's Digital Reference Shelf" for reviews of online and CD-ROM products; "Reference for Students" for reviews of reference materials suitable for use by children in school and public libraries; "Lawrence Looks at Books" for reviews of reference sources for public and academic library reference collections; and the "James Rettig Archives" for titles reviewed by James Rettig from 1997 to 1999. The Machine-Assisted Reference Section (MARS) of the Reference and User Services Association has begun a project to recognize annually the Best of Free Reference Web Sites (http://www.ala.org/rusa/mars/best1999.html).

Ideally, reviews describe, evaluate, and compare new reference sources so that librarians can make informed decisions about whether to purchase the titles for their reference collections. Some researchers who have completed systematic evaluations of the various reviewing tools have expressed dissatisfaction with the contents of many reviews. James Sweetland found a general lack of comparison within reviews.[36] Most reviews were generally favorable, with few mixed reviews and fewer wholly negative ones. Some reviews were descriptive rather than evaluative, and others made recommendations that did not follow from the text of the evaluation. Overall consensus among the reviewing sources covering the same title was low. Donald Dickinson has noted the lack of reviews of foreign-language reference sources in English-language reviewing media.[37]

Nevertheless, although reviews could be improved in content and coverage, they still offer the librarian some basis for assessing new reference sources. At present, coverage of print reference books is more comprehensive than coverage of newer media such as CD-ROMs, but the reviewing sources described in this section are trying to be more responsive to the need for reviews of reference sources in all formats. Other journals can be monitored to supplement the reviews found in the primary review journals. For example, *EContent* (formerly *Database*) regularly includes reviews of electronic resources, and *College & Research Libraries News* has both a regular column of Internet Reviews[38] and topical bibliographies of "Internet Resources" (also available on the Web at http://www.ala.org/acrl/resrces.html). Online bookseller sites such as Amazon.com reprint reviews from other sources as well as including reviews contributed by users of their sites.

Guides to Reference Sources

The best-known guide to reference sources in the United States is that published by the American Library Association. *Guide to Reference Books* has served librarians since 1902, with the eleventh edition published in 1996. This compilation is frequently referred to by the name of its editor: Alice Bertha Kroeger, Isadore Gilbert Mudge, Constance M. Winchell, Eugene P. Sheehy, and, most recently, Robert Balay have served in that capacity.[39] The *Guide* now provides bibliographic information and descriptions for 15,875 English- and foreign-language reference works in all fields through 1993. Arrangement is in five major parts: part A—general reference works; part B—humanities; part C—social and behavioral sciences; part D—history and area studies; and part E—science, technology, and medicine. Within each part, entries are classified first by subject and then by form. The table of contents displays the subjects in a classified arrangement, and there is an alphabetically arranged author/title/subject index. A bullet next to a title entry indicates that at least a portion of the source is available in electronic form. Entries include complete bibliographic information, publication history (where appropriate), notes or annotations, and often a Library of Congress call number. Periodic articles describing new reference sources appear in *College & Research Libraries*.[40]

The British counterpart to *Guide to Reference Books* was edited for a number of years by A. J. Walford, but now each volume has more than one individual responsible for its compilation. Unlike the one-volume format of the *Guide to Reference Books*, *Walford's Guide to Reference Material* appears in three volumes. Volumes 2 and 3 of the seventh edition appeared in 1998 and volume 1 of the eighth edition appeared in 1999. Thus, the three books of the set differ in currency. Volume 1 covers science and technology; volume 2 covers social and historical sciences, philosophy, and religion; and volume 3 covers generalia, language and literature, and the arts. Each volume has its own indexes, which include separate author/title and subject indexes and an online and database services index. *Walford's* bases the subject arrangement of volumes on the Universal Decimal Classification, with broad subject groupings comparable to those found in the Dewey Decimal Classification. Like the ALA *Guide*, *Walford's* is international in scope, but it has better coverage of British and European titles and more evaluative annotations. *Walford's* is also moving ahead with plans for a Web-based version, scheduled to be made available in fall 2000.[41] This will allow continuous updating of the entries and inclusion of more Web-oriented material, particularly subject gateways and portals.

Although both the ALA *Guide* and *Walford's* seek to encompass works from all subject areas, they cannot cover in depth the works in any particular subject area. For this purpose, the librarian must consult guides to the literature of particular subjects, such as Hans E. Bynagle's *Philosophy: A Guide to the Reference Literature*. Such works generally serve as introductions both to the subject area and to specialized reference works within each area.

Sample pages from the ALA *Guide* and *Walford's* are reproduced in Figures 13.1 and 13.2, page 320.

Figure 13.1 Entries from *Guide to Reference Books*. 11th edition, p. 126. Reprinted with permission of the American Library Association.

Idioms and usage

Allusions—cultural, literary, biblical, and historical : a thematic dictionary / Laurence Urdang and Frederick G. Ruffner, Jr., editors, David M. Glixon, assoc. ed. 2nd ed. Detroit : Gale, c1986. 634 p. **AC65**
For annotation, *see* BE74. PN43.A4

Britannica book of English usage / ed. by Christine Timmons and Frank Gibney. Garden City, N.Y. : Doubleday/ Britannica Books, 1980. 655 p. **AC66**
Made up in part by excerpts from articles in *Encyclopaedia Britannica* and partly by new contributions. In three main sections: (1) English today and how it evolved; (2) The basic tools [with subsections on grammar, spelling, pronunciation, words and dictionaries, the library, and abbreviations]; (3) Writing and speaking effectively. Bibliography; index. PE25.B7

Bryant, Margaret M. Current American usage. N.Y. : Funk & Wagnalls, [1962]. 290 p. **AC67**
A handbook which "attempts to bring together the most recent information about frequently debated points of usage in English speech and writing."—*Introd.* Debated points in current usage are discussed with citations to dictionaries, linguistic treatments, and articles in current periodicals, as well as to special investigations made especially for use in this book. PE2835.B67

Figure 13.2 Entries from *Walford's Guide to Reference Material*. Vol. 3, 7th edition, 1998, Generalia, Language and Literature, The Arts, p. 567. Reproduced with the permission of Library Association Publishing, London.

[5373]
Wired style: principles of English usage in the digital age. Hale, C., *ed.* San Francisco, HardWired, 1996. 158p. £12. ISBN: 1888869011.
A guide to online usage derived from the in-house style guide of the computer magazine *Wired*. 8 of the 10 chapters are specialized guides or glossaries for particular areas, such as acronyms ('FWIW') and colloquialisms ('spam').
Class No: 802.0-06

South Africa

[5374]
BEETON, D.R. *and* **DORNER, H. A Dictionary of English usage in Southern Africa.** Capetown, Oxford Univ. Press, 1975. xix,196p. ISBN: 0195700694.
*c.*6,000 entries covering local South African vocabulary and idiom; mistakes and problems, both characteristically South African and common to all English speakers; problems encountered by South Africans whose native tongue is not English; departures from standard English pronunciation characteristic of South Africa. Entries include symbols indicating language of origin of a term and its degree of acceptability, plus explanatory notes. Bibliography (3p.). *Class No:* 802.0-06(680)

USA

[5375]
COPPERUD, R.H. American usage and style: the consensus. New York, Van Nostrand Reinhold, 1970. vi,433p. $21.95. ISBN: 0422249068.
Revises, brings up to date, and consolidates 2 earlier works: *A Dictionary of usage and style* and *American usage: the consensus.*
*c.*3,500 entries, A-Z, in which the author, as well as offering his own advice, compares the judgements of 9 other usage guides and several general dictionaries. Bibliography of additional works consulted. *Class No:* 802.0-06(73)

For the reference librarian seeking listings of guides to English usage in *Walford's,* there are four entries in the index subordinate to the heading "English Language":

English Language
  Usage 5354-5373
    Australia 5381
    South Africa 5374
    USA 5375-5380

The librarian is directed to several entries, of which a subset deals with American English usage. These entries appear grouped at the end because the UDC classification number is more specific: 802.0-06(73) for American English and 802.0-06 for other works, including British English. Turning to the ALA *Guide*, one finds the following index entries:

English language
  idioms and usage, AC66, AC67, AC68, AC69, AC70, AC71, AC72, AC73, AC74, AC76, AC77, AC80, AC81, AC83, AC84, AC85, AC86, AC87, AC88, AC89, AC90
    dictionaries, AC78
    indexes, AC91

In this case, sources for American and British English are intermixed.

The ALA *Guide* and *Walford's* identify many sources likely to be found only in large academic libraries. There are more selective guides to reference sources for smaller libraries. One example is *Reference Sources for Small and Medium-Sized Libraries*, published by ALA. This compilation, last updated in 1999, has twenty-two sections representing the major subdivisions of the Dewey Decimal Classification and arranged in the order of that classification scheme. The first three sections cover general categories of tools, and the remaining sections cover sources for specific subject areas. Entries include Dewey and Library of Congress call numbers and alternative format icons (for CD-ROM and online) as well as complete bibliographic information and brief annotations. There is an author/title index.

James H. Sweetland has compiled the third edition (2000) of *Fundamental Reference Sources*, reflecting the major changes in reference sources since the second edition was published twenty years earlier. Chapters cover selected sources grouped by type, such as directories, biographical sources, encyclopedias, and indexing and abstracting services. Titles in electronic formats are included.

The American Library Association Guide to Information Access: A Complete Research Handbook and Directory, edited by Sandy Whiteley, provides an overview of "the printed and electronic sources librarians favor, the strategies they teach, and the pathways to the great networks of information they have helped create."[42] It is directed at all who conduct research, from high school students to professionals. Most of the book consists of topical chapters covering electronic and print information sources in areas such as film, gardening, and history. Introductory chapters explain research trends and resources, including the variety of electronic tools. There is a subject index.

Of particular interest to those in Canadian libraries is *Canadian Reference Sources: An Annotated Bibliography*. Its scope includes sources about Canadian people, institutions, organizations, publications, art, literature, languages, history, and religion; it is indexed by author, title, French subject, and English subject. Annotations are in English and French. The availability of nonprint formats is noted.

Two guides provide broad coverage of reference books for children. Barbara Ripp Safford's *Guide to Reference Materials for School Library Media Centers* includes more than 2,000 entries for books, CD-ROMs, and other electronic sources in all curriculum areas as well as extracurricular interests, providing for a wide range of age and reading levels. Entries include full bibliographic data, descriptions of sources, citations to reviews, and a code for grade level. There are author/title and subject indexes. In addition to reference works, this guide includes a section on collection management tools for school library media specialists. Carolyn Sue Peterson and Ann D. Fenton have compiled a work similar in scope, titled *Reference Books for Children*. It is more selective and not as current, covering about 1,000 titles. Annotated entries are grouped in the categories of general, humanities, recreation, social sciences, and sciences, with author/title and subject indexes.

Because the widely used guides to reference sources already described in this section provide only limited coverage of electronic sources, there is a need for directories of databases and Internet resources. These directories are useful sources of descriptions of databases, but they typically do not provide evaluative or comparative annotations. *Gale Directory of Databases*, formed from the merger of three titles (*Computer-Readable Databases, Directory of Online Databases*, and *Directory of Portable Databases*), provides extensive coverage of databases in all formats. Volume 1 is devoted to online databases; volume 2 divides the databases into five other media for distribution (CD-ROM, diskette, magnetic tape, handheld, and batch access). The directory is updated semiannually in an effort to keep pace with the rapid growth of sources in these formats. Entries in volume 1 are arranged alphabetically by database name; in volume 2 they are arranged by database name within each format. In the volumes for March 2000 nearly 6,100 online databases and nearly 7,800 databases on other media (from more than 3,600 producers and made available through more than 2,500 online services and vendors/distributors of database products) are described. Entries include information on such things as type of database, subjects covered, description of content, producer, vendor, language, geographic coverage, time span, and update frequency. A sample entry appears in Figure 13.3. If the database has a related print publication (or electronic publication in a different format), this is noted in the content note (or following "Alt. Formats"), as in the entry for *Library and Information Science Abstracts (LISA)* shown in Figure 13.3.

Each volume has subject, geographic, and master indexes as well as a directory of database producers with their associated databases. Volume 1 also includes an online services directory, and volume 2 has a directory of database vendors and distributors. The directory can also be searched online through Dialog and GaleNet. Such a directory is useful in identifying databases covering a particular subject area or containing a particular type of information. The information on producers and online services and vendors indicates how a library can acquire or gain access to these databases.

Although some directories provide descriptions of databases in several formats, other directories concentrate on CD-ROMs alone. One example is *CD-ROMs in Print*. The fourteenth edition of *CD-ROMs in Print* covers more than 17,000 CD-ROM titles. Arranged alphabetically by title, each main entry includes equipment specifications; pricing and subscription information; and a description indicating subject areas covered, time span, language, audience level, and multimedia content. A company directory provides full address and profile information for all companies mentioned in the title directory. An activity index groups companies by sector (e.g., content developer or distributor), and a geographic index lists companies by country internationally and by state within the United States. Separate indexes are included for multimedia, Macintosh, and electronic book and other formats. An audience level index identifies the target audience of each product, and the subject index classifies titles under nearly 200 different terms. A CD-ROM version of the directory is now available.

The proliferation of Internet resources has led to publication of many subject guides to selected Internet resources in print form. Subash Gandhi has compiled a bibliography of recently published guides showing the range of titles available.[43] The advantages of such directories include clear arrangement and organization of contents, well-developed subject headings, professional compilers, indexes, and ease of browsing. Disadvantages include problems of currency and cost. Such print guides are now often supplemented with an associated Web site to provide updates to links. One example of a guide is *Multicultural Resources on the Internet: The United States and Canada*, compiled by Vicki L. Gregory and colleagues. It cites Web resources dealing with multicultural issues likely to be of interest to an English-speaking audience in the United States and Canada. Entries in the book include title, URL, and a brief annotation and are divided by topic (e.g., business, fine arts) within a chapter for each ethnic group covered, ranging from African American to Jewish American to French Canadian. There is a site/sponsor index.

Figure 13.3 Entry from *Gale Directory of Databases*, Vol. 1, March 2000, p. 426. Copyright 2000 by Gale Group, Inc. Reprinted by permission of the Gale Group.

• 3616 • Library and Information Science Abstracts (LISA)

Bowker-Saur
Windsor Court, East Grinstead House
East Grinstead, W. Sussex RH19 1XA, England
Phone: 44 1342 326972 Fax: 44 1342 336198

Formerly Produced By: Library Association Publishing Ltd.

Former Database Name: Library Science Abstracts (LSA).

Type: Bibliographic.**Content:** Contains approximately 130,000 citations, with abstracts, to the worldwide journal and report literature and other selected documents in the areas of library and information science. Covers all aspects of librarianship, library services, promotion and use of libraries and library materials, library automation, information storage and retrieval, organization and administration, buildings and equipment, online databases, videotex, word processing, and electronic publishing. Corresponds to *Library & Information Science Abstracts.*

• LISA/Current Research—contains approximately 3000 citations, with summaries, to recently completed, ongoing, and proposed research projects worldwide, including investigations, surveys, and studies. Areas of study include online information retrieval, regional information networks, and handicapped/physically isolated users, among others. Includes project title and status, research team members, contact address, funding source, and duration of project. Corresponds to *Current Research in Library & Information Science.*

Subject Coverage: Librarianship, information science, micrographics, word processing, electronic publishing, viewdata and teletext, and the history of librarianship. **Lang:** English; some titles in English with abstracts in the original languages. **Geo. Coverage:** International. **Time Span:** 1969 to date. **Updating:** Monthly.

Online Availability:
Dial Up
• *The Dialog Corporation, DIALOG* (61: Contact Dialog for pricing information.).

Alt. Formats: *CD-ROM* (LISA).
Magnetic Tape (Library and Information Science Abstracts (LISA)).
Batch Access (Library and Information Science Abstracts (LISA)).

426

These guides to reference sources and directories of databases serve dual purposes: as collection evaluation checklists and selection tools for reference and collection development librarians, and as aids in reference work to identify appropriate reference sources to use in answering reference questions. In reference work, if the question is unlike one that a reference librarian has answered before, the librarian may not be able easily to identify a likely source without referring to a guide to reference sources or directory of databases. These lead-in tools can direct the librarian to one or more sources likely to provide an answer, as previously illustrated by the example on usage dictionaries. The remaining chapters in Part II consider each type of source in turn, describing their characteristics and appropriate search strategies.

SOURCES, COLLECTIONS, AND SERVICES IN TRANSITION

As the discussion in this chapter has made clear, one impact of technology on reference is the need to think in new ways about reference sources, collections, and the services they support. The familiar categories of reference sources (such as encyclopedias, dictionaries, directories) are still useful. Nevertheless, what Vannevar Bush termed "wholly new forms of encyclopedias . . . with a mesh of associative trails running through them"[44] are emerging both in the form of freely available Web resources and in newly aggregated offerings from publishers. For example, Gale Group's *Literature Resource Center* provides direct access to biographies, bibliographies, and critical analyses of authors from every age and literary discipline in a single Internet-searchable service, including links to related Web sites. The coverage of the electronic versions of texts found in *netLibrary* (http://www.netlibrary.com) includes a number of reference titles, which can be searched and manipulated in ways not possible with their print counterparts. As Ken Winter observes, emerging reference sources are "intricate text-and-image databases that harness the power of the Internet to deliver information in profoundly new ways."[45]

Reference collections and the reference collection development process also are becoming more complex. As Kathleen Kluegel states:

> the reference library is becoming an intersection of multiple collections through the Internet and the World Wide Web. Some of the collections have a physical dimension, composed of printed volumes or microform sets or CD-ROM workstations. Other collections are less tangible, being composed of bits on various computers and mainframes. Some of these collections are the result of internal selection processes, while others result from the selection processes of consortia and other cooperative arrangements among libraries.[46]

With the increasing reliance on networked access to information, selecting resources for reference is becoming both an acquisition activity and an access activity. Through building online directories to guide library users to available reference sources, both print and electronic, reference librarians are devising intellectual access systems that their user communities can find and use.

As the popular perception that "everything is on the Web" grows, reference librarians must find ways to show "which types of information resources answer which questions best."[47] As Jane Subramanian notes, many users have preconceived attitudes regarding the use of particular formats of indexes and other materials. These attitudes may interfere with the user's retrieval of needed resources due to the use of a preferred format rather than the best means of access for the information need.[48] Studies of the utility of freely available Internet resources in answering reference questions are beginning to appear,[49] but more analysis is needed to characterize strengths and weaknesses when compared to the resources acquired by librarians for inclusion in their reference collections. For example, Walter Minkel and Roxanne Hsu Feldman characterize the state of the Web for students' reference questions.[50] They note that the Web is particularly strong in such areas as news, science, medicine, and sports and recreation, but poor in providing free access to in-depth biographical information or literature still under copyright. As reference librarians develop and work with hybrid collections of purchased, licensed, and freely available Web resources, a better understanding of the questions most easily answered by each will emerge. The volume and diversity of information available on the Web opens new possibilities to both reference librarians and users. but both must continue to keep in mind that at present it can be hard to find good content; once found, such information may later disappear (or at least move); and some information found may be completely incorrect. Recalling *Harrod's* definition of a reference source as one used to obtain authoritative information, reference librarians and users alike must be vigilant in their search for credible information.[51]

NOTES

1. Heartsill Young, ed., *The ALA Glossary of Library and Information Science* (Chicago: American Library Association, 1983), 188.

2. Marcia J. Bates, "What Is a Reference Book? A Theoretical and Empirical Analysis," in *For Information Specialists: Interpretations of Reference and Bibliographic Work*, ed. Howard D. White, Marcia J. Bates, and Patrick Wilson (Norwood, N. J.: Ablex, 1992), 9-26.

3. Bill Katz, *Cuneiform to Computer: A History of Reference Sources* (Lanham, Md.: Scarecrow Press, 1998), 415p.

4. Ray Prytherch, comp., *Harrod's Librarians' Glossary and Reference Book,* 9th ed. (Aldershot, England: Gower, 2000), 618.

5. Michael D. G. Spencer, "Pamphlet Collection Development," in *Readings on the Vertical File*, ed. Michael D. G. Spencer (Englewood, Colo.: Libraries Unlimited, 1993), 21-28.

6. Pamela R. Cibbarelli, Elliot H. Gertel, and Mona Kratzert, "Choosing Among the Options for Patron Access Databases: Print, Online, CD-ROM, or Locally Mounted," *The Reference Librarian* 39 (1993): 85-97.

7. Sydney J. Pierce, "Introduction," *The Reference Librarian* 29 (1990): 1-8.

8. Mary Biggs and Victor Biggs, "Reference Collection Development in Academic Libraries: Report of a Survey," *RQ* 27 (Fall 1987): 67-79.

9. Christopher W. Nolan, *Managing the Reference Collection* (Chicago: American Library Association, 1999), 32-44.

10. Examples of reference collection policies can be found in: Daniel T. Richards and Dottie Eakin, *Collection Development and Assessment in Health Sciences Libraries* (Lanham, Md.: Medical Library Association and Scarecrow Press, 1997), 283-93.

11. Melissa Holmberg, "Using Publishers' Web Sites for Reference Collection Development," *Issues in Science & Technology Librarianship* 25 (Winter 2000). Available: http://www.library.ucsb.edu/istl/00-winter/article3.html.

12. Eleanor Mathews and David A. Tyckoson, "A Program for the Systematic Weeding of the Reference Collection," *The Reference Librarian* 29 (1990): 129-43.

13. Lynn Westbrook, "Weeding Reference Serials," *Serials Librarian* 10 (Summer 1986): 81-100.

14. William A. Katz, *Introduction to Reference Work*, 7th ed. (New York: McGraw-Hill, 1997), 2:254.

15. Jean C. McManus, "Archiving the Content of Print and Electronic Reference Works in the Digital Age: An Analysis and a Proposal," in *Finding Common Ground: Creating the Library of the Future Without Diminishing the Library of the Past* (New York: Neal-Schuman, 1998), 375-80.

16. For criteria for evaluating online databases, CD-ROMs, and Web resources, see the following: J. A. Large, "Evaluation of Electronic Media as Reference Sources," in *Encyclopedia of Library and Information Science*, ed. Allen Kent (New York: Marcel Dekker, 1991), 48: 116-29; Anne B. Piternick, "Decision Factors Favoring the Use of Online Sources for Providing Information," *RQ* 29 (Summer 1990): 534-44; Candy Schwartz, "Evaluating CD-ROM Products: Yet Another Checklist," *CD-ROM Professional* 6 (January 1993): 87-91; Nolan, "Criteria for Selecting Electronic Products," in *Managing the Reference Collection*, 111-45; James Rettig and Cheryl LaGuardia, "Beyond Cool: Reviewing Web Resources," *Online* 23 (July/August 1999): 51-55; and Richard Bleiler and Terry Plum, comps., "Selection Criteria," in *Networked Information Resources* (Washington, D.C.: Association of Research Libraries, 1999), 53-70.

17. Lynne M. Martin, "Evaluating OPACs, or, OPACS are Reference Tools, Too!" *The Reference Librarian* 38 (1992): 201-20.

18. Peggy Langstaff, "Getting the Picture—Along with the Words," *Publishers Weekly* 243 (April 29, 1996): 36-40.

19. Kayvan Kousha, "DVD: The Next Evolutionary Step for Publishing Multimedia Reference Sources," *Online & CD-ROM Review* 23 (June 1999): 203-5.

20. Péter Jacsó, "Content Evaluation of Databases," *Annual Review of Information Science and Technology* 32 (1997): 231-67.

21. Mary K. Taylor and Diane Hudson, " 'Linkrot' and the Usefulness of Web Site Bibliographies," *Reference & User Services Quarterly* 39 (Spring 2000): 273-77.

22. Mark Schumacher, "Accuracy of Reference Sources: The Example of Balzac," *RQ* 32 (Fall 1992): 26-29.

23. Pamela Cahn, "Testing Database Quality," *Database* 17 (February 1994): 23-30.

24. Marilyn Domas White, "The Readability of Children's Reference Materials," *The Library Quarterly* 60 (October 1990): 300-319.

25. David Isaacson, "Literary Style in Reference Books," *RQ* 28 (Summer 1989): 485-95.

26. "Checklist of Items for Inclusion in CD-ROM Vendor Documentation," *RQ* 33 (Winter 1993): 215-17.

27. Trisha L. Davis, "The Evolution of Selection Activities for Electronic Resources," *Library Trends* 45 (Winter 1997): 391-403.

28. Charles T. Townley and Leigh Murray, "Use-Based Criteria for Selecting and Retaining Electronic Information: A Case Study," *Information Technology & Libraries* 18 (March 1999): 32-39.

29. Péter Jacsó, "Be Savvy! Sometimes the Free Resources Are Better," *Computers in Libraries* 20 (May 2000): 56-58.

30. Elizabeth Thomsen, *Rethinking Reference: The Reference Librarian's Practical Guide for Surviving Constant Change* (New York: Neal-Schuman, 1999), 110.

31. See, for example, Judith Murray Griffiths, "Integrating the Web into Reference Services," *Colorado Libraries* 25 (Spring 1999): 10-14; Sue Scott, "Mapping the Internet: Applying Reference Skills to Tame the Web," *LASIE* 29 (September 1998): 20-26; Steven W. Sowards, "A Typology for Ready Reference Web Sites in Libraries," *First Monday* 3 (May 1998). Available: http://www.firstmonday.dk/issues/issue3_5/sowards/index.html.

32. Diane K. Kovacs, "Building a Core Internet Reference Collection," *Reference & User Services Quarterly* 39 (Spring 2000): 233-39.

33. Traugott Koch, "Quality-Controlled Subject Gateways: Definitions, Typologies, Empirical Overview," *Online Information Review* 24 (2000): 24-34; Emma Place, "International Collaboration on Internet Subject Gateways," *IFLA Journal* 26 (2000): 52-56.

34. James Rettig, "Reference Book Reviewing Media: A Critical Analysis," *Library Science Annual* 2 (1986): 13-29.

35. Helen K. Wright, "Reference Books Bulletin Editorial Review Board—ALA," in *Encyclopedia of Library and Information Science*, ed. Allen Kent (New York: Marcel Dekker, 1984), 37: 346-52.

36. James H. Sweetland, "Reference Book Reviewing Tools: How Well Do They Do the Job?" *The Reference Librarian* 15 (Fall 1986): 65-74.

37. Donald C. Dickinson, "The Reviewing of Foreign Language Reference Books: A Woeful Inadequacy," *RQ* 32 (Spring 1993): 373-80.

38. Sara Amato, "Internet Reviews," *College & Research Libraries News* 55 (February 1994): 89.

39. Stuart W. Miller, "Monument: *Guide to Reference Books*," in *Distinguished Classics of Reference Publishing*, ed. James Rettig (Phoenix, Ariz.: Oryx Press, 1992), 129-37.

40. For example, see Eileen McIlvaine, "Selected Reference Books of 1999/2000," *College & Research Libraries* 61 (September 2000): 452-63.

41. Moira Duncan, "To Infinity and Beyond," *Library Association Record* 102 (March 2000): 148-49.

42. Arthur Plotnik, "Prying with a Purpose," in *The American Library Association Guide to Information Access: A Complete Research Handbook and Directory*, ed. Sandy Whiteley (New York: Random House, 1994), xvii.

43. Subash Gandhi, "Internet Directories: A Subject Guide to Monographs," *Choice* 36 (April 1999): 1409-21.

44. Vannevar Bush, "As We May Think," *Atlantic Monthly* 176 (July 1945): 108.

45. Ken Winter, "From Wood Pulp to the Web: The Online Evolution," *American Libraries* 31 (May 2000): 70.

46. Kathleen M. Kluegel, "Reflections on Reference," in *Towards a New Vision of Reference: Kaleidoscopic Collections and Real Librarians*, ed. Kathleen M. Kluegel and Rob Richards (Chicago: Reference and User Services Association, American Library Association, 1998), 23.

47. Judith Metcalf, "Full Circle, Back to Selecting and Organizing," *American Libraries* 30 (May 1999): 42.

48. Jane M. Subramanian, "Patron Attitudes Toward Computerized and Print Resources: Discussion and Considerations for Reference Service," *The Reference Librarian* 60 (1998): 127-38.

49. Joseph R. Zumalt and Robert W. Pasicznyuk, "The Internet and Reference Services: A Real-World Test of Internet Utility," *Reference & User Services Quarterly* 38 (1998): 165-72.

50. Walter Minkel and Roxanne Hsu Feldman, *Delivering Web Reference Services to Young People* (Chicago: American Library Association, 1999), 121p.

51. Donald T. Hawkins, "What Is Credible Information?" *Online* 23 (September/October 1999): 87-89.

LIST OF SOURCES

American Libraries. Chicago: American Library Association, 1970– . 11 issues per year.

American Reference Books Annual. Edited by Bohdan S. Wynar. Englewood, Colo.: Libraries Unlimited, 1970– . Annual.

Best Reference Books, 1970–1980: Titles of Lasting Value Selected from American Reference Books Annual. Littleton, Colo.: Libraries Unlimited, 1981. 480p.

Best Reference Books, 1981–1985: Titles of Lasting Value Selected from American Reference Books Annual. Littleton, Colo.: Libraries Unlimited, 1986. 504p.

Best Reference Books, 1986–1990: Titles of Lasting Value Selected from American Reference Books Annual. Englewood, Colo.: Libraries Unlimited, 1992. 544p.

Booklist: Includes Reference Books Bulletin. Chicago: American Library Association, 1905– . Twice monthly September–June; monthly July–August. Also available on CD-ROM.

Books in Print with Book Reviews on Disc. [CD-ROM]. New Providence, N.J.: R. R. Bowker. Monthly.

Bynagle, Hans E. *Philosophy: A Guide to the Reference Literature.* 2d ed. Englewood, Colo.: Libraries Unlimited, 1997. 233p.

Canadian Reference Sources: An Annotated Bibliography/Ouvrages de Reference Canadiens: Une Bibliographie Annotée. Compiled by Mary E. Bond and Martine M. Caron. Vancouver, B.C.: UBC Press in association with the National Library of Canada, 1996. 1076p.

CD-ROMs in Print: An International Guide to CD-ROM, CD-I, 3DO, MMCD, CD32, Multimedia, Laserdisc and Electronic Products. 14th ed. Farmington Hills, Mich.: Gale Group, 2000. 1762p. Also available on CD-ROM.

Choice. Middletown, Conn.: Association of College and Research Libraries, 1964– . 11 issues per year.

ChoiceReviews.online. 1999– . Available: http://www.choicereviews.org.

EContent. Wilton, Conn.: Online, Inc., 1999– . (Formerly *Database*, 1978–1999.)

Gale Directory of Databases. Volume 1. *Online Databases.* Volume 2. *CD-ROM, Diskette, Magnetic Tape, Handheld, and Batch Access Database Products.* Farmington Hills, Mich.: Gale Group, 1993– . Semiannual. Also available online.

Gregory, Vicki L., Marilyn H. Karrenbrock Stauffer, and Thomas W. Keene, Jr. *Multicultural Resources on the Internet: The United States and Canada.* Englewood, Colo.: Libraries Unlimited, 1999. 366p.

Guide to Reference Books. 11th ed. Edited by Robert Balay. Chicago: American Library Association, 1996. 2020p.

Library Journal. New York: Cahners, 1876– . 20 issues per year.

Peterson, Carolyn Sue, and Ann D. Fenton. *Reference Books for Children.* 4th ed. Metuchen, N.J.: Scarecrow Press, 1992. 399p.

Recommended Reference Books for Small and Medium-sized Libraries and Media Centers. Edited by Bohdan S. Wynar. Englewood, Colo.: Libraries Unlimited, 1981– . Annual.

Reference & User Services Quarterly. Chicago: American Library Association, 1997– .(Formerly *RQ* 1960–1997.)

Reference Reviews. Farmington Hills, Mich.: Gale Group. Monthly. Available: http://www.galegroup.com/reference/reference.htm.

Reference Reviews Europe Annual. Florence, Italy: Casalini Libri, 1996- . Annual. Also available online.

Reference Sources for Small and Medium-Sized Libraries. 6th ed. Edited by Scott E. Kennedy. Chicago: American Library Association, 1999. 368p.

Safford, Barbara Ripp. *Guide to Reference Materials for School Library Media Centers.* 5th ed. Englewood, Colo.: Libraries Unlimited, 1998. 353p.

Sweetland, James H. *Fundamental Reference Sources.* 3d ed. Chicago: American Library Association, 2000. 384p.

Walford's Guide to Reference Material. 3 vols. London: Library Association, 1998– [7th ed. Volume 2: *Social and Historical Sciences, Philosophy and Religion,* 1998; Volume 3: *Generalia, Language and Literature, The Arts,* 1998; 8th ed. Volume 1: *Science and Technology,* 1999].

Whiteley, Sandy, ed. *The American Library Association Guide to Information Access: A Complete Research Handbook and Directory.* New York: Random House, 1994. 533p.

ADDITIONAL READINGS

Alexander, Janet E., and Marsha Ann Tate. *Web Wisdom: How to Evaluate and Create Information Quality on the Web.* Mahwah, N.J.: Lawrence Erlbaum Associates, 1999. 156p.

The authors offer a model of evaluation of Web sites that uses an approach of establishing authority, accuracy, objectivity, currency, and coverage. They further illustrate differences involved in assessing information quality in various types of pages (e.g., information pages versus entertainment pages). The final chapter provides guidance in creating effective Web pages and sites. A glossary and bibliography are also included.

Bates, Marcia J. "What Is a Reference Book? A Theoretical and Empirical Analysis." In *For Information Specialists: Interpretations of Reference and Bibliographic Work*, edited by Howard D. White, Marcia J. Bates, and Patrick Wilson. Norwood, N.J.: Ablex, 1992, 9-26.

Bates notes that reference books have traditionally been defined administratively (e.g., as books that are noncirculating) or functionally (e.g., as books used for reference) rather than descriptively (i.e., in terms of the essential characteristics that distinguish reference books from other books). This article develops and tests a descriptive definition.

Cassell, Kay Ann. *Developing Reference Collections and Services in an Electronic Age: A How-To-Do-It Manual for Librarians.* New York: Neal-Schuman, 1999. 150p.

This manual is designed to guide readers through collection development decisions, including the advantages and disadvantages of print versus electronic media. Cassell draws on her experience in both public and academic libraries in recommending ways of coping with and planning for future changes in reference collections.

Cooke, Alison. *Neal-Schuman Authoritative Guide to Evaluating Information on the Internet.* New York: Neal-Schuman, 1999. 169p.

This guide is divided into the following sections: the Internet and information quality; using search facilities to maximize quality information retrieval; assessing quality of any Internet information source; evaluating particular types of sources (e.g., organizational Web sites, databases, subject-based Web sites); an annotated bibliography helpful for its references to other discussions of evaluation; and a glossary.

Head, Alison J. *Design Wise: A Guide for Evaluating the Interface Design of Information Resources.* Medford, N.J.: CyberAge Books, 1999. 196p.

This guide provides very helpful checklists for evaluating the design of CD-ROMs, Web sites, and online commercial databases.

Katz, Bill, and Robin Kinder, eds. "The Publishing and Review of Reference Sources." *The Reference Librarian* 15 (Fall 1986): 1-336.

This collection of papers examines many facets of reference publishing and reviewing. Of particular interest are the papers in the section "Reviews and Evaluation of Reference Works," including "Evaluating Reference Books in Theory and Practice" by Norman Stevens; "Reference Book Reviewing Tools: How Well Do They Do the Job?" by James H. Sweetland; and "The Reference Reviewer's Responsibilities" by James Rettig.

Kluegel, Kathleen M., and Rob Richards, eds. *Towards a New Vision of Reference: Kaleidoscopic Collections and Real Librarians.* Chicago: Reference and User Services Association, 1998. 40p.

Based on papers presented at the American Library Association Annual Conference in June 1997, this collection focuses on three aspects of the topic of consortial collection development and management for service: reference service, consortial resource acquisition, and reference resource development. An annotated bibliography on collection development for reference, emphasizing networked resources, is also included.

Kovacs, Diane. *Building Electronic Library Collections: The Essential Guide to Selection Criteria and Core Subject Collections.* New York: Neal-Schuman, 2000. 217p.

The author provides a collection planning guide for collecting, evaluating, and selecting Web-based information resources. The first chapter provides a framework for planning and developing collections; subsequent chapters cover evaluation criteria and a recommended core for various topic areas, with Chapter 2 focusing on Web-based core ready-reference resources.

Nolan, Christopher W. *Managing the Reference Collection.* Chicago: American Library Association, 1999. 231p.

Nolan shows how to create "a lean, efficient reference collection that is based on actual user needs." He discusses developing reference collection development policies, selecting and managing electronic reference sources, and evaluating and weeding reference collections. The book concludes with a very helpful annotated bibliography, leading to key literature on reference collection management.

Pierce, Sydney J., ed. "Weeding and Maintenance of Reference Collections." *The Reference Librarian* 29 (1990): 1-173.

This issue attempts to remedy the limited treatment in the library literature to date of the topics of weeding and maintenance of reference collections. Articles are grouped in three sections. The first considers the impact of differing user groups and objectives on the reference collection; the second deals with policies for reference collection development; and the third covers evaluation and weeding of collections.

Reference Collection Development: A Manual. Chicago: Reference and Adult Services Division, American Library Association, 1992. 48p. (RASD Occasional Papers, no. 13).

Developed by the Reference Collection Development and Evaluation Committee of the Collection Development and Evaluation Section of RASD, this manual offers guidance in producing collection development policies for reference collections serving adults in academic and public libraries. The manual begins with a checklist for writing a reference collection development policy, then provides a model policy in outline, with illustrations and examples. Two complete policies, for a university library and a public library, are provided as appendices.

Rettig, James. "Every Reference Librarian a Reviewer." *RQ* 26 (Spring 1987): 467-76.

Rettig argues that all reference librarians are obligated to get to know the works in their collections as thoroughly as a reviewer must. This article describes this process with respect to reference tools in all formats, relating strengths and weaknesses to the situations that arise in dealing with the information needs posed by the library's users.

Slote, Stanley J. "Weeding Reference Collections." In *Weeding Library Collections: Library Weeding Methods.* 4th ed. Englewood, Colo.: Libraries Unlimited, 1997, 219-26.

Slote notes that the problems involved in weeding reference collections are made more complex by the diversity of types of materials they encompass. This chapter reviews methods of weeding the various categories of reference materials.

Spencer, Michael D. G., ed. *Readings on the Vertical File.* Englewood, Colo.: Libraries Unlimited, 1993. 174p.

Spencer has compiled a collection of articles covering every area of major concern pertaining to vertical files, from obtaining and selecting useful material, weeding, and record keeping to automating the vertical file index and evaluating its success. An appendix presents a sample vertical file selection policy and procedure policy manual.

Wells, Amy Tracy, Susan Calcari, and Travis Koplow. *The Amazing Internet Challenge: How Leading Projects Use Library Skills to Organize the Web.* Chicago: American Library Association, 1999. 279p.

This book includes case studies of twelve projects chosen for their international reputation as leaders in the delivery of selective, quality resources. The detailed profiles include information on the selection criteria used and the evaluation process employed in determining which resources to include. Projects profiled include Argus Clearinghouse, BUBL Information Service, INFOMINE, the Internet Public Library, and Librarians' Index to the Internet.

CHAPTER
14

DIRECTORIES

Susan Miller

USES AND CHARACTERISTICS

The need for information sources listing people or organizations in a systematic way may first have been met by the production of the *Domesday Book* in 1086 by order of William the Conqueror.[1] Used for tax purposes, this compilation of the wealth and people of England was arranged geographically by county and then by fief within the county.[2] Perhaps this listing was the first directory compiled, providing access to information regarding who held what property and where that person lived. Now directories cover all topics and geographic areas, ranging from commonly used titles such as *The World of Learning* and the *Encyclopedia of Associations* to highly specialized titles such as *American Art Directory* and *The Buddhist Directory*. Directories are available in such formats as print sources, CD-ROM, online databases, and files on the Internet. Directory-type information is also included in other types of reference sources, including almanacs, yearbooks, and guidebooks.

Defined by *The ALA Glossary of Library and Information Science* as "a list of persons or organizations, systematically arranged, usually in alphabetic or classed order, giving address, affiliations, etc., for individuals, and address, officers, functions, and similar data for organizations,"[3] directories are a very important type of reference source. They are used to locate organizations, institutions, and people. They are also used to verify the name of an organization or the spelling of a person's name, as well as to match individuals with organizations that can answer their information needs when they have to go beyond the resources of the library. Because directories encompass so many types of organizations, associations, institutions, and individuals, in many libraries they are the most often consulted type of reference source.

EVALUATION

When evaluating a directory, there are several criteria to consider. First is the *scope* of the directory: What organizations, geographical areas, or types of individuals are included in the work? The title often gives some insight into the scope of the source; however, more detailed information will be found in the preface, which should be closely examined. It is also important to determine how comprehensive the directory is within its stated scope. For example, a business directory may include all businesses in the geographical area covered, only those with an income greater than a specified dollar amount, or only those meeting some other criteria.

The *currency* of the information provided in the directory should also be examined. What is the frequency of publication? How often is the material actually updated? This is an important feature of directories, because they are often used to find the most up-to-date information on an organization, institution, or individual. How the information in the source is updated is also important in determining the *accuracy* of the directory. Many methods are used in updating records: verifying information by telephone, gathering data through forms sent in the mail, examining public records, or culling newspapers and journals. Often information on the currency and accuracy of the source is also included in its preface.

The directory's *format* is critical to its effective use by librarians and library users. One point to consider is the arrangement of the tool. Are the entries clearly arranged and consistent throughout the source? Does the source provide headers at the tops of pages for ease of use? The directory's indexes are a significant factor in providing access to the information it includes. Types of indexes can include, among others, a personal name index, a geographic index, a title or organization name index, and a subject index. Title or organization name indexes may be by actual title or organization name, or by keywords in the title or name (see Figure 14.1, which illustrates the multiple access points in a keyword index).

Figure 14.1 Example of keyword indexing in *Directories in Print*. From *Directories in Print*, by Dawn Conzert Dez Jardins, 16th Edition, Gale, 1998. Copyright 1998 by Gale Research, Inc. Reprinted by permission of the Gale Group.

Pacific Coast Studio Directory 6888
Pacific Design Center—Directory [California] C&SDIP
Pacific Egg and Poultry Association—Membership List 3944
Pacific Fishing—Yearbook Issue 2166
Pacific International Trapshooting Association—Yearbook 9627
Pacific Island and Australian Aboriginal Artifacts in Public Collections in the United States of America and Canada IDIP

Poughkeepsie-Hyde Park-Pleasant Valley, New York Cross Reference Directory C&SDIP
[Poultry]; American Silkie Bantam Club—Membership List 8742
Poultry Antiquities—Breeders Directory; Society for the Preservation of 9251
Poultry Association—Membership List; Pacific Egg and 3944
Poultry; Computer Software Directory for 3650

Egg Marketing—Directory of Processors and Further Processors Issue; Poultry & 3979
Egg Marketing—Egg Marketing Directory Issue; Poultry & 3980
Egg Marketing—Poultry Distributor Directory Issue; Poultry & 3981
Egg and Poultry Association—Membership List; Pacific 3944
Egg & Poultry Industries Issue; Poultry International—Who's Who International in the 3982

SELECTION

The process of selecting directory sources for a reference collection varies greatly from library to library and depends on many factors. Which directories are included in a collection is based on the community served, on the types of questions asked, and on the number of questions in a particular subject area. For example, research libraries and some special libraries may select more international sources than most public libraries would purchase. Public libraries may be more interested in business sources and telephone directories than a school library would be. Another factor in selection is the location of the library; this may dictate a concentration of sources dealing with a specific geographical area. Other considerations related to the library's location involve what collections are found nearby and whether the library has a formal network for the cooperative collection of sources. The budget available to the librarian and the cost of the directories considered for purchase must also be taken into account. Perhaps the librarian in a smaller library or in a library with funding problems will choose to purchase an annual directory only every other year.

Electronic Options

Another consideration for selection is the availability of the directory in nonprint format, either as a CD-ROM product, a commercial online database available from a vendor such as Dialog, or a free database accessible on the Internet. There are instances in which an electronic source is a better choice than trying to locate the information in a print source, because online databases and CD-ROM products often contain more current information than their print counterparts. If a source is published annually, but the database has quarterly reloads, the online version may be a more accurate source of information. The online database and CD-ROM can often be searched more efficiently, because some elements or fields of the record are indexed electronically but are not indexed in the print version. One example of this is the *American Library Directory*, which has no library type index in the print version but allows for searching the library type field in the electronic versions. Searching electronically often allows keyword searching that the print version cannot provide unless it includes a keyword title or name index. The advantage of this technique is that exact names or titles need not be known, but can be found with keyword searching.

Another benefit of online and CD-ROM searching is the ability to combine fields or terms using Boolean logic, a concept discussed further in Chapter 5. Boolean logic allows search terms to be combined to form a set specific to the library user's needs. For example, when searching for a company name in *D&B—Dun's Electronic Business Directory*, a large number of matches may occur when keywords are used. Using the Boolean operator AND, this set can be combined with a geographical location, narrowing the number of hits so the appropriate business can be identified.

An obvious consideration when using electronic sources is the cost involved for hardware, software, and online service charges. This issue must be weighed against the advantages of speed and the currency of information accessed. Each reference department should formulate policies regarding when and how often it is appropriate to use commercial online searching.

As more and more directories appear as free sites on the Internet, this availability also affects which directories are selected for purchase for the reference collection. It may be appropriate in some cases to provide a link at public terminals to a free directory on the Internet, such as the *AnyWho Toll Free Directory*, and cancel the order for a print version. Adding sites to the library's home page is an efficient way to provide access to directory-type information. For example, the Reference link in Yahoo! (http://dir.yahoo.com/Reference) provides an excellent means for finding Web sites that provide business and telephone directories. A comparable site for locating directories on the Web is the *Internet Public Library's Reference Center* (http://www.ipl.org/ref/). Identifying useful sites on the Internet is yet another important facet of the selection process. Further discussion of the selection process is found in Chapter 13.

IMPORTANT GENERAL SOURCES

The directories discussed in the following sections include a sampling of major directories in the areas of libraries, publishing, education and research, foundations and grants, business, associations, and government. Telephone directories and a representative group of specialized directories are also discussed. One general title that does not fit into any one of these areas, but lists Canadian organizations in all fields, is the *Canadian Almanac & Directory*, an extremely useful annual publication discussed more fully in Chapter 15.

Directories of Directories

Directories of directories provide listings and descriptions of various directories. These sources are a good starting point when the library user needs a specific directory but does not know the exact title, or when the user wants to know if a particular *type* of directory exists, such as a directory of psychologists.

Directories in Print gathers information on all types of directories of the United States and worldwide that are national or regional in scope. State, city, and local directories have now also been added. It provides coverage of directory-type sources, including commercial directories, lists of cultural institutions, directories of trades and professions, rosters of professional and scientific societies, biographical directories, and many other lists and guides on various topics. The common element of these various sources is that they include addresses. Nonprint formats of directories, such as microform and electronic, are also included. *Directories in Print* also provides information on the status of out-of-print directories.

Directories in Print consists of two volumes: a volume of descriptive entries and an index volume. A supplement, published between editions of the main set, gives descriptions of newly published directories and serves as an update to the main edition. The index volume provides a subject index, a title and keyword index, and an alternative formats index. The latter includes directories in formats other than print, such as audiocassette, Braille, CD-ROM, online database, diskette, and magnetic tape. The main entry volume is arranged by general subject areas; in each of these sections the entries are listed alphabetically by title of the directory. Each entry describes what the directory covers, languages of the text, frequency of publication, and what information the entries in the directory include. Other information provided includes how to order the directory and whether the publication is available in electronic format, as well as the URL of the publisher's home page.

Directories in Print is a good starting point when a library user needs address information on a specialized group of people, such as architects or candy brokers, or on a type of industry, such as the tool or real estate industry. The subject index supports searching under various subject headings to see what directories exist in these areas. The title and keyword index enables the user to browse actual titles of directories arranged by important words in their titles. This index is useful when individuals are searching for a known directory but do not know the complete title, or if they want to browse titles under a keyword to determine what directories are available in that subject area. *Directories in Print* is available on Dialog and GaleNet as part of the *Gale Database of Publications and Broadcast Media*, where the file is updated semiannually. It is also available on GaleNet as one component of *Gale's Ready Reference Shelf*.

A database of more than 10 directories published by the Gale Group, *Gale's Ready Reference Shelf* combines many of the most popular Gale directories. Directories currently included in this Web site are *Directories in Print*, *Directory of Special Libraries and Information Centers*, *Encyclopedia of Associations* (all series), *Gale Directory of Databases*, *Gale Guide to Internet Databases*, *Gale Directory of Publications and Broadcast Media*, *Publishers Directory*, *Research Centers Directory*, *International Research Directory*, *Government Research Directory*, *Newsletters in Print*, and *Encyclopedia of American Religions*. The database is organized into three files: organizations, publications, and databases. The three parts are searchable individually or as a whole. Search options include name, location, subject, free-text, or a combination.

Library Directories

Directories of libraries and subject collections are valuable sources for identifying the locations, professional staff, and special collections of libraries all over the world. They also provide the added benefit of connecting the library user to information experts in all subject areas and geographical locations.

The main print source to consult for basic factual information on libraries in the United States, Canada, Mexico, and regions administered by the United States is the *American Library Directory*. This two-volume set is a standard tool used by all sizes and types of libraries. Coverage of the directory includes public libraries; college, university, and community college libraries; armed forces and government libraries; law, medical, and religious libraries; and special libraries, which span industry, company, foundation, and association libraries. Also included are library networks, consortia, and library schools. The directory has been revised annually since 1978; from 1908 to 1978 it was published biennially.

Arrangement of *American Library Directory* is geographical; entries are listed by state or province, by city within the state, and then alphabetically within the city. An organization index and personnel index are provided. Entries contain a great deal of information: the name and address of the library, the library's Internet address, number of staff, income and expenditure figures, library holdings, special collections, automation networks in which the library participates, and branches of the library. This information is obtained either from the library itself or from public sources. The directory also contains a general information section providing, for example, lists of library schools and training courses, libraries that serve persons with visual or mobility impairments, libraries that serve deaf persons and persons with hearing impairments, and addresses of U.S. armed forces libraries overseas.

American Library Directory is available electronically on Dialog and NEXIS. The online records are identical to those found in the print format, and all fields are searchable. The entire database is updated annually. The database contains three subfiles: library records containing complete descriptions of libraries in the United States, Canada, and Mexico; consortia/network records; and library school records. Indexed fields found in the online format and not in the print format include the library's publications and subject interests. *American Library Directory* is also available as a CD-ROM product, either combined with *World Guide to Libraries* or as a separate database.

World Guide to Libraries provides address; Internet address where available; telephone, telex, and fax numbers; the name of the director; important holdings; and collection statistics for libraries worldwide. Many types of libraries are listed, including national, university and college, school, government, ecclesiastical, corporate, special, and public libraries. Inclusion is determined by number of book holdings, except in Third World countries, where libraries with lesser holdings have also been included. Entries are arranged by country, then by type of library. An alphabetical index is provided.

A listing of library collections that are limited by subject matter or form is the *Directory of Special Libraries and Information Centers*. Collections found in resource centers, research libraries, archives, information centers, special collections, and documentation centers located in the United States, Canada, and worldwide are within the scope of this directory. It is a good source to consult when trying to find information on a special type of collection rather than on a particular library. The descriptions of the collections, arranged in alphabetical order by library name, provide name and address of the library or information center, parent organization, principal subject keyword for the main subject of the collection, head of the library, founding date, number of staff, size of the collection, whether the library is automated, Internet address, and principal members of the professional staff. Geographic, personnel, and subject indexes are provided. These indexes allow the user to locate specific libraries when only a general geographical location is known, to determine where a librarian is located when only the librarian's name is known, or to locate libraries that collect extensively in a specific subject area. This directory is updated annually, with a supplemental volume published between the annual editions. It is also available online through GaleNet as part of *Gale's Ready Reference Shelf*.

The format and arrangement of the *Directory of Special Libraries and Information Centers* and the *American Library Directory* differ. Because the *American Library Directory* is geographically arranged with no subject index, it is not possible to search by subject. *Directory of Special Libraries and Information Centers* is arranged alphabetically and includes subject, geographic, and personnel indexes, providing more access points to the entries.

Another guide to libraries by special book collections is *Subject Collections*. Limited in scope to the United States and Canada, this source serves as a directory to special book collections of university, college, and public libraries; special libraries; and museums. *Subject Collections* has been published irregularly since 1958. It is a helpful source when the user wants to find the names and locations of libraries that have important collections in a specific subject area.

An excellent Web site for finding library Internet addresses is *Libweb: Library Servers via WWW*. This site provides links to over 3,700 Web pages from libraries in more than 100 countries.

Publishing and Book Trade Directories

Questions concerning addresses and telephone numbers of publishers and various aspects of the publishing business are commonly asked at the reference desk. Publishing directories provide this information and other types of information on the publishing industry on both national and international levels.

Literary Market Place is the business directory of the American book publishing industry. Published annually, it contains entries related to all aspects of publishing in the United States. Information is found under main subject groupings, with related sections listed in the table of contents under these groupings. Subjects covered include book publishers, both United States and Canadian, and foreign publishers with U.S. offices; book clubs; book distributors and literary agents; book trade organizations and events; and literary awards. Services and suppliers are listed, as well as book manufacturers and paper merchants. Generally, entries include name, address, telephone number, key personnel, and some descriptive information. Volume 2 of the directory includes an industry "yellow pages" (an alphabetical listing of all companies and personnel), and a directory of publishers' toll-free numbers. Information in the industry yellow pages includes e-mail and Internet addresses. Using the yellow pages, the user can find the section in the main volume where a specific company is listed. Using the section index, the user can locate information on companies or services of a specific type. *Literary Market Place* can be found on the Web together with International Literary Market Place.

International Literary Market Place covers information about the publishing world for more than 180 countries. This annual source has six sections subarranged by country: publishing; manufacturing; book trade information; literary associations and prizes; book trade calendar; and library resources. This source can be used to find the major libraries of a given country or to locate a listing of the main publishers in that country. One comprehensive index of all entries, by organization name, is provided.

Publishers Directory provides comprehensive coverage of U.S. and Canadian publishing organizations. A wide range of presses is represented, including major commercial publishers, literary and alternative small presses, scholarly publishers, museums, associations and societies, religious organizations, government agencies, and corporations. Also included are producers of databases, software, audiocassettes, and curriculum materials. Entries are arranged alphabetically by name of publisher and provide full contact information, including toll-free and fax numbers as well as e-mail addresses and Web URLs. Indexes provide access by subject or area of specialization and geographical area; there is also an alphabetical list of main entries that includes all imprints, affiliates, and former names associated with that publisher.

Another source that can be consulted for information on publishing companies is the publishers' volume of *Books in Print*. Publishers included are those that have books listed in the author, title, and subject volumes of *Books in Print*. The first section lists publishers' and distributors' name abbreviations in alphabetical order as they are listed in *Books in Print*. The abbreviated name is followed by the full form of the company's name, International Standard Book Number (ISBN) prefixes, business affiliation, editorial address, telephone and fax numbers, e-mail address, Web site, and ordering/distribution address and telephone number.

The next main section of the volume lists publishing companies alphabetically by their full company name and provides the same information as the entries previously mentioned. The subsequent section is a handy one; it lists publishers and distributors with toll-free telephone and fax numbers. Following this is a listing of wholesalers and distributors with ordering information. A geographic index to wholesalers and distributors is provided, allowing the user to see these companies arranged by state. A section of publishers added since the last published edition of *Books in Print* is also provided. The last section is a listing of inactive or out-of-business publishers. For a complete discussion of all volumes of the *Books in Print* set, see Chapter 20.

Although *Literary Market Place* deals mainly with the book publishing industry, *American Book Trade Directory* places its emphasis on retailers and wholesalers of books in the United States and Canada. This annual directory of booksellers is arranged geographically by state or province, then by city. It lists all types of bookstores, including antiquarian, college, educational, general, mail order, paperback, religious, used, and special subject. The directory is divided into four main sections: retailers and antiquarians, wholesalers of books and magazines, book trade information, and dealers in foreign language books. The section on wholesalers gives information on wholesalers, jobbers, and distributors of trade books and magazines. Also included in this section is a list of national distributors of paperbacks and wholesale remainder dealers. The section on dealers in foreign language books provides access to foreign book dealers, and the section on book trade information includes book exporters and importers. Entries in *American Book Trade Directory* may be found by consulting either the complete alphabetical index of all entries or the index by type of store, which lists bookstores by the specialty topic covering at least 50 percent of that store's stock.

Publishers, Distributors & Wholesalers of the United States lists more than 100,000 active publishers, distributors, wholesalers, software firms, audiocassette producers, museum and association imprints, and trade organizations that publish in the United States. The main section of the volume is the company name section; arranged alphabetically, it provides name, the name abbreviation used in many R. R. Bowker bibliographies, ISBN prefix, business affiliation, editorial address and telephone number, ordering/distribution address and telephone number, and imprints with their name abbreviations. Cross-references are provided from imprints and variant names to the main company name. The next section, the key to abbreviations, is helpful when a library user has an abbreviated publisher's name and needs the full name of the company. The ISBN prefix index is arranged numerically by the publishers' and distributors' prefixes. The corresponding company's full name is then given so the library user can look in the name index for the full entry. Other sections include a list of publishers' and distributors' toll-free telephone and fax numbers, an index of wholesalers and distributors, a geographic index, and an index of publishers by fields of activity. The online version on Dialog, *Publishers, Distributors, and Wholesalers of the U.S.*, has monthly updates and thus is likely to be more current than the print counterpart.

An excellent Internet site for searching information on publishers worldwide is *Publishers' Catalogues Home Page*. This site allows searching by format such as books, movies, audio books, and video games and by keyword in publisher name. A geographic index by country is also searchable. The United States publishers' sites also include university presses.

Education/Research Directories

Directories of educational institutions, secondary schools, community colleges, universities, and research centers are frequently consulted, particularly in academic libraries. They are used primarily for addresses of institutions and individuals. Education and research center directories provide addresses, telephone numbers, and often brief background information on the institution. In addition, the Internet can often be used to determine a faculty member's e-mail address.

Directories of Educational Institutions

The World of Learning is an annually published directory of international scope that provides information on learned societies, research institutions, libraries, museums, and universities. Arranged alphabetically by country, it is a good source of information on institutions of higher education in most countries. The general format within each country section consists of subject divisions such as academies, learned societies, research institutes, libraries and archives, museums and art galleries, universities, schools of art and music, and colleges of technology. Under these broad categories, the names of the institutions are listed.

The amount of data provided on a specific institution varies greatly. The minimum information in an entry consists of the address and telephone number of the institution, museum, library, or learned society. The entries can also include the number of teaching staff, number of students, titles of the institution's publications, affiliated institutions, names of faculty members, and the institution's e-mail address. The entries for libraries and archives may provide details on the collections. Museum and art gallery entries often supply information on displays or areas of collection. A comprehensive alphabetical index of institutions is provided at the end of the volume. For those interested in detailed information on U.S. museums, the *Official Museum Directory* can be consulted. Volume 1 is arranged by city within state; entries provide address, personnel profile, collections, facilities, activities, publications, hours and admission prices, and membership costs. Indexes provide access by institution name, personnel, category, and collections. Volume 2 is a directory of products and services for museums.

The universities and institutions of higher education of more than 170 countries and territories, excluding Commonwealth countries and the United States, are represented in the *International Handbook of Universities.* Information on degree-granting institutions at the university level is presented by country. As in *The World of Learning*, entries in the *International Handbook of Universities* vary greatly in the amount of information given. The briefest entry has address and telephone number and lists departments of the institution. More complete descriptions include deans' names, number of staff, dates of the academic calendar, admission requirements, fees, language used for instruction, and types of degrees and diplomas offered. A comprehensive alphabetical index of institutions is provided at the end of the volume.

Although many similarities exist between *The World of Learning* and *International Handbook of Universities*, there are several reasons why the former is often preferred over the latter. One valuable feature of *The World of Learning* is that it lists the faculty of many educational institutions. Also, *The World of Learning* includes libraries and museums as well as universities. The information may be more current in *The World of Learning* because it is published annually, while *International Handbook of Universities* is irregularly published.

Commonwealth Universities Yearbook is an annually published set with information arranged in alphabetical order by country. Within each country section is a narrative about each of the country's universities. Following this introductory section, the university information is outlined. In addition to standard directory data such as address and telephone number, the teaching staff of the school is listed by department. General information on the institution is then provided, including admission information, first degrees offered, higher degrees offered, fees, dates of the academic year, and publications of the institution. Indexes to the set are found in volume 2, including an index to institutions, an index to academic units, and indexes to research interests and personal names. *Commonwealth Universities Yearbook* is the only one of the international education directories discussed in this chapter that provides access to entries by personal names.

The *National Faculty Directory* is an alphabetical list with departmental affiliations and institutional addresses of more than 690,000 members of teaching faculties at community colleges, four-year colleges, and universities in the United States and at selected Canadian institutions. The *National Faculty Directory* is compiled from current class schedules and academic catalogs. A supplement volume lists new faculty members whose names did not appear in the most recent edition and other changes for faculty who are listed in the current edition.

Many sources exist for locating directory-type information for colleges and universities in the United States and Canada. One of the most frequently consulted sources for this type of information is *The College Blue Book*, available in print and on CD-ROM. *The College Blue Book* is a five-volume set with data on nearly 3,000 two- and four-year universities, colleges, and specialized institutions. Volume 1 provides narrative descriptions of the colleges and universities. Volume 2 lists tabular data in concise, easy-to-read summaries regarding such topics as enrollment, admission policies, student/faculty ratio, and calendar system of the institution. Volume 3 is arranged by degree offered for nearly 4,500 subject areas and lists the institutions offering each degree. Occupational education is listed in volume 4, describing almost 7,000 trade, technical, and business schools, as well as community colleges. Volume 5 provides scholarship, fellowship, grant, and loan information from corporate, government, and voluntary sources.

The HEP Higher Education Directory is a listing of accredited institutions of postsecondary education for the United States and its territories. This annual directory has four main parts: a directory portion and three indexes. The directory is arranged alphabetically by state, then alphabetically by institution name. Data provided in each entry include address, telephone number, and Internet address of the institution; size of enrollment; annual fees for undergraduate students; general programs offered; and a list of administrative and academic officers. The first index is of key administrators, with their most direct telephone number listed and a cross-reference to their institution. The second is an index of regional, national, professional, and specialized accreditation status arranged alphabetically by state; a page number is also provided for the institution's main entry. The third index is an alphabetical index of institutions by school name to be used when a person does not know in which state a college or university is located. Other information provided includes lists of the U.S. Department of Education offices, statewide agencies of higher education, and higher education associations.

For information on secondary and postsecondary schools in the United States, a standard source is *Patterson's American Education.* Part 1 of this directory includes entries for public, private, and church-affiliated secondary schools. These entries are organized alphabetically by state, then by community. Information found in the listings includes county name, community population, school district name, total district student enrollment, and a list of the community schools with their addresses. The second section arranges postsecondary schools by discipline and then alphabetically by state. Addresses of the institutions are listed here along with telephone numbers and, in some cases, Internet addresses. An alphabetical index is included for Section 2.

American School Directory is an Internet site providing access to all 108,000 K–12 schools in the United States. The search engine at this site allows either a specific school's home page or the Web sites of all schools within a city, county, state, or zip code to be located. Possible links from each school's home page include directory-type information (such as address, name of superintendent, and telephone number), an alumni directory, a local map showing the school's location, and the school's calendar.

Directories of Research Centers

The *Research Centers Directory*, an annual two-volume set, serves as a guide to more than 14,000 university-related and other nonprofit research organizations in the United States and Canada. Many types of research facilities fall under the scope of this directory: research institutes and centers; laboratories; experiment stations; and facilities affiliated with universities, hospitals, foundations, and other nonprofit entities. All areas of research are covered, including agriculture, business, education, the humanities, religion, labor and industrial relations, medicine and life sciences, physical sciences, engineering, and technology. For the purposes of this directory, the term *research* includes fundamental and applied studies as well as data-gathering and synthesis activities.

Research centers in the fields of life sciences, physical sciences, engineering, private and public policy and affairs, and social and cultural studies are covered in volume 1. Entries are arranged alphabetically by research center name within each general subject area. Four indexes are located in volume 2. The first is a subject index that lists general subjects in alphabetical order, followed by corresponding numbers of the entries arranged by the state in which they are located. This is helpful if the library user does not know the name of the research center but does know the subject area of research conducted by the center. The second is a geographic index with entries arranged alphabetically by state or province and city. The third index is a personal name index, giving the person's institutional affiliation and the entry numbers. The fourth is a master index arranged by research center name and by keywords within the center name. This index is useful if one or more keywords from the center's name are known, because each center is listed several times, once under each appropriate keyword.

Entries are clearly arranged and provide many details about each research center. After institution name, research center name, address, e-mail and Web address, and telephone and fax numbers, the director of the center is listed. A second section provides organizational notes, such as when the center was founded, former names of the center, sources of support, number of staff, affiliated centers, and memberships of the center. Next is a section describing research activities and fields within the scope of the institution. Other information provided includes a list of publications of the institution, dates of meetings of the research center, and whether the center has a library collection.

New Research Centers, a supplement to this publication, appears between the annual editions of the main work. The purpose of the supplement is to list research centers that are newly formed or that have been identified recently. The arrangement of the supplement is identical to that of the main volumes. It includes a master index, subject index, geographic index, and personal name index.

Broader in scope, both geographically and by type of research institution, than the *Research Centers Directory*, *International Research Centers Directory* covers all countries (except the United States) and all categories of research, including government, university, independent nonprofit, and commercial. The organizations are arranged by name within the same broad topics as *Research Centers Directory*. The entries follow the same format as those in the *Research Centers Directory*, giving general directory information, organizational notes, research activities and field, and publications and services. Contact information includes phone, fax, telex, e-mail, and Web addresses when available. Four indexes are provided: a subject index, providing access to centers by field of study; a country index, grouping centers by country; a personal name index; and a master, or keyword index, based on research center names. *New Research Centers* serves as a supplement to this directory as well as to *Research Centers Directory*.

As *Research Centers Directory* provides information on university and nonprofit-oriented research institutions in the United States, *Government Research Directory* provides the same type of information for more than 4,700 research centers of the U.S. and Canadian federal governments. Included in this publication are government research and development centers, test facilities, experiment stations, and laboratories in the areas of agriculture, business, education, energy, engineering, the environment, medicine, the humanities, and basic and applied sciences. Arrangement is alphabetical by name within agency (e.g., Department of Agriculture) with subject, geographic, and master indexes.

These three directories have been combined into a single online database, *Research Centers and Services Directories*, available through Dialog and GaleNet. This provides the capability of searching many parts of each directory entry, including names of personnel, publications and services, and research activities. All three directories can be searched simultaneously, or the search can be limited to a particular directory. This database is reloaded semi-annually.

Foundation and Grants Directories

Foundation and grants directories outline the interests of various foundations and grant-making institutions and the kinds of activities they support. Directories of this type also show which foundations give money to a particular nonprofit entity and how much they give. These are valuable tools in both academic and public libraries to help users identify appropriate sources of possible funding for research or community projects.

A major source of information on nongovernmental grant-making foundations in the United States is *The Foundation Directory*. It contains entries on nearly 8,000 foundations with at least $2 million in assets or $200,000 in annual giving. *The Foundation Directory* is now published annually, with updated information originating from written reports sent by the foundations or from the most current public records available. To identify new foundations for inclusion, Foundation Center staff monitor journal and newspaper articles and press releases. The new entries are then sent to each foundation for verification.

The Foundation Directory is arranged alphabetically by state, then alphabetically by foundation name within the state. Entries include the foundation's name and address, funding interests, contact person, officers and trustees, and financial data for the last year available. Other information, such as restrictions on giving programs, publications offered by the foundation, and application procedures, is included where applicable.

The Foundation Directory is a good source for a wide range of inquiries regarding foundations. The entries can be used to answer questions regarding what type of support a foundation will give or for what purposes or activities money will be given. Entries also show the number of grants given by a particular foundation and specify the grants with the highest and lowest dollar amounts. Arrangement of the indexes in the directory allows foundations to be studied geographically and also by types of support given. The index to donors, officers, and trustees enables the user to find the foundation connected with a particular individual. The foundation name index cross-references foundations with their state locations. Through the subject index, library users can find foundations grouped by the purposes and activities for which those foundations give grant money.

The Foundation Directory, Part 2 provides information on the second-tier U.S. grant-making foundations. It includes entries on private and community foundations making grants from $50,000 to $199,999 annually. A companion volume to *The Foundation Directory*, it has a similar entry format.

The Foundation Directory Supplement updates the information in both *The Foundation Directory* and *The Foundation Directory, Part 2*. It is published six months after these two volumes. It provides complete, revised entries for foundations that have reported substantial changes in personnel, name, address, program interests, or other areas.

The Dialog database of *The Foundation Directory* is much broader in scope than the printed source. This database includes information from the print versions of *The Foundation Directory* and *The Foundation Directory, Part 2*, *New York State Foundations*, *Guide to U.S. Foundations*, and *National Directory of Corporate Giving*. The Dialog database is updated semi-annually and reflects data available for the current fiscal year. *FC Search: The Foundation Center's Database on CD-ROM* provides access to the above print equivalents, with the addition of *The Foundation Grants Index* and *The Foundation Grants Index Quarterly*. The disc provides profiles of more than 53,000 U.S. foundations, corporate givers, and public charities, and descriptions of more than 200,000 newly reported grants.

The Foundation Center Online is the Web site of The Foundation Center. The site includes practical information for grant-seekers and provides links to Web sites of more than 1,500 grantmaker Web sites. Information on Foundation Center libraries around the country and instruction on how to conduct funding research is also provided. The site also provides access to *The Foundation Directory Online*, a subscription service for searching the directory.

The Foundation Grants Index is a list of the grants awarded by more than 1,000 foundations. This annual publication includes grants of $10,000 or more. The arrangement is alphabetical by state within subject category, with foundations listed alphabetically within each state. The grants are listed in alphabetical order by the name of the recipient organization. These entries include amount awarded, name and location of the recipient, purpose for which the grant was used, and date it was awarded. *The Foundation Grants Index* is a useful tool to determine specific projects for which a foundation has given, to ascertain the current giving trends of a specific foundation, and to assist fund-seekers in determining what foundations would be likely to support their projects. Indexes to the main section on grants awarded provide access in a number of ways, including by grant recipient, subject, and recipient categories.

The online version of *The Foundation Grants Index* is available on Dialog. The file cumulates grant records published in *The Foundation Grants Index Annual* and *The Foundation Grants Index Quarterly* issues. Quarterly reloads keep the online source up-to-date.

An additional source for matching grant-giving organizations with grant-seeking institutions is *Annual Register of Grant Support*. Covering a broad scope of grant support programs, this tool outlines programs of governmental agencies, public and private foundations, community trusts, unions, and educational and professional associations. This source is used by academic scholars and researchers, as well as by those in the fields of business, civic improvement, and social welfare. *Annual Register of Grant Support* is divided into major areas of giving interest: humanities, international affairs and area studies, special populations, urban and regional affairs, education, multiple-discipline sciences, social sciences, physical sciences, life sciences, and technology and industry. These areas are further subdivided into more specific giving areas. Entries for the grant-awarding sources give the name, address, and e-mail address of the source, when it was founded, names of programs, purpose of the programs, eligibility, financial data, and number of awards in the past year. Indexes allow the user to find grant-awarding sources by subject, organization and program, geographical area (state), or personnel of the grant-making body. An added feature of this source is an introductory section that describes program planning and proposal writing.

An annual source that matches grant programs with those individuals seeking funding for research projects is *Directory of Research Grants*. Sponsoring organizations listed include business and professional organizations, foundations, and governmental agencies. Grant programs are listed alphabetically. These entries provide data on the grant-awarding organization's interests, eligibility requirements, restrictions, application and review procedures, and deadlines. Internet addresses are available in many of the grant program entries. A subject index allows grant-seekers to see a list of funding sources in their areas of interest. Other indexes cover sponsoring organizations, grants by program type, and geographic location.

The foundation directories discussed here have different approaches. *The Foundation Directory*, *Annual Register of Grant Support*, and *Directory of Research Grants* give mostly information on the foundations themselves, while *The Foundation Grants Index* provides examples of actual grant amounts awarded by the foundations. *Directory of Research Grants* lists institutions giving specifically for research, while the other three directories list institutions with broader giving interests. Sources outlining current funding interests include *The Foundation Grants Index* and *Annual Register of Grant Support*; these are good sources for determining the most up-to-date giving patterns of major foundations.

GRANTS, an online database available from Dialog, is the source for listings of thousands of available grants offered by federal, state, and local governments; commercial organizations; associations; and private foundations. All grants included in the database carry application deadlines up to six months ahead. Each entry includes full description, qualifications, money available, and renewability. This database is updated monthly. *GRANTS* is also available on CD-ROM, which is updated every two months.

Foundations On-line on the Web provides access to numerous grant-giving institutions. This site allows browsing of the directory, choosing a listed foundation, and searching any organization's information page or home page. Home pages may contain downloadable information such as grant applications, periodical and financial reports, and e-mail capabilities. Most foundation home pages include guidelines for grant seekers, areas of interest of the foundation, restrictions on grants awarded, types of grants awarded, and deadlines for grant applications. Other links provided include a fund-raising events directory and a listing of fund-raising consultants.

Business Directories

Directories of businesses are used to find a company's location, the appropriate contact person at a particular business, general background on a corporation, the correct name of the company, or product information of the company. They also answer questions regarding which companies provide a particular service for consumers and businesspersons in the community. Business directories are likely to have either an online or CD-ROM equivalent, and in some cases both formats exist in addition to the paper version.

Standard & Poor's Register of Corporations, Directors and Executives is an annual directory of more than 75,000 leading public and private U.S., Canadian, and international corporations. It is arranged in three volumes. Volume 1 contains an entry for each corporation in alphabetical order. Entries include addresses and telephone numbers; Web addresses; names, titles, and functions of the company's officers, directors, and other principals; names of the company's accounting firm, law firm, and primary bank; stock exchange on which the company's stock is traded; and a description of the company's products and services. Also included in each entry are the company's division names and subsidiary listings. Volume 2 is an alphabetical listing of directors and executives, naming their affiliations with various companies and giving their business, home, and e-mail addresses. When available, year and place of birth, college attended, and fraternal memberships are also listed. Volume 3 contains indexes by Standard Industrial Classification, geographical location, subsidiaries and divisions linked to the parent company, obituaries of individual executives within the past year, new individual additions, and new company additions.

Standard & Poor's Register—Corporate is available online on Dialog. This database provides business facts on more than 100,000 leading public and private U.S. companies. A CD-ROM product, *Standard & Poor's Corporations*, consists of data from Standard & Poor's Corporate Descriptions, Register, and Compustat services. The data are organized into three files: Public Companies, Private Companies, and Executives. The Private Companies file provides information on more than 55,000 leading private corporations. The Executives file provides extensive personal and professional data on more than 70,000 key business executives. The Public Companies file contains business and financial information for 12,000 publicly traded U.S. and non-U.S. companies. *Standard & Poor's Register—Biographical* is also available online from Dialog. It provides both professional and personal information on key executives of public and private U.S. and non-U.S. companies with sales of $1 million and over. The file corresponds with the print publication *Standard & Poor's Register of Corporations, Directors and Executives*, volume 2. The file is updated semi-annually.

Dun & Bradstreet's *Million Dollar Directory* is a five-volume set containing information on more than 160,000 top U.S. public and privately held businesses. To be included, a business must have $9,000,000 or more in sales volume, and must be a headquarters or single-location business with more than 180 employees. Types of businesses included are agriculture, mining, construction, manufacturing, transportation, wholesale and retail trade, finance, insurance, real estate, and business services. Educational service and government agencies are generally not included. Within the five-volume set, the first three volumes list businesses alphabetically. Volumes 4 and 5 provide indexes by industry classification system and by geographical location.

Many types of data are given in each business entry: headquarters address and telephone number, stock exchanges used, company officers and directors, and members of the board of directors. Information included when available is telex number; whether the company is publicly owned; and the company's banking, accounting, and legal firm relationships. Some entries also show the company logo. *Million Dollar Directory* is also available on CD-ROM as *D&B Million Dollar Disc*, which is updated quarterly. *D&B Million Dollar Disc* contains more than 285,000 records on leading private and public U.S. companies, as well as business biographical information on major officers.

Million Dollar Directory has a broader scope than *Standard & Poor's Register of Corporations, Directors and Executives*, covering almost three times as many companies. An advantage of *Standard & Poor's Register* is the biographical information for directors and executives not found in the *Million Dollar Directory*.

D&B—Dun's Market Identifiers is a database that provides information on more than 10 million U.S. companies, including public, private, and government organizations. Address, product, financial, and marketing information are provided for public and private companies of a commercial or industrial nature. This Dialog database is updated monthly. Also available from Dialog is *D&B—Canadian Dun's Market Identifiers*, giving information on over 900,000 public and privately held Canadian companies. This database is updated quarterly.

D&B Business Locator CD-ROM is a listing of companies on CD-ROM that provides business locations and company identification for more than 11 million U.S. businesses. Entry information includes full business name and address, telephone number, and cross-references to the U.S. parent company. *D&B Business Locator CD-ROM* is updated quarterly.

An online database with no print equivalent is *D&B—Dun's Electronic Business Directory* (available on Dialog and other vendors). This directory of over 9.7 million U.S. businesses and professionals is reloaded quarterly, and it covers both private and public businesses of all sizes and types. The major industry groups included are agriculture, business services, communications, construction, finance, insurance, manufacturing, mining, professional services, real estate, retail, transportation, and utilities. Information provided for each company includes address, telephone number, and number of employees. *D&B—Dun's Electronic Business Directory* is a good source to search when an address is needed for a company but the general geographical location is not known, making it impossible to search in a telephone directory.

A Web site offered by Dun & Bradstreet, *D&B Companies Online*, provides information on more than 100,000 public and private U.S. companies. Search criteria for this site include company name, city, state (all states can be searched simultaneously), industry (all industry types can be searched simultaneously), ticker symbol, and URL of the company. Links provided also allow browsing by category of industry, such as natural resources, industrial technology, manufacturing, education and social services, and computers and software. Further industry subcategories are available from these links. Information listed for each company includes company address and telephone number, trade names used, the company's industry type, whether the company is public or private, a link to the company's home page, ticker symbol, and stock exchange used. For a fee, Dun & Bradstreet company reports can be requested directly from this page.

Thomas Register of American Manufacturers is an annually published set providing information on products and services of more than 156,000 U.S. companies. The set is divided into three main sections: products and services, company profiles, and the catalog files.

The volumes of company profiles list the companies alphabetically and give brief directory information such as address, telephone and fax numbers, and type of product or service offered. More extensive information is listed for some companies, providing the chair or president's name, subsidiaries and divisions of the company, and a complete product line. When pertinent, cross-references are given to the catalog files volumes, which reproduce the actual up-to-date product catalog data for more than 2,000 of the companies. These catalogs are arranged alphabetically by company name. The products and services volumes provide a subject approach to the *Thomas Register*. Arranged alphabetically by product and service type, manufacturers or sources are listed alphabetically by state and then by city. Indexes for the entire set include a product index and a trademark and brand names index.

Thomas Register Online, available on Dialog, corresponds to the print versions of *Thomas Register of American Manufacturers* and *Thomas Food Industry Register*. This database allows the searcher to identify nearly 200,000 U.S. and Canadian manufacturers of particular products, find trade names of products, develop targeted prospect lists, and find ownership of more than 110,000 active trade names. The Dialog database is updated quarterly, making it more current than the print set. *Thomas Register* is also available on CD-ROM and for free on the Web.

The five-volume *Directory of Corporate Affiliations* includes U.S. public and private companies, international public and private companies, and a master index. This directory provides, at a glance, "family tree" listings of parent companies, affiliations, and divisions. Corporate profiles list a company's net worth, annual sales, number of employees, year founded, and a description of the business. Indexes include a company name index, brand name index, geographic index, industry classification index, and corporate responsibilities index.

Directory of Corporate Affiliations, on Dialog and NEXIS, corresponds to the print source. Each parent company record contains the complete company hierarchy. Each affiliate record contains that portion of the company's hierarchy in which the affiliate is located. This information is also available on CD-ROM as *Corporate Affiliations Plus*. Both the *Corporate Affiliations* database and the *Corporate Affiliations Plus* CD-ROM are updated quarterly, and thus may contain more current information than the print version.

A source that helps put an individual in touch with the business community of a specific geographical area is the *World Chamber of Commerce Directory*. Published annually, it is arranged alphabetically by state, then by city. Contact person, address, and telephone number of that city's chamber of commerce are given. Other sections include state boards of tourism, convention and visitors' bureaus, Canadian chambers of commerce, and U.S. chambers of commerce abroad. This directory is also a good source for addresses and telephone numbers of foreign chambers of commerce located in the United States, as well as foreign embassies in this country and U.S. embassies abroad. The directory is also freely available on the Web.

A new source for finding U.S. and Canadian business and organization sites on the Internet is *Web Site Source Book*. This directory is organized alphabetically and contains a subject index. Entries contain Web site addresses, e-mail addresses, mailing addresses, telephone numbers, fax numbers, and toll-free numbers.

Box 14.1 Yahoo! Directory Searching

A library user came to the reference desk asking for a directory of music CD mail order companies. He had heard that a favorite musician of his, Bela Fleck, had recently released a new CD, but he did not know the title. The librarian decided to try Yahoo!, knowing a wealth of directories could be found at that site. After accessing Yahoo! at http://www.yahoo.com, she clicked on Reference, and then clicked on Directories, then Company Directories. Because Yahoo! is arranged by categories, she could then click on Music as a directory subject. Under Music, Music Mail Order Companies were listed. She and the library user looked at the options and chose *CD Universe*, which allowed for searching by artist, CD title, or song title. They entered Bela Fleck in the search box. This search resulted in a listing of many CDs for "Bela Fleck and the Flecktones." In browsing down the list, they spotted "Left of Cool," with a *NEW* banner beside it, and year of release noted as 1998. It was on sale, so the library user placed the order over the Internet, saving a trip to a CD store to try to find the new title.

Association Directories

Association directories are an indispensable means of connecting individuals with the appropriate organization for answering their information needs, on the local, national, or international level. Questions about addresses, telephone numbers, or names of executive officers are frequently asked. Other inquiries include information on publications of the organization and when or where the organization's annual conference is held. Some association-oriented questions are best answered by a telephone call to the association. This is also an efficient means (and sometimes the only means) of finding a local chapter of a national association.

The main source to consult for information about U.S. nonprofit membership organizations of national scope is *Encyclopedia of Associations: National Organizations of the U.S.* Published annually, this set contains entries for nearly 23,000 trade, business, and agricultural organizations; educational and cultural organizations; social, health, and public affairs organizations; labor unions; athletic and avocational organizations; Greek societies; fan clubs; and other groups consisting of voluntary members. The first two parts (volume 1, parts 1 and 2) contain details on the organizations, arranged by subject. Volume 1, part 3 is the organization name and keyword index. Volume 2 contains a geographic index by state and an executive index to chief executive officers of organizations listed.

The information provided for the various organizations is extensive. In addition to address, e-mail address, telephone number, and acronym of the organization, entries include founding date of the organization, name and title of the chief official, number of staff, annual budget of the organization, and number of members. The main body of the entry, the description of the association, outlines its purpose and activities and states the general type of membership. The frequency and dates of conventions and meetings are included, as well as titles of the organization's publications. Another useful feature is the outlining of the organization's computerized services, including online database searching provided and automated mailing list capabilities.

A companion set to the *Encyclopedia of Associations: National Organizations of the U.S.* is *Encyclopedia of Associations: International Organizations.* Arranged in the same format, this directory is a guide to international nonprofit membership organizations, including multinational and binational groups, and national organizations based outside the United States. The two-volume set is composed of one volume of entries and a second volume of indexes. The indexes include a geographic index, an index of names of executive officers, and a keyword index to organization names. The entries are arranged in the same format as the entries in the *Encyclopedia of Associations: National Organizations of the U.S.*, but also provide the organization's foreign-language name, working languages, and geographical scope.

Another set of volumes in the *Encyclopedia of Associations* series is the five-volume set of *Regional, State, and Local Organizations.* These volumes cover all 50 states, divided into five broad geographic areas: Great Lakes, Northeastern, Southern and Middle Atlantic, South Central and Great Plains, and Western. The scope of this set encompasses nonprofit membership organizations with interstate, intrastate, state, or local interest. Each volume is arranged alphabetically by state and city and includes an organization name and keyword-in-name index. Again, entries follow the same format as the other volumes in the *Encyclopedia of Associations* series and have generally the same fields of data.

Encyclopedia of Associations is available for online searching on Dialog and NEXIS. Corresponding to the print publications of *National Organizations of the U.S.*, *International Organizations*, and *Regional, State, and Local Organizations*, the database is a comprehensive file of more than 160,000 nonprofit member organizations. The database is reloaded annually and updated with inter-edition supplements between reloads. *Associations Unlimited*, the CD-ROM version of the database, offers the *Encyclopedia of Associations* series in its entirety. In addition, information is included on 300,000 nonprofit organizations, agencies, and service providers that are not membership organizations but provide many of the same services. Full-text reproduction of association membership applications and other promotional material are given in the CD-ROM product. This database is also offered through GaleNet, allowing direct access to the Internet address of the association selected.

Yearbook of International Organizations attempts to cover international organizations according to a broad range of criteria. This source may provide information on organizations not included in *Encyclopedia of Associations: International Organizations.* The first volume is arranged alphabetically by name of the organization. Entry information includes address, telephone and fax numbers, when the organization was founded, aims of the organization, structure, and languages used. Volume 2 provides a country directory of secretariats and membership, volume 3 has a subject directory and index, and volume 4 contains an international organization bibliography and listing of resources. *Yearbook of International Organizations* combined with *Who's Who in International Organizations* is available on CD-ROM as *Yearbook Plus: International Organizations and Biographies.* This product is updated annually.

The primary purpose of the *Associations Canada: The Directory of Associations in Canada/Le Répertoire des Associations du Canada* is to provide an authoritative listing of active associations in Canada serving the interests of the general public or the more specialized interests of the arts, business, industry, trade, labor, and the professions. Listings for almost 20,000 associations are found, with many of the new listings representing associations active on issues of current concern such as multiculturalism, free trade, and the peace movement. Also included are international associations with offices or branches in Canada, foreign-based associations with offices or branches in Canada, national associations, international associations, and provincial associations. Indexes are arranged by keywords, acronyms, personal names, and geographic location. A section of discontinued listings is provided. This title is also available on CD-ROM and online.

The Internet Public Library's *Associations on the Net* (AON) is a collection of over 2,000 Internet sites providing information about a wide variety of professional and trade associations, cultural and art organizations, political parties and advocacy groups, labor unions, academic societies, and research institutions. This site is organized by subject.

Government Directories

Government directories fall mainly into two categories: those published privately and those published by governments. This discussion covers only privately published sources; for directories published by government agencies, see Chapter 22.

A source that leads one through the labyrinth of governmental structure is the *Worldwide Government Directory*. It offers contact information on the governmental leadership of 199 countries and territories. The country section lists the head of state and cabinet ministers of the executive branch, legislative bodies, the judiciary, state agencies and corporations, the central bank, and various branches of each country's armed forces. A section of general data follows; it includes name of the capital city, official languages used, ethnic composition of the country, religious affiliations of the population, and type of local currency. International and regional memberships of the country are provided. There is also a section on the correct form of address for the officials of each country. Following this section is a directory of international organizations, providing address and personnel information on such entities as the World Bank and the United Nations Children's Fund.

For information on the executive branch of the U.S. government, Congress, or the related private, nonprofit organizations in the Washington, D.C., area, a useful source is *Washington Information Directory*. This annual directory is arranged by subject, with information organized by 20 main topics, under which applicable agencies of the federal government, Congress, and private, nonprofit organizations are outlined. Several strategies can be used to find information in *Washington Information Directory*. Individuals can be found through the name index; to locate a particular agency or organization, a subject/keyword index is provided. The table of contents lists the general headings, allowing users to search by subject, which can help them find agencies with an interest in a given topic by browsing through the possible options of information sources. Structures of government agencies are provided in the form of organizational charts scattered throughout the text.

Information on personnel at the federal, state, municipal, and county levels is provided in four directories published by Carroll Publishing. *Carroll's Federal Directory* includes entries on the executive, legislative, and judicial branches of the federal government. *Carroll's State Directory* lists executive, legislative, and judicial officials for the 50 states and the District of Columbia, Puerto Rico, and the American territories. *Carroll's Municipal Directory* provides names, titles, addresses, and telephone numbers of officials in approximately 7,900 cities, towns, townships, and villages. *Carroll's County Directory* includes names, addresses, and telephone numbers of primary government officials for all U.S. counties. Each of these directories is updated at least twice per year; each has a personal name index. *Carroll's Federal Directory* also includes a department and agency keyword index. Each of the four directories is available on CD-ROM and online by subscription.

Telephone and Fax Directories

Telephone directories are an excellent primary source for local information. Typically, a telephone directory is used to find names, addresses, and telephone numbers for individuals and businesses in a specific geographical area. Such directories may also provide additional information about a community, such as street maps, local history, calendars of cultural and sporting events, zip codes, shopping guides, and seating charts of auditoriums and stadiums. A type of telephone directory known as a *city directory* or *cross-reference directory* allows a telephone number to be verified by looking up an address rather than a name of a person or business. Some telephone directories on CD-ROM and on the Internet also allow this type of searching.

The breakup of the monopoly of AT&T in the United States in December 1983 led to the emergence of regional telephone companies, each of which produces its own telephone directories. One impact of this breakup for libraries is that telephone directories are no longer provided free of charge.

One alternative to the purchase of telephone directories from the regional companies is to purchase *Phonefiche*, telephone directories on microfiche from UMI. With *Phonefiche*, the entire content of the directory is reproduced on microfiche. The total collection available covers over 90 % of the U.S. population. The microfiche is produced and distributed immediately after the paper version is available, so the information is as current as the print directory. Many different subscription packages are available: categories of cities by various population sizes, packages of all directories for a given state or for all state capitals, and packages for up to 14 major metropolitan areas and various regions. Individual directories may also be purchased. Some directories of countries outside the United States are also available; larger academic and public libraries may find these useful.

One advantage of the microfiche versions of telephone directories is the amount of space saved. Nearly 2,600 directories covering 50,000 communities fit into nine 16-inch microfiche trays. This also allows for back issues of directories to be kept, and there is no binding expense. Another advantage of microfiche is that the directories can all be ordered from one source with one subscription payment.

A disadvantage to the microfiche is the resistance many people have to using this format. The microfiche can be difficult to read and cannot be reproduced without a microfiche printer. Also, there is the consideration of the cost of a microfiche reader and printer. For these reasons, some libraries purchase a combination of microfiche for lesser-used geographical locations and paper telephone directories for more frequently consulted cities.

Another alternative to the purchase of print telephone books is to purchase telephone directories available on CD-ROM. One of these CD-ROM products is *PhoneDisc*, which offers several packages of residential listings, business listings, and combinations of both. All *PhoneDisc* products have mail features to create and sort mailing lists from the CD-ROMs.

For libraries with adequate Internet access for their library users, white pages services on the Web may satisfy most inquiries for telephone directory information. Services such as *WhoWhere* provide telephone numbers, addresses, and e-mail addresses, searching all of the U.S. at once. *InfoUSA.com* links to maps and yellow pages information and features reverse number access, finding name and address based on the telephone number searched. *Telephone Directories on the Web* provides over 400 links to directories from all parts of the world.

Business Phone Book USA lists addresses, telephone numbers, fax numbers, toll-free numbers, e-mail addresses, and Web addresses for nearly 138,000 businesses, industries, professions, associations and organizations, educational and cultural institutions, and government agencies in the U.S. and Canada. This directory is divided into two volumes: white pages with alphabetical entries by organization name and yellow pages with classified entries by subject. There is now a section of brand name indexes by product name, manufacturer, and product type.

Facsimile transmission devices (fax machines) give the user the ability to transmit written or print communication quickly, and are popular in today's fast-paced world. *National E-Mail and Fax Directory* gives access to almost 50,000 e-mail addresses and more than 160,000 fax numbers for major U.S. companies, law firms, government agencies, media and publishing agencies, financial institutions, leading manufacturers and corporations, and libraries. The directory is arranged in two sections: alphabetical listings and subject listings. Entries include complete address, fax numbers, voice phone numbers, and e-mail address (where applicable).

Specialized Directories

The specialized directories discussed in this section are limited in scope to a specific segment of the population, such as Asian Americans. These directories represent a sample of the many types of specialized directories now available.

Asian Americans Information Directory is a comprehensive guide to resources for and about Asian Americans. It provides detailed information about a wide range of print sources and organizations concerned with Asian-American life and culture. Types of resources listed include embassies and consulates, broadcast media, videos, and government agencies and programs. *Asian Americans Information Directory* contains more than 5,200 entries, organized into sections by nationality or ethnic group (e.g., East Indian, Hmong, Pacific Islander, Thai). Within each section, listings are arranged into categories by type of information source. A master name and keyword index provides a single alphabetical arrangement of all resources mentioned in the descriptive listings.

African Americans Information Directory is a guide to approximately 5,300 organizations, agencies, institutions, programs, and publications concerned with African-American life and culture. The entries include such categories as awards, honors, and prizes; newsletters and directories; radio and television stations; and colleges and universities. A master name and keyword index is provided.

Hispanic Americans Information Directory is similar in arrangement to both the *Asian Americans Information Directory* and the *African Americans Information Directory*. Nearly 5,400 organizations, agencies, institutions, programs, and publications relating to Hispanic Americans are listed in this directory. Information ranges from the top 500 Hispanic-owned companies to videos on the creative arts and crafts of Mexico. The directory contains a master name and keyword index.

A wealth of information sources on Native Americans past and present can be found in *Native Americans Information Directory*. This directory is arranged into three broad sections covering North American Indians, Native Alaskans, and Native Hawaiians. More than 5,200 entries are arranged within nationality by type of information resource, including national organizations, museum collections, research centers, and newspapers. Descriptive information provides complete contact data: name, address, telephone number, and contact person. A name and keyword index includes former and alternative tribal names.

Women's Information Directory is a guide to more than 6,000 organizations, agencies, institutions, programs, and publications concerned with women in the United States. This directory contains information about a wide range of sources, such as women's studies programs, research centers, federal agencies, advertising organizations and programs, publications, consultants, and electronic resources. A master name and keyword index provides access to all organizations, publications, and other entries in the directory.

SEARCH STRATEGIES

Strategies reference librarians use for finding directory information for users are varied, as often more than one source will answer a given information need. An essential component of the librarian's search strategy is a thorough knowledge of available directories, both print and electronic. The librarian must also be aware of the limitations of the collection and know when it is appropriate to refer the user to a source outside the collection. Awareness of free Web sites such as the *Internet Public Library* and subscription resources such as *Gale's Ready Reference Shelf* expand the possibilities of searching beyond the physical walls of the library. The availability of electronic database searching at the reference desk adds another element affecting search strategy, because an electronic directory often provides the quickest route to the information needed by the user.

The first step in establishing a strategy is to determine the user's need. Does this person really want just the telephone number for a company, or the name of a company officer as well? Will the address of an association suffice, or would the user also like to know background information on the association? Ascertaining the exact information need of the questioner will assist the librarian in choosing the appropriate reference source.

Once the librarian has chosen a directory to consult, there are various ways of using the source. The librarian should already be aware of the directory's basic organization. Many directories are composed of a straightforward alphabetical arrangement of entries. If indexes are provided, they are often the quickest route to information. Keyword indexes are especially helpful, allowing one to look under a topical term rather than under an exact title or name. A personal name index, if provided, frequently offers the way to find both an individual and the entry for the organization that employs that person. Here again, personal names are more likely to be access points in an electronic database than in a print source.

When using electronic directories, the key to an efficient and effective search is the librarian's knowledge of the content and structure of the database or Web site. This is attained through practice and through a review of database documentation. Searching aids can be found in the form of online Bluesheets for searching Dialog, electronic help or print documentation for searching CD-ROM databases, and on-screen help when searching directory Web sites. The librarian should know which fields are searchable and how to combine terms from different fields using Boolean logic to reduce the retrieved entries to the most exact matches possible. Otherwise, time and possibly money will be lost looking at irrelevant records. In searching the Internet, it is important that the librarian have a thorough knowledge of the various browsers and search engines used to access the Web.

The preface of a print source provides insight into the content, scope, and use of the source. Scanning the preface can help determine whether one is using the proper source for the information needed. The preface often includes a sample entry, with all of the parts of the entry labeled. An example of such an entry is found in Figure 14.2.

Figure 14.2 "Sample Entry" page from *The Foundation Directory*. Reprinted by permission from *The Foundation Directory*. Copyright 1998 by The Foundation Center, 79 Fifth Ave., New York, NY 10003.

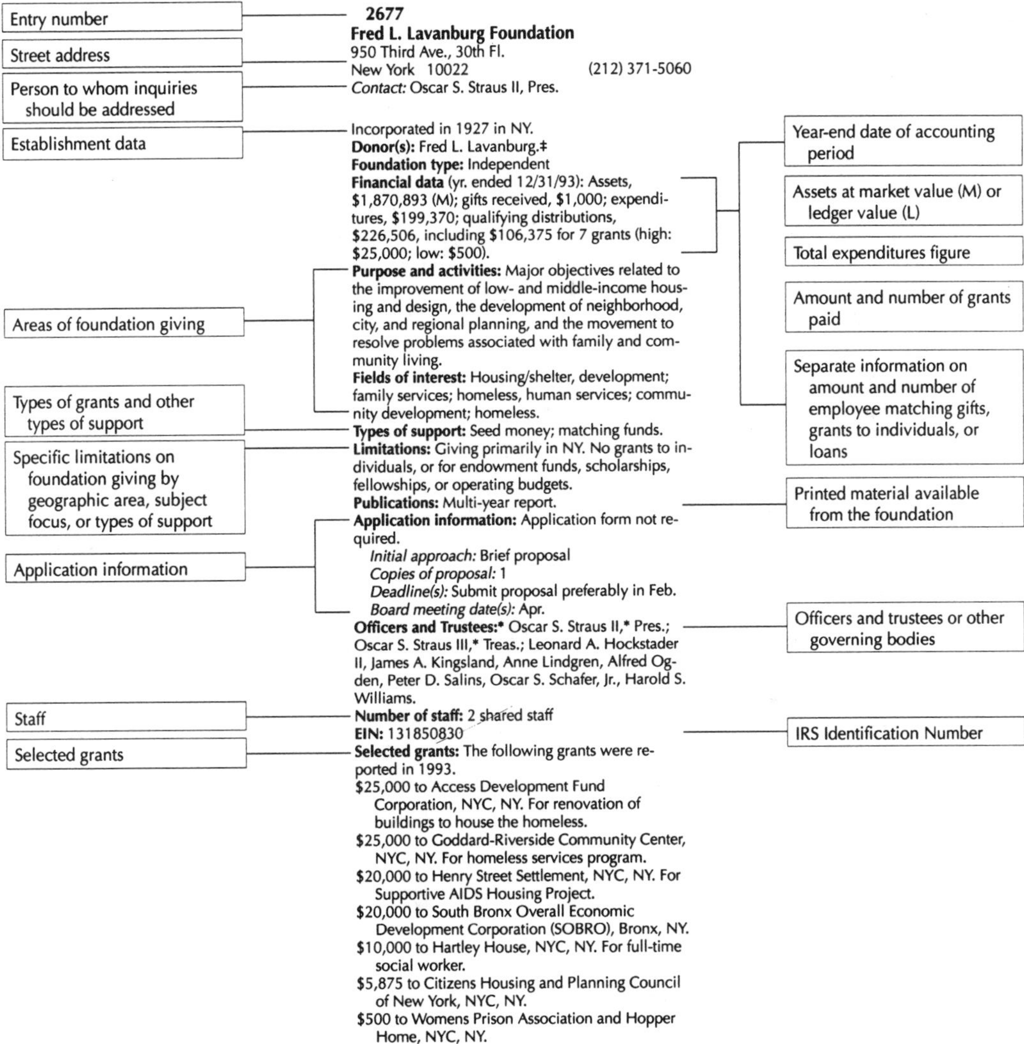

Sample Entry

Entry number — **2677**

Fred L. Lavanburg Foundation

Street address — 950 Third Ave., 30th Fl.
New York 10022 (212) 371-5060

Person to whom inquiries should be addressed — *Contact:* Oscar S. Straus II, Pres.

Establishment data — Incorporated in 1927 in NY.

Donor(s): Fred L. Lavanburg.‡

Foundation type: Independent

Financial data (yr. ended 12/31/93): Assets, $1,870,893 (M); gifts received, $1,000; expenditures, $199,370; qualifying distributions, $226,506, including $106,375 for 7 grants (high: $25,000; low: $500). — Year-end date of accounting period; Assets at market value (M) or ledger value (L); Total expenditures figure; Amount and number of grants paid; Separate information on amount and number of employee matching gifts, grants to individuals, or loans

Areas of foundation giving — **Purpose and activities:** Major objectives related to the improvement of low- and middle-income housing and design, the development of neighborhood, city, and regional planning, and the movement to resolve problems associated with family and community living.
Fields of interest: Housing/shelter, development; family services; homeless, human services; community development; homeless.

Types of grants and other types of support — **Types of support:** Seed money; matching funds.

Specific limitations on foundation giving by geographic area, subject focus, or types of support — **Limitations:** Giving primarily in NY. No grants to individuals, or for endowment funds, scholarships, fellowships, or operating budgets.

Printed material available from the foundation — **Publications:** Multi-year report.

Application information — **Application information:** Application form not required.
Initial approach: Brief proposal
Copies of proposal: 1
Deadline(s): Submit proposal preferably in Feb.
Board meeting date(s): Apr.

Officers and trustees or other governing bodies — **Officers and Trustees:*** Oscar S. Straus II,* Pres.; Oscar S. Straus III,* Treas.; Leonard A. Hockstader II, James A. Kingsland, Anne Lindgren, Alfred Ogden, Peter D. Salins, Oscar S. Schafer, Jr., Harold S. Williams.

Staff — **Number of staff:** 2 shared staff

IRS Identification Number — **EIN:** 131850830

Selected grants — **Selected grants:** The following grants were reported in 1993.
$25,000 to Access Development Fund Corporation, NYC, NY. For renovation of buildings to house the homeless.
$25,000 to Goddard-Riverside Community Center, NYC, NY. For homeless services program.
$20,000 to Henry Street Settlement, NYC, NY. For Supportive AIDS Housing Project.
$20,000 to South Bronx Overall Economic Development Corporation (SOBRO), Bronx, NY.
$10,000 to Hartley House, NYC, NY. For full-time social worker.
$5,875 to Citizens Housing and Planning Council of New York, NYC, NY.
$500 to Womens Prison Association and Hopper Home, NYC, NY.

For a complete listing of data elements, see "How to Use *The Foundation Directory Part 2*" in the Introduction.

Symbols

‡ Indicates individual is deceased.
(L) Ledger value of assets.
(M) Market value of assets.
* Officer is also a trustee or director.

In addition to knowing the structure of print and online directories and understanding the scope of the user's request, creativity on the part of the librarian is required. The use of alternative sources, such as tapping the expertise of a colleague or making a telephone call to an association or institution, can be important elements of an effective search strategy for locating directory information.

Box 14.2 Search Strategy: Locating Associations

A library user had just checked out the book *Summerhill* by A. S. Neill. She had not yet read the book but thought it had something to do with self-regulated schools in England, and she wanted to know if a center for that type of education existed in the United States. Because the librarian had no knowledge of the information discussed in *Summerhill,* he first located the title in the library's catalog to establish subject tracings. The subjects "Education—Experimental methods" and "Free schools" were both used for the title *Summerhill.*

The librarian took these subject headings to the name and keyword index volume of the *Encyclopedia of Associations: National Organizations of the U.S.* Several pages of listings were found under "Education" but "Education, Experimental" was not a subject heading. A search under the heading "Experimental Education" yielded no results.

Checking *Encyclopedia of Associations* again, this time under "Free schools," the librarian found that nothing was listed. At this point he decided to try other terminology to express the same topic. A search under the topic "Alternative Education" in the name and keyword index showed 16 names of associations. The librarian chose the one most likely to match the user's needs, and looked up the entry information. Because *Encyclopedia of Associations* groups entries by subject area, the library user was able to choose one or two appropriate associations from the several listed.

NOTES

1. Joseph R. Strayer, ed., *Dictionary of the Middle Ages* (New York: Scribner, 1982), 24:237-39.

2. Adrian Room, ed., *Dictionary of Britain* (New York: Oxford University Press, 1986), 81.

3. Heartsill Young, ed., *The ALA Glossary of Library and Information Science* (Chicago: American Library Association, 1983), 75.

LIST OF SOURCES

African Americans Information Directory, 1998-99. 4th ed. Detroit: Gale Research, 1998. 560p.

American Art Directory, 1999-2000. 57th ed. New Providence, N.J.: National Register Publishing, 1999. 970p.

American Book Trade Directory, 2000-2001. 46th ed. New Providence, N.J.: R. R. Bowker, 2000. 1801p.

American Library Directory, 2000-2001. 53d ed. 2 vols. New Providence, N.J.: R. R. Bowker, 2000. Also available on CD-ROM and online.

American School Directory. Available: http://www.asd.com.

Annual Register of Grant Support, 2000. 33d ed. New Providence, N.J.: R. R. Bowker, 2000. 1344p.

AnyWho Toll Free Directory. Available: http://www.anywho.com.

Asian Americans Information Directory, 1994-95. 2d ed. Edited by Charles B. Montney. Detroit: Gale Research, 1994. 577p.

Associations Canada: The Directory of Associations in Canada/Le Répertoire des Associations du Canada, 2000/2001. 21st ed. Toronto: Micromedia, 2000. 1685p. Also available on CD-ROM and online.

Associations on the Net. Available: http://www.ipl.org/ref/AON.

Associations Unlimited. [CD-ROM]. Farmington Hills, Mich.: Gale Group. Semi-annual. Also available online.

Books in Print: Publishers, 1999–2000. 52d ed. New Providence, N.J.: R. R. Bowker, 1999. 2704p.

The Buddhist Directory. Compiled by Peter Lorie and Julie Foakes. Boston: Charles E. Tuttle, 1997. 424p.

Business Phone Book USA, 2000. 22d ed. 2 vols. Detroit: Omnigraphics, Inc., 2000. Also available on CD-ROM.

Canadian Almanac & Directory. Toronto: Canadian Almanac & Directory Publishing, 1848– . Annual.

Carroll's County Directory. Washington, D.C.: Carroll Publishing, 1984– . Semi-annual. Also available on CD-ROM and online.

Carroll's Federal Directory. Washington, D.C.: Carroll Publishing, 1980– . Bimonthly. Also available on CD-ROM and online.

Carroll's Municipal Directory. Washington, D.C.: Carroll Publishing, 1984– . Semi-annual. Also available on CD-ROM and online.

Carroll's State Directory. Washington, D.C.: Carroll Publishing, 1980- . 3 per year. Also available on CD-ROM and online.

The College Blue Book. 27th ed. 5 vols. New York: Macmillan Reference USA, 1999. Also available on CD-ROM.

Commonwealth Universities Yearbook, 2000. 75th ed. 2 vols. London: Association of Commonwealth Universities, 2000.

Corporate Affiliations Plus. [CD-ROM]. New Providence, N.J.: National Register Publishing. Quarterly.

D&B Business Locator CD-ROM. [CD-ROM]. Parsippany, N.J.: Dun & Bradstreet Information Services. Quarterly.

D&B Companies Online. Available: http://www.companiesonline.com.

D&B Million Dollar Disc. [CD-ROM]. Parsippany, N.J.: Dun & Bradstreet Information Services. Quarterly.

D&B—Canadian Dun's Market Identifiers. Parsippany, N.J.: Dun & Bradstreet Information Services. Available online.

D&B—Dun's Electronic Business Directory. Parsippany, N.J.: Dun & Bradstreet Information Services. Available online.

D&B—Dun's Market Identifiers. Parsippany, N.J.: Dun & Bradstreet Information Services. Available online.

Directories in Print. 18th ed. 2 vols. Edited by Dawn Conzett DesJardins. Farmington Hills, Mich.: Gale Group, 2000.

Directory of Corporate Affiliations, 2000. 5 vols. New Providence, N.J.: National Register Publishing, 2000. Also available online.

Directory of Research Grants, 2000. 25th ed. Phoenix, Ariz.: Oryx Press, 2000. 1246p.

Directory of Special Libraries and Information Centers. 24th ed. 3 vols. Edited by Marc Faerber and Matthew Miskelly. Farmington Hills, Mich.: Gale Group, 2000.

Encyclopedia of Associations: International Organizations. 35th ed. 2 vols. Edited by Tara E. Sheets. Farmington Hills, Mich.: Gale Group, 2000. Also available on CD-ROM and online.

Encyclopedia of Associations: National Organizations of the U.S. 35th ed. 3 vols. Edited by Tara E. Sheets. Farmington Hills, Mich.: Gale Group, 1999. Also available on CD-ROM and online.

Encyclopedia of Associations: Regional, State, and Local Organizations. 10th ed. 5 vols. Edited by Ken Karges. Farmington Hills, Mich.: Gale Group, 2000. Also available on CD-ROM and online.

FC Search: The Foundation Center's Database on CD-ROM. [CD-ROM]. New York: Foundation Center. Semi-annual.

The Foundation Center Online. Available: http://fdncenter.org.

The Foundation Directory, 2000. 22d ed. Edited by David G. Jacobs. New York: Foundation Center, 2000. 2638p. Also available online.

The Foundation Directory, Part 2. Edited by Melissa Lunn. New York: Foundation Center, 2000. 1759p.

The Foundation Directory Supplement. New York: Foundation Center, 2000. 902p.

The Foundation Grants Index, 2000. 28th ed. Edited by Rebecca MacLean. New York: Foundation Center, 1999. 2902p. Also available online.

Foundations On-line. Available: http://www.foundations.org.

Gale Database of Publications and Broadcast Media. Farmington Hills, Mich.: Gale Group. Available online.

Gale's Ready Reference Shelf. Farmington Hills, Mich.: Gale Group. Available online.

Government Research Directory, 2000. 13th ed. Edited by Donna Batten. Farmington Hills, Mich.: Gale Group, 2000. 853p.

GRANTS. [CD-ROM]. Phoenix, Ariz.: Oryx Press. Bimonthly. Also available online.

The HEP 2000 Higher Education Directory. 18th ed. Edited by Mary Pat Rodenhouse and Constance Healy Torregrosa. Falls Church, Va.: Higher Education Publications, 1999. 812p.

Hispanic Americans Information Directory, 1994-95. 3d ed. Edited by Charles B. Montney. Detroit: Gale Research, 1994. 515p.

InfoUSA.com. Available: http://www.infousa.com.

International Handbook of Universities. 15th ed. New York: Grove's Dictionaries, 1998. 2474p.

International Literary Market Place, 2000. New Providence, N.J.: R. R. Bowker, 1999. 1593p.

International Research Centers Directory, 2000. 13th ed. Edited by Donna Wood. Farmington Hills, Mich.: Gale Group, 2000. 1300p.

Libweb: Library Servers via WWW. Available: http://sunsite.berkeley.edu/Libweb.

Literary Market Place, 2000. 2 vols. New Providence, N.J.: R. R. Bowker, 1999.

Literary Market Place Online. Available: http://www.literarymarketplace.com.

Million Dollar Directory. 5 vols. Parsippany, N.J.: Dun & Bradstreet Information Services, 1998.

National E-Mail and Fax Directory, 2000. Edited by Sheila Dow. Farmington Hills, Mich.: Gale Group, 1999. 2041p.

National Faculty Directory, 2000. 31st ed. 3 vols. Farmington Hills, Mich.: Gale Group, 2000.

Native Americans Information Directory. 2d ed. Detroit: Gale Research, 1998. 371p.

New Research Centers. 26th ed. Edited by Donna Wood. Farmington Hills, Mich.: Gale Group, 2000. 120p.

Official Museum Directory, 2000. 30th ed. 2 vols. New Providence, N.J.: National Register Publishing, 1999.

Patterson's American Education 2000. 96th ed. Mount Prospect, Ill.: Education Directories, 2000. 940p.

PhoneDisc. [CD-ROM]. Bethesda, Md.: PhoneDisc Corporation.

Phonefiche. [microfiche]. Ann Arbor, Mich.: UMI.

Publishers' Catalogues Home Page. Available: http://www.lights.com/publisher.

Publishers Directory. 22d ed. Edited by Louise Gagné. Farmington Hills, Mich.: Gale Group, 2000. 2083p.

Publishers, Distributors, & Wholesalers of the United States, 2000–2001. 2 vols. New Providence, N.J.: R. R. Bowker, 2000. Also available online.

Research Centers and Services Directories. Farmington Hills, Mich.: Gale Group. Available online.

Research Centers Directory. 26th ed. 2 vols. Edited by Donna Wood. Farmington Hills, Mich.: Gale Group, 2000.

Standard & Poor's Corporations. [CD-ROM]. New York: Standard & Poor's Corporation. Monthly.

Standard & Poor's Register—Biographical. New York: Standard & Poor's Corporation. Available online.

Standard & Poor's Register—Corporate. New York: Standard & Poor's Corporation. Available online.

Standard & Poor's Register of Corporations, Directors and Executives. 3 vols. New York: McGraw-Hill, 2000.

Subject Collections. 7th ed. 2 vols. Compiled by Lee Ash and William G. Miller. New Providence, N.J.: R. R. Bowker, 1993.

Telephone Directories on the Web. Available: http://www.teldir.com/eng.

Thomas Register of American Manufacturers. 90th ed. 33 vols. New York: Thomas Publishing, 2000. Also available on CD-ROM, online, and at http://www.thomasregister.com.

Washington Information Directory, 2000-2001. Washington, D.C.: Congressional Quarterly, 2000. 993p.

Web Site Source Book. 5th ed. Detroit: Omnigraphics, 2000. 2200p.

WhoWhere. Available: http://www.whowhere.lycos.com.

Women's Information Directory. Detroit: Gale Research, 1993. 795p.

World Chamber of Commerce Directory, 2000. Loveland, Colo.: World Chamber of Commerce Directory, 2000. 440p. Also available: http://chamber-of-commerce.com/search.htm.

World Guide to Libraries. 14th ed. 2 vols. München: K. G. Saur, 1999.

The World of Learning. 50th ed. London: Europa, 1999. 2135p.

Worldwide Government Directory. Washington, D.C.: Keesings Worldwide, 2000. 1564p.

Yearbook of International Organizations, 1999-2000. 36th ed. 4 vols. Edited by Union of International Associations. München: K. G. Saur, 1999.

Yearbook Plus: International Organizations and Biographies. [CD-ROM]. München: K. G. Saur, 1999.

ADDITIONAL READINGS

Andrews, Phyllis M. "Grant Information Online." *Database* 16 (April 1993): 38-45.

Andrews describes how to search online for funding from private and government sources using *The Foundation Grants Index* (Dialog File 27), *The Foundation Directory* (Dialog File 26), and *GRANTS* (Dialog File 85).

Ernest, Douglas, Jr., Joan Beam, and Jennifer Monath. "Telephone Directory Use in an Academic Library." *Reference Services Review* 20 (Spring 1992): 49-56.

This article examines the history of telephone directory collections in both public and academic libraries and describes and analyzes a survey of telephone directory collection use.

Grogan, Denis. *Encyclopedias, Yearbooks, Directories and Statistical Sources.* London: Clive Bingley, 1987. 170p. (Grogan's Case Studies in Reference Work, v. 2).

Although this text focuses primarily on British sources, the search strategies and discussions of directories are useful and instructional. Pages 111-134 deal with directories.

Helmer, Dona. "Sources on Grants, Funding, and Financial Aid." *Booklist* 94 (July 1998): 1900-1903.

This annotated bibliography provides information on the types of resources available on grants and funding opportunities. Sources marked with an asterisk suggest a basic collection of grant information for most libraries.

Lavin, Michael R. "A Clash of Titans: Comparing America's Most Comprehensive Business Directories." *Database* 21 (June/July 1998): 44-48.

The Dialog databases *American Business Directory* (File 531) and *D&B—Dun's Market Identifiers* (File 516) are evaluated for accuracy, timeliness, completeness of entries, and comprehensiveness of company coverage.

Notess, Greg R. "Internet Ready Reference Sources." *Database* 19 (April/May 1996): 88-91.

The focus of this article is a few selected Internet business directories for ready-reference use. Included in the discussion are *Central Source Yellow Pages, NYNEX Interactive Yellow Pages, Hoover's Online,* and the *United States Postal Service Address and ZIP Code Information* page.

Ojala, Marydee. "Locating Companies with DIALOG's Company Name Finder." *Database* 15 (April 1992): 87-91.

This article describes an efficient way to search for company information online in a world where company names are not standardized.

Pack, Thomas. "A Guided Tour of the Internet Public Library." *Database* 19 (October/November 1996): 52-56.

Thomas Pack describes the contents and uses of the Internet Public Library, cyberspace's unofficial library, maintained by the University of Michigan's School of Information. The IPL site contains Internet directories in the areas of business and associations.

Sternberg, Hilary. "Internet Resources for Grants and Foundations." *College & Research Libraries News* 58 (May 1997): 314-17.

This article lists important Internet sites for the identification of grant and foundation funding. A section of the sites are directories. Note that this column is featured in each issue of *C&RL News*; each one is devoted to a different subject area. This is a good source to scan for finding directory sites on the Internet.

Tobin, Carol M. "The Book That Built Gale Research: The *Encyclopedia of Associations*." In *Distinguished Classics of Reference Publishing*, edited by James Rettig. Phoenix, Ariz.: Oryx Press, 1992.

This chapter is a description of the evolution of the *Encyclopedia of Associations*, including such topics as the method of compilation and computerized production of this directory.

CHAPTER

15

ALMANACS, YEARBOOKS, AND HANDBOOKS

Laura R. Lucio and Sandra L. Wolf

USES AND CHARACTERISTICS

Almanacs, yearbooks, and handbooks provide concise factual information about current and historical events; organizations, people, places, and things; and statistical trends. The information in these tools is almost always available in other sources. Newspapers and journals report current events; encyclopedias and history books record historical facts; many sources, including directories and encyclopedias, supply information about organizations, people, and things; atlases and gazetteers, as well as other sources, present information about places; and government publications are invaluable sources of statistics and statistical trends. And now, of course, the World Wide Web provides access to all of these types of sources and more.

But surprisingly, almanacs, yearbooks, and handbooks are often the fastest and easiest way to locate concise facts or summaries. They consolidate information, summarizing and synthesizing it. In the hands of skilled librarians, information can be quickly retrieved. These tools, however, are not as useful if detailed or analytical discussion is sought, or primary sources are required. Reference librarians must evaluate the information needs of users and employ their knowledge of reference works to determine which type of reference tool will supply the most satisfactory answer.

Almanacs

Almanacs appeared first in the sixteenth and seventeenth centuries as calendars, containing days, weeks, and months, and astronomical data such as the phases of the sun and moon, home remedies, and folk wisdom. The first American almanac was published in 1639, but the most famous early North American almanac is Benjamin Franklin's *Poor Richard's Almanack*, which was published from 1732 to 1748. The *Old Farmer's Almanac* continues to be published as a surviving example of this type of almanac and is also available on the Web.

In the nineteenth century, American newspapers began to publish almanacs. These almanacs developed from the newspapers' need for easy access to accurate, factual information about political, historical, and current events[1] and were more like contemporary almanacs discussed in this chapter. These latter-day almanacs include some astronomical and calendar data but more important, are compendia of current and retrospective statistics and facts.

Although most almanacs are broad in geographical and subject coverage, many of the best-known general almanacs emphasize a particular country or state. Although the contemporary almanac consists of fact rather than folklore, the most famous general almanacs are still rooted in popular culture, which explains many aspects of their content. Sports, entertainment, practical information such as zip codes and first aid treatment, and business addresses are all part of the contents. An almanac is the place to find answers to questions such as:

- What is a hurricane?
- How many calories are in a tablespoon of butter?
- Who was the youngest president of the United States?
- What is the address of the Special Libraries Association?
- What percentage of adult Americans smoke?
- Where can one find a map showing international time zones?
- What is the population of Australia?
- How many seasons was Michael Jordan a scoring leader in the National Basketball Association?

Yearbooks

Most almanacs are issued annually, and in this respect they are like yearbooks. However, *yearbooks,* or *annuals* as they are sometimes called, stress events and statistics for a single year, usually the year preceding the publication date, whereas almanacs also have historical facts and statistics. Nomenclature for reference books is not consistent; almanacs may be called yearbooks and vice versa. Encyclopedias often issue yearbooks that supplement the main set and chiefly review a specific year. These yearbooks contain a chronology of the year, biographies of newsmakers, obituaries, sports news, current statistical data, and articles about events of the year. A general yearbook is the place to find information such as:

- An obituary for a person who died during the year
- A description of a disaster that occurred during the year
- The winner of a major athletic event that happened during the year
- Discussion of a current controversial social problem
- Chronology of important political happenings.

Although a general almanac also provides some of the same information, the yearbook's presentation of the information is different. Obituaries in the encyclopedia yearbook are longer and may include a photograph. Yearbooks regularly index personal names, while almanacs, in book format, index personal names sparingly. Yearbooks usually contain longer descriptions of events and more analysis and evaluation, and articles are almost always signed. Yearbooks customarily have larger and more readable type than almanacs in book format. Because almanacs and yearbooks are different, they fill different information needs. Almanacs are full of bits of data. A library user who simply wants to know if someone has died in the previous year will be content with information easily located by a reference librarian aware that almanacs index deaths under "obituaries" instead of personal names. A general almanac will satisfy a sports fan wanting box scores from the most recent World Series, but a yearbook will be a more suitable tool for a fan wanting a game-by-game description of the series.

Handbooks

Some yearbooks provide information about people, events, and trends in a single area. These yearbooks are similar to another category of reference work, the handbook. The *handbook*, or *manual* as it is sometimes called, serves as a handy guide to a particular subject. Often, large amounts of information about a subject are compressed into a single volume. A selection of handbooks, common to many general reference departments, is discussed in this chapter, but this selection represents a small sample of the handbooks available. Because handbooks often include examples, illustrations, or both, users may wish or need to look at these titles themselves. A handbook reviews a particular topic in a factual and comprehensive way. Handbooks provide answers to questions such as:

- Are there any adverse side effects to this drug?
- What happened in history on November 23, my birthday?
- Is the Sears Tower the world's tallest building?
- How do I format a bibliography?
- What do I wear to a formal evening wedding?

EVALUATION

In evaluating almanacs, yearbooks, and handbooks, accuracy, comprehensiveness, currency of information, and ease of use are all important to both user and librarian.

Accuracy

Accuracy is the single most important characteristic of works that present factual information. Reference librarians can test the accuracy and reliability of almanacs, yearbooks, and handbooks by reading reviews written by knowledgeable reviewers, by comparing data in different sources, and by relying on personal expertise. The longtime reputation of a work is also a guide, subject to continual re-evaluation. Errors occur in even the most prestigious works. These errors should be corrected in subsequent editions or by addenda.

Indexing

The index in a fact book should be helpful, accurate, and internally consistent in style and terminology, and it should complement the overall arrangement of the work. Some yearbooks include a cumulative index that covers more than the current volume. This is an extremely useful feature if, for example, the exact date of an event is unknown.

Documentation

Many almanacs, yearbooks, and handbooks are composed, at least in part, of secondhand information. The statistics should be recent and from identified sources. Identification should be complete enough to lead to the original source where additional information might be located. Reference works without documentation are of questionable reliability.

Comprehensiveness

Almanacs, yearbooks, and handbooks are a source of information on a single subject or many subjects. They should be comprehensive within their stated scope; if they are not, they have little value.

Uniqueness

A certain amount of overlap in reference collections is desirable, because users' needs vary in terms of the amount and presentation of information. Nonetheless, the reference work should provide either some unique information or a unique approach to information.

Format

Almanacs, yearbooks, and handbooks should be organized in a logical manner, one that the user can understand. Because many of these publications are inexpensive, they are sometimes less physically attractive than other types of reference books, but readability is still an important consideration. Currently, some familiar reference works are being marketed as online or CD-ROM databases or both. These electronic formats enable greater flexibility and ease of use. They may enhance traditional indexing through the use of keyword searching, not just of an index but of the full (complete) text as well. For example, users can find personal names in reference works that do not index personal names and, through the use of Boolean logic, combine terms and concepts.

Currency

A fact book containing current data is already out-of-date by the time it is published. This is an inherent limitation of this kind of reference tool. However, within the limitations of their publishing schedules, fact books should be continually updated. Electronic editions can be updated more frequently, but this varies.

SELECTION

Reference librarians need reference works that answer the information demands of their users. Most libraries can benefit from a general almanac. A paperbound edition of one of the best-known U.S. almanacs costs about $10. Every general reference collection in an academic or public library needs at least one almanac, and even specialized libraries have an occasional demand for information in an almanac. Research has also shown that if one almanac is good, several may be better, because each almanac has unique data and features.[2]

Although almanacs and encyclopedia yearbooks include some of the same information, they present this information differently. Some users need the longer explanation and description that encyclopedia yearbooks include. For this reason, an encyclopedia yearbook is a useful addition to general reference collections. These yearbooks, however, are published to meet the needs of owners who rarely buy a new set of encyclopedias. Therefore, libraries that routinely acquire the latest revision of major encyclopedias every few years may decide not to buy yearbooks for every set of encyclopedias.

Almanacs and encyclopedia yearbooks consist of information that is more extensively treated in other sources. The decision of whether to rely on the almanac and yearbook to supply information or to purchase specialized sources depends on the frequency of demand for more facts in greater depth than the almanac and yearbook supply. For example, *The World Almanac* has a list of "Associations and Societies." This list provides the founding date, address, and number of members of approximately a thousand organizations. *Encyclopedia of Associations* (discussed in Chapter 14) provides more information about more organizations. Most general reference collections own *Encyclopedia of Associations,* but small or specialized libraries may find that *The World Almanac* meets most of their needs.

Referral is another way of responding to a request that cannot be answered using the library's collection. The availability of other reference collections and services in a community can be tapped, and it may not be necessary to duplicate little-used reference tools. The Web can also expand the resources of libraries. For example, the *Stumpers-L* electronic discussion group provides a place to post questions for hard-to-find answers. The electronic discussion group is archived, and users can check the archive to see if a question has already been answered. The *Internet Public Library* is another useful resource.

Almanacs, yearbooks, and handbooks tend to offer very good value at a low cost. (However, even the least expensive, most useful tool is a poor investment if no one wants the information it contains.) Nevertheless, cost may be a determinant. Some general reference departments in public and academic libraries and many school libraries can afford to purchase a moderately priced yearbook like *The Statesman's Yearbook* but not the more expensive *Europa World Year Book*.

Characteristics of users, such as age, education, and occupation, influence decisions about which works to purchase. Various types of libraries have some of the same almanacs, yearbooks, and handbooks, but there are significant differences in emphasis between these types. Public libraries often get requests for information about how to make or repair household items and machinery. Automobile repair manuals, as an example, are in demand, and all but the smallest public library will have at least one such manual. Reference works relating to hobbies and games—bird watching, various kinds of collecting, craft work, card games, and the like—are standard tools in public library reference departments. Other common specialized almanacs, yearbooks, and handbooks in public libraries relate to questions of health, investments, consumer affairs, legal matters, and popular entertainment.

Academic libraries have some of the same works, although not nearly as many. Academic collections, as might be expected, concentrate on scholarly and educational sources and have many almanacs, yearbooks, and handbooks that support teaching and research. School libraries generally have smaller collections, and the intellectual level of the student body affects the books selected. Some almanacs, yearbooks, and handbooks are available in youth editions. Special libraries have as many specialized handbooks in their field as budgets will allow.

Electronic Options

The acquisition of an electronic edition of an almanac, yearbook, or handbook depends on several factors. Does the electronic edition improve the ability to retrieve information? Is it more current? Is it frequently used? Can it be easily integrated into the existing workspace? Is it part of a larger electronic product? For example, yearbooks are frequently part of the electronic edition of their parent encyclopedia. Since many of these tools are available from different vendors offering different interfaces, a secondary decision may be necessary to determine which version to acquire. Compatibility with other electronic products may determine vendor selection. Many other factors influence the acquisition of electronic tools. The reliability and completeness of information is important, but enhanced search capabilities, including the presence of hyperlinks and full text, are also important. Online searching using vendors such as Dialog may be an alternative to purchase, if occasional use of a tool is all that is required.

The cost of online and CD-ROM databases and the equipment needed to access them may deter some libraries from acquiring almanacs, yearbooks, and handbooks in these formats. Many libraries belong to consortia that acquire electronic products at discounted rates. Decisions of which tools to purchase are often taken out of the local librarian's control. The Web offers an abundance of free information. There are, however, problems in the use of the Web as a substitute for other sources. The authority for information on a Web site is critical. In addition, surfing the Web is time-consuming and sometimes counterproductive. Librarians expected to use the Web as a routine source for information need to acquire and continually upgrade their knowledge of what is available.

IMPORTANT GENERAL SOURCES

The reference collections in most libraries will contain almanacs, yearbooks, and handbooks. In this section, some examples of these genres are discussed. The examples were chosen either because they are widely used classics or because they are illustrative of subject-specific almanacs, yearbooks, and handbooks.

Almanacs

The World Almanac and Book of Facts began in 1868 as a publication of the *New York World* newspaper. Although it prominently bears the date of the following year, the almanac is published annually at the end of November. In election years (i.e., every two years), the cut-off date for news is the November election, and in off years, baseball's World Series in late October is the last event covered.[3] A series of colored plates of countries' flags, a map of world time zones, and maps of various parts of the world are in the center of the almanac. Millions of copies of *The World Almanac* are sold each year, and it annually makes the *New York Times* "Paperback Best Sellers" list in the "Advice, How-to and Miscellaneous" category.

Mastery of indexes is the key to using almanacs and other fact books as reference works. *The World Almanac* has three indexes: a general index in the front, a quick reference index on the last page, and a quick thumb index that utilizes black marks on the fore-edge of the volume to indicate the location of some sections of the almanac. The back cover of the paperback and the book jacket of the hardcover edition have the list of headings for the quick thumb index. Although these sections have varied somewhat from year to year, they often include the year in review, astronomy and calendar, noted personalities, nations of the world, and sports. A user can find the population of Australia, for example, by using the quick thumb index to turn to "nations of the world," an alphabetically arranged summary of information about countries of the world, including the United States. The general index consists of topical subject headings and includes only a few personal names. The quick reference index is composed of keywords for some of the most sought-after information in the almanac. Those who understand the organization of the almanac will find this index easier to use for quick reference, but less complete than the general one. The print is larger and the terms more to the point in the quick reference.

The World Almanac is now available electronically on OCLC FirstSearch and FACTS.com. The availability in electronic format of fact books such as *The World Almanac* enhances search capabilities by making additional words in the text searchable. However, in some cases, the paper edition is faster and easier to use. The general index of the paper edition includes many subentries that do not appear in the electronic editions. The definition of a "hurricane," the calories in a tablespoon of "butter," and the percent of adult Americans who smoke can be easily ascertained through the use of the general index, because "hurricane," "butter," and "smoking" are appropriately subdivided by "definition," "nutritive value," and "adult," respectively. The electronic edition relies on keyword searching. The question about the youngest president is an example of the way that the electronic editions can provide more or different information. The name of the youngest president in the history of the U.S. can be found by consulting the "Presidential Facts" section of the paper edition of *The World Almanac.* It is easily located in the general index under "Presidents, U.S.," subdivided "miscellaneous facts," or in the quick reference index under "Presidents, U.S." The answer given is Theodore Roosevelt. The electronic version gives the same answer. However, keyword searching on the phrase "youngest president" in the electronic version reveals that although Roosevelt was the youngest president to *hold* the office, John F. Kennedy was the youngest president *elected* to office.

Other questions raised earlier in this chapter can also be easily answered by the almanac. A map of international time zones can also be found in the general index under "Time," subdivided by "zones (map)." The OCLC FirstSearch version of *The World Almanac* does not include graphics. The information about Michael Jordan can also best be found through use of the general index. The data on Jordan appear twice, once in a chart of NBA scoring leaders, located either by searching the index under "basketball," subdivided "NBA," or under the National Basketball Association, and the other time in a brief biography of Jordan found in the "Sports Personalities, Noted" section. Jordan's name does not appear in the general index, but keyword searching under his name in the electronic edition quickly retrieves the same information. The phrase "noted personalities" is used to index biographical information in the almanac. Biographical information is arranged by categories of people. "Widely Known Americans of the Present," "Noted African Americans of the Past," "Poets Laureate," and "Noted Writers of the Past" are but a few of the categories represented.

Beginning in 2000, *The World Almanac Reference Database@FACTS.com* (http://www.facts.com/fdcrs) offers an enhanced electronic version of *The World Almanac* with monthly updating, full-text searching, photos and other graphics, and links to other Web sites. This is part of a subscription site created for schools and libraries.

The World Almanac is a respected reference source that sits next to the telephone at the reference desk in many libraries. Sometimes the almanac is a better-than-average source of information. For example, the table listing calories is very good (see Figure 15.1) for one part of this table. Derived from a U.S. Department of Agriculture publication, the table includes a household measure, the tablespoon, and a scientific measure, the gram. However, occasionally the information in the almanac is incorrect. As an example, when the Special Libraries Association moved from New York to Washington, D.C., in late 1985, a change in address did not appear in the almanac until the 1988 (i.e., 1987) edition.

Figure 15.1 Calorie chart from *The World Almanac*. Reprinted with permission from *The World Almanac and Book of Facts*. Copyright © World Almanac Education Group. All rights reserved.

FOOD	Measure	Grams	Food Energy (calories)	Protein (grams)	Fat (grams)	Saturated fats (grams)	Carbohydrate (grams)	Calcium (milligrams)	Iron (milligrams)	Sodium (milligrams)	Vitamin A (I.U.)	Ascorbic Acid (milligrams)
DAIRY PRODUCTS												
Cheese, cheddar, cut pieces	1 oz.	28	115	7	9	6.0	T	204	0.2	176	300	0
Cheese, cottage, small curd	1 cup	210	215	26	9	6.0	6	126	0.3	850	340	T
Cheese, cream	1 oz.	28	100	2	10	6.2	1	23	0.3	84	400	0
Cheese, Swiss	1 oz.	28	95	7	7	4.5	1	219	0.2	388	230	0
Half-and-half	1 tbsp.	15	20	T	2	1.1	1	16	T	6	70	T
Cream, sour	1 tbsp.	12	25	T	3	1.6	1	14	T	6	90	T
Milk, whole	1 cup	244	150	8	8	5.1	11	291	0.1	120	310	2
Milk, nonfat (skim)	1 cup	245	85	8	T	0.3	12	302	0.1	126	500	2
Milkshake, chocolate	10 oz.	283	355	9	8	4.8	60	374	0.9	314	240	0
Ice cream, hardened	1 cup	133	270	5	14	8.9	32	176	0.1	116	540	1
Sherbet	1 cup	193	270	2	4	2.4	59	103	0.3	88	190	4
Yogurt, fruit-flavored	8 oz.	227	230	10	2	1.6	43	345	0.2	133	100	1

The World Almanac, however, was not the only reference work that did not have the correct address. Good reference librarians can guard against this type of error by updating heavily used reference works. Most of the time the question of whether or not to use the almanac depends not on accuracy but on the amount of information the user needs. A general or special encyclopedia or encyclopedia yearbook has more information and a helpful bibliography. In addition, persons doing research generally prefer to use primary sources or a secondary source that is more detailed than an almanac.

Information Please Almanac has been published annually since 1947 by a series of publishers with variant titles. Its most recent title is *The Time Almanac*. "Information Please" was the name of a famous quiz program. The *Information Please Almanac* is very similar to the *World Almanac* both in content and style. The print in *Information Please Almanac* is more readable than that of *The World Almanac*, and *Information Please* indexes more personal and place names. Each almanac has some information the other almanac does not. *Information Please Almanac*, for instance, has a crossword puzzle guide and a writer's guide but does not have a list of calories.

In 1998, the *Information Please Almanac* appeared as part of a Web site, *Infoplease.com*, that also includes the *Random House Webster's College Dictionary* and *The Columbia Encyclopedia* (6th ed.). In addition, the *ESPN Information Please Sports Almanac, Information Please Kids' Almanac, Information Please Girls' Almanac*, and the *A&E Entertainment Almanac from Information Please* are included. The site is continuously updated, offering more recent information than can be found in the paper edition.

Two prestigious American newspapers, the *New York Times* and the *Wall Street Journal*, began to compile almanacs in 1997. The *New York Times Almanac* is very similar to *The World Almanac* and *Information Please Almanac*. The *Wall Street Journal Almanac* is divided into ten theme chapters, including the U.S. economy, technology and science, living in America, media and entertainment, and sports. Each chapter begins with a brief essay, followed by many easy-to-read graphs, tables, and charts that are helpful in interpreting long-range trends. The focus is primarily the U.S. economy, but useful information on education, sports, and entertainment is also included. A good index at the end of the volume includes personal names.

The question "What percentage of Americans smoke?" illustrates the way in which two almanacs can differ. *The World Almanac* presents the information in a table that occupies less than a quarter of a page, while the same information is presented in the *Journal Almanac* in three separate charts and graphs that occupy an entire page (see Figure 15.2, below and page 365).

There are also many almanacs that focus on countries or regions. *Whitaker's Almanack* was founded in London in 1868 by the publisher Joseph Whitaker. It emphasizes the United Kingdom in the way that *The World Almanac* and *Information Please Almanac* emphasize the United States. For this reason, it is a useful source for current information about the United Kingdom. For example, it lists historic landmarks, museums, and monuments, giving where appropriate a brief history, hours open, and admission charge. Other features include sections on British taxation, laws, and passport regulations. The almanac has extensive coverage of the British nobility, including a list of the English kings and queens, a list of peers and their heirs, orders of chivalry, and a list of baronetage and knightage. *Whitaker's* has a very extensive index, although personal names are generally not included. The *Cambridge Factfinder* has some of the same information as *Whitaker's*, but includes more illustrations and features a thorough 100-plus page index. The *Factfinder* may substitute for *Whitaker's* if it is updated on a regular basis.

Figure 15.2 Comparison of statistics on smokers from *The World Almanac* and the *Wall Street Journal Almanac*. Reprinted with permission from *The World Almanac and Book of Facts*. Copyright © World Almanac Education Group. All rights reserved.

Cigarette Use in the U.S., 1985-98

Source: Substance Abuse and Mental Health Services Administration (SAMHSA), U.S. Dept. of Health and Human Services
(percentage reporting use in the month prior to the survey; figures exclude persons under age 12)

Characteristic	1985	1996	1997	1998	Characteristic	1985	1996	1997	1998
TOTAL	**38.7**	**28.9**	**29.6**	**27.7**	**Age group**				
Sex					12-17	29.4	18.3	19.9	18.2
Male	43.4	31.1	31.2	29.7	18-25	47.4	38.3	40.6	41.6
Female	34.5	26.7	28.2	25.7	26-34	45.7	35.0	33.7	32.5
Race/Ethnicity					35 and older	35.5	27.0	27.9	25.1
White	38.9	29.8	30.5	27.9	**Education**(2)				
Black	38.0	30.4	29.8	29.4	Non-high school graduate	37.3	36.5	40.0	36.9
Hispanic	40.0	24.7	27.4	25.8	High school graduate	37.0	36.8	36.1	34.3
Other	(1)	17.2	18.8	23.8	Some college	32.6	27.5	29.5	29.2
					College graduate	23.0	17.5	17.1	15.2

(1) No estimate reported. (2) Estimates for Education are for persons aged 18 and older.

Figure 15.2—Continued

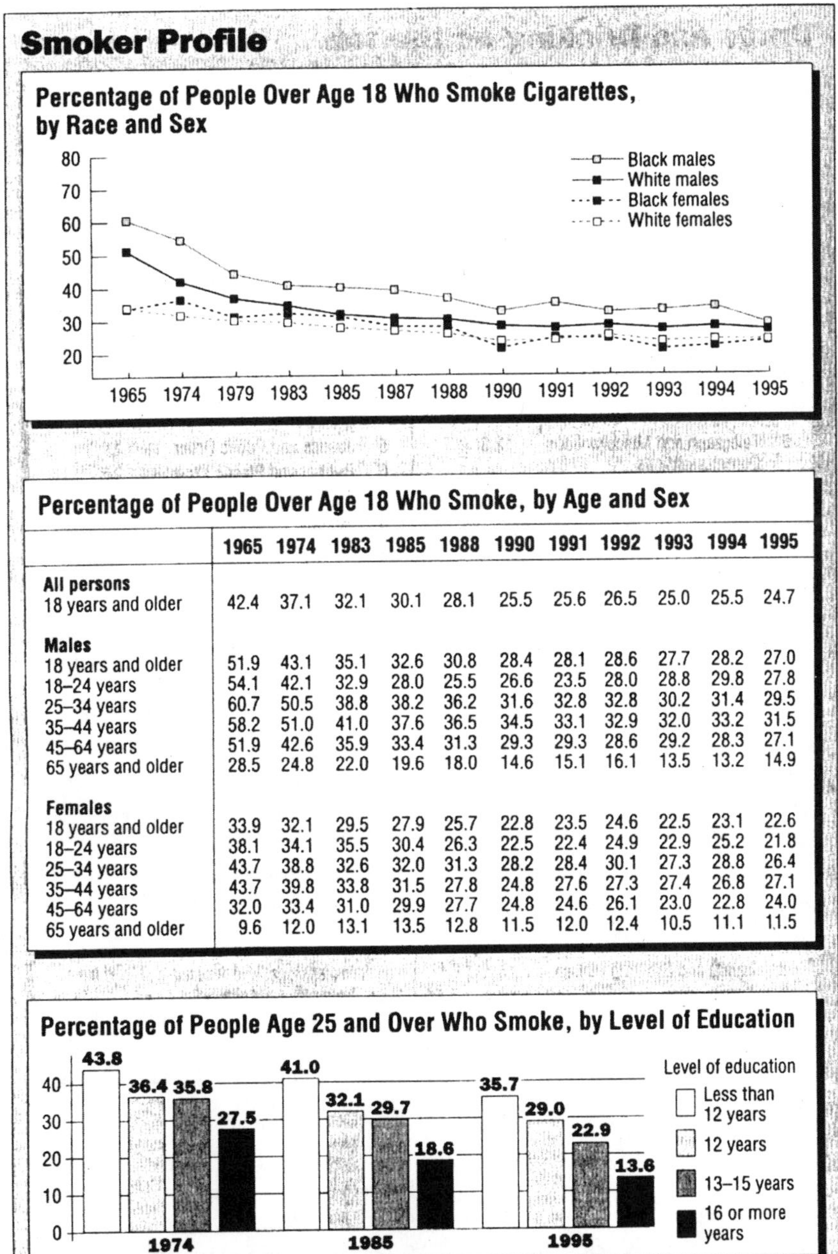

Smoker Profile

Percentage of People Over Age 18 Who Smoke Cigarettes, by Race and Sex

Percentage of People Over Age 18 Who Smoke, by Age and Sex

	1965	1974	1983	1985	1988	1990	1991	1992	1993	1994	1995
All persons											
18 years and older	42.4	37.1	32.1	30.1	28.1	25.5	25.6	26.5	25.0	25.5	24.7
Males											
18 years and older	51.9	43.1	35.1	32.6	30.8	28.4	28.1	28.6	27.7	28.2	27.0
18–24 years	54.1	42.1	32.9	28.0	25.5	26.6	23.5	28.0	28.8	29.8	27.8
25–34 years	60.7	50.5	38.8	38.2	36.2	31.6	32.8	32.8	30.2	31.4	29.5
35–44 years	58.2	51.0	41.0	37.6	36.5	34.5	33.1	32.9	32.0	33.2	31.5
45–64 years	51.9	42.6	35.9	33.4	31.3	29.3	29.3	28.6	29.2	28.3	27.1
65 years and older	28.5	24.8	22.0	19.6	18.0	14.6	15.1	16.1	13.5	13.2	14.9
Females											
18 years and older	33.9	32.1	29.5	27.9	25.7	22.8	23.5	24.6	22.5	23.1	22.6
18–24 years	38.1	34.1	35.5	30.4	26.3	22.5	22.4	24.9	22.9	25.2	21.8
25–34 years	43.7	38.8	32.6	32.0	31.3	28.2	28.4	30.1	27.3	28.8	26.4
35–44 years	43.7	39.8	33.8	31.5	27.8	24.8	27.6	27.3	27.4	26.8	27.1
45–64 years	32.0	33.4	31.0	29.9	27.7	24.8	24.6	26.1	23.0	22.8	24.0
65 years and older	9.6	12.0	13.1	13.5	12.8	11.5	12.0	12.4	10.5	11.1	11.5

Percentage of People Age 25 and Over Who Smoke, by Level of Education

Note: Data for 1992 and beyond are not strictly comparable with data for earlier years.

Sources: Centers for Disease Control and Prevention, National Center for Health Statistics

The bilingual (English/French) *Canadian Almanac & Directory* is introduced by a contents page that outlines its ten sections. The sections, containing statistical and directory information about various aspects of Canadian society, are independently paginated. A large percentage of the content is directory information, including an extensive directory of Web sites. A keyword index appears at the end of the volume, which is sent to press in November of the year prior to the date of publication. Many U.S. states have almanacs or yearbooks that describe their government, environment, population, and other facts and statistics about the state. The *Texas Almanac*, now available both in print and online on GaleNet, is one example of this kind of almanac.

Box 15.1 Almanac Search Strategy

An undergraduate student approached the librarian on duty at the reference desk. "I have just spent two hours on the Web searching for a list of counties which comprise South Texas. Can you tell me how to find a list?" The librarian asked the student to show him her Web search strategy. The student had searched for the words "South Texas counties" on Yahoo! and Lycos. These sites located a number of groups, such as the Boys Scouts of America, that had regional organizations for South Texas. The counties listed in these sites were not consistent. The librarian suggested a search of AltaVista. The first result on AltaVista was from a Texas genealogical site that had two good maps, but the maps included different counties. At this point, the librarian walked over to the reference shelf and looked in the *Texas Almanac* under "Counties" in the Table of Contents. He quickly located a table near the end of the chapter that classifies counties by geographical region, as used by the Secretary of State in reporting election results. None of the Web lists corresponded to this official list, which the student used for her assignment.

Numerous specialized almanacs are published, although some of these could easily be called either handbooks or yearbooks. A few examples give an indication of the wide variety available. The *International Motion Picture Almanac* is a compilation of biographical, organizational, and statistical information concerning the motion picture industry, primarily in the United States. British, Irish, and Canadian film industries are reviewed, and basic information on the world market is provided. A table of contents and subject index are included. The *Almanac of American Politics* provides biographical information and political records of state governors and members of Congress. Published every two years, it is organized by state and, within each state, by congressional district. *Places Rated Almanac,* by David Savageau, ranks a group of U.S. cities according to climate, housing, health care, crime, transportation, education, the arts, recreation, and economics. It provides considerable data about cities, although the ratings are controversial. *The Bowker Annual Library and Book Trade Almanac* consists of reports written by library and information industry professionals about events of the previous year, topics of current importance, and activities of national associations and government agencies. In addition, it includes statistics, directories, awards, and other information of interest to librarians. The *NEA Almanac of Higher Education* highlights current information on employment conditions in higher education, including national salary data, trends in bargaining, and faculty workload. Two media giants publish sports almanacs: The *Sports Illustrated Sports Almanac* and the *ESPN Information Please Sports Almanac* include extensive statistics and coverage of sporting events for the preceding year. Commentaries are written by staff of the respective organizations.

Gale Group publishes a series of almanacs that describe the history and culture of American ethnic and racial minorities: *The African American Almanac, The Hispanic American Almanac, The Native North American Almanac,* and *The Asian American Almanac.* These reference works contain a vast amount of information about the present condition and past history of their respective groups, including heavily illustrated biographical information as well as photographs of famous places and events. The works also have some information related to the roots of the groups covered. For example, *The African American Almanac* has a section profiling the various countries in Africa. Each has a comprehensive index. These almanacs are also published as multivolume sets that begin with the words "Reference Library of," for example, *Reference Library of Hispanic America.* Gale Group also produces *DISCovering Multicultural America*, both on CD-ROM and online through GaleNet, that includes information on all four ethnic groups.

Yearbooks

Britannica Book of the Year updates the *New Encyclopaedia Britannica* (discussed in Chapter 18) and is a chronicle of the events of a given year. The updating aspect occupies a relatively small part of the total text, and the majority of each yearbook is, in fact, a review of happenings in the previous year. In addition, about a third of each volume provides a largely statistical description of the nations of the world, called "Britannica World Data." Besides "Britannica World Data," *Britannica Book of the Year* has a section of images of the year and a section on people of significance in the previous year as well as obituaries for prominent people who died during the previous year. Special reports appear throughout "The Year in Review" and provide several-page discussions of topics of current interest. A cumulative, decennial index is an important feature of *Britannica Book of the Year,* because it allows the user to locate information when the exact year is not known. Unlike many almanac indexes, yearbook indexes also contain personal names. In the decennial index the date of the yearbook is indicated by boldface type followed by a page number; for example, **89**:14 refers to page 14 of the 1989 yearbook. The *Britannica Book of the Year* is included in *Britannica Online* (discussed in Chapter 18). Articles from the yearbook are identified in the "search results" list after performing a search. The online edition offers the advantage of single stop searching, but is not necessarily more current than the paper version.

Other encyclopedia annuals are similar in content and format to *Britannica Book of the Year* and have much in common with the almanacs previously discussed in this chapter. Both almanacs and this type of yearbook list such things as winners of sporting events, disasters (see Figure 15.3), election results, and awards. Biographies in the yearbooks are more detailed and often include a photograph. Articles in *Britannica Book of the Year* are signed.

Figure 15.3 "Disasters" from *Britannica Book of the Year, 2000.* Reprinted with permission from *Britannica Book of the Year*, 2000. © 2000 Encyclopaedia Britannica, Inc.

DISASTERS

explosions in a crowded market; at least 56 persons died, and 348 were injured.

October 30, Inchon, S.Kor. A fire swept through a crowded tavern that illegally catered to minors, killing 55 persons, most of them teenagers, and injuring at least 70.

Marine

February 7, Off the coast of Tambelan Islands, Indon. A passenger ship with 332 persons aboard sank in rough seas after the ship's pumps broke down; there were 20 survivors.

March 6, Off the coast of Palm Beach, Fla. Two fishing boats overloaded with Haitians attempting to reach the U.S. capsized and sank, killing some 40 persons.

March 7, Off the coast of Freetown, Sierra Leone. A boat overloaded with traders and their goods sank in rough seas; at least 100 persons lost their lives.

March 22, Off the coast of Tombo, Sierra Leone. A motorized canoe that was carrying some 200 persons, about twice its capacity, capsized and sank; at least 150 persons drowned; the passengers were refugees who were returning to Tombo after having fled fighting in the port a week earlier.

March 26, Eastern India. A storm caused a passenger boat to capsize in the Tileya Dam reservoir in Bihar; 27 persons were missing in the accident, and all were presumed drowned.

Britannica Book of the Year is a useful reference tool. It is physically attractive and easy to read, and the decennial index is an excellent feature. The yearbook, however, does have some limitations. It covers a complete calendar year and is slower to be published than the almanacs. It does not include directories, and the amount of retrospective data is limited. Because libraries often shelve *Britannica Book of the Year* with the *New Encyclopaedia Britannica*, it is not as accessible as some of the other fact books that are usually shelved at the reference desk. Nonetheless, this as well as other encyclopedia yearbooks help stretch the reference collection and are valuable in helping students, especially those in junior and senior high school.

Facts On File World News Digest with Index, a yearbook in the making, is a weekly digest of information published in newspapers. Information about political, social, cultural, and athletic events is summarized in the weekly classified digest. Classifications such as "World Affairs," "Finance," "Science," "Arts," and "Sports" are used as headings. Lists of best-selling records, movies, and books are included, as are obituaries of notable people. The digests have references to related stories. Each weekly issue of *Facts On File* is placed in a yearly loose-leaf volume that includes a quick reference world atlas.

A color-coded index is issued twice a month, with each index superseding the previous one; this index is replaced by a quarterly cumulative index that is in turn replaced by an annual index. The text of *Facts On File* is divided into three columns and further subdivided by letters that appear on the margins. The index refers first to the date of the event (not the publication date of *Facts On File*) and then to one of the pages numbered continuously throughout the year, the margin letter, and column number. The index entry "8-26, 735G3" refers to page 735, margin letter G, column 3. The date (8-26) in the citation is helpful in identifying the time of an event but is not necessary to locate a specific item. Items are indexed under personal names, place names, subject or subjects, and, where appropriate, title. The same news item is usually indexed in several ways. For example, an obituary of a business leader is indexed under personal name; under the heading "Death," which is subdivided by an alphabetical list of personal names; and under "Business and Industry," subdivided by obituaries. Five-year cumulative indexes are issued for *Facts On File*, which has been published since 1940. An annual bound volume called *Facts On File Yearbook* is also published. *Facts On File* in paper is an excellent resource. However, its index is daunting and it may be necessary to consult more than one year to find certain kinds of information.

Facts On File World News CD-ROM eliminates these problems. The CD-ROM version offers easy access to all of *Facts On File* from 1980. It also provides important indexing features not available in paper. The Main Menu offers a keyword search and a subject index to find news stories, but also offers three additional options that are great resources for students trying to decide on research topics: "Key Events," "Key Issues," and "Key People" list hot topics in the news suitable for student papers. There is also an index to photos, maps, and documents. Online access is provided through various vendors including OCLC Firstsearch, and the publisher provides access at the FACTS.com site (http://www.facts.com).

Facts that appear in *Facts On File* also appear in encyclopedia yearbooks and almanacs, but because *Facts On File* is issued throughout the year, it is much more up-to-date. Another advantage to the digest is that it can serve as an index to other newspapers and news magazines. Traditionally, newspaper indexes (discussed in Chapter 21) are slow to be published, and finding a specific bit of news can be time-consuming. Because *Facts On File* gives specific dates for events, it aids users in locating newspaper articles. Although news magazines are indexed in periodical indexes, these indexes are not as detailed as the *Facts On File* index. Of course, *Facts On File* does not have the information organized in the concise way that almanacs do.

At first glance, *Europa World Year Book* and *The Statesman's Yearbook* are similar. Both consist of an initial section on international organizations, followed by alphabetically arranged countries of the world. They both aim to give a concise but complete description of organizations and countries and to emphasize the political and economic aspects of the world. However, each has unique characteristics.

Europa is published annually in two thick volumes. Volume I, usually published in May, contains international organizations and the first part of the alphabetically arranged survey of countries; volume II, published in August, contains the second part of the alphabet. International organizations are described in terms of structure, function, and activities. Names of important officials, budget information, and addresses are given. Information about individual countries is divided into three parts: introductory survey, statistical survey, and directories. The introductory survey has short essays on location, climate, recent history, government, defense, economic affairs, welfare, and education. The brief statistical survey provides summary data about the country and is followed by separate directories for government, the press, religion, finance, and other areas. Entries for some of the industrialized countries include directories for periodicals, banks, and trade unions. The directory also has either a summary of, or the complete constitution for, each country.

The inclusion of this varied information makes the *Europa World Year Book* a one-stop reference work. The yearbook contains a short index to territories of the world. Statistical tables compare life expectancy, population, gross national product, and other topics among countries of the world. Each yearbook also contains a page or so of updated information received after the publication has been sent to press. *Europa World Year Book* obtains information from the institutions listed, as well as from many other sources, such as national statistics offices, government departments, and diplomatic missions. Statistical information is also taken from United Nations publications and from *The Military Balance*, published by the International Institute for Strategic Studies. The publisher of *Europa World Year Book* also publishes eight regional surveys: *The Far East and Australasia*; *The Middle East and North Africa*; *South America, Central America, and the Caribbean*; *Central and South-Eastern Europe; Eastern Europe, Russia and Central Asia; The USA and Canada*; *Western Europe*; and *Africa South of the Sahara*. These surveys are similar in content to *Europa World Year Book* but include more information and a bibliography. The publication schedules range in frequency from annual to triennial.

The Statesman's Yearbook, published annually since 1864, is a compact 1,600- to 1,700-page book. It does not have, as *Europa World Year Book* does, a description of the recent history of each country or directory information, although it does list the ambassadors to each country from Great Britain and the United States, as well as each country's United Nations ambassador. *The Statesman's Yearbook* does have some special features. There are lists of books about each country. The place and international organizations index is helpful in finding specific information, and *The Statesman's Yearbook* describes each state in the United States separately, something that *Europa World Year Book* does not do.

Although the *CIA World Factbook* provides only brief data and small maps for each country and does not compare in coverage to *Europa* or *Statesman's*, it is available for free on the Web. The *Canada Year Book* serves as an example of a yearbook featuring one country. Profusely illustrated, it combines statistical data and short descriptions about every aspect of Canadian life.

As is true for almanacs, there are many yearbooks on special topics. Sometimes topical yearbooks update either a special or a general encyclopedia. The *McGraw-Hill Yearbook of Science and Technology*, for example, is an annual review and supplement to the *McGraw-Hill Encyclopedia of Science and Technology* (discussed in Chapter 18). The yearbook updates the most recent edition of the encyclopedia and is arranged alphabetically by topic. Practitioners and researchers write entries. Bibliographies, cross-references, and an index are also included. Another example, *The World Book Health and Medical Annual*, one of the special yearbooks issued by *World Book Encyclopedia* (discussed in Chapter 18), focuses on current topics of popular interest relating to health and medicine.

Other yearbooks review the activities or the organization of groups. *Yearbook of American and Canadian Churches* and *Yearbook of the United Nations* are examples. These annuals furnish statistics, directories, facts, and trends about a specific group and are often published as a handbook for the group's members. For example, the *Yearbook of American and Canadian Churches*, prepared and edited at the National Council of the Churches of Christ in the U.S.A., has directories and statistics of religious denominations and affiliated organizations in North America. *Yearbook of the United Nations* summarizes events of the previous year, provides texts of important UN documents such as the "UN Charter," and lists member nations and important officeholders.

Box 15.2 Yearbook Search Strategy

An author writing a science fiction story about space flight wanted information about recent space expeditions. The librarian showed the writer entries under "space exploration" in recent *Britannica Book of the Year* volumes. Although she found these articles helpful, the author wanted more technical information. When the librarian showed her the *McGraw-Hill Yearbook of Science and Technology*, she found exactly the information she wanted. She did, however, have to look through several years, sometimes under "space flight" and sometimes under more specific topics, because coverage and indexing varied from year to year.

Handbooks

That famous trivia book, *Guinness World Records* (formerly *The Guinness Book of Records*), is also a useful reference work. The first American edition of *Guinness* was published in 1956, and it has appeared annually since that time. A hurdle to using *Guinness* as a reference tool is in understanding what a record means. The records in the book are for every type of extreme: largest-smallest, worst-best, widest-narrowest, oldest-newest, and the like. The reference librarian will find the subject index essential when using *Guinness*. The subject index, which does not include personal names, lists many specific terms in boldface type, in some cases also subdividing the term using normal typeface. The subdivisions are particularly important for terms such as *depth*, *prolific*, *span*, and *weight*, which are cues to records.

Another record book, Joseph Nathan Kane's *Famous First Facts*, is an alphabetical subject list of "First happenings, discoveries, and inventions in American history."[4] The fifth edition of this venerable reference book covers first events to 1997. Firsts included are quite diverse, from the invention of the tape measure to the first appearance of billiards in the United States. Five indexes—by subject, years, days of the month, personal names, and geographical areas—expand the usefulness of the work. *Famous First Facts* can be used to establish historical fact, to identify anniversaries, and to gather information about a specific place or time. The index to days of the month serves as a "book of days" for the United States. It is now also available on CD-ROM and online on WilsonWeb.

There are, of course, other "books of days." *Chase's Calendar of Events* lists birthdays of famous people (living and dead), festivals, historical anniversaries, special events, and the like for every day of the year. Brief biographical information is included with each name, and the name and telephone number of event organizers are given where applicable. *Chase's* also lists the winners of many popular awards, such as TV's Emmy Awards. Aside from the detailed index, the accompanying CD-ROM offers enhanced searching capabilities, as well as scheduling and grouping features. *The Folklore of World Holidays*, also arranged by the Gregorian calendar, describes customs associated with holidays around the world. The Web has a number of sites that serve as "books of days." *Any Day in History* lists famous people who were born or died on a given date, religious observances, and holidays. *Today in History*, from the Library of Congress, is a site that highlights an event from American history with digitized items from the American Memory historical collections.

The New York Public Library Desk Reference is a compilation of information frequently requested at library reference desks. "Religions," "Etiquette," "Personal Finances," and "Libraries and Museums" are a few of the chapter headings in this single-volume work. An important feature of *The New York Public Library Desk Reference* is its listing of additional sources of information at the end of each chapter. The source list consists of a directory of related organizations and a bibliography of reference works.

A standard handbook in almost all reference collections is the style manual. Many publishers and organizations prescribe a particular bibliographic style. *The Chicago Manual of Style*, one of the most common, is consulted by writers and by librarians helping writers to determine the format of bibliographies and footnotes. Although most people consult it for this reason, the work also includes a considerable amount of other helpful information of interest to authors and others concerned with publishing, such as the bookmaking process, copyright law, and the rules of spelling and grammar. *The Chicago Manual of Style* has a glossary of technical terms, a bibliography, and an index. The manual is subdivided into numbered paragraphs. The paragraph numbers appear on the left-hand margin of a page. References in the index, except for tables and figures, are to paragraph numbers rather than page numbers. *A Manual for Writers of Term Papers, Theses and Dissertations,* by Kate L. Turabian, is adapted from *The Chicago Manual of Style* but is aimed primarily at students. Other commonly required style manuals are the *MLA Handbook for Writers of Research Papers,* by Joseph Gibaldi, and the *Publication Manual of the American Psychological Association.*

Authors are increasingly citing electronic publications. The bibliographic conventions for these sources are continuously under development as new types of formats emerge. Some publications have developed bibliographic styles exclusively for electronic publications. Xia Li and Nancy Crane's *Electronic Styles* is divided into two parts, APA-embellished style and MLA-embellished style. Another useful source that focuses on electronic style and the Internet is Janice R. Walker and Todd Taylor's *The Columbia Guide to Online Style.* It is divided into two sections, "Citation" and "Production." This print source will stay current via a Web site containing updates that can be viewed at no extra charge.

Because many library users ask for assistance in solving practical problems of day-to-day living, etiquette books are a part of most public and academic library reference collections. Long considered the standard, *Emily Post's Etiquette*, currently edited by Peggy Post, has a subject arrangement divided into categories such as "Forms and Formality" and "Entertaining." It has an excellent index. *Miss Manners' Guide for the Turn-of-the-Millennium* is one of several additional or alternative guides. *Miss Manners,* written by Judith Martin, is also organized by subject and well indexed but differs from *Emily Post's Etiquette* in that it consists of letters written to "Miss Manners" and her responses to the letters. Not everyone is amused by the quaintly flippant style of "Miss Manners," but she does seem more aware of contemporary lifestyles than does Post.

When Henry M. Robert discovered that associations, societies, and other organized groups needed rules of etiquette to govern their conduct at meetings, he wrote his classic reference work on parliamentary procedure, *Robert's Rules of Order.* Originally published in 1876, many editions have appeared since then. *The Scott, Foresman Robert's Rules of Order Newly Revised* is preferred by many because of its easy-to-use format and excellent index. Another edition, *Robert's Rules of Order,* Modern edition, has been revised by Darwin Patnode in more contemporary English.[5]

Questions about sickness, health, and medicine are commonplace in many reference departments. Although reference librarians should not attempt to provide medical advice, a number of handbooks assist the user in understanding health-related issues. Merck Research Laboratories has published a consumer edition of their famous *The Merck Manual of Diagnosis and Therapy* (now also freely available on the Web). *The Merck Manual of Medical Information,* Home edition, offers straightforward discussions of diseases and other health problems. It describes symptoms and suggests possible treatments. Another excellent handbook, *Mayo Clinic Family Health Book,* describes various parts of the body and their diseases or ailments. Written in easy-to-understand language, *Mayo Clinic Family Health Book* is abundantly illustrated and has a comprehensive index. The information it provides is also online at the *Mayo Clinic Health Oasis. The Columbia University College of Physicians and Surgeons Complete Home Medical Guide, The American Medical Association Family Medical Guide*, and *Johns Hopkins Family Health Book* are three other reliable sources.

Physicians' Desk Reference (*PDR*), a handbook intended for physicians, is also at home in a general reference department. It is a compilation of product information on package inserts found in all available prescription drugs. Data comply with FDA (Food and Drug

Administration) regulations and are fairly uniform and concise. *PDR* is alphabetically arranged by manufacturer and then by trade name of drugs, and access is provided by several indexes at the beginning of the book. There are indexes to manufacturers, product names, product categories, and generic and chemical names. The product identification section of the work shows pictures of the different drugs and aids in verifying the name of a particular drug. *Physicians' Desk Reference* is available as the *PDR Electronic Library on CD-ROM.* The CD-ROM version also contains the complete text of *PDR for Nonprescription Drugs, PDR Guide to Drug Interactions, Side Effects, Indications, and Contraindications* and *PDR for Ophthalmology*, and is updated three times a year. *The Merck Manual of Diagnosis and Therapy* and *Stedman's Medical Dictionary* are also available as options on the CD-ROM. The latter sources are fully integrated into the database. *Physicians' Desk Reference* is also available to consumers on *PDR.net* (http://www.pdr.net) for a fee. A more limited drug index, the *RxList—The Internet Drug Index* is available without charge. *RxList* provides information about 300 generic drugs and cross-indexes brand names to the generic descriptions. Entries include warnings, adverse reactions, dosage and administration, and references. Because the searching by keyword produces limited results, the most effective way to search is under drug names.

Box 15.3 Handbook Search Strategy

A user headed toward the public library after having been advised by his doctor to consider drug therapy, in addition to diet, to help lower his elevated cholesterol level. The librarian found a reference in the *Physicians' Desk Reference* "product category" index from cholesterol reducers to cardiovascular agents—antilipemic agents. Several types of cholesterol-reducing drugs were listed under antilipemic agents. The user was able to consult the listed references to learn more about the drugs, including warnings about possible negative effects. If the user had known the specific name of a drug, he could have also consulted *RxList—The Internet Drug Index.*

Legal and business questions also occur frequently at the reference desk. There are many guides, such as *The Legal Researcher's Desk Reference* and Stephen Elias's *Legal Research: How to Find and Understand the Law,* that help librarians locate information. These tools, however, usually require more effort than users want to make. Examples of books designed for the average user include Robert W. Schachner's *How and When to Be Your Own Lawyer*, the American Bar Association's *Family Legal Guide*, and *The Court TV Cradle-to-Grave Legal Survival Guide.* Handbooks such as *Hoover's Handbook of American Business* are useful guides to business. *Hoover's Handbook* profiles over 700 companies. The profiles contain descriptions of each enterprise, its management, key competitors, and history of sales and growth. Hoover's also publishes the *Hoover's Handbook of World Business.* The Web site *Hoover's Online* combines its series of handbooks and offers free but limited access to company information, with full profiles and additional features available to subscribers.

Hobbies and special interests bring many users to the reference desk. Handbooks on topics such as genealogy, sports, and films are invaluable aids in helping them. *The Researcher's Guide to American Genealogy,* by Val D. Greenwood, is considered by many to be the best single guide to genealogical research. It explains both the principles of genealogical research and the use and value of specific records. David Wallechinsky's *The Complete Book of the Olympics* answers many questions about the Olympic Games. This handbook not only summarizes Olympic records in every competitive sport, it also provides descriptions and stories of human interest for each event. Although *The Complete Book of the Olympics* is updated every four years, it does not include records of the latest Olympic games and is valuable for retrospective rather than current information. Students of film and movie buffs will find answers to many of their questions in *Halliwell's Who's Who in the Movies.* The alphabetically arranged guide includes short biographies of actors, directors, writers, and other film-related persons; definitions of terms; plots of selected movies; descriptions and examples of movie genres and themes; and more. Information ranges from a country-by-country breakdown of national film industries to lists of prize-winning films. The *Internet Movie Database* is a comprehensive Web source with similar information, with extensive links to other related Web sites. Librarians may also want to refer users to *Leonard Maltin's Movie and Video Guide* for quick plot summaries, basic movie credits, and video availability. Published annually and arranged alphabetically by title, the *Guide* includes a star index and a director index.

Handbooks also solve educational, professional, or research problems. In the sciences, the *CRC Handbook of Chemistry and Physics,* published since 1913, is a basic reference work for chemistry and physics. Composed primarily of tables, it describes or defines the structure, formulas, and phenomena of chemistry and physics. Physicists, chemists, and students of physics and chemistry use the handbook for research and study, and reference librarians consult it to answer questions for them. CRC Press also produces *CRC Handbook on CD-ROM* and provides online access via the Web.

The Science and Technology Desk Reference is a different sort of science reference book. Compiled by the Science and Technology Department at Carnegie Library of Pittsburgh, *Desk Reference* provides answers to frequently asked or hard-to-answer questions. The questions answered are the kind that an average citizen or amateur scientist might ask. Arranged by subject, such as "Animal World," "Cars, Boats, Planes, Trains," "Health and Medicine," and "Weather," each answer has a citation to its source of information.

Literary handbooks are commonplace in most reference departments. *Benét's Reader's Encyclopedia* is a useful one-stop guide to authors, titles, plots, characters, literary terms, movements, and other information sought by book enthusiasts. Oxford University Press produces a series of respected handbooks, "The Oxford Companion to . . . ." Some of these companions, such as *The Oxford Companion to American Literature* and *The Oxford Companion to Canadian Literature,* serve as comprehensive guides to the literature of a particular country. These guides include historical themes and trends; biographies of writers; summaries of plots; and descriptions of literary awards, journals, societies, and so forth. *The Oxford Companion to the English Language* is a fascinating compendium of information about English, including histories of the countries where English is spoken. All the companions are arranged alphabetically by topic, with cross-references where necessary.

Librarians' responses to *Masterplots* and its confusing array of subsets vary. This famous, sometimes infamous, reference work summarizes the plots of major literary works, but it also offers critical assessments of the same works. The full text of the more than 80 volumes of all *Masterplots* series is available on *Masterplots Complete CD-ROM,* allowing users to search by title, author, locale, genre, subject, and principal characters. Whether it is a prop for lazy students or an aid to research, it remains a staple in many reference collections.[6]

SEARCH STRATEGIES

The first step in developing a search strategy is to determine the nature of the question. The sources described in this chapter provide simple, factual answers and in some cases lead users to more complex or authoritative sources. If an almanac, yearbook, or handbook is an appropriate choice to answer a user's question, the librarian draws on a thorough personal knowledge of the collection to choose a source. Wise decisions depend on knowledge gained from previous use and continual re-examination of these reference works. The scope of the work, its strengths and weaknesses, publishing schedule, special features, and indexes are all factors to be considered. As more and more "fact books" appear in electronic formats, choice of format must also be considered. If the librarian keeps in mind that current, accurate information is the goal of every reference transaction, some of the decisions will be easy to make.

Other factors influence the choice of source. If current information is required, frequently updated databases or Web sites are preferable. For difficult or hard-to-find information, the search capabilities of electronic resources make them better choices. On the other hand, for quick facts or simple information, books are often faster. Reference works with a national or regional slant usually have more information about these geographic areas than other sources and may be better sources for questions about those areas. It is important to remember, especially when relying on fact books, that more than one source can answer the same question. Often, comparing information in two or more sources may be the best way to serve the user.

The effective use of almanacs, yearbooks, and handbooks requires both patience and imagination. Successful search strategies can be written down and shared with colleagues. "The Exchange," a column in *Reference & User Services Quarterly* (formerly *RQ*) that contained "tricky questions, notes on unusual information sources, and general comments concerning reference problems and their solutions,"[7] offers insight into search strategies and identifies novel information contained in familiar sources. Entries for the column, which ceased in summer 1999, are indexed on the Web (http://www.ala.org/rusa/rusq/exchange_index.html). Reviews such as those in the *Reference Books Bulletin* section of *Booklist* also aid in the successful use of these sources. New technology can enhance the use of older sources, and an effort should be made to keep abreast of developments. There is no single magic formula to apply to the use of these reference works. This makes using them a challenge, but a rewarding one.

Box 15.4 Search Strategy: Locating Information About a Country

A high school student in a social studies course is engaged in a semester study of Liberia, requiring at least twenty-five different sources. He needs to discover information about the culture and language, geography, history, and political climate of the country. He begins by looking for Liberia on the Web using Yahoo! Yahoo! presents a number of sites by category. When reviewing the sites, he finds useful information in about half a dozen. The most useful is the *CIA World Factbook*. However, many of the other sites are from personal Web pages or from biased sources. Because he does not find enough information to complete his project, he consults his high school librarian for additional help. The librarian refers him to the *Infoplease* Web site and the high school's access to *Britannica Online*. Although he cannot rely on general encyclopedia articles, he finds that both of these sites give him additional resources to consult. Selected Internet links featured on *Britannica Online* include some that did not turn up in the Yahoo! search; the *Infoplease* search furnishes him with a list of books about Liberia. He goes to the public library to search for the books and to seek help from a reference librarian. One of the Web sites he located was about the colonization of Africa, and he wants more information on this topic. The librarian feels that *The African American Almanac* will be a good starting point. For more information about English as it is spoken in Liberia, she recommends *The Oxford Companion to the English Language*. Further, she suggests that the student consult *Facts On File World News CD-ROM*, where he finds useful information about current political, social, and economic events of the country. Because he is also interested in locating primary sources, he asks the librarian for the name and address of Liberian newspapers. She recommends that he look in the *Europa World Year Book*. She also suggests that he write to the Liberian Embassy in Washington, D.C., and that the address for the embassy can be located in *The Statesman's Yearbook*, but he tells her that he has already located the embassy's Web site. This background reading and research enable him to prepare to search the periodical indexes described in Chapter 21.

NOTES

1. Margaret Morrison, "All Things to All People: *The World Almanac*," in *Distinguished Classics of Reference Publishing*, ed. James Rettig (Phoenix, Ariz.: Oryx Press, 1992), 313-21.

2. Julie E. Miller and Jane G. Bryan, "Wealth of Information: A Review of Four 1979 Almanacs," *Reference Services Review* 7 (July/September 1979): 77-78.

3. "Answers to a Manufacturing Task That Aren't in *The World Almanac*," *Publishers Weekly* 227 (March 1, 1985): 66.

4. Joseph Nathan Kane, Steven Anzovin, and Janet Podell, *Famous First Facts*, 5th ed. (New York: H. W. Wilson, 1997), [title page].

5. Sarah B. Watstein, "Demystifying Parliamentary Procedure: *Robert's Rules of Order*," in *Distinguished Classics of Reference Publishing*, ed. James Rettig (Phoenix, Ariz.: Oryx Press, 1992), 211-19.

6. Mary Ellen Quinn, "Reference Tools for Literary Criticism: A Selected Guide," *Booklist* 85 (February 1, 1989): 915-16.

7. Charles Anderson, "The Exchange," *Reference & User Services Quarterly* 37 (Fall 1997): 15.

LIST OF SOURCES

Africa South of the Sahara. London: Europa, 1971– . Annual.

The African American Almanac. 8th ed. Edited by Jessie Carney Smith. Farmington Hills, Mich.: Gale Group, 2000. 1360p.

Almanac of American Politics. Washington, D.C.: National Journal, 1972– . Biennial.

The American Medical Association Family Medical Guide. 3d ed. New York: Random House, 1994. 880p.

Any Day in History. Available: http://www.scopesys.com/anyday.

The Asian American Almanac. Detroit: Gale Research, 1995. 834p.

Benét's Reader's Encyclopedia. 4th ed. New York: HarperCollins, 1996. 1144p.

The Bowker Annual Library and Book Trade Almanac. New Providence, N.J.: R. R. Bowker, 1989– . Annual. (Formerly *Bowker Annual of Library and Book Trade Information*, 1955–1988.)

Britannica Book of the Year. Chicago: Encyclopaedia Britannica, 1938– . Annual. Also available online.

Cambridge Factfinder. 4th ed. Edited by David Crystal. New York: Cambridge University Press, 2000. 912p.

Canada Year Book. Ottawa: Statistics Canada, 1906– . Annual.

Canadian Almanac & Directory. Toronto: Micromedia, 1848–. Annual.

Central and South-Eastern Europe. London: Europa, 2000.

Chase's Calendar of Events. Chicago: Contemporary Books, 1995–. Annual. (Formerly *Chase's Annual Events*, 1954–1994.) Also available on CD-ROM.

The Chicago Manual of Style. 14th ed. Chicago: University of Chicago Press, 1993. 921p.

CIA World Factbook. Available: http://www.odci.gov/cia/publications/factbook/index.html.

The Columbia University College of Physicians and Surgeons Complete Home Medical Guide. 3d rev. ed. New York: Crown Publishers, 1995. 932p.

The Court TV Cradle-to-Grave Legal Survival Guide: A Complete Resource for Any Question You Might Have about the Law. Boston: Little, Brown, 1995. 504p.

CRC Handbook of Chemistry and Physics. Boca Raton, Fla.: CRC Press, 1913– . Annual. Also available on CD-ROM and online.

DISCovering Multicultural America. [CD-ROM]. Detroit: Gale Research, 1996. Also available online.

Eastern Europe, Russia and Central Asia. London: Europa, 2000. 592p.

Elias, Stephen. *Legal Research: How to Find and Understand the Law*. 7th ed. Berkeley, Calif.: Nolo Press, 1997. (various pagings).

ESPN Information Please Sports Almanac. New York: Hyperion ESPN Books, 1998– . Annual. (Formerly *The Information Please Sports Almanac*, 1990–1997.)

Europa World Year Book. 2 vols. London: Europa, 1989– . Annual. (Formerly *Europa Year Book*, 1926–1929; *Europa, the Encyclopedia of Europe*, 1930–1958; *Europa Year Book*, 1959–1988.)

Facts On File World News CD-ROM. [CD-ROM]. New York: Facts On File, 1980.

Facts On File World News Digest with Index. New York: Facts On File, 1940– . Weekly. Also available online.

Family Legal Guide. Rev. ed. New York: Times Books, 1994. 732p.

The Far East and Australasia. London: Europa, 1969– . Annual.

The Folklore of World Holidays. 2d ed. Edited by Robert H. Griffin and Ann H. Shurgin. Detroit: Gale Research, 1998. 841p.

Gibaldi, Joseph. *MLA Handbook for Writers of Research Papers*. 5th ed. New York: Modern Language Association of America, 1999. 332p.

Greenwood, Val D. *The Researcher's Guide to American Genealogy*. 3d ed. Baltimore, Md.: Genealogical Publishing, 2000. 662p.

Guinness World Records. New York: Bantam, 1956– . Annual. (British edition began publication in 1955. Previous title: *Guinness Book of Records*.)

Halliwell, Leslie. *Halliwell's Who's Who in the Movies*. 13th ed. Edited by John Walker. New York: HarperPerennial, 1999. 584p.

The Hispanic American Almanac: A Reference Work on Hispanics in the United States. 2d ed. Edited by Nicolas Kanellos. Detroit: Gale Research, 1997. 811p.

Hoover's Handbook of American Business. Austin, Tex.: Hoover's Business Press, 1992– . Annual.

Hoover's Handbook of World Business. Austin, Tex.: Hoover's Business Press, 1992– . Annual.

Hoover's Online. Available: http://www.hoovers.com.

Infoplease.com. Available: http://www.infoplease.com.

Information Please Almanac. New York: Houghton Mifflin, 1947– . Annual. (Also issued as *Information Please Almanac: Atlas & Yearbook*. Now titled *The Time Almanac*.)

International Motion Picture Almanac. New York: Quigley, 1929– . Annual.

Internet Movie Database. Available: http://www.imdb.com.

Internet Public Library. Available: http://www.ipl.org.

Johns Hopkins Family Health Book. Edited by Michael J. Klag. New York: HarperCollins, 1999. 1657p.

Kane, Joseph Nathan, Steven Anzovin, and Janet Podell. *Famous First Facts.* 5th ed. New York: H. W. Wilson, 1997. 1122p. Also available on CD-ROM and online.

The Legal Researcher's Desk Reference. Teaneck, N.J.: Infosources, 1990– . Annual.

Leonard Maltin's Movie and Video Guide. New York: Penguin Group, 1993– . Annual. (Formerly *Leonard Maltin's TV Movies and Video Guide*, 1987–1992.)

Li, Xia, and Nancy Crane. *Electronic Styles: A Handbook for Citing Electronic Information.* 2d ed. Medford, N.J.: Information Today, 1996. 213p.

Martin, Judith. *Miss Manners' Guide for the Turn-of-the-Millennium.* New York: Pharos Books, 1989. 742p.

Masterplots: 1,801 Plot Stories and Critical Evaluations of the World's Finest Literature. Rev. 2d ed. 12 vols. Edited by Frank N. Magill. Pasadena, Calif.: Salem Press, 1996.

Masterplots Complete CD-ROM. [CD-ROM]. Pasadena, Calif.: Salem Press, 1999.

Mayo Clinic Family Health Book. 2d ed. New York: William Morrow, 1996. 1438p.

Mayo Clinic Health Oasis. Available: http://www.mayohealth.org.

McGraw-Hill Yearbook of Science and Technology. New York: McGraw-Hill, 1962– . Annual.

The Merck Manual of Diagnosis and Therapy. 17th ed. Whitehouse Station, N.J.: Merck Research Laboratories, 1999. 2833p. Also available: http://www.merck.com/pubs/mmanual.

The Merck Manual of Medical Information. Home ed. Whitehouse Station, N.J.: Merck Research Laboratories, 1997. 1509p.

The Middle East and North Africa. London: Europa, 1948– . Annual.

The Native North American Almanac. Detroit: Gale Research, 1994. 1275p.

NEA Almanac of Higher Education. Washington, D.C.: NEA Communications Services, 1984– . Annual.

The New York Public Library Desk Reference. 3d ed. New York: Macmillan, 1998. 1040p.

New York Times Almanac. New York: Penguin Group, 1998– . Annual.

Old Farmer's Almanac. Dublin, N.H.: Yankee Publishing, 1792– . Annual. Also available: http://www.almanac.com.

The Oxford Companion to American Literature. 6th ed. Edited by James David Hart. New York: Oxford University Press, 1995. 779p.

The Oxford Companion to Canadian Literature. 2d ed. General editors, Eugene Benson and William Toye. New York: Oxford University Press, 1997. 1199p.

The Oxford Companion to the English Language. Edited by Tom McArthur. New York: Oxford University Press, 1992. 1184p.

PDR Electronic Library on CD-ROM. [CD-ROM]. Montvale, N.J.: Medical Economics Data, 1999–.

Physicians' Desk Reference. Montvale, N.J.: Medical Economics, 1946– . Annual. Also available online.

Post, Peggy. *Emily Post's Etiquette.* 16th ed. New York: HarperCollins, 1997. 845p.

Publication Manual of the American Psychological Association. 4th ed. Washington, D.C.: American Psychological Association, 1994. 368p.

Robert's Rules of Order. Modern ed., completely rev. by Darwin Patnode. Nashville, Tenn.: T. Nelson, 1989. 155p.

RxList—The Internet Drug Index. Available: http://www.rxlist.com.

Savageau, David. *Places Rated Almanac.* 6th ed. Foster City, Calif.: IDG Books, 2000. 684p.

Schachner, Robert W. *How and When to Be Your Own Lawyer: A Step-By-Step Guide to Effectively Using Our Legal System.* 2d ed. Garden City Park, N.Y.: Avery, 1999. 416p.

The Science and Technology Desk Reference. 2d ed. [Edited by the Carnegie Library of Pittsburgh Science and Technology Department.] Detroit: Gale Research, 1996. 795p.

The Scott, Foresman Robert's Rules of Order Newly Revised. 9th ed. Edited by Sarah Corbin Robert and others. Glenview, Ill.: Scott, Foresman, 1990. 706p.

South America, Central America, and the Caribbean. London: Europa, 1986– . Annual.

Sports Illustrated Sports Almanac. Boston: Little, Brown, 1992– . Annual.

The Statesman's Yearbook. Edited by Barry Turner. New York: St. Martin's Press, 1864– . Annual.

Stumpers-L. [Electronic discussion group]. Available: http://www.cuis.edu/ ~ stumpers.

Texas Almanac. Dallas: Dallas Morning News, 1857– . Biennial. Also available online.

The Time Almanac. Boston: Information Please, 1999– . Annual. (Also titled *Information Please Almanac.*)

Today in History. Available: http://lcweb2.loc.gov/ammem/today/today.html.

Turabian, Kate L. *A Manual for Writers of Term Papers, Theses and Dissertations.* 6th ed. Revised by John Grossman and Alice Bennett. Chicago: University of Chicago Press, 1996. 308p.

The USA and Canada. London: Europa, 1990– . Triennial.

Walker, Janice R., and Todd Taylor. *The Columbia Guide to Online Style.* New York: Columbia University Press, 1998. 218p.

Wall Street Journal Almanac. Edited by the staff of the Wall Street Journal. New York: Ballantine Books, 1998– . Irregular.

Wallechinsky, David. *The Complete Book of the Olympics.* 2000 ed. London: Aurum Press, 2000. 880p.

Western Europe. London: Europa, 1989– . Irregular.

Whitaker's Almanack. London: J. Whitaker, 1869–. Annual.

The World Almanac and Book of Facts. Mahwah, N.J.: World Almanac Books, 1868–1876, 1886– . Annual. Also available online.

The World Almanac Reference Database @FACTS.com. Available online.

The World Book Health and Medical Annual. Edited by World Book staff. Chicago: World Book, 1986– . Annual.

Yearbook of American and Canadian Churches. Nashville, Tenn.: Abingdon, 1915– . Annual.

Yearbook of the United Nations. Dordrecht, The Netherlands: Martinus Nijhoff, 1946/47– . Annual.

ADDITIONAL READINGS

"Encyclopedia Annuals and Yearbooks." *Booklist* 90 (February 15, 1994): 1101-6.

From time to time, *Reference Books Bulletin* in *Booklist* publishes an analysis of encyclopedia yearbooks. Major English-language yearbooks are individually discussed using the most recent yearbook as an example. The latest review appeared in 1994, by Rashelle S. Karp, and the one previous to that appeared in 1985.

Greenberg, Carol A. "The Literature of Etiquette & Manners in the U.S." *AB Bookman's Weekly* 90 (October 19, 1992): 1358-64.

Greenberg offers a short history of etiquette and manners books from early to modern times. She stresses the variety of etiquette books and the revived interest in them that is currently taking place in our culture.

Grefrath, Richard W. "Eating Clams with Your Fingers: A Survey of Contemporary Etiquette Books." *Collection Building* 6 (Winter 1985): 10-16.

Grefrath has very decided opinions with which the reader may or may not agree. Nonetheless, this article is a useful description and bibliography of contemporary etiquette books.

Grogan, Denis. *Encyclopedias, Yearbooks, Directories and Statistical Sources*. London: Clive Bingley, 1987. 170p. (Grogan's Case Studies in Reference Work, v. 2).

Grogan uses the case study method to illustrate both search strategy and the content of ready-reference works. Although the sample questions are oriented to the United Kingdom, the discussion of the search process is informative.

Katz, Bill. *Cuneiform to Computer: A History of Reference Sources*. Lanham, Md.: Scarecrow Press, 1998. 417p.

This book emphasizes the use of reference sources throughout history. Almanacs, for example, date back to mid-1100 B.C.E. and handbooks to 200 B.C.E. The book contains a chapter titled "The Reference of Time: Almanacs, Calendars, Chronologies, and Chronicles." Another relevant chapter is "Ready Reference Books: Handbooks and Manuals." This chapter discusses yearbooks as well.

"Legal Reference Books of [given year]." *Law Library Journal*.

This feature has appeared annually in *Law Library Journal* since about 1989. It recently underwent a name change. Previously it was titled "Best Legal Reference Books of [given year]." Each year a team of experts with various law-related backgrounds compiles the list and provides valuable recommendations on many titles. Over the years, some particularly useful categories relating to legal handbooks and guides have been included, such as "Self-Help" and "Laypersons and the Law."

McCulley, Lucretia. "Basic International Reference Sources." *Reference Services Review* 13 (Fall 1985): 31-36.

This is a comparative review of thirteen sources for data about the nations of the world. *Europa World Year Book* and *The Statesman's Yearbook* are included in the survey.

Miller, Julie E., and Jane G. Bryan. "Wealth of Information: A Review of Four 1979 Almanacs." *Reference Services Review* 7 (July/September 1979): 67-78.

Even though the information is very out-of-date, the authors of this article provide an excellent framework for analyzing the organization and content of almanacs.

Mulac, Carolyn. "Style Manuals Revisited." *Booklist* 93 (May 1, 1997): 1511-16.

Mulac updates the reader on the changes taking place within the genre of style manuals, including transformations made to the standards. Other manuals are discussed by subject, including science and technology and government and electronic sources, as well as manuals found on the Web.

Perkins, Maureen. *Visions of the Future: Almanacs, Time, and Cultural Change 1775–1870*. Oxford: Clarendon Press, 1996. 270p.

Perkins has written a thought-provoking book about the history and use of almanacs. It is a detailed work covering Australian and English almanacs, with such chapter titles as "Almanacs, Astrology, and the Stationers' Company," "Comic Almanacs," and "Australian Almanacs and Popular Culture." This source would be useful for anyone who wanted to explore the boundaries of the use and history of almanacs outside the United States.

Quinn, Mary Ellen. "Reference Tools for Literary Criticism: A Selected Guide." *Booklist* 85 (February 1, 1989): 915-18.

"Surveys and Digests," "Compilations of Reprints of Criticism," and "Biobibliographic Sources" are described, and coverage and relationship to other works are explained.

Remington, Tracy L., and Mary J. Ferrill. "First Aid for the Reference Librarian: Responding to Consumer Healthcare Questions." *RQ* 36 (Spring 1997): 348-59.

This article serves as a "medical resource guide" that almost any reference librarian would find useful when asked to suggest medical sources. It could also function as a guide for building a core medical collection in a public library. Remington and Ferrill discuss five medical subject areas and provide a handy table that summarizes points made throughout the article.

Rettig, James. *Distinguished Classics of Reference Publishing.* Phoenix, Ariz.: Oryx Press, 1992. 356p.
This wonderful history of famous reference books includes the following works discussed in this chapter: *The Chicago Manual of Style*, *Emily Post's Etiquette*, *Guinness Book of Records*, *Robert's Rules of Order*, *The Statesman's Yearbook*, and *The World Almanac.*

Rogers, Stephen W. "Did Anything Else Ever Happen on December Seventh? A Review of Books of Days." *Reference Services Review* 14 (Spring 1986): 17-33.
This is a very thorough comparison of the contents of "Books of Days." The author also discusses other reference works, such as encyclopedias and almanacs, that list important happenings on a given date. Examples from different works are given, as well as a summary chart that compares features of the works reviewed.

CHAPTER

16

BIOGRAPHICAL SOURCES

Constance A. Fairchild and
Richard E. Bopp

USES AND CHARACTERISTICS

Biography, the history of the lives of individuals, has had a fascination for readers and researchers since earliest times. The collective biographies written by Plutarch (A.D. c.50–c.125) and Suetonius (A.D. c.70–c.140) remain among the most popular of classical writings almost 2,000 years after they were written. The nineteenth-century social critic and biographer Thomas Carlyle wrote that "the Life of the lowest mortal, if faithfully recorded, would be interesting to the highest."[1] Setting aside the elitism inherent in that statement, it is true that stories in the media about oppressed or underprivileged individuals attract a great deal of interest. However, it is usually prominent individuals about whom information is requested at the reference desk. Carlyle's larger point—that interest in the lives of others is a universal phenomenon—could easily be verified by reference librarians. One of the most consistent features of reference work has been the high demand for information about people. Sometimes this information is sought to satisfy curiosity; at other times it is needed for a school assignment or research project or to prepare remarks introducing a guest speaker. Among questions encountered at a public or academic library reference desk are: "How many of Stephen King's books have been made into movies?" or "Where can I find a summary of opera singer Kathleen Battle's career?" Answers to these and similar questions can be found in the sources discussed in this chapter, most of which are likely to be found in college and university library reference collections, as well as those of most public libraries.

Questions requiring one or two specific facts about an individual are probably the most common type of biographical reference question received in most libraries. Other requests may be for information on a person's writings, place of birth, date of death, or career history. Biographical sources providing factual information may be called *direct* sources, because they supply the information itself rather than referring the user, through bibliographic citations, to other sources where the information may be found. Direct sources may offer brief, basic biographical data (*Who's Who*), or they may provide lengthy biographical essays (*Current Biography* and *Dictionary of American Biography*). Although the distinction is not always clear, biographical sources providing brief data about individuals are generally referred to as *biographical directories*, while those offering more detailed information, usually in essay form, are often called *biographical dictionaries*.

Other biographical questions, unlike the queries mentioned above, may not be answered by a single source. These require the librarian to locate more extensive summaries of a person's life and career. When the librarian is not sure which source will provide the information requested, or if several direct sources have been tried to no avail, indirect sources may lead to the solution of the problem. *Indirect* sources list bibliographic citations referring the user to other works that may contain the information sought. They generally give only enough factual information (e.g., full name, birth and death dates) to identify each individual. These sources, for example *Biography Index,* usually are indexes to other sources. Some are both direct and indirect. *Contemporary Authors*, for example, gives fairly extensive information about individuals and sometimes lists other sources where further information can be found.

In addition to being direct or indirect, biographical sources may be further divided into *current*, those about living persons, or *retrospective*, those about people from the past. Some biographical tools provide data on both types of individuals. Some ready-reference sources such as "Who's Who" titles list only persons known to be living at the time of publication, while others include only deceased persons. For this reason the first question often asked by the reference librarian is, "Do you know if this person is still living?" Of course, very recently deceased individuals will still be listed in the latest editions of current sources. It takes some time for these individuals to appear in retrospective sources.

Scope and coverage vary among sources. The most narrow titles focus on one area of human endeavor, or on one profession or academic field. An example of this type is *Who's Who in Economics.* Other, broader sources cover several related fields. Two well-known sources of this type are *Directory of American Scholars* and *American Men and Women of Science* (discussed later in this chapter). An even broader class includes prominent persons from all fields residing in a specific country. These titles commonly begin "Who's Who in" or "Who Was Who in." They contain brief factual information about prominent persons—living and deceased, respectively—in the given country ("America" or "American" in these titles often means North America). Comprehensive, multivolume retrospective sources providing fairly lengthy essays have been compiled for many Western countries. Several of these titles, covering the United States, Canada, or Great Britain, are discussed in this chapter. Also discussed are obituary sources, another important type of retrospective biographical tool.

Finally, there are international biographical sources. These may be direct sources such as the *Encyclopedia of World Biography* or indirect tools like *Biography and Genealogy Master Index.* Indirect sources tend to be international in coverage. The relative number of non-American or non-Western persons included in these tools should be considered when evaluating them.

EVALUATION

As with other reference tools, biographical sources must be evaluated based on ease of use, accuracy of information, and the degree to which they achieve comprehensiveness within their stated scope. For current sources, the main consideration is up-to-date information. Retrospective tools, which are often used for research, are more valuable if they give sources for further reading.

Scope

The first question usually asked when evaluating a biographical reference tool is, "Who is included in this work?" This leads immediately to the further question, "What are the criteria for inclusion?" In other words, what is the intended scope of the work, and how is it determined whether a specific individual fits within that scope? Generally, biographical sources do not seek to include everyone who meets the most basic criterion indicated by the title (e.g., residents of a certain country; members of a particular gender, ethnic group, or profession). Rather, they try to include only those individuals in that group who have *reference interest* because of their position, achievements, or historical significance.

The question of reference interest brings up the problem of *vanity books*, or biographical directories published as profit-making ventures and generally sold only to the biographees themselves. These often have titles that include such words as "distinction" or "outstanding personalities." Reference librarians should be aware of the existence of these, because library users will inquire about the validity of questionnaires they may receive, and sometimes will want to know why the books are not in the library. These books do not have a well-defined scope and may include anyone who submits a questionnaire or agrees to purchase the book. Lack of reviews in the library literature and absence of holdings in major library collections, as determined from online catalogs, can be used to argue against purchasing these books.

Comprehensiveness

Scope and criteria for inclusion are generally spelled out in the book's prefatory material. How the criteria are defined and applied will determine how *comprehensive* the work will be within its stated scope. It is important that as many as possible of those individuals who meet the criteria be included, or the reference value of the work will be reduced. Of course, this is not always easy to determine, because criteria often are stated in general terms. *American Men and Women of Science* lists "those who have made significant contributions in their field."[2] "Significant contributions" are difficult to define precisely. However, one can check to see if all individuals who hold comparable positions or with similar accomplishments are included. Also, it can be determined if certain groups or fields of activity are under- or overrepresented. This kind of evaluation is more difficult with retrospective sources, because the importance or even existence of positions and professions changes with time, and it requires considerable research to identify individuals who are likely candidates for inclusion.

Whatever criteria are used, it is important that the work's scope and criteria for inclusion be in harmony. If the scope is broad, as in *Who's Who in America*, the criteria must be strictly applied, thus keeping to a manageable number the people to be included. On the other hand, if the scope is fairly narrow, then the criteria can be applied more liberally so that the work will be comprehensive within its stated scope. *Directory of American Scholars*, for example, profiles scholars who are currently active in the humanities and can be expected to list everyone who meets that broad definition. Its success at achieving that goal should not be difficult to evaluate by librarians making spot checks to find persons known to be working in the fields covered. Likewise, *Who's Who in America* should, ideally, include everyone who meets its narrower criteria—holder of one of a list of positions stated in its "Standards of Admission" (see Figure 16.1, page 384), or one who has demonstrated "significant achievement."[3] How comprehensive it is with regard to the second criterion, however, will depend on how carefully and objectively that criterion is applied. If it is not strictly applied, uneven rather than comprehensive coverage will be the result. Considering the size of this task in a biographical directory that may list anywhere from 20,000 to 80,000 individuals, it is strange to find reviewers who occasionally criticize a title because one or two individuals deemed important by the reviewer have been missed. If a large number of eligible persons known to the evaluator are missing, then the work may be considered to be lacking in comprehensiveness.

Accuracy

Accuracy of the information presented in biographical entries is of paramount importance in a reference work. There are basically only two sources of this information: the biographees themselves and writings about those individuals (*secondary sources*). Although the biographees are undoubtedly in the best position to provide accurate information, they may rely on their memories (which are not always reliable) for some facts, they may omit facts they regard as unfavorable, or they may not return the questionnaire at all. Most current sources, nevertheless, rely on biographees for their information, and some may check secondary sources to verify that information. Publishers of retrospective biographical tools must obtain their information either from secondary sources or from the writings and papers of the biographee. Secondary sources used by reputable scholars and publishers should be free of personal bias, but determining accuracy requires careful and objective research. When faced with conflicting facts from different biographical sources, librarians can consult other sources to try to determine the truth, or they can choose between the conflicting facts based on the nature and reputation of the titles involved. Either way, it is often difficult to be absolutely sure that one has determined which is the accurate information. In these situations, the librarian can only present the conflicting facts to the user and explain why one set of facts is, in the librarian's informed judgment, more likely to be correct.

Figure 16.1 "Standards of Admission" from *Who's Who in America*, 47th edition, Volume 1, 1992-1993. Reprinted by permission of Marquis Who's Who, a member of the Lexis-Nexis group.

Standards of Admission

The foremost consideration in determining who will be admitted to the pages of *Who's Who in America* is the extent of an individual's reference interest. Reference value is based on either of two factors: 1) the position of responsibility held or 2) the level of significant achievement attained in a career of noteworthy activity. The majority of biographees qualify for admission on the basis of the first factor, a specific position of responsibility. Incumbency in the position makes the person someone of high reference interest. The factor of position includes the following categories:

1. High-ranking members of the executive, legislative, and judicial branches of the United States government. This group includes, for example, the President of the United States, members of Congress, cabinet secretaries, chief administrators of selected federal agencies and commis sions, and justices of the federal courts.

2. Military officers on active duty with the rank of Major General or higher in the Army, Air Force, and Marine Corps, and of Rear Admiral or higher in the U.S. Navy.

3. Specified state government officials. Among these are governors, lieutenant governors, secretaries of state, attorneys general and treasurers. Also included under this standard are presidents of state senates, state university system administrators, chief state health officers and officials of American territories.

4. Judges of state and territorial courts of the highest appellate jurisdiction.

5. High-level officials of principal cities, based on population. These officials include mayors, police chiefs, school superintendents, and other selected positions.

6. Leading government officials of Canada and Mexico. In Canada, this group includes the prime minister, premiers of the provinces, ministers of departments of the federal government, and justices of the highest courts. Examples in the Mexican government are the president of the country and cabinet secretaries of the national government.

7. Principal officers of major national and international businesses as defined by several quantitative criteria.

8. Ranking administrative officials of major universities and colleges. Some of the officers included in this category are president, provost, dean, and selected department heads.

9. Heads of leading philanthropic, cultural, educational, professional, and scientific institutions and associations. These institutions include, for example, selected foundations, museums, symphony orchestras, libraries, and research laboratories.

10. Selected members of certain honorary and professional organizations, such as the National Academy of Sciences, the National Academy of Design, the American College of Trial Lawyers, and the Royal Society of Canada.

11. Chief ecclesiastics of the principal religious denominations.

12. Recipients of major national and international awards, such as the Nobel and Pulitzer Prizes, the Academy Awards, and the Antoinette Perry, or Tony Awards. Also included are winners of important professional awards, such as the American Institute of Architecture's Gold Medal for Architecture.

Admission by the second factor—significant achievement—is based on the application of objective criteria established for each field. An artist whose works hang in major museums qualifies for admission for noteworthy accomplishment. The professor who has made important research contributions in his field is of reference interest because of his outstanding achievements. Qualitative standards determine eligibility for every field.

In many instances there is considerable overlap between the two factors used for inclusion in *Who's Who in America.* For example, the head of a major library is in the book because of position, but reaching that responsibility also signifies important achievement. Similarly, a state governor not only holds a position that warrants inclusion; attaining that post also represents significant achievement in the political world. In both cases the reference value of the biographical sketch is significant. Whether the person has been selected because of position or as a mark of achievement, the biographee in *Who's Who in America* has noteworthy accomplishments beyond those of the vast majority of contemporaries.

Currency

A major factor determining the accuracy of a biographical source is its *currency*. In a highly mobile society, it is difficult to provide biographical information that is absolutely up-to-date. The editors of biographical directories who rely on data provided by the biographees themselves face a dilemma when individuals to be listed do not return their questionnaires. The data from a previous edition might be used, or it may be possible to update that information through research in other sources. Out-of-date information sometimes survives, leading to inaccuracies regarding an individual's current position, family status, or address. Comparing entries for the same individual in different biographical tools will occasionally reveal errors of this nature. Publication frequency is another factor in maintaining current information about biographees. Many biographical directories are revised every year or every other year. Their electronic counterparts, when available, are sometimes updated only when a new print edition is prepared and may, therefore, be no more current than the print volumes. Biographical dictionaries are revised less frequently, and are more likely to contain out-of-date material. However, dictionaries that are published serially, as are *Contemporary Authors* and *Current Biography*, will often publish entirely new or revised entries on prominent individuals whose earlier entries have become dated. Electronic versions of these dictionaries will bring up all the entries for an individual together, making it unnecessary to search through several volumes.

References

Another feature of some biographical sources is the inclusion of *references for further reading*. Generally, sources that provide biographical essays list the sources from which that information was obtained. Some also list sources not used, to enable the reader to conduct further research. If these are critical sources or book-length studies, they can be particularly valuable. The most recent studies are desirable, but older, standard biographies of the individual may contain valid factual information that has been overlooked by later biographers. Biographers are often selective about information that they include or omit, so researchers need to look at several sources to have a comprehensive picture of the individual.

Format

Almost as important as accuracy and currency of information provided in biographical tools is the *format* in which this information is presented. If a particular title is poorly organized, or if the access points (e.g., indexes, cross-references) are inadequate, users may never find the information they are seeking, even if it is, in fact, buried somewhere within the book. When speaking of access points, it is clear that electronic reference tools offer a definite advantage over print sources. Electronic retrieval in both CD-ROM and online databases allows one to retrieve biographical entries for persons with common characteristics, such as the same birth date or place, the same educational background or occupation, or receipt of the same honor or award. In addition, one can print full entries or only the parts of entries in which one is interested. A great deal of flexibility is available with this kind of tool, and this flexibility has been used to improve, to some extent, the access points in print sources. Several print biographical tools now provide electronically generated indexes by geographic area or occupation or both. However, it is doubtful that a print source could ever offer as many retrieval points as its electronic counterpart.

Electronic searching also permits one to simultaneously search entries from many different print editions or volumes of a specific biographical tool. For example, one can search all editions of *Biography and Genealogy Master Index* (1975–present) in the electronic version available online at GaleNet or Dialog. In similar fashion, in the electronic versions of *Biography Index* (available online from various vendors or on CD-ROM), one can search a database that corresponds to several annual volumes of the print version. This saves the librarian or user an enormous amount of time, and the references can be printed in one comprehensive list. Recent electronic offerings from H. W. Wilson and the Gale Group carry this aggregation even further. *Wilson Biographies Plus Illustrated* features the combined coverage of more than 100 print reference sources, and *Biography Resource Center* combines more than 50 of Gale Group's biographical reference sources with selected articles from more than 250 full-text periodicals and entries from Marquis Who's Who biographical sources.

Another aspect of format is the ease with which one can interpret data contained in the entries. With the essay form of entry, ease of interpretation refers primarily to the clarity and grace found in the writing style of the author. As in any written text, the information should be presented in a concise and unambiguous fashion; it should also not be disorganized or awkward. In biographical directories, a great deal of information may be packed into brief entries, and abbreviations are almost always employed. A list of abbreviations and their meanings should be placed where they can easily be found by the user.

SELECTION

Although criteria for evaluating biographical reference sources are fairly objective, selection decisions must be subjectively based on the needs of a library and its user groups. The amount of money the library can allocate to reference materials, and the uniqueness of the information provided by particular tools, also play a role in the selection process.

Needs of Users

Before one purchases a biographical reference tool, several factors must be considered. Perhaps the most important is the *needs of one's users*. These can be ascertained in several ways (see Chapters 10 and 13). School and academic library users will need as many biographical sources as possible: dictionaries, for the completion of class assignments, and directories, for finding information about professional colleagues or well-known persons. In special libraries, the latter interest generally predominates, so biographical directories will be in the highest demand, particularly those covering the specific occupations to which the library's users belong. In public libraries, where users are more diverse, both types are needed. In smaller public libraries, national sources such as *Who's Who in America* and *Newsmakers* may suffice, supplemented by the "Who's Who" for that library's region. In academic libraries, large public libraries, and some secondary school libraries, international biographical sources are essential. Current biographical sources will be in demand in all types of libraries. Retrospective biographical tools are required in school and academic libraries for research purposes. They may be used for general information and for research in public libraries, but are less often used in most special libraries.

Cost

For most libraries, the overriding consideration is likely to be *cost*. Many smaller libraries unable to afford a large set like *American National Biography* may purchase *Who Was Who in America* instead. Even larger libraries may be unable to afford all of the specialized directories available for individual nations, depending instead on *The International Who's Who* and/or *Who's Who in the World* for coverage of foreign individuals of note. Similarly, *Almanac of Famous People* might be a good choice for libraries unable to afford *Biography and Genealogy Master Index*.

Uniqueness

Uniqueness of a biographical title must be assessed before selecting it for one's collection. The two international directories just mentioned each contains unique entries, but there is considerable overlap between them with regard to the individuals included. Where such overlap exists, many librarians will have to choose only one of the two or more titles that offer similar coverage. In situations such as this, it is best to rely on reviews in professional journals before reaching a decision.

IMPORTANT GENERAL SOURCES

Of the many available biographical reference tools, discussion in this chapter focuses on those that, because of their broad coverage, are likely to be heavily used in general reference collections. A limited number of more specialized sources are also described briefly to illustrate the variety of such sources and their scope. Further information on specialized sources can be obtained from the guides to biographical reference tools listed in the "Additional Readings" for this chapter.

Librarians should also acquire a current catalog from each of the major publishers of biographical reference sources, namely, H.W. Wilson, Reed Elsevier (and its subsidiaries, Marquis Who's Who and R. R. Bowker), and Gale Group (and its subsidiary, St. James Press). Other publishers of important biographical reference tools can be identified in the "List of Sources" at the end of this chapter.

Current Biographical Directories

The one biographical source that every library providing reference service is likely to have is *Who's Who in America*. Published biennially from 1899 to 1994 and annually beginning with 1994, it provides, in the 54th edition, salient biographical facts about approximately 120,000 individuals whose "Reference value is based on either of two factors: 1) the position of responsibility held or 2) the level of significant achievement attained in a career of noteworthy activity."[4] These general "Standards of Admission" have remained relatively constant during this prestigious work's long history.[5] And, as with many reference sources, the "America" in *Who's Who in America* includes Canada and Mexico.

It is important to note that inclusion in *Who's Who in America* is based on achievement and not simply on wealth or notoriety. Following the example of *Who's Who in America*, most other current biographical directories have established the same criteria for inclusion. Among the 12 types of positions that automatically qualify an individual for inclusion in *Who's Who in America* are leading government jobs at the national or state level, high administrative positions in major universities and colleges, and leading positions in large businesses (the full list is printed in the prefatory section of each edition). Persons selected for one edition are generally listed again in succeeding editions. The editors identify possible new listees by careful searching in newspapers and journals. A few individuals who have retired may be dropped, on the supposition that they are no longer subjects of substantial reference interest. They are listed in a "Retiree Index" that refers the user to an entry for them in an earlier edition. A separate list identifies those who have died since publication of the previous edition.

As with most current biographical directories, the information provided for individuals is obtained, whenever possible, from questionnaires sent to those individuals. If the individual does not respond, the publisher's staff will gather the information as best they can from other sources. An asterisk at the end of an entry lets the user know that information in that entry was prepared in that way by the publisher. When this is the case, frequently changing information, such as address or current position, may not be as up-to-date or accurate as an entry for which the biographee supplied the information. The data presented in *Who's Who in America* are arranged in 20 data fields (see Figure 16.2). The many abbreviations are explained in a table. A few entries conclude with brief, personal thoughts by the biographee, a recent addition apparently designed to bring a personal touch to the collection of dry facts presented in the rest of the entry.

Figure 16.2 "Key to Information" in *Who's Who in America*, 47th edition, Volume 1, 1992-1993. Reprinted by permission of Marquis Who's Who, a member of the Lexis-Nexis group.

Key to Information

[1] GIBSON, OSCAR JULIUS, [2] physician, medical educator; **[3]** b. Syracuse, N.Y., Aug. 31, 1937; **[4]** s. Paul Oliver and Elizabeth H. (Thrun) G.; **[5]** m. Judith S. Gonzalez, Apr. 28, 1968; **[6]** children: Richard Gary, Matthew Cary, Samuel Perry. **[7]** BA magna cum laude, U. Pa., 1960; MD, Harvard U., 1964. **[8]** Diplomate Am. Bd. Internal Medicine, Am. Bd. Preventive Medicine. **[9]** Intern Barnes Hosp., St. Louis, 1964-65, resident, 1965-66; clin. assoc. Nat. Heart Inst., NIH, Bethesda, Md., 1966-68; chief resident medicine U. Okla. Hosps., 1968-69; asst. prof. community health Okla. Med. Ctr., 1969-70, assoc. prof., 1970-74, prof., chmn. dept., 1974-80; dean U. Okla. Coll. Medicine, 1978-82; v.p. med. staff affairs Bapt. Med. Ctr., Oklahoma City, 1982-86, exec. v.p., 1986-88, chmn., 1988—; **[10]** mem. governing bd. Ambulatory Health Care Consortium, Inc., 1979-80; mem. Okla. Bd. Medicolegal Examiners, 1985—. **[11]** Contbr. articles to profl. jours. **[12]** Bd. dirs., v.p. Okla. Arthritis Found., 1982—; trustee North Central Mental Health Ctr., 1985—. **[13]** Served with U.S. Army, 1955-56. **[14]** Recipient R.T. Chadwick award NIH, 1968; Am. Heart Assn. grantee, 1985-86, 88. **[15]** Fellow Assn. Tchrs. Preventive Medicine; mem. Am. Fedn. Clin. Research, Assn. Med. Colls., AAAS, AMA, Masons, Shriners, Sigma Xi. **[16]** Republican. **[17]** Roman Catholic. **[18]** Avocations: swimming, weight lifting, travel. **[19]** Home: 6060 N Ridge Ave Oklahoma City OK 73126 **[20]** Office: Bapt Med Ctr 1986 Cuba Hwy Oklahoma City OK 73120

KEY

[1] Name
[2] Occupation
[3] Vital Statistics
[4] Parents
[5] Marriage
[6] Children
[7] Education
[8] Professional certifications
[9] Career
[10] Career Related
[11] Writings and creative works
[12] Civic and political activities
[13] Military
[14] Awards and fellowships
[15] Professional and association memberships, Clubs and Lodges
[16] Political affiliation
[17] Religion
[18] Avocations
[19] Home address
[20] Office address

Who's Who in America is usually the first source to consult when basic biographical data on a prominent American are required. A careful study of the positions that automatically ensure inclusion, along with a good working knowledge of the kinds of data that are and are not provided, will give the reference librarian greater confidence that turning to this source will provide the answer.

Who's Who in America can be searched effectively online as well. Editions of this work dating back to 1985, as well as the 17 regional and topical Marquis "Who's Whos" (some discussed later in this chapter) are available online on Dialog and NEXIS as *Marquis Who's Who.* This database is updated semi-annually, making it more current than the print source. When searching online, one can combine elements from more than one part of the record to retrieve, for example, all members of a particular religious denomination who work in a specific occupation, or all persons who were born in a particular state who have a degree from a specific academic institution. Care must be taken when searching geographic, occupational, and other fields in this database because not every individual in a particular occupation will be indexed under the same term. For example, one history teacher may enter "educator" on the data form, while another may enter "historian."

Despite its comprehensiveness, *Who's Who in America* cannot list all Americans who might be the subject of reference questions. Persons of local or regional interest are often omitted. To provide better coverage at this level, Marquis Who's Who publishes four regional biographical directories modeled on *Who's Who in America*, one each for the East, Midwest, West, and South/Southwest. Adjacent areas of Canada or Mexico are included in each regional *Who's Who*. Each title lists some 16,000 to 25,000 persons. Selection criteria and data provided are the same as in the parent title, but overlap with that work is kept to a minimum. New editions are published every other year.

Several topical "Who's Whos," also published by Marquis, provide more in-depth coverage of fields such as finance and industry, law, entertainment, and religion. These titles, along with *Who's Who in America*, *Who's Who of American Women*, and the four regional directories, form *The Complete Marquis Who's Who* on CD-ROM, providing biographical data for more than 790,000 individuals.

Several works have been introduced in recent years to provide more comprehensive coverage of prominent U.S. and Canadian women and minority group members. *Who's Who of American Women* has appeared approximately every two years since 1958 and lists almost 34,000 women. The entries in *Who's Who of American Women* have the same criteria and contain the same information found in entries in *Who's Who in America*. Geographic and occupational indexes are included.

Another work that supplements *Who's Who in America* is *Who's Who Among African Americans*. It lists more than 20,000 African Americans living in the United States. Standards of admission are similar to those used for *Who's Who in America*, with information generally supplied by the biographee, but entries are more detailed than one would find in *Who's Who in America*. Also, headings within each entry, such as "Education," are printed in bold uppercase letters, allowing the user to more easily find a particular kind of data, such as career history. An obituaries section provides complete entries for persons who have died since their names appeared in the previous edition, and there are geographic and occupational indexes. *Who's Who Among African Americans* can be searched on NEXIS as part of the *Gale Biographies* database.

Other biographical directories providing expanded coverage for ethnic or racial minorities are *Who's Who Among Hispanic Americans*, first published in 1991, and *Who's Who Among Asian Americans, 1994–1995*, which profiles Americans of Asian or Pacific Island descent. Both are published by Gale Group. Selection of entries is based on position held or contributions and achievements. Each entry gives the standard personal and career data found in other biographical directories. As with *Who's Who Among African Americans*, field labels in these two works are printed in boldface uppercase letters, making them easier to use than the Marquis Who's Who directories, in which the entire entry is set in the same type size and style. Both of these titles provide occupational, geographic, and ethnic/cultural heritage indexes including, where relevant, the country from which an individual emigrated. Obituaries are given for individuals who have died since publication of the previous edition. Both can be searched online on NEXIS, as part of the *Gale Biographies* database.

Two annual biographical directories focus solely on prominent Canadians. *Canadian Who's Who* has individuals chosen for inclusion "on merit alone," with a broad range of social and occupational backgrounds represented. Entries resemble those in *Who's Who in America*, but are sometimes longer. *Who's Who in Canada* focuses more on business and political leaders, and includes fewer women. Photographs are included for many of the biographees. *Canadian Who's Who* is the more important source for a reference collection, because it includes many more entries and does a better job of including prominent Canadians from all types of occupations. It is also available on CD-ROM.

The British counterpart to *Who's Who in America* antedates its American imitation by some 50 years. First published in 1849, and the first biographical directory of its kind, it bears the simple title, *Who's Who*. As Ann Ricker notes, early editions merely listed nobility and those holding royal court positions, with no biographical data provided.[6] It was in 1897 that *Who's Who* first offered biographical information about those it listed and broadened its scope to include those who, by their abilities (not just by birth or position), had achieved national prominence. This expanded version provided the model for *Who's Who in America*.[7]

Today's criteria for inclusion in *Who's Who* are as stated in the 2000 edition: "The book aims to list people who, through their careers, affect the political, economic, scientific, and artistic life of the country."[8] This scope allows for the listing of a relatively large number of prominent foreigners. An estimated 30 percent of entries in the 1990 edition were for non-British persons.[9] The information provided is similar to that provided in *Who's Who in America*, with emphasis on educational background and career history. Current address, and in many cases, telephone number, are given. For subjects who are authors or performers, an extensive list of major works is included. As in the book's American counterpart, avocational interests are also listed. Whenever possible, all data are provided by the biographee.

The arrangement of *Who's Who* is alphabetical by surname, and there are no indexes. Special sections include a list of abbreviations, a list of individuals who have died since the publication of the previous edition, and a section on the royal family, in which very brief biographical data are provided. *Who's Who* has always been published annually. A CD-ROM, *Who's Who 1897–1998* is now available and includes *Who's Who 1998* as well as *Who Was Who* (discussed later in this chapter).

Large libraries will purchase current biographical sources covering many countries in addition to those of North America and the British Isles. Similar biographical directories in English or other languages exist for a number of Western European nations, along with titles covering multination areas such as Scandinavia. There are also biographical directories for some countries in Asia, Africa, South America, and the Pacific, although these tend to be updated less frequently than those for European countries.

Smaller libraries lacking funds to buy individual country directories can rely on international directories to provide information on prominent persons from other parts of the world. The two major current sources are *The International Who's Who*, published annually by Europa, and *Who's Who in the World*, published approximately every other year by Marquis Who's Who.

Who's Who in the World lists individuals from virtually every nation in a format almost identical to that of *Who's Who in America*, with the same types of data in the entries. There are a list of abbreviations employed and a list of rules used to alphabetize complex and compound names, but, unfortunately, no list of those who have died since publication of the previous edition. There is also an occupational index. *Who's Who in the World* is included in *The Complete Marquis Who's Who on CD-ROM*.

The annual *The International Who's Who* lists fewer persons but is often more current than *Who's Who in the World*. The usefulness of *International Who's Who* as a reference work is enhanced by a separate section containing biographical entries for reigning royal families throughout the world and a list with the date of death of individuals who have died since the publication of the previous edition. Information is easier to read and is more detailed than that in *Who's Who in the World*, and frequently includes a telephone number and current address. A CD-ROM version is now available.

Two specialized directories useful for finding biographical information on contemporary scholars are *American Men and Women of Science* and *Directory of American Scholars*. *American Men and Women of Science* lists "living scientists in the physical and biological fields, as well as public health scientists, engineers, mathematicians, statisticians, and computer scientists."[10] Since its first publication in 1906, it has provided biographical data on more than 300,000 prominent North American scientists and engineers. Its purpose, as stated in the preface, is to help scientists learn more about their colleagues and their colleagues' professional and research activities.

To be included, individuals must be actively engaged in scientific work, must have conducted research (which is usually published, but may not be if it is classified), or must have attained a "position of substantial responsibility requiring scientific training or experience."[11] Information is provided by the biographee whenever possible and includes both personal and professional data. A current mailing address is given, and beginning with the 19th edition, some e-mail addresses and fax numbers are provided.

American Men and Women of Science can be searched electronically on Dialog, as part of the *Bowker Biographical Directory,* and on NEXIS. Each element in the entry is searchable by keyword. The database contains entries only from the most recent edition of its print counterpart. The Web version from Bowker beginning fall 2000 includes updates since the most recent print edition (http://www.amws.com).

For libraries unable to afford *American Men and Women of Science*, Marquis Who's Who offers a one-volume biographical directory, *Who's Who in Science and Engineering*, published biennially. It provides standard biographical data, supplied in most cases by the person profiled, for scientists, doctors, and engineers. Inclusion is based on standard Marquis criteria. A separate listing of scientific awards and their recipients is included, as are professional and geographical indexes. A few scholars working in the social sciences or humanities are included if their work is regarded as important for those working in the "hard" sciences. Although most entries are for Americans, important scientists from more than 70 other countries are profiled as well. Because of this broad coverage, many libraries owning *American Men and Women of Science* will also purchase *Who's Who in Science and Engineering.*

Directory of American Scholars provides similar information about scholars in the humanities. The most recent edition is the 9th (1999). One must have published scholarly works in the humanities to be listed. Each volume covers several fields, with entries in one alphabetical list, and has a geographic index arranged by town name, giving the names and subject area of biographees in the United States and Canada. Volume 4 contains an alphabetical index to the entire set.

Biographical directories for specific professions or occupations are in demand in larger libraries and in special libraries that focus on specific professions. Examples of these include *Who's Who in American Art* and *Who's Who in American Politics*, both from Marquis. Publication schedules for such directories vary. Both are also searchable online as part of the *Bowker Biographical Directory* on Dialog, the same file containing entries from *American Men and Women of Science.*

Current Biographical Dictionaries

Since 1940, *Current Biography* has offered librarians and users readable, objective, and carefully researched biographical essays about newsworthy persons in a broad range of fields. Although some of the information presented is obtained from the individuals themselves, the essays are based primarily on articles that have appeared in newspapers and magazines. The style of the essays is analytical within a narrative context. Generally, a chronological overview of the individual's life is given, with the major focus on the contributions, achievements, or events that have brought that person to prominence. Details of the individual's private life (e.g., family, appearance, interests) are well integrated with a complete history of the public career. Each essay includes a photograph of the biographee and a list of the articles and, occasionally, books upon which the essay is based. For library users wanting a life history without reading a full biography, *Current Biography* is an excellent choice. It is also an excellent choice when an individual is looking for more specific biographical data than is found in most biographical directories, such as a person's height, dress, or general lifestyle. Although some prominent individuals from other nations are included, most entries are for Americans.

Each issue contains about 20 alphabetically arranged biographical essays, a number of short obituary notices of previous biographees, and a cumulative index for the year's issues to that point. Each obituary provides references both to a full-length article in an earlier issue of *Current Biography* and to a *New York Times* obituary. At the end of each year, the essays from the 11 monthly issues are cumulated in one alphabet in the *Current Biography Yearbook.* The yearbook provides an index by profession for the current year, as well as a cumulative index to yearbooks since the last separately issued cumulation. Cumulative indexes covering longer periods are published every 10 years or so.

Periodically, new essays for earlier biographees appear in *Current Biography* with a note that the earlier essay has been superseded. Although this policy of printing new, updated essays is helpful, it also reveals a weakness of "current" sources such as this—that the essays they provide can become outdated within a few years.

Originally titled *Contemporary Newsmakers*, *Newsmakers* was introduced in 1985 by Gale Group. *Newsmakers* is designed to complement and supplement Gale's *Contemporary Authors* (discussed later) by providing biographical information about prominent individuals who are not writers. Like *Current Biography*, *Newsmakers* covers all fields, from government and business to entertainment and sports. It provides slightly better coverage in fields such as sports and popular music. Business leaders are also well represented. For this reason, it is an important reference source for public libraries, although students at all levels will use it in school and college libraries for information on prominent individuals in popular culture.

Newsmakers is published in three quarterly paperback issues, each containing about 50 entries and about 10 or 12 fairly lengthy obituaries. Each entry begins with a listing of personal and career directory information. The main part of the entry, "Sidelights," consists of a signed narrative and analytical essay on the individual's life and career similar in style and content to *Current Biography*. The information is gathered primarily from newspaper and magazine articles, which are cited in the final section of each entry, "Sources." At the end of each year, a hardcover cumulated volume is published, adding about 50 entries and indexes by nationality, subject, and occupation as well as a cumulative name index covering the entire set, 1985 to the present. The cumulated volume also includes obituary notices, which are longer and more detailed than those provided in *Current Biography*. *Newsmakers* is part of the *Gale Biographies* database on NEXIS.

Although there is overlap between *Newsmakers* and *Current Biography*, having access to both sets increases the reference librarian's chances of finding a well-written, objective account of the life and career of any of the hundreds of individuals whose prominence in a given field makes them likely subjects of reference questions.

A similar title for students in middle or secondary schools is *Biography Today*, from Omnigraphics. Like *Newsmakers*, *Biography Today* is published in three softbound issues and one bound, cumulative volume annually. Each issue contains entries for 12 to 15 persons judged to be of current interest to young people. Every entry has numerous subdivisions, with headings like "Youth" and "Career Highlights," to make specific information easy to locate, along with at least one illustration. Each issue and the annual bound volume have numerous cumulated indexes, such as name, places of birth, and birthday indexes.

Gale Group, publisher of *Newsmakers*, began a current biographical series entitled *Contemporary Black Biography* in 1992. Three volumes are added to this series each year. Each volume includes biographical essays for about 65 prominent individuals of African heritage, most of whom are from the United States. Cumulative name, occupation, nationality, and subject indexes are provided in each volume.

Although probably not a favorite reference tool among beginners because it is made up of several separate series, *Contemporary Authors* has proven its worth to reference librarians. One of its strongest assets is that the term *authors* is very liberally interpreted to include not only writers of books, but also media writers (e.g., scriptwriters), journalists, critics, musicians, and many individuals whose prominence is in fields other than writing, such as politics and sports. Entries requiring revision are rewritten in a timely fashion. These features make *Contemporary Authors* an obvious first choice for many reference librarians faced with a question about the life or works of a twentieth-century writer.

Contemporary Authors contains three types of entries: brief entries providing basic personal and career information; sketches with the same data and a biographical essay, which may extend over several double-columned pages; and obituaries composed of a brief notice of an individual's life and important writings. All three types contain references for further reading or research and are arranged in one alphabetical sequence for ease of use.

The organization of the *Contemporary Authors* set is unusually complex. GaleNet, an online source from Gale Group, solves many problems by bringing up the most complete and up-to-date entry for an individual from *Contemporary Authors*, including some data more current than the print version. There is also a CD-ROM version. If *Contemporary Authors* is not available in electronic form it is advisable to spend some time studying the print set to familiarize oneself with the coverage of the various parts. Comparison of the Original Volumes, New Revision series, First Revisions series, Autobiographical series, and Bibliographical series, as well as the indexes is necessary if one is to use the set successfully. Citations to entries in other Gale publications, such as the *Dictionary of Literary Biography* series (also in GaleNet), a massive retrospective set with international coverage, are also included in the *Contemporary Authors* index. Although the inclusion of these citations enriches the *Contemporary Authors* index considerably, it makes an already complex reference tool more difficult to master.

The Gale Group publication comparable to *Contemporary Authors* but aimed primarily at secondary school students is *Something About the Author*. This set offers information similar to *Contemporary Authors* for authors and illustrators of works for children and young adults. It is heavily illustrated. Several volumes are published each year, and each volume contains a cumulative index to the entire set.

A growing number of specialized biographical dictionaries provide essay-length treatment of contemporary writers, artists, musicians, scholars, and other professionals. For example, H. W. Wilson has published two volumes of *World Artists*, covering 1950–1980 and 1980–1990. St. James Press has published several specialized current biographical dictionaries, such as *Contemporary Designers* and *Contemporary Composers*. Gale Group has an ongoing series, *Contemporary Theatre, Film & Television* (1984–). Because some of the information in these titles can also be found in more general works, libraries usually purchase them only if user demand for biographical information is high and the budget for the reference collection is sufficient to absorb the cost.

Retrospective Biographical Dictionaries—Universal

Encyclopedia of World Biography (2d ed., 1998), one of the largest modern biographical reference tools, was compiled for students in secondary schools and colleges. The selection of names was made with curriculum needs in mind. An effort was made to ensure that Asian and African historical figures were well represented among those persons, both living and dead, selected for inclusion. Articles from the 1973 edition have been updated and over 500 new biographees have been added.

This encyclopedia is composed of 16 volumes of text, a seventeenth volume containing an index, and a supplementary volume 18. Unlike the first edition, the articles are no longer signed. Entry length varies, portraits are included whenever possible, and there are numerous other illustrations. Each essay concludes with a further reading section, and some have "Additional Sources" containing citations to journals and Internet Web sites. The consolidated index is arranged alphabetically with entries for people, places, occupations, and so forth. A CD-ROM version is also available.

A more specialized multivolume biographical dictionary aimed at an educated audience is *Dictionary of Scientific Biography*. This work covers physical and biological sciences and mathematics. Medicine, technology, and the social sciences generally are not included. *Dictionary of Scientific Biography* is international in scope, although the history of science in the Western world predominates. This imbalance is partially corrected by essays in the first supplement (volume 15) on the history of science in non-Western cultures. The second supplement (volumes 17–18) adds essays on twentieth-century scientists not included in the original set.

Dictionary of Scientific Biography provides scholarly and readable essays on several thousand prominent scientists from the past, written by contemporary scientists or historians of science from around the world. The essays are all based on extensive study of the relevant primary and secondary literature and constitute, in some cases, a significant contribution to existing knowledge about the individual. Focus is on the career and scientific contributions of each biographee, rather than on details of personal or family life. Each essay is followed by an extensive bibliography listing published works, locations of papers, secondary literature, and any bibliographies devoted to that individual. The index (volume 16) is very detailed, with many subject terms in specific areas, such as "fluids" or "retina," corporate names such as Johns Hopkins University, and the names of scientific journals and societies.

Dictionary of Scientific Biography is used frequently by reference librarians in academic and research libraries. For libraries where less information is sought, *Concise Dictionary of Scientific Biography*, published in 1981, can be used instead of the longer set. It contains entries for all the individuals in *Dictionary of Scientific Biography* and its first supplement. The essay format is preserved for significant figures, while other entries are reduced to one paragraph.

Another option for libraries that cannot afford or do not need the massive *Dictionary of Scientific Biography* is the two-volume *The Biographical Dictionary of Scientists*, the third edition of which appeared in 2000. *The Biographical Dictionary of Scientists* profiles some 1,280 important scientists from ancient times to the present. All scientific fields are represented. Entries are generally several paragraphs in length. Unique features of this reference tool include chronologies of scientific discoveries and separate sections providing brief histories of the various branches of science, a glossary of scientific terms, and lists of Nobel prize winners. There is also a subject index.

For ready-reference purposes, three standard universal biographical sources offering briefer information are *Merriam-Webster's Biographical Dictionary*, *Cambridge Biographical Encyclopedia*, and *New Century Cyclopedia of Names.*

Merriam-Webster's Biographical Dictionary (1995) is the most recent revision of a dictionary originally published in 1943. It gives more emphasis to historical figures from all parts of the world. This dictionary offers short, one-paragraph descriptions with a guide to the pronunciation of the surname, dates of birth and death, and significant events in the individual's career. If appropriate, nicknames and pseudonyms are provided, which is very useful because both are often requested by users. *Composite entries* for families are used occasionally, in which the heading is either the name of the most famous member of the family or the surname by itself. In the case of popes, kings, and other rulers, the composite entry is headed simply by the common personal name. There are numerous cross-references from variant names, pseudonyms, and titled names to the form of the name under which the entry appears (e.g., "Eliot, George. See Mary Ann Evans"). Lists of abbreviations and pronunciation symbols are provided at the front of the volume.

Another useful one-volume biographical dictionary is the *Cambridge Biographical Encyclopedia* (2d ed., 1998). It is the successor to *Chambers Biographical Dictionary,* with information taken from the Chambers and Cambridge in-house database. It includes many individuals in the area of popular culture (e.g., sports and music) and emphasizes the twentieth century, women, African Americans, and other minorities. Important biographical facts are given in one-paragraph entries. Although most biographees are deceased, a small number of living persons are also profiled.

New Century Cyclopedia of Names, published in 1954, is broader in coverage than other biographical reference works, having entries for places, events, literary works, and fictitious and mythological characters, as well as for important people from the past. As the preface states, it provides "the essential facts about more than 100,000 proper names of every description" of interest to persons "in the English speaking world."[12] Although many non-Western names are included, they are likely to be those of interest to British and American citizens. Although now over 45 years old, the work's exceptionally broad scope makes it a valuable reference tool, particularly when users are uncertain as to whether the historical names they seek represent persons who actually lived or mythological or fictitious characters.

Like *Merriam-Webster's Biographical Dictionary*, *New Century Cyclopedia of Names* provides guidance on the pronunciation of surnames and gives the place and date of the person's birth and death. Some entries are significantly longer than those found in *Merriam-Webster's,* giving a detailed outline of the person's life and career and a list of significant writings, while other entries offer only a short summary. Historical appendices in volume 3 are out-of-date and must be supplemented by more recent sources.

Retrospective Biographical Dictionaries—National

United States

Until 1999 the most authoritative source for extensive biographical information about prominent deceased Americans was the *Dictionary of American Biography*, published by Scribner under the auspices of the American Council of Learned Societies, and often referred to simply as the *DAB*. In the 1980s it was felt by many scholars that the *DAB* was too dated and lacked diversity with regard to minorities, women, and occupations. The American Council of Learned Societies, in cooperation with Oxford University Press, developed the 24-volume *American National Biography*, published in 1999 and made available online in 2000 for a fee (http://www.anb.org). This work extends in time from the earliest European explorations to people who died as recently as December 1995. There are approximately 17,500 biographies, including 6,000 that do not appear in the *DAB*, of persons from a broad range of social, cultural, ethnic, and other areas. Each entry aims to present accurate biographical data and summarize the subject's significance in American history. The signed entries are quite long and have short bibliographies.

Although *American National Biography* has the most recent scholarship and diversity, researchers should still consult the *DAB* as one of their sources for biographical information about persons who happen to be included in both titles. Comparison of entries shows that the *DAB* has information that is not duplicated in the newer work. As Francine Fialkoff noted in her essay comparing the two works, "With their comprehensive look at the past from different perspectives and their preeminent scholarship, the two sets complement each other rather than merely compete."[13]

Like *Who's Who in America*, the *DAB* was inspired by a famous British work, the *Dictionary of National Biography* (*DNB*, discussed later). The original 20 volumes of the *DAB* were published between 1928 and 1936, and the index was published in 1937. It was updated by supplements giving coverage through 1980. The *DAB* supplements have ceased, but Scribner has started a new series, *The Scribner Encyclopedia of American Lives 1981–*, that in effect continues to update the *DAB*.

Entries are arranged alphabetically by surname in one alphabet throughout the original 20-volume set and also in each supplement. The essays are quite readable and vary in length from a couple of paragraphs to several pages. Although the focus is on the individual's public life, private and family life are not slighted. All entries were written by scholars, many of whom were eminent in the field of historical writing. Each entry concludes with a list of sources. These are now quite dated and must be updated by reference to more recent bibliographical sources, even though some of the sources listed are still useful.

National Cyclopedia of American Biography offers, in its 76 volumes, biographical essays on nearly 70,000 Americans, more than three times the number included in the *DAB*. This work, although lacking the critical approach and scholarly tone of the *DAB*, has many unique and important features. From its beginning in 1891, it sought to include businesspersons, engineers, inventors, and others who had been neglected in favor of clerics, statesmen, and literary figures in traditional biographical sources. It also included living persons and individuals with regional as well as national eminence. Line drawn portraits or photographs, some of them full-page, accompany each entry whenever possible. Biographees are grouped by occupation rather than alphabetically so that, for instance, the sketches of Supreme Court justices of a given period appear together.

Volumes of *National Cyclopedia of American Biography* appeared in one numbered series until 1926. After that the Permanent Series, containing only deceased persons, continued the numbered series, while a new Current Series, covering living individuals, was published simultaneously, using letters rather than numbers. The last volume in the set, published in 1984, was numbered N63, indicating that the two series had again merged (and were now closed). Most essays in the Current Series were revised and transferred to the Permanent Series upon the death of the biographees.

Biographies in both series are based on information supplied by the biographees and their families, supplemented by research done by the anonymous writer of the essay. The entries vary in length from one paragraph to several pages. Often several generations of the biographee's family are discussed, making it a useful source for genealogists tracing prominent family members. There are no bibliographies or suggestions for further reading.

The two series and the lack of an alphabetical arrangement make it necessary to use the separately published index containing subject terms and place, corporate, and personal names. This index also makes it possible to use the *National Cyclopedia of American Biography* for ready-reference questions, such as "Who developed the first liquid India ink?," and for research into the history of institutions and organizations.

To meet the demand for scholarly biographies of American women and African Americans, two titles modeled on the *DAB* have been published. The *DAB* provided entries for only 81 African Americans; the *Dictionary of American Negro Biography* (*DANB*) offers scholarly accounts of the lives of several hundred historically significant African Americans. Many of these individuals made important contributions to the (segregated) Negro community, rather than to the white society at large and had local rather than national eminence.

The signed essays vary in length from one-half page to several pages. Both public and private lives, including family information, of the biographees are chronicled; for writers, significant works are discussed. The essays are very well written, and each concludes with a list of sources upon which the account is based. Arrangement of the volume is alphabetical with no indexes.

A larger work, providing scholarly essays on historically significant American women, is *Notable American Women*. This set was published in two installments: the first three volumes, published in 1971, have the subtitle "1607–1950." Volume 4, "The Modern Period," published in 1980, focuses on women who died between 1951 and 1975. The compilation of this reference work was underwritten by Radcliffe College and was inspired by that college's important collection of women's studies materials, now called the Arthur and Elizabeth Schlesinger Library. The entire set was put together under the guidance of impressive scholarly advisory boards. It is valuable for ready-reference purposes as well as for research in women's history.

Modeled on the *DAB*, each entry in *Notable American Women* contains a fairly lengthy life history (generally a page or two of small print in double columns). Personal and career events are presented in a smooth, easy-to-read narrative. Biographees included must have had U.S. citizenship or have lived here and contributed to U.S. society in a way that transcends purely local significance. Each entry concludes with a list of primary and secondary sources for further research. Many vocations are represented among the women, and indexes by occupation are provided. Both volume 1 and volume 4 contain introductory chapters that offer an overview of women's history during the periods covered.

This title, like the *DAB*, *DANB*, and *National Cyclopedia of American Biography*, was published as a reference work and aid to research. However, these works are so well written and engaging that, unlike most reference books, they can also be read simply for pleasure.

An important retrospective source that many will consult, but few will read for pleasure, is *Who Was Who in America*. In 2000 this set numbered 11 volumes, each of which reproduces entries from *Who's Who in America* or one of its regional counterparts for individuals who are recently deceased. In addition, a "Historical Volume, 1607–1896," covers important Americans who died before the existence of *Who's Who in America*. A new volume with a new cumulative index is added to *Who Was Who in America* every four or five years. With a single search one can locate an individual entry anywhere in the set. *Who Was Who in America* is often the logical first choice for basic factual data about deceased prominent Americans.

The most comprehensive retrospective biographical tool covering the United States is a microfiche set titled the *American Biographical Archive,* which has appeared in two series. At a price of over $10,000, few libraries will own it, but all reference librarians should be aware of its existence for referral purposes. The *Archive* reproduces facsimile entries from U.S. and Canadian biographical sources, most of which were published before 1900 and are not owned by many libraries. Arrangement is alphabetical by name, so that if a particular individual was profiled in several source works, all of those entries appear together. A print 10-volume index comes with the set or may be purchased separately. Reference librarians having access to the index but not the microfiche can use the index to refer users to the exact fiche number at a library that owns the set. Also, the fiche number can be used to obtain the needed information by telephone or e-mail. Because the index contains birth and death dates and the occupation of the biographee, it can be used by itself to answer this type of question.

A similar work focusing on African Americans is *Black Biographical Dictionaries, 1790–1950*. Here, organization is not by name but by the biographical source, so the index must be used, and one must often refer to more than one fiche to find all of the entries for a particular individual. Some 350 printed biographical sources are reproduced in this set.

Canada

The major source for historically important Canadians is the *Dictionary of Canadian Biography* (*DCB*). The 14 volumes of this work published to date cover Canadian history from 1000 to 1920. Unlike the *DAB* and *DNB* (but like its Australian counterpart, *Australian Dictionary of Biography*), the *DCB* is arranged chronologically rather than alphabetically. Each volume contains essays about individuals who contributed to a specific period of Canadian history. The first four volumes (1000–1800) also provide background essays discussing the period covered by each volume.

Entries in the *DCB* average several hundred words in length, and all conclude with citations for further reading and research. There is a general bibliography at the end of each volume along with geographic and name indexes to that volume. A separately published index volume covers volumes 1–12. The name indexes are very comprehensive; they provide page number references to all names mentioned in each essay, regardless of whether those individuals are themselves the subject of an entry. For example, the British author Charles Dickens is included in the name index although he has no entry in the *DCB*.

Great Britain

Covering prominent deceased persons from Great Britain and Ireland as well as those from British colonies and non-British citizens who lived in England and contributed to its history, the *Dictionary of National Biography* (*DNB*) was originally published from 1885 to 1901. A year later, a supplement appeared, containing 1,000 individuals who were omitted from the original set or who were recently deceased, including Queen Victoria and William E. Gladstone, two preeminent nineteenth-century figures. Since that date, 10 other supplements have been published, which together treat individuals who died between 1901 and 1990. The latest supplement has a comprehensive index for all the supplements. A separate work, *Concise Dictionary of National Biography*, serves as an index to the original set and all of its supplements, while also giving a brief overview of the life of each individual. The *Concise DNB* offers, as of the 1992 edition, a brief history for each biographee who died before 1986 (this title is periodically revised). No citation is given to the longer entries in the original set and its supplements, but one can generally tell, by the date of death, where the full entry will be. There are no subject or corporate name indexes to the *DNB*. Thus, unlike some other biographical dictionaries, it cannot be effectively used for questions dealing with subjects rather than persons. However, the set is now available on CD-ROM, making keyword searching a possibility.

As of 1996, *DNB* (including the recently published *Missing Persons* volume) offered biographical essays about 37,986 individuals. These essays average about a page in length, although many are shorter and some are much longer (that on Queen Victoria covers over 100 pages). Each essay includes pertinent facts and dates from the subject's personal and public lives. The essays are quite readable, although those in the original set are written in a style rather different (some would say more elegant) than that commonly employed today. All are written by scholars and end with a list of sources upon which the essay is based. Bibliographical references are also sometimes given in the text of the article and not repeated at the end.

In 1993, a new volume of *DNB,* with the subtitle "Missing Persons," appeared. This alphabetically arranged work provides short essays on the lives of 1,086 individuals from all periods of British history who are now considered important but "had failed to come to the editors' attention for various reasons."[14] This work is not indexed in the *Concise DNB.*

Who Was Who performs the same service for Great Britain that *Who Was Who in America* provides for the United States. Entries that appeared in *Who's Who* during an individual's life are transferred to *Who Was Who* after that person dies. The date of death is added, and any necessary corrections are made. The first volume of *Who Was Who* covered the period 1897–1916. The publication schedule settled into a pattern of one volume every 10 years until the 1991–1995 volume, when the publication schedule was changed to five years in response to demand and also to coincide with publication of the CD-ROM, *Who's Who 1897–1996: One Hundred Years of Biography.* The CD-ROM, now updated to cover the period through 1998, contains all of the published *Who Was Who* volumes as well as *Who's Who 1998.* A cumulated print index of *Who Was Who* volumes (1897–1990) was published separately in 1991.

For comprehensive research collections, *British Biographical Archive* on microfiche reproduces entries from more than 300 British biographical works originally published between 1601 and 1926. It is arranged just like *American Biographical Archive.* A print 7-volume index covers the entire set, providing access to fiche number. It can thus be useful to libraries that do not own the microfiche collection but can obtain copies from a library that does. *British Biographical Archive: Series II* adds individuals from the late nineteenth and twentieth centuries.

Reference librarians in large academic and public libraries will also need to consult retrospective biographical sources for other nations, many of which are in languages other than English. Many of these are described in *Guide to Reference Books.*[15]

Indirect Sources

Indirect biographical sources, which cite sources where information about individuals may be found rather than providing that information directly, are helpful in several ways. If librarians are not sure which title is a likely source for the answer to a biographical question, or if they have tried one or several titles without success, they can consult an indirect source to identify relevant titles. Or, if the direct sources already checked provide only a partial answer to the question, an indirect source can lead to other titles with more detailed information. Finally, an indirect source is the best place to start a search for information about an individual if a number of different articles or books are requested by a user who is seeking extensive information or a variety of perspectives. In all these situations, indirect sources serve essentially as indexes to biographical reference tools and to a broader range of biographical literature.

Among indirect sources, *Biography and Genealogy Master Index* (*BGMI*) offers the most comprehensive current and retrospective coverage. In its print form, it has appeared in eight base volumes (1980) and annual updates. The annual updates can, at considerable cost, be replaced by five-year cumulated indexes. Online on Dialog or GaleNet, all volumes are searchable in one database (called *Biography Master Index* on Dialog), updated annually. Whether in print or electronic form, this title provides citations to more than 12 million entries in several hundred biographical sources. These sources are of all kinds: directories and dictionaries, annual publications, and nonserial titles. American biographical tools are the most common, but sources covering other countries are indexed as well. *BGMI* even indexes another indirect source, *Biography Index.*

Of course, many of the 12 million citations to be found in *BGMI* are duplications, in that they refer the user to a number of similar entries in different works or in different editions of the same work. For example, an online search for biographical entries about Bob Dylan would produce several dozen citations, including more than a few for *Who's Who in America* (different editions) and several more for *The International Who's Who*, which would give the reader essentially the same information as the entries in *Who's Who in America*. However, one can find information about Bob Dylan fairly easily; the greatest value of *BGMI* is for locating information about less-famous individuals, when the librarian is not sure where to begin searching for information.

In all of its versions (print or online), *BGMI* lists names exactly as they appear in the indexed sources. The same individual may be represented under more than one form of his or her name, such as with and without middle name or initial, or under both given name and nickname. For example, former President Carter is listed under "James E.," "James Earl," "James E., Jr.," and "James Earl, Jr." in one column, and under "Jimmy" and "Jimmy, Jr." in another column (see Figure 16.3). These variations can be identified in the print volumes with *careful study*; when searching online, one would need to use the Expand command (or its equivalent) to browse the name index and identify them.

Figure 16.3 Multiple entries in *Biography and Genealogy Master Index.* Selection from *Biography and Genealogy Master Index* 1996-2000, Volume 1, edited by Frank V. Castronova. Copyright © 2000 by Gale Group, Inc. Reprinted by permission of the Gale Group.

Carter, James E. 1924- *EncAPoR, PacWarE*
Carter, James E. 1944- *WhoTech* 95
Carter, James E., Jr. 1924- *ColdWRG*
Carter, James E(dward) 1935- *WhoWrEP* 95
Carter, James Earl *BioIn* 21, 22
Carter, James Earl 1924- *BioIn* 18, 19, 20, 23, *CamDcAB, EncAB-H* 1996, *EncWB* 98*[port], EncyDCo, HealPre*
Carter, James Earl, Jr. 1924- *AmDec* 1970*[port], SmATA* 79*[port], Who* 98, 99
Carter, James Earl, Jr. 1943- *WhoAfA* 9, 10, 11
Carter, James Edward 1929- *AmMWSc* 95, 98
Carter, James Edward 1935- *WhoAm* 95, 96, *WhoWest* 96
Carter, James Edward, Jr. 1906- *WhoAfA* 9
Carter, James Edward, Jr. 1906-1993 *WhAm* 11, *WhoAfA* 10N
Carter, James Edward, III 1938- *WhoAfA* 9, 10, 11
Carter, James Folger 1949- *WhoMedH* 99
Carter, James Gordon 1795-1849 *AmNatBi*
Carter, James H. 1935- *AmBench* 97, *WhoAm* 99, *WhoAmL* 96, 98, *WhoAmP* 95, 97, *WhoMW* 96, 98
Carter, James Hal, Jr. 1943- *WhoAm* 95, 96, 97, 98, 99, *WhoAmL* 96, 98
Carter, James Harrison 1945- *WhoAm* 97, 98, 99, *WhoSSW* 95, 97, *WhoWor* 96, 97, 98
Carter, Jefferson *DrAPF* 97
Carter, Jeffrey D.R. 1963- *DrAS* 99H, 99P
Carter, Jennifer Lynn 1964- *WhoWor* 99
Carter, Jerald S. *AmBench* 97
Carter, Jeremy Mackay 1958- *WhoAmL* 98
Carter, Jerry Dale 1951- *St&PR* 96, 97, 98, 99
Carter, Jerry Williams 1941- *WhoWor* 95, 99
Carter, Jesse Benedict 1872-1917 *AmNatBi*
Carter, Jesse Lee, Sr. 1926- *WhoAfA* 9, 10, 11
Carter, Jill Anne 1960- *WhoAmW* 99
Carter, Jill Herron 1959- *WhoMW* 98
Carter, Jim *See* Chuck Wagon Gang *BgBkCoM*
Carter, Jim 1948- *BioIn* 23
Carter, Jimmy *NewYTBS* 95*[port]*, 96*[port]*, *SmATA* 79 *See Also* Five Blind Boys of Alabama *ConMus* 12
Carter, Jimmy 1924- *AmJust[port], Benet* 96, *BioIn* 18, 19, 20, 21, 22, 23, *CamBiEn, ChamBiD, EncCW[port], EncVieW, EnvEnDr, FacPr* 93*[port], HeroCon, HisEAAC, IntWW* 97, *LegTOT, News* 95*[port]*, 95-1*[port], PresAR* 1996*[port], Pres* 96*[port], USGovLe[port], WhoAm* 95, 96, 97, 98, 99, *WhoAmP* 95, 97, *WhoIntA* 2, *WhoSSW* 95, 97, 99, *WhoWor* 95, 96, 97, 98, 99, *WrDr* 96, 98, 99
Carter, Jimmy, Jr. 1924- *IntWW* 98
Carter, Joan *WhsWeAm* 98

Entries in each volume of the print series are listed alphabetically by surname and consist of the person's name, birth date (and death date if the citation is to a retrospective source), and an abbreviation for the title where the entry will be found. The user must search the bibliographic key to source codes at the beginning of the volume to find the full title for the work cited. The difficulty in using *BGMI* in its print version is in knowing which volume to search first. If the individual about whom information is requested is deceased, the base set may be the best place to start. For someone currently in the news, the latest annual update would be the preferred starting point. In either situation, one may need to look through several volumes before locating a specific individual.

When access to Dialog or GaleNet is available, an online search is the most efficient way to use *BGMI*. The online database contains the entire *BGMI* set, allowing one to search the base set and all of the annual updates simultaneously. Using the Expand command in Dialog, entries for all versions of the individual's name can be located. In GaleNet possible alternative forms of the name should be searched. In cases in which multiple citations are retrieved (as in the Bob Dylan search), the librarian can advise the user as to which source appears most relevant to the user's specific need. In the online search, full titles of publications are displayed with the entries, eliminating the search through a list of source codes.

Another publication by Gale Group, *Almanac of Famous People*, offers a less comprehensive but cheaper alternative to *BGMI*. *Almanac of Famous People* is both a direct and an indirect source of information about prominent persons. Based on some of the same sources as *BGMI*, it indexes each source selectively, including only those individuals who have achieved fame. Although it lists persons from all historical eras and places, there is a heavy emphasis on twentieth-century figures. Only birth and death dates, occupation, and a descriptive phrase indicating the person's chief accomplishment are provided. Citations have source codes similar to those used in *BGMI*. *Almanac of Famous People* is revised every few years. It is searchable online on NEXIS as part of *Gale Biographies*.

Both *BGMI* and *Almanac of Famous People* index primarily other reference works. For biographical information in general scholarly and popular literature, the best source is *Biography Index*. Produced by H. W. Wilson, publisher of a number of standard indexes in various fields (see Chapter 21), *Biography Index* appears quarterly with annual and biennial cumulations. It provides references to biographical articles in periodicals; book-length individual and collective biographies; entries in reference works; and essays such as interviews, obituaries, and book reviews. Biographical articles cited are from periodicals indexed in one of the other Wilson topical indexes. Many of these are of a popular nature, but citations from scholarly journals are also included. The articles and books indexed in *Biography Index* discuss persons from all historical periods and the present.

Arrangement is alphabetical by surname of the individual. Each entry gives name and occupation, and many give birth date and, if applicable, death date. This information helps to distinguish the individual from others with the same or a similar name. Citations provide standard bibliographical information, such as author, title, and publication data, including year of publication and (for periodical articles) volume and page numbers. There is also a professional/occupational index.

Biography Index is available both in CD-ROM format and online from several vendors. The major difference between the online and CD-ROM versions of *Biography Index* is currency. The online database is updated monthly, while new CD-ROM discs are sent to subscribers quarterly. Both databases begin with July 1984 data, which means that print volumes must be searched for articles and books indexed before that date. Beginning fall 2000 the H. W. Wilson Company's *Biography Reference Bank* combines *Biography Index* with *Wilson Biographies Plus Illustrated* on WilsonWeb.

Obituaries

Obituary articles from national or regional newspapers can be valuable sources of information about prominent, and sometimes not-so-prominent, individuals. Obituary articles are news stories written by newspaper staff, not notices placed in the newspaper by family members or funeral homes. Obituary articles often provide biographical data about persons of regional interest who would not be found in standard biographical reference tools. In fact, obituary articles may be the only readily available published source of information on the lives of such individuals. These are indexed in print newspaper indexes and sometimes in local library card files.

For prominent Americans and a few individuals from other countries, access to obituary articles is provided by the *New York Times Obituaries Index*. Two volumes of this index have been published to date; the first covers the period from 1858 to 1968, while the second covers 1969 to 1978. These volumes index articles in the *New York Times* that report the death of individuals, provide pertinent facts about their lives, and list important contributions they made during their careers. *New York Times Obituaries Index* lists all names that appeared under the heading "Deaths" in the main index to the newspaper. The 1969 to 1978 volume includes reprints of obituary stories for 50 prominent persons.

Each alphabetical entry consists of the name of the deceased and a reference to the year, date, section, page, and column of the *New York Times*. Some names are listed twice or more; in these cases, there was more than one story (e.g., one on the death and one on the funeral). For individuals who have died since 1978, the user must consult the heading "Deaths" in the annual cumulated index to the *New York Times*.

The *New York Times Biographical Service* serves as a current biographical source as well as a source of obituary articles. It reprints biographical articles that appeared in the newspaper during the month covered by each issue. Because many of the articles reprinted are obituaries, it can profitably be used to supplement the *New York Times Obituaries Index*. An advantage is that the articles are right there, saving the user the trouble of going back through past years of the newspaper. *Biographical Service* articles are arranged chronologically in each monthly issue. Each issue contains its own alphabetical index, for the year to date, with an annual index in December. It is also available online on NEXIS.

SEARCH STRATEGIES

The strategy employed in dealing with a biographical reference question will vary depending on the nature of the reference collection to which the librarian has access. For instance, in a library where online searching is not an option, print tools alone must suffice. Similarly, where, for budgetary reasons, sets such as *BGMI* or *Contemporary Authors* are not options, other titles must be used in their place.

Even given identical collections, however, librarians will differ in their approach to the same question. Some will go immediately to a direct source for the answer, while others will search *BGMI* or *Almanac of Famous People* to see where entries about an individual are located. Each reference librarian develops personal strategies for different kinds of questions. Consequently, the strategies outlined here generally suggest more than one possible path to the answer.

Ready-Reference Questions

Ready-reference questions usually involve straightforward factual questions about an individual's life or career. For example, the library user may need a date (e.g., birth, death, year of graduation); a list of degrees, honors, children, or publications; or descriptive information about the individual, such as height, marital status, or current address.

As with any reference question, the first step is to get as much information as possible from the inquirer. Is the person still alive? What nationality is he or she? Is he or she an author, politician, scholar, etc.? This information tells the librarian whether to look in a current or retrospective source, and further, what kind of source to use. For example, in dealing with a request for information about a physicist, two obvious possibilities would be *American Men and Women of Science* and *Dictionary of Scientific Biography*; which one is used would depend upon the answers to the librarian's queries about the nationality of the physicist and whether the physicist is still alive. For an American physicist of some renown, *Who's Who in America* or *Who's Who in Science and Engineering* may also provide the required information.

Of course, a search of *BGMI*, online or in print form, would be likely to lead to one or more sources where information about the individual can be found. An advantage of this approach is that *BGMI* lists all editions of a title containing entries for that person. In the case mentioned above, if the physicist died recently, neither *Dictionary of Scientific Biography* nor the latest edition of *American Men and Women of Science* would have an entry. *BGMI*, however, would indicate to the librarian which earlier editions of *American Men and Women of Science* contain an entry for the physicist. It might also give the librarian an immediate second source to check, should the first not contain the answer.

General Background Questions

General background questions usually arise out of curiosity and a desire for more information about an individual's life and career. The librarian must generally supply a fair amount of descriptive and evaluative discussion, rather than merely a fact or two. The search can often be confined to one or two sources that produce good overviews of the person's life, although sometimes a user will want references for further reading.

Frequent subjects of questions like this are modern authors and political leaders. For authors, *Contemporary Authors* is the obvious choice; for a writer of books for children or young adults, *Something About the Author* would also be a logical choice. If the author is very well known, an essay about that person's life might be found in *Current Biography*. This source is also good for political figures. One of the cumulative indexes would be the best place to look in this case. Because political leaders are often the subjects of magazine articles, the librarian could also consult *Biography Index* to locate articles in periodicals.

In cases where neither the user nor the librarian knows very much about the subject, a search of *Almanac of Famous People* or *BGMI* is the safest place to begin. Here again, the advantages of online searching are apparent. If the name is a common one, or if the questioner is unsure of the spelling—as may be the case with a non-English name—the Expand command on *Biography Master Index* on Dialog will display an alphabetically arranged list of names from which the correct one can usually be identified. However, one must always remember that the same person's name may appear in more than one form.

When background information is sought for an historical figure, the first job of the librarian is to try to determine the nationality of the individual. This may lead directly to the *American National Biography* or *DNB*, or to a similar source for another country. If the nationality is not known, it can be found if the person is listed in *Almanac of Famous People*, *Merriam-Webster's Biographical Dictionary*, or *New Century Cyclopedia of Names*. Another good possibility in this situation is the *Encyclopedia of World Biography*, because it is international in scope and both current and retrospective in approach. General or topical encyclopedias should also be tried for background information on historical figures, if strictly biographical sources fail to produce the needed information. The index should always be used in this situation, in case the individual does not have a biographical entry but is discussed in a topical entry.

Research Questions

When library users—particularly students at any level—conduct research about a particular individual, they generally need to consult more than one kind of source, such as a reference source for basic information about the person's life, and secondary sources, such as books and journal articles, for more detail and an interpretive approach. College students will also be expected to find primary sources, such as correspondence, speeches, or other writings. For this, indirect sources such as *Biography Index* are particularly valuable. Also important are those direct sources, such as *Encyclopedia of World Biography* and *Dictionary of Scientific Biography*, that provide extensive evaluative essays and also list sources for further research. For research on a living individual, the user will find good essays and lists of magazine articles about the individual in *Current Biography* and *Newsmakers*. *BGMI* and *Almanac of Famous People* are less useful, because they index reference works rather than periodical literature, but if the librarian does not find the person sought in any of the sources just mentioned, a search in one of these tools may at least lead to some information.

Biographical information about an individual can be found on the Internet, but it requires some perseverance on the part of the searcher because it is difficult to locate more than a small amount of information on any one Web site. Living persons may have home pages with personal information, and prominent people will appear in full-text newspapers, but often the searcher must follow up numerous links to obtain information. Two sites that provide quick but brief information on historical figures are *Biographical Dictionary* and

Biography.com. World Biographical Index contains over 2.5 million short biographical entries for historical figures from many parts of the world. A well-organized site intended mainly for genealogists, but useful for all researchers because of its broad scope, is *Cyndi's List of Genealogy Sites on the Internet.* This site has links to many genealogical sites as well as full-text newspapers, books, geographical sources, obituaries, etc. *Lives, the Biography Resource* is an extensive guide to all types of biographical sites on the Web. Searchers on the Internet should expect to use many of the same search strategies as searchers of print works when tracking down information.

Genealogists are a specialized group of researchers who often need narrative biographical information to fill out information about family members that they have found in specialized genealogical sources. Genealogical research has become increasingly sophisticated with more emphasis on primary sources such as the census and land records, but many genealogists obtain unverified information from CD-ROMs and the Internet that can be augmented from standard print biographical sources. A reference library that does not specialize in genealogical material can still provide service to genealogists by guiding them to the same biographical sources used by students and other researchers. Conversely, students and historians can profit by using genealogical sources and techniques. A working family pedigree with verified dates and places can be essential in resolving inconsistencies that turn up in biographical research on individuals.

Research questions may require the librarian to go beyond the sources discussed in this chapter. General and subject encyclopedias or specialized biographical dictionaries such as Fitzroy Dearborn's *Dictionary of Women Artists* can be used to get individuals started in their research. Many of these can be identified in the *Guide to Reference Books* or Robert Slocum's *Biographical Dictionaries and Related Works.*[16] In addition, the librarian may suggest that the user consult the card or online catalog, a topical index, or a specialized bibliography. If the subject's career is in a certain field—music, for example—bibliographies, indexes, and subject headings in that field can be identified that will lead the user beyond biographical reference materials to the sources needed for further research.

Box 16.1 Search Strategy: Information About a Popular Novelist

A public library user asked at the reference desk for information about the life and writings of Ellis Peters, creator of the popular medieval sleuth, Brother Cadfael. Because the library had access to GaleNet the librarian selected *Contemporary Authors* and typed in "Ellis Peters." The database automatically did a cross-reference to "Edith Mary Pargeter," the real name of the author, and displayed an entry updated to reflect her death in 1995. Had the librarian used the print volumes of *Contemporary Authors* he would have had to consult five different volumes to obtain the same information. In addition, the user was able to take away an 11-page printout of the article in GaleNet.

NOTES

1. *The Works of Thomas Carlyle* (New York: Scribner, 1898–1901), 28:86.

2. *American Men and Women of Science, 1998–99*, 20th ed. (New Providence, N.J.: R. R. Bowker, 1998), 1:vii.

3. *Who's Who in America, 2000*, 54th ed. (New Providence, N.J.: Marquis Who's Who, 1999), 1:viii.

4. Ibid.

5. Ann Ricker, "*Who's Who in America*," *Reference Services Review* 8 (October/December 1980): 11.

6. Ibid., 8.

7. Ibid., 9.

8. *Who's Who 2000* (London: A & C Black, 2000), 9.

9. Linda K. Simons, "Afternoon Tea, Parliament, and . . . *Who's Who*," in *Distinguished Classics of Reference Publishing*, ed. James Rettig (Phoenix, Ariz.: Oryx Press, 1992), 309.

10. *American Men and Women of Science,* 1:vii.

11. Ibid.

12. *New Century Cyclopedia of Names* (Englewood Cliffs, N.J.: Prentice-Hall, 1954), 1:vii.

13. Francine Fialkoff, "Dueling Dictionaries," *Library Journal* 123 (November 15, 1998): 54.

14. *The Dictionary of National Biography: Missing Persons*, ed. C. S. Nicholls (New York: Oxford University Press, 1993), v.

15. Robert Balay, ed., *Guide to Reference Books*, 11th ed. (Chicago: American Library Association, 1996), 281-317.

16. Ibid.; Robert B. Slocum, *Biographical Dictionaries and Related Works*, 2d ed., 2 vols. (Detroit: Gale Research, 1986).

LIST OF SOURCES

Almanac of Famous People. 6th ed. 2 vols. Detroit: Gale Research, 1998.

American Biographical Archive. 1,842 microfiche. New York: K. G. Saur, 1986-1991. Series 2. 734 microfiche. 1993-1996.

American Biographical Index. 2d cum. and enl. ed. 10 vols. München: K. G. Saur, 1998.

American Men and Women of Science, 1998–99. 20th ed. 8 vols. New Providence, N.J.: R. R. Bowker, 1998. Also available online.

American National Biography. 24 vols. New York: Oxford University Press, 1999. Also available online.

Australian Dictionary of Biography. 14 vols. and index (of volumes 1–12). Carlton, Victoria: Melbourne University Press, 1966–1996.

Biographical Dictionary. Available: http://www.s9.com/biography.

The Biographical Dictionary of Scientists. 3d ed. 2 vols. New York: Oxford University Press, 2000.

Biography.com. Available: http://www.biography.com.

Biography and Genealogy Master Index. 2d ed. Farmington Hills, Mich.: Gale Group, 1980– . Annual. Also available online and on microfiche as *Bio-Base.*

Biography Index. New York: H. W. Wilson, 1946– . Quarterly, with annual cumulations. Also available on CD-ROM and online.

Biography Reference Bank. New York: H. W. Wilson. Available online.

Biography Resource Center. Farmington Hills, Mich.: Gale Group. Available online.

Biography Today. Detroit: Omnigraphics, 1992– . Three issues annually, plus annual hardbound cumulation.

Black Biographical Dictionaries, 1790–1950. 1,068 microfiche. Alexandria, Va.: Chadwyck-Healey, 1987.

Black Biography, 1790–1950: A Cumulative Index. 3 vols. Alexandria, Va.: Chadwyck-Healey, 1991.

Bowker Biographical Directory. New Providence, N.J.: R. R. Bowker. Available online. (Includes data from *American Men and Women of Science*, *Who's Who in American Art*, and *Who's Who in American Politics*.)

British Biographical Archive. 1,236 microfiche. New York: K. G. Saur, 1984–1989; index, 1991. Series II. 632 microfiche. 1991–1994.

British Biographical Index. 2d cum. and enl. ed. 7 vols. München: K. G. Saur, 1998.

Cambridge Biographical Encyclopedia. 2d ed. New York: Cambridge University Press, 1998. 1179p.

Canadian Who's Who, 2000. Vol. 35. Toronto: University of Toronto Press, 2000. 1394p. Also available on CD-ROM.

The Complete Marquis Who's Who on CD-ROM. [CD-ROM]. New Providence, N.J.: Marquis Who's Who.

Concise Dictionary of National Biography. 3 vols. New York: Oxford University Press, 1992.

Concise Dictionary of Scientific Biography. New York: Scribner, 1981. 773p.

Contemporary Authors. Farmington Hills, Mich.: Gale Group, 1962– . Irregular, but multiple volumes per year. Also available on CD-ROM and online.

Contemporary Black Biography. Farmington Hills, Mich.: Gale Group, 1992– . Three volumes per year.

Contemporary Composers. Detroit: St. James Press, 1992. 1019p.

Contemporary Designers. 3d ed. Detroit: St. James Press, 1997. 981p.

Contemporary Theatre, Film & Television. Farmington Hills, Mich.: Gale Group, 1984– . Irregular.

Current Biography. New York: H. W. Wilson, 1940- . Monthly, with an annual cumulative yearbook. Also available on CD-ROM and online.

Cyndi's List of Genealogy Sites on the Internet. Available: http://www.CyndisList.com.

Dictionary of American Biography. 20 vols. and Index. New York: Scribner, 1928–1937. Supplements, 1944-80. Index, 1996.

Dictionary of American Negro Biography. New York: W. W. Norton, 1982. 680p.

Dictionary of Canadian Biography. 14 vols. and Index (of volumes 1–12). Toronto: University of Toronto Press, 1966–1998 (further volumes in preparation). Published in French as *Dictionnaire Biographique du Canada*.

Dictionary of Literary Biography series. Farmington Hills, Mich.: Gale Group, 1978– . Irregular. Also available online.

Dictionary of National Biography. 22 vols. London: Smith, Elder, 1908–1909. (Reprint). Supplements, 1912– . Also available on CD-ROM.

Dictionary of National Biography: Missing Persons. New York: Oxford University Press, 1993. 768p.

Dictionary of Scientific Biography. 18 vols. New York: Scribner, 1970–1980, 1990.

Dictionary of Women Artists. 2 vols. Chicago: Fitzroy Dearborn, 1997.

Directory of American Scholars. 9th ed. 4 vols. Farmington Hills, Mich.: Gale Group, 1999.

Encyclopedia of World Biography. 2d ed. 18 vols. Detroit: Gale, 1998. Also available on CD-ROM.

Gale Biographies. Farmington Hills, Mich.: Gale Group. Available online. (Includes data from *Almanac of Famous People*, *Contemporary Theatre, Film & Television*, *Newsmakers*, *Who's Who Among African Americans*, *Who's Who Among Asian Americans*, *Who's Who Among Hispanic Americans*, and several other biographical sources.)

The International Who's Who, 2001. 64th ed. London: Europa, 2000. 1743p. Also available on CD-ROM.

Lives, the Biography Resource. Available: http://amillionlives.com.

Marquis Who's Who. New Providence, N.J.: Reed Elsevier. Available online.

Merriam-Webster's Biographical Dictionary. Rev. ed. Springfield, Mass.: Merriam-Webster, 1995. 1170p.

National Cyclopedia of American Biography. 76 vols. and index. New York: J. T. White, 1891–1984.

New Century Cyclopedia of Names. 3 vols. Englewood Cliffs, N. J.: Prentice-Hall, 1954.

New York Times Biographical Service. New York: Arno Press, 1970–. Monthly. Also available online.

New York Times Obituaries Index, 1858–1968. New York: New York Times, 1970. 1136p.

New York Times Obituaries Index, 1969–1978. New York: New York Times, 1980. 131p.

Newsmakers. Farmington Hills, Mich.: Gale Group, 1988– . Three issues yearly, with an annual yearbook.

Notable American Women: 1607–1950. 3 vols. Cambridge, Mass.: Belknap Press of Harvard University Press, 1971.

Notable American Women: The Modern Period. Cambridge, Mass.: Belknap Press of Harvard University Press, 1980. 773p.

The Scribner Encyclopedia of American Lives, 1981– . New York: Scribner, 1998– . Irregular.

Something About the Author. Farmington Hills, Mich.: Gale Group, 1971– . Irregular.

Who Was Who, 1897–1995. 9 vols. and index (1897–1990). London: A & C Black, 1929–1995. Irregular.

Who Was Who in America, 1897–1998. 13 vols. and index (1607–2000). Chicago; New Providence, N.J.: Marquis Who's Who, 1942–1998. Irregular.

Who Was Who in America: Historical Volume, 1607–1896. Rev. ed. Chicago: Marquis Who's Who, 1967. 689p.

Who's Who 1897-1998 [CD-ROM]. Oxford: Oxford University Press, 1999.

Who's Who, 2000. London: A & C Black, 2000. 2278p.

Who's Who Among African Americans,. 12th ed. Farmington Hills, Mich.: Gale Group, 1999. 1626p.

Who's Who Among Asian Americans, 1994-1995. Detroit: Gale Research, 1994. 779p.

Who's Who Among Hispanic Americans, 1994–95. 3d ed. Detroit: Gale Research, 1994. 990p.

Who's Who in America, 2000. 54th ed. 3 vols. New Providence, N. J.: Marquis Who's Who, 1999.

Who's Who in American Art, 1999–2000. 23d ed. New Providence, N. J.: Marquis Who's Who, 1999. 1525p.

Who's Who in American Politics, 1999–2000. 17th ed. 2 vols. New Providence, N. J.: Marquis Who's Who, 1999.

Who's Who in Canada, 2000. 91st ed. Toronto: Global Press, 2000. 632p.

Who's Who in Economics: A Biographical Dictionary of Major Economists, 1700–1986. 2d ed. Cambridge, Mass.: MIT Press, 1986. 935p.

Who's Who in Science and Engineering, 2000–2001. 5th ed. New Providence, N.J.: Marquis Who's Who, 1999. 1,500p.

Who's Who in the East, 1999-2000. 27th ed. New Providence, N.J.: Marquis Who's Who, 1998. 1197p.

Who's Who in the Midwest, 1998–1999. 26th ed. New Providence, N. J.: Marquis Who's Who, 1998. 698p.

Who's Who in the South and Southwest, 1999-2000. 26th ed. New Providence, N.J.: Marquis Who's Who, 1998. 800p.

Who's Who in the West, 2000–2001. 27th ed. New Providence, N.J.: Marquis Who's Who, 1999. 788p.

Who's Who in the World, 2000. 17th ed. New Providence, N. J.: Marquis Who's Who, 1999. 2552p.

Who's Who of American Women, 2000–2001. 22nd ed. New Providence, N. J.: Marquis Who's Who, 2000. 1705p.

Wilson Biographies Plus Illustrated. New York: H. W. Wilson. Available online.

World Artists, 1950–1980. New York: H. W. Wilson, 1984. 928p.

World Artists, 1980–1990. New York: H. W. Wilson, 1991. 432p.

World Biographical Index. München: K. G. Saur. Available: http://www.saur-wbi.de.

ADDITIONAL READINGS

Cimbala, Diana J., Jennifer Cargill, and Brian Alley. *Biographical Sources: A Guide to Dictionaries and Reference Works.* Phoenix, Ariz.: Oryx Press, 1986. 146p.

This work is an annotated bibliography of 689 biographical reference works arranged under some 30 subject headings. Annotations range in length from two lines to three paragraphs.

Clarke, Jack. "Biographical Directories, the Fine Line Between Vanity and Pride." *RQ* 22 (Fall 1983): 76-78.

This brief article provides useful information on "nearly five hundred biographical directories of a questionable reference value that are published irregularly in the United States alone." The goal is to prepare reference librarians to deal with questions about these publications from persons who have been invited to be in one.

England, Claire. "The Dictionary of Canadian Biography: A Major Bicultural Source." *Reference Services Review* 21 (Summer 1993): 71-76.

England describes the origins of the *Dictionary of Canadian Biography*, its unique chronological organization, and the nature of the 6,250 entries it included in its first 12 volumes (covering Canadian history to 1900).

Grogan, Denis. *Biographical Sources.* London: Clive Bingley, 1987. 154p. (Grogan's Case Studies in Reference Work, v. 6).

Grogan discusses numerous biographical reference works through 107 scenarios that demonstrate strategies for dealing with a variety of biographical reference questions.

Jarboe, Betty M. *Obituaries: A Guide to Sources.* 2d ed. Boston: G. K. Hall, 1989. 362p.

Jarboe's bibliography is a valuable resource for genealogists as well as for individuals conducting biographical research. It lists sources that provide obituaries or death notices. Its scope ranges from international obituary sources to sources of local death notices. Of particular value are the citations to sources containing death notices from local newspapers and a list of libraries that have collections of death notices from their areas.

Rettig, James, ed. *Distinguished Classics of Reference Publishing.* Phoenix, Ariz.: Oryx Press, 1992. 356p.

This interesting and unique collection of essays provides information on the historical background, origins, creation, and development of about 30 of the most important reference works in the English language. A foreword by Charles Scribner, Jr., describes the origins and publication of the *Dictionary of Scientific Biography.* In addition there are essays on the *Dictionary of National Biography* and *Who's Who.*

Schellinger, Paul E., ed. *St. James Guide to Biography.* Chicago: St. James Press, 1991. 870p.

This guide is composed of bibliographical essays that compare and evaluate the book-length biographies that have been written about some 700 historical figures. Dates of birth and death and occupation are given, and biographies of each individual are discussed. This book can be helpful with research questions, and it can also be used by librarians to refresh their memories regarding the qualities of a good biography.

Slocum, Robert B. *Biographical Dictionaries and Related Works.* 2d ed. 2 vols. Detroit: Gale Research, 1986.

This work lists, with brief annotations, some 16,000 biographical reference works under three broad headings: "Universal Biography," "National or Area Biography," and "Biography by Vocation." Both the table of contents and the subject index are very detailed, allowing one to locate, for example, biographical sources on French musicians. However, many of the specialized sources included in this bibliography will be found only in large research libraries.

Szucs, Loretto Dennis, and Sandra Hargreaves Luebking. *The Source: A Guidebook of American Genealogy.* Rev. ed. Salt Lake City: Ancestry, 1997. 834p.

This is an extremely detailed guide to the use and interpretation of major unpublished record sources such as family, cemetery, church, census, and the military and of published city directories, newspapers, biographies, etc. There are chapters on special kinds of research and appendices giving addresses for vital records and genealogical societies. The revised edition includes information on databases, indexes, and ethnic origins.

Wick, Robert L., and Terry Ann Mood, eds. *ARBA Guide to Biographical Resources, 1986–1997.* Englewood, Colo.: Libraries Unlimited, 1998. 604p.

This guide covers the entire spectrum of biographical sources (serial and nonserial) published during the period 1986–1997. Most originally appeared in *American Reference Books Annual.* There are 1,180 titles. Each entry gives complete bibliographic information with price and critical evaluation.

Wynar, Bohdan S., ed. *ARBA Guide to Biographical Dictionaries.* Littleton, Colo.: Libraries Unlimited, 1986. 444p.

This guide reproduces, with necessary updating and some revisions, evaluations that originally appeared in *American Reference Books Annual* for 718 biographical dictionaries. Indexes and other indirect sources are excluded. Evaluations include, in many cases, references to reviews in library science periodicals such as *Booklist* and *Library Journal.*

CHAPTER

17

DICTIONARIES

Constance A. Fairchild

USES AND CHARACTERISTICS

Dictionaries are used to define words; to verify spelling, syllabication, or pronunciation; to check on usage; or to determine the etymological history of a word. To some degree, they also standardize the language based on current usage.

Word lists were used in ancient Greece and Rome, but the dictionary concept first took form in the Middle Ages when scholars started inserting *glosses*—marginal or interlinear notes—into Latin manuscripts to define terms or to render them in vernacular Teutonic, Romanic, and Celtic tongues. These glosses are philologically very important and represent the oldest rudiments of bilingual, or dual-language, dictionaries.[1]

The Latin term *dictionarius* did not appear until around 1225, when the English grammarian John of Garland (Joannes de Garlandia) used the word as the title of a collection of Latin words arranged by subject for the use of learners.[2] Compilers of early word books favored a subject arrangement because the philosophy of scholarship dictated that knowledge be grouped into topical divisions. Alphabetization was rejected because related topics were separated, a problem that can now be resolved by computerization. The orderly convenience of the alphabet was recognized by early printers, but alphabetization of reference books was not established until around the year 1600.

Today, dictionaries are consulted chiefly by persons who are writing or editing manuscripts, although they may also be used for puzzle solving, for clarifying the meaning of words in texts, or purely for satisfying intellectual curiosity. Persons outside the library frequently call upon librarians to look in unabridged dictionaries (which tend to be found mainly in libraries), because these dictionaries are considered to be the ultimate authority for spelling and usage in manuscripts. They also have definitions for words not found in the desk dictionaries used in home and office.

Dictionaries may be either *descriptive*, recording how the language is actually used, or *prescriptive*, advocating how it ought to be used. There are proponents of each approach, with those in favor of the descriptive philosophy claiming that language is always changing, and that dictionaries should therefore reflect these changes. This is the philosophy governing the compilation of all major dictionaries today. Those who follow the prescriptive approach say that it is the major role of dictionaries to set standards, support traditional usage, and prevent contamination of the language by slang and jargon. This philosophy was followed by early dictionary compilers, but has now been largely abandoned by the compilers of unabridged dictionaries. Some desk dictionaries and specialized usage dictionaries still maintain the more conservative prescriptive approach. Users who expect hard-and-fast rules for such perennially controversial topics as split infinitives will be disappointed. Even the conservative *The New Fowler's Modern English Usage* (3d ed.) concludes that "No absolute taboo should be placed on the use of simple adverbs between the particle *to* and the verbal part of the infinitive."[3]

Contemporary dictionary compilers recognize that the descriptive philosophy, strictly defined, does not reflect social attitudes toward the words being described. Therefore modern dictionaries also include some indication of social usage to satisfy users who expect the dictionary to be the final authority on acceptability.

Kinds of Information Found in Dictionaries

A basic dictionary contains an alphabetical list of words with their definitions. Usually the linguistic derivation of the word, the part of speech, syllabication and hyphenation, variant spellings, and pronunciation are also indicated. Entries may also include inflected forms, run-on or derivative entries, etymologies or word histories, synonyms and antonyms, usage or status labels, usage notes, illustrative quotations and examples, and pictorial illustrations. General dictionaries—that is, those covering all subjects—may also have special features, such as gazetteers, lists of proper names, maps, and glossaries of foreign words. This nonlexical material is not central to the purpose of the dictionary and may be added by the publisher to inflate the size and make the dictionary more attractive to buyers.

Types of Dictionaries

An *unabridged* dictionary, one that is not derived or condensed from a larger work, attempts to include all the words in the language that are in use at the time the dictionary is compiled. This, of course, is an impossible goal, as no single compilation can ever include every word that is in use at any one time. These dictionaries are large single-volume or multivolume works that sacrifice convenience for comprehensiveness. The necessity for overcoming inconvenience has given rise to the *abridged*, or desk-sized, dictionary, a selective compilation often based on a larger dictionary. Desk dictionaries are compiled for a certain level of student use, with the college level being the one in general use by adults. Etymological dictionaries, slang dictionaries, thesauri, dual-language, dialect, and usage dictionaries are specialized types that serve different purposes. (See Box 17.1.) Individual titles of these specialized types are discussed later in this chapter.

Box 17.1 Specialized Dictionaries

Etymological dictionary. An etymological or diachronic dictionary gives the history of individual words with linguistic derivation and examples from writings of the past.

Slang dictionary. A slang dictionary defines terms used in ordinary, informal speech. These terms may include jargon, obscenities, or ephemeral words that go in and out of use quickly.

Thesaurus. A thesaurus contains synonyms and antonyms, usually without definitions. Its purpose is to provide writers with alternate or more specific words.

Dual-language dictionary. A dual-language dictionary has two sections, the first being a dictionary of terms in one language with definitions in a second language. The second section is the reverse, with terms in the second language and definitions in the first language.

Dialect dictionary. A dialect dictionary gives regional variants and usage for words within a language. It may include some slang.

Usage dictionary. A usage dictionary prescribes how a word should be used, based on the way it has been used in the past.

EVALUATION

When evaluating dictionaries, an assessment of their authority and accuracy is essential. More so than most types of reference tools, however, dictionaries tend to be prepared for a specific audience (e.g., high school students) or to fulfill a specific purpose (e.g., identifying and defining slang expressions). Therefore, it is also critical to judge the degree to which dictionaries have succeeded in fulfilling their purpose or in effectively meeting the needs of the group to which they are addressed. Here, comparing their scope, format, and ease of use with similar works is often helpful in the evaluation process.

Format

Large unabridged dictionaries are only infrequently published. They do not present many problems in evaluation, because there are so few, and those few are extensively reviewed in the library media. The unabridged dictionary should be a reasonably comprehensive compilation of the words in use in the language at the time of compilation. Current unabridged dictionaries contain between 300,000 and 600,000 entries. They include frequently encountered abbreviations and acronyms, idiomatic expressions, technical terminology, new coinages, nonstandard speech, foreign phrases and loanwords (foreign words that have been incorporated into the English language), and obsolete terms. There may also be lists of synonyms and antonyms, quotations, pictures, and etymologies.

There has been a change in the philosophy of unabridged dictionaries since the eighteenth century, when the first comprehensive dictionaries of English appeared. Early compilers hoped to establish standards of correctness in spelling and usage and to omit anything that was "low" or vulgar.[4] This attitude persisted to the mid-twentieth century, when the realities of language evolution and change convinced dictionary compilers that usage was a more important consideration governing inclusion than an academic standard of correctness. Slang terms and technical jargon now have their place in the unabridged dictionary and can be used as an indication of the currency of the compilation.

Comprehensiveness, of course, means an almost unmanageable size, so practicality has brought about the abridged, or desk, dictionary. Desk dictionaries must be judged on effectiveness of purpose as stated in the title or introduction. A high school-level dictionary should include words likely to be used in writing by a high school student. A college desk dictionary is the level of dictionary used by college students and other adults. A reputable desk dictionary with 50,000 to 200,000 entries is sufficient for most people.

Recent technology has brought into being CD-ROMs, diskettes, and online databases as reference tools. It is also possible to search many full-text English and foreign language dictionaries on the Internet. One must use caution with Internet sources because some full-text books, if they have dates indicated, are older editions that are no longer under copyright. These may have some historical interest but are not valid for current reference work. In general, Internet sources should be evaluated for use in the same way that print sources are evaluated for the collection. If they are out-of-date, poorly edited, or undocumented, they should be used with caution.

The chief advantages of an electronic format are multiple access points and time saved by computer searching and printing. In the most sophisticated electronic dictionaries, the techniques of keyword and Boolean searching (see Chapter 5) make it possible to find and search words in definitions as well as entry words. Authors whose cited quotations are used as examples can be found and the citations listed. In works having dated quotations, it is possible to find all the words used in a certain time span. Computerization in all of its forms is changing the approaches to dictionary compilation, because it is now technically possible to convert information from publishers' databanks directly into searchable databases without a print intermediary.

Scope

The scope of a dictionary is stated in its preface or introduction. Dictionaries intended for college-level use should include linguistic derivation and a brief historical definition as well as current usage. Pronunciation guides are a necessity in all general-language dictionaries, although standard pronunciation as used by radio and television announcers may not reflect regional variations. Additional lists, such as geographical and proper names, are helpful to the home user who may not have an extensive reference collection, but they are of less use in a library. Illustrations also add interest and information to the dictionary, especially small line drawings accompanying individual definitions. Large color plates are attractive, but not as necessary as the small illustrations.

Comparison with Others of Similar Coverage

To compare two or more dictionaries of the same type, one should pick a group of common words and compare the treatment given to each one in each dictionary. Look for clarity in definitions, accuracy, and comprehensibility in the pronunciation system. There should be verbal examples that explain how the words are actually used. It is a good idea to pick some uncommon words to test the breadth of inclusion in each dictionary. See if the abbreviations used in the entries are well defined and if the abbreviations list is in an obvious place, such as the bottom of the page. Size of print may also be a consideration for young children and older users.

Authority

It is difficult to judge the qualifications of individual compilers, because general-language dictionaries tend to be compiled by the editorial staffs of publishers. The authority and reputation of the publisher are consequently the most important factors in judging the quality of a dictionary. Publishers' reputations are built on earlier editions or on similar types of publications, and this should be taken into consideration. However, a good first edition does not always mean that the second has been satisfactorily edited and updated. An unknown publisher may put out a very good dictionary, or a well-known publisher can produce a mediocre one. To aid in making a judgment, reference librarians should learn the names of the most authoritative North American dictionary publishers, which are (in alphabetical order) Gage Educational Publishing (Canada), Harcourt Brace, HarperCollins, Houghton Mifflin (publisher of the American Heritage dictionaries), Macmillan USA, Merriam-Webster, Oxford University Press, Random House, and World Book.[5]

Accuracy

There are two types of accuracy to consider: spelling and definition. Accuracy in spelling has become a matter of usage rather than academic rule. In evaluating the currency of spelling in a recent dictionary, one should check words that have been modernized (e.g., "airplane" rather than "aeroplane"). Dictionaries are frequently used as authorities for such things as hyphenation, although this changes through evolution as well, with formerly hyphenated words becoming one (e.g., "on-line" to "online").

Definitions should reflect the meaning or meanings of words in clear, unambiguous terms. A definition should not use the word being defined or any word based on the same root to explain the meaning, because this does not give users any more information than they already have.[6] Illustrative examples or quotations from literature can help define the word in context.

Currency

Usage is continually changing. Slang terms can become standard usage, and standard words can take on new connotations that the user did not intend. This is particularly true in areas of popular culture, such as pop music, and in sexual terminology. Explicit definitions of sex words are a problem area in general dictionaries, because publishers are sometimes reluctant to include words that are considered vulgar or obscene. These words are often well defined in slang dictionaries. Writers in particular must be careful about current usage in this regard, and they are not well served by an out-of-date dictionary. Editorial policies often determine the inclusion or exclusion of recent words, based on perceived usage or a particular audience focus, such as on high school or undergraduate college students.

Indexing

General dictionaries, because of their alphabetical arrangement, do not require indexes. Indexes are most important in quotation books, because of the variety of approaches that can be used. A good quotation book should have an author index, if the arrangement is not alphabetical by author, and a keyword phrase index. The phrase index is very important, because keywords by themselves cause time-consuming effort when one is following up multiple references only to find out in the end that the desired phrase is not in the book.

SELECTION

Selection of a new dictionary for an existing collection requires some consideration of the needs of users served by the library, the age and condition of the dictionaries already in the collection, and the amount of money that can be put into new acquisitions. There is a natural tendency to replace an outdated edition with a newer one of the same title, but this should not be done automatically without giving some consideration to new titles in the field that may be just as good or better. Access to dictionaries on the Internet can be a consideration, but the drawbacks of Internet searching mentioned elsewhere in this chapter make it imperative that a collection of current print dictionaries be maintained in the library. Because desk dictionaries are compiled for specific age groups and levels of sophistication, the reference librarian must be aware of this when selecting a dictionary. High school-level dictionaries do not belong in college collections, although students may request them because of familiarity with titles used in high school. College-level dictionaries, however, may be useful in high school libraries, particularly for advanced students. Dictionary buying guides and reviews will indicate the level of specific dictionaries. Scholars and others exploring unfamiliar topics will require specialized subject dictionaries such as *The New Harvard Dictionary of Music* or *Brewer's Dictionary of Phrase & Fable*, foreign-language dictionaries, and unabridged compilations, such as the *Oxford English Dictionary*. Figure 17.1, page 414, illustrates the difference in treatment of the same word in an unabridged dictionary and a specialized music dictionary.

Unabridged dictionaries may seem expensive initially, but because they are so infrequently issued, experience shows that they will be used until they fall apart. The long useful life of the dictionary will justify the cost. The other types of dictionaries are also heavily used in libraries, justifying the extra cost for a hardbound edition. Paperback dictionaries have limited vocabulary coverage and treatment, in addition to having a shorter shelf life, and are not as satisfactory for library use as the hardbound editions. Smaller dictionaries are vulnerable to theft from reference collections, so it may be necessary to increase security to keep them. Also, be wary of dictionaries with the word *illustrated* in the title. These are usually desk dictionaries with attractive pictures added, and a greatly increased price, without any additional text. Certain standard tools, such as *Webster's Third New International Dictionary of the English Language, Unabridged* or Bartlett's *Familiar Quotations*, are used over and over again and are considered basic to any reference collection. Library users come to know them by name and expect to find them in any library, whether academic or public. These will be discussed later in this chapter.

Figure 17.1 Comparison of entries from *The Random House Webster's Unabridged Dictionary*, 2d ed., rev. and updated. New York: Random House, 1997, p. 162; and Randel, Don Michael, ed., *The New Harvard Dictionary of Music*. Cambridge, Mass.: Belknap Press of Harvard University, 1986, p. 76, for the word "band." Note that the specialized music dictionary gives only the meanings that relate to music. Reprinted by permission.

band[1] (band), *n.* **1.** a company of persons or, sometimes, animals or things, joined, acting, or functioning together; aggregation; party; troop: *a band of protesters.* **2.** *Music.* **a.** a group of instrumentalists playing music of a specialized type: *rock band; calypso band; mariachi band.* **b.** a musical group, usually employing brass, percussion, and often woodwind instruments, that plays esp. for marching or open-air performances. **c.** See **big band. d.** See **dance band. 3.** a division of a nomadic tribe; a group of individuals who move and camp together and subsist by hunting and gathering. **4.** a group of persons living outside the law: *a renegade band.* **5. to beat the band,** *Informal.* energetically; abundantly: *It rained all day to beat the band.* —*v.t.* **6.** to unite in a troop, company, or confederacy. —*v.i.* **7.** to unite; confederate (often fol. by *together*): *They banded together to oust the chairman.* [1480–90; < MF *bande* < It *banda;* c. LL *bandum* < Gmc; akin to Goth *bandwa* standard, BAND[2], BAND[3], BEND[1], BOND[1]]
—**Syn. 1.** gang, group; body; set; society, association, assembly. See **company.**

Band [Fr. *bande;* Ger. *Kapelle;* It., Sp. *banda*]. (1) Any instrumental ensemble larger than a chamber ensemble, including, especially in British usage, the orchestra. Early ensembles bearing the name include the 17th-century **Vingt-quatre violons du roi* (*La grande bande*) and the 24 fiddlers of Charles II (The King's Private Band). (2) An ensemble of wind instruments, sometimes also with percussion. See Brass band, Military music, Symphonic band. (3) Any ensemble other than one of the traditional combinations of Western art music, sometimes identified by the type of instrument(s) included or by the repertory performed, e.g., accordion band, jazz band, dance band, *big band, *string band, *jug band, *bluegrass band, *rock band. (4) [It.] The brass and percussion sections of the orchestra.

There is a confusing proliferation of general English-language dictionaries available from bookstores, supermarkets, and remainder houses. Dictionary publishers themselves frequently publish a number of titles that are similar. One area of confusion is in the designation "Webster" in the title. There is no copyright on the use of "Webster," and anyone can claim to be publishing a dictionary in the direct tradition of Noah Webster himself. Several publishers have a "Webster's Unabridged" that purports to be a great bargain at a greatly reduced price. One should not buy one of these without first examining a copy, as they are, at best, large desk dictionaries. They may also be reissues of older material from other sources.[7]

When in doubt, the best policy is to read reviews and stay with the standard titles. Dictionary buying guides that compare several titles, such as *Encyclopedias, Atlases & Dictionaries* or *Kister's Best Dictionaries for Adults & Young People: A Comparative Guide* can often clear up the confusion. There are very few bargains in the dictionary world.

IMPORTANT GENERAL SOURCES

This section focuses on several kinds of dictionaries and related tools that are found in typical school, public, or academic library reference collections. Under each category, a few of the most widely used titles are described. For information on titles not discussed here, the reader can consult one of the guides to dictionaries listed in the Additional Readings.

Unabridged Dictionaries

There are only three good unabridged English-language dictionaries: *Webster's Third New International Dictionary of the English Language, Unabridged*; *The Random House Webster's*

Unabridged Dictionary, 2d ed., rev. and updated; and *Funk & Wagnalls New Standard Dictionary of the English Language*.

Webster's Third, originally published in 1961, has been updated periodically by the addition of new words in the form of an addendum, but it is in need of a complete revision. However, it remains the most prestigious dictionary published in North America and is considered by most users to be the final authority for spelling and definition. In defining usage it has become outdated, reflecting the usage of the 1950s.[8] However, *Merriam-Webster's Dictionary of English Usage* is an up-to-date dictionary that deals with many of the disputed usages in *Webster's Third* and provides recent usage notes from Merriam-Webster's files.

When *Webster's Third* first appeared, reviewers complained about permissiveness in the change from a prescriptive to a descriptive philosophy in compiling the third edition. There were scathing reviews in the *New York Times* and in other newspapers and magazines (see Box 17.2). Some critics also disliked the fact that the biographical section and gazetteer of the previous edition had been omitted. However, these changes just follow in the tradition of change and updating that has gone on since Merriam-Webster bought Noah Webster's copyright in 1843, and other reviewers recognized this (see Box 17.3).

Box 17.2 A Prescriptive View

In its review of *Webster's Third New International*, the *Washington Sunday Star* of September 10, 1961, held a staunchly prescriptive view:

It "Ain't" Good

"The Merriam-Webster unabridged dictionary, in its first completely new edition since 1934, contains a number of startling revisions. They are revisions likely to shock more than a few of us who happen, for better or worse, to be traditionalists congenitally opposed to change just for change's sake. In that respect, perhaps the most shocking thing in the whole book is that it takes a rather respectful view of 'ain't' as a word that is now 'used orally in the U.S. by cultivated speakers.'

"This is certainly a far cry from the dictionary's 1934 edition, which bluntly—and correctly, in our view—brands 'ain't' as a 'dialectal' and 'illiterate' expression employed by people on the fringes of polite society. But now, along with a lot of other vulgarisms that have become respectable, this basically unpleasant, unnecessary and grammatically gauche word has been more or less legitimatized by the Merriam-Webster people."

James Sledd and Wilma R. Ebbitt,
Dictionaries and That Dictionary[9]

Box 17.3 A Descriptive View

A more liberal, descriptive point of view was taken by Norman E. Isaacs, writing in *The Louisville Times* of October 18, 1961:

And Now, the War on Words

"As if we do not have enough warring, we have another now on words. It has burst full-blown over the publication of the *Webster's Third New International Dictionary*, . . .

"What annoys the traditionalists is Webster's acceptance of words like *double-domes, yakking, confabbing*, and *finalize*, to mention only a mere scattering. Presumably, the critics might well sanction such new entries as *teaching fellow, carbon 14, traffic island*, and even *crop duster*. Why include such words and set phrases and object to others like *litter bug, elbow bending, two-way stretch*, or *greasy spoon*? Are these not also part of the American language?

> "The *New York Times* shudders over 'finalize.' I confess to irritation, too. But it must be admitted that it arrives from an established principle that earlier resulted in 'colonize' and 'clockwise'. . . .
>
> "The net is that we have a new dictionary and it will become the accepted authority, despite all the literary hassles that will ensue. It is not a revision of the old unabridged. It has taken 27 years to compile. It includes 50,000 new words and phrases, with another 50,000 new meanings added."
>
> James Sledd and Wilma R. Ebbitt,
> *Dictionaries and That Dictionary*[10]

Noah Webster published his first unabridged dictionary in 1828. The first Webster's dictionary published by Merriam was in 1847, and the first unabridged dictionary of the current series, the *Webster's New International*, appeared in 1909. *Webster's Second* was published in 1934. Periodic supplements, the latest called *12,000 Words: A Supplement to Webster's Third New International Dictionary*, are published separately or as addenda in recent printings. The Merriam-Webster staff is continually collecting citations and examples of language to be added into the addendum with each new printing. A CD-ROM version is now also available.

In *Webster's Third*, the first element in an entry is the pronunciation. Etymologies are listed immediately after the pronunciation, followed by the definitions and illustrative quotations. Synonyms are listed at the end of the entry. Three kinds of status labels indicate obsolete, slang, and dialect terms. Pronunciation given is that of educated people, and there is no "preferred" pronunciation listed first.

The *Random House Webster's Unabridged Dictionary* (2d ed. rev. and updated, 1997), is the smallest of the three unabridged dictionaries, but it is more current than *Webster's Third*. Its coverage of the language reflects the mid-1980s rather than the 1950s. The revised and updated edition has a separate section of new words from the 1990s taken from the in-house *Random House Living Dictionary Database*. It is descriptive in its approach, but has numerous usage notes. Valuable features are the inclusion of approximate dates when a word or phrase first entered the language and identification of vocabulary specifically of American origin. The illustrative quotations are made up by the editorial staff and vary in their clarity and usefulness. Because it is so up-to-date, most libraries should have a copy of the *Random House* in addition to *Webster's Third*, and reference librarians should make it the first choice for recent definitions, spelling, and hyphenations, unless the user specifically requests *Webster's Third*. Random House also issues the dictionary on CD-ROM.

Funk & Wagnalls New Standard Dictionary of the English Language is badly out-of-date, and has not been published since 1965. It was originally published in 1913 as a thorough revision of an earlier work published in 1893. Successive printings had new words inserted in the text and, finally, a supplement of new words. Since 1958, the Funk & Wagnalls name has been used on a desk dictionary published under a succession of titles, the latest being *Funk & Wagnalls New International Dictionary of the English Language* (comprehensive ed., 1999). It is not comprehensive, however, having about half as much text as the *New Standard*.

Etymological Dictionaries

The *Oxford English Dictionary* (*OED*), 2d ed., published in the spring of 1989, is a completely updated version of the first edition, completed in 1928, and its four supplements. About 5,000 new words and meanings were added, new definitions were added to the old ones, and the old phonetic system devised by Sir James Murray, the original compiler, was replaced by the International Phonetic Alphabet. The *OED* is considered the premier source for etymology, and its definitions and quotations take on encyclopedic proportions. It is a massive, scholarly compilation, usually consulted for its extensive etymologies that record the history of words and meanings in use since 1150 and trace their evolution through dated citations, or quotations, from standard literature. It can be used as a quotation dictionary and often is, particularly by writers and speakers. It has no biographical or geographical material, and no special features outside its main lexicon. Although the *OED* is compiled in England, words from other English-speaking countries are well represented.

The size of the print set (20 volumes in the main set plus an additions series) and its more-than-$2,000 cost make it a work that is usually available for consultation only in libraries. However, it has become widely available in electronic form either on CD-ROM or on a fee basis via the Web (http://www.oed.com). The Web version is regularly updated.

The *Oxford English Dictionary on CD-ROM* (2d ed.) originally appeared in 1992, amid enthusiastic reviews. As is the case with all CD-ROM products, the advantages of computerized access are keyword and Boolean searching and a variety of customized printouts. The CD-ROM allows searching of quotations by keyword and date, thus supporting extensive searches that are not possible with the print volumes.

Another choice for libraries not having the resources to purchase the 20-volume *OED* is *The New Shorter Oxford English Dictionary on Historical Principles*, a 1993 abridgment in two volumes, based on the second edition of the *OED*. Many of the entries are shortened, and the etymologies are not as extensive, but it is an excellent etymological dictionary in its own right. A CD-ROM version is also available.

A good, single-volume, U.S. etymological dictionary is the *Barnhart Dictionary of Etymology*, edited by Robert K. Barnhart. It focuses on a core vocabulary of 30,000 words basic to contemporary English, paying particular attention to the way the language is written and spoken in the United States today. Semantic development of each word is traced from the first recorded appearance, as determined by modern scholarship, to the present time. Linguistic derivations are spelled out without the use of abbreviations, making the entries clear and readable.

William Craigie and James Hulbert's *A Dictionary of American English on Historical Principles* (1938–1944) and Mitford Mathews's *A Dictionary of Americanisms on Historical Principles* (1951) cover the historical derivations of words originating in the United States or having a greater currency here than elsewhere. Both are out-of-date (see discussion of *Dictionary of American Regional English* later in this chapter).

Desk Dictionaries

Merriam-Webster's Collegiate Dictionary (10th ed., 1993) is the update of *Webster's Ninth New Collegiate Dictionary* and is considered a classic of its type. The tenth edition represents an extensive revision and updating in both the entries section and the special sections. Merriam-Webster is considered one of the foremost dictionary publishers in the United States and has an immense citation bank (master collection of words and definitions that is continually enlarged by the addition of new words found by the editorial staff) to draw on for its dictionaries. The *Collegiate Dictionary* is an adult-level dictionary based on the *Webster's Third New International*, with definitions somewhat simplified and shortened. Many technical, archaic, variant, and esoteric terms found in the parent dictionary are omitted from the collegiate version.

The entries include part of speech, pronunciation, inflections, etymology, definitions, and notes on usage and synonymy. The date of the first instance of use of the word is given with a discussion of the current use of the word. Definitions are precise and clear, and there is considerable emphasis on contemporary pronunciation and definitions. There are an extensive section of explanatory notes at the beginning and a short pronunciation key on each right-hand page. There are separate lists of abbreviations and symbols for chemical elements, foreign words and phrases, biographical names, geographical names, and signs and symbols, as well as a handbook of style. These are of more use in the home than in the library, where other standard tools provide this information. Illustrations are kept to a minimum.

Merriam-Webster's Collegiate Dictionary is available on CD-ROM as a single title or packaged with other titles. Beginning in 1998 it has been available in its entirety at no charge on the Web. Electronic versions include all the text from the print version. Some versions have multimedia features such as sound and graphics that are not supported by all types of software, and search results may vary because of this.

The American Heritage Dictionary of the English Language (4th ed., 2000); *Random House Webster's College Dictionary* (2d ed., 1997); and the *Webster's New World College Dictionary* (4th ed., 1999), are also popular, authoritative desk dictionaries with many similarities to the *Webster's Collegiate* and to each other. The lexical content of the leading desk dictionaries is so similar that selecting a desk dictionary becomes a matter of personal preference.

The *American Heritage* is heavily illustrated and is noted for its attractive and easy-to-read page layout. The first edition of this dictionary, which appeared in 1969, was noted for its etymologies and for being the first general dictionary to include obscenities. The second edition had briefer definitions and etymologies than the previous edition or than either the *Merriam-Webster's Collegiate* or the *Webster's New World*. Shortening the definitions and the etymologies was not an improvement, and many users preferred the original edition. In the third edition the editors decided to return to the fuller definitions of the popular first edition and added many regional terms that had not previously been included. A panel of linguistic experts prescribes usage labels. A revision of the appendix of Indo-European roots of the 1969 edition appears in the fourth edition together with a new appendix of Semitic roots. The Indo-European roots appendix lists and defines the ultimate ancestral root and allocates the various words derived from the root to the Indo-European language family, such as Germanic or Celtic, that preceded the English word. The *American Heritage* (4th ed.) emphasizes contemporary usage and is strong in recent scientific and technical terms. A CD-ROM edition is also available and this edition is freely accessible on the Web.

The *Random House Webster's College Dictionary* (2d ed.) is also based on a well-respected larger dictionary, *The Random House Webster's Unabridged Dictionary*. The *Random House Webster's College Dictionary* was developed from the *Living Dictionary Database*, which is edited online and is remarkably up-to-date. A comparison of entries in *The Random House Webster's Unabridged Dictionary* with those in the *Random House Webster's College Dictionary* shows that the entries in the desk dictionary are not just "cut down"; in some cases they are rewritten or are eliminated entirely. This dictionary has been criticized for being overly politically correct, including such awkward terms as *womyn*, *heightism*, and *waitperson*.[11] It follows the descriptive approach of the parent *Random House Webster's Unabridged*. There are prefix tables for commonly used prefixes, such as *re-* and *pro-*, in their respective alphabetical sections, and a guide for writers and a pronunciation table at the end. It can also be searched at no cost on the Web.

Webster's New World College Dictionary is highly regarded. Based on an electronic database of words begun in 1980, it was updated for the fourth edition with thousands of new words and meanings ranging from technical terminology to the jargon of professional sports and slang terms. Formerly titled *Webster's New World Dictionary of the American Language*, it is published by Macmillan USA. It has no relation to the Merriam-Webster line of dictionaries, and has been a separate publication in its own right since 1951. Its major emphasis is on English as it is spoken and written in the United States, with good coverage of American idioms and slang. The etymologies are particularly good.

Third Barnhart Dictionary of New English, edited by Robert K. Barnhart, is a desk dictionary that emphasizes the new words of the 1980s. Each entry includes the year of the earliest appearance of the word as far as the editors can ascertain, along with the definition and relevant quotations.

High School- and Elementary School-Level Dictionaries

Dictionaries for high school use tend to be abridged, simplified editions of the larger dictionaries intended for adults. High school libraries should also have at least one adult-level dictionary for use by advanced students.

The American Heritage Concise Dictionary (3d ed.) is an abridged version of the 1992 *American Heritage Dictionary of the English Language* and retains many of its features. The definitions have been revised to be simpler and easier to read, and the typeface and the illustrations are larger. Biographical and geographical entries are included in the main alphabet, while etymologies are in a separate appendix. The etymologies are based on those in the parent work. A panel of writers, editors, and speakers determined the usage notes that appear in the text.

This dictionary does not try to be comprehensive, but it is very complete for a concise edition. Many advanced scientific and technical terms found in the parent work are excluded, and the meanings for those that remain are considerably rewritten and condensed. The language of the concise edition is simpler and more direct than in the other American Heritage dictionaries. This is a dictionary that can be understood by readers with unsophisticated or limited vocabularies. Pronunciation follows the standard American Heritage system. Usage notes are much more condensed than in the parent dictionary and are less prescriptive. The illustrations are large and excellent and add considerably to the reader's understanding of words. There are also maps and portraits. This dictionary has been favorably reviewed and is a good buy for the high school library.

Another highly respected dictionary that is suitable for high schools is the *World Book Dictionary*, edited by Clarence Barnhart and Robert K. Barnhart. It is published by World Book, publishers of the *World Book Encyclopedia*, and is designed to complement the encyclopedia. This title is part of the Thorndike-Barnhart dictionary series, and is a large, annually updated work in two volumes that approaches the size of the unabridged dictionaries. The Thorndike-Barnhart lexicographical file is large and extensive, and the breadth of the dictionary reflects this. It has a large assortment of foreign words and phrases and a selection of British terms. Entries are in simplified language, and obscenities are omitted. Biographical and geographical names are also excluded. The dictionary has a number of special features, including a lengthy introduction that summarizes the history of the English language, how to write effectively, how to use alternate language systems such as Braille and Morse Code, and how to use the dictionary. This dictionary is well designed and easy to read; its only real drawbacks are the two-volume format and the relatively high cost compared with other desk dictionaries.

Elementary school-level dictionaries are colorful, are often arranged by broad topics, and give a simplified definition, the part of speech, and sometimes the pronunciation of the word being defined. The color illustrations take up a larger proportion of the page space than those in dictionaries for older users. Age levels are usually specified. Some of the most popular are the following titles: *The American Heritage First Dictionary* and *Macmillan First Dictionary* (ages 5-9); *Macmillan Dictionary for Children* (also available on CD-ROM), *Thorndike-Barnhart Children's Dictionary*, and *The American Heritage Children's Dictionary* (ages 8-12); and *Thorndike-Barnhart Student Dictionary* and *Webster's New World Student's Dictionary* (junior high-level). An October 2000 article in *Booklist* reviews these and similar dictionaries for elementary and high school-aged children.[12]

Foreign-Language/English-Language Dictionaries

The foreign-language/English-language (dual) dictionary is a popular type of reference book that is particularly important in academic reference collections. These dictionaries are generally issued in series by major publishers, with the same format throughout the series. The major publishers are all British, perhaps reflecting a greater concern and expertise with multilingualism in Great Britain.

The Cassell's series, published in England and issued in the United States by Macmillan, are the best known of the dual-language dictionaries for European languages. These handy, one-volume works are large enough to include most of the foreign words and idiomatic phrases that the user is likely to want. The dictionary is divided in half, the first half consisting of the foreign words with English equivalents, and the second half consisting of English words with their foreign equivalents. Slang words, colloquialisms, and pronunciation guides are included. The individual entries give pronunciation, part of speech, definition, inflection, compounds, and idioms. Geographical names are incorporated into the alphabetical listing.

HarperCollins, Oxford University Press, and Cambridge University Press are other highly respected publishers of dual-language dictionaries. Oxford in particular specializes in non-European languages and has a whole range of dictionaries in African and Asian tongues, as well as in ancient Greek and Latin. Cambridge has a number of multivolume dictionaries that provide a more extensive vocabulary than Cassell's or HarperCollins.

A large number of dual-language dictionaries in many languages can be accessed on the Internet. A good source for these is *yourDictionary.com*. This site has links to more than 1500 free online dictionaries in more than 230 different languages. Unfortunately, as in many electronic sources, these dictionaries are usually identified only by title, and it is difficult to tell when and by whom they were published in print. However, this is not a serious concern for most users of the site, and the convenience of having so many dictionaries available for quick lookups is a considerable advantage in libraries unable to afford a large dual-language dictionary collection.

Box 17.4 Search Strategy: A Translation Problem

A library user came to a small public library with a decoratively painted breadboard that she had recently purchased in an antique shop. The board had an inscription that read: *Giv os idag vort daglige brød*. From the floral design on the board the woman thought that the inscription was either Swedish or Norwegian, but she wasn't sure which one. Because the library had no Scandinavian dual-language dictionaries, the librarian quickly accessed *yourDictionary.com* on the Internet and tried searching the words *daglige* and *brød* in several Swedish and Norwegian dictionaries that were listed there. The dictionaries revealed that the words were Norwegian for "Give us this day our daily bread."

Dictionaries of Slang and Dialect

Slang and dialect dictionaries are compiled because standard dictionaries frequently omit colloquial and vulgar terms or do not define them with enough depth. Dialect dictionaries explore regional differences in spelling, pronunciation, and usage. These types of dictionaries are almost entirely descriptive, with every nuance of meaning considered valid as long as it is used by someone.

Dictionary of American Regional English is an ambitious scholarly project sponsored by the American Dialect Society, edited by Frederic G. Cassidy, and published by Belknap Press of Harvard University Press. It was scheduled to be completed in approximately the year 2000 in five volumes, with a supplement summarizing the questions that were asked and the answers that were obtained by the dictionary's field workers. As of 1999, three volumes had been published. The dictionary's purpose is to obtain and document, as comprehensively as possible, a record of regional American English in 1,000 selected communities and to record folk language that is learned at home or in the community rather than from school, books, or other sources of formal communication. Vocabularies of in-groups, such as criminals, along with other types of jargon, particularly those of highly specialized or esoteric occupations, are omitted. Included are vocabularies of widespread occupations that involve entire communities or regions, such as farming, lumbering, mining, and homemaking. The language of children's games is included, because it is usually of folk origin, has been preserved orally, and shows great regional differences.

Some entries contain deliberately distorted explanatory maps (see Figure 17.2) that indicate the frequency and density of the population using the word or phrase by enlarging or compressing the size of the states. In this example, the term *banana pepper* is used by more people in the states of the Mississippi River Valley and farther east, so these states appear larger on the map. Dots indicate the location of individual informants who reported use of the term. A separate map section will be included in the final volume.

Figure 17.2 Entries and map from *Dictionary of American Regional English.* Reprinted by permission of the publishers from *Dictionary of American Regional English,* Volume 1, Frederic G. Cassidy, Editor, Cambridge, Mass.: The Belknap Press of Harvard University Press, Copyright © 1988 by the President and Fellows of Harvard College. Reprinted by permission.

banana pepper n **widely scattered exc NEast, West** See Map
A banana-shaped pepper, usu yellow.
1965–70 *DARE* (Qu. I22a, . . *Different kinds of peppers—small hot*) 14 Infs, **esp Sth, S Midl,** Banana pepper; **AL6,** Banana pepper—shaped like a banana and red; (Qu. I22b, . . *Large hot*) 37 Infs, **widely scattered exc NEast, West,** Banana peppers; **CT2,** Banana peppers—built like a banana; hot, long ones; **GA85,** Banana peppers—thicker than a finger; **IL41,** Banana peppers—long, yellow, not too hot; **IL117,** Hot banana peppers; **KY28,** Banana—hots; **OK43,** Banana peppers are sometimes sweet; long but pretty thin, fairly small; (Qu. I22c, . . *Small sweet*) 15 Infs, **esp Sth,** Banana peppers; **AL11,** Banana peppers—green and yellow; **MS59,** White banana pepper; (Qu. I22d, . . *Large sweet*) 19 Infs, **chiefly Missip Valley,** Banana peppers; **LA2,** Called banana pepper in the store—same as wax pepper; **NC81,** Banana peppers—yellow and long, a little hot; **TN26,** Banana peppers—tolerable long yellow pepper.

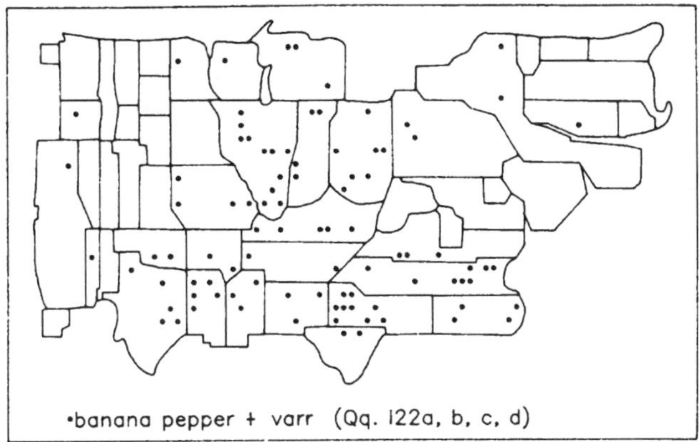

Box 17.5

Search Strategy: In Search of the Elusive Banana Pepper

A gardener came into the public library in a large midwestern city trying to find out just what kind of plant produces the fruit popularly known in her neighborhood as a banana pepper. Gardening books were not much help. The reference librarian, knowing that popular names of plants are often regional, checked the *Dictionary of American Regional English* and determined that the term was commonly used in her area for any long, yellow pepper. The gardener was then able to select the proper seeds from her seed catalog.

Entries are in strict alphabetical sequence, letter by letter. Spelling is based on *Webster's Third New International*. Phrases and compounds are included as well as single words. Parts of speech, pronunciation, etymology, geographical and usage labels, cross-references, dated quotations, and research notes obtained by the field workers are included. The field workers were graduate students in English language and linguistics who interviewed 2,777 people in 1,000 communities and phonetically transcribed their speech. The pronunciation key fills 13 pages, reflecting the importance of exact comprehension of the nuances of regional speech.

Dictionary of American Regional English does not have any current competitors. Two out-of-print dictionaries, William Craigie and James Hulbert's *A Dictionary of American English on Historical Principles* (1938–1944) and Harold Wentworth's *American Dialect Dictionary* (1944), will be surpassed by the sheer scope and diversity of the newer work when it is completed. The Craigie and Hulbert work is still useful for historical research, however, because it includes some standard words, such as aborigine, that do not appear in *Dictionary of American Regional English.* The Wentworth compilation has been used as a source by the compilers of *Dictionary of American Regional English* and will be obsolete when the new compilation is finished.

Slang dictionaries are made up entirely of words used in colloquial speech and include many terms considered derogatory or vulgar. These words are increasingly found in general dictionaries as well, but the good slang dictionaries are still the handiest source and frequently give better, more complete definitions. The standard in this field is Eric Partridge's *Dictionary of Slang and Unconventional English*, originally published in 1937 and now in its eighth edition. Partridge was Australian, and his compilation emphasizes British slang, but he ranged far over the English-speaking world for his sources. Although many of the words in his dictionary are now found in the *Oxford English Dictionary* with better etymologies, Partridge's dictionary is still considered the most scholarly of the slang dictionaries because of its historical approach and its many quotations with citations to sources. The frequently updated editions keep the dictionary current with recent slang.

American slang has been covered since 1960 by Harold Wentworth and Stuart Berg Flexner's *Dictionary of American Slang* (3d ed., 1995), edited by Robert Chapman. It covers all periods of American history but emphasizes modern slang. Quotations and citations to sources are also an important part of the definitions in this dictionary.

The multivolume *Random House Historical Dictionary of American Slang* began publication in 1994 and is a comprehensive compilation of slang terms from many sources using the historical principles made famous by the *OED.* It has many citations from *Dictionary of American Regional English* and *Dictionary of American Slang* as well as standard English-language and usage dictionaries. Its coverage extends back over 300 years of American history.

Slang and jargon of specialized groups also have special dictionaries. Among these are Eric Partridge's *A Dictionary of the Underworld, British & American*; *Newspeak: A Dictionary of Jargon*, by Jonathon Green; and *Thesaurus of American Slang*, edited by Robert Chapman. *Thesaurus of American Slang* combines the slang dictionary and thesaurus format, providing an incredible array of colorful synonyms for common four-letter words.

Thesauri and Usage Guides

A *thesaurus* is a very specialized dictionary that deals only with word synonyms (same meaning) and antonyms (opposite meaning). The first English-language synonym and word finding list, the Reverend John Trusler's *The Difference between Words Esteemed Synonymous in the English Language*, was published in 1766. The modern thesaurus was developed by Peter Mark Roget, an English doctor, who first published his work in 1852 at age 73. Today the name Roget, like the name Webster, is not copyrighted and can be used by anyone.

The standard thesaurus in the Roget tradition now in use is *Roget's International Thesaurus* (5th ed., 1992), published by HarperCollins. The distinctive feature of this thesaurus is its arrangement. Words are arranged according to 15 primary classes of categories designated as living things, language, arts, and so forth. Within these categories, words are grouped by the ideas they convey, with synonyms and antonyms appearing in close proximity. There are many cross-references and no definitions in the usual sense, although the many synonyms serve to make the meaning clear. There is a comprehensive alphabetical index. This thesaurus is used mainly by writers and crossword puzzle enthusiasts. A writer must already have a good vocabulary and a sense of subtle variations in connotation to use it effectively, because connotative meanings are not provided. For example, in Figure 17.3, under *46 compose*, the user must know that in music *harmonize* and *adapt* do not mean the same thing as *compose*, even though all are listed as synonyms in the same entry, and must understand all three activities to convey the correct meaning. It is a good idea to use *Roget's* in conjunction with a standard dictionary that gives definitions to make sure that the synonym selected actually conveys the intended meaning.

Figure 17.3

Definition from *Roget's International Thesaurus* by Peter Mark Roget. Entries from page 494:46-48 from *Roget's International Thesaurus,* 5th edition by Peter Mark Roget. Copyright © 1992 by HarperCollins Publishers, Inc. Reprinted by permission of HarperCollins Publishers, Inc.

46 compose, write, arrange, score, set, set to music, put to music; musicalize, melodize, **harmonize; orchestrate;** instrument, instrumentate; **adapt,** make an adaptation; transcribe, transpose

ADJS **47 musical, musically inclined,** musicianly, with an ear for music; virtuoso, virtuose, virtuosic; **music-loving,** music-mad, musicophile, philharmonic; absolute, aleatory

48 melodious, melodic; **musical,** music-like; **tuneful,** tunable; fine-toned, **pleasant-sounding,** agreeable-sounding, pleasant, appealing, agreeable, catchy, singable; **euphonious** *or* euphonic, **lyric, lyrical,** melic; **lilting,** songful, songlike; **sweet, dulcet,** sweet-sounding, achingly sweet, sweet-flowing; honeyed, mellifluent, mellifluous, mellisonant, music-flowing; rich, mellow; sonorous, canorous; golden, golden-toned; silvery, silver-toned; sweet-voiced, golden-voiced, silver-voiced, silver-tongued, golden-tongued, music-tongued; ariose, arioso, cantabile

Roget's II: The New Thesaurus (3d ed.), published by Houghton Mifflin in 1995, attempts to overcome this definition problem by providing definitions and illustrative examples. A separate Category Index has synonym lists with corresponding antonyms. It does away with the need to use another dictionary for definitions, but does not have the comprehensiveness of *Roget's International*. This format has not been as popular with users, who seem to prefer the masses of undefined synonyms provided by *Roget's International*. An electronic version can be searched at no charge on the Web.

Merriam-Webster's Dictionary of Synonyms is entirely in conventional dictionary format. Each entry gives a definition followed by a list of analogous terms (synonyms) and lists of antonyms and contrasted words. Published by Merriam-Webster in 1984, it is both current and comprehensive, although it does not have the sheer quantity of words found in *Roget's International*.

The *Harcourt Brace Student Thesaurus* for elementary students ages 8 to 13 provides a good introduction to the thesaurus format and is an aid for writers of school papers. It provides related terms, usage statements, and antonyms.

Automated thesauri that are a part of word processing programs are becoming quite popular with both children and adults. Users can point to or click on words to make a window pop up listing synonyms for the highlighted word. They are now a common writing tool of students and adults alike.

Related somewhat to the thesauri in intent are the usage dictionaries, of which the best known is *The New Fowler's Modern English Usage*, originally written by H. W. Fowler in 1926. The third revised edition, edited by R. W. Burchfield and published by Oxford University Press, appeared in 2000. Fowler's dictionary is entirely prescriptive in its approach, as one would expect, and deals extensively with grammar and syntax. Definitions are supplemented with discussion analyzing how words should be used, pointing out clichés and common errors in somewhat scathing terms. The intent of this dictionary is to make writers and others aware of the principles of good usage and good writing.

Harper Dictionary of Contemporary Usage (2d ed., 1985), by William and Mary Morris, is a work that points out inaccuracies and improper usage as determined by a panel of 166 writers, editors, news broadcasters, and other language experts. It contains discussions with panel members and examples of correct usage based on the standards of those who use English well. *Harper Dictionary* puts emphasis on American usage.

A recent work that has no modern counterpart, but which closely resembles in concept and format a seventeenth-century lexical encyclopedia—the *Academy of Armory* (1688), compiled by Randle Holme—is the *Random House Word Menu* (rev. ed.), by Stephen Glazier. This is a classified list of words and short definitions that was compiled over a period of eight years and originally appeared as a software product titled *Inside Information.* The revised edition was published by Random House in 1997. It has seven general categories and numerous subcategories of related terms with definitions, but no lists of synonyms as are found in Roget. The word lists include such things as breeds of domestic animals and names of all the muscles and bones in the human body.

Abbreviations and Acronyms Dictionaries

Abbreviations dictionaries are very important tools in the reference collection because writers at every level, from journalists to academicians, persist in using abbreviations and acronyms without definitions. Abbreviations are used as a form of literary or bibliographic shorthand, to the confusion of many readers who often cannot remember, or never knew, what they stand for. Some, such as SPEBSQSA (Society for the Preservation and Encouragement of Barber Shop Quartet Singing in America), have become famous as mind-teasers in their own right.

As is the case with quotation books, one can almost never have too many abbreviations dictionaries. However, one title is the first choice for abbreviations questions: *Acronyms, Initialisms & Abbreviations Dictionary* and its companion, *Reverse Acronyms, Initialisms & Abbreviations Dictionary*, published annually by the Gale Group. This is a multivolume set and includes abbreviations of periodical titles, acronyms for societies and institutions, and commonly used abbreviations in every subject area. The major disadvantage of such a large compilation is the large number of entries under some abbreviations (see Figure 17.4 under TU). It is necessary to know the context of the abbreviation to select the correct entry.

Reverse Acronyms reverses the procedure by listing the name of the organization or term and giving the accepted abbreviation. Coverage of these two titles focuses on North America and Western Europe. The Gale Group also publishes a separate work, *Periodical Title Abbreviations*, which consists of periodical abbreviations only, but the abbreviations in this work are included in the larger *Acronyms, Initialisms & Abbreviations Dictionary.* Purchasing the former is an expensive duplication if one already owns the latter, more comprehensive work.

Figure 17.4

Entries in *Acronyms, Initialisms & Abbreviations Dictionary.* Selections from *Acronyms, Initialisms & Abbreviations Dictionary 2000,* by Mary Rose Bonk, Volume 1, Part 3, Gale, 2000. Copyright 2000 by Gale Group, Inc. Reprinted by permission of the Gale Group.

TU............... Societe Tunisienne de l'Air [*Tunisia*] [*ICAO designator*]
TU............... Take-Up (IAA)
TU............... Tanking Unit (AAG)
TU............... Tanners' Union [*British*]
TU............... Tape Unit
TU............... Task Unit [*Military*]
TU............... Taxicrinic Unit [*Computer science*]
TU............... Technical Service Unit [*Military*]
TU............... Technical Utilization (NAKS)
TU............... Technische Universitat [*Technical University*] [*German*]
TU............... Technology Utilization
TU............... Temporary Unit (BCP)
TU............... Tenebrio Unit [*Endocrinology*]
TU............... Terminal Unit
TU............... Testo Unico [*Consolidated Statutes*] [*Italian*] (ILCA)
TU............... Test Unit
TU............... Texas Utilities Co. (EFIS)
TU............... Thank You [*Communications operator's procedural remark*]
TU............... Thermal Unit
TU............... Thiouracil [*Biochemistry*] (MAE)
TU............... Thulium [*Symbol is Tm*] [*Chemical element*] (ROG)
TU............... Time-of-Update
TU............... Timing Unit
TU............... Todd Unit [*Medicine*] (MAE)
TU............... Torah Umesorah - National Society for Hebrew Day Schools [*Defunct*] (EA)
TU............... Toxic Unit [*Medicine*]

There are many abbreviations dictionaries for specialized subject areas, and abbreviations are also found in general dictionaries and periodical indexes. Large computer databases indexing the journal literature, such as BIOSIS, have print lists of the journal abbreviations used in their databases.

Electronic Dictionaries

Several software vendors have produced electronic reference and writing aids. These may be more useful for the home user than for the library, but it is a good idea to be aware of them. Electronic dictionaries are often packaged with other electronic reference sources such as encyclopedias on CD-ROM. Individual dictionaries on CD-ROM are discussed elsewhere in this chapter. Increasingly, commonly used sources are also being made available via the Web.

Quotation Books

Quotation questions tend to come from persons writing speeches or essays or from persons wanting the author, source, or correct wording of a quotation for some other purpose. Quotations as received by reference librarians are frequently garbled or inaccurate, but a well-indexed quotation book can often solve the problem.

The standard in the vast field of quotation books is Bartlett's *Familiar Quotations*, originally compiled by John Bartlett in Cambridge, Massachusetts, in 1855. It is now in its sixteenth edition, published in 1992. Quotations are included on the basis of familiarity and worth, as determined by the editors, and each new edition has quotations added and removed. The sixteenth edition has an increased emphasis on popular culture, with the addition of many quotations from movies and television. Bartlett's has a chronological arrangement, with authors arranged by birth date and their quotations by date of publication. The earliest attributed quotation in Bartlett's is from the ancient Egyptian "Song of the Harper" (c. 2650–2600 B.C.E); the last ones are from the television series *Monty Python's Flying Circus* (1969–1974) and *Sesame Street* (1969–). There is an alphabetical index of authors and an extensive keyword phrase index.

Librarians themselves occasionally compile quotation books. *Respectfully Quoted: A Dictionary of Quotations Requested from the Congressional Research Service* was compiled by reference librarians in the Library of Congress from the requests that they have received over the years from members of Congress and others in the government. It gathers a good selection of quotations from government officials as well as from perennially elusive texts. Because it was compiled from a list of actual reference questions, it is likely to include more quotations that have relevance to politics and current affairs than do other quotation books. *The New York Public Library Book of Twentieth-Century American Quotations* is a compilation of quotations from files compiled by librarians of that library. It is arranged into 40 major topics, with separate author and subject indexes, and is strong on recent events.

There are a number of other highly respected quotation books, some with general coverage and many with coverage of specialized groups such as women or the military. Many of these have insufficient indexes, which makes them less desirable than Bartlett's despite having a good range of quotations. A popular title using a subject arrangement is Burton Stevenson's *The Home Book of Quotations*. This has quotations classified under broad subject terms such as "game" or "garden." Although it has a good phrase index, the author index can be frustrating because heavily quoted authors are cited by page numbers only, with no further indication of the contents of the quotation. Stevenson is strong on quotations from literature, particularly poetry, and the phrase index makes tracking down this type of question relatively easy. The subject arrangement has little use when a specific quotation is sought. It is difficult to browse through quotations from a single author, as is possible with an author arrangement such as that found in Bartlett's.

The Columbia Dictionary of Quotations by Robert Andrews is a recent compilation of 18,000 quotations in a topical arrangement. It has 11,000 quotations that are unique to this book, and the emphasis is on twentieth-century quotations from contexts other than literature. The author index refers to topic headings only, with no further identification of the quotations being sought.

Some other quotation books cite sources poorly or not at all, giving the user only part of the information sought. The user must also bear in mind that all quotations in English from non-English sources are translations, so there may be variations in wording from one book to another.

Quotation books are also available in electronic form. *Quotations Database*, with material from *The Oxford Dictionary of Quotations*, is available online through Dialog. *The Oxford Dictionary* has primarily a literary orientation. The database includes the quotation accompanied by the author's name, birth and death dates, and the source of the quotation. All words from the quotations are searchable, allowing more complete identification of quotations containing particular words or phrases than is possible in a print quotation book. Because it includes only the one work, the database has limited usefulness as a source for elusive quotations. Quotations can also be found on the Internet through *yourDictionary.com*, mentioned earlier in this chapter, but many quotation Web sites are not searchable and tend to be lists of favorite quotations compiled by individuals.

SEARCH STRATEGIES

As with all areas of reference work, the strategy of answering dictionary-related questions is often dictated by the nature of the question itself. The questioner may specify the source to be used: "Please tell me how *Webster's Third* spells this word" or even "Is this word in *Webster's Third*?" Students may come looking specifically for an etymological (or more commonly, an "entomological") dictionary. Librarians soon learn to repress any comments about insects and steer them directly to the *Oxford English Dictionary*.

An interesting problem sometimes arises with regard to the date of the dictionary being used in relation to the information being sought. Editors of manuscript diaries, letters, and personal narratives frequently have to define words found in these manuscripts in the context of the period in which they were written. In this case, a dictionary written during the period in question or a dictionary such as the *OED*, with extensive quotations from the period, may serve better than a modern one.

Box 17.6 Search Strategy: A Question of Wills

Jane, a graduate assistant working for Professor White in the History Department, came to the reference desk with a problem that had arisen in connection with the manuscript of an eighteenth-century will that the professor was editing for a book. In the will, the deceased had left "a pair of stillyards" to his oldest son, and nothing in the context of the will gave a clue as to what this was. A quick check of *Webster's Third* and *The Random House Webster's Unabridged Dictionary* proved fruitless, so the reference librarian suggested the *OED*. The *OED* gave two possibilities, both with examples from the eighteenth century (definitions given here are paraphrased from the *OED*):[13]

> *still-yard*, or *stillion*. A stand for a cask used in distilling.
>
> *stillyard*, or *steelyard*. A balance consisting of a lever with unequal arms, used for weighing. Also *a pair of steelyards*.

Although the cask stands could be used in pairs, the more likely answer was the weighing instrument, since it probably was a valuable item and likely to be mentioned in a will. In this case, it was necessary for Jane to consider the quotations from the eighteenth century and to make a decision based on the context in which the term in question had originally been found.

The availability of dictionaries on the Internet has freed librarians from the limitations imposed by their on-site collections. Caution must be observed in using Internet sources because many are older works in the public domain or the unedited creations of individuals. As a practical consideration, the handiness of the single-volume print dictionary is still unrivaled for fast checks of definitions and spelling or for extensive translation projects. Electronic sources are most useful when they access multivolume works or include many titles.

A representative selection of the sources discussed in the previous section should answer most of the general lexicographical questions that come up. Specialized vocabulary questions may require the use of specialized dictionaries or subject encyclopedias. When more information than a simple dictionary definition is required, or information of a very technical nature is needed, a subject dictionary should be consulted. Scientific and medical terms sometimes require a subject specialist to interpret the dictionary. Telephoned questions can be very tricky in this regard, because it is difficult for the nonspecialist to read chemical formulas and unfamiliar terminology to a phone caller. If feasible, it is sometimes better to suggest that the caller consult the books in person or discuss the question directly with a subject specialist.

Librarians soon adopt a strategy such as: first stop, *Webster's Third* or *Random House Webster's*; second stop, *OED*; and so on, for definition questions. Questions involving quotations can be much more difficult, with a typical strategy involving Bartlett's first, followed by a sweep of quotation books, one after another, until the quotation is located or the available sources exhausted. In addition to the general quotation books, there are many specialized titles on subjects such as the military, sports, politics, or quotations by women. These should also be considered if the quotation is of a topical nature. Electronic sources such as the *Quotations*

Database and the electronic versions of the *OED* can make the search much faster if they contain the quotation being sought.

Desk dictionaries and thesauri are generally consulted by library users as writing aids while they are in the library, although a desk dictionary by the telephone on the reference desk is handy for librarians answering telephone questions. The use of foreign-language, slang, usage, and abbreviations dictionaries is directly dictated by the question, which may be "How do you say 'third' in German?" or "What does PMLA stand for?"

There is no substitute for actual use of reference books in enabling a librarian to become familiar with their contents. Browsing through dictionaries or following a subject of interest through several often reveals features that are not indicated by the title. For example, *Dictionary of American Regional English* is an excellent source for folklore concerning individual wild plants. Unfamiliar terms used in popular song titles and lyrics can be found in Partridge's *Dictionary of Slang and Unconventional English.* Most dictionaries are not used to their fullest capacity. The wise reference librarian knows and uses these valuable tools daily.

NOTES

1. *Benét's Reader's Encyclopedia*, 4th ed. (New York: HarperCollins, 1996), 404.

2. *Oxford English Dictionary*, 2d ed. (New York: Clarendon Press/Oxford University Press, 1989), 4:625. "Dictionarius: a repertory of dictiones, phrases or words."

3. R. W. Burchfield, ed., *The New Fowler's Modern English Usage*, 3d ed. (New York: Clarendon Press/Oxford University Press, 1996), 738.

4. James Root Hulbert, *Dictionaries: British and American*, rev. ed. (London: Andre Deutsch, 1968), 99. "The purpose of the dictionary-maker then was to present what was correct in the spelling, meaning, and use of words, actually to omit anything that was 'low', and, from the time the dictionaries of Sheridan and Walker appeared, to set a standard of elegance and excellence in pronunciation."

5. Ken Kister, "Dictionaries Defined," *Library Journal* 117 (June 15, 1992): 46.

6. Hulbert, *Dictionaries*, 68: "[I]f I had written: a good definition is one that defines the meaning of a word, I should have dodged the issue or begged the question. The reader would have got no real information, nothing that he did not know before he read my discussion. Yet such slipshod definitions find place in dictionaries."

7. Ken Kister, "The Big Dictionaries: Hoards and Hordes of Words," *Wilson Library Bulletin* 62 (February 1988): 41, 43. "Some of our best and worst dictionaries bear the name *Webster*. The same is true of *Roget* when it comes to thesauri and synonym dictionaries." The worst of the dictionaries is the heavily promoted *Webster's New Universal Unabridged Dictionary*. This was originally published in 1941 and has been little changed since then.

8. Ibid., 40.

9. James Sledd and Wilma R. Ebbitt, *Dictionaries and That Dictionary, A Casebook on the Aims of Lexicographers and the Targets of Reviewers* (Chicago: Scott, Foresman, 1962), 55-56.

10. Ibid., 79-80.

11. Kister, "Dictionaries Defined," 44.

12. Terri Tomchyshyn, "Children's Dictionaries," *Reference Books Bulletin* in *Booklist* 97 (October 15, 2000): 475-77.

13. *Oxford English Dictionary*, 2d ed. (New York: Clarendon Press/Oxford University Press, 1989), 16: 611, 698, 699, 700.

LIST OF SOURCES

Acronyms, Initialisms & Abbreviations Dictionary. Farmington Hills, Mich.: Gale Group, 1960– . Annual.

The American Heritage Children's Dictionary. Rev. ed. Boston: Houghton Mifflin, 1998. 856p. Also available on CD-ROM.

The American Heritage Concise Dictionary. 3d ed. Boston: Houghton Mifflin, 1994. 952p.

The American Heritage Dictionary of the English Language. 4th ed. Boston: Houghton Mifflin, 2000. 2111p. Also available on CD-ROM and online at http://www.bartleby.com/61.

The American Heritage First Dictionary. Boston: Houghton Mifflin, 1998. 377p.

Andrews, Robert. *The Columbia Dictionary of Quotations*. New York: Columbia University Press, 1993. 1092p.

Barnhart Dictionary of Etymology. Edited by Robert K. Barnhart. New York: H. W. Wilson, 1988. 1284p.

Bartlett, John. *Familiar Quotations*. 16th ed. Boston: Little, Brown, 1992. 1405p.

Burchfield, R. W., ed. *The New Fowler's Modern English Usage*. 3d rev. ed. New York: Clarendon Press/Oxford University Press, 2000. 873p.

Cassidy, Frederic G., ed. *Dictionary of American Regional English*. Cambridge, Mass.: Harvard University Press, vol. 1– . 1985– .

Craigie, William A., and James R. Hulbert, eds. *A Dictionary of American English on Historical Principles*. 4 vols. Chicago: University of Chicago Press, 1938–1944.

Dictionary of American Slang. 3d ed. Edited by Robert L. Chapman. New York: HarperCollins, 1995. 617p.

Funk & Wagnalls New International Dictionary of the English Language. 2000 ed. 2 vols. New York: Ferguson Publishing, World Publishers Guild, 1999.

Funk & Wagnalls New Standard Dictionary of the English Language. New York: Funk & Wagnalls, 1965. 2816p.

Glazier, Stephen. *Random House Word Menu*. Rev. ed. New York: Random House, 1997. 767p.

Green, Jonathon. *Newspeak: A Dictionary of Jargon*. Boston: Routledge & Kegan Paul, 1984, 1985. 263p.

Harcourt Brace Student Thesaurus. 2d ed. San Diego: Harcourt Brace, 1994. 312p.

Macmillan Dictionary for Children. 3d rev. ed. New York: Simon & Schuster Books for Young Readers, 1997. 864p. Also available on CD-ROM.

Macmillan First Dictionary. New York: Macmillan, 1990. 402p.

Mathews, Mitford M., ed. *A Dictionary of Americanisms on Historical Principles*. 2 vols. Chicago: University of Chicago Press, 1951.

Merriam-Webster's Collegiate Dictionary. 10th ed. Springfield, Mass.: Merriam-Webster, 1993. 1559p. Also available on CD-ROM and online at http://m-w.com/dictionary.htm.

Merriam-Webster's Dictionary of English Usage. Springfield, Mass.: Merriam-Webster, 1994. 978p.

Merriam-Webster's Dictionary of Synonyms. Springfield, Mass.: Merriam-Webster, 1984. 909p.

Morris, William, and Mary Morris. *Harper Dictionary of Contemporary Usage*. 2d ed. New York: Harper & Row, 1985. 641p.

The New Shorter Oxford English Dictionary on Historical Principles. Edited by Lesley Brown. 2 vols. New York: Clarendon Press/Oxford University Press, 1993. Also available on CD-ROM.

The New York Public Library Book of Twentieth-Century American Quotations. Edited by Stephen Donadio. New York: Warner Books, 1992. 622p.

The Oxford Dictionary of Quotations. 5th ed. New York: Oxford University Press, 1999. 1152p.

Oxford English Dictionary. 2d ed. 20 vols. New York: Clarendon Press/Oxford University Press, 1989. Additions series, v. 1– . 1993– . Also available online.

Oxford English Dictionary on CD-ROM. [CD-ROM]. 2d ed. Version 2.0. New York: Oxford University Press, 1999.

Partridge, Eric. *Dictionary of Slang and Unconventional English.* 8th ed. New York: Macmillan, 1984. 1400p.

Partridge, Eric. *A Dictionary of the Underworld, British & American, Being the Vocabularies of Crooks, Criminals, Racketeers, Beggars and Tramps, Convicts, the Commercial Underworld, the Drug Traffic, the White Slave Traffic, Spivs.* 3d ed. London: Routledge & Kegan Paul, 1968. 886p.

Periodical Title Abbreviations. 12th ed. 3 vols. Farmington Hills, Mich.: Gale Group, 2000.

Quotations Database. New York: Oxford University Press. Available online.

Randel, Don Michael, ed. *The New Harvard Dictionary of Music.* Cambridge, Mass.: Belknap Press of Harvard University, 1986. 942p.

Random House Historical Dictionary of American Slang. New York: Random House, v. 1– . 1994– .

Random House Unabridged Dictionary. [CD-ROM]. 2d ed. New York: Random House, 1993.

Random House Webster's College Dictionary. 2d ed. New York: Random House, 1999. 1571p. Also available: http://www.funkandwagnalls.com/dictionary.

The Random House Webster's Unabridged Dictionary. 2d ed., rev. and updated. New York: Random House, 1997. 2230p.

Respectfully Quoted: A Dictionary of Quotations Requested from the Congressional Research Service. Washington, D.C.: Library of Congress, 1987. 520p.

Reverse Acronyms, Initialisms & Abbreviations Dictionary. Farmington Hills, Mich.: Gale Group, 1972– . Annual.

Roget's II: The New Thesaurus. 3d ed. Boston: Houghton Mifflin, 1995. 1200p. Also available: http://www.bartleby.com/62.

Roget's International Thesaurus. 5th ed. New York: HarperCollins, 1992. 1141p.

Room, Adrian, ed. *Brewer's Dictionary of Phrase & Fable.* 16th ed. New York: HarperCollins, 1999. 1298p.

Sader, Marion, and Amy Lewis, eds. *Encyclopedias, Atlases & Dictionaries.* New Providence, N.J.: R. R. Bowker, 1995. 495p.

Stevenson, Burton Egbert. *The Home Book of Quotations.* 10th ed. New York: Dodd, Mead, 1967. 2816p.

Thesaurus of American Slang. Edited by Robert L. Chapman. New York: Harper & Row, 1989. 489p.

Third Barnhart Dictionary of New English. Edited by Robert K. Barnhart. New York: H. W. Wilson, 1990. 565p.

Thorndike, E. L., and Clarence L. Barnhart. *Thorndike-Barnhart Children's Dictionary.* Updated ed. Glenview, Ill.: Scott Foresman-Addison Wesley, 1999. 823p.

Thorndike, E. L., and Clarence L. Barnhart. *Thorndike-Barnhart Student Dictionary*. Rev. ed. Glenview, Ill.: Scott Foresman-Addison Wesley, 1997. 1302p.

12,000 Words: A Supplement to Webster's Third New International Dictionary. Springfield, Mass.: Merriam-Webster, 1986. 212p.

Webster's New World College Dictionary. 4th ed. New York: Macmillan USA, 1999. 1716p.

Webster's New World Student's Dictionary. Rev. ed. New York: Macmillan USA, 1996. 1040p.

Webster's Third New International Dictionary of the English Language, Unabridged. Springfield, Mass.: Merriam, 1961, 1996. 2783p. Also available on CD-ROM.

Wentworth, Harold. *American Dialect Dictionary*. New York: Thomas Y. Crowell, 1944. 747p.

World Book Dictionary. Millennium ed. Edited by Clarence L. Barnhart and Robert K. Barnhart. 2 vols. Chicago: World Book, 2000.

yourDictionary.com. Available: http://www.yourdictionary.com.

ADDITIONAL READINGS

Amato, Kimberly, and Karen Moranski. "Oxford English Dictionary: CD-ROM and Second Edition." *Reference Services Review* 18 (Spring 1990): 79-82, 86.

Amato and Moranski examine the advantages and problems of electronic access to the dictionary through the medium of CD-ROM and describe the merits of the second edition of the *OED*.

Berg, Donna Lee. *A Guide to the Oxford English Dictionary*. New York: Oxford University Press, 1993. 206p.

Part One of this two-part handbook to the *OED* is a step-by-step guide to the information found in typical *OED* entries. Part Two is a companion to the *OED* in dictionary format covering history, terminology, and persons who were influential in producing the dictionary.

Bibel, Barbara, and Victor Or. "Bilingual Dictionaries." *Reference Books Bulletin* in *Booklist* 92 (June 1 & 15, 1996): 1750-1752, 1754, 1756, 1758, 1760.

This is an extensive annotated list by language of dual-language print dictionaries. Most have been published since 1990 and are considered by the authors to be the best ones available for the languages most commonly spoken in the United States.

Grogan, Denis. *Dictionaries and Phrase Books*. London: Clive Bingley, 1987. 153p. (Grogan's Case Studies in Reference Work, v. 5).

Grogan gives students examples of reference questions involving the use of dictionaries and phrase books.

Hulbert, James Root. *Dictionaries: British and American*. Rev. ed. London: Andre Deutsch, 1968. 109p.

Hulbert gives a short history of English-language dictionaries with a discussion of the features of good dictionaries and how they are used. It is a good background source in spite of its age.

Isaacson, David. "New Word Sources: A Selective Annotated Bibliography." *Reference Services Review* 25 (Summer 1997): 53-64, 72.

This article surveys dictionaries that include definitions of recently coined words. It provides excellent descriptions of standard as well as specialized works.

Kabdebo, Thomas. *Dictionary of Dictionaries and Eminent Encyclopedias*. 2d ed. New Providence, N.J.: Bowker-Saur, 1997. 418p.

This is an annotated bibliography, arranged in dictionary format, of recent English-language dictionaries by topic and includes bilingual and electronic dictionaries. It replaces Kabdebo's earlier *Dictionary of Dictionaries*.

Kister, Kenneth F. *Kister's Best Dictionaries for Adults & Young People: A Comparative Guide.* Phoenix, Ariz.: Oryx Press, 1992. 438p.

This guide describes and evaluates all major U.S. dictionaries, along with Canadian and British English dictionaries. Coverage includes electronic dictionaries. It replaces Kister's earlier *Dictionary Buying Guide.*

Loughridge, Brendan. *Which Dictionary?: A Consumer's Guide to Selected English-Language Dictionaries, Thesauri and Language Guides.* London: Library Association, 1990. 177p.

This guide to dictionaries published in the United Kingdom includes standard, abridged, pocket, usage, regional, and learner's dictionaries, as well as thesauri. It is similar to *Kister's Best Dictionaries for Adults & Young People: A Comparative Guide,* listed above.

McArthur, Tom. *Worlds of Reference.* New York: Cambridge University Press, 1986. 230p.

This is a history of reference books from ancient to modern times. Chapters 10 and 11 cover the roots of lexicography, early alphabetization, and the emergence of English-language dictionaries.

The Reader's Adviser, A Layman's Guide to Literature. 14th ed. 6 vols. New Providence, N.J.: R. R. Bowker/Reed Reference Publishing, 1994.

Volume 1, chapter 3, has an annotated list of currently available English- and foreign-language dictionaries.

Rettig, James, ed. *Distinguished Classics of Reference Publishing.* Phoenix, Ariz.: Oryx Press, 1992. 356p.

These historical essays on classic reference works include several dictionaries such as the *OED* and the Merriam-Webster titles as well as Bartlett's *Familiar Quotations* and *Roget's Thesaurus.* The bibliographic publication histories are very useful.

Sader, Marion, and Amy Lewis, eds. *Encyclopedias, Atlases & Dictionaries.* New Providence, N.J.: R. R. Bowker, 1995. 495p.

This replaces two earlier books by Bowker, *General Reference Books for Adults* and *Reference Books for Young Readers,* and includes books in print as of spring 1994. Dictionaries are discussed and evaluated in Part Four—Dictionaries, Part Five—Electronic Reference Works, and Part Six—Large-Print General Reference Works.

Shipps, Anthony W. *The Quote Sleuth: A Manual for the Tracer of Lost Quotations.* Urbana, Ill.: University of Illinois Press, 1990. 194p.

Chapters on quotation compilations, concordances, English-language dictionaries containing quotations, poetry indexes, and single-author quotation books with tips for using them effectively are found in this manual.

Tomchyshyn, Terri. "Children's Dictionaries." *Reference Books Bulletin* in *Booklist* 97 (October 15, 2000): 475-77.

The author reviews 22 dictionaries designed for children in elementary grades, junior high, or high school. The annotations, which are detailed and evaluative, are arranged under four headings: Kindergarten to Grade 3; Grades 3-6; Grades 6-9; and High School.

Whiteley, Sandy, ed. *Dictionaries for Adults and Children.* Chicago: Booklist, American Library Association, 1991. 48p.

This is a reprint of two articles previously published in *Reference Books Bulletin*: "Desk Dictionaries," by Rashelle Karp (February 1, 1991) and "Children's Dictionaries," by Frances Corcoran (June 15, 1991). It contains comparative reviews of dictionaries in print and criteria for selection.

CHAPTER

18

ENCYCLOPEDIAS

Holly Crawford

USES AND CHARACTERISTICS

People seek general information on many topics, and often they go to a library to find that information. That library could be the local public library, a school media center, or a business information center located within a large corporation. The library could even be virtual, with access gained by using either the Internet or a stand-alone computer workstation. Typically, people have a broad idea of what subject information they seek and will commonly ask librarians general questions in an effort to narrow their focus. For example, a middle school student charged with the task of writing a term paper on Ellis Island might visit the school's media specialist and ask: "Do you have any books about Ellis Island?" A purchasing analyst with a Fortune 500 company might call his firm's information resource center and ask: "Where can I find a general overview of TQM (total quality management)?" And, a retired person living in Connecticut might approach the local public librarian and say: "I want to learn about the art of Bonsai; what sources can you recommend?" Although no single source exists to answer all of these questions, one type of reference tool—the encyclopedia—has historically endeavored to do just that. Whether the encyclopedia be a single volume on one specific subject, or a multivolume work such as the *New Encyclopaedia Britannica*, the goal remains implicit: to provide a summarized compendium of multidisciplinary knowledge in a verifiable, organized, and readily accessible manner that allows its users to meet their information needs first on a general level and then on a specific level by pointing them to more detailed sources of information. Kenneth Kister reinforces this: "Encyclopedias, in short, aim to encompass and codify that knowledge and information educated people deem essential or universally worth knowing."[1]

Jacques Barzun notes that "encyclopedias should be 'learned' and not blindly used: The childhood faith in *the* encyclopedia that happened to be the one large book of knowledge in the house should be replaced by a discriminating acquaintance with others."[2] Barzun's comments aptly describe the mixed perceptions many people have of encyclopedias. Although few would dispute their convenience, others, particularly those in academe, may not view them as scholarly works and may encourage students not to overuse them when engaging in research.

Given the varied role of encyclopedias and because they provide summary information, it is valuable to categorize the types of questions best answered through their use:

1. Ready-Reference Information: "What is the size of Jupiter? Where can I find a picture of a koala bear? Where can I see the Periodic Table of Elements?" These are types of questions suited to the encyclopedia.

2. General Background Information: "How does photosynthesis work? What construction techniques were used to build the Golden Gate Bridge?" As in the case of locating answers to ready-reference questions, one can also consult encyclopedias to garner background information. They are unique in that they give definitions, explain phenomena, and provide illustrations. They often list cross-references to related information located in other parts of the encyclopedia or include bibliographic citations to similar, yet more in-depth information found in outside sources.

3. "Preresearch" Information: Encyclopedias provide a useful launch point for learning basic research skills and for embarking on research itself. For a novice researcher, the encyclopedia provides an introduction to the organization and procurement of information. It allows the novice to make connections between topics and to see that all information lies in a broader context. Through this understanding, novices can readily seek out more substantive and focused sources of information, thus embarking on a path that could make them better researchers.

Kinds of Information Contained in Encyclopedias

Encyclopedias provide a well-organized overview of *selected* topics of major importance. They deliver a survey presentation, a snapshot of how topics are and were. Encyclopedias are written in an objective rather than an analytical style, imitating the textbook rather than the scholarly monograph. Although most people are familiar with the traditional, multivolume encyclopedia (like the *New Encyclopaedia Britannica*), other equally important types exist.

Single-Volume Encyclopedias

Single-volume encyclopedias like *The Cambridge Encyclopedia* deliver condensed, factual information, often with accompanying illustrations. Typically arranged in dictionary format without an index, single-volume encyclopedias are inexpensive alternatives to multivolume sets. They can be readily purchased by individuals for home use or by libraries seeking cost-effective ways of augmenting their core or ready-reference collections. Desktop versions, when available, are even more compact and inexpensive.

Encyclopedias for Children and Young Adults

Browsing through the children's section of any public library or large local bookstore, one will find several encyclopedias for children. Sometimes parents will use these encyclopedias as teaching tools for their pre-school-aged children. However, children most commonly learn about encyclopedias in elementary school. Children's encyclopedias tend to place more emphasis on format, illustrations, and pedagogical tools, perhaps as a way of making it easier for children to learn how to use them. Typically, the format of these encyclopedias mirrors those targeted to adults. The principal difference between the two lies in content. Children's encyclopedias are written for young readers, a domain that contains a variety of abilities and audiences. Consequently, one finds a variety of titles to choose from in both print and electronic formats. For example, World Book's *Childcraft* targets elementary school students, whereas Grolier's *Academic American Encyclopedia* targets young adults in grades 9 and up. *School Library Journal* regularly reviews[3] reference books written for children and young adults and occasionally highlights specific genres like encyclopedias, devoting pages to comprehensive and candid reviews of the latest versions.

Subject Encyclopedias

Subject encyclopedias, unlike their single- or multivolume counterparts having a broader scope, give more in-depth coverage to a specific field of knowledge. For help in choosing subject encyclopedias for purchase, one can consult the *ARBA Guide to Subject Encyclopedias and Dictionaries*. In addition, *Kister's Best Encyclopedias: A Comparative Guide to General and Specialized Encyclopedias* and Mirwis's *Subject Encyclopedias* provide an objective overview of subject encyclopedias.

Varying in price and size, subject encyclopedias can deliver depth and breadth of information not covered in general encyclopedias and can easily be used to augment the reference collection of a library. Inexpensive single-volume titles such as the *Encyclopedia of African-American Civil Rights: From the Emancipation to the Present* or the *Encyclopedia Sherlockiana: An A-Z Guide to the World of the Great Detective,* although highly specialized, can function as cost-effective alternatives that facilitate ready-reference access to subjects under-represented in the overall library collection. Some mid-sized sets, such as the *Gale Encyclopedia of Multicultural America* or *The Asian American Encyclopedia*, can also add immediate depth to a library's circulating collection, which may not represent these subjects adequately. And, unlike single-volume titles, multivolume sets can address their subjects in greater detail. Such titles can rival general multivolume encyclopedias in price. *McGraw-Hill Encyclopedia of Science and Technology* is a case in point. The 20-volume eighth edition lists at $1,995 in mid-2000. Finally, several subject encyclopedias, such as *The Simon and Schuster D-Day Encyclopedia: A Multimedia Exploration!*, have CD-ROM counterparts, which also vary in price.

Encyclopedia Yearbooks and Supplements

With the advent of electronic encyclopedias, yearbooks and supplements have become an even more important feature of encyclopedia publishing. Yearbooks have always functioned as "year-in-review" reference tools, providing users with either chronological or topical reports of the events and/or people that shaped the world in a given year. Yearbooks, such as the 2000 *Britannica Book of the Year*, also include a plethora of statistical data rivaling the information contained in *The World Almanac and Book of Facts*. It is important to note that yearbooks do not act as encyclopedia updates (although some, like *Britannica*, include articles that update those contained in the parent set); instead they are tools that complement the information contained within the encyclopedia, whether it be in print, on CD-ROM, or online.

Supplements, on the other hand, are designed to update print and CD-ROM encyclopedias, which are "current" only on the day they go to press. Web-based encyclopedias have no need for supplements, because information can theoretically be updated on a minute-by-minute basis. Although this level of currency makes Web encyclopedias attractive, subscribers have to be aware that they pay a premium for this service in their yearly access fees (generally higher than the cost of print or CD-ROM encyclopedias and their associated supplements).

Foreign-Language Encyclopedias

Foreign-language encyclopedias can provide a wealth of information about a particular country or culture and are invaluable additions to academic libraries. Like their American counterparts, foreign-language encyclopedias appear as single- or multivolume entities. Some, like Encyclopaedia Britannica's *Enciclopedia Hispanica*, are modeled after those published in the United States. Others, like the *Grand Usuel Larousse: Dictionnaire Encyclopédique*, use a format unique to their content. Some countries like Ukraine (*Encyclopedia of Ukraine*) and Japan (*Japan: An Illustrated Encylopedia*—the successor to the *Kodansha Encyclopedia of Japan*) publish English-language versions of their national encyclopedias that can be considered subject encyclopedias on other countries.

EVALUATION

Like dictionaries, encyclopedias are published to meet the general information needs of a particular group, such as school children or scholars. Unlike dictionaries, encyclopedias typically contain lengthy essays, compact factual discussions, and a variety of tools that teach research skills. Consequently, the writing style and syndetic structure of encyclopedias assume great importance when one attempts to assess their usefulness. Format, accuracy and objectivity, currency, and ease of use are other factors to keep in mind when evaluating specific titles.

Using Reviewing Tools

When evaluating any reference work for acquisition, librarians use a variety of reputable reviewing sources, including reviews written in scholarly journals or trade magazines (in either print or electronic form), books, or even colleagues. Before purchasing any encyclopedia, one should consult three widely accepted works, which contain hundreds of reviews of encyclopedias: *Kister's Best Encyclopedias: A Comparative Guide to General and Specialized Encyclopedias, Subject Encyclopedias,* and the *ARBA Guide to Subject Encyclopedias and Dictionaries. Booklist* annually publishes its encyclopedia update in *Reference Books Bulletin,* in addition to regular reviews of new titles. Given the increase in the number of encyclopedias for children and adults appearing in electronic format, it is likely that more and more journals will devote additional space to this topic in future issues. One should also consult other journals for reviews. Reputable titles like *Choice* and discipline-specific journals often include reviews of encyclopedias and can provide more in-depth or subject-specific insights than those found in *Booklist.* Trade magazines should not be discounted, either. *PC World* and *ZDNet-PC Magazine* regularly review new electronic products including CD-ROM and online encyclopedias. Finally, one can also speak to colleagues in similar institutions to ascertain their opinions before purchasing a new encyclopedia.

Scope

Focus or Purpose

The *focus* or *purpose* of an encyclopedia is generally found in its prefatory remarks. There, its editors should clearly delineate its intended audience, its scope, and its format. For example, with regard to content, the editors of the *Encyclopedia of African-American Culture and History* state: "It was the Board's opinion that it was far more important to reserve space for information about a wide range of African Americans and to preserve a record of achievement not covered elsewhere."[4] Reviews often describe the focus or purpose of encyclopedias and even point out where emphasis is placed. Some encyclopedias, such as Microsoft's *Encarta,* a CD-ROM product, place more emphasis on the visual than on the textual. *New Encyclopaedia Britannica,* on the other hand, values textual content above all.

Subject Coverage

With regard to multivolume general encyclopedias, coverage should be even across all subjects; however, it is important to note that some subjects, by their very nature, demand greater emphasis. It would also be naïve to assume that general encyclopedias do not have inherent biases. General encyclopedias published in the United States would contain far more information about the United States than they would about any other country. When assessing whether an encyclopedia is balanced with respect to subject coverage, one merely has to examine the length and depth of articles written on a variety of subjects. One also must take into account the extent to which current affairs are covered, and how.

Audience

Subject matter and age determine an encyclopedia's *audience*. Clearly, Routledge's *International Encyclopedia of Business and Management* sees its audience as adults who have a personal or professional interest in business. *Encyclopaedia Britannica* is appropriate for readers at the ninth grade level and above. *World Book*, however, states that its articles "meet the reference and study needs of students in elementary school, junior high school, and high school. Librarians, teachers, and the general public likewise turn to *World Book* to satisfy their everyday reference needs."[5] Although Microsoft's *Encarta* comes as standard equipment on many PCs today, thus implying that it is an encyclopedia appropriate for all age levels, older students and adults may find its content less substantive than that of *Britannica Online*.

Arrangement and Style

General multivolume encyclopedias typically follow a common format: alphabetical arrangement with associative cross-references and indexes. Alphabetization can vary between the word-by-word method, where *San Salvador* comes before *sandman*, and the letter-by-letter method, where *sandman* comes before *San Salvador*. In traditional print sets, bibliographies often follow articles or sections within long articles. Online versions, such as *Britannica Online*, take a different approach, building extensive bibliographies within the text and adding thousands of hypertext links.

Presentation style varies from encyclopedia to encyclopedia. Titles such as *Encyclopedia Americana* (the oldest American encyclopedia, first published in 1829) and *New Encyclopaedia Britannica's Macropaedia* emphasize breadth and depth. *Academic American* focuses on brevity and coverage of many topics. *World Book* touts its *Research Guide and Index,* which covers over 200 reading and study guides. The writing style of an encyclopedia must also be considered. Is it appropriate to the audience? Is it objective? Does it engage the reader?

The arrangement and style of an encyclopedia should enhance, not detract from, its content and accessibility. Because arrangement and style vary from title to title, evaluators should consider their diverse user needs and choose a variety of encyclopedias to meet those information needs.

Format

The *physical format* of an encyclopedia is inextricably intertwined with its accessibility and overall usefulness. An encyclopedia whose physical format looks daunting or appears confusing in spite of its content may dissuade potential users from choosing it. On the other hand, slick packaging might tell another tale: Looks can be deceiving. The key to evaluating an encyclopedia in terms of its physical format lies in understanding one's target audience. With regard to adult general encyclopedias, a plethora of photographs and illustrations and a dearth of content might indicate a lack of substance; however, in the case of encyclopedias for children, this scenario would be welcome, particularly if the photographs and illustrations are current and targeted to a child's viewpoint. Page layout also figures prominently. Minimal or excessive "white space," poor placement of illustrations, incorrect choice of fonts for headers and text, and densely-written user guides would again detract from content, no matter how scholarly or substantive it may be.

With the advent of CD-ROM and online encyclopedias, physical format now can be seen as having two facets: outside packaging and interface design. Plastic containers and glossy illustrations replace book bindings. Query boxes and radio buttons replace indexes and cross-references. Despite the shift in format, some of the criteria used to assess the physical format of a print encyclopedia apply when evaluating electronic versions. In the case of electronic versions, however, another variable comes into play: the computer screen and one's interaction with it. Today's CD-ROM and online versions of encyclopedias bear little resemblance to their ancestors, which were known for their non-intuitive interfaces and emphasis on showcasing the latest advancement in technology. Electronic versions now typically contain the full-text of their print counterparts with a variety of multimedia enhancements. Designers seem to be achieving a better balance between content and media and to be putting more effort into developing products that are as readily usable as print versions.

When evaluating media, it is important to ask what contribution their inclusion makes to the overall efficacy of the encyclopedia. Do video clips or sounds enhance the reference value of the encyclopedia, or are they merely intrusive? Do images, sounds, and text work together to provide a rich and substantive learning experience, or do they act disharmoniously, distracting the user from finding information or understanding better how the product works?

User-friendliness, or more specifically, the interface design of an electronic encyclopedia, plays the greatest role in terms of usability and accessibility. An interface may be at the "cutting edge" of technology, but if few can use it, what value does it have? Why should function be sacrificed in the name of form? Interfaces for electronic encyclopedias must be as intuitive as the usage guides and indexes included in their print counterparts. They must readily and effortlessly guide their users to desired information. The best online encyclopedia interfaces tend to mimic intuitive, yet simply constructed Web sites such as Yahoo's home page. With extensive online help features and a sparing use of graphics and search buttons, these interfaces do not intimidate even novice or computer-phobic users.

Ease of access to information in electronic encyclopedias is theoretically superior to locating information in print versions. With the presence of robust, Boolean-based search engines, the inclusion of controlled vocabulary, and the presence of quality authority control and indexing and abstracting, one can, in effect, access any word contained in an electronic encyclopedia through keyword searching. Using Boolean operators such as *and*, *or*, *not*, and *adj* (adjacent) can make a search more precise and productive; however, because many users do not have experience using Boolean logic, several current versions of electronic encyclopedias allow for *natural language* searching, where the users type in a question such as "What was England's role in the American Civil War?" and the search engine returns articles containing any of the question's key words (England, American, Civil, and War). Although this latter method lacks precision and yields a number of *false drops*, the users will presumably retrieve some relevant articles that could lead them to other related information. Some electronic encyclopedias even rank retrieved articles for relevance, thus allowing users to quickly discard irrelevant information.

One of the greatest advantages of electronic encyclopedias lies in their ability to be accessed by several people simultaneously. Whether it be a CD-ROM product mounted on a multi-use workstation or an online product accessed through a public access catalog or remotely through the World Wide Web, electronic encyclopedias have the ability to serve the information needs of a variety of people located in a variety of places. Although a library, in particular, would support such broad access, costs of providing such access play an important factor in determining if an institution should purchase an electronic encyclopedia instead of the print version. Libraries must own, maintain, and routinely upgrade computer hardware and, with respect to online encyclopedias, must have Internet access. Also, space considerations and user needs must be taken into account. If money or space were not considerations, libraries would certainly own both print and electronic versions of encyclopedias to best meet the needs of all users.

Some libraries now place all of their electronic reference tools under one Web-based umbrella. *WebLuis,* the online public access catalog for the Florida university system, allows Web access to university library catalogs, a variety of databases provided by FirstSearch and RLIN, and *Britannica Online*. Although the general public can access the library catalog, only registered members of the Florida university community can access, via patron identification number, the fee-based databases or reference tools.

Uniqueness

An encyclopedia is *unique* if it contains features that set it apart from other encyclopedias. The inclusion of a variety of reading guides and study aids makes *World Book* unique. The effective blending of sound, images, and text distinguishes Microsoft's *Encarta. New Encyclopaedia Britannica* has a *Propaedia*, a single volume that acts as an outline of knowledge. An encyclopedia can also be unique within the context of a library's reference collection. The presence of certain subject encyclopedias may bolster areas underrepresented in the circulating collection or may augment the broad, general information contained in a traditional, multivolume set like *Academic American*. Electronic encyclopedias might add further depth to a collection and provide users, especially those familiar with computers, with alternative means for accessing information.

Authority

As with any reference source, *authority*, or the staff responsible for the content, has immense value when one chooses to use or purchase the source. An examination of a source's prefatory remarks can reveal much about its authority and, thus, its worthiness. With regard to encyclopedias, the editorial board and contributors are deemed to be specialists in their respective fields. In the case of general, multivolume, adult-level encyclopedias, the editorial staff serves to review and revise authors' contributions so that they conform to the editorial guidelines typically set forth by the publishers. For example, there must be conformity in style and length. Author credit appears either at the beginning or at the end of each article and a separate list of authors and their credentials generally follows the prefatory remarks. Some articles may not provide an author credit; therefore, one might conclude that the editorial staff, in concert with a subject expert, wrote those pieces.

Accuracy

Accuracy and Reliability of Information

Although one would like to believe otherwise, reference works such as encyclopedias contain errors and misinformation. Copy editors overlook typographical errors and even the most diligent editors and authors can get their facts wrong. As with any source, librarians should not assume complete accuracy and reliability. Instead, they should choose an encyclopedia wisely and be mindful that they should look at other sources to verify information located in that encyclopedia.

Objectivity

Because encyclopedias have numerous contributors and because, in the case of general encyclopedias, they cover a broad range of subjects, users may initially assume that encyclopedias maintain an objective viewpoint. However, without examining an encyclopedia's prefatory material as well as its text and images, a librarian would be naïve to make such an assumption. Although the publishing industry has made great strides in the past decade to eliminate gender and racially biased language or stereotyped images from their publications, bias has not been eliminated entirely.

When reviewing an encyclopedia, a librarian should pay careful attention to what an article includes or omits. A librarian should also be concerned with balanced coverage and language. With respect to controversial issues such as the death penalty or abortion, does the article present both sides? Is inflammatory or neutral language used? A librarian must also consider photographs, illustrations, sounds, and digital images when evaluating an encyclopedia for objectivity. Do images portray women solely in traditional settings? Do multimedia encyclopedias developed in the United States devote equal media space to all ethnic groups?

Currency

Encyclopedias, like computers, lose value soon after they are purchased. Given the lengthy lead times for publication of print works, one could even posit that print encyclopedias lose value while in press. This poses a greater problem for publishers of multivolume sets than it does for those who produce single-volume or subject encyclopedias. It is a Herculean and economically infeasible task to revise a multivolume general encyclopedia yearly. Consequently, complete currency cannot be achieved with every annual update.

Electronic encyclopedias often provide a solution to the problem of currency. Online encyclopedias, in particular, have no limitations, other than those imposed by their producers, on the level and frequency of updates. CD-ROM versions, however, are limited by production schedules, cost, and space constraints. Kenneth Kister notes, "Like books, CD-ROMs can accommodate only so much content, and multimedia enhancements require huge amounts of memory that can quickly fill up a disc. When new content is added, something must be deleted or, barring that, a new disc created, diminishing a product's ease of use."[6]

Indexing (Access)

With regard to print encyclopedias, indexing remains the key means of *accessing* information. As pointed out in Chapter 4, indexes are tools that point users to required information. Reading guides, tables of contents, cross-references, and bibliographies should not be discounted.

Most encyclopedias have separate indexes, but tend to differ in terms of scope and subject subdivision. In the right half of Figure 18.1, the volume and the page numbers of the major references to "Irish language" are indicated following the main heading, preceded by an *or* reference to "Erse language, *or* Gaeilge language, *or* Gaelic language." References to specific uses of Irish language are indented underneath. A few entries above, "Irish Land League" is followed by a *see* reference to the term that is used in the index, "Land League." Some children's sets enhance accessibility with the inclusion of an index at the end of each volume. These indexes refer to pages within the volume as well as to related information in other volumes.

Internal cross-references also appear with varying levels of uniformity. In the example in the left half of Figure 18.1, "Irish Free State" and "Irish Gaelic language" are followed by clearly indicated *see* references. Within the text of the "Irish Literary Renaissance" article, the user is expected to understand that the capitalization of "YEATS" indicates that another article appears under this heading. Some encyclopedias present cross-references in a *see also* list at the end of articles. Other titles provide both internal cross-referencing and separate lists of related articles. With regard to electronic versions, internal hyperlinking appears to have replaced the *see also*; however, most products have separate indexes similar to those seen in their print counterparts. Again, the difference lies in the user's ability to click on an index term and go directly to the article or illustration and back to the index again with ease. With multivolume print sets, the user must constantly go back and forth between the index and the content volumes themselves, a method that often proves tiresome and inefficient.

Figure 18.1 Examples of encyclopedia cross-referencing and indexing. From the *Academic American Encyclopedia*, 1999 Edition. Copyright 1999 by Grolier Incorporated. Reprinted by permission.

Irish Free State: see IRELAND, HISTORY OF.

Irish Gaelic language: see CELTIC LANGUAGES.

Irish Literary Renaissance

The Irish Literary Renaissance, also known as the Irish Revival and the Celtic Renaissance, was a literary movement sparked by a growing consciousness of a Celtic identity separate from English influence; it was bound up with Ireland's struggle for political independence. Beginning toward the end of the 19th century and continuing into the early decades of the 20th century, it was inspired by the past glories of the Gaelic bards, Irish mythology and legends, and the simplicity of peasant folkways. Among its most gifted writers were the poets William Butler YEATS, George William RUSSELL (pseudonym, Æ), and Padraic COLUM; the prose writers George MOORE and James STEPHENS; and the dramatists John Millington SYNGE, Lady GREGORY, Lennox ROBINSON, and Sean O'CASEY. The revival restored and preserved a literary past and led to the creation of an indigenous contemporary literature.

The renaissance began when the Gaelic League was formed in 1893 to rekindle interest in Ireland's cultural past and particularly in Gaelic language and literature. Such works as *The Ballad Poetry of Ireland* (1845) by Charles Gavan Duffy (1816–1903), the seminal two-volume *History of Ireland* (1878 and 1880) by Standish James O'Grady (1846–1928), and *A Literary History of Ireland* (1892) by Douglas Hyde (1860–1949) supplied an historical perspective for the movement. In 1888, Yeats collected and edited *Poems and Ballads of Young Ireland*, and in 1891–92 he was instrumental in founding the Irish Literary Society, which gave the movement a creative center. In mystical poems such as those in *The Wanderings of Oisin* (1889), in symbolic plays like *The Land of Heart's Desire* (1894), and in stirring essays Yeats invoked the spirit of Irish myth and legend. In 1899, Yeats, Moore, Lady Gregory, and Edward Martyn (1859–1924) established the Irish Literary Theatre, a forerunner of the ABBEY THEATRE, where the plays of the movement were presented.

Bibliography: Boyd, E., *Ireland's Literary Renaissance* (1916; repr. 1968); Fallis, R., *The Irish Renaissance* (1967); Todd, L., *The Language of Irish Literature* (1989); Vance, N., *Irish Literature* (1990).

Irish Land Acts (Br.-Irish hist.)
history of
Ireland **21**:1014:2a
United Kingdom **29**:83:2b, 85:1a
role of
Gladstone **5**:293:3a
Parnell **9**:165:3a
Irish Land League (Irish agrarian org.): *see* Land League
Irish Land Purchase Act (1903): *see* Wyndham Land Purchase Act
Irish language, *or* Erse language, *or* Gaeilge language, *or* Gaelic language **6**:384:2b
major ref. in Languages of the World **22**:667:2b, 669:2a
classification **3**:17:2b; **5**:334:1b
development of dictionary by Royal Irish Academy **18**:286:1a
linguistic affinities with Scottish Gaelic **10**:566:3a
revival by Gaelic League **22**:670:1b
status in
Ireland **21**:1001:1b, 1004:2a
Northern Ireland **29**:130:1a
symbolization of independence and patriotism **22**:565:1b
use of ogham writing **8**:885:2a
for a list of related subjects see PROPAEDIA: Section 514
Irish languages (Celt.): *see* Goidelic languages

SELECTION

Purchasing an encyclopedia, whether it be a print, CD-ROM, or online version, is a major investment in terms of cost; with a print set, space constraints also can be an issue. With recent advances in technology and requests to make information widely accessible, many libraries are no doubt feeling pressured to purchase electronic encyclopedias. Part of this pressure also comes from publishers of encyclopedias, who see print encyclopedias as an endangered species. Alex Soojung-Kim Pang, author of "The Work of the Encyclopedia in the Age of Electronic Reproduction" observes: "The world in which printed encyclopedias were produced and consumed has vanished. The economics that control and constrain the production of encyclopedic knowledge have likewise changed radically."[7]

Electronic Options

Electronic versions of encyclopedias, especially those that are Web-accessible, have become more common and cost-effective since 1995. Their presence has also begun to change the nature of encyclopedia publication. Some publishers, such as Encyclopaedia Britannica, continue to publish and sell their multivolume print encyclopedias while simultaneously producing CD-ROM and DVD versions and offering both free and fee-based online versions. Funk & Wagnalls, however, ceased publishing a print version in 1997 and now offers only CD-ROM and online editions. It is unclear if other encyclopedia publishers will follow Funk & Wagnalls's lead. What is clear is that electronic versions have become commonplace in libraries. Users, especially younger ones, expect libraries to have resources such as encyclopedias either on CD-ROM or accessible through a Web-linked kiosk. Many universities have included Web-based encyclopedias in their suite of resources together with their online catalogs because of their ability to be accessed by a large number of users locally and remotely. What also makes many Web-based encyclopedias so attractive is their level of interactivity, inclusion of engaging multimedia tools, and links to a wealth of information located on the Web. Whereas print versions of encyclopedias provide users with a discrete amount of information, electronic versions can provide seemingly unbounded access. With some encyclopedia producers now offering free online access to their encyclopedias, libraries can choose to spend moneys previously earmarked for the purchase of print encyclopedias on other items.

The other electronic alternative, an encyclopedia on CD-ROM or DVD, is also a good choice and often a better one than online encyclopedias, some of which have currency and server stability problems. Nearly all of the CD-ROM/DVD encyclopedias offer multimedia (e.g., sound and video clips, Web links) and all cost less than $100.00 (as of 2000). Although fewer users can access CD-ROM/DVD encyclopedias at one time, their selection may be the best a library can make.

Cost alone, however, is not reason enough for a librarian to select an electronic version of an encyclopedia. Other factors such as available shelf space, preservation goals, and type and number of users figure into the calculus. It is incumbent upon the librarian to choose an encyclopedia that best addresses all of these issues. Table 18.1 is a chart of several common encyclopedia titles available today, showing alternative formats.

Determining Need in Different Library Settings

The needs of a library's users determine which encyclopedias a librarian should select for purchase. A business information center would probably not need *Childcraft*, just as a small public library probably would not purchase the *McGraw-Hill Encyclopedia of Science and Technology*. Librarians at large academic or public libraries face a different problem: how best to serve the varied needs of a large and diverse population.

Regardless of where they are located, people who seek information fall into one of three information-seeking categories: learners, users with general needs, and users with scholarly or specialized needs. These categories are not mutually exclusive and it is not uncommon to find a modicum of overlap. A doctor who consults a drug encyclopedia while at work might visit the local public library to obtain information about organic gardening.

Learners

Anyone can be a *learner*, and publishers of encyclopedias generally target their products to this individual. Encyclopedias play a didactic role regardless of the age of the learner. They provide a range of tools that can help a wide variety of people learn how to access, synthesize, and in some cases, analyze information. Encyclopedias also tend to present information clearly and briefly so that the learner will not feel overwhelmed or intimidated. Children's encyclopedias are probably the best examples of encyclopedias geared to learners. They provide

Table 18.1 Encyclopedia Format Comparison Chart

Encyclopedia	Print Edition	CD-ROM/DVD Editions	Online Editions
Academic American (Grolier)	2000 Edition (revised and updated)	Grolier Multimedia Encyclopedia on CD-ROM(c)	Grolier Multimedia Encyclopedia Online http://go.grolier.com
Childcraft (World Book)	2000 Edition (revised and updated)	Not available in either format	Not available online
Compton's Encyclopedia (Compton's Books and The Learning Company)	2001 Edition (revised and updated)	Compton's Interactive Encyclopedia 99 (c)	Compton's Encyclopedia Online http://www.comptons.com/encyclopedia
Encarta (Microsoft)	Not available	Microsoft Encarta Encyclopedia Deluxe 2001 (c)	Microsoft Encarta Online http://encarta.msn.com
Encyclopedia Americana (Grolier)	Year 2000 Edition (revised and updated)	Encyclopedia Americana 1999 (c)	Encyclopedia Americana Online http://go.grolier.com
Funk & Wagnalls (Versaware Technologies)	Ceased publication in 1997	Funk & Wagnalls Multimedia Encyclopedia 1999 (c,d)	Funk & Wagnalls Online http://www.funkandwagnalls.com
The New Book of Knowledge (Grolier)	Year 2000 Edition (revised and updated)	Not available in either format	The New Book of Knowledge Online and NBK News http://go.grolier.com
New Encyclopaedia Britannica (Encyclopaedia Britannica)	15th Edition, 1999 (revised and updated); 2000 Book of the Year available	Britannica CD 2000 Deluxe (c)	Britannica Online http://www.britannica.com (free version) Encyclopaedia Britannica Online http://www.eb.com (fee version)
World Book (World Book, Inc.)	2000 Edition (revised and updated)	World Book Millennium 2000 (c); World Book Macintosh Edition (c); World Book Discoveries (d) NOTE: (c) = CD-ROM format (d) = DVD format	World Book Online http://www.worldbookonline.com

only the most basic information, include a multitude of illustrations, and use vocabulary that allows children not only to expand their own vocabulary but also to locate information in other sources. Adult encyclopedias can also aid learners. Research and study skills guides can act as mini-refresher courses for an older adult who is returning to college after graduating from high school thirty years earlier, or they can help a high school senior choose a topic for a term paper.

Users with General Needs

People who need brief factual information or leads to sources about a particular topic qualify as users with *general* needs. Unlike learners, general users will not consult an encyclopedia's research guides but rather will focus on locating information quickly and easily. To meet those needs, librarians should acquire encyclopedias whose emphasis is on breadth of subject coverage as opposed to those that emphasize scholarly depth and treatment of subject matter.

Users with Scholarly or Specialized Needs

Although users with *scholarly* or *specialized* needs might find some information of value in a general, multivolume encyclopedia, it appears more likely that subject encyclopedias would be a better choice. A doctoral candidate in library history would obviously benefit by access to the *Encyclopedia of Library History*, and the library and information science librarian would undoubtedly choose that for inclusion in the reference collection. Because the University of California at Davis has the only undergraduate program in enology in the United States, it would necessarily follow that its university library would acquire encyclopedias about wine and wine-making.

Which subject encyclopedias a librarian chooses to acquire depends entirely on the needs of the library's users. However, it would be foolish for most public and academic libraries not to include a variety of subject encyclopedias in their collections. New titles can always be added when user needs change.

Cost

Cost plays a major role in the acquisition of any library material. Encyclopedias, by their very nature, can be viewed as investment pieces, and their acquisition should not be a cavalier matter. As is the case with most reference sources, publishers price encyclopedias according to their use. Academic and nonprofit institutions buy at a discount; commercial or individual users pay retail price. Annual updates and supplements are often purchased as separate items. Some publishers of multivolume sets such as the *McGraw-Hill Encyclopedia of Science and Technology* even offer compact, one-volume versions containing material extracted from the larger set. As of 2000, McGraw-Hill offered several compact volumes, including the *McGraw-Hill Encyclopedia of Engineering* and the *McGraw-Hill Encyclopedia of Physics*. These one-volume titles allow a smaller library to grow or vary its collection cost-effectively.

With regard to print encyclopedias, there is a tacit understanding that they lose their usefulness, especially with regard to currency, within a short period of time. Before the current trend of moving to electronic encyclopedias, libraries typically followed a pattern whereby they would purchase a new multivolume set on a fairly regular schedule determined by user needs and the amount of revision work undertaken by encyclopedia publishers from year to year.

Impact of Format on Costs

For years, librarians could only purchase print encyclopedias. Multivolume general sets cost the most and had limited shelf lives. However, once a library made the purchase, it owned it outright and could provide unlimited access to it. The downside lay in having to make this investment over and over because encyclopedias lose their currency rather quickly. With the advent of CD-ROM technology, libraries now theoretically have a lower-cost alternative to print encyclopedias. Moreover, libraries that choose CD-ROM encyclopedias instead of print versions can readily afford to purchase new CD-ROM encyclopedias every year, thus making a significant improvement in the area of currency. Like their print counterparts, the purchase of a CD-ROM gives the purchaser a de facto site license that permits unlimited access for an indefinite period of time. What is important to consider with regard to CD-ROMs is that they require expensive computer hardware to run them. In addition, given the current obsolescence rate of personal computers, librarians now have the added problem of upgrading or replacing this equipment every two to four years to keep up with the system requirements that new and improved software always requires. Therefore, librarians need to examine a variety of issues before deciding whether to abandon print encyclopedias in favor of CD-ROM counterparts.

Online encyclopedias add a different dimension to the equation. Previously, online encyclopedias, like other online databases housed under a system like Dialog, charged hourly connect fees in addition to the Internet connect fees incurred by a "networked" library. With fees prohibitive for the small library, online encyclopedias were not a viable alternative to print or CD-ROM versions. Today, it is not uncommon to see online encyclopedias included as one of the choices provided by an academic or large public library Web-based online public catalog. Online encyclopedia producers can even negotiate a site-specific contract. Often public and academic libraries form consortia that allow for the purchase of an online encyclopedia site license for a yearly flat fee. All the members of a consortium can access the encyclopedia electronically, yet no single member carries the burden of paying the fee.

In October 1999 Encyclopaedia Britannica made a bold move: Through its electronic resources division Britannica.com began to offer the full text of *Encyclopaedia Britannica* online at no cost. Although other encyclopedia producers have yet to follow suit, the issue of access is far from solved. As in the case of CD-ROMs, access to online encyclopedias entails a costly and long-term investment in computer hardware. Again, it is important to weigh potential benefits and liabilities before purchasing and/or accessing any encyclopedia, whether it be print, CD-ROM, or online.

IMPORTANT GENERAL SOURCES

This section focuses on general encyclopedias typically purchased by school, public, or academic libraries. Although there are many subject encyclopedias, only three that have broad coverage are discussed. For further titles not described in this section, the reader is referred to sources listed in the additional readings.

Encyclopedias for Children and Young Adults

Although targeted at primary and secondary school students, *World Book Encyclopedia* prides itself as being suitable as a "family reference tool" that is also used by "librarians, teachers, and the general public to satisfy their everyday reference needs."[8] The 2000 revision of *World Book* contains twenty-two volumes, more than 14,000 pages, over 17,000 signed articles, and 28,000 illustrations (photographs, maps, charts, timelines, graphs, diagrams, and art). The 2000 edition contains 112 new articles, 1,500 revised articles, and more than 160 new or revised maps. More than 3,700 authors contributed to this revision.

World Book's strength lies in its ability to help a wide variety of users find information quickly and effectively. All subjects are arranged alphabetically using the word-by-word method. Cross-references also play a significant role in this alphabetical arrangement. With two exceptions, every article that begins with a letter of the alphabet will be located in a single volume devoted to that letter. Topics and subtopics are shown in boldface within or beside articles, and page numbers and guide words appear at the top of every page. Articles vary in length and treatment depending on the subject matter and intended audience. The "mouse" article targets young readers and includes age-specific vocabulary, whereas the "cell" article targets advanced readers. Many of the lengthier articles, like the "leaf" article, use a graduated approach; that is, its authors use simple concepts and vocabulary at the beginning of the article and build toward incorporating more advanced ideas and vocabulary at its conclusion. Technical terms such as those found in the "moon" article are italicized and their meanings given within the context of the sentence or within parentheses. Related reading lists often appear at the end of articles and are often split into two levels, easy and advanced.

World Book conveys a lot of its information in tables, graphs, and charts, which are set apart from the text on a given page. This method makes the layout more visually appealing and acts as a vehicle for helping its readers digest what they have read thus far. The "tree" article has a section on "How a Tree Grows," complete with capsulized information and a large-scale detailed illustration of the cross-section of a tree. The illustrated timeline within the "History of Classical Music" section not only shows significant dates but provides factoids about specific musical milestones and beautiful illustrations depicting the development of musical instruments throughout the ages.

Another great strength of *World Book* is its ability to be used as a learning and instructional tool. Lengthy articles are often followed by an outline of the article for quick review purposes, related entries, and a list of study questions. This format mimics that often found in primary and middle school textbooks. Volume 22 contains over 200 research guides and a 150,000-entry index. It also includes an instructional section, "A Student Guide to Better Writing, Speaking, and Research Skills." Students can take advantage of this section to get advice on how to prepare for an oral report or how to use other reference sources.

World Book is also available as a CD-ROM called *World Book Millennium*. There are several editions of this product, including the *Standard Edition* and the *Deluxe Edition*. Viewed as favorably by librarians as its print counterpart, it is compatible with Windows 95/98/NT. These CD-ROM products are unique in that they contain the complete text of the print counterpart plus audio, video, animation, pictures, maps, and links to Internet sources. The *Standard Edition* includes every article from the *World Book Encyclopedia* plus thousands more and a feature called "Surf the Millennium," which allows users to search on simulated Web sites for each century. It also includes a free year of updates, plus a 60-day subscription to *World Book Online*. The *Deluxe Edition* has all of the aforementioned features plus more multimedia (videos, maps, 360-degree panoramas, photos, and sound) as well as a homework tool kit and research wizards. World Book also offers a DVD version, *Discoveries*, but that does not derive its content from *World Book Encyclopedia*. Instead, World Book takes its content from "one of Europe's best-selling encyclopedias" (but fails to identify the actual source) and offers its users a plethora of images, sounds, and animation. Users can search thematically, chronologically, or via subject. Also included are tips for research reports. World Book has also developed a version for the Macintosh, aptly titled *World Book Macintosh Edition*. It includes all articles contained in the print version, but also has features not offered in the Windows version, such as virtual reality tours, a quiz wizard, and a distance calculator. Macintosh users also get a year's online subscription. *World Book Online* contains the complete contents of the print set plus 3,700 more articles, as well as links to periodical articles and Web sites.

Since 1922, *Compton's Encyclopedia* has remained consistent in terms of its original objectives. Aimed at upper-elementary and middle-school-aged children, *Compton's* can be used in school or at home. The 2001 edition has 26 volumes, containing more than 37,000 articles covering over 11,000 pages and 22,500 illustrations, of which 67% are in color. The editors significantly added to and updated the Fact-Index, the 26th volume of the set, which contains the index to the entire set; over 30,000 brief articles; and many tables, graphs, and charts.

Other notable features include "Exploring," a list of questions that introduce each volume; timelines; "Here and There," a guide that organizes information in each volume and lists, by subject, articles and page numbers; and "Previews," tables of contents in longer articles that help users find major subdivisions located within those articles.

Compton's strength lies in its emphasis on being used as a curricular tool. Many of the articles conclude with bibliographies of related sources whose reading levels are aimed at eight-to-fourteen-year-olds. However, the numerous pictures, some of which are marginal in quality, tend to distract the user's attention from the textual content. At the beginning of each volume, users can find a study guide containing study questions within specific subject areas. The study guide also includes page numbers within the volume where users can locate the requisite answers.

In 1989 Compton's introduced the first CD-ROM version not only of its own encyclopedia, but of any encyclopedia. Given its long-term experience with this medium, one would expect consistency of quality, particularly with respect to the most recent releases. *Compton's Interactive Encyclopedia 1999 Edition* has a user-friendly interface and a powerful Boolean-based search engine that provides search results as a user's search progresses. Like other CD-ROM encyclopedias, *Compton's* also incorporates videoclips, sound clips, and Web links to many of its articles.

The multimedia aspect of *Compton's* tends to disappoint, especially when one considers its history and compares it to newer competitors like *World Book*, *Encarta*, and *Grolier's*. Péter Jacsó describes some of these shortcomings in his June 1999 "CD-ROM Currents" column for *Computers in Libraries*: "*Compton's* may have the most pictures among the encyclopedias, but quantity is at the expense of quality. There are still lots of mediocre pictures from an unidentified collection."[9] *Compton's* also provides a freely accessible online version. One can search for keywords or Boolean combinations of terms, browse an alphabetical list of articles, examine articles in broad topic areas (e.g., Geography, Living Things), or use a search wizard.

Unlike *Compton's*, which is more often used by teachers and librarians as a teaching tool, Grolier's twenty-one-volume *The New Book of Knowledge* (*NBK*) can be used by elementary and middle-school students as a self-teacher. It includes a variety of activity projects as well as stories and poems that users can read aloud. Revised every October since its inception in 1911, content is determined by the editorial staff, who review public school curricula to identify trends that should be addressed in the next revision of *NBK*. Since 1992, *NBK* has been undergoing a major overhaul with respect to content, layout, and images. Subject areas receiving special attention include children's literature, health, and U.S. government. Volumes B, C, N, and T have also been targeted for significant revision. For the 2000 edition, the editors revised over 5,500 pages of text and added 4,400 new photographs, illustrations, and maps. Illustrations now make up 40% of the content, of which 90% are in color. The editors included 1,870 new and/or revised articles. The volume entitled "Home and School Reading and Study Guides" (written for parents and teachers) recommends more than 5,000 fiction and nonfiction children's and young adult titles. It strives to relate encyclopedia content to elementary school curricula and includes twelve activities that teach basic research skills. Attractive in appearance and child-focused in layout (larger fonts than those used in standard encyclopedias), the 2000 revision of *The New Book of Knowledge* has made special efforts to make better use of outlines, charts, graphs, and timelines. The one area that the editors have chosen not to change is the index. Unlike all other encyclopedias, every volume of *NBK* contains an index—printed on blue paper to separate it from the volume's contents—which is cross-referenced to the contents of the entire encyclopedia. To make *NBK* even more child-friendly, its editors have put keywords in boldface, used non-glare paper, and made each volume a stand-alone (letters of the alphabet are not split between volumes). In addition, all of the indexes are brought together in Volume 21 to form an 85,000-entry cumulative index. Volume 21 also has a section called "Dictionary Entries," a series of short biographies or factoids on different topics.

In 1998, *NBK* introduced an online counterpart, *The New Book of Knowledge Online*. Broken into two sections—NBK News and the encyclopedia—*NBK Online* mimics the best features of the print version of *NBK* and adds many multimedia tools to enhance a child's learning experience. A large font size, an uncluttered interface, and a simple navigation feature make it easy for children to move readily between sections. NBK News includes NewScoops (weekly current events stories), lesson plans, Word Challenge (an interactive vocabulary builder), links to related encyclopedia articles, crafts, puzzles, games, and a teacher's guide. NBK News is updated weekly, and news stories are archived for future access. The encyclopedia section has over 9,000 articles, 8,300 article-to-article links, and over 11,000 illustrations. It is organized with alphabetical browse, subject browse, and search functions. Users can search via article titles or via full text. Picture quality is excellent and links to Web sites have been screened by *NBK's* editors. *NBK* is also available through the *Grolier Online* gateway (discussed in the following section).

Although several smaller multivolume sets are also available for children and young adults, the best is clearly *The Oxford American Children's Encyclopedia,* published by Oxford University Press and aimed at children aged eight to thirteen. Revised in 1999, this highly regarded nine-volume set reflects a global perspective in tone and subject coverage. It also provides broader coverage of international issues than do its American counterparts. Its layout demonstrates a good balance between form and function, and its evenhanded use of graphics complements the text. The 1999 revision places great emphasis on science and technology. It also includes a gazetteer, a world history timeline, extensive cross-references, and numerous photos and illustrations. Articles contain word definitions so that users can expand their vocabulary. Reasonably priced, *The Oxford American Children's Encyclopedia* remains a logical choice for school-aged children.

Another thoughtful print encyclopedia for children is *The World Book Student Discovery Encyclopedia.* Designed for elementary-school-aged children, its thirteen volumes have an alphabetical arrangement, color-coded articles, and colored backgrounds for special feature articles. Most articles are brief and cover no more than half a page. Photos and/or illustrations often accompany the articles; most relate well to their associated subject matter. The editors also took care to place articles into categories most children would understand. Therefore, an article about North American Indians would come under Indians—North American. There are few cross-references, and this poses an occasional problem (oil, for example, is not cross-referenced with petroleum). The 2000 edition covers 2,464 pages and costs under $400.

There are several single-volume encyclopedias available for children and young adults as well. The 1998 edition of *The Kingfisher Children's Encyclopedia* contains over 400 brief, alphabetically arranged entries on a broad range of subjects. The *DK Children's Illustrated Encyclopedia* contains hundreds of well-crafted illustrations and sharp photographs, as well as 450 main entries. One single-volume encyclopedia—*Oxford Family Encyclopedia*—targets secondary school students, although the prefatory matter indicates that college students and families might find it useful. First published in 1997, this encyclopedia places emphasis on six core subjects: science, technology, English, history, humanities, and contemporary politics. It contains 13,000 entries, 2,500 biographical profiles, and over 1,100 illustrations. A ready-reference guide of tables and charts follows the main entries. Written beautifully and demonstrating sophistication with respect to design, *Oxford Family Encyclopedia* should become a favorite of users.

Although there are several encyclopedias on CD-ROM aimed at elementary school children, many tend to be mediocre. Therefore, parents, librarians, and teachers may be well-advised to consider introducing younger students to CD-ROMs such as *Microsoft Encarta* and *World Book Millennium Edition,* which traditionally target an older audience. Although the vocabulary may be too advanced for some young readers, parents, teachers, and librarians can still make use of the multimedia aspects of these CD-ROMs.

Encyclopedias for Adults

The most commonly known encyclopedias for adults include *New Encyclopaedia Britannica, Encyclopedia Americana, Academic American Encyclopedia,* and *Funk & Wagnalls New Encyclopedia.* The differences among these four general, multivolume sets lie in length, presentation, style, and size. The first two titles listed qualify as full-length sets and the last two as mid-length.

The largest of the multivolume English-language general encyclopedias, *New Encyclopaedia Britannica* is considered by many to be the most scholarly. On October 19, 1999, Encyclopaedia Britannica Inc.'s electronic resources division, Britannica.com, announced that it would make the entire text of *Encyclopaedia Britannica* available free of charge within the company's Web site. Encyclopaedia Britannica continues to publish a print edition and its publisher Paul Hoffman has stated: "There is a place for books alongside all of the digital formats, and many people around the world still want books."[10] The 1999 revision, published in fall 1998, contains thirty-two volumes and comes in three parts: the *Propaedia*, the *Micropaedia*, and the *Macropaedia*. The single-volume *Propaedia* (volume 30) acts as an "outline of knowledge." The twelve-volume *Micropaedia* serves as the ready-reference portion of the encyclopedia, and the seventeen-volume *Macropaedia* contains lengthy, detailed articles. The *Index* to the 1999 set comes in two volumes. CD-ROM and online versions are also available and purchasers can also buy *Britannica Book of the Year* separately.

The *Propaedia* serves as "a topical guide to the contents of *Encyclopaedia Britannica*, enabling the reader to carry out an orderly plan of reading in any field of knowledge or learning chosen for study in some depth."[11] Although this is indeed correct, the *Propaedia*, or "outline of knowledge," can seem daunting to the uninitiated. It has a unique structure that allows the user to find relationships and connections within and across disciplines and thus to relevant information in the *Micropaedia* and *Macropaedia*. Broken into 10 parts, 41 divisions, and 177 sections, this structure can act as a study guide. The *Propaedia* also contains lists of the approximately 4,300 contributing authors of signed articles and the 2,600 *Micropaedia* subject experts who did not also contribute signed articles. In comparison, *Britannica's Index* includes over 215,000 entries with more than 500,000 references and cross-references and provides ready access to the information contained in the *Micropaedia* and the *Macropaedia*. Whereas the *Index* tells the user where to find information, the *Propaedia* tells the user what information can be found.

The 1999 revision of *Britannica's Micropaedia* has 64,254 brief entries designed primarily for ready-reference. These entries are arranged alphabetically using the word-by-word method. The *Micropaedia* can be used as a resource on its own or as a support resource for the *Macropaedia*. Several entries conclude with bibliographies of scholarly research material. The structure of the *Micropaedia* facilitates easy access to the information contained within. Entries for individuals follow certain conventions. For example, individuals of Eastern origin will have their entries listed with the surname preceding the personal name (Deng Xiaoping, Nguyen Cao Ky). Certain titles, such as those for institutions or structures, also receive special treatment with regard to entry arrangement (the Tower of London is listed as London, Tower of). Cross-references have several functions within the *Micropaedia*. They can act as referents to alternate names or spellings or operate as *see also*, *see under*, *q.v.* (quo vide—"which see," singular), or *qq.v.* (quae vide—"which see," plural) within or following the conclusions of articles. Page format tends toward the crowded, with little white space, use of smallish fonts, and illustrations.

Britannica's Macropaedia has 672 detailed survey articles averaging 26 pages in length. Some articles even exceed 100 pages. A bibliography follows every article. Like the *Micropaedia*, page layout tends to be dense, although sidebars help to break it up. The *Macropaedia* incorporates larger illustrations and several color-insert plates; however, *Britannica*, in spite of adding more graphics to the 1999 version, will never rival *World Book* in terms of number of photographs, images, and illustrations used.

Another tool connected to *Britannica* is its *Book of the Year*. Purchased separately, this single volume includes vast statistical information in the "World Data" section, a collection of current facts and figures for 217 countries and dependencies of the world. Because *Britannica* does not cover statistical information in depth in its *Propaedia*, *Micropaedia*, and *Macropaedia*, it is imperative for libraries to order *Book of the Year*. *Book of the Year* also contains a series of articles on recent noteworthy events. Further information about yearbooks can be found in Chapter 15.

Although locating information in the *New Encyclopaedia Britannica* can be difficult or intimidating for some, the depth and breadth of scholarship contained within outweigh these difficulties. Nevertheless, because CD-ROM and online versions eliminate the need to move through multiple print volumes, libraries that can afford to purchase and maintain a computer network may want to consider switching from the print set to an electronic version to give users easier access to information housed in what many deem the premier English-language encyclopedia produced today.

New Encyclopaedia Britannica, as mentioned earlier, also comes in CD-ROM and Web versions. *Britannica CD 2000 Deluxe Edition*, a reasonably priced product, requires a Pentium processor PC running either Windows 95 or 98. It contains the entire text of the *New Encyclopaedia Britannica*, the 1999 *Britannica Book of the* Year, more than 125,000 Internet links via *Britannica Online*, photos, maps, illustrations, and *Merriam-Webster's Collegiate Dictionary*, 10th edition.

Britannica Online, the Web version of *New Encyclopaedia Britannica*, maintains the high standards that are the hallmark of the print version and augments what is available in the print edition. Using a Netscape Windows format, *Britannica Online* contains over 72,000 entries, a wealth of graphics, images, tables, and figures, along with a powerful Boolean-based search engine that can be readily used by novice or advanced searchers. *Britannica Online* also differs from the print version in terms of new features offered. Included are a browsable *Propaedia* (a hierarchical list of subjects that allows the user to scan quickly the scope, contents, and organization of the *Encyclopaedia Britannica*); *Merriam-Webster's Collegiate Dictionary*, a *Week in Review* section (for current events); full text articles from magazines such as *The Economist*, *Commonweal*, *Time*, and *Discover;* and searchable and extensive databases of the nations of the world and *Britannica Book of the Year* articles. There are two versions of the online service, one free and one fee-based. The former has banner ads and has a less-robust Boolean-based underlying search engine. The latter contains no ads, allows searching by all Boolean operators, and provides alternate search terms. In an effort to make the textual content of *New Encyclopaedia Britannica* more accessible, Britannica.com introduced, in May 2000, *Britannica Traveler*, a wireless Web-clipping application for use in the Palm family of personal digital assistants. For a nominal monthly fee, users can access the entire 45-million word encyclopedia.

First published by Grolier in 1980, *Academic American* contrasts greatly with *New Encyclopaedia Britannica*. Focusing more on breadth of coverage than on detail, *Academic American* (2000) has more than 45,000 articles compared to 672 in *Britannica's Macropaedia*. It also comprises only thirty volumes and its index contains fewer than 250,000 entries. This does not mean that *Academic American* is not, in and of itself, a fine general encyclopedia; it is a mid-length encyclopedia, whereas *Britannica* is a full-length one.

Placing information in context or depicting cross-discipline relationships does not figure in the scope and treatment of *Academic American*. Bibliographies accompany only half of the articles, yet there are thousands of cross-references sprinkled throughout. The editorial staff sees its mission as disseminating information clearly and succinctly, and it appears to do it rather well; overall, the information seems factual and up-to-date. For the 2000 version, 5,750 new and revised articles were added as well as 114 new subjects and 660 photographs, illustrations, and maps. Its Periodic Table contains Element 112. The 23,000 illustrations (75% in color)—one-third of the space used in the entire encyclopedia—make *Academic American's* layout more attractive and less compact in terms of density of text on a page than *Encyclopaedia Britannica*.

Academic American is available as a CD-ROM and online under the title *Grolier Multimedia Encyclopedia*. Using a Boolean-based search engine and an easy-to-use interface, the *Grolier Multimedia Encyclopedia* on CD-ROM provides a wonderful partnership between text and media. The 2000 edition continues to make use of article hotlinks, addressing one of Péter Jacsó's earlier complaints: "Hotlinks to articles are now indicated by highlighting the word or phrase in an article that links to another article. For example, in the article about Franz Liszt, the phrase "Hungarian music" is highlighted, meaning that there is an article titled "Hungarian music" that you can jump to."[12] One can also search Internet sites by using the

Grolier Internet Index, which is updated monthly. With a few minor exceptions, the online version mirrors the CD-ROM, but it has the advantage of being more current and the possibility of being accessed by a larger number of simultaneous users.

The first encyclopedia published in the United States (1829), *Encyclopedia Americana* prides itself on its focus on U.S. history, geography, and biography as well as on science and technology. This is not to say that it sacrifices coverage of other countries or topics to make room for these emphases; *Encyclopedia Americana* is second only to *Britannica* in terms of depth and breadth. Several articles run to 100 pages (many even have their own table of contents), cross-references are numerous, and bibliographies appear at the end of longer articles as well as at the end of major sections within them. Like *Britannica, Encyclopedia Americana* uses illustrations sparingly; the majority are black and white even though more color photographs were added in 1999. But, unlike *Britannica,* only a fraction of *Encyclopedia Americana's* articles are signed. The thirty-volume 1999 version includes 45,000 articles; 23,000 illustrations (20 % in color); 1,300 maps; and a 353,000-entry index. Despite its philosophy of "continuous revision," *Encyclopedia Americana's* currency appears to be a weak point. For example, the coverage in the "American Literature" section ends in the late 1960s. No mention of the 1994 Northridge earthquake is made in the article on "California." This problem is less apparent in the CD-ROM version. *Encyclopedia Americana* on CD-ROM ranks alone with *Encyclopaedia Britannica* in terms of comprehensive coverage. Not only does it include the information contained in the thirty-volume print set, it also houses *Merriam Webster's Collegiate Dictionary, 10th Edition, Chronology of World History* (produced by Helican Publishing Company), and Academic Press's *Dictionary of Science and Technology.* In addition, the *Grolier Internet Index* links more than 30,000 *Americana* articles to carefully chosen Web sites. And, like *Britannica* on CD-ROM, content, not the latest multimedia advancement, is showcased.

An online version of *Encyclopedia Americana* is offered, and online subscription rates vary according to the number of users. As is the case for most online encyclopedias, a subscription commitment gives the purchaser a substantial discount on the print version. *Encyclopedia Americana Online* allows keyword and Boolean-based searches; provides quarterly updates of encyclopedia articles and monthly updates of hypertext links; and includes access to *The Americana Journal,* a searchable current events database. It also offers over 6,000 bibliographies; 155,000 links to Web sites; and access to *The American Heritage Dictionary of the English Language, Third, Roget's II: The New Thesaurus, Third Edition,* and the contents of seventy-five magazines and journals. It should be noted that *Encyclopedia Americana* is one of a suite of online products offered through the *Grolier Online* gateway. In 1997 Grolier Inc. combined *Encyclopedia Americana* and *Grolier Multimedia Encyclopedia* for delivery on the Web. Selected in 1997 as the recipient of *Booklist's* "Reference Source of the Year" award, *Grolier Online* stays true to the standards established by its print counterparts. Although not as comprehensive in coverage as *Britannica Online,* it provides its users with access to information beyond that currently available in print versions. Since 1997, Grolier has added other products to its gateway, including *The New Book of Knowledge, Nueva enciclopedia Cumbre en línea, The New Book of Popular Science,* and *Lands and Peoples.*

For several years, *Funk & Wagnalls New Encyclopedia* had been known as the "supermarket" encyclopedia. However, when Microsoft decided to use its content as the foundation for its *Encarta* encyclopedia on CD-ROM, that stigma began to fade. Moreover, it also signaled the demise of the print version; *Funk & Wagnalls* issued its last edition in 1996.

Versaware Technologies, the company licensing *Funk & Wagnalls,* continues to produce CD and DVD versions titled *Funk & Wagnalls Multimedia Encyclopedia.* Compatible with Windows 95/98, the 1999 edition contains 27,500 articles, 9,000 illustrations, 553 maps, 46 videos, 51 animations, and 390 sounds. Content comes from the 1996 print edition; articles are revised and/or added when the need arises. For the 1999 edition, the editors added 200 new articles.

In late 1998, Versaware launched a free online version of *Funk & Wagnalls New Encyclopedia.* Under continuous redesign since then, the July 2000 edition showcases two areas, *Knowledge Center* and *Versabook Store.* The latter allows users to download e-books for a fee;

the former contains the entire encyclopedia, a dictionary, a media gallery, the Reuters News Center, a thesaurus, and an atlas. Users can search the various online resources simultaneously or choose to focus the search on one part such as the encyclopedia.

What differentiates this Web version from others, however, is the addition of a chat room for students and teachers and several aids for writing term papers. The interface is very engaging and easy to navigate. Searching the site is extremely easy and works primarily by keyword searching, although advanced Boolean searching is also available. The online help guides are extensive.

Microsoft Encarta Encyclopedia Deluxe 2001 [CD-ROM] has more than 42,000 articles (2,000 of which are new); 18,000 historical archive articles from 1938 to 1999; 21,500 Web links and "Further Reading" lists; 2,500 sound clips; and over 170 videos and animations. New features seen in this edition include a "Web Center," which extends searches conducted in *Encarta* into the World Wide Web; "Encarta Today," which places current events information collected from the Web into the "Encarta Encyclopedia" home screen; and "Researcher," which collects information from *Encarta* and the Web and cites sources as one searches. *Encarta 2001* retains several successful features such as natural language searching (introduced in 2000), a dynamic timeline, a curriculum guide, and access to *Encarta Online*. *Encarta* also comes in seven foreign editions, each of which is tailored to a specific country, region, or language group. With respect to interface design, *Encarta 2001* is the most user-friendly of all CD-ROM encyclopedias. It readily merges browsability, superior multimedia (including new panoramic and collage images), and online searching capabilities so that the user can easily access high-quality content. Monthly downloads from the Microsoft *Encarta* Web site are easy and quick. The only weakness noted appears to be the need to switch among three discs to take full advantage of all the multimedia. Not to be outdone by Web competitors like *Britannica Online*, Microsoft also has *Encarta Online Deluxe*, a Web-based version of *Encarta Encyclopedia Deluxe 2001*. All *Encarta* products are competitively priced.

With regard to encyclopedias written for a Canadian audience, *The Canadian Encyclopedia* does an admirable job of including information on a wide variety of Canadian personalities, places, events, and achievements. Each of the more than 10,000 articles is signed by its author. The CD-ROM version includes the full text of the encyclopedia in both English and French, French/English and English/French dictionaries, and other reference aids such as thesaurus, stylebook, and Internet links and updates. Although written in English, the *Canadian Encyclopedia* contains articles about and references to French-Canadian issues.

It should also be noted that there are a few free encyclopedias available on the Web. Although most focus on a specific subject or genre, some, like *Encyclopedia.com* (launched in 1998 by Infonautics Corporation) are true multisubject encyclopedias. *Encyclopedia.com* is actually the *Concise Columbia Electronic Encyclopedia* (3d ed.). Unabridged, it allows users free access to over 17,000 articles. Microsoft's *Encarta* is also available for free on the Web, but it is an abridged version.

Single-Volume Encyclopedias

Although the format of single-volume encyclopedias has become increasingly popular over the past few years, there are not many current editions or revisions from which to choose. Some print standards, like *The Random House Encyclopedia* (1990), have not been recently revised. The newest edition of *The Columbia Encyclopedia* (2000) includes more than 50,000 articles with nearly 1,500 new entries as well as fully updated existing entries and geographical entries that reflect the most recent political changes. This edition is also freely available on the Web. The third edition of *The Cambridge Encyclopedia* appeared in 1998. According to its publisher, Cambridge University Press, "the main aim of *The Cambridge Encyclopedia* is to provide a succinct, systematic, and readable guide to the facts, events, issues, beliefs, and achievements which make up the sum of human knowledge."[13] A daunting task, this encyclopedia nevertheless lives up to its aims: 1,302 pages long, it contains 36,000 entries, of which 26,000 are main entries presented in alphabetical order and 10,000 are ready-reference entries located in a 128-page guide at the back of the encyclopedia.

Subject Encyclopedias

Although there are numerous high-quality subject encyclopedias, the limits of a single chapter allow for discussion of only three important multidisciplinary titles: the *Gale Encyclopedia of Multicultural America*, *Encyclopedia of Multiculturalism*, and the *McGraw-Hill Encyclopedia of Science and Technology*.

Published in 2000 to meet the need for information about ethnicities in the United States, the second edition of the *Gale Encyclopedia of Multicultural America* contains over 100 signed articles, each of which focuses on a specific ethnic, ethnoreligious, or Native American group in the United States. The editorial staff used 1990 U.S. Census statistics in tandem with recommendations from an advisory board (made up of librarians and scholars well-versed in multiculturalism) as the basis for determining which groups would merit examination. Consequently, lesser-known groups such as Hmong-Americans and Ojibwa receive overdue recognition. Articles or essays range in length from 3,000 to 20,000 words and are arranged alphabetically.

Students looking for more detailed treatments would necessarily look to the *Encyclopedia of Multiculturalism,* published by Marshall Cavendish. First published in 1994 as a six-volume set, two additional volumes or supplements were published in 1998. The publisher aims to collect substantive information about groups of people (and specific issues related to those people) traditionally excluded from or marginalized by mainstream reference sources. The supplements include 584 new entries as well as updated appendixes, which include a timeline, a filmography, subject and resource lists, and a general index.

At the other end of the size and cost spectrum falls the twenty-volume *McGraw-Hill Encyclopedia of Science and Technology*. Unsurpassed in scope and coverage, the eighth edition, published in 1997, contains over 10% more coverage than the seventh edition, with 7,100 entries (of which 1,600 are new or revised) and over 13,000 illustrations (nearly 1,800 are new additions). Over 3,500 individuals contributed to this edition; 19 have won the Nobel Prize. In spite of having so many world-renowned experts, the *McGraw-Hill Encyclopedia of Science and Technology* is written to accommodate a wide variety of readers, from the layperson to the specialist. Specific disciplines, such as meteorology and physics, are covered in broad, survey articles. Each entry begins with a definition and a general overview of the topic. The entry then progresses from the general to the specific in an effort to provide comprehensive coverage of the topic. Bibliographies typically come at the end of an article. Pure science remains the focus of the eighth edition; there are no articles devoted to sociological, historical, and biographical aspects of science or technology. Over 60,000 cross-references are included. Perhaps the best feature of this subject encyclopedia is its organization. One can locate information using four methods: find an article alphabetically in its appropriate volume; consult the 170,000-entry index; browse the "Topical Index" (a list of all titles contained within a specific discipline); and use the "Study Guides." The last three features are found in Volume 20. The "Study Guides" are essentially outlines of six major disciplines: biology, chemistry, engineering and technology, geosciences, health, and physics. They aid students in their studies and also act as reference tools. A CD-ROM version (*McGraw-Hill Multimedia Encyclopedia of Science and Technology*, version 2.0, based on the eighth edition) is also available.

Supplementing the *McGraw-Hill Encyclopedia of Science and Technology* is the single-volume *McGraw-Hill Yearbook of Science and Technology*. Since 1962, these yearbooks have reviewed the previous year's scientific accomplishments and advancements. The 2000 edition of the *Yearbook* does not deviate from this tradition, and librarians would be well advised to purchase this volume as a means of maintaining currency in this area. If currency and space are of concern, McGraw-Hill's *AccessScience* might be a better choice. Launched in September 1999, *AccessScience* gives subscribers Web access to a fully searchable *McGraw-Hill Encyclopedia of Science and Technology*. Textual content is based on the 1997 print edition;

however, new and revised entries are added frequently, in some cases daily. Users can read breaking science news stories, view science research updates, and read more than 2,000 biographies of scientists. *AccessScience* offers competitive subscription rates based on the population size of a specific organization.

SEARCH STRATEGIES

As is the case with any reference source, knowledge of how and when to use that source plays a key role with respect to locating required information quickly and efficiently. Given the unique role of encyclopedias, having an understanding of how to use them properly has greater significance. Because no two encyclopedias are alike in terms of format and scope, librarians need to become familiar with as many as possible to best guide users in their selection. No one encyclopedia can meet every information need. Therefore, a librarian must conduct a reference interview with the user to ascertain what information is specifically needed. If the librarian determines that encyclopedias would be the best source, the information need can then be categorized into one of the three areas discussed earlier in this chapter: ready-reference, general background information, or preresearch information. Once categorization has been determined, a librarian can then choose an encyclopedia or encyclopedias that would best allow the user to locate the needed information.

With the advent of electronic encyclopedias, especially those in CD-ROM format or mounted on the World Wide Web, search strategies with regard, first, to selection of an encyclopedia and, second, to locating information contained within the encyclopedia have become more complex. First, users need to have some computer experience to conduct even the most simple searches. Although all electronic encyclopedias have some sort of help tool, a novice computer user would benefit from librarian instruction. The librarian can demonstrate how the search engine works and how to submit keyword queries so that the user can retrieve some relevant information. However, because all electronic encyclopedias are based on some form of Boolean searching, users can only exploit them fully if they understand the logic behind this method. Keyword searching is an easy way to locate some information, but more precise Boolean-based searching will yield retrieval sets that have a higher relevancy rate. Again, users, whether they be computer novices or experts, are encouraged to seek help from a librarian when using electronic encyclopedias for the first time.

Which Encyclopedia Should I Use?

Following are examples of questions users might ask librarians with regard to encyclopedias. Because encyclopedias are now available in four formats (print, CD-ROM, DVD, and online), the question itself will help the librarian determine not only which encyclopedia to choose, but in which format:

"Why are relations between the United States and Iraq strained?" This question requires an answer grounded in both past and current events. A Web-based encyclopedia such as *Britannica Online* would be the best choice if it is available because it contains the in-depth articles from the print edition of the *New Encyclopaedia Britannica* as well as up-to-date, brief entries.

A sixth grader asks: "I am writing a report about Martin Luther King. My teacher said that he wrote a speech about a dream. Where can I find it?" Not only would *Microsoft Encarta Encyclopedia Deluxe* provide an article about Dr. King as well as the text of his "I Have a Dream Speech," it would also include a video clip of Dr. King delivering that speech. The student would benefit from reading and listening to this speech and might gain a better understanding of the impact Dr. King had on U.S. history.

Nearly all university freshmen take a rhetoric and composition class during their first semester. Typically, their teachers have them write a position piece about a controversial topic such as gun control or the death penalty. A common question might be: "I have to write a paper about the history of gun control in the United States. Where would I find some good introductory material?" Because these students will be conducting preresearch, two print encyclopedias, *New Encyclopaedia Britannica* and the *Encyclopedia Americana,* would be good places to start. *Encyclopedia Americana* takes pride in its focus on American history. Because the possession of guns has figured in U.S. history since its founding, this encyclopedia would provide the student with a good historical overview. The *Index* and *Micropaedia* of the *New Encyclopaedia Britannica* would provide, respectively, locations of information about gun control in the *Macropaedia* as well as ready-reference or broad topical information.

"Where can I read about the structure of DNA?" Because of the specificity of this question, a subject encyclopedia would be the first place to look. In particular, the *McGraw-Hill Encyclopedia of Science and Technology* best lends itself to this question because it is the standard for in-depth information on science and technology. For younger patrons, *World Book* or *Compton's* would provide comparable information written at a level they would better understand.

NOTES

1. Kenneth F. Kister, "Questions and Answers about Encyclopedias," in *Kister's Best Encyclopedias: A Comparative Guide to General and Specialized Encyclopedias,* 2d ed. (Phoenix, Ariz.: Oryx Press, 1994), 3.

2. Jacques Barzun, *The Modern Researcher,* 5th ed. (New York: Houghton Mifflin, 1992), 73.

3. Stephen Del Vecchio, "Out for a Spin: A School Librarian Test Drives 14 CD-ROM Encyclopedias," *School Library Journal* 43 (September 1997): 118-24.

4. *Encyclopedia of African-American Culture and History* (New York: Simon & Schuster Macmillan, 1996), vii.

5. *World Book Encyclopedia* (Chicago: World Book, 1996), iv.

6. Kenneth F. Kister, "Encyclopedists Head for Cyberspace," *Library Journal* 123 (November 15, 1998): S4.

7. Alex Soojung-Kim Pang, "The Work of the Encyclopedia in the Age of Electronic Reproduction," *First Monday* 3 (September 1998). Available: http://www.firstmonday.dk/issues/issue3_9/pang/index.html.

8. *World Book Encyclopedia*, iv.

9. Péter Jacsó, "CD-ROM Currents," *Computers in Libraries* 19 (June 1999): 31.

10. *Library Hotline* 28 (September 13, 1999): 5.

11. *New Encyclopaedia Britannica Propaedia* (Chicago: Encyclopaedia Britannica, 1995), 4.

12. Péter Jacsó, "The 1997 Editions of General Interest Encyclopedias," *Computers in Libraries* 17 (February 1997): 30.

13. *The Cambridge Encyclopedia,* 3d ed. (New York: Cambridge University Press, 1998), iii.

LIST OF SOURCES

Academic American Encyclopedia. 21 vols. Danbury, Conn.: Grolier, 2000.

AccessScience. New York: McGraw-Hill. Available: http://www.accessscience.com (subscription required).

The African American Encyclopedia. Edited by Michael W. Williams. 8 vols. New York: Marshall Cavendish, 1996.

ARBA Guide to Subject Encyclopedias and Dictionaries. 2d ed. Edited by Susan C. Awe. Englewood, Colo.: Libraries Unlimited, 1997. 482p.

The Asian American Encyclopedia. Edited by Franklin Ng. 6 vols. New York: Marshall Cavendish, 1995.

Britannica Book of the Year. Chicago: Encyclopaedia Britannica, 1938– . Annual.

Britannica CD 2000 Deluxe Edition. [CD-ROM]. Chicago: Encyclopaedia Britannica, 2000.

Britannica Macropaedia, Britannica Micropaedia, and *Britannica Propaedia.* See *New Encyclopaedia Britannica.*

Britannica Online. Chicago: Encyclopaedia Britannica, 2000. Available: http://www.eb.com (subscription); http://www.britannica.com (free).

The Cambridge Encyclopedia. 3d ed. Edited by David Crystal. New York: Cambridge University Press, 1998. 1302p.

The Canadian Encyclopedia. Edited by James H. Marsh. Toronto, Ont.: McClelland & Stewart, 2000. 2573p. Also available on CD-ROM.

Childcraft: The How and Why Library. 15 vols. Chicago: World Book, 1997.

The Columbia Encyclopedia. 6th ed. New York: Columbia University Press, 2000. 3156p. Also available: http:/wwww.bartleby.com/65.

Compton's Encyclopedia & Fact Index. 26 vols. Chicago: Compton's Books, 2001.

Compton's Encyclopedia Online. Available: http://www.comptons.com/encyclopedia.

Compton's Interactive Encyclopedia 1999 Edition. [CD-ROM]. Minneapolis, Minn.: The Learning Company, 1999.

The Concise Columbia Encyclopedia. 3d ed. New York: Columbia University Press, 1994. 973p.

DK Children's Illustrated Encyclopedia. 2d rev. ed. New York: DK Publishing, 1998. 644p.

Enciclopedia Hispanica. 18 vols. Barcelona: Encyclopaedia Britannica Publishers, 1995.

Encyclopaedia Britannica Macropaedia, Britannica Micropaedia, and *Britannica Propaedia.* See *New Encyclopaedia Britannica.*

Encyclopedia Americana. 30 vols. Danbury, Conn.: Grolier, 1999.

Encyclopedia Americana 1999. [CD-ROM]. Danbury, Conn.: Grolier, 1999.

Encyclopedia Americana Online. Available: http://go.grolier.com (subscription required).

Encyclopedia of African-American Civil Rights: From the Emancipation to the Present. New York: Greenwood, 1992. 658p

Encyclopedia of African-American Culture and History. Edited by Jack Salzman, David Lionel Smith, and Cornel West. 5 vols. New York: Simon & Schuster Macmillan, 1996.

Encyclopedia of Library History. Edited by Wayne A. Wiegand and Donald G. Davis. New York: Garland, 1994. 707p.

Encyclopedia of Multiculturalism. 8 vols. New York: Marshall Cavendish, 1994, 1998.

Encyclopedia of Ukraine. 5 vols. Toronto, Ont.: University of Toronto Press, 1984–1993.

Encyclopedia Sherlockiana: An A-to-Z Guide to the World of the Great Detective. Edited by Matthew Bunson. New York: Macmillan, 1994. 326p.

Encyclopedia.com. Available: http://www.encyclopedia.com.

Funk & Wagnalls Multimedia Encyclopedia. [CD-ROM/DVD]. New York: Versaware Technologies, 1999.

Funk & Wagnalls New Encyclopedia. 29 vols. New York: Funk & Wagnalls, 1997.

Funk & Wagnalls Online. Available: http://www.funkandwagnalls.com.

Gale Encyclopedia of Multicultural America. 2d ed. Edited by Robert Dassanowsky and Jeffrey Lehman. 3 vols. Farmington Hills, Mich.: Gale Group, 2000.

Grand Usuel Larousse: Dictionnaire Encyclopédique. 5 vols. Paris: Larousse, 1997.

Grolier Multimedia Encyclopedia Online. Available: http://go.grolier.com (subscription required).

Grolier Multimedia Encyclopedia 2000. [CD-ROM]. Danbury, Conn.: Grolier Interactive, 2000.

International Encyclopedia of Business and Management. 6 vols. New York: Routledge, 1996.

Japan: An Illustrated Encyclopedia. 2 vols. Tokyo: Kodansha, 1993.

The Kingfisher Children's Encyclopedia. Edited by Jennifer Justice. New York: Kingfisher, 1998. 468p.

Kister's Best Encyclopedias: A Comparative Guide to General and Specialized Encyclopedias. 2d ed. Edited by Kenneth F. Kister. Phoenix, Ariz.: Oryx Press, 1994. 506p.

McGraw-Hill Encyclopedia of Engineering. 2d ed. Edited by Sybil P. Parker. New York: McGraw-Hill, 1993. 1414p.

McGraw-Hill Encyclopedia of Physics. 2d ed. Edited by Sybil P. Parker. New York: McGraw-Hill, 1993. 1624p.

McGraw-Hill Encyclopedia of Science and Technology. 8th ed. Edited by Sybil P. Parker. 20 vols. New York: McGraw-Hill, 1997.

McGraw-Hill Multimedia Encyclopedia of Science and Technology. [CD-ROM]. New York: McGraw-Hill, 2000.

McGraw-Hill Yearbook of Science and Technology 2000. New York: McGraw-Hill, 1999. 482p.

Microsoft Encarta Encyclopedia Deluxe 2001. [CD-ROM]. Redmond, Wash.: Microsoft, 2001.

Microsoft Encarta Online. Available: http://encarta.msn.com.

The New Book of Knowledge. 21 vols. Danbury, Conn.: Grolier, 2000.

The New Book of Knowledge Online. Available: http://go.grolier.com (subscription required).

New Encyclopaedia Britannica. 15th ed. 32 vols. Chicago: Encyclopaedia Britannica, 1999.

The Oxford American Children's Encyclopedia. 9 vols. New York: Oxford University Press, 1999.

Oxford Family Encyclopedia. London: George Philip Ltd., 1997. 744p.

The Random House Encyclopedia. Rev. ed. New York: Random House, 1990. 2912p.

The Simon and Schuster D-Day Encyclopedia: A Multimedia Exploration! [CD-ROM]. New York: Simon & Schuster, 1996.

Subject Encyclopedias: User Guide, Review Citations, and Keyword Index. Edited by Allan N. Mirwis. 2 vols. Phoenix, Ariz.: Oryx Press, 1999.

World Book Discoveries. [DVD]. Chicago: World Book, 2000.

World Book Encyclopedia. 22 vols. Chicago: World Book, 2000.

World Book Macintosh Edition. [CD-ROM]. Chicago: World Book, 1999.

World Book Millennium Edition. [CD-ROM]. Chicago: World Book, 2000.

World Book Online. Available: http://www.worldbookonline.com (subscription required).

The World Book Student Discovery Encyclopedia. 13 vols. Chicago: World Book, 2000.

ADDITIONAL READINGS

American Reference Books Annual. Edited by Bohdan S. Wynar. Englewood, Colo.: Libraries Unlimited, 1970– . Annual.

This work examines all categories of reference works, covering general encyclopedias in three-, four-, and five-year cycles. Initial reviews give detailed background about an encyclopedia, whereas subsequent reviews focus solely on updates and revisions undertaken.

ARBA Guide to Subject Encyclopedias and Dictionaries. 2d ed. Edited by Susan C. Awe. Englewood, Colo.: Libraries Unlimited, 1997. 482p.

The second edition of this *ARBA* guide maintains a tradition of reviewing excellence begun in 1986. Signed articles on several selected works published between 1968 and 1997 make this a valuable resource for librarians.

Encyclopedias, Atlases & Dictionaries. Edited by Marion Sader and Amy Lewis. New Providence, N.J.: R. R. Bowker, 1995. 495p.

Essentially a hybrid of *Encyclopedias, Atlases, and Dictionaries* (1988) and *General Reference Books for Adults* (1991), this source includes three categories of reference sources: encyclopedias, atlases, and dictionaries. It reviews over 200 general encyclopedias and includes a lengthy overview (and accompanying chart) about the current state of general encyclopedias.

Grogan, Denis. *Encyclopedias, Yearbooks, Directories, and Statistical Sources.* London: Clive Bingley, 1987. 170p. (Grogan's Case Studies in Reference Work, v. 2).

Because of its methodology—the use of case studies to teach search strategies when using encyclopedias—this source remains a standard in spite of its publication date. Student librarians or new professionals will appreciate Grogan's candor and examples of how to evaluate an encyclopedia for objectivity and reliability.

Guide to Reference Books. 11th ed. Edited by Robert Balay. Chicago: American Library Association, 1996. 2020p.

This comprehensive and authoritative guide to all types of reference sources includes many annotated entries on general and subject encyclopedias.

Jacsó, Péter. "Péter's Picks and Pans." *EContent.* Bimonthly.

EContent, formerly *Database Magazine,* includes a bimonthly review of electronic resources written by University of Hawaii professor Péter Jacsó. More often than not, Jacsó's column spotlights encyclopedias (online, CD-ROM, and DVD versions). His reviews are in-depth and very timely. *EContent*'s Web site (http://www.ecmag.net) lists the contents of current and earlier columns.

Katz, Bill. *Cuneiform to Computer: A History of Reference Sources.* Lanham, Md.: Scarecrow Press, 1998. 417p.

For those interested in the origins and evolution of encyclopedias (as well as other reference sources), this book provides an in-depth overview.

Kister, Kenneth F. *Kister's Best Encyclopedias: A Comparative Guide to General and Specialized Encyclopedias.* 2d ed. Phoenix, Ariz.: Oryx Press, 1994. 506p.

Although somewhat dated, this source provides the reader with sound criteria for selecting subject encyclopedias. Its first chapter, "Questions and Answers About Encyclopedias," remains especially useful in training librarians or teachers how to choose encyclopedias.

Mirwis, Allan N. *Subject Encyclopedias: User Guide, Review Citations, and Keyword Index.* 2 vols. Phoenix, Ariz.: Oryx Press, 1999.

A welcome addition to existing resources on subject encyclopedias, the two-volume *Subject Encyclopedias* examines, in detail, 1,000 subject encyclopedias presently available. Not only does this work provide comparative information, it also gives the author's ratings, bibliographic information, awards received, review citations, and Library of Congress and Dewey Decimal classification numbers.

Purchasing an Encyclopedia: 12 Points to Consider. 5th ed. Chicago: ALA Press, 1996. 43p.

This short book provides readers with reviews by the editorial staff of *Reference Books Bulletin*, guidelines for choosing encyclopedias, and comparative features and price charts. Librarians should consult the latest edition of this useful work.

Recommended Reference Books for Small and Medium-sized Libraries and Media Centers. 20th ed. Edited by Bohdan S. Wynar. Englewood, Colo.: Libraries Unlimited, 2000. 309p.

This title is a wonderful resource for librarians and school media specialists who work in small institutions. Although it covers all types of reference sources, the encyclopedias section thoughtfully discusses which encyclopedias would be most appropriate, and why, for the small or medium-sized library or media center.

Reference Books Bulletin. Chicago: American Library Association, 1983– . 22 issues per year.

RBB appears as a separate section in every issue of *Booklist*. It devotes one issue annually to the review of encyclopedias; see, for example, *Booklist* 97 (September 15, 2000): 264-84. Other issues often include lengthier reviews of a newly released title.

CHAPTER

19

GEOGRAPHICAL SOURCES

David A. Cobb

USES AND CHARACTERISTICS

Geographical sources are most often used to answer location questions: "Where is Frankfurt, Germany, where my grandmother was born?" or "Where is the location of yesterday's environmental catastrophe?" Although these are the types of questions asked most often, readers should not have the false impression that geography only refers to specific places or that those answers will only be found in traditional print reference volumes. Geographers study spatial problems involving environmental issues, regional planning, medical geography, political geography, mapping, and the general relationship between humans and their physical world. It is beyond the scope of this chapter to discuss specialized works of geography in great detail, but readers are encouraged to pursue further studies if they should find themselves in charge of administering even a small geography collection or acquiring materials in geography.

The publications discussed in this chapter represent the basic sources used in an average academic or large public library. For larger academic libraries that have greater financial resources, reference is made to additional sources. Similarly, it is impossible to discuss more than a few of the many resources that are now available via the Internet and Web. The most dramatic change for geographical sources is the amount of digital data widely available and the number of electronic map products available via the Web and on commercial CD-ROM.

Because many librarians will not be able to answer all geographical questions using the sources in their own collections, they should identify the closest large collection of geographical and cartographic materials in their state or region. David Cobb's *Guide to U.S. Map Resources* is the most comprehensive listing of such collections in the United States, providing information on nearly 1,000 individual map collections. The geographical and cartographic collections in this guide are the locations to which one may direct questions requiring more detail or expertise.

Librarians must always justify the cost of their materials, and geographical sources have suffered in the library environment because of their cost, size, and storage requirements. Quality atlases, which often cost over $100, create an added burden on budgets that are usually already unable to meet demands. The recent increase in the number of quality atlases and political changes in an ever-changing world make it even more difficult for the reference librarian to make choices among geographical materials. Although it may be impossible to purchase all the different atlases, an alternative solution would be to purchase one or two titles annually and thus develop a well-rounded collection over several years.

Oversized materials, and particularly geographical atlases and maps, present obvious storage problems for the average reference department. The increasing availability of maps and atlases through the U.S. Government Printing Office's (GPO's) depository library program (see Chapter 22) has exacerbated this problem. All too often, oversized atlases are filed on bottom shelves, only to be forgotten. The acquisition of oversized atlases is more cost-effective if they are stored (preferably horizontally) on middle shelves where they can be seen and used more frequently.

Almost all maps, especially oversized maps, present a unique problem for the library because they require specialized storage equipment. Ideally, large atlases should be stored on oversized atlas shelves, and maps should be placed in either vertical or horizontal cases designed specifically for map storage. Unfortunately, these may be luxury items for some libraries. Maps can always be placed in large flat boxes and stored on top of filing cabinets to provide protection from light and dust. If a library's collection of maps grows to several hundred, metal map cases are the alternative of choice.

The primary purpose for the majority of geographical sources is to help one locate places. All of the sources described in this chapter locate something, tell something about a location, or show how to get there. Another general characteristic of geographical sources is that they usually deal with a time period, either current or historical. Although currency is very often important, historical and out-of-date information is also often critical to a reference question. In addition, some geographical sources deal with thematic or subject information. Examples of thematic information are a population atlas, a geological map, or an electronic road atlas.

Location questions can be grouped into three general categories: current events, recreation, and business. Current events are one of the strongest reasons for maintaining up-to-date geographical sources. Just as last night's talk-show novel will be requested in the library the next day, so too will information on yesterday's volcanic eruption, earthquake, revolution, or other human or physical disaster. Human society has become more global than ever, and the media bring the world's crises and disasters into the living room. It is the library's role to provide additional information on this global society. Current detailed geographical sources are one important means to accomplish this.

Recreation has become an important part of many lives, and travel is now more common than it was in the past. The result is that a larger segment of the population is interested in information, not only on the local, state, or national park, but also on cities and regions all over the world. The amount of travel literature available today is more than any library can possibly accumulate, but an attempt should be made to provide a collection of travel literature for user needs.

Finally, business travel is also more common, and the information required to answer these questions is related to travel literature. This particular type of travel requires more information on cities and detailed information regarding subjects such as hotels and restaurants.

Another category of questions concerns historical geography. This can be divided into genealogy, military history, and place name changes. All three of these areas are covered in many specialized sources that cannot be described in this chapter. Many genealogy questions are specific. For example, the user may want a map of the town where an ancestor lived in southern Germany in 1860. Few libraries can provide this information, and referral to a more specialized map collection may be required. However, often a quality atlas or an older atlas in the collection may show the location of the town. The most valuable asset in answering these questions may be a late nineteenth- or early twentieth-century atlas. Age should not be a primary criterion when weeding geographical sources because historical sources are especially valuable for these questions. Most historical atlases provide some treatment of military history, and there are also large atlases that restrict themselves to a particular war or country (e.g., the American Civil War), if more specialized information is needed. Similarly, place name changes can present a special problem for the general reference librarian; Eastern Europe presents particularly difficult challenges no matter how many sources the library has. Again, older atlases are excellent sources for early place names. Gazetteers, which list place name locations, are also discussed later in this chapter.

The types of geographical sources considered in this chapter include maps, atlases, gazetteers, travel literature, and a few general sources. Maps are purposely listed first, because too many libraries tend to forget them, for reasons already mentioned. Nevertheless, maps generally provide more detailed information on a specific area, and provide more comprehensive thematic coverage, than do atlases. The advantage of atlases, however, is that they can provide the whole world, or a single country or state, in one volume at a nominal cost. Individual atlases may cover many types of subjects and offer basic reference information on geological features, the oceans, space, or the historical geography of a particular country. Gazetteers are also important reference tools because they provide information on geographical place names. Some gazetteers simply give precise locational information, such as latitude and longitude; others describe the locations and give information on population, climate, economy, and notable tourist attractions. The titles making up travel literature have grown considerably in the last few years because of the travel patterns of society. Fortunately, there are many good options available from which libraries and individuals can choose. The section covering other geographical sources briefly describes the genre of titles that relate to geography, such as climatic information, political/geographical information on individual countries, mileage guides, and geographical dictionaries.

EVALUATION

Although atlases may be evaluated using criteria applicable to other reference books, there are criteria unique to atlases. Maps also must be evaluated differently than other reference sources. The criteria to be considered when evaluating atlases and maps include scale and projection, color and symbols, publisher/authority, indexing, and currency. These criteria are equally important when evaluating digital cartographic formats.

Scale and Projection

Scale and *projection* are the two most common characteristics that make cartographic materials different from all other library materials. These two concepts are difficult for many persons to understand and are also difficult to explain. Essentially, *scale* is the ratio of the distance on the map to the actual distance on the face of the Earth. Maps must be drawn to scale so that accurate comparisons may be made between the map and the corresponding distance on the Earth. This scale may be given as a verbal scale (e.g., 1 inch equals 4 miles); a representative fraction (e.g., 1:253,440); or a graphic scale or bar scale normally found below the map. The verbal and representative fraction examples here are the same, because there are 253,440 inches in 4 miles. Scale is the most important element of a map because it defines the amount of information that can be shown as well as the size of the geographical area (see Figure 19.1). Maps are generally classed by scale: large-scale maps are normally 1:100,000 or larger, medium-scale maps are between 1:100,000 and 1:1,000,000, and smaller-scale maps are 1:1,000,000 or smaller. Note the cartographic aberration that, as the number increases, the scale is considered smaller rather than larger, and vice versa.

A good map or atlas—even in electronic form—will always identify the scale, and the librarian must decide the appropriate scale for the user or library. Topographic maps, with large scales of 1:50,000, are excellent sources for geographical place names but would be the wrong choice for someone looking for a country's administrative boundaries. A smaller geographical area is shown on a 1:50,000-scale map; therefore, such a map is very detailed in the amount of data it shows. A more appropriate scale for administrative divisions would be 1:250,000 or even 1:500,000. It is important that maps in an atlas not vary their scales greatly. Quality atlases make an attempt to map nations and states at similar scales. An inferior atlas may show each U.S. state on its own page, which leads the user to believe that all states are "page-size." Similar examples should be carefully reviewed when looking at world atlases.

Map projection is one of the most complicated aspects of cartography, and scholars continue to discuss the value of one projection over another. Suffice it to say that when a spherical globe is drawn on a flat piece of paper (*projected*), there will be some distortion and unavoidable error. Certain projections are better suited to large-scale maps and others to small-scale maps. Furthermore, some projections are preferred for their mapping characteristics (e.g., equal area, navigation, least distortion). The map user should be aware of these distortions

Figure 19.1 Comparison of various map scales. (From Morris Thompson, *Maps for America*, U.S. Department of the Interior, 1987.)

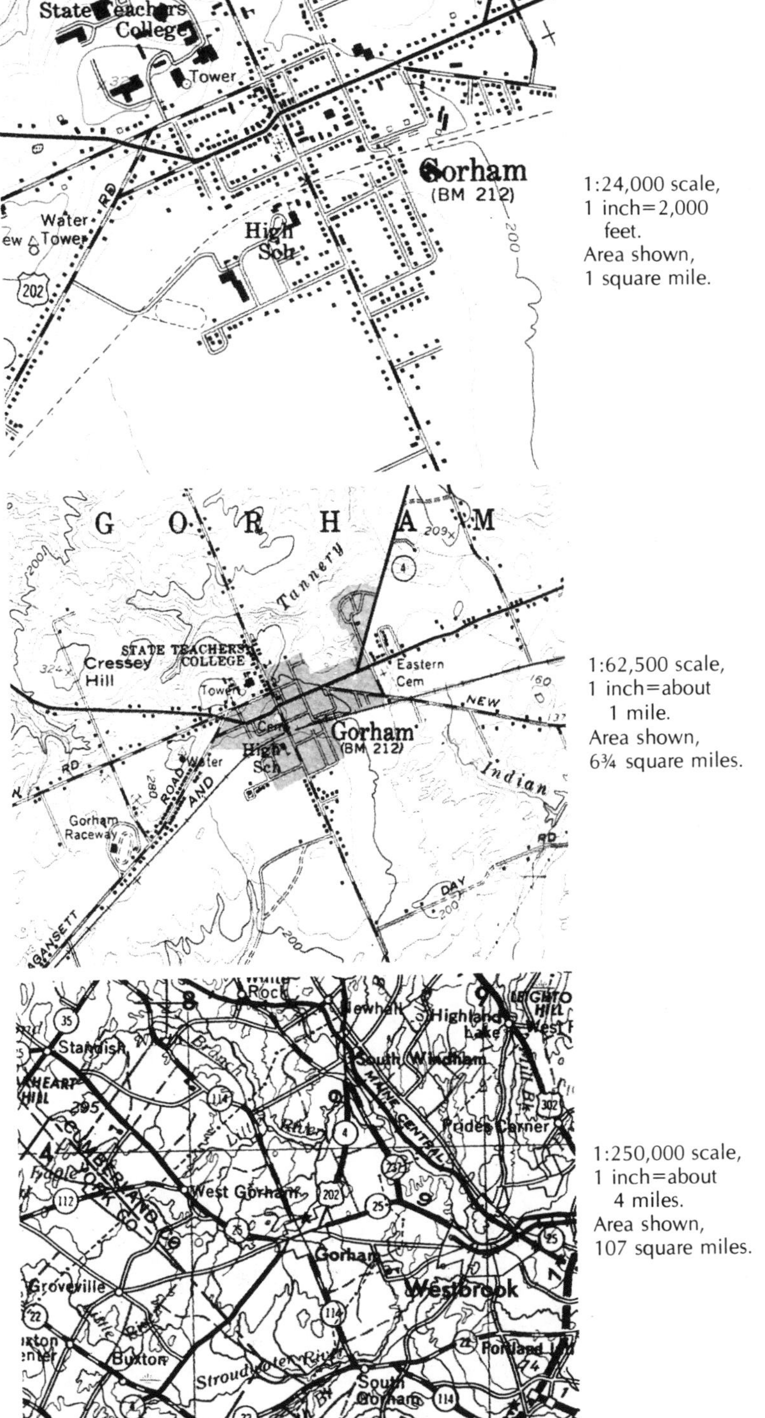

and differences. A current globe will decrease the degree of distortion found in many maps and atlases. One of the well-known examples of distortion is the "large" Greenland on the Mercator projection world map. Find such a map and compare it to a globe to see how projections can slant one's understanding of the Earth. It is difficult for the average user, or librarian, to be aware of the many characteristics of the various projections used. *Map Appreciation*, by Mark Monmonier and George Schnell, provides an expert and clear explanation of this mapping concept.[1]

Color and Symbols

Color is used on maps in many different ways and for different purposes. The simplest of maps use color to show political boundaries: for example, France, green; Germany, yellow; and Italy, blue. Color is also used on many government maps to show standard types of information. The U.S. Geological Survey, for example, uses five basic colors on its topographic maps. Brown is used to show contours (altitude lines), their elevations, and certain unverified altitude heights. Blue shows lakes, rivers, canals, and other waterways. Black indicates roads, buildings, railroads, and other human impact on the land. Red is another "culture color," showing road classifications for major highways, some administrative boundaries, and built-up areas in the center of many cities. Green displays vegetation, such as woodland, vineyards, and orchards.

Color may also be used to show land heights, ocean depths, or gradients on a thematic map. An example of the latter might be the use of color shading to indicate population distribution from an inner city to its suburbs. Many atlas maps use color to portray the varying land heights in a country or across Europe, for example. Usually, deeper colors are used to show the highest land, with pastel shades used for lowlands and coastal plains. Another subtle use of color is the shading that creates shadows along the eastern side of mountains, assuming a light source from the northwest. The results create an easy-to-read relief map. Figure 19.2 shows the relationship between shaded relief and contour elevations. Excellent examples of this

Figure 19.2 Shaded relief and contours. (From Morris Thompson, *Maps for America,* U.S. Department of the Interior, 1987.)

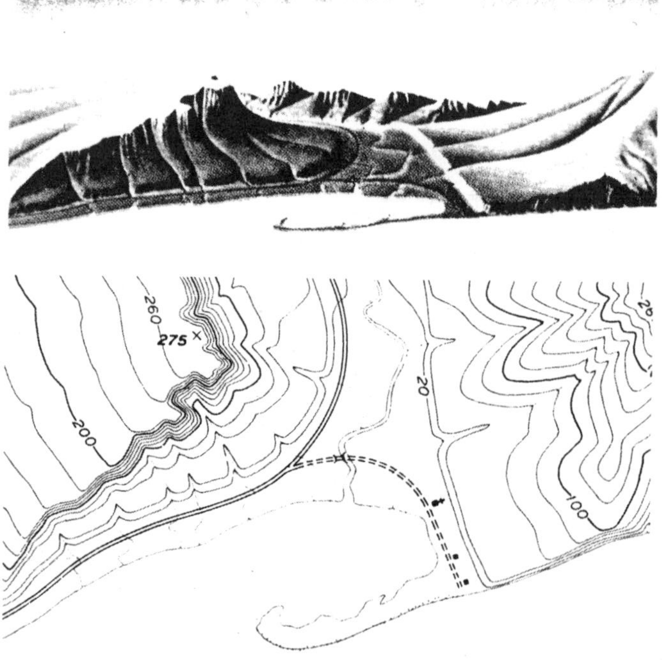

map type are the many country maps produced by the Central Intelligence Agency and distributed by the GPO.

Symbols on a map allow it to communicate its information to the reader. Users must not expect too much from a map, which can only communicate effectively when it is not cluttered. The scale of the map controls the number of symbols. To state the obvious, a map of Denver will show far more detail and symbols for that city than will a map of Colorado. A successful map differentiates between geographical features. For example, there should be a clear indication of the difference between such symbols as roads and railroads, external and internal boundaries, and rivers and canals. Each map or atlas should provide a key or index to its symbols. The first question that should be asked of a map is: "Is it too cluttered?" A map that attempts to provide too much information can be as misleading as a map that shows very little.

Publisher/Authority

As with any area of publishing, there are reputable map and atlas publishers and those that are less so. On the whole, few publishers produce inferior products because they face a marketplace that has become far more qualified to evaluate their products. Nevertheless, librarians need to be familiar with the literature and study reviews of maps and atlases, as they would for other reference materials.

With very few exceptions, national mapping agencies (see *World Mapping Today* and *Inventory of World Topographic Mapping*) produce high-quality, current, authoritative maps for their nations. These agencies, such as the U.S. Geological Survey, the Ordnance Survey in Great Britain, and Natural Resources Canada, are sources of quality mapping products at reasonable costs for their countries. Unfortunately, they are often overlooked.

Commercial map products are more difficult to evaluate if the librarian is not familiar with the firm or its products. The major U.S. firms that produce both maps and atlases are Rand McNally, C. S. Hammond, and the National Geographic Society. The number of smaller firms producing high-quality products is growing rapidly and includes such companies as DeLorme, Raven, Northern Cartographic, and ADC. The international market is equally prolific, although several large firms again stand out: John Bartholomew in Scotland, Kummerly & Frey of Switzerland, and Michelin of France. Numerous smaller firms also produce maps, especially city maps of individual foreign countries. Finally, although good maps are available from many sources, it is prudent to purchase materials from established, reputable dealers. There are now several Web map sites that offer maps from several publishers and range from the more general offerings of Omni Resources (http://www.omnimap.com) to the large-scale topographic map series offered by MAPSWAP (http://www.mapswap.nl) in the Netherlands.

Indexing/Place Names

The heart of an atlas or a map is the map itself. By analogy, then, the brain is the index or guide to that atlas or map. An atlas without an index to the maps, their locations, and the place names they contain is of questionable value as a reference tool. Similarly, a map of a city without an index to its streets or geographical features is equally suspect. How is the index to be used? Does the index locate the feature on the map with grid references or exact coordinates, as well as references to page number? Does the index include all of the place names on the map? Does the index include not only cities and towns, but also national parks, administrative divisions, and mountains? It is important to find an atlas/map that indexes as many of these features as possible. A publisher's higher-priced atlas or map is usually the best buy, because it offers more information, more maps, and a larger index.

Currency

After scale, currency is probably the most important criterion for geographical source material. Because the world is changing so rapidly, it is imperative that libraries be able to provide current information. A world atlas that is five years old portrays enough obsolete information that it should be used only for historical purposes. So many changes occur annually: place name changes, new roads, railroad abandonment, boundary changes (e.g., the former Soviet Union and Yugoslavia), new dams, and power lines. There are also many subtle changes that occur within cities that can be shown only on the most detailed of maps, including growth of the city's boundaries, its suburbs, and redevelopment projects, including the replacement of old buildings with new ones.

SELECTION

Geographical sources vary extensively. Each library must determine the needs of its users and the community that it is trying to serve. A large academic library will require a greater complexity of geographical sources for its users than will a smaller, rural public library. The academic library may require several world atlases as well as selected national atlases to supplement its map collection, whereas a small public library may be satisfied with a new world atlas every few years. No library can satisfy all of its users all of the time, and it is imperative that librarians communicate among themselves to become aware of expertise that is available to them. This may be especially important with geographical sources, as very few libraries have large, comprehensive collections in this area.

The library must also decide, within its collection development guidelines, whether it will collect primarily ready-reference materials or develop a more comprehensive collection for in-depth research purposes. A ready-reference collection may consist of only 100 titles,[2] whereas research collections may include tens of thousands of maps and hundreds of atlases. The basic collection is the focus in this chapter; there are many sources one can refer to for the development of larger collections.

Finding appropriate selection tools for geographical sources is perhaps the most difficult task in this area of collection development. Although *American Reference Books Annual*, *Publishers Weekly*, *Choice*, and other reviewing sources include atlas reviews, it is not possible to use only the standard tools for current awareness of geographical sources. As in other fields, there is a specialized literature of unique publications. A current and regular listing of current cartographic publications appears in *base line*, the newsletter of the American Library Association's Map & Geography Round Table.[3] Published six times annually, this small newsletter contains information in each issue on new publications. Other publications useful for selection purposes are included in the "List of Sources" in this chapter. Several Web sources also announce new cartographic publications, such as *Oddens' Bookmarks* and Omni Resources (http://www.omnimap.com).

Another useful guide is David Cobb's *Guide to U.S. Map Resources.* With over 950 entries, it is the most comprehensive source describing U.S. map collections. It provides information on special collections and area and subject strengths, as well as addresses, telephone numbers, and so forth. Libraries are encouraged to review this volume to locate the nearest research library map collection and to develop contacts for interlibrary loan and assistance with research questions.

Format

The choice of format is quickly becoming a dilemma for those using geographical sources. Maps and atlases are now being offered as print publications, on diskettes, and as CD-ROMs. In addition, numerous Web sites are being developed that offer maps. With these formats come the demands for additional library equipment, personal computers with large hard drives, CD-ROM drives, Zip drives, scanners, and color printers.

The newer digital products range from the simplest diskette programs to complex combinations of geographical data and boundaries using compression technology. An example of the first is *Centennia*. It allows the user to view the boundaries of Europe and the Middle East from the year 1000 C.E. to the mid-1990s. A user can select boundaries for a particular year, compare boundaries, or allow the boundaries to move forward in time with a "movie" option. The major limitation of such products is their inability to interact with other data that a user may have or wish to map. Nevertheless, they are reasonably priced (ca. $50) and provide color graphic maps that can be reproduced for applications such as term papers. Essentially, they provide a variety of international and domestic document information in map form. The more complex electronic maps are issued on CD-ROM; DeLorme's *Street Atlas USA* is an excellent example that is suitable for almost every library. Using a complicated Census mapping database (the TIGER street file boundaries), DeLorme has created a seamless street and road map for the entire United States that is very easy to use. The next step is to consider the use of geographical information systems (GIS), discussed later in this chapter.

IMPORTANT GENERAL SOURCES

As mentioned earlier in this chapter, categories of geographical sources that librarians find useful in reference work include atlases, travel guides, gazetteers, and maps. In this section, major publishers and their geographical products are discussed, as well as a selection of the most useful gazetteers and geographical dictionaries. Three distinct types of atlases are identified, and a few of the best of each type are described. Finally, mention is made of some important geographical sources that do not fit into any of these categories.

Maps

Even though individual maps may present storage problems, libraries should not forego them entirely in favor of atlases. The major disadvantage of the atlas map is its small scale and inability to depict many geographical regions with sufficient detail. Local detail is usually provided only through individual maps, unless one is fortunate enough to live in a large metropolitan area that has its own street atlas. Some of the sources for maps that should be collected and included in all library collections are described here.

The U.S. Geological Survey (USGS) is the national agency officially responsible for domestic mapping. It creates maps at many scales, prints maps for other agencies of the federal government, and produces maps both on printed paper and in electronic formats. Libraries should focus on providing coverage of the local area at various scales to show varying amounts of detail. Libraries may request the free state indexes and other information for their states by calling 1-888-ASK-USGS. This number may also be used to ask any questions regarding maps or map products. Libraries, including public and school, should purchase maps covering their cities or towns at the following scales: 1:250,000 (one sheet); 1:100,000 (one to two sheets); and 1:24,000 (one to six sheets). These maps provide valuable information on the town and surrounding area: topography, drainage systems, transportation, woodland coverage, and other physical and cultural features. An electronic option worth considering is DeLorme's *Topo USA,* which provides complete topographic coverage of the United States on six CD-ROMs for under $100. For those libraries unable to store nearly 60,000 + paper maps or acquire the map cases to store them in, this is an alternative that should receive serious consideration. Libraries located in coastal cities or near the Great Lakes are encouraged to contact the National Ocean Service in Riverdale, Maryland, for information on nautical charts of their local areas. These charts are valuable for boaters, fishermen, and others interested in the coastline environment.

A variety of commercial sources also produce local maps that are useful when answering reference questions on local streets, public buildings, schools, and so forth. Companies such as Rand McNally, American Map, and Champion Maps produce numerous maps for local government agencies and chambers of commerce. Once again, DeLorme's *Street Atlas USA* provides a viable option for libraries wishing to offer street-level access for cities and towns in the United States. Realistically, this product provides the average library with more street detail than they could ever hope to collect in paper form. And yet, librarians should remember that paper maps for their local area are still important primary sources. All libraries should maintain contacts with local tourism offices for new publications, including maps; regular visits to local bookstores also can provide information on new maps.

Some of the most important, and often overlooked, sources for local information are local governments and regional agencies. Most municipal governments and regional agencies produce maps for planning and now digital data for electronic mapping and analysis. Sadly, many of these items are simply discarded once they are out-of-date (including the old digital data information). It is important to maintain contacts with these agencies, as their discards can be a valuable source of information for libraries. Although maps and aerial photographs are seldom free, these items are usually available for reasonable reproduction costs. Besides the usual chamber of commerce maps, libraries are encouraged to seek out aerial photographs and maps showing neighborhoods, school districts, and parks, as well as examples of out-of-date maps to show the changing landscapes within their geographical area.

Electronic Map Products

Additional products are appearing that provide greater detail and allow some interaction with the map display and printed output. It is important to maintain currency with electronic titles. The most up-to-date and comprehensive guide to electronic map resources is *Oddens' Bookmarks*. Its recent reorganization, and links to over 11,000 sites, make this Web site even more valuable as a thorough listing whether one is looking for historical or current sites. One of the most popular programs is DeLorme's *Street Atlas USA,* a CD-ROM that can display all of the streets and rural roads in the United States. Version 8.0 includes over 500,000 new streets and street names. Its software allows the user to zoom into features, streets, and city blocks across the United States. One can search maps by place name, zip code, telephone area code, and more. Each map has a scale bar and geographical coordinates in the map margin. *Street Atlas USA* allows one to highlight routes, add text, fill shaded areas, measure distances between specified points, and print maps in black-and-white or color.

Street Atlas USA is derived from the TIGER/Line file database (see Chapter 22), compiled for the U.S. Census. This program is one of the most geographically detailed, is very quickly learned by the average user, and is a very popular program whenever introduced. It is appropriate for all libraries.

Box 19.1 Map Search Strategy

A traveling businesswoman asked a reference librarian in a public library for city maps. She had client addresses and wanted to make her hotel reservations nearby. The librarian's first response was to refer to the current general atlases, but none of them provided maps detailed enough for such a query. A quick check of the current *Rand McNally Road Atlas* was more useful for major cities but the businesswoman requested more detail. The librarian then remembered a new CD-ROM product that had just arrived in the library: *Street Atlas USA*. She was able to quickly search the city maps for Waukegan, Illinois; Bozeman, Montana; and Boise, Idaho. By adjusting the magnification, the needed detail was found for each city, and a printed copy could be provided to the woman for further reference.

A useful electronic world atlas is Microsoft's *Encarta Interactive World Atlas*. This is another quickly learned program that provides quality maps for students with homework assignments, travelers, users of current maps for world events, and for general home and library use. This world atlas provides more detail than a print world atlas, with more than 1.8 million place names. In addition, it is a multimedia product with hundreds of images and audio clips.

The next level of data and software begins to bring libraries near or into the development and maintenance of geographical information systems (GIS). Although this requires sophisticated equipment and additional training and staff expertise, GIS has the potential to offer sophisticated enhancements to existing numeric data and geographical datasets to create unique and specialized reference services. Libraries are encouraged to pursue this path if it conforms with their primary mission. The Association of Research Libraries (ARL) sponsored such an initiative in cooperation with a leading GIS firm, Environmental Systems Research Institute (ESRI). As an outgrowth of this project, ESRI has provided many ARL libraries with training, various datasets, and software (e.g., *ArcView GIS*) so libraries can evaluate the use and impact of GIS technology in a public reference and research environment.[4]

Another example of mapping software that is reasonably priced for nonprofit agencies is *MapInfo*. Its basic package comes with sample world and U.S. maps and data. This sample package may be sufficient for many libraries, but there are also large amounts of data that are available for libraries to add.

Atlases

Atlases, like maps, can be divided into three groups: current, historical, and thematic. Current atlases are needed for up-to-date information on geographical and political changes in the world. Historical atlases are necessary for the study of boundary changes, military campaigns, early exploration, and similar topics. Thematic, or subject, atlases emphasize a specific subject or region. Examples include national atlases, population atlases, and geological atlases.

General World Atlases

The finest general world atlas available is *The Times Atlas of the World*. The *Times* is regarded as the highest quality English-language world atlas, providing balanced geographic coverage. The scales of many maps are generally larger and show greater detail than the *Hammond* or *Oxford* atlases discussed below. The *Times Atlas's* 123 map pages, produced by the highly respected firm of John Bartholomew, provide excellent regional maps to answer all but the most specialized reference questions. This atlas is divided into three general sections: an introductory section including general physical information and thematic world maps, a series of regional maps showing political and physical features, and a final section that is a large index-gazetteer with more than 200,000 names. Locations are indexed by map page, a map-page grid system, and latitude and longitude.

Three additional atlases that deserve attention are the *Hammond Atlas of the World*, Rand McNally's *The New International Atlas*, and the *Atlas of the World*, by Oxford University Press. Each of these atlases has advantages and should be seriously considered for inclusion in reference collections. Hammond's atlas contains 160 pages of maps and was one of the earliest computer-generated atlases. The *Hammond Digital Cartographic Database*, used to create this atlas, was developed by Hammond over the last several years and contains the latitude and longitude of significant geographical features and a new map projection that displays truer dimensions and angles of the Earth's continents.

The physical and political maps of the *Hammond* atlas indicate relief using shading. Included in its appendixes are a large gazetteer, statistical tables, and the population of major cities. The results are crisp, easy-to-read maps, uncluttered place names, good choice of color throughout, and an affordable price for public and school libraries.

The *Atlas of the World*, in contrast, represents a more traditional atlas like the *Times*. Its use of color tints to show relief results in large patches of purples and browns to show mountains. To its credit, it provides an encyclopedia of geographical information in its introductory pages, with color maps illustrating climate, the greenhouse effect, health, population and migration, global conflicts, and more. This atlas also has a large collection of world metropolitan maps and a separate index to the place names on these maps.

The New International Atlas is Rand McNally's international effort to create a quality world atlas for the American market, and they have succeeded. It opens with world thematic maps showing various characteristics worldwide, then moves to continental maps, then to regional maps, and then to various appendixes. It too includes a large gazetteer and uses very effective shading to show relief.

Historical Atlases

The Times Atlas of World History broke a long tradition of Eurocentricity, or emphasis on the history of Europe, by presenting a more balanced view of history that is worldwide in conception. The maps begin with one showing human origins, move through the early civilizations, and conclude with a group entitled "The Age of Global Civilization," which takes users into the 1980s. This is the first historical atlas to incorporate new mapping techniques and includes information on social history and cultural achievements of different civilizations. It also provides an index to historical place names and a glossary giving supplementary information about some individuals, peoples, and events.

The *Historical Atlas of the United States* provides a unique and current perspective on America's history. In addition to hundreds of maps, this atlas incorporates more than 450 photographs, 80 graphs, and 140,000 words of text. It is an interesting volume that interweaves the historical timeline of American history throughout its chapters: "Land," "People," "Boundaries," "Economy," "Networks," and "Communities." The atlas also includes a useful bibliography and index.

Kenneth Martis's *The Historical Atlas of Political Parties* offers a wealth of information in a political atlas. Its multicolored maps, combined with judicious text and tables, provide an authoritative record and geographical understanding of American political history.

The significant three-volume *Historical Atlas of Canada* must also be mentioned here. Too often, such projects are restricted to a single volume, and their reference and scholarly value are somewhat diminished; not so with this exquisite Canadian effort. Bringing together scholars from many disciplines, this collaborative effort has resulted in a publication recommended for all libraries whose users are interested in Canada and Canadian history. Volume I includes topics on Canada's early prehistory and settlement to 1800; volume II focuses on the nineteenth century, 1800–1891; and volume III reviews the changes in the twentieth century, 1891–1961.

Perhaps the grandest historical atlas underway remains the *Tübinger Atlas des Vorderen Orients,* which has been regularly issuing separate maps since the mid-1970s. A sampling of map titles will give some idea of its comprehensiveness: "Middle East Vegetation," "Lebanon House Types," "Iran in the 2nd Millennium B.C.," and "Pastoral Migration Systems." The maps and scholarship are of the highest quality, and this atlas has become the most important source for the historical geography of the Middle East.

Many other historical atlases concentrate on either particular periods in history or particular regions. Examples of the former are Martin Gilbert's *Atlas of the Holocaust* and *The Times Atlas of the Second World War*. Regional atlases are appearing with greater frequency today. Gerald Hanson's *Historical Atlas of Arkansas*, Iwo Pogonowski's *Poland, A Historical Atlas*, Michael Crowder's *Historical Atlas of Africa*, and the *Historical Atlas of Massachusetts* are significant examples of the proliferation of this atlas type.

Thematic Atlases

The National Atlas of the United States of America is included in this category because it focuses on a specific nation. Even though this atlas has long been out-of-print, it provides a cornucopia of knowledge about the United States through its many statistical and graphic maps. Although much of the economic and social information is now out-of-date, many of the sections (e.g., general reference maps, landforms, climate, history) are still valuable for reference purposes. An updated version is now being compiled digitally and the information is provided on the Web.

In spite of the ever-increasing popularity of the Internet and its various geographic Web travel sites, librarians still consult the venerable road atlas. The *Rand McNally Road Atlas* (2000) is in its seventy-sixth edition and features over 400 maps, including city maps, and is updated annually. Each year it shows thousands of changes, including new roads, construction hot lines, and new travel Web sites. The most recent addition to this market is the *National Geographic Road Atlas.* This atlas includes over 350 maps plus travel planning information, city maps, and national park maps. It is published in a spiral binding that allows the maps to be viewed completely flat.

Mark Mattson's *Atlas of the 1990 Census* is an excellent graphic depiction of the social context of America's population. Using 1990 Census data, this atlas reveals the population distribution patterns by regions. The atlas examines population distributions primarily in terms of counties and larger cities and towns. The volume also includes sections on households, housing, race and ethnicity, economy, and education. It is expected that similar titles will appear soon after the 2000 Census is completed.

The *Atlas of North America* is included here not for its regional perspective, but for its unique blend of traditional maps and satellite imagery. Library users often ask for examples of satellite imagery and how it may be used. This atlas, with its numerous examples of remote sensing, is an excellent source for answering such questions. It includes examples of black-and-white, natural-color, and infrared images, plus geographical information on North America, making it a valuable regional reference source as well.

The *National Atlas of Canada* has taken a unique path in deciding to issue the maps separately and is a good example that the United States could follow. The format allows individual maps to be updated as needed and the atlas to continue and expand in a changing environment. Like similar national atlases, this series of maps reveals the country's social, economic, and physical characteristics. Existing maps show election results, population density, native populations, farm types, and climatic regions, to name a few topics covered. The Canadians also are offering much of their digital information via their Web site.

There are numerous titles available in thematic atlas publishing, and a library's budget and collection development goals will define the depth of coverage in this area. Examples of additional titles are Dan Smith's *The State of the World Atlas*; John Keegan and Andrew Wheatcroft's *Zones of Conflict: An Atlas of Future Wars*; Ewan Anderson's *An Atlas of World Political Flashpoints*; Gerard Chaliand and Jean-Pierre Rageau's *Strategic Atlas*; the *Nunavut Atlas*, an atlas of land ownership and wildlife data used to assist the Inuit in preparing for negotiations to establish the Tungavik Federation of Nunavut; and Patrick Moore's *Atlas of the Universe.*

A new genre of thematic atlases has recently appeared and represents a new trend in atlas publishing. These atlases usually focus on a theme or historical time period. They are further characterized by commentary, illustrations, photographs, and relative paucity of maps. These books are more aptly described as popular histories illustrated with maps rather than as atlases. Nevertheless, for the less specialized library they can offer an economical option, by combining a historical volume and maps. Examples of these are Nicholas de Lange's *Atlas of the Jewish World*; *Atlas of the Christian Church*; Francis Robinson's *Atlas of the Islamic World since 1500*; Rafic Boustani and Philippe Fargues's *The Atlas of the Arab World*; and Angus MacKay's *Atlas of Medieval Europe.*

Gazetteers

Gazetteers may be the most often used geographical reference source. A gazetteer is usually a list of geographical names or physical features, or both, either appended to an atlas or published as a separate volume. There are two types of gazetteers: locational and descriptive. *Locational* gazetteers usually provide information precisely locating the feature, either by atlas page and grid index or by even more precise latitude and longitude on the Earth's surface. *Descriptive* gazetteers may provide some or all of the above information and then describe the place. Such a description may include such features as a brief history, commodity production, population, and altitude.

Almost every atlas includes a gazetteer as an appendix used to locate the place names in that volume. Therein lies its limitations. Atlas gazetteers are useful for locating major towns, cities, administrative divisions, and physical features. Questions requiring information on those cities beyond the scope of the normal world atlas will require a more detailed volume, such as a gazetteer.

A standard library gazetteer in the past has been *The Columbia-Lippincott Gazetteer of the World*. Although its 130,000 entries made it one of the most comprehensive descriptive gazetteers, it has become too outdated (1961) to be used for current reference. Fortunately, *The Columbia Gazetteer of the World*, a new three-volume, 160,000-entry work, will take its place as the standard general library reference gazetteer. The old gazetteer had been unmatched in scope, detail, and usefulness, but this new edition is completely revised and updated, with over 25,000 new entries. As a descriptive gazetteer no other single resource resembles this title in scope, coverage, and amount of detail about so many places. Nevertheless, librarians should not discard the 1961 volume because its value for historical information (including its earlier historical editions) will continue to be significant for many reference questions.

Similar in format, as it provides descriptive information for locations, is the third edition of *Merriam-Webster's Geographical Dictionary*, which has been completely revised. This has become a "best buy" for U.S. libraries, although it is restricted by having fewer than 50,000 entries. Its inclusion of over 250 maps showing national and international boundaries, cities, physical features, and national parks is very useful. Its lists of administrative divisions for major countries and U.S. states also make it a useful world gazetteer for smaller libraries.

The newest, and potentially most valuable, gazetteer for U.S. libraries is the U.S. Geological Survey's *The National Gazetteer of the United States of America*. When completed, this series of gazetteers will have a single volume for each state and, presumably, another one or two for territories and possessions. It is being published as a part of the Survey's Professional Paper Series, and each volume will have the number designation "1200" followed by the two-letter code for the subject state. The series is available to depository libraries as a separate item and is for sale from the USGS to all other libraries. *The National Gazetteer of the United States of America, Concise 1990* is a single-volume general gazetteer derived from the individual state volumes and is recommended for all libraries. The state gazetteers are derived from the *Geographic Names Information System* (*GNIS*). In cooperation with the U.S. Board on Geographic Names (BGN), this database contains information about nearly 2 million physical and cultural geographic features in the United States. It includes the following information: federally recognized feature name, feature type, elevation, estimated population, state and county in which the feature is located, latitude and longitude, on which 7.5-minute topographic map the feature is located, and links to sites offering map viewers. This database includes names found on various maps and public documents but excludes railroads, streets, and roads. These gazetteers will become the most comprehensive listing of geographical information for each state as they are published. Their detail can be illustrated by comparing the Indiana volume, with 23,000 entries, to *Merriam-Webster's*, which has approximately 47,000 entries to cover the entire world. The entire *GNIS* database is currently available on the Web.

The *Omni Gazetteer of the United States of America* is an impressive, although expensive, reference source ($1,400) that includes 1.5 million place names in its eleven volumes. The first nine volumes are regional divisions of the United States; these volumes are available separately ($150); volume 10 is a detailed national index, and volume 11 contains appendixes locating other national information. Although it does include information not found in the *USGS Geographic Names Information System,* the entire set is needed by only the largest of research libraries. A suggested alternative is to acquire the regional volume for one's area and then use the *GNIS* Web site that will provide national coverage at a bargain price.

An important set of gazetteers is the series of foreign country volumes produced by the U.S. Board on Geographic Names and published by the then-named Army Map Service and Defense Mapping Agency. Similar to the USGS volumes, these are locational gazetteers providing latitude and longitude for geographical places. These are the best volumes for locating any place-name information for foreign countries. Most of these titles have been distributed to libraries through the GPO depository library program. This dataset is also now available on the newly named *National Imagery and Mapping Agency GEOnet Names Server* Web site.

The *Rand McNally Commercial Atlas and Marketing Guide* contains a wealth of economic information in addition to large maps for each state. It is noted in this context because it has long been considered an unofficial gazetteer for the United States. The annual editions include more than 125,000 principal cities, towns, and inhabited places. Furthermore, each entry includes information on population, elevation, zip code, airlines, railroads, and so forth.

Travel Guides

Travel literature continues to proliferate at an unprecedented rate as publishers attempt to provide sources for a large number of travelers, both domestic and international. It is difficult for libraries to decide among the multiplicity of choices for travel guides to various regions of the United States or to other countries. There is also considerable duplication, as publishers try to take advantage of a growing market. The traditional areas of Europe, the Caribbean, and the United States are the mainstays of the U.S. travel industry, but many firms are now producing guides for Eastern Europe, the former Soviet Union, and adventure travel locations, expecting increased travel in these areas.

Librarians are encouraged to refer to the *Publishers Weekly* annual issues on travel literature, usually appearing in May. These articles provide descriptions of sources for both foreign and domestic travel and list the major publishers and their specialties. The accompanying advertisements are useful for reviewing the most current titles for selection.

An article by Carolyn Anthony provides an interesting division of travel literature into four general categories.[5] First are the popular annuals—Fodor, Frommer, and Birnbaum—that cover all topics, including passports, restaurants and hotels, and car rentals. Most of these guides are revised annually by local authorities and provide reliable, up-to-date information on restaurants, accommodations, and sightseeing. They usually provide current pricing for a variety of budgets. A second group—"Let's Go" from the Harvard Student Agencies, "Shoestring Guides" from Lonely Planet, and business traveler guides—is aimed at particular groups or types of traveler. These guides may target adventurous travelers looking for out-of-the-way locations, special groups such as students and budget travelers, business travelers who intend to extend their stays for short vacations, or upscale travelers looking for premier accommodations and sightseeing. Third, there is a growing literature for the specialized traveler: guides to museums, cathedrals, pubs, and similar tourist attractions. Guides in this category include "maverick" guides, trail guides, diving and snorkeling guides, and so forth. Finally, there is a resurgence in the literary travel book for the armchair tourist who enjoys taking an imaginary trip or to satisfy curiosity.

As one might suspect, the increasing use of personal computers has resulted in the introduction of electronic travel guides. Some incorporate navigation technology, while others simply pinpoint locations. There are several alternatives available from a variety of Web sites, including *MapQuest* and *Yahoo! Maps.* These sites are usually quite user-friendly and offer a variety of options for trip planning: identification of the quickest, shortest, or most scenic route; production of a map and directions for a specific trip; and/or the provision of detailed plans of individual cities.

Although not yet widely used in libraries, such software packages and data are introduced here in view of the increasing distribution of electronic data from both federal and state governments as well as many commercial geo-spatial datasets. Libraries and librarians also have the opportunity to provide a technical bridge to the efficient use and enhancement of these data, and that bridge may indeed be GIS and electronic mapping.

Other Geographical Sources

Geography's supplementary reference sources, like those of so many disciplines, are turning to the digital world and the Web. Several sources for travel have already been mentioned, such as *MapQuest, Street Atlas USA,* and *Yahoo! Maps.* These sources have largely replaced several print publications of the past such as Rand McNally's *Standard Highway Mileage Guide.* Now distances worldwide can be queried using a Web site (http://www.indo.com/distance). The answer to one of the more ubiquitous questions asked—"Where is the nearest ATM?"—is now available on the Web (http://www.visa.com/pd/atm/main.html), and zip code information is available from the postal service (http://www.usps.gov/ncsc/lookups/lookup_ctystzip.html).

It is now possible to check on local environmental hazards using the U.S. Environmental Protection Agency's *Enviro Mapper* Web site (http://www.epa.gov/enviro/html/em/index.html). For those interested in the activities of the U.S. Geological Survey, there is a very informative Web site (http://info.er.usgs.gov) that provides detailed information about mapping and several other programs including the dissemination of digital information. Similarly, with the arrival of a decennial year the importance of the Census grows. Its distribution of statistical information can be tracked by viewing its Web site (http://www.census.gov) for specific geographical information in addition to population data.

A new product from GeoLytics that has made the 1990 Census data easily accessible is *Census CD + Maps.* It has brought Census data, geographical boundaries, and a simple mapping program onto one CD-ROM. This one CD is the most efficient and most complete source for information about the people, housing, and economy of the United States. This product creates data reports and color maps easily. It includes demographic information to the neighborhood level (block groups) from the 1990 Census, along with current estimates and population projections. *Census CD + Maps* brings together valuable information into an easily used format and at a very reasonable price ($500 in 1999), making it affordable for many libraries.

Another of the new datasets can be found at ESRI's Web site *ArcData Online* (http://www.esri.com/data/online/index.html). The site offers access to an ever-increasing amount of free and commercial data that integrate with ESRI GIS products. The Perry-Castañeda Map Library at the University of Texas offers a spectacular collection of online maps from government sources on its Web site (http://www.lib.utexas.edu/Libs/PCL/Map_collection/Map_collection.html). This site is especially cognizant of world affairs and provides maps for current world crises. One of the most comprehensive Web sites is Matt Rosenberg's *Guide to Geography* (http://geography.about.com/science/geography). This Web site provides hundreds of netlinks to other sites and is updated and revised continually. Its "In the Spotlight" section focuses on world crisis areas and provides links to maps and geographical information.

A useful publication on foreign countries is *Background Notes*, compiled by the U.S. Department of State. It is a series of brief, authoritative pamphlets on selected countries and geographical entities that includes information on history, geography, culture, government, politics, and economics. These pamphlets also include base maps (easily photocopied) for each country, showing cities, rivers, railroads, roads, and airports. The series now includes approximately 170 titles, which are updated every few years. These *Notes* are now available on the Department of State Web site. The Web version, however, does not include the very useful maps.

A geographical dictionary is useful for any reference collection. Many specialized terms developed for the lexicon of this field are not included in standard dictionaries. Audrey

Clark's *Longman Dictionary of Geography* is a compact volume incorporating terms from both physical and human geography, including definitions for terms such as *bathymetric*, *gobolala*, *portulano*, and *zymogenous*. Similarly, *The Weather Almanac* provides information on U.S. weather and weather fundamentals. This volume summarizes many U.S. government documents and provides weather information using maps and statistical tables. The *Almanac* includes topics such as storms and severe weather phenomena, retirement and health weather, air pollution, weather fundamentals, record-setting weather, round-the-world weather, and detailed weather data for 108 selected U.S. cities. Additional weather information is available on various Web sites, including *The Weather Channel*.

An additional, and increasingly useful, source for geographic information is the MAPS-L listserv. MAPS-L is like many listservs, providing access to reference expertise in a specific area, in this case the area of geography, maps, and map librarianship. Its significance lies in its members in many countries, working in a variety of libraries, large and small, who can provide valuable reference expertise through electronic communication. One may subscribe to MAPS-L by sending the following message to Listserv@uga.cc.uga.edu: "SUB FIRSTNAME LASTNAME."

SEARCH STRATEGIES

Geographical sources should be used when the question asked involves location. Such questions could be as simple as "I need to know where Vilnius is" or "Could I have a map showing Beethoven's birthplace?" They may also be more complicated, such as a request for information on the distribution of radioactive waste from a specific nuclear arsenal or power plant. Both cases require maps and other reference sources as well, which may be more easily accessible in a smaller library where all of these sources are grouped together. Reference librarians must become thoroughly familiar with basic mapping concepts, such as scale and projection, and must understand how these concepts are represented in general and historical maps. This knowledge will allow the librarian to focus on finding the needed information without having to struggle to interpret mapping symbols.

Map reference work also requires a reference interview. Most users are unfamiliar with the resources of the map collection and, therefore, generally ask for maps of a much larger area rather than for one of a specific area that they would really prefer. For example, a map librarian may encounter a genealogist requesting a map of Germany, when the user really needs a detailed map of the outskirts of Hanover, Germany. Too often, users ask for general maps because they do not know the resources of the library and are not sufficiently questioned by the librarian so that they can be helped to use those resources correctly. Conversing with the user better defines the query so that the appropriate map will be retrieved. Similarly, users will often consult an atlas in an attempt to locate a particular place name; if they fail to find it, they may leave, believing that the library does not have the answer. Again, a discussion with the user would probably lead the librarian to examine a gazetteer, which has considerably more place names for an area, to provide the answer to such a question.

One of the more difficult concepts for many map users to accept is that it may be possible to use a map of a larger area to answer a question for a smaller one. This is especially important for libraries that do not have large, detailed collections of maps for foreign countries. An example would be a question on the location of Angel Falls, Venezuela. Although the collection may not contain maps of Venezuela, a map of northern South America or of the whole continent may provide the correct location. Similarly, users may ask for a small map of a particular country but be shown only a wall-sized map that is too large. Again, using the above example, a map of South America would be able to provide a Venezuelan map for the user at a smaller size.

A "sliding-scale" concept should be used when answering geographic reference questions. The reference interview allows the librarian to ask specific questions to define the appropriate type of map to be used to answer the question. For example, suppose a user asks for a railroad map of Europe. Although the library has such a map, further questioning reveals that the user is really looking for railroads in Germany, and additional questions reveal that the user really wants to know if there is a subway system in Berlin. This question is probably going to require a different map than a railroad map of Europe. Librarians should let their minds "slide" through the various kinds of maps in the collection as the discussion with the user progresses. Users often do not define their questions before they approach the library; thus, the librarian must help clarify questions so that appropriate reference sources can be used to answer them.

Today's cartographic reference services must also include knowledge of Internet sources and an ability to search and find the increasing amount of cartographic information available via the Web. Using *Oddens' Bookmarks*, a reference librarian can search for current maps, historical maps, location of map libraries, online atlases, and online gazetteers and distance calculators, and may even download maps for a user's query. For example, *Oddens'* has been used to search for historical maps for areas from Atlanta to Zurich and has led users to identify locations of historic railroad roundhouses in Atlanta and an early baseball field in Boston. Each of these latter cases used the Library of Congress *Panoramic Maps 1847–1929* Web site to view historical landscapes (http://lcweb2.loc.gov/ammem/pmhtml/panhome.html).

Box 19.2

Search Strategy: A Map of Oberweis

A user entered the map library one afternoon to inquire if the library had any maps of Germany, as she was tracing her family history. A brief reference interview revealed that she was really looking for a detailed map that would show the town of Oberweis. The librarian first checked the gazetteer in *The Times Atlas of the World*, only to discover that this town was not listed. Two additional world gazetteers were also consulted, the *Columbia Gazetteer of the World* and *Merriam-Webster's Geographical Dictionary*, with no success. It became apparent that this was a small village that would require a specialized place name gazetteer, usually available only in research collections. Fortunately, the librarian had access to such tools in the collection, and the town was located in *Müllers Grosses Deutsches Ortsbuch*, which included a brief description of the village. An additional source, *Gazetteer to AMS 1:25,000 Maps of West Germany*, volume 2, also listed Oberweis and provided location information: latitude/longitude and an individual map number for libraries having this map series. The user not only found the location of the small village but also was able to view a detailed map (1:25,000) revealing the plan of the town. This map provided the user with the necessary information to locate her family's birthplace.

NOTES

1. Mark Monmonier and George A. Schnell, *Map Appreciation* (Englewood Cliffs, N.J.: Prentice-Hall, 1988), 15-25.

2. David A. Cobb, "Developing a Small Geographical Library with Special Emphasis on Indiana," *Focus on Indiana Libraries* 26 (Fall 1972): 114-20.

3. American Library Association, Map & Geography Round Table, *base line*, 1980– . Six times per year.

4. Prudence S. Adler and Donna P. Koepp, "Association of Research Libraries Geographic Information Systems Literacy Project," *Meridian* 7 (1992): 45-46.

5. Carolyn Anthony, "The World in the '90s," *Publishers Weekly* 237 (January 19, 1990): 20-30.

LIST OF SOURCES

Anderson, Ewan W. *An Atlas of World Political Flashpoints.* London: Pinter Reference, 1993. 243p.

ArcView GIS. [CD-ROM]. Redlands, Calif.: Environmental Systems Research Institute, 1999.

Atlas of North America: Space-Age Portrait of a Continent. Washington, D.C.: National Geographic Society, 1985. 264p.

Atlas of the Christian Church. Edited by Henry Chadwick and G. R. Evans. New York: Facts on File, 1987. 240p.

Atlas of the World. 7th ed. New York: Oxford University Press, 1999. 304p.

Background Notes. Washington, D.C.: U.S. Government Printing Office, 1954–. Irregular. Also available: http://www.state.gov/www/background_notes/index.html.

Boustani, Rafic, and Philippe Fargues. *The Atlas of the Arab World.* New York: Facts on File, 1991. 144p.

Census CD + Maps. [CD-ROM]. East Brunswick, N.J.: GeoLytics, 1999.

Centennia. [diskette]. Chicago: Clockwork Software, 1993.

Chaliand, Gerard, and Jean-Pierre Rageau. *Strategic Atlas.* 3d ed. New York: HarperCollins, 1992. 223p.

Clark, Audrey N. *Longman Dictionary of Geography, Human and Physical.* Essex, England: Longman, 1985. 724p.

The Columbia Gazetteer of the World. 3 vols. New York: Columbia University Press, 1998.

Crowder, Michael. *Historical Atlas of Africa.* Essex, England: Longman, 1985. 156p.

Gazetteer to AMS 1:25,000 Maps of West Germany. 3 vols. Washington, D.C.: U.S. Army Map Service, 1954.

Geographic Names Information System. Available: http://mapping.usgs.gov/www/gnis.

Gilbert, Martin. *Atlas of the Holocaust.* New York: Pergamon Press, 1993. 282p.

Guide to U.S. Map Resources. 2d ed. Compiled by David A. Cobb. Chicago: American Library Association, 1990. 495p.

Hammond Atlas of the World. 2d ed. Maplewood, N.J.: Hammond, Inc., 1998. 312p.

Hanson, Gerald T. *Historical Atlas of Arkansas.* Norman, Okla.: University of Oklahoma Press, 1989. 142p.

Historical Atlas of Canada. 3 vols. Toronto, Ont.: University of Toronto Press, 1987–1993.

Historical Atlas of Massachusetts. Edited by Richard Wilkie and Jack Tager. Amherst: University of Massachusetts Press, 1991. 152p.

Historical Atlas of the United States. Rev. ed. Washington, D.C.: National Geographic Society, 1988. 289p.

Inventory of World Topographic Mapping. Edited by Rolf Böhme. 3 vols. London: Elsevier, 1989–1993.

Keegan, John, and Andrew Wheatcroft. *Zones of Conflict: An Atlas of Future Wars.* New York: Simon & Schuster, 1986. 158p.

Lange, Nicholas de. *Atlas of the Jewish World.* Oxford: Phaidon, 1984. 240p.

MacKay, Angus. *Atlas of Medieval Europe*. New York: Routledge, 1997. 271p.

MapInfo. [CD-ROM]. Troy, N.Y.: MapInfo Corporation, 1997.

MapQuest. Available: http://www.mapquest.com.

Martis, Kenneth C. *The Historical Atlas of Political Parties in the United States Congress, 1789–1989*. New York: Macmillan, 1989. 518p.

Mattson, Mark T. *Atlas of the 1990 Census*. New York: Macmillan, 1992. 168p.

Merriam-Webster's Geographical Dictionary. 3d ed. Springfield, Mass.: Merriam-Webster, 1997. 1361p.

Microsoft Encarta Interactive World Atlas. [CD-ROM]. Redmond, Wash.: Microsoft, 2000.

Moore, Patrick. *Atlas of the Universe*. New York: Cambridge University Press, 1998. 288p.

Müller, Friedrich. *Müllers Grosses Deutsches Ortsbuch....* Wuppertal, Germany: Post- und Ortsbuchverlag, 1996/97. 1266p.

National Atlas of Canada. 5th ed. Ottawa, Ont.: Canada Geographical Services Division, 1987– . Also available: http://atlas.gc.ca/english.

The National Atlas of the United States of America. Washington, D.C.: U.S. Geological Survey, 1970. 417p. Updates available: http://www.nationalatlas.gov.

The National Gazetteer of the United States of America. Washington, D.C.: U.S. Geological Survey, 1982–. (USGS Professional Paper 1200).

The National Gazetteer of the United States of America, Concise 1990. Washington, D.C.: U.S. Government Printing Office, 1990. 526p. (USGS Professional Paper 1200-US).

National Geographic Road Atlas. Mountville, Pa.: MapQuest.com in association with National Geographic Maps and Melcher Media, 1998-. Annual.

National Imagery and Mapping Agency GEOnet Names Server. Available: http://164.214.2.59/gns/html/index.html.

The New International Atlas. 25th anniversary ed. Chicago: Rand McNally, 1996. 1200p.

Nunavut Atlas. Edited by Rick Riewe. Edmonton, Alb.: Canadian Circumpolar Institute, 1992. 259p.

Oddens' Bookmarks. Available: http://oddens.geog.uu.nl/index.html.

Omni Gazetteer of the United States of America. Edited by Frank R. Abate. 11 vols. Detroit, Mich.: Omnigraphics, 1991.

Pogonowski, Iwo. *Poland, A Historical Atlas*. New York: Hippocrene Books, 1987. 321p.

Rand McNally Commercial Atlas and Marketing Guide. Chicago: Rand McNally, 1876– . Annual.

Rand McNally Road Atlas. Chicago: Rand McNally, 1926– . Annual.

Robinson, Francis. *Atlas of the Islamic World since 1500*. New York: Facts on File, 1982. 238p.

Smith, Dan. *The State of the World Atlas*. 6th ed. London: Penguin, 1999. 144p.

Street Atlas USA. [CD-ROM Version 8.0]. Yarmouth, Maine: DeLorme, 1999.

The Times Atlas of the Second World War. Edited by John Keegan. New York: Harper & Row, 1989. 254p.

The Times Atlas of the World. 10th ed. with revisions. London: Times Books, 1999. 220p.

The Times Atlas of World History. 4th ed. Edited by Geoffrey Parker. London: Times Books, 1993. 360p.

Topo USA. [CD-ROM Version 2.0]. Yarmouth, Maine: DeLorme, 1999.

Tübinger Atlas des Vorderen Orients. Wiesbaden, Germany: Dr. Ludwig Reichert Verlag, 1977– .

The Weather Almanac. 9th ed. Edited by Richard A. Wood. Farmington Hills, Mich.: Gale Group, 1999. 738p.

The Weather Channel. Available: http://weather.com.

World Mapping Today. Edited by R. B. Parry and C. R. Perkins. 2d ed. London: Bowker-Saur, 2000. 1064p.

Yahoo! Maps. Available: http://maps.yahoo.com.

ADDITIONAL READINGS

American Library Association, Map & Geography Round Table. *base line.* 1980– . Six times per year.

This newsletter provides current information on cartographic materials, other publications of interest to map and geography librarians, meetings, related government activities, and map librarianship.

Buisseret, David, ed. *From Sea Charts to Satellite Images: Interpreting North American History through Maps.* Chicago: University of Chicago Press, 1990. 324p.

This work provides an introduction to the use of cartography in historical research, with a series of essays describing different map types prevalent in the United States.

Cobb, David A. "Reference Service and Map Librarianship." *RQ* 24 (1984): 204-9.

Cobb defines both the uniqueness of map reference service and the many similarities it shares with general reference service.

Larsgaard, Mary Lynette. *Map Librarianship: An Introduction.* 3d ed. Englewood, Colo.: Libraries Unlimited, 1998. 487p.

This text constitutes the most comprehensive description of map librarianship, including information on collection development, cataloging, reference, and care of maps. The appendixes provide useful information for those just beginning to work with maps.

Monmonier, Mark, and George A. Schnell. *Map Appreciation.* Englewood Cliffs, N.J.: Prentice-Hall, 1988. 431p.

Written by two geographers, this book provides an excellent explanation of the different types of maps (e.g., photomaps, population maps, political maps, computer maps).

Seavey, Charles A. "Map Collection Development Planning: Mapkeeper and Library Administrator Working Together Can Tailor a Rational Acquisition Policy." *Information Bulletin* (Western Association of Map Libraries) 15 (1984): 268-79.

This is an excellent article for the librarian wishing to develop a collection development policy for the map collection.

Special Libraries Association, Geography and Map Division. *Bulletin.* 1947– . Quarterly.

This journal presents original articles on research problems, technical services, and other aspects of cartographic and geographic literature.

Western Association of Map Libraries. *Information Bulletin.* 1969– . Three times per year.

This lively journal includes articles, announcements, and news regarding new maps, atlases, and related publications.

Wood, Denis. *The Power of Maps.* New York: Guilford Press, 1992. 248p.

The author challenges traditional cartographic ideas and lays a framework for the map as an influential communication medium.

CHAPTER

20

BIBLIOGRAPHIC SOURCES

Carol Bates Penka

USES AND CHARACTERISTICS

Knowledge of bibliographic sources is essential for both librarians and scholars. Bibliographies are used to answer a wide variety of questions and to further research by identifying resources on various topics. A historian studying the Civil War may seek a better understanding of plantation life by locating and reading novels written by women in the South during that time period. A school librarian may wish to select books on dinosaurs for the library's collection to satisfy the scientific interests of the students in the school. A rare-book librarian may need to study books published in a particular place during a particular period to identify a fragment of a work. A library user wants to read the best translation of a literary work originally published in German. In each case, a bibliographic source would be consulted to achieve the desired result.

In addition, many of the most challenging questions that a reference librarian faces deal with bibliographic puzzles involving the verification of incomplete or inaccurate information. A user wants to find a particular book in the library. The librarian must then determine the following:

1. Do the library's records show that the library owns the book?
2. If not, is the user looking for a book that really exists—that is, has it actually been published?
3. Is the user's information correct, or only partially correct? For example, could the author's name be a pseudonym or perhaps misspelled, thus rendering the search of the library's catalog fruitless?
4. If the information is not completely correct, did the user get the information about the book title from a print source, or has it perhaps been garbled in an oral communication?

The librarian must decide what path to take to re-create the information in correct form or to verify that the information is correct. A seemingly simple question—does the library own this book?—may turn into a puzzle requiring the skills of a legendary detective and the use of multiple bibliographic sources.

"The term *bibliography* can have two definitions: there is bibliography itself, an activity, and there is a bibliography, the product of this activity."[1] Bibliographies generally belong to two groups. *Enumerative* or *systematic* bibliographies are concerned with the listing of books and other documents. The second group of bibliographies, which are composed of several subtypes, are concerned primarily with the study of books as physical objects. Some define the cultural impact of texts as yet a third type of bibliographical study. In this chapter the focus is bibliographic products that meet the first definition.

In the print environment, the usual definition of enumerative bibliography refers to a list of works compiled on some common organizing principle, such as authorship, subject, place of publication, chronology, or printer/publisher. The primary arrangement of the list is usually alphabetical, although a subject classification scheme, such as the Dewey Decimal Classification, may be used. Secondary arrangement schemes may also be employed. To illustrate, a bibliography of writings by Ernest Hemingway (author approach, with primary arrangement by title) may be secondarily arranged by the dates the works were published. Indexes to the main listings are usually included to provide access points not covered by the primary and secondary arrangements. For example, the Ernest Hemingway bibliography would probably include an index of the publishers of the works listed and an index to the type of literature, such as short stories, novels, etc. Currently, most print bibliographic sources are derived or printed from an electronic database and may be sold in either or both formats. The two formats may or may not be identical in content.

Electronic resources differ from print sources and, with a few exceptions, provide a superior bibliographic product. The internal file structure of the electronic database, which is invisible to the user, is usually based on the date/time the item was entered into the database. Each record is identified by a unique accession number assigned to the record at the time of its entry into the database. Most fields or elements of the bibliographic record are searchable by keyword or phrase, although fields can be made "display only" (not searchable). Using the Boolean operators *and, or,* and *not,* the searcher is able to perform extremely precise queries based on the information needs of the moment. Other commands may limit the search to particular publication years, publishers, formats, languages, or other factors. Depending on the capabilities of the database, a search for all books published in Canada in the 1980s on the subject of immigration could be conducted quickly and easily. Because of the limited number of access points, the same search in a print source would be difficult and time-consuming, if not impossible. The printout from the computer search could be produced as an author list, a title list, a list in chronological or reverse chronological order, or in any number of other ways. In cases where it is not illegal to do so, search results downloaded from a computer search can become a freestanding database searchable in a similar fashion to the larger database from which it was derived.

Electronic databases have proven their superiority for both users and compilers. For users the electronic product is superior because of the ease of producing precise, customized search results. Perhaps the greatest advantage of an electronic catalog from the compiler's perspective is the fact that future additions and corrections can be made, location symbols added, and re-sequencing accomplished with relative ease and low cost.[2]

The theory of bibliographic control is discussed more fully in Chapter 4. This chapter discusses the concepts necessary for the study of bibliographies. The process of providing bibliographic control generally means providing two different kinds of access to information: bibliographic access (i.e., letting the user know of the existence of the work), and physical access (i.e., letting the user know where the work can be found). In the current library environment, both types of access can be provided by a wide variety of methods.

To achieve the aims of bibliographic control—providing bibliographic and physical access—three major types of reference sources have evolved: bibliographies, library catalogs, and bibliographic utilities. The firm distinctions between types of sources are rapidly disappearing in the electronic environment.

Distinctions between types of bibliographic sources are often made based on the bibliographic level of material that is listed and whether the physical location of the work is indicated. Does the bibliography or catalog include journal articles and book chapters, or are only whole books listed? In general, bibliographies list works or parts of work regardless of their physical location; library catalogs aim to list the works located in one or more libraries. Bibliographic utilities serve both functions, providing complete machine-readable cataloging copy and a list of libraries that own the item reflected in the catalog record.

The desire to achieve universal bibliographic control (UBC) is shared by librarians and scholars alike. "Simply put, the ideal of UBC is that each document should be cataloged once in its country of origin and that cataloging should be made available to libraries around the world."[3] On a more theoretical level, Patrick Wilson, in *Two Kinds of Power,* defines universal bibliographic control as the creation of an "exhaustive inventory" of all the works that have ever been published.[4] Although extremely noble, these aspirations toward UBC are unattainable. However, we are now able to go a long way toward achieving this aim through the cooperative efforts of national libraries, national standards organizations, and the efforts of the bibliographic utilities in various countries.

Types of Bibliographies and Catalogs

Bibliographies and catalogs fall into several basic types, and one should study these basic distinctions before reading about specific tools.

National bibliographies list the materials published in a particular country. In addition, the scope of the work may be enlarged to include works written about the country or in the language of the country, regardless of the place of publication. Because the intent is that the publication be as comprehensive as possible, material written by the citizens of the country, wherever published, may also be included.

Often, national bibliographies are published under the auspices of the national library or other governmental agency charged with the responsibility for the production of the national bibliography. Usually this entity is the recipient of copies received to satisfy the provisions of legal deposit. Under legal deposit, certain libraries or agencies are entitled by law to receive one or more copies of certain types of publications printed or published in the country. Often legal deposit is required for copyright protection under copyright law, but the two do not always go together. For example, in Canada copyright protection is separated from legal deposit requirements, and there is no system of legal deposit in the United States.

Print versions of current national bibliographies usually appear weekly or monthly, with both annual and multiyear cumulations. Electronic versions may be updated as often as daily. In many cases, retrospective national bibliographies, which give a record of the country's publishing history over a long period of time, have also been published.

The terms *current* and *retrospective,* as applied to bibliographies, refer to the time period covered by the items selected for inclusion in the bibliography. Current bibliographic sources list books or other items close to the time at which they are published. A retrospective bibliography covers materials published during an earlier time period. Compilations of current bibliographic sources turn into retrospective sources when the time period covered recedes into the past.

Trade bibliographies are produced by commercial publishers and serve to provide the information necessary to select and acquire recently published materials. Usually the materials included in trade bibliographies are trade books—those intended for sale to the general public and generally available for sale in bookstores—as opposed to mass market books, which are sold in grocery stores or on newsstands. Nontrade publications, such as textbooks, government documents, encyclopedias, and dissertations, are not listed in trade bibliographies. As a consequence, they must be acquired directly from the publisher or specialized dealers. They may, however, be listed in the national bibliography of the country in which they are produced. The predominant form of trade bibliography is the in-print list, such as R. R. Bowker's *Books in Print* (*BIP*). In-print lists show which titles are currently available from publishers. In another form, trade bibliographies such as *American Book Publishing Record* provide lists of books as they are published. The various electronic products discussed later in the chapter are blurring the distinctions between types of bibliographic publications, but these distinctions should still be understood.

Library catalogs exist to serve the users of a particular library by listing the holdings and location of materials held in that library. The term *online public access catalog,* or OPAC, refers to an electronic catalog designed for end users, as opposed to a version of the catalog that may be used by reference librarians or staff in other units. OPACS generally have user-friendly interfaces. Union catalogs (or union lists) identify the material held in the collections of more than one library. Such shared cataloging networks as OCLC and RLIN (often referred to as bibliographic utilities) serve as union catalogs for their member libraries. The geographic area covered by union lists may vary from local to multi-national. In the case of serials, it is quite common to find not only the lists of libraries holding a particular title but also a record of which volumes each library holds.

Bibliographies of bibliographies are lists of bibliographies that have been created as a means of bibliographic control. They are usually general in scope and offer a good starting place when trying to locate a list of works on a particular subject.

Subject bibliographies, as the name implies, are lists of materials that relate to a particular topic. Some authorities consider national bibliographies that include material written about a country as being subject bibliographies rather than true national bibliographies.

Kinds of Information Contained in Bibliographies and Library Catalogs

The data elements in a bibliography entry depend largely on the intent of the publication. Current national bibliographies exist in part to facilitate the international exchange of cataloging data in a standardized format. Therefore, the entries reflect the information available in machine-readable cataloging records. In addition to author, title, and publication data, each entry usually includes subject headings, contents notes, and suggested classification numbers. Name entries, both personal and corporate, are standardized with appropriate *see* references from alternate forms of the name. Ordering information such as price is often included.

Because trade bibliographies are produced for the use of book dealers, they contain information that is essential for book purchases. Examples include price, availability, publishers' addresses, and International Standard Book Number (ISBN). The ISBN is a code number assigned by the publisher to provide unique identification of a particular work. There will be, for example, different ISBNs for the cloth and paperback versions of the same title. The ISBN consists of a country code, a publisher identifier, a title identifier, and a checkdigit. For example, the ISBN for the second edition of this textbook is 1-56308-129-6 for the paperback edition and 1-56308-130-X for the hardback edition. The International Standard Serial Number serves a similar role, uniquely identifying each serial title with an eight-digit number.

Use of bibliographies will depend on the type of information needed. If one needs simply to verify the existence of an item, a source giving short entries may be sufficient. If one needs both to identify and to locate copies, a union list is necessary. If the intent is to purchase materials, information such as price, ISBN, and availability is definitely required.

EVALUATION

Evaluation of general bibliographies and library catalogs is primarily concerned with the following criteria: authority, scope of the bibliography, arrangement of contents, frequency of publication, and currency of the included material. These criteria are used to evaluate the bibliography itself. Additional criteria should be considered when choosing a bibliography for inclusion in a collection, and these are discussed in the section on selection.

Authority

Authority concerns the qualifications of the compiler or sponsor of the bibliography. Compiling a national or trade bibliography is a massive undertaking. It usually involves the resources of a major publisher, national library, or governmental agency. Therefore, the issue of authority usually concerns the compilers of subject bibliographies or resources found on the Internet. Do the compilers have the educational background or academic stature to justify their roles in compiling these bibliographies? Does the organization sponsoring the bibliography have a particular political agenda or viewpoint?

Scope

The scope of any reference tool is of primary importance when evaluating its usefulness. "The domain or set of items in the bibliographic universe from which a bibliography's content is selected and drawn defines the outer limits of the scope of a bibliography. Ordinarily, the domain will be larger than the number of items actually listed, as some principle of selection is applied to define and restrict the bibliography's scope."[5] The scope of the bibliography, meaning the domain of items selected for inclusion, should be stated by the compilers in the preface or introduction. Furthermore, any exclusion of materials, for reasons such as place of publication, language, time, type of materials, level of bibliographic unit, format, or subject, should also be noted. The librarian will need to make frequent use of the introductory material, because this type of information is not always immediately apparent simply from reading the entries in the body of the work. For example, the *Union List of Serials* does not contain entries for newspapers, a fact not readily discernible simply from scanning the listings.

Reading the introductory material is essential, but it may not be enough. Commercial publishers may not be too eager to point out the limitations of their publication, and the introductions to national bibliographies are often in a language unfamiliar to the librarian. Therefore, it is also essential to consult guides to the tools of reference work that give clear and concise descriptions of the coverage, accuracy, intent, and scope of the bibliographic sources. Balay's *Guide to Reference Books, Walford's Guide to Reference Material* (the British counterpart to Balay), and *Canadian Reference Sources* serve this purpose. (These sources are discussed more fully in Chapter 13.) Other, more specialized tools exist for specific types of bibliographies, and a selection of these tools is listed in the "Additional Readings" section at the end of this chapter.

When a bibliography or catalog includes coverage dates in its title, the librarian must learn what those dates mean. In some cases, the dates may indicate the years in which the items included were published. In the case of the *National Union Catalog,* the dates mean the years in which the cataloging copy was reported to the Library of Congress. On the other hand, the title of the printed catalog of the New York Public Library includes the dates 1911–1971. Here 1911 refers to the date of the founding of the library and has no relation to the dates of the publications listed in the catalog.

Similarly, the word "international" may be included in a title merely as a selling point. The true geographical coverage of an international or regional work must be determined by reading introductory material and examining the contents for depth of inclusion from the countries or areas intended to be covered. The coverage may be uneven, or spotty entries from a few countries may be included to justify the use of the word "international."

Arrangement

The titles discussed in this chapter vary widely in the primary form of arrangement. Some catalogs have author, title, and subject entries in separate alphabetical sequences. Dictionary catalogs interfile all three types of entries in a single alphabetical listing. A classified subject catalog arranges the contents by subject according to a classification scheme. The index/register arrangement consists of a register that contains the complete bibliographic descriptions of all entries arranged in accession number order. Alphabetical indexes contain a brief bibliographic description and the register (or accession) number that locates the complete entry in the register. The register is never superseded. Cumulated indexes are published at regular intervals. Practically any combination of arrangement and subarrangement is possible. In each case, indexes, which complement the primary arrangement, are essential to enhance the effectiveness of access. Any of these arrangements may be helpful at a given time, depending on the user's need. In reference work, the librarian needs to be aware of the possible arrangements and to make the appropriate choice of tools depending on the information at hand and the information to be located.

Currency

Currency refers to the delay—or lack thereof—between the date of publication and the time at which the publication is entered in the bibliography. Obviously, publications designed for the book trade should offer the most recent information to fulfill the intent of their publication: providing current information on currently available materials. Book trade publications may also list publications announced for publication but not yet published.

Countries that maintain no formal system of legal deposit are at a disadvantage in trying to keep up with publishing output in the areas of their coverage. In addition, bibliographies produced in developing countries where the production of a national bibliography is a major undertaking have perhaps the greatest problem with currency. In regions such as Latin America or Africa, where a prompt book order is necessary to obtain one of the few copies produced before the title goes out of print, national bibliographies are rarely produced fast enough to be of help in acquisitions. Librarians must rely on the services of book jobbers in the region and other means to supplement information obtained in national and trade bibliographies.

SELECTION

The selection of a particular bibliographic source for inclusion in a library's collection depends on the mission of the library and on its collection development policies. Library units using bibliographic tools may well stretch across administrative or budgetary divisions in the library. Therefore, the reference department may be called upon to purchase and house a title that is more frequently used by catalogers or subject bibliographers than by reference librarians. Yet all concerned may feel that the title should be in the reference department because of the use of the material by so many different personnel in the library: acquisitions, cataloging, interlibrary loan, reference, and subject bibliographers. Reference librarians can be encouraged by the knowledge that all sources are eventually used for reference purposes. Often, reference library budgets are increased in anticipation of this demand on their monetary resources by other departments.

Many of the sources discussed in this chapter would be found in most libraries. Current sources, such as *Books in Print,* are essential tools for selection and acquisitions in both public and academic libraries of all sizes. National and trade bibliographies of foreign countries, however, are most often found in large research libraries. Nevertheless, large public libraries maintaining foreign-language collections would frequently need at least some of these foreign sources, particularly in-print lists.

Most often the choice is fairly clear-cut: Only one source will fill a particular need. Therefore, the most frequent decisions to be made involve choice of format (print or microfilm versus electronic access), number of copies, and the retention of those copies.

The selection of format involves weighing several factors concerned with use of the item. In general, providing electronic access offers the greatest advantage to users. The first and most obvious advantage is the enhanced searching capability provided by electronic access. The ability to search a database by phrase or keyword and to combine the resultant sets using Boolean searching techniques simply cannot be matched by the indexes in a print product. Search sets may also be limited by other criteria such as date, language, or year. Unless mounted as a stand-alone CD-ROM, electronic products are accessible through the Web or local area networks to multiple users at the same time. These users may be located anywhere in the world.

Cost must also be considered when selecting which form of a bibliography or catalog to purchase. So many factors come into the equation that it is hard to generalize; each library's situation is unique. The use of electronic access involves the purchase and upkeep of supporting equipment (computers, CD-ROM drives, networks) in addition to the cost of the bibliographic product itself. The exact cost of electronic access will vary depending on the number of simultaneous users allowed and whether the product will be networked or run on a standalone computer. Moreover, the cost of some products varies depending on the size of the library's overall budget. In much the same way, bibliographic sources (both print and electronic) produced by the H. W. Wilson Company are sold on a service basis, under which the price depends on the size of the library's book budget. In some cases, the cost of an electronic product is discounted if the library also subscribes to the paper version. Relative costs are discussed in Chapters 5 and 13.

Small libraries of all types generally keep only the latest edition of a bibliographic source. They would simply be overrun if they retained superseded issues or volumes. Large academic or research libraries retain all copies of bibliographic tools to provide for a historical perspective on publishing. In other cases, if libraries require that payment of lost book fees reflect the actual price of the book at the time of its publication, historical publishing information is needed for accounting purposes. However, the choice of format complicates this issue. Libraries that provide access to bibliographic information via the Web are actually leasing access to that data, but they do not own the material. Indeed, the data do not even reside on computers owned by the library itself. Suppliers of CD-ROM versions of bibliographic tools often require return of the superseded disc when a new one is issued. If a subscription to the CD-ROM product is canceled, contracts often require the return of all discs. The provision of online access thus does not guarantee the archival coverage that will form the basis of future historical research. To ensure a retrospective collection, a library must often acquire either a microform or a print copy of the same title acquired electronically. To do so is an expensive proposition. Among the current issues facing librarians today are: How many times and in how many formats should a library buy the same data? And how many libraries should do so? Should libraries cooperatively provide for historical access rather than having each library do so individually? And how will this cooperation be coordinated and under whose auspices?

IMPORTANT GENERAL SOURCES

The following discussion covers those bibliographic compilations that provide the most comprehensive coverage of books or serials or both. For the United States, both current and retrospective sources are described; for Canada, Great Britain, and France, only current bibliographies are included. Works providing information about materials currently available from commercial publishers (in-print lists) are discussed, as are a few of those that offer lists of recommended works in a particular area or for a specific group of users. The printed catalogs of a few of the world's largest libraries, as well as a selection of bibliographies of bibliographic materials, are also included.

Shared Cataloging Networks

The most important bibliographic sources in today's library have neither a long history nor a traditional format. Shared cataloging networks (often called bibliographic utilities), such as OCLC and RLIN, were established about 30 years ago to provide machine-readable cataloging records and holdings information for their member libraries. Their services have expanded to support resource sharing through interlibrary loan and document delivery (see Chapter 7). Cooperative research projects extend the scope of the organizations.

Both OCLC and RLIN provide services not just to libraries for the use of librarians (e.g., cataloging, interlibrary loan, and document delivery), but also directly to end users. In doing so, bibliographic utilities are not only revolutionizing access to the bibliographic universe, they are also rapidly changing the interactions between libraries and their users.

Begun in 1967, the Online Computer Library Center (OCLC) provided, as of 2000, bibliographic records and holdings information for more than 36,000 libraries in 74 countries. Although the numbers obviously change daily, by 2000, the database contained more than 43 million records for books, serials, audiovisual materials, maps, archives/manuscripts, sound recordings, music scores, and computer files. The date ranges of records entered into the system extend from almost 800 records from the 2000 B.C.E. to 1 B.C.E. time period to more than 6 million for the 1990s. Retrospective conversion projects, whereby some of the world's leading libraries enter newly created machine-readable records for older materials into the system, make the shared cataloging networks the first bibliographic source of choice for materials from all time periods, not just from the period since 1971 when computerized cataloging began.

Access to the OCLC Online Union Catalog (WorldCat) and its other services is provided by several different systems, each to be used for specific purposes. The Prism service provides access for cataloging and resource sharing (interlibrary loan and the production of union catalogs). The FirstSearch service is aimed at end users who may access not only WorldCat but also other databases of indexes, abstracts, and full texts. FirstSearch, which is menu-driven, also allows users to search their own catalog for holdings and then to input an interlibrary loan request if their library does not own the item.

The Research Libraries Information Network (RLIN) is the shared cataloging network operated by the Research Libraries Group (RLG), a nonprofit membership corporation composed in 2000 of 161 institutions, including university libraries, archives, museums, and other research or educational bodies. RLG focuses its attention on the development of cooperative solutions to the problems of information access, information delivery, preservation, and the management of digital information. The services offered by RLIN are similar in structure to those of OCLC. The central RLIN bibliographic database is a union catalog of more than 105 million items held in RLG member institutions, plus an additional 100 libraries that use RLIN. In addition, it includes records that describe works cataloged by the Library of Congress, the National Library of Medicine, the U.S. Government Printing Office, CONSER (Conversion of Serials Project), the British Library, the British National Bibliography, and the National Union Catalog of Manuscript Collections. RLIN also offers access to CitaDel, a service providing access to 13 databases of journals, newspapers, conference proceedings, dissertations, and other publications, which are indexed at the individual article level. These databases include *Avery Index to Architectural Periodicals, Chicano Database, FRANCIS,* and *Inside Information Plus* from the British Library. Special databases of interest to scholars complement the other files offered. The *English Short Title Catalogue, Hand Press Book Database,* and *SCIPIO: Art and Rare Book Sales Catalogs* are examples. Eureka is RLIN's Web-based search interface, and Zephyr is a service that allows users of local online catalogs to search the RLIN database using the same commands as their local system. Using Ariel, RLG's document transmission software for the Internet, libraries can scan articles or images and transmit the electronic image over the Internet directly to either their users' personal computers or a receiving library (see Chapter 7).

United States Bibliography

The study of bibliography in the United States is complicated by several factors. First, there is no official list of books published in the United States. Second, there is no law requiring that publishers donate books under legal deposit in the United States. Third, legal deposit is not required for copyright protection under U.S. law. The retrospective coverage of publishing in the United States must be pieced together by using many sources. The earlier sources were produced by individual bibliographers, and they reflect their compilers' biases and idiosyncrasies. More recently, commercial publishers have dominated the field. Currently, the products and services of the Library of Congress and the shared cataloging networks, OCLC and RLIN, are the dominant elements in the provision of bibliographic control in the United States.

For most bibliographic quests, a search of OCLC or RLIN is the first order of business. The speed, ease of searching, and depth and breadth of coverage make searching the bibliographic utilities the first choice in almost all cases. A reference librarian, however, still needs a thorough knowledge of these early bibliographic sources (see Figure 20.1). To answer a question, the librarian may need to look at several tools and may well find pieces of the bibliographic puzzle in each of them. A knowledge of these sources will assist the librarian in deciding which tools to examine and, in some cases, may narrow the search to only one tool that will give a particular type of information. For example, a bibliographic description of a book published in 1857 might be found in the *National Union Catalog* or in OCLC, but the price is likely to be found only in Roorbach's *Bibliotheca Americana.*

Figure 20.1 Timeline of major sources for American bibliography.

CHRONOLOGY OF AMERICAN RETROSPECTIVE BIBLIOGRAPHY

1492 — 1639 — 1800 — 1820 — 1830 — 1846 — 1861 — 1871

Sabin, J. Bibliotheca Americana .... (1492)——(1868)

Evans, C. American Bibliography .... (1639)——(1800)

Shaw, R. American Bibliography .... (1800)——(1819)

Shoemaker, R. Checklist of American Imprints... .... (1820)——(1829)

Checklist of American Imprints .... (1830)——(1846)

Roorbach, O. Bibliotheca American .... (1820)——(1861)

Kelly, J. American Catalogue of Books .... (1861)——(1871)

1876 — 1899 — 1910 — 1928 — 1977 — Present

American Catalogue .... (1876)——(1910)

United States Catalog .... (1899)——(1928)

Cumulative Book Index .... (1928)——(1999)

American Book Publishing Record Cumulative .... (1876)——(1977)

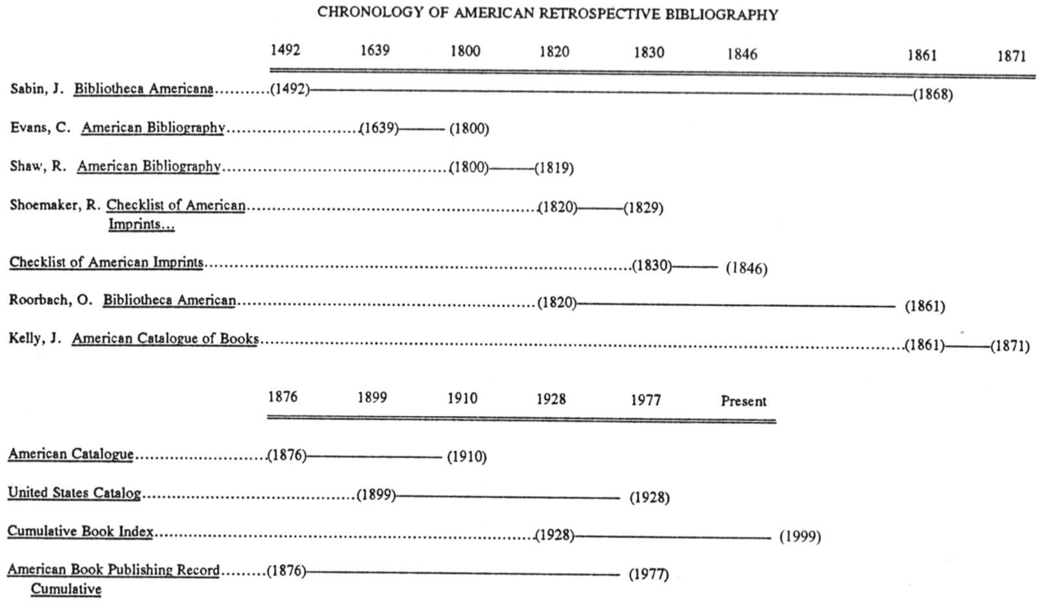

United States Retrospective Bibliography (to 1876)

Charles Evans's *American Bibliography* lists books, pamphlets, and periodicals published in the United States from 1639 through 1800. It is the most important of the bibliographies covering this period. The titles included are arranged in chronological order by date of publication. Evans made every effort to include all publications and to give a complete bibliographic description of each item. Each volume includes an index of authors and anonymous titles and a list of printers and publishers. The fourteenth volume, published in 1959, provides a cumulative author-title index to the whole set. The references in the index are to the item numbers assigned to each entry, not to pages. Library locations are given, by code, for each item listed. Figure 20.2 shows a typical entry from the *American Bibliography.* An electronic version of the bibliography is produced on CD-ROM by NewsBank Readex in conjunction with the American Antiquarian Society.

Figure 20.2 Entry from *American Bibliography,* showing "Evans number." Charles Evans: AMERICAN BIBLIOGRAPHY, Peter Smith Publisher, Inc. Gloucester, MA 1942.

37339 DWIGHT, TIMOTHY 1752–1817
A DISCOURSE, DELIVERED AT NEW-HAVEN, FEB. 22, 1800; ON THE CHARACTER OF GEORGE WASHINGTON. . . .
Printed by Thomas Green and Son, New-Haven: 1800. pp. 55. 8vo.
Cover title: "Dr. Dwight's discourse, Feb. 22, 1800. Also, Gen. Washington's Farewell address." AAS, BA, BPL, CHS, CSL, G[r]L, HEH, JCB, LCP, LOC, MFM, MHS, NL, NYPL, NYSL, PL, P[r]U, RU, WC, WL, YC.

Early American Imprints: Series I, Evans is a microform set of the full texts of the nonserial titles listed in Evans's work. It is also available from NewsBank Readex. The microforms are filed in order by the item numbers in the Evans bibliography. The cataloging records for these microform copies have now been entered in the OCLC database as part of the Major Microforms Project, and the American Antiquarian Society has fully cataloged *Series I* in RLIN.

Ralph R. Shaw and Richard H. Shoemaker continued the Evans bibliography with *American Bibliography: A Preliminary Checklist for 1801–1819.* This 23-volume set includes 19 annual volumes and 4 additional volumes containing addenda, as well as author, title, publisher, and geographic indexes. Library locations for copies are given whenever possible. A microform reprint set of the full texts of the contents, *Early American Imprints Series II, Shaw-Shoemaker* is also available from NewsBank Readex. The set is arranged by the Shaw-Shoemaker numbers. The series continues with Shoemaker's *A Checklist of American Imprints for 1820–1829* and *A Checklist of American Imprints for 1830–*. As of 2000, coverage extended through 1846.

Orville Roorbach's *Bibliotheca Americana . . . 1820–1861* and James Kelly's *The American Catalogue of Books . . . Jan. 1861 to Jan. 1871* are trade bibliographies listing books published during the periods covered. They are alphabetical lists by author and title and give publisher and price information. Neither title is as complete or as accurate as one would like, but they are the only general bibliographies that cover the period.

Joseph Sabin's *Bibliotheca Americana* is an extremely valuable bibliography of books relating to the United States from its European discovery to 1868. It lists books, pamphlets, and periodicals published in the Western Hemisphere as well as elsewhere. Sabin differs from the titles discussed previously in that the emphasis is on complete bibliographic description. Therefore, contents notes and varying editions are frequently included. The entries also often give locations of copies and references to reviews. Primary Source Media is currently filming items listed in Sabin and is producing *The Sabin Collection Catalog on CD-ROM.* Cataloging records are available on RLIN.

United States Retrospective Bibliography (since 1876)

To counter the weakness in U. S. national bibliography, R. R. Bowker produced *American Book Publishing Record Cumulative, 1876–1949,* published in 1980, and *American Book Publishing Record Cumulative, 1950–1977,* published in 1978. Both sources have the same type of arrangement and scope. The main arrangement is by Dewey Decimal Classification, with separate volumes for fiction and juvenile fiction. These volumes are followed by author and title indexes. They do not include periodicals, government publications, theses, or a few other types of publications. The information in these bibliographies is taken from many sources, and the great value of the cumulation is the unique subject access combined with multiyear coverage.

The *American Catalogue of Books,* published by Publishers Weekly, covers the period 1876 to 1910 in volumes spanning varying numbers of years. Each volume provides author, title, and subject access to all books that were in print at the time the volume was published. *United States Catalog* was an in-print list published by H. W. Wilson in four editions from 1899 to 1928. Supplements to the *United States Catalog,* entitled *Cumulative Book Index,* were published in the years between editions. *Cumulative Book Index* is also the title of H. W. Wilson's bibliography of works in English published from 1928 to 1999.

Current United States Bibliography

Current bibliographic sources are heavily used in any library because they list works at the time they are published. These sources serve as selection aids for librarians, who are always eager to keep up-to-date collections. In addition, reference librarians use them to answer reference questions, including the verification and identification of bibliographic citations. Also, access to books by subject allows both librarians and users to determine those books that have been published on the topic of interest.

Cumulative Book Index (CBI), produced by the H. W. Wilson Company, ceased publication in March 2000 with the appearance of its 1999 cumulation. *CBI* had been published continuously since 1933, with coverage from 1928. Each volume was a listing of works in the English language that were published anywhere in the world, although it was most complete for the United States. *CBI* was arranged by author, title, and subject, in one alphabetical sequence. Information provided for each publication included full bibliographic description, price, ISBN or ISSN, and Library of Congress card number. Each volume also contained a directory of publishers and distributors that included addresses and other information such as ISBN prefixes. *CBI* was the most inclusive bibliography of works in English, and it may remain useful for verification of older titles not found elsewhere.

American Book Publishing Record (*ABPR*), a monthly publication from R. R. Bowker, provides full cataloging information for approximately 5,000 new titles as they are published. It does not include government publications, subscription books, dissertations, or pamphlets under 49 pages in length. It is arranged by Dewey Decimal Classification, with author and title indexes complementing the primary arrangement. In addition, the subject guide, which is arranged alphabetically, directs the user from the traced subject headings to the corresponding Dewey Decimal Classification numbers. The annual *ABPR,* published in March, is compiled from the 12 monthly issues. Five-year cumulations are available for 1970–1974, 1975–1979, and 1980–1984, with only annual cumulations available from 1985.

Current Bibliographies from Great Britain, France, and Canada

British National Bibliography (*BNB*), the national record of publishing in the United Kingdom and the Republic of Ireland, has been published by the British Library since 1950. Its content is based on the books received by the Legal Deposit Office of the British Library under the Copyright Act of 1911. It also contains advance notification of forthcoming titles that is supplied by publishers under the Cataloging in Publication (CIP) program. Cataloging in Publication is a program through which participating publishers provide galley proofs or the frontmatter of their books to the national library or other centralized catalog agency. A cataloging record is then prepared and returned to the publisher. The cataloging record becomes a part of the book and is published on the verso of the title page. CIP originated in the Library of Congress in 1971, and the program now operates internationally. The British Library catalogs *BNB* entries in the MARC21 format according to the second edition of the *Anglo-American Cataloguing Rules.* Full subject access is provided by Library of Congress Subject Headings and Dewey Decimal Classification numbers. In addition, such essential ordering information as ISBN and price is included as part of the entry.

BNB is available in print, on microfiche, and as an electronic file. Electronically, *BNB* can be purchased on CD-ROM or accessed online as *BNBMARC* (via the British Library's Blaise system). In all formats except CD-ROM the *BNB* is updated weekly. Print and microfiche editions have annual cumulations. Multiyear cumulations in various formats cover differing periods of time. The *1950–84 Author/Title Cumulation* on microfiche provides access in a single alphabetical sequence to 2.5 million entries. The 1981–1992 microfiche cumulation arranges 500,000 entries in classified subject order with author and title indexes.

The *British National Bibliography* (*BNB*) on CD-ROM is published by the British Library's National Bibliographic Service and is distributed in the United States by Chadwyck-Healey. The CD-ROM provides access to more than 1.7 million records. The current file includes all records from 1986 to the present on one CD-ROM. It is updated monthly, with each issue cumulating the file and replacing the previous disc. The backfile contains records from 1950 to 1985 on one CD-ROM. Twenty-five searchable indexes provide access by such record elements as author, title, keywords, series, subject, publication details, and Dewey class number. Boolean operators can be used to optimize search results. Cataloging records for items listed in the *BNB* can also be found in both RLIN and OCLC.

The current national bibliography of France is the *Bibliographie Nationale Française* (*BNF*) (until 1990, *Bibliographie de la France*), which records titles received by the Bibliothèque Nationale de France through legal deposit. It has been continuously published since 1811, although the frequency, arrangement, and supplements have varied through the years. Now published as a biweekly title, *BNF* has four supplements listing publications in series, official publications, music, and maps and atlases. Its primary arrangement is by Universal Decimal Classification (UDC). (The Universal Decimal Classification began as a French translation of the Dewey Decimal Classification. It contains the same basic arrangement but is much more detailed than Dewey.) Author and title indexes, published in each issue, complement the classified arrangement, and cumulations of the indexes are published three times a year on microfiche. An annual cumulative index is issued in print.

Bibliographie Nationale Française on CD-ROM contains all French MARC (machine-readable cataloging) records of titles received by the Bibliothèque Nationale de France since 1970 on two discs. Records are taken from the *Bibliographie de la France;* its supplement *Publications Officielles;* and, for new titles not yet listed, the legal deposit records. Searching capabilities are similar to other national bibliographies on CD-ROM distributed by Chadwyck-Healey. Publication is bimonthly, with each issue cumulating the file and replacing all previous discs.

Canadiana, the current national bibliography of Canada, lists and describes a wide variety of publications produced in Canada, including books, periodicals, pamphlets, educational kits, theses, microforms, government documents, sheet music and scores, sound recordings, video recordings, and CD-ROM and other electronic documents. Canadian publishers are required to send two copies of these items to the National Library of Canada as they are published. In Canada, legal deposit of Canadian publications is not related to copyright, but it is required by law. In addition, *Canadiana* lists titles published outside Canada that are of special interest because they are about Canadian topics or because they are written by Canadian authors. *Canadiana,* which is produced by the National Library of Canada/Bibliothèque nationale du Canada, is available as an online service, on microfiche, or on CD-ROM. Online access is provided through the National Library of Canada's *AMICUS* database.

Canadiana on microfiche (1992–) consists of two noncumulating registers of full MARC records: Register 1 lists Canadian imprints; Register 2 records foreign imprints written by Canadian authors or having Canadian subject content. Twelve monthly indexes cumulate entries from the previous months, and the December issue cumulates index entries for the previous year. The indexes provide access to the registers by the following: author, titles, and series; English subject headings; French subject headings; ISBNs, ISSNs; and Dewey Classification numbers. Multiyear cumulations of *Canadiana* (microfiche) are also available, priced and sold separately by Bibliographic Services of the National Library of Canada.

From 1950 until December 1991, a print version of *Canadiana* was published 11 times a year with annual cumulations. It succeeded the *Canadian Catalogue of Books,* which had been published from 1921 to 1949.

Coverage of *Canadiana* on CD-ROM (2000 release) differs from the print and microfiche editions of *Canadiana* in three important ways. First, the CD-ROM includes cataloging records created between 1973, the year in which the Library began cataloging with an online system, and June 2000. Second, authority files are included along with the bibliographic databases as one integrated package. Third, the scope of the national bibliography now extends beyond the works in the collections of the National Library of Canada to include records from other important databases, such as the National Archives of Canada's *Carto-Canadiana. Carto-Canadiana* is a list of cartographic materials produced by Canadian agencies, both governmental and non-governmental, which are held in the National Archives of Canada. The list contains full cataloging records for maps, atlases, and globes in a variety of formats, including microform and electronic. Further releases will include bibliographic records for items published before 1973 as well as older *Canadiana* materials from other databases.

Canadiana, both CD-ROM and microfiche versions, is created from machine-readable cataloging records found in and selected from the *AMICUS* database. *AMICUS* is the bilingual information system of the National Library of Canada. The database is continuously updated and contains over 9 million cataloging records for books, serials, sound recordings, theses, microforms, and other publications. The Library's fee-based search service, Access AMICUS, allows Canadian libraries and researchers to search the *AMICUS* database at a moderate cost.

Sources of Purchasing Information

In-print lists identify titles that are currently available from publishers. Because books may remain in print for a number of years, the current list can also be useful in identifying material published much earlier. In reference work, in-print lists are often used to determine if an announced book has been published, if a later edition of a work has been published, or what volumes of a series are still in print. Subject specialists use in-print lists as a way of determining what is being published in the subject area they cover. Virtually every in-print list is available in electronic format, with the enhanced access that Boolean logic and keyword searching allow.

The primary advantage of the in-print list is that it consolidates book purchasing information from thousands of publishers in one integrated list. Other resources, however, are rivaling the in-print list in usefulness. Almost all publishers worldwide now produce catalogs available through the Internet. Frequently these electronic catalogs produce more accurate, up-to-date information than that available from in-print lists. Several Internet resources provide Web-accessible directories of these publishers' catalogs; the NorthernLight and Yahoo! search engines are examples. AcqWeb, the Web site (http://www.library.vanderbilt.edu/law/acqs/acqs.html) for acquisitions librarians maintained by Vanderbilt University, provides a directory of publishers. In addition, vendors such as the Academic Book Center and Martinus Nijhoff International have Internet-accessible databases for their customers to use in purchasing books and serials. Other book vendors such as Casalini Libri, Purvill Libros, and Otto Harrassowitz have become OCLC selection vendors. Selection vendors load minimal-level cataloging records for the books they sell into OCLC WorldCat. This process allows libraries to use the OCLC interlibrary loan module to send orders for acquisition purposes to these vendors.

R. R. Bowker has been producing reference materials for the U.S. market since 1872 and has totally dominated the in-print list field for over 50 years. The publishing company maintains electronic contact with publishers regarding the status of books: date of publication, availability, price, etc. From the database thus developed, a family of in-print products, both print and electronic, is produced. The electronic products are available via Web access, CD-ROM, site licenses for local tape loading, or through bibliographic utilities such as OCLC.

Books in Print (*BIP*) is an annual listing of books available from U. S. publishers. It is a nine-volume set with separate author and title sections. Each entry includes price, ISBN, publisher, binding, and other ordering information. Volume 9, a separate stand-alone *Publishers Index,* lists more than 63,000 publishers and their addresses. The lists are compiled from information provided by publishers. *BIP* is a list of what publishers report is in print at a given moment. Because data are collected from thousands of sources, errors of omission and commission are not uncommon. No attempt is made to standardize the form of an author's name. It is, therefore, possible to have a single author listed in more than one form, so one must be careful when searching the author volume. The works of an author whose name is listed as both W. Kenneth Smith and as Kenneth Smith would be entered far apart in the alphabetical listings.

Subject Guide to Books in Print arranges the contents of *BIP* according to the Library of Congress Subject Headings assigned to the books. Although *BIP* and the *Subject Guide* are separate publications, most libraries subscribe to both titles because both are necessary for acquisitions and reference work.

Two titles supplementary to *BIP* add unique features to the main set. The annual volumes of *BIP* are updated by the *Books in Print Supplement,* which appears in March six months after the main volumes are published in September. *Forthcoming Books* is a bimonthly supplement that lists new books in print as well as books projected to be published within the next several months. Both works are not only useful for selection and ordering but are also frequently used to confirm that a requested title has not yet appeared.

In addition to the print volumes, the information is accessible through a multitude of other delivery and format options: CD-ROM, site licensing, subscription online services such as Ovid and from Bowker on the Web (http://www.booksinprint.com/bip). *Books in Print on Disc* (U.S. and Canadian editions) can be purchased with monthly, quarterly, twice a year, or annual updates. *Books in Print with Book Reviews on Disc* (with separate U. S. and Canadian editions) combines the print status of the book with reviews of it from standard book reviewing sources such as *Library Journal, Choice, Kirkus Reviews,* and *School Library Journal.* The *Books Out of Print* database is now available on the Web by subscription (http://www.bowker.com/bop) and on CD-ROM as *Books Out of Print Plus.*

Whitaker's Books in Print (until 1989 *British Books in Print*) is published annually and lists titles available from publishers in the United Kingdom. It is arranged by author, title, and subject in one alphabet and includes a list of publishers and their addresses. Unlike its U.S. equivalent, *Whitaker's* does list some government publications. *Whitaker's Books in Print* is available on microfiche with complete quarterly updates. It is also published on CD-ROM as *BookBank* and as part of *Bowker/Whitaker Global Books in Print on Disc,* a joint venture of R. R. Bowker and J. Whitaker. This product strives to be the most complete listing of English-language titles. With more than 3 million titles, it encompasses the in-print and forthcoming databases from R. R. Bowker for U. S. and Canadian titles, from Whitaker for British titles, from D. W. Thorpe for New Zealand and Australian titles, and from K. G. Saur for English-language titles published internationally. A Web version is planned. *Whitaker's Books in Print* is also available online on Dialog as *British Books in Print* with weekly updates.

Canadian Books in Print (*CBIP*) is a print reference tool intended primarily to bridge the gap between Bowker's *Books in Print* and *Whitaker's Books in Print.* As such, it includes all English-language titles currently in print bearing the imprint of Canadian publishers or originated by the Canadian subsidiaries of international publishing firms. Not included are maps, sheet music, newspapers, periodicals and catalogs, microfiche, and annuals not considered to be of general interest. A selection of federal and provincial government publications considered of interest to the general public and generally available in bookstores is included. *Canadian Books in Print: Author and Title Index* is issued annually in a hardcover edition, followed by complete microfiche supplements in April, July, and October. *Canadian Books in Print: Subject Index* is published annually in hardcover only. *Books in Print on Disc* (Canadian Edition) and *Books in Print with Book Reviews on Disc* (Canadian Edition) are updated monthly, and both mirror their U. S. counterparts.

Foreign in-print lists are invaluable for verifying titles for selection, as well as for locating publishers' addresses. The French books-in-print list is *Les Livres Disponibles,* an annual publication with books listed in separate author, title, and subject volumes. Another useful reference tool, *International Books in Print,* is now published annually and lists more than 280,000 books published in English in non-English-speaking countries. It can be used, for example, to find information about an English-language work published in Denmark. Its list of publishers and their addresses contains some that are difficult to locate elsewhere. *International Books in Print Plus* on CD-ROM, updated annually, is published by K. G. Saur and is available from R. R. Bowker. It is also available on CD-ROM as part of *Bowker/Whitaker Global Books in Print on Disc.*

Library Catalogs

In reference work, library catalogs are used most often for verification purposes, but those that include a subject approach can also be used as subject bibliographies. The catalogs of some special libraries also include indexing at the article level for periodicals in the fields covered. This is particularly important because there may not have been a journal index for the subject involved during the time period covered by the catalog.

Although hundreds of library catalogs have been published, few are still being printed today. Production costs have made printed library catalogs prohibitively expensive. The storage space required to house them is excessive even in the largest of libraries. These catalogs are now much more likely to appear in electronic format, where they can be accessed via the Internet, on CD-ROM, as computer output microforms, or as part of the larger database in a bibliographic utility.

It is important to note here that libraries gradually began to use machine-readable cataloging in the late 1960s.The cataloging of materials in non-Roman alphabets did not begin until the late 1970s. Large libraries did not go back and create machine-readable cataloging copy for materials acquired earlier. It was simply too expensive to do so. Only now in the late 1990s are research libraries conducting widespread massive retrospective conversion projects, allowing libraries such as Princeton and Yale to convert earlier holdings to machine-readable cataloging. The reference librarian, when looking at the librarian's own catalog as well as remote electronic catalogs, must determine what materials have been converted. In other words, what precisely is being searched? Without this information it is impossible to evaluate the results of a search that had negative results.

Individual library catalogs may be searched using the Web, although a few still require earlier technologies. The application of common standards allows users to search remote catalogs without knowing the exact search syntax required by the remote catalog. Z39.50, discussed further in Chapters 6 and 7, is a national standard defining a protocol for computer-to-computer information retrieval. The MARC communications format is an international standard for representing and exchanging bibliographic data in machine-readable form. The Library of Congress maintains a Z39.50 gateway to individual library catalogs on the LC Web page (http://lcweb.loc.gov/z3950/). In addition, several library consortia have produced gateways that allow searchers to search multiple libraries' catalogs simultaneously. The Committee for Institutional Cooperation's CIC Virtual Electronic Library (see Chapter 7) is an example of such unified data access. Another example is Gabriel, the gateway to Europe's national libraries (http://portico.bl.uk/gabriel).

Most often it is preferable to search the bibliographic utilities rather than individual library catalogs. However, the presence of locally produced cataloging copy that might not be present in the utilities occasionally merits searching catalogs individually. Subject bibliographers may wish to search a local collection to determine their holdings in a particular area of strength. An example of such a collection might be that of a local historical society library. In addition to the online catalog, conditions of use, hours of operation, and other worthwhile information may be found on a library's Web site.

United States

Whether one is the sole librarian in a small public library or one of many reference librarians in a large academic library, one needs to be familiar with the *National Union Catalog* (*NUC*) and its publishing history. In a nation that has no official national bibliography, no system of legal deposit, and a "multiplicity of bibliographic structures,"[6] the products and services of the Library of Congress are, next to the bibliographic utilities, the most important resource for bibliographic methods of research.

NUC began as the actual card catalog of the Library of Congress. Later, when increased access to the card catalog was deemed desirable, more than 1,000 depository (duplicate) sets of cards were distributed to and maintained by large research libraries throughout the United States. The first printed book catalog version of the card set, *The Library of Congress Catalog: A Cumulative Catalog of Books Represented by Library of Congress Printed Cards,* was published in 1942 under the sponsorship of the Association of Research Libraries. This set represented cataloging done at the Library of Congress, at some libraries of government departments, and at 1,500 research libraries. Cards printed from 1898 to July 31, 1942 were reproduced. Its supplement included cards produced from August 1, 1942, to December 31, 1947; the next cumulation was *Library of Congress Author Catalog . . . 1948–1952.* In 1953 the scope was enlarged to include cataloging entries and holdings information of additional contributing North American libraries, and, consequently, the title of the catalog was changed to *National Union Catalog* (*NUC*).

The publication of the Library of Congress catalog has continued to the present, with additional title changes reflecting its variations in scope, frequency, and format. For an extended description of the publishing history of *NUC*, see the entry for it in Balay's *Guide to Reference Books.*[7]

The large retrospective set now in use is *National Union Catalog, Pre-1956 Imprints.* For this set the entries are photocopies of catalog cards. Location symbols for research libraries in the United States and Canada that own a particular title are added to the bottom of the card. *NUC, Pre-1956 Imprints* is an author, or main entry, catalog. Necessary cross-references are included, but subject headings are not. Furthermore, only selected added entries are included. Thus, a knowledge of the cataloging code that governs the choice and form of the main entry is necessary to use *NUC* effectively. For almost all entries in *NUC, Pre-1956,* this means using the *ALA Cataloging Rules for Author and Title Entries,* 1949 edition. For example, general rule 92 stated, "Enter an institution (using the latest name) under the place in which it is located."[8] Therefore, Southern Methodist University in Dallas, Texas, was entered under Dallas. Similarly, many subdivisions of governments were entered first under the largest unit of a government agency, with subdivisions for the successive layers of government structure. Subsequent cataloging codes have allowed for entry under the smallest subdivision of a government agency that can logically stand alone, and for entry directly under the name of an institution (e.g., Southern Methodist University).

Because the set was published over a period of 12 years, supplementary volumes were necessary almost immediately. These volumes (686 to 754) add titles identified after publication began and add locations to titles published earlier. *NUC, Pre-1956* was continued as *National Union Catalog* through 1982. Five-year cumulations, except for 1978 to 1982, have been published.

Beginning in 1983, the national union catalogs have been published in microfiche, with no print version available. The microfiche edition uses the register/index form of arrangement. Full bibliographic records appear only once—in the register—and they are numbered sequentially. Separate alphabetically arranged indexes for names, titles, subjects, and series provide access points to the register. The indexes supply a brief cataloging record and the item number under which the full record can be found in the register. Although briefer than the register records, index entries frequently provide sufficient bibliographic information to complete a search. The full record in the register provides complete cataloging information as well as information such as ISBN, price, and suggested Dewey Decimal Classification number. With this arrangement, the indexes can be cumulated without having to reprint the full record. *National Union Catalog: Books* provides bibliographic records for books, pamphlets, manuscripts, map atlases, monographic microform publications, and monographic government publications. Records for all non-Roman-language materials are in romanized form only, however. With the publication of the 1990 edition, *National Union Catalog: Books* no longer includes records for books from OCLC and RLIN. The national union catalogs of the Library of Congress also include the following titles in microfiche: *National Union Catalog: Audiovisual Materials, National Union Catalog: Cartographic Materials,* and *The Music Catalog.*

Library of Congress cataloging records are also available electronically from the MARC (MAchine Readable Cataloging) Distribution Service (MDS), which is part of the Cataloging Distribution Service (CDS) of the Library of Congress. Records are available on nine-track tape reel, tape cartridge, or via Internet ftp (file transfer protocol). Most libraries will, however, simply access OCLC or RLIN for LC's cataloging output.

The *Library of Congress Online Catalog* (http://catalog.loc.gov/) is a database of approximately 12 million records representing books, serials, computer files, manuscripts, cartographic materials, music, sound recordings, and visual materials in the Library's collections. The online catalog also provides references, notes, circulation status, and information about materials still in the acquisitions stage. The catalog is available for searching 7 days a week, 24 hours a day. Research tools, specialized databases, legislative information, and full-text digital resources are also available through the LC Web site (http://www.loc.gov).

Great Britain and France

The library catalogs of Great Britain and France follow similar publishing patterns to those in the United States. The British Library's *General Catalogue of Printed Books to 1975* (*BLC*) is the latest edition of this catalog. Editions published before the establishment of the British Library in 1972 were known as the *British Museum Catalogue.* As of 1999 published supplements brought the coverage of the print version to the end of 1998. This catalog is an invaluable source of bibliographic data because it lists the holdings of one of the world's largest libraries. Because the British Library is a depository for all materials copyrighted in the United Kingdom, its catalog is the most complete record of such publications.

The catalog is arranged by main entry in one alphabetical sequence. Most entries are personal authors, but corporate author and title entries are included where necessary. Serials are included, but they are listed under "periodical publications." Newspapers are not included, but the British Library has published a catalog of its newspaper library.[9]

The completeness of the bibliographic description provided varies a good deal, depending on when the book was cataloged. In the supplements, complete MARC records are the rule. Figure 20.3 shows entries from the *BLC* to 1975 and its 1986–1987 supplement, illustrating the differences in format and amount of information given. Note that the newer entries give complete cataloging information.

A subject approach to the catalog was provided under the title *Subject Index of the Modern Works Added to the Library,* which appeared in multivolume sets published from 1906 to 1985. These indexes excluded "pure" literature and personal names, which were included in the *General Catalogue.* The early catalogs are rather difficult to use because the material is arranged in very broad subjects that are then subdivided. The subjects are in alphabetical rather than classified order.

A massive retrospective conversion project was undertaken at the British Library between 1987 and 1991 to convert the entire British Library *General Catalogue of Printed Books to 1975* to machine-readable form. Such conversion does not merely change the format of the catalog, it also enhances use of the catalog by making almost all elements of the entries searchable.

Figure 20.3 Entries from British Library's *General Catalogue of Printed Books to 1975* and from the 1986–1987 supplement. Reprinted with permission of Bowker (London, England).

LEMON (ABRAHAM) Report of the proceedings upon a criminal information against A. Lemon, T. Turner, B. Wilson, J. Webster, J. R. Mulleneux, and C. Rowlinson, for a conspiracy and riot at the Theatre Royal, Liverpool ... at the Summer Assizes for ... Lancaster ... 14th September 1810; taken in short hand by Mr. Farquharson. *Liverpool*, 1810. 8°. **1131. d. 18.**

LEMON (ALFRED D.) *See* CUMMING (J. G.) The great Stanley ... A narrative ... illustrated from Manx scenery and antiquities, by A. D. L., *etc.* 1867. 8°. **10816. bb.27.**

LEMON (ANTHONY)

—— **Postwar industrial growth in East Anglian small towns: a study of migrant firms, 1945–1970.** *Oxford*, [1975]. ISBN 0 901691 12 7 **P. 805/202. (12.)**

pp. 40; maps. 30 cm. (University of Oxford. School of Geography. Research papers. no. 12 ISSN 0305 8190.) □

LEMON, Anthony
Apartheid in transition / Anthony Lemon. - Aldershot : Gower, 1987.
[410]p : ill ; 22cm. - Includes bibliography and index.
0-566-00635-9 YC.1987.a.8439
White voters and political change in South Africa, 1981-1983 / A. Lemon. - Oxford : School of Geography, University of Oxford, 1984.
40p : ill,maps ; 22cm. - (Research paper ; 32). - Bibliography: p39-40.
B86-26660 P.805/202

LEMON, Charles
A leaf from an unopened volume, or, The manuscript of an unfortunate author : an Angrian story / by Charlotte Brontë ; newly transcribed and edited by Charles Lemon. - Haworth : Brontë Society, 1986.
xvi,66p : ill,facsims,1geneal.table ; 21cm.
0-9505829-2-1 YC.1986.a.4005

LEMON, Daphne Violet
The stars in Orion : Tuapeka then and now / Daphne Lemon. - Dunedin : J. McIndoe, 1979.
64 p. : maps.
0-908565-89-5 X.800/43123

The British Library's OPAC 97 service (http://opac97.bl.uk/), which is partially funded by sponsorship from Amazon.com.uk, provides free access via the Web to more than 8.5 million records in a number of catalogs that cover major Reference and Document Supply collections of the British Library in London and Boston Spa. (At present individual collections have their own separate catalogs.) Blaise (the British Library Automated Information Service) is a fee-based service that offers information professionals access to over 18.5 million bibliographic records (http://www.bl.uk).

Catalogue Général des Livres Imprimés from the Bibliothèque Nationale in Paris is the most important source for French publications. It is an alphabetical list of books by personal author only. It does not include entries for anonymous works, serials, or works of corporate authorship. The catalog was published from 1897 to 1981, so there is a great difference in the dates of coverage in different parts of the alphabet. Even in the volumes published after 1960, nothing is included that was published after 1959. A supplement covering 1960 to 1969 has been published that includes entries for corporate authors and anonymous works, as well as for personal authors. Because of the unevenness in coverage over time, the Bibliothèque Nationale has published a microfiche supplement that brings all parts of the original up to 1959.

Three catalogs of the Bibliothèque Nationale de France (http://www.bnf.fr) are available on the Internet. *BN-OPALE,* a telnet-accessible online catalog of the Bibliothèque Nationale de France, includes 2 million bibliographic entries for books acquired since 1970, journals since 1960, and computer files since 1984. The *BN-OPALINE* catalog, also available through telnet, contains 460,000 bibliographic entries for such specialized collections as maps, prints and photographs, and music scores. *BN-OPALE PLUS,* which has been available on the Internet since May 1999, provides Web access to 7 million bibliographic records. Additional resources were to be added in 2000.

Canada

The National Library of Canada (http://www.nlc-bnc.ca) was established by Parliament in 1953 to acquire, preserve, and promote the published heritage of Canada for all Canadians, both now and in the years to come. The *National Library Catalogue* contains 2 million records and is available electronically in two ways: resAnet, a Web interface, provides access to brief records, and The National Library Catalogue Z39.50 is available with Z39.50 client software. The *National Library Catalogue* is a subset of the *AMICUS* database. The full *AMICUS* database, which contains the holdings of over 500 Canadian libraries, including the *National Library Catalogue,* can be accessed for a fee.

Serial and Newspaper Sources

The term *serial* can be extremely confusing to the neophyte. It simply means "a publication that is issued in successive parts, usually at regular intervals, and, as a rule, intended to be continued indefinitely."[10] Types of serials include periodicals, annuals (e.g., reports, yearbooks), proceedings, and transactions of societies. Irregular serials are issued irregularly at unspecified intervals. The term *periodical* refers to a type of serial that has a distinctive title intended to appear in successive (usually unbound) numbers or parts at stated or regular intervals and, as a rule, for an indefinite time. Each part generally contains articles by several contributors. Each serial title is assigned an ISSN that is unique to that title. If the serial title changes, a new ISSN must be assigned to the new title.

Two types of sources are discussed in this section. One is lists of serial titles that are currently being published. The other is union lists that include the location and holdings of each title listed. In these examples, *location* means a library in the United States or Canada; *holdings* means a record of which volumes or years each library holds.

Retrospective and Union Lists

Union List of Serials in Libraries of the United States and Canada (*ULS*) lists serials published before 1950. It is arranged in alphabetical order by main entry. Although the holdings information is limited to libraries located in the United States and Canada, the serials may be published in any country, making this work international in its coverage. Each entry includes a detailed publication history of the title and notes any variation that has occurred in the title. *ULS* contains no newspapers and very few government publications. Figure 20.4 illustrates a typical entry from *ULS.* Note the library locations and the holdings shown. The symbols used are the same as those used in the *National Union Catalog.*

New Serial Titles (*NST*) continued *ULS.* Its first cumulation covers serials that began publication between 1950 and 1970. Since that time, there have been several multiyear cumulations. In 1981, *NST* expanded its entries to include complete cataloging information; the entries were produced from OCLC tapes and are the reproduction of the OCLC record (see Figure 20.5). *NST* ceased publication with the 1999 cumulation.

American Newspapers, 1821–1936 is similar in format to *ULS* in that it lists locations in the United States and Canada and gives a complete bibliographic description of each title. However, entries are arranged by place of publication. Detailed holdings for each location are included. Because there has been no supplement, other titles must be used to identify more current holdings and to locate descriptions of titles that began publication after 1936.

Newspapers in Microform: United States and *Newspapers in Microform: Foreign Countries* are union lists for Canadian and U.S. libraries. In addition to listing libraries where the newspaper can be consulted or borrowed, sources for purchasing microform copies are indicated. Both of these titles, like *American Newspapers,* are arranged by the place of publication of the newspaper. A title index is provided.

Figure 20.4 Entry from *Union List of Serials.* Reprinted with permission of The H. W. Wilson Company.

AMERICAN water works association
Index: 1881-1939
Journal. 1,Mr 1914+
Supersedes its Proceedings

AAP [16+]
ArU 17+
AzU 31+
C 1+
CCC 1-24[28-29]
CL 1+
CLU [1-31]+
CPT [1-20]22+
CSf 4+
CSfM 1+
CSt 1+
CU 1+
CaEU 29+
CaM 1-26
CaME 1-3,24+
CaON 29+
CaSU 4+
CaTU 1+
CaWU 1+
CoD 1+
CoU 1+
Ct 6-25,28-31
CtHT 1-3
CtU 17+
DA 1-[24-27]+

DES 1-29
DGS 1+
DH 3+
DLC 1+
DP 1+
FU 1+

MoSB 1+
MoSW 1914+
MoU 1+
MsSM 27+
N 1+
NB 1+
NBu 2,15+
NBuG 1+
NIC 1+
NN 1+
NN-M 1+
NNA 3-[7]+
NNC 1+
NNCC 1+
NNCoC 1-17,29+
NNE 1+
NNQ 30+
NR 10-12,15+
NStC 22-28
NTR 1+
NcD 1+
NcRS 1+
NcU 1-[9]-[15]+
NdU 1+
NhD 1+
NjHoS 4+
NjP 1+
NjR 1+
NjT 1-12
OC 1-21,23+
OCl 1-[11]+
OClW 8-[23]

GAT 1+
ICA 1+
ICJ 1+
ICW 1+
IEN-M [21-22]
IU 1+
IaAS 1+
IaU 1+
IdU 27+
InU 33+
KMK 1+
KU 1+
KyU 1+
LU 1-[22-26]30+
MAA 29+
MB 1+
MBM 2-7,9
MCM 1+
MH 1+
MH-M 10-25
MMeT [1-4]
MWiW 1+
MdBE 1+
MdBJ 1+
MeU 1-12,15+
MiD 1+
MiDU 22+
MiEM 8-[11]17-30
MiGr [1-3]
MiMiD [17]+
MiU 1+
MnM 14+
MnS 1-4,8-9
MnSJ 1+
MnU 1+

MoK 11-18
MoRM 1+
MoS 1+

ODa 14+
OO 2[5,9-13]
OT 1+
OU 1+
OkS 19+
OkU 1-8
OrCA 1+
OrP 1+
OrU 1-22
PBL 1+
PP 1+
PPD 9+
PPF 6+
PPi 1+
PPiM 12+
PSt 2+
PU 1+
ScCc 12+
TC [23-24]
TNV 1-2,4,7-9,13-[22]-28
TU 1+
TxCM [1-2]-[12]-[18-28]+
TxDaM 18+
TxH 11+
TxU 1+
ULA 29+
UU 1+
VU [6-21]-30
Vt 1-22
VtU 1-10,12+
WM 1+
WU 1+
WaS 1+
WaSp 4+
WaU 1+
WvU 1+

AU 1-35
CLSU 33+
CtU 1-[16]+
DSG 33
H 35+
IEN 1+
InTR 31+
MiEM 8-12,15+

MtBC [4-7]-[11-14]25+
NBuG 1-34
NRU 1-[30]
RPB 26,33
ScU 33+
TxCM [1-2]-[12]-[23-26]+
TxLT 32+

Figure 20.5 Entry from *New Serial Titles,* published by the Library of Congress, Washington, D.C.

Journal (American Water Works Association)
Journal / American Water Works Association. — Vol. 40, no. 1 (Jan. 1948)- — [New York, N.Y.] : The Association, [c1948-
v. : ill. ; 23-28 cm.
Monthly.
Title from cover.
Imprint varies: Denver, CO,
Supplements accompany some numbers.
Indexes:
Vols. 32 (1940)-47 (1955) (includes index to former title). 1 v.; v. 48 (1956)-57 (1965). 1 v.
Annual special no. published separately with title: AWWA ... buyers' guide and publications catalog.
Running title: Journal AWWA
Continues: Journal of the American Water Works Association.
ISSN 0003-150X = Journal - American Water Works Association.
1. Water-supply engineering—Periodicals. I. American Water Works Association. II. AWWA ... buyers' guide and publications catalog. III. Title: Journal AWWA.
TD201.A512 86-641260
628.1'05—dc19
AACR 2
CSt DLC ICRL InU KMK MChB MoSU PU RPB-S

At some point, weakness in a particular bibliographic area is usually addressed by a new product. As can be seen from the above descriptions, bibliographic coverage of newspaper holdings in the United States is one such weak area. The United States Newspaper Program (USNP) is a cooperative project planned by the National Endowment for the Humanities, the Library of Congress, the Organization of American Historians, and the Council on Library Resources. The project seeks to identify newspapers published in the United States and its Trust Territories, to identify the repositories in those areas that collect those newspapers, and finally to list summary holdings of those repositories. Participants in the program use the OCLC Cataloging and Union List services to create an online database of newspaper bibliographic, location, and holdings information. *United States Newspaper Program National Union List* (*USNP NUL*) is computer output microfiche of the online (*USNP NUL*) cataloging records database available from OCLC. It first became available in 1985, and the fifth edition was published in January 1999. The arrangement of the list is alphabetical by title; indexes by date, intended audience, language, and place of publication are included. The most current information is, of course, available online through OCLC.

Current Lists

Ulrich's International Periodicals Directory is a guide to more than 164,000 currently available periodicals, and, since 1993, newspapers. The arrangement is by broad subject area, with separate indexes providing access to title, ISSN, online and CD-ROM availability, online vendors, title changes, and refereed serials. Entries include the information needed to order the title: publisher, address, price, and ISSN. In addition, frequency, beginning date, circulation figures, advertising rates, and telephone and fax numbers are usually included. Ulrich's has several other features that greatly increase its usefulness in the reference collection. Each entry lists the indexes and online databases that cover the contents of the periodical. This feature allows the librarian or other user to locate the complete citation for an article in a periodical by identifying the index or database where the citation can be found. Another valuable feature is the list of cessations, which lists periodicals that have ceased publication since the previous edition. Since 1988, *Ulrich's* has incorporated *Irregular Serials and Annuals* in its coverage and title, thus providing publication and ordering information for most directories, almanacs, and yearbooks.

Ulrich's is available electronically in four different ways. Through online vendors such as Dialog, LEXIS-NEXIS, or Ovid, *Ulrich's* is updated monthly. The CD-ROM version, *Ulrich's on Disc,* which contains critical evaluations from *Magazines for Libraries* and *Library Journal,* is updated quarterly. An *Ulrich's* Web site with subscription access is now available (http://www.bowker.com/ulrichs). Site licensing enables libraries to mount the information on local OPACs (online public access catalogs).

EBSCO Publishing, a sister division of EBSCO Subscription Services, has produced *The Serials Directory,* now in its fourteenth edition. This international directory covers more than 178,500 titles, including newspapers. Each entry provides more than 50 elements of information, including publisher's name and address, telephone and fax numbers, price, editor's name, CODEN designators, classification numbers, and so forth. Of particular use to librarians are the designations indicating whether the journal is peer-reviewed, accepts book reviews, or accepts advertising. The electronic version of *The Serials Directory* includes the same information as the print version, plus historical data for an additional 20,000 serials. It is available online through EBSCOhost and on CD-ROM.

Newspapers currently published in the United States and Canada are listed in the *Gale Directory of Publications and Broadcast Media.* This directory has been published annually since 1880 (until 1982, as *Ayer Directory of Publications*). Because it has been published for such a long time, back volumes are an excellent source for historical information on U.S. newspapers. In addition to newspapers, the *Gale Directory* includes information about magazines, journals, college publications, radio and television stations, and cable. *Ulrich's,* because it is international in scope, lists more periodicals than does the *Gale Directory*, but *Ulrich's* does not include broadcast media.

The *Gale Directory* is published in four volumes. The first two volumes are arranged geographically, with the titles listed alphabetically under the place of publication. In addition to information that can be used for ordering, such as address and price, the entries include information specific to newspapers, such as circulation figures, number of columns, size, and advertising rates. The third volume includes statistical tables and indexes. In addition to the publishers index and master name and keyword index, there are several different subject or type listings, such as Jewish publications, free newspapers, and radio format. The fourth volume has a regional market index and maps. Tables are provided showing statistics by type of publication and geographical region. The maps section includes maps for individual states and provinces, and shows the cities and towns in which the titles listed in the directory are published. This directory is also available online as part of the *Gale Database of Publications and Broadcast Media* (see Chapter 14).

A series of publications from Oxbridge Communications replicates the coverage offered by other periodical directories and expands coverage into other areas such as newsletters. *The Standard Periodical Directory* includes more than 75,000 North American periodicals; *The National Directory of Magazines* provides production specifications and rates for over 20,000 U.S. and Canadian publications; and the *Oxbridge Directory of Newsletters* covers over 20,000 newsletters, loose-leafs, bulletins, and fax letters. All these titles are produced in print and on CD-ROM and are accessible on the Web through the MediaFinder subscription service. The strength of these sources lies in the provision of narrower, more numerous subject categories (more than 250) and in the listing of some unique titles not found in other sources.

Bibliographies of Bibliographies

Bibliographies of bibliographies are usually general in scope and are used to identify bibliographies on a specific subject. The major titles of the genre are Theodore Besterman's *A World Bibliography of Bibliographies* (often referred to as Besterman) and *Bibliographic Index*. Besterman includes more substantial bibliographies, but it is not current. *Bibliographic Index* is current and provides information appropriate to any level of inquiry.

Besterman lists in five volumes separately published bibliographies only. It is international in scope and arranged by subject. The last volume is an index that includes authors, titles, and subjects. The last edition covers material through 1963. It has been supplemented by Alice F. Toomey's *A World Bibliography of Bibliographies, 1964–1974*. The supplement, compiled from Library of Congress printed cards, is arranged by subject, based on Library of Congress Subject Headings. In 1998 K. G. Saur began publishing the massive 12-volume *International Bibliography of Bibliographies 1959–1988*, which is intended to serve as yet another supplement to Besterman.

Bibliographic Index is a subject index to bibliographies that have been published in books, pamphlets, and more than 2,700 periodicals. H. W. Wilson began publishing the index in 1937. It currently appears in two paperbound issues per year and an annual permanent clothbound cumulation, which includes four additional months of coverage. This is an excellent source for beginning a search for scholarly and popular works in many subjects. *Bibliographic Index* includes material published in English and other Western European languages. Each entry gives complete information on the bibliography and tells if it is annotated. The arrangement is by Library of Congress Subject Headings.

Recommended Lists

Recommended lists are highly selective, evaluative bibliographies. They list only the best titles published in a particular area. The evaluative nature of recommended lists saves the librarian time by eliminating from consideration lesser titles that have been found lacking in some way. The compiler of the bibliography, however, should always carefully define the criteria used to evaluate materials. Quality is a very subjective measure. Because of this fact, selection of materials by a group of qualified experts is perhaps the most frequently used method of compiling such lists. However, the number of copies sold can be a valid criterion for lists of popular reading material.

Recommended lists are used by librarians in three integral ways: building a collection to meet the needs of users, measuring (evaluating) the library collection against these standard lists, and advising readers. In carrying out these activities, one must keep in mind that recommended lists are created for an average collection, whereas the librarian is collecting for a particular library with a unique user population.

The term *readers' advisory service* is usually used in the public library context. In reality, all reference interviews essentially provide a bridge between the reader and the sources required to meet the reader's information needs. The difference may be that the true readers' advisory service offered in public libraries is an expanded reference service that includes advice on the selection of recreational reading titles. To assist in this type of service some recommended lists offer indexing by criteria not often used in other types of bibliographies. Primary examples are lists of fiction and nonfiction by age or reading level, and lists of fiction by genre, geographic area, or historical period. Finding books on astronomy written for the layperson in a collection that contains both technical and nontechnical works would be extremely time-consuming without the use of these special indexes.

The Reader's Adviser is the prime example of the "best books" type of bibliography. Bessie Graham published the first edition in 1921 as an outgrowth of the bookselling course that she taught at the William Penn Evening High School in Philadelphia. By the fourteenth edition, published in 1994, *The Reader's Adviser* had grown to an encyclopedic six volumes used not only by booksellers but also by librarians and general readers. "Each volume is designed to carry the users from the general to the specific—from overarching reference guides, critical histories, and anthologies about a genre or a field to the lives and works of its leading exemplars."[11] Subject specialists make the selections of entries, and separate editors are assigned to the work as a whole, to individual volumes, and to the various sections. Annotated bibliographies cover broad subject areas: British and American literature, world literature in English translation, philosophy, religion, the Bible, science, technology, medicine, arts, history, and social sciences. Most books listed are in print; only major works in a subject are listed if they are out-of-print. Volume 6 provides name, title, and general subject indexes to the entire set, and also supplies a directory of publishers.

H. W. Wilson publishes the *Wilson Standard Catalogs,* which are lists of recommended books for particular audiences. These titles are used for collection development, book selection and acquisition, and readers' advisory services. A subscription to the catalogs brings an initial hardcover volume followed by four annual paperbound supplements. Two of the titles are used by public libraries: *Public Library Catalog* and *Fiction Catalog. Public Library Catalog* lists adult nonfiction, in-print titles arranged by Dewey Decimal Classification; it includes annotations. *Fiction Catalog* is an annotated bibliography arranged by author with title and subject indexes. With this catalog it is possible to identify novels about specific places or historical periods, for example. Another popular use is to locate genre fiction, such as spy novels or murder mysteries. The other three standard catalog titles in this series are aimed at school libraries: *Children's Catalog, Middle & Junior High School Library Catalog,* and *Senior High School Library Catalog.* Electronic editions of the *Wilson Standard Catalogs* became available online through WilsonWeb in 2000.

Magazines for Libraries is an annotated listing by subject of more than 8,000 periodicals, both print and electronic journals. Selection is limited to those titles considered to be the most useful for the average elementary or secondary school, public, academic, or special library. The title also serves as a readers' advisory tool for the user who wants to select a magazine in a subject area of particular interest. With the publication of the tenth edition in 2000, new sections were added to address current interests, with 158 subject categories ranging from antiquities to women's studies.

SEARCH STRATEGIES

Verification is necessary when trying to identify, and eventually to locate, a given item. Often the bibliographic information presented by a library user to the reference librarian is so incomplete that a good deal of ingenuity must be used to locate a copy. The sources of incomplete citations can vary from partial information gathered from a chance reference on a television or radio talk show to a poorly constructed bibliography in a scholarly book. Practice and experience make the process easier, but there are a number of factors to keep in mind when deciding where to start.

If the incomplete citation lacks a date, it is best to start looking in a cumulated list that will allow searching a number of years simultaneously. Shared cataloging networks such as OCLC and RLIN are especially useful in cases like this, because of the wide range of dates covered. Unfortunately, a citation lacking a date frequently also lacks some other important element.

When selecting the bibliography or catalog to use for verification, the librarian needs to keep in mind the stated purpose of the tools. National bibliographies usually list materials published during the time period covered. Most library catalogs list material cataloged during the stated time. Thus, a title published in 1850, but not cataloged and reported to *NUC* until 1965, would not have appeared in *NUC* until the 1963–1967 cumulation.

Using *New Serial Titles* presents some of the same concerns. That is, a serial that began publication in 1975 may very well not appear until the 1981–1985 cumulation. In addition, the librarian needs to keep in mind the changes in rules of entry that have occurred over time. The examples given in Figures 20.4 and 20.5 show the same serial title cataloged at different times.

Box 20.1 Search Strategy: A Book on Homeschooling

An out-of-town researcher appeared at a university library's reference desk. A colleague at her home institution had recommended a book by Eva Boyd. The book was about a single mother who homeschooled her son, who then completed college by age 17. She remembered neither the date of publication nor the title of the book. The first step was searching the university library's own catalog. Because the university had a strong collection in the field of education, it was assumed that the book would turn up immediately as the result of an author search. No author with the name of Eva Boyd appeared in the list of authors. A widening of the OPAC search to include the holdings of all libraries in the state resulted in one book by Eva Jolene Boyd on the subject of stagecoach travel in the American West, *That Old Overland Stagecoaching.* A search of OCLC WorldCat and Bowker's *Books in Print* on the Web turned up more books by the same Eva Jolene Boyd. A perusal of the print *Subject Guide to Books in Print* under the subject Home Schooling was unsuccessful. Finally, the librarian searched the Web site of Amazon.com, an Internet bookseller. The librarian chose this site because it would list the most popular titles on the subject. A search of the site for books on the subject of Home Schooling revealed a book by Eva Seibert, titled *About Face.* The book description indicated that the book was a self-published, autobiographical account of how both sons of a single mother were homeschooled and admitted to college by the time they were 12. This search strategy illustrates a somewhat atypical search, but also shows the lengths to which a good reference librarian will go to find the answer to a user's question. (549 books are listed in Amazon.com under the subject heading Home Schooling. Fortunately, *About Face* shows up early in the listings.) A subject search of WorldCat under Home Schooling produces a set of 1,241 records. However, a subject search of Home Schooling and keyword author Eva produces only one citation: *About Face* by Eva Seibert. The alternative title is "How both sons of a single mother were homeschooled and admitted to college by the time they were twelve."

The search in Box 20.1 illustrates several points. First, one should note that current English usage indicates that the word *homeschooling* should be spelled as one word, yet the Library of Congress Subject Headings uses two words. The listings in WorldCat and *Books in Print* use LCSH. When one goes back and checks the electronic *Books in Print* entry for the book, the entry shows only one subject heading: Education—Aims and Objectives. At no place in the *Books in Print* entry does the concept "home schooling" appear. Had the librarian relied on only one source, this query would never have been answered.

Further questioning of the library user indicated that Eva Boyd married again after rearing her boys and before publishing the book. Thus Eva Seibert is a later form of her name. She has written only under the name Eva Seibert; therefore, there is no *see* reference from the earlier form of name to the later form. Most users would not be aware of the earlier form of her name.

This case shows how resourceful and creative reference librarians must be when tackling complex bibliographic questions. Name and title variations, or uncertainties regarding specific editions of works or which libraries might own these editions, are just a few of the difficulties that may arise from a seemingly simple request for a book or journal article. Often, the librarian must carefully question the user and consider all available resources to successfully answer bibliographic reference questions.

NOTES

1. D. W. Krummel, *Bibliographies: Their Aims and Methods* (London: Mansell Publishing, 1984), 4.

2. Robert W. Melton, " 'The Baby Figure of the Giant Mass': Pollard & Redgrave's and Wing's Short-Title Catalogues," in *Distinguished Classics of Reference Publishing,* ed. James Rettig (Phoenix, Ariz.: Oryx Press, 1992), 254.

3. Glen Holt, "Catalog Outsourcing: No Clear-Cut Choice," *Library Journal* 120 (September 15, 1995): 34.

4. Patrick Wilson, *Two Kinds of Power: An Essay on Bibliographic Control* (Berkeley, Calif.: University of California Press, 1968), 13.

5. Mary Ellen Soper, "B. Procedures or Processes," in *The Librarian's Thesaurus: A Concise Guide to Library and Information Terms* (Chicago: American Library Association, 1990), 44.

6. Doralyn J. Hickey, "Theory of Bibliographic Control in Libraries," in *Prospects for Change in Bibliographic Control* (Chicago: University of Chicago Press, 1977), 28.

7. Robert Balay, ed., *Guide to Reference Books,* 11th ed. (Chicago: American Library Association, 1996), AA106-AA114.

8. *ALA Cataloging Rules for Author and Title Entries,* 2d ed. (Chicago: American Library Association, 1949), 151.

9. British Library, Colindale, *Catalogue of the Newspaper Library, Colindale.* 8 vols. (London: British Museum Publications, 1975).

10. Heartsill Young, ed., *The ALA Glossary of Library and Information Science* (Chicago: American Library Association, 1983), 203.

11. Marion Sader, "Preface," in *The Reader's Adviser: A Laymen's Guide to Literature,* 14th ed. (New Providence, N.J.: R. R. Bowker, 1994), xvii.

LIST OF SOURCES

American Book Publishing Record. New Providence, N.J.: R. R. Bowker, 1960- . Monthly.

American Book Publishing Record Cumulative, 1876–1949. 15 vols. New York: R. R. Bowker, 1980.

American Book Publishing Record Cumulative, 1950–1977. 15 vols. New York: R. R. Bowker, 1978.

American Catalogue . . . 1876–1910. 8 vols. in 13 pts. New York: Publishers Weekly, 1880–1911.

American Newspapers, 1821–1936. New York: H. W. Wilson, 1937. 791p.

Ayer Directory of Publications. Philadelphia: Ayer, 1880–1982. Annual.

Besterman, Theodore, comp. *A World Bibliography of Bibliographies and of Bibliographical Catalogues, Calendars, Abstracts, Digests, Indexes, and the Like.* 4th ed. 5 vols. Lausanne, Switzerland: Societas Bibliographica, 1965–1966.

Bibliographic Index: A Cumulative Bibliography of Bibliographies. New York: H. W. Wilson, 1937– . 3 issues per year.

Bibliographie Nationale Française. Paris: Bibliothèque Nationale, 1990– . Biweekly with annual indexes. (Title varies: 1811–1989, *Bibliographie de la France.*) Also available on CD-ROM.

Books in Print. New Providence, N.J.: R. R. Bowker, 1948– . Annual with semiannual supplements. Also available online.

Books in Print on Disc. [CD-ROM]. New Providence, N.J.: R. R. Bowker. Monthly, quarterly, semiannual, or annual.

Books in Print with Books Reviews on Disc. [CD-ROM]. New Providence, N.J.: R. R. Bowker. Monthly, quarterly, semiannual, or annual.

Books Out of Print Plus.[CD-ROM]. New Providence, N.J.: R. R. Bowker. Quarterly. Also available online.

Bowker/Whitaker Global Books in Print on Disc. [CD-ROM]. New Providence, N.J.: R. R. Bowker. Monthly.

British Library. *General Catalogue of Printed Books to 1975.* 360 vols. London: K. G. Saur, 1979–1987. Also available on CD-ROM.

British Library. *General Catalogue of Printed Books 1976–1982.* 50 vols. London: K. G. Saur, 1983.

British Library. *General Catalogue of Printed Books 1982–1985.* 26 vols. London: K. G. Saur, 1986.

British Library. *General Catalogue of Printed Books 1986–1987.* 22 vols. London: K. G. Saur, 1988.

British Library. *General Catalogue of Printed Books 1988–1989.* 28 vols. London: K. G. Saur, 1990.

British Library. *General Catalogue of Printed Books 1990–1992.* 27 vols. London: K. G. Saur, 1993.

British Library. *General Catalogue of Printed Books 1993–1994.* 27 vols. London: K. G. Saur, 1995.

British Library. *General Catalogue of Printed Books 1995–1996.* 27 vols. London: K. G. Saur, 1997.

British Library. *General Catalogue of Printed Books 1997–1998.* 27 vols. London: K. G. Saur, 1999.

British Library. *Subject Index of the Modern Works Added to the Library.* London: British Library, 1906–1985.

British National Bibliography. London: British Library, 1950– . Weekly with annual cumulative volumes. Also available on CD-ROM and online.

Canadian Books in Print: Author and Title Index. Toronto: University of Toronto Press, 1968– . (Coverage from 1967). Annual with quarterly microfiche supplements.

Canadian Books in Print: Subject Index. Toronto: University of Toronto Press, 1974– . (Coverage from 1975). Annual.

Canadian Catalogue of Books: Published in Canada, About Canada, as well as Those Written by Canadians, with Imprint 1921–1949. 2 vols. Toronto: Toronto Public Libraries, 1959.

Canadian Reference Sources: An Annotated Bibliography/Ouvrages de Reference Canadiens: Une Bibligraphie Annotée. Compiled by Mary E. Bond and Martine M. Caron. Vancouver, B.C.: UBC Press in association with the National Library of Canada, 1996. 1076p.

Canadiana: Canada's National Bibliography/La bibliographie nationale du Canada, 1950–1991. Ottawa: National Library of Canada, 1953–1991.

Canadiana. [Microfiche]. Ottawa: National Library of Canada, 1973– . Also available on CD-ROM and online.

Children's Catalog. 17th ed. New York: H. W. Wilson, 1996. 1373p. Annual supplements. Also available online.

Cumulative Book Index. A World List of Books in the English Language. New York: H. W. Wilson, 1933–1999. (Coverage from 1928).

Evans, Charles, comp. *American Bibliography; A Chronological Dictionary of All Books, Pamphlets, and Periodical Publications Printed in the United States of America from the Genesis of Printing in 1639 Down to and Including the Year 1800.* 14 vols. Chicago: printed for the author, 1903–1959. Also available on CD-ROM.

Fiction Catalog. 13th ed. New York: H. W. Wilson, 1996. 973p. Annual supplements. Also available online.

Forthcoming Books. New Providence, N.J.: R. R. Bowker, 1966– . Bimonthly. (Online as part of *Books in Print*; also available on CD-ROM as part of *Books in Print on Disc*).

France. Bibliothèque Nationale. *Catalogue Général des Livres Imprimés: Auteurs.* 231 vols. Paris: Impr. Nationale, 1897–1981.

France. Bibliothèque Nationale. *Catalogue Général des Livres Imprimés: Auteurs, Collectivités-Auteurs, Anonymes, 1960–1969.* 27 vols. Paris: Impr. Nationale, 1972–1978.

France. Bibliothèque Nationale. *Catalogue Général des Livres Imprimés, 1897–1959, supplement sur fiches.* Paris: Chadwyck-Healey France, 1986. 2,890 microfiche.

Gale Directory of Publications and Broadcast Media. Farmington Hills, Mich.: Gale Group, 1990– . Annual. (Continues *Gale Directory of Publications* and *Ayer Directory of Publications.*) Also available online.

Guide to Reference Books. 11th ed. Edited by Robert Balay. Chicago: American Library Association, 1996. 2020p.

International Bibliography of Bibliographies 1959–1988. München: K. G. Saur, 1998-. 12 vols. planned.

International Books in Print, English-Language Titles Published Outside the U. S. A. and the United Kingdom. München: K. G. Saur, 1979– . Annual. Also available on CD-ROM.

Kelly, James, comp. *The American Catalogue of Books (Original and Reprints), Published in the United States from Jan. 1861 to Jan. 1871.* 2 vols. New York: John Wiley, 1866–1871.

Les Livres Disponibles. Paris: Cercle de la Librairie, 1971– . Annual.

Magazines for Libraries. 10th ed. New Providence, N.J.: R. R. Bowker, 2000. 1645p.

Middle & Junior High School Library Catalog. 7th ed. New York: H. W. Wilson, 1995. 1008p. Annual supplements. Also available online.

Music, Books on Music, and Sound Recordings. Washington, D. C.: Library of Congress, 1978–1989.

The Music Catalog: 1981–1990. Washington, D. C.: Library of Congress, 1991. Microfiche.

The Music Catalog on CD-ROM. [CD-ROM]. Washington, D. C.: Library of Congress. 1994-. Semiannual.

The National Directory of Magazines. New York: Oxbridge, 1987– . Annual. Also available on CD-ROM and online.

National Union Catalog of Manuscript Collections. 1959/1961–1993. Washington, D. C.: Library of Congress, 1962–1993.

National Union Catalog, Pre-1956 Imprints. A Cumulative Author List Representing Library of Congress Printed Cards and Titles Reported by Other American Libraries. 754 vols. London: Mansell, 1968–1981.

National Union Catalogs in Microfiche. Washington, D. C.: Library of Congress, 1983– . Irregular. (Includes *National Union Catalog: Audiovisual Materials, National Union Catalog: Books, National Union Catalog: Cartographic Materials, The Music Catalog,* and *National Union Catalog Register of Additional Locations.*)

New Serial Titles: A Union List of Serials Commencing Publication After Dec. 31, 1949. Washington, D.C.: Library of Congress, 1953–1999.

Newspapers in Microform: Foreign Countries, 1948–1983. Washington, D.C.: Library of Congress, 1984. 504p.

Newspapers in Microform: United States, 1948–1983. 2 vols. Washington, D.C.: Library of Congress, 1984.

Oxbridge Directory of Newsletters. New York: Oxbridge Communications, 1979– . Annual. (Continues *Standard Directory of Newsletters.*) Also available on CD-ROM and online.

Public Library Catalog. 11th ed. New York: H. W. Wilson, 1999. 1456p. Annual supplements. Also available online.

The Reader's Adviser: A Laymen's Guide to Literature. 14th ed. 6 vols. New Providence, N.J.: R. R. Bowker, 1994.

Roorbach, Orville Augustus, comp. *Bibliotheca Americana . . . 1820–1861.* 4 vols. New York: Roorbach, 1852–1861.

Sabin, Joseph, comp. *Bibliotheca Americana. A Dictionary of Books Relating to America, from Its Discovery to the Present Time.* 29 vols. New York: Sabin, 1868–1892.

Senior High School Library Catalog. 15th ed. New York: H. W. Wilson, 1997. 1312p. Annual supplements. Also available online.

The Serials Directory. 14th ed. 5 vols. Birmingham, Ala.: EBSCO Publishing, 2000. Also available on CD-ROM and online.

Shaw, Ralph R., and Richard H. Shoemaker, comps. *American Bibliography: A Preliminary Checklist for 1801–1819.* 23 vols. New York: Scarecrow Press, 1958–1983.

Shoemaker, Richard, comp. *A Checklist of American Imprints for 1820–1829.* 10 vols. New York: Scarecrow Press, 1964–1971. (Continued by *A Checklist of American Imprints for 1830–* . Metuchen, N.J.: Scarecrow Press, 1972– .)

The Standard Periodical Directory. 22d ed. New York: Oxbridge Communications, 1999. 2335p. Also available on CD-ROM and online.

Subject Guide to Books in Print. New Providence, N.J.: R. R. Bowker, 1957– . Annual.

Toomey, Alice F., comp. *A World Bibliography of Bibliographies, 1964–1974: A List of Works Represented by Library of Congress Printed Cards. A Decennial Supplement to Theodore Besterman, A World Bibliography of Bibliographies.* 2 vols. Totowa, N.J.: Rowman & Littlefield, 1977.

Ulrich's International Periodicals Directory, Including Irregular Serials and Annuals. 39th ed. 5 vols. New Providence, N.J.: R. R. Bowker, 2000. Annual. Also available online.

Ulrich's on Disc. [CD-ROM]. New Providence, N. J.: R. R. Bowker. Quarterly.

Union List of Serials in Libraries of the United States and Canada. 3d ed. 5 vols. New York: H. W. Wilson, 1965.

United States Catalog: Books in Print. 4 vols. New York: H. W. Wilson, 1899–1928.

United States Newspaper Program National Union List. 5th ed. Dublin, Ohio: OCLC, 1999. 102 microfiche.

Walford's Guide to Reference Material. [7th ed. Volumes 2 and 3, 1998; 8th ed. Volume 1, 1999]. 3 vols. London: Library Association, 1998–1999.

Whitaker's Books in Print. London: Whitaker, 1874– . Annual. (Title varies: 1962–1988, *British Books in Print.*) Also available on CD-ROM and online.

ADDITIONAL READINGS

Bell, Barbara L. *An Annotated Guide to Current National Bibliographies.* 2d rev. ed. München: K. G. Saur, 1998. 487p.

This bibliography lists national bibliographies for 181 countries. The introduction includes a valuable discussion of bibliographic control and a selective but extensive bibliography lists books, articles, and conference papers dealing with various aspects of current national bibliography.

Bourne, Ross. "National Bibliographies—Do They Have a Future?" *Alexandria* 5, no. 2 (1993): 99-109.

The author discusses the conditions affecting the future of national bibliographic agencies and their products: economic conditions, legal deposit, technology, and others.

Krummel, D. W. *Bibliographies: Their Aims and Methods.* London: Mansell Publishing, 1984. 192p.

This basic text discusses the various types of bibliographic study and the evaluation of bibliographies.

Lawrence, John R. M. " 'The Bibliographic Wonder of the World': The National Union Catalog." In *Distinguished Classics of Reference Publishing.* Edited by James Rettig. Phoenix, Ariz.: Oryx Press, 1992. 161-73.

Lawrence provides a readable account of the publishing history of the *National Union Catalog.*

Lombard, Petro M., and Joan F. De Beer. "National Libraries Around the World, 1998–1999: A Review of the Literature." *Alexandria* 12 (2000): 3-32.

This literature review article is a recurring feature of *Alexandria, The Journal of National & International Library and Information Issues.*

Madsen, Mona. "The National Bibliography in the Future: New Recommendations." *Alexandria* 12 (2000): 45-50.

Madsen discusses revised recommendations for the national bibliography emerging from an International Conference on National Bibliographic Services held in November 1998. The new recommendations emphasize the importance of legal deposit regulations and take into account today's new technologies and media as they relate to coverage and production of the national bibliography.

Soper, Mary Ellen, Larry N. Osborne, and Douglas L. Zweizig. *The Librarian's Thesaurus.* Chicago: American Library Association, 1990. 164p.

Section B, by Soper, presents an excellent overview of the concepts of bibliography and bibliographic control.

Wainwright, Eric. "The National Library in an Electronic Age: Dinosaur or Catalyst?" *Alexandria* 5, no. 2 (1993): 111-18.

Wainwright discusses factors affecting national library directions: economic growth, technological development, social equity, and justice.

CHAPTER
21

INDEXES AND ABSTRACTS

Linda C. Smith

USES AND CHARACTERISTICS

A library's catalog, whether in card format or online, generally does not provide access to the entire contents of a library's collection. The catalog may confirm the holdings of a periodical title but not its contents; a poetry collection but not individual poems; the title of an author's collected works but not an individual essay; and newspaper titles but not individual news stories. Indexes and abstracts can be used to more fully reveal resources not covered in the general catalog as well as listing additional resources not held in a given library's collection. With the availability of online catalogs and indexes and abstracts in electronic form, more efforts are being made to provide direct links between them. For example, when the user of an index locates the record of a journal article likely to be of interest, information about the library's holdings of that journal title should be directly accessible. As more material becomes available in electronic form, mechanisms for index entries to link directly to the full texts of the publications indexed are likewise being developed.

Indexes such as periodical indexes usually list the authors, titles, or subjects of publications without comment. Abstracts, on the other hand, present a brief summary of content. Most abstracts are descriptive, but a few abstracting services contain evaluative abstracts, including the abstractor's critical comments, in the summary. Many abstracting services at present rely on author abstracts (or translations thereof) rather than having staff read each article and abstract it (a very costly practice). Abstracts serve as an aid in assessing the content of a document and its potential relevance. Although indexes and abstracts existed before 1900, there was a dramatic growth in their number during the twentieth century, as the scholarly community demanded improved access to a growing number of publications.

Two trends raise questions about the future of indexes and abstracts.[1] On the one hand, there is the growing popularity of table of contents services providing subject access to periodical article titles (sometimes supplemented with annotations appearing on journal contents pages). Such services lack the controlled vocabulary subject indexing characteristic of most print subject indexes and their electronic counterparts. On the other hand, a growing number of publications are in full text online or on CD-ROM, with the entire text searchable for occurrences of the keywords sought. Nevertheless, Dennis Auld argues that the skills of classifying, indexing, aggregating, and structuring content still are needed in the Web environment.[2] Indexes and abstracts are often thought of as *value-added* services because a human indexer or abstractor has analyzed the document content and developed a document surrogate including assigned indexing terms and (often) an abstract. It is assumed that this effort benefits the user by improving retrieval performance, enabling the identification of the best set of items for the user's purposes. More research is needed to determine how tables of contents and full text compare with established indexes and abstracts (and their electronic counterparts) in their usefulness for reference work.

Publishers of indexes and abstracts are introducing a number of enhancements to better meet user needs: (1) addition of newspaper, newswire, and radio and television transcript indexing to indexes formerly limited to coverage of periodicals; (2) inclusion of abstracts in what were formerly only indexing services; (3) inclusion of at least some full-text articles in what were formerly only abstracting services; (4) marketing of different subsets of a service to meet the needs of different sizes and types of libraries; (5) creation of rich networks of links between indexes and multiple full text resources; and (6) enhanced retrospective coverage available in electronic form. As noted in Chapter 7, library users increasingly demand rapid access to full texts, and indexes and abstracts are evolving to support that. This has led to what can seem to be a bewildering array of choices for librarians seeking to make selections among competing indexes and abstracts, increasing the need for careful evaluation.

EVALUATION

As reference librarians use the tools in reference work, they evaluate indexes and abstracts and choose those that will best reveal the contents of their own collections or that will refer users to needed information beyond library walls. Important characteristics to consider are format (print, CD-ROM, locally loaded, or online), scope, authority, accuracy, arrangement, and any special features that enhance effectiveness or ease of use.

Many of the indexes and abstracts discussed in this chapter are devoted to a particular type of publication: periodicals, newspapers, dissertations, or pamphlets. More specialized services devoted to indexing and abstracting the literature of a discipline often try to encompass many different types of publications to provide more comprehensive coverage in one source. Other differences arise if there are restrictions on place and language of publication of the source materials. Some indexes and abstracts cover only English-language material; others try to identify material relevant to a particular subject area in any language and from any part of the world. There may also be differences in the level of material covered. Some indexes of science materials may focus on the popular science literature while others cover the scholarly research literature. In print indexes and abstracts, introductory matter may provide a clear statement of materials covered. For electronic databases, it is necessary to rely on database descriptions found in directories or in documentation provided by the database producer or vendor/aggregator. Many publishers of periodical indexes are now posting lists of journals covered on their Web sites, making comparison among competing services easier.

Format

As explained in Chapter 5, many indexes and abstracts now exist in electronic form. A large number of the databases that were accessible in the 1970s and 1980s only by searching remote vendors online are now also available on CD-ROM, on magnetic tape for loading locally, or online from the producer via the Web. Some still have a print counterpart; others exist only in electronic form. The print format may still lend itself best to browsing, especially for abstracts; but the electronic forms usually have much more powerful search capabilities, with more access points and the possibility of refining searches by using Boolean logic to combine terms. Because most databases do not cover the literature before the mid-1960s, searches of indexes and abstracts for much of the older literature must rely on the print versions. Although most databases contain the same records as their print counterparts, some databases include more or combine the records from several print counterparts in a single database. Thus, when comparing alternative formats for a particular index or abstract, the librarian should study available documentation to determine the extent of correspondence between the content of each format and to understand the search capabilities of each.

The readability of entries is important, whether the index is in print or in electronic form. Indexes vary in type size, use of boldface, and other aspects of presenting entries. Extensive use of abbreviations may make the entries hard to interpret without frequent reference to lists of abbreviations and symbols elsewhere in the set. For example, an index might read "Dickens, Charles 3(221–27)." Somewhere in the index will be a key revealing that Charles Dickens is to be found in volume three, pages 221–27. This key is a relatively simple one. Other indexing schemes can be so obscure that an in-depth study must be undertaken before a reference can be understood.

Scope

Several characteristics define the scope of indexes and abstracts. The time covered does not necessarily coincide with the period of publication because the publisher may go back and index some older material valuable to the users of the index. For example, *Science Citation Index* has now extended its coverage back to 1945, although it originally began publication in the 1960s. Related factors are the frequency of publication and cumulation. Frequency of publication also affects currency; a monthly publication is likely to be more current than a quarterly one. Frequency of cumulation affects the ease with which retrospective searching can be done. If an index is semimonthly but cumulates only annually, for example, then many individual issues must be searched until the annual cumulation is issued. An advantage of searching indexes and abstracts online or on CD-ROM is that the contents are automatically cumulated.

Types of materials covered are another aspect of scope. Indexes and abstracts differ in the number of publications covered and the depth or specificity of the indexing. General periodical indexes tend to index all substantive articles from the periodicals selected for indexing, whereas subject-specific indexes and abstracts are more likely to index selectively from a much larger list of periodicals, with indexers identifying those articles of most relevance to the subject scope of the service. Some indexes and abstracts are more inclusive in the types of articles indexed, indexing such things as letters to the editor and editorials, whereas other services restrict their coverage to research articles. As the number of electronic journals has grown, publishers of indexes and abstracts have had to develop criteria for covering such titles. As Brian Quinn notes, electronic journals may have difficulty gaining acceptance into the mainstream of academic research and scholarship unless they are covered in major indexes.[3]

Authority

Considerations in assessing the authority of indexes and abstracts are the reputation of the publisher or sponsoring organization and the qualifications of the editorial staff. Publishers of indexes include commercial firms, professional associations, and government agencies. The H. W. Wilson Company is one of the longest-established commercial firms and has a well-deserved reputation for the quality of its indexes.[4] As reference librarians use various indexes, the authority of the indexers will usually reveal itself over time.

Accuracy

The quality of indexing and accuracy of bibliographic citations are as important in print indexes and abstracts as they are in electronic databases. Important selection criteria may include questions such as: Are all authors associated with an indexed item included in the author index? Are all major facets of the content of the article represented by entries in the subject index? Accuracy can also apply to both author and subject indexing. Author names should be spelled in the index as they are spelled in the work. Unfortunately, indexing guidelines for some indexes and abstracts dictate that only initials of given names be retained, even when a fuller form of the name appears on the original publication. This can make it difficult when searching authors to distinguish between different authors who share a common surname and initials. Accuracy of subject indexing depends on the indexer's ability to represent the content of a publication using terminology drawn from the controlled vocabulary to be used in indexing. Cross-references should be included where needed to lead from a form not used to the proper form or to link related terms. Some indexes include augmented titles, where the indexer supplements the original title with additional terms to characterize the article's content more completely. Abstracts should provide an accurate summary of the original article's content.

Arrangement

Arrangement of entries determines one possible approach to the items indexed. Although indexes generally employ an alphabetical arrangement, abstracts often appear in a classified arrangement that makes it easier to browse entries for related material. If additional indexes are present, they offer other access points to the publications indexed. Access points in print sources are generally limited to subject, author, and (occasionally) title. Indexes and abstracts in electronic form generally offer many additional options for searching, such as keywords from title and abstract, journal title, and author affiliation. The arrangement may not be critical because the search engine will instantly reveal the location of a term no matter where it is in an entry.

Special Features

When indexes and abstracts are evaluated, any special features that enhance their usefulness should be noted. Examples include a list of periodicals or other sources indexed and a published list of subject headings. The list of sources indexed is helpful in providing a clear indication of the materials covered as well as complete bibliographic information for those not available locally. This can be helpful in acquiring documents, whether ordering copies for inclusion in the library's collection or making requests through interlibrary loan or a document delivery service. A published list of subject headings can help in formulating effective search strategies in print and electronic indexes and abstracts, because the user can see a comprehensive list of terms available to the indexer and thus have a better chance of locating the appropriate terms to search. This is especially the case for those lists of subject headings that include scope notes or instructions for indexers, explaining how particular terms are to be used in indexing (and hence in searching). A growing number of indexing and abstracting services are developing approaches to ease the task of locating the full text of documents covered by their services. In some cases the full text of documents is available online or on CD-ROM, as page images or searchable full text. Copies of other documents can be ordered directly from the indexing and abstracting service, with various alternatives for rapid delivery.

SELECTION

Indexes and abstracts are often expensive reference tools, no matter what format is selected. Selection of titles for a particular collection must take into account the characteristics of that collection as well as the needs of users for access beyond what is already provided by the library's catalog.

Directories of periodicals can be used to identify available indexes and abstracts. *Ulrich's International Periodicals Directory*, described in Chapter 20, has a section on abstracting and indexing services, with entries for a few general services and cross-references to many more subject-specific services with entries elsewhere in the directory. In addition, for each periodical listed in the directory, *Ulrich's* provides an indication of the indexes and abstracts that include the periodical in their coverage—meaning inclusion of at least some of the periodical's articles as entries in the index or abstract. In using such information, it should be noted that a study by Jonathan D. Eldredge suggests that such a directory may under-report index coverage.[5] *Magazines for Libraries* provides descriptions of many of the more widely held titles in its section on abstracts and indexes. *Gale Directory of Databases* provides good coverage of indexes and abstracts in electronic form.

Needs of Users

Indexes and abstracts selected for a particular library collection should reflect the types of information and publications that library users wish to access. They should allow more complete use of the local collection as well as identification of publications of possible value available elsewhere. General periodical indexes, table-of-contents services, and newspaper indexes could be useful in libraries of all types. Selection of periodical indexes devoted to particular subject areas will reflect the subject interests of the library's users. Citation indexes, with their emphasis on scholarly literature, will be of most use in academic and special libraries. Indexes to special types of materials, except for *Vertical File Index*, are also likely to be found most often in academic and special libraries. Selection of indexes to reviews should reflect user demand for this information. Indexes to literary forms can prove useful wherever collected works and anthologies make up part of the collection. Fortunately the availability of so many indexes and abstracts in electronic form has meant that access to at least a portion of most indexes is possible online even if the library does not have a subscription to the print version. Usage of indexes and abstracts in electronic form can be measured, providing a tool to guide choice of which resources to retain and which to cancel when licenses come up for renewal.[6]

The availability of CD-ROM versions or magnetic tapes (to be locally loaded) has complicated the selection decision, because now the library can acquire many indexes in print form, on CD-ROM, to be locally loaded, or in more than one of these formats. When resources to purchase indexes and abstracts are limited, librarians must determine whether duplication of some titles in different formats is justified. A growing number of articles discuss issues involved in the decision to cancel print indexes[7] and the selection among electronic alternatives.[8]

In addition to providing access to online databases through commercial vendors, librarians now have the opportunity to use specialized indexes and abstracts developed by libraries and other organizations and made available online through the Web.[9] Such databases include indexes to regional magazines, local newspaper indexes, or specialized subject indexes.

Cost

The discussion of alternative formats in Chapter 13 identifies a number of factors affecting the cost of using indexes and abstracts in the various formats: in print, on CD-ROM, or online. Some publishers of indexes and abstracts offer discounted pricing on a second format if one format is already part of the library's collection. A complete analysis of cost factors for each format has to take into account subscription prices for print and CD-ROM versions, binding and shelving costs for print copies, equipment costs for using CD-ROM or online databases, and per search charges or subscription costs for online access. The tradeoffs may be different for different indexes as each publisher develops its own pricing policy. Increasingly libraries are gaining access to electronic versions through participation in consortial licensing arrangements, which may reduce the price paid by each participating library.

In a discussion of cost of indexes, it is important to describe the service basis of charging for some of the print indexes published by the H. W. Wilson Company. To make the indexes available to the widest possible audience, such indexes are priced so that each subscriber is charged according to the amount of service provided. For periodical indexes such as *Business Periodicals Index*, *General Science Index*, *Humanities Index*, and *Social Sciences Index*, subscribers pay an amount determined by the number of indexed periodicals they hold. A library holding only a few of the indexed periodicals would pay less than a library holding most of the titles. For some book indexes, such as *Book Review Digest*, the price of the index paid by a particular library reflects that library's expenditure for books. The idea underlying this approach is that the users of a library with a large collection derive more benefit from the index than the users of a library with a small collection. This principle is also reflected in instances where online subscription rates are determined in part by the number of users served by the library, with those serving more users paying a higher rate.

Uniqueness

Uniqueness relates to both the coverage and arrangement of the indexes and abstracts being considered for selection. Although overlap in sources indexed is one indicator of the degree of uniqueness of indexes, the access points and search capabilities provided by the indexes must also be considered. Two indexes could cover many of the same periodicals, but the subject indexing provided may give the user different ways of approaching the content in each. Thus examination of overlap in materials covered must be supplemented by an assessment of the approaches provided to those materials by the different indexes.

Full Text Coverage

Given the growing demand for the full text of periodicals, newspapers, and other publications in electronic form, criteria for selecting these resources deserve special consideration. Unfortunately "full text" does not have a standard definition when applied to electronic publications with print counterparts. At the article level, "full text" may include the main text but not any sidebars or illustrations. At the issue level, "full text" may include major articles, but omit such things as letters to the editor, short columns, book reviews, and advertisements. At the journal level, one expects "full text" to cover all the issues of the publication, including any supplements. As Walt Crawford notes, these differences may result in a loss of important context for the content.[10] A related issue is how errors, corrections, and retractions are handled.[11]

Systematic comparisons of available full-text databases are beginning to appear, providing a framework for selecting among available alternatives.[12] Factors to consider include which titles are covered in various subject areas (and whether any are unique, not covered elsewhere), coverage dates, currency, policy on inclusion of article types and illustrations, whether text is searchable or only displayable, indexing, output formats, screen design, and pricing. Delivery of full text in a Web environment also opens up the possibility of creating links among articles, reflecting the relationships among them. CrossRef (http://www.crossref.org) is one example of a project to create live reference links among journal articles available in electronic form from different publishers. Another recent development, the SFX (http://www.sfxit.com) framework, extends the linkages possible to include full-text repositories, abstracts and indexes, online catalogs, and citations appearing in research articles on the Web.

As journal publishers experiment with the electronic medium, the situation becomes even more complex. Electronic journals now range "from simplistic (and quite old-fashioned looking) ASCII texts to complex multimedia and interactive electronic journals."[13] Because of possible differences between the electronic and print versions of the same title, indexing and abstracting services may have difficulty deciding which is the authoritative version to index. Reference librarians also need to be aware of the different models of supplying full text that have emerged in the Web environment: publisher-supplied full text; third-party, or aggregator-supplied full text (e.g., *Wilson Omnifile*), and distributed, "linked" full text, in which an indexing or abstracting service links to publisher-supplied full text.[14]

IMPORTANT GENERAL SOURCES

This chapter describes some of the most widely held general periodical indexes, table of contents services, newspaper indexes, broad subject periodical indexes, citation indexes, indexes for special types of materials, indexes of reviews, and indexes for different literary forms. Most abstracting services lie outside the scope of this chapter because they are devoted to the literature of a specific subject area. However, a number of general periodical indexes are now enhanced with the inclusion of abstracts (described below). Selection among competing products should include evaluation of the quality of the abstracts as well as the indexing.[15]

General Periodical Indexes

General periodical indexes are held by all types of libraries. They index periodicals covering current events, hobbies, popular culture, and school curriculum-related areas. The *Readers' Guide to Periodical Literature* has filled this need since 1900.[16] The main body of the index consists of subject and author entries to articles from 270 English-language periodicals arranged in one alphabet (see Figure 21.1).

Figure 21.1 Entries from *Readers' Guide to Periodical Literature,* May 2000. Reprinted with permission of The H. W. Wilson Company.

FREEDOM MARCHES *See* Civil rights demonstrations
FREEDOM OF INFORMATION
See also
Classified information
Government and the press
Journalistic ethics
FREEDOM OF INFORMATION ACT (1966)
Fears recede over access to research data. I. Goodwin. *Physics Today* v52 no12 p48-9 D 1999
No secrets [Shelby amendment] T. Beardsley. *Scientific American* v281 no6 p58 D 1999
FREEDOM OF RELIGION *See* Religious liberty
FREEDOM OF SPEECH
See also
Freedom of the press
Libel and slander
Antitrust cops shouldn't police free expression. M. France. il *Business Week* no3668 p88 F 14 2000
Dissing John Rocker [question whether baseball should punish him for expressing his beliefs] J. Leo. il *U.S. News & World Report* v128 no6 p14 F 14 2000
Free speech on the Net? Not quite [companies suing over statements made anonymously online] M. France. il *Business Week* no3670 p93-4 F 28 2000
He said, they said. P. Mushnick. por *TV Guide* v48 no8 p56 F 19-25 2000
Kids' beat [free speech issues and video games] M. W. Lynch. *Reason* v31 no9 p20 F 2000
Loose lips sink Web sites? [Blueovalnews.com vindicated after exposing Ford secrets] J. Koch. il *Hot Rod* v53 no1 p18 Ja 2000
Talk is cheap [Supreme Court and campaign finance reform] J. Rosen. *The New Republic* v222 no7 p20-2 F 14 2000
Teaching core democratic values? D. Barlow. *The Education Digest* v65 no5 p35-40 Ja 2000
The unremarked victims of the war on drugs [content of TV shows] R. Norton. il *Fortune* v141 no4 p74 F 21 2000
Watch what you say [restrictions on free speech by American left] J. Leo. il *U.S. News & World Report* v128 no11 p18 Mr 20 2000
FREEDOM OF TEACHING *See* Academic freedom
FREEDOM OF THE PRESS
See also
College newspapers—Censorship
Government and the press
Libel and slander
Democracy in infancy. M. Frankel. il *The New York Times Magazine* p17-18 Ja 23 2000

Since 1976 each issue has included a listing of citations to book reviews, arranged by author of the book reviewed, following the main body of the index. An *Abridged Readers' Guide* covering 82 periodicals selected from those in the unabridged edition is available for use in school and small public libraries.

Extensive cross-references lead the user from a term not used to the proper term (for example, "Freedom of religion, *See* Religious liberty") and from a term to related terms (for example, "Freedom of speech, *See also* Freedom of the press, Libel and slander"). Specific aspects of a subject are indicated by subdivisions under the main heading. Under authors and subjects, titles are arranged in alphabetical order by the first word, disregarding initial articles. Under personal names, titles *by* an author precede those *about* an author. When titles are not sufficiently descriptive of an article's content, supplementary notes are added in brackets following the original title (as in "Free speech on the Net? Not quite [companies suing over statements made anonymously online]"). Subdivisions of a subject are arranged alphabetically under the subject, with geographical subheads following the other subdivisions in a separate alphabet. The instructions for use explain how to locate reviews of ballet, books, dance, motion pictures, musicals, opera, radio programs, sound recordings, television programs, theater, videodiscs, and videotapes, together with how to locate the index entries for fiction, poems, and short stories. The subject headings try to make use of common language, so that users can easily find the topics sought.

Readers' Guide is published monthly, with quarterly cumulations and an annual bound cumulation. Since 1952 the Committee on Wilson Indexes of the American Library Association's Reference and User Services Association has advised the publisher on indexing and editorial policy for *Readers' Guide* and other Wilson indexes.[17] In the 1970s a few other general periodical indexes were introduced, such as *Access: The Supplementary Index to Periodicals*, an author and subject index to more than 100 periodicals not indexed in *Readers' Guide* but commonly held in libraries. *Alternative Press Index*, which began publication in 1969, seeks to provide subject indexing for more than 250 journals and newspapers covering alternative or radical points of view. The National Information Services Corporation publishes a CD-ROM version with coverage beginning in 1991, and also provides online access.

During the 1980s the H. W. Wilson Company introduced a number of additions to the *Readers' Guide* family, and competitors emerged with new products taking advantage first of CD-ROM technology and now the Web. Wilson's *Readers' Guide Abstracts* provides summaries of the articles indexed in *Readers' Guide* and can be purchased on CD-ROM or accessed online with coverage from 1983. More recently the full text of many of the periodicals indexed has been part of the CD-ROM and online versions. For example, *Readers' Guide Full Text: Mega Edition* has full text coverage of more than 140 periodicals from January 1994. *Readers' Guide for Young People*, designed for students in grades 4 through 8, has full text coverage of more than 60 periodicals from January 1995. The electronic version of *Readers' Guide* now also includes indexing of *The New York Times*. Enhanced retrospective coverage is planned, with coverage from 1969 to 1982 to be available in June 2001 and coverage from 1890 to 1969 to be available in June 2002. *Readers' Guide* and other Wilson indexes are characterized by quality subject indexing and author name authority control.

The other major publishers of general periodical indexes include Gale Group (Infotrac), EBSCO Publishing, and ProQuest. They now market a family of databases on CD-ROM, from online vendors, and via the Web, with products ranging from those for school libraries to those intended for large academic and public libraries. Many of these products now provide the full text of articles from selected journals as well as citations and abstracts for articles from a larger number of journals. These competing products continue to change their coverage (both of titles indexed and titles available in full text) and search capabilities. Therefore, librarians need to follow these developments to determine which approaches to providing access to periodicals best meet the needs of the library's users and which are affordable. Publisher Web sites are very helpful for current listings of product offerings. H. W. Wilson Company (http://www.hwwilson.com), EBSCO Publishing (http://www.epnet.com), Gale Group (http://www.galegroup.com), and ProQuest (http://www.proquest.com), from Bell & Howell

Information and Learning should all be investigated. Increasingly these databases encompass material in addition to periodicals, such as transcripts of television and radio programs.

Major retrospective indexing projects are becoming available in electronic form, overcoming a longstanding weakness of most online indexes. *Poole's Plus* (http://www.poolesplus.net) is merging entries from nineteenth-century indexes to periodicals, newspapers, government documents, and books into a searchable database. *Periodicals Contents Index* from Chadwyck-Healey provides access to the tables of contents of more than 3,100 periodicals from 1770 to 1990, including titles in French, German, Italian, Spanish, and other Western languages as well as English. In a partnership with ProQuest, libraries can gain access to the full text of some of these periodicals through *Periodicals Contents Index Full Text*, including the full runs of over 250 journals in the humanities and social sciences.

Although indexes like *Readers' Guide* include some magazines of interest to children, *Children's Magazine Guide* provides a subject index specifically to 53 children's magazines (at the elementary and middle school level). In nine issues per year, it gives subject entries in a simple-to-read format, with cross-references to related topics. Some entries also include URLs and brief descriptions of related Web sites suitable for children (for example, an article on dinosaurs is followed by an entry for *The Dinosaur Interplanetary Gazette* at http://www.dinosaur.org).

Two indexes provide good coverage of Canadian periodicals. *Canadian Index* covers approximately 400 Canadian English-language and 50 Canadian French-language periodicals in all subjects. It also indexes 25 major foreign periodicals and 9 Canadian daily newspapers. It has three parts: subject, corporate name, and personal name indexes. It is also available online and on CD-ROM as part of *Canadian Business and Current Affairs* (*CBCA*). *Canadian Periodical Index* is a bilingual author and subject index to more than 400 English- and French-language periodicals, including more than 30 U.S. titles dealing with North American and international issues. Citations are listed under English subject headings only, with cross-references from French subject headings. The index is available in print, CD-ROM, and online formats. *CBCA Fulltext Reference* provides full-text access to over 180 general interest periodicals as well as indexing of more than 750 periodicals and 9 daily news sources.

Table of Contents Services

The idea of table of contents services is not a new one. *Current Contents*, now with seven different subject editions (covering agriculture, biology, and environmental sciences; arts and humanities; clinical medicine; engineering, computing, and technology; life sciences; physical, chemical, and earth sciences; and social and behavioral sciences), was introduced in a weekly print format by the Institute for Scientific Information (ISI) in 1958. These editions emphasize the scholarly literature, with each edition covering from 1,000 to 1,600 journals from around the world. Tables of contents are grouped in broad subject classes, and a simple keyword subject index provides access to article titles. *Current Contents Connect* combines all editions into a single database on the Web, and is also available from online vendors and on CD-ROM. Copies of documents indexed can be ordered through ISI's document delivery service, ISI Document Solution.

Although *Current Contents* has proved most useful in academic and special libraries, several other table of contents services have emerged in the past few years with coverage encompassing general interest as well as scholarly journals. Because they are coupled with document delivery services, their popularity reflects the growing pressure from library users for faster delivery of journal articles when local collections lack the needed materials. Major competitors include *UnCover*, OCLC's *ContentsFirst*, and the British Library Document Supply Centre's *Inside Information Plus*, made available by the Research Libraries Group's CitaDel. *UnCover* covers more than 18,000 periodicals, with very rapid updating. *Inside Information Plus* covers 21,000 titles, with particularly strong coverage of European titles. *ContentsFirst* covers more than 12,000 titles, with links to those full-text journals available in OCLC's *Electronic Collections Online*. Comparative studies of coverage, search features, and document delivery services have been published.[18] Given the growing emphasis in libraries on access to, rather than ownership of, journals, it is important for reference librarians to stay informed of enhancements to these services to determine which offer the best coverage and features to meet the library users' need for access to current periodicals.

Newspaper Indexes

General periodical indexes such as *Readers' Guide* include coverage of the major newsmagazines and selected newspapers, thus offering some access to information on current events at the national and international level. Many library users also want access to more extensive newspaper coverage of national and international topics, as well as regional and local news. The effect of technology on newspaper indexing has been considerable: Well-established newspaper indexes are now supplemented with indexes and abstracts available on CD-ROM or online and an increasing number of full-text newspapers in electronic form. More recently the Web has developed into a rich and diverse source of current news. These changes have made it possible to make much fuller use of news sources in answering reference questions, especially those on current events.

The best-known print newspaper index is the *New York Times Index*.[19] Because it includes abstracts of articles appearing in the newspaper, it can be used alone for a basic survey of the news, or it can be used to locate full articles in the original newspaper. Abstracts are classified under appropriate subject, geographic, organization, and personal name headings. They are sufficiently detailed that they may answer some questions without reference to the original *Times* articles. Headings are arranged alphabetically, and entries under them are arranged chronologically. Each entry is followed by a reference (date, section, page, and column) to the item it summarizes. Entries indicate if the original article includes illustrations or other special material. Cross-references are used to identify related material. In addition to serving as an index to *The New York Times*, the index can also be used to locate discussions of particular events in other newspapers that lack indexes. The *New York Times Index* can be used to identify the date of an event, and the corresponding issue of the local newspaper can be consulted for its discussion of that event. Issues appear semimonthly, with quarterly and annual cumulations. Because of the time lag in indexing, the index is not helpful in locating articles on very recent events. A separately published *Personal Name Index to the New York Times Index*, compiled by Byron A. Falk and Valerie R. Falk, eases the task of finding the issues of the *New York Times Index* in which an individual's name is mentioned.

Electronic newspaper resources include both indexes and the full text of newspaper articles. Gale Group (*National Newspaper Index*), ProQuest (*ProQuest Full-Text Newspapers*), EBSCO Publishing (*Newspaper Source*), and NewsBank (http://www.newsbank.com) all offer coverage of newspaper resources. *National Newspaper Index* indexes five major U.S. newspapers (*The New York Times*, *The Wall Street Journal*, *Christian Science Monitor*, *Los Angeles Times*, and *Washington Post*). *ProQuest Full-Text Newspapers* has the full text online of 150 national and international newspapers; libraries can select which titles to subscribe to. *Newspaper Source* contains the full text of the *Christian Science Monitor* from 1995 and abstracting and indexing for *The New York Times*, *The Wall Street Journal*, and *USA Today*, as well as newswire information. It also has the full text for 123 regional U.S. newspapers and 15 international newspapers. NewsBank's strength lies in the provision of access to articles from more than 500 U.S. regional newspapers. A number of other vendors offer full-text searching of selected newspapers, including LEXIS-NEXIS (http://www.lexis-nexis.com), Dialog (http://www.dialog.com), and Factiva (http://www.factiva.com).[20] *Canadian Newspapers*, one of the files on Dialog, includes the full text of 11 Canadian general circulation newspapers and one national business newspaper. Although there is some overlap in titles covered by the various vendors, each vendor provides access to some unique titles. In searching full-text files, it is important to use the most specific and unique words possible and to narrow the search by other criteria (such as date range) if possible. Full-text files generally do not predate the 1980s. Some full-text newspapers are also being distributed on CD-ROM.

Publishers are creating other specialized CD-ROM and online products to complement coverage of indexes for general newspapers. For example, *Ethnic NewsWatch* is a full-text database, available on CD-ROM, online, and via the Web, with articles from about 200 ethnic newspapers and magazines published in the United States, including African American, Caribbean, Hispanic, Native American, Asian American, Jewish, Arab/Middle Eastern, European American, and multiethnic publications. Spanish-language publications appear in Spanish. Indexing covers subjects, title, byline, article type, date, names, geographic location, ethnic group, publication name, and article keywords. A directory provides information on each publication and publisher. Enhancing retrospective news coverage, Chadwyck-Healey's *Historical Newspapers Online* allows users to search the indexes of *The Times* of London back to 1790 and *The New York Times* back to 1851.

At present news sources freely available on the Web are most valuable for the access they provide to very current news from around the world.[21] Newspapers, news magazines, wire services, and broadcast networks are among the sources of news on the Web. Useful directory sites for locating news sources include *AJR Newslink* (http://ajr.newslink.org) and the *Newspaper Association of America* (http://www.naa.org/hotlinks/index.asp).

Broad Subject Periodical Indexes

When the scope of a library's periodical collection exceeds that of the coverage of a general periodical index, the library should acquire one or more additional indexes. Most of the widely held titles are published by the H. W. Wilson Company, but one index commonly found in public and academic libraries is published by OCLC Public Affairs Information Service. Formerly titled *Public Affairs Information Service (PAIS) Bulletin*, *PAIS International in Print* now incorporates both the *Bulletin* and the *PAIS Foreign Language Index*. It appears monthly, with quarterly and annual cumulations. English-language sources are supplemented with material in French, German, Italian, Portuguese, and Spanish. Entries include English-language abstract-like notes and indications of special features, such as maps, charts, tables, and bibliographies. The scope of *PAIS* includes public policy, business, legal, economic, social science, and related literature. Compilers try to identify the public affairs information likely to be most useful to legislators, government officials, the business and financial community, policy researchers, and students. The listings encompass print materials in all formats: periodical articles, books, government documents (drawn from national and state governments and intergovernmental organizations), pamphlets, and the reports of public and private organizations; beginning in 1997 some Internet documents have also been indexed. Indexing of periodicals is selective; about 1,600 periodicals are scanned to identify articles within the scope of *PAIS*. In introducing a library user to this index, it is helpful to point out the types of publications indexed, as different strategies may be needed to locate periodicals, books, and documents in the library's collection.

The emphasis in *PAIS* is on factual and statistical information. An effort is made to represent the full range of positions on controversial subjects. The subject entries are drawn from a controlled vocabulary, *PAIS Subject Headings*, which includes more than 8,000 subject headings and cross-references displaying relationships among terms. Entries can appear under either subject or geographical headings, both of which may be subdivided. An author index is provided in the annual bound volume for entries that have either a personal or corporate author. The "Key to Periodicals Referenced" gives the abbreviated journal title, the full title, the frequency, price, and ISSN of the journal, as well as the address of the publisher. The "Directory of Publishers and Distributors" gives the abbreviated name, full name, and address. *PAIS* can also be searched on CD-ROM and online, with coverage from 1972. The CD-ROM is updated quarterly; online updates are made monthly. Beginning with 1996 a CD-ROM product titled *PAIS Select* provides the full text of some of the articles indexed in *PAIS International*.

The H. W. Wilson Company publishes indexes to periodicals in a variety of subject areas, such as *Social Sciences Index* and *General Science Index*, supplementing the coverage of general periodicals provided by *Readers' Guide*. One or more of these indexes are likely to be found in academic, public, and special libraries, with the choice depending on the subject strengths of the collection and interests of the library's users. They are all limited to English-language periodicals, but include some titles published outside the United States. Selection of periodicals for indexing is accomplished by subscriber vote, with an emphasis on the reference value of the periodicals under consideration. There is also an effort to give consideration to subject balance. Each issue has a list of periodicals indexed, with order information. A well-developed system of cross-references aids the search for articles on specific subjects in a particular index. Each of these indexes is available on CD-ROM with coverage from the early 1980s. In addition they can be searched online through various vendors and on the Web via WilsonWeb. Details of subject scope and lists of journals covered can be found at the H. W. Wilson Company Web site. As with *Readers' Guide,* the electronic versions of the subject indexes are now being augmented with abstracts and full text. For example, *Wilson Business Abstracts* began publication in 1991, the first of the Wilson subject titles to offer abstracts as an enhancement of the electronic version. *Wilson Business Full Text* now offers the full text of more than 260 periodicals back to January 1995, abstracting of 530 periodicals back to 1990, and indexing back to 1982.

Although ProQuest, the Gale Group, and EBSCO Publishing have emphasized multidisciplinary indexing and full-text products, they also have some databases covering more specific subject areas. For example, Bell & Howell Information and Learning's *ABI/INFORM* provides indexing and abstracting for more than 1,000 titles and the full text of about 400 of the major business publications; EBSCO's *Business Source Elite* provides indexing and abstracting for 1,650 titles, with nearly 970 in full text.

Citation Indexes

The periodical indexes described thus far allow the user to find articles written by the same author or indexed under the same subject heading. Citation indexes allow the user to locate items based on a different type of relationship: the links created when authors cite earlier works by other authors (or even some of their own previously published works). The primary use of a citation index is to find, for a particular publication known to the searcher, later items that have cited it. The Institute for Scientific Information (ISI) publishes three indexes that allow the user to carry out such searches in broad subject areas: *Science Citation Index*, *Social Sciences Citation Index*, and *Arts & Humanities Citation Index*.[22] Coverage includes journals and chapters in some multiauthored books. They are all structured in the same way, with four indexes: a "Source Index," "Citation Index," "Permuterm Subject Index," and "Corporate Index." The "Source Index" provides complete bibliographic information for each article indexed in a particular issue. It is arranged by author name, with cross-references from co-authors to first authors. Figure 21.2 shows some sample entries from the "Source Index." In addition to bibliographic and author address information, the entries in *Social Sciences Citation Index* and *Arts & Humanities Citation Index* contain a complete list of the references included in the source item's bibliography. To find complete journal titles, the complete list of periodicals elsewhere in the volume must be consulted to translate from abbreviated to full journal titles. The "Source Index" is used to find articles by known authors that have been published during the time period covered by the index.

Figure 21.3 shows sample entries from the "Citation Index," which allows one to find recent articles in which earlier works are cited. Entries are made for any author's work cited during the period covered by the index. In the example, an article by G. Renoux, published in 1973 in the *Bulletin of the World Health Organization*, was subsequently cited by A. Thelin writing in the *Scandinavian Journal of Social Medicine* in 1990. Cited publications can be of all types and from any time period. The "Source Index" must be consulted to get complete bibliographic information for the citing articles. Codes are used to indicate the type of source item (e.g., E = editorial) where applicable. The "Citation Index" is used to go from older, known publications to the more recent, related articles that cite them. Using the "Citation Index,"

Figure 21.2 Entries from "Source Index," *Social Sciences Citation Index.* Reprinted with permission of the Institute for Scientific Information, Philadelphia, PA 19104.

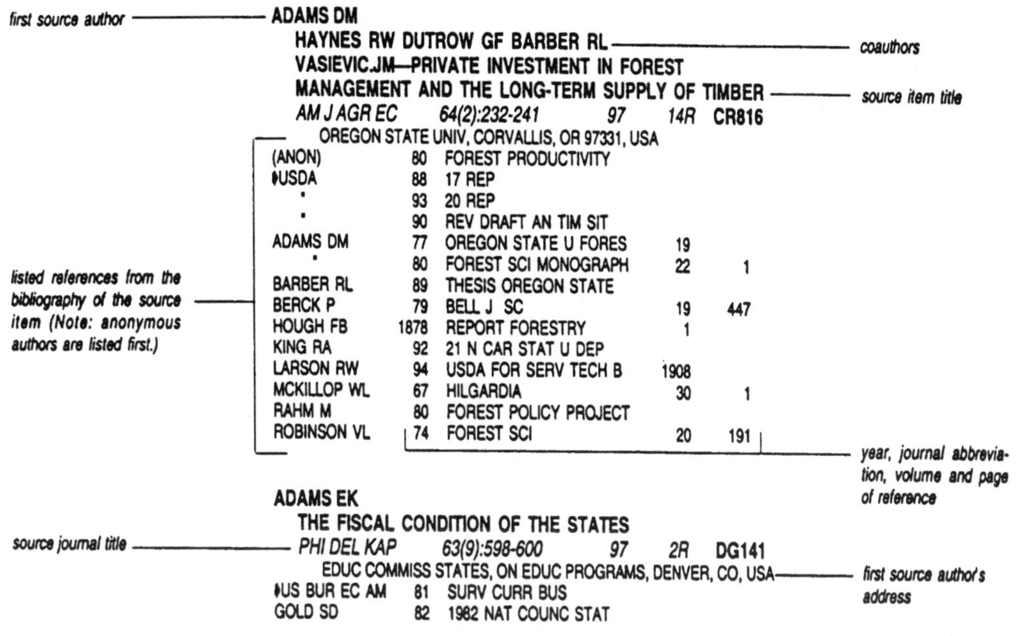

Figure 21.3 Entries from "Citation Index," *Social Sciences Citation Index.* Reprinted with permission of the Institute for Scientific Information, Philadelphia, PA 19104.

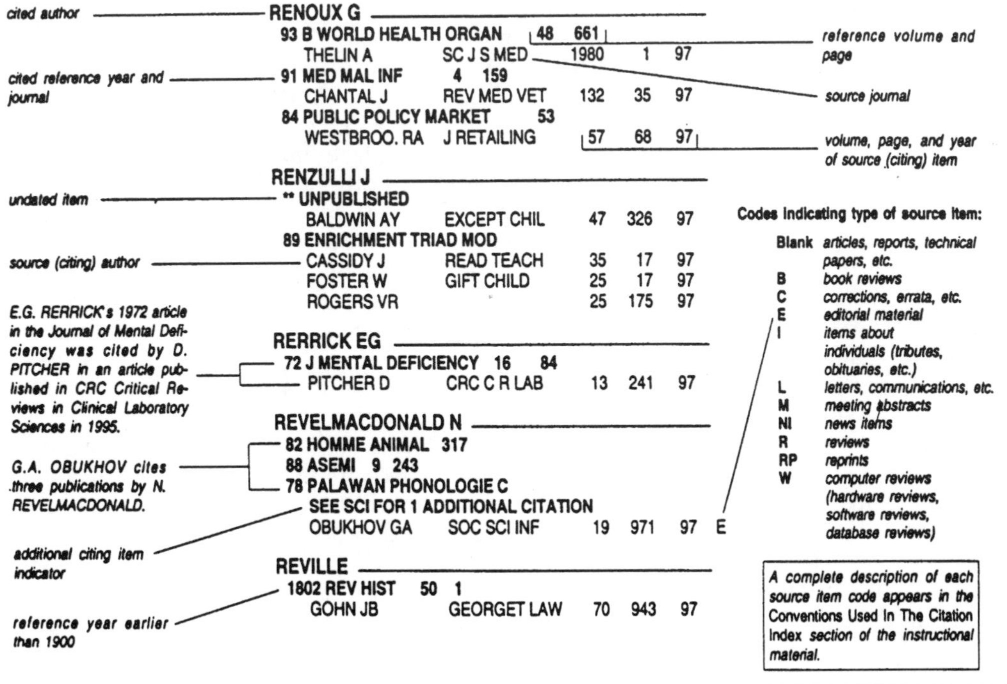

terminology problems may be avoided because earlier published works can be used to represent concepts or topics of interest. Citing publications are assumed to be related in some way to those earlier cited publications. Only first authors are listed in the "Citation Index" entries, so the first author of multiauthored papers must be known to use the paper as a starting point. *Arts & Humanities Citation Index* also includes entries for *implicit citations,* works of art or music that are discussed in the source article but not necessarily cited explicitly in an article's bibliography. Thus, one could look for entries in the "Citation Index" under Rembrandt or Mozart to find articles discussing their works.

The "Permuterm Subject Index" allows one to find articles with words related to the search topic in their titles. Entries are derived from keywords appearing in source article titles. The "Source Index" must be consulted to get complete bibliographic information for the articles. This index can be used in searching for newly coined terms that appear in article titles but that are not yet used in other indexes as subject headings. Because there is no vocabulary control, the user of the "Permuterm Subject Index" must look for synonyms and variant spellings of the terms sought. The effectiveness of this type of indexing depends on the quality of the titles and the ingenuity of the searcher.

The fourth index is the "Corporate Index," providing access to authors and their works by corporate or academic affiliation. It is arranged by geographic location and then by organization name. States of the United States appear in one alphabetical listing, followed by a separate list of other countries. There is also a list of organizations with cross-references to the geographic list. The "Source Index" must be consulted to get complete bibliographic information for the articles located in the "Corporate Index." This index can be used to find articles of interest when a corporate or academic institution is known to sponsor work on the topic.

All three citation indexes are international in scope, covering many journals published outside the United States as well as the major U.S. titles in each subject area. Source articles in languages other than English include a language code preceding the English translation of the title. *Science Citation Index* now covers the period back to 1945 and is updated bimonthly; *Social Sciences Citation Index* goes back to 1956 with current issues covering four-month intervals; and *Arts & Humanities Citation Index* has annual volumes for the period 1976–1988 and semiannual volumes beginning in 1989. All three indexes are available with more restricted time coverage online from various vendors (*SciSearch* from 1974, *Social SciSearch* from 1972, and *Arts & Humanities Search* from 1980). For the time period covered, these sources can be searched much more easily online than in print. Coverage is also more current online because updates are made weekly. CD-ROM editions are now available for all three titles as well. In addition to search capabilities found in print, the CD-ROMs have a "related records" feature, enabling the user to find articles related to a known article. Relatedness is determined by the number of references the articles share (a technique known as *bibliographic coupling*), rather than by having keywords in common. Both the CD-ROM and online versions of *Science Citation Index* and *Social Sciences Citation Index* have now been enhanced with English-language author abstracts where available in the source article as well as author keywords and keywords extracted from the titles of works cited by an article.[23] *ISI Basic Science Index* and *ISI Basic Social Sciences Index*, two Web-based indexes with more limited periodical coverage but retaining the citation searching capability, are designed especially for use by undergraduates.

The Web has inspired the most recent innovation in citation searching: ISI's *Web of Science*[24] supports simultaneous searching of all three citation indexes. Citation networks are an inherently hypertext approach to navigating the literature. This implementation has three types of internal links among records in the database: "cited references" lead to the items cited by a publication (going backward in time), "times cited" leads to the items citing a publication (going forward in time), and "related records" identify other publications that have overlapping items cited with the publication of interest. *Web of Science* also provides external links to the full text of journals articles indexed in the database.[25] If the library subscribes to a given journal, then the user can link from the record in *Web of Science* to the full text of the journal article.

Box 21.1 Search Strategy: The Indexable Web

A computer science student had heard about a study of search engines done in 1999 that found that only 42 percent of the Web is indexed by a combination of several major search engines. He knew the last names of the authors (Lawrence and Giles), but did not know their full names or where the study had been published. He was interested in finding more discussions of this topic but was having difficulty thinking of search terms that would locate what he wanted. He e-mailed the question to his college library's e-mail reference service. The librarian who handled the question recognized *Web of Science* as a likely tool to find an answer. Using truncation on each of the author names and combining them with AND in the search box for article author(s), she found the record for the original article: S. Lawrence and C. L. Giles, "Accessibility of Information on the Web," *Nature* 400 (July 8, 1999): 107–109. It had six cited references that would allow the student to locate earlier research, and it had already been cited 64 times, providing links to more recent research. She e-mailed the student instructions on how to locate the record and navigate the links in *Web of Science* and encouraged him to contact the reference desk again if he had further questions.

Indexes for Special Types of Materials

The indexes discussed thus far in this chapter provide good coverage of periodicals and newspapers, but are not helpful for gaining access to some other special types of materials that may be important in certain library collections. Academic library users frequently want access to dissertations; public and school library users often want to locate pamphlets on particular topics. Indexes devoted to these and other special types of materials, such as conference proceedings and research reports, can be useful for both collection development and reference work. This section describes the indexes for dissertations and pamphlets. Other indexes to special materials are described in more specialized guides to reference sources, such as the sections on conference literature, patents, and technical reports in *Using Science and Technology Information Sources*.[26]

Students have been earning doctoral degrees in U.S. universities for almost 140 years. Research for the doctorate is reported in dissertations, many of which are deposited with UMI in Ann Arbor, Michigan, to enable their use outside the institution in which the research was originally completed. UMI has developed several reference tools to aid librarians in providing more effective access to the dissertation literature. Print tools include *Comprehensive Dissertation Index* (*CDI*) and *Dissertation Abstracts International* (*DAI*).[27] *CDI* attempts to list every doctoral dissertation accepted in North America since 1861. The original set covers the period 1861–1972. This has been followed by multiyear cumulations and annual supplements. The set includes some coverage of dissertations accepted at universities outside North America. Titles are arranged by keyword in broad subject categories in the sciences or the social sciences and humanities. Entries give the full dissertation title, author, degree, date, institution, number of pages, a reference to the location in *DAI* where an abstract can be found, and an order number if it is available from UMI. Because dissertations usually have quite specific titles, this form of subject access works reasonably well. However, the lack of vocabulary control means that the user must identify any likely synonyms for the topic of interest to do a complete subject search. If the author is known, the author index can be used to identify the title of the dissertation.

DAI is published monthly in two parts ("A—The Humanities and Social Sciences" and "B—The Sciences and Engineering") and includes abstracts of doctoral dissertations submitted to UMI by participating institutions in North America. A third section ("C—Worldwide") is published quarterly and includes abstracts of dissertations in all disciplines from many institutions throughout the world. A list of participating institutions is included in each issue of *DAI*. Copies of dissertations may be purchased from UMI in microform or paper format;

dissertations published since 1997 are available through ProQuest Digital Dissertations (http://www.lib.umi.com/dissertations) in electronic form. Entries in *DAI* are grouped by author-selected subject, then alphabetically by author within subject. Each issue contains a keyword index and an author index to gain access to the classified abstracts.

Although *CDI* cumulations can make the task of searching several years for dissertations somewhat easier than searching year by year, the availability of *CDI* and *DAI* in electronic form on CD-ROM and online has considerably enhanced the search capabilities. The online database includes abstracts published since July 1980 as well as citations to dissertations back to 1861 in a single database. British and European dissertations are included in the database from January 1988 forward. Subject access is enhanced for those dissertations with abstracts because every word in the abstract is searchable in addition to the title keywords searchable in the print indexes. *Dissertation Abstracts Ondisc* has the same coverage as the online database, and it allows keyword searching. As more universities require students to submit dissertations in electronic form, libraries may have a role to play in storing, indexing, and preserving these titles.[28]

Vertical File Index is a subject index to current pamphlets and other inexpensive paper-bound items published in English in the United States or Canada. Selected nonbook materials such as charts, posters, and maps for classroom use are also listed. Under subject headings, entries are arranged alphabetically by the title of the pamphlet. Entries contain bibliographic and ordering information and many include an annotation. Each issue now includes a supplementary section, titled "References to Current Topics," that contains periodical citations to subjects of current interest. Each issue also includes a separate title index. *Vertical File Index* is issued monthly except in August. A subject index published in quarterly and semiannual numbers cumulates the subject headings used in preceding issues of the current volume. *Verical File Index* is useful in acquiring and organizing vertical file material.

Indexes of Reviews

Reference librarians are often asked to assist the user in locating reviews of books or nonprint materials, such as films and software. Although periodical indexes such as *Readers' Guide* can sometimes help with such requests, it may be more efficient and effective to use indexes specifically designed for this purpose.

The two tools most often used to locate book reviews are *Book Review Digest* and *Book Review Index*. *Book Review Digest*, with coverage since 1905, provides excerpts of and citations to reviews of current juvenile and adult fiction and nonfiction in the English language. Book reviews appearing in more than 110 selected periodicals in the humanities, social sciences, and general science from the United States, Canada, and Great Britain (e.g., *Canadian Literature*, *Political Science Quarterly*, *New Scientist*) as well as library reviewing media are included. Certain types of books (government publications, textbooks, technical books in the sciences and law) are excluded, but books on science for the general reader are included. Not all books reviewed in the indexed periodicals are included in *Book Review Digest*. To qualify for inclusion a book must have been published or distributed in the United States or Canada. A work of nonfiction must have received at least two reviews and a work of fiction must have received at least three reviews. All books reviewed in the *Reference Books Bulletin* section of *Booklist* are included, even if that is the only review received. Reviews must have appeared within 18 months after a book was published, and at least one review must be from a journal published in the United States or Canada. Excerpts from reviews accompany many of the citations to the original reviews, with more excerpts included for books of unusual importance or of a controversial nature.

The main body of *Book Review Digest* consists of listings in alphabetical order by the last name of the author (or by title when title is the main entry). Citations include bibliographic information, price, classification according to the Abridged Dewey Decimal Classification (for nonfiction titles), and subject headings from *Sears List of Subject Headings*. A descriptive note, including age or grade level for juvenile books, precedes the excerpts and review citations.

The excerpts and review citations are arranged by the name of the journals in which the reviews appeared. The name of the reviewer and the approximate number of words in the complete review are included as part of the citation to a review. A "Subject and Title Index" is included in each issue. Fiction and nonfiction for children and young adults are listed under the headings "Children's literature" and "Young adult literature," respectively. *Book Review Digest* is published monthly except February and July, with a bound annual cumulation. Coverage on WilsonWeb begins in 1983.

Because of differences in coverage and inclusion policies, *Book Review Index* often can identify one or more reviews of many books that *Book Review Digest* will not include. *Book Review Index* provides access to reviews of books and periodicals appearing in more than 500 publications and indexes reviews when they appear. It covers reviewing journals (such as *Booklist*), national publications of general interest (such as *Time*), scholarly and literary journals (such as *Journal of Sociology*), and electronic publications (such as *H-Net*). *Book Review Index* includes citations for reviews of any type of book that has been or is about to be published and is at least 50 pages long, although poetry and children's books may be shorter. All reviews in the journals indexed are cited. Citations for reviews of periodicals are included if the reviewer evaluated the publication as a whole. Reviews of audio books or electronic media are cited if they are presentations of previously published books. The definition of "review" used in compiling the index is broad; reviews are cited if they "provide a critical comment, a description of the book's contents, or a recommendation regarding the type of library collection for which a book is suited."[29] Entries in the main section of *Book Review Index* include the author's or the editor's name, the title being reviewed, an abbreviation identifying the reviewing source, the date and volume number of the source, and the page number on which the review appears. Reviews of reference works, periodicals, and books for children and young adults are coded to allow them to be distinguished easily (using *r*, *p*, *c*, and *y*). The title index, which follows the main body of the book, can be used to identify the main entry where the review citation will be found. A listing of all periodical abbreviations together with the full title appears in the front matter of each issue. In contrast to *Book Review Digest*, *Book Review Index* has neither a subject index nor digests of the book reviews indexed. *Book Review Index* appears three times per year with annual cumulations. There are also several multiyear cumulations. The entire run of *Book Review Index* can be searched online, with updates three times per year.

Entries for reviews of the *Encyclopedia of Folklore and Literature* listed in *Book Review Digest* and *Book Review Index* are shown in Figures 21.4 and 21.5, page 526. *Book Review Digest* includes excerpts of reviews from *Booklist*, *Choice*, and *Library Journal*. The 1999 cumulation of *Book Review Index* identifies five reviews (listed under the first editor's name as the entry point, rather than the title). As can be seen, the periodical titles are quite abbreviated, so the listing of periodical abbreviations may need to be consulted to decipher such titles as R&R Bk N (*Reference & Research Book News*).

In addition to looking for book reviews, library users may also be interested in locating reviews of other types of materials, such as nonprint media (film and video, audio) and computer software or CD-ROMs. *Media Review Digest* (*MRD*) is an annual index to and digest of reviews, evaluations, and descriptions of all forms of nonprint media appearing in more than 150 periodicals and reviewing services. The 1999 volume of *MRD* includes over 40,000 citations and cross-references to reviews and descriptions of films, videos, CD-ROMs, audiocassettes, and other media. Primary emphasis is placed on instructional and informational media. Sections cover film and video, audio, CD-ROM, and miscellaneous. Materials reviewed are listed alphabetically by title or other main entry. Entries include descriptive and cataloging information, audience level indications, review sources, review ratings (an indication of how positive or negative the original review was), and review digests (brief extracts from the original reviews). Indexes to the review listing include a general subject index for a broad-subject approach using about 90 subject headings, an alphabetical subject index using Library of Congress subject headings, a reviewer index to evaluators of feature films, and a geographical index to foreign feature films. The volume also includes a directory of producers and distributors.

Figure 21.4 Entry from *Book Review Digest 1999–2000.* Reprinted with permission of The H. W. Wilson Company.

ENCYCLOPEDIA OF FOLKLORE AND LITERATURE; editors, Mary Ellen Brown [and] Bruce A. Rosenberg; editorial assistants, Peter Hale [and] Kathy Sitarski. 766p il $99.50 1998 ABC-CLIO
803 1. Literature—Dictionaries 2. Folklore—Dictionaries
ISBN 1-57607-003-4 LC 98-19904

SUMMARY: This volume's "goal is to examine the relationship between folklore and literature. Many of the 350 entries treat individual authors like Chinua Achebe. . . . Margaret Atwood, Geoffrey Chaucer, Bob Dylan, and Herman Melville are among the others discussed. Coverage ranges from Aesop to modern times. In addition to authors, there are entries for scholars, theorists, and teachers. Forms such as archetype, epic, fakelore, and riddle have entries, as do specific works. . . . Latino, Native American, Scandinavian, Scottish, and Russian literatures receive attention, along with genres of tales specific to certain cultures. . . . Each entry includes a [bibliography]. . . . The introduction is preceded by an alphabetical list of entries, and a list of entries by category (authors, works, scholars/movements, concepts/themes, themes/characters)." (Booklist) Index.

REVIEW: *Booklist* v95 no8 p762 D 15 1998 (50-500w)
"Coeditors Brown and Rosenberg successfully address an enormous topic in this single volume. . . . There are a few entries for Asian authors and themes, but basically the work concentrates on European and Western themes, including classical Greek and Roman. Cross-referencing between entries is good. . . . An introductory overview of folklore's relationship to literature is worthwhile as background material. . . . A number of the same topics are covered in other reference books on folklore. However, this volume adds something new by focusing on the complex ways in which folklore forms the basis of and continues to influence literature. It will serve as a handbook for undergraduate college students and the general reader."

REVIEW: *Choice* v36 no6 p1038 F 1999. P. Mardeusz (50-500w)
"The essays vary not only in length, but in quality; excellent essays, like those for The Canterbury Tales and Hamlet, provide a solid introduction to the role folklore plays in those works, but that for 'Cinderella' is little more than an annotated bibliography and cannot compare with the intellectual insight found in the entry in Funk & Wagnalls Standard Dictionary of Folklore, Mythology, and Legend, ed. by Maria Leach (1949)."

REVIEW: *Libr J* v123 no17 p60 O 15 1998. Richard K. Burns (50-500w)
"[This] is an extraordinary model of scholarly order and presentation that includes a list of entries, a list of contributors, entries by category, references to the basic motif index, citations to the types of folktale, topical bibliographies, references to similar studies, and a thorough index. The signed articles feature selected lists of additional writing on topics that concentrate on folklore and literature as parallel forms of art. Thoroughgoing yet concise, this reference fills an important need."

Figure 21.5

Entry from *Book Review Index 1999,* by Charles B. Montney, Gale 2000.Copyright 2000 by Gale Group, Inc. Reprinted by permission of the Gale Group.

Brown, Mary Elizabeth - *The Scalabrinians in North America 1887-1934*
CHR - v84 - Ja '98 - p153+ [501+]
Brown, Mary Ellen - *Encyclopedia of Folklore and Literature*
r BL - v95 - D 15 '98 - p762+ [51-500]
r Choice - v36 - F '99 - p1038 [51-500]
r LJ - v123 - O 15 '98 - p60 [51-500]
r R&R Bk N - v14 - F '99 - p158 [51-500]
r SLJ - v45 - F '99 - p41 [51-500]

Software and CD-ROM Reviews on File is published monthly, with excerpts of software and CD-ROM reviews appearing in more than 100 print and online publications. Indexing includes program name, category of software, and software producer. Indexes cumulate each month, with the January-December index covering the entire volume. Software covered includes categories such as business, graphics, utilities, and development tools; CD-ROMs include education, games, and reference. Entries include producer, price, system requirements, publisher's description, and review extracts with an indication of review source and date.

Indexes for Different Literary Forms

Library collections in school, public, and academic libraries generally include many collected works: poetry anthologies, collections of plays or short stories, and collections of essays. Unless the contents of these volumes are analyzed during the cataloging process and the analytical entries made searchable directly in the library's catalog, the user of the catalog cannot easily determine whether the library holds an anthology that includes a particular play, short story, poem, or essay. The H. W. Wilson Company publishes three indexes that provide access to the contents of collections by author and subject: *Essay and General Literature Index*, *Play Index*, and *Short Story Index*. *Essay and General Literature Index* is an author and subject index to essays published in collections, with particular emphasis on materials in the humanities and social sciences. It is published semiannually, with an annual cumulation. Five-year cumulations are also published. Each issue includes a list of books indexed and a directory of publishers and distributors. *Essay and General Literature Index* is arranged in one alphabet and includes author entries, subject entries, and occasional title entries under significant phrases. Each entry includes the author and title of the essay together with brief information about the collection and the pages where the essay can be found. Entries under the name of a person follow the sequence: person's works, works about the person's life (listed under the subdivision "About"), and criticism of an individual work (listed under the subdivision "About individual works"). *Essay and General Literature Index* is available on CD-ROM and online from 1985.

Play Index is published at several-year intervals. The most recent volume, *Play Index, 1993–1997*, indexes 4,617 plays that were published during the period 1993–1997. The index covers both individual plays and plays in collections, written in or translated into English. Plays are tagged with *c* for children (through grade 6) or *y* for young people (grades 7 through 12), when those designations apply. The contents are in four parts. Part I is an author, title, and subject index, part II provides a cast analysis, part III has a list of collections indexed, and part IV provides a directory of publishers and distributors. In part I the most complete information is found under the author entries, which include name of the author, title of the play, a brief descriptive note, the number of acts and scenes, the size of the cast, and the number of sets and any dancing or music required. For separately published plays, bibliographic information is given; for plays in collections, the name of the collection is identified. Title entries give the name of the author, and subject entries give the name of the author and title of the play. This tool can be used to identify plays meeting certain requirements, such as subject and cast composition, as well as to identify one or more collections containing a play when the title or author are known.

Short Story Index appears annually, with five-year cumulations (the most recent covering 1994–1998). The 1994–1998 volume indexes 23,397 stories. About 83 percent of the stories appeared in 1,143 collections and the remainder appeared in 97 periodicals. Part I contains the index to short stories, with author, title, and subject entries. As in *Play Index*, the author entry provides the most complete information on where the story can be found. The stories in periodicals are indexed only by author and title. Part II is a list of collections indexed, part III is a directory of publishers and distributors, and part IV is a directory of periodicals. *Short Story Index* is also available on CD-ROM and online.

All three of these indexes to literary forms may be helpful in collection development as well as in reference, because order information is given for the indexed collections. Reference librarians often annotate the lists of collections in these indexes to indicate holdings and location information. This saves the user a step, because the library's catalog does not have to be consulted to determine this information once the collection containing an essay, play, or short story of interest has been identified.

Indexes to poetry anthologies are comparable to the indexes to collections in providing author, title, and subject indexing. In addition, indexes like *The Columbia Granger's Index to Poetry in Anthologies* also index poems by first line and last line, because that may be the information the user remembers rather than the poem's title.[30] The most recent edition of *The*

Columbia Granger's indexes anthologies published through January 31, 1997. More than 75,000 poems, drawn from 379 anthologies, are indexed in this edition. Several of the anthologies are collections of poetry translated from other languages. The list of anthologies has 40 titles (30 recommended, 10 highly recommended) suggested for first purchase. There are three indexes: title, first line, and last line; author; and subject. Titles, first lines, and last lines are arranged in one alphabetical listing. Titles are distinguished by initial capital letters on the important words and all first and last line entries are followed by the title of the poem, if there is a title. Entries in this index include the author of the poem and an abbreviated symbol for each anthology that includes the poem. This must be checked in the "List of Anthologies" to find the complete bibliographic information. Starting from the author or subject index involves two more steps, because each leads to the titles of poems that in turn must be looked up to find the symbols for the anthologies before turning to the list of anthologies. Because the most recent edition does not cover all anthologies indexed in the previous editions, the latter should be retained to allow access to poems found only in older anthologies.

Just as other types of indexes now have CD-ROM and online formats, indexes to literary forms are now available on CD-ROM and online. The *Columbia Granger's World of Poetry* includes 250,000 poem citations searchable by title, first line, last line, subject, and author as well as the full text of 13,000 poems, biographies and bibliographies on poets, commentaries on poems, and 7,500 excerpts from poems not included in full text. Another electronic poetry source, Roth Publishing's *Poem Finder* on the Web, includes entries for 750,000 indexed poems and 70,000 full-text poems in one resource. It indexes poetry from 3,500 anthologies, 5,000 single-author works, and 6,000 periodical issues. It is international in scope, covering all time periods. The user can search by any word(s) in a poem title, first line, last line, book title, author, or subject. The full-text poems can be searched by any word in the text, by author name, and by subject. Such literary databases enable the user to locate literary works using only bits of information.

SEARCH STRATEGIES

The reference interview is an important part of assisting library users in accessing indexes and abstracts. Many users may be familiar with only the *Readers' Guide* and ask for it by name. If the library has other indexes and abstracts available, it is important to determine the subject of interest and direct the user to the most appropriate indexes for the subject and type of material desired. The same phenomenon may occur in libraries with indexes on CD-ROM or linked from the online catalog: Because they are the most visible, they may be used even if other indexes in the collection would provide more appropriate sources for a particular search. Because CD-ROMs and online databases are often limited in the time period covered, library users must be aware that using only these tools for literature searching may lead to inadequate coverage of the published literature.[31]

If a library user is in search of an article that is known to have appeared in a certain periodical, but for which no other information is available, the librarian can consult either a cumulative index for the specific periodical (if one is available) or an index or abstract that covers the periodical. The entry for the periodical in *Ulrich's International Periodicals Directory* provides notations to indicate coverage by indexes and abstracts; the directory *Books and Periodicals Online* also provides this coverage information for both bibliographic and full-text databases. The directory *Fulltext Sources Online* will reveal which databases have periodicals, newspapers, newswires, newsletters, and television or radio transcripts in full text. *Dialog Journal Name Finder* is a helpful tool for identifying coverage of journal titles in online databases available on Dialog, because it lists not only which database(s) cover a particular journal, but also the number of articles indexed.[32] *Periodical Titles in OCLC FirstSearch* (http://www2.oclc.org/oclc/fs/fstitle/index.asp) gives journal title coverage for FirstSearch databases. A recently developed Web-based tool called *jake* (Jointly Administered Knowledge Environment, http://jake.med.yale.edu) provides information on journal coverage (both indexing and full text) by nearly 200 databases. Because many indexes and abstracts only cover periodical titles selectively, it may be necessary to look in more than one index to find the particular article sought. Indexes also differ in time lag for indexing the same article where there is an overlap in coverage.

For topical searches it is likewise necessary to identify the source(s) most likely to provide the best coverage of the topic. In online searching on Dialog, *DIALINDEX* can be used to determine the number of postings for a search statement in each database in a specified set.[33] Individual libraries are beginning to develop tools that can assist with database selection from among the databases available to library users.[34]

For the first-time user of an index, some instruction may be necessary. Although introductory material in the index should explain the scope and arrangement of entries and provide examples of searches, it may be more efficient for the librarian to tell the user the essential information directly, as users may not be willing to take the time to read through the instructions. This is also an opportunity to advise on search strategy, such as beginning with the most specific heading and proceeding to more general headings as needed. The purpose of cross-references should be explained. It may also be necessary to explain how to interpret the various components of a bibliographic citation as well as how to locate materials in the library's collection. If citations contain abbreviations, then the librarian should point out the section of the index where these abbreviations are interpreted.

Librarians must work to develop expertise in database coverage and search options if the available electronic resources are to be fully exploited. There is the added complexity of different interfaces when databases are licensed from different vendors. Chapters 4 and 5 provide additional discussion of search strategies for indexes and abstracts in both print and electronic form. Knowing the scope of the various indexes and abstracts is essential in selecting the most appropriate source(s) when verifying a citation or searching for information on a subject. Awareness of the conventions used by a particular database for author indexing is essential to doing a thorough search for works by an author. Familiarity with the approaches to subject indexing used in each index or abstract is necessary to select the source(s) most likely to have the terminology required in searching a particular subject. If the librarian is unfamiliar with the topic sought, it may be necessary first to check reference books such as encyclopedias and dictionaries to develop a list of related terms under which to search. As noted in Chapter 4, indexing vocabularies are not standardized, so it may be necessary to reformulate a subject search when checking multiple indexes and abstracts. Access to online and CD-ROM sources, as well as print indexes with keyword indexes, allows the use of terms appearing in titles and/or abstracts in addition to terms selected from controlled vocabularies. Database vendors are undertaking various approaches to assist users of their systems with cross-database searching,[35] so the task of successfully searching multiple databases may become easier in the future. In the meantime, reference librarians have an important role to play in assisting users with database selection and search strategy development.

Box 21.2 Search Strategy: Earth Day

A college student in an environmental policy class came to the reference desk looking frustrated. She explained that she was trying to locate sources that would be useful in writing a paper comparing the first Earth Day celebration with Earth Day 2000. She remarked that she usually had good success in searching *Readers' Guide* for periodical articles, but she was finding limited coverage of Earth Day 2000 and nothing about the first Earth Day celebration. She had also tried some Web searching using her favorite search engine but was overwhelmed with the amount of material that came back when she searched on "Earth Day." The librarian checked *Chase's 2000 Calendar of Events* and confirmed that the first Earth Day celebration took place on April 22, 1970; April 22, 2000 was the 30th anniversary. He explained that because the available databases had limited retrospective coverage, she would need to use print indexes to locate material contemporary with the first Earth Day. For Earth Day 2000 he suggested that the student might be more successful in online resources that index more sources or cover other types of literature.

Together they reviewed the organization of databases available through the library's online gateway. Under General Interest, the librarian pointed out that the student might be interested in exploring the discussion of Earth Day 2000 events in a range of literature, including alternative press, ethnic, and international sources as well as newspapers and magazines. He explained that "FT" next to a database name indicated that full text was available online; other indexes would give citations to material that could be located either in the library or requested through interlibrary loan. He suggested that *Alternative Press Index, Ethnic NewsWatch,* and EBSCO's *Academic Search Elite* and *Newspaper Source* would be good starting points for Earth Day 2000. They did a quick keyword search in each to get some idea of what could be found: *Alternative Press Index* included coverage of *Earth First! Journal; Ethnic Newswatch* included articles from African American, Jewish, and Native American publications; and the search on EBSCO databases yielded some news items from the Environmental News Network along with articles from a variety of journals. For the original Earth Day, he showed her how to use the 1970 *New York Times Index* (which provided a cross-reference from "Earth Day" to "U.S.—Environmental problems") and *Readers' Guide* (which provided a cross-reference from "Earth Day" to "Environmental movement—Earth Day"). A keyword title search on the online catalog turned up a recently published (1999) book by Mary Graham titled *The Morning after Earth Day: Practical Environmental Politics* that sounded promising as a source of background information. As an active member of the American Library Association, the librarian was aware that ALA's Social Responsibilities Round Table included a Task Force on the Environment. He entered the URL for the ALA Web site (http://www.ala.org) and quickly found the home page for SRRT/TFOE (http://www.ala.org/alaorg/rtables/srrt/tfoe), which had an entry for "Earth Day" under Key Issues. This led to a "CyberExhibit" commemorating the 30th anniversary of Earth Day, which included a number of helpful links to other Web resources. Satisfied that she had a number of promising leads to resources for her paper, the student went to one of the public terminals to spend time exploring the electronic sources in more depth before tracking down the older print materials.

NOTES

1. Deborah Lynne Wiley, "From Print to Internet . . . Can Traditional Abstracting and Indexing Services Survive?" *Database* 17 (December 1994): 18-24.

2. Dennis Auld, "The Future of Secondary Publishing," *Online & CD-ROM Review* 23 (1999): 173-78.

3. Brian Quinn, "Mainstreaming Electronic Journals Through Improved Indexing: Prospects for the Social Sciences," *Serials Review* 25, no. 2 (1999): 23-34.

4. *The H. W. Wilson Company: A Centennial Celebration 1898–1998* (Bronx, N.Y.: H. W. Wilson Company, 1998), 25p.

5. Jonathan D. Eldredge, "Accuracy of Indexing Coverage Information as Reported by Serials Sources," *Bulletin of the Medical Library Association* 81 (October 1993): 364-70.

6. International Coalition of Library Consortia, "Guidelines for Statistical Measures of Usage of Web-based Indexed, Abstracted, and Full-Text Resources," *Information Technology & Libraries* 18 (September 1999): 161-63.

7. Katie Clark, "To Cancel or Not to Cancel (Print Indexes)," *CD-ROM Professional* 5 (July 1992): 126-28; Margaret Sylvia and Marcella Lesher, "Making Hard Choices: Cancelling Print Indexes," *Online* 18 (January 1994): 59-64.

8. Richard W. Meyer, "Selecting Electronic Alternatives," *Information Technology & Libraries* 12 (June 1993): 173-80; Margaret Sylvia, "Too Many Concerns? Paper or Online, Local or Remote, Full Text or Index," in *Introducing and Managing Academic Library Automation Projects*, ed. John W. Head and Gerard B. McCabe (Westport, Conn.: Greenwood, 1996), 53-61; DeeAnn Allison, Beth McNeil, and

Signe Swanson, "Database Selection: One Size Does Not Fit All," *College & Research Libraries* 61 (January 2000): 56-63.

9. Greg R. Notess, "Offspring of OPACs: Local Databases on the Net," *Database* 16 (June 1993): 106-10; Bobb Menk, "Indexing a Local Newspaper on the Web," *Library Computing* 18 (1999): 151-59.

10. Walt Crawford, "Here's the Content—Where's the Context?" *American Libraries* 31 (March 2000): 50-52.

11. Nancy Garman, "Errors, Corrections, Retractions," *Online* 22 (September/October 1998): 6-7.

12. Steve Black, "An Assessment of Social Sciences Coverage by Four Prominent Full-Text Online Aggregated Journal Packages," *Library Collections, Acquisitions, & Technical Services* 23 (1999): 411-19; Patricia M. Brennan, Joanna Burkhardt, Susan McMullen, and Marla Wallace, "What Does Electronic Full-Text Really Mean? A Comparison of Database Vendors and What They Deliver," *Reference Services Review* 27, no. 2 (1999): 113-26; Rashelle Karp, "Comparing Three Full-Text Journal Services," *Booklist* 94 (May 15, 1998): 1646-50; Julie M. Still and Vibiana Kassabian, "Selecting Full-Text Undergraduate Periodicals Databases," *EContent* 22 (December 1999): 57-65; Karen Whisler, Marlene Slough, Nackil Sung, and Barbara Cressman, "Evaluating Selected Full-Text Databases for Collection Development," *Illinois Libraries* 80 (Fall 1998): 239-44.

13. Carol Tenopir, "Should We Cancel Print?" *Library Journal* 124 (September 1, 1999): 138.

14. Bette Brunelle, "Quieting the Crowd: The Clamour for Full Text," *Online & CD-ROM Review* 23 (1999): 297-302; Larry Krumenaker, " 'A Dillar, a Dollar . . .' Where's That Article, Scholar?" *Searcher* 7 (September 1999): 36-40; Carol Tenopir, "Linking to Full Texts," *Library Journal* 122 (April 1, 1998): 34-36.

15. Carol Tenopir and Péter Jacsó, "Quality of Abstracts," *Online* 17 (May 1993): 44-55.

16. Mary Biggs, " 'Mom in the Library': *The Readers' Guide to Periodical Literature*," in *Distinguished Classics of Reference Publishing*, ed. James Rettig (Phoenix, Ariz.: Oryx Press, 1992), 198-210.

17. Charles R. Andrews, "Cooperation at Its Best: The Committee on Wilson Indexes at Work," *RQ* 24 (Winter 1984): 155-61.

18. Janice M. Jaguszewski and Jody L. Kempf, "Four Current Awareness Databases: Coverage and Currency Compared," *Database* 18 (February/March 1995): 34-44; Scott Stebelman, "Analysis of Retrieval Performance in Four Cross-Disciplinary Databases: Article1st, Faxon Finder, UnCover, and a Locally Mounted Database," *College & Research Libraries* 55 (November 1994): 562-67.

19. Jo A. Cates, "The Record of Record: The *New York Times Index*," in *Distinguished Classics of Reference Publishing*, ed. James Rettig (Phoenix, Ariz.: Oryx Press, 1992), 174-79.

20. Larry Krumenaker and Jill Ann Hurst, "Check 'Em All: The Mathematics of Online Newspapers," *Searcher* 8 (May 2000): 38-47.

21. Greg R. Notess, "Searching for Current News," *Online* 22 (June/July 1999): 57-60; Peter Williams and David Nicholas, "The Migration of News to the Web," *Aslib Proceedings* 51 (April 1999): 122-34.

22. David A. Tyckoson, "Eugene Garfield's Contribution to Bibliography: *Science Citation Index*," in *Distinguished Classics of Reference Publishing*, ed. James Rettig (Phoenix, Ariz.: Oryx Press, 1992), 234-40.

23. Bonnie Snow, "SciSearch Changes: Abstracts and Added Indexing," *Online* 15 (September 1991): 102-6.

24. Harriet Oxley, "ISI Spins a Web of Science," *Database* 21 (April/May 1998): 37-40.

25. Helen Atkins, "The ISI Web of Science—Links and Electronic Journals," *D-Lib Magazine* 5 (September 1999). Available: http://www.dlib.org/dlib/september99/atkins/09atkins.html.

26. Ellis Mount and Beatrice Kovacs, *Using Science and Technology Information Sources* (Phoenix, Ariz.: Oryx Press, 1991), 189p.

27. Mary W. George, "Controlling the Beasties: *Dissertation Abstracts International*," in *Distinguished Classics of Reference Publishing*, ed. James Rettig (Phoenix, Ariz.: Oryx Press, 1992), 66-76.

28. Roy Tennant, "Accessing Electronic Theses: Progress?" *Library Journal* 125 (May 15, 2000): 30, 33.

29. "Introduction," *Book Review Index* 35 (1999): vii.

30. Milton H. Crouch, " 'Of Permanent Use and Usefulness': *Granger's Index to Poetry*," in *Distinguished Classics of Reference Publishing*, ed. James Rettig (Phoenix, Ariz.: Oryx Press, 1992), 113-16.

31. Jody Bales Foote, Mary M. Harrison, and Mark Watson, "Electronic Library Resources: Navigating the Maze," *Resource Sharing & Information Networks* 12, no. 2 (1997): 5-17; Thomas W. Conkling and Bonnie Anne Osif, "CD-ROM and Changing Research Patterns," *Online* 18 (May 1994): 71-74.

32. Deborah L. McMaster, "DIALOG Journal Name Finder: Online Journal Coverage Made Easier," *Online* 15 (July 1991): 24-27.

33. Terry Brainerd Chadwick, "DIALOG's Enhanced DIALINDEX," *Online* 15 (January 1991): 22-26.

34. Christy Hightower, Jennifer Reiswig, and Susan S. Berteaux, "Introducing Database Advisor," *College & Research Libraries News* 59 (June 1998): 409-12.

35. Jessica L. Milstead, "Cross-File Searching: How Vendors Help—And Don't Help—Improve Compatibility," *Searcher* 7 (May 1999): 44-55.

LIST OF SOURCES

ABI/INFORM. [CD-ROM]. Ann Arbor, Mich.: Bell & Howell Information & Learning. Also available online.

Abridged Readers' Guide to Periodical Literature, 1935– . New York: H. W. Wilson, 1936– . Monthly except June–August, with quarterly and annual cumulations. Also available online as part of *Readers' Guide to Periodical Literature.*

Access: The Supplementary Index to Periodicals. Evanston, Ill.: John Gordon Burke, 1975– . Two issues per year plus annual cumulations.

Alternative Press Index. Baltimore, Md.: Alternative Press Center, 1969– . Quarterly with annual cumulations. Also available on CD-ROM and online.

Arts & Humanities Citation Index, 1975– . Philadelphia: Institute for Scientific Information, 1978– . Semiannual. Also available on CD-ROM.

Arts & Humanities Search. Philadelphia: Institute for Scientific Information. Available online.

Book Review Digest. New York: H. W. Wilson, 1905– . Monthly except February and July, with quarterly and annual cumulations. Also available on CD-ROM and online.

Book Review Index. Farmington Hills, Mich.: Gale Group, 1965– . Three per year with annual cumulations. Multiyear cumulations, 1965–1984, 1985–1992, 1993–1997. Also available online.

Books and Periodicals Online. 2 vols. Washington, D.C.: Library Technology Alliance, 2000.

Business Periodicals Index. New York: H. W. Wilson, 1958– . Monthly except August, with quarterly and annual cumulations.

Canadian Business and Current Affairs (CBCA). [CD-ROM]. Toronto, Ont.: Micromedia. Also available online.

Canadian Index. Toronto, Ont.: Micromedia, 1993– . Monthly with semiannual cumulations.

Canadian Newspapers. Montreal, Quebec: Southam. Available online.

Canadian Periodical Index. Toronto, Ont.: Gale Canada, 1938– . Monthly with annual cumulations. Also available on CD-ROM and online.

CBCA Fulltext Reference. [CD-ROM]. Toronto, Ont.: Micromedia. Also available online.

Children's Magazine Guide. New Providence, N.J.: R. R. Bowker, 1948– . Nine issues per year and annual cumulation.

The Columbia Granger's Index to Poetry in Anthologies. 11th ed. Edited by Edith P. Hazen. New York: Columbia University Press, 1998. 2200p.

The Columbia Granger's World of Poetry. [CD-ROM]. New York: Columbia University Press, 1999.

Comprehensive Dissertation Index, 1861–1972. 37 vols. Ann Arbor, Mich.: UMI, 1973. Supplemented by ten-year cumulation 1973–1982, five-year cumulation 1983–1987, and annual supplements. Also available online as part of *Dissertation Abstracts Online*.

ContentsFirst. Dublin, Ohio: OCLC. Available online.

Current Contents. Philadelphia: Institute for Scientific Information, 1958– . Weekly. Also available on CD-ROM.

Current Contents Connect. Philadelphia: Institute for Scientific Information. Available online.

DIALINDEX. Cary, N.C.: The Dialog Corporation. Available online.

Dialog Journal Name Finder. Cary, N.C.: The Dialog Corporation. Available online.

Dissertation Abstracts International. Ann Arbor, Mich.: UMI, 1938– . Monthly with annual cumulated author and subject indexes. Also available online as part of *Dissertation Abstracts Online*.

Dissertation Abstracts Ondisc. [CD-ROM]. Ann Arbor, Mich.: UMI. Monthly. Also available online as *Dissertation Abstracts Online*.

Electronic Collections Online. Dublin, Ohio: OCLC. Available online.

Essay and General Literature Index, 1900– . New York: H. W. Wilson, 1934– . Semiannual with bound annual and five-year cumulations. Also available on CD-ROM and online.

Ethnic NewsWatch. [CD-ROM]. Stamford, Conn.: SoftLine Information. Also available online.

Falk, Byron A., Jr., and Valerie R. Falk. *Personal Name Index to the New York Times Index*, 1851– . Verdi, Nev.: Roxbury Data Interface, 1976– .

Fulltext Sources Online. Medford, N.J.: Information Today, 2000. 900p.

Gale Directory of Databases. Volume 1. *Online Databases*. Volume 2. *CD-ROM, Diskette, Magnetic Tape, Handheld, and Batch Access Database Products*. Farmington Hills, Mich.: Gale Group, 1993– . Semiannual. Also available online.

General Science Index. New York: H. W. Wilson, 1978– . Monthly except June and December, with quarterly and annual cumulations. Also available on CD-ROM and online.

Historical Newspapers Online. Alexandria, Va.: Chadwyck-Healey. Available online.

Humanities Index. New York: H. W. Wilson, 1974– . Quarterly with annual cumulations. (Formerly *International Index*, 1907–1965; *Social Sciences and Humanities Index*, 1965–1974.) Also available on CD-ROM and online.

Inside Information Plus. Boston Spa, England: British Library Document Supply Centre. Available online.

ISI Basic Science Index. Philadelphia: Institute for Scientific Information. Available online.

ISI Basic Social Sciences Index. Philadelphia: Institute for Scientific Information. Available online.

Magazines for Libraries. 10th ed. Edited by Bill Katz and Linda Sternberg Katz. New Providence, N.J.: R. R. Bowker, 2000. 1645p.

Media Review Digest, 1970– . Ann Arbor, Mich.: Pierian Press, 1971– . Annual.

National Newspaper Index. Farmington Hills, Mich.: Gale Group, 1979– . Available online.

New York Times Index. New York: Times, 1913– . Semimonthly with quarterly and annual cumulations.

Newspaper Source. Ipswich, Mass.: EBSCO Publishing. Available online.

PAIS Foreign Language Index. New York: Public Affairs Information Service, 1972–1990.

PAIS International. New York: OCLC Public Affairs Information Service. Available online.

PAIS International in Print. New York: OCLC Public Affairs Information Service, 1991– . Monthly with annual cumulation.

PAIS on CD-ROM. [CD-ROM]. New York: OCLC Public Affairs Information Service. Quarterly.

PAIS Select. [CD-ROM]. New York: OCLC Public Affairs Information Service. Semiannual.

PAIS Subject Headings. 2d ed. Edited by Alice Picon and Gwen Sloan. New York: Public Affairs Information Service, 1990. 536p.

Periodicals Contents Index. Alexandria, Va.: Chadwyck-Healey. Available online.

Periodicals Contents Index Full Text. Ann Arbor, Mich.: ProQuest. Available online.

Play Index, 1949– . New York: H. W. Wilson, 1953– . Irregular with multiyear volumes.

Poem Finder. Great Neck, N.Y.: Roth Publishing. Available online.

Poole's Plus. Reston, Va.: Paratext. Available online.

ProQuest Full-Text Newspapers. Ann Arbor, Mich.: ProQuest. Available online.

Public Affairs Information Service Bulletin. New York: Public Affairs Information Service, 1915–1990.

Readers' Guide Abstracts. [CD-ROM]. New York: H. W. Wilson. Monthly. Also available online.

Readers' Guide for Young People. New York: H. W. Wilson. Available online.

Readers' Guide Full Text: Mega Edition. [CD-ROM]. New York: H. W. Wilson. Monthly. Also available online.

Readers' Guide to Periodical Literature, 1900– . New York: H. W. Wilson, 1905– . Monthly with quarterly and annual cumulations. Also available on CD-ROM and online.

Science Citation Index, 1945– . Philadelphia: Institute for Scientific Information, 1961–. Bimonthly with annual and five- or ten-year cumulations. Also available on CD-ROM.

SciSearch. Philadelphia: Institute for Scientific Information. Available online.

Short Story Index, 1900– . New York: H. W. Wilson, 1953– . Semiannual with annual and five-year cumulations. Also available on CD-ROM and online.

Social Sciences Citation Index, 1956– . Philadelphia: Institute for Scientific Information, 1973– . Three times per year with annual and five-year cumulations. Also available on CD-ROM.

Social Sciences Index. New York: H. W. Wilson, 1974– . Quarterly with annual cumulations. (Formerly *International Index,* 1907–1965; *Social Sciences and Humanities Index,* 1965–1974.) Also available on CD-ROM and online.

Social SciSearch. Philadelphia: Institute for Scientific Information. Available online.

Software and CD-ROM Reviews on File. New York: Facts on File, 1985– . Monthly, with annual cumulation of indexes.

Ulrich's International Periodicals Directory, Including Irregular Serials and Annuals. 39th ed. 5 vols. Providence, N.J.: R. R. Bowker, 2000. Also available online.

UnCover. Denver, Colo.: The UnCover Company. Available online.

Vertical File Index, 1932/34– . New York: H. W. Wilson, 1935– . Monthly except August. Also available online.

Web of Science. Philadelphia: Institute for Scientific Information. Available online.

Wilson Business Abstracts. [CD-ROM]. New York: H. W. Wilson. Monthly. Also available online.

Wilson Business Full Text. [CD-ROM]. New York: H. W. Wilson. Monthly. Also available online.

Wilson Omnifile. [CD-ROM]. New York: H. W. Wilson. Monthly. Also available online.

ADDITIONAL READINGS

Anderson, James D. *Guidelines for Indexes and Related Information Retrieval Devices.* Bethesda, Md.: NISO Press, 1997. 53p.

This technical report provides guidelines for the content, organization, and presentation of indexes used for the retrieval of documents and parts of documents. It deals with the principles of indexing, regardless of the type of material indexed, the indexing method used, the medium of the index, or the method of presentation for searching.

Brennan, Patricia M., Joanna Burkhardt, Susan McMullen, and Marla Wallace. "What Does Electronic Full-Text Really Mean? A Comparison of Database Vendors and What They Deliver." *Reference Services Review* 27, no. 2 (1999): 113-26.

The authors provide criteria and guidelines to assist in the decision-making process for multidisciplinary electronic products.

Cleveland, Donald B., and Ana D. Cleveland. *Introduction to Indexing and Abstracting.* 3d ed. Englewood, Colo.: Libraries Unlimited, 2000.

The authors describe the types of indexes and abstracts, indexing and abstracting methods and procedures, and index evaluation. New chapters in this edition cover indexing and the Internet as well as Web resources for indexers and abstractors.

Chandler, Helen E., and Vincent de P. Roper. "Citation Indexing: Uses and Limitations." *The Indexer* 17 (October 1991): 243-49.

This article outlines the principles, uses, and limitations of citation indexing and explains the use of the citation indexes published by the Institute for Scientific Information in both print and online formats.

Courtois, Martin P., and Judith A. Matthews. "Tips for Searching the ISI Citation Indexes for Personnel Decisions." *Database* 16 (June 1993): 60-67.

Librarians may be asked to aid in the evaluation of an individual's publications by gathering data on how often and by whom they have been cited. This article reviews the pre-search interview, search, and post-search techniques that have proved useful in responding to such requests.

Grogan, Denis. *Periodicals and Their Guides.* London: Clive Bingley, 1987. 114p. (Grogan's Case Studies in Reference Work, v. 4).

The 58 cases in this volume have been chosen to demonstrate how abstracting and indexing services are used to exploit the information found in periodicals and newspapers. The cases include examples of terminological problems in subject searching, the difficulties of composite topics, the advantages and disadvantages of online and manual searching, author searching, and the use of citation indexes.

Hodge, Gail M., and Jessica L. Milstead. *Computer Support to Indexing.* Philadelphia: National Federation of Abstracting and Information Services, 1998. 118p.

Based on interviews with database producers, this report describes the current environment of database indexing; the use of indexing with metadata; plus the surrounding issues, policies, and developments with the advent of the Web.

Lancaster, F. W. *Indexing and Abstracting in Theory and Practice.* 2d ed. Champaign, Ill.: Graduate School of Library and Information Science, University of Illinois, 1998. 412p.

Intended as a text for students in library and information science, this book reviews indexing and abstracting theory together with a discussion of practice and sample exercises. Evaluation of indexes and abstracts is also emphasized. Chapters new to this edition cover multimedia and Internet sources.

Mann, Thomas. *The Oxford Guide to Library Research.* New York: Oxford University Press, 1998. 316p.

Several chapters in this guide provide helpful discussions on search strategy for effective use of indexes and abstracts in both print and electronic form. See in particular the chapters on "Subject Headings and Indexes to Journal Articles," "Keyword Searches," "Citation Searches," and "Related-Record Searches."

National Information Standards Organization. *Guidelines for Abstracts.* Bethesda, Md.: NISO Press, 1997. 14p.

Types of abstracts and their content are described, together with a list of selected readings on the subject of abstracting.

Puccio, Joseph A. *Serials Reference Work.* Englewood, Colo.: Libraries Unlimited, 1989. 228p.

This book is intended as a practical guide to the tools and techniques of serials reference work. Of particular interest are chapter 5 on periodical indexes and abstracts and chapter 12 on newspaper indexes and abstracts.

Tenopir, Carol, and Jeff Barry. "Database Marketplace 2000: Are Online Companies Dinosaurs?" *Library Journal* 125 (May 15, 2000): 44-50.

The latest in an annual survey of fee-based information companies highlights trends and provides comparative data about their offerings.

Wellisch, Hans H. *Glossary of Terminology in Abstracting, Classification, Indexing, and Thesaurus Construction.* 2d ed. Reston, Va.: American Society of Indexers, 2000. 77p.

The *Glossary* defines terms used in texts on abstracting, indexing, classification, and thesaurus construction, as well as terms for the most common types of documents and their parts. The definitions are derived from several authoritative sources.

CHAPTER

22

GOVERNMENT DOCUMENTS AND STATISTICS SOURCES

Mary Mallory and Eric Forte

USES AND CHARACTERISTICS

Government information is often perceived as a unique and separate area of reference service. Government documents have their own classification schemes, their own Internet domains, and often their own departments and librarians. Yet governments operate in nearly every discipline that is of importance or interest to their people, and government documents and information cover nearly every imaginable topic. These sources are used by the general public, by statisticians, social workers, scientists, students, teachers, politicians, parents—in short, by anyone who has a need for information. Virtually every library, regardless of its type, size, or location, uses government documents. Government documents are authoritative, comprehensive, inexpensive, and, because of the system of government documents depository libraries and the wealth of information on government Web sites, they are generally easy to obtain.

United States government documents are officially defined as "informational matter which is published as an individual document at Government expense, or as required by law."[1] Basic government information sources include laws and official records of government entities, such as the *Congressional Record*, the *United States Statutes at Large*, the *Federal Register*, the *Public Papers of the President*, and the *United States Reports*. Government information also includes information of a more administrative nature, such as the *Annual Report of the Department of Energy*,[2] and *Foreign Per Diem Rates*[3] for federal employee travel. In the course of carrying out their responsibilities, government agencies often produce statistical and economic data, such as reports from the Census of Population and Housing, the *Statistical Abstract of the United States*, and *Economy at a Glance*. Government information may be technical or scholarly in nature, as in the case of the range of research included in the United States Geological Survey's *Bulletins*[4] and *Professional Papers*,[5] or NASA-funded research in aeronautics and physics. Many documents are informational matter for general use, such as *Chances Are You Need a Mammogram: A Guide for Midlife and Older Women*[6] and *How to Apply for Social Security Retirement Benefits*.[7]

All of these documents are published by the U.S. Government Printing Office (GPO), the largest printing house in the world. Although documents originate in hundreds of government agencies and offices, almost all federal government printing is handled by GPO. It produces some of the most essential general reference sources for all libraries. It also publishes more esoteric scientific reports that are of limited general interest but vital to many academic or special libraries. Government documents exist in a variety of formats. Thousands are published in print and microfiche each year. In addition, the U.S. government has been at the forefront of electronic publishing, both on CD-ROM and online (mostly on the Web). Databases such as those included in *GPO Access* have in many aspects changed the way government documents reference service is conducted, and the ability to use emerging technologies is vital to the contemporary librarian working with government information.

This chapter focuses on the most indispensable government documents and information from the federal government, along with a number of nongovernmental or commercially published titles useful in accessing or locating government information. Selected state and intergovernmental sources (e.g., the United Nations and the Organisation for Economic Cooperation and Development) are highlighted. Sources for Canadian information are described in their own section. Because governments are arguably the most important publishers of statistics, a large section of this chapter will familiarize the reader with strategies and resources for statistical reference service. Strategies for reference service using government information and statistics are discussed throughout.

Organization of Documents

Federal government documents in physical formats use a unique classification called the Superintendent of Documents system, referred to as the SuDoc system. Unlike Dewey or Library of Congress (LC), the SuDoc system is based not on subject area, but on the issuing agency. Class numbers are based on agency, subagency, and publication type. For example, the SuDoc number for the *County and City Data Book*, C3.134/2:C83/2/998 is constructed as follows:[8]

C	Department of Commerce
3.	Bureau of the Census
134/	*Statistical Abstract of the United States*
2:	Supplement
C83/2/	*County and City Data Book*
998	1998 edition

SuDoc numbers are devised and assigned by GPO. Although some libraries classify and integrate their documents into their regular collections using LC or Dewey, the SuDoc system is universal and used in many standard bibliographies, such as *Monthly Catalog of United States Government Publications*, *CIS/Index*, and *PAIS International*. A library user can identify a government document and its SuDoc number via one of these bibliographies or indexes, then find that document in libraries across the country without needing to check local catalogs. The system also allows the user to browse an agency or subagency's publications and allows the librarian to eliminate one step in the cataloging process, getting the item to the shelf that much faster. The classification system chosen will, to some extent, determine how the collection is used and the extent to which reference service is provided by documents specialists or by general reference staff. For example, libraries with a separate documents collection, arranged by SuDoc, may be more likely to have a separate service point for the documents collection.

Most states and some intergovernmental entities and foreign governments use their own classification system. A library's decision to use these classification systems or to add these items to regular Dewey or LC collections may be based on numerous factors, including how many of these items a library collects and their level of use.

Although the SuDoc system is used for print, microfiche, and CD-ROM formats, the rules and policies for classifying online government information continue to evolve. URLs for government Web sites contain no unique style beyond generally using the .gov domain.[9] The GPO is aggressive in its cataloging of government information appearing on government Web sites, and these sites may often be identified by using the standard bibliographies and catalogs, discussed later in the chapter.

Uses of Documents

Librarians rely on the broad array of federal documents, including directories, yearbooks, handbooks, bibliographies, indexes and abstracts, geographical sources, and others, to answer factual questions about the government, its personnel, and its activities. Government documents also contain a wealth of historical and current information about the country and its citizens. Many of these documents are among the most important primary sources in various fields.

In many cases, users consult documents to conduct statistical or legislative research. Another major category of reference use of documents is *bibliographic verification*, or obtaining bibliographic information about a particular document. The question may take the form of: "What is the *Serial Set* volume number of House Document 91-102?" or "What series includes the title *House Bat Management*?" The sources used to answer such questions are unique to documents, and their mastery goes a long way to providing excellent documents reference service.

Documents are often indexed only in highly specialized tools, such as *CIS/Index* or the *Department of Energy Reports Bibliographic Database*.[10] Because these bibliographic tools are often specific to government information, users may be unfamiliar with the content, organization, and best approaches to using any given title. Documents librarians frequently find themselves in the position of teaching library users about unique reference sources and helping them to acquire government information access skills. It is important to be able to interpret all of the essential parts of the citations presented in such indexes, including information regarding series and subseries titles. Time may also be spent teaching some basics about the organization and operation of government (a mini civics class), which is often necessary to most clearly explain government information. This educational facet may require more time on the part of the librarian, but it is a necessary and rewarding aspect of documents librarianship. Instructional guides on numerous topics, prepared by documents librarians throughout the United States and Canada, have been compiled and made available via the *GODORT Handout Exchange*, an ongoing project of the American Library Association (ALA), Government Documents Round Table (GODORT), Education Committee. These can be good places to begin to learn about specific components of documents reference work or about specific resources.

EVALUATION

A government document may be the only source of authoritative information on a subject. Therefore, it can be difficult to find similar sources with which to compare its currency and accuracy. The *2000 Census of Population and Housing*, the 22nd decennial census, is a representative example. No other census or statistical survey contains the breadth and scope of this massive undertaking done to count the U.S. population. However, because the federal government is the largest collector of statistical data in the world, many trade publishers obtain their data from government sources, repackage the information, perhaps abridge or enhance the data, offer the data in an electronic medium, or add special features such as expanded indexing, data manipulation, or a better interface. Of course, the library will have to pay for these features. Evaluation of reference tools from the government or using government data, therefore, depends mainly on comparing features, format, indexing, ease of use, and price, as well as the inclusion of complete and accurate citations to the original sources.

Government-funded research and its report literature and administrative records of government agencies also present unique and original information. Geologists working for the United States Geological Survey (USGS), for example, have conducted much of the original research in American geology; therefore, the documents of the USGS are just as important to many geologists as the standard scholarly journals in geology.[11] These considerations must be accounted for in the evaluation process.

Additionally, materials may be published in print, microfiche, and electronic formats, and are listed in distinct bibliographies, catalogs, or databases. The materials budget, space constraints, and user demand, as well as the quality of the pertinent bibliographic tools, can influence choice of format.

Commercially-published reference sources that provide background, present additional factual information, and offer analyses on politics, socioeconomic matters, and public officials help to supplement the vast array of government-produced information tools. Examples include: *Congressional Quarterly's Politics in America*, which presents more detailed information about congressional districts than can be found in the *Official Congressional Directory*; and *Congressional Quarterly Weekly Report*, a weekly magazine that surveys current public policy, significant legislation, and other activities of Congress, and serves as a convenient source for obtaining specific information, such as bill or public law numbers, and roll-call votes. In some cases, an overview is what a user really wants, rather than the text of a bill itself or the in-depth details about proposed legislation that can appear in various congressional publications. Just as with any reference source, the documents librarian must always take into account the needs of the library's users when making choices regarding government and government-related materials.

Another situation in which evaluative considerations can become almost moot is when government information is produced in microfiche or electronic format only, assuming adequate equipment is available. The *Toxic Release Inventory (TRI)* CD-ROM is an example, although selected data on the disc are also distributed in print format. But if the user needs certain data on toxic emissions, the *TRI* on CD-ROM is simply the only choice.[12] Format can also be especially important for statistical data. Statistical products may be needed in electronic formats when users require flexibility and complexity in searching and analyzing data. For example, a library may select a print volume of *United States Census of Population and Housing* reports if its users require primarily ready-reference information. The library whose users are more inclined to be conducting in-depth research, however, may prefer an electronic version—perhaps repackaged by a commercial publisher—which offers added value in data extraction, manipulation, and downloading. The quality and effectiveness of database interfaces, plus the availability of adequate documentation, will also have an impact on format selection.

Often a government resource may be available in multiple formats. One example is congressional bills. Current bills are sent to most depositories in microfiche format (a few receive paper facsimiles), with an accompanying print index of bill numbers. There is no index by such elements as subject or congressperson. However, the congressional bills database on *GPO Access* allows much greater flexibility in searching and identifying current bills, whereas the privately produced *Congressional Universe* offers still greater search and retrieval by a variety of criteria. The ultimate choice of edition and format will depend to a large extent on local factors, chief among them user needs. Increasingly important are these considerations of media, especially that of tangible formats versus access via the Web.

SELECTION

The enormous variety of government publications requires librarians to employ several different strategies for identifying and selecting documents that will meet the needs of their users. Similarly, there is more than one method of acquiring government documents once they have been selected. This section describes the selection and acquisition processes commonly employed by librarians in obtaining government publications.

In the approximately fourteen hundred federal depository libraries, acquisition of depository materials is, in general, routine. Through the federal deposit system, the GPO makes thousands of federal publications available to libraries at no charge. There are at least two depositories in each congressional district. These may be public, university, college, or special libraries. A regional depository, of which there are approximately fifty, receives all materials available on deposit (in other words, everything GPO prints and is able to potentially distribute to libraries and the public) and acts as a resource library for other depositories in its geographic area, as well as for other nearby libraries that are not federal depositories. The rest are *selective depositories*, meaning that they receive materials in certain categories (for example, a category may contain only a certain title, several titles together, or all publications from a particular government office). Categories are delineated in the *List of Classes of United States Government Publications Available for Selection by Depository Libraries*, and chosen by a librarian or staff member for a library and its users through the *item selection* process. Although all selective depositories receive certain core government documents, the rest of the collection is based on these item selections, which are chosen to best meet the needs of the library's particular clientele and local community. All documents officially remain the property of the U.S. government, and the library must allow all citizens to access the documents collection.[13] Based on the categories of items a library has pre-selected, shipments of current documents are sent on a regular schedule.

In a depository library, alternative methods of acquisition are a consideration only for multiple copies or replacements, for titles that were not selected, and for nondepository publications (those not made available for distribution to depository libraries). In these cases, federal depositories follow the same procedures that nondepository libraries do to acquire materials. More often than not, this means purchasing items from the GPO.

To identify materials, a librarian may make use of standard collection development tools. The *Journal of Government Information,*[14] *Government Information Quarterly,* and *Library Journal*[15] all selectively review new documents. Frank Hoffmann and Richard Wood's *Guide to Popular U.S. Government Publications* and Gayle Hardy and Judith Schiek Robinson's *Subject Guide to U.S. Government Reference Sources* are authoritative, annotated guides to reference publications. One can also use one of several bibliographies from the GPO, which list government documents by subject but do not provide critical reviews. These include the *Sales Product Catalog* (formerly the *PRF*, or *GPO Sales Publications Reference File)* and the *Subject Bibliography* series, as well as newsletters or new book lists from various agencies (e.g., *Library of Congress Information Bulletin,*[16] *Census and You*[17]). The reference librarian can also build a collection based on the suggestions in the GPO's *Federal Depository Library Manual.*

In an informal sense, sometimes the best and only means by which to select new documents is to be attuned to the needs and tastes of library users and to be aware of current events. By carefully reading a daily newspaper and listening attentively to the media when one hears the phrase "in a government study released yesterday," librarians can learn about new sources and anticipate users' informational requests. These requests may be for specific facts or for the full text of the material mentioned in what are sometimes oblique references. In many cases, a letter or telephone call to the appropriate agency will procure the information required and/or a copy of that recently released study. Although the basic government information sources are easily identified and will be discussed later in this chapter, the less common sources that users of a particular library want will have to be identified through the librarian's alertness and sensitivity to their needs.[18]

To determine whether a federal government document is in stock and its price, use the *Sales Product Catalog.* All items sold by the GPO can be identified here, with price and ordering information. Although most standard government reference sources are available for sale through the GPO, numerous titles that are less in demand, are printed in smaller quantities, or may have special use in specific reference situations may be obtainable directly from the issuing agency at no charge. A phone call, e-mail, or postcard with the appropriate request will often secure a copy of these publications.

More detail about sources used to identify government publications is included in the "Catalogs and Bibliographies" section of this chapter.

IMPORTANT GENERAL SOURCES

Government-produced reference sources fall into many categories. Guides, or descriptive surveys of government information and its use, are essential tools for the continuing education of the government information librarian. Catalogs, indexes, bibliographies, and directories all provide comprehensive coverage to some aspect of government information. Other tools are unique to the world of government information, such as publications that provide broad coverage of the legislative and regulatory activities of the government. Statistical reference tools are also treated in this section because various U.S. government agencies, as well as those of other governments, compile and publish many significant sources of numerical data.

Guides

Guides to government information are useful both to newcomers to government information and to librarians who need to know when to use a particular type of source and how to use it. For example, when library users need to know details about an eighteenth-century report, a legislative document from the 100th Congress, or thirty years of data on the Gross Domestic Product, and librarians are uncertain about which source to consult for help in answering those questions, they can turn first to a guide to documents. This is analogous to consulting the *Guide to Reference Books*,[19] reading the annotations, and then choosing the source most likely to contain the answer to the question. The guides may provide information about government in general, publication practices of government agencies, or coverage of important sources. Even veteran government documents librarians make frequent use of one or more of these guides, which often serve as library and information science textbooks as well.

An informative and entertaining introduction and guide to government information is Judith Schiek Robinson's *Tapping the Government Grapevine: The User-Friendly Guide to U.S. Government Information Sources*, now in its third edition. As its subtitle implies, this highly readable volume is an excellent field manual for newcomers to the territory of government information. Seasoned users will also appreciate its well-organized format, clear prose, and humorous style. Basic information on federal government agencies, including their functions and publications, serves as a helpful introduction to documents librarianship and documents usage. A first-rate, selective bibliography is incorporated, covering documents reference materials. The graphics, flowcharts, and examples make this book as appealing as it is practical for learning how to access and provide government information.

Joe Morehead's *Introduction to United States Government Information Sources*, now in its sixth edition, is a well-known, comprehensive textbook. The sixth edition begins with a discussion of the issues surrounding the transition to electronic government information. It then presents the bibliographic structure of federal government publications and covers both current and historical reference sources. The GPO and the Federal Depository Library Program—knowledge of which is fundamental to understanding documents sources and how they are acquired and organized—are treated in separate chapters. Further chapters cover popular topics such as "Statistical Sources" and "Legislative Branch Information Sources," as well as some of the more specialized and difficult aspects of government information, such as "Intellectual Property" and "Geographic Information Sources." Valuable discussions on the technical report and periodical literature, and details on how to use the most important reference tools for identifying these, are included.

Another notable textbook treatment of government information is Edward Herman's *Locating United States Government Information: A Guide to Sources*. Managing to be both introductory and comprehensive, the second edition of this work features a separate, updated *Internet Supplement*, which keeps the main volume current regarding government Internet resources. These texts can lead a librarian to the answers for requests for government information, ranging from ready reference questions such as "Where can I locate a photograph of

Representative Lois Capps?" to in-depth needs such as "I would like to compile a legislative history of the Presidential Libraries Act, P. L. 99-323. Where do I start?"

Jean L. Sears and Marilyn K. Moody's *Using Government Information Sources* (3d ed.) offers actual search strategies for locating over fifty different categories of government-produced information. Unique in its encyclopedic coverage, this thorough volume can be used as a map for finding a known resource, information on government agencies, statistical sources, or titles on a subject, such as genealogy and data sources. Each chapter covers one subject and provides comprehensive coverage of the essential resources in that subject area. All the essential electronic sources and sites are included, and the index includes titles and topics. The format and breadth of this work ensure its continuing value for the documents or reference librarian.

Most of this chapter is concerned with government information that is designed for public use and relatively easy to access. Some government information, however, is considered by the government to be of a more private nature. Nonetheless, much of this information may be requested via the Freedom of Information Act. There are several resources to aid in this effort: *Your Right to Federal Records: Questions and Answers on the Freedom of Information Act and the Privacy Act* and *A Citizen's Guide on Using the Freedom of Information Act and the Privacy Act of 1974 to Request Government Records*, both from the U.S. Congress; and the FBI's *Freedom of Information Act Electronic Reading Room* Web site. Each of these sources outlines the procedures individuals can use to obtain access to federal records and/or agency files about themselves.

Government publications of other countries are covered in the valuable *Guide to Official Publications of Foreign Countries*, compiled by ALA/GODORT's (the Government Documents Round Table of the American Library Association) International Documents Task Force.[20] An excellent handbook to United Nations (UN) information, the European Union, and other international organizations is *International Information: Documents, Publications, and Electronic Information of International Governmental Organizations*, edited by Peter I. Hajnal.

Another commercially published tool, *State Reference Publications: A Bibliographic Guide to State Blue Books, Legislative Manuals and Other General Reference Sources*, edited by Lynn Hellebust, is useful for locating sources of information for each of the fifty states. Arrangement is by state and type of reference source.

A number of guides to government information that is accessible via the Internet have been published. Among the best is Bruce Maxwell's *How to Access the Federal Government on the Internet*, now in its fourth edition, which covers all the basic sites. New editions keep this work current, and its subject arrangement makes it useful to the librarian and layperson alike. James Evans's *Government on the Net* is unique in its coverage of both the basic federal government sources and related sites, such as those devoted to politics and public policy. It also includes a detailed listing of state, international, and foreign government sites.

It may be equally instructive to go to one of the many excellent Web sites that serve as guides to government information; most are maintained by working documents librarians. The best of these is Grace York's *University of Michigan Documents Center*. This site provides a comprehensive, annotated guide to government and related information on the Internet. It covers federal, state, international, and foreign resources, with special guides to important topics such as statistics and political science.

Although they are not instructional guides to government information, two more sites should be mentioned when discussing government information Web gateways: *Frequently Used Sites Related to U.S. Government Information*, a project of the GODORT's Federal Documents Task Force, covers all the major sites by topic, as does the *Government Information Web Page Template*, an effort of the Government Information Technology Committee of GODORT. The latter page pointedly does not try to be comprehensive, but rather identifies the most important sites for government information. Finally, many of the federal depository libraries maintain wonderful Web sites that can serve as guides to government information, often tailored to meet the needs of their particular community.[21]

Catalogs and Bibliographies

In providing government information reference service, catalogs and bibliographies serve several purposes: (1) to identify what publications a government agency or department has produced, (2) to find out what the government has published on certain subject matter, and (3) to determine format. Some catalogs and bibliographies may include Web addresses and SuDoc numbers. They may also indicate the depository status of an individual title or series, and these can be consulted to determine the likelihood of locating the item in a particular depository collection. Selective depositories choose categories of materials, series, and titles from the *List of Classes of United States Government Publications Available for Selection by Depository Libraries*, as previously mentioned. The *List of Classes'* print format edition is published and distributed semiannually, and updates appear in the *Administrative Notes Technical Supplement*.[22] Although not in the strict sense a catalog or bibliography, the *List of Classes* can be an invaluable tool in numerous reference situations. Format, frequency, and class number of materials, as well as the depository status, can be verified by checking this source. Publication class titles are arranged by SuDoc number stem; depository item selection numbers are provided. Lists of government authors and discontinued or revised classes are included as appendices.

Nondepository federal publications are also acquired by libraries. If an item is unavailable in a local depository collection, another more comprehensive collection of government documents may have it and/or the authoring agency may be able to provide a copy. Catalogs and bibliographies of government publications also function as selection aids and are useful in building a reference or specialized collection. Librarians can browse this type of tool for new titles or revised editions and to obtain bibliographic, URL, or ordering information.

The basic bibliographic tool for federal documents is the *Catalog of United States Government Publications* (for a sample entry, see Figure 22.1). Although it does not include all unclassified documents, the *Catalog* represents the most complete bibliography available.[23] The *Catalog*, one of the *GPO Access* "Finding Aids," is set up as a "search and retrieval service" and contains bibliographic records created since January 1994. It is updated on a daily basis. In addition to keyword, title, and SuDoc class number searches, the system supports depository item and GPO stock number searches. Searches can be limited by year of publication, and a multiple field search is also available. Either a brief or a full record can be displayed from the search results, and a direct link to a Web edition is incorporated into each record where appropriate. A "Locate Libraries" option is included. The traditional print version of the *Catalog* is titled *Monthly Catalog of United States Government Publications*, often referred to as *MOCAT*. Its emphasis recently has been on depository titles; in the past, coverage extended to selected nondepository publications. Published since 1895, *MOCAT* underwent significant format changes in July 1976 when GPO catalogers began to create machine-readable cataloging records (MARC format) based on the Anglo-American Cataloguing rules and other national standards, and these records became available electronically through OCLC. From 1976 through 1995, organization of entries was by SuDoc number; hence, agency publications were listed together. Indexes by author, title, title keyword, subject, series/report number, contract number, and sales stock number appeared in each monthly issue and were cumulated semiannually and annually. A classification number index appeared in the cumulations as well. In 1996, the GPO introduced a CD-ROM edition of MOCAT, as well as the *GPO Access* service. Still arranged in SuDoc number order, the print edition now consists of briefer entries and has a keyword title index only.[24]

The various search functions and types of indexes have specific uses. Keyword subject access or the subject index, which employs headings derived from the latest *Library of Congress Subject Headings*, is used by inquirers who want to know if the government has published anything on a particular topic, such as semiconductors, grizzly bears, or U.S. relations with Cuba. Title and author searches or indexes are generally used to verify a bibliographic citation or to identify a title when only part of the relevant information is known. Series/report number indexes help to draw together reports on a similar topic by a single agency; series

Figure 22.1 Entry from *Catalog of United States Government Publications.*

Falling through the net : defining the digital divide. [computer file] :. [3rd report] [1999] United States. C 60.2:N 38/3/999. [[0126-E-04 (online)]].
http://purl.access.gpo.gov/GPO/LPS3064

<001> ocm41869935
<005> 19991018081320.0
<040a> CUS
<040c> CUS
<040d> GPO
<035a> (GPO)apn99-027126
<043a> n-us---
<074a> 0126-E-04 (online)
<086a> C 60.2:N 38/3/999
<099a> C 60.2:N 38/3/999
<049a> GPOO
<245a> Falling through the net
<245h> [computer file] :
<245b> defining the digital divide.
<246a> Defining the digital divide
<250a> [3rd report]
<256a> Computer data
<260a> Washington, D.C. :
<260b> U.S. Dept. of Commerce, National Telecommunications and Information Administration,
<260c> [1999]
<538a> Mode of access: Internet via the NTIA web site. Address as of 10-15-99: http://www.ntia.doc.gov/ntiahome/fttn99/contents.html ; current access is available via PURL.
<500a> Title from title screen.
<590a> [cat:lww]
<650a> Telephone
<650z> United States.
<650a> Computer networks
<650z> United States.
<650a> Telecommunication policy
<650z> United States.
<650a> Online information services
<650z> United States.
<650a> Internet service providers
<650z> United States.
<710a> United States.
<710b> National Telecommunications and Information Administration.
<856u> http://purl.access.gpo.gov/GPO/LPS3064
<994a> 01
<994b> GPO
<990a> 00-00005

report numbers and other numerical identifiers can be searched as keywords. On occasion, when only a report number is cited in a journal article or monograph, this feature or these indexes may be critical in obtaining additional bibliographical details and ultimately locating a copy of a publication. An annual *Periodicals Supplement* and a *Serial Set Catalog*, the latter listing House and Senate committee reports and documents, have also been produced. Traditionally, the *Periodicals Supplement* has included only those titles that are issued three or more times a year, but as of 2001, all serials, regardless of frequency, will be included. The publication will also revert to its previous title of *Serials Supplement*.

In a library in which documents are not typically cataloged and entered into an online catalog, the *Catalog* may function as the primary access tool to the library's U.S. documents collection. Due to its comprehensive and varied search capabilities, the electronic equivalent of the *Catalog*—either the *GPO Access* service, the GPO's CD-ROM product, or a vendor database—is particularly useful in libraries in which documents have not been integrated into an online catalog. GPO cataloging records can also be accessed via OCLC to obtain complete bibliographic information, SuDoc numbers, and other details.

The series *Subject Bibliography: SB* comprises 150 irregularly revised lists of sales titles that range in subject matter from accounting and auditing to zip codes. The lists are composed of reference books, monographs, pamphlets, and periodicals, in varied formats. Entries in each bibliography are arranged alphabetically by title, and include date, pagination, SuDoc number, order information, price, and in some cases an annotation. In a reference setting, each bibliography provides a concise list of titles on a topic, including many current and some older sources. Information pertaining to important social, scientific, and legal issues; historical subjects and geographical areas; and agency publications can be accessed through this series. Examples of recently revised bibliographies include those on *Agriculture*, Subject Bibliography (SB) 162; the *Pacific Rim*, Subject Bibliography (SB) 318; and *Teaching*, Subject Bibliography (SB) 137. The complete set is available through *GPO Access*; an up-to-date "Subject Bibliographies Index" is part of the site (http://bookstore.gpo.gov/sb/sale180.html). These bibliographies are also published in paper format, and the most recent edition of the index is titled, "A Guide to U.S. Government Information: The Subject Bibliography Index." One caveat: Because the bibliographies cover only in-print sales publications, the *Catalog* or another subject-oriented guide should be consulted for additional titles.

The *U.S. Government Online Bookstore* is also available via *GPO Access* and includes links to several important sources. The *Sales Product Catalog (SPC)*, updated daily, is a database of government information products for sale by the Superintendent of Documents. It includes forthcoming titles as well as recently superseded or out of print items. *New Product Announcements* is also featured at this site (it replaces the now ceased print publication, *New Products from the U.S. Government*). These acquisition catalogs, which contain ordering information and forms, serve as current awareness tools. The Web-based *U.S. Government Subscriptions Catalog* (referred to as *U.S. Government Subscriptions* in its print version) contains a list of government periodicals and subscription services available for sale by the Superintendent of Documents, GPO. This quarterly publication includes annotations and is a convenient source for serial ordering information for standard titles.

Many agencies, bureaus, commissions, and offices include short or extensive, cumulative or evolving, lists of publications at their Web sites. Frequently, the full text of the publication is automatically retrievable. Three illustrative examples are (1) the National Council on Disability's *NCD Newsroom* (http://www.ncd.gov/newsroom/newsroom.html), with links to a publications list of a few dozen of the Council's major reports from 1986 to the present and a direct link to the full text of each report; (2) the Centers for Disease Control and Prevention's *Publications, Software and other Products* (http://www.cdc.gov/publications.htm), which contains a broad array of the organization's information resources, with links to the full text of publications, microdata, and free software to access and manipulate the microdata; and (3) the Federal Bureau of Investigation's *Freedom of Information Act Electronic Reading Room* (http://foia.fbi.gov/), where one can access FBI files on Bertolt Brecht, John Lennon, and Thurgood Marshall, among other prominent individuals, and also on incidents, groups, and institutions, such as the Highlander Folk School. The site includes "frequently requested" documents released under the Freedom of Information Act (FOIA). There are other large collections of archival materials on government Web sites that previously were only accessible at the National Archives and Records Administration in Washington, D.C., or in regional archives. The distinction between published government documents and information and archival records may disappear over time. It is crucial for anyone fielding government information requests to keep current on the rapidly evolving publishing and distribution cycles of government information and not to assume that certain kinds of information or records are not accessible on the Web. It is just as important to remember that just because something is not on the Web, that does not mean it is not available to the public. GPO Pathway Services' *Federal Agency Internet Sites* provides quick access to federal agency Web sites, and many have obvious links to bibliographies, catalogs, or publication lists. GPO and the Library of Congress (LC) provide excellent starting places for beginners; those seeking major government series, such as the *Congressional Record* or *Economic Indicators;* and anyone seeking an authoritative subject bibliography. Permanent entryways, such as the *GPO Access Database List* (http://www.access.gpo.gov/su_docs/db2.html), *Research Guides and Finding Aids* (http://lcweb.loc.gov/rr/bibguide.html), and *Internet Resource Pages Maintained by Library of Congress Reading Rooms* (http://lcweb.loc.gov/rr/eleclcrr.html), are particularly reliable.

The federal government produces specialized indexes to provide access to scientific and technical reports prepared as a result of government-funded or contract research. The National Technical Information Service (NTIS) maintains the *NTIS Electronic Catalog*, which provides free access to citations for its reports and products produced from 1990 to the present. Search capabilities are limited to titles and topics, and most records do not include abstracts. Online access to the full NTIS bibliographic database, 1964–current, is available through NTIS's *GOV.Research_Center* and through a number of other vendors, such as Cambridge Scientific Abstracts, by subscription.[25] The traditional, most comprehensive source was NTIS's *Government Reports Announcements and Index (GRAI)*, which ceased publication in 1994. These sources are crucial in verifying the accuracy of a citation and in obtaining NTIS accession and report numbers. A typical question arises when a library user has what appears to be a citation to a research report from a government agency and wants to know how to obtain a copy. If there is no indication that the title is available from the GPO, or if a search of the *Catalog of United States Government Publications* or the *SPC* is unsuccessful, the next step is to search the *NTIS Electronic Catalog*, or its predecessor *GRAI*. Through keyword, personal author, corporate author, and/or report/accession number searches, the user can find a complete bibliographic citation with all relevant report numbers, a detailed abstract, subject descriptors, and the price for a microfiche or paper copy, or a URL for the Web edition. Although the free *NTIS Electronic Catalog* does not include abstracts, these are available in the fee-based subscription services and in *GRAI*. Reports are available for purchase from NTIS. In cases where the publication year is unknown, the electronic services offer much speedier verification. Only a selected number of NTIS publications are distributed via the depository program. In December 1997, NTIS and the GPO established an interagency agreement that led to a pilot project to develop full-text online access to new "scientific, technical, and engineering information (STEI) products."[26] At present twenty-two libraries are participating in this project, making electronic editions of recent reports available to their constituencies. The fate of NTIS—it may close its doors, its operations could be transferred to another government agency, or it might be privatized—has been under discussion since August 1999, when Secretary of Commerce William M. Daley proposed closing the organization.[27]

When assisting users who need this type of technical report literature, whether it is in electronic, print, or microfiche format, it is important to remember that in most cases these titles are uncataloged and arranged by NTIS accession number in libraries. To locate a specific title, the *NTIS Electronic Catalog*, *GRAI*, or a comparable source must be checked. Thematic indexes such as the *NASA Center for AeroSpace Information Technical Report Server* are produced by agencies and also commercial firms. Their organization and usage are similar to the NTIS tool, but their subject coverage is narrower, and periodical citations may be included along with the references to research and development reports.

Declassified government information represents another substantial, normally uncataloged body of literature that has its own unique catalogs or access tools. Many declassified documents may be identified and accessed through the *Declassified Documents Reference System*, a privately produced database of full-text declassified documents, which generally cannot be identified using traditional government documents catalogs and indexes such as the *Catalog*. The *Digital National Security Archive* is a similar product.

Important bibliographies and catalogs of U.S. government information are produced by several commercial publishers. *Guide to Popular U.S. Government Publications*, compiled by Frank W. Hoffmann and Richard J. Wood, is one example. The fifth edition, published in 1998, covers recent important documents, a few "classics" from previous years, and some periodicals. This annotated listing encompasses a wide range of topics of particular interest to students, teachers, and the public. Books, journals, maps, posters, pamphlets, and media kits are listed by subject, and entries include complete bibliographic data, GPO item, shipping list, SuDoc numbers, and GPO ordering information. Sample subject divisions include aging and senior citizen issues, arts and humanities, business and international trade, consumer information and protection, grants, maps and atlases, public buildings, landmarks and historical sites, and travel. Within selected subject areas, more narrowly defined categories occur. For example, military affairs is divided into general, military history, Civil War, Gulf War, Korea, Revolutionary War, etc. An author/title/subject index is included. This single bibliography, which covers tangible formats, can be exploited by librarians and users alike to unearth a wealth of government information, especially for the uninitiated, and even on occasion, the experienced. A related title is *U.S. Government Directories, 1982–1995*, by Joyce A. McCray Pearson and Pamela M. Tull. This volume is arranged by subject and has descriptions of directories published by departments and agencies from 1982 through 1995. It is also indexed. These print resources have been standard in depositories and other libraries, and they are particularly useful in information settings that lack a federal depository collection.

CD-ROMs have become a standard publishing medium for the GPO and other federal agencies, as well as state governments. Fewer floppy disks are now being distributed, but DVDs are now being issued, and there is also talk of e-books. The unique issues related to these electronic products, such as hardware and software requirements, make specialized catalogs tailored to the needs of these formats very useful. GPO and government documents specialists, such as ALA/GODORT's Government Information Technology Committee (GITCO) members and the many librarians who contribute to the *GODORT Handout Exchange*, have undertaken projects to make these tangible e-resources more accessible to the entire depository library community and users of government information. GITCO's *How to Find Information about Government CD-ROM Products* (http://www.library.ucsb.edu/ala/gitco/cdromdoc/guide.html) is an especially handy, concise Web page that describes sources of information about CDs and floppy disks, and includes links to these. GITCO's own *CD-ROM Documentation Project* is in progress.[28] Several other catalogs of CD-ROMs exist, including the Committee on Institutional Cooperation (CIC) *CD-ROM Technical Documentation Project* (http://www.lib.umich.edu/libhome/Documents.center/cicdoc/cicdoc.htm), the GPO's list of in-stock titles (http://bookstore.gpo.gov/cdrom/index.html), and the *SIGCAT Disc Compendium* (http://www.sigcat.org/discs.htm). The latter, compiled by the Special Interest Group on CD/DVD Applications & Technology (SIGCAT),[29] is a 1996 compilation of over five hundred CD-ROM titles and includes discs published by federal agencies and those that contain a substantial amount of information from either federal or other government organizations. As a result, a selected number of private industry products appear in the compilation. The 1994 print format edition of this is titled *SIGCAT CD-ROM Compendium*, and both the GPO's Office of Electronic Information Dissemination Services and the U.S. Geological Survey Library, along with SIGCAT, contributed to this version. Abstracted entries are arranged alphabetically by CD-ROM title and include important details about the availability of documentation, software, technical requirements, local area network (LAN) information, vendor and source, frequency, price, and other facts. The depository status of titles is not noted. Separate source name and vendor name indexes are provided. The *SIGCAT CD-ROM Compendium* can be used for verification purposes, to gain a brief overview of the contents of a particular CD-ROM title, to determine equipment needs, and to obtain ordering information.

State government bibliographies have a venerable heritage as a separate publishing endeavor, beginning with R.R. Bowker's four-volume set, covering the years 1899 through 1908, titled *State Publications; a Provisional List of Official Publications of the Several States of the United States from Their Organization.* Adelaide Hasse's *Index of Economic Material in the Documents of the States of the United States*, 1908–1919, continued the tradition, and overlapping her efforts, from 1910–1994, the most comprehensive bibliography of state government information sources was the Library of Congress' *Monthly Checklist of State Publications*. The latter was compiled by Collection Services of the Library of Congress' Exchange and Gift Division. Typically, bibliographic information and price were given for monographs, annuals, and monographic series, arranged by state and issuing agency. The June and December issues contained periodicals; publications of associations of state officials and of regional organizations, library surveys, and other types of reports appeared in separate lists in the monthly issues. Beginning in January 1987, a subject index was included; an annual, cumulated version appeared the following year. This massive undertaking ceased in the mid-1990s, as state governments began to participate on a larger scale in Web publishing. *StateList: The Electronic Source for State Publication Lists*, however, aims to bring some organization to these efforts by providing links to state publication checklists and shipping lists from thirty states that are currently available on the Web.[30]

The amount and variety of state government information in electronic format has increased rapidly. Electronic access to legislative information, business and economic data, and agency reports is representative of the type of information that is currently available to the public. Utilizing these electronic sources to answer questions about state and local government issues has become the norm. Keeping informed about new developments in this area is obligatory for government information specialists. Announcements about such services are likely to appear on GOVDOC-L (a moderated electronic discussion list about government information), in Debora Cheney's column, "Regional, State, and Local News," published in the *Journal of Government Information*, and on state and local documents electronic discussion lists.[31]

Periodical Indexes

Governments publish a number of periodicals, some of which come up in reference queries. Examples from the federal government include titles such as *Survey of Current Business* (articles and data on the U.S. economy), *Monthly Labor Review* (articles and data on U.S. labor conditions),[32] and *Morbidity and Mortality Weekly Report* (articles and data on infectious diseases).[33] The articles in these periodicals are indexed right along with titles such as *Time* or the *New England Journal of Medicine* in many popular, general purpose periodical indexes. In addition, government periodicals are picked up by appropriate subject-based indexes.[34] For example, research articles from the National Institute of Environmental Health Sciences' *Environmental Health Perspectives*[35] are indexed in *Chemical Abstracts*,[36] among other science periodical databases. However, to find comprehensive coverage of this type of government material, including many significant but less well known and/or esoteric periodicals, indexing and abstracting tools that either emphasize government-sponsored serial titles or limit inclusion to such material should be consulted.

The *U.S. Government Periodicals Index* fills this role. It covers approximately 180 publications issued by federal government agencies and departments and may be used to locate literature on economic, social, and political issues, as well as articles of a technical or scientific nature. Whether seeking information on genetically altered food, the latest use of technology in schizophrenia research, or U.S.-China relations, it is conceivable that an article on such a topic appeared in a U.S. government-sponsored journal and has been indexed in *U.S. Government Periodicals Index*.

American Statistics Index (*ASI*) is an example of a highly specialized indexing and abstracting tool related to government information. This index offers access to the hundreds of statistical reports and other sources of statistical information, including those found in journals produced by the U.S. government that are frequently not covered in other indexing tools. *ASI* is discussed in greater detail in the "Statistical Sources" portion of this chapter.

PAIS International, from the Public Affairs Information Service, is an index to articles and other materials in international public affairs. *PAIS* covers topics in government, public policy, economics, political science, and international relations. As such, it should be no surprise that *PAIS* indexes the articles in a number of government journals, including those from the U.S. government, some foreign governments, and many international governmental organizations. *PAIS International* is discussed further in Chapter 21.

The above sources are private information providers whose periodical indexes include government titles. The U.S. government also produces several very important periodical indexes, including indexing for government *and* nongovernment titles.

MEDLINE, from the National Library of Medicine, is the standard index to periodical literature in medicine. *MEDLINE* is the electronic equivalent to *Index Medicus*. Those searching the current medical research literature in depth will likely make use of *MEDLINE*. Available via two free public databases, called *PubMed* and *Internet Grateful Med*, the *MEDLINE* database is also licensed by several private vendors, who may add special indexing or searching capabilities and then sell access.[37]

ERIC (Educational Resources Information Center) is the popular name for another long-running government-produced database to periodical literature. Produced by the U.S. Department of Education, Office of Educational Research and Improvement, and the National Library of Education, *ERIC* (which like *MEDLINE* is available both free and in various privately enhanced manifestations[38]) actually includes two distinct resources: *Resources in Education*, an index to documents such as reports and conference papers, and *Current Index to Journals in Education*, which indexes the contents of hundreds of education journals. As *ERIC*, these two databases may be searched concurrently to provide the premier index to education literature, covering everything from lesson plans and teaching styles to the latest research in education and child psychology.

A new notable government periodical database is *PubSCIENCE*. Launched in 1999 by the U.S. Department of Energy (DOE), it contains current article information taken from the journals of 35 participating science publishers, plus all the citations from the *DOE Reports Bibliographic Database*.[39] Most records include abstracts. Unlike *MEDLINE* or *ERIC*, *PubSCIENCE* is not quite the definitive index in all its many fields. As a government-funded effort, however, it is free, which alone makes it notable.

Finally, there is *AGRICOLA*, created by the National Agricultural Library. The records in this free database describe publications and resources encompassing all aspects of agriculture and allied disciplines, including plant and animal sciences, forestry, entomology, and more. *AGRICOLA* includes both monographs and journal articles.

General Facts and Directories

The official handbook of the federal government, the *United States Government Manual*, has been published annually since 1935. The *Manual* provides description, mission, and in some cases, organization charts (see Figure 22.2) for legislative, judicial, and executive agencies and offices, as well as for independent boards, commissions, committees, and quasi-official agencies. Entries give information on dates of establishment, key personnel, major subagencies, and programs and services. Often just as useful as the *Manual* are the various government Web sites. Many agency Web sites include their mission, along with the text of the laws that established them, and phone or e-mail directories of staff. Two excellent, comprehensive directories to government Web sites are *Federal Agency Internet Sites*, a joint project of the GPO and Louisiana State University, and the *Federal Web Locator*, run by the Center for Information Law and Policy.

Figure 22.2 Sample organizational chart from the *United States Government Manual.*

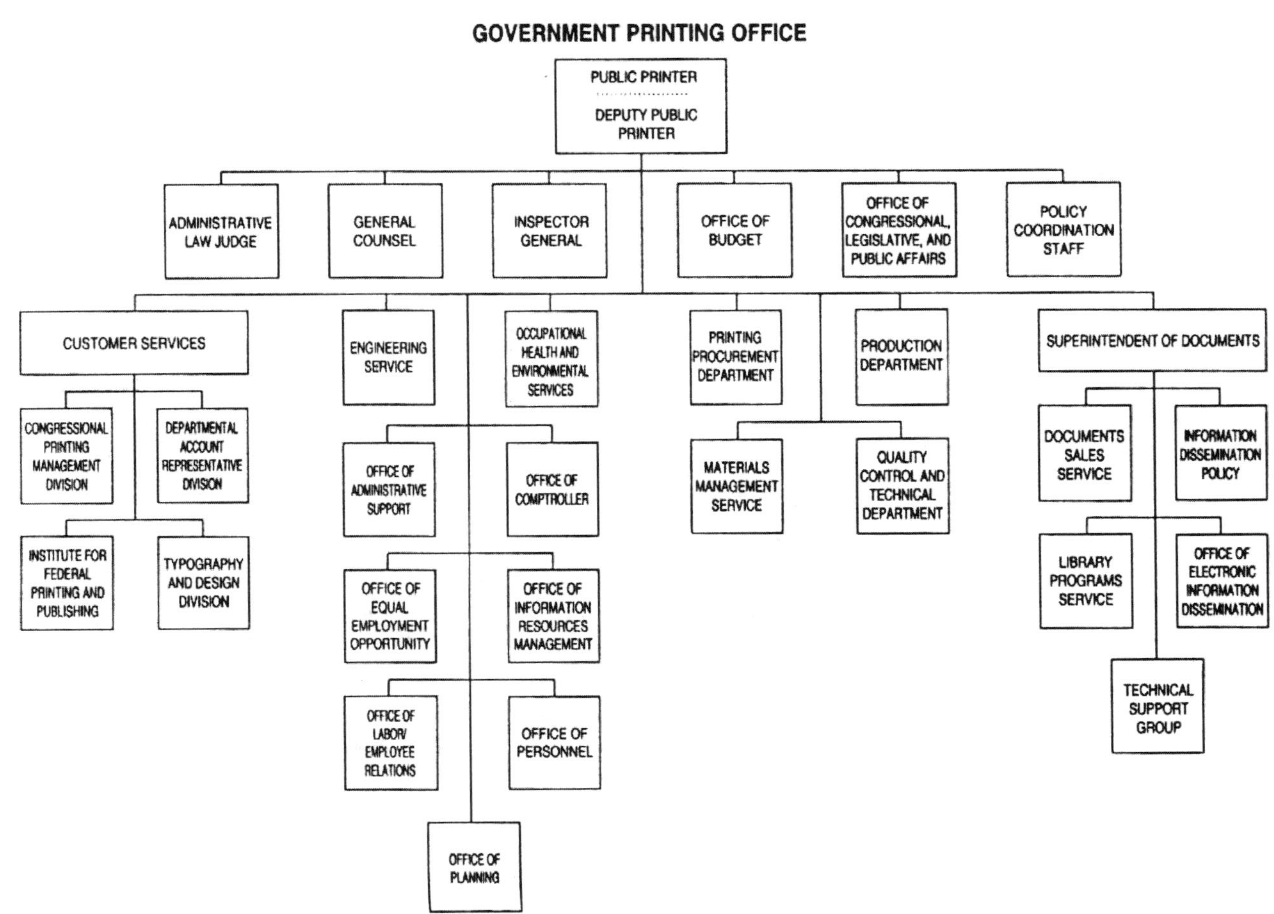

Another basic government handbook that covers most government offices is the *Official Congressional Directory*. It can be thought of as a directory published for the *use* of Congress, as well as *about* the Congress. A major portion of this handbook provides brief biographies and committee appointments of senators and representatives and directory information for them, their office staff, and congressional committee staff. Descriptions and maps of congressional districts are given, as are district zip codes. In addition, this title presents directory information for all major departments and many smaller agencies in which members of Congress have some interest. There are separate sections on the judiciary and the press galleries of Congress. It is an invaluable resource for details about the Capitol, including building floor plans. Although the *United States Government Manual* presents useful descriptions of agencies and their programs, the *Official Congressional Directory* usually provides more detailed personnel information. If a library user wants to know the address of the Government Printing Office, for example, one can consult either of these titles. If a user wants to know when the GPO was established, or how the Depository Library Program is administered, one must consult the *Manual*. On the other hand, if a very fine breakdown of the subagencies and names, addresses, and telephone numbers of department and section heads is required, turn to the *Official Congressional Directory*.

Various other directories are published commercially. Some are descriptive, such as the *Washington Information Directory*, which includes brief information about the programs or purpose of an agency or congressional committee, as well as the address, telephone number, and directors' names or committee members and staff. The *Washington Information Directory* also covers nongovernmental groups interested in federal activities; these include associations, lobbying organizations, and foundations. The *Congressional Staff Directory* and the *Congressional Yellow Book* are detailed directories to congresspeople and their staff. Both contain portraits of representatives and senators; information and maps from their districts; committee assignments; and the names, addresses, and phone numbers of staff.

Other directories provide similar information for other parts of government. The *Federal Yellow Book* and the *Federal Staff Directory* each provide names, titles, telephone numbers, and addresses of employees of the executive branch of government, including the president, the cabinet agencies, and all of the smaller and quasi-governmental entities associated with the federal government. The *Judicial Yellow Book* and the *Judicial Staff Directory* provide similar information for the federal and state judiciaries, and the *Federal Regional Yellow Book* is a directory of personnel at the many federal agency offices spread throughout the country. Each of the titles in the "yellow book" series mentioned above is updated quarterly, whereas those in the *Staff Directory* series are updated three times per year.

In addition to these comprehensive directories, individual federal agencies sometimes publish their own handbooks or manuals, which give the user more detailed information about the programs, services, and organization of an agency and also may provide factual material for reference purposes. An example is the *Social Security Handbook*, which tells what the Social Security Administration programs encompass and how to apply for benefits. Examples of the second type are *General Information Concerning Patents* (U.S. Patent and Trademark Office) and *Occupational Outlook Handbook* (Bureau of Labor Statistics). The former describes the process of patenting, in a question-and-answer format. The latter provides detailed descriptions of occupations and careers, informing the user about preparation for that career, salary expectations, job descriptions, and where to obtain additional information.

STAT-USA, an export information and statistics Web site from the Department of Commerce (discussed in more detail in the "Statistical Sources" section of this chapter), contains directory information. *STAT-USA* includes a list of American Chambers of Commerce Abroad, Country Directories of International Contacts, and State Trade Contacts, to name just a few of the listings.

The above titles are only a few examples of an enormous variety of sources useful in answering factual, ready-reference questions such as: "How can I determine if my invention is already patented?"; "Do I need a master's degree to be a medical technologist?"; "I'd like to contact my congressional representative, Christopher Shays, at his office in Washington, D.C.

Can you give me the phone number?"; or "What was Frederick Law Olmsted's involvement with the Capitol site?"

Most state governments publish directories to their state government offices. Also, the *State Yellow Book*, updated quarterly, is a directory of state government offices and personnel, with comprehensive coverage of all fifty states' governments. Like their federal counterparts, state agency Web sites are full of directory and other factual information. Excellent lists of links to state government Web sites include *State and Local Government on the Net*, from Piper Resources, and *State and Local Governments: A Library of Congress Internet Resource Page*, from the Library of Congress. Another "Yellow Book," the *Municipal Yellow Book*, compiles in one place the names and contact information for major officials of city and county governments.

Book of the States, published biennially, offers a wealth of factual information about individual states. *Book of the States* is the standard ready-reference source to check for recent information on state officials, state legislatures, and the state judiciary, as well as state elections and finances. Whether seeking information on the qualifications of secretaries of state, the methods for the removal of judges and filling of vacancies, or allowable state investments, this source is the place to start. The volume is indexed. Tables abound: state excise tax rates, motor vehicle laws, and time-series data on state minimum wages are examples. State mottoes, flowers, songs, birds, and so forth are also given.

For international and foreign governments and organizations, an excellent guide is the *Worldwide Government Directory*. This directory provides names, addresses, and telephone numbers for foreign governments and their major agencies, as well as major international intergovernmental organizations, from the United Nations to the North Atlantic Treaty Organization (NATO).

Linking users to the government information they require can occasionally involve making referrals to other documents librarians or to other collections of government information. Two directories that are useful for this purpose are the *Federal Depository Library Directory* and the *Directory of Government Document Collections & Librarians*. In addition, one may search depository library directory information via the GPO's Web site,[40] which has the added value of linking to the depository library Web site, if one exists.[41] Of course the best thing about knowing one's fellow government documents specialists is to be able to call on their expertise, which can also be tapped by using listservs such as GOVDOC-L. The cardinal rule in documents reference situations is, "If you can't answer the question or find the source, ask a colleague."

Laws and Legislative Information

The Legislative Process

United States national policies are rooted in statutory law promulgated by Congress. These public and private laws begin as legislative proposals. Legislative proposals do not always originate with Congress; however, only members of Congress may introduce bills and resolutions, and it is at this step that the formal life cycle of a measure begins. An overview of the usual sequence of events follows. Upon introduction, each House or Senate bill or resolution is published and numbered sequentially within a specific Congress. The number and session of the pertinent Congress is printed as part of the header, and, if provided, the bill's "Short Title" appears at the beginning of the bill text. Once a bill has been introduced, it is next referred to a congressional committee, the "nerve endings" of Congress.[42] In most cases, if the committee or a subcommittee holds hearings on the bill, a transcript of these will be published.

Further committee action may occur in the form of a bill "markup." If the committee decides to move the measure to the next stage, consideration by the full chamber, the bill is reported out of committee, and accompanied by a written Senate or House report. This report, "to accompany H.R. [bill no.]," will contain the latest version of the proposed legislation and may include more detailed information, such as an overview of the proposal, a cost estimate, and supplemental views. Committee roll-call votes on whether to report the bill are also incorporated into the report. More in-depth analyses about a policy, subject, or issue may also be authorized, and these studies are published as committee prints. The proposal may be debated on the floor of the chamber and then voted upon. If passed it would be sent to the other chamber and follow a similar path. Upon passage, it would be sent to the president for consideration.

As indicated above, there are numerous steps in the process by which a formal measure becomes a public law. The entire process is often referred to as its *legislative history*. Judith Schiek Robinson cites a potential 153 steps, as well as "the undocumented political activities interwoven at every stage."[43] At each stage of this activity, information results, and in most cases congressional publications are issued to disseminate that information. Bills and resolutions, hearings, reports and committee prints, floor debates, votes, presidential actions, laws, and other congressional publications are the tangible representations and textual records of the legislative process. These types of resources are fundamental to fielding a broad range of information queries, whether specific, general, or comprehensive in nature.

In addition, the House and Senate may order the printing of standard titles or request specialized materials, analyses, or studies, either monographic or serial in nature. Examples include the president's State of the Union message and the *Economic Report of the President*, an annual publication. Each of these congressional publications is numbered and categorized as a "congressional document," and these and the *reports* form what is known as the *Serial Set*. This long-standing, ongoing series has been compiled since 1789. "The current set consists of three categories of congressional publications issued in six discrete parts: House reports, Senate reports, House documents, Senate documents, Senate treaty documents, and Senate executive reports."[44]

By way of illustration, on January 6, 1999, Representative Heather Wilson, Republican, New Mexico, introduced "An Act to Preserve the Cultural Resources of the Route 66 Corridor and to Authorize the Secretary of the Interior to Provide Assistance." This bill was designated H.R. 66, 106th, 1st session, and referred initially to the House Committee on Resources. A hearing was held on March 11, 1999, by the House Subcommittee on National Parks and Public Lands. The House Committee on Resources reported the bill out of committee, and a House Report, entitled *Route 66 Corridor Act*, dated May 13, 1999, was issued. Discussion of the bill occurred in the House several times, and the House passed an amended version of the bill on June 30, 1999. The Senate passed the bill on July 27, 1999, and President Clinton signed it into public law on August 10, 1999, whereupon H.R. 66 became P. L. 106-45, Route 66 Corridor, Historic Preservation.

Guides and Indexes

Answering questions about legislation and public laws is a major component of government information reference service. A user may be looking for a specific fact, such as the date the president signed a bill into law, or may want to review a known discrete source, such as a Public Law, a House Resolution, or subcommittee hearings on a bill, such as the one above, from a recent Congress. Frequently the testimony of a particular individual is requested. A user may be interested in the status of proposed legislation or may want either a succinct overview or in-depth coverage of a particular social policy. Usually current information is needed, but historical queries are common. Standard congressional information tools may provide answers to ready-reference or basic requests, although in some cases congressional publications have to be consulted. Locating official versions of these publications, whether in print or electronic format, can be straightforward, as long as an accurate citation is available or can be fairly easily ascertained. Each legislative measure, i.e., a bill or resolution, has a legislative history, and the process of ascertaining this information or tracking current legislative proposals has become much less time-consuming and cumbersome as a result of the development of several excellent electronic tools and databases, including both free and fee-based resources.

The "Legislative" section of *GPO Access* is the premier permanent, no-fee electronic gateway to legislative actions, congressional publications, and related information. This official Web site's "History of Bills" section provides a concise listing of the steps through which each legislative measure proposed during the 98th and subsequent Congresses progressed. Another free, invaluable Web-based service is the Library of Congress's *THOMAS*. It also has the full text of most congressional publications, and its "Bill Summary and Status" section, which begins coverage with the 93rd Congress, 1973/74–present, includes more comprehensive bill tracking information. Bill number access is provided in *GPO Access* and *THOMAS*. Both services support keyword and phrase searching, and subject term searching or browsing is available in *THOMAS*. The latter is based on Legislative Indexing Vocabulary (LIV).[45] *THOMAS* has one additional unique and important feature: the option to search legislation by stage in the legislative process.[46] These up-to-date services contain bill summaries; *THOMAS* includes roll-call votes. Both provide excellent Web site user guides in the form of FAQ's and/or Help screens. *THOMAS* includes revised and updated copies of Charles W. Johnson's basic pamphlet on the legislative process, *How Our Laws Are Made*, Senate Document 105-14 (1997), and Robert B. Dove's *Enactment of a Law*. Both *GPO Access* and *THOMAS* can be utilized as an extended teaching tool with either the general public or students of almost any age who want to understand the workings of Congress, U.S. law-making, and the related information cycle.

The "Bill Summary and Status" section of *THOMAS* has replaced the former print serial, the *Digest of Public General Bills and Resolutions*, which the Library of Congress' Legislative Reference Service compiled from the 74th Congress, 1936, through the 101st Congress, 1990. Its print counterpart, *Major Legislation of the Congress*, which ran from the 97th Congress, 1982 through the 102nd Congress, 1992, has also been incorporated into *THOMAS*, as of the 104th Congress, 1995– .[47] The *Calendars of the United States House of Representatives and History of Legislation* and the *Senate Calendar of Business* are also helpful in obtaining bill and public law information. As of the 104th Congress, 1995– , these can be found on *GPO Access*. The timeliness, search and retrieval capabilities, and the availability of electronic full-text documents and transcripts have limited the value of the print format edition of these titles; however, they are still essential when investigating earlier legislation.

Another useful print resource is the *Congressional Index* from Commerce Clearing House, Inc. (CCH). This is a commercial looseleaf service, updated weekly, that has been produced since the 75th Congress, 1937/38. Public bills and resolutions are indexed by subject. The status tables indicate, by bill or resolution number, whether hearings have been held and reports issued, and follow through with information and dates on votes, vetoes, and public law numbers. *Congressional Index* covers all pending legislation, even when no publications have been issued after a bill's introduction and referral to committee. It is a convenient source for obtaining brief legislative histories for bills and resolutions proposed in pre-1970s Congresses. CCH products can be found in many depository, law, and public libraries.[48]

Congressional Information Service's (CIS) *Congressional Universe*,[49] and Congressional Quarterly's *CQ.com On Congress,* are Web-based subscription services offering near real-time access to congressional activity. Competitors, they both operate as guides and indexes to the legislative process and to the literature, serve as centralized locales for electronic versions of primary publications, and function as educational tools. The full text of bills, the *Congressional Record*, and other types of congressional materials are available, legislative histories or current status of bills are readily accessible, and voting records of members of Congress can quickly be obtained in these systems. *Congressional Universe* includes brief bill synopses, summaries, and/or digests, and *CQ.com On Congress* maintains bill digests.[50] Each features news services and transcripts of hearings, press briefings, and other events. The complexities of the legislative and regulatory process have created a legitimate demand among documents librarians in both small and large institutions for these types of resources. As with *GPO Access* and *THOMAS*, these value-added services can be used to answer basic questions—"What is the public law number of the legislation, originally proposed by then Senator Al Gore, called the 'High Performance Computing Act,' and has it been amended since it passed in December, 1991?"—and the more complex, such as, "I'd like to identify the legislation that has been proposed over the past five years related to public libraries and rural library services, examine some of the congressional publications relevant to a selected number of the bills that became public law, and compile a list of the senators and representatives who supported passage of these. I would also like to know whether or not the president signed these into law."

Congressional Universe is unique among these electronic services because it contains *CIS/Index*, a long-standing, comprehensive indexing and abstracting tool for congressional publications. Begun in 1970 by CIS, this multivolume series provides access to hearings, committee prints, and other types of congressional publications, including Senate and House Reports and Documents that form the *Serial Set,* from the 91st Congress, 1969 on. The comprehensive subject and name index directs the user to the relevant abstract. The abstract provides complete bibliographic information, details for purchase, and SuDoc classification number, followed by a detailed summary of the document's content. Of the aforementioned tools, this is the only resource at present that includes the formal titles of published hearings. This is pertinent for those who may want to access a library's holdings via an online catalog. All regional and many selective depository libraries house congressional hearings and maintain these collections over time. The source documents cited in the abstracts are available from the CIS for purchase on microfiche. Subscriptions to the monthly *Index* and the *Abstract* volumes in paper format are still available. The *Index* volumes are cumulated quarterly; yearly cumulations of the abstracts and indexes, plus a third volume, *Legislative Histories of U.S. Public Laws*, form *CIS/Annual*. Multiyear cumulations of the indexes are also available.[51]

If library users want discussion or background information on political activities, but not necessarily primary documents from Congress, they can consult *Congressional Quarterly Weekly Report* and *Congressional Quarterly Almanac*. These two major publications from Congressional Quarterly, Inc., cover Congress, the Supreme Court, the presidency, and politics. *Congressional Quarterly Weekly Report* discusses major legislation, events, and issues. It also furnishes roll-call votes. At the end of the year, information from *Congressional Quarterly Weekly Report* is reorganized by subject and summarized in chronological order in the *Almanac*. *Congressional Quarterly Weekly Report* and *Congressional Quarterly Almanac* provide the user with a well-organized, succinct, and readable account of national politics and congressional, presidential, and judicial consideration of major issues affecting the American public. The weekly source, as well as other CQ journals, is available as a separate Web subscription and in *CQ.com On Congress.*

Primary Sources

After reading about legislation in the *Congressional Quarterly* sources or having identified sources in *GPO Access*, *THOMAS*, or *Congressional Universe*, the next step for many users is to read the actual publications. These are available within the Web-based services in electronic format or in print or microfiche in most depository libraries. They will include: the *Congressional Record*, the transcripts of proceedings and debates from the floor of Congress; congressional bills, the form in which legislation is introduced; committee hearings, the testimony and discussion that occurs, as well as appendices of supplementary material; committee prints, research reports requested by a committee; congressional reports, a description, and frequently, detailed analysis of the legislation that is prepared when the bill is sent to the House or Senate floor; as well as congressional documents. Bills that become public laws are first printed separately as "Slip Laws." These are compiled in the *United States Statutes at Large* and then finally are codified in the *United States Code*. Full-text versions of the public laws are available on the Web in the aforementioned services. Dates of coverage vary however; for example, *Congressional Universe* includes 100th Congress, 2nd session, 1988– ; *THOMAS*, 101st Congress, 1989– ; and *GPO Access*, 104th Congress, 1995– . The *United States Code* is also included.

Box 22.1 Search Strategy: Tracking Current Legislation

A user heard that Congress had passed a law called "E-Sign," regarding digital signatures, and would like to read the text. A search of "e-sign" in *THOMAS's* current congress bill-text section yields no results; a search of "electronic signature" yields twenty-eight occurrences of that exact phrase. Of those, "Electronic Signatures in Global and National Commerce Act (Enrolled Bill; Sent to President; S.761.ENR)" is the only one that has been sent to the president, indicating that it has cleared both chambers of Congress and, unless there is a presidential veto, will become law. Note that legislation is often reported in the press at this stage, before the president has signed the legislation into law (although if there is reason to believe a veto may be coming, that fact is usually reported also). From this point in *THOMAS* the user may see the text of the bill and verify that this is indeed the desired law.

The user may also look at "Bill Summary and Status" to obtain information on related hearings and committee reports that are very useful in understanding Congress's intent in passing the legislation.

A nearly identical process would be followed to obtain the same information in another congressional resource, such as *GPO Access, Congressional Universe,* or *CQ.com On Congress.*

The example in Box 22.1 illustrates that a straightforward question may lead down several paths, requiring different approaches to related information. It is crucial to understand the user's specific information needs and tailor the search accordingly. Also, keep in mind that choosing the correct subject heading in various indexes requires some inventiveness and reliance on cross-references.

State governments are increasing the amount and expanding the accessibility of legislative information in electronic format. Gateways to these include *State Constitutions, Statutes and Related Legislative Information*, from Cornell University; the *State Web Locator*, compiled by Lori Hallman; and the Library of Congress Internet Resource Page, *State and Local Governments.* They serve as convenient pathfinders to the official home pages of the fifty states. A related source, *StateList: The Electronic Source for State Publication Lists*, provides links to the thirty state publication lists accessible via the Web.[52] Beginning dates of coverage vary widely, but many include recent listings. Fee-based subscription systems, such as CIS's *State Capital Universe*, also cover state legislative activity. West Group's *Westlaw* has files of codified legislation for the fifty states, as does LEXIS-NEXIS via products such as *LEXIS* and *Academic Universe*.[53]

Regulatory Documents

Rules and regulations constitute another principal type of legal document. United States executive agencies and departments are empowered by Congress and the president to issue detailed requirements pertaining to statutory law and its actual implementation. Considered "quasi-legislation or bureaucratic law,"[54] these administrative rulings, notices, and presidential executive orders and proclamations appear in the *Federal Register*, which is published daily Monday through Friday, excepting official holidays. *Final* rules (see Figure 22.3) are published here, as are *proposed* rules and regulations. The printing and distribution of these proposed regulations gives citizens, officials, and experts the opportunity to comment on and critique them in advance. It is just as common for users to seek proposed rules as final versions. For instance, in 1999, the Office of Energy Efficiency and Renewable Energy, U.S. Department of Energy, began the process of amending and revising the test procedures for dishwashers as a result of changes to the "Energy Policy and Conservation Act."[55] A "Notice of proposed rulemaking and public workshop" appeared initially, followed by a "Proposed rule; reopening of the comment period." The extension until February 14, 2000, came about as a result of issues raised during the public workshop. As of this writing, the final regulations have not yet been published.[56] *Federal Register* notices can be announcements of meetings, opinions, or other miscellaneous information, such as the availability of an environmental impact statement or a research grant. For example, on January 13, 2000, the Forest Service announced its intention to prepare an environmental impact statement for the Threemile Stewardship Project to be undertaken in the Ashland Ranger District, part of the Custer National Forest.[57] These are only two representative examples.

Figure 22.3 Notice in *Federal Register.*

SMALL BUSINESS ADMINISTRATION

13 CFR Part 120

Business Loan Program

AGENCY: Small Business Administration (SBA).

ACTION: Final rule.

SUMMARY: This final rule would implement Public Law 106–22, enacted on April 27, 1999, which establishes new rules for the loan loss reserve fund which an intermediary must maintain to participate in SBA's microloan program.

DATE: This rule is effective on April 3, 2000.

FOR FURTHER INFORMATION CONTACT: Jody Raskind, 202–205–6497.

SUPPLEMENTARY INFORMATION: Public Law 106–22, enacted on April 27, 1999, amended section 7(m) of the Small Business Act (15 U.S.C. 636(7)(m)) in order to change the requirements for the loan loss reserve fund (LLRF) which each intermediary in the SBA's microloan program must maintain. The LLRF is an interest-bearing deposit account at a bank. An intermediary must establish an LLRF to pay any shortage in its day-to-day revolving account caused by delinquencies or losses on microloans it makes to qualified small business borrowers. An intermediary must maintain the LLRF until it repays all obligations it owes to the SBA.

On July 26, 1999, SBA published a proposed rule in the **Federal Register** (64 FR 40310). Since SBA received no comments, it is publishing in final the rule as proposed and making it effective on the date of publication in the **Federal Register**.

Final rules and regulations, and presidential Executive Orders and Proclamations, are incorporated into the *Code of Federal Regulations (CFR)*, the "codification of the general and permanent rules published . . . by the Executive departments and agencies of the Federal Government."[58] The *CFR* is divided into fifty numbered titles, such as Title 3 The President, Title 17 Commodity and Securities Exchanges, Title 22 Foreign Relations, Title 29 Labor, and Title 40 Protection of Environment. The print edition is revised once a year, with one-fourth of the *CFR* being reissued each calendar quarter.[59] The monthly publication, *LSA, List of CFR Sections Affected*, is used to update the traditional edition of the *CFR* by citing amendments that appear in the daily *Federal Register*. If the relevant title and section appear in the *LSA*, the user will be referred to a page number in the *Federal Register*. *GPO Access* links to the daily *Federal Register*, the *CFR*, and the *LSA* from its "Regulatory" Web page. New *CFR* volumes are made available concurrent with the release of the paper editions; *GPO Access* contains a schedule regarding their availability at http://www.access.gpo.gov/nara/cfr/cfr-table-search.html#page1. The *LSA* on *GPO Access* provides access to the monthly *LSA* series, a current list of changes, and a special feature for those monitoring changes on a daily basis. Helpful instructions appear throughout, and page numbers can be "copied-and-pasted" into the "Retrieve a *Federal Register* Page (in PDF Format)" to access the initial pages of published amendatory actions.

In the same manner, the "CFR Parts Affected" list in the daily print edition of the *Federal Register* can be used to update the information provided in the *LSA*. The monthly cumulative and annual print format *Federal Register* indexes can be consulted, also.

When a library user needs regulations for an agency and its programs, the research may start with the *CFR* (see Box 22.2). It is possible to search the entire current *CFR* database by keyword or search or browse a single title or several in the current and the historical database. Another option would be to use the *CFR Index and Finding Aids*, a subject and agency index, which is revised annually. More detailed subject or topical access to the *CFR* is provided by CIS's *Index to the Code of Federal Regulations*. The *CFR* volumes contain only those final regulations in effect at the time of publication. Whether responding to a specific query, or assisting a user in conducting research, *LSA, List of CFR Sections Affected* must be consulted to determine if there are more recent rules and regulations than those in the latest edition of *CFR*. CIS's *Congressional Universe* includes regulatory information as well. Its version of the *Federal Register* is updated daily; the *CFR*, every two weeks. In Figure 22.4, page 560, the entry shows that 14 CFR 93—that is, CFR title 14, section 93—has been changed; in this case, the number of commercial air tours over the Grand Canyon National Park has been reduced. Native American tribes, environmentalists and conservationists, and the local business community contributed to this process, as did President Clinton.[60] Final regulations include the effective date; in this case, the regulation went into effect on May 4, 2000.

Box 22.2 Regulatory Search Strategy

A citizen calls who has heard the previous week that legislation has been passed that will ban the manufacturing of medical inhalers in the near future to protect the ozone. A search of *Congressional Universe's* "Bills" section and "Congressional Bills" on *GPO Access* resulted in no matches; however, a "by words in text" search for "inhalers" in *Congressional Universe's* or *GPO Access's Federal Register*, limited to the most recent volume, the current month, and the Environmental Protection Agency, located the pertinent final regulation. As it turned out, the U.S. government had forwarded to the Montreal Protocol's Secretariat nominations for production of certain compounds after 1995 for use in metered dose inhalers and other specified medical applications.

Figure 22.4 Entries in *Code of Federal Regulations. LSA, List of CFR Sections Affected* on *Congressional Universe* [a Congressional Information Service product]. Reprinted by permission.

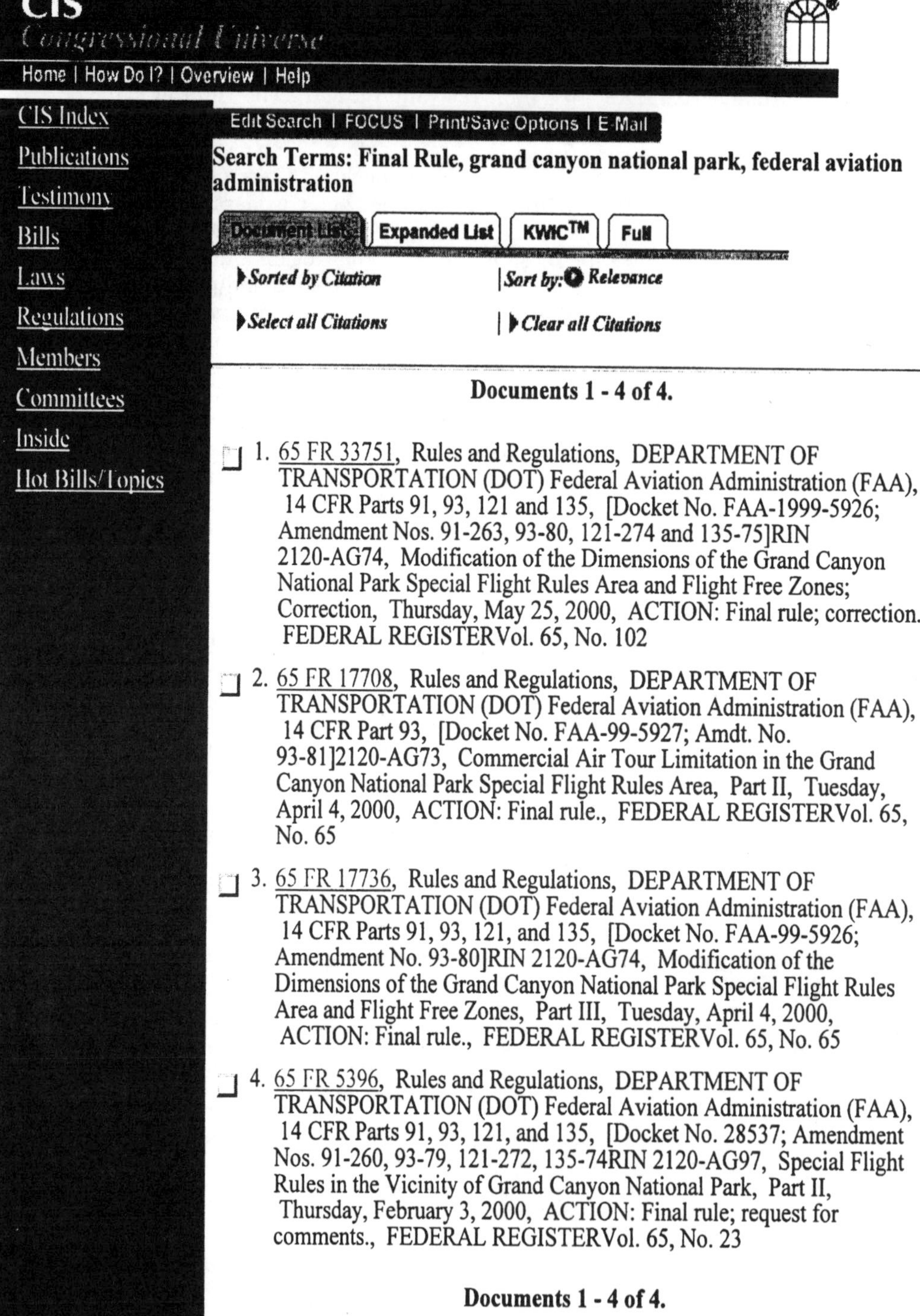

Search Terms: Final Rule, grand canyon national park, federal aviation administration

Documents 1 - 4 of 4.

1. 65 FR 33751, Rules and Regulations, DEPARTMENT OF TRANSPORTATION (DOT) Federal Aviation Administration (FAA), 14 CFR Parts 91, 93, 121 and 135, [Docket No. FAA-1999-5926; Amendment Nos. 91-263, 93-80, 121-274 and 135-75]RIN 2120-AG74, Modification of the Dimensions of the Grand Canyon National Park Special Flight Rules Area and Flight Free Zones; Correction, Thursday, May 25, 2000, ACTION: Final rule; correction., FEDERAL REGISTERVol. 65, No. 102

2. 65 FR 17708, Rules and Regulations, DEPARTMENT OF TRANSPORTATION (DOT) Federal Aviation Administration (FAA), 14 CFR Part 93, [Docket No. FAA-99-5927; Amdt. No. 93-81]2120-AG73, Commercial Air Tour Limitation in the Grand Canyon National Park Special Flight Rules Area, Part II, Tuesday, April 4, 2000, ACTION: Final rule., FEDERAL REGISTERVol. 65, No. 65

3. 65 FR 17736, Rules and Regulations, DEPARTMENT OF TRANSPORTATION (DOT) Federal Aviation Administration (FAA), 14 CFR Parts 91, 93, 121, and 135, [Docket No. FAA-99-5926; Amendment No. 93-80]RIN 2120-AG74, Modification of the Dimensions of the Grand Canyon National Park Special Flight Rules Area and Flight Free Zones, Part III, Tuesday, April 4, 2000, ACTION: Final rule., FEDERAL REGISTERVol. 65, No. 65

4. 65 FR 5396, Rules and Regulations, DEPARTMENT OF TRANSPORTATION (DOT) Federal Aviation Administration (FAA), 14 CFR Parts 91, 93, 121, and 135, [Docket No. 28537; Amendment Nos. 91-260, 93-79, 121-272, 135-74RIN 2120-AG97, Special Flight Rules in the Vicinity of Grand Canyon National Park, Part II, Thursday, February 3, 2000, ACTION: Final rule; request for comments., FEDERAL REGISTERVol. 65, No. 23

Documents 1 - 4 of 4.

Statistical Sources

Requests for statistics are among the most common of reference queries. Governments collect and analyze much statistical data in the course of satisfying the missions of their various agencies and branches. Indeed, the U.S. federal government is the largest statistics-gathering agency in the world. Data gathered and published include popular items such as population demographics and economic statistics as well as more esoteric items such as personal computer ownership and the flow rates for various rivers. A librarian can quickly and easily determine how many persons were arrested last year (by race and sex), as well as how many high school graduates went to college. If an event can be counted, it is likely that the government has reported it. This section identifies the major statistical reference sources and discusses strategies for their use.[61]

It is essential to note that to protect confidentiality, public data from the government never identify individuals by name. Companies or business establishments are identified by name only when the mission of the statistical program specifically calls for it—such as in company reports appearing in the U.S. Securities and Exchange Commission's *EDGAR* database.[62] This confidentiality sometimes results in suppression or deletion of data if the data could possibly be used to identify characteristics or information about a specific individual or business. For example, names from the *United States Census of Population and Housing* are kept secret for seventy-two years after each Census. Likewise, if there are only a handful of auto repair shops in Garfield County, Utah, all information about auto repair shops in Garfield County may be suppressed in *County Business Patterns, Utah*, to prevent a user from deducing data about a particular auto repair business.[63]

Indexes and Guides to Statistical Resources

Statistics come from numerous sources. In addition to the programs of the federal government, most state governments and foreign nations conduct various statistics-gathering programs. International organizations, such as the UN or World Bank, also gather statistics in the course of their operations. Private data publishers, industry or nonprofit organizations, and individual scholars may also collect data. With so many resources, an index of some kind is extremely helpful, especially for a library doing significant statistical research.

The standard statistical indexes are those published by Congressional Information Service (CIS). In essence, CIS attempts to identify all published statistical data and lead the user to the needed information. CIS produces three print statistical index products: the *American Statistics Index (ASI)*, which indexes and abstracts federal government statistical sources from 1973; the *Statistical Reference Index (SRI)*, which indexes and abstracts state, industry, and other non-federal statistical publications (about a thousand) from 1980; and the *Index to International Statistics (IIS)*, which indexes and abstracts international organizations' statistical sources (about two thousand) from 1983. CIS also has a Web product, via LEXIS-NEXIS, called *Statistical Universe.*[64] *Statistical Universe* combines the data from all three print publications into a single, searchable online database, which even includes some full-text reports.

Libraries may purchase any of the ongoing print editions of *ASI*, *SRI*, and *IIS*. Each print service consists of two complementary volumes: *Index* and *Abstracts*. Volumes are published annually and kept current with monthly updates. Additionally, multi-year cumulations are put together approximately every four years. The user begins with the index volume, browsing by CIS subject terms. Under the appropriate subject term, browse for content notes that appear to describe the specific data needed. From this content note in the *Index* volume, the user gets an abstract number. Following the abstract number leads to complete bibliographic information and a detailed abstract in the companion *Abstracts* volume (see sample abstract in Figure 22.5, page 562). These abstracts generally list every statistical table in the cited source. Abstracts in *ASI*, the federal government series, include a Superintendent of Documents (SuDoc) number and depository item number to assist in finding the actual publication in a federal depository library.

Figure 22.5 Abstract from *American Statistics Index* [a Congressional Information Service product]. Reprinted by permission.

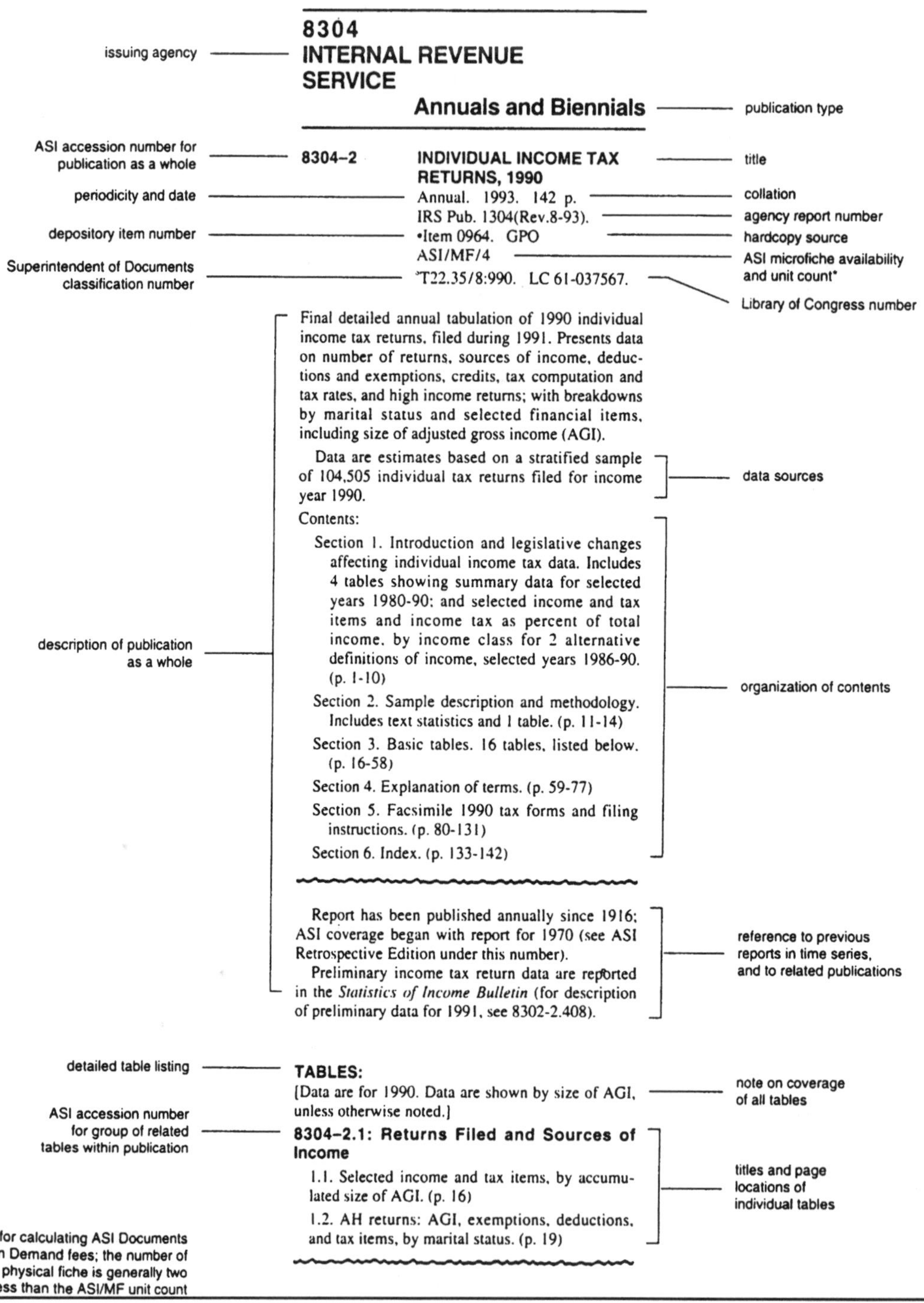

Sample Abstract—Individual Publication

8304
INTERNAL REVENUE SERVICE

Annuals and Biennials

8304–2 **INDIVIDUAL INCOME TAX RETURNS, 1990**
Annual. 1993. 142 p.
IRS Pub. 1304(Rev.8-93).
•Item 0964. GPO
ASI/MF/4
°T22.35/8:990. LC 61-037567.

Final detailed annual tabulation of 1990 individual income tax returns, filed during 1991. Presents data on number of returns, sources of income, deductions and exemptions, credits, tax computation and tax rates, and high income returns; with breakdowns by marital status and selected financial items, including size of adjusted gross income (AGI).

Data are estimates based on a stratified sample of 104,505 individual tax returns filed for income year 1990.

Contents:

Section 1. Introduction and legislative changes affecting individual income tax data. Includes 4 tables showing summary data for selected years 1980-90; and selected income and tax items and income tax as percent of total income, by income class for 2 alternative definitions of income, selected years 1986-90. (p. 1-10)

Section 2. Sample description and methodology. Includes text statistics and 1 table. (p. 11-14)

Section 3. Basic tables. 16 tables, listed below. (p. 16-58)

Section 4. Explanation of terms. (p. 59-77)

Section 5. Facsimile 1990 tax forms and filing instructions. (p. 80-131)

Section 6. Index. (p. 133-142)

Report has been published annually since 1916; ASI coverage began with report for 1970 (see ASI Retrospective Edition under this number).

Preliminary income tax return data are reported in the *Statistics of Income Bulletin* (for description of preliminary data for 1991, see 8302-2.408).

TABLES:

[Data are for 1990. Data are shown by size of AGI, unless otherwise noted.]

8304–2.1: Returns Filed and Sources of Income

1.1. Selected income and tax items, by accumulated size of AGI. (p. 16)

1.2. All returns: AGI, exemptions, deductions, and tax items, by marital status. (p. 19)

In addition to the subject-based indexing, each *Index* volume contains a "category" index section. The category index is useful for the person whose primary need is comparative data: For instance, someone needing comparative crime statistics for the states could use the *ASI* category index for "By State" and then browse the entries for crime. Similarly, one could browse the "By Sex" category index to find comparative data by sex for earnings or some other topic.

The breadth of the publications covered by the CIS indexes is far beyond what most library collections are likely to have. CIS does, however, publish a microfiche set of nearly every report included in the indexes. Libraries may purchase any of the three sets: the ASI Microfiche Library, the SRI Microfiche Library, and the IIS Microfiche Library (in the case of *ASI*, a depository library may purchase only fiche reports for nondepository items). The microfiche reports are numbered by CIS abstract number and are therefore simple to find from the abstract volumes.

By combining *ASI*, *SRI*, and *IIS* into one source, the Web-based *Statistical Universe* allows users to search all indexed statistical publications at once. This is almost the same as searching the index of thousands of statistical publications simultaneously. Users may search by CIS subject terms (the list of CIS subject terms may be browsed), titles, authors, publishers, and category for comparative statistics. It is also possible to expand a search to look for "all words in summary," which finds keywords anywhere in the abstracts and bibliographic information. Users may limit by date or by any combination of the three sources (see sample search, Figure 22.6).[65] Just like the print sources, the results include full bibliographic information, with SuDoc numbers for locating depository items in a depository library as well as an abstract number for finding the data in one of the CIS microfiche libraries.

Figure 22.6 Sample search on *Statistical Universe* [a Congressional Information Service product]. Reprinted by permission.

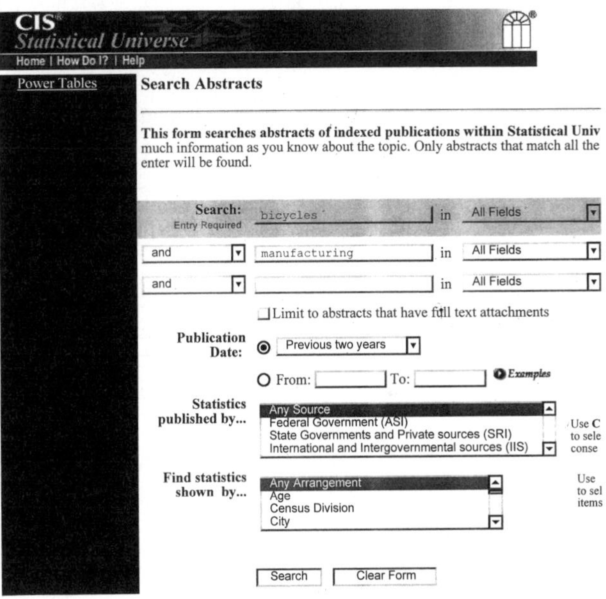

Many *Statistical Universe* entries include the full text of the statistical publication. The full text may be in ASCII text with GIF images of tables, PDF files (for use with Adobe Acrobat), and in many cases, spreadsheets for easy importing into other applications. Much of this full text is maintained at the system's data archive. In other cases, the full text appears on a statistical agency's Web site, to which *Statistical Universe* links. Finally, *Statistical Universe* includes the full text (with spreadsheet versions of the tables) for the *Statistical Abstract of the*

United States, the single most useful compilation of statistics that exists (discussed in more detail under "Important Statistical Sources" below).

Libraries are offered a variety of subscription options for *Statistical Universe* to meet their specific needs. Just as with the print volumes, a library may subscribe to the entire *Statistical Universe* database or only to a particular index within *Statistical Universe*. Some full text is included regardless of the subscription, but further, subject-based full-text modules may be added, which increase the amount of full text included as well as the price.

Although there is nothing quite like the breadth of coverage offered by the CIS statistical products, many libraries may not have the need for such comprehensive indexing or the budget to pay for it. Several other publications aid the librarian in gaining an understanding of the various statistical programs that exist while helping to identify specific statistical publications. A fine, comprehensive guide to statistical programs and sources is the two-volume set *Statistics Sources: A Subject Guide to Data on Industrial, Business, Social, Educational, Financial, and Other Topics for the United States and Internationally*, edited by Jacqueline Wasserman O'Brien and Steven R. Wasserman. Its 24th annual edition (2000) contains almost 100,000 citations to statistical sources covering the United States and the world, arranged alphabetically by subject. Particularly useful sections include the "Selected Bibliography of Key Statistical Sources" and an appendix that lists all cited sources alphabetically. A similar volume is *State and Local Statistics Sources*, edited by M. Balachandran and S. Balachandran. Although the latest edition (1993) is becoming a bit dated, this excellent work indexes 5,500 statistical publications, arranged by state and subject. Although neither of these volumes indexes each piece of statistical data that appears in a publication, as the CIS products do, they both use broader subject indexing to lead the user to statistical publications that cover a particular topic.

Nearly as important as a librarian's bibliographic knowledge of statistical sources are electronic skills. Government Web sites are the best and often the only way to find the most timely statistical information. The trend toward Web publishing has given the nondepository library access to government statistical data as never before. Providing statistical reference service in the electronic age requires not only an awareness of the government statistical sources available online, but also an unyielding commitment to ongoing training and awareness (see Chapter 9). Reading the relevant literature, whether professional journals or listservs (such as GOVDOC-L), and undertaking investigative studies is an indispensable part of this process. Although there is no substitute for an index as comprehensive as *Statistical Universe*, a librarian who combines a thorough knowledge of statistical programs and sources, current awareness of publishing trends, electronic skills, and an Internet connection can provide competent statistical reference service relying exclusively on freely available government Web resources.

The best index to federal government statistical data on the Web is *FedStats*, which aims to provide links to all federal statistical data on the Web. *FedStats* is an undertaking of the Federal Interagency Council on Statistical Policy. Users may browse *FedStats* by subject or search by keyword. For a broader guide to statistical information on the Web, users should consult a site such as the *University of Michigan Documents Center*, whose statistics section links to sites with government statistical data, information about statistics, microdata (the raw data resulting from the statistical gathering endeavor), and more. Librarians familiar with statistical programs and agencies may always go directly to the Web site of the various statistical agencies to browse for the needed statistical data.

Important Statistical Sources

For the library that can purchase only one statistical reference volume—or even only one government document—the *Statistical Abstract of the United States* is a likely choice. An annual compendium published by the Census Bureau, the *Statistical Abstract* compiles the most popular statistical data not only from all federal agencies, but from various nongovernmental publishers as well. A few of the topics included are births and birth rates, high school dropouts, arrests for drug crimes, attendance of performing arts, visitation of National Parks, voting patterns, federal aid to states and local governments, unemployment, women-owned businesses, and government spending by topic. The *Statistical Abstract* is also available on the Census Bureau Web site and as a CD-ROM, with the CD-ROM adding spreadsheet versions of nearly every table. To gain access to these statistics, begin by browsing the subject index. Subjects are arranged by broad heading over more specific subheadings. Beginning in 1987, index references are to table numbers, not page numbers. Many data tables are for the United States as a whole, but some tables provide state and metropolitan area data and there is a chapter that features comparative international statistics. Although the *Statistical Abstract* is often sufficient to answer a reference question, it also serves as a guide to historical or more detailed information. For more detailed information, each table includes a source note that provides the original source for the particular data. If desired one may then go to the original source—more often than not another government document—and usually find more detailed or complete data on the particular topic (see Figure 22.7 for sample table).

Figure 22.7 Table and notes from *Statistical Abstract of the United States*, 1998, p. 243.

Geography and Environment 243

No. 401. Emissions of Greenhouse Gases, by Type and Source: 1990 to 1996

[Emission estimates were mandated by Congress through Section 1605(a) of the Energy Policy Act of 1992 (Title XVI). Gases that contain carbon can be measured either in terms of the full molecular weight of the gas or just in terms of their carbon content]

TYPE AND SOURCE	Unit	1990	1991	1992	1993	1994	1995	1996, prel.
Carbon dioxide:								
Carbon content, total [1]	Mil. metric tons	1,373.7	1,360.2	1,379.9	1,411.6	1,433.5	1,444.6	1,495.9
Energy sources	Mil. metric tons	1,345.8	1.330.6	1,351.5	1,380.9	1,401.3	1,411.4	1,463.0
Methane:								
Gas, total [1]	Mil. metric tons	31.6	31.6	31.7	30.8	31.4	30.9	30.9
Energy sources	Mil. metric tons	12.1	12.0	12.0	11.1	11.4	11.2	11.6
Landfills	Mil. metric tons	11.1	11.0	10.9	10.8	10.7	10.6	10.4
Agricultural sources	Mil. metric tons	8.3	8.6	8.8	8.8	9.1	9.1	8.8
Nitrous oxide, total	1,000 metric tons	449	452	452	463	472	454	446
Agriculture	1,000 metric tons	164	167	168	176	179	159	146
Mobile sources	1,000 metric tons	150	148	150	147	147	148	148
Stationary combustion	1,000 metric tons	38	37	37	38	39	39	41
Industrial sources	1,000 metric tons	97	100	96	101	107	108	111
Nitrogen oxide, total [1]	Mil. metric tons	20.9	20.6	20.7	21.1	21.5	19.7	(NA)
Energy related	Mil. metric tons	19.8	19.5	19.7	20.1	20.3	18.8	(NA)
Stationary source fuel combustion	Mil. metric tons	10.4	10.3	10.4	10.6	10.5	9.1	(NA)
Transportation	Mil. metric tons	9.4	9.2	9.4	9.5	9.8	9.6	(NA)
Nonmethane volatile organic compounds (VOCs), total [1]	Mil. metric tons	21.4	20.8	20.3	20.5	21.1	20.7	(NA)
Energy related	Mil. metric tons	9.0	8.7	8.4	8.4	8.7	8.2	(NA)
Transportation	Mil. metric tons	8.1	7.8	7.5	7.5	7.9	7.6	(NA)
Industrial processes	Mil. metric tons	9.4	9.3	9.5	9.6	9.8	9.9	(NA)
Solid waste disposal	Mil. metric tons	2.1	2.1	2.1	2.1	2.1	2.2	(NA)
Carbon monoxide, total	Mil. metric tons	91.3	88.3	85.3	85.4	89.6	83.5	(NA)
Energy related	Mil. metric tons	74.9	74.4	72.9	72.9	74.7	70.9	(NA)
Transportation	Mil. metric tons	70.3	69.6	67.8	68.5	70.3	67.4	(NA)
Stationary source fuel combustion	Mil. metric tons	4.6	4.8	5.0	4.5	4.4	3.5	(NA)
Industrial processes	Mil. metric tons	4.7	4.6	4.7	4.8	4.9	5.2	(NA)
Chloroflurocarbons (CFCs) gases [2]	1,000 metric tons	223	201	173	149	113	105	73
Hydrofluorocarbons	1,000 metric tons	5	5	8	11	18	22	34
Hydrochloroflurocarbons (HCFCs) gases [3]	1,000 metric tons	74	89	101	118	135	129	146
Other chemicals:								
Carbon tetrachloride	1,000 metric tons	30	-	26	22	16	5	5
Methyl Cloroform	1,000 metric tons	316	224	215	122	78	46	26
Sulfur hexafluoride	1,000 metric tons	1	1	1	1	1	1	1

- Represents zero. NA Not available. [1] Includes minor sources not shown separately. [2] Covers principally CFC-11, CFC-12, and CFC-113. [3] Covers principally HCFC-22.

Source: U.S. Energy Information Administration, *Emissions of Greenhouse Gases in the United States, annual.*

Notes at the beginning of many *Statistical Abstract* tables cite related tables in *Historical Statistics of the United States: Colonial Times to 1970*. This two-volume set compiles popular statistical data from the earliest time it was available, includes an index, and presents comprehensive source notes from which the user can often track data to their earliest published sources. One should remember that statistics were gathered on a much smaller scale in the past, so *Historical Statistics* is unable to provide older data for many data items treated in the *Statistical Abstract*. Also useful in the *Statistical Abstract* are the appendices, which list major statistical publications of the federal agencies, states, and foreign countries.

For a broad range of statistical data on states, counties, and cities, consult the *County and City Data Book*, the *State and Metropolitan Area Data Book*, *USA Counties*, and the *American FactFinder*. Each of these Census Bureau compendiums compiles statistics from many agencies. Each includes data for major topics such as population, housing, retail trade, crime, agriculture, education, and employment. Generally, there is more information available for counties and metropolitan areas than for smaller cities. The *County and City Data Book* is available both in print and on CD-ROM.[66] *USA Counties* is only on CD-ROM. The *American FactFinder* is an evolving, interactive application on the Census Web site that will eventually serve as an interface to an even broader amount of census data.[67]

In addition to compiling statistics from many government agencies into the above compendiums, the Census Bureau gathers and publishes a wealth of information based on its own programs. The *United States Census of Population and Housing* remains its single largest endeavor. A population census has been conducted every ten years since 1790; housing data were added to the census in 1940. The original function of the *United States Census of Population and Housing* was to provide the official population counts to calculate each state's congressional apportionment. Although it still serves this purpose, its results are also important in the allocation of federal monies to states and metropolitan areas for various federal programs, and as an unparalleled statistical portrait of the country of vital use to researchers and general citizens alike. The *United States Census of Population and Housing* provides a representative picture of the U.S. population. It consists of a small number of questions asked of everyone and additional questions asked of a sample of the population, reporting data on age, race, sex, household relationships, income, employment, characteristics of housing, and other variables. Data are published for the nation as a whole, states, counties, metropolitan areas, cities, and several smaller geographic representations called Census Tracts, Block Numbering Areas, Block Groups, and Blocks. Small businesses and marketers especially make use of data for these smaller geographic areas.

The 1990 Census saw a large effort by the Census Bureau to make data available electronically as well as in print. A Web application and a series of CD-ROMs with software allowing selective data access make finding and manipulating data into other software applications easier than ever before. Current plans for the 2000 Census focus primarily on the electronic distribution of results, likely via both the Web and CD-ROM. Scaled down print editions containing the most popular and essential data will still be available. Although many depositories will have the complete set of the *United States Census of Population and Housing* volumes in all formats, a smaller, nondepository library may consider buying only a print volume or CD-ROM summarizing U.S. results and a similar volume for their own and neighboring states. Some libraries may choose to rely solely on what is available via the Web.

In addition to the large Census conducted every ten years, the Census Bureau conducts various surveys and makes statistical estimates and projections every year. Some of the results of these efforts are published in the topical series *Current Population Reports*. Reports in this series, which cover topics such as poverty, education, income, and various demographics, are now available primarily via the Census Web site. Other survey and sample results, such as the burgeoning *American Community Survey*, aim to update data from the decennial census.

Although not as large as the *United States Census of Population and Housing*, the *Economic Census* is conducted every five years and presents a statistical portrait of U.S. businesses. Businesses are counted and categorized by type, and data such as number of employees and net sales are collected. Data are available by type of business and for states and counties. The 1997 *Economic Census* marked the first time businesses were categorized using the *North American Industry Classification System (NAICS)* codes; previously, *the Standard Industrial Classification Manual (SIC)* codes were used.[68] The *NAICS* codes include categories for many new types of businesses, such as those engaged in activities based on various emerging technologies (e.g., Internet Service Providers). The results of the *Economic Census* are published in print, CD-ROM, and online formats, but the trend is clearly toward Web publishing (note that beginning with 1997, the agriculture portion of the *Economic Census* is published by the Department of Agriculture).

The annual *Economic Report of the President*, from the Council of Economic Advisors, includes a long discussion of current economic policy and trends, followed by a series of time-series tables of U.S. economic data on topics from GDP to employment to interest rates. For popular economic data, the *Economic Report of the President* may be the most useful general volume. Much of the information in the *Economic Report of the President* is collected from historical Bureau of Labor Statistics data and the monthly *Economic Indicators*, a congressional publication featuring official statistics mostly on macroeconomic topics.

Another wide-ranging statistical government source is the *STAT-USA* Web site, a product of the U.S. Department of Commerce. *STAT-USA* (and the related *National Trade Data Bank* and *USA Trade* CD-ROMs) is a clearinghouse of trade and economic information and data. It contains the full text of thousands of reports, including many key statistical titles. *STAT-USA*, although a government site, is required by law to be self-funding; therefore it must recoup its costs. Accordingly, it requires a fee to use. Depository libraries, however, are allowed a free logon with which users may access *STAT-USA* from within a depository library.

There are several other major agencies whose important statistical reports are used frequently for reference service. These include the Bureau of Labor Statistics, the National Center for Health Statistics, the National Center for Education Statistics, the Bureau of Justice Statistics, and the Bureau of Economic Analysis.

The Bureau of Labor Statistics (BLS) publishes numerous serial statistical products. Chief among these are the monthly *Consumer Price Index Detailed Report*, the source for official price and inflation data, and *Employment and Earnings*, the source for employment and unemployment statistics. A pioneer in Web publishing among statistical agencies, BLS's interactive Web site allows the user to access various specific data and also includes the eminently useful summary *Economy at a Glance*.

The National Center for Health Statistics (NCHS) publishes *Health, United States*, the *Vital Statistics of the United States*, and a series of reports and CD-ROMs based on various health surveys. *Health, United States* is an annual volume summarizing the health condition and trends of the nation. *Vital Statistics of the United States*, an annual volume supplemented by frequent updates, is the official source for fatality and natality data. For example, one may find deaths by cause by state, or births by characteristics of the baby and mother. The many surveys conducted by the National Center for Health Statistics—such as the *National Health Interview Survey*—form the basis of numerous reports on various topics relating to the health of the American people.

The National Center for Education Statistics (NCES) collects data about American education and its institutions. Popular volumes on education are the annuals *Digest of Education Statistics* and *Condition of Education*, which both present statistics on current education trends. The text of these volumes is also available on the NCES Web site, as are many other education reports.

Crime in the United States (also known as *Uniform Crime Reports*) and the *Sourcebook of Criminal Justice Statistics* are valuable statistical reports on American crime published by the Bureau of Justice Statistics (BJS). BJS also publishes a variety of smaller, single-topic statistical volumes on crime topics. Many are available via the BLS Web site.

The Bureau of Economic Analysis publishes economic data, including statistics on income and national accounts, in its monthly *Survey of Current Business*, its annual CD-ROM *Regional Economic Information System* (*REIS*), and in several other publications. *REIS*, with over twenty years of various economic data at the national, state, and county levels, is especially useful.

Several educational institutions have created useful Web interfaces to federal government statistical data and products. Oregon State University's *Government Information Sharing Project* offers the latest *Census of Population and Housing, Economic Census, USA Counties, Regional Economic Information System*, and other products. Among the many public resources available through the University of Virginia's Social Science Data Center are interfaces to *County Business Patterns*, the *County and City Data Book*, and *National Income and Product Accounts*. Also deserving special mention is the *United States Historical Census Data Browser*, a product of the Instructional Computing Group of Harvard University, in cooperation with the Inter-university Consortium for Political and Social Research at the University of Michigan, which makes selected data from the U.S. Census back to 1790 (the first census) available online.

All federal statistical data are in the public domain. This means that private publishers may use federal data to create their own statistical reference works. In fact, many excellent statistical reference sources are published in this way, as private publishers may repackage statistical data in formats that may be easier to use than official government documents. They also may publish data that are difficult to find or bring together statistics from government and nongovernment sources. Titles such as *CQ's State Fact Finder: Rankings Across America*, from Congressional Quarterly Books, and *State Rankings*, from Morgan Quitno Corp., compile statistics for states for numerous variables. Bernan Press produces a number of useful volumes using mostly federal government data, such as *Business Statistics of the United States, Handbook of U.S. Labor Statistics*, and George Kurian's *Datapedia of the United States 1790–2000: America Year by Year*. A number of useful volumes focus on specific demographic groups, such as Louise Hornor's *Black Americans: A Statistical Sourcebook,* and Frank Schick and Renee Schick's *Statistical Handbook on Aging Americans*. Another private product is *CensusCD + Maps*, a CD-ROM from GeoLytics, which compiles *United States Census of Population and Housing* data onto a single CD and adds a mapping component to create simple thematic maps.

These maps are based on the Census Bureau's *Topographically Integrated Geographic Encoding and Referencing System, TIGER.*[69] *TIGER* contains digital map information for all Census geographic entities, and may be used, along with the *United States Census of Population and Housing* data itself, with commercial GIS (Geographical Information System) applications. In its simplest form, GIS allows users to combine statistical data and maps to create thematic maps. For example, *LandView* (currently in its third release, *LandView III*) is a simple GIS-type program distributed via a set of CDs from the Environmental Protection Agency. The CDs contain the *LandView* program, selected *United States Census of Population and Housing* data, and several environmental variables. *LandView* then uses the data as the base for some simple thematic mapping. The Census Bureau has been developing mapping capabilities to use via the Web as well; see the *American FactFinder* for a nice thematic mapping program. Other agencies, especially the USGS, offer many spatial data resources.[70]

In addition to the many federal publications that feature statistics for states, state governments themselves collect and publish statistical data. One may identify these publications through an index such as the *Statistical Reference Index (SRI)*. Lacking the *SRI*, librarians should familiarize themselves with the major state government statistical publications available about their particular state.

International and foreign country data are compiled in many excellent sources. The *Statistical Abstract of the United States* contains a chapter of basic international statistics, with broader data on topics related to the United States (foreign aid, immigration, exports and imports). The *Index to International Statistics (IIS)* is an excellent way to identify international statistics. Major statistical publications of international organizations and foreign governments are also listed in *Statistics Sources* and in an appendix to the *Statistical Abstract of the United States*.

Box 22.3 Statistical Search Strategy

A user asks for "statistics about computers." The reference interview reveals that the user is specifically interested in data on use patterns of home personal computers. Begin with the most current *Statistical Abstract of the United States*. The index to the 1999 edition has "Personal Computers" cross-referenced to "Computers." Looking under "Computer Use" one sees a list of tables. The best one is Table 924, titled "Use of Home Computers," which features numbers and percentages of Americans using home computers by certain demographic characteristics. The source of this table is the 1999 *Digest of Education Statistics* (from the National Center for Education Statistics), so one can check that title for more detailed data. It includes tables 431 ("Access to home computers, by selected characteristics of students and other users: October 1997") and 432 ("Percent of home computer users using specific applications, by selected characteristics: October 1997"). Notes provided with these tables reveal that all of this information is based on *Current Population Survey (CPS)* responses; a particularly savvy user may want to access the raw data from the appropriate *CPS* via the Census Web site.[71] If the user still wants more, a search of *FedStats* also turns up several useful documents, including a number of tables from the Web version of the National Science Foundation's (NSF) *1998 Science and Engineering Indicators*,[72] another NSF document titled *Complex Picture of Computer Use in the Home Emerges*,[73] and a Census Bureau document, *Computer Use and Ownership*.[74] Finally, a search of *Statistical Universe* finds the above reports as well as a large number of further potential sources, mainly from private and industry publishers, and most on specific aspects of computer use.

Some of the best international statistics are those produced under the broad umbrella of the United Nations. The UN publishes numerous statistical volumes, highlighted by the *Statistical Yearbook* and *Demographic Yearbook*, each of which compile a number of useful demographic, social, and economic statistics for countries worldwide. Much information may also be found via the UN Web site, such as via *InfoNation*, an interactive application for finding popular statistical data for foreign nations.

Also worthy of special mention is the World Bank's *World Development Indicators*, among the most detailed statistical compilations for the world's nations. Social, demographic, and economic statistics are included, as well as data on environmental factors and government finance. *World Development Indicators* is available in print and on CD-ROM; the CD-ROM includes time-series for all available indicators and is the successor to the World Bank's *World Tables*.

In addition to the various international organizations' statistical volumes, many of the world's nations publish their own statistical compendiums, somewhat akin to the U.S. *Statistical Abstract of the United States*. Collections of these volumes may be purchased in a microfiche set called *Current National Statistical Compendiums* from Congressional Information Service (CIS). And although no nation can quite match the U.S. Census Bureau's wealth of information via the Web, statistical agencies of many nations do have evolving Web sites.

Finally, many private publications do an excellent job of gathering international and foreign statistics. Sources such as the *Europa World Year Book* and *The World Almanac and Book of Facts* (see Chapter 15) each contain summary statistics for the world and its nations, and also include a variety of other information.

Canadian Government Documents

Canadian government documents, like U.S. government documents, are current, accurate, inexpensive, and indispensable reference sources. They are administered and distributed through the National Library of Canada's Depository Services Program (DSP) in a fashion somewhat analogous to the GPO's Federal Depository Library Program. There are currently forty-eight *full* depository libraries in Canada, and one each in England, Germany, Japan, and the United States. The rest of the depositories are *selectives.* Canadian public libraries and also libraries of the country's educational institutions that are open to the public or their clientele minimally twenty hours per week and have one full-time employee are granted selective status. The Depository Service Program's *Depository Libraries* Web site, with various information about the program and documents, features an "About the Program" page (http://dsp-psd.pwgsc.gc.ca/dsp-psd/AboutDSP/dspcont-e.html) with links to pertinent information. Depository locations and addresses are also available via the DSP site. *What's Up Doc?*, the newsletter of the Depository Services Program, is published two to three times each year and distributed free. Its primary purpose is to provide administrative news, minutes from meetings, statistics regarding the depository program, and bibliographic information regarding ceased or reclassified titles.

The *Government of Canada Primary Internet Site (Canada Site)* is the nation's official Web site. From here, one may see the "Government at a Glance" pages (http://canada.gc.ca/howgoc/glance_e.html) for an orientation and links to the major national-level government entities, including Sovereign, the Governor General, Parliament, the Prime Minister and the Cabinet, and the Judiciary. One can also learn the organization of Canadian government through *How Government Works: A Primer*, developed by the Institute of Governance. This Web site describes itself as an insider's view on "who does what to whom and why." All materials at the *Government of Canada Primary Internet Site* can be accessed in either English or French.

Government Information in Canada, a quarterly e-journal of the University of Saskatchewan Libraries,[75] is an essential source for specialists and other librarians who want to keep informed about Canadian government information policies, depository library programs, and professional issues and innovations, as well as new resources and products. The *Depository Libraries* Web page also includes recent "Reports from the Depository Services Program" (http://dsp-psd.pwgsc.gc.ca/Rapports/index-e.html), which are helpful in understanding the current distribution mechanisms and anticipating future plans.

For background, a complete discussion of the early history, evolution, problems, and status of the Canadian Depository Library Program through the late 1980s can be found in Elizabeth Dolan's, *The Depository Dilemma: A Study of the Free Distribution of Canadian Federal Government Publications to Depository Libraries in Canada.* The author describes the official origins of the program, the role of various agencies, and pressures that combined to form the system in place until recently.

Identification and Selection of Canadian Documents

Following is a brief discussion of the identification and acquisition of some of the basic guides, indexes, and primary sources used for Canadian administrative, parliamentary, and statistical research.

The *Weekly Checklist of Canadian Government Publications* is the standard source for acquiring books and serial titles from federal departments, the Parliament, and Statistics Canada. The *Weekly Checklist*, produced by Canadian Government Publishing, which is part of the Communications Coordination Services Branch of the Public Works and Government Services Canada, includes both free and priced items. Full depositories receive a single copy in English and French of all items listed for distribution in the program, and selectives choose from the *Weekly Checklist*. Each library is responsible for claiming, processing, maintaining, and providing access to the publications received. Different types of materials are required to be kept for varying lengths of time. Retention and disposition guidelines are provided by the DSP (http://dsp-psd.pwgsc.gc.ca/dsp-psd/AboutDSP/retention-e.html). Selectors have fifty working days in which to place orders from date of issue. This process can be done over the Web or on paper (a print edition is still mailed). It is a useful acquisitions tool in nondepositories as well, and free publications can usually be obtained from the issuing agencies. Within the *Weekly Checklist,* URLs are provided in both formats.

Important General Canadian Sources

Canadian government reference sources fall into many of the same categories already discussed for U.S. federal sources. Like other titles treated in this text, they include directories, fact books, catalogs, and indexes, and, like U.S. federal reference materials, they are the authoritative sources for laws, regulations, and statistics. A selection of the most important sources are discussed in the following sections.

Guides: Canada

Canadian government publications are described in various specialized reference sources. One of these is *Canadian Official Publications*, by Olga B. Bishop, volume 9 of the Pergamon series Guides to Official Publications. This source offers very detailed annotations of parliamentary, administrative, and statistical publications. In addition to listing important titles, the author discusses the agencies responsible for the documents, as well as the publication history of long-standing series. The descriptive notes are particularly helpful. Karen F. Smith's succinct, excellent introduction to Canadian government documents and information, Chapter 15, "Foreign and International Documents," in *Tapping the Government Grapevine,* can be used to update Bishop's book. The ALA/Government Documents Round Table's *Guide to Official Publications of Foreign Countries* includes a Canada section, compiled by Carol Goodger-Hill and Doug Home. This core list of essential reference tools focuses on current resources and includes a selection of topical resources, such as publications on the economy, health, human rights, and the status of women.

The DSP's Web-based "Guides" (http://dsp-psd.pwgsc.gc.ca/dsp-psd/Reference/guides-e.html) include links to Help Sheets, Serials Information, and three primary categories of government Web sites: Government of Canada, Provincial Government, and Provincial Printers. These Guides are a key tool for anyone fielding Canadian government information requests, and also include links to comprehensive and vital library resources. *Canadian Government Information on the Internet*, by Anita Cannon, the DSP, and contributors, is an extensive guide to online Canadian government information, as is the National Library of Canada's *Canadian Information by Subject*. Fran Rose's compilation, *Some Canadian Academic and Government Libraries with Government Information Web Pages*, provides direct access to these institutional guides, with links to the Web pages of various government publications departments. The importance of networking and utilizing local resources cannot be overemphasized on the road to success as a government information specialist. For example, the University of Saskatchewan Libraries' Government Publications, Maps and Microforms Department maintains a particularly well-organized and well-designed *Federal Government of Canada* (http://moondog.usask.ca/govpub/federal.html) set of links, including direct access to national-level political parties. It provides one-stop access, whether the Bloc Québécois, the Green Party, or the Progressive Conservative Party is of interest.

ALA/GODORT International Documents Task Force's home page (http://govinfo.ucsd.edu/idtf) is another clearinghouse of instructional materials on foreign governments and links to important professional toolkits such as "Acquiring International Documents," by Chuck Eckman, and "Foreign Governments: Strategies for Locating Foreign Government Information on the Internet," by Helen Sheehy.

Canadian official publications are covered in some detail by general guides to reference sources, such as Balay's *Guide to Reference Books*. Guides for the documents of multiple foreign countries will also be useful, including the aforementioned *Guide to Official Publications of Foreign Countries* and, for historical works, Vladimir Palic's *Government Publications: A Guide to Bibliographic Tools*. A related ALA Government Documents Round Table reference book, edited by Marian Shaaban, is the *Guide to Country Information in International Governmental Organization Publications*. This annotated guide is helpful in determining appropriate sources in a reference situation, as well as for building a collection.

Catalogs and Indexes: Canada

The bibliographic control of Canadian documents remained in its nascency until the late 1920s. Publications for sale by the Department of Public Printing and Stationery were listed in the *Price List of Government Publications*, first published in 1895. A more complete catalog, the *Catalogue of Official Publications of the Parliament and Government of Canada*, was issued in 1928, and included all types of official publications, whether copies were available from the King's Printer or the issuing agency. In 1953, a formal system for control and recording of Dominion government publications was begun with the issuance of a daily checklist and monthly and annual catalogs titled *Canadian Government Publications*, which existed until 1978. The *Government of Canada Publications: Quarterly Catalogue* and its annual cumulation continued through 1992. The *Weekly Checklist of Canadian Government Publications*, mentioned above, was also a component of this series, and it remains current. A *Weekly Checklist of Canadian Government Publications Supplement*, for example, separate compilations of the Library of Parliament or federal government publications available via the Web, is produced and available in both print and electronic format. A *Weekly Checklist Catalogue* (http://dsp-psd.pwgsc.gc.ca/search_form-e.html) represents the DSP's searchable database of information—basically GILS records[76]—about Canadian government publications. Coverage begins in 1993, and it is updated on a weekly basis. As its name implies, its records come from the *Weekly Checklist*. Abstracts are included, as is ordering information. Hot links are also provided. The DSP's *Electronic Publications* (http://dsp-psd.pwgsc.gc.ca/dsp-psd/epubs-e.html) features fee-based sources, such as *Finance Canada*, although depositories may have free access. The DSP site also publishes the now Web-based *Consolidated List of Serials of the Government of Canada* to facilitate acquisitions and access.

Canadiana, the country's national bibliography, began in 1951. Issued by the National Library of Canada in parts, originally only dominion official publications were included. In 1954, provincial government publications were added to the multipart annual series. *Canadiana* is discussed in more detail in Chapter 20. For a detailed list of retrospective bibliographies of Canadian government publications, including titles that record provincial documents, consult Palic's *Government Publications: A Guide to Bibliographic Tools.*

Factual/Directory Information: Canada

Regularly revised directories, handbooks, and manuals are produced by the government as well as by commercial publishers. *Info Source* is the government's annual directory and organizational manual; it describes the executive and administrative departments. Addresses, phone numbers, and e-mail addresses are provided. The *Government of Canada Primary Internet Site* maintains a link to the primary types of "Directories" (http://canada.gc.ca/directories/direct_e.html) and to a "Programs and Services" index (http://canada.gc.ca/programs/program_e.html). It also includes sections "About Canada," "About Government," and the useful "InfoCentre" (http://canada.gc.ca/infocentre/), designed to provide "quick access to government of Canada information." The *Canada Year Book* is a well-indexed standard reference work that includes statistical tables and graphs, along with descriptive information concerning all aspects of Canada's natural resources, economic and social conditions, government organizations, finance, and industries. It is published biennially in both hardbound and CD-ROM formats. *Canada: A Portrait* is a collection of essays, including photographs, chronicling the country's "social, economic and intellectual life." It is also published biennially, is indexed, and complements the *Year Book*. Both volumes are available from Statistics Canada. *Canadian Almanac & Directory*, from Micromedia, is an expansive compendium of directory information for governmental and nongovernmental organizations, and it includes coverage for municipalities. From abbreviations and airline companies to the Yukon government and zoological gardens, it is a convenient source for quick facts, basic statistics, and street and e-mail addresses, as well as URLs, if available. Color plates of flags, arms and emblems, honors, and a map of Canada add to this important tool. Many of the sections have been revised to include the new territory of Nunavut. *Canadian Government Programs and*

Services, from CCH Canadian Ltd., is an updated, looseleaf reporting service that provides information on the latest changes in the organization of the government. Detailed information on the structure, functions, and responsibilities of the government's departments and agencies is presented.

Legislative Documents: Canada

The *Canadian Parliamentary Guide/Guide Parlementaire Canadien* is an annual title that details the current membership of the legislative and judicial branches of the government. It includes biographical information on the members of the Senate and House of Commons, the Supreme Court and Federal Court of Canada, and the provincial legislatures. Also listed are Canadian government representatives abroad and foreign representatives in Canada, members of boards and commissions, results of general elections dating back to 1867, members of the Privy council, and members of the Royal family.

For a detailed discussion of the process through which bills become laws, refer to a general guide such as Bishop's *Canadian Official Publications* or a pertinent Web site. For example, *Parliamentary Internet Parlementaire*, the Web site of Canada's Parliament, includes the section "Canada's Parliament; Democracy in Action" (http://www.parl.gc.ca/36/servpub/visitors/about/content-e.htm), which provides the basic steps in the legislative process. More detailed reference works, such as the "Standing Orders of the House of Commons," are accessible via the "Reference Works" page (http://www.parl.gc.ca/36/rm-ref-e.htm). The more extensive guides, such as Bishop's text or the several guides available via the "Reference Works" page, will either take the researcher through the parliamentary process and/or describe the role of primary sources, including *Bills of the House of Commons*; *Bills of the Senate of Canada*; *Debates of the Senate: Official Report; House of Commons Debates: Official Report* (both of which are referred to as Hansard after the first King's printer); *House of Commons Journals*; *House of Commons Votes and Proceedings*; *Journals of the Senate of Canada;* and *Minutes of the Proceedings of the Senate*. Bishop also discusses the *Canada Gazette*. As described in the *Guide to Official Publications of Foreign Countries,* the *Canada Gazette, Part I* contains government notices of a general nature, official proclamations, certain orders-in-council, and various other types of statutory notices; *Part II* gives the text of all regulations that must be reported according to the *Statutory Instruments Act (1971)* and certain other statutory instruments and documents. *Part III* publishes the text of the public acts of Canada, including a list of those acts that have been proclaimed from the date of the last issue of the *Canada Gazette Part III*. The purpose of this publication is to make available those acts that have received Royal Assent and will be published as the *Statutes of Canada* (also called *Acts of the Parliament of Canada*) at the end of the parliamentary session. Occasionally, *Part III* also includes the "Table of Public Statutes" from 1907 to the date of the current issue, which shows the chapters of the *Revised Statutes* and amendments to statutes, and a listing of acts and the ministers responsible for them. Bishop's guide also elaborates on the functions and relationships of the *Consolidated Regulations of Canada*, *Revised Statutes of Canada*, and the historical set of the *Statutes of Canada*. *Parliamentary Internet Parlementaire* also contains a section called "Parliamentary Business," which includes government bills from 1997 to the present, whereas the "Senators and Members" section lists both current and historical members of Parliament. Also useful in this section is "Bills: User Guide" (http://www.parl.gc.ca/36/2/parlbus/chambus/house/bills/guibill-e.htm).

Statistical Sources: Canada

Statistics Canada is the central federal government agency responsible for the collection, analysis, and publication of statistical data about Canada. Statistics Canada publishes several excellent catalogs of their own publications. These include *Historical Catalogue of Statistics Canada Publications, 1918–1980*, which provides information on all Statistics Canada titles ever published. Publication histories are included for recurring titles, as are brief abstracts.

Statistics Canada Catalogue is similar in format, but is a comprehensive listing of all currently available Statistics Canada publications. It is arranged by subject categories (e.g., general, manufacturing, commerce, education, health and welfare).

As mentioned earlier, the major official statistical reference work is the *Canada Year Book*. This is supplemented by *Historical Statistics of Canada*, edited by F. H. Leacy, which presents a broad spectrum of statistical time-series dealing with social and economic data covering the period from 1867 to 1974. The Statistics Canada Web site, available at http://www.statcan.ca/, contains a plethora of data and detailed information concerning *CANSIM*, a large database of Canadian socio-economic data.

A major census is taken every ten years in the year ending in "1." In addition, a less detailed census is taken decennially in the year ending in "6." Publications of these censuses are listed in the *Statistics Canada Catalogue* and in the *Historical Catalogue of Statistics Canada Publications, 1918–1980*. Micromedia Ltd. offers microfiche copies of census publications.

This discussion of Canadian documents has been necessarily brief. The reader is advised to consult the "List of Sources" and "Additional Readings" in this chapter for detailed information on research sources and their uses.

SEARCH STRATEGIES

As a rule, reference librarians should consider using government documents to answer questions pertaining to a government agency and its programs or personnel. Numerous directories are available from the government and from commercial publishers (see also Chapter 14); beyond those, very detailed information will be found in an agency's own directory, handbook, annual report, or Web site. If a user asks who the Surgeon General of the United States is, the first choice is the most up-to-date directory in the collection, probably the *United States Government Manual* or the *Federal Staff Directory,* the latter of which is updated frequently. It is important to keep in mind that changes in personnel can occur, whether due to the outcome of an election, new political appointment, or reorganization. However, if the user wants to know who was the Surgeon General during World War II, one can use an older edition of the *United States Government Manual* or the *Official Congressional Directory*. If the user wants to know who works for the Surgeon General in several subagencies, one would use the *Federal Staff Directory*. If the user wants to know when the Surgeon General's office was established and if it was ever organized differently, one would consult the *Government Manual*.

When looking for government publications on a particular subject, start the search in the *Catalog of United States Government Publications*. Specialized lists are published as individual *Subject Bibliography: SB* titles. Periodical articles are found through the *U.S. Government Periodicals Index* (1994– ; coverage October 1993–), *Index to U.S. Government Periodicals* (1970–1987), and *PAIS*, as well as *ASI*. If the topic sounds as though it might involve government-funded research, try to find citations in the *NTIS Electronic Catalog*. In any case, if the user knows of an issuing agency or source, use a Web site such as *Federal Agency Internet Sites* or the *Federal Web Locator* to find the home page of the appropriate source to see if there is "Publications" information there.

If the user has only a report number and wants to identify the document, try to determine the origin of the alphabetical part of the number (e.g., PHS for Public Health Service, EIA for Energy Information Administration, NTSB for National Transportation Safety Board). Knowing the issuing agency will help determine if the report is more likely to be an administrative or a research publication. Administrative reports can be identified by using the *Catalog*, whereas research and development reports will be identified in *NTIS*. Both of these sources include report number indexes. Specialized, topical indexes that include government reports are also an option.

If the user has a SuDoc number with no date, try the *Catalog* or a union catalog such as *WorldCat* via *OCLC FirstSearch*. If the report precedes 1976, when SuDoc number indexes were not produced, use the number to determine the issuing agency and consult the corporate author index. Many thousands of pre-1976 government documents have been cataloged and may be found via *WorldCat*. There may be occasions when a user knows only a common or unofficial name for a document, such as the "Warren Report" or the "Plum Book." *Popular Names of U.S. Government Reports* is a specialized index that gives the correct title of such publications along with the complete bibliographic citation. Also, many popular names are included in the "Notes" field of the MARC record, and may be identified via *WorldCat*.

Legislative reference service can most easily be accomplished by using online services such as *GPO Access*, *THOMAS*, *Congressional Universe*, or *CQ.com On Congress*, although the print *CIS/Index* remains invaluable for those who do not have access to it via *Congressional Universe*. Many users will find that the Congressional Quarterly products, such as *Congressional Quarterly Weekly Report*, give sufficient details to help them understand and trace a particular piece of legislation, but a depository library may also have the primary documents, bills, congressional reports and documents, hearings, committee prints, debates, and laws. Most of the source documents are best accessed through the indexes mentioned above. If someone wants to know the status of legislation that has been proposed in the current Congress to change the minimum wage, *Congressional Universe* or the "Major Legislation" section of *THOMAS* will identify, by subject, the bill number, provide a brief summary, and indicate if hearings were held and if the bill was reported out of committee. If the user needs historical background and wants to know who supported the legislation, use *Congressional Quarterly Weekly Report*. To find an abstract of relevant hearings with page references and names of witnesses, the *Congressional Universe* or *CIS/Index* is the best choice; lacking those resources, one may be able to identify the title and call number of the hearing via the *Catalog* or *WorldCat*. If a compiled legislative history is needed, *GPO Access*'s "History of Bills" would be one convenient source, as all the above services offer legislative histories. *Congressional Universe* or *CIS/Index* would be the best choice for legislative histories of older materials. *Congressional Universe* can also be used to quickly answer regulatory questions that might otherwise be particularly time-consuming. With sophisticated electronic systems, these types of questions can be answered fairly rapidly. Without these sources, it would be next to impossible, in some cases, to obtain an answer at all.

For statistical data, there is almost always an appropriate governmental source. The data will be reliable, complete, and usually up-to-date. It is always appropriate to start by trying the *Statistical Abstract of the United States*. Use the *Abstract* for complete data, and as an index to other sources. Remember that, as its title implies, it is an abstract; that is, the data tables presented are condensed from other sources, which can be traced through source notes. In addition, notes will frequently guide the user to *Historical Statistics of the United States: Colonial Times to 1970* for earlier data. If statistics are not found through these or other basic sources, such as *County and City Data Book* or *State and Metropolitan Area Data Book*, the librarian will consult *American Statistics Index,* if available either in print or via *Statistical Universe*. Additionally, the librarian may check *FedStats* for any Web-available statistics on the topic. A statistic has to be collected to be reported. Requests for statistical information that is difficult to define and/or measure may have to be reinterpreted. For example, if a user were interested in finding the "number of elderly people who enjoy traveling," the query may have to be modified to the "number of people in their sixties who take pleasure trips."

Government documents are treated like any other material in major indexes and catalogs. One can expect to find documents along with commercial publications by using standard indexes, such as *PAIS International in Print,* and shared catalogs, such as *WorldCat*. To facilitate access and use, documents should be cataloged and organized as essential sources like any other material in the library collection. They should not be viewed as being particularly problematic or even different simply because of origin. In the not so distant past, users who wanted to find government information had to deal with a card catalog containing dozens of drawers and thousands of cards that all began "U.S.—," or they had to limit most of their bibliographic searches in print tools to the *Catalog*, which had only limited indexing. Those difficulties are now mitigated by excellent commercially produced products, computerized bibliographic systems, and keyword access through a variety of electronic sources. The fundamental point to remember is that if something can be investigated, counted, legislated, or regulated, the government has probably published information about it. In the past, present, and future, whether the issue is personal or political, local or global, government information can frequently be crucial to decision making. With advanced technology government sources are more readily accessible. Finding this information can be structured and strategic, and simultaneously, serendipitous and idiosyncratic. Whether innate or acquired, flexibility, imagination, creativity, and insightfulness, plus healthy doses of tenacity and political awareness, are necessary traits for any government information professional. Skilled librarians, who can work with the enormous variety of information tools and sources and "extract the maximum value" for their users and community, will ensure public access to government information.[77]

NOTES

1. 44 U.S.C. §1901.

2. U.S. Department of Energy, *Secretary's Annual Report to Congress* (Washington, D.C.: GPO, 1978–). Annual.

3. U.S. Department of State, Office of Allowances, *Foreign Per Diem Rates,* http://www.state.gov/www/perdiems/index.html.

4. U.S. Geological Survey, *Bulletins* (Washington D.C.: GPO, 1883–). Monographic Series.

5. U.S. Geological Survey, *Professional Papers* (Washington D.C.: GPO, 1902–). Monographic Series.

6. U.S. National Institutes of Health, National Cancer Institute, *Chances Are You Need a Mammogram: A Guide for Midlife and Older Women* (Washington, D.C.: GPO, 1996), 14p.

7. U.S. Social Security Administration, *How to Apply for Social Security Retirement Benefits,* http://www.ssa.gov/retirement.html.

8. For more discussion of the Superintendent of Documents Classification system, see: U.S. Government Printing Office, *An Explanation of the Superintendent of Documents Classification System* (Washington D.C.: GPO, 1990), 14p.

9. Although the .gov extension is the standard for government Web sites, military organizations use .mil, and some quasi-governmental entities, such as the Smithsonian Institution, may use another domain, such as .org or .edu. Most international government organizations use .org, most state governments use some variation on their postal abbreviation and "us" (e.g., http://www.state.wi.us), and foreign nations' governments generally use their assigned country extension. See the "Directories" section of this chapter for lists of links to government entities.

10. U.S. Department of Energy, *Department of Energy Reports Bibliographic Database,* http://apollo.osti.gov/html/dra/dra.html.

11. Important, large series of USGS research documents include *Bulletins*, *Professional Papers*, *Monographs*, *Open-File Reports*, and *Water Supply Papers.*

12. U.S. Environmental Protection Agency, *Toxic Release Inventory* (Washington, D.C.: GPO, 1987–). Annual.

13. The laws regarding the U.S. depository library program are found at 44 U.S.C. §1901. For more details on the rules regulating depository libraries, see *Instructions to Depository Libraries*, available: http://www.access.gpo.gov/su_docs/fdlp/pubs/instructions/index.html; and U.S. Government Printing Office, *The Federal Depository Library Manual* (Washington, D.C.: GPO, revised 1993), 180p.

14. Prior to 1994, the *Journal of Government Information* was titled *Government Publications Review.* Each issue includes reviews, and annually an issue is devoted to recent notable documents. In addition to federal documents, it includes reviews for documents from local, state/provincial, and national governments as well as international organizations.

15. *Library Journal* prints the ALA/GODORT Notable Documents Panel's annual selection of excellent government information sources for federal, international, and state and local sources. The selections appear in the May 15 issue.

16. U.S. Library of Congress, *Library of Congress Information Bulletin* (Washington, D.C.: GPO, 1943–). Monthly. (Also available: http://purl.access.gpo.gov/GPO/LPS1457).

17. U.S. Bureau of the Census, *Census and You* (Washington, D.C.: GPO, 1988–). Monthly. (Formerly *Data User News*.) (Also available: http://purl.access.gpo.gov/GPO/LPS1679).

18. For two superb discussions on the role of the government information professional, see Kathleen M. Heim, "Attitudinal and Operational Considerations for Education in the Provision of Government Information," *Government Publications Review* 12 (March/April 1985): 131-36; and Bernadine E. Abbott Hoduski, "Political Activism for Documents Librarians," in *Communicating Public Access to Government Information, Proceedings of the 2nd Annual Library Government Documents and Information Conference*, ed. Peter Hernon (Westport, Conn.: Meckler, 1982), 1-11.

19. Robert Balay, *Guide to Reference Books*, 11th ed. (Chicago: American Library Association, 1996), 2020p.

20. This chapter makes occasional mention of the work of various committees and task forces of GODORT, the Government Documents Round Table of the American Library Association. For more information, see the GODORT Web site (http://www.lib.berkeley.edu/GODORT/).

21. A comprehensive directory of U.S. depository Web sites is Lily Wai's (University of Idaho), http://www.lib.uidaho.edu/govdoc/otherdep.html.

22. The *Documents Data Miner*, from Wichita State University, the National Institute for Aviation Research, and the Federal Depository Library Program, is an excellent tool to aid depository librarians in the item selection process and for other collection development and reference tasks, and includes a version of the *List of Classes*. It is available at http://govdoc.wichita.edu/ddm/GdocFrames.asp. Also, the *Federal Bulletin Board*, sponsored by the Superintendent of Documents, GPO, maintains an electronic version of the *List of Classes*, designed to be downloaded by documents librarians into collection development databases or other tools. It is available at ftp://fedbbs.access.gpo.gov/gpo_bbs/class/listclas.txt, monthly.

23. Background and history of the *Catalog of United States Government Publications* and its print predecessor, the *Monthly Catalog of United States Government Publications (MOCAT)*, is available at http://www.access.gpo.gov/su_docs/locators/cgp/a_catalog.html.

24. Production of the microfiche ceased after December 1995, and the magnetic tape version of MOCAT still exists in its present form.

25. *GOV.Research_Center* is a joint venture between NTIS and the National Information Services Corporation.

26. For background on the NTIS/GPO Depository Library Pilot Project, including a list of participants, see http://deplib.ntis.gov.

27. For background on the closure and possible future of NTIS and NTIS resources, see *Preliminary Assessment of NTIS Closure*, http://www.nclis.gov/govt/ntis/ntis.html.

28. For information about GITCO's *CD-ROM Documentation Project*, visit its home page at http://www.library.ucsb.edu/ala/gitco/cdromdoc/index.html. The actual database may be accessed at http://tango.lib.uiowa.edu:8003/govpubs/gitco.taf.

29. SIGCAT is the largest member of the Federation of Government Information Processing Councils; for information on the Councils, see http://www.fgipc.org.

30. For background about the *StateList* project and its predecessors, see *About the StateList Project*, http://www.law.uiuc.edu/library/check/project.htm.

31. There are numerous state and local groups and organizations of government information librarians. A small sampling is available at http://library.berkeley.edu/GODORT/profpage.html; to identify groups, however, the best way is simply to ask your local depository librarian.

32. U.S. Bureau of Labor Statistics, *Monthly Labor Review* (Washington, D.C.: GPO, 1918–). Monthly.

33. U.S. Centers for Disease Control and Prevention, *Morbidity and Mortality Weekly Report* (Washington, D.C.: GPO, 1952–). Weekly.

34. *Time* and the *Monthly Labor Review*, for example, are both indexed by the *Readers' Guide to Periodical Literature* (from the H. W. Wilson Co.), while *Morbidity and Mortality Weekly Report* and the *New England Journal of Medicine* are both indexed by *MEDLINE* (from the National Library of Medicine).

35. U.S. National Institute of Environmental Health Sciences, *Environmental Health Perspectives* (Washington, D.C.: GPO, 1972–). Monthly.

36. American Chemical Society, *Chemical Abstracts* (Columbus, Ohio: American Chemical Society, 1907–). Weekly. (Also available electronically via the SciFinder Scholar system; see http://www.cas.org/SCIFINDER/SCHOLAR/index.html).

37. For discussion of the issues of different public and private versions of the same database, see "Evaluation Criteria for Different Versions of the Same Database: A Comparison of *Medline* Services," by Betsy Anagnostelis and Alison Cooke, presented at Online Information 97: The 21st International Online Information Meeting, London, 9-11 December, 1997, and reproduced at http://biome.ac.uk/sage/iolim97.html.

38. A useful comparison chart of four *free* versions of *ERIC* may be found at http://www.accesseric.org:81/searchdb/dbchart.html.

39. U.S. Department of Energy, *Department of Energy Reports Bibliographic Database*, http://apollo.osti.gov/html/dra/dra.html.

40. This information may be searched at *Federal Depository Library Directory*, http://www.access.gpo.gov/su_docs/fdlp/tools/ldirect.html.

41. See Lily Wai's Web site, http://www.lib.uidaho.edu/govdoc/otherdep.html.

42. Judith Schiek Robinson. *Tapping the Government Grapevine: The User-Friendly Guide to U.S. Government Information Sources*, 3d ed. (Phoenix, Ariz.: Oryx Press, 1998), 90.

43. Ibid.

44. Joe Morehead, *Introduction to United States Government Information Sources*, 6th ed. (Englewood, Colo.: Libraries Unlimited, 1999), 146. Note that the legislative process is discussed in more detail in several of the titles listed in the "Guides" section, especially Morehead's and *Tapping the Government Grapevine*. For a book-length treatment, see Congressional Quarterly's *How Congress Works*, 3d ed. (Washington, D.C.: Congressional Quarterly, 1998), 184p.

45. See the list at http://thomas.loc.gov/liv/livtoc.html.

46. E.g., see the search page (http://thomas.loc.gov/bss/legstage.html).

47. Coverage for the 106th Congress can be found at http://thomas.loc.gov/bss/d106/hot-subj.html.

48. CCH is a major publisher of law and accounting resources. For information, see http://www.cch.com.

49. Note that although *Congressional Universe* itself is available to subscribers at http://web.lexis-nexis.com/congcomp, nonsubscribers may not access any information there. Information about *Congressional Universe* is available at CIS's Web site (http://www.cispubs.com).

50. These bill digests are from CRS, the Congressional Research Service. CRS, a department of the Library of Congress, is a nonpartisan research arm for Congress. Its reports are not part of the depository program, but selected reports have been made available by the Senate Democratic Policy Committee (http://www.senate.gov/ ~ < dpc/crs/index.html) and the National Library for the Environment (http://www.cnie.org/nle/crs_main.html).

51. The *CIS/Index* is available from the publisher on CD-ROM as *Congressional Masterfile* 2, which covers the period from 1970 to date, and it can also be searched online through Dialog. CIS has also produced *Congressional Masterfile 1*, a CD-ROM that provides retrospective access to congressional information from 1789 to 1969.

52. Sue Hemp, Priscilla McIntosh, Mary Mallory, and Rob Richards are the principal compilers of *StateList*. Hal Southern of the University of Illinois Law Library is uploading the files as needed.

53. *Westlaw*, from the West Group, and *LEXIS*, from the LEXIS-NEXIS Group, are the two major online legal information systems. These expensive services are available at many law libraries and at some larger academic and public libraries, although in most cases there are limits on use. *Academic Universe*, from LEXIS-NEXIS, is a product designed and priced for academic libraries that includes many legal materials, including state law. Little information is available free via any of these companies' Web sites.

54. Robinson, *Tapping the Government Grapevine,* 118.

55. 42 U.S.C. §6293.

56. 64 Fed. Reg. 187 (28 September 1999), 52248-259, and 65 Fed. Reg. 9 (13 January 2000), 2077. The latter refers back to 64 Fed. Reg. 187, but incorrectly cites p. 54428. Always beware and search thoroughly, and use your imagination.

57. 65 Fed. Reg. 9 (13 January 2000), 2111-112.

58. *GPO Access*, http://www.access.gpo.gov/nara/about-cfr.html#page1.

59. Titles 1-16, as of January 1; Titles 17-27, as of April 1; Titles 28-41, as of July 1; and Titles 42-50 as of October. 1.

60. On April 22, 1996, the president issued a Memorandum for the Heads of Executive Departments and Agencies; he specifically directed the Secretary of Transportation to issue regulations for the GCNP that would place appropriate limits on sightseeing aircraft to reduce the noise immediately. This memorandum may be found online as part of the *Weekly Compilation of Presidential Documents* (published by NARA, the National Archives and Records Administration), available via *GPO Access* at http://www.access.gpo.gov/nara/nara003.html.

61. For an in-depth discussion of federal statistics programs focusing on the nature and methodology of their collection, see Jean Slemmons Stratford and Juri Stratford's *Major U.S. Statistical Series: Definitions, Publications, Limitations* (Chicago: American Library Association, 1992), 147p.

62. The Securities and Exchange Commission (SEC) ensures that securities markets are fair and honest. It requires publicly traded companies to file various reports, some of which are made public via the EDGAR system. Securities laws are generally found in 15 U.S.C.; the SEC in particular is covered at 15 U.S.C. §78a-78jj.

63. The laws regarding privacy of Census information may be found at 13 U.S.C. §9.

64. Note that although *Statistical Universe* itself is available to subscribers at http://web.lexis-nexis.com/statuniv, nonsubscribers may not access any information there. Information about *Statistical Universe* is available at CIS's Web site (http://www.cispubs.com/).

65. Note that many database products, especially those available via the Web, are still evolving. *Statistical Universe*, for example, has gone through several significant redesigns to its interface in its relatively short lifespan. As of this writing, another major redesign was in the planning stages.

66. *County and City Data Book* is published every five years. A near-equivalent product, updated and published annually, is *County and City Extra*, from Bernan Press.

67. *American FactFinder* is the result of Census efforts to provide a Web-based data dissemination system. Eventually, it may be able to serve as a gateway to nearly all public census data.

68. For a discussion of NAICS, see Carole A. Ambler and James E. Kristoff's "Introducing the North American Industry Classification System," *Government Information Quarterly* 15, no. 3 (1998): 263-73.

69. For more information on TIGER, see the Census Bureau's *TIGER* Web site (http://www.census.gov/geo/www/tiger/index.html).

70. For a detailed overview of spatial data resources and use, see Mary Larsgaard, *Map Librarianship: An Introduction*, 3d ed. (Englewood, Colo.: Libraries Unlimited, 1998), 487p.

71. U.S. Census Bureau and U.S. Bureau of Labor Statistics, *Computer Ownership,* http://www.bls.census.gov/cps/computer/computer.htm.

72. U.S. National Science Foundation, *Science and Engineering Indicators: 1998,* http://www.nsf.gov/sbe/srs/seind98/.

73. U.S. National Science Foundation, *Complex Picture of Computer Use in the Home Emerges,* http://www.nsf.gov/sbe/srs/issuebrf/ib00314.htm.

74. U.S. Census Bureau, *Computer Use and Ownership,* http://www.census.gov/population/www/socdemo/computer.html.

75. Micromedia Ltd. is the principal sponsor of *Government Information in Canada.*

76. GILS stands for Government Information Locator Service. A GILS record describes information, including its format and accessibility, in a standardized manner to facilitate search and retrieval of information on a variety of computing systems. For more information about GILS, see *Global Information Locator Service* (http://www.usgs.gov/public/gils/locator.html).

77. Nancy M. Cline calls for a versatile staff who can handle government information in its changing formats and emphasizes the importance of building on that expertise, "to develop skilled librarians who can work with the increasing array of government databases and extract the maximum value from them for the institution's clientele. . . . in the future it may take a very different investment from libraries to provide access to its [the federal government's] many information products." Nancy M. Cline, "Government Documents: Assets or Liabilities? A Management Perspective," in *Management of Government Information*, ed. Diane H. Smith (Englewood, Colo.: Libraries Unlimited, 1993), 226-27.

LIST OF SOURCES

Academic Universe. Dayton, Ohio: LEXIS-NEXIS Group. Available: http://web.lexis-nexis.com/universe (by subscription only; for more information, see http://www.cispubs.com).

Administrative Notes. Washington, D.C.: GPO, 1980– . Monthly. *Technical Supplement*, 1994– . Also available: http://www.access.gpo.gov/su_docs/fdlp/pubs/index.html.

AGRICOLA (AGRICultural OnLine Access). Beltsville, Md.: National Agricultural Library. Available: http://www.nal.usda.gov/ag98.

American Community Survey. [CD-ROM]. Washington, D.C.: U.S. Census Bureau, 1996– . Also available: http://www.census.gov/acs/www.

American FactFinder. Washington, D.C.: U.S. Census Bureau. Available: http://factfinder.census.gov.

American Statistics Index (ASI). Bethesda, Md.: Congressional Information Service, 1973– . Monthly; quarterly cumulative index; annual. (Also available as part of *Statistical Universe.*)

Balachandran, M., and S. Balachandran, eds. *State and Local Statistics Sources.* 2d ed. Detroit: Gale, 1993. 1912p.

Bishop, Olga B. *Canadian Official Publications.* Oxford: Pergamon, 1981. 297p. (Guides to Official Publications, vol. 9).

Book of the States. Lexington, Ky.: The Council of State Governments, 1965– . Annual.

Bowker, R. R. (Richard Rogers). *State Publications; a Provisional List of Official Publications of the Several States of the United States from Their Organization.* New York: Publishers Weekly, 1899–1908. Issued in four parts.

Business Statistics of the United States. Lanham, Md.: Bernan Press, 1996– . Annual. (Continues *Business Statistics.* Washington, D.C.: U.S. Bureau of Economic Analysis, 1951–1992. Biennial.)

Calendars of the United States House of Representatives and History of Legislation. Washington, D.C.: GPO. Available: http://www.access.gpo.gov/congress/cong003.html. (Also available in print).

Canada. House of Commons. *Bills of the House of Commons.* Ottawa, Ont.: Queen's Printer, 1867– . Published individually.

Canada. House of Commons. *House of Commons Debates: Official Report (Hansard).* Ottawa, Ont.: Queen's Printer, 1875– . Daily.

Canada. House of Commons. *House of Commons Journals.* Ottawa, Ont.: Queen's Printer, 1867– . Annual.

Canada. House of Commons. *House of Commons Votes and Proceedings.* Ottawa, Ont.: Queen's Printer, 1867– . Daily.

Canada. Senate. *Bills of the Senate of Canada.* Ottawa, Ont.: Queen's Printer, 1867– . Published individually.

Canada. Senate. *Debates of the Senate: Official Report (Hansard).* Ottawa, Ont.: Queen's Printer, 1867– . Daily.

Canada. Senate. *Journals of the Senate of Canada.* Ottawa, Ont.: Queen's Printer, 1867– . Annual.

Canada. Senate. *Minutes of the Proceedings of the Senate.* Ottawa, Ont.: Queen's Printer, 1867– . Daily.

Canada: A Portrait. 52d ed.- . Ottawa, Ont.: Statistics Canada, 1989– . Biannual.

Canada Gazette: Parts I, II, and III. Ottawa, Ont.: Queen's Printer, 1867– (Part I); 1947– (Part II); 1974– (Part III).

Canada Year Book. Ottawa, Ont.: Statistics Canada, 1867– . Biennial. Also available on CD-ROM.

Canadian Almanac & Directory. Toronto: Micromedia, 1948– . Annual.

Canadian Government Information on the Internet. Ottawa, Ont.: Government of Canada Depository Services Program. Available: http://dsp-psd.pwgsc.gc.ca/dsp-psd/Reference/cgii_index-e.html.

Canadian Government Programs and Services. Don Mills, Ont.: CCH Canadian Ltd., 1973– .

Canadian Government Publications. 24 vols. Ottawa, Ont.: Supply and Services Canada, 1955–1978.

Canadian Information by Subject. Ottawa, Ont.: National Library of Canada. Available: http://www.nlc-bnc.ca/caninfo/ecaninfo.htm.

Canadian Parliamentary Guide/Guide Parlementaire Canadien. Ottawa, Ont.: Queen's Printer, 1912– . Annual. (Continues *Parliamentary Companion,* 1862–1911.)

Canadiana. Ottawa, Ont.: National Library of Canada, 1951– . Monthly with annual cumulations. Available on microfiche, CD-ROM, or online.

Catalog of United States Government Publications. Washington, D.C.: GPO. Available: http://www.access.gpo.gov/su_docs/locators/cgp/index.html. (Print equivalent is *Monthly Catalog of United States Government Publications.*)

Catalogue of Official Publications of the Parliament and Government of Canada. 11 vols. and supps. Ottawa, Ont.: King's Printer, 1928–1948.

CensusCD + Maps Version 3.0. [CD-ROM]. East Brunswick, N.J.: GeoLytics, 1999.

CIS/Index. Bethesda, Md.: Congressional Information Service, Inc., 1970– . Annual (*CIS Annual, Legislative Histories of U.S. Public Laws*), with monthly supplements. (Also available via *Congressional Universe*; parts also available on *Congressional Masterfile*).

A Citizen's Guide on Using the Freedom of Information Act and the Privacy Act of 1974 to Request Government Records: First Report. Washington, D.C.: GPO, 1999. 76p.

Code of Federal Regulations. Washington, D.C.: National Archives and Records Administration, 1949– . Revised annually. Also available at http://www.access.gpo.gov/nara/cfr/index.html and online from various commercial vendors.

Code of Federal Regulations. CFR Index and Finding Aids. Washington, D.C.: National Archives and Records Administration, 1977– . Annual.

Code of Federal Regulations. LSA, List of CFR Sections Affected. Washington, D.C.: National Archives and Records Administration, 1977– . Monthly. Also available: http://www.access.gpo.gov/nara/lsa/aboutlsa.html.

Condition of Education. Washington, D.C.: U.S. National Center for Education Statistics, 1975– . Annual.

Congressional Index. Chicago: CCH, 1937– . Weekly throughout session.

Congressional Masterfile, 1 and 2. [CD-ROM]. Bethesda, Md.: Congressional Information Service, 1995, 1998.

Congressional Quarterly Almanac. Washington, D.C.: Congressional Quarterly, 1945– . Annual.

Congressional Quarterly Weekly Report. Washington, D.C.: Congressional Quarterly, 1946– . Weekly. (Also available by subscription at http://www.cq.com).

Congressional Quarterly's Politics in America. Washington, D.C.: Congressional Quarterly, 1981– . Biennial.

Congressional Record. Washington, D.C.: U.S. Congress, 1873– . Daily when Congress is in session. Also available at http://www.access.gpo.gov/su_docs/aces/aces150.html, via *THOMAS*, and from various commercial vendors.

Congressional Staff Directory. Mt. Vernon, Va.: Staff Directories, Ltd., 1959– . Three times a year. (Also available by subscription at http://csd.cq.com).

Congressional Universe. Bethesda, Md.: Congressional Information Service. Available: http://web.lexis-nexis.com/congcomp (by subscription only; for more information, see http://www.cispubs.com).

Congressional Yellow Book. Washington, D.C.: Leadership Directories, 1976– . Quarterly. (Also available by subscription at http://www.leadershipdirectories.com).

Consolidated List of Serials of the Government of Canada. Ottawa, Ont.: Government of Canada Depository Services Program. Available: http://dsp-psd.pwgsc.gc.ca/dsp-psd/Consolidated/conlist-e.html.

Consolidated Regulations of Canada. 18 vols. Ottawa, Ont.: Queen's Printer, 1978. (Updated by *Canada Gazette, Part II*.)

Consumer Price Index Detailed Report. Washington, D.C.: U.S. Bureau of Labor Statistics, 1953– . Monthly.

County and City Data Book. Washington, D.C.: U.S. Bureau of the Census, 1994. 1062p. Also available on CD-ROM.

County and City Extra: Annual Metro, City and County Data Book. Lanham, Md.: Bernan Press, 1992– . Annual.

County Business Patterns. Washington, D.C.: U.S. Census Bureau, 1964– . Annual. Also available on CD-ROM and at http://www.census.gov/epcd/cbp/view/cbpview.html.

CQ.com On Congress. Washington, D.C.: Congressional Quarterly, Inc. (by subscription only; information available at http://www.cq.com/prodsandsubs/prodsandsubs.html#oncongress).

CQ's State Fact Finder: Rankings Across America. Washington, D.C.: Congressional Quarterly, Inc., 1993– . Annual.

Crime in the United States. Washington, D.C.: Federal Bureau of Investigation, 1930– . Annual. (Also known as *Uniform Crime Reports*.)

Current Index to Journals in Education. Phoenix, Ariz.: Oryx Press and Educational Resources Information Center (ERIC), 1969–1996. (Print version ceased; now available through *ERIC*.)

Current National Statistical Compendiums on Microfiche. Bethesda, Md.: Congressional Information Service, 1974– . Annual. (Coverage from 1970.)

Current Population Reports. Washington, D.C.: U.S. Census Bureau, 1946– . Irregular. Also available: http://www.census.gov/main/www/cprs.html.

Declassified Documents Reference System. Woodbridge, Conn.: Primary Source Media. (by subscription only; information available at http://www.ddrs.psmedia.com).

Demographic Yearbook. New York: United Nations, 1948– . Annual.

Depository Libraries. Ottawa, Ont.: Government of Canada. Available: http://dsp-psd.pwgsc.gc.ca/dsp-psd/AboutDSP/DepoNew/table-e.html.

Digest of Education Statistics. Washington, D.C.: U.S. National Center for Education Statistics, 1962– . Annual.

Digest of Public General Bills and Resolutions. Washington, D.C.: Library of Congress, Congressional Research Service, 74th Cong., 2d sess.–101st Congress, 2d sess., 1936–1990. Two cumulative issues, occasional supplements, and a final edition for each session. Ceased. Continued by "Bill Summary and Status" section of *THOMAS*.

Digital National Security Archive. Alexandria, Va.: Chadwyck-Healey. Available: http://nsarchive.chadwyck.com/ (information only; subscription needed to access actual database).

Directory of Government Document Collections & Librarians. 7th ed. Edited by Marianne Ryan Kapfer. Bethesda, Md.: Congressional Information Service, Inc., 1997. 624p.

Dolan, Elizabeth Macdonald. *The Depository Dilemma: A Study of the Free Distribution of Canadian Federal Government Publications to Depository Libraries in Canada*. Ottawa, Ont.: Canadian Library Association, 1989. 131p.

Dove, Robert B. *Enactment of a Law*. Washington, D.C.: Library of Congress. Available: http://thomas.loc.gov/home/enactment/enactlawtoc.html.

Economic Census. Washington, D.C.: U.S. Census Bureau, 1954– . Quinquennial (portions also available on CD-ROM and at http://www.census.gov/epcd/www/econ97.html).

Economic Indicators. Washington, D.C.: U.S. Congress, Joint Economic Committee, 1948– . Monthly.

Economic Report of the President. Washington, D.C.: Executive Office of the President, Council of Economic Advisers, 1947– . Annual. (Recent issues also available: http://w3.access.gpo.gov/eop).

Economy at a Glance. Washington, D.C.: U.S. Bureau of Labor Statistics. Available: http://www.bls.gov/eag/eag.map.htm.

EDGAR Database of Corporate Information. Washington, D.C.: U.S. Securities and Exchange Commission. Available: http://www.sec.gov/edgarhp.htm.

Employment and Earnings. Washington, D.C.: U.S. Bureau of Labor Statistics, 1954– . Monthly.

ERIC. Washington, D.C.: Educational Resources Information Center. Available: http://ericir.syr.edu/Eric/ or http://ericae.net/scripts/ewiz/. (Also available via ERIC Clearinghouse on Assessment and Evaluation at http://ericae.net/aesearch.htm).

Europa World Year Book. London: Europa, 1959– . Annual.

Evans, James. *Government on the Net*. Berkeley, Calif.: Nolo Press, 1997. 711p.

Everyone's United Nations. New York: United Nations, 1979– . Irregular.

Federal Agency Internet Sites. Washington, D.C.: GPO and Baton Rouge, La.: Louisiana State University Libraries. Available: http://www.access.gpo.gov/su_docs/locators/agency/index.html.

Federal Depository Library Directory. Washington, D.C.: GPO, 1996- . Irregular.

Federal Depository Library Manual. Washington, D.C.: GPO, revised 1993. 180p. Also available: http://www.access.gpo.gov/su_docs/fdlp/pubs/fdlm. ("Appendix A, Suggested Core Collection" also available: http://www.access.gpo.gov/su_docs/fdlp/pubs/fdlm/corelist.html; "Collection Development Guidelines for Selective Federal Depository Libraries" also available: http://www.access.gpo.gov/su_docs/fdlp/pubs/fdlm/coldev.html).

Federal Regional Yellow Book. Washington, D.C.: Leadership Directories, 1976– . Quarterly. (Also available by subscription at http://www.leadershipdirectories.com).

Federal Register. Washington, D.C.: National Archives and Records Administration, 1936– . Daily. Also available at http://www.access.gpo.gov/su_docs/aces/aces140.html and from various commercial vendors.

Federal Staff Directory. Mt. Vernon, Va.: Staff Directories, Ltd., 1982– . Three times a year. (Also available by subscription at http://fsd.cq.com).

Federal Web Locator. Chicago: The Center for Information Law and Policy. Available: http://www.infoctr.edu/fwl.

Federal Yellow Book. Washington, D.C.: Leadership Directories, 1976– . Quarterly. (Also available by subscription at http://www.leadershipdirectories.com).

FedStats. Washington, D.C.: Federal Interagency Council on Statistical Policy. Available: http://www.fedstats.gov.

Freedom of Information Act Electronic Reading Room. Washington, D.C.: Federal Bureau of Investigation. Available: http://foia.fbi.gov/room.htm.

Frequently Used Sites Related to U.S. Government Information. Nashville, Tenn.: ALA GODORT Federal Documents Task Force, comp. Available: http://www.library.vanderbilt.edu/central/staff/fdtf.html.

General Information Concerning Patents. Washington, D.C.: U.S. Patent and Trademark Office, 1997. 87p.

Geostat Interactive Data Resources. Charlottesville, Va.: University of Virginia, Geostat Geospatial and Statistical Data Center. Available: http://fisher.lib.virginia.edu/active_data.

GODORT Handout Exchange. Ann Arbor, Mich.: American Library Association, Government Documents Round Table, Education Committee. Available: http://www.lib.umich.edu/libhome/Documents.center/godort.html.

GOVDOC-L Discussion List (govdoc-l@lists.psu.edu). LISTSERV. January 16, 1990– . To subscribe to GOVDOC-L, send a command to listserv@lists.psu.edu. The text of the message should read SUB GOVDOC-L [Yourfirstname] [Yourlastname]. For more information, and to search the archives, see http://docs.lib.duke.edu/federal/govdoc-l/index.html.

Government Information in Canada. Saskatoon, Saskatchewan: University of Saskatchewan Libraries. Available: http://www.usask.ca/library/gic/index.html.

Government Information Quarterly. Greenwich, Conn.: JAI Press, 1984– . Quarterly. (Also available to subscribers at http://www.sciencedirect.com).

Government Information Sharing Project. Corvallis, Ore.: Oregon State University Libraries. Available: http://govinfo.kerr.orst.edu.

Government Information Web Page Template. Denton, Tex.: ALA GODORT Government Information Technology Committee, comp. Available: http://www.library.unt.edu/gpo/template/govinfo.html.

Government of Canada Primary Internet Site (Canada Site). Ottawa, Ont.: Government of Canada. Available: http://canada.gc.ca/main_e.html.

Government of Canada Publications: Quarterly Catalogue and Checklist of Canadian Government Publications. Ottawa, Ont.: Canadian Government Publications Centre, 1979–1992.

Government Reports Announcements and Index (GRAI). Springfield, Va.: National Technical Information Service, 1946–1994. Ceased. (Continued by *NTIS Electronic Catalog.*)

GPO Access. Washington, D.C.: GPO. Available: http://www.access.gpo.gov/su_docs/index.html.

GPO Access Legislative. Washington, D.C.: GPO. Available: http://www.access.gpo.gov/su_docs/legislative.html.

GPO Access Regulatory. Washington, D.C.: GPO. Available: http://www.access.gpo.gov/su_docs/regulatory.html.

GPO Sales Publications Reference File (PRF). Washington, D.C.: GPO, 1977–1997. Ceased. (Continued by *Sales Product Catalog.*)

Guide to Official Publications of Foreign Countries. 2d ed. By ALA GODORT International Documents Task Force. Bethesda, Md.: Congressional Information Service, Inc., 1997. 494p.

Hajnal, Peter I., ed. *International Information: Documents, Publications, and Electronic Information of International Governmental Organizations.* 2d ed. Englewood, Colo.: Libraries Unlimited, 1997. 528p.

Handbook of U.S. Labor Statistics. Lanham, Md.: Bernan Press, 1997– . Irregular. (Continues *Handbook of Labor Statistics.* Washington, D.C.: U.S. Bureau of Labor Statistics, 1924–1989. Irregular.)

Hardy, Gayle J., and Judith Schiek Robinson, eds. *Subject Guide to U.S. Government Reference Sources.* Englewood, Colo.: Libraries Unlimited, 1996. 358p.

Hasse, Adelaide Rosalia. *Index of Economic Material in the Documents of the States of the United States.* Washington, D.C.: Carnegie Institution of Washington, 1908–1919. Various volumes for individual states.

Health, United States. Washington, D.C.: U.S. National Center for Health Statistics, 1975– . Annual.

Hellebust, Lynn, ed. *State Reference Publications: A Bibliographic Guide to State Blue Books, Legislative Manuals and Other General Reference Sources.* Topeka, Kans.: Government Research Service, 1991– . Annual.

Herman, Edward. *Locating United States Government Information: A Guide to Sources.* 2d ed. Buffalo, N.Y.: W. S. Hein, 1997. 588p.

Herman, Edward. *Locating United States Government Information: A Guide to Sources.* 2d ed. *Internet Supplement.* Buffalo, N.Y.: W. S. Hein, 1999. 228p.

Historical Catalogue of Statistics Canada Publications, 1918–1980. Ottawa, Ont.: Statistics Canada, 1982. 337p.

Historical Statistics of the United States: Colonial Times to 1970. 2 vols. Washington, D.C.: U.S. Bureau of the Census, 1975.

History of Bills. Washington, D.C.: GPO. Available: http://www.access.gpo.gov/su_docs/aces/aaces200.html.

Hoffmann, Frank W., and Richard J. Wood. *Guide to Popular U.S. Government Publications.* 5th ed. Englewood, Colo.: Libraries Unlimited, 1998. 300p.

Hornor, Louise, ed. *Black Americans: A Statistical Sourcebook.* Palo Alto, Calif.: Information Publications, 1999. 311p.

How Government Works: A Primer. Ottawa, Ont.: Institute on Governance and Public Service Commission. Available: http://learnet.gc.ca/eng/lrncentr/online/hgw/index.htm.

Index Medicus. Bethesda, Md.: National Library of Medicine, 1960– . Monthly. Also available as *MEDLINE*, *PubMed*, and *Internet Grateful Med* (see below).

Index to International Statistics. Bethesda, Md.: Congressional Information Service, 1983– . Monthly; quarterly cumulative index; annual. (Also available as part of *Statistical Universe*).

Index to the Code of Federal Regulations. Englewood, Colo.: Information Handling Services, 1978– . Annual.

Index to U.S. Government Periodicals. Chicago: Infordata International, 1970–1987.

Info Source. Ottawa, Ont.: Government of Canada, 1991– . Annual.

InfoNation. New York: United Nations. Available: http://www.un.org/Pubs/CyberSchoolBus/infonation/e_infonation.htm.

Internet Grateful Med. Bethesda, Md.: National Library of Medicine. Available: http://igm.nlm.nih.gov.

Johnson, Charles W. *How Our Laws Are Made.* Washington, D.C.: Library of Congress. Available: http://thomas.loc.gov/home/lawsmade.toc.html. (Also available in print as Senate Document 105-14).

*Journal of Government Information,*Vol. 21- , January/February 1994– . New York: Pergamon Press, 1994– . Bimonthly. (Continues *Government Publications Review*, Vols. 1-20, 1973–1993. Also available to subscribers at http://www.sciencedirect.com.)

Judicial Staff Directory. Mt. Vernon, Va.: Staff Directories, Ltd., 1986– . Three times a year. (Also available by subscription at http://jsd.cq.com).

Judicial Yellow Book. Washington, D.C.: Leadership Directories, 1976– . Quarterly. (Also available by subscription at http://www.leadershipdirectories.com).

Kurian, George Thomas. *Datapedia of the United States, 1790–2000: America Year by Year.* Lanham, Md.: Bernan Press, 1994. 466p.

LandView III: Environmental Mapping Software. [11 CD-ROMs]. Washington, D.C.: U.S. Environmental Protection Agency and U.S. Bureau of the Census, 1997.

Leacy, F. H., ed. *Historical Statistics of Canada.* 2d ed. Ottawa, Ont.: Statistics Canada, 1983. 900p.

LEXIS. Dayton, Ohio: LEXIS-NEXIS Group. (Available by subscription only; see http://www.lexis.com for information).

Library Journal. Vol. 1- , 1876- . New York: Cahners. Semi-monthly, except in January, July, and August.

Library of Congress Subject Headings. 23d ed. 5 vols. Washington, D.C.: Cataloging Distribution Service, Library of Congress, 2000.

List of Classes of United States Government Publications Available for Selection by Depository Libraries. Washington, D.C.: GPO, 1960- . Semiannual. Has supplement: *Inactive or Discontinued Items from the 1950 Revision of the Classified List.* (Electronic version (delimited text file; see note 22) available at ftp://fedbbs.access.gpo.gov/gpo_bbs/class/listclas.txt).

Major Legislation of the Congress. Washington, D.C.: Congressional Research Service, 97th Cong., 2d sess.– 102d Congress, 2d sess., 1982–1992. Monthly. (Ceased in print; now available via *THOMAS*).

Maxwell, Bruce. *How to Access the Federal Government on the Internet.* 4th ed. Washington, D.C.: Congressional Quarterly, 1999. 328p.

MEDLINE. Bethesda, Md.: National Library of Medicine. Available: http://www.nlm.nih.gov/databases/freemedl.html.

Monthly Catalog of United States Government Publications. Washington, D.C.: GPO, 1895– . Monthly. Supplemented by *Periodicals Supplement and Serial Set Catalog.* (Also available on CD-ROM, and on the Web as *Catalog of United States Government Publications*).

Monthly Checklist of State Publications. Washington, D.C.: Library of Congress, 1910–1994. Monthly. Ceased.

Morehead, Joe. *Introduction to United States Government Information Sources.* 6th ed. Englewood, Colo.: Libraries Unlimited, 1999. 491p.

Municipal Yellow Book. Washington, D.C.: Leadership Directories, 1991– . Quarterly. (Also available by subscription at http://www.leadershipdirectories.com).

NASA Center for AeroSpace Information Technical Report Server. Hanover, Md.: NASA. Available: http://www.sti.nasa.gov/RECONselect.html.

National Center for Education Statistics. Washington, D.C.: U.S. National Center for Education Statistics. Available: http://www.nces.ed.gov.

National Center for Health Statistics. Washington, D.C.: U.S. National Center for Health Statistics. Available: http://www.cdc.gov/nchs.

National Health Interview Survey. [CD-ROM]. Hyattsville, Md.: U.S. National Center for Health Statistics, 1987– . Annual.

National Trade Data Bank (NTDB). [CD-ROM]. Washington, D.C.: U.S. Department of Commerce, 1990– . Monthly. (Also available via *STAT-USA* at http://www.stat-usa.gov).

New Product Announcements. Washington, D.C.: GPO. Available: https://orders.access.gpo.gov/su_docs/sale/market/index.html. (Formerly *New Products from the U.S. Government.*)

North American Industry Classification System. Washington, D.C.: U.S. Office of Management and Budget, 1998. 1247p. Also available: http://www.census.gov/epcd/www/naics.html.

NTIS Electronic Catalog. Springfield, Va.: National Technical Information Service. Available: http://www.ntis.gov/search.htm.

NTIS Gov. Research Center. Springfield, Va.: National Technical Information Service. Available: http://grc.ntis.gov.

O'Brien, Jacqueline Wasserman, and Steven R. Wasserman, eds. *Statistics Sources: A Subject Guide to Data on Industrial, Business, Social, Educational, Financial, and Other Topics for the United States and Internationally.* Farmington Hills, Mich.: Gale Group, 1962– . Annual.

Occupational Outlook Handbook. Washington, D.C.: U.S. Bureau of Labor Statistics, 1949– . Biennial. Also available on CD-ROM and at http://stats.bls.gov:80/ocohome.htm.

Official Congressional Directory. Washington, D.C.: GPO, 1887– . Biennial.

PAIS International in Print. New York: OCLC Public Affairs Information Service, 1991– . Monthly. (Formerly *Public Affairs Information Service Bulletin*, 1915–1990.) (Available online from several vendors; see http://www.pais.aa.psiweb.com/index.html).

Palic, Vladimir. *Government Publications: A Guide to Bibliographic Tools*. Washington, D.C.: Library of Congress, 1975. 441p.

Parliamentary Internet Parlementaire. Ottawa, Ont.: Canadian Senate, House of Commons and Library of Parliament. Available: http://www.parl.gc.ca.

Pearson, Joyce A. McCray, and Pamela M. Tull. *U.S. Government Directories, 1982–1995*. Englewood, Colo.: Libraries Unlimited, 1998. 159p.

Popular Names of U.S. Government Reports. 4th ed. Compiled by Bernard Bernier, Jr. and Karen Wood. Washington, D.C.: Library of Congress, 1984. 272p.

Price List of Government Publications. Ottawa, Ont.: King's Printer, 1895.

Public Papers of the President. Washington, D.C.: GPO, 1929–1933, 1945– . (Equivalent volumes for many earlier presidents and Franklin D. Roosevelt published by various private publishers.)

PubMed. Bethesda, Md.: National Library of Medicine. Available: http://www.ncbi.nlm.nih.gov/PubMed.

PubSCIENCE. Oak Ridge, Tenn.: DOE's Office of Scientific and Technical Information and Washington, D.C.: GPO. Available: http://pubsci.osti.gov.

Regional Economic Information System. [CD-ROM]. Washington, D.C.: U.S. Bureau of Economic Analysis, 1991– . Annual.

Resources in Education. Washington, D.C.: Educational Resources Information Center (ERIC). 1966– . (Continues *Research in Education*.) (Also available through *ERIC*).

Revised Statutes of Canada. 8 vols. Ottawa, Ont.: Queen's Printer, 1985.

Robinson, Judith Schiek. *Tapping the Government Grapevine: The User-Friendly Guide to U.S. Government Information Sources*. 3d ed. Phoenix, Ariz.: Oryx Press, 1998. 286p.

Sales Product Catalog. Washington, D.C.: GPO. Available: https://orders.access.gpo.gov/su_docs/sale/index.html. (Continues *GPO Sales Publications Reference File (PRF)*.)

Schick, Frank L., and Renee Schick, eds. *Statistical Handbook on Aging Americans*. Phoenix, Ariz.: Oryx Press, 1994. 335p.

Sears, Jean L., and Marilyn K. Moody. *Using Government Information Sources: Electronic and Print*. 3d ed. Phoenix, Ariz.: Oryx Press, 2000. 632p.

Senate Calendar of Business. Washington, D.C.: GPO. Available: http://www.access.gpo.gov/congress/cong004.html. (Also available in print).

Serial Set. Washington, D.C.: U.S. Congress, 1817– .

Shaaban, Marian, ed. *Guide to Country Information in International Governmental Organization Publications*. Washington, D.C.: ALA GODORT, 1996. 343p.

SIGCAT CD-ROM Compendium. Compiled by Special Interest Group on CD-ROM Applications and Technology (SIGCAT), GPO Office of Electronic Information Dissemination Services, and U.S. Geological Survey Library. Washington, D.C.: GPO, 1992–1994.

SIGCAT Disc Compendium. Washington, D.C.: Special Interest Group on CD-ROM Applications and Technology (SIGCAT). Available: http://www.sigcat.org/discs.htm. (Update of *SIGCAT CD-ROM Compendium.*)

Social Security Handbook. Washington, D.C.: U.S. Social Security Administration, 1960– . Irregular.

Some Canadian Academic and Government Libraries with Government Information Web Pages. Victoria, B.C.: McPherson Library, University of Victoria. Available: http://gateway2.uvic.ca/staff/frose/frclagpp.htm.

Sourcebook of Criminal Justice Statistics. Washington, D.C.: U.S. Bureau of Justice Statistics, 1973– . Annual.

Standard Industrial Classification Manual. Washington, D.C.: U.S. Office of Management and Budget, 1987. 705p. Also available: http://www.osha.gov/oshstats/sicser.html.

STAT-USA. Washington, D.C.: U.S. Department of Commerce. Available: http://www.stat-usa.gov. (Parts also available on CD-ROM as *National Trade Data Bank*).

State and Local Government on the Net. Minneapolis, Minn.: Piper Resources. Available: http://www.piperinfo.com/state/index.cfm.

State and Local Governments: A Library of Congress Internet Resource Page. Washington, D.C.: Library of Congress. Available: http://lcweb.loc.gov/global/state/stategov.html.

State and Metropolitan Area Data Book. Washington, D.C.: U.S. Bureau of the Census, 1997–1998. 177p.

State Capital Universe. Bethesda, Md.: Congressional Information Service. Available: http://web.lexis-nexis.com/stcapuniv (by subscription only; for more information, see http://www.cispubs.com).

State Constitutions, Statutes and Related Legislative Information. Ithaca, N.Y.: Legal Information Institute, Cornell Law School. Available: http://www.law.cornell.edu/statutes.html.

State Rankings: A Statistical View of the 50 United States. Lawrence, Kans.: Morgan Quitno Corp., 1990– . Annual.

State Web Locator. Chicago: Center for Information Law and Policy. Available: http://www.infoctr.edu/swl.

State Yellow Book. Washington, D.C.: Leadership Directories, 1989– . Quarterly. (Also available by subscription at http://www.leadershipdirectories.com).

StateList: The Electronic Source for State Publication Lists. Urbana-Champaign, Ill.: Documents and Law Libraries at the University of Illinois. Available: http://www.law.uiuc.edu/library/check/check.htm.

Statistical Abstract of the United States. Washington, D.C.: U.S. Census Bureau, 1878– . Annual. Also available on CD-ROM and at http://www.census.gov/statab/www.

Statistical Reference Index (SRI). Bethesda, Md.: Congressional Information Service, 1980– . Monthly; quarterly cumulative index; annual. (Also available as part of *Statistical Universe*).

Statistical Universe. Bethesda, Md.: Congressional Information Service. Available: http://web.lexis-nexis.com/statuniv (by subscription only; for more information, see http://www.cispubs.com). (For print equivalents, see *American Statistics Index, Index to International Statistics,* and *Statistical Reference Index.*)

Statistical Yearbook. New York: United Nations, Statistical Office, 1948– . Annual. Also available on CD-ROM.

Statistics Canada Catalogue. Ottawa, Ont.: Statistics Canada, 1922– . Title varies. Also available: http://www.statcan.ca:80/english/search/ips.htm.

Statutes of Canada. Ottawa, Ont.: Queen's Printer and Controller of Stationery. Sessional.

Stratford, Jean Slemmons, and Juri Stratford. *Major U.S. Statistical Series: Definitions, Publications, Limitations.* Chicago: American Library Association, 1992. 147p.

Subject Bibliography: SB. Washington, D.C.: GPO, 1975– . Revised irregularly. Also available: http://bookstore.gpo.gov/sb/index.html.

Survey of Current Business. Washington, D.C.: U.S. Bureau of Economic Analysis, 1921– . Monthly. (Recent issues also available at http://www.bea.doc.gov/bea/pubs.htm).

THOMAS. Washington, D.C.: Library of Congress. Available: http://thomas.loc.gov.

TIGER/Line: Topologically Integrated Geographic Encoding and Referencing Line. Washington, D.C.: U.S. Bureau of the Census, 1997.

United States Census of Population and Housing. Washington, D.C.: GPO, 1790– . Decennial. 1990– . Also available on CD-ROMs and at http://www.census.gov/main/www/cen1990.html.

United States Code. 1994 ed. with supplements. Washington, D.C.: GPO, 1994– . Also available on CD-ROM, at http://www.access.gpo.gov/congress/cong013.html, and from various commercial vendors.

United States Government Manual. Washington, D.C.: Office of the Federal Register, 1935– . Annual. Also available: http://www.access.gpo.gov/nara/nara001.html.

United States Historical Census Data Browser. Ann Arbor, Mich.: Inter-university Consortium for Political and Social Research (ICPSR) and Charlottesville, Va.: University of Virginia, Geostat Geospatial and Statistical Data Center. Available: http://fisher.lib.virginia.edu/census.

United States Reports. Washington, D.C.: U.S. Supreme Court, 1790– . Irregular.

United States Statutes at Large. Washington, D.C.: GPO, 1789– . Annual. (*Public Laws*—of which the *Statutes at Large* are a compilation—also available at http://www.access.gpo.gov/nara/nara005.html, via *THOMAS*, and from various commercial vendors.)

U.S. Bureau of Justice Statistics. Washington, D.C.: Bureau of Justice Statistics. Available: http://www.ojp.usdoj.gov/bjs.

U.S. Bureau of Labor Statistics. Washington, D.C.: Bureau of Labor Statistics. Available: http://www.bls.gov.

U.S. Government Online Bookstore. Washington, D.C.: GPO. Available: http://bookstore.gpo.gov/index.html.

U.S. Government Periodicals Index. Bethesda, Md.: Congressional Information Service, October–December, 1993– . Quarterly. (Previously available on CD-ROM. Web service available by subscription; see *CIS Government Periodicals Universe*, http://www.lexis-nexis.com/cispubs/new_product_announcements/gov_periodicals/Default.htm, for more information).

U.S. Government Subscriptions Catalog. Washington, D.C.: GPO. Available: http://bookstore.gpo.gov/subscriptions/index.html. (Available in print as *U.S. Government Subscriptions*).

USA Counties. [CD-ROM]. Washington, D.C.: U.S. Census Bureau, Economics and Statistics Administration, 1992– . Biennial.

USA Trade. [CD-ROM]. Washington, D.C.: U.S. Department of Commerce, 1998– . Monthly.

Vital Statistics of the United States. Washington, D.C.: GPO, 1937– . Annual.

Washington Information Directory. Washington, D.C.: Congressional Quarterly, 1980– . Annual.

Weekly Checklist of Canadian Government Publications. Ottawa, Ont.: Canadian Government Publishing. Available: http://dsp-psd.pwgsc.gc.ca/dsp-psd/Checklist/lists-e.html. (Includes Supplements "Library of Parliament publications accessible through the Depository Services Program Web site" and "Canadian federal government databases accessible through the Internet;" continues *Weekly Checklist of Canadian Government Publications,* Hull, Ont.: Supply and Services Canada.)

Westlaw. St. Paul, Minn.: West Group. (Available by subscription only; see http://www.westlaw.com for information).

What's Up Doc? Ottawa, Ont.: Canadian Government Publishing. Available: http://dsp-psd.pwgsc.gc.ca/dsp-psd/Whatsup/contents-e.html. (Continues *What's Up Doc?* Ottawa, Ont.: Canada Communication Group, Depository Services Program. Irregular.)

The World Almanac and Book of Facts. Mahweh, N.J.: World Almanac Books, 1868– . Annual. Also available online.

World Development Indicators. [CD-ROM]. Washington, D.C.: IBRD, World Bank, 1997– . Annual. (Current year data also available in print version).

WorldCat. Dublin, Ohio: OCLC. (Available by subscription via the *FirstSearch* service; see http://www.oclc.org for more information).

Worldwide Government Directory. Washington, D.C.: Keesings Worldwide, 2000. 1564p.

York, Grace. *University of Michigan Documents Center*. Ann Arbor, Mich.: University of Michigan Libraries. Available: http://www.lib.umich.edu/libhome/Documents.center/index.html.

Your Right to Federal Records: Questions and Answers on the Freedom of Information Act and the Privacy Act. Washington, D.C.: U.S. General Services Administration, 1996. 25p. Also available: http://www.pueblo.gsa.gov/cic_text/fed_prog/foia/foia.htm.

ADDITIONAL READINGS

American Library Association, Government Documents Round Table, Education Committee. *Government Information and Depository Management Clearinghouse*. Available: http://www.library.ucsb.edu/ala/clearing.html.

Currently maintained by Sherry DeDecker, this is an outstanding collection of tools, tutorials, and other types of training materials for government information librarians. This site should be reviewed regularly.

Berinstein, Paula. *Finding Statistics Online: How to Locate the Elusive Numbers You Need*. Edited by Susanne Bjørner. Medford, N.J.: Information Today, 1998. 356p.

This guide explains how to locate statistics, using both professional systems and services and the Internet. Discussion of the nature of statistics and how to evaluate their validity is also included.

Browning, Graeme. *Electronic Democracy: Using the Internet to Influence American Politics*. Edited and with a foreword by Daniel J. Weitzner. Wilton, Conn.: Pemberton Press, 1996. 185p.

As described by its editor, this is "a comprehensive guide through the newly emerging techniques of interactive politics online." All government information specialists need to keep current on the political scene at various levels of government, as well as information policy and technology.

Cheverie, Joan F., ed. *Government Information Collections in the Networked Environment: New Issues and Models*. Co-published simultaneously as *Collection Management* 23, no. 3 (1998). New York: Haworth Press, 1998. 118p.

This collection takes a look at the current state of affairs, It should be read along with another first-rate collection of articles on the role of information technology, *Depository Library Use of Technology: A Practitioner's Perspective*, edited by Jan Swanbeck and Peter Hernon (Norwood, N.J., Ablex, 1993, 260p.).

DttP: A Quarterly Journal of Government Information Practice and Perspective. Chicago: American Library Association, Government Documents Round Table. v. 1- , September 1972– . Quarterly.

Formerly *Documents to the People (DttP)*, this is the official publication of the Government Documents Round Table (GODORT), American Library Association (ALA). It is an important source for articles, news items, and other information on government publications, technical reports, and maps; related governmental activities; documents librarianship; and ALA/GODORT matters, as well as other professional organizations, such as the Council of Professional Associations on Federal Statistics.

Garner, Diane L., and Diane H. Smith. *The Complete Guide to Citing Government Information Resources*. Rev. ed. Washington, D.C.: Congressional Information Service, 1993. 222p.

This comprehensive manual provides complete details on how to cite U.S. federal, state, local, international, intergovernmental, and other representative national level government documents and electronic sources in bibliographies and footnotes. A detailed index gives the user quick access to hundreds of individual examples. More recent guides and collections of examples for electronic sources can be found on the Web itself. For an overall look at these, see "Citation Guides," *University of Michigan Documents Center*, by Grace York, available at http://www.lib.umich.edu/libhome/Documents.center/cite.html.

Government Technology. Folsom, Calif.: e.Republic, January 1995– . Monthly; semimonthly, February, May, August, and November. Available: http://www.govtech.net.

This useful magazine contains news and publication, conference, and product announcements. The focus is on state and local governments' use of technology. A free print subscription to the regular issues and supplements, such as *Visions*, is available; a complete set of previous issues is accessible and searchable at the Web site.

Hernon, Peter, John A. Shuler, and Robert E. Dugan. *U.S. Government on the Web: Getting the Information You Need*. Englewood, Colo.: Libraries Unlimited, 1999. 349p.

This guide to government information on the Web has some chapters on units of government (e.g., executive branch, legislative branch) and others covering special topics (e.g., Web pages for children). Initial chapters discuss the importance of government information, government structure, and search engines. Updates to sources cited in the text can be found at http://www.lu.com/lu/hernontoc.html.

Journal of Government Information: An International Review of Policy, Issues and Resources. New York: Pergamon Press, v. 21– , January/February 1994– . Bimonthly.

This journal continues *Government Publications Review* (1973–1993). Steven D. Zink serves as editor-in-chief, and Debora Cheney as associate editor. One can keep track of relevant reading material through Dena Holiman Hutto's outstanding feature article, "Recent Literature on Government Information" (see, for example, vol. 26, September/October 1999, pp. 525-75), and find the latest scholarship on "government policy, current practice, new developments, and history" in the field. The "Table of Contents," maintained by James M. Gravois, is available at http://www.lib.auburn.edu/madd/docs/jgi/contents.html, and the journal is also available to subscribers at http://www.sciencedirect.com.

Kelly, Melody Specht. *Uncle Sam's Net of Knowledge for Schools*. New York: Neal-Schuman, 1998. 349p.

This guide to Web-based and other types of federal information emphasizes resources for K–12 curriculum development and projects. Its coverage includes periodicals and reference resources, with subject scope ranging from fine arts to science.

O'Mahony, Daniel P. "The Federal Depository Library Program in Transition: A Perspective at the Turn of a Century." *Government Information Quarterly* 15, no. 1 (1998): 13-26.

O'Mahony provides an astute and highly readable discussion about maintaining public access as the cornerstone of a transformative federal government information dissemination system.

Ross, John M. *How to Use the Major Indexes to U.S. Government Publications*. Chicago: American Library Association, 1989. 37p.

The text clearly shows, in a step-by-step process, how to use six major reference sources: *American Statistics Index*, *CIS/Annual*, *CIS Legislative Histories of U.S. Public Laws*, *Congressional Record*, *Monthly Catalog of United States Government Publications*, and *Index to U.S. Government Periodicals*. Although the latter title is no longer published, it is of use in identifying older periodical literature.

Schreiber, Mae N. *International Trade Sources: A Research Guide*. New York: Garland Publishing, 1997. 327p.

Over 800 sources are included in this comprehensive, annotated bibliography. This excellent subject guide contains thirteen chapters, including periodicals and newspapers; electronic sources; regulations, laws, and agreements; and dictionaries. An instructive sample search is included as part of the introductory material. Specialized bibliographic sources such as this form an essential category of government information reference works.

Sheehy, Helen M., and Andrea Sevetson. "International Information Update: A Unique Period in Time: The Canadian Depository Services Program in Transition." *Journal of Government Information* 26 (March-April 1999): 165-69.

This article is a representative sample of this excellent regular feature by two international documents specialists. For further coverage of Canadian depositories, see also Liwen Qiu Vaughan and Elizabeth Dolan, "Electronic Dissemination of Government Information in Canada: Implications for Equitable Access," *Journal of Government Information* 25 (September/October 1998): 439-52.

Smith, Diane H., ed. *Management of Government Information Resources in Libraries*. Englewood, Colo.: Libraries Unlimited, 1993. 260p.

Written by experienced and dedicated professionals, this is an excellent text on organizing, accessing, and utilizing government information sources, suitable for students and practitioners alike. Ridley Kessler and Jack Sulzer's trenchant chapter, "The Politics of Documents Librarianship" includes a convenient list of key organizations in government information. A selected bibliography, covering literature from the 1980s and 1990s, concludes the volume.

"Special Issue, Symposium on the Decennial Census, U.S. Bureau of the Census." *Government Information Quarterly* 17, no. 2 (2000): 93-231.

This relevant and timely series of articles includes an introduction by Dr. Kenneth Prewitt, Director, United States Census Bureau.

Stubbs, Walter, and Eric Wettstein, "U.S. GPO CD-ROMs: Blessing or Curse?" *Journal of Government Information* 26 (March–April 1999): 131-63.

The authors give an important survey of federal depository library collections and their use.

Author/Title Index

Subject Index